M000272339

BREAST CANCER

Second Edition

Atlas of Clinical Oncology

Series Volumes

Blumgart, Jarnagin, Fong	*Hepatobiliary Cancer*
Cameron	*Pancreatic Cancer*
Carroll	*Prostate Cancer*
Char	*Cancer of the Eye and Orbit*
Clark, Duh, Jahan, Perrier	*Endocrine Tumors*
Eifel, Levenback	*Cervical, Vulvar, and Vaginal Cancer*
Ginsberg	*Lung Cancer*
Grossbard	*Malignant Lymphomas*
Ozols	*Ovarian Cancer*
Pollock	*Soft Tissue Sarcomas*
Poplack	*Childhood Leukemias*
Poplack	*Solid Tumors in Children*
Prados	*Brain Cancer*
Raghavan	*Germ Cell Tumors*
Rice	*Endometrial and Uterine Cancer*
Shah	*Head and Neck Cancer*
Shipley	*Urothelial Cancer*
Silverman	*Oral Cancer*
Sober, Haluska	*Skin Cancer*
Volberding, Palefsky	*Viral and Immunological Malignancies*
Wiernik	*Adult Leukemias*
Willett	*Colon and Rectal Cancer*
Winchester, Winchester	*Breast Cancer*

BREAST CANCER

Second Edition

David J. Winchester, MD, FACS
Associate Professor of Surgery
Northwestern University Fineberg School of Medicine
Chief, Division of General Surgery and Surgical Oncology
Evanston Northwestern Healthcare
Evanston, Illinois

David P. Winchester, MD, FACS
Professor of Surgery
Northwestern University Fineberg School of Medicine
Chairman, Department of Surgery
Evanston Northwestern Healthcare
Evanston, Illinois

Clifford A. Hudis, MD, FACS
Associate Professor of Medicine
Weill Medical School of Cornell University
Chief, Breast Cancer Medicine Service
Memorial Sloan-Kettering Cancer Center
New York, New York

Larry Norton, MD, FACS
Professor of Medicine
Weill Medical School of Cornell University
Deputy Physician-in-Chief for Breast Cancer Programs
Norma S. Sarofim Chair in Clinical Oncology
Memorial Sloan-Kettering Cancer Center
New York, New York

BC Decker Inc
Hamilton

BC Decker Inc
P.O. Box 620, L.C.D. 1
Hamilton, Ontario L8N 3K7
Tel: 905-522-7017; 800-568-7281
Fax: 905-522-7839; 888-311-4987
E-mail: info@bcdecker.com
www.bcdecker.com

05 06 07 08/WPC/9 8 7 6 5 4 3 2 1

ISBN 1-55009-272-3
Printed in the United States of America by Walsworth Publishing Company
Production Editor: Maria L. Reyes; Typesetter: Jansom; Cover Designer: Lisa Mattinson

Sales and Distribution

United States
BC Decker Inc
P.O. Box 785
Lewiston, NY 14092-0785
Tel: 905-522-7017; 800-568-7281
Fax: 905-522-7839; 888-311-4987
E-mail: info@bcdecker.com
www.bcdecker.com

Canada
BC Decker Inc
50 King St. E.
P.O. Box 620, LCD 1
Hamilton, Ontario L8N 3K7
Tel: 905-522-7017; 800-568-7281
Fax: 905-522-7839; 888-311-4987
E-mail: info@bcdecker.com
www.bcdecker.com

Foreign Rights
John Scott & Company
International Publishers' Agency
P.O. Box 878
Kimberton, PA 19442
Tel: 610-827-1640; Fax: 610-827-1671
E-mail: jsco@voicenet.com

Japan
Igaku-Shoin Ltd.
Foreign Publications Department
3-24-17 Hongo
Bunkyo-ku, Tokyo, Japan 113-8719
Tel: 3 3817 5680; Fax: 3 3815 6776
E-mail: fd@igaku-shoin.co.jp

UK, Europe, Scandinavia, Middle East
Elsevier Science
Customer Service Department
Foots Cray High Street
Sidcup, Kent
DA14 5HP, UK
Tel: 44 (0) 208 308 5760
Fax: 44 (0) 181 308 5702
E-mail: cservice@harcourt.com

Singapore, Malaysia, Thailand, Philippines, Indonesia, Vietnam, Pacific Rim, Korea
Elsevier Science Asia
583 Orchard Road
#09/01, Forum
Singapore 238884
Tel: 65-737-3593; Fax: 65-753-2145

Australia, New Zealand
Elsevier Science Australia
Customer Service Department
STM Division
Locked Bag 16
St. Peters, New South Wales, 2044
Australia
Tel: 61 02 9517-8999
Fax: 61 02 9517-2249
E-mail: stmp@harcourt.com.au
www.harcourt.com.au

Mexico and Central America
ETM SA de CV
Calle de Tula 59
Colonia Condesa
06140 Mexico DF, Mexico
Tel: 52-5-5553-6657
Fax: 52-5-5211-8468
E-mail:
editoresdetextosmex@prodigy.net.mx

Brazil
Tecmedd Importadora E Distribuidora
De Livros Ltda.
Avenida Maurílio Biagi, 2850
City Ribeirão, Ribeirão Preto – SP –
Brasil
CEP: 14021-000
Tel: 0800 992236; Fax: (16) 3993-9000
E-mail: tecmedd@tecmedd.com.br

India, Bangladesh, Pakistan, Sri Lanka
Elsevier Health Sciences Division
Customer Service Department
17A/1, Main Ring Road
Lajpat Nagar IV
New Delhi – 110024, India
Tel: 91 11 2644 7160-64
Fax: 91 11 2644 7156
E-mail: esindia@vsnl.net

To our families, for their understanding and support, and to your patients, who endure the challenges presented by this disease.

Contents

Preface

The organization of this book reflects the stepwise evaluation and treatment of the patient with breast cancer. It emphasizes the importance of early detection, but highlights the increasing emphasis on risk assessment and reduction. The treatment of breast cancer has evolved from radical mastectomy for all patients to a tailored approach with the selective use of multiple treatment modalities in accordance with the patient's risk of recurrence.

Despite shifting efforts to identify high-risk patients and address risk with preemptive strategies, there remains a worldwide educational challenge to adopt early-detection guidelines for screening. Although there is continuing progress in implementing mortality-reducing screening mammography, as reflected by the increased prevalence of preinvasive breast cancer and by falling breast cancer mortality, the full spectrum of disease is still a challenge to the medical community. The high prevalence of breast cancer continues to drive improvements in prevention, detection, diagnostic evaluation, disease characterization, multimodal therapy, and quality-of-life issues. Providing equal access to these improvements remains a challenge.

One of the most important advances in the understanding of breast cancer has been the identification of genetic mutations, which provides the opportunity to intervene with chemopreventive strategies or surgical procedures to dramatically reduce the risk of cancer. Diagnostic imaging continues to provide increased precision and resolution, resulting in an enhanced ability to preserve tissue and identify otherwise unrecognized disease. Minimally invasive surgery, including sentinel node biopsy, has progressed to a point where the role of the standard axillary dissection has become increasingly limited. The selection of breast conservation patients continues to be refined by improved diagnostic imaging and emerging patterns defined by molecular profiles.

Adjuvant systemic therapy has also become significantly more precise with the improved clarity in the molecular characterization of tumors. New and improved categories of antiestrogen therapies have emerged, along with numerous highly effective chemotherapy regimens, including trastuzumab therapy. Proven as a highly effective drug in the metastatic setting, trastuzumab has recently emerged as one of the most significant advances in the adjuvant therapy of breast cancer, providing dramatic reductions in recurrence and mortality rates for suitable patients. Such advances underscore the importance of understanding breast cancer on the molecular level in order to develop improved therapies. Molecular markers now provide more than prognostic value and have become critical determinants in the selection of adjuvant therapy.

Improved therapies for breast cancer have lessened the physical and psychological burdens of the disease. Immediate reconstruction, microvascular surgery, and tissue expanders have also significantly improved cosmetic outcome. Tissue damage has become less common with minimally invasive surgery and the targeted delivery of radiation therapy. Proactive and preemptive prevention and treatment of lymphedema have helped to control the physical and mental consequences of the more radical treatments that remain necessary for a subset of patients.

It is the goal of this book to identify significant improvements in breast cancer prevention, diagnosis, and treatment and to help accelerate the dispersion of this knowledge to an ever-broadening spectrum of scientists and physicians who are dedicated to the prevention and treatment of one of the most common afflictions to strike women. We wish to thank our distinguished authors for their timely and expert contributions to this effort.

DJW
DPW
CAH
LN

Contributors

Stefan Aebi, MD
Inselspital
Bern, Switzerland
Management of Locoregional Recurrences

Banu Arun, MD
The University of Texas
M.D. Anderson Cancer Center
Houston, Texas
Breast Cancer Risk Assessment and Management

Kristen A. Atkins, MD
University of Virginia
Charlottesville, Virginia
Unusual Breast Histology

Kirby Bland, MD
University of Alabama at Birmingham
Birmingham, Alabama
Anatomy of the Breast, Axilla, and Thoracic Wall

William D. Bloomer, MD, FACR, FACRO
Northwestern University
Feinberg School of Medicine
Chicago, Illinois
Breast Cancer in the Irradiated Breast

David R. Brenin, MD, FACS
University of Virginia
Charlottesville, Virginia
Unusual Breast Histology

John Ralph Broadwater, MD
The University of Arkansas for Medical Sciences
Little Rock, Arkansas
Axillary Staging and Therapeutics

Aman U Buzdar, MD
The University of Texas
M.D. Anderson Cancer Center
Houston, Texas
Endocrine Therapy of Early and Advanced Breast Cancer

Hiram S. Cody III, MD, FACS
Weill Medical College of Cornell University
New York, New York
Breast Cancer in the Previously Augmented Breast

William L. Donegan, MD
Medical College of Wisconsin
Milwaukee, Wisconsin
History of Breast Cancer
Male Breast Cancer

Stephen B. Edge, MD
State University of New York at Buffalo
Buffalo, New York
The Evolving Concept of the Breast Center

Michael J. Edwards, MD
The University of Arkansas for Medical Sciences
Little Rock, Arkansas
Axillary Staging and Therapeutics

Joseph L. Feldman, MD
Northwestern University
Feinberg School of Medicine
Chicago, Illinois
Lymphedema

Geoffrey Fenner, MD, FACS
Evanston Northwestern Healthcare
Evanston, Illinois
Evolution in Breast Reconstruction

RICHARD FINE, MD
University of Tennessee College of Medicine
Chattanooga, Tennessee
Diagnostic Techniques

BRUNO D. FORNAGE, MD
The University of Texas
M.D. Anderson Cancer Center
Houston, Texas
Sonography of Breast Cancer

WILLIAM J. GRANDISHAR, MD
Northwestern University
Feinberg School of Medicine
Houston, Texas
Surveillance Strategies for Breast Cancer Survivors

NEAL HANDEL, MD
University of California Los Angeles
Los Angeles, California
Oncoplastic Surgery of the Breast

EMER O. HANRAHAN, MB, MRCPI
The University of Texas
M.D. Anderson Cancer Center
Houston, Texas
Pregnancy and Breast Cancer

BRYAN T. HENNESSY, MD
The University of Texas
M.D. Anderson Cancer Center
Houston, Texas
Adjuvant Chemotherapy

TARA L. HUSTON, MD
New York Presbyterian Hospital
New York, New York
Image-Guided Ablation for Breast Cancer

RESHMA JAGSI, MD, DPHIL
University of Michigan
Ann Arbor, Michigan
Novel Radiation Therapy Techniques

JACQUELINE SARA JERUSS, MD, PHD
University of Texas
M.D. Anderson Cancer Center
Houston, Texas
Molecular Basis of Breast Cancer

Malcolm Kell, MD
Temple University School of Medicine
Philadelphia, Pennsylvania
Multifocal, Multicentric, and Bilateral Breast Cancer

TIMOTHY KENNEDY, MD
Northwestern University
Feinberg School of Medicine
Chicago, Illinois
Evaluation and Surgical Management of Stage I and II Breast Cancer

DANIEL B. KOPANS, MD, FACR
Harvard Medical School
Boston, Massachusetts
Diagnostic Breast Imaging

HELEN KRONTIRAS, MD
University of Alabama at Birmingham
Birmingham, Alabama
Anatomy of the Breast, Axilla, and Thoracic Wall

HENRY M. KUERER, MD, PHD, FACS
The University of Texas
M.D. Anderson Cancer Center
Houston, Texas
Breast Cancer Risk Assessment and Management

MICHAEL A. LACOMBE, MD
Northwestern University
Feinberg School of Medicine
Chicago, Illinois
Breast Cancer in the Irradiated Breast

HENRY T. LYNCH, MD
Creighton University Medical Center
Omaha, Nebraska
Genetics, Natural History, and DNA-Based Genetic Counseling in Hereditary Breast Cancer

Jane F. Lynch
Creighton University Medical Center
Omaha, Nebraska
Genetics, Natural History, and DNA-Based Genetic Counseling in Hereditary Breast Cancer

Helen Mabry, MD
St. John's Health Center
John Wayne Cancer Institute
Santa Monica, California
Ductal Carcinoma In Situ

Heather R. Macdonald, MD
University of Souther California
Los Angeles, California
Ductal Carcinoma In Situ

Catherine A. Madorin,
Emory University School of Medicine
Atlanta, Georgia
Hormone Therapy and Breast Cancer

Colleen M. McCarthy, MD
Memorial Sloan-Kettering Cancer Center
New York, New York
Breast Cancer in the Previously Augmented Breast

Laura P. McGartland, MD, MS
Northwestern University
Feinberg School of Medicine
Chicago, Illinois
Surveillance Strategies for Breast Cancer Survivors

Babak J. Mehrara, MD
Weill Medical College of Cornell University
New York, New York
Breast Cancer in the Previously Augmented Breast

S. Brenda Moorthy, DO
Comprehensive Breast Center of Arizona
Phoenix, Arizona
Ductal Carcinoma In Situ

Monica Morrow, MD
Temple University School of Medicine
Philadelphia, Pennsylvania
Multifocal, Multicentric, and Bilateral Breast Cancer

Sabin B. Motwani, MD
The University of Texas
M.D. Anderson Cancer Center
Houston, Texas
Radiation Therapy in Early and Advanced Breast Cancer

Thomas A. Mustoe, MD, FACS
Northwestern University Medical School
Chicago, Illinois
Evolution in Breast Reconstruction

Lisa A. Newman, MD, MPH, FACS
University of Michigan
Ann Arbor, Michigan
Locally Advanced Breast Cancer
Breast Cancer and Multiethnic/Multiracial Populations

Jacobo Nurko, MD
The University of Arkansas for Medical Sciences
Little Rock, Arkansas
Axillary Staging and Therapeutics

Lori J. Pierce, MD
University of Michigan
Ann Arbor, Michigan
Novel Radiation Therapy Techniques

Andrea L. Pusic, MD, MHS
Memorial Sloan-Kettering Cancer Center
New York, New York
Breast Cancer in the Previously Augmented Breast

Philip N. Redlich, MD, PhD
Medical College of Wisconsin
Milwaukee, Wisconsin
Male Breast Cancer

Aysegul A. Sahin, MD
University of Texas
M.D. Anderson Cancer Center
Houston, Texas
Pathology of Invasive Breast Cancer

Mitchell Schnall, MD, PhD
University of Pennsylvania Health System
Philadelphia, Pennsylvania
Magnetic Resonance Imaging

Stephen F. Sener, MD
Northwestern University
Feinberg School of Medicine
Chicago, Illinois
Role of Screening in Breast Cancer Mortality Reduction

Ruth Silverman,
Buffalo Grove, Illinois

Melvin J. Silverstein, MD
Keck School of Medicine
University of Southern California
Los Angeles, California
Ductal Carcinoma In Situ
Oncoplastic Surgery of the Breast

Rache M. Simmons, MD
New York Presbyterian Hospital
New York, New York
Image-Guided Ablation for Breast Cancer

Robert A. Smith, PhD
American Cancer Society
Atlanta, Georgia
Role of Screening in Breast Cancer Mortality Reduction

Eric A. Strom, MD
The University of Texas
M.D. Anderson Cancer Center
Houston, Texas
Radiation Therapy in Early and Advanced Breast Cancer

Toncred Marya Styblo, MD
Emory University School of Medicine
Atlanta, Georgia
Hormone Therapy and Breast Cancer

Richard L Theriault, DO, MBA
The University of Texas
M.D. Anderson Cancer Center
Houston, Texas
Pregnancy and Breast Cancer

Vicente Valero, MD
The University of Texas
M.D. Anderson Cancer Center
Houston, Texas
Adjuvant Chemotherapy

Victor G. Vogel, MD, MHS, FACP
University of Pittsburgh School of Medicine
Magee-Womens Hospital
Pittsburgh, Pennsylvania
Epidemiology of Breast Cancer

Irene Wapnir, MD
Stanford University School of Medicine
Stanford, California
Management of Locoregional Recurrences

David J. Winchester, MD, FACS
Northwestern University
Feinberg School of Medicine
Chicago, Illinois
Evaluation and Surgical Management of Stage I and II Breast Cancer
Lymphedema

David P. Winchester, MD, FACS
Northwestern University
Feinberg School of Medicine
Chicago, Illinois
Staging and Histologic Grading

William C. Wood, MD
Emory University School of Medicine
Atlanta, Georgia
Hormone Therapy and Breast Cancer

1

History of Breast Cancer

WILLIAM L. DONEGAN

The story of breast cancer is told in the acts and artifacts of the human struggle against disease. It is an epic tale that follows the concepts of illness from the work of evil spirits or of offended gods to the results of identifiable physical causes, and the healing arts from mysticism to the tools of modern science. The following is a brief history of breast cancer in the Western world.

PREHISTORY AND THE ANCIENT WORLD

Prior to recorded history, life was undoubtedly short, and as cancer is predominantly a disease of maturity one suspects that cancer was a poor competitor among causes of mortality. The study of primitive peoples indicates that for the ill, rituals, potions, and recipes at the hands of magicians, witch doctors, and folk healers were the usual recourses. In ancient Babylon (2100–689 BC) it was common practice to place the ailing in public places for the recommendations of passersby, but professional healers were also recognized. The Code of Hammurabi, inscribed on a pillar in Babylon, indicated that healers were paid fees for their services and were penalized for surgical deaths with amputation of their hands.[1]

Before the third millennium BC, physicians had learned the futility of treating certain tumors of the breast. Among the eight extant Egyptian medical papyri, *The Edwin Smith Surgical Papyrus* is believed to contain the first reference to breast cancer (Figure 1–1). This surgical text, penned in hieratic script, is the incomplete and fragmented copy of an original document that probably dates back to the pyramid age of Egypt (3000–2500 BC) and was possibly written by Imhotep, the physician-architect who practiced medicine and designed the step pyramid in Egypt in the 30th century BC.[2] It provides the earliest references to suturing of wounds and to cauterization with fire drills. More pertinently, it includes the diagnosis and treatment of eight cases of ailments of the "breast," meaning of the bones and soft tissues

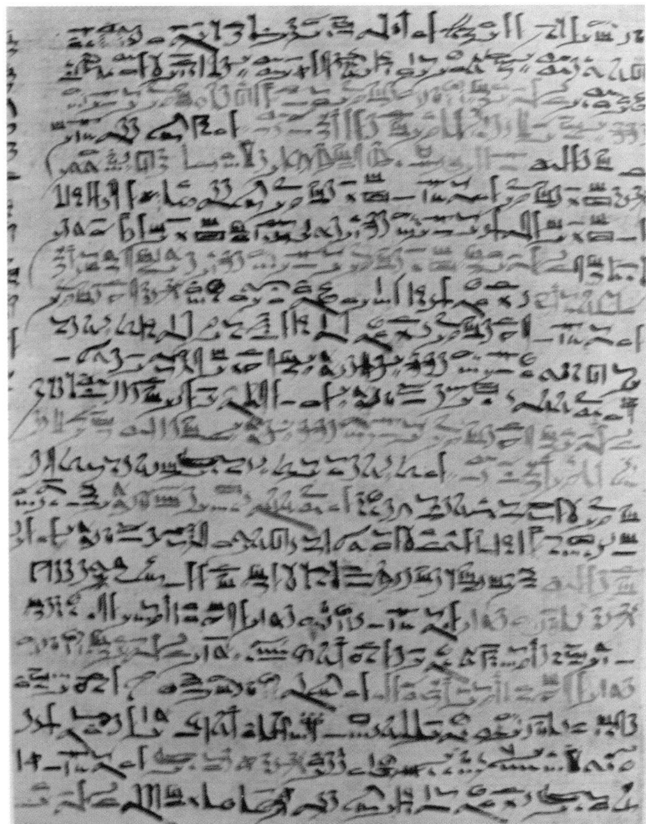

Figure 1–1. Column VIII of *The Edwin Smith Surgical Papyrus*, a copy of the first document believed to describe cancer of the breast, circa 3000 BC. Used with permission from The Classics of Surgery Library.[2]

of the anterior thorax, all in men and most due to injuries. One of the five cases relating to soft tissues (Case 45) describes "bulging tumors" in the breast. The author writes that if the tumors have spread over the breast, are cool to the touch, and are bulging, there is no treatment. Whether this case was a rare cancer of the male breast is conjectural, but in stark contrast to the physician's active recommendations for the other cases, he recognized this one as sinister; and his conviction that no treatment would help appears to have been based on established practice.

GREEK AND ROMAN PERIOD (460 BC–475 AD)

Ancient Greece was pervaded by a rich mythology based on a belief in close associations between humans and gods. Historians speculate that the god of medicine, Aesculapius, may have had origin in a physician who lived around the time of the siege of Troy (≈1300 BC) and to whom were attributed miracles of healing. In the *Iliad*, Homer mentioned Aesculapius' two sons as "good physicians" who had come to join the siege.[3] On the seal of the American College of Surgeons, Aesculapius is pictured seated, holding his staff entwined with a serpent, the symbol of life and wisdom. Early Greeks sought cures by sleeping in the abaton at the temples of Aesculapius and enjoying the associated baths and recreations, forerunners of modern health spas. Votive offerings in the form of breasts found at such sites offer evidence that some came hoping for cure of breast disease (Figure 1–2).

Greek medicine and surgery became the most sophisticated of its time. In the course of his conquests, Alexander the Great of Macedonia (356–323 BC) founded the city of Alexandria on the Nile delta in 332 BC, and a famous medical school arose there around 300 BC. The library at Alexandria was the largest of its time, housing more than 700,000 scrolls. Many prominent Greek and Roman physicians studied, taught, and practiced in Alexandria. The study of anatomy was based on dissection of human bodies and surgery flourished; vascular ligatures were used.

Physicians of the Hellenistic period provide vivid accounts of breast cancer. The Greek term "karkinoma" was used to describe malignant growths and "scirrhous" to describe particularly hard, solid tumors. "Cacoethes" referred to an early or a probable malignancy. A "hidden" cancer was one not ulcerating the skin. In an anecdote, Herodotus (484–425 BC), historian of the wars between Greece and Persia, claimed that Democedes, a Persian physician living in Greece, cured the wife of Persian King Darius of a breast tumor that had ulcerated and spread.

Hippocrates (460–375 BC), whose legacy, the *Corpus Hippocraticum*, may have been the work of more than one person, was the most prominent of Greek physicians. He maintained that every disease was distinctive and arose from natural causes, not from gods or spirits.[4] He also believed in the power of nature to heal and in a humoral origin of disease. In his view, a balance of the four bodily fluids, blood, phlegm, yellow bile, and black bile (later linked to sanguine, phlegmatic, choleric, and melancholy dispositions by Galen) was necessary for good health. Hippocrates described cases of breast cancer in detail. One of his case histories was of a woman of Abdera who had a carcinoma of the breast with bloody discharge from her nipple. Attaching a beneficial effect to the bleeding, he noted that when the discharge stopped, she died. Similarly, Hippocrates associated cessation of menstrual bleeding with breast cancer and sought to restore menstruation in young sufferers. His detailed description of the inexorable course of advancing breast cancer rings true today. He said that

Figure 1–2. Votive offerings from an Etruscan temple include a vagina, a uterus, an ear, an eye, and a breast (lower central). Reproduced with permission from Lyons AS and Petrucelli RJ.[6]

hard tumors appear in the breast, become increasingly firm, contain no pus, and spread to other parts of the body. As the disease progresses, the patient develops bitter taste, refuses food, develops pain that shoots from the breast to the neck and shoulder blades, complains of thirst, and becomes emaciated. From this point death was certain. He advised no treatment for hidden breast cancers because treatment was futile and shortened the patient's life.

In the ascendant Roman Empire, physicians were guided largely by Greek medicine. Around 30 AD, the Roman physician Aulus Cornelius Celsus (42 BC–37 AD) noted that the breasts of women were frequent sites of cancer. Celsus described breast cancer in his manuscript, *De Medicina*, and defined four stages. The first was cacoethes, followed by carcinoma without skin ulceration, carcinoma with ulceration, and, finally, "thymium," an advanced exophytic and sometimes bleeding lesion, the appearance of which suggested to him the flowers of thyme. Celsus recommended excision for the cacoethes but no treatment for other stages. In situations of uncertainty, the tumor was treated first with caustics, and if the symptoms improved, it was a cacoethes; if they worsened, it was a carcinoma. Some masses for which treatment was successful might have been fibroadenomas, phyllodes tumors, or even tuberculosis.

Leonides, a surgeon of the Alexandrian school, described surgical removal of breast cancers during this time.[4] Leonides said that with the patient supine he cut into the sound part of the breast and used a technique of alternately cutting and cauterizing with hot irons to control bleeding. The resection was carried through normal tissues wide of the tumor and customized to the extent of involvement. The operation was concluded with a general cauterization to destroy any residual disease. Poultices were then applied to the wound to promote healing. He explained that excision was used selectively for tumors in the upper part of the breast of limited extent, and he specifically advised against surgery if the whole breast was hardened or if the tumor was fixed to the chest wall. Leonides was perhaps the first to record that breast cancers spread to the axilla. Complete and thorough excision of breast malignancies has been a cardinal principle of surgery since the time of Leonides.

The teachings of the Greek physician, Galen of Pergamum (129–200 BC), on the subject of breast cancer reached far beyond his time. Born of a wealthy and educated family in Asia Minor, he traveled and studied widely. Galen became surgeon to gladiators in Pergamum and finally practiced in Rome, attending the emperor Marcus Aurelius. His vast experience, clinical acumen, investigative approach to knowledge, and prolific, authoritative writings (400 treatises) gained Galen enormous respect. For the next 1,500 years, Galen's teachings guided medical practice, and his animal dissections provided the bases for human anatomy and physiology.

Galen revered Hippocrates and adopted his humoral theory of disease. In Galen's view, breast cancer was a systemic disease caused by an excess of black bile in the blood (ie, melancholia). Black bile was formed in the liver from blood elements and absorbed in the spleen; malfunction of either of these organs caused an excess of black bile, which thickened the blood, and where black bile accumulated, carcinoma developed as hard, non-tender tumors that ulcerated if the bile was particularly acrid. Like Hippocrates, he noted that carcinomas were predisposed to accumulate in the breasts of women who had ceased to menstruate, a recurring theme and doubtless a reference to the frequency of cancer in postmenopausal women. This observation supported Galen's belief that menstruation, and the practice of bleeding, served to clear the body of excess black bile. He likened the dilated veins that radiated from carcinomas to the legs of a crab; as a result, the crab became a symbol for cancer. Leonides had also likened cancers to crabs, but rather because the tenacious adherence to surrounding tissues mimicked the crab's pinchers. For early cancers, Galen recommended purging, bleeding, diet, and topicals. Ulcerating cancers were treated with caustics or cleansed and treated with zinc oxide.

In operating for breast cancer, Galen's approach was less modern than that of Leonides before him. Galen condemned the use of ligatures, and although he was aware of the dangers of excessive blood loss, he preferred to let the blood run unchecked and to express the dark, dilated veins in order to rid them of the morbid black bile. The cancer was removed at the boundary between diseased and healthy parts, sparing the cautery out of concern for destroying too much tissue. After Galen, medicine languished into a contented observance of his teachings, and the Middle Ages intervened, temporarily halting further medical progress.

MIDDLE AGES (476–1500 AD)

The Middle Ages, a period of roughly 1,000 years, began with the collapse of the Roman Empire in 476 and ended with the Renaissance and discovery of the New World in 1492. With the Middle Ages came feudalism, bubonic plague, crusades, and the age of faith. Papal influence spread in the form of the Holy Roman Empire, and human dissection was prohibited by Papal decree; opposition to church doctrine constituted heresy. To save his soul, the astronomer Copernicus (1473–1543 AD) was forced to rescind his thesis that the earth circled the sun rather than the reverse, and the physician Michael Servetus (1511–1553), discoverer of the pulmonary circulation, was burned alive for heresy. Meanwhile, monastic scribes in Christian Europe quietly preserved medical knowledge, principally that of Galen, by copying and illuminating surviving ancient manuscripts, manuscripts that were in little demand during an era of widespread illiteracy. Monks dispensed folk remedies, and surgery was discouraged. Amputation of the breast was depicted by the church as a form of torture in the story of St. Agatha, the patron saint of breast disease[5] (Figure 1–3). Many miraculous cures were attributed to saints. Faith healing by the laying on of hands was among the remedies, a practice that endured to recent times. Folk medicine included application of fresh bisected puppies and cats.

After the death of the prophet Muhammad (570–632 AD), the rise of Islam resulted in the Arab conquest of the southern shores of the Mediterranean from Persia to Spain, bringing to an end the medical center in Alexandria. Medical documents that survived were translated into Arabic for study and preserved; translated later from Arabic into Latin, the language of medicine in Europe, they re-entered the continent. In addition to preserving the past, Arabic medicine was noted for expertise in pharmacy and for establishing fine hospitals. Among the most influential physicians of this period were Avicenna (980–1037 AD), the Jewish physician Maimonides (1135–1204 AD) and Albucasis (936–1013).[6] Avicenna's reputation rivaled that of Galen, but he had no new insights about breast cancer. Albucasis in Moorish Spain favored the cautery and caustic applications for treatment of breast cancer but admitted that he had never cured a case of breast cancer and knew of no one who had. Caustic paste (a mixture of zinc chloride, stibnite, and *Sanguinaria canadensis*) was used for treatment of breast cancer in the United States as late as the 1950s.[7] The paste was applied to the involved breast to cause progressive tissue necrosis, which was then cut away or allowed to slough and to heal by granulation. Continued use of charms, prayers, medicaments, and caustics in conjunction with surgery and modern methods is a reminder that treatments for breast cancer progressed through history not by substitution, but by addition.

Figure 1–3. Saint Agatha, the patron saint of breast disease, was martyred for her Christian beliefs. Her torture included amputation of the breasts shown here in a painting by Anthony Van Dyck.[5]

In the late Middle Ages, Henri de Mondeville (1260–1320 AD), surgeon to the king of France, refined Galen's black bile theory with a distinction between black bile from the liver, which caused a hard tumor in the breast (a sclerosis), and twice combusted black bile derived from breakdown of the other three other body humors, which caused a true cancer. He described true breast cancer as ulcerated with thick margins and having an offensive odor. The treatment: diet and purging, with operation only if the cancer could be completely excised; de Mondeville appreciated that incomplete removal often resulted in a non-healing wound.[8]

RENAISSANCE (SIXTEENTH TO EIGHTEENTH CENTURIES)

The Middle Ages ended with the Renaissance. This period of approximately 200 years, also known as The Enlightenment, saw a rejection of medieval values and a rebirth of interest in secular art, in science, and in exploration of the world and the human body. With the Renaissance came badly needed formal training for physicians. The University of Salerno, founded around 1200 AD, was the first organized medical school in Europe. Free of clerical influence and progressive for its time, Salerno served as the precursor of prominent schools of medicine in France, England, and elsewhere on the continent. The Royal College of Physicians was established in London in 1518, and the first medical journal, the *Ephemerides*, appeared in 1670.

Surgeons became more respectable. Traditionally unlettered craftsmen whose operations were directed by physicians, surgeons became independent practitioners. Incorporated as barber-surgeons in England since 1461, surgeons were officially separated from barber guilds in 1745. The French Academie de Chirurgie, established in 1731, produced the first journal for surgeons, *Memoires*, which in 1757 published Henri LeDran's thesis that breast cancer had a local origin, providing an impetus for surgical cure.[9]

The Renaissance in medicine brought a critical reexamination of anatomy and physiology and a decline of Galen's authority. Publication of Andreas Vesalius's *De Humani Corporis Fabrica* in 1543 marked the beginning. This volume of anatomical drawings, based on the young professor of surgery at Padua's own dissections of human cadavers, illustrated the errors of Galen's anatomy and stimulated further interest in human anatomy.[10] The *Fabrica* provided no useful details of the female breast. However, 300 years later, Sir Astley P. Cooper (1768–1841), surgeon to Guy's Hospital in London, illustrated with desiccated specimens the suspensory ligaments of the breast that bear his name. The Parisian anatomist Marie-Philibert-Constant Sappey (1810–1896) illustrated the lymphatics of the breast, a name that endures as Sappey's subareolar plexus.[11,12]

Each anatomic discovery generated new theories about breast cancer, but to little advantage. John Hunter (1728–1793), the father of investigative surgery, conceived that coagulation of lymph rather than black bile was responsible for carcinoma of the breast and the associated cancerous nodes. Boerhaave of Leyden (1668–1738) postulated that neural fluid "liquor nervorum" might be the instigator of breast cancer, whereas others believed that inspissated milk within the mammary ducts generated cancers. Trauma to the breast was believed to cause leakage into the tissues, which created irritation, induration, and malignant change. Observing the rapid growth of ulcerating breast cancers, Claude-Nicholas le Cat (1700–1768) in Rouen postulated that exposure to air was a stimulant to cancers, a tenacious idea persisting in some laity today. Anecdotes of multiple-affected family members supported the suspicion that breast cancer was infectious long before the hereditary aspect of the disease became known in the twentieth century. The deadly spread of malignancy was attributed to circulating humors or to a general diathesis. The suspicion of a "cancer prone" personality lingers but remains unconfirmed by modern psychological research.[13]

Breast lumps continued to fuel controversy about the nature of a "schirrous," the hard tumor that generated concern for patient and physician. Whether schirrous was benign, a stage of cancer, or a precursor that became cancer by a process of "acrimony" remained in doubt. Observation or immediate treatment divided opinions. Opinions on the worth of surgery varied. Extended survival of occasional untreated cases, coupled with the considerable risk and poor results of mastectomy, supported a nihilistic attitude among many physicians. Others shared the opinion of Nicolaes Tulp (1593–1674) of Amsterdam, who saw the need for early surgery. "The sole remedy is a timely operation," he said.[4] For the most part, the fearsome prospect of an operation was delayed until bulky growth, pain, or ulceration made obvious both the diagnosis and the need. Informed surgeons recognized tumor attachment to the chest wall, sternal pain due to deep invasion or involvement of the internal mammary nodes (described by Petrus Camper in 1777), poor general health, or a diathesis-revealing "melancholy" appearance as contraindications to mastectomy.

Without anesthesia or antisepsis, mastectomies were a painful and dangerous ordeal customarily carried out in the patient's home. The procedure varied from impalement of the breast with needles and ropes for traction followed by swift amputation through the base, leaving a large open wound as illustrated by Johann Scultetus (1595–1645) in his *Armamentarium Chirurgicum*, to the alternative of incising the skin and enucleating the tumor by hand.[4] The prevailing opinion was to leave the wound open to minimize the risk of infection. From 2 to 10 minutes were required for the operation, depending on the technique. Ligatures, if used, were led out through the wound to be withdrawn later, after necrosis or infection loosened them. Painful re-explorations of the wound on subsequent days were performed to inspect for infection or to remove additional tumor; the major threats were secondary hemorrhage or potentially fatal infection. In various illustrations, the patient's hands were tied behind her back or assistants restrained her while another assistant caught jets of blood in a pan. A cauterizing iron provided hemostasis, and steam issued from the wound where it seared the flesh. The company included a dour, attending physician and often an anguished family standing in witness. Students of breast cancer should not miss the touching account of such an operation in Scotland told by John Brown.[14] The rigors of surgery were such that alternative treatment with compression of the breast using metal plates or strapping, not entirely devoid of pain and occasional necrosis, continued to survive into the nineteenth century.

Expert surgeons operating in major centers during these times enlarged mastectomies to include all morbid parts. In Paris, Jean Louis Petit (1674–1750) removed both the breast and diseased nodes in his operations, and in 1774, Bernhard Perilhe reported removing the pectoralis major muscle as well. A healed wound was the customary end point for declaring a surgeon's success; few bothered with further follow-up. In a report by Richard Wiseman (1622–1676), surgeon to Charles II, among twelve mastectomies, two patients (17%) died from the operation, eight died shortly afterwards from progressive cancer, and two of the 12 were declared "cured" for undisclosed lengths of time.[4]

NINETEENTH CENTURY

From the oncologic standpoint, the nineteenth century was truly a giant step forward. Major advances were made in human pathology and in the safety of surgery. Hand washing was promoted by the Hungarian physician Ignac Semmelweis (1818–1865) and by Oliver Wendell Holmes, MD (1809–1894), Professor of Anatomy and Physiology at Harvard University. Building on Louis Pasteur's (1822–1895) discovery of "putrefying" bacteria, Joseph Lister (1827–1912) in Glasgow introduced surgical antisepsis with carbolic acid spray in 1867.[15] Adoption of aseptic techniques (ie, steam sterilization) first by Ernst von Bergmann of Berlin in 1886, the surgical mask by the Pole Johannes von Mikuliez-Radecki in 1886, and sterile rubber surgical gloves by William S. Halsted in 1890 further reduced contamination.[16] Successful demonstration of general anesthesia by William T. Morton in Boston in 1846 allowed unprecedented development of surgery; operations became more acceptable, and for the first time surgeons could concentrate on precision rather than haste. Blood transfusions became safe after 1900 when Karl Landsteiner in Austria discovered blood groups. All of the current technology for treatment of breast cancer had their beginnings in this century; only chemotherapy remained for development in the years to come.

The microscope was the key to progress in pathology. Building on Anton van Leewenhoek's (1674–1723) work with lenses, perfection of the compound achromatic microscope in Germany opened the world of microscopic anatomy, and Germany was the center of this new science under the leadership of Johannes Müller at the University of Berlin.

Early in the century, the microscopic work of Matthias Schleiden (1804–1881), a botanist at the University of Jena, and of Theodor Schwann (1810–1882), working in Müller's laboratory, established that both plants and animals were composed of living cells with the nucleus as the essential feature. Robert Hooke (1655–1703) earlier had coined the word "cell" from the structure he saw in cork. "The cells are organisms," said Schwann, "and animals as well as plants are aggregates of these organisms…" These two researchers destroyed the existing humoral and the competing solidistic concepts of tissue composition. Johannes Müller (1801–1859) was first to report that cancers also were composed of living cells. In his landmark publication of 1838, *Uber den feinen Bau und die Formen der krankhaften Geschwülste*, Müller noted the similarity of cells in a "scirrhus" of the breast and its metastases in the ribs and noted that cancer cells had lost the proportions of normal cells[17] (Figure 1–4). Rudolph Virchow, also of Berlin, Müller's former student and the founder of cellular pathology, is responsible for the dictum that "all cells come from cells." His lectures, *Die Cellularpathologie*, published in 1858, laid to rest the notion of spontaneous generation of living cells from a liquid "blastema." But Virchow did not make the connection between migrating malignant cells and metastases; he thought that axillary metastases arose from cells in the nodes responding to "hurtful ingredients" or "poisonous matter" from the cancer in the breast.[18] Müller was perhaps the first to suspect that spread of malignant cells constituted the mechanism of metastasis, later confirmed by the microscopic work of Carl Thiersch (1822–1895) and Wilhelm von Waldeyer (1836–1921).[4] These insights supported the concept that breast cancer spread from a local origin.

Noteworthy clinical observations were also being made. Alfred Velpeau was the first to describe breast cancer en cuirasse, the deadly form that spreads across the chest like a breast plate.[19] Velpeau's *Traite des maladies du sein,* published in 1854, was a comprehensive review of breast disease of the time. Across the English Channel in London, Sir James Paget made a brief (1,050 words) but enduring report in 1874 describing changes on the nipple that preceded breast cancer and continue to bear his name. He said, "… certain chronic affections of the skin of the nipple and areola are very often succeeded by the formation of sirrhous cancer in the mammary gland…within at the most two years, and usually within one year."[20] Paget's observation remains as valuable today as when it was first made.

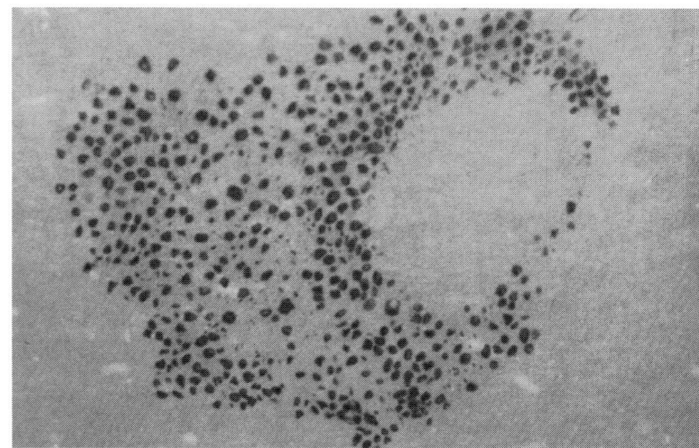

Figure 1–4. Figure 9, Table I, from Johannes Müller's *Uber den feinen Bau und der Formen dei Krankhafte Geschwülste*, 1838, illustrating for the first time the cellular structure of breast cancer. Reproduced from Müller J.[17]

Charles Moore (1821–1870) at the Middlesex Hospital in London deserves credit for the en bloc principle of resection. Moore was convinced that the piecemeal mastectomies of his day spread the "elements" of cancer in the surgical wound and accounted for the local reappearance of cancer in, or adjacent to, the scar. In 1867 he published a strong argument for removal of the whole breast intact in every case.[21] He also recommended removal of axillary nodes and the pectoral muscles if they were involved. William M. Banks in Liverpool carried mastectomy a step further in 1882 by practicing routine removal of axillary lymph nodes.[22]

Similar initiatives were occurring in Germany. Ernst G.F. Küster (1839–1922) in Berlin was performing routine axillary clearance and reported that it virtually eliminated recurrences in the axilla. In 1875 Richard von Volkmann (1830–1889) was routinely removing the pectoralis major fascia, and Küster's assistant Lothar Heidenhain (1860–1940) held the muscle itself suspect. Their microscopic studies of mastectomy specimens showed extension of cancer to the deep pectoral fascia, and occasionally to the muscle itself, when it had not been suspected. Samuel W. Gross at Jefferson Medical College in Philadelphia (1837–1879) attributed a 3-year survival of 19.4% to routinely removing not only the whole breast but the pectoralis fascia and axillary contents.[4]

The events in Germany influenced William S. Halsted (1852–1922), Professor of Surgery at Johns Hopkins Hospital in Baltimore, to devise what became known as the radical mastectomy. He reported the operation in 1894 almost simultaneously with a similar report by Willy Meyer in New York.[23] Through a large "tear-drop" incision, Halsted removed en bloc the breast complete with its skin, the axillary lymph nodes, "a part, at least" of the pectoralis major muscle (the sternal portion) and "usually" cleared the supraclavicular region. Halsted had adopted this "complete" operation 5 years earlier, and emphasized that the pectoralis major muscle must be removed in all cases to obtain a secure tumor-free deep surgical margin. He explained that von Volkmann had removed the pectoral muscles in 38 cases with reduction in local recurrences. As Moore before him, Halsted wrote that the crux of the operation was "to remove in one piece all of the suspected tissues" lest the wound become infected by the division of tissues or lymphatics invaded by the disease, and lest shreds or pieces of cancerous tissue be overlooked in a piecemeal extirpation. It is clear from Halsted's descriptions that the supraclavicular clearance initially was a removal of tissues superior to the axillary vessels in the course of the axillary dissection, later a formal dissection through a cervical incision and ultimately an excursion that he abandoned. The complete operation resulted in a large open wound left to heal by granulation. Two years later he began to close the wound with a split-thickness skin graft, a technique developed by Thiersch (Figure 1–5). Eventually primary closure of skin became more popular.

Whether radical mastectomy resulted in improved local control is unclear. Halsted recognized "local" as recurrences in the surgical area within 3 years of operation (6% in his cases); "regionary" recurrences, by his definition, appeared after 3 years or in the skin away from the scar. The German literature did not distinguish local from regionary recurrences. By counting both, and making the unlikely assumptions that cases were comparable and had equal periods of follow-up, his recurrence rate was 20% compared to 55 to 82% for his German counterparts. Halsted disregarded that local and/or regionary recurrences totaled 58% when von Volkmann had removed the pectoralis major muscle and 60% when he had not, a negligible difference.

Halsted had no surgical deaths despite having "old" patients. "Their average age is nearly 55 years," he said. "They are no longer very active members of society." This comment is strange to modern ears, but the average life span at the time was 47 years. For fear of spreading cancer with a biopsy, diagnosis was almost always clinical, established histologically after the operation. In doubtful cases Halsted said, "The excision of a specimen for

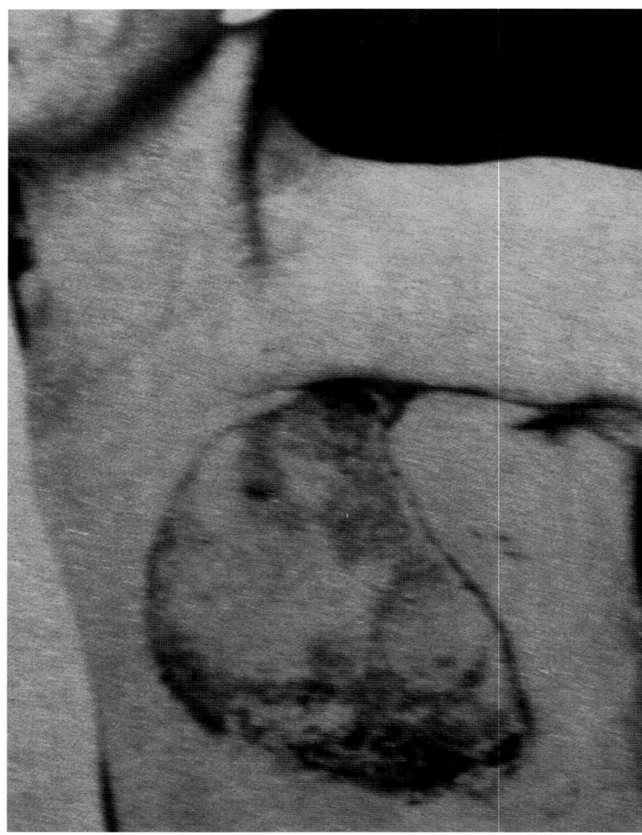

Figure 1–5. William S. Halsted's radical mastectomy. A case pictured in 1912. The operation resulted in a large wound closed with skin grafts. Reproduced with permission from the Classics of surgery library. Surgical papers. William Stewart Halsted. Vol. 2. Special Edition. Birmingham (AB): L. B. Adams Jr. 1984; Figure 2, Plate LX. p. 82.

macroscopic or microscopic is never resorted to except just before operation."[24]

Radical surgery had intellectual support from W.S. Handley's theory of permeation, which held that breast cancer spread centrifugally in continuity, and lymph nodes provided mechanical barriers. Blood vascular spread was insignificant; tumor emboli were destroyed by clot.[25] Halsted's operation was used, with mixed results, for the next 80 years.

Cushman D. Haagensen (d 1990) was both a staunch supporter and a critic of radical mastectomy.[19] His book *Diseases of the Breast,* published in 1956, is a classic. Haagensen's careful analysis of cases treated at Presbyterian Hospital in New York City resulted in eight "criteria of inoperability" to discourage inappropriate use of the operation. He also standardized physical breast examination and originated the Columbia Clinical Classification (CCC) staging system. After the CCC, staging systems became increasingly sophisticated and eventuated in the current Tumor, Node, Metastasis system initially adopted in 1954 by the International Union Against Cancer. Prior to randomized clinical trials, staging provided the principal means for comparing different methods of treatment.

As the nineteenth century came to a close, mastectomy appeared better than no treatment but still cured less often than not. The actuarial survival of Halsted's first fifty cases 5 years from the first symptom (40.4%) was greater than twice that of untreated patients in the Middlesex Hospital Charity Ward in London admitted between 1805 and 1933, which was 18%.[26,27]

Two events of this time were momentous for the future treatment of breast cancer. The first was the discovery of x-rays, and the second was the discovery that breast cancer was hormone dependent. Discovery of x-rays by Wilhelm Conrad Röntgen in Würzburg in 1895 provided the basis for radiotherapy and mammography. The mysterious ray, designated "x," not only penetrated tissues but also killed cancers. One year after Röntgen's discovery, x-rays were used to treat three cases of breast cancer, two by Hermann Goeht in Hamburg and one by Emile Herman Grubbé in Chicago.[4] All three had advanced, inoperable cancers and died shortly afterwards. With the development of dosimetry, improvements in instrumentation and appropriate safeguards, radiation therapy became an effective local treatment of inoperable cancers, and a postoperative (and sometimes preoperative) supplement to mastectomy that ultimately enabled breast-conserving surgery. The discovery of radium in 1898 by Pierre and Marie Curie added interstitial radiation to therapeutic options. Geoffrey Langdon Keynes in London (1932) used radium as the sole treatment of operable cases.[28] The obvious benefit of ionizing irradiation was in reducing the bulk of large cancers and in reducing recurrence in treated fields. An inferred influence on survival proved elusive.

The hormonal treatment of breast cancer began with oophorectomy. In 1899 Albert Schinzinger (1827–1911) in Freiburg commented on the poor prognosis of young women with breast cancer and proposed castration to age them and slow down the malignant growth. Independent of this suggestion, George Thomas Beatson (1848–1933) of Glasgow performed the first castration for breast cancer 7 years later. Beatson knew by his studies of lactation that castration or rebreeding of cows shortly after they calved prolonged milk production, both measures having in common the interruption of ovarian function. Since the hyperplastic cells of lactation decomposed into milk, he reasoned that castration might make the hyperplastic cells of breast malignancy do so as well. The reasoning was wrong, but the result was gratifying. In 1896 he reported temporary tumor regression after oophorectomy in three cases of advanced breast cancer. Beatson's discovery established the palliative value of oophorectomy, and for a period it became a regular adjuvant to mastectomy by some surgeons.[29] Secondary endocrine surgery with adrenalectomy and hypophysectomy developed as sequels to oophorectomy, but in time endocrine surgery was replaced by hormone therapy (Henry Starling described hormones in 1905) and, ultimately, by pharmacologic methods of reducing estrogen production or its effects with luteinizing hormone-releasing hormone agonists, estrogen receptor modulators and aromatase inhibitors. Discovery of intracellular estrogen receptors (ER) in breast cancers by Elwood Jensen in Chicago in 1967 was another milestone in hormone therapy, permitting patients who could benefit from hormone therapy to be distinguished from those who could not.[30]

TWENTIETH CENTURY

The next 100 years resulted in a retreat from radical surgery and the introduction of mammography and chemotherapy. Research confirmed a hereditary component of breast cancer. As important as all else came a demand for scientific evidence to support claims of efficacy and to supplant the anecdotes and polemics of the past. Cooperative groups of clinician investigators amassed large numbers of patients for study, and randomized, controlled clinical trials with sophisticated statistical analysis of data became commonplace. Breast cancer was recognized as a major health problem in the Western world, stimulating a concerted effort against it.

In the early decades, many sought to improve the results of radical surgery with "extended" radical mastectomies. Margottini and Veronesi in Milan, Caseres in Peru, and Urban and Sugarbaker in the United States removed the internal mammary nodes. Dahl-Iverson in Copenhagen removed the supraclavicular and internal mammary nodes and Wangenstein in Minnesota added removal of mediastinal nodes. Other than showing that extra-axillary nodes often contained metastases and that their removal improved regional tumor control, cures were not increased, and these extensions were eventually abandoned in favor of chest wall and regional irradiation. As Handley's permeation theory lost credence, D. H. Patey and R. S. Handley in London felt justified in preserving the pectoralis major muscle unless it was directly involved by cancer, an operation they called the "conservative" radical mastectomy. With the support of surgeons in the United States such as Hugh Auchincloss Jr. in New York, this operation eventually prevailed in 1979 as the "modified" radical mastectomy.[31]

Mammography, unarguably the most important advance to date in the detection of breast cancer, developed in parallel with surgery. Even early physicians had recognized that small breast cancers were the most curable. Mammography allowed many breast cancers to be detected when clinically occult, including ductal carcinoma in situ, which was regularly curable. Film-screen mammography involved penetrating the breast with x-rays to activate a rare earth screen that glowed in response. This screen exposed a transparent, photosensitive film in the same cassette which, when developed, provided an image in various shades of gray for interpretation. In Robert Egan's *History of Mammography,* he gives Stafford L. Warren at Rochester Memorial Hospital in Rochester, New York, credit for early explorations of mammography beginning in 1926 but also mentioned that the German surgeon, Albert Salomon, performed studies with radiographs of breasts resected for carcinoma as early as 1913 before his work was apparently interrupted by World War I.[32] The technique met resistance despite such advocates as Jacob Gershon-Cohen in Philadelphia and Charles M. Gros in Strasbourg until Egan, while a radiologist at M. D. Anderson Hospital in Houston, Texas, developed the soft tissue technique that allowed mammography to move forward.

An early randomized trial of screening with mammography and physical examination in New York by Sam Shapiro and Philip Strax in 1963 demonstrated that 30% of cancers could be detected by mammography alone, and deaths from cancers among screened women were reduced 30% compared with unscreened. After a host of radiologists was trained in the technique of mammography, a demonstration project, the Breast Cancer Detection Demonstration Project (BCDDP), begun in 1973 and sponsored by the National Cancer Institute and the American Cancer Society (ACS), screened 283,222 asymptomatic women. The BCDDP established the feasibility of mass population screening. Multiple randomized clinical trials of screening followed, showing that regular mammograms could detect 85 to 90% of asymptomatic breast cancers with a reduction of breast cancer mortality. Periodic mammograms and physical examinations for detection of breast cancer in asymptomatic women 40 years of age and older received endorsement by the NCI, ACS, and numerous professional groups.[33]

Mammography was followed by a number of innovative means for imaging the breast. Xeromammography appeared briefly.[34] This dry-process technique recorded all structures in the breast with equally good detail and could be examined without view boxes, but it disappeared from use after further improvements in film-screen mammography. Enduring adjuncts to mammography were ultrasonography and magnetic resonance imaging (MRI). Ultrasonography came into use in the 1950s. As well as allowing for the distinction between cysts and solid masses, it could characterize solid masses and permitted irradiation-free, real-time, guided needle biopsy of suspicious lesions. Malignant lesions detected by other means were not always visible on ultrasonography, and results were highly operator-dependent, making it unsuited for population screening. MRI proved valuable in special situations.

As the twentieth century advanced, opposition to radical surgery grew. Kaae and Johansen in Denmark and Robert McWhirter in Scotland maintained that simple mastectomy with regional irradiation was the equal of radical mastectomy, and preferable.[35] McWhirter protested that the selective use of radical mastectomy made the results look better but offered no overall increase in cures. George Crile Jr. in Cleveland argued for conservative surgical treatment based on a biological view of breast cancer, largely immunologic.[36] Most compelling, however, was that radical surgical removal of tissues had reached its limits with no decrease in mortality rates. In 1939 Gray showed that early lymphatic spread to axillary nodes was by embolism rather than by permeation, and blood vascular spread was increasingly accepted as the mechanism of general dissemination.[37,38]

Bernard Fisher, Professor of Surgery at the University of Pittsburgh and a researcher in the biology of metastasis, became the intellectual leader and the most compelling spokesman for the need to critically re-evaluate the treatment of breast cancer. Fisher's laboratory investigations indicated that lymph nodes were not effective barriers to cancer spread. Referring to Halsted's rationale for radical mastectomy, Fisher wrote in 1970 that, "...either the original surgical principles have become anachronistic or, if they are still valid, they were conceived originally for the wrong reasons."[39] Much like a modern Galen, Fisher asserted that breast cancer was a systemic disease and that its course was determined by a biologic struggle between tumor and host. Fisher implied that viable cancer cells always, or almost always, disseminated before diagnosis. His thesis presented two testable hypotheses: (1) variations in local treatment were unlikely to influence cure, and (2) effective systemic treatment was necessary to improve cure rates. As Chairman of the National Surgical Adjuvant Breast and Bowel Project (NSABP), Fisher was able to implement large, randomized, controlled clinical trials to test these concepts and to stimulate others to do the same (Figure 1–6). The results confirmed the observations of Moore, Küster, and Halsted, namely, that limited operations resulted in poor local and regional control, and that patients with recurrence fared poorly.[40–42] As predicted, they also confirmed that whether the regional nodes or the whole breast were removed, overall cure rates among different

Figure 1–6. Bernard Fisher MD, modern researcher in the biology of breast cancer who revised Halstedian concepts, (fourth from the right in the front row) with early members of the NSABP at a group meeting in Florida, May 1978.

treatment groups proved similar. The explanation offered was that failure of local control indicated incurability at the outset. But the need to retreat ("salvage") was distressing for all, and as local or regional recurrence might jeopardize cure for some, optimum tumor control at the outset remained a priority.

The greatest impact of these trials was on management of the breast itself. As confidence grew in irradiation for controlling occult regional metastases, the question was whether irradiation could do the same for occult tumor in the breast. Selected cases so treated by F. Baclesse in France, Ruth Guttman in the United States, Sakan Mustakallio in Finland, and others had suggested this was the case as early as 1965.[43] After an initial but unsatisfactory beginning at Guy's Hospital in London, controlled trials of breast conservation started in Milan, Italy, in 1973 by Umberto Veronesi and by the NSABP in 1976.[44,45] These trials established that excision of the primary tumor, "lumpectomy," followed by whole breast irradiation was as effective as total mastectomy for both local and ultimate disease control of most early-stage cases and was an obvious cosmetic improvement. Based on these outcomes, in 1990 the NCI sanctioned breast-conserving surgery as the preferred treatment of stage I and II breast cancers.[46]

Axillary sentinel lymph node biopsy (SLNB) was rapidly adopted after it was introduced in 1997, making routine axillary lymph node dissection unnecessary. Axillary dissection could be reserved instead for cases in which the SLNB showed nodal metastases, thereby sparing many the morbidity of this operation.[47] Surgical treatment of the breast and the regional nodes could be customized to individual needs, and with the combination of SLNB and breast conservation, the surgical component of multidisciplinary treatment reached a minimum.

Chemotherapy developed in parallel with changes in local treatment. Its beginnings can be traced to the use of mustard gas in World War I. Exposure caused depression of bone marrow and lymphoid tissue followed by death from pneumonia. The effects on tissues were similar to those of ionizing radiation and suggested usefulness against lymphomas. Experiments with animals followed, and, indeed, nitrogen mustard produced regression of implanted lymphoma in mice. In 1942 it was first used to treat human lymphoma at Yale University; the results of which were not reported by Goodman and Philips until 1946, a delay necessitated by the need for wartime secrecy. Reference is sometimes made in texts to events surrounding explosion of mustard agent (dichloroethyl sulfide) bombs aboard the S.S. John Harvey on December 2, 1943, in Bari Harbor, Italy, during WW II as the stimulus for research into chemotherapy, but this event followed the clinical investigations at Yale University.[48] Continued development produced such therapeutically useful alkylating agents as busulfan, cyclophosphamide and chlorambucil. Additional agents with various mechanisms of cytotoxicity followed. None proved toxic specifically for cancer cells or free of undesirable side effects, and none cured overt breast cancers, but their judicious use proved clinically useful. Systemic "chemotherapy," a word coined by the researcher Paul Erlich, often produced temporary regression and occasionally complete disappearance of advanced breast cancers.[49] Initial trials of intravenous, perioperative triethlylene-thiophosphoramide (Thio-TEPA) in the late 1950s, intended to destroy tumor cells released during mastectomy, were failures, but extended adjuvant treatment with L-phenylalanine mustard directed against occult micrometastases improved the survival of patients with early stage breast cancer.[50,51] A similar approach using combinations of drugs with different mechanisms of action (eg, cyclophosphamide, fluorouracil, and methotrexate (CMF), and doxorubicin combinations) proved more effective, securing adjuvant chemotherapy an established place in multidisciplinary treatment. With the addition of chemotherapy, treatment of breast cancer truly became a coordinated effort of specialists, bringing to bear a medley of surgery, radiation therapy, and systemic chemohormonal therapy on the local and systemic components of the disease.

As the twentieth century closed, breast cancer was recognized as a disorder of unrestrained cell growth, but its instigation remained an enigma. A virus caused the disease in mice, but apparently not in humans; ingestion of aromatic hydrocarbons (dimethylbenzanthracene) produced it in rats. In humans, exposure to ionizing radiation increased risk, as evidenced in survivors of the atomic bombing of Hiroshima during WW II and the recipients of multiple fluoroscopies incident to treatment of pulmonary tuberculosis, information spurring closer regulation of mammography and other radiological procedures. Hormone replacement therapy to alleviate menopausal symptoms also increased risk, prompting cautions about exposure to exogenous estrogens.[52] The discovery of predisposing mutations in *BRCA1* and *BRCA2* genes of families prone to breast cancer confirmed genetic transmission and provided a means to identify individuals at great risk.[53,54] Among preventive strategies, early castration was effective but unacceptable; in 1998 tamoxifen, a synthetic estrogen receptor modulator, became the first drug proven to lower risk and the first approved for this use.[55] Prophylactic mastectomies offered almost total protection, and became an option for women especially in need.[56]

Breast cancer remained a daunting problem as science and medicine reached the third millennium AD, but a problem more accurately defined than ever before and upon which all the tools of modern science were brought to bear. Research explored cellular growth factors and intracellular signaling pathways that might be exploited against it. For practicing physicians radiotherapy, medical oncology, surgical oncology, and even breast surgery had become specialties. Cancer institutes dotted the country. For the record, in the United States in 2004 an estimated 217,000 women continued to develop breast cancer each year and 40,000 died of it annually. With screening and modern therapy, the death rate had begun to decline and overall relative survival 5 years after diagnosis, cured and uncured, was 86.6%.[57]

COMMENT

The sometimes heroic, often tragic, and always poignant story of breast cancer is incomplete; happy will be the day when the final chapter is written. When that day comes, it may not get the attention it deserves. It will come in familiar voices on the nightly news: "Today doctors at (some) medical center announced that a (vaccine?) prepared from the (prions?) of breast cancer resulted in immediate and total disappearance of all signs of the disease in eleven advanced cases. Further studies are planned to follow up this promising development. In international news…" Reactions will be mixed. Most will notice without comment. Skeptics will quip, "Yeah, another breakthrough!" But it will be true. Others, robbed of loved ones, will hesitate in melancholy reflection. More than suspected will reap the rewards, and after more than 5,000 years of telling, the story of breast cancer will have been told.

ACKNOWLEDGMENT

The author wishes to thank Judith H. Donegan, MD, PhD, for constructive criticism of the manuscript.

REFERENCES

1. Encyclopedia Britannica, 15th ed. Encyclopedia Britannica, Inc. Chicago: Encyclopedia Britannica Inc.; 1978. Macropedia. Vol 11 p. 823.
2. Breasted JH, editor. The Edwin Smith Surgical Papyrus. Chicago, IL: The University of Chicago Press; 1930, Special Edition. 1984. The Classics of Surgery Library. Division of Gryphon Editions, Ltd. Birmingham (AB). Frontispiece.
3. Homer. Iliad. Translated by WHD Rouse. New York: A Signet Classic. New American Library; 1966. p. 36.
4. De Moulin D. A short history of breast cancer. Boston: Martinus Nijhoff; 1983. p. 1–107.
5. Lewison EF. Saint Agatha the patron saint of diseases of the breast in legend and art. Bull History of Medicine 1950;24:409–20.
6. Lyons AS, Petrucelli RJ. Medicine. An illustrated history. New York: Harry N. Abrams Publishers; 1978. p. 294–317.
7. Hoxey HM. You don't have to die. New York: Milestone Books Inc; 1956. p. 47.
8. Yalom M. A history of the breast. New York: Alfred A. Knopf; 1997. p. 211.
9. LeDran HF. Memoires avec un précis de plusieurs observations sur le cancer. Memories de l'academie royale de chirurgie 1757;3:1–54.
10. Saunders JB deC M, O'Malley CD. The anatomical drawings of Andreas Vesalius. New York: Bonanza Books; 1982. p. 172–3.
11. Cooper AP. The anatomy and diseases of the breast. Philadelphia: Lea and Blanchard; 1845.
12. Sappey MPC. Anatomie, physiologie, pathologie des vaisseaux lymphatique considérés chez l'homme et les vertébrés. Paris: A Delahaye and E Lecrosnier; 1874.
13. Lillberg K, Verkasalo PK, Kaprio J, et al. Personality characteristics and the risk of breast cancer: a prospective cohort study. Int J Cancer 2002;100 361–6.
14. Robbins G, editor. Silvergirl's surgery—the breast. Austin: Silvergirl Inc.; 1984. p. 25–9.
15. Garrison FH. An introduction to the history of medicine. 4th ed. Philadelphia: WB Saunders, Co.; 1929. p. 588–9.
16. Encyclopedia Britannica, 15th ed. Chicago: Encyclopedia Britannica Inc.; 1978. Macropedia Vol 11 p. 837.
17. Müller J. Uber den feinen Bau und der Formen dei Krankhafte Geschwülste. Berlin: G Reimer; 1838.
18. Virchow R. Cellular pathology. Birmingham; The Classics of Medicine Library, Division of Gryphon Editions, Ltd.; 1978. p. 66.
19. Haagensen CD. Diseases of the breast, 2nd ed. Philadelphia: W. B. Saunders Co; 1971. p. 394–5.

20. Paget J. On disease of the mammary areola preceding cancer of the mammary gland. St. Bartholomew Hospital Reports;1874:vol. 10; p. 75–8.
21. Moore C. On the influence of inadequate operations on the theory of cancer. Royal Medical and Chirugical Society. London. Med Chir Trans 1867;32:245–80.
22. Banks WM. Free removal of mammary cancer with extirpation of the axillary glands as a necessary accompaniment. Paper read before the British Medical Association at Worcester. 1882.
23. Halsted WS. The results of operations for the cure of cancer of the breast performed at the Johns Hopkins Hospital from June 1889 to January 1894. Johns Hopkins Hospital Reports. Baltimore 1894–95;4:297–350.
24. Halsted WS. The results of radical operations for the cure of cancer of the breast. Trans Am Surg Assoc 1907;25:61–79. Reprinted in: Surgical papers of William Stuart Halsted Birmingham (AL): Gryphon Editions; 1984. p 80.
25. Handley WS. Cancer of the breast and its operative treatment. London: John Murray; 1906.
26. Bloom, HJG, Richardson WW, Harries EJ. Natural history of untreated breast cancer (1805-1933). Comparison of untreated and treated cases according to histological grade of malignancy. Brit Med J 1962;I:213–21.
27. Donegan WL. Staging and prognosis. In: Donegan WL, Spratt JS, editors. Cancer of the breast, 5th ed. Philadelphia: W.B. Saunders Co; 2002. p. 478.
28. Keynes GL. The radium treatment of carcinoma of the breast. Brit J Surg 1942;19:415–80
29. Horsley JS III, Horsley GW. Twenty years experience with prophylactic bilateral oophorectomy in the treatment of carcinoma of the breast. Ann Surg 1962;155:935.
30. Jensen EV, DeSombre ER, Jungblut PW. Estrogen receptors in hormone responsive tissues and tumors. In: Wissler RW, Dao TL, Wood S Jr., editors. Endogenous factors influencing host-tumor balance. Chicago: University of Chicago Press; 1967.
31. Special Report: Treatment of primary breast cancer. N Engl J Med 1979;301:340.
32. Egan RL. Mammography, 2nd ed. Springfield: Charles C Thomas; 1972. p. 3–22.
33. NCI statement on mammography screening. Available at: http://www.cancer.gov/newscenter/mammstatement31jan02 (accessed Jan 4, 2005).
34. Wolfe JN. Xeroradiography of the breast. Springfield: Charles C Thomas; 1972. p. 3–5.
35. McWhirter R. Simple mastectomy and radiotherapy in the treatment of breast cancer. Br J Radiol 1955;28:128.
36. Crile G Jr. A biological consideration of treatment of breast cancer. Springfield, IL: Charles C. Thomas;1967.
37. Gray JH. The relation of lymphatic vessels to the spread of cancer. Br J Surg 1939;26:462.
38. Ewing J. Neoplastic diseases, 4th ed. Philadelphia: W. B. Saunders Co; 1940. p. 63–74.
39. Fisher B. The surgical dilemma in the primary therapy of invasive breast cancer: a critical appraisal. Current problems in surgery. Chicago: Year Book Medical Publishers Inc.;1970.
40. Fisher B, Montague E, Redmond C, et al. Comparison of radical mastectomy with alternative treatments for primary breast cancer. Cancer 1977;39:2827–39.
41. Veronesi U, Valagussa P. Inefficacy of internal mammary node dissection in breast cancer surgery. Cancer 1981;47:170–5.
42. Fisher B, Redmond D, Poisson R, et al. Eight-year results of a randomized clinical trial comparing total mastectomy and lumpectomy with or without irradiation in the treatment of breast cancer. N Engl J Med 1989;320:822–8.
43. Baclesse F. Five-year results in 431 breast cancers treated solely by roentgen rays. Ann Surg 1965;61:103–4.
44. Veronesi U, Volterrani F, Luini A, et al. Quadrantectomy versus lumpectomy for small size breast cancer. Eur J Cancer 1990;26:671–3.
45. Fisher B, Anderson S, Redmond CK, et al. Reanalysis and results after 12 years of follow-up in a randomized clinical trial comparing total mastectomy with lumpectomy with or without irradiation in the treatment of breast cancer. N Engl J Med. 1995;333:1456–61.
46. Treatment of Early-Stage Breast Cancer. NIH Consens Statement Online 1990 Jun 18–21 [cited 2005 October 26];8: 1–19.
47. Guilliano AE, Jones RC, Brennan M, Statman R. Sentinel lymphadenectomy in breast cancer. J Clin Oncol 1997; 15:2245–50.
48. Papac RJ. Origins of cancer therapy. Yale J Biol and Med 2002;74:391–8.
49. DeVita VT. Principles of chemotherapy. In: DeVita VT Jr, Hellman S, Rosenberg SA, editors. Cancer—principles and practice of oncology. Philadelphia: J. B. Lippincott Co; 1982. p. 132–3.
50. Noer RJ. Adjuvant chemotherapy. Thio-tepa with radical mastectomy in the treatment of breast cancer. Am J Surg 1963;106:405–12.
51. Fisher B, Fisher ER, Redmond C. Ten-year results from the National Surgical Adjuvant Breast and Bowel Project (NSABP) clinical trial evaluating the use of L-phenylalanine mustard (L-PAM) in the management of primary breast cancer. J Clin Oncol 1986;4:929–41.
52. Chlebowski RY, Hendrix SL, Langer RD, et al. Influence of estrogen plus progestin on breast cancer and mammography in healthy postmenopausal women: the Women's Health Initiative Randomized Trial. JAMA 2003;289:3243–53.
53. Friedman LS, Ostermeyer EA, Szabo CI, et al. Confirmation of *BRCA1* by analysis of germline mutations linked to breast and ovarian cancer in ten families. Nat Genet 1994;8:399–404.
54. Futreal PA, Liu Q, Shattuck-Eidens D, et al. *BRCA1* mutations in primary breast and ovarian carcinomas. Science 1994;266:120–2.
55. Fisher B, Constantino JP, Wickerham DL, et al. Tamoxifen for prevention of breast cancer: report of the National Surgical Adjuvant Breast and Bowel Project P-1 Study. J Natl Cancer Inst 1998;90:1371–88.
56. Hartmann LC, Schaid DJ, Woods JE, et al. Efficacy of bilateral prophylactic mastectomy in women with a family history of breast cancer. N Engl J Med 1999;340:77–84.
57. American Cancer Society 2004 statistics. Available at: http://www.cancer.org/downloads/MED/Page4.pdf (accessed Jan 11, 2005).

2

Anatomy of the Breast, Axilla, and Thoracic Wall

HELEN KRONTIRAS
KIRBY I. BLAND

GROSS ANATOMIC STRUCTURE OF THE BREAST

Form and Size

The breast is located within the superficial fascia of the anterior thoracic wall. It consists of 15 to 20 lobes of glandular tissue of the tubuloalveolar type. Each lobe is supported by fibrous connective tissue that forms a framework. Adipose tissue fills the space between the lobes.[1] Although a distinct capsule around the components of the breast is not present, subcutaneous connective tissue surrounds the gland and extends as a septum between the lobes and lobules, providing support for the glandular elements. The deep layer of the superficial fascia that lies on the posterior surface of the breast rests on the pectoral fascia of the thoracic wall. A distinct space, the retromammary bursa, can be identified anatomically on the posterior aspect of the breast between the deep layer of the superficial fascia and the deep investing fascia of the pectoralis major and contiguous muscles of the thoracic wall (Figure 2–1).[2] The retromammary bursa contributes to the mobility of the breast on the thoracic wall. Fibrous thickenings of the connective tissue interdigitate between the parenchymal tissue of the breast, extending from the deep layer of the superficial fascia (hypodermis) and attaching to the dermis of the skin. These suspensory structures, called Cooper's ligaments, insert perpendicular to the delicate superficial fascial layers of the dermis, providing support and mobility.

At maturity, the glandular portion of the breast has a unique and distinctive protuberant conical form. The base of the cone is roughly circular. There is tremendous variation in the size of the breast. Commonly, breast tissue extends into the axilla as the axillary tail (of Spence). A typical nonlactating breast weighs between 150 and 225 g, whereas the lactating breast may exceed 500 g.[3,4]

The breast of the nulliparous female has a typical hemispheric configuration with distinct flattening above the nipple. The multiparous breast, which has experienced the hormonal stimulation associated with pregnancy and lactation, is usually larger and more pendulous. As noted, during pregnancy and lactation, the breast increases dramatically in size and becomes more pendulous. With increasing age, the breast usually decreases in volume, becomes somewhat flattened and pendulous, and is less firm.

Extent and Location

The mature female breast extends inferiorly from the level of the second or third rib or to the inframammary fold, which is at about the level of the sixth or seventh rib, and laterally from the lateral border of the sternum to the anterior edge of the latissimus dorsi muscle or the anterior or midaxillary line. The deep or posterior surface of the breast rests on portions of the deep investing fasciae of the

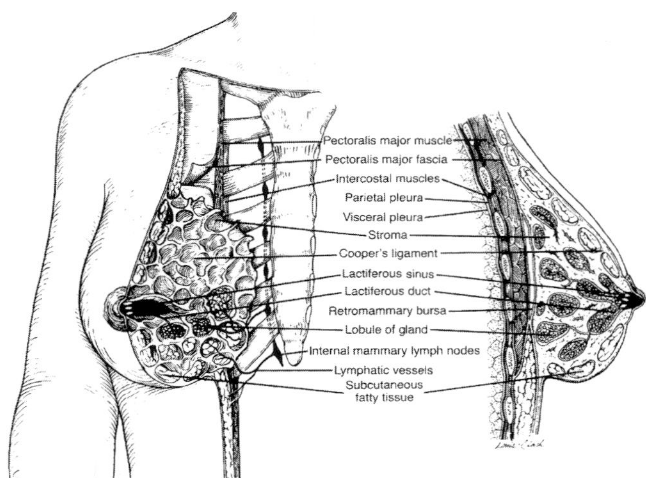

Figure 2–1. A tangential view of the breast on the chest wall and a sectional (sagittal) view of the breast and associated chest wall. The breast lies in the superficial fascia just deep to the dermis. It is attached to the skin by the suspensory ligaments of Cooper and is separated from the investing fascia of the pectoralis major muscle by the retromammary bursa. Cooper's ligaments form fibrosepta in the stroma that provides support for the breast parenchyma. From 15 to 20 lactiferous ducts extend from lobules comprised of glandular epithelium to openings located on the nipple. A dilation of the duct, the lactiferous sinus, is present near the opening of the duct in the subareolar tissue. Subcutaneous fat and adipose tissue, distributed around the lobules of the gland, give the breast its smooth contour and, in the nonlactating breast, account for most of its mass. Lymphatic vessels pass through the stroma surrounding the lobules of the gland and convey lymph to collecting ducts. Lymphatic channels ending in the internal mammary (or parasternal) lymph nodes are shown. The pectoralis major muscle lies adjacent to the ribs and intercostal muscles. The parietal pleura, attached to the endothoracic fascia, and the visceral pleura, covering the surface of the lung, are shown. Reproduced with permission from Romrell LJ, Bland KI.[2]

pectoralis major, serratus anterior, and external abdominal oblique muscles, and the upper extent of the rectus sheath. The axillary tail (of Spence) of the breast extends into the anterior axillary fold. The upper half of the breast, and particularly the upper outer quadrant, contains more glandular tissue than does the remainder of the breast.

MICROSCOPIC ANATOMIC STRUCTURE OF THE BREAST

The epidermis of the nipple and areola is somewhat wrinkled and highly pigmented. It is covered by keratinized, stratified squamous epithelium. The deep surface of the epidermis is invaded by unusually long dermal papillae that allow capillaries to bring blood close to the surface, giving the region a pinkish color in young, fair-skinned individuals. At puberty, the pigmentation of the nipple and areola increases, and the nipple becomes more prominent. During pregnancy, the degree of pigmentation increases, and the areola enlarges. Deep to the areola and nipple, bundles of smooth muscle fibers are arranged circumferentially and radially in the dense connective tissue and longitudinally along the lactiferous ducts that extend up into the nipple. These muscle fibers are responsible for the erection of the nipple that occurs in response to various stimuli.[5]

The areola contains sebaceous glands, sweat glands, and accessory areolar glands (of Montgomery). The accessory areolar glands of Montgomery are intermediate in their structure between true mammary glands and sweat glands and produce small elevations on the surface of the areola. The sebaceous glands (which usually lack associated hairs) and sweat glands are located along the margin of the areola. Whereas the tip of the nipple contains numerous free sensory nerve cell endings and Meissner's corpuscles in the dermal papillae, the areola contains fewer of these structures.[6] Neuronal plexuses are also present around hair follicles in the skin peripheral to the areola, and pacinian corpuscles may be present in the dermis and in the glandular tissue.

Each lobe of the mammary gland ends in a lactiferous duct (2 to 4 mm in diameter) that opens through a constricted orifice (0.4 to 0.7 mm in diameter) onto the nipple (see Figure 2–1). Beneath the areola, each duct has a dilated portion, the lactiferous sinus. Near their openings, the lactiferous ducts are lined with stratified squamous epithelium. The epithelial lining of the duct shows a gradual transition to two layers of cuboidal cells in the lactiferous sinus and then becomes a single layer of columnar or cuboidal cells through the remainder of the duct system. Myoepithelial cells of ectodermal origin lie within the epithelium between the surface epithelial cells and the basal lamina.[7] These cells, arranged in a basketlike network, are present in the secretory portion of the gland but are more apparent in the larger ducts. They contain myofibrils and are strikingly similar to smooth muscle cells in their cytology. In light microscopy, epithelial cells are characteristically seen to be attached to an underlying layer called the basement membrane. With electron microscopy, the substructure of the basement membrane can be identified.

The inner layer of the basement membrane is called the basal lamina. In the breast, the parenchymal cells of the tubuloalveolar glands, as well as the epithelial and myoepithelial cells of the ducts, rest on a basement membrane or basal lamina. The integrity of this supporting layer is of significance in evaluating biopsy specimens of breast tissue. Changes in the basement membrane have important implications in immune surveillance, transformation, differentiation, and metastasis.[8–12]

The morphology of the secretory portion of the mammary gland varies greatly with age and during pregnancy and lactation (Figure 2–2). In the inactive gland, the glandular component is sparse and consists chiefly of duct elements. During the menstrual cycle, the inactive breast undergoes slight cyclical changes.

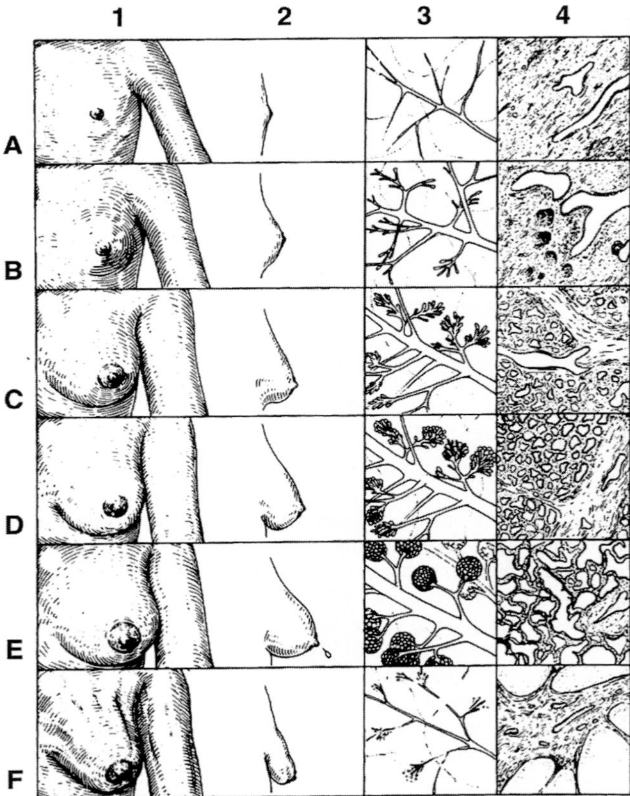

Figure 2–2. Schematic drawing illustrating mammary gland development. Anterior and lateral views of the breast are shown in columns 1 and 2. The microscopic appearances of the ducts and lobules are illustrated in columns 3 and 4, respectively. Panels: *A,* prepubertal (childhood); *B,* puberty; *C,* mature (reproductive); *D,* pregnancy; *E,* lactation; *F,* postmenopausal (senescent) state. Reproduced with permission from Romrell LJ and Bland KI.[2]

Early in the cycle, the ductules appear as cords with little or no lumen. Under estrogen stimulation, at about the time of ovulation, secretory cells increase in height, lumens appear as small amounts of secretions accumulate, and fluids and lipid accumulate in the connective tissue. Then, in the absence of continued hormonal stimulation, the gland regresses to a more inactive state through the remainder of the cycle.

THORACIC WALL

The thoracic wall is composed of both skeletal and muscular components. The skeletal components include the 12 thoracic vertebrae, the 12 ribs and their costal cartilages, and the sternum. The intercostal spaces are the spaces between the ribs. These spaces are filled with the external, internal, and innermost or intimal intercostal muscles and the associated intercostal vessels and nerves (Figure 2–3). The intercostal veins, arteries, and nerves pass in the plane that separates the internal intercostal muscle from the innermost (or intimal) layer. The endothoracic fascia, a thin fibrous layer of connective tissue forming a fascial plane continuous with the most internal component of the investing fascia of the intercostal muscles and the adjacent layer of the periosteum, marks the internal limit of the thoracic wall. The parietal pleura rests on the endothoracic fascia.

The 11 pairs of external intercostal muscles, whose fibers run downward and forward, form the most superficial layer (Figure 2–4). The muscle begins posteriorly at the tubercles of the ribs and extends anteriorly to the costochondral junction. Between the costal cartilages, the muscle is replaced by the external intercostal membrane. The fibers of the 11 pairs of internal intercostal muscles run downward and posteriorly. The muscle fibers of this layer reach the sternum anteriorly. Posteriorly, the muscle ends at the angle of the ribs, and then the layer continues as the internal intercostal membrane. The innermost intercostal muscles (intercostales intimi) form the most internal layer and have fibers that are oriented more vertically but almost in parallel with the internal intercostal muscle fibers. The muscle fibers of this layer occupy approximately the middle half of the intercostal space. This is the least well developed of the three layers. It can best be dis-

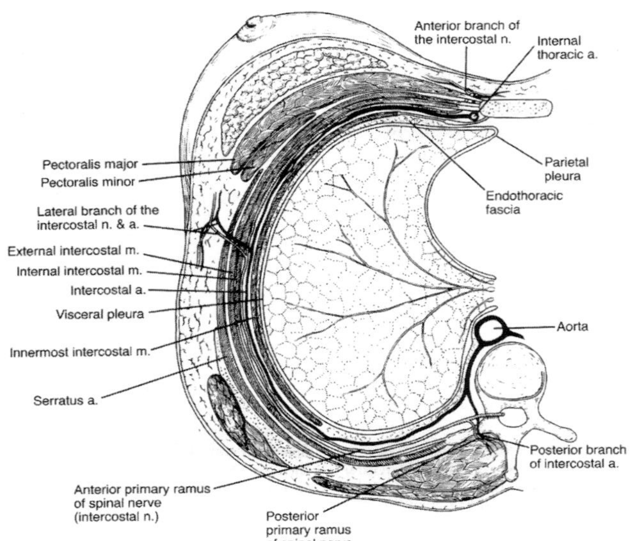

Figure 2–3. Cross-section of the breast and chest wall illustrating the layers of the thoracic wall and paths of blood vessels and nerves. The intercostal muscles occur in three layers: external, internal, and innermost. The intercostal vessels and nerves pass between the internal and innermost layers. The posterior intercostal arteries arise from the aorta and pass anterior to anastomose with the anterior intercostal arteries that are branches of the internal thoracic artery. The veins are not shown but follow the course of the arteries. The intercostal nerves are direct continuations of the anterior primary rami of thoracic spinal nerves. They supply the intercostal muscles and give anterior and lateral branches that supply the overlying skin, including that of the breast. The breast lies superficial to the pectoralis major muscle and the underlying pectoralis minor muscle. The serratus anterior muscle originates from eight or nine fleshy digitations on the outer lateral surface of the ribs and inserts on the ventral surface of the medial (vertebral) border of the scapula. Parietal pleura attaches to the endothoracic fascia that lines the thoracic cavity. Visceral pleura covers the surface of the lungs. The thin channels in the substance of the lung represent lymphatic channels that convey lymph to pulmonary lymph nodes located in the hilum of the lung. Lymphatic channels draining the thoracic wall and overlying skin and superficial fascia are not illustrated but follow the path of the blood vessels that supply the region (see text). Reproduced with permission from Romrell LJ and Bland KI.[2]

tinguished by the fact that its fibers are separated from the internal intercostals by the intercostal vessels and nerves.

The subcostalis and transversus thoracis muscles are located on the internal surface of the thoracic wall. They occur in the same plane as the innermost intercostal muscles and are considered anterior and posterior extensions of this layer. The subcostal muscles are located posteriorly and have the same orientation as the innermost intercostal muscles. They are distinct because they pass to the second or third rib below (ie, they pass over at least two intercostal spaces). Anteriorly, the transversus thoracis muscles form a layer that arises from the lower internal surface of the sternum and extends upward and laterally to insert on the costal cartilages of the second to sixth ribs (Figure 2–5). These fibers pass deep to the internal thoracic artery and accompanying veins. All of these muscles are innervated by the intercostal nerves associated with them.

The superficial muscles of the pectoral region include the pectoralis major and minor muscles and the subclavius muscle. The pectoralis major muscle is a fan-shaped muscle with two divisions. The clavicular division (or head) originates from the clavicle and is easily distinguished from the larger costosternal division that originates from the sternum and costal cartilages of the second through sixth ribs.

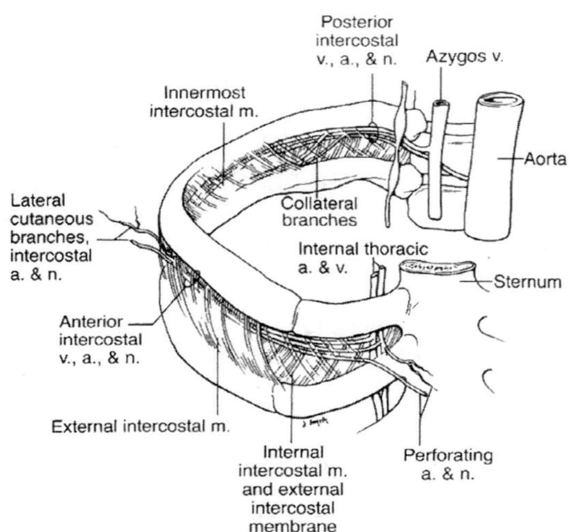

Figure 2–4. A segment of the body wall illustrating the relationship of structures to the ribs. Two ribs are shown as they extend from the vertebrae to attach to the sternum. The orientation of the muscle and connective tissue fibers is shown. The external intercostal muscle extends downward and forward. The muscle layer extends forward from the rib tubercle to the costochondral junction, where the muscle is replaced by the aponeurosis, called the external intercostal membrane. The internal intercostal muscle fibers with the opposite orientation can be seen through this layer. The innermost intercostal muscle fibers are present along the lateral half of the intercostal space. The intercostal nerve and vessels pass through the intercostal space in the plane between the internal and innermost (or intima of the internal) intercostal muscle layers. Anterior intercostal arteries arise from the internal thoracic artery; anterior intercostal veins join the internal thoracic vein. Posterior intercostal arteries arise from the aorta; posterior intercostal veins join the azygos venous system on the right and the hemiazygos system on the left. Lymphatics follow the path of the blood vessels. Anteriorly, lymphatics pass to parasternal (or internal mammary) nodes that are located along the internal mammary vessels; posteriorly, they pass to intercostal nodes located in the intercostal space near the vertebral bodies. Reproduced with permission from Romrell LJ and Bland KI.[2]

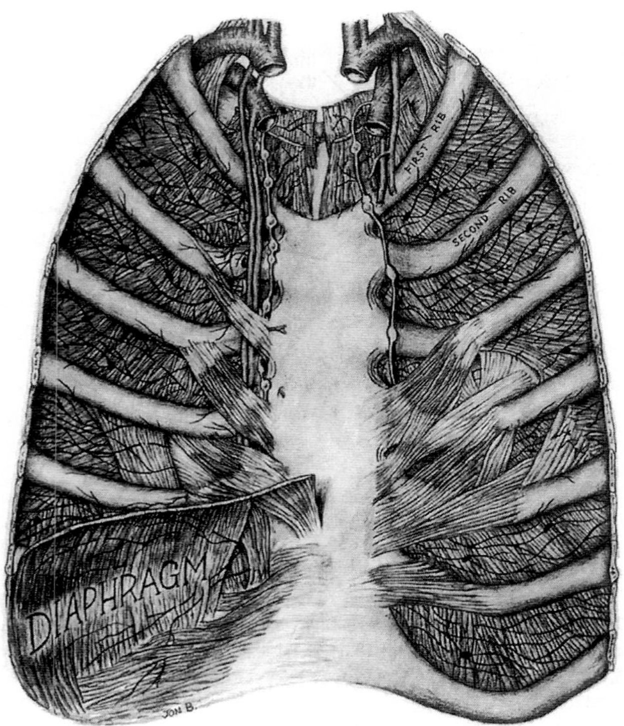

Figure 2–5. The anterior thoracic wall as viewed internally. The internal thoracic arteries and veins can be seen as they pass parallel to and about 1 cm from the sternal margin. Except in the upper two or three intercostal spaces, the transversus thoracic muscle lies deep to these vessels. The internal thoracic lymphatic trunks and associated parasternal lymph nodes accompany these vessels. Lymphatic channels located in the intercostal spaces convey lymph from the thoracic wall anteriorly to the parasternal nodes or posteriorly to the intercostal nodes. Reproduced with permission from Romrell LJ and Bland KI.[2]

The fibers of the two divisions converge laterally and insert into the crest of the greater tubercle of the humerus along the lateral lip of the bicipital groove. The cephalic vein serves as a convenient landmark defining the separation of the upper lateral border of the pectoralis major muscle from the deltoid muscle. The cephalic vein can be followed to the deltopectoral triangle, where it pierces the clavipectoral fascia and joins the axillary vein. The pectoralis major muscle acts primarily in flexion, adduction, and medial rotation of the arm at the shoulder joint. This action brings the arm across the chest. In climbing, the pectoralis major muscles, along with the latissimus dorsi muscles, function to elevate the trunk when the arms are fixed. The pectoralis major muscle is innervated by both the medial and the lateral pectoral nerves, which arise from the medial and lateral cords of the brachial plexus.

Located deep to the pectoralis major muscle, the pectoralis minor muscle arises from the external surface of the second to the fifth ribs and inserts on the coracoid process of the scapula. Although its main action is to lower the shoulder, it may serve as an accessory muscle of respiration. It is innervated by the medial pectoral nerve.

The subclavius muscle arises from the first rib near its costochondral junction and extends laterally to insert into the inferior surface of the clavicle. It functions to lower the clavicle and stabilize it during movements of the shoulder girdle. It is innervated by the nerve to the subclavius muscle, which arises from the upper trunk of the brachial plexus.

FASCIAL RELATIONS OF THE BREAST AND THORACIC WALL

The breast is located in the superficial fascia in the layer just deep to the dermis, the hypodermis. In approaching the breast, a surgeon may dissect in a bloodless plane just deep to the dermis. This dissection leaves a layer 2 to 3 mm in thickness in thin individuals in association with the skin flap. The layer may be several millimeters thick in obese individuals. The blood vessels and lymphatics passing in the deeper layer of the superficial fascia are left undisturbed.

Anterior fibrous processes, the suspensory ligaments of Cooper, pass from the septa that divide the lobules of the breast to insert into the skin. The posterior aspect of the breast is separated from the deep, or investing, fascia of the pectoralis major muscle by a space filled with loose areolar tissue, the retromammary space or bursa (see Figure 2–1). The existence of the retromammary space and the suspensory ligaments of Cooper allow the breast to move freely against the thoracic wall. The space between the well-defined fascial planes of the breast and pectoralis major is easily identified by the surgeon removing a breast. Connective tissue thickenings, called posterior suspensory ligaments, extend from the deep surface of the breast to the deep pectoral fascia.

It is important to recognize, particularly with movements and variation in the size of the breast, that its deep surface contacts the investing fascia of other muscles in addition to the pectoralis major. Only about two-thirds of the breast overlies the pectoralis major muscle. The lateral portion of the breast may contact the fourth through seventh slips of the serratus anterior muscle at its attachment to the thoracic wall. Just medial to this, the breast contacts the upper portion of the abdominal oblique muscle, where it interdigitates with the attachments of the serratus anterior muscle. As the breast extends to the axilla, it has contact with deep fascia present in this region.

BLOOD SUPPLY OF THE BREAST AND THORACIC WALL

The breast receives its blood supply from (1) perforating branches of the internal mammary artery; (2) lateral branches of the posterior intercostal arteries; and (3) several branches from the axillary artery, including highest thoracic, lateral thoracic, and pectoral branches of the thoracoacromial artery (Figure 2–6).[13–15]

The lateral thoracic artery gives branches to the serratus anterior muscle, both pectoralis muscles, and the subscapularis muscle. The lateral thoracic artery also gives rise to lateral mammary branches that wrap around the lateral border of the pectoralis major muscle to reach the breast.

The intercostal arteries originate in two groups: the anterior and the posterior intercostal arteries. The anterior intercostals are usually small paired arteries that extend laterally to the region of the costochondral junction. The anterior intercostal arteries of the upper five intercostal spaces arise from the internal thoracic (or mammary) artery; those of the lower six intercostal spaces arise from the musculophrenic artery. The posterior intercostal arteries, except for the first two spaces, arise from the thoracic aorta. The posterior intercostals for the first two spaces arise from the superior intercostal artery, which is a branch of the costocervical trunk.

The thoracodorsal branch of the subscapular artery is not involved in the supply of blood to the breast, but it is important to the surgeon who must deal with this artery during the dissection of the axilla. The central and scapular lymph node groups are intimately associated with this vessel.

A fundamental knowledge of the pattern of venous drainage is important because carcinoma of

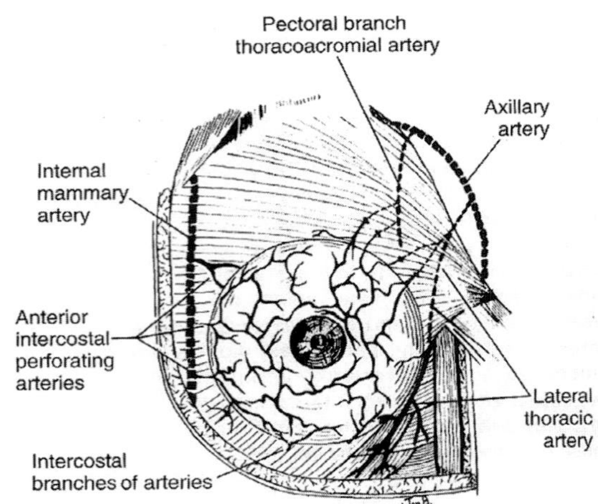

Figure 2–6. Arterial distribution of blood to the breast, axilla, and chest wall. The breast receives its blood supply via three major arterial routes: (1) medially from anterior perforating intercostal branches arising from the internal thoracic artery, (2) laterally from either pectoral branches of the thoracoacromial trunk or branches of the lateral thoracic artery (the thoracoacromial trunk and the lateral thoracic arteries are branches of the axillary artery), and (3) from lateral cutaneous branches of the intercostal arteries that are associated with the overlying breast. The arteries indicated with a dashed line lie deep to the muscles of the thoracic wall and axilla. Many of the arteries must pass through these muscles before reaching the breast. Reproduced with permission from Romrell LJ and Bland KI.[2]

the breast may metastasize through the veins and because lymphatic vessels often follow the course of the blood vessels. The veins of the breast basically follow the path of the arteries, with the chief venous drainage toward the axilla. The superficial veins demonstrate extensive anastomoses that may be apparent through the skin overlying the breast. The distribution of these veins has been studied by Massopust and Gardner[16] and Haagensen[17] using photographs taken in infrared light. Around the nipple, the veins form an anastomotic circle, the circulus venosus. Veins from this circle and from the substance of the gland transmit blood to the periphery of the breast and then into vessels joining the internal thoracic, axillary, and internal jugular veins.

The three groups of deep veins that drain the breast (Figure 2–7) and serve as vascular routes include the following:

1. The intercostal veins, which traverse the posterior aspect of the breast from the second to the sixth intercostal spaces and arborize to enter the vertebral veins posteriorly and the azygos vein centrally to terminate in the superior vena cava.

2. The axillary vein, which may have variable tributaries that provide segmental drainage of the chest wall, pectoral muscles, and the breast.
3. The internal mammary vein perforators, which represent the largest venous plexus to provide drainage of the mammary gland. This venous network traverses the rib interspaces to enter the brachiocephalic (innominate) veins. Thus perforators that drain the parenchyma and epithelial components of the breast allow direct embolization to the pulmonary capillary spaces to establish metastatic disease.[17,18]

Three principal groups of veins are involved in the venous drainage of the thoracic wall and the breast: (1) perforating branches of the internal thoracic vein, (2) tributaries of the axillary vein, and (3) perforating branches of posterior intercostal veins. Metastatic emboli traveling through any of these venous routes will pass through the venous return to the heart and then be stopped as they reach the capillary bed of the lungs, providing a direct venous route for metastasis of breast carcinoma to the lungs.

The vertebral plexus of veins (Batson's plexus) may provide a second route for metastasis of breast carcinoma via veins.[19–21] This venous plexus surrounds the vertebrae and extends from the base of the skull to the sacrum. Venous channels exist between this plexus and veins associated with thoracic, abdominal, and pelvic organs. These vessels provide a route for metastatic emboli to reach the skull, vertebrae, ribs, pelvic bones, and central nervous system.

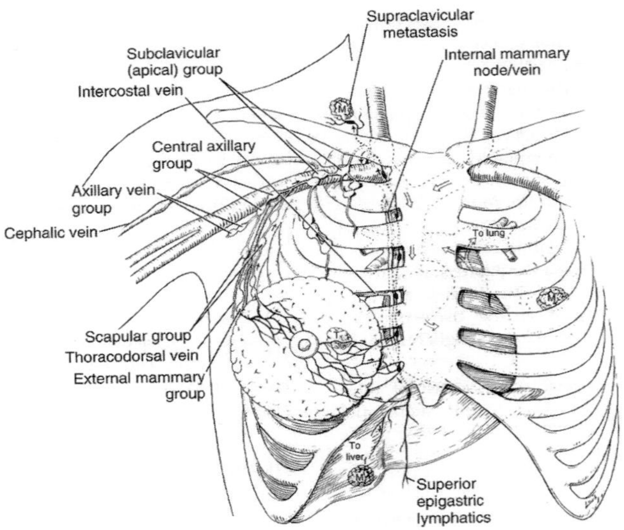

Figure 2–7. Venous drainage of the breast and its relationship to the lymphatics. Lymphatic vessels parallel the course of the three major groups of veins serving the breast and provide routes for metastasis: intercostal, axillary, and internal mammary veins. Visceral metastases to the liver or lungs are possible via vessels providing venous or lymphatic drainage of the breast because these structures communicate with the major venous trunks. Reproduced with permission from Romrell LJ and Bland KI.[2]

INNERVATION OF THE BREAST

Sensory innervation of the breast is supplied primarily by the lateral and anterior cutaneous branches of the second through sixth intercostal nerves (see Figure 2–4). These sensory nerves of the breast originate principally from the fourth, fifth, and sixth intercostal nerves, although the second and third intercostal nerves may provide cutaneous branches to the superior aspect of the breast. These intercostal nerves are direct continuations of the ventral primary rami of the upper 11 thoracic spinal nerves. As the nerves pass anteriorly, they give branches to supply the intercostal muscles. In addition, each nerve gives a relatively large lateral cutaneous branch. The lateral branches of the intercostal nerves exit the intercostal space at the attachment sites of the slips of serratus anterior muscle. The nerves divide into anterior and posterior branches as they pass between the muscle fibers. As the anterior branches pass in the superficial fascia, they supply the anterolateral thoracic wall; the third through sixth branches, also known as lateral mammary branches, supply the breast. The lateral branch of the second intercostal nerve is of special significance because a large nerve, the intercostal brachial, arises from it. This nerve, which can be seen during surgical dissection of the axilla, passes through the fascia of the floor of the axilla and usually joins the medial cutaneous nerve of the arm. If this nerve is injured during surgery, the patient will have loss of cutaneous sensation from the upper medial aspect of the arm and floor of the axilla.

The anterior branches of the intercostal nerves exit the intercostal space near the lateral border of the sternum to allow arborization of the nerve branches medially and laterally over the thoracic wall. The branches that course laterally reach the medial aspect of the breast and are sometimes called medial mammary nerves.

AXILLA

Boundaries of the Axilla

The axilla is a pyramidal compartment between the upper extremity and the thoracic walls (Figure 2–8). It is described as having four walls, an apex, and a base. The curved base is made of axillary fascia and skin. Externally, this region, the armpit, appears dome-shaped (and covered with hair after puberty). The apex is not a roof but an aperture that extends into the posterior triangle of the neck through the cervicoaxillary canal. The cervicoaxillary canal is bounded anteriorly by the clavicle, posteriorly by the scapula, and medially by the first rib. Most structures pass through the cervical axillary canal as they course between the neck and upper extremity. The anterior wall is made up of the pectoralis major and minor muscles and their associated fasciae. The posterior wall is composed primarily of the subscapularis muscle, located on the anterior surface of the scapula, and to a lesser extent by the teres major and latissimus dorsi muscles and their associated tendons. The lateral wall is a thin strip of the humerus, the bicipital groove, between the insertions of the muscles of the anterior and posterior walls. The medial wall is made up of serratus anterior muscle that covers the thoracic wall in this region (over the upper four or five ribs and their associated intercostal muscles).

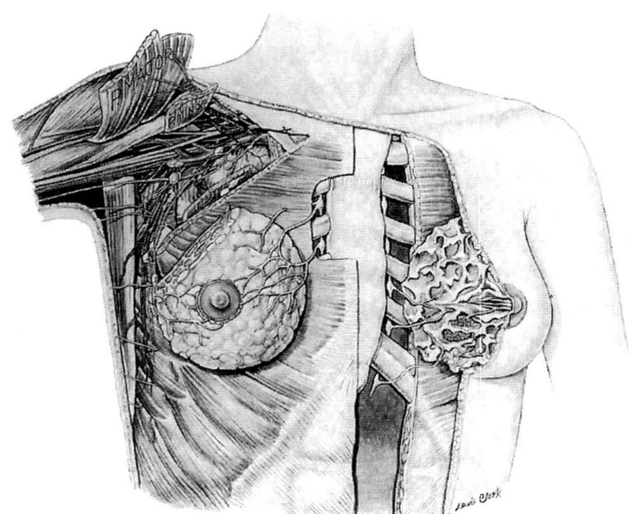

Figure 2–8. The anterior chest illustrating the structure of the chest wall, breast, and axilla. See text for details of the structure of the axilla and a description of its contents. On the right side, the pectoralis major muscle has been cut lateral to the breast and reflected laterally to its insertion into the crest of the greater tubercle of the humerus. This exposes the underlying pectoralis minor muscle and the other muscles forming the walls of the axilla. The contents of the axilla, including the axillary artery and vein, components of the brachial plexus, and axillary lymph node groups and lymphatic channels, are exposed. On the left side, the breast is cut to expose its structure in sagittal view. The lactiferous ducts and sinuses can be seen. Lymphatic channels passing to parasternal lymph nodes are also shown. Reproduced with permission from Romrell LJ and Bland KI.[2]

Contents of the Axilla

The axilla contains the great vessels and nerves of the upper extremity. These, along with the other contents, are surrounded by loose connective tissue. Figure 2–8 illustrates many of the key relationships of structures within the axilla. The vessels and nerves are closely associated with each other and are enclosed within a layer of fascia, the axillary sheath.

This layer of dense connective tissue extends from the neck and gradually disappears as the nerves and vessels branch.

The axillary artery may be divided into three parts within the axilla: (1) The first segment, located medial to the pectoralis minor muscle, gives one branch, the supreme thoracic artery that supplies the thoracic wall over the first and second intercostal spaces. (2) The second part, located posterior to the pectoralis minor muscle, gives two branches, the thoracoacromial trunk and the lateral thoracic artery. The thoracoacromial trunk divides into the acromial, clavicular, deltoid, and pectoral branches. The lateral thoracic artery passes along the lateral border of the pectoralis minor on the superficial surface of the serratus anterior muscle. Pectoral branches of the thoracoacromial and lateral thoracic arteries supply both the pectoralis major and minor muscles and must be identified during surgical dissection of the axilla. The lateral thoracic artery is of particular importance in surgery of the breast because it supplies the lateral mammary branches. (3) The third part, located lateral to the pectoralis minor, gives off three branches, the anterior and posterior circumflex humeral arteries, which supply the upper arm and contribute to the collateral circulation around the shoulder, and the subscapular artery. Although the latter artery does not supply the breast, it is of particular importance in the surgical dissection of the axilla. It is the largest branch within the axilla, giving rise after a short distance to its terminal branches, the subscapular circumflex and the thoracodorsal arteries, and it is closely associated with the central and subscapular lymph node groups. In the axilla, the thoracodorsal artery crosses the subscapularis and gives branches to it and to the serratus anterior and the latissimus dorsi muscles.

The axillary vein has tributaries that follow the course of the arteries just described. They are usually in the form of venae comitantes, paired veins that follow an artery. The cephalic vein passes in the groove between the deltoid and pectoralis major muscles and then joins the axillary vein after piercing the clavipectoral fascia.

Throughout its course in the axilla, the axillary artery is associated with various parts of the brachial plexus (Figure 2–9). The cords of the brachial plexus are named according to their relationship with the axillary artery—medial, lateral, and posterior—rather than their anatomic position in the axilla or on the chest wall. The lateral cord gives four branches, namely, the lateral pectoral nerve, which supplies the pectoralis major; a branch that communicates with the medial pectoral nerve, which is called the ansa pectoralis[22]; and two terminal branches, the musculocutaneous nerve and the lateral root of the

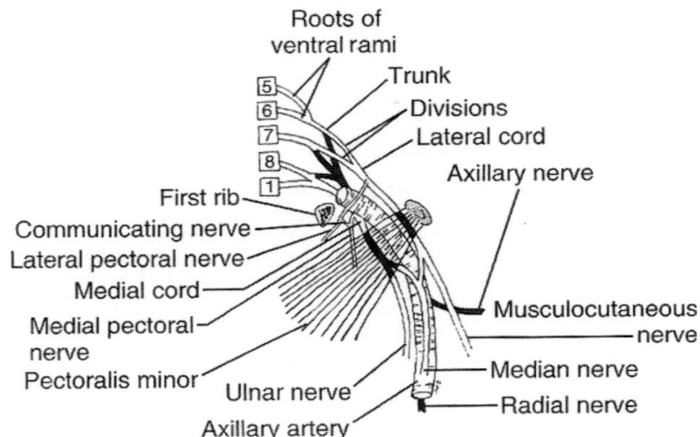

Figure 2–9. Schematic drawing of the brachial plexus illustrating its basic components. The cords are associated with the axillary artery and lie behind the pectoralis minor muscle. The names of the cords reflect their relationship to the artery. Reproduced with permission from Romrell LJ and Bland KI.[2]

median nerve. Injury to the medial or lateral pectoral nerves, or the ansa pectoralis,[21] which joins them, may lead to loss of muscle mass and fatty necrosis of the pectoralis major or minor muscles,[23] depending of the level of nerve injury.

The medial cord usually gives five branches, the medial pectoral nerve (which supplies both the pectoralis major and minor), the median brachial cutaneous nerve, the medial antebrachial cutaneous nerve, and two terminal branches—the ulnar nerve and the lateral root of the median nerve. The posterior cord usually has five branches. Three of these nerves arise from the posterior cord in the superior aspect of the axilla—the upper subscapular, the thoracodorsal, and the lower subscapular; the cord then divides into its two terminal branches, the axillary and radial nerves.

Two additional branches of the brachial plexus, the long thoracic and intercostobrachial nerves, are of particular interest to surgeons because they are vulnerable to injury during axillary dissection. The long thoracic nerve is located on the medial wall of the axilla. It arises in the neck from the fifth, sixth, and seventh roots of the brachial and then enters the axilla through the cervicoaxillary canal. It lies on the surface of the serratus anterior muscle, which it supplies. The long thoracic nerve is covered by the serratus fascia and is sometimes accidentally removed with the fascia during surgery. This results in paralysis of part or all of the serratus anterior muscle. The functional deficit is an inability to raise the arm above the level of the shoulder or extreme weakness when one attempts this movement (winged scapula). A second nerve, the intercostobrachial, is formed by the joining of a lateral cutaneous branch of the second intercostal nerve with the medial cutaneous nerve of the arm. This nerve supplies sensation to the skin of the floor of the axilla and the upper medial aspect of the arm. Sometimes, a second intercostobrachial nerve may form an anterior branch of the third lateral cutaneous nerve. This nerve may be injured in axillary dissection, resulting in numbness of the skin of the floor of the axilla and the medial aspect of the arm.

Lymph nodes are present in the axilla. They are found in close association with the blood vessels. The lymph node groups and their location are described in the section on the lymphatic drainage of the breast.

Axillary Fasciae

The anterior wall of the axilla is composed of the pectoralis major and minor muscles and the fascia that covers them. The fasciae occur in two layers: (1) a superficial layer investing the pectoralis major muscle, called the pectoral fascia, and (2) a deep layer that extends from the clavicle to the axillary fascia in the floor of the axilla, called the clavipectoral (or costocoracoid) fascia. The clavipectoral fascia encloses the subclavius muscle located below the clavicle and the pectoralis minor muscle (Figure 2–10A and B).

The upper portion of the clavipectoral fascia, the costocoracoid membrane, is pierced by the cephalic vein, the lateral pectoral nerve, and branches of the thoracoacromial trunk. The medial pectoral nerve does not pierce the costocoracoid membrane but enters the deep surface of the pectoralis minor supplying it and passes through the anterior investing layer of the pectoralis minor to innervate the pectoralis minor. The lower portion of the clavipectoral fascia, located below the pectoralis minor muscle, is sometimes called the suspensory ligament of the axilla or the coracoaxillary fascia.

Halsted's ligament, a dense condensation of the clavipectoral fascia, extends from the medial end of the clavicle and attaches to the first rib (see Figures 2–8 and 2–10A). The ligament covers the subclavian artery and vein as they cross the first rib.

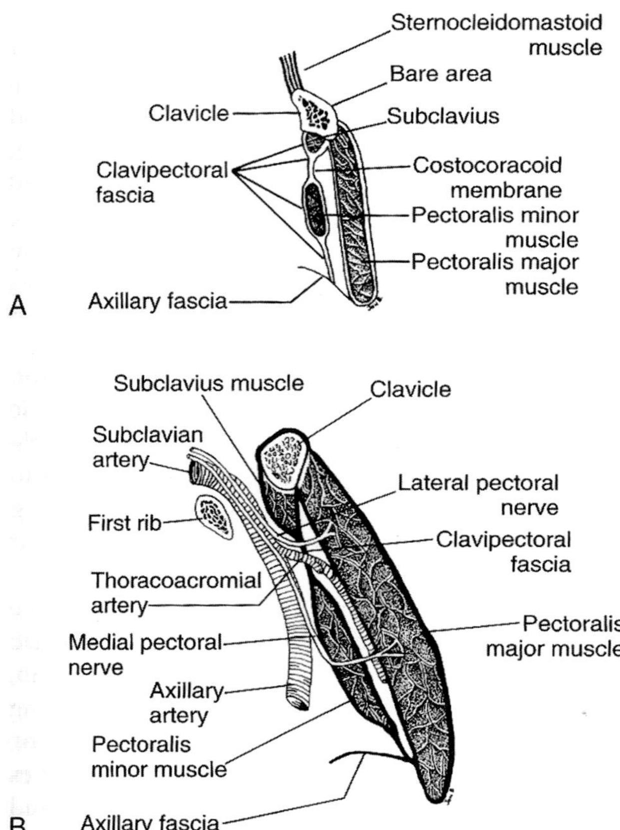

Figure 2–10. Sagittal sections of the chest wall in the axillary region. *A*, The anterior wall of the axilla. The clavicle and three muscles inferior to it are shown. *B*, Section through the chest wall illustrating the relationship of the axillary artery and medial and lateral pectoral nerves to the clavipectoral fascia. The clavipectoral fascia is a strong sheet of connective tissue that is attached superiorly to the clavicle and envelops the subclavius and pectoralis minor muscles. The fascia extends from the lower border of the pectoralis minor to become continuous with the axillary fascia in the floor of the axilla. Reproduced with permission from Romrell LJ and Bland KI.[2]

LYMPHATIC DRAINAGE OF THE BREAST

Lymph Nodes of the Axilla

The primary route of lymphatic drainage of the breast is through the axillary lymph node groups (see Figures 2–8 and 2–11). Therefore, it is essential that the clinician understand the anatomy of the grouping of lymph nodes within the axilla. Unfortunately, the boundaries of groups of lymph nodes found in the axilla are not well demarcated. Thus, there has been considerable variation in the names given to the lymph node groups. Anatomists usually define five groups of axillary lymph nodes.[24,25] Surgeons usually identify six primary groups.[16] The most common terms used to identify the lymph nodes are indicated as follows:

1. The axillary vein group, usually identified by anatomists as the lateral group, consists of four to six lymph nodes that lie medial or posterior to the axillary vein. These lymph nodes receive most of the lymph draining from the upper extremity (Figure 2–12). The exception is lymph that drains into the deltopectoral lymph nodes, a lymph node group sometimes called infraclavicular. The deltopectoral lymph nodes are not considered part of the axillary lymph node group but rather are outlying lymph nodes that drain into the subclavicular (or apical) lymph node group (see later discussion).
2. The external mammary group, usually identified by anatomists as the anterior or pectoral group,

consists of four or five lymph nodes that lie along the lower border of the pectoralis minor in association with the lateral thoracic vessels. These lymph nodes receive the major portion of the lymph draining from the breast. Lymph drains primarily from these lymph nodes into the central lymph nodes. However, lymph may pass directly from the external mammary nodes into the subclavicular lymph nodes.

3. The scapular group, usually identified by anatomists as the posterior or subscapular group, consists of six or seven lymph nodes that lie along the posterior wall of the axilla at the lateral border of the scapula in association with the subscapular vessels. These lymph nodes receive lymph primarily from the inferior aspect of the posterior neck, the posterior aspect of the trunk as far inferior as the iliac crest, and the posterior aspect of the shoulder region. Lymph from the scapular nodes passes to the central and subclavicular nodes.
4. The central group (both anatomists and surgeons use the same terminology for this group) consists of three or four large lymph nodes that are embedded in the fat of the axilla, usually posterior to the pectoralis minor muscle. They receive lymph from the three preceding groups and may receive afferent lymphatic vessels directly from the breast. Lymph from the central nodes passes

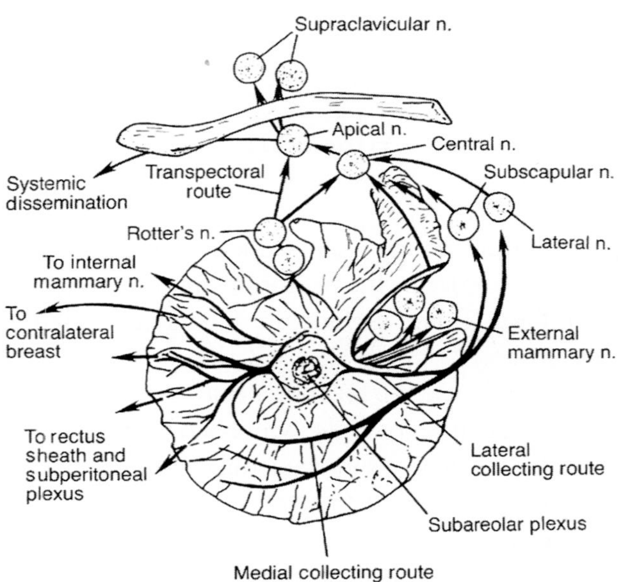

Figure 2–11. Schematic drawing of the breast identifying the position of lymph nodes relative to the breast and illustrating routes of lymphatic drainage. The clavicle is indicated as a reference point. See the text to identify the group or level to which the lymph nodes belong. Level I lymph nodes include the external mammary (or anterior), axillary vein (or lateral), and scapular (or posterior) groups; level II, the central group; and level III, the subclavicular (or apical). The arrows indicate the routes of lymphatic drainage (see text). Reproduced with permission from Romrell LJ and Bland KI.[2]

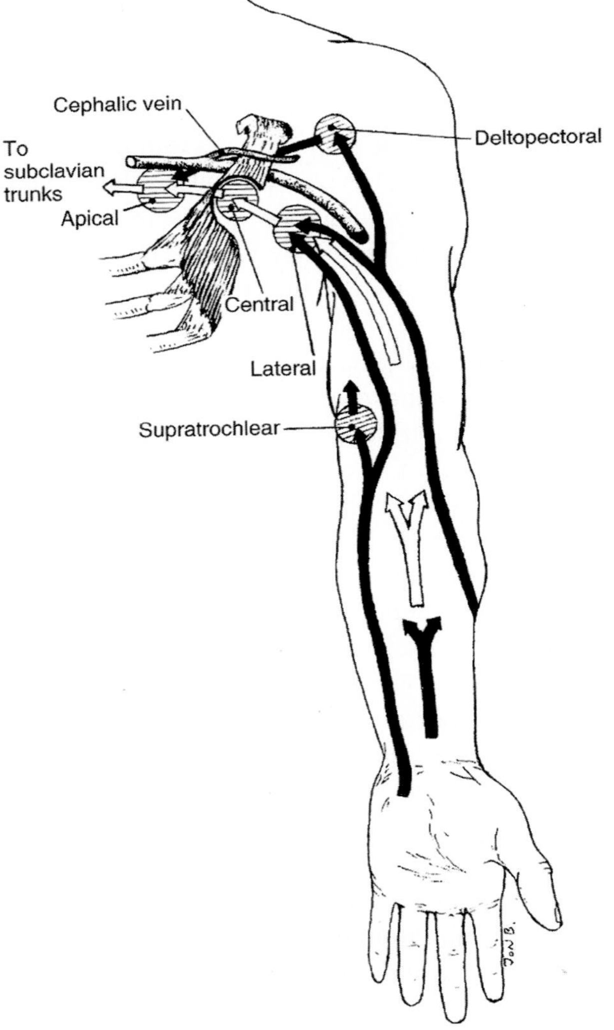

Figure 2–12. Schematic drawing illustrating the route of lymphatic drainage in the upper extremity. The relationship of this drainage to the major axillary lymph node groups is indicated by the arrows. All the lymph vessels of the upper extremity drain directly or indirectly through outlying lymph node groups into the axillary lymph nodes. The outlying lymph nodes are few in number and are organized into three groups: (1) supratrochlear lymph nodes (one or two, located above the medial epicondyle of the humerus adjacent to the basilic vein), (2) deltopectoral lymph nodes (one or two, located beside the cephalic vein where it lies between the pectoralis major and deltoid muscle just below the clavicle), and (3) variable small isolated lymph nodes (few and variable in number; may be located in the cubital fossa or along the medial side of the brachial vessels). Note that the deltopectoral lymph node group drains directly into the subclavicular, or apical, lymph nodes of the axillary group. Reproduced with permission from Romrell LJ and Bland KI.[2]

directly to the subclavicular (apical) nodes. This group is often superficially placed beneath the skin and fascia of the mid axilla and is centrally located between the posterior and anterior axillary fold. This nodal group is commonly palpable because of its superficial position and allows the clinical estimation of metastatic disease.[17,18]

5. The subclavicular group, usually identified by anatomists as the apical group, consists of 6 to 12 lymph nodes located partly posterior to the upper border of the pectoralis minor and partly superior to it. These lymph nodes extend into the apex of the axilla along the medial side of the axillary vein. They may receive lymph directly or indirectly from all the other groups of axillary lymph nodes. The efferent lymphatic vessels from the subclavicular lymph nodes unite to form the subclavian trunk. The course of the subclavian trunk is highly variable. It may directly join the internal jugular vein, the subclavian vein, or the junction of these two; likewise, on the right side of the trunk, it may join the right lymphatic duct, and on the left side, it may join the thoracic duct.
6. Efferent vessels from the subclavicular lymph nodes may also pass to deep cervical lymph nodes.
7. The interpectoral or Rotter's group,[26] a group of nodes identified by surgeons[21] but usually not by anatomists, consists of one to four small lymph nodes that are located between the pectoralis major and minor muscles in association with the pectoral branches of the thoracoacromial vessels. Lymph from these nodes passes into central and subclavicular nodes.

Surgeons also define the axillary lymph nodes with respect to their relationship with the pectoralis minor muscle (Figure 2–13).[18,26,27] These relationships are illustrated schematically in (Figure 2–14). Lymph nodes that are located lateral to or below the lower border of the pectoralis minor muscle are called level I and include the external mammary, axillary vein, and scapular lymph node groups. Those lymph nodes located deep or posterior to the pectoralis minor muscle are called level II and include the central lymph node group and possibly some of the subclavicular lymph node group.

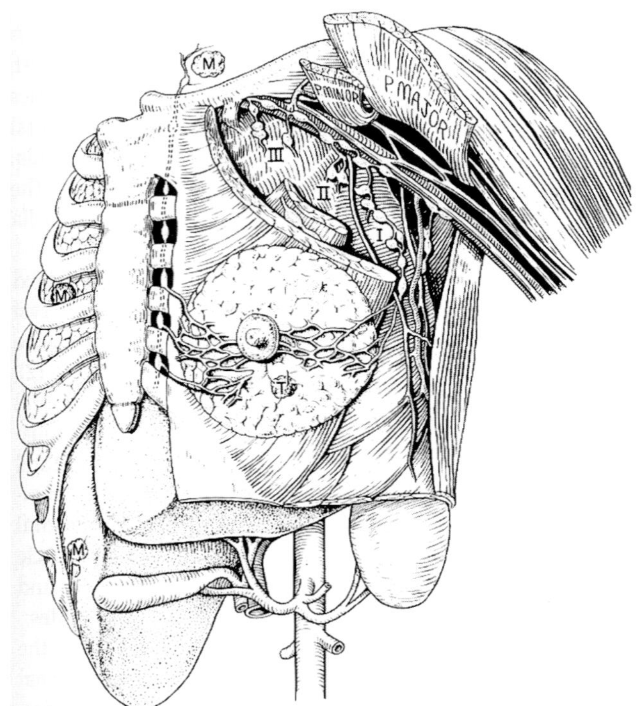

Figure 2–13. Lymphatic drainage of the breast. The pectoralis major and minor muscles, which contribute to the anterior wall of the axilla, have been cut and reflected. This exposes the medial and posterior walls of the axilla, as well as the basic contents of the axilla. The lymph node groups of the axilla and the internal mammary nodes are depicted. Also shown is the location of the long thoracic nerve on the surface of the serratus anterior muscle (on the medial wall of the axilla). The scapular lymph node group is closely associated with the thoracodorsal nerve and vessels. The Roman numerals indicate lymph node groups defined in Figure 2–14. Reproduced with permission from Romrell LJ and Bland KI.[2]

Those lymph nodes located medial or superior to the upper border of the pectoralis minor muscle are called level III and include the subclavicular lymph node group.

Surgeons use the term prepectoral or intramammary to identify a single lymph node that is only rarely found in the subcutaneous tissue associated with the breast or in the breast itself in its upper outer sector.[17] Haagensen reports finding only one or two prepectoral nodes each year among the several hundred mammary lesions studied.

Lymph Flow

Metastatic dissemination of breast cancer occurs predominantly by lymphatic routes that are rich and extensive and arborize in multiple directions through

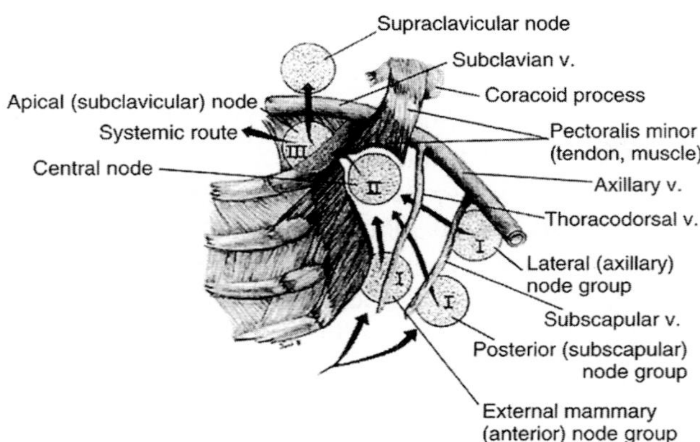

Figure 2–14. Schematic drawing illustrating the major lymph node groups associated with the lymphatic drainage of the breast. The Roman numerals indicate three levels or groups of lymph nodes that are defined by their location relative to the pectoralis minor. Level I includes lymph nodes located lateral to the pectoralis minor; level II, lymph nodes located deep to the muscle; and level III, lymph nodes located medial to the muscle. The arrows indicate the general direction of lymph flow. The axillary vein and its major tributaries associated with the pectoralis minor are included. Reproduced with permission from Romrell LJ and Bland KI.[2]

skin and mesenchymal (intraparenchymal) lymphatics. The delicate lymphatics of the corium are valveless; flow encompasses the lobular parenchyma and, thereafter, parallels major venous tributaries to enter the regional lymph nodes. This unidirectional lymphatic flow is pulsatile as a consequence of the wavelike contractions of the lymphatics to allow rapid transit and emptying of the lymphatic vascular spaces that interdigitate the extensive periductal and perilobular network. As a consequence of obstruction to lymph flow by inflammatory or neoplastic diseases, a reversal in lymphatic flow is evident and can be appreciated microscopically as endolymphatic metastases of the dermis or breast parenchyma. This obstruction of lymphatic flow accounts for the neoplastic growth in local and regional sites remote from the primary neoplasm.

Lymphatic flow is typically unidirectional, except in the pathologic state, and has preferential flow from the periphery toward larger collecting ducts. Lymphatic capillaries begin as blind-ending ducts in tissues from which the lymph is collected; throughout their course these capillaries anastomose and fuse to form larger lymphatic channels that ultimately terminate in the thoracic duct on the left side of the body or the smaller right lymphatic duct on the right side. The thoracic duct empties into the region of the junction of the left subclavian and internal jugular veins, whereas the right lymphatic duct drains into the right subclavian vein near its junction with the internal jugular vein.

Haagensen emphasized that lymphatics of the dermis are intimately associated with deeper lymphatics of the underlying fascial planes, which explains the multidirectional potential for drainage of superficial breast neoplasms. Preferential lymphatic flow toward the axilla is observed in lesions of the upper anterolateral chest. In addition, at the level of the umbilicus, tributaries diverge such that chest and upper anterior and lateral abdominal wall lymph also enter channels of the axilla. Thus, carcinomatous involvement of skin, even of the inframammary region, has preferential flow to the axilla rather than to the groin.[17]

Anson and McVay[18] and Haagensen[17] acknowledged two accessory directions for lymphatic flow from breast parenchyma to nodes of the apex of the axilla: the transpectoral and retropectoral routes (see Figure 2–11). Lymphatics of the transpectoral route (ie, interpectoral nodes) lie between the pectoralis major and minor muscles. The transpectoral route begins in the loose areolar tissue of the retromammary plexus and interdigitates between the pectoral fascia and breast to perforate the pectoralis major muscle and follow the course of the thoracoacromial artery and terminate in the subclavicular (level III) group of nodes.

The second accessory lymphatic drainage group, the retropectoral pathway, drains the superior and internal aspects of the breast. Lymphatic vessels from this region of the breast join lymphatics from the posterior and lateral surface of the pectoralis major and minor muscles. These lymphatic channels terminate at the apex of the axilla in the subclavicular (level III) group. This route of lymphatic drainage is found in approximately one third of individuals and is a more direct mechanism of lymphatic flow to the subclavicular group. This accessory pathway is also the major lymphatic drainage by way of the external mammary and central axillary nodal groups (levels I and II, respectively).[17,18]

The recognition of metastatic spread of breast carcinoma into internal mammary nodes as a primary route of systemic dissemination is credited to the British surgeon R. S. Handley.[28] Extensive investigation confirmed that central and medial lymphatics of the breast pass medially and parallel the course of major blood vessels to perforate the pectoralis major muscle and thereafter terminate in the internal mammary nodal chain.

The internal mammary nodal group (see Figures 2–5 and 2–13) is anatomically situated in the retrosternal interspaces between the costal cartilages approximately 2 to 3 cm within the sternal margin. These nodal groups also traverse and parallel the internal mammary vasculature and are invested by endothoracic fascia. The internal mammary lymphatic trunks eventually terminate in subclavicular nodal groups. The right internal mammary nodal group enters the right lymphatic duct, and the left enters the main thoracic duct (Figure 2–15). The presence of supraclavicular nodes results from lymphatic permeation and subsequent obstruction of the inferior, deep cervical group of nodes of the jugular-subclavian confluence. In effect, the supraclavicular nodal group represents the termination of efferent trunks from subclavian nodes of the internal mammary nodal group. These nodes are situated beneath the lateral margin of the inferior aspect of the sternocleidomastoid muscle beneath the clavicle.[29–32]

Cross-communication from the interstices of connecting lymphatic channels from each breast provides ready access of lymphatic flow to the opposite axilla. This observation of communicating dermal lymphatics to the contralateral breast explains the rare metastatic involvement of the opposite breast and axilla. Structures of the chest wall, including the internal and external intercostal musculature (see Figure 2–4), have extensive lymphatic drainage that parallels the course of their major intercostal blood supply. As expected, invasive neoplasms of the lateral breast that involve deep musculature of the thoracic cavity will have preferential flow toward the axilla. Invasion of medial musculature of the chest wall allows preferential drainage toward the internal mammary nodal groups, whereas bidirectional metastases may be evident with invasive central or subareolar cancers.

The lymphatic vessels that drain the breast occur in three interconnecting groups[33]: (1) a primary set of vessels originates as channels within the gland in the interlobular spaces and along the lactiferous ducts; (2) vessels draining the glandular tissue and overlying skin of the central part of the gland pass to an interconnecting network of vessels located beneath the areola, called the subareolar plexus[34]; and (3) a plexus on the deep surface of the breast communicates with minute vessels in the deep fascia underlying the breast. Along the medial border of the breast, lymphatic vessels within the substance of the gland anastomose with vessels passing to parasternal nodes.

Using autoradiographs of surgical specimens, Turner-Warwick[33] demonstrated that the main lymphatic drainage of the breast is through the system of lymphatic vessels occurring within the substance of the gland and not through the vessels on the superficial or deep surface. The main collecting trunks run laterally as they pass through the axillary fascia in the substance of the axillary tail. The subareolar plexus plays an essential part in the lymphatic drainage of the breast.[33] Using vital dyes, Halsell and colleagues[35] demonstrated that this plexus receives

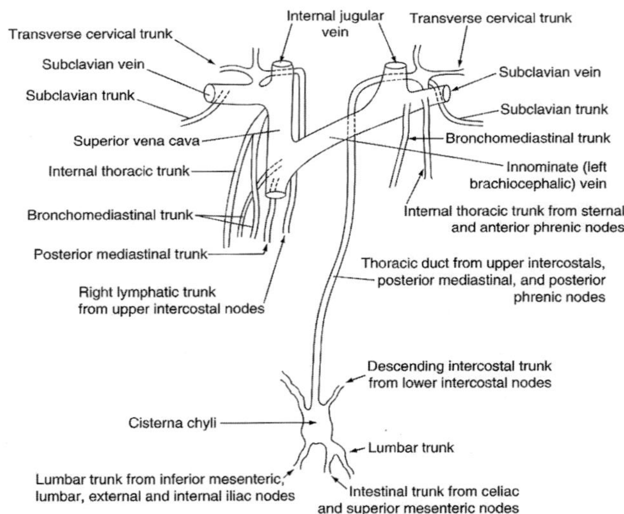

Figure 2–15. Schematic of the major lymphatic vessels of the thorax and the root of the neck. The thoracic duct begins at the cisterna chyli, a dilated sac that receives drainage from the lower extremities and the abdominal and pelvic cavities via the lumbar and intestinal trunks. Lymph enters the systemic circulation via channels that join the great veins of the neck and superior mediastinum. The lymphatic vessels demonstrate considerable variation as to their number and pattern of branching. A typical pattern is illustrated here. Most of the major trunks, including the thoracic and right lymphatic ducts, end at or near the confluence of the internal jugular with the subclavian. Reproduced with permission from Romrell LJ and Bland KI.[2]

lymph primarily from the nipple and the areola and conveys it toward the axilla. The lymphatics communicating with minute vessels in the deep fascia play no part in the normal lymphatic drainage of the breast and provide an alternative route only when the normal pathways are obstructed.

More than 75% of the lymph from the breast passes to the axillary lymph nodes (see Figure 2–11). Most of the remainder of the lymph passes to parasternal nodes. Some authorities have suggested that the parasternal nodes receive lymph primarily from the medial part of the breast. However, Turner-Warwick[33] reported that both the axillary and the parasternal lymph node groups receive lymph from all quadrants of the breast, with no striking tendency for any quadrant to drain in a particular direction.

Other routes for the flow of lymph from the breast have been identified. Occasionally, lymph from the breast reaches intercostal lymph nodes located near the heads of the ribs. Lymphatic vessels reach this location by following lateral cutaneous branches of the posterior intercostal arteries. Lymph may pass to lymphatics within the rectus sheath or subperitoneal plexus by following branches of the intercostal and musculophrenic vessels. Lymph may pass directly to subclavicular, or apical, nodes from the upper portion of the breast.

The skin over the breast has lymphatic drainage via the superficial lymphatic vessels, which ramify subcutaneously and converge on the axillary lymph nodes. The anterolateral chest and the upper abdominal wall above the umbilicus demonstrate striking directional flow of lymph toward the axilla. Below the umbilicus (the umbilicus establishing a "watershed"), superficial lymphatics carry lymph to the inguinal lymph node groups. It is important to recognize that the skin of the inframammary region drains into the axillary lymph nodes and not into the inguinal nodes. Lymphatic vessels near the lateral margin of the sternum pass through the intercostal space to the parasternal lymph nodes, which are associated with the internal thoracic vessels. Some of the lymphatic vessels located on adjacent sides of the sternum may anastomose in front of the sternum. In the upper pectoral region, a few of the lymphatic vessels may pass over the clavicle to inferior deep cervical lymph nodes.

REFERENCES

1. Cowie AT. Overview of mammary gland. J Invest Dermatol 1974;63:2.
2. Romrell LJ and Bland KI. Anatomy of the breast, axilla, chest wall and related metastatic sites. In: KI Bland, EM Copeland III, editors. The Breast: comprehensive management of benign and malignant diseases. 3rd ed. Philadelphia: Saunders; 2004. p. 21–42.
3. Spratt JS. Anatomy of the breast. Major Probl Clin Surg 1979;5:1.
4. Spratt JS Jr, Donegan WL. Anatomy of the breast. In: Donegan WL, Spratt JS Jr, editors. Cancer of the breast. 3rd ed. Philadelphia: WE Saunders; 1979.
5. Giacometti L, Montagna W. The nipple and areola of the human female breast. Anat Rec 1962;144:191.
6. Sykes FA. The nerve supply of the human nipple. J Anat 1969;105:201.
7. Radnor CJP. Myoepithelium in the prelactating and lactating mammary glands of the rat. J Anat 1972;112:337.
8. Hoffman S, Dutton SL, Ernst H, et al. Functional characterization of antiadhesion molecules. Perspect Dev Neurobiol 1994;2:101.
9. Stampfer MR, Yaswen P. Culture systems for study of human mammary epithelial cell proliferation, differentiation and transformation. Cancer Surv 1993;18:7.
10. Thompson EW, Yu M, Bueno J, et al. Collagen induced MMP-2 activation in human breast cancer. Breast Cancer Res Treat 1994;31:357.
11. Verhoeve D, Van-Marck E. Proliferation, basement membrane changes, metastasis and vascularization patterns in human breast cancer. Pathol Res Pract 1993;189:851.
12. Waugh D, Van Der Hoeven E. Fine structure of the human adult female breast. Lab Invest 1962;11:220.
13. Cunningham L. The anatomy of the arteries and veins of the breast. J Surg Oncol 1997;9:71.
14. Maliniac JW. Arterial blood supply of the breast. Arch Surg 1943;47:329.
15. Sakki S. Angiography of the female breast. Ann Clin Res 1974;6(Suppl 12):1.
16. Massopust LC, Gardner WD. Infrared photographic studies of the superficial thoracic veins in the female. Surg Gynecol Obstet 1950;91:717.
17. Haagensen CD. Anatomy of the mammary glands. In: Haagensen CD, editor. Diseases of the breast. 3rd ed. Philadelphia:WE Saunders;1986.
18. Anson BJ, McVay CB. Thoracic walls: breast or mammary region. In: Surgical Anatomy. Vol. 1, Philadelphia: WB Saunders; 1971.
19. Batson OV. The function of the vertebral veins and their role in the spread of metastases. Ann Surg 1940;112:138.
20. Batson OV. The role of the vertebral veins and metastatic processes. Ann Intern Med 1942;16:38.
21. Henriques C. The veins of the vertebral column and their role in the spread of cancer. Ann R Coll Surg Engl 1962;31:1.
22. Grife RM, Sullivan RM, Colborn GL, The ansa pectoralis: anatomy and applications. Gainesville (FL): American Association of Clinical Anatomists; 2002.
23. Moosman DA. Anatomy of the pectoral nerves and their preservation in modified mastectomy. Am J Surg 1980; 139:883.

24. Gray H. The lymphatic system. In: Clemente CD, editor. Anatomy of the human body. 30th ed. Philadelphia: Lea & Febiger; 1985.
25. Mornard P. Sur deux cas de tumeurs rnalignes des mammelles axillaires aberrantes, Bull Mem Soc Chir Paris 1929;21:487.
26. Grossman F. Ueber die Axil/aren Lymphdrusen Inaug Dissert. Berlin: C. Vogt; 1986.
27. Copeland EM III, Bland KI. The breast. In: Sabiston DC Jr. editor. Essentials of surgery, Philadelphia: WB Saunders; 1987.
28. Handley RS, Thackray AC. The internal mammary lymph chain in carcinoma of the breast. Lancet 1949;2:276.
29. Stibbe EP. The internal mammary lymphatic glands. J Anat 1918;52:527.
30. Soerensen B. Recherches sur la localisation des ganglions lymphatiques parasternaux par rapport aux espaces intercostaux. Int J Chir 1951;11:501.
31. Putti F. Richerche anatomiche sui linfonodi mammari intemi. Chir Ital 1953;7:161.
32. Arao A, Abrao A. Estudo anatomico da cadeia ganglionar mamaria interna em 100 casos. Rev Paul Med 1954;45:317.
33. Turner-Warwick RT. The lymphatics of the breast. Br J Surg 1959;46:574.
34. Grant RN, Tabah EJ, Adair FF. The surgical significance of subareolar lymph plexus in cancer of the breast. Surgery 1953;33:71.
35. Halsell JT, Smith JR, Bentlage CR, et al. Lymphatic drainage of the breast demonstrated by vital dye staining and radiography. Ann Surg 1965;162:221.

3

The Evolving Concept of the Breast Center

STEPHEN B. EDGE

Medical care in the United States has historically been directed by physicians working in solo practice. For most aspects of medical care, the individual physician had the breadth and depth of knowledge to define treatment requirements and execute the treatment plan without substantial input from colleagues. The physician was a distinct business entity without broad oversight. As necessary, the physician engaged other similarly independent components of the health care system including other physicians and used hospitals for surgical care or other inpatient services. This system generally worked well. Indeed, the high standards of care now enjoyed in the developed world were established in such a care environment.

Over the last few decades, a number of factors led to the need for change in this treatment paradigm. Medical care became more complicated and technically specialized, making it impossible for any individual to diagnose and treat all aspects of a given disease. The care for cancer is a good example of this shift. All aspects of cancer care have become more technically demanding and subspecialized. Technical fields ranging from primary care, imaging, many aspects of surgical care, the nuances of systemic therapy, and the administration of radiation therapy require specialized training and expertise. Each patient requires the input of multiple physicians as well as professionals from other health disciplines. In particular, advances in breast care in the 1970s led to the need for input by specialists of multiple disciplines early in the care of patients with breast cancer. Mammography screening became available, and studies emerged showing its effectiveness. Surgical care shifted from radical mastectomy toward breast conservation, requiring coordination with radiation oncology, and clinical trials demonstrated the effectiveness of adjuvant systemic therapy.

Another major factor affecting change in the organization of medical care has been the clear recognition that all patients did not receive a high quality of care under the past system, and that simple passive continuing education was insufficient to yield uniform high-quality outcomes.[1,2] Disparities in care have been identified in the treatment of all cancer types. The quality of care is affected by patient factors, provider characteristics, and the organization of the health care system. Most disturbing are the disparities in care related to race, ethnicity, and wealth.[3] Variation in the application of cancer care affects outcomes that range from survival and cancer recurrences to organ preservation, quality of life, satisfaction, and cost.[4]

A further factor contributing to change in the delivery systems for cancer care has been consumerism. The treatment of breast cancer, in particular, is one where the public is expecting increased sophistication from their treatment specialists. In addition, consumers want patient-centered care programs. Increasingly knowledgable patients demand a better coordination of their care as well as the support services beyond those available in physician offices.

Furthermore, there is increasing oversight of cancer care from health care institutions, health payers, employers, and government. The extent of such oversight has intensified since publication of reports from the Institute of Medicine, challenging the health care system to bridge the "quality chasm."[5] A concrete example is the direct legislative quality mandate regulating mammography services in the United States, the Mammography Quality Standards Act (MQSA).[6] Congress enacted the MQSA to address real variation in the quality of mammography. It sets technical and professional standards that must be met by any provider of mammography, if they wish to receive payment for patients covered under federal health coverage programs including Medicare. Given that Medicare is the single largest payer, these standards are ipso facto requirements for all mammography providers. Although meeting documentation requirements for MQSA adds workload, even for high-quality centers, it can be reasonably argued that this legislative intervention was the primary factor leading to a marked overall improvement in the quality of mammography, and has likely saved the lives of thousands of American women.[7]

The increasing complexity of care and required oversight, the need for financially efficient health systems, and documented disparities in care have led to the development of new organizational models of cancer care. Increasingly, health care is organized in systems that coordinate and often employ providers of all disciplines. Among these developments that are most critical to cancer care has been the establishment of the multidisciplinary team approach. Under this model, specialists from all health disciplines collaborate in a real or virtual team to determine the required treatment course and administer the care of each patient.

The cancer type that has seen the most rapid move toward establishment of multidisciplinary teams in coordinated centers is breast cancer.[8] The first reports of breast centers were published in the mid-1980s. Premiere early centers included the academic center at the University of Michigan, and the private centers in Van Nuys, California, and Rochester, New York.[9–13]

In the United States, there has been little coordination of the models used. In Europe, the European Society of Mastology provided a blueprint for coordinated efforts to regionalize breast care into specialty units. The stated goals are to make breast specialist care available to all women in Europe, to define standards for care, and to recommend standards for accreditation of breast care programs; to assure that "Breast disease be cared for by specialists in breast disease working in teams."[14] The concern is that many hospitals claim to have specialists but only a few have specialized units. The expectation is to develop region-wide standards and to achieve a critical mass of care to assure the success of teams. Similar standards and quality initiatives are now underway under the auspices of national organizations including the National Consortium of Breast Centers.[15]

This chapter will review the different models of breast care centers, examine the objectives and organization of each, and review data defining whether such centers provide a higher quality of care and generate better outcomes. This chapter is not intended to serve as a primer for those developing a breast center. Such planning requires careful medical and financial coordination, multidisciplinary strategic planning, community-wide consensus building, and careful review of the available primary literature.

ORGANIZATIONAL MODELS AND GOALS OF BREAST CENTERS

The term "breast center" is applied to a wide variety of organizational models that provide professional services focusing on breast disease. Breast centers range from the offices of independent solo mammographers providing screening services and single surgeons providing breast care to centers embedded within major academic cancer centers that provide comprehensive services for breast imaging, diagnosis, high-risk evaluation, surgery, radiation, and systemic therapy coupled with teaching and clinical and translational research. Centers may be loose or virtual professional associations in a community, or they may occupy a distinct physical plant. The center may be virtual, freestanding, or housed in a hospital or large health system. Financial organizational models range from independent private enterprises to integrated staff models embedded in large health systems and academic environments.

TYPES OF BREAST CENTERS

The general types of breast centers may be classified as discussed below and in Table 3–1, as outlined by the National Consortium of Breast Centers.[15]

Breast Screening Centers

A breast screening center provides only screening mammography services. This requires mammography equipment and the services of a radiologist. Screening services may be provided with a radiologist on site, or with delayed screening reading, requiring callback or referral for screening examinations that show abnormalities. This is often the most cost-effective model for providing screening services in smaller health centers and hospitals. However, there is considerable patient inconvenience and anxiety inherent to a system that requires a second appointment to evaluate abnormalities identified at screening.

Diagnostic Mammography Centers

A diagnostic mammography center requires additional imaging equipment, including ultrasound, and will generally offer the capability of performing image-guided biopsy and image-guided localization for affiliated surgeons. These services require the on-site presence of the radiologist because of the interactive process of diagnostic breast imaging, with additional mammogram views and ultrasound performed as needed, based on the results of screening images. The volume requirements to support the presence of a full-time radiologist are sufficient to limit such centers to larger health care institutions or active free-standing centers. It is necessary to perform 10,000 screening mammograms to detect 30 to 50 breast cancers. In this process, there will be about 500 diagnostic evaluations. This volume is approximately that needed to support one full-time mammographer. A hospital system may maintain a single diagnostic center at one central location, serving the diagnostic needs of a number of peripheral screening centers.

Screening and Diagnostic Mammography Centers

A screening and diagnostic mammography center provides full services, including high-volume screening and complete diagnostic services. These tend to be larger centers, often with one or more radiologists that devote most or all of their professional efforts to mammography. These centers provide full breast ser-

Table 3–1. TYPES OF BREAST CENTERS AND PROFESSIONAL STAFFING

Types of Centers	Professional Disciplines
Breast screening center	Radiology/mammography Surgery (general surgery/surgical oncology)
Diagnostic mammography center	Medical oncology Radiation oncology
Screening and diagnostic mammography center	Pathology/cytology Medical genetics
Breast problem clinic	General internal medicine/family medicine Gynecology
Breast cancer treatment center	Nursing Advanced practice nursing
Cancer risk assessment clinic	Physician assistant Genetic counseling Psychology/psychiatry Social work Patient educator Clinical research nurse Pharmacy

Adapted from National Consortium of Breast Centers, Inc.[15]

vices, often including full physical examination services with patient counseling. Some of the first US breast centers were established by radiologists dedicated to providing such patient-centered services, including providing women with immediate results.[16] Indeed, the capacity to provide complete diagnostic results to women on the day of their screening mammography, including a consultation regarding the results, alleviating much of the enormous anxiety induced by screening callbacks, and diagnostic evaluation, is one of the distinct advantages of a comprehensive screening and diagnostic center.

Breast Problem Clinics

A breast problem clinic provides services for evaluation of abnormalities identified on personal or professional physician examination, or by breast imaging. These services may be provided by a breast specialist radiologist, a surgeon with special expertise in breast diseases, or another nonimaging breast specialist such as an internist, family practitioner, or gynecologist with a special interest in breast care and diagnosis. For example, the high-quality and efficient breast cancer intake center for diagnostic evaluation at the Mayo Clinic is staffed by general internists with special interest and experience in breast care. A breast problem clinic may be physically located in or adjacent to a mammography unit, or in a separate location.

Breast Cancer Treatment Center

A breast cancer treatment center provides services for full diagnosis and treatment of breast cancer. These centers may be limited to specialists of one discipline, house the separate practices of providers of different disciplines, or integrate in a staff model system the providers of radiology, pathology, surgery, radiation, medical oncology, and other specialties into a multidisciplinary service. Generally, such centers provide value-added and support services, and quality oversight systems that are not available to physicians in nonintegrated practices. These include case conferences, ongoing data management for case evaluation and reporting, clinical research support, patient support, education and outreach, and psychosocial support programs. These centers may be established in any type of health center, including private practice and tertiary academic systems. They are ideally suited to providing teaching for professionals in all medical specialties and allied disciplines.

Cancer Risk Assessment Clinics

A cancer risk assessment clinic provides services for the evaluation of cancer risk and implementation of prevention strategies, usually with special emphasis on risk associated with inherited susceptibility. Risk assessment clinics are often closely associated with oncology providers (surgical, gynecological, or medical) and medical geneticists, and are most often located in academic centers. They provide comprehensive genetic counseling with certified genetics counselors, as well as preventive services. Cancer risk assessment programs are often comprehensive centers providing services to assess and manage risks of cancer risk syndromes affecting all organ syndromes. Most notable is the need for collaborative efforts of the breast and gynecologic services in breast cancer risk evaluation centers because of the linkage of breast and ovarian cancers in cancer inherited susceptibility syndromes.

Many organizations offer centers that span these service models. Clinical care may be provided in a single administrative unit with screening, diagnostic, comprehensive treatment, genetic, and support services. Conversely, an organization may separate these services physically and administratively but still coordinate their services to provide the entire spectrum of breast care.

STAFFING AND VALUE-ADDED SYSTEMS OF BREAST CENTERS

An advantage of breast centers that may lead to higher patient satisfaction, service efficiency, higher quality of care, and improved outcome is that these centers have highly specialized personnel that devote most or all of their professional efforts to breast disease and work in a collaborative model. Table 3–1 lists many of the disciplines that may be integrated into a breast care system. The physician may remain the "captain of the ship," but must embrace the professional expertise of colleagues from other disciplines. The breast center brings together a sufficient "critical mass" of volume of care not possible in the office of a single physician, and the center makes integrating efforts from all these professionals economically and logistically possible.

These added services may improve quality measured in patient satisfaction, time to service, and increased levels of adherence to established standards of care and outcome. The value-added services include integrated physician service, rapid patient access, immediate diagnosis including the option of "one-stop" centers for evaluation and biopsy, psychosocial support education programs, community outreach, patient navigation, genetic services, lymphedema treatment, nutritional and exercise support, and community education (Table 3–2). In addition, comprehensive programs provide strong platforms for education of health professionals and for clinical and translation research.

A key value to breast centers is the ability to provide rapid access for consultation and early biopsy where necessary. Many believe that such rapid access is critical for women undergoing a stressful experience of abnormalities on mammography or physical examination with the potential diagnosis of breast cancer. Indeed, stress related to a breast abnormality may be equal or greater to that of the cancer diagnosis. Furthermore, because of its common nature, and because most breast abnormalities prove not to be cancerous and require no further treatment nor referral, there is often little attention paid to provide emotional support services for the large number of women who have suspicious breast lesions. Breast centers of all types are more suited to provide rapid service, in some cases offering same-day biopsy for abnormal mammograms. Comprehensive centers allow physicians to work efficiently by providing services outside traditional specialty boundaries. In many excellent breast diagnostic centers, well-trained and dedicated radiologists provide comprehensive breast examination and biopsy services without involving specialists of other disciplines, most notably excluding the surgeon. Only those cases diagnosed with cancer or that need surgical excision for specific benign lesions are even referred to the surgeon. Conversely, in other centers, surgeons perform image-guided biopsy. Both alternatives can be implemented with high quality and allow patients rapid patient service without the delays associated with referral among different specialists.

Although the ability to obtain rapid diagnostic services is assumed to improve the psychological impact of finding a breast abnormality, there are few data to demonstrate whether women who have this rapid referral and biopsy have better psychological or emotional outcomes than those treated in a more traditional system. Indeed, rapidity of diagnosis is now being considered as a quality measure for national accountability in the management of breast cancer. The Institute of Medicine recently recommended measures of the quality of cancer care. One

Table 3–2. VALUE-ADDED SERVICES OF A COMPREHENSIVE BREAST CENTER
Integrated services for primary breast diagnosis and treatment
Radiology, pathology, surgical, medical, radiation oncology, nursing
Rapid access; rapid diagnosis and consultations
Research support and quality management
Clinical research—clinical trials availability
Support of translational and supportive care research
Coordination of collection of biologic specimens
Data collection for quality oversight and cancer registry support
Clinical services to augment primary treatment services
Medical genetics/genetics counseling
Physical therapy
Lymphedema management
Psychology/psychiatry
Social services/counseling
Support services
Education resource center
Patient navigation services
Support group—sponsored and referrals
Wig and prosthetic support—sponsored and referral
Survivorship support
Community support/activities
Educational outreach—general and targeted populations
Coordination of community screening outreach
Support of breast cancer advocacy
Professional education
Pre- and postgraduate medical education in oncology disciplines
Pre- and postgraduate medical education in primary care
Nursing and advanced practice nursing education
Ancillary personnel education
Forums including multidisciplinary conferences—case review and education

measure calls for women with a BIRAD 4 or 5 mammogram to undergo biopsy within 14 days of the abnormal mammogram.[17] In Great Britain, the National Health Service implemented a national mandate in 1999 to reduce wait times for major cancer referrals to 2 weeks or less.[18–20] Suspected breast cancer was among the conditions addressed by this initiative. The data on referral times by breast centers are provided to the public on the Internet (see <http://www.publications.doh.gov.uk/cancer/waitingtimes.htm>; last accessed April 10, 2005). The program has met limited success in reducing wait time, because reduction in wait time for initial consultation may be offset by delays in starting treatment.[20] Despite this lack of clear evidence, the intuitive value of rapid diagnosis has been a core objective in the development of many breast centers.

Breast centers also add value by coordinating the services of specialists of multiple disciplines. For diagnostic services, this may include radiologists and breast surgeons. In comprehensive centers, this may include all oncology disciplines. Each center operationalizes this in different ways. In some centers, patients see staff from one discipline, as defined by the specific requirements of that visit. For example, patients with newly diagnosed cancers see the surgical staff and are referred to the medical and radiation oncology staff after surgery or if presurgical therapy is warranted. In some centers, all such patients are seen at the initial visit by staff from all treatment disciplines who then collectively develop a treatment plan. There are inherent strengths and weaknesses of each organizational model. For example, the former may be more time and cost efficient, and with appropriate quality review may lead to identical treatment plans as the latter model. The second model may be difficult to implement because of scheduling the physician time, especially outside the academic health system, and may be inefficient for both patients and staff. Regardless of the operational model, the value of care coordination in the center seems inherently apparent, but as discussed below, there are few data demonstrating that this results in improved outcomes for cancer patients.

Another value-added aspect of breast centers is the availability of other services that complement the primary diagnostic services and cancer treatment. These services include comprehensive risk evaluation programs, lymphedema prevention and treatment, psychological support, social services, patient navigation, support groups, and patient education. Increasingly, these services are integral to breast care.[21] In the private practice model, such services may be available, but only by separate referral to other independent practitioners, a complicated process that may limit use of the service.

Breast centers also provide the volume of cases necessary to implement and support clinical trial research. Breast cancer is a disease of which there is a large body of high-level evidence that identifies the best treatment options. This evidence was developed through large-scale clinical trials. Because patients on clinical trials receive either the currently known best available care or a new treatment that preliminary evidence suggests will be better, many experts feel that patients receive the highest quality of care when enrolled in a clinical trial. However, pitifully few cancer patients in the United States enroll in such trials, markedly slowing the advance of cancer treatment.[22] One of the barriers to clinical trial enrollment is the organizational requirement to provide the support necessary to meet the data collection needs of the study, and to meet the procedural requirements of the regulatory environment governing clinical trials. Although critically important to assuring human research subject protection, these regulations, coupled with the inadequate financial support for clinical trial research, make clinical trials onerous to the independent physician. Therefore, most patients on clinical trials are entered through large practice centers that have sufficient case volume to make the research enterprise economically viable.

Breast centers also provide patients with the added value of quality assurance oversight. The basis of quality assurance is collecting patient information for subsequent quality review. Like the clinical research enterprise, establishing and maintaining quality assurance databases require a major initial and ongoing investment that may be out of the reach of independent physicians. Another core element of quality assurance is education and dialogue with all professionals in the program. Breast centers specifically conduct ongoing education. Most have a weekly conference at which cases are discussed and treatment plans are reviewed. The breast conference may include all cases treated at the center, or may focus on select cases chosen for presentation because they are either complicated or have specific educational value. However, the regular interaction of professionals and the dialogue on current treatment and developing advances in treatment are key elements in maintaining a high level of care.

OBJECTIVES FOR ESTABLISHING A BREAST CENTER

A successful breast center should be established after careful examination of community needs and thorough defining of the objectives for the center. Failure to identify the goals, or basing a center on goals that are solely altruistic, is a recipe for failure. Centers may be based on a wide range of goals. Among these are enhanced quality of care in diagnosis and cancer treatment, improved efficiency of care, enhanced practice management for participating providers, improved financial performance, and increased regional market share to improve profitability of the physicians, hospital, or health system.

Given the competitive environment of health care delivery in major population centers in the United States, this last goal for the establishment of breast centers must not be discounted. Regardless of whether centers improve the quality, efficiency, and coordination of the care, adequate financial performance is required for the success of any center. Furthermore, even without meeting the objectives of improved quality, the center may provide a better care delivery product that attracts patients, resulting in market shifts. In the United States, such competition is expected and rewarded in all industries, including health care. Even among providers and organizations that give an equally high quality of medical care, it is not unreasonable for organizations to compete on the basis of the quality of care delivered including patient support, location, ease of access, and other amenities. Further recognizing and articulating the financial goals for the center makes it more likely to achieve these and other goals, and to achieve longevity in providing high-quality services to the community.

Reimbursement for breast care is generally considered to be low compared to other services of similar intensity, and generally decreasing levels of reimbursement have strained the financial viability of breast cancer care, even leading to the demise of one of the early leading centers.[13] Services with particularly low reimbursement include breast screening, diagnostic services and surgery. It is especially difficult to provide screening mammography in a cost-effective manner.[23,24] Reimbursement levels for screening mammography may be barely sufficient or insufficient to cover the expense of providing this service, even with the rate increase approved for Medicare by the Center for Medicare and Medicaid Services (CMS) in 2002. One financial analysis of mammography services at seven academic institutions found that all of them provided mammography services at a loss.[25]

The cost of providing any service includes fixed overheads (equipment, space, insurance, personnel) and the marginal costs of supplies for each iteration of the service. The best way to achieve cost efficiency for a service with a low margin is to increase the productivity of personnel and facilities. Increased productivity is best achieved by defining the work flow and optimizing the use of the professional expertise of each member of the team. In breast centers, revenue is generated by physicians providing medical services. Assuring their freedom from nonmedical tasks improves productivity for the entire center. Higher volumes may be achieved by organizational solutions that delegate nonphysician-specific tasks to nonphysician employees and optimizing the time for keeping records through the use of short, templated reports.[16,24]

In addition, the coordination and combination of services in a center allows it to provide a comprehensive service, even if a single component is not itself profitable, as that element contributes to the overall success of the program. For example, mammography is a key component of breast cancer care. A breast center cannot function without high-quality imaging and will lose market share to other practitioners if mammography is not provided. Mammography itself may be at best only marginally, if at all, profitable. However, without mammography, the center will not succeed. The overall financial performance of a center may be positive even with losses in mammography. A detailed analysis of the financial performance of an academic breast center performing 10,000 screening examinations per year found that significant losses in mammography were more than offset by the positive financial impact of the other services provided at the center, including surgery, radiation, and chemotherapy.[26]

The breast surgeon in a single specialty practice faces similar challenges. Reimbursement for breast surgery is relatively low compared to reimbursement for major gastrointestinal, vascular, and thoracic surgeries. Economic viability for a breast surgical practice may only be accomplished by increasing the volume of and diversifying services. Although formal economic studies of this issue have not been published in the United States, a European study demonstrated that cost efficiencies were enhanced in breast surgery by increasing caseload to approximately 150 new breast cancer cases per year.[27]

Another means to enhance the financial performance of a center is to increase the volume of services with higher reimbursement. Centers need to critically assess the value of such technologies when introducing them into practice to avoid the overuse of a service of marginal medical value, or in which providers are not well qualified to enhance financial performance. An example that raised such concerns occurred in the early 1990s, when surgeons were losing breast diagnostic surgical biopsy procedures to other specialists performing image-guided needle biopsy. Many surgeons had learned the technique of image-guided needle biopsy and offered these procedures in competition with radiology colleagues. This move in breast surgery was one of the driving forces behind the founding of the American Society of Breast Surgeons, an organization that has matured into a major academic outlet for breast surgeons as well. Many surgeons became quite expert in these techniques and provided high-quality services. However, without oversight, there was concern that less experienced surgeons, especially those working outside a collaborative arrangement with a radiologist, might provide services of inferior quality. Furthermore, the availability of the less morbid needle biopsy raised concerns over the potential for overuse of breast biopsy for lesions of low suspicion that would otherwise require only short-term imaging follow-up. At some centers, this would be manifested in a low rate of biopsies positive for cancer. Ideally, 30 to 40% of image-guided biopsy should prove to be malignant. Lower positive rates suggest an overuse of breast biopsy. A recent study confirmed that increased use of core biopsy in a large academic practice resulted in a doubling of the rate of biopsy procedures, with a concomitant decrease in the positive rate.[28] Data comparing practice in the United States with that in the United Kingdom have suggested that a doubling of the biopsy rate in the United States did not increase the rate of detection of early breast cancer.[29] One community-wide study showed that the positive rate for breast biopsies in the mid-1990s varied among centers, ranging from 40 to as low as 7%.[30] Concerns over the quality of image-guided biopsy led the American College of Surgeons to collaborate with the American College of Radiology to establish credentialing standards for surgeons and radiologists performing these procedures, either independently or in collaborative practice environments.[31]

Financial pressures may also lead to the overuse of unproven technologies with high profit margins. For example, a new technology available to augment mammography interpretation is computer-assisted diagnosis (CAD) of scanned mammogram images. Large studies of CAD are inconclusive about its value at improving the sensitivity of mammography, particularly in high-volume mammography centers.[32] However, reimbursement for mammography with CAD is higher than for mammography alone. One group recommended the use of CAD in a breast center to improve financial performance.[33]

Other quality concerns in breast practice may stem from financial pressures. Despite widespread availability of needle biopsy, and the recognition that needle biopsy is preferred over surgical biopsy, many surgeons still perform surgical excision for mammography-detected abnormalities. The use of surgical biopsy in place of needle biopsy increases the number of trips to surgery and the number of billable operations performed by a surgeon. Similarly, indiscriminate use of central venous access devices increases the financial performance of a breast surgical practice. Central venous access is not required for many or most women receiving chemotherapy, but in many practices, most women receive these devices. Indiscriminate use of central venous access devices in all patients may not be quality care, but may improve the bottom line for the surgeon. Therefore, it is extremely important for breast centers to critically analyze their treatment practices to assure that services are appropriately applied.

A key financial benefit of breast centers is to centralize services and increase volume. Centers aim to increase the number of patients seen, drawing patients from other providers and centers in their community, and expanding the geographic base of their practice. There are few data on the large-scale effects of centers on the patterns of care and referral on a regional level. Anecdotally, referral patterns in large population centers have concentrated the care of a large fraction of breast cancer patients into the hands of a few centers and providers. This is best documented in the number of breast cancer cases treated annually by individual surgeons. In the late 1980s in New York State, approximately 3,000 surgeons performed surgery on at least one patient among the 12,000 cases of breast cancer diagnosed annually.[34] The most recent data show that the large majority of surgeons treat only a few cases, and that the majority of cases in New York are treated by less than 100 surgeons.[35] Similarly, in Los Angeles in the 1990s, most surgeons treated only a few cases (median number per surgeon < 5), and only a minority of surgeons treated many cases, suggesting a similar concentration of cases in centers.[36]

QUALITY OF CARE AND OUTCOME

The most common stated goal among breast centers is to improve quality. There is clear documentation that the quality of breast cancer care varies widely.[4,37] The degree to which breast centers have been successful in improving quality is not well documented. Quality is difficult to quantify, and it may be hard to determine if improvements in quality of care are because of the new organizational model with the breast center or because of general improvements in health care delivery among all providers.

There are two key dimensions of quality in a breast center. One is the quality of the medical care delivered, be it imaging, biopsy, or a component of cancer care. The other dimension is the quality of the patient experience. Although the stated objective may be to improve the quality of delivered care, a major impact of a breast center may be in improving the patient experience and satisfaction with care.

The most widely accepted definition from the Institute of Medicine states is that quality is, "the degree to which health services for individuals and populations increase the likelihood of desired health outcomes and are consistent with current professional knowledge."[38] This definition encompasses many dimensions of quality: quality does not achieve good outcome for all; quality is an issue for individuals and populations; quality standards are constantly changing. A more functional definition of quality is "doing the right thing at the right time."

QUALITY MEASURES

A key issue is how to quantify quality. Subjectively, we may recognize poor quality in individual cases or from specific providers. However, measuring quality on a broader scale requires accepted and validated measures for which the data to apply the measures are available. Quality may be measured in three domains, including the structure of the health care systems and care models, the outcome of care, and the processes of care. The primary outcomes of cancer care include survival, cancer recurrence, and preservation of organ function. Processes of cancer care refer to the performance of expected treatment as defined by accepted standards of care. These standards are consensus standards as defined in cancer care by professional societies and the National Cancer Institute, and codified in practice guidelines such as those developed by the National Comprehensive Cancer Network.[39]

Outcomes in cancer care may not be as useful as process measures for ongoing quality evaluation. The major outcomes in cancer care require many years of follow-up. Specifically, mortality and cancer recurrence in breast cancer may not occur for 5 to 10 years. This time frame makes these measures of no value in quality improvement. Furthermore, mortality and recurrence may be insensitive to variations in quality. In a disease such as breast cancer, where the benefit of therapy is often measured in the improvement in survival of a few percent (eg, the addition of a taxane to anthracycline-based chemotherapy), or even in only an improvement of disease-free survival where an overall survival benefit has not been demonstrated (eg, the use of anastrozole in place of tamoxifen in adjuvant therapy), it may be impossible to differentiate good from bad quality on the basis of outcomes. Therefore, measures of the processes of care may be of more value in assessing quality.

Unfortunately, there are no accepted and validated sets of process measures for breast cancer care. Measures for cancer care must address common issues of significant burden, and must be clinically relevant, amenable to change, backed by strong evidence, free of confounding factors, and measurable with available or readily collectable data.[40]

Basic measures of the breast cancer care widely used include measures of the population of patients treated, such as the proportion of those diagnosed with early-stage disease, those that receive breast-conserving therapy, and the percentage that receive adjuvant systemic therapy. Another approach is to derive process measures for all aspects of care from comprehensive practice guidelines. For each patient that fits the cancer stage and treatment of a component of a guideline, the care is determined to be "concordant" with the guideline or "nonconcordant." This allows detailed dissection of the care provided with a means to identify areas for improvement of quality. The most widely used guidelines for this purpose are the comprehensive cancer guidelines of the NCCN.[15]

There have been attempts at developing comprehensive panels of quality measures for breast cancer care. However, most of these have been based largely on the opinion of the members of the organizations developing the measures. Virtually none of the measures have been validated so that they can reliably be applied to compare providers or practices, or be used to direct care or payment. These panels of measures generally cover aspects of care ranging from screening and diagnosis to treatment of early-stage and advanced cancers. For example, in 2000, the Rand Corporation published sets of measures for multiple cancer types, including breast cancer.[41] These cover breast diagnostic care and treatment, but have not been validated in practice. Many aspects of care addressed in these measures are not codified in any existing administrative, medical record, or registry system. This highlights the problem of balancing the need for in-depth data to assess quality, with the need to have reasonable data requirements for data collection.[42]

In 2005, the Institute of Medicine published a set of measures commissioned by the Georgia Cancer Coalition to assess the quality of cancer care.[17] However, the measures were developed by a panel of national authorities and are not Georgia-specific. The breast cancer quality measures from this project are shown in Table 3–3. These range from population measures of breast cancer mortality and the use of screening, to assessment of specific processes of care for defined subset of patients.

Other organizations are developing quality measures in 2005. The National Quality Forum, under contract from the CMS, the National Cancer Institute, and the Agency for Healthcare Research and Quality, is developing a panel of quality measures for breast, colorectal, and prostate cancers, as well as cross-cutting domains, including pain management and palliative care. The American Society of Clinical Oncology is developing quality measures based on its program examining the care of breast and colon cancer patients, and has established a separate program for assessing quality in medical oncology offices.

Quality measurement programs that are specific to breast centers have been previously described. Most rely on data collection in the center, with reporting of proportions of patients receiving care concordant with a variety of process measures with ongoing review for improvement of quality.[43–45] A multicenter quality evaluation program is under development for pilot testing in 2005 through the National Consortium of Breast Centers.[15]

DATA FOR QUALITY MEASUREMENT

The availability of detailed data on care is a key element to measuring quality. Collecting community-wide data on cancer treatment is a daunting task, limited both by resources and collective commitment. Kahn and colleagues set forth a model, highlighting

Table 3–3. BREAST QUALITY MEASURES FROM INSTITUTE OF MEDICINE, 2005

Domain of Care	Description of Quality Measures
Preventing cancer	Breast cancer incidence rate
Detecting early cancer	Breast screening rate Proportion of breast cancer cases diagnosed at an early stage Incidence of advanced-stage breast cancer
Diagnosing cancer	Timely breast cancer biopsy after a category 4 or 5 abnormal mammogram—biopsy performed within14 days of the date of mammogram Needle biopsy performed before breast cancer surgery Tumor-free surgical margins in breast-conserving surgery (BCS) Appropriate histologic assessment of stage I and stage II breast cancers Pathology reports on invasive breast cancer surgical specimens that include College of American Pathologists data elements Breast cancer cases in which pathologic staging preceded chemotherapy and radiation treatment
Treating cancer	Cancer patients in treatment who participate in clinical trials Adjuvant radiation after BCS for women under age 70 years Adjuvant hormonal therapy for hormone receptor-positive invasive breast cancer Adjuvant combination chemotherapy for women under age 71 years with hormone receptor-negative stage I to stage III breast cancers Follow-up mammography after treatment for breast cancer Cancer pain assessment Prevalence of pain among cancer patients Cancer deaths in hospice per 100 cancer deaths Breast cancer 5- and 10-year survival rates Breast cancer deaths per 100,000 females per year

Adapted from Assess the Quality of Cancer Care; An Approach to Measurement in Georgia.[17]

four key components necessary to measure quality: case identification, source of data, data-collection strategies, and availability of a care management model of measures.[42] They specifically cautioned that the extent of resources needed to establish and maintain an ideal quality measurement program makes it necessary to make trade-offs between the validity and the resource burden of measurement.

Even though community-wide data may not be available for comparison, it is important for a breast center to collect data on all patients treated at the center for quality assurance. These data should include (at a minimum) demographics, risk factors and family history, comorbidity and concurrent illness, imaging history, mode of diagnostic testing, cancer staging and pathology characteristics, type of treatment for local and systemic therapies, and follow-up information. Additional data may include measures of quality of life, satisfaction with care, clinical trial management systems, and databases for specific research studies. This information can then be used for an ongoing evaluation of quality, and research in patterns of care and translational research.

One notable example of a system specific to breast cancer is the breast cancer outcomes database of the NCCN. This system collects data similar to the cancer registry, but is more granular, is collected close to the point and time of service, and is audited for completeness and quality of data. Data collection began in 1998, and as of 2005, data have been collected on over 20,000 breast cancer patients treated at comprehensive cancer centers across the United States. The primary purpose of this database is to benchmark care against practice guidelines, and to study factors affecting variation in practice.[46,47]

The data sets for breast centers overlap with other health system data systems. Whereas the data required for management of a breast center are greater than that needed for MQSA certification or cancer registry, the data collected for the breast center should ideally be coordinated and linked with such data sets, and with other health system data, including electronic health records and financial data systems. Breast cancer data are collected in hospital and population cancer registries. Hospital cancer registries at hospitals participating in the approvals programs of the Commission on Cancer of the American College of Surgeons are the most comprehensive.[4] These include data on the type of cancer; comorbidity based on discharge diagnosis codes; treatment including surgery, radiation, and systemic therapy; and follow-up data on cancer recurrence and survival. Although rapidly improving over the last few years, the use of cancer registries suffers from variably incomplete data on care that occurs outside of the hospital.[48] This is especially significant for diseases like breast cancer, where care is administered mostly in the outpatient setting. Population registries are used mostly for identifying population trends in cancer incidence and mortality. They are less useful to monitor quality of care because of limited applicable data, and because the data are not available for 1 to 3 years after diagnosis. However, breast centers should be aware of other data systems within their community and look to collaborate with other programs to enhance available data and minimize the duplication of data collection.

It is important that breast centers maintain data systems for quality management. However, an individual center's data system does not allow a center to compare its care with that administered elsewhere in their community. Such comparisons require consistent and high-quality data on the entire community of patients with breast disease and not only on the convenience cohort of patients treated at the center. For many reasons, including access, insurance coverage, cultural barriers, and referral bias, the population of patients at a given breast center is unlikely to be representative of the community of breast disease patients, and crude comparisons with rudimentary community data are not likely to be valid. Unfortunately, breast centers are often tempted to use these data in misleading marketing campaigns, with claims that their center provides better care.

There is a growing need for data to be accessible to the public for the purpose of holding institutions and hospitals accountable for their performance and to allow consumers to choose providers or hospitals. Because breast cancer is so prevalent, such reporting by breast centers is likely to be required. To date, there are limited publicly available data for such purposes. However, an idea of how such reporting might appear can be obtained from the American College of Surgeons National Cancer Data Base. In collaboration with the American Cancer Society, the ACoS makes NCDB available for public use at its web site.[49] An example of the type of data available on breast cancer surgery are shown in Figure 3–1. The proportion of patients receiving different types of breast cancer surgery is shown comparing three types of ACoS approved cancer centers: Community Centers, Comprehensive Community Centers, and Teaching/Research Centers. For simplicity, Figure 3–1 only shows crude rates for all cancers. However the currently available website allows stratification by variables including stage of disease, age, race and other factors. Other functions allow viewing of data on survival and recurrence. At the current time, the only data available to the public are aggregate data based on type of cancer center. Each participating cancer center can access data on itself for comparison to other centers in its state or region. Under its current plan, the ACoS is looking to establish public access to data on volume, patterns of care, and outcomes on specific hospitals. It is highly likely that other groups ranging from non-profit groups such as ACoS to health payers and for-profit data mining organizations will establish similar reporting systems for the public in the near future.

DO BREAST CENTERS PROVIDE BETTER CARE?

The absence of reliable community-wide data on cancer care and the lack of accepted measures of quality make it difficult to determine whether care in breast centers is better than that from doctors in practices outside of the center. The available literature mostly reviews the patterns of care in centers and compares that care to data from prior time periods at that institution or from the patterns of care in prior years reported from population registries. Although such data are provocative, they do not provide definitive evidence that cancer center care is better.

Early data suggesting improved treatment at breast centers came from the University of Michigan for patients treated from 1985 to 1991.[9,10] These reports demonstrated rates of breast-conserving surgery to be well above the national average, and

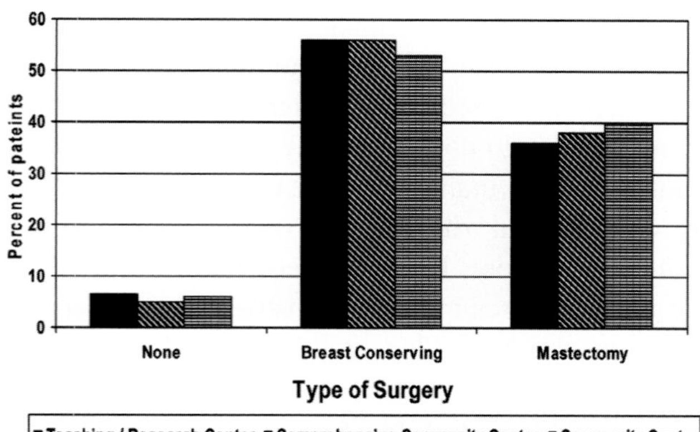

Figure 3–1. Public reporting of breast cancer treatment data: Pattern of breast surgery comparing cancer center types in 2001. Publicly available data from National Cancer Database <http://web.facs.org/ncdbbmr/ncdbbenchmarks.cfm> (accessed August 6, 2005).

the value in clinical trials, education, and support of basic research. The breast center at the Henry Ford Hospital also demonstrated benefits compared to patients treated before the implementation of the center, with improved satisfaction and reduced time to completed treatment.[50]

Another approach taken to demonstrate improved quality of care in breast centers is to examine the frequency with which treatment recommendations are changed for patients who come to the center for a second opinion. For example, the University of Pennsylvania multidisciplinary team disagreed with outside treatment recommendations in 43% of cases.[51] Changes included breast-conserving surgery in place of mastectomy, need for re-excision, additional work-up, and major change in pathology. A similar report from the Lynn Sage Breast Center at Northwestern University found that treatment recommendations were changed in 20% of cases.[52]

Another important measure of the quality of care is patient satisfaction with care. The majority of studies examining this question show higher levels of patient satisfaction with breast center care, though again, most do not have a comparison of breast center with non-breast center patients. For example, the one-stop diagnostic clinics in place in the United Kingdom provide high levels of satisfaction.[53] However, an interesting randomized trial suggested that women treated with one-stop clinics did not reduce short term anxiety compared to traditional systems of evaluation.[54]

These data provide limited proof that the care administered at a breast center is of higher quality or provides better outcomes. A recent systematic review evaluating diagnostic assessment units in oncology identified only 20 articles examining the outcomes of patients treated in such units for all of oncology.[55] The majority were in breast cancer, many of which are reviewed above. The review concluded that the promise of these oncology units is apparent, but that more rigorous evaluations are needed.

An indirect inference of the value of breast center care comes from data that demonstrate that women treated by more specialized providers, or those with higher case volumes, have better outcomes. There are compelling data on the relationships between outcome and case volume. Although this does not directly identify care provided at breast centers versus outside of such centers, high-volume providers are more likely to work in settings that include multidisciplinary care or formal breast center structures.

It is likely that an association between specialization and/or annual case volume and outcome exists for all specialties, including breast imaging, surgery, pathology, radiation oncology, and medical oncology. This has led to specialty training in breast disease, breast surgery, breast imaging, and breast pathology. Data to demonstrate this relationship are most available on the case volume of surgeons. As noted above, the majority of surgeons that perform surgery for breast cancer treat very few cases of breast cancer annually. The median number of cases per surgeon per year in New York in the early 1990s was 4.[34] In the Los Angeles area in the late 1990s, over half the surgeons who operated on breast cancer treated only one patient.[36] Only a handful of surgeons treat more that 20 to 30 cases per year. The large number of low-volume surgeons treat a substantial fraction of breast cancer patients. In New York State in 2002, 25% of all breast cancer operations were done by surgeons who did only 1 operation, and 50% were done by surgeons who did 5 or fewer.[35] Only 76 surgeons in New York, a state with a population of 19 million and 13,000 breast cancers annually, performed more than 50 operations. Most of these surgeons work at well-recognized multidisciplinary breast centers that are associated with major teaching hospitals and regional cancer centers.

A number of studies have demonstrated that women treated by surgeons with higher patient volume have better outcomes than those treated by low-volume surgeons. In Yorkshire, England, patients treated by surgeons with more than 30 cases per year had significantly improved survival than those treated by surgeons with fewer cases.[56] Women treated in general surgery offices were less likely to be treated with guideline-appropriate care than those treated in breast centers. Women treated by high case-load surgeons in Western Australia in the 1990s were more likely to have breast-sparing surgery, receive radiation, and be alive, compared with women treated by surgeons with low case loads.[57] A similar relationship was found between surgeon and hospital case volume in the mid-1990s in Los Angeles.[36] In New York in the late 1980s, a significant association was noted between hospital case volume and 5-year survival rates, controlling for stage, age, race, and socioeconomic status.[34]

FACTORS IN ESTABLISHING A BREAST CENTER

Although the data demonstrating the value of breast centers in providing better cancer treatment outcomes are limited, the benefits seem to be clear from the available data. Breast centers must set the standard for breast cancer care, including a commitment to multidisciplinary care, patients support, teaching, and research. As part of this commitment, breast centers should also perform ongoing audits of the care that they provide, with careful investigation of the barriers to quality of care. The current effort of the National Consortium of Breast Centers in a multicenter quality evaluation program is one excellent example of the types of effort possible.[15]

Future efforts should focus on assuring that all patients receive the best available breast cancer care. This requires coordinated action from professional organizations and government. At the regional level, those establishing breast centers should engage all community-wide constituencies. They should inventory available resources, the sites where cancer is treated, and ongoing collaborative efforts. They should define community-wide data collection systems to track cancer care.

The same organizational solution may not meet the needs of different communities. An important issue in breast cancer management is to recognize that many women do not have ready access to multidisciplinary care. In many urban areas, access is restricted by cultural and financial barriers.[3] Similar access issues face those living in remote or rural areas. Major differences in the administration of breast cancer care have been identified between those in rural and in urban areas in both the United Kingdom and the United States.[58–60] Such issues must be addressed when planning and organizing a breast center.

Many factors will continue to spur the development of the multidisciplinary model for breast cancer care. Breast cancer is the most common cancer that affects women, and with the aging population, the absolute numbers of cases will rise. This population is increasingly demanding high-quality, coordinated, and sophisticated care. Breast medicine requires the input of many specialties where the depth of knowledge and expertise are increasingly demanding. Financial pressures will increasingly require coordination and centralization of breast services. Those developing breast centers must pay careful attention to community needs and access for at-risk populations to assure that all women have access to the best possible breast care.

REFERENCES

1. McGlynn EA, Asch SM, Adams J, et al. The quality of health care delivered to adults in the United States. N Engl J Med 2003;348:2635–45.
2. Hewitt M, Simone JV, editors. Ensuring quality cancer care. Washington (DC): National Academy Press; 1999.
3. Hurd TC, James T, Foster JM. Factors that affect breast cancer treatment: underserved and minority populations. Surg Oncol Clin N Am 2005;14:119–30, vii.
4. Edge SB, Cookfair DL, Watroba N. The role of the surgeon in quality cancer care. Curr Probl Surg 2003;40:511–90.
5. Crossing the quality chasm: a new health system for the 21st century. Washington (DC): National Academy Press; 2001.
6. Birdwell RL, Wilcox PA. The mammography quality standards act: benefits and burdens. Breast Dis 2001;13:97–107.
7. Pisano ED, Schell M, Rollins J, et al. Has the mammography quality standards act affected the mammography quality in North Carolina? AJR Am J Roentgenol 2000;174:1089–91.
8. Link JS. History and overview of comprehensive interdisciplinary breast centers. Surg Oncol Clin N Am 2000;9:147–57.
9. Harness JK, Bartlett RH, Saran PA, et al. Developing a comprehensive breast center. Am Surg 1987;53:419–23.
10. August DA, Carpenter LC, Harness JK, et al. Benefits of a

multidisciplinary approach to breast care. J Surg Oncol 1993;53:161–7.
11. Chang AE. Multidisciplinary cancer clinics: their time has come. J Surg Oncol 1998;69:203–5.
12. Roux S, Logan-Young W. Private practice interdisciplinary breast centers: their rationale and impact on patients, physicians, and the health care industry: a bicoastal perspective. Surg Oncol Clin N Am 2000;9:177–98.
13. Silverstein MJ. The Van Nuys Breast Center: the first free-standing multidisciplinary breast center. Surg Oncol Clin N Am 2000;9:159–75.
14. The requirements of a specialist breast unit. Eur J Cancer 2000;36:2288–93.
15. National Consortium of Breast Centers, Inc. Available at: http://www.breastcare.org (accessed July 4, 2005).
16. Logan-Young W. The breast imaging center. Successful management in today's environment. Radiol Clin North Am 2000;38:853–60.
17. Eden J, Simone JV, editors. Assess the quality of cancer care; an approach to measurement in Georgia. Washington (DC): The National Academy Press; 2005.
18. Cant PJ, Yu DS. Impact of the '2 week wait' directive for suspected cancer on service provision in a symptomatic breast clinic. Br J Surg 2000;87:1082–6.
19. Khawaja AR, Allan SM. Has the breast cancer 'two week wait' guarantee for assessment made any difference? Eur J Surg Oncol 2000;26:536–9.
20. Robinson D, Bell CM, Moller H, Basnett I. Effect of the UK government's 2-week target on waiting times in women with breast cancer in southeast England. Br J Cancer 2003;89:492–6.
21. Rabinowitz B. Psychologic issues, practitioners' interventions, and the relationship of both to an interdisciplinary breast center team. Surg Oncol Clin N Am 2000;9:347–65.
22. Murthy VH, Krumholz HM, Gross CP. Participation in cancer clinical trials: race-, sex-, and age-based disparities. JAMA 2004;291:2720–6.
23. Farria D, Feig SA. An introduction to economic issues in breast imaging. Radiol Clin North Am 2000;38:825–42.
24. Feig SA. Economic challenges in breast imaging. A survivor's guide to success. Radiol Clin North Am 2000;38:843–52.
25. Enzmann DR, Anglada PM, Haviley C, Venta LA. Providing professional mammography services: financial analysis. Radiology 2001;219:467–73.
26. Chen SL, Clark S, Pierce LJ, et al. An academic health center cost analysis of screening mammography: creating a financially viable service. Cancer 2004;101:1043–50.
27. Pagano E, Ponti A, Gelormino E, et al. An economic evaluation of the optimal workload in treating surgical patients in a breast unit. Eur J Cancer 2003;39:748–54.
28. Gur D, Wallace LP, Klym AH, et al. Trends in recall, biopsy, and positive biopsy rates for screening mammography in an academic practice. Radiology 2005;235:396–401.
29. Smith-Bindman R, Chu PW, Miglioretti DL, et al. Comparison of screening mammography in the United States and the United Kingdom. JAMA 2003;290:2129–37.
30. McKee MD, Cropp MD, Hyland A, et al. Provider case volume and outcome in the evaluation and treatment of patients with mammogram-detected breast carcinoma. Cancer 2002;95:704–12.
31. Bassett L, Winchester DP, Caplan RB, et al. Stereotactic core-needle biopsy of the breast: a report of the Joint Task Force of the American College of Radiology, American College of Surgeons, and College of American Pathologists. CA Cancer J Clin 1997;47:171–90.
32. Gur D, Sumkin JH, Rockette HE, et al. Changes in breast cancer detection and mammography recall rates after the introduction of a computer-aided detection system. J Natl Cancer Inst 2004;96:185–90.
33. Kolb GR. New tools for cost-effective delivery of breast imaging. Radiol Manage 2002;24:22–6, 28, 30.
34. Roohan PJ, Bickell NA, Baptiste MS, et al. Hospital volume differences and five-year survival from breast cancer. Am J Public Health 1998;88:454–7.
35. Breast cancer surgery performed by individual doctors in New York in 2002 (inpatient and outpatient) and 1999 and 1997 (inpatient only). Available at: http://www.healthcarechoices.com.breastsurdrny/breastsurdrny.htm (accessed July 4, 2005).
36. Skinner KA, Helsper JT, Deapen D, et al. Breast cancer: do specialists make a difference? Ann Surg Oncol 2003; 10:606–15.
37. Malin JL, Schuster MA, Kahn KA, Brook RH. Quality of breast cancer care: what do we know? J Clin Oncol 2002; 20:4381–93.
38. Institute of Medicine. Medicare: A strategy for quality assurance. Volume 1. Committee to design a strategy for quality review and assurance in Medicare. Lohr K, ed. Washington, DC: National Academy Press; 1990.
39. The NCNN Clinial Practice Guidelines in Oncology. Available at: http://www.nccn.org/professionals/physician_gls/default.asp (accessed July 4, 2005).
40. Mandelblatt JS, Ganz PA, Kahn KL. Proposed agenda for the measurement of quality-of-care outcomes in oncology practice. J Clin Oncol 1999;17:2614–22.
41. Quality of care for oncologic conditions and HIV: a review of the literature and quality indicators. Santa Monica (CA): The Rand Corporation; 2000.
42. Kahn KL, Malin JL, Adams J, Ganz PA. Developing a reliable, valid, and feasible plan for quality-of-care measurement for cancer: how should we measure? Med Care 2002;40 Suppl 6:III73–85.
43. Coleman C. Building quality into comprehensive breast care: a practical approach. Surg Oncol Clin N Am 2000;9:319–37.
44. Hughes KS, Barbarisi LJ, Rossi RL, et al. Using continuous quality improvement (CQI) to improve the care of patients with breast cancer. Adm Radiol J 1997;16:19–27.
45. Kollias J, Bochner MA, Gill PG, et al. Quality assurance in a multidisciplinary symptomatic breast assessment clinic. ANZ J Surg 2001;71:271–3.
46. Niland JC. NCCN outcomes research database: data collection via the Internet. Oncology (Huntingt) 2000;14:100–3.
47. Edge SB, Niland JC, Bookman MA, et al. Emergence of sentinel node biopsy in breast cancer as standard-of-care in academic comprehensive cancer centers. J Natl Cancer Inst 2003;95:1514–21.
48. Malin JL, Kahn KL, Adams J, et al. Validity of cancer registry data for measuring the quality of breast cancer care. J Natl Cancer Inst 2002;94:835–44.
49. American College of Surgeons NCDB Benchmark Reports –

Patterns of Care for Selected Cancers and Treatments 1997–2001. Available at: http://web.facs.org/ncdbbmr/ncdbbenchmarks.cfm (accessed August 6, 2005).

50. Gabel M, Hilton NE, Nathanson SD. Multidisciplinary breast cancer clinics. Do they work? Cancer 1997;79:2380–4.
51. Chang JH, Vines E, Bertsch H, et al. The impact of a multidisciplinary breast cancer center on recommendations for patient management: the University of Pennsylvania experience. Cancer 2001;91:1231–7.
52. Clauson J, Hsieh YC, Acharya S, et al. Results of the Lynn Sage Second-Opinion Program for local therapy in patients with breast carcinoma. Changes in management and determinants of where care is delivered. Cancer 2002;94:889–94.
53. Berry MG, Chan SY, Engledow A, et al. An audit of patient acceptance of one-stop diagnosis for symptomatic breast disease. Eur J Surg Oncol 1998;24:492–5.
54. Dey P, Bundred N, Gibbs A, et al. Costs and benefits of a one stop clinic compared with a dedicated breast clinic: randomised controlled trial. BMJ 2002;324:507–11.
55. Gagliardi A, Grunfeld E, Evans WK. Evaluation of diagnostic assessment units in oncology: a systematic review. J Clin Oncol 2004;22:1126–35.
56. Sainsbury R, Haward B, Rider L, et al. Influence of clinician workload and patterns of treatment on survival from breast cancer. Lancet 1995;345:1265–70.
57. Ingram DM, McEvoy SP, Byrne MJ, et al. Surgical caseload and outcomes for women with invasive breast cancer treated in Western Australia. Breast 2005;14:11–7.
58. Sainsbury R, Rider L, Smith A, MacAdam A. Does it matter where you live? Treatment variation for breast cancer in Yorkshire. The Yorkshire Breast Cancer Group. Br J Cancer 1995;71:1275–8.
59. Baldwin LM, Taplin SH, Friedman H, Moe R. Access to multidisciplinary cancer care: is it linked to the use of breast-conserving surgery with radiation for early-stage breast carcinoma? Cancer 2004;100:701–9.
60. Elliott TE, Elliott BA, Renier CM, Haller IV. Rural-urban differences in cancer care: results from the Lake Superior Rural Cancer Care Project. Minn Med 2004;87:44–50.

4

Epidemiology of Breast Cancer

VICTOR G. VOGEL

DEMOGRAPHICS AND DESCRIPTIVE STATISTICS

Breast cancer is the most common form of cancer and is the second leading cause of cancer death among women in the United States. It is estimated that in the year 2005, more than 212,000 American women will be diagnosed with breast cancer and approximately 41,000 women will die from this disease.[1] Both incidence (Figure 4–1) and death from all malignancies (Figure 4–2) are greatest in African Americans than in white or other ethnic groups in the United States. US incidence rates of breast cancer are 20 to 40% higher in white women than in non-white women; however, US incidence rates are higher in young (< age 40 yr) black women than in young white women (Figure 4–3). In 1990 the majority of the 300,000 breast cancer deaths worldwide occurred in developed countries, yet annual mortality rates ranged from 27 in 100,000 women in northern Europe, to 4 in 100,000 women in Asia. Studies of increasing breast cancer rates among first-generation daughters of Japanese American women suggest that environmental and lifestyle factors are of greater significance than are genetic factors in explaining international differences in breast cancer risk.[2–4] The identification of potentially modifiable risk factors for breast cancer, therefore, provides opportunities for breast cancer prevention among women both at average and high risk.

RISK FACTORS FOR BREAST CANCER

Few breast cancer risk factors have prevalence in the population of greater than 10 to 15%, although some are associated with very large relative risks (eg,

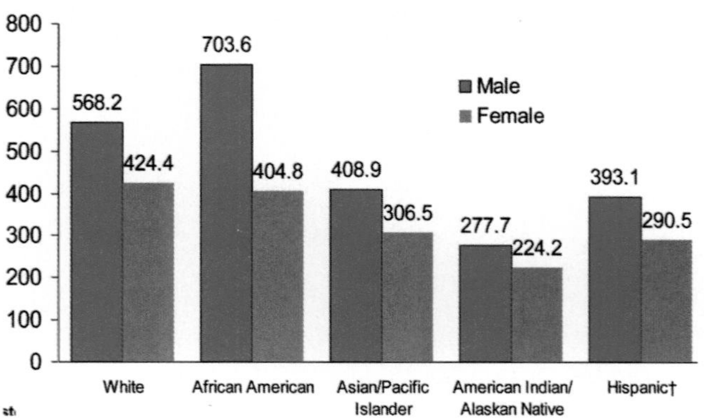

Figure 4–1. Cancer incidence rates by race and ethnicity in the United States 1992–1999. Data are from the National Cancer Institute Surveillance, Epidemiology and End Results (SEER) Program of the National Cancer Institute.

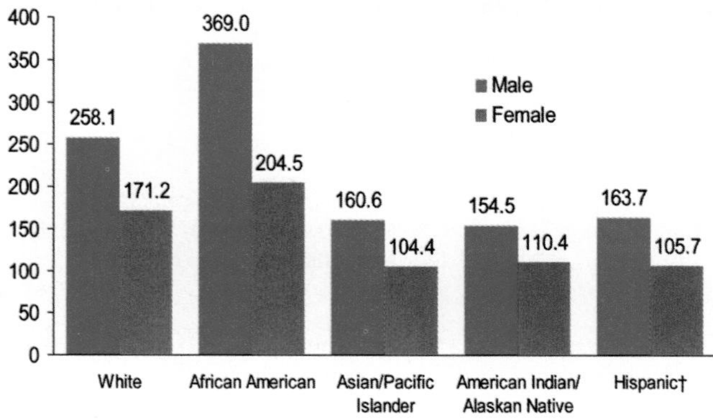

Figure 4–2. Cancer death rates by race and ethnicity in the United States 1992–1999. Data are from the National Cancer Institute Surveillance, Epidemiology and End Results (SEER) Program of the National Cancer Institute.

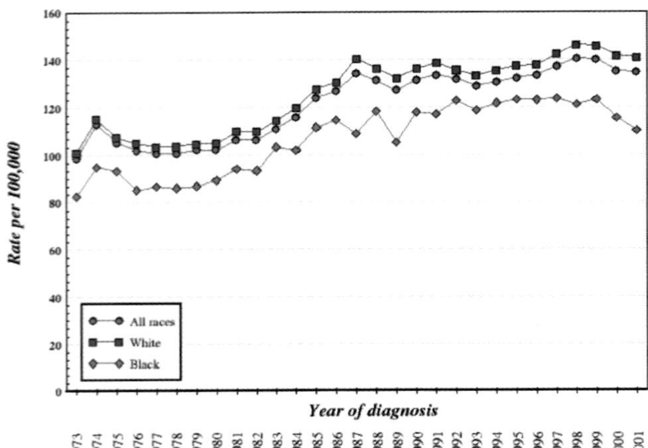

Figure 4–3. Age-adjusted breast cancer incidence rates, United States females, 1973–2001, by race. Data are from the National Cancer Institute Surveillance, Epidemiology and End Results (SEER) Program of the National Cancer Institute.

mutated genes, cellular atypia). Age is one of the most important risk factors for breast cancer.[5] Although age-adjusted incidence rates continue to rise, breast cancer mortality has fallen in the past decade in the United States.[1] Common clinical risk factors for breast cancer are shown in Table 4–1, along with the magnitude of their associated risks and the strength of the evidence that establishes them as risk factors for breast cancer. Traits associated with large relative risks are rare; common risk factors are associated with relative risks < 2.0, so the attributable risk for any particular risk factor is small.[6] Estimates of the summary attributable risk for breast cancer range from only 21 to 55%, leaving most of this attributable risk for the disease unexplained. Nevertheless, it is instructive to examine what is known regarding risk factors for breast cancer. We concentrate here on new and recently identified traits, factors, and exposures.

Breast cancer occurs over 100 times more frequently in women than in men. In the United States in 2003, about 1,300 new cases of male breast cancer were expected to be diagnosed, and approximately 400 deaths occurred as a result of male breast cancer.[7] Genetics may contribute to the etiology of male breast cancer, with increased risk linked to a familial history of breast cancer and in patients with Klinefelter's syndrome.

BENIGN BREAST DISEASE

One accepted hypothesis about the origin of breast cancer is that cells progress through sequential changes over a period of years. Benign breast lesions can be classified according to their histologic appearance. Benign breast lesions thought to impart no increased risk of breast cancer include adenosis, duct ectasia, simple fibroadenoma, fibrosis, mastitis, mild hyperplasia, cysts, and metaplasia of the apocrine or squamous types.[6,8] Lesions associated with a slight increase in the subsequent risk of developing invasive breast cancer include complex fibroadenoma, moderate or florid hyperplasia with or without atypia, sclerosing adenosis, and papilloma. Atypical hyperplasia of the ductal or lobular type is associated with a four- to fivefold increased

Table 4–1. CLASSICAL RISK FACTORS FOR BREAST CANCER: RELATIVE AND POPULATION ATTRIBUTABLE RISKS

Risk Factor	Comparison Category	Risk Category	Relative Risk	Prevalence (%)	Population Attributable Risk*
Age at menarche	16 yr	< 12 yr	1.3	16	0.05
Age at menopause	45–54 yr	> 55 yr	1.5	6	0.03
Age when first child born alive	< 20 yr	Nulliparous or > 30 yr	1.9	21	0.16
Benign breast disease	No biopsy or fine-needle aspiration	Any benign disease	1.5	15	0.07
		Proliferative disease	2.0	4	0.04
		Atypical hyperplasia	4.0	1	0.03
Family history of breast cancer	No first-degree relative affected	Mother affected	1.7	8	0.05
		Two first-degree relatives affected	5.0	4	0.14

Adapted from Harris JR, Lippman ME, Veronesi U, et al. Breast cancer. Part 1. N Engl J Med 1992;327:319–28.
*Population attributable risk = [prevalence × (relative risk - 1)] _ {[prevalence × (relative risk - 1)] + 1}.

risk of developing subsequent breast cancer, and this risk increases to approximately 10-fold if it is also associated with a family history of invasive breast cancer in a first-degree relative[9] (Figure 4–4).

The number of epidemiologic studies linked with the presence of benign breast disease and the subsequent risk of developing invasive malignancy is large.[10–13] One of the first studies to examine the relationship between proliferative benign breast disease with and without atypical hyperplasia and the subsequent risk of breast cancer was conducted among 121,700 US registered nurses followed up from 1976 to 1986.[12] The adjusted relative risks for breast cancer, compared with women with no proliferative disease, were 1.6 for proliferative disease without atypia (95% CI 1.0–2.5) and 3.7 for atypical hyperplasia (95% CI 2.1–6.8). Breast cancer risk was more strongly associated with atypical hyperplasia among premenopausal (relative risk [RR] = 5.9, 95% CI 2.9–13.2) than postmenopausal women (RR = 2.3, 95% CI 0.9–5.9), but the association of breast cancer risk with proliferative disease without atypia did not differ across menopausal status. These results confirmed the marked increase in breast cancer risk among women with atypical hyperplasia, particularly in premenopausal women.

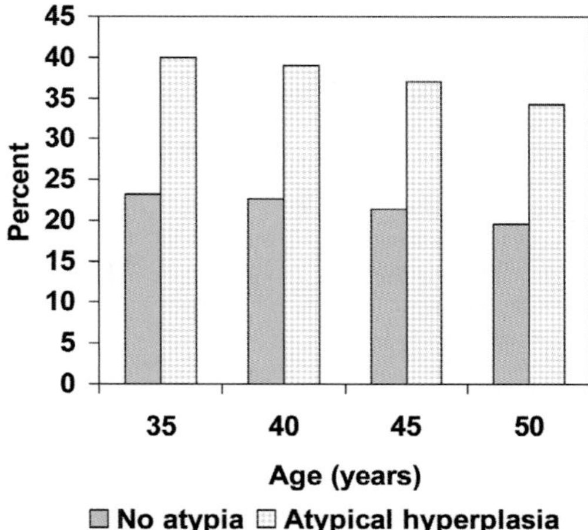

Figure 4–4. Lifetime risk (to age 90) by current age of developing invasive breast cancer following a breast biopsy showing either atypical lobular or ductal hyperplasia or no atypia.

NEWER RISK FACTORS FOR BREAST CANCER

The field of breast cancer epidemiology is an evolving body of knowledge. Newer and more recently identified risk factors for breast cancer are listed in Table 4–2 and are discussed individually in the sections that follow.

Anthropometry

The identification of potentially modifiable risk factors for breast cancer, such as alcohol consumption, physical activity, and certain anthropometric factors, provides opportunities for risk-reducing interventions among women at both average and high risk for breast cancer.[14]

Epidemiologic evidence implicates anthropometric risk factors in breast cancer etiology, but the results of these studies are conflicting. For postmenopausal women, an increased risk of breast cancer is found with increasing levels of all the anthropometric variables including height, weight, body mass index (BMI; weight in kilograms/[height in meters]^2), waist-to-hip ratio, waist circumference, and weight gain (Figure 4–5). The positive association between obesity and breast cancer among postmenopausal women may be limited to those who have never taken hormone replacement therapy (HRT).[15] Weight loss may decrease risk, particularly if it occurs later in life, but this observation has not been tested in clinical trials.

BMI shows significant inverse and positive associations with breast cancer among both pre- and postmenopausal women, and these associations are nonlinear. In a pooled analysis from seven prospective cohort studies on the relationship between weight, height, and breast cancer risk, premenopausal women with a BMI exceeding 31 kg/m^2 had an RR of breast cancer of only 0.54 when compared with premenopausal women with a BMI of $<$ 21 kg/m^2 (Figure 4–6).[16] In postmenopausal women, the relative risks did not increase further when BMI exceeded 28 kg/m^2.

Recent results from the Women's Health Initiative observational study confirmed the effect of increasing BMI on breast cancer risk among postmenopausal women, but only among those women who had never taken HRT.[15] The elevation in risk associated with increasing BMI appears to be most marked among younger postmenopausal women.

Table 4–2. RECENTLY INVESTIGATED EPIDEMIOLOGIC RISK FACTORS FOR BREAST CANCER

Risk Factor	Effect	Odds Ratio (OR) or Relative Risk (RR)
Breastfeeding	Favorable	For every 12 mo of breastfeeding: OR = 0.96
Preeclampsia	Favorable	ORs range from 0.3–0.8
Induced abortion	Null	RR = 1.00 (0.94–1.06)
Anthropometry (body mass index)		
Premenopausal	Favorable	RR = 0.5
Postmenopausal	Unfavorable	RR = 1.3–2.5
Endogenous hormones	Unfavorable	For increasing quintiles of free estradiol vs lowest quintile: OR (postmenopausal) = 1.3
Exogenous hormones		
Oral contraceptives	Null (after cessation of use)	RR = 1.2 (1.15–1.33) RR = 1.1 (0.94–1.32)
HRT	Unfavorable	Hazard ratio = 1.26 (1.00–1.59)
Mammographic breast density	Unfavorable	RR = 4–6
Bone mineral density	Unfavorable	For the highest quartile vs. the lowest quartile: RR = 2.7
Bone fracture	Favorable	For history of fracture vs. no fracture in past 5 yr: OR = 0.8
Biologic growth factors		
TGF-β_1	Favorable	Protective effect for women lacking common TGF-β_1 genetic polymorphism vs women with the common variant: hazard ratio = 0.4
IGF-I	Unfavorable	Top vs. bottom tertile of IGF-I: RR = 3
Alcohol consumption	Unfavorable	For 12 g/d vs. nondrinkers: RR = 1.06 HRT for ≥ 5 yr plus ≥ 20 g/d: RR = 2
Smoking		
Premenopausal	Unfavorable	OR (parous) = 1.7 OR (nulliparous) = 7
Postmenopausal	Favorable	OR = 0.5
Breast implants	No effect or favorable	RR = 0.7
Diet	Null	Fats compared with equivalent energy intake from carbohydrates for an increment of 5% of energy
Exercise/physical activity	Favorable	ORs are variable with an average risk reduction of 30–40%
Phytoestrogens	Null	For the highest vs lowest quartile: OR = 1.0 (0.8–1.3)
Ionizing radiation	Positive	OR = 1.4 (1.2–1.8) RR = 4.1 (2.5–5.7)
Environmental toxins		
eg, dichloroethene, chlordane, dieldrin, PCB congeners, etc.	Null	
Electromagnetic fields	Null	
HIV infection	Uncertain	OR = 0.2

Adapted from Gierach G, Vogel V. Epidemiology of breast cancer. In: Singletary SE, Robb GL, Hortobagyi GN, editors. Advanced therapy of breast disease. 2nd ed. Hamilton: BC Decker; 2004. p. 58–63.

HIV = human immunodeficiency virus; HRT = hormone replacement therapy; IGF-I = insulin-like growth factor I; OR = odds ratio; PCB = polychlorinated biphenyls; RR=relative risk; TGF-β_1 = transforming growth factor β_1.

Change in BMI since age 18 years, maximum BMI, and weight were also associated with breast cancer risk in HRT nonusers. The association between BMI and breast cancer appears to vary by menopausal status and HRT. Weight control may thus reduce the risk of breast cancer among postmenopausal women, but this hypothesis requires confirmation in prospective clinical trials. Among elderly women older than 75 years, in whom the age-specific incidence of breast cancer is already high, obesity increases the risk of breast cancer by more than 40%.[17]

Endogenous Hormones

Most risk factors for breast cancer appear to be associated with ovarian function, and many may be associated with concentrations of endogenous and exogenous hormones.[18] Exposure to estrogen over prolonged durations and in higher concentrations has been consistently related to an increased risk of breast cancer in many epidemiologic studies.[19] The roles of progestins, androgens, and insulin-like growth factors are less clearly established.

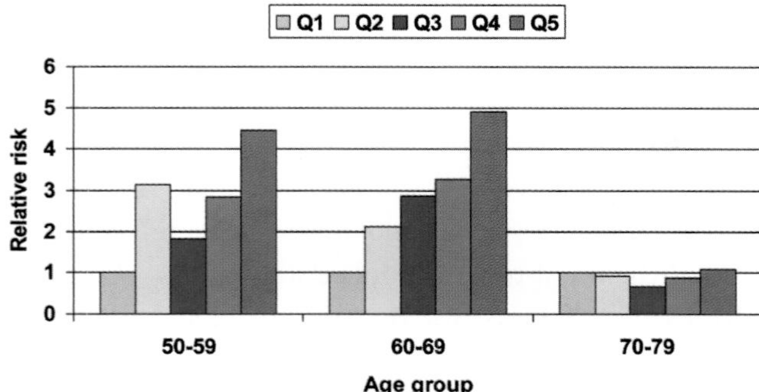

Figure 4–5. Relative risk of developing invasive breast cancer by ten-year age groups stratified by quintiles of body size. The referent group is quintile 1 (Q1) Body mass index (BMI = weight in kg/[height in meters]^2) ≤ 22.6; Q2 > 22.6–24.9; Q3 BMI > 24.9–27.4; Q4 BMI > 27.4–31.1; Q5 BMI > 31.1. There is no apparent effect of body size on the risk of breast cancer among women older than 70 years.

A review of nine prospective studies of endogenous hormone concentrations and breast cancer risk[18] showed that the risk for breast cancer increased significantly with increasing concentrations of all sex hormones examined. The RRs for women with increasing quintiles of estradiol concentrations relative to the lowest quintile were 1.42 (95% CI 1.04–1.95), 1.21 (95% CI 0.89–1.66), 1.80 (95% CI 1.33–2.43), and 2.00 (95% CI 1.47–2.71; p for trend < .001); the RRs for women with increasing quintiles of free estradiol were 1.38 (95% CI 0.94–2.03), 1.84 (95% CI 1.24–2.74), 2.24 (95% CI 1.53–3.27), and 2.58 (95% CI 1.76–3.78; p for trend < .001). The magnitudes of risk associated with the other estrogens and with the androgens were similar.

In the Multiple Outcomes of Raloxifene Evaluation (MORE) Study, those in the highest tertile (top third of the sample) of estradiol levels (≥ 12 pmol/L) had a twofold increased risk of invasive breast cancer compared with that in women with lower levels (Figure 4–7).[20] The selective estrogen receptor modulator raloxifene significantly reduced breast cancer risk in both the low- and high-estrogen subgroups for all risk factors examined. In studies of women at very high risk for breast cancer, endogenous serum hormone levels do not appear to further stratify women into differing risk groups. Taken together, these studies suggest that increased lifetime endogenous estrogen exposure appears to increase breast cancer risk.

Estrogen Metabolism

Although the evidence linking estrogen and breast cancer is compelling, there is growing evidence that the way estrogen is metabolized is associated with the risk of breast cancer.[21–24] Both 16-hydroxyestrone and 16-hydroxyestradiol strongly activate the classic estrogen receptor and, similar to estradiol, can stimulate uterine tissue growth.[21] On the other hand, the 2-hydroxymetabolites do not appear to promote

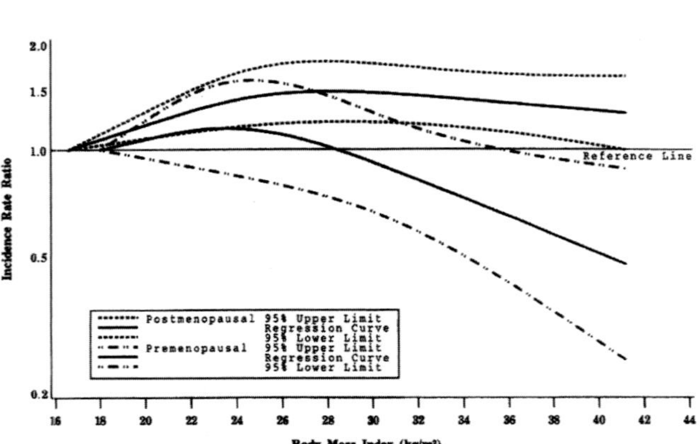

Figure 4–6. Regression curves with 95% intervals showing the relationship between body mass index and the relative incidence of breast cancer stratified by menopausal status in multiple published studies. The descending curve is for premenopausal women. From the Pooling Project of Diet and Cancer.[16]

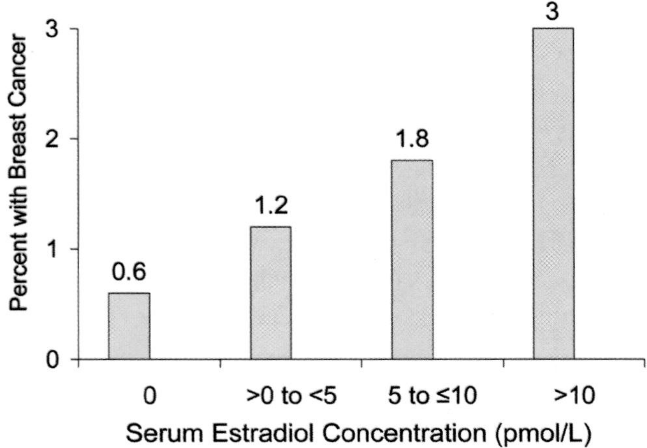

Figure 4–7. Relationship between baseline serum estradiol levels and the risk of breast cancer during 4 years of follow-up among postmenopausal women in the placebo arm of Multiple Outcomes Raloxifene Evaluation (MORE) trial.[20]

cellular proliferation and may even have antiestrogenic effects.[25]

Breastfeeding

In addition to the protective effect of parity on breast cancer, breastfeeding appears to contribute to a reduced risk. As duration of breastfeeding increases, the risk of breast cancer decreases, although parity may be a confounding factor. Hypothesized mechanisms for the protective effect of breastfeeding include the decline in estrogen production related to the suppression of ovulatory cycles and an increased secretion of prolactin.[26,27] The RR of breast cancer decreased by 4.3% (95% CI 2.9–5.8) for every 12 months of breastfeeding, and decreased by 7.0% (95% CI 5.0–9.0) for each birth. It is possible that the cumulative incidence of breast cancer in developed countries would be reduced by more than half, from 6.3 to 2.7 per 100 women by age 70 years, if women had the average number of births (6.5 versus 2.5) and lifetime duration of breastfeeding (24 versus 3 mo per child) that had been prevalent in developing countries until recently. Strong epidemiologic evidence does not exist for a relationship between being breast-fed in infancy and breast cancer incidence in adult life.[28]

Preeclampsia

Preeclampsia, a common complication of pregnancy, may be a particularly sensitive marker for endogenous hormonal factors associated with the development of breast cancer. Available data suggest that both a personal and maternal history of preeclampsia are inversely and independently associated with subsequent breast cancer risk.[29] Preeclampsia may be a novel marker of endogenous hormonal factors, including reduced levels of estrogens and insulin-like growth factor I (IGF-I) and elevated levels of progesterone, androgens, and IGF-I binding protein, that are related to breast cancer development. These factors may act both individually and synergistically to decrease breast cancer risk.

Induced Abortion

It has been hypothesized that an interrupted pregnancy might increase a woman's risk of breast cancer owing to the proliferation of breast cells without the later protective effect of differentiation, but induced abortion in a large national registry was not associated with an increased risk of breast cancer.[29] The relative risk of breast cancer increased with increasing gestational age of the fetus at the time of the most recent induced abortion: < 7 weeks, 0.81 (95% CI 0.58–1.13); > 12 weeks, 1.38 (95% CI 1.00–1.90) (reference category, 9–10 weeks). Induced abortions appear to have no overall effect on the risk of breast cancer.[30]

Bone Mineral Density

Bone mineral density (BMD) may be one of the best surrogate measures of lifetime estrogen exposure, and fractures in postmenopausal women may reflect lower estrogen levels across the lifespan.[31] Compared with women without a fracture in the previous 5 years, the odds of breast cancer for women with a history of fracture were significantly decreased in one study (OR = 0.80, 95% CI 0.68–0.94). Height loss (≥ 2.5 cm) and recent fracture history were associated with the lowest risk of breast cancer (OR = 0.62, 95% CI 0.46–0.83). In another study, women with the highest BMD and those with a family history of breast cancer experienced a significantly greater therapeutic benefit with raloxifene, compared with the effect in the two-thirds of patients who had a lower BMD or no such family history.[20] Another prospective study demonstrated that elderly women with high BMD had an increased risk of breast cancer, especially advanced cancer, compared with the risk in women with low BMD.[32] These findings suggest that osteoporosis may confer a protective effect on invasive breast cancer. These data suggest that the endogenous hormonal factors associated with increased fracture risk are related to a decreased risk of breast cancer.

Biologic Growth Factors

Epidemiologic studies of biologic growth factors and breast cancer risk are few, and the data are inconsistent in pre- and postmenopausal women. Increased expression of transforming growth factor β_1 (TGF-β_1), a potent inhibitor of mammary cell lines, is protective against early breast cancer development in animals,[33] and about 85% of the women carry at least one T allele for the TFG-β_1 gene, whereas the remainder had the C/C genotype. Risk of breast cancer was similar in the women with the T/T genotype and in women with the T/C genotype but was significantly lower in women with the C/C genotype. Women with the C/C genotype had a significantly lower risk of developing breast cancer compared with women with the T/T or T/C genotype (hazard ratio = 0.36, 95% CI 0.17–0.75). The findings suggest that the TGF-β_1 genotype is associated with the risk of breast cancer in white women ages 65 years or older. Because the T allele is the common variant and relates to an increased risk, it may be associated with a significant proportion of breast cancer cases.

Insulin resistance may also be a risk factor for breast cancer, possibly through increased levels of estrogens or IGF-I (Figure 4–8). Insulin resistance has been associated with obesity, hypertension, dyslipidemia, and impaired glucose tolerance. Increased levels of IGF-I may increase breast cancer risk through the induction of cell proliferation and inhibition of apoptosis in the human breast epithelium.[34] The biologic activity of IGF-I largely depends on its absolute tissue level, in addition to the levels of at least six IGF binding proteins (IGFBPs). Several epidemiologic studies have demonstrated an increased risk of breast cancer in women with elevated plasma IGF-I levels,[35–37] but many studies are hindered by low sample sizes and an inability to establish a temporal relationship between IGFs and breast cancer owing to a lack of a prospective study design.

Exogenous Hormones: Oral Contraceptives and Hormone Replacement Therapy

In the general population, oral contraceptive (OC) use is weakly associated with breast cancer risk, but the association among women with a familial predisposition to breast cancer is less clear. OCs may be associated with risk of breast cancer in *BRCA1* mutation carriers, but data for *BRCA2* mutation carriers are limited.

The Collaborative Group on Hormonal Factors in Breast Cancer[38] reanalyzed about 90% of the worldwide epidemiologic evidence on the relationship between risk of breast cancer and use of hormone replacement therapy (HRT). Among current users of HRT, or those who ceased use 1 to 4 years previously, the risk of having breast cancer diagnosed increased by 2.3% for each year of use.

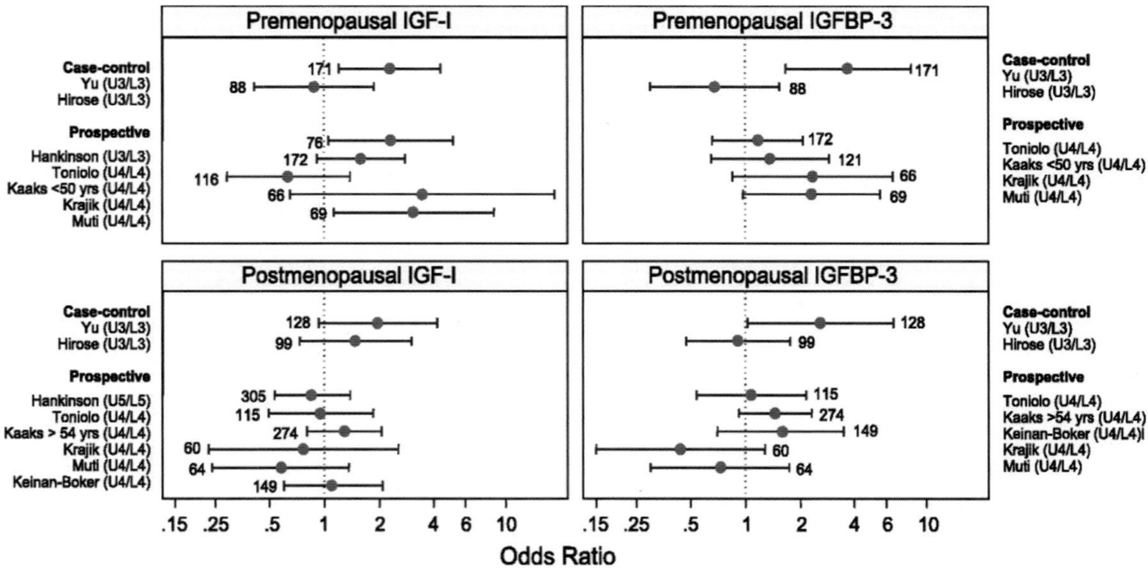

Figure 4–8. Meta-analysis of serum levels of insulin-like growth factor I (IGF-I) and insulin-like growth factor binding protein 3 (IGFBP-3) by menopausal status and risk of breast cancer. The number of cases in each study is shown next to the study result bar. Comparisons are for the upper versus. the lower tertile, quartile, or quintile as indicated.

The Women's Health Initiative, a randomized controlled primary prevention trial in which 16,608 postmenopausal women ages 50 to 79 years with an intact uterus at baseline were recruited, confirmed these results.[39] Participants received conjugated equine estrogens 0.625 mg daily plus medroxyprogesterone acetate 2.5 mg daily in one tablet (n = 8,506) or placebo (n = 8,102). After slightly more than 5 years of follow-up, the risk of breast cancer increased by 26%, with an absolute excess risk of 8 more breast cancers per 10,000 person-years attributable to estrogen plus progestin.

The primary outcome was coronary heart disease (CHD) (nonfatal myocardial infarction and CHD death), with invasive breast cancer as the primary adverse outcome. After slightly more than 5 years of follow-up, the risk of coronary heart disease was increased by 29%; breast cancer by 26%; stroke by 41%; and pulmonary embolism by 213%. The risks of both colorectal cancer and hip fracture were both reduced by more than 30%. Absolute excess risks per 10,000 person-years attributable to estrogen plus progestin were 7 more CHD events, 8 more strokes, 8 more pulmonary embolisms, and 8 more invasive breast cancers (Figure 4–9), whereas absolute risk reductions per 10,000 person-years were 6 fewer colorectal cancers and 5 fewer hip fractures. Overall health risks exceeded benefits from use of combined estrogen plus progestin for an average 5-year follow-up among healthy, postmenopausal US women.

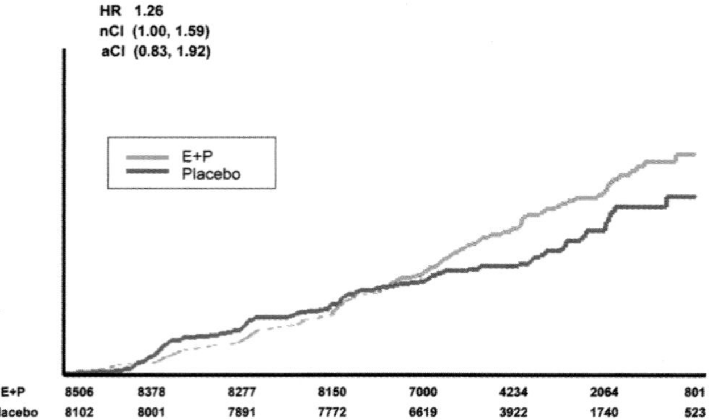

Figure 4–9. Kaplan-Meier estimates of the cumulative hazard for invasive breast cancer among postmenopausal women with a uterus taking conjugated equine estrogens plus medroxyprogesterone acetate versus placebo in the Women's Health Initiative.[39]

A large meta-analysis that combined individual data on 53,297 women with breast cancer and 100,239 women without breast cancer from 54 epidemiologic studies conducted in 25 countries showed that women had a slight but significant increased risk of breast cancer while taking OCs, as compared with the risk among nonusers (RR = 1.24, 95% CI 1.15–1.33).[40] Reassuringly, the risk diminished steadily after cessation of use, with no increase in risk 10 years after cessation of OC use, irrespective of family history of breast cancer, reproductive history, geographic area of residence, ethnic background, differences in study designs, dose and type of hormone, and duration of use. More recent population-based studies of the risk of breast cancer among former and current users of OCs do not suggest that these drugs increase risk.[41,42] Use of OCs by women with a family history of breast cancer was not associated with an increased risk of breast cancer, nor was the initiation of OC use at a young age.

A matched case-control study of women with known deleterious *BRCA1* and/or *BRCA2* mutations further examined the association among women at high risk for breast cancer.[43] Among *BRCA2* mutation carriers, ever use of OCs was not associated with an increased risk of breast cancer (OR = 0.94, 95% CI 0.72–1.24). On the contrary, for *BRCA1* mutation carriers, ever use of OCs was associated with a modestly increased risk of breast cancer (OR = 1.20, 95% CI 1.02–1.40) when compared with the risk in never-users. Further analyses demonstrated that for *BRCA1* mutation carriers, the increased risk of early-onset breast cancer was also found among women who first used OCs before 1975, who used them before age 30 years, or who used them for ≥ 5 years.

Therefore, most epidemiologic studies have shown little or no increased risk for breast cancer associated with OC use, but the evidence suggests that OCs may increase breast cancer risk in certain subgroups of women: those who have a first-degree relative with breast cancer or who are *BRCA1* mutation carriers. The data also indicate that recent OC use may increase breast cancer risk in very young women, and that risk may be increased in women who have used earlier formulations of OCs.

Hormone Replacement Therapy

Published single-cohort observational studies,[44] several meta-analyses,[45–48] and the combined reanalysis of epidemiologic studies[38] all indicate that increased risk of developing invasive breast cancer occurs among current users of HRT (especially those who have used HRT for 5 or more years). However the risk of breast cancer is no higher among former users who had stopped taking hormones more than 5 years previously than the risk among never-users. These observations suggest that the major effect of HRT on the breast may be through the promotion of cancer growth rather than through directly genotoxic effects.[49]

Among current users of HRT, or those who ceased use 1 to 4 years previously, the risk of having breast cancer diagnosed increased by 2.3% for each year of use; the relative risk was 1.35 for women who had used HRT for 5 years or longer. This increase is comparable with the effect on breast cancer of delaying menopause, since among never-users of HRT the relative risk of breast cancer increases by a factor of 2.8% for each year older at menopause. Five or more years after cessation of HRT use, there was no significant excess of breast cancer overall or in relation to duration of use.

Of the many factors examined that might affect the relation between breast cancer risk and use of HRT, only weight and BMI had a material effect: the increase in the risk of breast cancer associated with long durations of use in current and recent users was greater for women of lower than of higher weight or BMI. There were no marked variations in the results according to hormonal type or dose but little information was available about long durations of use of any specific preparations. Cancers diagnosed in women who ever use HRT tend to be less advanced clinically than those diagnosed in never-users. In North America and Europe, the cumulative incidence of breast cancer between the ages of 50 and 70 in never-users of HRT is about 45 per 1,000 women. The cumulative excess numbers of breast cancers diagnosed between these ages per 1,000 women who began use of HRT at age 50 and used it for 5, 10, and 15 years, respectively, are estimated to be 2, 6, and 12.

Whether HRT affects mortality from breast cancer is not known, although some data suggest a more favorable outcome among users of HRT following a diagnosis of breast cancer.[50] Data that are contradictory of assumptions widely held among clinicians demonstrate reduced mortality from breast cancer among women who were current users of estrogen replacement therapy (ERT) when they were diagnosed with node-negative breast cancer. The rate ratio of breast cancer mortality associated with current use of ERT compared with nonuse at diagnosis was 0.5 (95% CI, 0.3 to 0.8), an effect greater than the benefits reported with the use of tamoxifen in early breast cancer. This effect was also seen among women with a hysterectomy who took estrogen alone in the Women's Health Initiative trial.[51] Recent reviews of multiple retrospective studies of the influence of HRT on the prognosis of invasive breast cancer call into question whether prognosis is improved among women taking HRT at the time of diagnosis.[52] The issue remains unresolved.

Mammographic Breast Density

The radiographic appearance of a mammogram is determined by the relative amounts of radiolucent fat and radiodense epithelial/fibrous tissue. Mammographic density is a measure of the radiodense area on the mammogram. A number of different classification schemes have been used to characterize the amount of mammographic density.[53,54] Published studies have concluded that, regardless of the method used to classify them, mammographic density is an independent predictor of breast cancer risk, with risk increasing with increasing density. Furthermore, the magnitude of this increase in risk is greater than that associated with nearly all other breast cancer risk factors. The three most conclusive studies to date[55–57] suggest that women with the greatest breast density have a four- to sixfold increased risk of breast cancer compared with women with the least dense breasts.

Exercise and Physical Activity

Evidence for an association between physical activity and breast cancer is not entirely consistent.[58] Many studies have observed a reduction in breast cancer risk in women who were most physically active, and the risk reduction averaged between 30 and 40%. An inverse dose-response relationship between increasing activity levels and decreased breast cancer risk was found in 20 of 23 studies that examined this trend. Only two studies observed an opposite trend such that breast cancer risk increased with increasing physical activity levels; the remaining study found no association at all. Based upon the results of the observational studies, controlled clinical trials are needed to elucidate the mechanisms by which physical activity may influence breast cancer risk.

Alcohol Consumption

A meta-analysis of epidemiologic studies carried out through 1999 examined the dose-response relationship and assessed whether effect estimates differed according to various study characteristics.[59] Overall, there was an increase in the RR of breast cancer with alcohol consumption, but the magnitude of the effect was small; in comparison with nondrinkers, women averaging 12 g/d of alcohol consumption (approximately one typical drink) had an RR of 1.10. The findings of five US cohort studies published since 1990 yielded an RR of 1.06 (95% CI 1.00–1.11) for consumers of 12 g/d compared with nondrinkers. Cohort studies with < 10 years of follow-up gave estimates 11% higher than did cohort studies with longer follow-up periods. No meaningful differences were seen in relation to menopausal status or type of beverage consumed.

In a second meta-analysis that reviewed human and animal investigations published since 1995, the authors reported that alcohol-related breast cancer risk may be associated with endogenous hormone levels.[60] Recent results from 44,187 postmenopausal women participating in the Nurses' Health Study are consistent with the hypothesis that the use of alcohol increases the risk for breast cancer through a hormonal mechanism.[61] Self-reported alcohol consumption and postmenopausal hormone use (type and regimen unspecified) were associated with an increased incidence of breast cancer. Risk for breast cancer was about 30% higher in women who currently used postmenopausal hormones for 5 or more years and did not drink alcohol (RR = 1.32, 95% CI 1.05–1.66). Those who never used postmenopausal hormones but drank ≥ 20 g (1.5 to 2 drinks) or more alcohol daily had an increased risk of 28% (RR = 1.28, 95% CI 0.97–1.69); however, this risk was not statistically significant. Current users of postmenopausal hormones for ≥ 5 years who also consumed ≥ 20 g of alcohol daily had an RR for breast cancer nearly twice that of nondrinking nonusers of postmenopausal hormones (RR = 1.99, 95% CI 1.42–2.79).

Smoking

The role of active and passive smoking in breast cancer remains controversial, largely owing to the fact that breast cancer is hormone dependent and cigarette smoking appears to have antiestrogenic effects in women.[62,63] There are at least 11 studies that have compared passive and active smoking exposures to a referent category of those women who had never smoked nor lived with a smoker.[64] Of the 11 studies reviewed, all ORs were > 1.0 five found significantly increased ORs of ≥ 1.5 for passive smokers versus unexposed, and six reported significantly increased ORs of ≥ 1.4 for active smokers versus unexposed, suggesting a similar strength of association for active or passive smoking and breast cancer risk. A recent review by the state of California summarizes the recent literature and supports a 25% increase in the lifetime risk of breast cancer among women who are passive smokers.[65]

Breast Implants

Researchers have consistently found no persuasive evidence of a causal association between breast implants and cancer of any type. The results of a meta-analysis obtained by combining epidemiologic studies support the overall conclusion that breast implants do not pose any additional risk for breast cancer or for other cancers. [66]

Diet

No study has shown a significant association between breast cancer and dietary fat when comparing the highest with the lowest category of total fat intake.[67] A collaborative pooled analysis has been conducted of the large prospective studies published through 1995 that included a total of 4,980 cases of breast cancer among 337,819 women.[68] In addition to providing great statistical precision, the pooled analysis allowed standard analytic approaches to be applied to all studies, an examination of a wider range of fat intake, and a detailed evaluation of interactions with other breast cancer risk factors. Overall, no association was observed between intake of total, saturated, monounsaturated, or polyunsaturated fat and risk of breast cancer, even in women with fat intake as low as 20% of total energy intake. A recent update of the pooled data has continued to support an overall lack of association.[69] Prospective randomized data from the National Institutes of Health's Women's Health Initiative should provide a definitive answer to this question in the next few years.

Dietary Micronutrients

The consumption of vegetables and fruit may protect against some types of cancer, but research evidence is not compelling for breast cancer.[70] Data linking carotenoids to breast cancer risk are conflicting. The risk of developing breast cancer in the highest fifth was approximately half of that of women in the lowest fifth for beta-carotene (OR = 0.41, 95% CI 0.22–0.79), lycopene (OR = 0.55, 95% CI 0.29–1.06), and total carotene (OR = 0.55, 95% CI 0.29–1.03). There was a trend toward protective association for other micronutrients in both cohorts, although none was statistically significant. These observations offer limited evidence that carotenoids may protect against the development of breast cancer and may have public health relevance for people with markedly low intakes.

Phytoestrogens

Phytoestrogens are compounds derived from plants that have estrogenic properties, but research on the relationship between phytoestrogens and breast cancer risk has been limited in scope. Many experimental but few epidemiologic studies have suggested that dietary sources of phytoestrogens have inhibitory effects on breast cancer. The low rates of breast cancer in Asia have stimulated the examination of the effects of traditional soy foods (eg, tofu), soy protein, and urinary excretion of phytoestrogens on breast cancer risk in Asian women. Two recent population-based case-control studies have suggested that soy food consumption in adolescent Asian women is associated with a reduced risk of breast cancer later in life, although supporting data from prospective studies are needed.[71,72]

In contrast, phytoestrogens appeared to have little effect on breast cancer risk in a case-control study of non-Asian Americans.[73] Whether greater consumption of phytoestrogens would reduce the incidence of breast cancer remains unknown.

Ionizing Radiation

There is a well-established relationship between exposure to ionizing radiation and the risk of developing breast cancer.[74, 75] Excess breast cancer risk has been consistently observed in association with a variety of exposures, such as the Hiroshima or Nagasaki atomic explosions, fluoroscopy for tuberculosis, and radiation treatments for medical conditions (eg, Hodgkin's disease). Although risk is inversely associated with age at radiation exposure, exposures past the menopausal age seem to carry a low risk. Although an estimate of the risk of breast cancer associated with medical radiology puts the figure at < 1% of the total,[75,76] certain populations such as ataxia-telangiectasia heterozygotes may be at increased risk from usual sources of radiation exposure.[77]

Environmental Toxins

Whether environmental contaminants increase breast cancer risk is unknown. The association between breast cancer with endogenous estrogen or hormonally related events has led to the hypothesis that exposures to exogenous estrogen agonists or antagonists in the environment may increase the risk of breast cancer.[78] Although a few studies support this hypothesis, the vast majority of epidemiologic studies do not. Several studies have sought to determine whether breast cancer risk is increased in relation to exposure to organochlorines (eg, polychlorinated biphenyls [PCBs], dioxins, organochlorine pesticides such as DDT, lindane, hexachlorobenzene), compounds with known estrogenic characteristics that were extensively used in some areas of the United States until the 1970s. The few available studies of occupational exposure to PCBs and dioxins have not supported a causal association with breast cancer. Most studies have been conducted among white women in developed countries where heavy pesticide spraying is no longer in use. Overall, the evidence does not support an association between environmental exposure to organochlorines and breast cancer risk. Additional studies of recent and ongoing exposures may be informative.

Two investigations from the Long Island Breast Cancer Study Project (LIBCSP), mandated by the US Congress in 1993, demonstrated no association between increased rates of breast cancer and exposure to some pesticides and industrial chemicals (including DDT and PCBs), and only a possible weak association with exposure to chemicals found in air pollution known as polycyclic aromatic hydrocarbons.[79,80] In one LIBCSP substudy, no substantial elevation in the risk of breast cancer was observed in relation to the highest quintile of lipid-adjusted serum levels of *p,p*'-bis(4-chlorophenyl)-1,1-dichloroethane, chlordane, dieldrin, the sum of the four most frequently occurring PCB congeners, and other PCB congener groupings. No dose-response relationships were apparent; nor was risk increased in relation to organochlorines among women who had not breast-fed or were overweight, were postmenopausal, or were long-term residents of the geographic area studied. Organochlorine exposure was not associated with diagnosis of cases with invasive versus in situ disease, or with hormone receptor-positive tumors. These findings do not support the hypothesis that organochlorine compounds increase breast cancer risk.

Electric and Magnetic Fields

Most large studies have failed to find strong consistent associations between electromagnetic fields (EMF) and breast cancer risk.[81,82] Because of the fact that exposures to EMF are common and difficult to assess, studies exploring the relationship between EMF and breast cancer risk have a high likelihood of misclassification of exposure. A hypothesis for a melatonin-mediated effect of EMF on breast cancer risk has yet to be substantiated.

REFERENCES

1. American Cancer Society. Cancer Facts and Figures 2005. Atlanta: American Cancer Society, 2005.
2. Lacey JV Jr, Devesa SS, Brinton LA. Recent trends in breast cancer incidence and mortality. Environ Mol Mutagen 2002;39:82–8.
3. Johnson JW. Transactions of the sixty-third annual meeting of the South Atlantic Association of Obstetricians and Gynecologists. The millennial mark: presidential address. Am J Obstet Gynecol 2001;185:261–7.
4. Deapen D, Liu L, Perkins C, et al. Rapidly rising breast cancer incidence rates among Asian-American women. Int J Cancer 2002;99:747–50.
5. Alberg AJ, Singh S. Epidemiology of breast cancer in older women: implications for future healthcare. Drugs Aging 2001;18:761–72.
6. Vogel VG. Breast cancer risk factors and preventive approaches to breast cancer. In: Kavanagh JSS, Einhorn N, DePetrillo AD, editors. Cancer in women. Cambridge (MA): Blackwell Scientific Publications Inc; 1998. p. 58–91.
7. Sasco AJ, Lowenfels AB, Pasker-de Jong P. Review article: epidemiology of male breast cancer. A meta-analysis of published case-control studies and discussion of selected aetiological factors. Int J Cancer 1993;53:538–49.
8. Fitzgibbons PL, Henson DE, Hutter RV. Benign breast changes and the risk for subsequent breast cancer: an update of the 1985 consensus statement. Cancer Committee of the College of American Pathologists. Arch Pathol Lab Med 1998;122:1053–5.
9. Vogel V. Atypia in the assessment of breast cancer risk: implications for management. Diagn Cytopathol 2004;30: 151–7.
10. Dupont WD, Page DL. Risk factors for breast cancer in women with proliferative breast disease. N Engl J Med 1985;312:146–51.
11. Dupont WD, Page DL, Parl FF, et al. Long-term risk of breast cancer in women with fibroadenoma. N Engl J Med 1994; 331:10–5.
12. London SJ, Connolly JL, Schnitt SJ, et al. A prospective study of benign breast disease and the risk of breast cancer. JAMA 1992;267:941–4.
13. Colditz GA, Rosner BA, Speizer FE. Risk factors for breast cancer according to family history of breast cancer. For the Nurses' Health Study Research Group. J Natl Cancer Inst 1996;88:365–71.
14. Brewster A, Helzlsouer K. Breast cancer epidemiology, prevention, and early detection. Curr Opin Oncol 2001;13: 420–5.
15. Morimoto L, White E, Chen Z, et al. Obesity, body size, and risk of postmenopausal breast cancer: the Women's Health Initiative (United States). Cancer Causes Control 2002;13:741–51.

16. van den Brandt PA, Spiegelman D, Yaun SS, et al. Pooled analysis of prospective cohort studies on height, weight, and breast cancer risk. Am J Epidemiol 2000;152:514-27.
17. Sweeney C, Blair CK, Anderson KE, et al. Risk factors for breast cancer in elderly women. Amer J Epidemiol 2004; 160:868–75.
18. Hilakivi-Clarke L, Cabanes A, Olivo S, et al. Do estrogens always increase breast cancer risk? J Steroid Biochem Mol Biol 2002;80:163–74.
19. The Endogenous Hormones and Breast Cancer Collaborative Group. Endogenous sex hormones and breast cancer in postmenopausal women: reanalysis of nine prospective studies. J Natl Cancer Inst 2002;94:606–16.
20. Lippman ME, Krueger KA, Eckert S, et al. Indicators of lifetime estrogen exposure: effect on breast cancer incidence and interaction with raloxifene therapy in the Multiple Outcomes of Raloxifene Evaluation Study participants. J Clin Oncol 2001;19:3111–6.
21. Fishman J, Martucci C. Biological properties of 16 alpha-hydroxyestrone: implications in estrogen physiology and pathophysiology. J Clin Endocrinol Metab 1980;51:611–5.
22. Bradlow HL, Telang NT, Sepkovic DW, et al. 2-hydroxyestrone: the 'good' estrogen. J Endocrinol 1996;150 Suppl: S259–65.
23. Bradlow HL, Hershcopf RJ, Martucci CP, et al. Estradiol 16 alpha-hydroxylation in the mouse correlates with mammary tumor incidence and presence of murine mammary tumor virus: a possible model for the hormonal etiology of breast cancer in humans. Proc Natl Acad Sci U S A 1985;82:6295–9.
24. Bradlow HL, Hershcopf R, Martucci C, et al. 16 alpha-hydroxylation of estradiol: a possible risk marker for breast cancer. Ann N Y Acad Sci 1986;464:138–51.
25. Schneider J, Huh MM, Bradlow HL, et al. Antiestrogen action of 2-hydroxyestrone on MCF-7 human breast cancer cells. J Biol Chem 1984;259:4840–5.
26. Tryggvadottir L, Tulinius H, Eyfjord JE, et al. Breastfeeding and reduced risk of breast cancer in an Icelandic cohort study. Am J Epidemiol 2001;154:37–42.
27. Collaborative Group on Hormonal Factors in Breast Cancer. Breast cancer and breastfeeding: collaborative reanalysis of individual data from 47 epidemiological studies in 30 countries, including 50302 women with breast cancer and 96973 women without the disease. Lancet 2002;360: 187–95.
28. Michels K, Trichopoulos D, Rosner B, et al. Being breastfed in infancy and breast cancer incidence in adult life: results from the two nurses' health studies. Am J Epidemiol 2001;153:275–83.
29. Innes KE, Byers TE. Preeclampsia and breast cancer risk. Epidemiology 1999;10:722–32.
30. Melbye M, Wohlfahrt J, Olsen JH, et al. Induced abortion and the risk of breast cancer. N Engl J Med 1997;336:81–5.
31. Newcomb PA, Trentham-Dietz A, Egan KM, et al. Fracture history and risk of breast and endometrial cancer. Am J Epidemiol 2001;153:1071–8.
32. Zmuda JM, Cauley JA, Ljung BM, et al. Bone mass and breast cancer risk in older women: differences by stage at diagnosis. J Natl Cancer Inst 2001;93:930–6.
33. Ziv E, Cauley J, Morin PA, et al. Association between the T29->C polymorphism in the transforming growth factor beta1 gene and breast cancer among elderly white women: the Study of Osteoporotic Fractures. JAMA 2001;285:2859–63.
34. Kaaks R, Lundin E, Rinaldi S, et al. Prospective study of IGF-I, IGF-binding proteins, and breast cancer risk, in northern and southern Sweden. Cancer Causes Control 2002;13:307–16.
35. Hankinson SE, Willett WC, Colditz GA, et al. Circulating concentrations of insulin-like growth factor-I and risk of breast cancer. Lancet 1998;351:1393–6.
36. Petridou E, Papadiamantis Y, Markopoulos C, et al. Leptin and insulin growth factor I in relation to breast cancer (Greece). Cancer Causes Control 2000;11:383–8.
37. Bohlke K, Cramer DW, Trichopoulos D, et al. Insulin-like growth factor-I in relation to premenopausal ductal carcinoma in situ of the breast. Epidemiology 1998;9:570–3.
38. Collaborative Group on Hormonal Factors in Breast Cancer. Breast cancer and hormone replacement therapy: collaborative reanalysis of data from 51 epidemiological studies of 52,705 women with breast cancer and 108,411 women without breast cancer. Lancet 1997;350:1047–59.
39. Writing Group for the Women's Health Initiative. Risks and benefits of estrogen plus progestin in healthy postmenopausal women: principal results from the Women's Health Initiative randomized controlled trial. JAMA 2002;288:321–33.
40. Collaborative Group on Hormonal Factors in Breast Cancer. Breast cancer and hormonal contraceptives: collaborative reanalysis of individual data on 53 297 women with breast cancer and 100 239 women without breast cancer from 54 epidemiological studies. Lancet 1996;347:1713–27.
41. Hankinson SE, Colditz GA, Manson JE, et al. A prospective study of oral contraceptive use and risk of breast cancer (Nurses' Health Study, United States). Cancer Causes Control 1997;8:65–72.
42. Marchbanks PA, McDonald JA, Wilson HG, et al. Oral contraceptives and the risk of breast cancer. N Engl J Med 2002;346:2025–32.
43. Narod SA, Dube MP, Klijn J, et al. Oral contraceptives and the risk of breast cancer in BRCA1 and BRCA2 mutation carriers. J Natl Cancer Inst 2002;94:1773–79.
44. Colditz GA, Hankinson SE, Hunter DJ, et al: The use of estrogens and progestins and the risk of breast cancer in postmenopausal women. N Engl J Med 1995;332:1589–93.
45. Dupont WD, Page DL: Menopausal estrogen replacement therapy and breast cancer. Arch Intern Med 1991;151:67–72.
46. Steinberg KK, Thaker SB, Smith SJ, et al: A meta-analysis of the effect of estrogen replacement therapy on the risk of breast cancer. JAMA 1991;265:1885–90.
47. Silero-Arenas M, Delgado-Rodriguez M, Rodrigues-Canteras R, et al: Menopausal hormone replacement therapy and risk of breast cancer: A meta-analysis. Obstet Gynecol 1992;79:286–94.
48. Colditz GA, Egan KM, Stampfer MJ: Hormone replacement therapy and risk of breast cancer: Results from epidemiologic studies. Am J Obstet Gynecol 1993;168:1473–80.
49. Colditz GA. Relationship between estrogen levels, use of hormone replacement therapy, and breast cancer. J Natl Cancer Inst 1998;90:814–23.

50. Schairer C, Gail M, Byrne C, et al: Estrogen replacement therapy and breast cancer survival in a large screening study. J Natl Cancer Inst 1999;91:264–70.
51. The Women's Health Initiative Steering Committee. Effects of conjugated equine estrogen in postmenopausal women with hysterectomy: The Women's Health Initiative Randomized Controlled Trial. JAMA 2004;291:1701–12.
52. Antoine C, Liebens F, Carly B, et al. Influence of HRT on prognostic factors for breast cancer: a systematic review after the Women's Health Initiative trial. Human Reproduct 2004;19:741–86.
53. Saftlas AF, Hoover RN, Brinton LA, et al. Mammographic densities and risk of breast cancer. Cancer 1991;67:2833–8.
54. Boyd NF, Lockwood GA, Martin LJ, et al. Mammographic densities and breast cancer risk. Breast Disease 1998;10:113–26.
55. Brisson J, Merletti F, Sadowsky NL, et al. Mammographic features of the breast and breast cancer risk. Am J Epidemiol 1982;115:428–37.
56. Boyd NF, Byng J, Jong R, et al. Quantitative classification of mammographic densities and breast cancer risks: results from the Canadian National Breast Screening Study. J Natl Cancer Inst 1995;87:670–5.
57. Byrne C, Schairer C, Wolfe J, et al. Mammographic features and breast cancer risk: effects with time, age and menopause status. J Natl Cancer Inst 1995;87:1622–9.
58. Friedenreich CM, Orenstein MR. Physical activity and cancer prevention: etiologic evidence and biological mechanisms. J Nutr 2002;132(11 Suppl):3456S–64S.
59. Ellison RC, Zhang Y, McLennan CE, et al. Exploring the relation of alcohol consumption to risk of breast cancer. Am J Epidemiol 2001;154:740–7.
60. Singletary KW, Gapstur SM. Alcohol and breast cancer: review of epidemiologic and experimental evidence and potential mechanisms. JAMA 2001;286:2143–51.
61. Chen WY, Colditz GA, Rosner B, et al. Use of postmenopausal hormones, alcohol, and risk for invasive breast cancer. Ann Intern Med 2002;137:798–804.
62. Egan KM, Stampfer MJ, Hunter D, et al. Active and passive smoking in breast cancer: prospective results from the Nurses' Health Study. Epidemiology 2002;13:138–45.
63. Russo IH. Cigarette smoking and risk of breast cancer in women. Lancet 2002;360:1033–4.
64. Morabia A. Smoking (active and passive) and breast cancer: epidemiologic evidence up to June 2001. Environ Mol Mutagen 2002;39:89–95.
65. California Air Resources Board. Proposed Identification of Environmental Tobacco Smoke as a Toxic Air Contaminant. Available at: http://www.arb.ca.gov/toxics/ets/dreport/dreport.htm (accessed April 1, 2005).
66. Hoshaw SJ, Klein PJ, Clark BD, et al. Breast implants and cancer: causation, delayed detection, and survival. Plast Reconstr Surg 2001;107:1393–1407.
67. Willett WC. Diet and breast cancer. J Int Med Res 2001; 249:395–411.
68. Hunter DJ, Spiegelman D, Adami HO, et al. Cohort studies of fat intake and the risk of breast cancer-a pooled analysis. N Engl J Med 1996;334:356–61.
69. Smith-Warner SA, Spiegelman D, Adami HO, et al. Types of dietary fat and breast cancer: a pooled analysis of cohort studies. Int J Cancer 2001;92:767–74.
70. Smith-Warner SA, Spiegelman D, Yaun SS, et al. Intake of fruits and vegetables and risk of breast cancer: a pooled analysis of cohort studies. JAMA 2001;285:769–76.
71. Shu XO, Jin F, Dai Q, et al. Soyfood intake during adolescence and subsequent risk of breast cancer among Chinese women. Cancer Epidemiol Biomarkers Prev 2001; 10:483–8.
72. Wu AH, Wan P, Hankin J, et al. Adolescent and adult soy intake and risk of breast cancer in Asian-Americans. Carcinogenesis 2002;23:1491–6.
73. Horn-Ross PL, John EM, Lee M, et al. Phytoestrogen consumption and breast cancer risk in a multiethnic population-The Bay Area Breast Cancer Study. Am J Epidemiol 2001;154:434–41.
74. Tokunaga M, Land CE, Yamamoto T, et al. Incidence of female breast cancer among atomic bomb survivors, Hiroshima and Nagasaki, 1950–1980. Radiat Res 1987;112:243–72.
75. Boice JD Jr. Radiation and breast carcinogenesis. Med Pediatr Oncol 2001;36:508–13.
76. Evans JS, Wennberg JE, McNeil BJ. The influence of diagnostic radiography on the incidence of breast cancer and leukemia. N Engl J Med 1986;315:810–5.
77. Swift M, Morrell D, Massey RB, et al. Incidence of cancer in 161 families affected by ataxia-telangiectasia. N Engl J Med 1991;325:1831–6.
78. Calle EE, Frumkin H, Henley SJ, et al. Organochlorines and breast cancer risk. CA Cancer J Clin 2002;52:301–9.
79. Gammon MD, Santella RM, Neugut AI, et al. Environmental toxins and breast cancer on Long Island. I. Polycyclic aromatic hydrocarbon DNA adducts. Cancer Epidemiol Biomarkers Prev 2002;11:677–85.
80. Gammon MD, Wolff MS, Neugut AI, et al. Environmental toxins and breast cancer on Long Island. II. Organochlorine compound levels in blood. Cancer Epidemiol Biomarkers Prev 2002;11:686–97.
81. Bernstein L. The roles of physical activity and electric blankets in breast cancer occurrence. Epidemiology 2001; 12:598–600.
82. Erren TC. A meta-analysis of epidemiologic studies of electric and magnetic fields and breast cancer in women and men. Bioelectromagnetics 2001;Suppl 5:S105–19.

5

Genetics, Natural History, and DNA-Based Genetic Counseling in Hereditary Breast Cancer

HENRY T. LYNCH
JANE F. LYNCH

Breast cancer is a major public health problem with its estimated incidence in the United States of 217,440 in 2004 expected to far surpass that of lung cancer for women. Its mortality is estimated at more than 40,580 in 2004, which will exceed the number of deaths from colorectal cancer (CRC) in women.[1] Lifetime projections indicate that about one in eight women in the general population will develop breast cancer during their lifetime. Of these, about 5 to 10% of the total breast cancer burden will be hereditary, and, when based upon the above incidence figures, it will have affected approximately 10,872 to 21,744 patients during 2004. An additional 15 to 20% of the newly diagnosed breast cancer patients will be referred to as "familial breast cancer." This is a crude classification which is defined as the index patient (proband) with carcinoma of the breast, plus one or more of her first- and/or second-degree relatives also manifesting breast cancer. Lacking, however, is the segregating pattern within the family of breast cancer and/or other tumors that are integral to the specific hereditary cancer syndrome, particularly carcinoma of the ovary in the hereditary breast-ovarian cancer (HBOC) syndrome,[2,3] or others that are consonant with one of several hereditary breast cancer syndromes.[4–6] In this familial breast cancer category, a first-degree relative of a person affected by breast cancer will have a lifetime risk of about two times that of the general population risk for developing this disease. Although the remainder of the population will be classified as "sporadic," another crude term in that it simply implies an absence of breast cancer among the patient's first- and second-degree relatives, it must be realized that this may be due to incomplete family history; failure to examine other cancers that could constitute a hereditary breast cancer syndrome, such as ovarian, colon, or prostate cancer; false paternity; or simply lack of patient's cooperation in compiling the family history.[3]

Hereditary cancer, once considered to be a rarely occurring clinical problem, has, thanks to prodigious advances in molecular genetics and coupled with the discovery of cancer-causing germline mutations, emerged as a major public health problem. The clinical translation of the significance of cancer "running in families" has become a source of major contention as a result of a veritable explosion of knowledge about cancer causality at the molecular level during the past decade.[7] In turn, the lay media have helped to educate patients about the significance of genetics in medicine, with particular attention to cancer. The demand for information has increased greatly among the laity. Consequently, physician interest has become more strongly devoted to these concerns of their patients.[8]

At the clinical level, the increasing awareness of the "familial" and "hereditary" burden of cancer has contributed heavily to both physician and laity concern about "cancer risk." For example, present estimates, albeit conservative, suggest that approximately 15 to 20% of virtually all varieties of cancer will show familial clustering, whereas an additional 5 to 10% will show a primary hereditary etiology (Figure 5–1).

The epidemiology of breast cancer has been intensively investigated. Studies of Western women have shown that an excessive lifetime number of ovulations, as evidenced by early menarche (< age 13) and late age of menopause (> age 50),[9,10] increases the breast cancer risk. Early first full-term pregnancy, particularly that occurring before age 20, provides protection, but first full-term pregnancy occurring after age 30 increases the patient's lifetime breast cancer risk. Nulliparity, tallness, obesity, and alcohol consumption have also been implicated in increasing breast cancer risk.[9]

GENETICS

The combination of carcinoma of the breast and ovary in families, now known as the HBOC (hereditary breast and ovarian cancer) syndrome, was first reported in the early 1970s.[2,6,11] The molecular genetic discoveries that confirmed beyond any doubt the hereditary basis for hereditary breast cancer (HBC) and HBOC have progressed at an explosive rate, particularly over the past decade. This avalanche of knowledge was heralded by the gene linkage study of Hall and colleagues,[12] which identified a locus on chromosome 17q for families with site-specific breast cancer. Subsequently, Narod and colleagues[13] reported that this same breast cancer susceptibility locus was responsible for the HBOC syndrome. The culprit gene, now known as *BRCA1*, was then cloned.[14] This was rapidly followed by the discovery, through linkage analysis, of a second breast cancer susceptibility locus on chromosome 13q, known as *BRCA2*,[15] and its subsequent cloning.[16]

Approximately 45% of all hereditary breast cancer-prone families, including those characterized as HBOC, are due to mutations of the *BRCA1* gene,[17] whereas a slightly lower percentage is due to *BRCA2* mutations. Initial studies estimated that carriers of the *BRCA1* germline mutation harbor a lifetime risk for breast cancer of about 85%[17,18] and a risk for ovarian cancer that ranges between 40 and 66%.[17,18] Carriers of the *BRCA2* mutation harbor a lifetime risk of breast cancer of about 85%, comparable to its *BRCA1* counterpart, but their risk for ovarian cancer is somewhat lower (10 to 20%).[17,18] In further contrast to *BRCA1*, male *BRCA2* mutation carriers have an approximate 7% lifetime risk for breast cancer. Other cancers occurring in excess in *BRCA2* mutation carriers include carcinoma of the pancreas, head and neck, prostate, colorectum, and cutaneous and intraocular malignant melanoma.

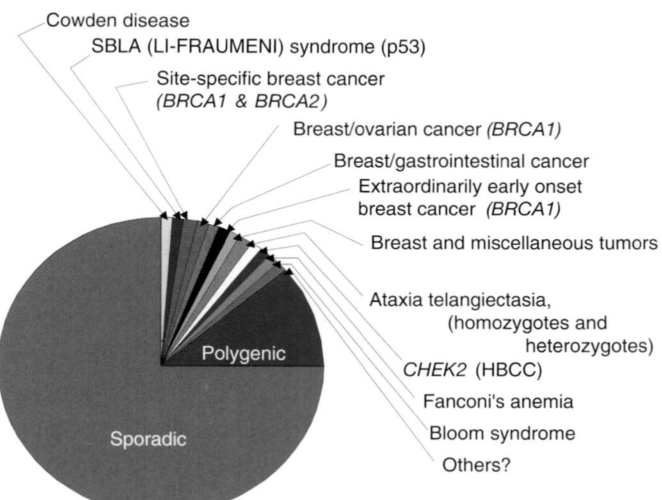

Figure 5–1. Circle graph showing relative frequencies of sporadic, polygenic (familial), and hereditary breast cancers.

These initial estimates of breast and ovarian cancer gene penetrance risks in *BRCA* mutation carriers were based upon publications of highly extended pedigrees that were selected because of their profound familial cancer aggregation, and, thereby, were biased in the direction of cancer excess. In contrast, recent observations of breast and ovarian cancer occurrence in the Ashkenazi Jewish founder mutations (185delAG and 5382insC mutations on the *BRCA1* gene, and 6174delT on the *BRCA2* gene) indicate that the lifetime risk for breast cancer is only 56%, and that of ovarian cancer 16%.[19]

Claus and colleagues[20] examined the family history of carcinoma of the breast and ovary in a data set which involved 4,730 cases with breast cancer and 4,688 controls who were enrolled in the Cancer and Steroid Hormone Study. Attention was given to the association between family history of carcinoma of the breast and/or ovary and breast cancer risk when controlling for the carrier status of *BRCA1* and *BRCA2* mutations. The question they examined pertained to whether the family history of carcinoma of the breast remained a predictive risk factor once the carrier status for *BRCA1* and/or *BRCA2* was given consideration. They found that among those women, "...with a moderate family history of breast cancer (ie, predicted noncarriers of *BRCA1* and/or *BRCA2* mutations), family history remains a factor in predicting breast cancer risk. In families with breast and ovarian cancers, the aggregation of these two cancers appears to be explained by *BRCA1/BRCA2* mutation-carrier probability." This study clearly enunciates the need for obtaining a well-orchestrated cancer family history for the assessment of breast/ovarian cancer risk.[8]

In the past, the prediction of a patient's lifetime breast cancer risk was based upon the patient's position in the pedigree, namely, having one or more first-degree relatives with a cancer syndrome in the direct genetic lineage of an HBC or HBOC family, and, therein, the most precise estimate possible was 50%. However, the identification of the mutations for *BRCA1*[14] and *BRCA2*,[16] in the context of the penetrance of these genes, dramatically changed these relatively crude estimates and now enables physicians and genetic counselors to predict a patient's lifetime risk for carcinoma of the breast and ovary with great precision.

OVARIAN CARCINOMA

Any discussion of the genetics of carcinoma of the breast must include ovarian cancer. This disease will affect approximately 1% of women in the United States during their lifetime, where it accounts for about 16,090 deaths annually[1] with a 5-year survival rate of < 30%. The biological mechanism of transforming benign ovarian cells to carcinoma remains elusive, although it likely involves a multistep process requiring an accumulation of genetic lesions involving different gene classes.

As mentioned, the genetic epidemiologic association of ovarian cancer with breast cancer was first reported in the early 1970s in a series of breast cancer-prone pedigrees[2,6,11]; both *BRCA1* and *BRCA2* mutations were subsequently found to predispose to ovarian as well as breast cancer in the HBOC syndrome.[13] In *BRCA1*, the lifetime risk for ovarian cancer is in the range of approximately 50%, whereas in *BRCA2* the lifetime ovarian cancer risk is about 20%. Ovarian carcinoma is also an integral lesion in Lynch syndrome II.[21] Lynch and colleagues[22] have provided an extensive review of the genetics of ovarian cancer.

HETEROGENEITY AND HEREDITARY BREAST CANCER

Virtually all forms of hereditary cancer show significant genotypic and phenotypic heterogeneity. For example, breast cancer occurs in significant excess in disorders associated with extra breast cancer sites, such as Li-Fraumeni syndrome (Figure 5–2), Blooms syndrome, Cowden disease, ataxia telangiectasia, the breast-gastrointestinal tract cancer syndrome, extraordinarily early-onset breast cancer (Figure 5–3), Lynch syndrome, and the HBOC syndrome (Figure 5–4). Undoubtedly, other tumor combinations and/or hereditary syndromes which will qualify as hereditary breast cancer are yet to be identified. Space does not allow a discussion of each of these breast cancer-associated disorders (for more detail, see Lynch and colleagues[23]).

Clearly, it is no longer appropriate to characterize hereditary breast cancer as a generic term. Rather, one must be more precise and denote the particular breast cancer-associated syndrome relating to a particular

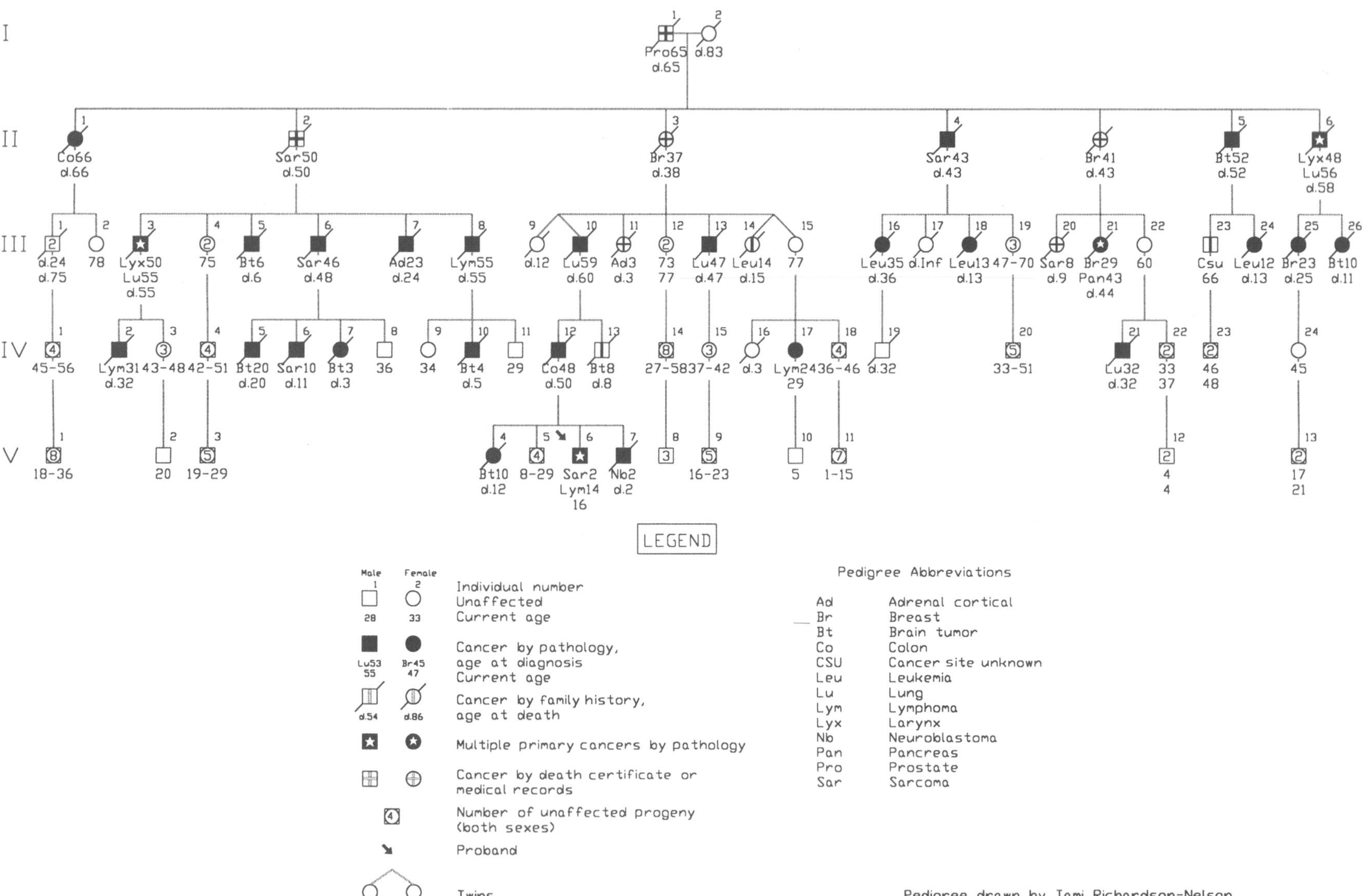

Figure 5–2. Updated pedigree of a family with sarcoma, breast cancer, brain tumors, lung cancer, laryngeal cancer, and adrenocortical carcinoma (SBLA syndrome). Reproduced with permission from Lynch et al.[66]

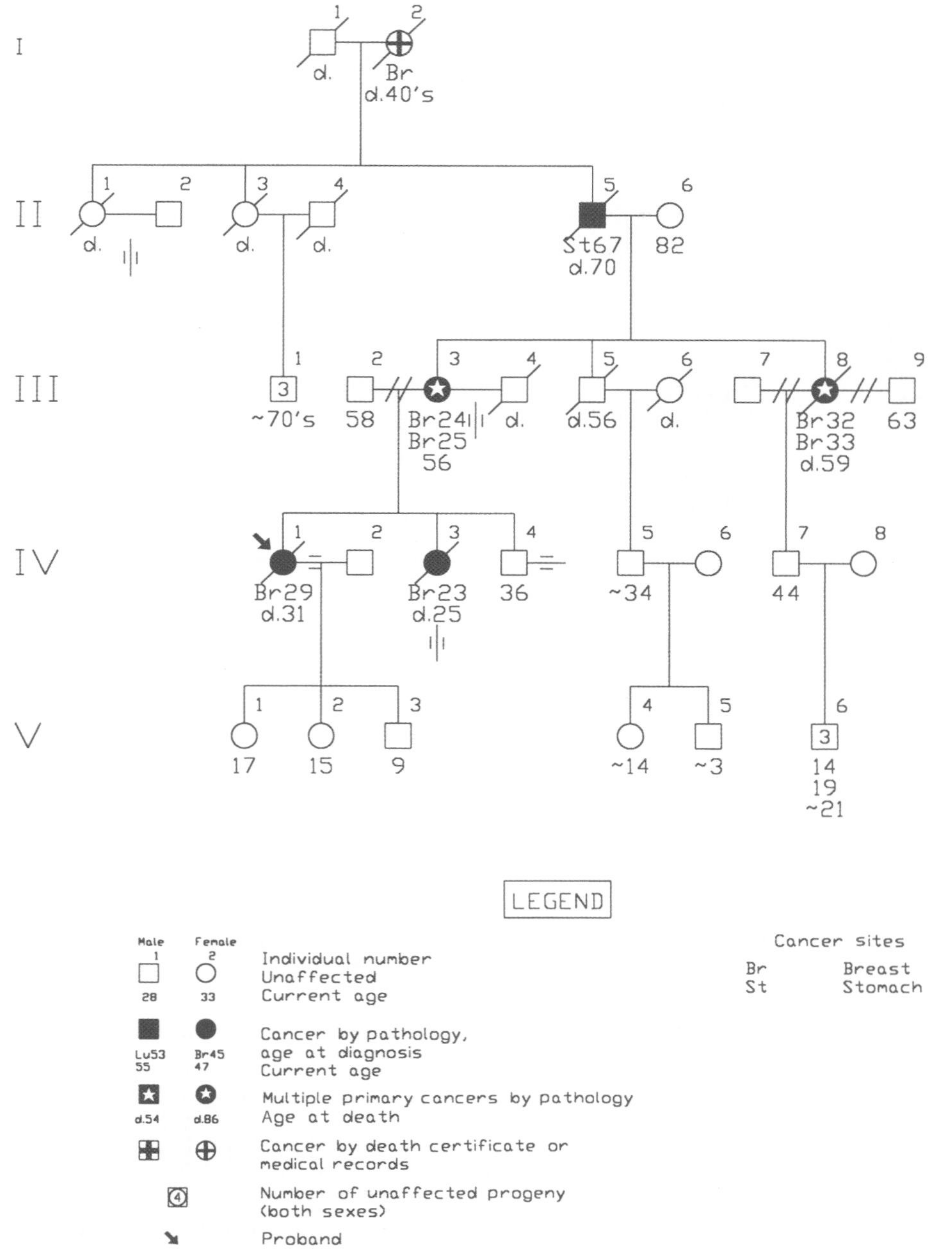

Figure 5–3. Pedigree of a family showing extremely early age of onset of hereditary breast cancer. Reproduced with permission from Lynch et al.[86]

patient/family. Such syndrome identification is important not only for molecular genetic assessment but also for targeted surveillance and management purposes.

ASSESSMENT OF BREAST CANCER-PRONE FAMILIES

The search for a deleterious cancer-causing germline mutation should be performed only when there are personal or family history features suggestive of a hereditary cancer syndrome.[24] Therefore, to establish a hereditary breast cancer syndrome diagnosis, a detailed collection of a patient's cancer family history, with as much pathology corroboration as possible, is mandatory for consideration of DNA testing. Given this rationale, the family history may potentially constitute the most cost-beneficial component of a patient's medical workup. When a can-

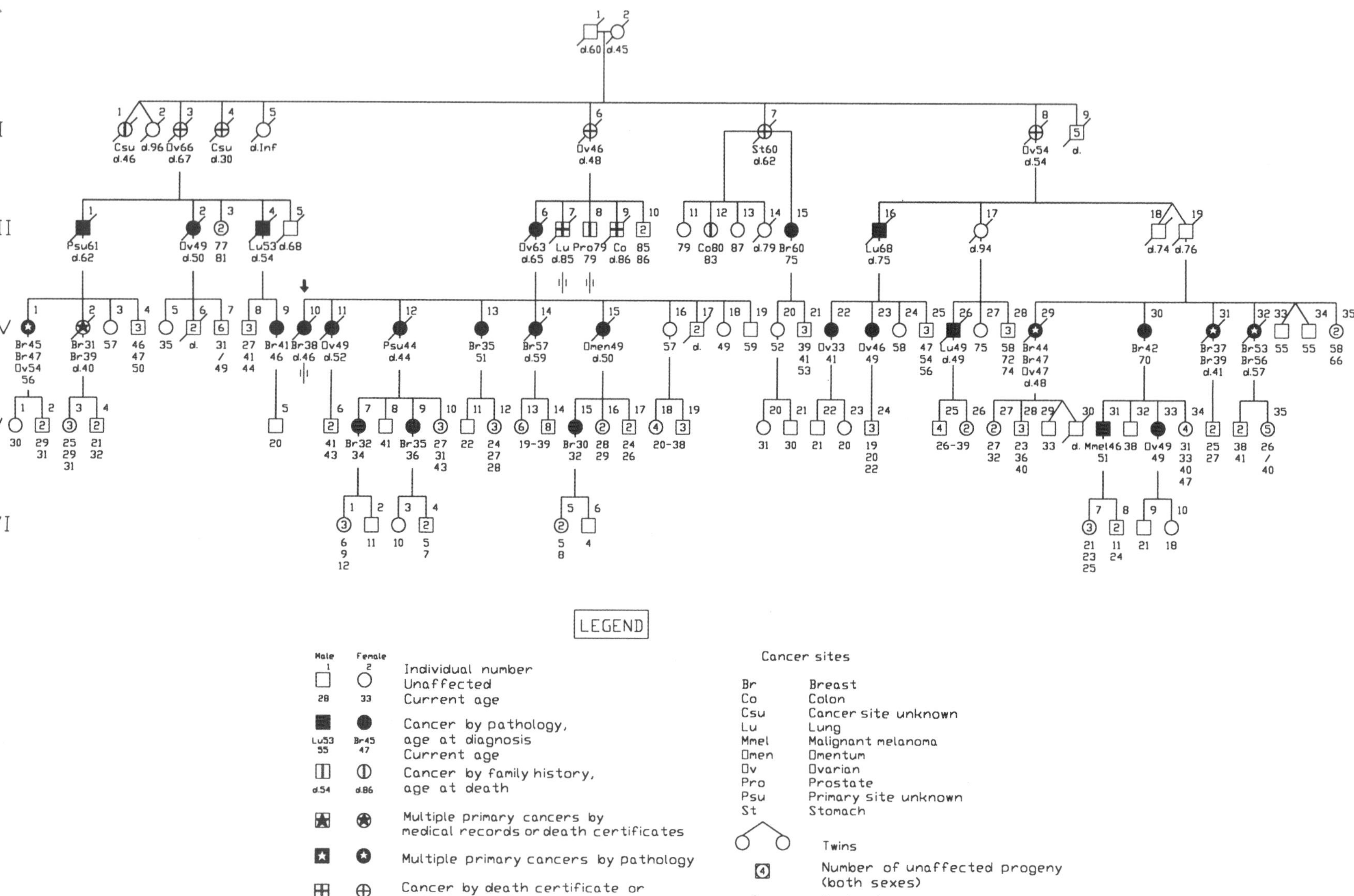

Figure 5–4. Updated pedigree of a large hereditary breast-ovarian cancer family. Adapted with permission from Lynch et al.[87]

cer causing mutation is identified, this information can, in concert with genetic counseling, be used effectively to benefit the patient and the patient's family members.

The family history is indispensable in this effort.[8] Once the family history is meticulously compiled, with as much verification as can be obtained, one can then cast this knowledge in the form of a cancer family pedigree, which often will depict a particular patient's lifetime cancer destiny. This effort can be readily accomplished through collecting information through four generations, namely the patient, his or her siblings, progeny, and maternal and paternal lineages (aunts and uncles and both sets of grandparents), which collectively constitutes the modified nuclear pedigree (Figure 5–5). This amount of information can often lead to the recognition of a hereditary predisposition to cancer.

NATURAL HISTORY

Building the case for hereditary cancer is frequently based upon the cardinal clinical features of hereditary cancer, namely, early age of cancer onset, a specific pattern of multiple primary cancers (such as breast and ovarian cancer), often vertical transmission of cancer, and increased number of cancer occurrences (Table 5–1). It is virtually axiomatic that the larger the breast cancer-prone family, the greater the number of expected carcinomas of the breast or ovary, or other patterns of cancer combinations that may constitute a specific hereditary cancer syndrome. One can then be more confident of a likely hereditary etiology, particularly when there is substantial evidence of the aforementioned cardinal features of hereditary cancer. In such a setting, there will be an increased probability that a germline mutation, such as one for HBOC (*BRCA1*, *BRCA2*), will be found. On the other hand, when dealing with families that are small, there may be a limited number of patients with cancer, a deficit of females, or the few cancers that are occurring may be in the paternal lineage. The overall effect is that it may become exceedingly difficult to predict whether such a small family should be a candidate for searching for a mutation in *BRCA1* or *BRCA2* for the HBOC syndrome, *p53* as in the Li-Fraumeni syndrome,[25,26] or mutations associated with other hereditary syndromes that predispose to breast cancer.[3]

SURVEILLANCE AND MANAGEMENT FOR HEREDITARY BREAST CANCER

When the diagnosis of a hereditary breast cancer-prone syndrome has been established, the surveillance and management strategies are then melded to the natural history of the particular HBC syndrome.

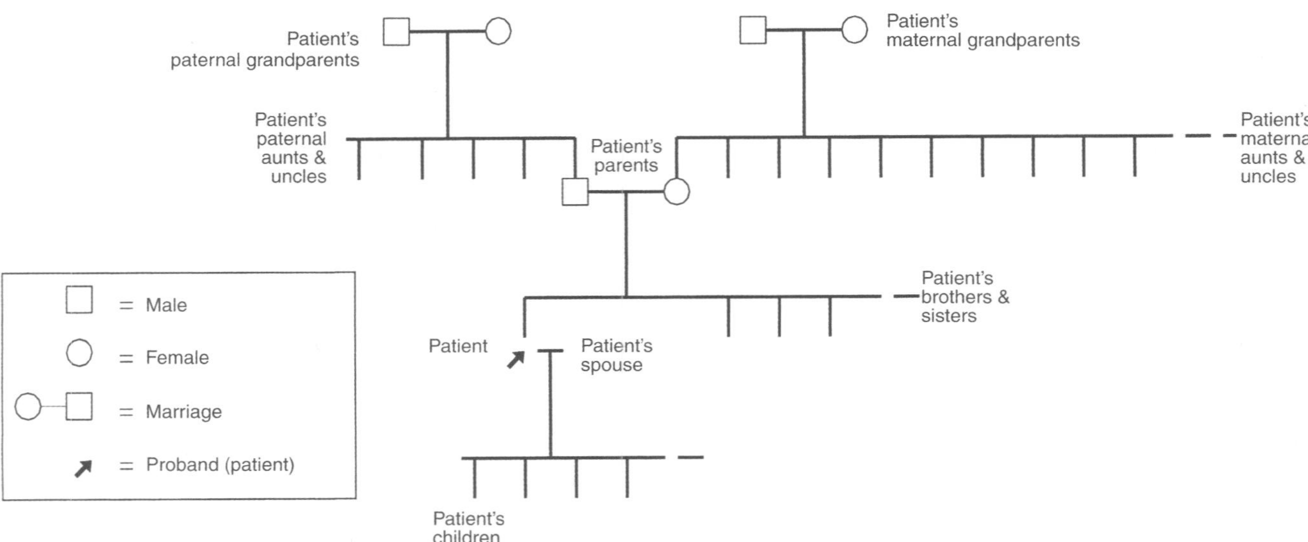

Figure 5–5. Patient's modified nuclear pedigree.

Table 5–1. ESTIMATED PROBABILITY OF BRCA1 MUTATION BASED ON FAMILY HISTORY

Family History	Probability of *BRCA1* Mutation, %
Single affected person	
Breast cancer at < 30 years of age	12
Breast cancer at < 40 years of age	6
Breast cancer at 40 to 49 years of age	3
Ovarian cancer at < 50 years of age	7
Sister pairs	
Both with breast cancer at < 40 years of age	37
Both with breast cancer at 40 to 49 years of age	20
Breast cancer at < 50 years of age, ovarian cancer at < 50 years of age	46
Both with ovarian cancer at < 50 years of age	61
Families	
Breast cancer only, three or more cases at < 50 years of age	40
Two or more breast cancers and one or more ovarian cancers	82
Two or more beast cancers and two or more ovarian cancers	91

Reprinted with permission from Weber B. Breast cancer susceptibility genes: current challenges and future promises. Ann Intern Med 1996;124:1088–90.

In these cases, we recommend that patients receive intensive education regarding the natural history, genetic risk, and availability of DNA testing such as *BRCA1*, *BRCA2*, or *p53*, depending upon the hereditary breast cancer syndrome of concern. We initiate such education between ages 15 and 18 years but do not perform any DNA testing until the patient is 18 years of age and has given informed consent. We then provide instruction in breast self-examination (BSE) with physician assessment of their performance. Although the effectiveness of BSE has been controversial, it can be effective if the woman is taught how to perform this procedure and demonstrates proficiency in performing the procedure on return medical visits. When patients reach the age of 20 years, we begin semiannual breast examination by the physician and at age 25 initiate annual mammography. Given the problem of dense breasts in these young women, magnetic resonance imaging (MRI) might be offered.[27]

With respect to ovarian cancer, we discuss transvaginal ovarian ultrasound, Doppler color blood flow imaging, and CA 125, with their limitations, and initiate this screening at age 30 and perform it annually. The option of prophylactic bilateral oophorectomy is also discussed. If the patient is interested in this option and has completed her child bearing, prophylactic oophorectomy can be performed between the ages of 35 and 45 years.

Breast Cancer Prevention in *BRCA1/BRCA2* Mutation Carriers

Calderon-Margalit and Paltiel[27] examined evidence for the efficacy of surveillance and early detection, bilateral prophylactic mastectomy, prophylactic oophorectomy, and chemoprevention in preventing breast cancer and improving survival in *BRCA1* or *BRCA2* mutation carriers. Their study involved a critical review of pertinent articles from 1998 to 2004 identified through MEDLINE, PubMed, and references from retrieved articles. None of this current evidence was based upon randomized investigations, although the efficacy of surveillance for early detection of breast cancer among *BRCA1* and *BRCA2* carriers is yet to be clarified. Findings showed that screening with clinical breast examination and mammography showed lower sensitivity in *BRCA1* or *BRCA2* mutation carriers as opposed to the general population. They suggest that MRI screening might offer higher sensitivity rates as opposed to mammography. Reduction in the risk of breast cancer by as much as 89.5 to 100% was found through prophylactic mastectomy, even in the face of this procedure being the least acceptable to high-risk women. Tamoxifen use was associated with breast cancer prevention among *BRCA2*, but not *BRCA1*, carriers; note that *BRCA1* carriers show a lower rate of estrogen receptor (ER) positivity than do *BRCA2* mutation carriers. In *BRCA1* or *BRCA2* carriers with breast cancer, tamoxifen was associated with prevention of secondary breast cancer (odds ratio [OR] = 0.50, 95% CI: 0.28–0.89). In addition, "prophylactic oophorectomy was associated with hazard ratios for breast cancer of 0.47 (95% CI: 0.29–0.77) and 0.32 (95% CI: 0.08–1.20), in retrospective and short follow-up prospective cohort studies, respectively." The authors concluded the need for more studies in order to determine which of these four strategies, alone or in combination, might prove to be most efficacious for breast cancer prevention and improvement of survival among patients harboring *BRCA* mutations.

PROPHYLACTIC MASTECTOMY

In a landmark retrospective study, Hartmann and colleagues[28] studied 214 women with a breast cancer-positive family history who underwent bilateral prophylactic mastectomy at the Mayo Clinic between 1960 and 1993. These women were divided into high-risk versus moderate-risk groups based on their family history. To predict the number of breast cancers expected in these two groups had prophylactic mastectomies not been performed, the researchers used a nested-sister control study for the high-risk group and the Gail model for the moderate-risk group. The moderate-risk group showed an 89.5% reduction ($p < .001$) in breast cancer occurrence from the expected prediction, and the high-risk group showed a > 90% reduction in the instance of breast cancer with follow-up to the end of the study. Breast cancer mortality was also reduced significantly in both groups. Seven breast cancers occurred in their study after subcutaneous bilateral mastectomy; there were none after total mastectomy.[28]

Subsequently, they performed a prospective study of this same cohort of high-risk women.[29] They identified 26 of the women with an alteration in *BRCA1* or *BRCA2* and, herein, 18 of the mutations were considered to be deleterious whereas 8 were of uncertain clinical significance. Importantly, none of these 26 women has developed breast cancer for a median of 13.4 years of follow-up.[29] Therefore, prophylactic mastectomy appears to reduce the long-term risk of breast cancer in those women with a *BRCA1* or *BRCA2* mutation. These authors concluded that their results suggest that the risk of breast cancer is reduced by approximately 90 to 100% in the *BRCA1* or *BRCA2* mutation carriers following prophylactic mastectomy.

A prospective study by Meijers-Heijboer and colleagues[30] also showed significant benefit of prophylactic mastectomy among *BRCA1/2* mutation carriers. These investigators studied 139 women with a *BRCA1* or *BRCA2* mutation who were part of a prospective study of the effectiveness of prophylactic mastectomy in a breast-cancer surveillance program at the Rotterdam Family Cancer Clinic in The Netherlands. Seventy-six of these women eventually underwent prophylactic mastectomy, and 63 declined that surgery in preference to regular surveillance. Cox proportional-hazards method evaluated the incidence of breast cancer as a time-dependent covariate for the effect of mastectomy on the incidence of breast cancer. Findings disclosed an absence of breast cancer among those undergoing prophylactic mastectomy during a follow-up of 2.9 (± 1.4) years whereas, in comparison, eight breast cancers developed in those women who elected regular surveillance after a mean follow-up of 3.0 (± 1.5) years ($p = .003$; hazard ratio, 0; 95% CI, 0 to 0.36). The authors concluded that "...in women with a *BRCA1* or *BRCA2* mutation, prophylactic bilateral total mastectomy reduces the incidence of breast cancer at 3 years of follow-up." It was of particular interest that of the eight cancers identified in the screening group, four were identified between screening sessions, consonant with so-called interval cancers, and herein "the interval from screening to diagnosis was 2 to 5 months." Cancers in the remaining four patients were detected during a screening session. Thus, it is possible that some were "missed lesions" versus accelerated breast carcinogenesis.

A significantly greater number of women in the prophylactic mastectomy group, as opposed to those in the surveillance group, had undergone a premenopausal oophorectomy (44 versus 24 [58% versus 38%], $p = .03$). Thus, there was likely a protective effect from prophylactic oophorectomy, consistent with the findings of Rebbeck and colleagues,[31] discussed subsequently.

Given the assumption that within 10 years breast cancer will develop in approximately 25% of the women undergoing regular surveillance, these authors[30] estimated that 10 to 20% of high-risk women who choose surveillance instead of prophylactic mastectomy will die of breast cancer within 20 years, and 35 to 50% of women under surveillance who develop primary breast cancer will die of distant metastases within 10 to 15 years.[32,33]

Meijers-Heijboer and colleagues[30] also suggest that the use of high-resolution imaging as well as more frequent screening might be effective in early breast cancer detection among women with a *BRCA1* or *BRCA2* mutation. Specifically, in their study MRI was performed in six women at the time of breast cancer diagnosis, and it detected all six cancers. In contrast, mammography was diagnostic in only two of the eight women with breast cancer.

Schrag and colleagues[34] discuss the decision analysis involved in prophylactic mastectomy and oophorectomy and life expectancy outcome among patients with *BRCA1* and *BRCA2* germline mutations. They found that, on average, a 30-year-old woman harboring such a mutation would gain from 2.9 to 5.3 years of life expectancy from prophylactic mastectomy and from 0.3 to 1.7 years from prophylactic oophorectomy. These findings were dependent upon their cumulative risk of cancer. Gains in life expectancy would also decline with age at the time of prophylactic surgery. They would be minimal for a 60-year-old woman. Importantly, in women aged 30, an oophorectomy may be delayed for 10 years with minimal loss of life expectancy. This would allow women to complete their families. These investigators concluded that "on the basis of a range of estimates of the incidence of cancer, prognosis, and efficacy of prophylactic surgery, our model suggests that prophylactic mastectomy provides substantial gains in life expectancy and prophylactic oophorectomy more limited gains for young women with *BRCA1* or *BRCA2* mutations."

Should these findings regarding prophylactic mastectomy affect the management of a patient with HBOC, particularly one who is harboring a *BRCA1* or *BRCA2* germline mutation, as opposed to a patient with the more common sporadic form of this disease? We have taken the position that, because of the early age of breast cancer onset and the excess lifetime risk for bilaterality, coupled with the potential deficiency of repair of radiation-induced DNA damage,[35] the high-risk patient should be given the *option* of total mastectomy as opposed to conservative ("lumpectomy") management, and, when ipsilateral breast cancer is present, she should seriously consider contralateral prophylactic mastectomy, assuming that her ipsilateral breast cancer is likely to have adequate control.

A woman's personal decision about prophylactic bilateral mastectomy is key to its ultimate acceptability. But many issues impact upon this decision. What will be the public health impact of Hartmann and colleagues'[28,29] findings given the enormous magnitude of breast cancer in the general population, particularly in women in Western highly industrialized nations? How will women determine if they are at high risk? Will physicians take family histories that are sufficiently detailed to enable them to make hereditary risk determinations? Are there enough genetic counselors who are sufficiently knowledgeable about cancer genetics and the pros and cons of prophylactic bilateral mastectomy (as well as prophylactic bilateral oophorectomy), particularly the potential physical and psychologic sequelae, to adequately and responsibly advise their clients? Indeed, should offering such options be the responsibility of the non-medically trained genetic counselor? Are the skills of these counselors being sufficiently used? Will insurers defray the cost of genetic counseling, genetic testing, and prophylactic surgery? Will there be insurance discrimination? Will women accept the loss of sexual stimulation following prophylactic bilateral mastectomy, particularly with sacrifice of the nipple areola complex, and/or the change in their body image because of disfigurement? What will be the spouse response? Only time will tell.

PROPHYLACTIC OOPHORECTOMY

Rebbeck and colleagues[31] examined the efficacy of bilateral oophorectomy in *BRCA* mutation carriers and its reduction in risk of gynecologic cancer, as well as breast cancer, in women who harbor these mutations. The study involved 551 women with disease-associated germline *BRCA1* or *BRCA2* mutations. The incidence of ovarian cancer was determined in

259 women who had undergone bilateral prophylactic oophorectomy and in 292 matched controls who had not undergone this procedure. In a subgroup of 241 women without a history of breast cancer or prophylactic mastectomy, the incidence of breast cancer was determined in 99 women who had undergone bilateral prophylactic oophorectomy and 142 matched controls. Post-operative follow-up for both groups was at least 6 years. The results were extremely striking and statistically significant. Specifically, only six women who underwent prophylactic oophorectomy (2.3%) were found to have stage I ovarian cancer at the time of the procedure, whereas two women (0.8%) received a diagnosis of papillary serous peritoneal carcinoma 3.8 and 8.8 years after bilateral prophylactic oophorectomy. Furthermore, "among the controls, 58 women (19.9%) received a diagnosis of ovarian cancer, after a mean follow-up of 8.8 years. With the exclusion of the six women whose cancer was diagnosed at surgery, prophylactic oophorectomy significantly reduced the risk of coelomic epithelial cancer (hazard ratio, 0.04; 95% CI, 0.01–0.16). Of 99 women who underwent bilateral prophylactic oophorectomy and who were studied to determine the risk of breast cancer, breast cancer developed in 21 (21.2%) as compared with 60 (42.3%) in the control group (hazard ratio, 0.47; 95% CI, 0.29–0.77)." Rebbeck and colleagues concluded that prophylactic oophorectomy not only reduced the risk of coelomic epithelial cancer but also the risk of breast cancer in those women harboring *BRCA1* or *BRCA2* mutations.

GENOTYPE–PHENOTYPE DIFFERENCES

More than 200 different *BRCA1* germline mutations have been identified in HBOC families. Certain types of these mutations may give rise to differing patterns of cancer occurrence. Gayther and colleagues[36] suggest that the position of the *BRCA1* mutation has a significant influence on the ratio of breast to ovarian cancer in HBOC kindreds. Specifically, they reported that mutations in the 3′ third of the gene are associated with a lower proportion of ovarian cancer. However, these findings must be viewed cautiously. For example, Serova and colleagues[37] were unable to confirm these findings.

In the case of *BRCA2*, Gayther and colleagues[38] found that "truncating mutations in families with the highest risk of ovarian cancer relative to breast cancer are clustered in a region of approximately 3.3 kb in exon 11 ($p = .0004$)." Further research in this area may establish links between specific mutations and specific cancer risk that will prove to be extremely useful for genetic counseling. However, until confirmation of these genotype–phenotype findings is more firmly established, it is prudent to refrain from introducing this preliminary information into the genetic counseling setting.

Most of the hereditary breast and ovarian cancer cases will harbor a *BRCA1* or *BRCA2* germline mutation. However, because of the high prevalence of carcinoma of the breast and ovary in the general population, coupled with the previously mentioned fact that approximately 5 to 10% of the total breast cancer burden will be hereditary, one should expect to encounter (albeit rarely) families where both *BRCA1* and *BRCA2* mutations are segregating.

Interestingly, Ramus and colleagues[39] reported a patient from a Hungarian family who manifested both breast and ovarian cancer and was found to have truncating mutations in *both* the *BRCA1* and *BRCA2* genes. This patient "carried the 185delAG mutation in *BRCA1* as well as the 6174delT mutation in *BRCA2*. Both of these mutations are common in Ashkenazi Jewish breast cancer patients.[40–42] Recently, Liede and colleagues[43] identified an Ashkenazi Jewish kindred with three mutations, namely *BRCA1* 185delAG, *BRCA1* 5382insC, and *BRCA2* 6174delT. Each founder mutation has been shown to have a frequency of approximately 1% in the Ashkenazi population.[44–46]

PATHOLOGY OF BREAST CANCER IN CONCERT WITH *BRCA1* OR *BRCA2* MUTATIONS

Pathology studies have shown differences between *BRCA1*- and *BRCA2*-related breast cancers when compared with sporadic controls. Specifically, Marcus and colleagues[47–49] have shown that *BRCA1* HBC has a highly distinctive pathology phenotype, consisting of an increased number of aneuploid cancers, more medullary carcinomas, and high proliferation rates as measured by DNA flow cytometry and mitotic grade. They also show a lesser occurrence of ductal carcinoma in situ (DCIS) than in nonfamilial cases. In alluding to high S-phase fraction in HBC and attributing it to the *BRCA1*-linked subset, it was suggested that the mutation resulted in enhanced cellular proliferation.[50] This prediction was borne out by the demonstration of the antiproliferative effect of *BRCA1* mRNA protein in vitro and in vivo[51–53] after the gene was cloned.

We have proposed a model for the *BRCA1* pathophenotype that considers the tumors to be in an advanced state of genetic evolution.[47] With respect to antiestrogen hormonal management, it is important to know that breast cancers in *BRCA1* mutation carriers are frequently ER negative.

In contrast, "other" HBCs (cases from HBC families with no *BRCA1* mutations, no 17q linkage, and a paucity of ovarian cancer affecteds, or with *BRCA2* mutations or 13q linkage) appear to lack the systematic high grade, aneuploidy, and high proliferation of *BRCA1* HBCs, and they are not deficient in situ carcinoma.[47,48] This "other" group also has more invasive lobular, tubular, tubulolobular, and cribiform special type carcinomas, which we have designated as the "tubular-lobular group" (TLG). Indeed, the excess of TLG and "no special type" (NST) invasive carcinomas with TLG "features" (10 to 50% tumor composition) parallels a trend for more lobular neoplasia (lobular carcinoma in situ and atypical lobular hyperplasia) in "other" HBCs. These features are present in the subset of mutation-confirmed *BRCA2* HBC cases in the "other" HBC group,[49] which suggests that TLG carcinomas and lobular neoplasia are signatures of the *BRCA2* HBC phenotype.[49] In contrast, *BRCA1* HBC cases manifest a *deficit* of TLG carcinomas and lobular neoplasia.[49] Armes and colleagues[54] confirm an excess of TLG carcinoma (in their cases, pleomorphic lobular carcinomas) in *BRCA2* HBC in a population-based study of *BRCA2* cases that were not specifically recruited from large HBOC families.

The pathophenotype of *BRCA2* HBC may be more heterogeneous than *BRCA1* HBC when the amount of high-grade carcinoma in the syndrome is considered. There have been reports of *BRCA2* families with predominantly high grade carcinomas.[55,56] However, we have not seen high-grade predominance in the four *BRCA2* families we have studied nor as the average phenotype of the "other" HBC group in which most Creighton *BRCA2* families would reside.[49] Similarly, the Breast Cancer Linkage Consortium has not observed unusually high grades in its *BRCA2* family series.[57] The higher grades reported from Iceland[56] and, to a lesser extent, from the Linkage Consortium,[57,58] may well be associated with a site on the *BRCA2* gene, in these cases the 999del5 mutation.[54]

Lakhani and colleagues[58] confirmed many of the original observations of Marcus and colleagues.[49,50,59] Specifically, Lakhani and colleagues showed that "cancers associated with *BRCA1* mutations exhibited higher mitotic counts ($p = .001$), a greater proportion of the tumor with a continuous pushing margin ($p < .0001$), and more lymphocytic infiltration ($p = .002$) than sporadic (ie, control) cancers. Cancers associated with *BRCA2* mutations exhibited a higher score for tubule formation (fewer tubules) ($p = .0002$), a higher proportion of the tumor perimeter with a continuous pushing margin ($p < .0001$), and a lower mitotic count ($p = .003$) than control cancers." These authors concluded that this histopathology information may improve the classification of breast cancers in those patients showing a positive family history for this disease. Specifically, employing multifactorial analysis results from their previous estimates, they found that 7.5% of individuals with breast cancer in Britain who had been diagnosed between the ages of 20 and 29 years harbor a *BRCA1* mutation.[60] Furthermore, "assuming that the odds ratios from our analysis are independent of age, only about 2% of case subjects in this age group in whom the mitotic count is below 5 per 10 hpf, without continuous pushing margins, and in whom there is no lymphocytic infiltrate would be expected to carry a *BRCA1* mutation. By contrast, about 45% of case subjects in the 20- to 29-year-old group with 20 to 39 mitoses per 10 hpf, continuous pushing margins occupying more than 75% of the tumor perimeter, and a prominent lymphocytic infiltrate would be expected to be *BRCA1* carriers. The corresponding proportions based on mitotic count would be 4% and 16%."

OTHER MUTATIONS

CHEK2

De Bock and colleagues[61] investigated a cohort of 1,084 consecutive patients with primary breast cancer and identified 34 with *CHEK2**1100delC mutation (3.1%), and 102 patients lacking that mutation. All patients were stratified by age and date of diagnosis of the first primary breast cancer within a period of one year. Mutated alleles of *BRCA1*, *BRCA2*, and *p53* were absent. They found this mutation to be associated with breast cancer occurring in multiple-case families wherein *BRCA1* and *BRCA2* had been excluded. They postulated that this gene is involved in cell cycle control and DNA repair through its ability to phosphorylate *p53*, Cdc25c, and BRCA1, a function which is abrogated by the 1100delC mutation. They estimated that the mutation has a population frequency of approximately 1%, and it has been suggested to confer an approximately two-fold relative risk of breast cancer. There were significant unfavorable differences found in the mutation carriers with respect to cancer-free survival ($p = .005$), contralateral breast cancer-free survival ($p = .001$), and distant metastasis-free survival ($p = .04$). No difference in overall survival has yet been determined. Contralateral breast cancer occurred in 26% (9% in the noncarriers) and distant metastasis in 43% (28% of the noncarriers), the highest relative risk pertaining to contralateral breast cancer in mutation carriers.

CHEK2 mutations are associated with a positive family history of breast cancer unrelated to *BRCA1/2* mutations, and this mutation may act together with another as-yet-unidentified breast cancer susceptibility gene. Because these are frequently steroid receptor-positive tumors, they appear more like *BRCA2* tumors than *BRCA1*-related tumors. *CHEK2* mutation carriers also appear to be at an increased risk for distant metastasis and have proved to be more malignant relative to other breast tumors. DNA testing for this mutation has not yet been introduced into daily clinical management of breast cancer patients.

Cybulski and colleagues[62] note that the CHEK2 protein participates in the DNA damage response in many cell types, and thereby they consider it a good candidate for a multi-site cancer susceptibility gene. They ascertained the prevalence of three founder alleles present in Poland, two of which resulted in truncated CHEK2 protein whereas a third is a missense substitution of an isoleucine for a threonine. They went on to ascertain the prevalence of each of these alleles in 4,008 cancer cases and 4,000 controls, all from Poland. The mutation was present in the majority of cancer sites; specifically, positive associations with protein truncating alleles were found for the following: "…cancers of the thyroid OR 4.9; $p = .0006$), breast (OR 2.2; $p = .02$), and prostate (OR 2.2; $p = .04$). The missense variant I157T was associated with an increased risk of breast cancer (OR 1.4; $p = .02$), colon cancer (OR 2.0; $p = .001$), kidney cancer (OR 2.1; $p = .0006$), prostate cancer (OR 1.7; $p = .002$), and thyroid cancer (OR 1.9; $p = .04$)." Therefore, these authors postulate that the whole tumor spectrum attributable to the *CHEK2* germline mutations may be much in excess of that previously considered.

These authors also provide a provocative statement relevant to the possible discovery of a third rare high-risk breast cancer gene following the discovery of *BRCA1* and *BRCA2* in 1994 and 1995 respectively. They note that such an identification of a rare high-risk breast cancer gene would follow the *BRCA1/BRCA2* discovery or, at least, the common variants of these genes, which may confer a modest cancer risk. Nevertheless, to date these genes remain undiscovered. Furthermore, these authors state, "arguably, the most important discovery of a breast cancer gene in the past 8 years has been *CHEK2*, which is typical of a third category of genes; mutations in genes in this category are rare and are associated with moderate penetrance. It is difficult to study these genes because very large sample sizes are needed to identify significant relevant risks."

Li-Fraumeni Syndrome

Li-Fraumeni syndrome (LFS) is inherited as an autosomal dominant.[63,64] Its incidence is unknown. Mutations in the *p53* gene on chromosome 17p31 are found in about 70% of classic LFS families,[25,26] but *p53* has been ruled out in some classic families,[65] suggesting that this syndrome is genetically heterogeneous. Genetic testing for *p53* mutations is available.

The tumor spectrum in LFS was characterized by Lynch and colleagues[66] with the acronym SBLA (*s*arcoma, *b*reast, brain tumors, *l*eukemia, lymphoma, laryngeal carcinoma, lung cancer, *a*drenal cortical carcinoma). Melanoma, germ cell tumor, and pancreatic, gastric, and prostatic carcinomas have also been described in LFS. The clinical diagnosis requires one patient with sarcoma under age 45, a first-degree relative with any type of cancer under age 45, and a third affected family member with sarcoma (any age) or other cancer (less than 45 years old). However, its extensive genotypic and phenotypic heterogeneity must be considered when evaluating suspect families.[67]

The risk of developing noncutaneous malignancy is 50% by age 30 and 90% by age 70. Hisada and colleagues[68] studied the incidence of second and third primary cancers in members of 24 LFS kindreds. The cumulative probability of a second primary was 57% at 30 years after the first cancer diagnosis. Sarcomas and carcinoma of the breast accounted for 46 of the 72 cancers identified. Brain tumors may show an extraordinarily high frequency in certain families.[67] Breast cancer may show remarkably early age of onset in some LFS families.

Annual physical examinations with blood cell counts are advised for LFS patients. Careful attention should be given to sites known to be at risk in LFS. Annual mammography and clinical breast examination and frequent breast self-examination starting at age 25 are particularly important.

GENETIC COUNSELING

Genetic counseling is mandatory for patients who are at high risk for breast cancer (or any type of hereditary cancer) and are contemplating DNA testing in the search for specific germline mutations.[24] Counseling should take place *prior* to the collection of DNA and at the time of disclosure of results. When possible, the ideal individual for initial gene testing in a family where a hereditary form of breast cancer is considered likely would be one who has had a syndrome cancer, particularly if diagnosed at an early age, and who is in the direct line of descent of the putative syndrome cancer expression. The clinician's task during the genetic counseling process is to help answer the patient's crucial questions which may arise during the genetic testing process. Importantly, patients need to decide whether to be tested for the presence of a germline mutation, such as *BRCA1* or *BRCA2*, once the facts are understood. They should be made aware of the potential for fear, anxiety, apprehension, intrafamily strife, as well as insurance/employment discrimination. Finally, they need to become knowledgeable about the best type of medical management for them, based upon the test result.

Figure 5–6 is an algorithm depicting the process used by the Creighton cancer genetic research team to ascertain, test, and counsel HBC/HBOC-prone families. Detailed information about the natural history of HBC/HBOC is provided, and the pros and cons of DNA testing are discussed. This program has involved more than 2,000 members of 29 large families with *BRCA1* mutations and 8 families with *BRCA2* mutations.[69] According to their self-reports, although most of these individuals freely chose to be tested, occasionally they reported pressure within the family either for or against their being tested. The same study showed the two primary reasons for deciding to be tested were to help their children and to aid in their own health management. Among those who declined to receive their test results, responses to an anonymous questionnaire disclosed various reasons for declining, including fear of insurance discrimination, which was cited by 37% of this group, and fear of the consequences of a positive result, cited by 20%.

The emotional responses to disclosure of germline mutation results cannot always be anticipated. The data for the Creighton study just discussed[69] show that the majority of patients who were negative for a *BRCA* mutation expressed relief. However, some individuals may experience disbelief or survivor guilt. Those who were told they did have the germline mutation expressed a variety of reactions, including acceptance because the results were expected, relief of anxiety with the removal of uncertainty about their genetic risk status, a positive attitude in terms of prevention, feel-

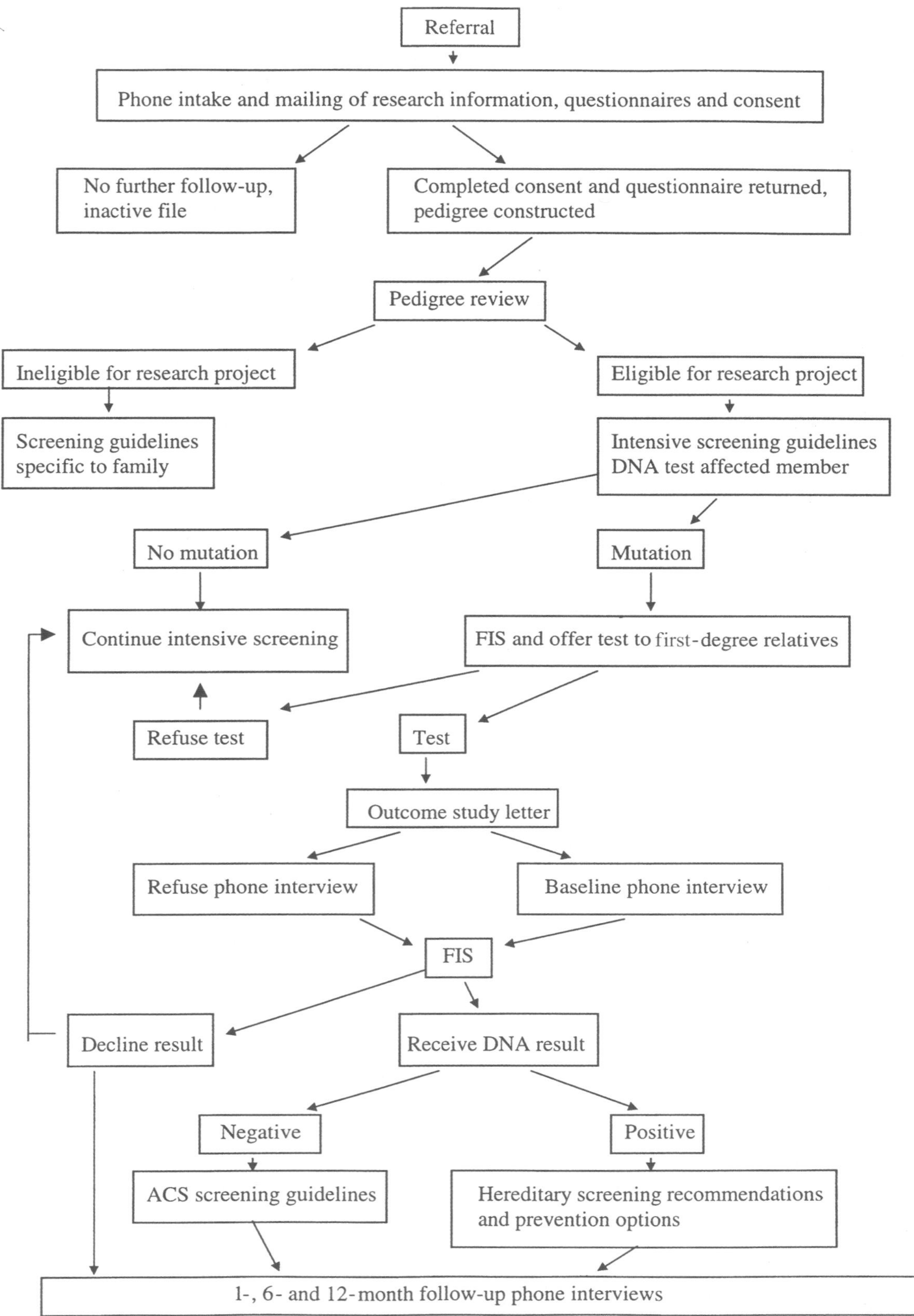

Figure 5–6. Algorithm for education and assessment of *BRCA1* and *BRCA2* families. Reproduced with permission from Lynch et al.[88]

ings of sadness, or even anger. The genetic counselor must be responsive to all of these emotions.

At a baseline interview in a study by Lerman and colleagues,[70] breast-ovarian cancer-related stress symptoms were predictive of the onset of depressive symptoms in family members who were invited but declined testing. "Among persons who reported high baseline levels of stress, depression rates in decliners increased from 26% at baseline to 47% at one-month follow-up; depression rates in noncarriers decreased and in carriers showed no change (OR for decliners vs noncarriers = 8.0; 95% CI 1.9-33.5; $p = .0004$). These significant differences in depression rates were still evident at the six-month follow-up evaluation ($p = .04$)." It was concluded that in *BRCA1*/*BRCA2*-linked families, individuals showing high levels of cancer-related stress who ultimately declined genetic testing appeared to be at increased risk for depression. It was reasoned that they could derive benefit through education and counseling even though they might ultimately decline to be tested; these are the individuals who require monitoring for the potential occurrence of adverse psychological effects.

It remains elusive whether family members of HBOC kindreds manifest psychological distress in concert with genetic testing. The question, therefore, emerges as to whether pre-test counseling can ameliorate some of the anxiety and provide the at-risk patient with a better sense of well-being. Another question pertains to the effectiveness of genetic counseling and DNA testing with respect to the action, that is, compliance with breast and ovarian cancer screening and whether or not patients with germline mutations heed the option of prophylactic bilateral mastectomy or patients with ipsilateral breast cancer undergoing contralateral prophylactic mastectomy, and, finally, whether these patients may elect bilateral prophylactic oophorectomy.[31]

In an attempt to answer these questions, McInerney-Leo and colleagues[71] studied 212 members of 13 HBOC families who were offered *BRCA1/2* testing, given a previously identified mutation in the family. Patients were educated and then randomized to one of two counseling interventions: problem-solving training (PST) intervention or client-centered counseling, and then followed at 6 months after receipt of test results and at the equivalent time for those participants who chose not to undergo testing. Psychological testing was utilized for measuring depressive symptoms as well as intrusive thoughts, cancer worries, and self-esteem. Those who chose testing versus those who did not, in addition to those who received positive and negative test results, were compared with each other. One hundred eighty-one participants underwent genetic testing (85%) and therein 47 (26%) were identified as *BRCA1/2* mutation carriers. In those randomized to PST, there was a greater reduction in depressive symptoms as opposed to those who were randomized to client-centered counseling ($p < .05$ and $p = .02$, respectively). Individuals with a past history of cancer ($n = 22$) were found to be more likely to have an increase in breast cancer worries when compared to those who had never been diagnosed with cancer ($p < .001$). It was, therefore, concluded that a problem-solving intervention may help to enhance psychological wellbeing following testing. Furthermore, a prior history of cancer may increase psychological distress associated with genetic testing.

An important genetic counseling question is: Do patients who receive information about their genetic risk status, including the presence of a *BRCA1*/*BRCA2* germline mutation, heed surveillance and management recommendations? These recommendations include the need for increased frequency of mammography, breast self-examination, and physician breast examination. Recommendations for ovarian screening include transvaginal ovarian ultrasonography, Doppler color blood flow imaging, and CA 125. However, patients must be thoroughly educated about the limitations of ovarian cancer screening. The option of prophylactic mastectomy and/or prophylactic oophorectomy should also be discussed during genetic counseling sessions.[28,29,31]

Preliminary data show that psychological assessment 6 months following *BRCA1*/*BRCA2* testing among unaffected individuals (both male and female) from HBOC families did not reflect adverse psychological effects. However, with respect to screening, rates of adherence to mammography recommendations among mutation carriers were not found to be increased. It was also noted that carriers of deleterious genes who said they would consider prophylactic surgery nevertheless showed low rates of actually adopting such options. However, these observations were based upon short-term experience and, clearly, longer-term data will be required in order to determine how often women may opt for prophylactic surgery.[72]

Insurance and Employment Discrimination

Because there are a limited number of certified genetic counselors who have sufficient knowledge of oncology to engage effectively in genetic counseling of cancer-prone families, the American Society of Clinical Oncology (ASCO) has recommended that, whenever possible, physicians should perform genetic counseling.[73] In its published position[73] on genetic testing for cancer susceptibility, ASCO recognizes that the clinical oncologists' role should be to document the family history of cancer, provide counseling with respect to a patient's inordinate lifetime cancer risk, and provide options for prevention and early detection to those families for whom genetic testing may aid in the genetic counseling process. Informed consent by the patient is considered to be an integral part of the process of genetic predisposition testing, on either a clinical or research basis. Predisposition testing should be performed on patients for whom there is a strong family history of cancer that is consonant with a likely hereditary etiology, where the results can be adequately interpreted, and where there is a potential to aid in the medical management of the patient and/or family members.

ASCO also recognizes the need to strengthen regulatory authority over laboratories that provide cancer predisposition tests that will ultimately be used in making informed clinical decisions. In the interest of protecting patients and their families, ASCO endorses the adoption of legislation to prohibit discrimination by insurance companies or employers based on an individual's susceptibility to cancer. Finally, ASCO and the American Cancer Society prudently endorse the need for all individuals at hereditary risk for cancer to have, in concert with medical care, appropriate genetic counseling which should be covered by public and private third-party payers.

Cost Effectiveness of Genetic Counseling and Screening in HBOC

There have been limited studies showing the cost benefit of genetic counseling and screening in high-risk HBOC patients. Balmaña and colleagues[74] noted the need to screen women more frequently at a younger age, as opposed to the general population, and the possibility of their undergoing genetic counseling, both of which are options for their management. In an analysis of the benefits and costs of their clinical program in familial breast cancer, they carried out a cost-effectiveness analysis of such procedures. This involved 143 high-risk families which were registered in their database. Their findings disclosed that the cost-effectiveness ratio of their familial breast cancer genetic counseling and screening program was 4,294 euros per life-year gained. In their setting, according to their model, results suggested that their program of genetic testing and screening for breast cancer in this high-risk population may be cost effective.

RADIATION EFFECTS AND *BRCA1* AND *BRCA2* MUTATIONS

Questions have been raised relevant to a potential carcinogenic risk of radiation exposure for women who harbor the *BRCA1* or *BRCA2* mutations. Scully and colleagues[35] raised the possibility that there may be an interaction between *BRCA1* and *BRCA2* gene products with respect to proteins involved in the repair of radiation-induced DNA errors. However, this issue remains controversial owing to lack of confirmation of this risk in the past by other investigators.[75] Nevertheless, recent evidence has indicated that both *BRCA1* and *BRCA2* are associated with defective repair of radiation-induced DNA damage.[35,76]

In a study by Chabner and colleagues[75] of 201 patients, 29 of whom had positive family histories of breast cancer (a mother or sister previously diagnosed before the age of 50 years, or ovarian cancer at any age) and who had undergone breast-conserving surgery and radiation therapy for early-stage breast cancer, there was no evidence associated with a higher rate of "...local recurrence, distant failure, or second (non-breast) cancers in young women with an FH [family history] suggestive of inherited breast cancer susceptibility compared with young women without an FH." As expected, the patients with a positive FH showed an increased risk of contralateral breast cancer. This matter of contralateral breast cancer must be given careful consideration when counseling women with positive family histories who are considering the option of breast-conserving surgery and radiation therapy versus modified radical mastectomy. Given these findings, Chabner and colleagues[75] conclude that "young women can be offered conservative surgery and radiation therapy as a reasonable option at breast cancer diagnosis." However, the investigators appropriately call attention to the limitations in their study: a relatively short follow-up time, small size of their cohort, and the absence of specific genetic findings on their patients, including an absence of *BRCA1* or *BRCA2* mutation findings.

POTENTIAL FOR TARGETED *BRCA1/BRCA2* MUTATION THERAPY

In addition to identifying cancer risk status through mutations such as *BRCA1* and *BRCA2*, this knowledge has the potential to provide individualized highly targeted molecular genetic therapies based upon mutation discoveries.[77] Specifically, once the functions of cancer susceptibility genes have been identified, knowledge as to how such gene-determined biochemical functions can be employed for targeted radiation and chemotherapy should emerge.

One provocative example of this phenomenon has been discussed in the recent report of Kennedy and colleagues[78] regarding *BRCA1* and its chemotherapy effect. These authors discuss the major role of *BRCA1* in responding to DNA damage by its participation in cellular pathways for DNA repair, mRNA transcription, cell cycle regulation, and protein ubiquitination. In this context, we find that "most chemotherapeutic agents function by directly or indirectly damaging DNA, the role of BRCA1 as a regulator of chemotherapy-induced DNA damage has been the subject of an increasing number of investigations..." These authors reviewed the preclinical and clinical evidence showing how the "level of BRCA1 function in an individual patient's tumor can guide the choice of chemotherapeutic agents for breast and ovarian cancer." This evidence was found to support the loss of *BRCA1* function in association with sensitivity to DNA-damaging chemotherapy and therein it may, in turn, be associated with resistance to spindle poisons. Given this background, the authors recommend that prospective clinical studies be undertaken to investigate "the role of BRCA1 in the response to chemotherapy."

Abbott and colleagues[79] examined the protein product of the *BRCA2* gene in terms of its having an important role in mediating repair of double-strand breaks in DNA. They identified a human pancreatic carcinoma cell line which lacked one copy of the *BRCA2* gene and contained a mutation (617delT) in the remaining copy.[80] In vitro and in vivo experiments in this cell line, as well as with other carefully matched cell lines, were performed. They then examined double-strand break repair with attention given to sensitivity to drugs and radiation effects that induce double-strand breaks. Their findings disclosed that "*BRCA2*-defective cells are unable to repair the double-strand DNA breaks induced by ionizing radiation. These cells were also markedly sensitive to mitoxantrone, amsacrine, and etoposide... (two-sided $p = .002$) and to ionizing radiation (two-sided $p = .001$). Introduction of antisense *BRCA2* deoxyribonucleotides into cells possessing normal *BRCA2* function led to increased sensitivity to mitoxantrone (two-sided $p = .008$). Tumors formed by injection of *BRCA2*-defective cells into nude mice were highly sensitive (> 90% tumor size reduction, two-sided $p = .002$) to both ionizing radiation and mitoxantrone when compared with tumors exhibiting normal *BRCA2* function." These authors concluded that these *BRCA2*-defective cancer cells were highly sensitive to agents that contribute to double-strand breaks in DNA.

CONCLUSION

It is necessary to keep an open mind about the pros and cons of DNA testing and genetic counseling and its translation into medical practice by the basic scientist, medical, and molecular geneticist, physician, genetic counselor, and ethicist. For example, how does one interpret some of the ethical positions of today suggesting that genetic testing be limited to a research setting or even curtailed until specific benefit of such DNA testing can be more fully established?

We are thankful that this is becoming a distinctly minority concern, but its full answer must await the expected molecular advances in DNA technology. Meanwhile, we are in the midst of prodigious advances in science and technology (ie, better surveillance, more effective surgical management, including data supporting prophylactic surgery and improved molecular genetic technology with lower cost for germline mutation discovery) which may help to resolve some of the concerns about molecular genetic testing that cause certain physicians, basic scientists, and ethicists to believe it should be limited. How does one educate ethicists about newly emerging benefits of molecular genetic testing which could prove to be lifesaving? Molecular genetic advances are occurring at such a rapid pace that it is exceedingly difficult to keep physicians fully informed of this progress.

The lay press strives to keep the public fully informed about the impact that new gene discoveries may have on patients and their close relatives. Unfortunately, certain members of the media have overinterpreted the benefit of germline testing and have not fully dealt with some of its drawbacks. In turn, some molecular genetic laboratories have made testing appear to be the panacea for cancer control. Some may offer molecular testing without sufficient evidence that the family of concern merits testing. Genetic counseling may not be provided to those being tested. In spite of these misgivings, we believe that hereditary breast and ovarian cancer patients, when properly counseled and DNA tested, will benefit immensely during this exciting era of molecular genetics.

Patients must be encouraged to meticulously examine their family histories of cancer. Should they be found to harbor a germline cancer predisposing mutation, this knowledge may be used to encourage screening and detect cancer at an early stage so that a cure might be possible and/or cancer prevented through the option of prophylactic surgery.

Finally, coming full circle on the crucial importance of a family history, we conclude with the charge of Guttmacher and colleagues,[8] who emphasize the importance of a well-orchestrated family history in this fast-moving era of genomic medicine. Such a family history may provide extremely important clues to the presence of an extraordinarily high risk of CRC in the case of FAP or the Lynch syndrome, for breast cancer in the hereditary breast-ovarian cancer syndrome, as well as for a host of other hereditary cancers as well as for countless hereditary non-cancer disorders. But, given this note of extreme preventive value, the family history, unfortunately, is often undervalued in the medical evaluation of patients. How can we reconcile this medical deficiency? How can we make the collection and utilization of a family history more efficient and physician-friendly? One point raised by Guttmacher and colleagues[8] is the use of interactive software[81] that enables patients to record their family history on a computer[82,83] and thereby eliminate the precious time involved in the process which clinicians may spend in organizing these data. Guttmacher and colleagues[8] also call attention to newly-evolving computer-based tools[84] that may increase the accuracy of this information so that patients can enter the data "…not only in the clinic but also in their own homes and over a span of time, thus allowing better access to records and family members than patients have during an office visit." It is equally important that clinicians understand the natural history and differential diagnosis of hereditary cancer as well as hereditary non-cancer syndromes, so that the family history can be used more efficiently for diagnosis and prevention for the individual patient and his or her family. Thus, Guttmacher and colleagues discuss the augmentation of "genetic literacy," which has become an increasingly important part of overall health care literacy in the interest of early diagnosis and prevention. Even knowing the presence of a germline mutation such as *BRCA1*, it is important to realize that a positive family history of breast and/or ovarian cancer will accentuate a patient's risk for breast or ovarian cancer.[85]

When considering the overall mounting rise in health care costs, one must appreciate the potential health care thriftiness emanating from a well-designed family history, where workups can be more directed toward targeted clinical and pathology features, for example, multiple colonic adenomas in FAP, right-sided colon cancer proclivity and accelerated carcinogenesis in the Lynch syndrome, and the combination of breast and ovarian cancer in harbingers of *BRCA1* or *BRCA2* germline mutations.

ACKNOWLEDGMENTS

This chapter was supported by revenue from Nebraska cigarette taxes awarded to Creighton University by the Nebraska Department of Health and Human Services. Its contents are solely the responsibility of the authors and do not necessarily represent the official views of the State of Nebraska or the Nebraska Department of Health and Human Services.

Support was also received from NIH Grant #1U01 CA86389 and through a grant awarded by the Jacqueline Seroussi Memorial Foundation.

REFERENCES

1. Jemal A, Tiwari RC, Murray T, et al. Cancer statistics, 2004. CA Cancer J Clin 2004;54:8–29.
2. Lynch HT, Krush AJ. Carcinoma of the breast and ovary in three families. Surg Gynecol Obstet 1971;133:644–8.
3. Lynch HT, Snyder CL, Lynch JF, et al. Hereditary breast-ovarian cancer at the bedside: role of the medical oncologist. J Clin Oncol 2003;21:740–53.
4. de Jong MM, Nolte IM, te Meerman GJ, et al. Genes other than *BRCA1* and *BRCA2* involved in breast cancer susceptibility. J Med Genet 2002;39:225–42.
5. Lynch HT, Lynch J, Conway T, et al. Hereditary breast cancer and family cancer syndromes. World J Surg 1994;18:21–31.
6. Lynch HT, Krush AJ, Lemon HM, et al. Tumor variation in families with breast cancer. JAMA 1972;222:1631–5.
7. Vogelstin B, Kinzler KW, editors. The genetic basis of human cancer. New York: McGraw-Hill; 1998.
8. Guttmacher AE, Collins FS, Carmona RH. The family history—more important than ever. N Eng J Med 2004;351: 2333–6.
9. MacMahon B, Trichopoulos D, Brown D, et al. Age at menarche, urine estrogens and breast cancer risk. Int J Cancer 1982;30:427–31.
10. Apter F, Reinila M, Vikho R. Some endocrine characteristics of early menarche, a risk factor for breast cancer, are preserved into adulthood. Int J Cancer 1989;44:783–7.
11. Lynch HT, Guirgis HA, Albert S, et al. Familial association of carcinoma of the breast and ovary. Surg Gynecol Obstet 1974;138:717–24.
12. Hall JM, Lee MK, Newman B, et al. Linkage of early-onset breast cancer to chromosome 17q21. Science 1990;250: 1684–9.
13. Narod SA, Feunteun J, Lynch HT, et al. Familial breast-ovarian cancer locus on chromosome 17q12-q23. Lancet 1991;388:82–3.
14. Miki Y, Swensen J, Shattuck-Eidens D, et al. A strong candidate for the breast and ovarian cancer susceptibility gene *BRCA1*. Science 1994;266:66–71.
15. Wooster R, Neuhausen SL, Mangion J, et al. Localization of a breast cancer susceptibility gene, *BRCA2*, to chromosome 13q12-13. Science 1994;265:2088–90.
16. Wooster R, Bignell G, Lancaster J, et al. Identification of the breast cancer susceptibility gene *BRCA2* [published erratum appears in Nature 1996;379:749]. Nature 1995;378:789–92.
17. Easton DF, Bishop DT, Ford D, Crockford GP. The Breast Cancer Linkage Consortium. Genetic linkage analysis in familial breast and ovarian cancer: results from 214 families. Am J Hum Genet 1993;52:678–701.
18. Easton DF, Ford D, Bishop DT. The Breast Cancer Linkage Consortium. Breast and ovarian cancer incidence in *BRCA1* mutation carriers. Am J Hum Genet 1995;56:265–71.
19. Struewing JP, Hartge P, Wacholder S, et al. The risk of cancer associated with specific mutations of *BRCA1* and *BRCA2* among Ashkenazi Jews. N Engl J Med 1997;336:1401–8.
20. Claus EB, Schildkraut J, Iversen ES Jr, et al. Effect of *BRCA1* and *BRCA2* on the association between breast cancer risk and family history. J Natl Cancer Inst 1998;90:1824–9.
21. Watson P, Lynch HT. Extracolonic cancer in hereditary nonpolyposis colorectal cancer. Cancer 1993;71:677–85.
22. Lynch HT, Casey MJ, Lynch J, et al. Genetics and ovarian carcinoma. Sem Oncol 1998;25:265–81.
23. Lynch HT, Marcus JN, Lynch JF, et al. Breast cancer genetics: heterogeneity, molecular genetics, syndrome diagnosis, and genetic counseling. In: Bland KI, Copeland EMI, editors. The breast: comprehensive management of benign and malignant disorders. Vol. 1. 3rd ed. St. Louis: Saunders; 2004. p. 376–411.
24. American Society of Clinical Oncology. American Society of Clinical Oncology policy statement update: genetic testing for cancer susceptibility. J Clin Oncol 2003;21:2397–406.
25. Malkin D, Li FP, Stron LC, et al. Germ line *p53* mutations in a familial syndrome of breast cancer, sarcomas and other neoplasms. Science 1990;250:1233–8.
26. Malkin D, Jolly KW, Barbier N, et al. Germline mutations of the *p53* tumor-suppressor gene in children and young adults with second malignant neoplasms. N Engl J Med 1992;326:1309–15.
27. Calderon-Margalit R, Paltiel O. Prevention of breast cancer in women who carry *BRCA1* or *BRCA2* mutations: A critical review of the literature. Int J Cancer 2004;112:357–64.
28. Hartmann LC, Schaid DJ, Woods JE, et al. Efficacy of bilateral prophylactic mastectomy in women with a family history of breast cancer. N Engl J Med 1999;340:77–84.
29. Hartmann LC, Sellers TA, Schaid DJ, et al. Efficacy of bilateral prophylactic mastectomy in *BRCA1* and *BRCA2* gene mutation carriers. J Natl Cancer Inst 2001;93:1633–7.
30. Meijers-Heijboer H, van Geel B, van Putten WLJ, et al. Breast cancer after prophylactic bilateral mastectomy in women with a *BRCA1* or *BRCA2* mutation. N Engl J Med 2001;345:159–64.
31. Rebbeck TR, Lynch HT, Neuhausen SL, et al. Prophylactic oophorectomy in carriers of *BRCA1* or *BRCA2* mutations. N Engl J Med 2002;346:1616–22.

32. Verhoog LC, Brekelmans CTM, Seynaeve C, et al. Survival in hereditary breast cancer associated with germline mutations of *BRCA2*. J Clin Oncol 1999;17:3396–402.
33. Verhoog LC, Brekelmans CTM, Seynaeve C, et al. Survival and tumour characteristics of breast-cancer patients with germline mutations of *BRCA1*. Lancet 1998;351:316–21.
34. Schrag D, Kuntz KM, Garber JE, Weeks JC. Decision analysis—effects of prophylactic mastectomy and oophorectomy on life expectancy among women with *BRCA1* or *BRCA2* mutations. N Engl J Med 1997;336:1465–71.
35. Scully R, Chen J, Plug A, et al. Association of *BRCA1* with Rad51 in mitotic and meiotic cells. Cell 1997;88:265–75.
36. Gayther SA, Warren W, Mazoyer S, et al. Germline mutations of the *BRCA1* gene in breast and ovarian cancer families provide evidence for a genotype-phenotype correlation. Nat Genet 1995;11:428–33.
37. Serova O, Montagna M, Torchard D, et al. A high incidence of *BRCA1* mutations in 20 breast-ovarian cancer families. Am J Hum Genet 1996;58:42–51.
38. Gayther SA, Mangion J, Russell P, et al. Variation of risks of breast and ovarian cancer associated with different germline mutations of the *BRCA2* gene. Nat Genet 1997;15:103–5.
39. Ramus SJ, Friedman LS, Gayther SA, Ponder BAJ. A breast/ovarian cancer patient with germline mutations in both *BRCA1* and *BRCA2*. Nat Genet 1997;15:14–5.
40. Tonin P, Moslehi R, Green R, et al. Linkage analysis of 26 Canadian breast and breast-ovarian cancer families. Hum Genet 1995;95:545–50.
41. Neuhausen S, Gilewski T, Norton L, et al. Recurrent *BRCA2* 617delT mutations in Ashkenazi Jewish women affected by breast cancer. Nat Genet 1996;13:126–8.
42. Couch FJ, Farid LM, DeShano ML, et al. *BRCA2* germline mutations in male breast cancer cases and breast cancer families. Nat Genet 1996;13:123–5.
43. Liede A, Metcalfe K, Offit K, et al. A family with three germline mutations in *BRCA1* and *BRCA2*. Clin Genet 1998;54:215–8.
44. Struewing JP, Abeliovich D, Peretz T, et al. The carrier frequency of the *BRCA1* 185delAG mutation is approximately 1 percent in Ashkenazi Jewish individuals. Nat Genet 1995;11:198–200.
45. Roa BB, Boyd AA, Volcik K, Richards CS. Ashkenazi Jewish population frequencies for common mutations in *BRCA1* and *BRCA2*. Nat Genet 1996;14:185–7.
46. Oddoux C, Struewing JP, Clayton CM, et al. The carrier frequency of the *BRCA2* 6174delT mutation among Ashkenazi Jewish individuals is approximately 1%. Nat Genet 1996;14:188–90.
47. Marcus JN, Watson P, Page DL, et al. Hereditary breast cancer: pathobiology, prognosis, and *BRCA1* and *BRCA2* gene linkage. Cancer 1996;77:697–709.
48. Marcus JN, Page DL, Watson P, et al. *BRCA1* and *BRCA2* hereditary breast carcinoma phenotypes. Cancer 1997; 80(Suppl):543–56.
49. Marcus JN, Watson P, Page DL, et al. BRCA2 hereditary breast cancer pathophenotype. Breast Cancer Res Treat 1997;44:275–7.
50. Marcus JN, Watson P, Page DL, Lynch HT. The pathology and heredity of breast cancer in younger women. J Natl Cancer Inst Monogr 1994;16:23–34.
51. Thompson ME, Jensen RA, Obermiler PS, et al. Decreased expression of *BRCA1* accelerates growth and is often present during sporadic breast cancer progression. Nat Genet 1995;9:444–50.
52. Rao VN, Shao N, Ahmad M, Reddy ESP. Antisense RNA to the putative tumor suppressor gene *BRCA1* transforms mouse fibroblasts. Oncogene 1996;12:523–8.
53. Holt JT, Thompson ME, Szabo CI, et al. Growth retardation and tumour inhibition by *BRCA1*. Nat Genet 1996;12:298–302.
54. Armes JE, Egan AJM, Southey MC, et al. The histologic phenotypes of breast carcinoma occurring before age 40 years in women with and without *BRCA1* or *BRCA2* germline mutations: a population-based study. Cancer 1998;83:2335–45.
55. Collins N, McManus R, Wooster R, et al. Consistent loss of the wild type allele in breast cancers from a family linked to the *BRCA2* gene on chromosome 12q12-13. Oncogene 1995;10:1673–5.
56. Sigurdsson H, Agnarsson BA, Jonasson JG, et al. Worse survival among breast cancer patients in families carrying the *BRCA2* susceptibility gene [abstract]. Breast Cancer Res Treat 1996;37(Suppl):33.
57. Breast Cancer Linkage Consortium. Pathology of familial breast cancer: differences between breast cancers in carriers of *BRCA1* or *BRCA2* mutations and sporadic cases. Lancet 1997;349:1505–10.
58. Lakhani SR, Jacquemier J, Sloane JP, et al. Multifactorial analysis of differences between sporadic breast cancers and cancers involving *BRCA1* and *BRCA2* mutations. J Natl Cancer Inst 1998;90:1138–45.
59. Eng C, Li FP, Abramson DH. Mortality from second tumors among long-term survivors of retinoblastoma. J Natl Cancer Inst 1993;85:1121–6.
60. Ford D, Easton DF, Peto J. Estimates of the gene frequency of *BRCA1* and its contribution to breast and ovarian cancer incidence. Am J Hum Genet 1995;57:1457–62.
61. de Bock GH, Schutte M, Krol-Warmerdam EMM, et al. Tumour characteristics and prognosis of breast cancer patients carrying the germline *CHEK2**1100delC variant. J Med Genet 2004;41:731–5.
62. Cybulski C, Górski B, Huzarski T, et al. *CHEK2* is a multiorgan cancer susceptibility gene. Am J Hum Genet 2004; 75:1131–5.
63. Li FP, Fraumeni JF. Soft-tissue sarcomas, breast cancer, and other neoplasms: a familial syndrome? Ann Intern Med 1969;71:747–52.
64. Li FP, Fraumeni JF. Familial breast cancer, soft-tissue sarcomas, and other neoplasms. Ann Intern Med 1975;83:833–4.
65. Evans SC, Mims B, McMasters KM, et al. Exclusion of a *p53* germline mutation in a classic Li-Fraumeni syndrome family. Hum Genet 1998;102:681–6.
66. Lynch HT, Mulcahy GM, Harris RE, et al. Genetic and pathologic findings in a kindred with hereditary sarcoma, breast cancer, brain tumors, leukemia, lung, laryngeal, and adrenal cortical carcinoma. Cancer 1978;41:2055–64.
67. Lynch HT, McComb RD, Osborn NK, et al. Predominance of brain tumors in an extended Li-Fraumeni (SBLA) kindred, including a case of Sturge-Weber syndrome. Cancer 2000;88:433–9.
68. Hisada M, Garber JE, Fung CY, et al. Multiple primary can-

cers in families with Li-Fraumeni syndrome. J Natl Cancer Inst 1998;90:606–11.

69. Lynch HT, Watson P, Tinley S, et al. An update on DNA-based *BRCA1/BRCA2* genetic counseling in hereditary breast cancer. Cancer Genet Cytogenet 1999;109:91–8.
70. Lerman C, Hughes C, Lemon SJ, et al. What you don't know can hurt you: adverse psychologic effects in members of *BRCA1*-linked and *BRCA2*-linked families who decline genetic testing. J Clin Oncol 1998;16:1650–4.
71. McInerney-Leo A, Biesecker BB, Hadley DW, et al. *BRCA1/2* testing in hereditary breast and ovarian cancer families: Effectiveness of problem-solving training as a counseling intervention. Am J Med Genet 2004;130A:221–7.
72. Lerman C, Narod S, Schulman K, et al. *BRCA1* testing in families with hereditary breast-ovarian cancer: a prospective study of patient decision-making and outcomes. JAMA 1996;275:1885–92.
73. American Society of Clinical Oncology. Statement of the American Society of Clinical Oncology: genetic testing for cancer susceptibility. J Clin Oncol 1996;14:1730–6.
74. Balmaña J, Sanz J, Bonfill X, et al. Genetic counseling program in familial breast cancer: Analysis of its effectiveness, cost and cost-effectiveness ratio. Int J Cancer 2004;112:647–52.
75. Chabner E, Nixon A, Gelman R, et al. Family history and treatment outcome in young women after breast-conserving surgery and radiation therapy for early-stage breast cancer. J Clin Oncol 1998;16:2045–51.
76. Lim DS, Hasty P. A mutation in mouse Rad51 results in early embryonic lethal that is suppressed by a mutation in *p53*. Mol Cell Biol 1996;16:7133–43.
77. Livingston DM. Genetics is coming to oncology. JAMA 1997;277:1476–7.
78. Kennedy RD, Quinn JE, Mullan PB, et al. The role of *BRCA1* in the cellular response to chemotherapy. J Natl Cancer Inst 2004;96:1659–68.
79. Abbott DW, Freeman ML, Holt JT. Double-strand break repair deficiency and radiation sensitivity in *BRCA2* mutant cancer cells. J Natl Cancer Inst 1998;90:978–85.
80. Goggins M, Schutte M, Lu J, et al. Germline *BRCA2* gene mutations in patients with apparently sporadic pancreatic carcinomas. Cancer Res 1996;56:5360–4.
81. Progeny Software homepage. Available at: http://www.progeny2000.com. (accessed November 4, 2004).
82. Acheson LS, Stange KC, Zyzanski SJ, Wiesner GL. Validation of the GREAT system for automated collection of the cancer pedigree [abstract]. Am J Hum Genet 2002; 71(Suppl):182.
83. American Medical Association. Adult family history form. American Medical Association, 2004. Available at: http://www.ama-assn.org/ama/pub/category/13333.html (accessed June 30, 2005).
84. Yoon P, Scheuner M. The Family History Public Health Initiative in genomics and population health: United States 2003. Atlanta: Centers for Disease Control and Prevention, Office of Genomics and Disease Prevention; 2004.
85. Antoniou A, Pharoah PD, Narod S, et al. Average risks of breast and ovarian cancer associated with *BRCA1* and *BRCA2* mutations detected in case series unselected for family history: a combined analysis of 22 studies. [Erratum in: Am J Hum Genet 2003;73:709] Am J Hum Genet 2003;72:1117–30.
86. Lynch HT, Conway T, Watson P, et al. Extremely early onset hereditary breast cancer (HBC): surveillance/management implications. Nebr Med J 1988;73:97–100.
87. Lynch HT, Harns RE, Organ CH Jr, Lynch JF. Management of familial breast cancer. Case reports, pedigrees, genetic counseling, and team concept. Arch Surg 1978;113:1061–7.
88. Lynch HT, Watson P, Shaw TG, et al. Clinical impact of molecular genetic diagnosis, genetic counseling, and management of hereditary cancer. Part I: Studies of cancer in families. Cancer 1999;86(Suppl 1):2449–56.

6

Molecular Basis of Breast Cancer

JACQUELINE SARA JERUSS

BACKGROUND

Every year, approximately 44,000 women die of breast cancer in the United States. After lung cancer, breast cancer is the most common cause of cancer death in women. Breast cancer incidence in men is a much rarer event, with approximately 1,300 new cases diagnosed each year.[1] The overall lifetime risk for an American woman to develop breast cancer is 1 in 8.[2] Despite a decline in breast cancer-associated mortality in many countries, the incidence of early-stage disease is on the rise.[1] Improved detection and reporting have played a significant role in this increased incidence, yet molecular and epigenetic determinants may contribute as well. Simultaneously, therapeutic options have been rapidly expanding and include surgical, radiotherapeutic, oncologic, immunologic, and genetic strategies. Therapeutic targets are now being identified for both cancer prevention and treatment. Individualization of treatment regimens to maximize response, to minimize morbidity and mortality, and to prevent the recurrence of breast cancer have become the new therapeutic goal. Endocrine therapy for breast cancer has been centered primarily on tamoxifen and other selective estrogen receptor (ER) modulators. The roles of other hormonal influences, genetic mutations, and growth factors in breast cancer pathogenesis and therapeutics are currently being actively explored. Ultimately, the future of breast cancer management lies in the innovation of molecular diagnostics that will further reveal the interrelatedness of known tumor markers, permit the discovery of novel tumor markers, and enable the development of new therapeutic options.

Normal Development of the Mammary Gland

Mammary gland structure and function vary throughout menarche, pregnancy, lactation, involution, and menopause. Most of what is known of normal mammary gland development has been learned from the mouse model.[3] The overall organization of the mouse and human mammary glands are similar. In both organisms, the mammary gland is comprised of diverse groups of various cell types, including epithelial cells, fibroblasts, adipocytes, and endothelial cells. The two types of epithelial cells, myoepithelial and luminal epithelial cells, in addition to the mammary stromal compartment, make up the network of branching ducts that weave their way through the collagen-rich stromal scaffold of the mammary gland fat pad. The luminal epithelial cells form a continuous lining of each duct and alveolus. At the basal surface of the luminal epithelial cell layer are supporting myoepithelial cells. Finally, each ductal branch ends in a collection of spherical lobules referred to as acini or alveoli.

In the human female, few structural changes occur in the breast from birth to puberty.[4] At the time of puberty, the female breast begins to respond to the production of the ovarian steroid hormone estrogen (E2). Under the influence of E2, the mammary epithelium branches into multiple ducts with terminal alveoli, known as terminal ductal lobular units. After puberty, there is only a minimal amount of alveolar proliferation. Thus, in the pre-pregnant state, there is a higher number of ductal structures per lobular unit in the mammary gland. At the time of pregnancy, the mammary gland is stimulated by increased levels of ovarian E2, which controls ductal elongation; progesterone, which increases ductal side branching; and prolactin from the pituitary, which is responsible for alveolar development.[5] These hormonal stimuli result in the epithelial expansion of preexisting alveoli, and it is at this time that the lobules attain their secretory capacity. Thus, it is only through the cooperative action of the ovarian hormones, in the presence of prolactin, that the mammary gland can produce milk for lactation.[6] After birth, the lactating mammary gland losses its sensitivity to E2. During involution, the mammary gland again responds to estrogenic stimuli, the secretory alveoli collapse, and the gland reverts to a structure similar to, but more complicated than, the pre-pregnancy state.[7]

Breast Cancer

There are several hypotheses regarding the inception of breast cancer. Many heritable breast cancers result from genetic mutations in genes important for DNA repair. Sporadic tumors may arise within a continuum of disease, beginning with atypical hyperplasia and progressing to carcinoma in situ and ultimately to invasive disease.[8] Alternatively, certain breast cancers may arise de novo, as a consequence of crucial clonal deletions or other genetic abnormalities. Approximately 30% of breast tumors have major genetic alterations including DNA amplification and loss of heterozygosity.[9] It has been postulated that ER negative tumors evolve from cancers that were once ER positive but, over time, have lost the genetic machinery to express the ER during the cellular dedifferentiation of advancing disease. Simultaneously, it has also been proposed that ER positive and ER negative tumors arise from distinct and variant cell types at their inception.[10] Much of the research on the molecular basis of breast cancer has thus far focused on changes in hormone sensitivity, genetic mutations, and growth factor/signal transduction pathways. Specific therapies are being developed that target each of these mechanisms. As molecular techniques for oncologic research continue to evolve, the significance of these different influences in the treatment of disease will become even more clearly elucidated.

HORMONAL INFLUENCES

Estrogen and Breast Cancer

Estrogen is a known mammary epithelial cell carcinogen.[11] The carcinogenic effects of E2 vary with patient age, dose, and duration of exposure.[10,12–14] Estrogenic control over several G1 cell-cycle regulators and growth factors has been demonstrated both in vivo and in vitro.[15,16] Estrogenic promotion of cellular proliferation, in particular, is believed to put responsive ductal cells at risk for carcinogenesis by facilitating or even inducing the acquisition of genetic changes during cell cycle progression.[16,17] The clinical prevention of breast cancer by the antiestrogen tamoxifen serves as proof of principle for this concept.[18,19] Endogenous modifiers of hormonal levels include age, body habitus, and physical activity.[20] Exogenous factors, such as plant derived steroids (phytoestrogens) and vitamin D_3, may also modify hormonal levels and breast cancer risk.[12,21–23] Pre- and peri-pubertal exposure to a diet high in soy has been shown to decrease mammary carcinogenesis in both rat model systems and in humans.[12,24,25] The phytoestrogens most prevalent in soy, daidzein and genistein, are capable of binding to the ER and acting as selective E2 receptor modulators (SERMS).[26] Additionally, vitamin D receptor expression in normal mammary tissue is thought to act as an antiestrogen and preserve cellular function, whereas animal studies have shown that vitamin D mitigates breast cancer development.[23]

Estrogen receptors are expressed in approximately 10% of normal breast tissue, whereas ER positivity is found in up to 60 to 70% of breast cancers.[27,28] There are two known variants of the E2 receptor, ERα and ERβ. The ERα receptor is primarily implicated in mammary gland development, whereas ERβ is more involved in lobuloalveolar development [29] ERα and ERβ are encoded by different genes on chromosomes 6q and 14q, respectively.[29] These receptors, along with receptors for progesterone, thyroid hormone, vitamin D, and vitamin A, are steroid nuclear receptors that function as transcription factors upon ligand binding (Table 6–1).[27] The ER contains two sites, the N-terminal activating function (AF)-1 region and the C-terminal AF-2, that are involved in the transcriptional activation of the receptor.[30]

Table 6–1. HORMONAL INFLUENCES AND GROWTH FACTORS

Hormonal Influences and Growth Factors		Signaling
Hormonal influences	ERa/ERb	1. Nuclear steroid receptors 2. MAPK/PI-3K
	PR-A/PR-B	
Growth factors	EGFR	1. Receptor tyrosine Kinase Superfamily 2. MAPK/PI-3K
	erbB-2	
	TGF-β/Activin	1. TGF-β superfamily/smad signaling 2. MAPK/PI-3K
	IGF	1. Insulin-like growth factor family 2. MAPK/PI-3K

Prior to ligand binding, the ERs are bound to heat shock proteins in the cell cytoplasm.[31] Upon ligand binding, the steroid receptor detaches from the heat shock protein and homodimerizes. The ligand-bound ER homodimer then binds to estrogen response elements (ERE) within the promoters of E2-responsive genes, leading to their transcriptional activation.[27] Gene transcription can further be modified by interactions between the ER and coactivators or corepressors at the nuclear level, thus permitting tremendous variability in E2 actions at the gene level.[32,33] Finally, estrogenic action has also been linked to the classic signal transduction mitogen activated protein kinase (MAPK)/extracellular signal-regulating kinase (ERK) and phosphatidylinositol-3 kinase (PI-3K)/Akt pathways, though evidence for this is controversial.[34] It is thus likely that although the loss of ER expression in breast cancer portends a poor prognosis, alterations in the nuclear milieu of estrogenic coactivators and corepressors may also significantly influence the pathogenic properties of E2 in breast cancer cells.[35] Several different mutations in ERα and ERβ have been described. The significance of these mutations has been the subject of a great deal of intensive research in both breast cancer progression as well as resistance to hormonal therapies. Thus far, it has been hypothesized that ER mutations may permit unbridled cellular expansion or act in a dominant negative manner, preventing ER signaling from occurring and enabling hormone independence and the progression of cellular dedifferentiation and malignancy.[29]

Primarily, E2 is thought to be carcinogenic in that it functions as a cell cycle mitogen, driving cellular proliferation. Specifically, E2 is thought to govern the G1 to S phase cell cycle transition.[36] Under estrogenic stimulation, breast cells are forced to undergo rapid proliferation, compromising DNA repair mechanisms and allowing for the accumulation of genetic mutations. Under the continued influence of E2, cells with acquired mutations are further expanded, ultimately leading to oncogenic transformation.[30] The mitogenic genes, c-Fos and c-Myc, which are important to G1 cell cycle progression, contain EREs and respond to E2 in breast cancer cells. Additional work demonstrates an association between estrogenic stimulation and expression of cyclin D1.[34] Cyclin D facilitates ER signaling, which may help to explain the poor prognostic significance of cyclin D amplification and overexpression found in 20% and 50% of breast cancers respectively.[27,37]

Estrogen responsive genes also include transforming growth factor (TGF)-α, insulin-like growth factor-I (IGF-I), epidermal growth factor receptors (EGFR), and cathepsin D, as well as histone H1 family members and histone deacetylase 5, which affect chromatin structure and facilitate transcription.[27,33] A procarcinogenic, cooperative effect between E2-driven c-Myc and TGF-α expression has been demonstrated, which involves TGF-α induced $BclX_L$, and resistance to apoptosis by c-Myc. Furthermore, these gene products activate cyclin-dependent kinases (cdk), resulting in further G1 to S phase cell cycle stimulation and chromosomal abnormalities.[30] Breast cancer cells coexpressing ER and the EGF receptor, ErbB-2, develop an E2-independent growth pattern over time. These data imply that ErbB-2 expression may ultimately facilitate breast cancer progression despite estrogenic resistance.[38] In addition, histone deacetylase inhibitors (HDACi) inhibit cellular proliferation in ER positive and ER negative breast cancer cells, with ER positive cells showing greater sensitivity. The antiproliferative effect of HDACi is associated with cyclin-dependent kinase inhibitor (cdki) p21 expression, which is higher in ER positive breast cancer cells.[33] This data and the loss of cellular HDACi points towards a mechanism for the aggressive nature of the ER negative breast cancer.

The success of the antiestrogen tamoxifen in breast cancer treatment has served to confirm the promoter role of E2 in breast cancer. Tamoxifen has been shown to both reduce the risk of breast cancer in high-risk patients, as well as to lower the risk of breast cancer recurrence in ER positive patients, when used in the adjuvant setting.[39] The use of tamoxifen in ER positive breast cancer patients has been shown to lower the risk of death by 28% and the risk of contralateral breast cancer by 47%.[40] Tamoxifen exerts its action as a SERM, which has antiestrogenic actions in the breast but has estrogenic effects in bone and the uterus and on cholesterol levels.[40] SERMs alter the action of E2 binding to ERα and ERβ by directly binding to the ER, disrupting normal signal transduction, and potentially modulating the association of ER with coactivators and corepressors.[40] The clinical success of hormonal modulation underscores the importance of hormonal treatments as part of the therapeutic armamentarium in cancer care. Further research on the precise mechanisms of E2-driven cellular proliferation and dedifferentiation will hopefully provide additional therapeutic options for breast cancer treatment via hormonal manipulation.

Progesterone and Breast Cancer

The regulatory action of progesterone in breast cancer is still largely undefined, and its role in cancer progression is controversial.[16] There are two progesterone receptors (PR), PR-A and PR-B, each transcribed from unique promoters on the same gene, and both PRs are expressed in normal mammary tissue.[31,41,42] These receptors have a structure and signaling motif similar to the ERs.[43] Progesterone has been postulated to enable cells to reach a cell cycle check point in G1, while preventing senescence.[44] PR positive cells may then be able to respond to further growth directives from additional growth factors. Thus, progesterone-responsive cells may be more likely than PR negative breast cancer cells to respond to ligands, such as TGF-β, by staying in G1.

Interestingly, recent work has indicated that the effects of progesterone in breast cancer may be attributable to dual functions of PR as a cytoplasmic signaling molecule, primarily via the MAPK pathway, and as a canonical nuclear transcription factor acting through binding to progesterone response elements (PREs). This research has implicated PR signaling through MAPK to be the primary mechanism for cellular proliferation in breast cancer, as PR mutant cells that were unable to stimulate MAPK did not stimulate cell cycle progression.[43] Conversely, studies using the well-differentiated breast cancer cell line T47D have shown that progesterone offsets the mitogenic effects of E2. Further, in the ER/PR negative metastatic breast cancer cell line MDA-MD-231, overexpression of PR-A or PR-B and treatment with progesterone was able to reduce cellular proliferation, with concomitant increased cdki p21 expression, decreased c-Myc expression, and decreased cellular invasion.[42] Also, upregulation of PR expression has recently been found in the normal epithelium of patients with *BRCA1* mutation-associated cancers. As a consequence, altered expression of the PR receptor is being pursued as a potential mechanism for tumorigenesis in *BRCA1* patients.[45] Presently, there remains much to be elucidated about the role of progesterone in breast cancer, both as a steroid receptor and as a growth factor capable of cross-talk with other crucial signaling pathways.

GROWTH FACTORS AND SIGNAL TRANSDUCTION

Several growth factors have been implicated in essential autocrine and paracrine stimulation of normal ductal and lobuloalveolar growth, and thus the derangement of these growth factor signals has proven deleterious to the mammary gland (see Table 6–1). EGF is a paracrine mediator of E2 action on ductal growth and appears to exert its action on ductal epithelium via mediators produced in the mammary stroma.[46] TGF-β has been implicated in the maintenance of normal spatial patterning in mammary gland development. In pregnancy, TGF-β may function in a capacity that allows for development of lobuloalveolar units, while repressing hyperplasic growth. TGF-β plays a primary role in post-lactational mammary gland involution.[47,48] The systemic actions of growth hormone (GH) on normal ductal development also modulate other paracrine mediators. Specifically, IGF-I is produced in response to GH acting on the mammary stroma. Additionally, the down regulation of IGF-I is necessary for mammary gland involution.[49,50] Hepatocyte growth factor/scatter factor (HGF/SF) has recently been shown to mediate a signal from the stroma to its receptor, c-met, in mammary epithelial cells. HGF/SF has additionally been associated with epithelial cell growth and development.[51] The interplay of growth factors in breast cancer evolution and progression is proving to be incredibly complex as the ability to study cancer on a molecular level becomes more sophisticated.

Epidermal Growth Factor Receptors

The EGFR family is composed of four receptors: EGFR, erbB-2, erbB-3, and erbB-4. These receptors are transcribed from different genes, yet they are highly homologous. The EGFRs are transmembrane proteins belonging to the receptor tyrosine kinase (RTK) superfamily.[52–54] Signal transduction is initiated by ligand binding (with the exception of erbB-2) and homo- and heterodimerization, which then leads to receptor autophosphorylation and the phosphorylation of cytoplasmic proteins that mediate downstream signal transduction.[52–55] Members of the EGFR superfamily influence diverse cellular processes, including cell cycle progression, cellular proliferation, angiogenesis, and tumor cell metastasis.[56–60]

EGFR may be mutated or overexpressed in infiltrating ductal and medullary cancers.[1] Specifically, the extracellular ligand binding domain may be mutated in breast cancer; mutations in these regions in EGFR and erbB-2 have been linked to disease.[1] The EGFR inhibitor, ZD1839 (Iressa), blocks cell proliferation in breast cancer cells and is associated with an increase in cdki p27 expression. Of particular significance is the ability of this inhibitor to act in ER negative breast cancer cells and to prevent resistance in ER positive cells treated with tamoxifen. This finding is exciting in that it points towards a mechanism for breast cancer treatment in ER negative and tamoxifen-resistant breast cancers.[59] EGFR also cooperates with cytokine signaling which has augmented cell migration in breast cancer T47D cells.[61]

Overexpression and amplification of the erbB-2 (*HER2/neu*) proto-oncogene is independently associated with patient prognosis.[62] The *erbB-2* gene is located on human chromosome 17q21 and encodes an orphan receptor transmembrane protein.[52,53,63] ErbB-2 gene expression is commonly amplified, and the protein p185 is overexpressed in one-third of invasive breast cancers.[64] Amplification and overexpression of this gene have been linked both to poor prognosis and to chemotherapy response.[65] Study of the *neu* gene, the rat proto-oncogene equivalent of human erbB-2, has revealed a mutation in the receptor transmembrane domain, which renders the receptor constitutively active, giving the receptor its oncogenic potential.[66] Additionally, the erbB-2 receptor has the capacity to homodimerize to facilitate signal transduction, and it also has the highest affinity for other erbB family members in the formation of heterodimers. Variable receptor combinations ultimately dictate the nature and amplification of the signal transduced.[52–54] In breast cancer cells, erbB-2/erbB-3 heterodimers act as cell cycle mitogens through inhibition of the cdki p27, which permits cdk2 to act unopposed, and G1 to S cell cycle transition to be amplified.[52–54]

ErbB-2 has been shown to interact with several different signaling pathways, including MAPK and PI-3K, which are both involved in cellular proliferation.[67] Additional evidence has found cross-talk between the erbB-2 and ER signaling pathways that rendered erbB-2/ER-positive breast cancer cells tamoxifen resistant and in which tamoxifen actually acted as an E2 agonist. Tyrosine kinase inhibition was able to restore tamoxifen action in these cells, suggesting a direct role for erbB-2 signaling in the cell response to tamoxifen.[68]

In 1998, trastuzumab (Herceptin), a monoclonal antibody that binds the erbB-2 receptor, became available for treatment of breast cancer. This therapy has been effective for a subset of erbB-2 positive patients. Trastuzumab resistance has not been found at the level of receptor binding or dephosphorylation, but it has been found at the level of cytoplasmic signal transduction.[52–54] Additional monoclonal antibodies are currently being studied that act synergistically with trastuzumab to more successfully block signaling through erbB receptors.[69] Further work will be required to determine alternative therapeutic mechanisms to capitalize on the modulation of this receptor's activity.[1]

Transforming Growth Factor-β

Members of the TGF-β superfamily of growth factors share significant structural and functional homology, and several of these growth factors have crucial roles in mammary gland physiology.[70] The biological actions of the molecules in this superfamily are dynamic and contribute to a wide variety of cellular processes, such as cellular proliferation, differentiation, motility, adhesion, and apoptosis.[71] There are over 40 members of this superfamily, including activin and its structural homolog, inhibin, the TGF-β isoforms 1-3, bone morphogenic proteins, and müllerian inhibiting substance or antimüllerian hormone.[72]

Essentially, the entire TGF-β superfamily signaling system is a variation on a single theme of ligand binding to heteromeric complexes of type II and type I serine/threonine kinase receptors.[73,74] The signal generated by the TGF-β 1-3 isoforms is transduced via the Smad pathway. Activin and TGF-β each signal through a specific set of type II and type I receptors, (activin: ActRIIA/ActRIIB and ActRIB; TGF-β: TβRII and TβRI), both type I receptors have very similar kinase domains and both phosphorylate Smad 2 and Smad 3 to transduce a signal intracellularly. Phosphorylated Smad 2/3 interacts with Smad 4 to facilitate the modulation of DNA transcription in the nucleus. Whereas the signaling mechanisms of both activin and TGF-β are nearly identical, the actions of these ligands are not the same. Differences in the relative expression and bioavailability of the activin and TGF-β signal transduction components, the action of cell-specific coactivators and corepressors that interact with the Smad proteins, and the modulation of the canonical activin/TGF-β signaling pathway by other signaling pathways may confer the unique actions of these different ligands in vivo.[74-76]

Known Associations of TGF-β Superfamily Signaling Mutations with Breast Cancer

Previous work has correlated the presence of a cytosine to adenine transversion mutation in the *TβRI* gene in breast cancer lymph node metastasis.[77] This gene mutation results in a serine to tyrosine substitution at codon 387, which alters TGF-β ligand signaling found in patients with tumor metastases to the lymph nodes.[77] TβRII receptor expression is decreased in tumor tissue relative to its expression in normal and benign breast tissue, and has an inverse correlation to tumor grade. These studies support the rationale that loss of TGF-β signaling correlates to aggressive malignancy.[78,79] Studies that focused on the downstream signaling components of the TGF-β pathway have implicated Smad 4 as a tumor suppressor which, when mutated in the C-terminal domain, has tumorigenic potential.[80] When wild-type Smad 4 was transfected into a TGF-β insensitive breast cancer cell line, the growth inhibitory response to TGF-β treatment was restored.[81] Recently, a large study identified a group of breast cancer patients who lacked phosphorylated Smad 2 (phosphoSmad 2) as having a particularly malignant course, whereas an additional study found loss of nuclear Smad 3 to be associated with higher grade, larger size, and hormone receptor negative cancers.[82,83] With accumulating evidence pointing towards both TGF-β superfamily receptor and Smad mutations in aggressive breast cancer, the goal of localizing unique risk factor components throughout this superfamily has become crucial.

Several co-activators and co-repressors of Smad signaling have been identified, and these coregulatory molecules may be intimately associated with the actions of the TGF-β superfamily in breast cancer. Oncogenic Ras interferes with the nuclear activation of Smad 2 and 3 through ERK MAP kinases in mammary epithelial cells.[84,85] Increased amounts of oncogenic Ras correlates to high tumor grade.[85] Possibly, elevated levels of oncogenic Ras in high grade disease are responsible for lower levels of activated functional nuclear Smads in those cancers. The oncoproteins Ski and SnoN modulate Smad function through a transcriptional corepressor N-CoR.[86,87] The oncoprotein Evi-1 interacts with the nuclear Smad3/4 complex to repress Smad 3 interaction with its cognate DNA Smad binding element (SBE).[88] Moreover, cytoplasmic Smad 3 co-factors, E2F4/5 and p107, act in concert with Smad 4 to bind a Smad-E2F site on c-Myc. This transcription complex represses the cell cycle mitogen, c-Myc, suggesting that disruption or loss of any components within this complex could lead to the loss of cell cycle control detected in aggressive cancers.[89,90] Together, these data suggest that modulation of the canonical TGF-β superfamily signaling pathway by various intracellular factors may promote oncogenesis (Figure 6–1).

Additional work has described a nuclear Smad complex that includes Smad 3 and the transcription factor Sp1. Acting in concert, Smad 3 and Sp1 mediate transcription of the crucial cdki p15, whose promoter contains both Sp1 and Smad 3 binding sites. Specifically, it is thought that Sp1-driven transcription of cdki p15 is Smad dependent.[91] Additionally, c-Myc has the ability to join the Smad 3/Sp1 complex and inhibit its activity, thereby blocking cdki p15 transcription. Thus, Smad 3 can potentially act in a dual capacity to both block c-Myc transcription and mediate cdki p15 production to actualize G1 arrest. It is therefore possible that loss of Smad 3 in cancer cells could induce a very thorough and potent cell cycle release and facilitate oncogenic progression (Figure 6–2).

There are several possible mechanisms for Smad deregulation, both cytoplasmic and nuclear, that may lead to loss of cell cycle arrest in breast cancer cells. As stated, Smad 3 deregulation in the cell cytoplasm may be induced by overexpression of Ras, which is overexpressed in up to 70% of breast cancers and has been shown to block Smad 3 signaling through cytoplasmic phosphorylation and inactivation.[84,92] When Smad 3 phosphorylation sites for Ras were mutated, the TGF-β growth arrest response was restored to Ras-transformed cells.[84] Finally, signal transduction can be mutated and partially lost, as is seen in the mutation of the TβRII receptor in certain patients with hereditary nonpolypopsis colorectal cancer. These patients were found to have TGF-β signaling

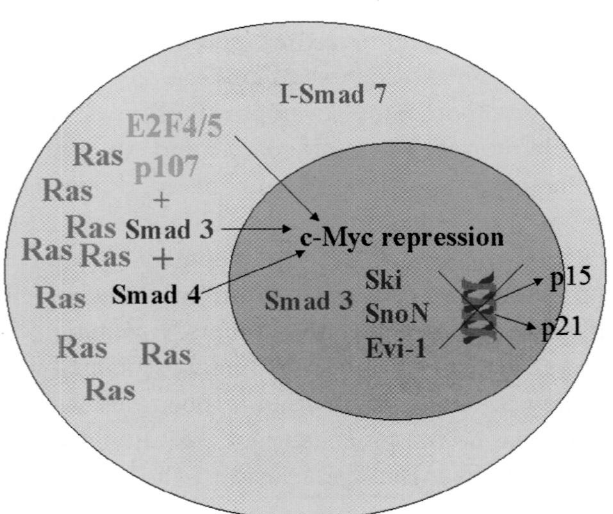

Figure 6–1. Several cell signaling events may be deranged in breast cancer leading to disruption of TGF-β signaling. Oncogenic Ras interferes with nuclear activation of Smad signaling in the cell cytoplasm. Cytoplasmic Smad 3 co-factors E2F4/5 and p107 act in concert with Smad 4 to bind a Smad E2F site on c-Myc, thereby repressing c-Myc. Disruption of any member of this complex could lead to loss of cell cycle control. Nuclear oncoproteins Ski, SnoN, and Evi-1 prevent Smad 3 from initiating transcription, providing further mechanisms for signaling deregulation at the nuclear level.

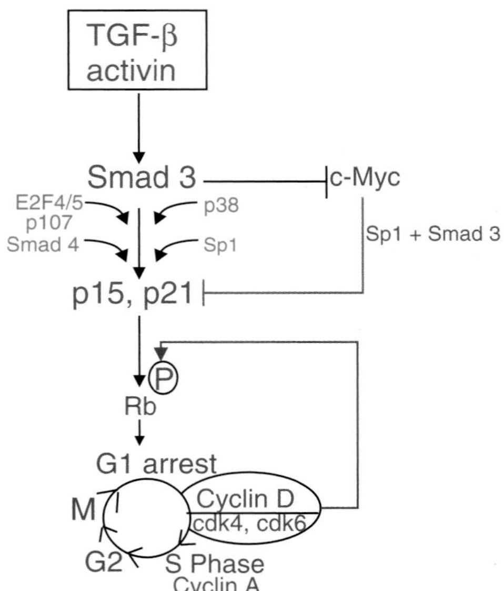

Figure 6–2. Cytoplasmic and nuclear Smad co-factors E2F4/5 and p107, Smad 4, Sp1, and cross-talk involving p38 from the MAPK pathway are involved in both cdkis p15 and p21 expression, as well as c-Myc repression. The cdkis prevent Rb phosphorylation by inhibiting cyclin D, cdk4, and cdk6 from complexing. Overexpression of c-Myc in complex with Smad 3 and Sp1 can prevent expression of cdkis p15 and p21. Also, overexpression of cyclin D can squelch cdki mediated hypophosphorylation of Rb. Both Ras and neu, which are overexpressed in breast cancer, may drive cyclin D promoter activation.

capable of inducing expression of plasminogen activator inhibitor-1 promoter (PAI-1), but not cdki p15.[93] Additionally, overexpression of c-Myc in 30% of breast cancers presents another potential mechanism for overwhelming nuclear Smad signaling and promoting cell cycle progression.[91]

TGF-β has been shown to mediate cancer progression through epithelial to mesenchymal transition, where epithelial cells lose their normal cell-cell interactions and phenotype in favor of mesenchymal characteristics that exhibit poorer cellular contact and improved motility.[94] This may be facilitated through Smad-independent TGF-β signaling mechanisms. Motility in breast cancer MDA-MB-231 cells was found to be mediated by a pathway involving TGF-β signaling thorough the PI-3K and MAP kinase pathways, where TβRI signaling, and not Smad 2, 3, or 4, permitted cell motility.[95] Evidence of TGF-β signaling through the PI3K-Akt pathway to promote cell survival in breast cancer MDA-MB-231 cells has also been demonstrated. Transfection of MDA-MB-231 cells with the inhibitory TGF-β type III receptor, betaglycan, or treatment with the PI3K inhibitor, LY294002, restores growth arrest and apoptosis in these cells.[96] Collectively, this data indicates that the nuclear status of Smads may be a marker of cancer prognosis, and, furthermore, modulation of the TGF-β signaling pathway may be a key therapeutic strategy.

Insulin-like Growth Factor

The IGF family is composed of two ligands, IGF-I and IGF-II, as well as two cell membrane receptors, IGF-IR and IGF-IIR, and IGF binding proteins (IGFBP) 1 through 6. IGFBP proteases are partially responsible for the concentration of active IGF, which binds IGF receptors and triggers the cellular responses to these ligands.[97] Ligand binding results in receptor phosphorylation and stimulation of signal transduction pathways including PI-3K and MAPK.[98] A plethora of hormones and growth factors, including E2, growth hormone, and EGF, influence the expression of the IGF ligands, receptors, and binding proteins.[97]

The ligands have been found to be mitogenic in several cancer cell lines, including breast cancer, and the presence of E2 augments this mitogenic effect. The addition of IGFBP-1 to MCF-7 breast cancer cells was found to block IGF-1–induced mitogenic effects in these cells, thus implying that the relative ratio of binding proteins to ligands in breast cancer might influence oncogenic progression.[99] Additionally, overexpression of the IGF-IR receptor has been associated with cellular transformation to an anchorage independent phenotype.[98] Although cancer research on the IGF family is thus far compelling, both in terms of the role of this family in oncogenesis and for potential therapeutic targeting, much of the data on this growth factor remains controversial. Further work will be necessary to ultimately reveal the significance of IGF in the molecular pathogenesis of breast cancer.

GENETICS

Heritable genetic mutations are thought to be responsible for 5 to 10% of newly diagnosed breast cancer; *BRCA1* and *BRCA2* are the two genes that have been most strongly linked to breast cancer development (Table 6–2).[100] Patients with Li-Fraumeni syndrome who have mutations of the *p53* gene, Cowden syndrome involving mutations of the *PTEN* gene, Peutz-Jeghers syndrome, and ataxia telangiectasia also have an increased risk of developing breast cancer.[101,102] Although the development of breast cancer is likely the result of both genetic and environmental factors, autosomal dominant inheritance of *BRCA1/2* genes has an associated lifetime risk of 55 to 85% for breast cancer development.[103] Patients with *BRCA1/2* mutations tend to be younger, with high grade, ER/PR negative tumors.[98] Mutations of these genes have also been strongly associated with the development of ovarian cancer, as well as melanoma, colon, prostate, pancreas, stomach, and gall bladder cancer.[102] Because of the widespread

Table 6–2. GENETIC RISK FACTORS

***BRCA1* Mutation**
BRCA2 mutation
Li-Fraumeni syndrome (*p53* gene mutation)
Cowden syndrome (*PTEN* gene mutation)
Peutz-Jeghers syndrome
Ataxia telangiectasia

impact of *BRCA1* and *2* on overall regulation of cell growth and differentiation, these proteins have been thought of globally as shepherds of normal cellular function.[101,104] Further understanding of the implications of genetic mutation in breast cancer may ultimately shed greater light on the pathogenic evolution of this disease.

BRCA1

The *BRCA1* gene is located on chromosome 17q21. Whereas eight clinically relevant mutations were first associated with the gene, several more have since been described. Most of the mutations are either frameshift or missense mutations.[100] Attempts to study BRCA1 homozygous deletions and mutations in a murine model have generally resulted in embryonic lethality, indicating a crucial role for the BRCA1 protein in murine development. [105] The normal BRCA1 protein is involved in DNA repair mechanisms important for homologous recombination and transcriptional regulation, as well as cell cycle control and ubiquitination.[106] Specifically, the BRCA1 protein has been shown to facilitate repair of DNA double strand breaks caused by ionizing radiation and to inhibit S phase progression by enabling dephosphorylation of the retinoblastoma (Rb) protein, E2F binding, and possible cdk2 repression.[98] Furthermore, interaction between the BRCA1 protein and *p53* has been shown to induce transcription of cdki p21. Mutations of the *BRCA1* gene can directly inhibit *p53* transcription, whereas other *BRCA1* mutations function as dominant negative inhibitors of *p53*.[98] One key function of *p53* is G1 to S-phase cell cycle control. Disruption of *p53* function may allow for both the persistence of cells with DNA mutations and the inhibition of damaged cells from undergoing apoptosis. Normal BRCA1 protein function has also been associated with c-Myc repression. Mutations in *BRCA1* may thus lead to tumorigenesis through the loss of normal cellular function and subsequent accumulation of cells with the ability to transcend normal cell cycle control mechanisms.[105]

Further evidence of the impact of *BRCA1* on transcription regulation stems from the interaction of the protein with RNA polymerase II, several transcription factors, and RNA helicase A.[100] *BRCA1* induction of cellular apoptosis has also been demonstrated through modulation of the c-Jun N-terminal kinase/stress-activated protein kinase (JNK/SAPK) and GADD45 pathways. Additional evidence has also pointed toward a role for *BRCA1* in the regulation of chromatin structure which may affect gene expression.[98]

BRCA2

The *BRCA2* gene is located on chromosome 13q12-13, and mutations of this gene render a lifetime risk of breast cancer, similar to mutations of the *BRCA1* gene of 60 to 85%. Ovarian cancer risk association with *BRCA2* gene mutation is lower than with *BRCA1*, but male carriers of the *BRCA2* gene have a 6% lifetime risk of developing breast cancer, whereas male carriers of *BRCA1* do not have a known associated risk.[100] Although several hundred *BRCA2* mutations have been identified, primarily those that lead to truncated protein products, missense mutations, and overexpression of BRCA2 protein have been found to have clinical relevance.[100] Overexpression of BRCA2 has been found to repress *p53*.[105] The BRCA2 protein has also been associated with DNA repair mechanisms; specifically, this protein has been shown to bind Rad51, which is important for meiotic and mitotic recombination, as well as double strand break repairs. BRCA2 has also been associated with proliferating nuclear cell antigen (PCNA), also important to DNA repair and replication.[100,105,107] The data on the BRCA2 protein and cell cycle control is less well understood than that of BRCA1 but points significantly toward cooperation of the protein with RAD51 to help mediate the G2/M cell cycle checkpoint.[105] As new factors are revealed that modify BRCA function, phenomena such as incomplete disease penetrance may ultimately be explained. Patients with BRCA mutations who remain disease free may be compensating through the redundancy or cooperation of other signaling pathways or co-factors. Consequently, the disease state would indicate a patient's inability to compensate for the loss of crucial BRCA co-factors or signaling molecules in the face of BRCA1/2 mutations.

ON THE HORIZON

The advent of advanced molecular diagnostic techniques, such as fluorescence in situ hybridization (FISH), comparative genomic hybridization (CGH), spectral karyotyping (SKY), and cDNA microarray analysis, has made it possible to identify several new genetic abnormalities in breast cancer that will ultimately facilitate a better understanding of cancer pathogenesis (Table 6–3).[108,109] CGH analysis of breast tumors has identified several chromosomes that are commonly gained or lost in disease.[109,110] Array-based techniques have allowed for the localization of gene amplification regions in disease as well. Study of preinvasive lesions using these advanced molecular techniques has also shed light on the potential genetic continuum of these lesions in breast cancer pathogenesis.[108]

SUMMARY

Breast cancers are evaluated most consistently by stage and pathologic grade, which examine the macro- and microanatomic nature of cancer. The significance of stage and grade lies in their contribution to the determination of disease prognosis and treatment. Currently, the accuracy of stage and grade is not refined, which results in subsets of patients being under- or overtreated, both of which may lead to untimely death. Consequently, new methods for evaluating breast cancer are necessary to bring this crucial refinement to disease prognosis and treatment. An additional molecular staging of breast cancer may help to facilitate this refinement, and currently clinical trials are starting to examine the utility of signature gene profile DNA microarrays as a novel means for establishing breast cancer prognosis.[111–113] Several molecular markers of breast cancer have been studied; today, hormone and erbB-2 receptor status are measured routinely. Whereas hormone receptor negativity portends a worse prognosis, those patients who retain tumor suppressant TGF-β/Smad signaling may fare better than those who do not. This type of thinking will expand the conventional staging and grading of breast cancer to include an organized molecular staging of disease that accounts for growth factor signaling and cross-talk of signal transduction pathways. The hope is that molecular staging will lead to more thoughtful, accurate, and individualized treatment of the patient. This will ultimately facilitate the additional development of individualized prognostic markers to guide adjuvant therapy. More optimistically, this may also help to identify new predictive markers and the discovery of new therapies, thereby contributing to the ongoing and incredibly complex pursuit of a breast cancer cure.

Table 6–3. CURRENT MOLECULAR DIAGNOSTIC TECHNIQUES

Current Molecular Diagnostic Techniques
Fluorescence in situ hybridization (FISH)
Comparative genomic hybridization (CGH)
Spectral karyotyping (SKY)
cDNA/ Tissue microarrays

REFERENCES

1. Thor AD, Jeruss JS. Prognostic and predictive markers in breast cancer. In: Bonadonna G, Hortobagyi GN, Gianni AM, editors. Textbook of breast cancer a clinical guide to therapy. 2nd ed. London: Martin Dunitz; 2001. p. 63–84.
2. Willett WC, Rockhill B, Hankinson SE, et al. Nongenetic factors in the causation of breast cancer. In: Harris JR, Lippman ME, Morrow M, Osborne CK, editors. Diseases of the breast 3rd ed. Philadelphia: Lippincott Williams and Wilkins; 2004. p. 223–76.
3. Schmeichel KL, Weaver VM, Bissell MJ. Structural cues from the tissue microenvironment are essential determinants of the human mammary epithelial cell phenotype. J Mammary Gland Biol Neoplasia 1998;3:201–13.
4. Hansen RK, Bissell MJ. Tissue architecture and breast cancer: the role of extracellular matrix and steroid hormones. Endocr Relat Cancer 2000;7:95–113.
5. Shillingford JM, Hennighausen L. Experimental mouse genetics— answering fundamental questions about mammary gland biology. Trends Endocrinol Metab 2001;12:402–8.
6. Hadley ME. Growth hormones. In: Corey PF, editor. Endocrinology. 5th ed. New Jersey: Prentice-Hall, Inc.; 2000. p. 277–311.
7. Ronnov-Jessen L, Petersen OW, Bissell MJ. Cellular changes involved in conversion of normal to malignant breast: importance of the stromal reaction. Physiol Rev 1996; 76:69–125.
8. Fu M, Wang C, Zhang X, Pestell RG. Acetylation of nuclear receptors in cellular growth and apoptosis. Biochem Pharmacol 2004;68:1199–208.
9. Lerebours F, Bertheau P, Bieche I, et al. Two prognostic groups of inflammatory breast cancer have distinct genotypes. Clin Cancer Res 2003;9:4184–9.
10. Russo J, Hu YF, Yang X, Russo IH. Developmental, cellular, and molecular basis of human breast cancer. J Natl Cancer Inst Monogr 2000;27:17–37.
11. Liehr JG. Genotoxicity of the steroidal oestrogens oestrone and oestradiol: possible mechanism of uterine and mam-

mary cancer development. Hum Reprod Update 2001; 7:273–81.
12. Shu XO, Jin F, Dai Q, et al. Soyfood intake during adolescence and subsequent risk of breast cancer among Chinese women. Cancer Epidemiol Biomarkers Prev 2001;10:483–8.
13. Key T, Appleby P, Barnes I, Reeves G. Endogenous sex hormones and breast cancer in postmenopausal women: reanalysis of nine prospective studies. J Natl Cancer Inst 2002;94:606–16.
14. Toniolo PG, Levitz M, Zeleniuch-Jacquotte A, et al. A prospective study of endogenous estrogens and breast cancer in postmenopausal women. J Natl Cancer Inst 1995;87:190–7.
15. Russo IH, Russo J. Role of hormones in mammary cancer initiation and progression. J Mammary Gland Biol Neoplasia 1998;3:49–61.
16. Foster JS, Henley DC, Ahamed S, Wimalasena J. Estrogens and cell-cycle regulation in breast cancer. Trends Endocrinol Metab 2001;12:320–7.
17. Dees C, Foster JS, Ahamed S, Wimalasena J. Dietary estrogens stimulate human breast cells to enter the cell cycle. Environ Health Perspect 1997;105 Suppl 3:633–6.
18. Lippman SM, Brown PH. Tamoxifen prevention of breast cancer: an instance of the fingerpost. J Natl Cancer Inst 1999;91:1809–19.
19. Tamoxifen for early breast cancer: an overview of the randomised trials. Early Breast Cancer Trialists' Collaborative Group. Lancet 1998;351:1451–67.
20. Matthews CE, Fowke JH, Dai Q, et al. Physical activity, body size, and estrogen metabolism in women. Cancer Causes Control 2004;15:473–81.
21. Middleton E Jr, Kandaswami C, Theoharides TC. The effects of plant flavonoids on mammalian cells: implications for inflammation, heart disease, and cancer. Pharmacol Rev 2000;52:673–751.
22. Yamamoto S, Sobue T, Kobayashi M, et al. Soy, isoflavones, and breast cancer risk in Japan. J Natl Cancer Inst 2003; 95:906–13.
23. Welsh J, Wietzke JA, Zinser GM, et al. Vitamin D-3 receptor as a target for breast cancer prevention. J Nutr 2003; 133:2425S–33S.
24. Murrill WB, Brown NM, Zhang JX, et al. Prepubertal genistein exposure suppresses mammary cancer and enhances gland differentiation in rats. Carcinogenesis 1996;17: 1451–7.
25. Lamartiniere CA, Cotroneo MS, Fritz WA, et al. Genistein chemoprevention: timing and mechanisms of action in murine mammary and prostate. J Nutr 2002;132:552S–8S.
26. Rastogi P, Lo S, Vogel VG. Chemoprevention: clinical aspects. In: Harris JR, Lippman ME, Morrow M, Osborne CK, editors. Diseases of the breast. 3rd ed. Philadelphia: Lippincott Williams and Wilkins; 2004. p. 363–80.
27. Hanstein B, Djahansouzi S, Dall P, et al. Insights into the molecular biology of the estrogen receptor define novel therapeutic targets for breast cancer. Eur J Endocrinol 2004;150:243–55.
28. Tobias JS. Endocrine approaches for the treatment of early and advanced breast cancer in postmenopausal women. Int J Biochem Cell Biol 2004;36:2112–9.
29. Herynk MH, Fuqua SA. Estrogen receptor mutations in human disease. Endocr Rev 2004;25:869–98.
30. Dickson RB, Stancel GM. Estrogen receptor-mediated processes in normal and cancer cells. J Natl Cancer Inst Monogr 2000;27:135–45.
31. Flototto T, Niederacher D, Hohmann D, et al. Molecular mechanism of estrogen receptor (ER)alpha-specific, estradiol-dependent expression of the progesterone receptor (PR) B-isoform. J Steroid Biochem Mol Biol 2004; 88:131–42.
32. Nagai MA, Da Ros N, Neto MM, et al. Gene expression profiles in breast tumors regarding the presence or absence of estrogen and progesterone receptors. Int J Cancer 2004; 111: 892–9.
33. Margueron R, Duong V, Castet A, Cavailles V. Histone deacetylase inhibition and estrogen signalling in human breast cancer cells. Biochem Pharmacol 2004;68:1239–46.
34. Gaben AM, Saucier C, Bedin M, et al. Mitogenic activity of estrogens in human breast cancer cells does not rely on direct induction of mitogen-activated protein kinase/extracellularly regulated kinase or phosphatidylinositol 3-kinase. Mol Endocrinol 2004;18:2700–13.
35. Weldon CB, Elliott S, Zhu Y, et al. Regulation of estrogen-mediated cell survival and proliferation by p160 coactivators. Surgery 2004;136:346–54.
36. Chen X, Danes C, Lowe M, et al. Activation of the estrogen-signaling pathway by p21(WAF1/CIP1) in estrogen receptor-negative breast cancer cells. J Natl Cancer Inst 2000; 92:1403–13.
37. Yu Q, Geng Y, Sicinski P. Specific protection against breast cancers by cyclin D1 ablation. Nature 2001;411:1017–21.
38. Ellis M. Overcoming endocrine therapy resistance by signal transduction inhibition. Oncologist 2004;9(Suppl 3):20–6.
39. Decensi A, Robertson C, Viale G, et al. A randomized trial of low-dose tamoxifen on breast cancer proliferation and blood estrogenic biomarkers. J Natl Cancer Inst 2003;95: 779–90.
40. Jordan VC, Gapstur S, Morrow M. Selective estrogen receptor modulation and reduction in risk of breast cancer, osteoporosis, and coronary heart disease. J Natl Cancer Inst 2001;93:1449–57.
41. Clarke RB, Anderson E, Howell A. Steroid receptors in human breast cancer. Trends Endocrinol Metab 2004;15:316–23.
42. Sumida T, Itahana Y, Hamakawa H, Desprez PY. Reduction of human metastatic breast cancer cell aggressiveness on introduction of either form a or B of the progesterone receptor and then treatment with progestins. Cancer Res 2004;64:7886–92.
43. Skildum A, Faivre E, Lange CA. Progesterone receptors induce cell cycle progression via activation of mitogen activated protein kinases. Mol Endocrinol 2004;2:327–39.
44. Groshong SD, Owen GI, Grimison B, et al. Biphasic regulation of breast cancer cell growth by progesterone: role of the cyclin-dependent kinase inhibitors, p21 and p27(Kip1). Mol Endocrinol 1997;11:1593–607.
45. King TA, Gemignani ML, Li W, et al. Increased progesterone receptor expression in benign epithelium of *BRCA1*-related breast cancers. Cancer Res 2004;64:5051–3.
46. Silberstein GB. Postnatal mammary gland morphogenesis. Microsc Res Tech 2001;52:155–62.

47. Silberstein GB, Daniel CW. Reversible inhibition of mammary gland growth by transforming growth factor-beta. Science 1987;237:291–3.
48. Nguyen AV, Pollard JW. Transforming growth factor beta3 induces cell death during the first stage of mammary gland involution. Development 2000;127:3107–18.
49. Neuenschwander S, Schwartz A, Wood TL, et al. Involution of the lactating mammary gland is inhibited by the IGF system in a transgenic mouse model. J Clin Invest 1996; 97:2225–32.
50. Richert MM, Wood TL. The insulin-like growth factors (IGF) and IGF type I receptor during postnatal growth of the murine mammary gland: sites of messenger ribonucleic acid expression and potential functions. Endocrinology 1999;140:454–61.
51. Niranjan B, Buluwela L, Yant J, et al. HGF/SF: a potent cytokine for mammary growth, morphogenesis and development. Development 1995;121:2897–908.
52. Ross JS, Fletcher JA. The HER-2/neu oncogene in breast cancer: prognostic factor, predictive factor, and target for therapy. Oncologist 1998;4:237–52.
53. Walker RA. The erbB/HER type 1 tyrosine kinase receptor family. J Pathol 1998;185:234–5.
54. Olayioye MA, Neve RM, Lane HA, Hynes NE. The ErbB signaling network: receptor heterodimerization in development and cancer. Embo J 2000;19:3159–67.
55. Olayioye MA. Update on HER-2 as a target for cancer therapy: intracellular signaling pathways of ErbB2/HER-2 and family members. Breast Cancer Res 2001;3:385–9.
56. Timms JF, White SL, O'Hare MJ, Waterfield MD. Effects of ErbB-2 overexpression on mitogenic signalling and cell cycle progression in human breast luminal epithelial cells. Oncogene 2002;21:6573–86.
57. Zwick E, Bange J, Ullrich A. Receptor tyrosine kinase signalling as a target for cancer intervention strategies. Endocr Relat Cancer 2001;8:161–73.
58. Lane HA, Beuvink I, Motoyama AB, et al. ErbB2 potentiates breast tumor proliferation through modulation of p27(Kip1)-Cdk2 complex formation: receptor overexpression does not determine growth dependency. Mol Cell Biol 2000;20:3210–23.
59. Lu C, Speers C, Zhang Y, et al. Effect of epidermal growth factor receptor inhibitor on development of estrogen receptor-negative mammary tumors. J Natl Cancer Inst 2003;95:1825–33.
60. Tommasi S, Fedele V, Lacalamita R, et al. Molecular and functional characteristics of erbB2 in normal and cancer breast cells. Cancer Lett 2004;209:215–22.
61. Hynes NE, Horsch K, Olayioye MA, Badache A. The ErbB receptor tyrosine family as signal integrators. Endocr Relat Cancer 2001;8:151–9.
62. Forozan F, Veldman R, Ammerman CA, et al. Molecular cytogenetic analysis of 11 new breast cancer cell lines. Br J Cancer 1999;81:1328–34.
63. Kauraniemi P, Barlund M, Monni O, Kallioniemi A. New amplified and highly expressed genes discovered in the ErbB2 amplicon in breast cancer by cDNA microarrays. Cancer Res 2001;61:8235–40.
64. Bankfalvi A, Simon R, Brandt B, et al. Comparative methodological analysis of erbB-2/HER-2 gene dosage, chromosomal copy number and protein overexpression in breast carcinoma tissues for diagnostic use. Histopathology 2000;37:411–9.
65. Lakhani SR. Molecular genetics of solid tumours: translating research into clinical practice. What we could do now: breast cancer. Mol Pathol 2001;54:281–4.
66. Xie D, Shu XO, Deng Z, et al. Population-based, case-control study of HER2 genetic polymorphism and breast cancer risk. J Natl Cancer Inst 2000;92:412–7.
67. Hibshoosh H, Mansuklani MM. Molecular pathology of breast cancer. In: Bonadonna G, Hortobagyi GN, Gianni AM, editors. Textbook of breast cancer a clinical guide to therapy. 2nd ed. London: Martin Dunitz; 2001. p. 49–62.
68. Shou J, Massarweh S, Osborne CK, et al. Mechanisms of tamoxifen resistance: increased estrogen receptor-HER2/neu cross-talk in ER/HER2-positive breast cancer. J Natl Cancer Inst 2004;96:926–35.
69. Nahta R, Hung MC, Esteva FJ. The HER-2-targeting antibodies trastuzumab and pertuzumab synergistically inhibit the survival of breast cancer cells. Cancer Res 2004;64:2343–6.
70. Yue J, Mulder KM. Transforming growth factor-beta signal transduction in epithelial cells. Pharmacol Ther 2001; 91:1–34.
71. Massague J. TGF-beta signal transduction. Annu Rev Biochem 1998;67:753–91.
72. Lebrun JJ, Vale WW. Activin and inhibin have antagonistic effects on ligand-dependent heteromerization of the type I and type II activin receptors and human erythroid differentiation. Mol Cell Biol 1997;17:1682–91.
73. Lagna G, Hata A, Hemmati-Brivanlou A, Massague J. Partnership between DPC4 and SMAD proteins in TGF-beta signalling pathways. Nature 1996;383:832–6.
74. Chen YG, Hata A, Lo RS, et al. Determinants of specificity in TGF-beta signal transduction. Genes Dev 1998;12: 2144–52.
75. Piek E, Moustakas A, Kurisaki A, et al. TGF-(beta) type I receptor/ALK-5 and Smad proteins mediate epithelial to mesenchymal transdifferentiation in NMuMG breast epithelial cells. J Cell Sci 1999;112:4557–68.
76. Whitman M. Smads and early developmental signaling by the TGFbeta superfamily. Genes Dev 1998;12:2445–62.
77. Chen T, Carter D, Garrigue-Antar L, Reiss M. Transforming growth factor beta type I receptor kinase mutant associated with metastatic breast cancer. Cancer Res 1998;58: 4805–10.
78. Gobbi H, Arteaga CL, Jensen RA, et al. Loss of expression of transforming growth factor beta type II receptor correlates with high tumour grade in human breast in-situ and invasive carcinomas. Histopathology 2000;36:168–77.
79. Pouliot F, Labrie C. Expression profile of agonistic Smads in human breast cancer cells: absence of regulation by estrogens. Int J Cancer 1999;81:98–103.
80. Shi Y, Hata A, Lo RS, et al. A structural basis for mutational inactivation of the tumour suppressor Smad4. Nature 1997;388:87–93.
81. de Winter JP, Roelen BA, ten Dijke P, et al. DPC4 (SMAD4) mediates transforming growth factor-beta1 (TGF-beta1) induced growth inhibition and transcriptional response in breast tumour cells. Oncogene 1997;14:1891–9.

82. Xie W, Mertens JC, Reiss DJ, et al. Alterations of Smad signaling in human breast carcinoma are associated with poor outcome: a tissue microarray study. Cancer Res 2002;62:497–505.
83. Jeruss JS, Sturgis CD, Rademaker AW, Woodruff TK. Down-regulation of activin, activin receptors, and Smads in high-grade breast cancer. Cancer Res 2003;63:3783–90.
84. Kretzschmar M, Doody J, Timokhina I, Massague J. A mechanism of repression of TGFbeta/ Smad signaling by oncogenic Ras. Genes Dev 1999;13:804–16.
85. Kretzschmar M. Transforming growth factor-beta and breast cancer: transforming growth factor-beta/SMAD signaling defects and cancer. Breast Cancer Res 2000;2:107–15.
86. Luo K, Stroschein SL, Wang W, et al. The Ski oncoprotein interacts with the Smad proteins to repress TGFbeta signaling. Genes Dev 1999;13:2196–206.
87. Stroschein SL, Wang W, Zhou S, et al. Negative feedback regulation of TGF-beta signaling by the SnoN oncoprotein. Science 1999;286:771–4.
88. Kurokawa M, Mitani K, Imai Y, et al. The t(3;21) fusion product, AML1/Evi-1, interacts with Smad3 and blocks transforming growth factor-beta-mediated growth inhibition of myeloid cells. Blood 1998;92:4003–12.
89. Chen CR, Kang Y, Siegel PM, Massague J. E2F4/5 and p107 as Smad cofactors linking the TGFbeta receptor to c-myc repression. Cell 2002;110:19–32.
90. Chen CR, Kang Y, Massague J. Defective repression of c-myc in breast cancer cells: A loss at the core of the transforming growth factor beta growth arrest program. Proc Natl Acad Sci U S A 2001;98:992–9.
91. Feng XH, Liang YY, Liang M, et al. Direct interaction of c-Myc with Smad2 and Smad3 to inhibit TGF-beta-mediated induction of the CDK inhibitor p15(Ink4B). Mol Cell 2002;9:133–43.
92. Oh AS, Lorant LA, Holloway JN, et al. Hyperactivation of MAPK induces loss of ERalpha expression in breast cancer cells. Mol Endocrinol 2001;15:1344–59.
93. Lu SL, Kawabata M, Imamura T, et al. Two divergent signaling pathways for TGF-beta separated by a mutation of its type II receptor gene. Biochem Biophys Res Commun 1999;259:385–90.
94. Lehmann K, Janda E, Pierreux CE, et al. Raf induces TGF-beta production while blocking its apoptotic but not invasive responses: a mechanism leading to increased malignancy in epithelial cells. Genes Dev 2000;14:2610–22.
95. Dumont N, Bakin AV, Arteaga CL. Autocrine transforming growth factor-beta signaling mediates Smad- independent motility in human cancer cells. J Biol Chem 2003;278: 3275–85.
96. Lei X, Bandyopadhyay A, Le T, Sun L. Autocrine TGFbeta supports growth and survival of human breast cancer MDA-MB-231 cells. Oncogene 2002;21:7514–23.
97. Yu H, Rohan T. Role of the insulin-like growth factor family in cancer development and progression. J Natl Cancer Inst 2000;92:1472–89.
98. Pavelic K, Gall-Troselj K. Recent advances in molecular genetics of breast cancer. J Mol Med 2001;79:566–73.
99. McGuire WL Jr, Jackson JG, Figueroa JA, et al. Regulation of insulin-like growth factor-binding protein (IGFBP) expression by breast cancer cells: use of IGFBP-1 as an inhibitor of insulin-like growth factor action. J Natl Cancer Inst 1992;84:1336–41.
100. Martin AM, Weber BL. Genetic and hormonal risk factors in breast cancer. J Natl Cancer Inst 2000;92:1126–35.
101. Cipollini G, Tommasi S, Paradiso A, et al. Genetic alterations in hereditary breast cancer. Ann Oncol 2004;15(Suppl1): I7–113.
102. Marchetti P, Di Rocco CZ, Ricevuto E, et al. Reducing breast cancer incidence in familial breast cancer: overlooking the present panorama. Ann Oncol 2004;15(Suppl 1): 127–34.
103. Halbert CH. Decisions and outcomes of genetic testing for inherited breast cancer risk. Ann Oncol 2004;15(Suppl 1): 135–9.
104. Balmain A, Gray J, Ponder B. The genetics and genomics of cancer. Nat Genet 2003;33(Suppl):238–44.
105. Zheng L, Li S, Boyer TG, Lee WH. Lessons learned from *BRCA1* and *BRCA2*. Oncogene 2000;19:6159–75.
106. Ohta T, Fukuda M. Ubiquitin and breast cancer. Oncogene 2004;23:2079–88.
107. Shamoo Y. Structural insights into *BRCA2* function. Curr Opin Struct Biol 2003;13:206–11.
108. Reis-Filho JS, Lakhani SR. The diagnosis and management of pre-invasive breast disease: genetic alterations in pre-invasive lesions. Breast Cancer Res 2003;5:313–9.
109. Popescu NC, Zimonjic DB. Chromosome and gene alterations in breast cancer as markers for diagnosis and prognosis as well as pathogenetic targets for therapy. Am J Med Genet 2002;115:142–9.
110. Cingoz S, Altungoz O, Canda T, et al. DNA copy number changes detected by comparative genomic hybridization and their association with clinicopathologic parameters in breast tumors. Cancer Genet Cytogenet 2003;145: 108–14.
111. Branca M. Genetics and medicine. Putting gene arrays to the test. Science 2003;300:238.
112. Simon R, Mirlacher M, Sauter G. Tissue microarrays in cancer diagnosis. Expert Rev Mol Diagn 2003;3:421–30.
113. Cleator S, Ashworth A. Molecular profiling of breast cancer: clinical implications. Br J Cancer 2004;90:1120–4.

7

Breast Cancer Risk Assessment and Management

BANU ARUN
HENRY KUERER

Breast cancer is the most common cancer in women and the second leading cause of cancer deaths among women in the United States. In 2004, more than 200,000 women were diagnosed with breast cancer, and more than 40,000 died of this disease.[1]

Recently, a decrease in breast cancer mortality has been reported,[2] which can be attributed to improvements in adjuvant therapy as well as screening mammography. Furthermore, clinical management now focuses on the identification of high-risk women and risk-reduction strategies.

BREAST CANCER RISK

One of the known factors associated with increased breast cancer risk is family history. About 5 to 10% of breast cancers are due to inherited genetic mutations,[3,4] Mutations in the recently cloned *BRCA-1* and *BRCA-2* genes account for 60 to 70% of all hereditary breast cancers.[5] Women with mutations in these genes have an approximate 50 to 80% lifetime risk of developing breast cancer.[6,7] Germline mutations in genes, such as the tumor suppressor gene *p53* (Li-Fraumeni syndrome),[8] *PTEN* (Cowden disease),[9,10] and *STK11/LKB1* (Peutz-Jeghers syndrome),[11] are also associated with increased hereditary breast cancer risk. But most women with a family history do not have genetically inherited disease, and the risk of breast cancer in these individuals is lower. For example, a 30-year-old woman with a mother and sister diagnosed with unilateral breast cancer has up to an 18% lifetime risk of breast cancer.[12]

Several epidemiologic studies suggest an association between ovarian hormones and the risk of breast cancer. Prolonged estrogen exposure, such as early menarche,[13] late menopause,[14] nulliparity, and late age at first pregnancy are associated with increased risk of breast cancer.[15] Interestingly, it was shown that early first pregnancy is not protective in *BRCA1* or *BRCA2* mutation carriers.[16] The relationship between breast cancer risk and abortion[17,18] and lactation and breast cancer risk[19] is controversial, with recent data suggesting that prolonged lactation can actually reduce breast cancer risk.[20]

The exogenous use of hormones and breast cancer risk has been studied extensively. One recent meta-analysis revealed that the use of hormone replacement therapy was associated with a small increased risk.[21] Another meta-analysis revealed essentially the same results; in this particular report, the increased risk was noted in patients who used estrogen for at least 5 years.[22] And the Women's Health Initiative Placebo Controlled Trial evaluated the risks and benefits of estrogen plus progestin in 16,600 healthy postmenopausal women.[23] The primary outcome of this study was coronary heart disease, with invasive breast cancer as the primary adverse outcome. At a mean of 5.2 years of follow-up, the estimated hazard ratio for breast cancer risk was 1.26 (CI: 1.00–1.59). A slight increase risk of breast cancer has been also shown with oral contraceptive use, especially if it is used before first birth.[24,25] However, other studies have not confirmed these results.[26]

Certain proliferative breast diseases are associated with an increased risk of breast cancer. The RR for developing subsequent breast cancer is 4.5- to 5-fold in individuals who have a diagnosis of atypical hyperplasia.[27] Lobular carcinoma in situ (LCIS) is also a known risk factor; the RR for developing breast cancer in women with the diagnosis of LCIS is about 7 to 9 times that of the normal population, with an absolute lifetime risk of 20%.[28] Furthermore, women with a diagnosis of ductal carcinoma in situ (DCIS) or invasive cancer have a 1% risk of developing contralateral breast cancer per year.[29,30]

IDENTIFICATION OF HIGH-RISK INDIVIDUALS

Since breast cancer risk reduction strategies will be essentially applied to "healthy" individuals, the risk and benefit ratio of these strategies needs to be carefully calculated. With the help of epidemiologic studies evaluating risk factors for breast cancer, models have been developed to identify women at increased risk. The Gail model is the most commonly used model, which used data from 4,496 matched pairs of cases in the Breast Cancer and Diagnosis and Demonstration Project.[31] The risk factors for this model include age at menarche, age at first live birth, number of previous breast biopsies, and number of first-degree relatives with breast cancer. This model has been validated by two subsequent studies.[32,33] However, it does not take into account the risk for individuals who have second-degree relatives diagnosed with breast cancer or relatives diagnosed with ovarian cancer. It also underestimates the risk of individuals with a history of LCIS or DCIS and may overestimate the risk in women with nonproliferative disease at biopsy. Therefore, this model may not be appropriate for all individuals. Other models, such as the Claus model, may be more appropriate.[34]

Recently, a new risk-assessment tool, ductal lavage, has been developed and is now an FDA-approved risk-assessment tool for breast cancer. This procedure was developed to enhance the efficiency of collecting breast epithelial cells for cytologic analysis. The rationale for this technique is based upon several assumptions. Because most invasive breast cancers are ductal in origin[35] and are believed to result from progressive molecular and morphologic changes, including, in the early phases, the phenotypic appearance of cellular atypia,[36] the identification of atypia in the ducts may represent a precursor lesion and a marker of risk.[37–39] Women with cellular atypia detected by cytologic examination of breast specimens (collected by random fine needle or nipple aspiration) have a 4.9- to 5-fold increase in the RR of developing breast cancer as compared to women without cellular atypia.[37–39] Because the cellular yield with nipple aspiration is usually not optimal and fine needle aspiration and core biopsies are more invasive procedures, ductal lavage provides a less invasive method of collecting epithelial cells for cytological analysis. A recent study reported that ductal lavage is a safe and well-tolerated procedure and a more sensitive method of detecting cellular atypia than nipple aspiration in women who were high risk as defined by the Gail model.[40] In fact, the median cell yield was 13,500 epithelial cells per duct, compared to 120 cells by nipple aspiration. More importantly, in 78% of the cases, the specimen was adequate for cytologic analysis. This procedure could be potentially used to stratify women at increased risk and help to define an optimal strategy for screening, chemoprevention with tamoxifen, or prophylactic surgery. However, long-term studies comparing cellular atypia defined by ductal lavage are not available to confirm equivalency to atypia defined by percutaneous biopsy or excisional biopsy.

RISK MANAGEMENT OPTIONS

Screening

In general, screening recommendations for average-risk individuals include monthly self-breast examinations, yearly clinical breast examinations, and yearly mammograms. Screening mammography reduces breast cancer mortality in women older than 50 years of age,[41,42] but its effectiveness for younger women remains controversial.[43,44] The recommendations for follow-up of individuals with an inherited predisposition to breast cancer, as recommended by the Cancer Genetics Studies Consortium, include monthly self-breast examination beginning at age 18 to 21 years, annual or semiannual clinical breast examination beginning at age 25 to 35 years, and annual mammography beginning at age 25 to 35 years.[45] Recommendations for optimal screening and frequency have not been well described in prospective studies with mortality end points and are largely based on expert opinion.[46,47] Brekelmans and colleagues recently reported on the surveillance of 128 individuals with known *BRCA1* and *BRCA2* mutations, which were followed with at least annual mammograms, annual clinical breast examinations, and monthly self breast examinations.[47] Within a median follow-up of 3 years, 9 breast cancers developed in mutation carriers, with 4 being interval cancers not detected during the course of screening. Another recent study reported on 165 *BRCA1* and *BRCA2* mutation carriers who were followed with monthly self breast examination, clinical breast examination 2 to 4 times per year, and annual mammograms.[48] At a mean follow-up of 24 months 12 breast cancer cases developed; 6 (50%) were interval cancers. Five cancers were detected on self-examination and 1 by physical examination. The remaining 6 cases were detected by routine mammograms; 3 were invasive cancers and 3 were DCIS. The finding of DCIS in this and two other studies[49,50] is of interest, implying the presence of a non-invasive phase in a subset of patients that can be identified by radiologic screening. Nevertheless, at this point, with standard annual screening, interval cancers remain an important problem. Interval cancer detection may be delayed by dense breast tissue, limiting the visualization of an already existing malignancy or an aggressive tumor with a high growth rate, developing subsequent to the prior mammogram. The mammographic screening interval or the complementary addition of alternative screening modalities such as magnetic resonance imaging (MRI) remains unclear and needs further evaluation. A number of studies have suggested that screening with MRI may benefit women at high risk.[49–51] A group of 236 women with *BRCA1* or *BRCA2* mutation were followed with annual mammography, ultrasonography, MRI, and biannual physical examination,[52] and 22 cancers were identified. MRI was more sensitive for detecting breast cancers than ultrasound, mammogram, or clinical breast examination alone. Another group of 1,909 high-risk women, including 358 with germline mutations, were screened with yearly mammography, MRI, and biannual clinical breast examination.[53] The sensitivity for detecting invasive breast cancer was higher for MRI when compared to mammography or clinical breast examination. Whether MRI provides a meaningful clinical benefit and will improve survival remains unanswered. Although early in its evaluation, MRI appears to be a useful screening modality for high-risk patients.

Chemoprevention

Tamoxifen

Currently, tamoxifen is the first and only drug to be approved for the risk reduction of breast cancer in high-risk individuals.[54,55]

The study that led to the approval was the phase III National Surgical Adjuvant Breast and Bowel Project (NSABP) chemoprevention trial (BCPT-P1), which randomized 13,388 women at high risk for breast cancer to tamoxifen versus placebo.[54] Eligible women had to be 60 years or older, or between ages 35 and 59 and have a diagnosis of LCIS or a projected 5-year risk of developing breast cancer greater than 1.66%, according to the modified Gail model.[31] After a median follow-up of 54 months, a 49% reduction in the incidence of invasive breast cancer ($p < .00001$), and a 50% reduction of noninvasive cancer ($p < .0001$) occurred among those receiving tamoxifen. A subset analysis revealed that women with LCIS had a 56% reduction of risk, and women with atypical hyperplasia had an 86% reduction in the occurrence of breast cancer. The decreased risk occurred in women of all ages and in all risk groups except those developing ER-negative breast cancers. Tamoxifen appeared to reduce the incidence of osteoporotic fractures of the hip, spine, and radius but did not reach statistical significance.[54] No difference was seen in the incidence of myocardial infarction, angina, coronary artery bypass, or angioplasty.

In contrast, the Royal Marsden trial did not show a reduction in the incidence of breast cancer among women who took tamoxifen at 70 months' follow-up.[56] This study included 2,471 women with a family history of breast cancer. There were 34 cases of breast cancer in women who took tamoxifen versus 36 cases in the placebo group (RR 1.06, 95% confidence interval [CI] 0.7–1.7, $p = .8$).

In an Italian study, 5,408 hysterectomized women were randomized to tamoxifen versus placebo. At a median follow-up of 46 months, no statistically significant difference in the incidence of breast cancer was evident between women who took tamoxifen versus those who took placebo.[57] However, these women had a low or normal risk of developing breast cancer. For example, 48.3% of the women had had a previous bilateral oophorectomy, a known risk-reduction intervention.[58] An unplanned subgroup analysis in this trial showed that the incidence of breast cancer was reduced among women who took tamoxifen and hormone replacement therapy (HRT). An update at a median 81.2 months of follow-up showed no significant difference in breast cancer incidence between women given tamoxifen and those given placebo.[59] However, a benefit favoring tamoxifen was seen among women who used HRT; the cumulative incidence of breast cancer was 0.92% among those who used HRT versus 2.58% among those assigned to the placebo group.

Recently, investigators re-analyzed their data to evaluate the risk reduction of tamoxifen for estrogen receptor (ER)-positive breast cancers. Factors indicating increased risk of developing ER-positive breast cancer include reproductive and hormonal characteristics, such as height, age at menarche, nulliparity, age at first birth, and not having undergone oophorectomy. Only 702 women (13%) in the study were considered to be high risk. Tamoxifen was shown to reduce the incidence of breast cancer among these women as compared to a low-risk group (3 breast cancer cases in high-risk group versus 15 in the low-risk group, $p = .003$). The overall risk of breast cancer in the high-risk group was three times higher than that in the low risk group (hazard ratio = 3.32, 95% CI 1.78 to 6.17). Tamoxifen use decreased the incidence of breast cancer by 82% in the high-risk group but not in the low-risk group (tamoxifen = 31, placebo = 30; $p = .89$).

Finally, the IBIS -I (International Breast Cancer Intervention Study) trial randomized 7,152 women, aged 35 to 70 years who were at increased risk of breast cancer, to receive either tamoxifen or placebo for 5 years.[56] At a median follow-up of 50 months, a 32% reduction in the odds of developing breast cancer in the tamoxifen group was found. Eligibility included a twofold RR for breast cancer for women aged 45 to 70 years, a fourfold RR for women aged 40 to 44 years, and a 10-fold RR for women aged 35 to 39 years. Risk factors included family history, nulliparity, lobular carcinoma in situ, atypical hyperplasia, and benign breast biopsies.

A direct comparison of these studies is difficult owing to several differences, such as variations in baseline risk, the entry criteria, the number of participants, and compliance issues. The NSABP P1 trial used the validated Gail risk model, whereas the IBIS-I trial did not. As noted, the Italian trial consisted of a low-risk cohort and the Royal Marsden trial included a higher-risk cohort with younger women with a family history of breast cancer. Nevertheless, what emerges from these trials is that tamoxifen reduces the incidence of breast cancer.

Several questions remain unanswered at this time. An increase in survival with a reduction in the incidence of breast cancer remains unproven. Targeting a population that would derive the greatest benefit with tamoxifen will require additional study. The risks and benefits of tamoxifen should be weighed carefully as the target population is still considered "healthy." Side effects of tamoxifen in the NSABP trial included an increased risk of endometrial cancer with a RR in the tamoxifen group of 2.5, and increasing to 4.01 in women 50 years or older. Deep vein thrombosis and pulmonary emboli were also seen more often in the tamoxifen group, with women 50 years or older at a higher risk (RR 1.71 for deep vein thrombosis, 3.00 for pulmonary emboli)[54] (Table 7–1). An apparent increase in the risk of stroke among women taking tamoxifen did not reach statistical significance. A marginally significant increase in the occurrence of cataract formation and the risk of requiring cataract surgery was noted for the tamoxifen group.[54] Other side effects included increased hot flashes and vaginal discharge. No difference was noted between groups in effects such as irregular menses, weight gain, skin changes, fluid retention, or nausea.[54] The IBIS investigators also reported a range of side effects, including an increased rate of thromboembolic events, an appar-

Table 7–1. NUMBER OF EVENTS AMONG WOMEN PARTICIPATING IN THE NSABP P-1 BREAST CANCER PREVENTION TRIAL

Event	Placebo (n = 6,131)	Tamoxifen (n = 6,101)
Invasive breast cancer	175	89
Noninvasive breast cancer	69	35
Endometrial cancer	15	36
Deep vein thrombosis	22	35
Pulmonary emboli	6	18
Stroke	24	38
Deaths	71	57
ER-positive breast cancers	130	41
ER-negative breast cancers	31	38
Unknown hormone receptor status	14	10
Lobular carcinoma in situ	18	8
Atypical hyperplasia	23	3

ER = estrogen receptor; NSABP = National Surgical Adjuvant Breast and Bowel Project. Reproduced with permission from Singletary SE, Robb GI, Hortobagyi, editors. Advanced therapy of breast disease. 2nd ed. Hamilton (ON): BC Decker; 2004.

ent (but not statistically significant) increase in the incidence of endometrial cancer, and an increase in the occurrence of hot flashes. Most worrisome in the IBIS study was a significant increase in the total number of non-breast cancer–related deaths among women taking tamoxifen. The causes of death formed a broad range, with no clear dominance of any one category, suggesting that this finding might have resulted from random chance. Nevertheless, this finding heightens concern for the safety of tamoxifen in the prevention setting. Perhaps a more targeted population needs to be defined to optimize the benefits and limit the risks of tamoxifen. As noted previously, the re-analysis of the Italian trial results identified a subgroup of women who are at increased risk of developing ER-positive breast cancer, and those women derived the most benefit from tamoxifen.[59] Other data from the same investigators[59] suggest that women who took, or are taking, HRT are candidates for tamoxifen because their risk/benefit ratio is smaller than those who have never taken HRT. A recently developed methodology indicated that tamoxifen is beneficial for younger women with an elevated risk of breast cancer and for women older than 50 years if their short-term risk is 1% per year for women with a uterus and 0.5% per year for women without a uterus.[60]

The impact of tamoxifen on women with a high genetic risk, such as *BRCA1* or *BRCA2* mutation carriers, is currently being evaluated. In this effort, *BRCA1* and *BRCA2* gene sequencing was performed on all breast cancer cases (n = 288) in women who participated in the NSABP-P1 trial, and 19 cases were found to have the *BRCA1* or *BRCA2* mutation.[61] Five out of 8 patients with *BRCA1* mutations received tamoxifen, and 3 out of 11 patients with *BRCA2* received tamoxifen. Results showed that 83% of *BRCA1* breast tumors were ER-negative, whereas 76% of *BRCA2* breast tumors were ER-positive. This study suggests that tamoxifen reduces breast cancer incidence in *BRCA2* carriers but not in *BRCA1* carriers. However, firm conclusions cannot be drawn as the sample size is low. In contrast, another study showed that tamoxifen reduces the risk of contralateral breast cancer in women with a *BRCA1* or *BRCA2* mutation.[62] A group of 209 women with a *BRCA1* or *BRCA2* mutation and bilateral breast cancer were compared with 384 women with a *BRCA1* or *BRCA2* mutation and unilateral breast cancer, and in a matched case-control study, history of tamoxifen use for the first breast cancer was obtained. Their results revealed that tamoxifen use reduced the risk of contralateral breast cancer by 50% in women with a *BRCA1* or *BRCA2* mutation. Furthermore, studies have shown that bilateral prophylactic oophorectomy reduces the risk of breast cancer in *BRCA1* or *BRCA2* mutation carriers, indicating again the efficacy of antihormonal intervention,[63,64] At this point, it remains unknown whether tamoxifen can reduce the risk of breast cancer in *BRCA*1 mutation carriers.

In conclusion, tamoxifen is the only drug to be approved for the reduction of breast cancer in high-risk individuals.[55] But, before making the decision to use tamoxifen to reduce the risk of breast cancer, potential benefits must be weighed against potential side effects, taking risk of breast cancer, age, race, and comorbid conditions into consideration.

Raloxifene

Raloxifene is a selective estrogen receptor modulator (SERM), which is currently being considered for breast cancer prevention.[65] The promising data for this agent comes from The Multiple Outcomes of Raloxifene Evaluation (MORE) trial, which randomized 7,704 postmenopausal women with osteoporosis and no history of breast or endometrial cancer to placebo, 60, or 120 mg raloxifene daily. The risk of breast cancer was reduced by 76% at 3 years.[66] The second database pooled all placebo-controlled raloxifene trials and included 10,553 women monitored for an average of 3 years. Raloxifene-treated patients had a 54% reduction in the incidence of breast cancer.[67] There was no increased risk of endometrial cancer in the raloxifene group as compared to the placebo group. Currently, raloxifene is being tested against tamoxifen as a chemopreventive agent for breast cancer in high-risk postmenopausal women in a large-scale national trial (NSABP-P2, STAR Trial). The primary end point of this study is to demonstrate superior efficacy of either agent or their equivalence in reducing the incidence of primary breast cancer. Inclusion criteria for this trial includes women greater than 35 years of age and postmenopausal, a history of LCIS, or a 5-year risk of invasive breast cancer of at least 1.67% as determined by the Gail model. Subjects are randomly assigned to receive either 20 mg tamoxifen or 60 mg raloxifene daily. This trial has reached accrual, and data analysis is in progress.

Aromatase Inhibitors

Aromatase inhibitors are a group of potential agents that can be considered for the use of chemoprevention. The aromatase inhibitors block the conversion of androgens to estrogens. Aromatase activity, by increasing local estrogen synthesis, may play an early role in breast cancer carcinogenesis[68]; in fact, in vivo models have shown that aromatase expression in breast tissue can induce the development of premalignant lesions.[69] Recently, results of three adjuvant hormonal trials with anastrazole, letrozole, or exemestane have demonstrated a 50 to 58% reduction in primary contralateral breast cancer in women treated with the aromatase inhibitors versus tamoxifen.[70–72] The NSABP-B35 is currently investigating anastrazole versus tamoxifen in patients with DCIS. IBIS-II is evaluating anastrazole versus placebo in high-risk women. The only concern with these agents is the effects of estrogen depletion in target organs, such as the cardiovascular system and bones. Perhaps this could be overcome with lower doses of these potent agents, which might inhibit local estrogen synthesis in the breast without decreasing ovarian estrogen production.[73]

Prophylactic Mastectomy

Reduction of breast cancer risk by prophylactic mastectomy has been studied in retrospective and prospective studies.[48,74–77] Despite a major risk reduction, a very limited possibility of developing cancer remains after surgery owing to residual microscopic glandular tissue. Prophylactic mastectomy is considered in genetically high-risk individuals as well as in women with lower risk such as those with a positive family history of breast cancer, a history of multiple breast biopsies, or the presence of nodular and dense breast tissue that would obscure radiographic or physical findings. Most studies evaluating the benefit of prophylactic surgery have consisted of women at increased risk of breast cancer. Hartman and colleagues studied 639 women with a family history of breast cancer who underwent bilateral prophylactic mastectomy, of which 214 were considered high risk and 425 moderate risk. Breast cancer incidence in the high-risk group (Table 7–2) was compared to a control group consisting of the probands' sisters (n = 403) who had not undergone prophylactic mastectomy. The study showed a 90% reduction in the incidence of breast cancer in the prophylactic mastectomy group[74] (Table 7–3). Interestingly, all of those developing breast cancer had undergone a bilateral subcutaneous mastectomy between 2 and 25 years following mastectomy (Table 7–4). None of the women undergoing a bilateral total mastectomy developed breast cancer. The same investigators reported on the effect of bilateral mastectomy in a subset of 26 women who were found to be *BRCA1* or *BRCA2* mutation carriers. At a median follow-up of 13.4 years, none developed breast cancer.[75] A prospectivestudy reported on 76 women with *BRCA1* or *BRCA2* mutation who underwent prophylactic mastectomy and 63 women with *BRCA1* or *BRCA2* mutation who chose surveillance. At 2.9 years of follow-up, no breast cancer occurred in women who had prophylactic mastectomy, whereas 8 breast cancers occurred in the surveillance group.[76] And finally, another prospective

Table 7–2. CRITERIA FOR HIGH-RISK CASES
Two or more first-degree relatives with breast cancer
One first-degree relative and two or more second- or third-degree relatives with breast cancer
One first-degree relative with breast cancer before the age of 45 yr and one other relative with breast cancer
One first-degree relative with breast cancer and one or more relatives with ovarian cancer
Two second- or third-degree relatives with breast cancer and one or more with ovarian cancer
One second- or third-degree relative with breast cancer and two or more with ovarian cancer
Three or more second- or third-degree relatives with breast cancer
One first-degree relative with bilateral breast cancer

Reproduced with permission from Singletary SE, Robb GI, Hortobagyi, editors. Advanced therapy of breast disease. 2nd ed. Hamilton (ON): BC Decker; 2004.

study reported on the effect of prophylactic mastectomy in 194 individuals with a *BRCA1* or *BRCA2* mutation, 29 of whom opted for prophylactic mastectomy. Even though the follow-up was short (mean, 24 months), none of these individuals developed breast cancer, whereas 12 breast cancers were identified in the group opting surveillance.[48] Another study evaluated 483 women with germline *BRCA1/2* mutations. At a mean follow-up of 6.4 years, breast cancer was diagnosed in 2 of 105 women (1.9%) who had bilateral prophylactic mastectomy and in 184 (48.7%) of 378 matched controls who did not have surgery. Bilateral prophylactic mastectomy reduced the risk of breast cancer by approximately 95% in women with prior or concurrent bilateral prophylactic oophorectomy and by approximately 90% in women with intact ovaries.[77] Based upon abundant data, bilateral prophylactic mastectomy is an extremely effective risk-reduction strategy. Women choosing this option have their risk lowered to a level well below that of the average American woman. These data also suggest that if prophylactic surgery is performed, a total mastectomy with removal of the nipple-areolar complex is a more effective intervention than a subcutaneous mastectomy.[74]

Table 7–3. EXPECTED AND OBSERVED BREAST CANCER EVENTS AFTER BILATERAL PROPHYLACTIC MASTECTOMY		
Event	Moderate Risk (n = 425)	High Risk (n = 214)
Incidence		
Expected	37.4	30–53*
Observed	4	3
Reduction	89.5%	90–94.3%
95%CI	73-97%	71–99%
Deaths		
Expected	10.4	11–31*
Observed	0	2
Reduction	100%	89.7%
95% CI	70–100%	31.4–98.8%

*Range based on three different statistical approaches
Reproduced with permission from Singletary SE, Robb GI, Hortobagyi, editors. Advanced therapy of breast disease. 2nd ed. Hamilton (ON): BC Decker; 2004.

Prophylactic Oophorectomy

The efficacy of prophylactic oophorectomy in breast cancer risk reduction has been shown in several studies. Brinton and colleagues reported a 45% reduction in breast cancer risk in women who underwent prophylactic oophorectomy before the age of 40 years, as compared with women who underwent natural menopause.[78] Parazzini and colleagues reported a 20% risk reduction after prophylactic oophorectomy in premenopausal women.[79] In another study, a 50% reduction in breast cancer risk was observed in women less than 50 years undergoing prophylactic oophorectomy, although a risk reduction was not seen in women 50 years and older.[58] Breast cancer risk

Table 7–4. POSTPROPHYLACTIC MASTECTOMY BREAST CANCERS		
Location of Cancer	Years since Mastectomy	Risk*
Left breast	15	Moderate
Chest wall	2	Moderate
Left breast above areola	5	Modeerate
Chest wall	25	Moderate
Bone marrow	12	High
Left lateral side of chest wall	3	High
Left nipple	6	High

*Based on family history
Reproduced with permission from Singletary SE, Robb GI, Hortobagyi, editors. Advanced therapy of breast disease. 2nd ed. Hamilton (ON): BC Decker; 2004.

reduction has been observed with oophorectomy in premenopausal patients, even with the use of hormonal replacement therapy.[80] Prophylactic oophorectomy has also been studied in genetically high-risk patients.[81] Rebbeck and colleagues reported that breast cancer risk was reduced by at least 50% in women with a *BRCA1* mutation (*n* = 43) who underwent prophylactic oophorectomy, compared with women who did not undergo surgery (*n* = 79).[82] A recent, multicenter retrospective study revealed a 53% risk reduction in individuals with a *BRCA1* or *BRCA2* mutation who underwent prophylactic oophorectomy.[64] Of 99 women who underwent prophylactic oophorectomy, 21 developed breast cancer, as compared to 60 breast cancers developing in 142 matched controls. Recently, the results of a prospective study in *BRCA1* and *BRCA2* mutation carriers, with a mean follow-up of 24.2 months, was reported.[63] Three breast cancers occurred in 69 individuals who had prophylactic salpingo-oophorectomy group, compared to 8 breast cancers in 62 individuals who opted for surveillance.

PSYCHOSOCIAL ASPECTS

The psychosocial aspects of risk assessment and the decision process for risk reduction strategies are relevant for high-risk individuals. The reaction to a positive genetic test result leads to a stressful cascade of issues. Individuals who underestimate their emotional response to test result disclosure experience greater psychological distress at 6 months.[83] The presence of cancer-related stress symptoms at baseline in family members with *BRCA1*- and *BRCA2*-linked cancers was strongly predictive of depression in those who were invited but declined testing. The depression rate of these individuals was not only increased compared to non-carriers but also, when compared to mutation carriers who had decided to be tested, pointed out that dealing with uncertainty is more difficult than knowing about a positive test result.[84]

Risk reduction options for high-risk women include a conservative approach with screening or a prevention approach with tamoxifen or surgery. The decision process is affected by risk perception and patients' preference to their management approach. In one study, for example, 19% of 333 women stated that they would consider prophylactic mastectomy if they tested positive, and 54% reported being unsure. Variables correlating with the potential decision for mastectomy included age, risk estimate, and breast cancer anxiety; younger women with higher risk and higher levels of anxiety were more likely to consider prophylactic mastectomy.[85] Other studies have evaluated the perception of prophylactic mastectomy in *BRCA1* or *BRCA2* mutation carriers. In two studies, the acceptance for prophylactic mastectomy was 3 to 8%,[86,87] whereas a study from Rotterdam in 139 unaffected *BRCA1* or *BRCA2* mutation carriers reported an acceptance rate of 55%.[76] A recent study in 194 *BRCA1* or *BRCA2* mutation carriers reported that 29 (15%) women opted for prophylactic mastectomy.[48] The differences in the acceptance rate in these studies are unclear, but cultural differences may play an important role. Furthermore, advances in skin-sparing mastectomy with autologous reconstruction have made this option more desirable for high-risk patients.

CONCLUSIONS

Breast cancer risk reduction options include screening, chemoprevention, and prophylactic surgery. Guidelines for screening include monthly self-breast exams, annual clinical breast exams, and yearly mammograms. The frequency of mammography and the long-term benefit of MRI for genetically high-risk women has not yet been determined.

Tamoxifen is the only chemopreventive agent approved for the risk reduction of breast cancer in high-risk women as defined by the Gail model (> 1.66%) and in postmenopausal women age 60 and older. The risk-benefit ratio in elderly women remains to be carefully assessed. Previous history of thromboembolic events or premalignant changes in the uterus are contraindications. Although tamoxifen is indicated in women with a 5-year projected risk of > 1.66% (by the Gail model); especially in postmenopausal women, the benefit/ratio is higher if estimated risk of breast cancer is > 0.5% per year without a uterus or >1% per year with a uterus. To overcome menopausal symptoms caused by tamoxifen in hysterectomized women, HRT has been routinely included for patients in European centers with no apparent loss of efficacy in early clinical trials. The benefit of tamoxifen in *BRCA1* mutation carriers seems to be less likely as compared to *BRCA2* mutation carriers; however, definitive conclusions have not been reached. Raloxifene is a potential but unapproved chemoprevention agent and is currently under study in the STAR trial. Until results are available, it should not be prescribed. Current research is focusing on the development of other less toxic agents, such as aromatase inhibitors. Furthermore, since tamoxifen has been shown to reduce ER-positive breast cancer risk and has no effect on the occurrence of ER-negative breast cancers, there is an obvious need to develop chemopreventive agents that target ER-negative breast cancer. One potential non-hormonal agent is the selective cyclooxygenase-2 (COX-2) inhibitor, celecoxib,[88,89] currently under investigation in phase II breast cancer chemoprevention trials.[90] Other promising agents for the prevention of ER-negative breast cancers include polyamine biosynthesis inhibitors (DFMO),[91] vitamin D analogues, retinoids, cyclin-dependent kinase inhibitors,[92] telomerase inhibitors,[93] isoflavonoids,[94] demethylating agents,[95] and molecular chemopreventive approaches including targeted gene therapy for *BRCA1* mutation carriers.[96]

Although the Gail risk model is a commonly used risk assessment tool, it may provide an inaccurate estimate of breast cancer risk in certain circumstances. Therefore, more accurate risk assessment models need to be developed, potentially incorporating tissue-based risk markers.

Prophylactic mastectomy and oophorectomy are highly effective management options. The decision process requires an extensive discussion and education, at times requiring several visits with the genetic counseling team, the medical oncologist, the surgical oncologist, the gynecologist, and the plastic surgeon. Factors affecting this decision include the estimated risk, the physical, mental, and cosmetic aspects of the surgery and recovery, and the patient's choice between early detection and prevention.

REFERENCES

1. Jemal A, Tiwari RC, Murray T, et al. Cancer statistics, 2004. CA Cancer J Clin 2004;54:8–29.
2. Hortobagyi GN. Treatment of breast cancer. N Engl J Med 1998;339:974–84.
3. Newman B, Austin MA, Lee M, et al. Inheritance of human breast cancer: evidence for autosomal dominant transmission in high-risk families. Proc Natl Acad Sci U S A 1988; 85:3044–8.
4. Yang X, Lippman ME. *BRCA1* and *BRCA2* in breast cancer. Breast Cancer Res Treat 1999;54:1–10.
5. Ford D, Easton DF, Stratton M, et al. Genetic heterogeneity and penetrance analysis of the *BRCA1* and *BRCA2* genes in breast cancer families. The Breast Cancer Linkage Consortium. Am J Hum Genet 1998;62:676–89.
6. Easton DF, Bishop DT, Ford D, et al. Genetic linkage analysis in familial breast and ovarian cancer: results from 214 families. The Breast Cancer Linkage Consortium. Am J Hum Genet 1993;52:678–701.
7. Struewing JP, Hartge P, Wacholder S, et al. The risk of cancer associated with specific mutations of *BRCA1* and *BRCA2* among Ashkenazi Jews. N Engl J Med 1997;336:1401–8.
8. Malkin D, Li FP, Strong LC, et al. Germline *p53* mutations in a familial syndrome of breast cancer, sarcomas, and other neoplasms. Science 1990;250:1233–8.
9. Li J, Yen C, Liaw D, et al. *PTEN*, a putative protein tyrosine phosphatase gene mutated in human brain, breast, and prostate cancer. Science 1997;275:1943–7.
10. Liaw D, Marsh DJ, Li J, et al. Germline mutations of the *PTEN* gene in Cowden disease, an inherited breast and thyroid cancer syndrome. Nat Genet 1997;16:64–7.
11. Chen J, Lindblom A. Germline mutation screening of the *STK11/LKB1* gene in familial breast cancer with LOH on 19p. Clin Genet 2000;57:394–7.
12. Anderson DE, Badzioch MD, Bilaterality in familial breast cancer patients. Cancer 1985;56:2092–8.
13. MacMahon B, Cole P, Lin TM, et al, Age at first birth and breast cancer risk. Bull World Health Organ 1970;43:209–21.
14. Trichopoulos D, MacMahon B, Cole P. Menopause and breast cancer risk. J Natl Cancer Inst 1972;48:605–13.
15. Lowe CR, MacMahon B. Breast cancer and reporoduction, Lancet. 1970;2:1137.
16. Jernstrom H, Lerman C, Ghadirian P, et al. Pregnancy and risk of early breast cancer in carriers of *BRCA1* and *BRCA2*. Lancet 1999;354:1846–50.
17. Newcomb PA, Storer BE, Longnecker MP, et al. Pregnancy termination in relation to risk of breast cancer. JAMA 1996;275:283–7.
18. Melbye M, Wohlfahrt J, Olsen JH, et al. Induced abortion and the risk of breast cancer. N Engl J Med 1997;336:81–5.
19. Layde PM, Webster LA, Baughman AL, et al. The independent associations of parity, age at first full term pregnancy, and duration of breastfeeding with the risk of breast cancer. Cancer and Steroid Hormone Study Group. J Clin Epidemiol 1989;42:963–73.
20. Newcomb PA, Storer BE, Longnecker MP, et al, Lactation and a reduced risk of premenopausal breast cancer. N Engl J Med 1994;330:81–7.
21. Sillero-Arenas M, Delgado-Rodriguez M, Rodigues-Canteras R, et al. Menopausal hormone replacement therapy and breast cancer: a meta-analysis. Obstet Gynecol 1992;79:286–94.
22. Steinberg KK, Thacker SB, Smith SJ, et al. A meta-analysis of the effect of estrogen replacement therapy on the risk of breast cancer. JAMA 1991;265:1985–90.
23. Risks and benefits of estrogen plus progestin in healthy postmenopausal women: principal results From the Women's

Health Initiative randomized controlled trial. JAMA 2002;288:321–33.
24. Meirik O, Lund E, Adami HO, et al. Oral contraceptives and breast cancer. Lancet 1986;2:1272–3.
25. Oral contraceptive use and breast cancer risk in young women. UK National Case-Control Study Group. Lancet 1989;1:973–82.
26. Malone KE, Daling JR, Weiss NS. Oral contraceptives in relation to breast cancer. Epidemiol Rev 1993;15:80–97.
27. Page DL, Dupont WD. Benign breast disease: indicators of increased breast cancer risk. Cancer Detect Prev 1992;16: 93–7.
28. Grooff PN, Pamies RJ, Hunyadi S. Lobular carcinoma in situ: what clinicians need to know. Hosp Pract 1993;28:122–30.
29. Chen Y, Thompson W, Semenciw R, et al. Epidemiology of contralateral breast cancer. Cancer Epidemiol Biomarkers Prev 1999;8:855–61.
30. Broet P, de la Rochefordiere A, Scholl SM, et al. Contralateral breast cancer: annual incidence and risk parameters. J Clin Oncol 1995;13:1578–83.
31. Gail M, Brinton L, Byar D, et al. Projecting individualized probabilities of developing breast cancer for white females who are being examined annually. J Nat Cancer Inst 1989;81:1879–86.
32. Spiegelman D, Colditz GA, Hunter D, et al. Validation of the Gail et al model for predicting individual breast cancer risk. J Natl Cancer Inst 1994;86:600–7.
33. Bondy ML, Lustbader ED, Halabi S, et al. Validation of a breast cancer risk assessment model in women with a positive family history. J Natl Cancer Inst 1994;86:620–5.
34. Claus EB, Risch N, Thompson WD. Autosomal dominant inheritance of early-onset breast cancer. Implications for risk prediction. Cancer 1994;73:643–51.
35. Wellings SR. A hypothesis of the origin of human breast cancer from the terminal ductal lobular unit. Pathol Res Pract 1980;166:515–35.
36. Waldman FM, DeVries S, Chew KL, et al. Chromosomal alterations in ductal carcinomas in situ and their in situ recurrences. J Natl Cancer Inst 2000;92:313–20.
37. Wrensch MR, Petrakis NL, King EB, et al. Breast cancer incidence in women with abnormal cytology in nipple aspirates of breast fluid. Am J Epidemiol 1992;135:130–41.
38. Fabian CJ, Kimler BF, Zalles CM, et al. Short-term breast cancer prediction by random periareolar fine-needle aspiration cytology and the Gail risk model. J Natl Cancer Inst 2000;92:1217–27.
39. Dupont WD, Parl FF, Hartmann WH, et al. Breast cancer risk associated with proliferative breast disease and atypical hyperplasia. Cancer 1993;71:1258–65.
40. Dooley WC, Ljung BM, Veronesi U, et al. Ductal lavage for detection of cellular atypia in women at high risk for breast cancer. J Natl Cancer Inst 2001;93:1624–32.
41. Kerlikowske K, Grady D, Rubin SM, et al. Efficacy of screening mammography. A meta-analysis. JAMA 1995; 273:149–54.
42. Fletcher SW, Black W, Harris R, et al. Report of the International Workshop on Screening for Breast Cancer. J Natl Cancer Inst 1993;85:1644–56.
43. Taubes G. The breast-screening brawl. Science 1997;275: 1056–9.
44. Kopans DB. An overview of the breast cancer screening controversy. J Natl Cancer Inst Monogr 1997;(22):1–3.
45. Burke W, Daly M, Garber J, et al. Recommendations for follow-up care of individuals with an inherited predisposition to cancer. II. *BRCA1* and *BRCA2*. Cancer Genetics Studies Consortium. JAMA 1997;277:997–1003.
46. Eisinger F, Alby N, Bremond A, et al. Recommendations for medical management of hereditary breast and ovarian cancer: the French National Ad Hoc Committee. Ann Oncol 1998;9:939–50.
47. Brekelmans CT, Seynaeve C, Bartels CC, et al. Effectiveness of breast cancer surveillance in *BRCA1/2* gene mutation carriers and women with high familial risk. J Clin Oncol 2001;19:924–30.
48. Scheuer L, Kauff N, Robson M, et al. Outcome of preventive surgery and screening for breast and ovarian cancer in BRCA mutation carriers. J Clin Oncol 2002;20:1260–8.
49. Stoutjesdijk MJ, Boetes C, Jager GJ, et al. Magnetic resonance imaging and mammography in women with a hereditary risk of breast cancer. J Natl Cancer Inst 2001; 93:1095–102.
50. Warner E, Plewes DB, Shumak RS, et al. Comparison of breast magnetic resonance imaging, mammography, and ultrasound for surveillance of women at high risk for hereditary breast cancer. J Clin Oncol 2001;19:3524–31.
51. Kuhl CK, Schmutzler RK, Leutner CC, et al. Breast MR imaging screening in 192 women proved or suspected to be carriers of a breast cancer susceptibility gene: preliminary results. Radiology 2000;215:267–79.
52. Warner E, Plewes DB, Hill KA, et al. Surveillance of *BRCA1* and *BRCA2* mutation carriers with magnetic resonance imaging, ultrasound, mammography, and clinical breast examination. JAMA 2004;292:1317–25.
53. Kriege M, Brekelmans CT, Boetes C, et al. Efficacy of MRI and mammography for breast-cancer screening in women with a familial or genetic predisposition. N Engl J Med 2004;351:427–37.
54. Fisher B, Costantino JP, Wickerham DL, et al. Tamoxifen for prevention of breast cancer: report of the National Surgical Adjuvant Breast and Bowel Project P-1 Study. J Natl Cancer Inst 1998;90:1371–88.
55. Chlebowski RT, Col N, Winer EP, et al. American society of clinical oncology technology assessment of pharmacologic interventions for breast cancer risk reduction including tamoxifen, raloxifene, and aromatase inhibition. J Clin Oncol 2002;20:3328–43.
56. Powles T, Eeles R, Ashley S, et al. Interim analysis of the incidence of breast cancer in the Royal Marsden Hospital tamoxifen randomised chemoprevention trial. The Lancet 1998;352:98–101.
57. Veronesi U, Maisonneuve P, Costa A, et al. Prevention of breast cancer with tamoxifen: preliminary findings from the Italian randomised trial among hysterectomised women. Italian Tamoxifen Prevention Study. Lancet 1998;352:93–7.
58. Schairer C, Persson I, Falkeborn M, et al. Breast cancer risk associated with gynecologic surgery and indications for such surgery. Int J Cancer 1997;70:150–4.
59. Veronesi U, Maisonneuve P, Rotmensz N, et al. Italian randomized trial among women with hysterectomy: tamoxifen and hormone-dependent breast cancer in high-risk women. J Natl Cancer Inst 2003;95:160–5.
60. Gail MH, Costantino JP, Bryant J, et al. Weighing the risks and benefits of tamoxifen treatment for preventing breast cancer. J Natl Cancer Inst 1999;91:1829–46.

61. King MC, Wieand S, Hale K, et al. Tamoxifen and breast cancer incidence among women with inherited mutations in *BRCA1* and *BRCA2*: National Surgical Adjuvant Breast and Bowel Project (NSABP-P1) Breast Cancer Prevention Trial. JAMA 2001;286:2251–6.
62. Narod SA, Brunet JS, Ghadirian P, et al. Tamoxifen and risk of contralateral breast cancer in *BRCA1* and *BRCA2* mutation carriers: a case-control study. Hereditary Breast Cancer Clinical Study Group. Lancet 2000;356:1876–81.
63. Kauff ND, Satagopan JM, Robson ME, et al. Risk-reducing salpingo-oophorectomy in women with a *BRCA1* or *BRCA2* mutation. N Engl J Med 2002;346:1609–15.
64. Rebbeck TR, Lynch HT, Neuhausen SL, et al. Prophylactic oophorectomy in carriers of *BRCA1* or *BRCA2* mutations. N Engl J Med 2002;346:1616–22.
65. Arun B, Anthony M, Dunn B. The search for the ideal SERM. Expert Opin Pharmacother 2002;3:681–91.
66. Cummings SR, Eckert S, Krueger KA, et al. The effect of raloxifene on risk of breast cancer in postmenopausal women: results from the MORE randomized trial. Multiple Outcomes of Raloxifene Evaluation. JAMA 1999;281:2189–97.
67. Jordan VC, Glusman JE, Eckert S, et al. Incident primary breast cancers are reduced by raloxifene: integrated data from multicenter double blind, randomized trials in 12,000 postmenopausal women [abstract 466]. Proc Am Cancer Soc Clin Oncol 1998;17:122a.
68. Bulun SE, Price TM, Aitken J, et al. A link between breast cancer and local estrogen biosynthesis suggested by quantification of breast adipose tissue aromatase cytochrome P450 transcripts using competitive polymerase chain reaction after reverse transcription. J Clin Endocrinol Metab 1993;77:1622–8.
69. Tekmal RR, Ramachandra N, Gubba S, et al. Overexpression of int-5/aromatase in mammary glands of transgenic mice results in the induction of hyperplasia and nuclear abnormalities. Cancer Res 1996;56:3180–5.
70. Anastrozole alone or in combination with tamoxifen versus tamoxifen alone for adjuvant treatment of postmenopausal women with early breast cancer: first results of the ATAC randomised trial. Lancet 2002;359:2131–9.
71. Goss PE, Ingle JN, Martino S, et al. A randomized trial of letrozole in postmenopausal women after five years of tamoxifen therapy for early-stage breast cancer. N Engl J Med 2003;349:1793–802.
72. Coombes RC, Hall E, Gibson LJ, et al. A randomized trial of exemestane after two to three years of tamoxifen therapy in postmenopausal women with primary breast cancer. N Engl J Med 2004;350:1081–92.
73. Santen RJ, Yue W, Naftolin F, et al. The potential of aromatase inhibitors in breast cancer prevention. Endocr Relat Cancer 1999;6:235–43.
74. Hartmann LC, Schaid DJ, Woods JE, et al. Efficacy of bilateral prophylactic mastectomy in women with a family history of breast cancer. N Engl J Med 1999;340:77–84.
75. Hartmann LC, Sellers TA, Schaid DJ, et al. Efficacy of bilateral prophylactic mastectomy in *BRCA1* and *BRCA2* gene mutation carriers. J Natl Cancer Inst 2001;93(21):1633–7.
76. Meijers-Heijboer H, van Geel B, van Putten WL, et al. Breast cancer after prophylactic bilateral mastectomy in women with a *BRCA1* or *BRCA2* mutation. N Engl J Med 2001;345:159–64.
77. Rebbeck TR, Friebel T, Lynch HT, et al. Bilateral prophylactic mastectomy reduces breast cancer risk in *BRCA1* and *BRCA2* mutation carriers: the PROSE Study Group. J Clin Oncol 2004;22:1055–62.
78. Brinton LA, Schairer C, Hoover RN, et al. Menstrual factors and risk of breast cancer. Cancer Invest 1988;6:245–54.
79. Parazzini F, Braga C, La Vecchia C, et al. Hysterectomy, oophorectomy in premenopause, and risk of breast cancer. Obstet Gynecol 1997;90:453–6.
80. Meijer WJ, van Lindert AC. Prophylactic oophorectomy. Eur J Obstet Gynecol Reprod Biol 1992;47:59–65.
81. Struewing JP, Watson P, Easton DF, et al. Prophylactic oophorectomy in inherited breast/ovarian cancer families. J Natl Cancer Inst Monogr 1995;17:33–5.
82. Rebbeck TR, Levin AM, Eisen A, et al. Breast cancer risk after bilateral prophylactic oophorectomy in *BRCA1* mutation carriers. J Natl Cancer Inst 1999;91:1475–9.
83. Dorval M, Patenaude AF, Schneider KA, et al. Anticipated versus actual emotional reactions to disclosure of results of genetic tests for cancer susceptibility: findings from *p53* and *BRCA1* testing programs. J Clin Oncol 2000;18:2135–42.
84. Lerman C, Hughes C, Lemon SJ, et al. What you don't know can hurt you: adverse psychologic effects in members of *BRCA1*-linked and *BRCA2*-linked families who decline genetic testing. J Clin Oncol 1998;16:1650–4.
85. Meiser B, Butow P, Friedlander M, et al. Intention to undergo prophylactic bilateral mastectomy in women at increased risk of developing hereditary breast cancer. J Clin Oncol 2000;18:2250–7.
86. Wagner TM, Moslinger R, Langbauer G, et al. Attitude towards prophylactic surgery and effects of genetic counseling in families with BRCA mutations. Austrian Hereditary Breast and Ovarian Cancer Group. Br J Cancer 2000;82:1249–53.
87. Lerman C, Narod S, Schulman K, et al. *BRCA1* testing in families with hereditary breast-ovarian cancer. A prospective study of patient decision making and outcomes. JAMA 1996;275:1885–92.
88. Arun B, Goss P. The role of COX-2 inhibition in breast cancer treatment and prevention. Semin Oncol 2004;31:22–9.
89. Howe LR, Subbaramaiah K, Brown AM, et al. Cyclooxygenase-2: a target for the prevention and treatment of breast cancer. Endocr Relat Cancer 2001;8:97–114.
90. Arun B, Valero V, Cook E, et al. Phase II chemoprevention trial of celecoxib using ductal lavage. Breast Cancer Res Treat 2003;71:126a.
91. Meyskens FL Jr, Gerner EW. Development of difluoromethylornithine (DFMO) as a chemoprevention agent. Clin Cancer Res 1999;5:945–51.
92. Brown PH, Lippman SM. Chemoprevention of breast cancer. Breast Cancer Res Treat 2000;62:1–17.
93. Herbert BS, Wright WE, Shay JW. Telomerase and breast cancer. Breast Cancer Res 2001;3:146–9.
94. Barnes S. The chemopreventive properties of soy isoflavonoids in animal models of breast cancer. Breast Cancer Res Treat 1997;46:169–79.
95. Yang X, Yan L, Davidson NE. DNA methylation in breast cancer. Endocr Relat Cancer 2001;8:115–27.
96. Fan S, Wang J, Yuan R, et al. *BRCA1* inhibition of estrogen receptor signaling in transfected cells. Science 1999;284:1354–6.

8

Role of Screening in Breast Cancer Mortality Reduction

STEPHEN F. SENER
ROBERT A. SMITH

DESIGN OF CLINICAL TRIALS FOR THE EARLY DETECTION OF BREAST CANCER

Classic Study, Up-Front, and Closeout Designs

Screening programs are based on the premise that detecting cancers in asymptomatic patients at an early stage, when combined with effective treatment, may lead to longer survival and lower mortality rates. However, it is theoretically possible that treatment of some small screen-detected cancers might not lead to increased benefit, either because these lesions may have never progressed or have already spread to regional lymph nodes or beyond at the time of diagnosis. These fundamental issues about the efficacy of early detection were at the crux of clinical trials designed to evaluate the benefit of screening for breast cancer.

In the classic design of a therapeutic clinical trial, there are study and control groups. In this model, patients in the control group have their usual medical care and may not derive benefit from enrollment in the study. However, there are two experimental designs for early detection trials in which subjects derive potential benefit, even if they are assigned to the control group. As described by Hu and Zelen, these are called the up-front design (UFD) and the closeout design (COD), both of which have been used in randomized breast cancer screening trials.[1] In trials using the UFD, every subject receives an initial early detection exam; whereas in trials using the COD, subjects in the control group receive an early detection exam at the same time as those in the study group receive their last exam.

In trials using the UFD, the initial exam may be different from the screening exam offered to the study group. Thus, for a breast cancer screening trial, the initial exam might be a clinical breast exam (CBE), whereas the exams in the study group might consist of a CBE plus a mammogram. Then, when analyzing the data, a decision must be made whether to drop or keep all subjects who had a positive initial exam, that is the prevalent cases. If the drop option is used, then the trial will define the benefit of periodic screening exams in a population of subjects with no detectable cancer at the onset of the trial. If the keep option is used, subjects are randomized to control or study groups regardless of the result of the initial exam. Indeed, there are trials in which the result of the initial exam is not known at the time of randomization. The trial will then define the benefit of additional screening exams after an initial exam. If a third group consisting of usual care only is added to the UFD, then the comparisons can define the incremental benefits for detecting prevalent cases and for periodic screening exams versus care without screening.

The probability that a trial can observe a given percentage reduction in mortality is referred to as the power. Hu and Zelen have determined that the power of the UFD is reduced compared to that of the classic trial design, and that in general the drop option provides greater power than the keep option. To obtain the maximum power with the drop and keep options requires longer follow-up times in UFD trials than in classic design trials. In addition, the power increases with the number of screening exams, but the required follow-up time is lengthened.

Data from studies using a COD may be analyzed either by comparing all breast cancer deaths in each group over the duration of the study or by including only deaths from cases diagnosed up to and including the last exam in the study group. Unless the sensitivity of the closeout exam is very high, the false-negative rate of the exam will lead to a higher number of undetected cancers in the control than the study group, simply because there will be a greater number of cases in the previously unscreened group. These cases can still be included in the data analysis, provided that follow-up is sufficiently long enough to identify the missed cancers.

These principles become important when analyzing the results of randomized breast cancer screening trials, such as the Canadian National Breast Screening Study.[2] The Canadian study of breast cancer screening in women 40 to 49 years of age (at the time of entry) randomized subjects to receive annual mammograms and CBE versus usual care. It used an UFD in which all subjects received an initial exam consisting of a CBE. At the time of randomization, the results of CBE were allegedly unknown to the study coordinators, so all subjects were allotted to the control or study group independent of the results of the physical exam. Hence, the data were analyzed using the keep option, and prevalent cases were retained in their respective study or control groups. In the first analysis of end results, with mean follow-up of 8.5 years, the authors concluded that there was no significant difference in breast cancer mortality between the control and study groups. However, Hu and Zelen have stated that if the prevalent cases had been dropped, the power of the trial could have been raised. This issue is important because the results of the Canadian Trial have been controversial, owing to a surprisingly high imbalance in the rate of advanced breast cancer detected in the group invited to screening compared with the control group.

The Stockholm Mammography Breast Screening Trial for women aged 40 to 64 years was begun in 1981.[3,4] The study group had approximately 40,000 women invited to screening, and the control group had 20,000 age-matched randomly selected women. The trial used a COD, providing two mammograms over a 4-year period to the study group and a mammogram to the control group at the end of the trial. Data analysis included mortality for cases diagnosed up to and including the second exam in the study group and the single exam in the control group. Although the study originally had a classic design, the final study COD was set up to define the magnitude of benefit from the screening program versus a single delayed exam. Thus, the addition of the COD screening significantly diminished the power of the study by reducing the number of potential deaths in the control group.

Controversial Areas in Early Detection Trial Design: Methods of Randomization and End Point Evaluation

The eight randomized trials of screening for breast cancer have shown a significant reduction in breast cancer mortality associated with an invitation to screening.[5] However, Olsen and Götzsche called the evidence for benefit into question in a meta-analysis of these trials, citing methodological flaws in the randomization processes and in the classification of the cause of death.[6–8] These authors have also stated their view that the end point for screening trials should be all-cause mortality rather than breast cancer mortality. Although some individuals have embraced the conclusions of Olsen and Götzsche's analysis, formal reviews of their methodology and critiques have shown their conclusions to be largely unsubstantiated.

Using the Swedish Two-County Trial as an example, approximately 77,000 women aged 40 to 74 years (study group) were invited to have single-view mammograms every 24 or 33 months depending on age at entry. The control group was comprised of approximately 56,000 age-matched women who were not invited to receive mammograms. The trial, begun in 1977, used the method of cluster randomization, in which women in geographic regions were randomized, with the selections being stratified by residency (urban or rural), socioeconomic factors, and sample size. The COD was employed, with women in the control group being invited to mammographic screening at the end of the trial. The trial end point was mortality from breast cancer. With follow-up through 1998, there was a 32% reduction in age-adjusted breast cancer mortality associated with an invitation to screening.[9]

Subsequent to the criticisms of Olsen and Götzsche, Duffy and colleagues re-analyzed the data, taking into account variations between clusters and the longer follow-up time in the group invited to screening. The authors demonstrated that cluster randomization was efficient, that differences in the classification of the cause of death between the original trial's end point committee and an independent overview committee were not significant, and that death from breast cancer (not all-cause mortality) was the appropriate end point for breast cancer screening trials.[10,11] Indeed, it has been estimated that it would require a screening trial of more than one million women in each arm to detect a statistically significant difference in all-cause mortality between subjects invited to screening and control groups.[12,13] Furthermore, if one were going to use all-cause mortality as the end point, the appropriate comparison would be not the entire cohort, but only those women diagnosed with breast cancer in the invited versus control groups. Such an analysis has demonstrated that in breast cancer patients there was a 13% reduction in all-cause mortality risk associated with an invitation to screening.[14] Because breast cancer is a leading cause of death in the age group being screened, it logically followed that a reduction in breast cancer mortality would translate into a reduction in the risk of dying from any cause.

RESULTS FROM RANDOMIZED CLINICAL TRIALS

Evidence supporting the efficacy of mammographic screening for breast cancer has been derived from the eight randomized clinical trials which have been done to date, summarized in Table 8–1.[9,15–20] Although there were differences in study designs and attendance rates, the common theme in all of the trials was that the data were analyzed according to a classic intention-to-treat analysis, that is, whether the subjects were invited or not invited to be screened, not whether they actually were screened or not screened. Significant efforts have been expended to provide rebuttals to the various criticisms of the methodologies employed in these trials.[21] Follow-up in the eight trials now ranges from 12 to 20 years.

The trials demonstrated that there were reductions in breast cancer mortality associated with an invitation to screening of 20% (RR = 0.80, 95% CI = 0.73–0.86) overall in women 40 to 74 years, of 15% (RR = 0.85, 95% CI = 0.73–0.98) in women 40 to 49 years, and of 22% (RR = 0.78, 95% CI = 0.70–0.85) in women 50 to 74 years.[22] The results were consistent with the observation that those trials that had the greatest reductions in the relative risk of having node-positive cancer also had the greatest reductions in breast cancer mortality.[23]

Because all eligible participants were included in these analyses, the results were predicated on the invitation or intention-to-treat method. However, the actual attendance rates for all screening rounds aver-

Table 8–1. STUDY DESIGN AND OVERALL RESULTS FOR BREAST CANCER MORTALITY IN EIGHT RANDOMIZED CLINICAL TRIALS OF SCREENING FOR BREAST CANCER

Study (yr)	Age Range (yr)	Study Group	No. Subjects	Relative Risk
HIP (1963)[15]	40–64	M+CBE	60,995	0.78
Malmö (1976)[16]	43–70	M	60,076	0.78
Two-County (1977)[9]	40–74	M	133,065	0.68
Edinburgh (1978)[17]	45–64	M+CBE	44,268	0.78
Stockholm (1981)[16]	40–64	M	60,117	0.90
NBSS-1 (1980)[18]	40–49	M+CBE	50,430	0.97
NBSS-2 (1980)[19]	50–59	M+CBE	39,405	1.02
Gothenburg (1982)[20]	39–59	M	51,611	0.79
Overall			499,967	0.80

Adapted from Smith RA et al.[22] The control group in each trial consisted of usual care with the exception of NBSS-2, in which the control group received CBE. In NBSS-1 and 2, subjects invited to both screening and control groups also received instruction in breast self-exam. CBE = clinical breast exam;
M = mammographic exam.

aged only about 75%. Non-attendance in the Malmö Screening Trial was associated with unfavorable socioeconomic factors and a higher risk of more advanced cancer at the time of diagnosis than that in subjects attending screening.[24] Further, there was considerable crossover from the "usual care" control group, such that a fraction of subjects assigned to usual care actually received mammograms. Specifically, in Canadian NBSS-1 and -2, those assigned to usual care had access to universal health care, including mammography services. In those studies, 26% (NBSS-1) and 17% (NBSS-2) of those assigned to the control group actually received a screening mammogram outside of the NBSS.[18] Although tumors detected by mammography alone were smaller than those detected by clinical examination alone, with this level of contamination in the control group, it is not surprising that an analysis of tumor size by method of detection failed to demonstrate an overall difference in the median tumor size in the screened versus usual care cohort. There was a similar 24% contamination rate for control group women in the Malmö Screening Trial.[25] Thus, it is clear that results from randomized trials have underestimated the reduction in breast cancer mortality associated with the use of screening mammography.

EVIDENCE FROM COMMUNITY SERVICE SCREENING PROGRAMS

Subsequent to demonstrating that the use of screening mammography led to a reduction in breast cancer mortality, community service screening programs were introduced in many countries. However, measuring the efficacy of screening in service settings has become much more complex because of heightened public awareness of screening and breast cancer, improvements in diagnostic technology, and advances in treatment. Duffy and colleagues evaluated breast cancer mortality for women 40 to 69 years in prescreening and screening epochs in seven Swedish counties, screening approximately one-third of the eligible Swedish population over a maximum of a 40-year time span in community service programs.[26] The mortality reduction for breast cancer in all seven counties combined for women actually exposed to screening compared to the prescreening era was 44% (RR = 0.56, 95% CI = 0.50–0.62). During the screening era, there was a 39% mortality reduction for screened compared with unscreened women (RR = 0.61, 95% CI = 0.55–0.68). During the same time period, there was a 30% reduction in mortality associated with an invitation to screening provided in an ongoing randomized screening trial. Thus, reductions in breast cancer mortality demonstrated in randomized clinical trials have been obtained in nonresearch, organized service screening programs.

In the United States, the use of mammography gained acceptance during the mid- to late 1970s. Subsequent to the results of the randomized trial done by the Health Insurance Plan (HIP), 280,000 women were screened from 1973 to 1980 in the Breast Cancer Detection Demonstration Project.[27] This program, sponsored jointly by the American Cancer Society and the National Cancer Institute, provided clear evidence that screening mammographic techniques used in the United States were able to detect small, non-palpable cancers as well as a higher incidence of node-negative cancers. Data from the Behavioral Risk Factor Surveillance System (BRFSS) of the National Center for Chronic Disease Prevention and Health Promotion (Centers for Disease Control and Prevention) demonstrated that the median percentage of US women at or over 40 years of age not having a mammogram within the last two years dropped from 41.7% in 1990 to 27.2% in 1999.[28] And, in 2000 the BRFSS estimated that 62.6% of US women over 40 years of age had a mammogram within the last year.

The results of population-based service screening programs have been demonstrated by State departments of public health. For example, in Michigan during the 1990s, the percentage of women 50 years of age or older who reported having a mammogram within the last two years went from 60% to over 80%. As a consequence of this aggressive screening program throughout Michigan's 85 counties, the number of counties reporting node-negative breast cancer rates over 50% increased from 41 in 1987 to 76 in 1997.[28] Also, in Rhode Island, an aggressive mammogram promotional campaign was initiated in 1986. The rate of biennial mammographic screening for women 40 years of age and older went from approximately 40% in 1985 to greater than 75% in 2001.[29] It was interesting that there was no significant change in the overall incidence of invasive cancer during the study period. However, the median tumor size decreased from 2.0 to 1.5 cm, and there were significant reductions in the rate of node metastases and in the number of women presenting with stage III and IV cancers. These results were accompanied by a 25% reduction in breast cancer mortality from 1987 to 2001. In a companion report by the same authors, it was noted that 73% of the deaths from breast cancer in Rhode Island from 1995 to 2001 occurred in the 16% of women not participating in regular mammographic screening.[30] And, more than half of the (few) deaths that occurred in women participating in regular screening programs were true interval cancers.

EFFECTS OF MAMMOGRAPHIC DETECTION ON YOUNGER AND OLDER WOMEN

In 1992, Mandelblatt and colleagues addressed the interaction of mammographic detection of breast cancer and level of comorbidity in predicting risk of death among older women, using existing data from randomized trials to develop a Markov model.[31] The authors concluded that screening led to breast cancer mortality reduction at all ages studied, and that there was no inherent reason to impose an upper age limit for screening mammography, except perhaps for the oldest women with significant comorbidities. Satariano and Ragland demonstrated that the level of comorbidity predicted the 3-year survival rates independent of the breast cancer stage at diagnosis.[32] Subsequently, McPherson and colleagues performed a retrospective cohort analysis of 5,186 patients aged 65 years and older with invasive breast cancer diagnosed from 1986 through 1994.[33] Comorbidity coding was done using a modification of the Charlson Co-Morbidity Index, and the mean comorbidity score increased linearly with age. Mammographic detection was associated with mortality risk reduction for older women of all ages, including those with mild to moderate levels of comorbidity. But, for women with severe or multiple significant comorbidities, mammographic detection of breast cancer was not associated with improvement in overall survival. In addition, increasing comorbidity was associated with significantly increased risk of death in women with local or regional disease but not in those with distant disease. Thus, the poor survival of older women with metastatic breast cancer was not altered by comorbid disease. And, to illustrate the converse, McCarthy and colleagues demonstrated that, after adjusting for comorbidity, older women who did not obtain regular screening mammography had a threefold higher risk of dying from breast cancer than women who did receive regular screening.[34]

For women in their forties, breast cancer remains the leading cause of death.[35] Despite the growing body of evidence which has demonstrated the effectiveness of screening mammography in reducing breast cancer mortality for women 40 to 49 years of age, for some the subject remains a topic of debate. Whereas screening women in their 40s was controversial due to smaller mortality reductions observed in trials, additional concerns have included lower sensitivity and specificity compared with women 50 years and older.[36] However, comparing women under age 50 with those over age 50 obscures the gradual trend of increasing efficiency of screening with increasing age. Further, in clinical trials and observational studies, the detection of small, node-negative (early stage) cancers has been shown to be a surrogate marker for decreased mortality risk, regardless of age at diagnosis.[9,27] In a health care setting where at least biennial screening mammography was a covered benefit for all women ages 40 to 49 years, Buseman and colleagues demonstrated that women who were regularly screened were less likely to be diagnosed at late stage (stage III and IV) than women who were not regularly screened (RR = 0.56, 95% CI = 0.32–0.97).[37] Further, as Tabar and colleagues demonstrated in an analysis of the effectiveness of service screening in two Swedish counties, mortality reductions were similar in women diagnosed with breast cancer during their forties compared with women in their fifties if they were screened at a short interval.[38] Despite the areas of controversy, one thing remains clear: the vast majority of women with small, node-negative cancers identified by screening have benefited from the process of early detection.

PRIMARY FACTOR IN DECLINING BREAST CANCER MORTALITY RATES: EARLY DETECTION OR ADJUVANT THERAPY?

Even with a 36.8% increase in the incidence of invasive breast cancer from 1980 to 1999, mortality rates for breast cancer in the United States remained stable until 1989. From then through 1995, there was a nationwide average mortality decline of 1.6% per year, followed by an average decline of 3.4% per year from 1996 through 1999.[39] Feig has estimated that, for this time period, breast cancer mortality rates were 39% lower than expected on the basis of the increased incidence of invasive cancer.[40] There has been considerable discussion as to whether this mortality reduction can be attributed to advances in systemic adjuvant therapy, more aggressive implementation of screening programs, or a combination of both.[41,42] Because of the implications for national policy and resource allocation, it is important to differentiate between these factors.

The National Institutes of Health 2000 consensus statement on the use of adjuvant therapy for breast cancer reaffirmed that the four reliable prognostic features were size, node status, grade, and hormone receptor status.[43] As previously described in this chapter, results from randomized screening trials and service screening programs have demonstrated a decrease in tumor size and node-positive rates associated with screening. In geographic regions of the United States where aggressive screening programs have been used, the median diameter of invasive breast cancer has decreased to 1.5 cm and the rate of node-positive cancers has dropped to 30%.[29] More than 30% of cancers treated in these areas were classified T1a and T1b, and Cady has estimated that within 10 years this proportion will be 50% if screening rates continue to increase.[44]

The hallmark of systemic adjuvant treatment for breast cancer has been the proportional reduction in mortality of about 25% with tamoxifen and about 33% with polychemotherapy. However, in the Swedish two county studies, it was estimated that there was a 50 to 67% proportional mortality reduction by screening 85% of women aged 40 to 74 years at 30-month intervals.[45] The largest absolute effect on mortality reduction with systemic adjuvant treatment would be in patients with larger, node-positive cancers. As smaller cancers with a reduced risk of metastases were discovered with screening, the absolute impact of adjuvant therapy on mortality would become far less, although the proportional impact would remain the same. In the Swedish report, with a 30-month interval between screenings, 39% of cancers were discovered in the interval between screenings. With annual screening of 90% of this population, only 11% of cancers would have been detected in the interval between screenings and the mean tumor diameter would have been about 1 cm, with a node-positive rate of about 10%. Although it is clear that both early detection and adjuvant therapy have contributed to mortality reductions, the greatest potential to reduce breast cancer deaths is through the contribution of screening to reduce the incidence rate of advanced disease. Thus, the comparative effects on population mortality of screening versus adjuvant treatment have been quite different and have become more pronounced as screening programs have become more successful. The key issue for the contribution of screening to reduce deaths from breast cancer is high rates of participation in screening and adherence to recommended screening intervals, whereas the key issue for adjuvant therapy is the proportion of patients at high risk for metastases who actually receive adjuvant therapy.[44]

SCREENING INTERVALS

The primary reason that 1- to 2-year screening intervals have been recommended by guideline review groups is that observed breast cancer mortality reductions have been demonstrated in randomized trials of women 40 to 69 years of age which used intervals of 1 year, 2 years, or longer. However, an

Table 8–2. MEAN SOJOURN TIMES FOR BREAST CANCER ACCORDING TO THE AGE OF THE PATIENT

Age of Women (yr)	Mean Sojourn Time (yr)
40–49	2.4
50–59	3.7
60–69	4.2
70–79	4.0

Adapted from Tabar et al.[9]

Table 8–3. AMERICAN CANCER SOCIETY GUIDELINES FOR EARLY BREAST CANCER DETECTION, 2003

Women at Average Risk
• Begin mammography at age 40. • For women in their twenties and thirties, it is recommended that clinical breast examination be part of a periodic health examination, preferably at least every 3 years. Asymptomatic women aged 40 and over should continue to receive a clinical breast examination as part of a periodic health examination, preferably annually. • Beginning in their twenties, women should be told about the benefits and limitations of breast self-examination (BSE). The importance of prompt reporting of any new breast symptoms to a health professional should be emphasized. Women who choose to do BSE should receive instruction and have their technique reviewed on the occasion of a periodic health examination. It is acceptable for women to choose not to do BSE or to do BSE irregularly. • Women should have an opportunity to become informed about the benefits, limitations, and potential harms associated with regular screening.
Older Women
• Screening decisions in older women should be individualized by considering the potential benefits and risks of mammography in the context of current health status and estimated life expectancy. As long as a woman is in reasonably good health and would be a candidate for treatment, she should continue to be screened with mammography.
Women at Increased Risk
• Women at increased risk of breast cancer might benefit from additional screening strategies beyond those offered to women of average risk, such as earlier initiation of screening, shorter screening intervals, or the addition of screening modalities other than mammography and physical examination, such as ultrasound or magnetic resonance imaging. However, the evidence currently available is insufficient to justify recommendations for any of these screening approaches.

Adapted from Smith RA et al.[5]

important factor in determining the interval between screening examinations is the mean sojourn time, the average time during which the tumor is detectable by mammography but remains nonpalpable. Using the Swedish two-county trial data, Tabar and colleagues have reported that sojourn times were 2.4 years for women 40 to 49 years of age, 3.7 years for women 50 to 59 years of age, 4.2 years for women 60 to 69 years of age, and 4.0 years for women 70 to 79 years of age[9] (Table 8–2). Whereas sojourn times determined by Markov models have been shown to increase with increasing age of women being screened, they are only an approximation of the time intervals which should not be exceeded. The optimal time interval would be the longest time which allowed routine screening to detect the vast majority of tumors while small, nonpalpable, and node-negative.

The observations that there were higher incidences of interval cancers in younger than older women and in women with increased versus decreased mammographic density have led to the conclusion that, while screening at a 1-year interval is likely more beneficial than longer intervals for all women, there clearly is more benefit to annual screening in younger than older women.[20, 46–48]

CONCLUSIONS

During the last 5 years, data supporting the efficacy of screening mammography have undergone intensive re-examination, and the benefits of regular screening have been reaffirmed (Table 8–3).[5] However, the ultimate potential of this screening tool has yet to be realized, a concept perhaps best embodied by a quote from Spencer and colleagues: "If 90% of American women between the ages of 40 and 75 years were given annual screening mammograms, breast cancer mortality would likely be reduced by two-thirds."[30]

REFERENCES

1. Hu P, Zelen M. Experimental design issues for the early detection of disease: novel designs. Biostatistics 2002; 3(3):299–313.
2. Miller AB, Baines CJ, Wall C. Canadian National Breast Screening Study: 1. Breast cancer detection and death rates among women aged 40–49 years. Can Med Assoc J 1992;147:1459–76.
3. Frisell J, Eklund G, Hellstrom L, et al. Randomized study of mammography screening: preliminary report on mortality in the Stockholm Trial. Breast Cancer Res Treat 1991; 18:49–56.
4. Frisell J, Lidbrink E, Hellstrom L, Rutqvist LE. Follow-up after 11 years—update of mortality results in the Stock-

holm mammographic screening trial. Breast Cancer Res Treat 1997;45:263–70.
5. Smith RA, Saslow D, Sawyer KA, et al. American Cancer Society guidelines for breast cancer screening: update 2003. CA Cancer J Clin 2003;53:141–69.
6. Gotzche PC. Is screening for breast cancer with mammography justifiable? Lancet 2000;355:129–34.
7. Olsen O, Gotzsche PC. Cochrane review on screening for breast cancer with mammography. Lancet 2001;358: 1340–2.
8. Olsen O, Gotzsche PC. Screening for breast cancer with mammography (Cochrane Review). In: The Cochrane Library. Issue 3. Chichester, UK. John Wiley and Sons; 2004.
9. Tabar, L, Vitak B, Chen HH, et al. The Swedish Two-County Trial twenty years later: updated mortality results and new insights from long-term follow-up. Radiol Clin North Am 2000;38:625–51.
10. Duffy SW, Tabar L, Vitak B, et al. The Swedish Two-County Trial of mammographic screening: cluster randomization and end point evaluation. Ann Oncol 2003;14: 1196–8.
11. Nystrom L, Larsson LG. Breast cancer screening with mammography. Lancet 1993;341:1531–2.
12. Duffy SW, Tabar L, Smith RA. The mammographic screening trials: commentary on the recent work by Olsen and Gotzsche. CA Cancer J Clin 2002;52:68–71.
13. Gail MH, Katki HA. Re: all-cause mortality in randomized trials of cancer screening. J Natl Cancer Inst 2002;94:862, discussion, 865–6.
14. Tabar L, Duffy SW, Yen MF, et al. All-cause mortality among breast cancer patients in a screening trial: support for breast cancer mortality as an end point. J Med Screen 2002;9:159–62.
15. Shapiro S. Periodic screening for breast cancer: The HIP randomized controlled trial. Health Insurance Plan. J Natl Cancer Inst Monogr 1997;22:27–30.
16. Nystrom L, Andersson I, Bjurstam N, et al. Long-term effects of mammography screening: updated overview of the Swedish randomized trials. Lancet 2002;359:909–19.
17. Alexander FE, Anderson TJ, Brown HK, et al. 14 years of follow-up from the Edinburgh randomized trial of breast cancer screening. Lancet 1999;353:1903–8.
18. Miller AB, To T, Baines CJ, Wall C. Canadian National Breast Screening Study 1: Breast cancer mortality after 11 to 16 years of follow-up. A randomized screening trial of mammography in women 40 to 49 years. Ann Intern Med 2002;137:305–12.
19. Miller AB, To T, Baines CJ, Wall C. Canadian National Breast Screening Study 2: 13-year results of a randomized trial in women aged 50 to 59 years. J Natl Cancer Inst 2000;92:1490–9.
20. Bjurstam N, Bjorneld L, Warwick J, et al. The Gothenburg Breast Screening Trial. Cancer 2003;97:2387–96.
21. Freedman DA, Petitti DB, Robins JM. On the efficacy of screening for breast cancer. Int J Epidemiol 2004;33: 43–55.
22. Smith RA, Duffy SW, Gabe R, et al. The randomized trials of breast cancer screening: what have we learned? Radiol Clin N Am 2004;42:793–806.
23. Smith RA, Saslow D, Andrews-Sawyer K, et al. American Cancer Society guidelines for breast cancer screening: update 2003. CA Cancer J Clin 2003;53(3):141–69.
24. Zackrisson S, Andersson I, Manjer J, Janzon L. Non-attendance in breast cancer screening is associated with unfavourable socio-economic circumstances and advanced carcinoma. Int J Cancer 2004;108:754–60.
25. Moss SM. Breast carcinoma mortality rates and screening. Cancer 1997;79:1–2.
26. Duffy SW, Tabar L, Chen HH, et al. The impact of organized mammography service screening on breast carcinoma mortality in seven Swedish counties. Cancer 2002;95:458–69.
27. Smart CR, Byrne C, Smith RA, et al. Twenty-year follow-up of breast cancers diagnosed during the Breast Cancer Detection Demonstration Project. CA Cancer J Clin 1997;47:134–49.
28. Behavioral Risk Factor Surveillance System. National Center for Chronic Disease Prevention and Health Promotion. Available at: http://www.cdc.gov/nccdphp/brfss/trends (accessed, October 2004).
29. Coburn NG, Chung MA, Fulton J, Cady B. Decreased breast cancer tumor size, stage, and mortality in Rhode Island: an example of a well-screened population. Cancer Control 2004;11:222–30.
30. Spencer DB, Potter JE, Chung MA, et al. Mammographic screening and disease presentation of breast cancer patients who die of disease. Breast J 2004;10:298–303.
31. Mandelblatt JS, Wheat ME, Montane M, et al. Breast cancer screening for elderly women with and without co-morbid conditions: a decision analysis model. Ann Intern Med 1992;116:722–30.
32. Satariano WA, Ragland DR. The effect of co-morbidity on 3-year survival of women with primary breast cancer. Ann Intern Med 1994;120:104–10.
33. McPherson CP, Swenson KK, Lee MW. The effects of mammographic detection and co-morbidity on the survival of older women with breast cancer. J Am Geriatr Soc 2002;50:1061–8.
34. McCarthy EP, Burns RB, Freund KM, et al. Mammography use, breast cancer stage at diagnosis, and survival among older women. J Am Geriatr Soc 2000;48:1226–33.
35. Jemal A, Tiwari R, Murray T, et al. Cancer statistics 2004. CA Cancer J Clin 2004;54:8–29.
36. Sener SF, Winchester DJ, Winchester DP, et al. The spectrum of mammographically detected breast cancers. Am Surg 1999;65:731–6.
37. Buseman S, Mouchawar J, Calonge N, Byers T. Mammography screening matters for young women with breast carcinoma. Evidence of downstaging among 42-49 year old women with a history of previous mammography screening. Cancer 2003;97:352–8.
38. Tabar L, Yen MF, Vitak B, et al. Mammography service screening and mortality in breast cancer patients: 20-year follow-up before and after introduction of screening. Lancet 2003;361(9367):1405–10.
39. Ries L, Eisneer M, Kosary C, et al. SEER Cancer Statistics Review, 1973-1999. Bethesda, MD: National Cancer Institute; 2002.
40. Feig SA. Effect of service screening mammography on population mortality from breast carcinoma. Cancer 2002; 95:451–7.

41. Berry DA. Benefits and risks of screening mammography for women in their forties: a statistical appraisal. J Natl Cancer Inst 1998;90:1431–9.
42. Baum M, Tobias JS. Effect of screening programmes on mortality from breast cancer. Investment in treatment would be more cost effective. Br Med J 2000;321(7275):1528.
43. National Institutes of Health. Adjuvant therapy for breast cancer. NIH consensus statement. 2000;17:1–23.
44. Sener SF, Cady B, Merkel D. Primary factor in declining breast cancer mortality rates: early detection or adjuvant therapy? Cancer Pract 2002;10:45–7.
45. Tabar L, Vitak B, Chen HH, et al. Beyond randomized controlled trials: organized mammographic screening substantially reduces breast cancer mortality. Cancer 2001;91:1724–31.
46. Andersson I, Janzon L. Reduced breast cancer mortality in women under age 50: updated results from the Malmo Mammographic Screening Program. J Natl Cancer Inst Monogr 1997;22:63–7.
47. Michaelson JS, Halpern E, Kopans DB. Breast cancer: computer simulation method for estimating optimal intervals for screening. Radiology 1999;212:551–60.
48. Field LR, Wilson TE, Strawderman M, et al. Mammographic screening in women more than 64 years old: a comparison of 1- and 2-year intervals. AJR Am J Roentgenol 1998;170:961–5.

9

Diagnostic Breast Imaging

DANIEL B. KOPANS

The most important advance in breast cancer care in the past 50 years has been the development of x-ray mammography. Not only has the earlier detection of breast cancer resulted in decreased deaths from these malignancies, but by finding breast cancers at a smaller size and earlier stage, mammography screening has permitted the substitution of lumpectomy and radiation therapy rather than the need for removal of the breast.

Mammography screening is the most highly evaluated imaging test in medical history. Although it was shown in the 1970s that x-ray mammography could detect cancers at a smaller size and earlier stage than clinical examination and the usual care, questions were raised as to whether or not this actually saved lives.[1] This resulted in the performance of seven randomized, controlled trials to eliminate any biases that potentially compromised the analysis of survival and historic data. Although many of these trials were too small to provide statistically significant results, two trials (the Health Insurance Plan study and The Swedish Two-County Trial) had sufficient numbers to show statistically significant mortality reduction of 20 to 30% for women invited to be screened.[2] Combining all of the trials in a meta-analysis has shown clear evidence of mortality reduction.[3]

What is often overlooked is the fact that most of the trials measured the results of "invitation to screening." Women were randomly divided and then those allocated to screening were invited to be screened (The National Breast Screening Studies of Canada involved volunteers who were first examined and then allocated to be screens or controls). Analysis of data by "invitation to screening" is required to avoid bias, but it dilutes the results. Women who were randomly allocated to the group invited for screening are counted as having been screened even if they refused the invitation. More importantly, to avoid self-selection bias, women who refused to be screened and died of breast cancer have still been counted as deaths in the screening group. Similarly, women who were allocated to the control group, who had mammograms outside the trial that saved their lives, were still counted as unscreened women. This is necessary to prevent possible biases, but it should be remembered that this results in a probable underestimation of the mortality benefit.

When all of the trials are combined into meta-analyses, the strength of the benefit becomes even greater, showing a decrease in cancer deaths from "invitation to screening," for women of ages 40 to 74 years, of approximately 25%.[3] Despite proof from the most rigorous studies available, numerous controversies have developed over the years. The most intense debate was over whether or not screening benefited women of ages 40 to 49 years. This debate was the result of improper data analysis and medical journal publication bias.[4–6] The data clearly showed that there is a benefit for screening women of ages 40 to 69 years and that the age of 50 years is an arbitrary threshold that has absolutely no biologic or scientific relevance.[7] Analysts should cease suggesting that the data for women of ages 40 to 49 years is less conclusive than for women of ages 50 years and over. If anything, the data are more conclusive among the younger women.

In 2000 and 2002, analysts associated with the Cochrane Collaboration suggested that there was no benefit from screening for women at any age.[8,9] It turned out that they were inexperienced in the analysis of cancer screening data and made numerous mistakes in their analysis. In addition to all of the preceding reviews, subsequent reviews confirmed the benefit of mammography screening.[10–12]

Once a test has been shown in randomized, controlled trials to decrease cancer deaths, it remains to be shown that the benefit will accrue for screening in the general population. Several studies in Sweden, one in the Netherlands, one in Copenhagen, and data in the United States have shown that when screening has been introduced into the general population, the breast cancer death rate falls.[13–17] Since these studies only measured death rate, they were not compromised by the number of cancers detected and the possible misleading effect of finding nonlethal cancers. It is fairly clear that the reduction in breast cancer deaths is a direct result of the introduction of mammography screening.

The success of mammography has been a major triumph. However, the war against breast cancer has clearly not been won. There are still many cancers that are not detected sufficiently early by mammography to result in a cure for all women. This has stimulated efforts to develop additional methods for detecting breast cancers that are not detected early enough, or detected at all, by mammography. Screening using ultrasonography and magnetic resonance imaging (MRI) holds great promise. However, since there are breast cancers that are never lethal, and others that are metastatic long before any test can detect them, ultrasonography and MRI need to be properly validated before they are introduced for general screening, just as mammography was validated.[18] Until proper validation is achieved, ultrasonography and MRI should not be used for screening outside of properly performed clinical trials.

TECHNIQUES FOR SCREENING

In order to reduce the cost of screening and increase its efficacy, screening mammography should be performed in a highly efficient fashion. The Swedish screening trials have shown that separating screening from diagnosis is the most efficient approach. Women attend screening centers, where two views of each breast, the medial lateral oblique (MLO) and craniocaudal (CC) views, are obtained and the patient leaves. The images (film/screen or digital) are then read at a later time in batches. This not only makes image interpretation very efficient and reduces the number of false-positive studies, but it permits double reading, which has been shown to increase the number of cancers detected.[19–20] Every observer, no matter how skilled, will fail to see significant abnormalities that are visible in retrospect.[21] Having a second reader who may see cancers missed by the first reader reduces the chance that cancers will be overlooked. Although double reading is desirable, it is not reimbursed, and requires additional effort. Consequently, it is not the standard of care. Some have found that computer-aided detection may have some value as a substitute for a second human reader, but it is also not the standard of care, although some insurers will reimburse for its use.[22,23] Some radiologists have been urged to read online in order to give the patient her report before she leaves the screening center. Not only does online reading increase the extra views that radiologists order with no increased benefit, but online reading pressures radiologists to read quickly, leading to increased errors.[24] Although the psychology is clearly different, mammography screening is a "Pap" test of the breast. There is no urgency to read the study immediately. Screening interpretation is best performed after the patient has left, as noted above.

When screening mammograms are read in batches, approximately 5 to 10% of women will be recalled for an additional evaluation based on an abnormal screening examination. In our practice, approximately 8% of women are recalled. Among these, additional mammographic evaluation shows that 25% of those recalled (2% of the total number of women screened) are negative and were due to a benign overlap of normal structures. Approximately 1% of the women screened (15% of the 8% who are recalled) are found to have a benign change (cyst or benign calcifications). Another 4% of the women screened (50% of those recalled) are found to have probably benign lesions that are placed in a short-interval follow-up category, whereas approximately

1.5% of women screened (15% of those recalled) are recommended for a biopsy for an indeterminate lesion. Among the 15 of 1,000 women who are screened and recommended for a biopsy, approximately 25% (3 to 4 per 1,000) will be found to have breast cancer. This number is approximate and will vary depending upon the age and prior probability of breast cancer in the population being screened. It will also vary depending on whether the women are being screened for the first time (prevalence screen) or they are being screened repetitively (incidence screens). At the prevalence screen, approximately 8 to 10 cancers can be expected per 1,000 women being screened, whereas an incidence screen is more likely to detect 2 to 4 cancers per 1,000 women screened. The percentage of ductal carcinoma in situ (DCIS) will also vary, but in modern screening programs, approximately 20 to 30% of the cancers detected will be DCIS. The yield of cancers will also vary depending on how frequently the women attend screening. The number of cancers detected by the screen will increase as the time between screens increases, as cancers begin to build up to detectable levels between screens.

Approximately 20% of the cancers detected in a given year will be missed at the screening, but will become clinically evident in the period before the next screen (interval cancers). The longer the time between screens, the greater will be the number of interval cancers.[25,26]

ANALYZING THE MAMMOGRAM

Mammographic interpretation should be systematic. The images should be placed in the same position on view boxes or digital monitors so that previous studies can be compared with the present study and so that the left breast can be compared with the right. The breast is fairly stable from year to year, so that changes for one year to another need to be assessed to determine whether or not additional evaluation is needed. We believe that the present examination should be compared with one that was obtained at least 2 years prior to the present study, if it is available. Changes can be subtle from one year to the next, but they become more apparent when studies of several years apart are compared.

Difference in symmetry can be important. Most asymmetries are due to a normal variation. Large areas of asymmetry that are not new, have no architectural distortion, do not contain suspicious calcifications, are not forming a mass, and are not palpable, are also normal variations and need no further evaluation (Figure 9–1).[27] Asymmetries that could be forming a mass should be evaluated.

On the screening study, the radiologist looks for new densities, new or enlarging masses, areas of architectural distortion, and suspicious clustered calcifications. It has become the standard to recall women with these findings for additional evaluation, as noted below.

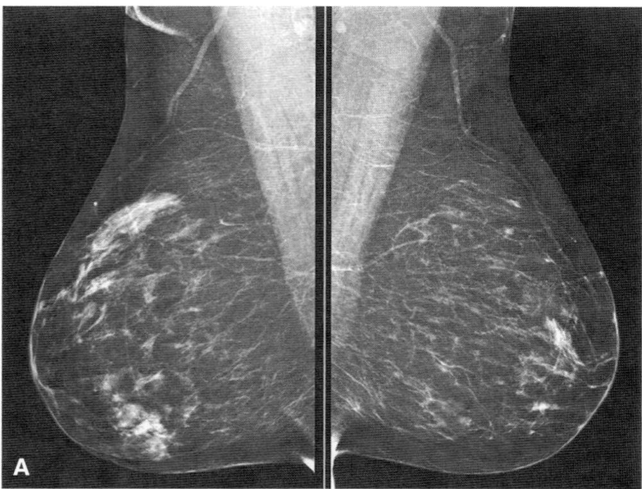

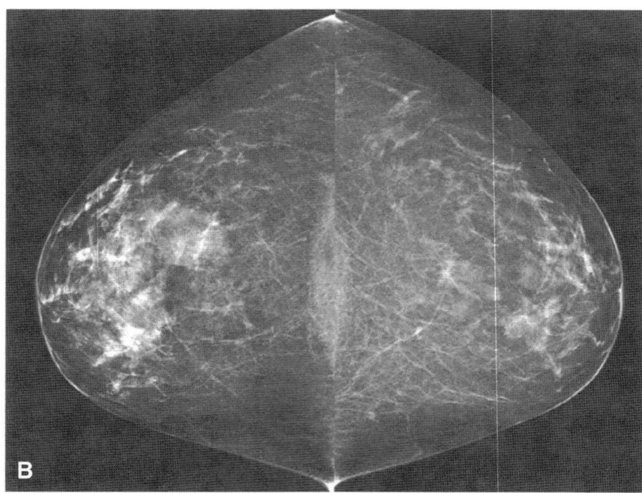

Figure 9–1. *A* and *B*, Benign asymmetric breast tissue in the upper outer quadrant on the right.

If a patient presents with a palpable abnormality, then the standard MLO and CC images are obtained of both breasts, and a spot compression tangential view of the area of clinical concern is then obtained to try to push the area of concern into the subcutaneous fat to better appreciate its shape and margins. If a palpable abnormality is evident, then ultrasound may also be used to evaluate the finding. It is important for the clinician to be sure that the patient can feel the area of concern so that she can identify it for the x-ray technologist and radiologist to facilitate the evaluation of the correct area of concern.

DIAGNOSTIC MAMMOGRAPHY

Screening is the evaluation of healthy women in an effort to detect cancer at a smaller size and earlier stage before it becomes clinically evident, with the goal of saving lives. Diagnostic mammography is the evaluation of areas of concern detected clinically (by the patient or her physician/health care provider), or findings detected at screening mammography, in an effort to determine their significance. Although imaging tests are used every day for the "diagnostic" evaluation of breast problems, the true efficacy of these tests is difficult to establish. Unlike screening, where the bottom line of saving lives can be tested and proven, the use of mammography, ultrasonography, and MRI to assist in managing breast problems is based on predominantly anecdotal information. For example, most would recommend a mammogram for any woman of age 30 years or over, who was being evaluated for a sign or symptom that raised the possibility of cancer. Although it is routinely performed, the rationale is tenuous. It is unclear that this will actually save any lives. The real reason for doing the mammogram in any woman with a sign or symptom of possible breast cancer is actually to "screen" both breasts for occult unsuspected cancer that is not clinically evident.[28] Diagnostic mammography is used every day, but since mammography is not a very accurate way of separating benign from malignant lesions, the efficacy of diagnostic mammography is anecdotal. In fact, the efficacy of diagnostic mammography is tenuous, as shown by the following analysis.

Assume a woman presents with a palpable lump. A mammogram is obtained.

1. Often, the lump is not even visible on the mammogram. If the lesion is clinically suspicious and is not a cyst by ultrasonography or aspiration, then a biopsy is indicated despite the mammographic results. In this case, the mammogram adds little to the diagnosis. Its main use is for screening the rest of the breast and the contralateral breast for unsuspected cancer.
2. The lump may be visible by mammography, but its appearance is indeterminate. If the lesion is clinically suspicious and is not a cyst by ultrasonography or aspiration, then a biopsy is indicated despite the mammographic results. In this case the mammogram adds little to the diagnosis. Its main use is for screening the rest of the breast and the contralateral breast for unsuspected cancer.
3. The lump may have a classic appearance of a benign calcifying fibroadenoma (Figure 9–2), mixed radiographic density hamartoma (Figure 9–3), or fat lesion such as fat necrosis or a lipoma. The appearance of these lesions can be

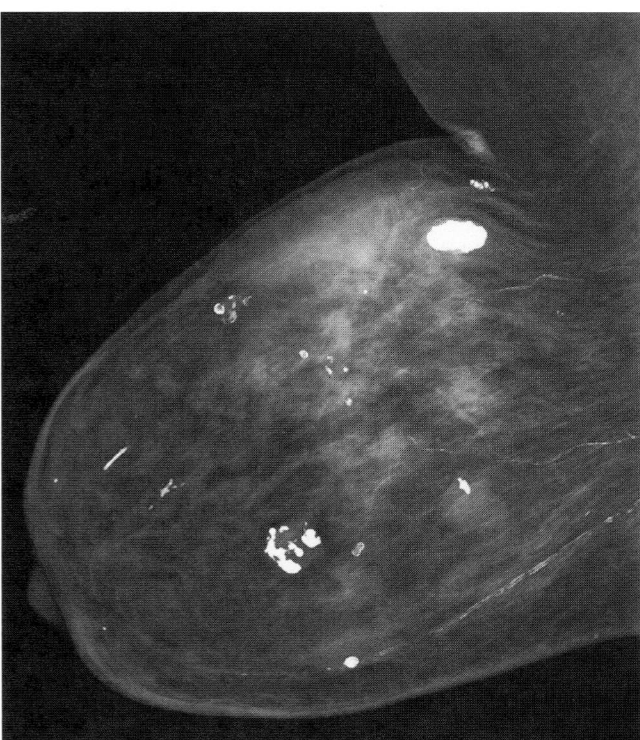

Figure 9–2. Typical "popcorn" shaped benign calcified fibroadenoma.

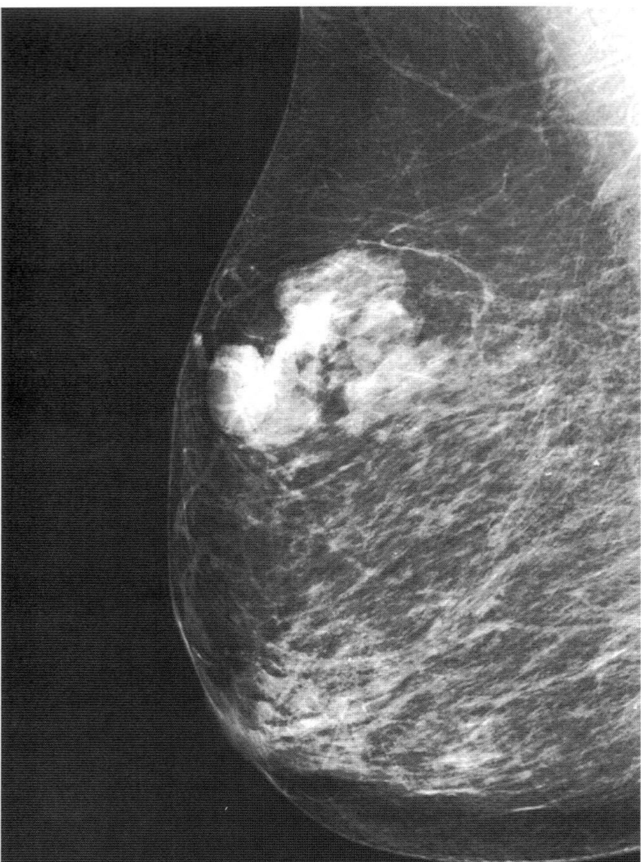

Figure 9–3. Benign hamartomas have mixed x-ray attenuation with fat and fibroglandular tissue mixed together in a lesion defined by a pseudocapsule.

used to avoid a biopsy, so that in these cases, the diagnostic mammogram is very helpful, but these lesions are seen, at most, a few times each year. Once again, the main value from the mammogram is for screening the rest of the breast and the contralateral breast for unsuspected cancer.

4. The lump has a classic appearance of breast cancer (Figure 9–4) and biopsy is clearly required. In this case, the mammographic findings could prevent a delay in diagnosis by making it clear that a biopsy is needed. However, in the author's experience, when the appearance of the palpable lesion is malignant by mammography, it is usually very suspicious on the clinical breast examination and would not be ignored.

The preceding text is an objective summary of mammography as a diagnostic test in the evaluation of women with signs or symptoms of breast cancer. It is clear that the value of mammography is primarily for screening, even in the "symptomatic" individual. By understanding its limitations, mammography can be used appropriately in this setting.

Most diagnostic mammography is used to evaluate lesions that have been detected by mammographic screening and that are not clinically evident. In this context, the diagnostic mammogram is used for the following:

1. To determine whether or not the finding is real, or merely a superimposition of normal structures
2. To evaluate the margins of masses to decide whether or not they can be followed safely or may represent a possible malignancy and need to be biopsied[29]
3. To evaluate the morphology and distribution of calcifications to determine whether or not they need to be biopsied

The radiologist can avoid problems by following the simple rules outlined below. The clinician should understand these rules so that he/she will understand why the radiologist may have recalled the patient for additional evaluation.

1. Find it
2. Is it real?
3. Where is it?
4. What is it?
5. What should be done about it?

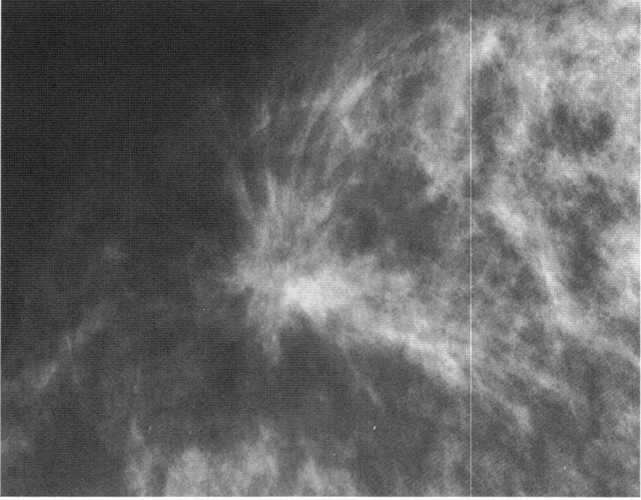

Figure 9–4. Classic invasive ductal carcinoma. Irregular in shape with spiculated margins.

Find it. This of course pertains to screening, where the radiologist is trying to filter out women who may have cancer from the thousands who do not. The first task is to find abnormalities on the screening mammogram that might represent cancer. Many findings on a mammogram are clearly benign, and do not require recall for additional evaluation (Figure 9–5). The experienced radiologist can evaluate these on the screening mammogram and is able to dismiss them as benign without requiring any further evaluation. Other findings are not clearly benign, and may be indications of malignancy. Fortunately, as noted above, most

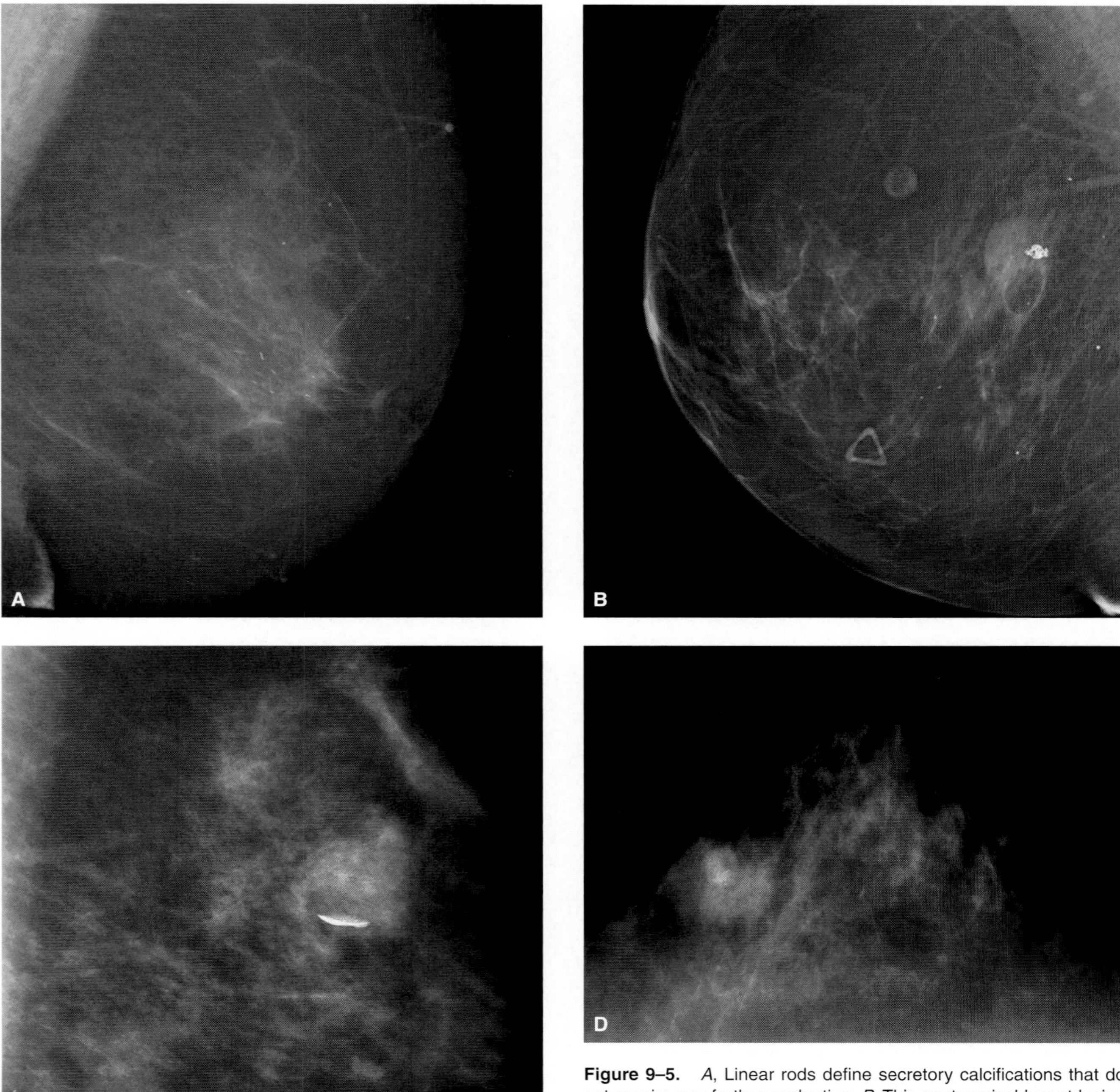

Figure 9–5. *A*, Linear rods define secretory calcifications that do not require any further evaluation. *B*, This postsurgical lucent lesion is a form of fat necrosis that requires no intervention. *C*, Calcifications that layer in the dependent portion of cysts as seen in the horizontal magnification mammogram, and appear (*D*) amorphous on the craniocaudal projection are benign.

women who are recalled from screening have benign findings, but some require a biopsy. Once findings that might represent malignancy are found, the patient is recalled from screening for additional evaluation.

Is it real? Superficially, this seems like a trivial issue. However, it is fairly common to have findings that look like possible cancer on the screening mammograms, but that actually turn out to be a benign superimposition of normal structures on additional evaluation (Figure 9–6). Sickles has called these "summation shadows." In our practice, these account for 25% of the women whom we recall from screen-

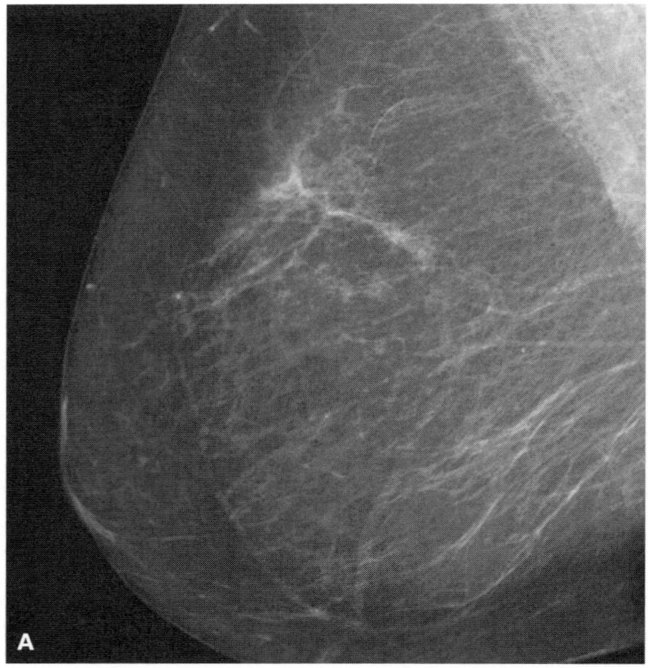

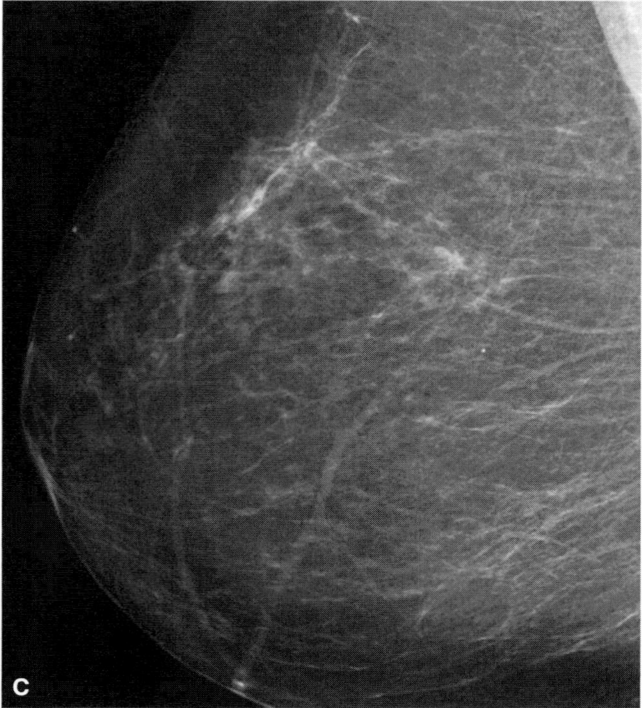

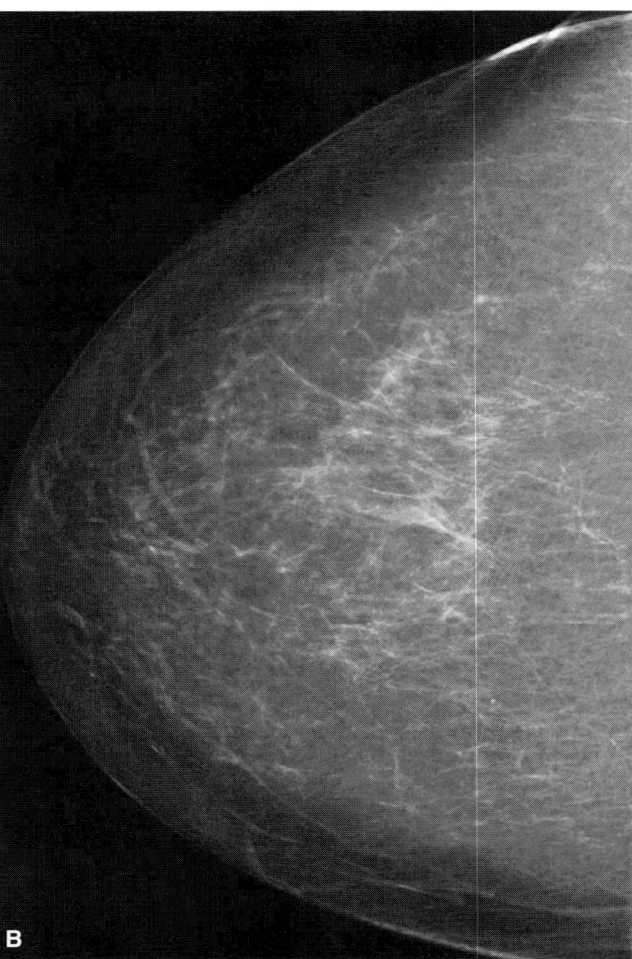

Figure 9–6. *A–C*, The suggested abnormality on the (*A*) MLO projection proved to be nothing more than superimposed normal tissues when additional images were obtained (*B*, *C*).

ing. Usually, all that is needed to confirm or eliminate a real lesion is a few extra mammographic projections.

Although cancer is sometimes only visible in one mammographic projection, but not in another, it is usually evident in two projections. If there is any question as to whether or not a finding seen in only one projection is a real lesion, the rule that we have developed is that the radiologist should return to the projection on which the lesion was seen, and modify that projection slightly to see if the finding persists when the x-rays follow a different path through the breast. If there appears to be a lesion on the MLO projection, then the radiologist should have the technologist obtain a straight lateral image. If the potential lesion is seen on the CC projection, but not the MLO, then rolled views are useful for determining whether or not it is real.[30–32] Spot compression can be used to spread structures apart by bringing greater pressure to bear on a small portion of the breast under suspicion. This can cause overlapping tissues to spread apart and confirm that what was seen at screening was a benign superimposition of normal structures, and the patient can return to annual screening.

Where is it? If it is clear from the screening study, or based on additional imaging, that a true lesion is present, then its location in the breast must be determined. This is needed for accurate evaluation and is, of course, necessary if a biopsy is to be performed. Our rule of thumb is, "Do I know where this lesion is with sufficient accuracy that I could put a biopsy needle or localization needle in it?"

Additional mammographic projections can be used to triangulate a lesion and determine its three-dimensional location.[31–33]

What should be done about it? Once a finding on screening mammography has been verified as being real on diagnostic mammography, and its location has been determined, then the radiologist must decide what should be done to determine whether or not it is a breast cancer.

What additional imaging is used? When the patient is recalled for additional imaging, this usually means a modification of the standard mammographic projections. The extreme lateral portions of the breast may not be included on the standard MLO and CC screening projections, and exaggerated CC views may help identify lesions laterally, or those adjacent to the sternum. Rolled views reorient the structures and can reveal that what was thought to be a finding was actually nothing more than the superimposition of normal structures.

One of the other reasons for recalling a patient for additional imaging is to assess a real finding to determine one of three possibilities:

1. The lesion is of sufficient concern that it needs to be biopsied to establish a firm diagnosis.
2. The lesion is probably benign, but its stability over time would be more reassuring. Lesions that fall in to the category "probably benign, short interval follow-up is recommended" are those that have a < 2% risk of being malignant. In his original study, Sickles placed a variety of lesions in this category and had the patients return at 6 months, 12 months (for follow-up and bilateral screening), 24 months (for follow-up and bilateral screening), and 36 months (for follow-up and bilateral screening).[30] Lesions that were stable over the follow-up period were classified as benign and returned to annual screening. He found that by using his criteria, the lesions that were followed had a < 2% chance of malignancy. Our short-interval follow-up at the Massachusetts General Hospital has been every 6 months for a total of 2 years. If the "probably benign" lesion is unchanged at that time, then the patient is returned to annual screening.
3. The lesion is not real or clearly benign, and no further evaluation is needed.

A recall from screening for additional evaluation allows the radiologist to obtain a better understanding of the finding that was detected at screening. The additional mammograms may establish what appeared to have been a vague density at screening to be a true mass on diagnostic evaluation. Spot compression, or merely changing the standard projection, may allow the radiologist to see the margins of a lesion more clearly. Round, oval, or slightly lobulated masses that have sharply defined "circumscribed" margins are almost always benign (Figure 9–7). Generally, mammography cannot differentiate a cyst from a solid mass, so additional imaging often

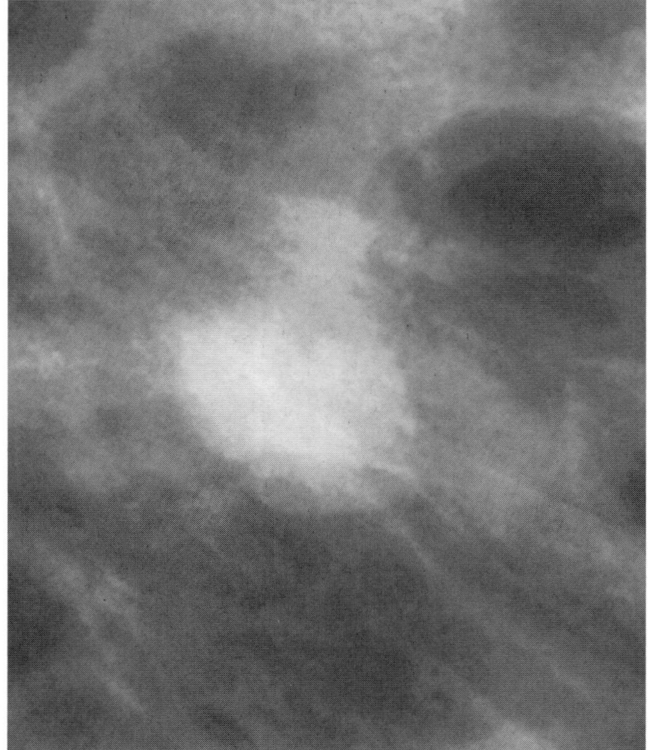

Figure 9–7. Circumscribed mass is a benign fibroadenoma.

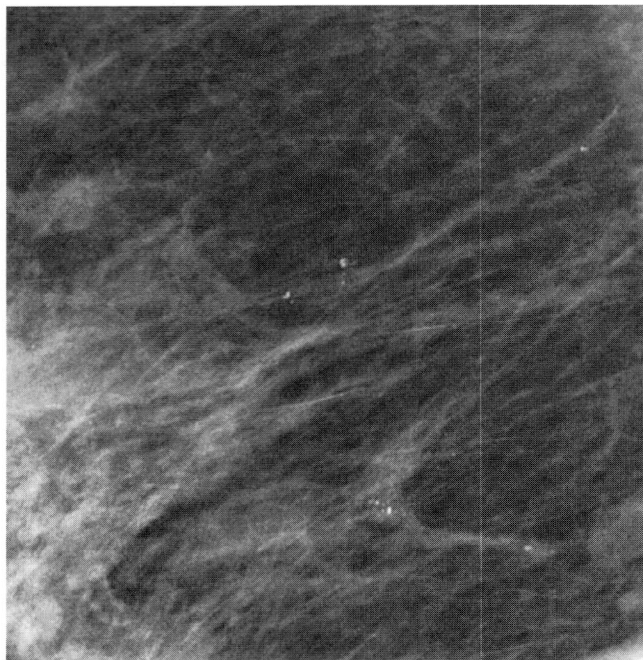

Figure 9–8. Clustered calcifications are indeterminate and should be biopsied. These were due to ductal carcinoma in situ.

includes ultrasonography to make this important distinction. If a lesion is clearly a simple cyst by ultrasonography, then no further intervention is needed. Lesions that have irregular shapes and ill-defined margins are much more likely to be malignant. Additional imaging can help to make a more accurate assessment of a lesion's margins than can be made on the screening images.

If calcifications are detected at screening, then additional imaging is obtained to evaluate the distribution and morphology of the calcifications. Clustering of calcifications is one important criterion that distinguishes malignant from benign calcifications (Figure 9–8). Calcium deposits are extremely common in the breast, and scattered calcifications can be seen in virtually every mammogram (see Figure 9–9). Although nature clearly does not recognize numbers, the definition of a cluster being 5 or more particles in a cubic centimeter of tissue has held up over the years. There are likely cancers that identify themselves by 1, 2, 3, or 4 calcifications, but these are exceedingly rare. As the number of particles in a cluster increases, the likelihood of associated malignancy also increases. Malignant calcifications also tend to be extremely small. Each particle, as seen on a mammogram, if due to a malignancy, tends to be 0.5 mm or less in diameter. Calcifications that are 1 mm or larger are virtually always benign. Calcifications associated with cancer are almost always in intraductal cancer (DCIS). Even when there is an associated invasive component, the calcifications seen by mammography are in the DCIS. Clusters of small calcifications can also be seen in benign entities such as fibrocystic tissue, adenosis, and fibroadenomas. The radiologist often cannot distinguish deposits caused by benign lesions from those caused by cancer, and biopsy is frequently needed to make the diagnosis. Stereotactically guided core needle biopsy with vacuum assistance has become the usual method to make a diagnosis. If an image-guided core biopsy cannot be performed, then accurate needle localization using methods that permit the guide wire to be placed through or alongside the targeted lesion should be used to guide the surgical biopsy.[33] "Freehand" needle localization from the front of the breast, required by some surgeons who do not understand the issues involved in needle localization, is dangerous and inaccurate, and should only be used as a last resort in

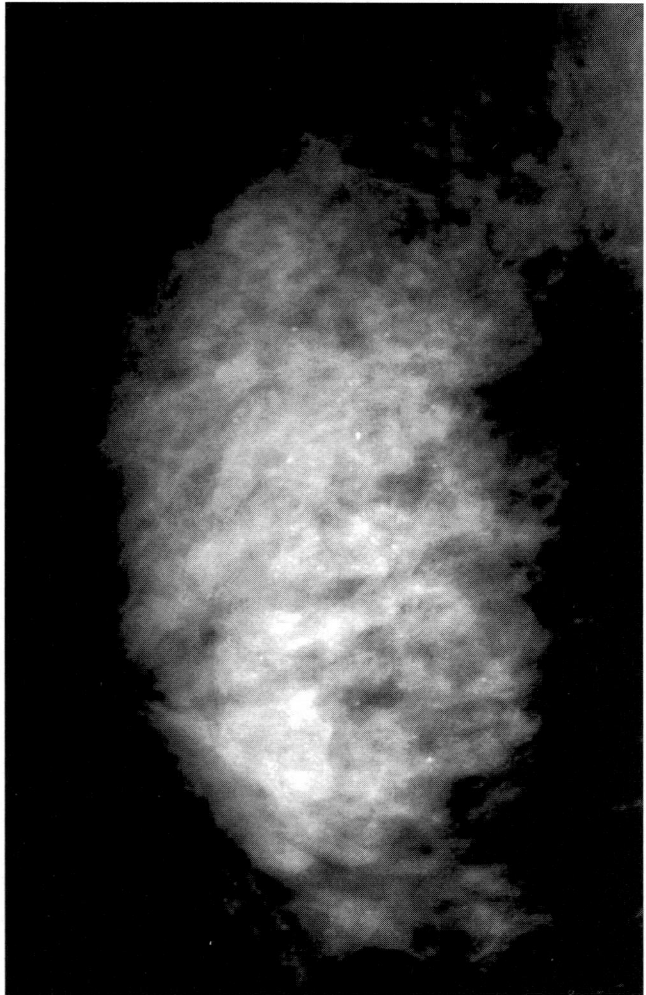

Figure 9–9. Diffusely scattered calcifications are benign.

place of parallel to the chest wall grid localization. If all of the calcifications are removed at core biopsy, then a clip should be placed at the site that had contained the calcifications, in case a rebiopsy or surgical excision is needed. When all types of clustered calcifications are counted, only about 25% of biopsied clusters prove to be associated with malignancy.

Other distributions of calcification that raise concern are those that form linear branching deposits (Figure 9–10). DCIS can fill ducts spreading up and down branches. When tumor cells die, they can become calcified, and the calcifications can form in the ducts, producing a linear distribution. These are often quite characteristic. When there is DCIS throughout a segment of breast tissue, the distribution of calcifications can be "segmental" (Figure 9–11). Calcifications that are distributed over a large portion of the breast are called "regional," and are rarely associated with malignancy. Calcifications that are diffusely scattered throughout the breast are almost always due to a benign process.

Figure 9–10. Fine linear branching calcifications are virtually always due to ductal carcinoma in situ.

The morphology of the particles making up clusters of calcifications is important. Benign calcifications tend to be round and regular (Figure 9–12), whereas pleomorphic calcifications that vary in size are more likely to be due to cancer (Figure 9–13). In addition to assessing the distribution of calcifications, the radiologist evaluates their morphology, trying to determine how best to manage them. One

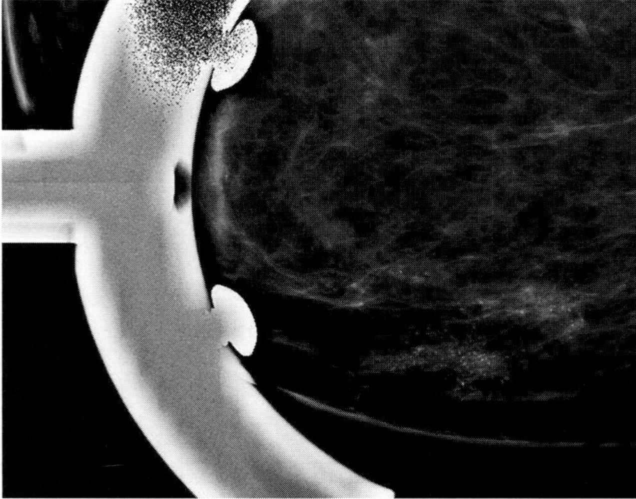

Figure 9–11. Calcifications whose distribution appears to define a breast segment should raise suspicion. These were due to ductal carcinoma in situ.

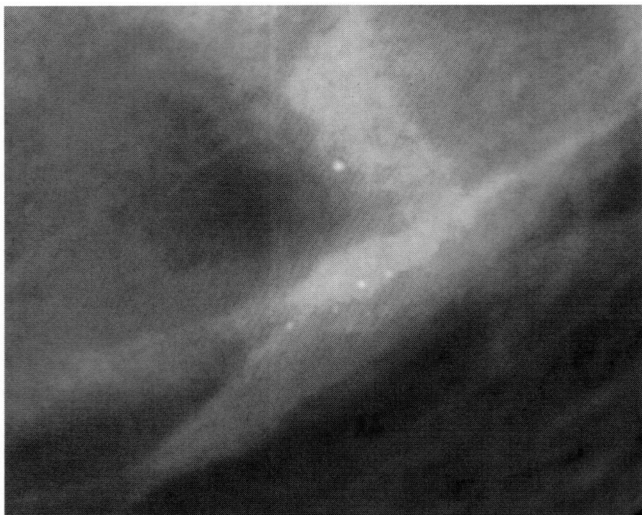

Figure 9–12. Round and regular calcifications are almost always due to a benign process.

of the reasons to recall a patient from screening for additional evaluation is to obtain magnification mammograms. Magnification mammography actually provides higher spatial resolution and a better signal-to-noise ratio. This provides greater clarity to the image than contact images and allows the radiologist to better assess the significance of calcifications. Magnification mammography is achieved by elevating the breast away from the imaging detector and closer to the focal spot of the x-ray device. Because the x-ray beam is divergent, this spreads the shadow of the structures over a larger area of the detector, improving the signal-to-noise ratio and providing higher spatial resolution. The morphologic details of calcifications are better appreciated on magnification mammograms. For example, cancer does not form calcifications with radiolucent centers. Therefore, if calcifications can be shown to have lucent centers, then malignancy is excluded.

One of the important criteria used to differentiate benign from malignant calcifications is the demonstration of calcifications settling in the dependent portions of small cysts. This "milk of calcium" represents small deposits that the radiologist can characterize as benign by the fact that that they form a cup-shaped layer in the dependent portion of cysts, conforming to the inner wall of the cyst, as seen in the horizontal beam lateral magnification mammogram (see Figure 9–5C). When analyzing calcifications, a magnification CC projection and a magnification horizontal beam lateral projection provide the best information.

Magnification mammography is also used to evaluate the morphology of masses. The shape and margin of the mass help to determine its significance. If the margins of a round, oval, or smoothly lobulated mass are sharply defined, then the mass is very unlikely to be malignant (Figure 9–14). The margins of a mass are better seen using magnification mammography.

Spot compression uses a small compression paddle to press on an area of the breast where a lesion is suspected. This can be done based on mammographic suspicions, or a clinical suspicion. Using the same compression force over a smaller area

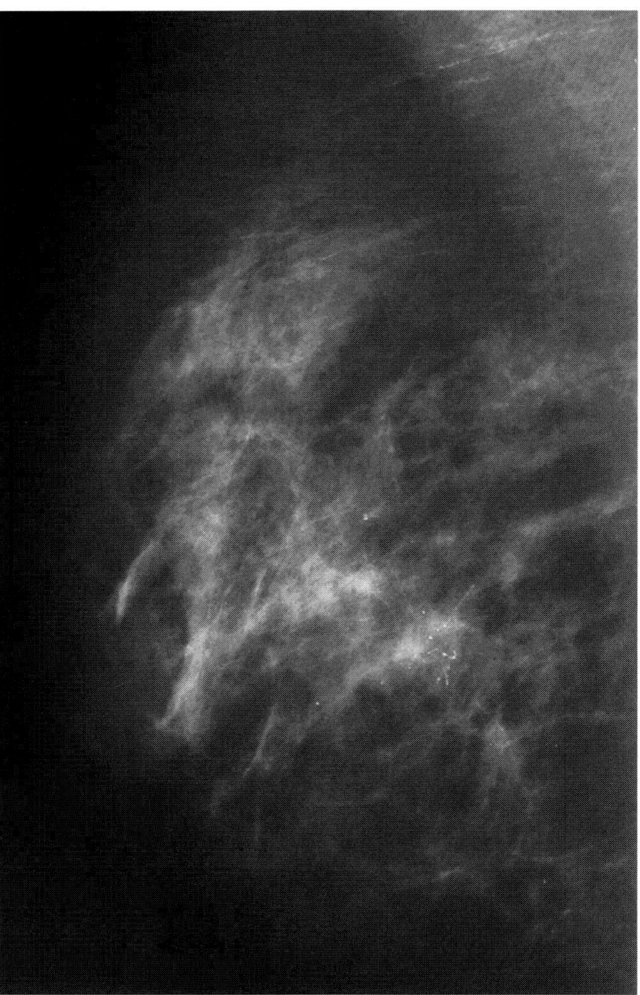

Figure 9–13. Pleomorphic calcifications are often associated with ductal carcinoma in situ with or without invasion.

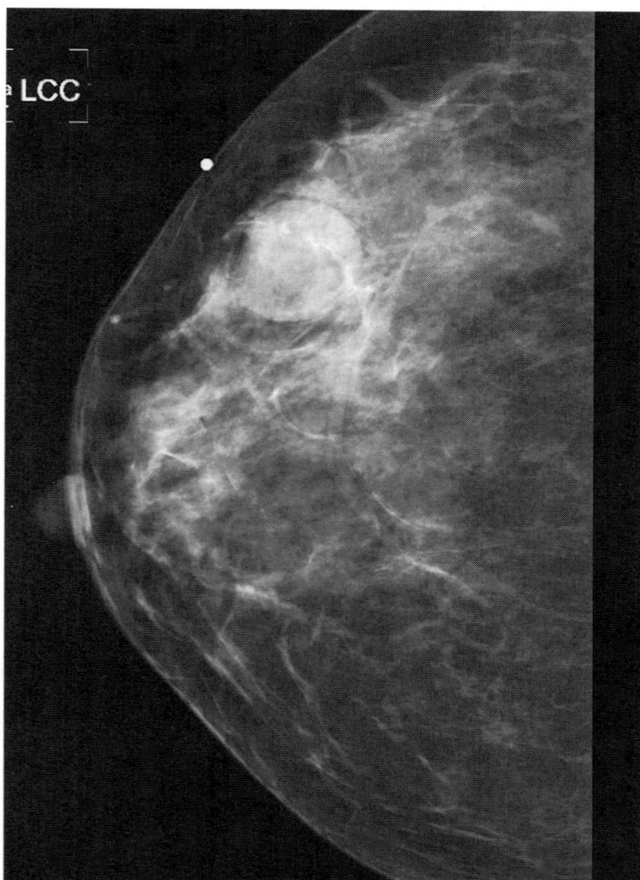

Figure 9–14. Circumscribed benign lesion proved to be a cyst.

brings greater pressure to bear on the tissues. Spot compression can be used to spread overlying structures that can obscure the detail of a mass or calcifications. Spot compression of a palpable abnormality can be used to push it into the subcutaneous fat and provide a better view of its margins. The technique is frequently used with magnification to improve the clarity with which a possible lesion can be seen.

When Should Ultrasonography be Used to Evaluate the Breast?

Mammography does not find all cancers, and the cancers that are found by mammography are not all found sufficiently early to result in a cure. Efforts have been made to find other imaging tests that can find the cancers that are missed by mammography. Years ago, ultrasonography was unable to find cancers that were occult to mammography, but with the marked improvements in technology that have taken place over the past 20 years, there are cancers that can be found by ultrasonography alone.[34] Unfortunately, the studies that have been published to date were not blinded, so the exact percentage of cancers that can be detected only by ultrasound is not known.[35–38] Perhaps of greater importance is the fact that even if ultrasonography can detect cancers missed by mammography, there are no data to know whether or not this results in lives saved. The same questions that were raised with regard to mammography screening need to be addressed with regard to ultrasonography screening.[39] Until a true benefit has been shown, there is potential to provide only harm, since false-positive ultrasonography studies are common and the potential for unnecessary treatment is high. Until there is clear proof of a benefit, ultrasonography should not be used to screen for breast cancer.

Ultrasonography, however, is extremely useful in helping to deal with breast problems. When a round, oval, or lobulated lesion is detected by mammography, ultrasonography can quickly dispel concern about its significance by showing that it is a simple cyst (Figure 9–15). If a lesion is a simple cyst by ultrasonography, then there is no need for follow-up or intervention. The only reason to aspirate a cyst is if there is any concern that it might not be a simple

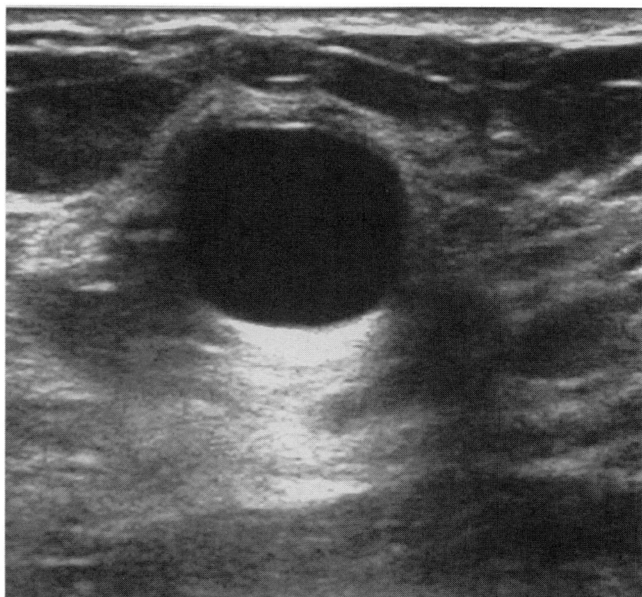

Figure 9–15. Ultrasound shows a round, sharply defined lesion with no internal echoes and good through transmission of sound. This is a simple cyst and requires no further intervention.

cyst, or if it is causing symptoms that bother the patient (pain or a lump). The same is true for palpable lumps. If it is a simple cyst by ultrasonography, then no further intervention is needed.

Since the first use of breast ultrasonography, investigators have tried to use the test to differentiate benign from malignant lesions to avoid biopsies. The most widely cited paper by Stavros and colleagues grouped criteria that had been unsuccessful at differentiating lesions in the past and claimed that they were highly accurate in differentiating benign from malignant lesions using ultrasonography. The problem is that they had an undefined population. If a large number of women in their twenties were included in the study, then the prior probability of cancer would be very low and the statistics would be meaningless. Furthermore, they included women who had obvious cancers by mammography. The fact that ultrasonography showed irregularly shaped spiculated masses had no differential significance, and again contaminated the conclusions. The real problem is the well-defined round, oval, or lobulated masses that are usually benign, but on occasion can be a well-defined invasive ductal carcinoma (usually not otherwise specified).[40] Although the odds are in favor of a circumscribed lesion that is round, oval, or smoothly lobulated, with a homogeneous internal echo texture and a well-defined margin, as being benign (Figure 9–16), the occasional cancer can have this appearance. All solid masses should be biopsied.

In fact, the ability to monitor and guide core biopsies of breast lesions in real time is one of the major advantages of breast ultrasonography. Transducers permit the visualization of biopsy needles, and lesions can be sampled under ultrasound guidance with minimum of trauma to the patient and with a fairly high degree of accuracy. Ultrasound-guided core needle biopsy has become the first-line biopsy technique for both nonpalpable as well as palpable breast masses.

One of the controversies that has recently evolved is the interpretation of imaging-guided biopsies. Several retrospective studies have suggested that if an imaging-guided core needle biopsy reveals lobular neoplasia (atypical lobular hyperplasia or lobular carcinoma in situ) as the worst lesion at pathology, then surgical excision should be undertaken since, in these studies, excision reveals breast cancer in a fairly high percentage of women.[41] The problem is that these studies have all been retrospective, and the reasons that the women were re-excised were not provided. For example, if a woman had a spiculated lesion and the core biopsy showed that the worst pathology was atypical lobular hyperplasia (ALH) or lobular carcinoma in situ (LCIS), then the biopsy would be clearly discordant and excision would, not surprisingly, reveal a breast cancer. Retrospective reviews do not take this into account. In fact, it may not be the LCIS or ALH that is the issue. We have noted for years, but never made much out of the fact that, periodically, when we did needle localizations to biopsy calcifications, the pathologist would inform us that the calcifications were in benign tissue, but there was a cancer in the adjacent tissue. We attributed this to coincidence, but a large number of the women who were rebiopsied following a core biopsy, in the cases cited above, had been biopsied for calcifications. These relationships need to be worked out in careful prospective study. Until the relationships are clear, I would only recommend excision for discordance and not as a routine when ALH or LCIS are found at core biopsy.

Guide Placement

Real-time ultrasound monitoring is also used to position wires to guide the surgeon for the removal of lesions in the following circumstances:

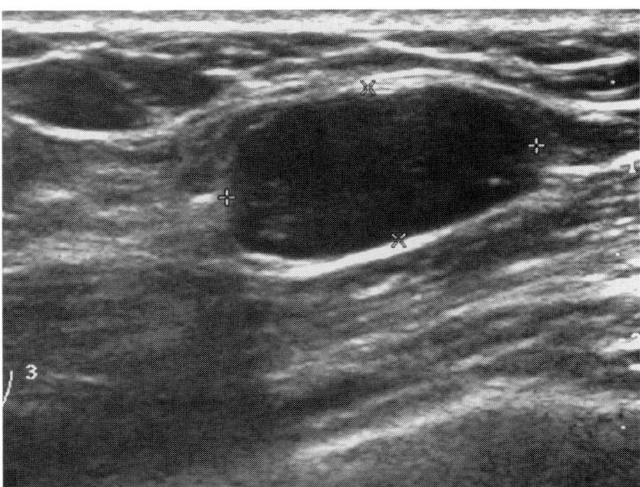

Figure 9–16. Fibroadenomas by ultrasound usually are oval in shape with sharply defined margins and a uniform internal echotexture. Some believe that if these characteristics are present along with a fine echogenic border that a biopsy is not needed.

1. A lesion is not amenable to imaging-guided needle biopsy.
2. The core biopsy was not concordant with the imaging analysis.
3. The core biopsy revealed atypical ductal hyperplasia, and excision is undertaken since many of these will be converted to DCIS with more tissue.
4. The lesion is a known malignancy and the surgeon needs guidance to remove it.

Magnetic Resonance and Breast Evaluation

The same issues that were raised above with regard to ultrasonography screening apply to the use of MRI for breast cancer screening as well. At least one study was properly conducted in a blinded fashion and it showed that cancers that were not detected by mammography could be detected in "high-risk" women.[42] This is an important observation, but it does not answer the key question: Does finding cancers with MRI reduce the death rate from breast cancer? Unfortunately, the only way to determine whether or not screening with MRI can save lives is in the same way that it had to be shown for mammography: through the use of randomized, controlled trials. Unless surrogate end points are discovered that exactly predict breast cancer deaths, there is no way to avoid the randomized, controlled trial. Those who advocate using MRI to screen "high-risk" women are overlooking the fact that MRI can likely detect cancers that are missed by mammography in women who are not at elevated risk. The issue needs to be addressed, because there are no data to define where "high risk" begins, and there are no data to conclude that women cannot all benefit from MRI screening.

MRI for breast evaluation should be used with caution. It is an extremely powerful test, but it can cause more problems than it solves. There are no agreed upon pulse sequences and methods of evaluating the breast with MRI, so it is difficult to transfer the results obtained by one group to be used by others. The literature would support the use of breast MRI in the following circumstances:

1. *Implant evaluation*. Most agree that MRI is useful and probably the best way to evaluate the integrity of silicone gel implants. Collapse of the silicone rubber envelope into the silicon is clearly evident by MRI and an accurate indication of intracapsular rupture.[43] Since it has been established that ruptured implants are not likely the cause of systemic problems, the importance of implant evaluation has diminished, but if a rupture is questioned, then MRI is the best way to evaluate implant integrity.[44]
2. *Search for a primary breast cancer*. Usually, when a woman develops metastatic breast cancer, the location of her primary has already been well established. Periodically, a woman will present with metastatic disease with an unknown primary. When axillary adenopathy is the presenting lesion, breast cancer is likely. Occasionally, the primary is palpable in the breast, or is evident by mammography, but sometimes the primary cannot be detected. In this situation, MRI of the breast can often show the lesion, so conservative therapy can be employed and the breast can be conserved.[45]
3. *Monitoring neoadjuvant chemotherapy*. Neoadjuvant chemotherapy is being used with increasing frequency and with evolving indications. A number of studies have shown that MRI is probably the most accurate imaging test for monitoring these women, in terms of reflecting what is ultimately found at pathology.[46,47] Clips should be placed in the lesion prior to the institution of therapy, so that the previous center of the lesion can be identified, should the therapy result in a complete elimination of any visible cancer. A clip that causes a small signal void on MRI should be used so that its location can be determined, but will not obscure large volumes of tissue on MRI.
4. *Problem solving*. This is a valuable role for MRI, but one that is difficult to prove and quantify. It should be used sparingly. MRI is highly sensitive to the detection of breast cancer, but its specificity is low and many lesions that "light up" on MRI are not cancer. Even normal hormone fluctuations of the menstrual cycle can cause normal tissues to mimic the enhancement patterns of cancer. In our experience, premenopausal women should, whenever possible, be scanned between days 3 to 11. Others suggest that the sec-

ond week of the cycle is the safest with regard to the hyperemia that can confound MR imaging with gadolinium.[48] There can be a large number of false positives with MRI, and anyone using breast MRI consistently should develop the ability to biopsy breast lesions under MR guidance.

MRI is useful to locate a suspicious mammographic lesion that cannot be located by mammography or ultrasonography. MRI may determine its three-dimensional location (Figure 9–17).

5. *Determining the extent of a known cancer*. This is a highly controversial use of breast MRI. In the early years of conservation therapy, women who had a lumpectomy and irradiation had a fairly high recurrence rate of 1 to 2 percent per year, with up to 20% recurring in the breast at 10 years. These rates were measured at a time when little attention was being paid to margin status and radiation techniques. More recently, several studies have shown that MRI can find unsuspected foci of cancer elsewhere in the breast of women with known malignancy and some have suggested this may account for a portion of local recurrences.[49–51] By finding these lesions, some clinicians expect that their recurrence rates will go down because they convert many of these women to mastectomy. The problem with this approach is that more modern data suggest that with attention to clear margins at surgery, and thoughtful and complete irradiation, the recurrence rates have dropped dramatically. At the Massachusetts General Hospital, with clear margins at excision, the recurrence rates are down to <2% at 10 years (unpublished data). This has been achieved, apparently, without knowing about the additional foci of cancer, and yet they do not seem to be causing recurrences. A randomized, controlled trial needs to be performed to determine whether the MRI localization of additional foci of cancer decreases the risk of local recurrence or simply decreases the rate of breast conservation. The last 40 years were spent trying to reduce the rate of mastectomy. It would be a shame to increase it again without evidence that shows that the MRI revelation of other tumor foci is important information.
6. *MRI and partial breast irradiation*. The above discussion takes on a different meaning with regard to the more recent efforts to limit the amount of radiation needed to conservatively treat the breast. Partial breast irradiation will do just that; only a portion of the breast around the tumor will be irradiated. In this situation, MRI may be extremely important in defining the extent of cancer, since unsuspected tumor outside the treatment field will likely result in recurrence.

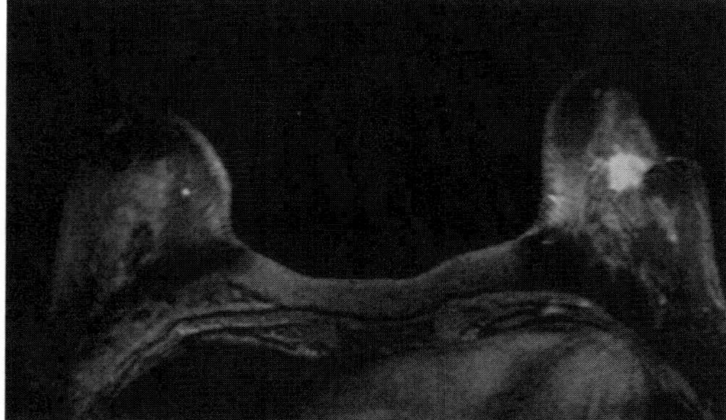

Figure 9–17. MRI can help define the three-dimensional location of a lesion as with the cancer seen here in the left breast that could not be triangulated by mammography and ultrasound but seen clearly on MRI.

Which Lesions Should be Biopsied?

There is no universal agreement over which lesions seen by mammography should be biopsied. The radiologist must determine the likelihood of malignancy. If it is sufficiently high, then most would recommend a biopsy. Based on Sickles' work, in which lesions with a 2% or lower risk of cancer can be safely followed, a risk of > 2% seems to be the threshold that most radiologists probably use, although since many lesions have a much higher risk, the overall yield of cancers found at mammography is much higher. A nonpalpable lesion that is biopsied has a 25 to 30% chance of being cancer. The percentage is much higher when the lesion has classic cancer changes such as an irregular shape with spiculated margins (Figure 9–18), or pleomorphic calcifications in a fine linear branching pattern (Figure 9–19). Nonspecific clustered calcifications and round, oval, or smoothly lobulated masses have a lower likelihood of malignancy.

Certainly, solid masses with ill-defined or spiculated margins should be biopsied. A solitary group

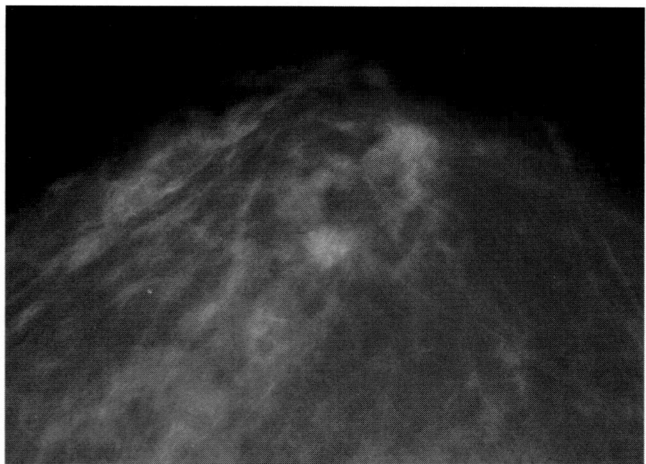

Figure 9–18. Classic spiculated cancer.

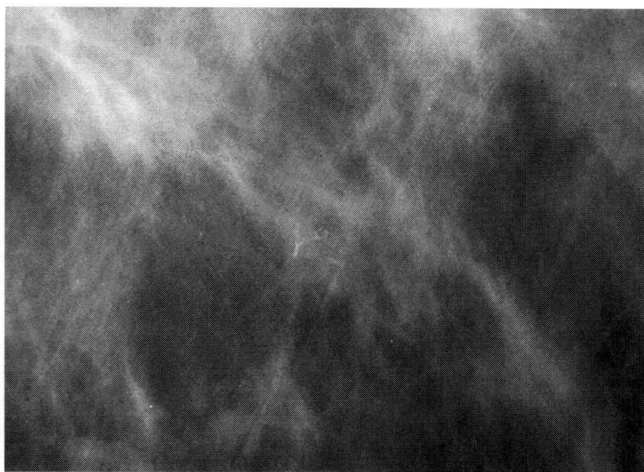

Figure 9–19. Calcifications of high-grade DCIS.

of clustered, pleomorphic, and heterogeneous calcifications (5 or more in a cubic centimeter of tissue) should be biopsied. Mammographic interpretation follows receiver operating characteristic (ROC) curves.[52,53] These link true positives and false positives. Assuming that radiologists understand the criteria for possible malignancy, they will operate on the same ROC curve. This means that the only way they can increase their true-positive rate is to increase their false-positive calls, and the only way to reduce false positives is to increase the false negatives (allow borderline lesions through and miss some cancers). In a review by Sickles and colleagues, the yield of cancers referred for diagnostic evaluation from screening and referred on for biopsy was demonstrated to be between 30 and 35%.[54]

The Breast Imaging Reporting and Data System of The American College of Radiology

The American College of Radiology (ACR) understands that the clear communication of mammography results to the clinician is critical, to reduce the chance that miscommunication delays the care of a patient. Consequently the ACR, with input from the American College of Surgeons, the American Medical Association, and other organizations developed the Breast Imaging Reporting and Data System (BIRADS). This provides an organization for the mammography report, a dictionary of terminology that should be used (the BIRADS lexicon), and final assessment categories. The latter consist of seven assessment categories that should be used to succinctly summarize the mammography findings. Because of the importance of clear communication, the US Food and Drug Administration, having received a mandate from Congress under the Mammography Quality Standards Act, requires that all mammography reports have a final summary statement that is based on the BIRADS categories listed below. BIRADS has proven to be quite successful and the ACR is developing a similar reporting system for breast ultrasonography as well as for breast MRI.

The mammography report should provide several facts. In addition to noting any comparison to previous studies, BIRADS requires that the report include a statement of the general breast tissue type with four categories that are similar to those that were originally described by Wolfe[55]:

1. "The breast is almost entirely fat (< 25% fibroglandular)."
2. "There are scattered fibroglandular tissue (approximately 25 to 50% fibroglandular)."
3. "The breast tissue is heterogeneously dense, which could obscure detection of small masses (approximately 51 to 75% fibroglandular)."
4. "The breast tissue is extremely dense. This may lower the sensitivity of mammography (> 75% fibroglandular)."

If an implant is present, then it should be stated in the report.[56]

These descriptions of tissue patterns are provided as an indication of the likely sensitivity of the test, acknowledging that mammography is less sensitive in the dense breast and alerting the referring physician as to the type of breast being evaluated.[57,58]

The radiologist should then describe significant findings and provide an impression.

Once significant findings have been described, a final assessment that summarizes the findings and classifies the study as 1 of 6 possible decision categories should be provided.

0. *Need additional imaging evaluation*. The patient must be recalled for additional evaluation (eg, magnification mammography, rolled views, ultrasonography) before a final assessment can be rendered. This category actually means that the study is incomplete until additional imaging is completed and a final assessment can be rendered.
1. *Negative*. The vast majority of screening mammograms are in this category. There is nothing on the mammogram to suggest the presence of malignancy.
2. *Benign finding(s)*. This category is used when a benign finding that the observer wishes to report appears on the mammogram, but the finding has no likelihood of malignancy and there is no need for further evaluation. This might include a fat-containing lesion, such as a lipoma or an oil cyst, or calcifications, such as secretory or vascular, that might be confusing to the untrained observer or have some implications for the management of a palpable finding.
3. *Probably benign—short-interval follow-up suggested*. This category should only be used for a finding whose characteristics suggest that it is almost certainly benign, but because a very small possibility exists (2% or less) that it is a malignant tumor, and it is thought to be prudent to follow up at a shorter interval to assess its stability. Approaches to such lesions have been described.[59,60] One of the common lesions that fits into this category is the solitary circumscribed mass. Sickles, who has done the most work in this area, has shown that if a mass found on a prevalence (first) mammogram is round, oval, or lobulated and has well-defined margins over 75% of its surface in two magnification projections, then it can be safely followed at short interval. As noted earlier, his follow-up consisted of a mammogram at 6 months and then 3 additional years of annual mammograms, not just as screening mammograms but as highly recommended annual follow-up mammograms. Our own short-interval follow-up is more intensive, with mammography every 6 months but for a total of 2 years (stability of a cancer for more than two years is extremely rare). The principle behind short-interval follow-up is the fact that if a lesion has a low probability of cancer based on its morphology, and given that the probability of cancer being stable over time is also very low, then the probability of a lesion with low-probability morphology as well as stability being a cancer is extremely low (the probabilities are multiplicative). Follow-up is done to try to detect the few cancers that have benign morphology, as early as possible, while trying to avoid unnecessary traumatic intervention.
4. *Suspicious abnormality—biopsy should be considered*. Most impalpable lesions that come to biopsy fall into this category. The range of "suspicious" is determined by the interpreter. BIRADS now suggests that the interpreter might wish to divide this category into 3 subcategories (A, B, and C) to better alert the referring physician as to the level of concern.
   i. Category 4A indicates a lesion that the radiologist feels should be biopsied, but believes that the probability of malignancy is low. An example of this is a solid circumscribed mass where the core biopsy is expected to show a fibroadenoma, but the radiologist wishes to exclude a less common, circumscribed malignancy or phyllodes tumor.
   ii. Category 4B indicates a lesion of intermediate suspicion. An example of this might be a cluster of calcifications whose shapes are slightly irregular and could well be due to DCIS, but are most likely to be due to fibrocystic tissue.
   iii. Category 4C indicates a lesion of concern, but one that does not have the classic morphology of a malignancy.

5. *Highly suggestive of malignancy—appropriate action should be taken.* Although mammography cannot provide histologic diagnoses, there are many lesions whose morphology is so characteristic that the diagnosis of malignancy is almost certain. An irregular spiculated mass, for example, is virtually always a cancer. It goes without saying that a lesion in this category requires intervention.
6. *Known biopsy; proven malignancy—appropriate action should be taken.* This simply means that there is evidence of a known cancer on the mammogram. For example, patients who are being followed while on neoadjuvant chemotherapy, whose cancer is not removed from the breast during the treatment, would fall into this category. The statement will be modified in the next iteration of BIRADS to read something like, "There is evidence of the known cancer. There is no evidence of new or additional disease."

BIRADS also explains how radiologists should be monitoring their practices. It is important to determine, among other facts,

1. how many women are being screened,
2. how many women are being called back from screening for additional imaging,
3. how many women are being advised to have a biopsy,
4. how many women have a biopsy,
5. what percentage of the above result in cancer being detected, and
6. what the size and stage distribution are of the cancers being diagnosed.

There are no absolute numbers that can be assigned to each of these categories as being ideal, since the prior probability and kinds of cancers being detected will vary with the population being screened. The following are some ranges that make reasonable targets for mammography screening programs in which women ages 40 years and over are being screened.

1. Approximately 6 to 8% of women are recalled for additional evaluation.
2. Approximately 1 to 2% of women screened will be advised to have a biopsy.
3. Approximately 25% of the women who have a biopsy will be diagnosed with breast cancer
4. Ideally, 30 to 50% of the invasive cancers detected by screening will be 1 cm or smaller.
5. Twenty to 30% of the cancers will be DCIS.
6. Fewer than 20% of women with invasive cancer will have positive axillary lymph nodes.

THE FUTURE

X-ray mammography is the only test that has been shown in properly performed randomized, controlled trials to lower the death rate for breast cancer. It is likely that further decreases in the death rate will be achieved by screening with ultrasonography, and even more likely with MRI, but this needs to be proved. The development of digital detectors to replace film has provided the opportunity to make significant improvements in x-ray mammography. We have developed the Digital Breast Tomosynthesis (DBT). DBT is performed by positioning the breast as for an ordinary mammogram. The x-ray tube is then moved through an arc above the breast, and in our prototype system, 11 images are made, each from a different point on the arc, and each one at a fraction of a mammographic dose. From these 11 images, slices thorough the breast can be "synthesized" at 1 mm separation, with the in-plane resolution being the same as the digital detector.[61] DBT eliminates superimposed normal tissue structures in the breast so that cancers become more conspicuous (Figure 9–20) and benign lesions are more easily determined to be benign. By eliminating overlapping structures, 25% of women who would usually be called back because superimposed structures falsely suggested a lesion, will not be called back. DBT will increase the sensitivity and specificity of mammography screening.

CONCLUSION

Although it has taken years to prove, in countries where it has been introduced, mammography screening has had a major impact on the death rate from breast cancer. It has certainly not eliminated deaths from breast malignancy, but it has helped to reduce the rate of death for the first time in 50 years. It is

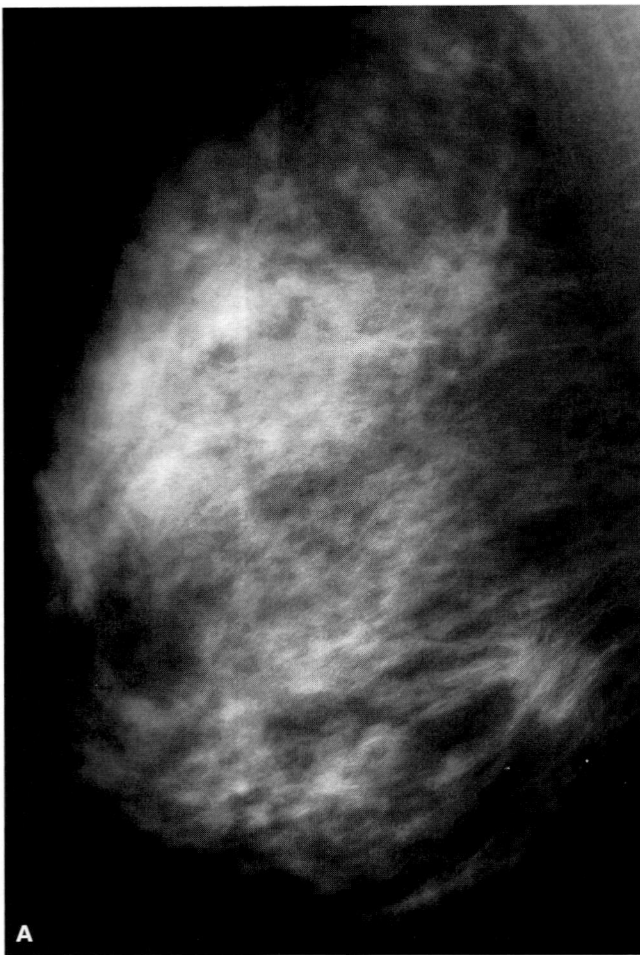

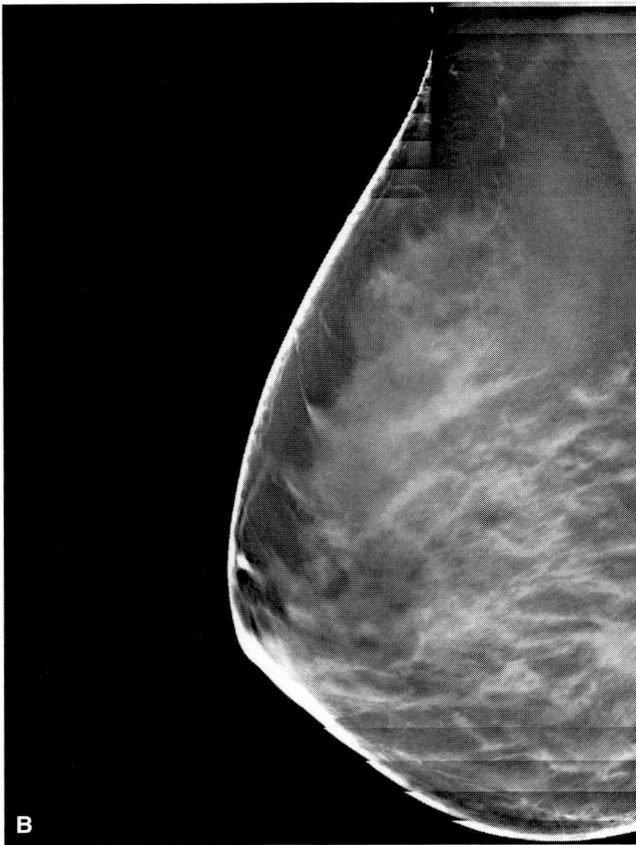

Figure 9–20. *A,* Standard 2D projection image from a film/screen mammogram. *B,* A slice from the DBT study that has eliminated the superimposition of normal tissues so that the lesion is more easily seen on DBT at the lower back portion of the breast.

my hope that our understanding of cancer and normal tissues at the molecular level will ultimatelypermit us to prevent or universally cure breast malignancies. However, until the breakthroughs are made, early detection offers hope to many, and improved early detection can expand the number of women who benefit from it. Laboratory research is critical, but incremental improvements are made by clinical research and development.

REFERENCES

1. Baker LH. Breast Cancer Detection Demonstration Project: five-year summary report. CA Cancer J Clin 1982;32: 194–225.
2. Shapiro S. Screening: assessment of current studies. Cancer 1994;74:231–8.
3. Duffy SW, Tabar L, Smith RA. The Mammographic Screening Trials: commentary on the recent work by Olsen and Gotzsche. CA Cancer J Clin 2002;52:68–71.
4. Kopans DB, Feig SA. The Canadian National Breast Screening Study: a critical review. AJR Am J Roentgenol 1993; 161:755–60.
5. Kopans DB, Halpern E, Hulka CA. Statistical power in breast cancer screening trials and mortality reduction among women 40–49 with particular emphasis on the National Breast Screening Study of Canada. Cancer 1994;74: 1196–203.
6. Kopans DB. The breast cancer screening controversy: lessons to be learned. J Surg Oncol 1998;67:143–50.
7. Kopans DB. Bias in the medical journals: informed decision making—women and their physicians should be informed that the age of 50 is arbitrary and has no demonstrated influence on breast cancer screening. AJR Am J Roentgenol. [In press]
8. Gotzsche PC, Olsen O. Is screening for breast cancer with mammography justifiable? Lancet 2000;355:129–34.
9. Olsen O, Gotzsche PC. Cochrane review on screening for breast cancer with mammography. Lancet 2001;358: 1340–42.
10. European Institute of Oncology. Global summit on mammographic screening. 2002 June 3–5. Milan, Italy.
11. Knottnerus JA. Report to the Minister of Health, Welfare,

and Sport. The benefit of population screening for breast cancer with mammography. Health Council of the Netherlands. P.O. Box 16052 NL-2500 BB The Hague. Publication No. 2002/03E.

12. Kopans DB. The most recent breast cancer screening controversy about whether mammographic screening benefits women at any age: nonsense and nonscience. AJR Am J Roentgenol 2003;180:21–6.
13. Tabar L, Vitak B, Tony HH, et al. Beyond randomized controlled trials: organized mammographic screening substantially reduces breast carcinoma mortality. Cancer 2001;91:1724–31
14. Duffy SW, Tabar L, Chen H, et al. The impact of organized mammography service screening on breast carcinoma mortality in seven Swedish counties. Cancer 2002;95:458–69.
15. Otto SJ , Fracheboud J, Looman CWN, et al, and the National Evaluation Team for Breast Cancer Screening. Initiation of population-based mammography screening in Dutch municipalities and effect on breast-cancer mortality: a systematic review. Lancet 2003;361:411–7.
16. Copenhagen after introduction of mammography screening: cohort study. BMJ 2005;330:220.
17. Kopans DB. Beyond randomized, controlled trials: organized mammographic screening ubstantially reduces breast cancer mortality. Cancer 2002;94:580–1.
18. Kopans DB, Monsees B, Feig SA. Screening for cancer—when is it valid? Lessons from the mammography experience. Radiology 2003;229:319–27.
19. Bird RE. Professional uality assurance for mammographic screening programs. Radiology 1990;177:587.
20. Anderson EDC, Muir BB, Walsh JS, Kirkpatrick AE. The efficacy of double reading mammograms in breast screening. Clin Radiol 1994;49:248–51.
21. Kopans DB. Double reading. Radiol Clin North Am 2000;38:719–24.
22. Birdwell RL, Ikeda DM, O'Shaughnessy KF, Sickles EA. Mammographic characteristics of 115 missed cancers later detected with screening mammography and the potential utility of computer-aided detection. Radiology 2001;219:192–202.
23. Karssemeijer N, Otten JD, Verbeek AL, et al. Computer-aided detection versus independent double reading of masses on mammograms. Radiology 2003;227:192–200.
24. Ghate SV, Soo MS, Baker JA, et al. Comparison of recall and cancer detection rates for immediate versus batch interpretation of screening mammograms. Radiology 2005; 235:31–5.
25. Tabar L, Faberberg G, Day NE, Holmberg L. What is the optimum interval between mammographic screening examinations? An analysis based on the latest results of the Swedish Two-county Breast Screening Trial. Br J Cancer 1989;55:547–51.
26. Moskowitz M. Breast cancer: age-specific growth rates and screening strategies. Radiology 1986;161:37–41.
27. Kopans DB, Swann CA, White G, et al. Asymmetric breast tissue. Radiology 1989;171:639–43.
28. Kopans DB, Meyer JE, Cohen AM, Wood WC. Palpable breast masses: the importance of preoperative mammography. JAMA 1981;246:2819–22.
29. Sickles EA. Periodic mammographic follow-up of probably benign lesions: results of 3184 consecutive cases. Radiology 1991;179:463–8.
30. Swann CA, Kopans DB, McCarthy KA, et al. Practical solutions to problems of triangulation and preoperative localization of breast lesions. Radiology 1987;163:577–9.
31. Sickles EA. Practical solutions to common mammographic problems: tailoring the examination. AJR Am J Roentgenol 1988;151:31–9.
32. Kopans DB. Breast imaging. 2nd ed. Philadelphia (PA): J.B. Lippincott Co.; 1997.
33. Kopans DB, Meyer JE, Lindfors KK, McCarthy KA. Spring-hookwire breast lesion localizer: use with rigid compression mammographic systems. Radiology 1985;157:537–8.
34. Kopans DB, Meyer JE, Lindfors KK. Whole breast ultrasound imaging. Four year follow up. Radiology 1985;157:505–7.
35. Kaplan SS. Clinical utility of bilateral whole-breast ultrasound in the evaluation of women with dense breast tissue. Radiology 2001;221:641–9.
36. Kolb TM, Lichy J, Newhouse JH. Comparison of the performance of screening mammography, physical examination, and breast US and evaluation of factors that influence them: an analysis of 27,825 patient evaluations. Radiology 2002;225:165–75.
37. Crystal P, Strano SD, Shcharynski S, Koretz MJ. Using sonography to screen women with mammographically dense breasts. AJR Am J Roentgenol. 2003;181:177–82.
38. Leconte I, Feger C, Galant C, et al. Mammography and subsequent whole-breast sonography of nonpalpable breast cancers: the importance of radiologic breast density. AJR Am J Roentgenol 2003;180:1675–9.
39. Kopans DB. Sonography should not be used for breast cancer screening until its efficacy has been proven scientifically. AJR Am J Roentgenol 2004;182:489–91.
40. Rubens JR, Kopans DB. Medullary carcinoma of the breast: is it overdiagnosed? Arch Surg 1990;125:601–4.
41. Foster MC, Helvie MA, Gregory NE, et al. Lobular carcinoma in situ or atypical lobular hyperplasia at core-needle biopsy: is excisional biopsy necessary? Radiology 2004;231:813–9.
42. Kriege M, Brekelmans CT, Boetes C, et al; Magnetic Resonance Imaging Screening Study Group. Efficacy of MRI and mammography for breast-cancer screening in women with a familial or genetic predisposition. N Engl J Med. 2004;351:427–37.
43. Gorczya DP, Sinha S, Ahn CY, et al. Silicone breast implants in vivo: MR imaging. Radiology 1992;185:407–10.
44. Summary of report of National Science Panel. Silicone breast implants in relation to connective tissue diseases and immunologic dysfunction. Commissioned by U.S. District Judge Sam C. Pointer, Jr. Federal Courthouse, Birmingham, Alabama. Available at: http://www.fjc.gov/BREIMLIT/SCIENCE/summary.htm (accessed October 2005).
45. Morris EA, Schwartz LH, Dershaw DD, et al. MR imaging of the breast in patients with occult primary breast carcinoma. Radiology 1997;205:437–40.
46. Giles R, Guinebretiere JM, Toussaint C, et al. Locally advanced breast cancer: contrast-enhanced subtraction MR imaging of response to preoperative chemotherapy. Radiology 1994;191:633–8.
47. Yeh E, Slanetz P, Kopans DB, et al. Prospective comparison

of mammography, sonography, and MRI in patients undergoing neoadjuvant chemotherapy for palpable breast cancer. AJR Am J Roentgenol 2005;184:868–77.

48. Kuhl CK, Bieling HB, Gieseke J, et al. Healthy premonopausal breast parenchyma in dynamic contrast-enhanced MR imaging of the breast: normal contrast medium enhancement and cyclical-phase dependency. Radiology 1997;203:137–44.
49. Boetes C, Mus RDM, Holland R, et al. Breast tumors: comparative accuracy of MR imaging relative to mammography and US for demonstrating extent. Radiology 1995;197:743–7.
50. Bedrosian I, Mick R, Orel SG, et al. Changes in the surgical management of patients with breast carcinoma based on preoperative magnetic resonance imaging. Cancer 2003; 98:468–73.
51. Hata T, Takahashi H, Watanabe K, et al. Magnetic resonance imaging for preoperative evaluation of breast cancer: a comparative study with mammography and ultrasonography. J Am Coll Surg 2004;198:190–7.
52. D'Orsi CJ, Getty DJ, Swets JA, et al. Reading and decision aids for improved accuracy and standardization of mammographic diagnosis. Radiology 1992;184:619–22.
53. Barlow WE, Chi C, Carney PA, et al. Accuracy of screening mammography interpretation by characteristics of radiologists. J Natl Cancer Inst 2004;96:1840–50.
54. Sickles EA, Miglioretti DL, Ballard-Barbash R, et al. Performance benchmarks for diagnostic mammography. Radiology 2005;235:775–90.
55. Wolfe JN. Breast patterns as an index of risk for developing breast cancer. AJR Am J Roentgenol 1976;126:1130–9.
56. D'Orsi CJ, editor. The American College of Radiology breast imaging reporting and data system. 2nd ed. Reston (VA): American College of Radiology; 1995.
57. Holland R, Hendriks JHCL, Mravunac M. Mammographically occult breast cancer: a pathologic and radiologic study. Cancer 1983;52:1810–9.
58. Bird RE, Wallace TW, Yankaskas BC. Analysis of cancers missed at screening mammography. Radiology 1992;184: 613–7.
59. Sickles EA. Periodic mammographic follow-up of probably benign lesions: results of 3184 consecutive cases. Radiology 1991;179:463–8.
60. Varas X, Leborgne F, Leborgne JH. Non-palpable, probably benign lesions: role of follow-up mammography. Radiology 1992;184:409–14.
61. Niklason LT, Christian BT, Niklason LE, et al. Digital tomosynthesis in breast imaging. Radiology 1997;205: 399–406.

10

Sonography of Breast Cancer

BRUNO D. FORNAGE

The major goal of breast imaging is to detect a focal lesion and determine if it is benign or malignant, preferably without having to perform a biopsy. As a rule, sonography (US) cannot depict isolated microcalcifications that would indicate the presence of an early intraductal carcinoma; these remain the domain of mammography. In contrast, with the use of state-of-the-art high-resolution ultrasound transducers, masses—cystic or solid, large or small—are reliably identified, and US can now play a significant role in the diagnosis and management of breast masses, in general, and of breast cancer, in particular.

During the last two decades, we at The University of Texas M. D. Anderson Cancer Center have used US not only to identify and characterize breast lesions but also, in cases of newly diagnosed breast cancer, to refine the local and regional staging and to routinely evaluate the cancer's response to therapy.

This chapter discusses the current roles of US in breast cancer and also describes the experience at M. D. Anderson Cancer Center with ultrasound-guided interventional procedures from needle biopsy to percutaneous ablation of breast masses.

RECENT DEVELOPMENTS IN ULTRASOUND EQUIPMENT AND SCANNING TECHNIQUES

Recent advances in ultrasound equipment used for breast imaging include very-high-frequency and multi-array transducers that operate at peak frequencies of up to 15 MHz and provide exquisite spatial resolution. Such transducers now allow visualization of cancers as small as a few millimeters (Figure 10–1).

In addition, extended-field-of-view technology, which is now available on most high-end scanners, allows the operator to "stretch" the standard sonogram to build a static picture with a much wider field of view than that available with standard real-time transducers.[1] One advantage of obtaining sonograms of the entire breast is to be able to scan through a lesion and the nipple and to measure the distance from that lesion to the nipple for optimal correlation with the location of that lesion on mammograms (Figure 10–2).[2]

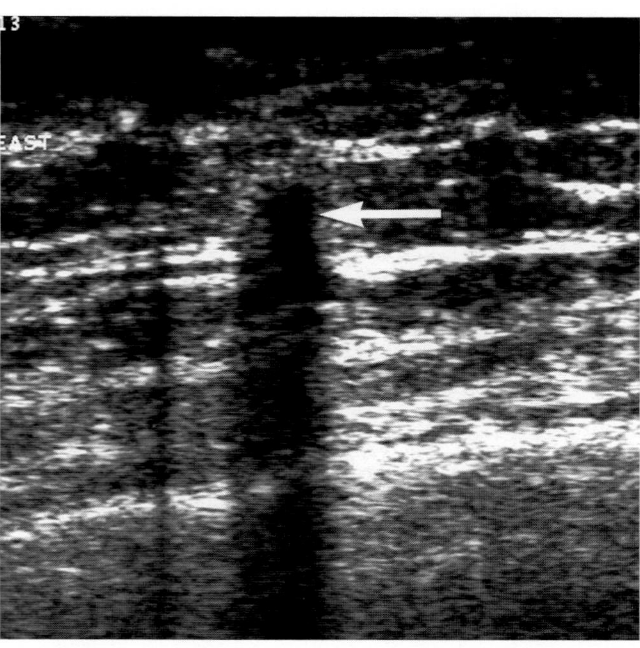

Figure 10–1. Sonogram shows the spiculated margins of a tiny (3 mm) infiltrating ductal carcinoma (arrow). Note the associated acoustic shadowing.

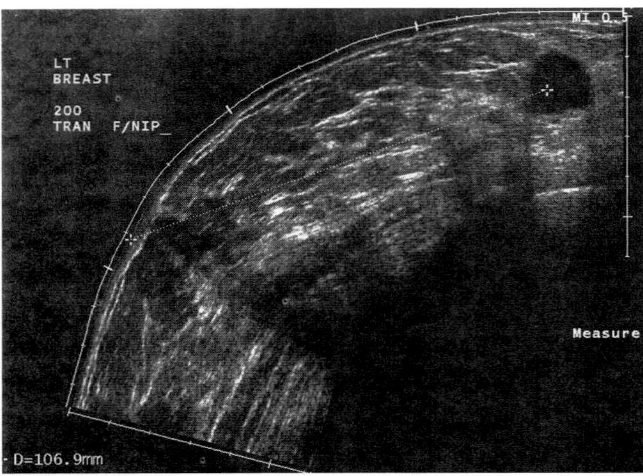

Figure 10–2. Extended-field-of-view sonogram through the lesion and the nipple allows measurement of the distance (10.7 cm) between the nipple and the tumor, a critical parameter to describe the location of the tumor and ensure proper correlation with the mammographic location.

Another image-processing technique, real-time compound scanning, which was initially predicted to provide higher-quality images than those attainable with conventional US, has not proved beneficial. In fact, in our experience, the significant blurring associated with this new technique has actually had a negative effect on image quality.

Tissue harmonic imaging has been shown to increase the spatial resolution slightly and to boost the contrast, which may improve the delineation of poorly defined cancers (Figure 10–3).[3,4]

Three-dimensional US is still investigational, but it is expected to change the way breast sonograms will be acquired, displayed, and interpreted in the not-too-distant future.[5] It may also facilitate the guidance of interventional procedures.[6]

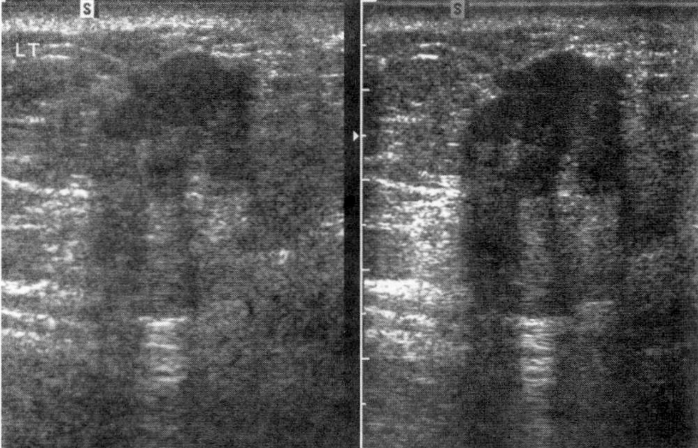

Figure 10–3. Comparison between conventional (fundamental) sonographic imaging (left) and tissue harmonic imaging (right) shows the better delineation of the margins of the tumor achieved with tissue harmonic imaging.

Another newly developed type of equipment that combines sonographic and mammographic images and is capable of accurately correlating the two has recently generated some interest. The obvious advantage of such equipment is its accurate topographic correlation between the two images, but its drawbacks include the operator's inability to tweak the image by optimizing the probe's position and difficulties in performing ultrasound-guided procedures.

Recently, elasticity imaging with ultrasound, or elastography, has emerged. This is a promising practical method for representing the hardness of a breast lesion in quasi–real time and in side-by-side comparison with conventional sonograms.[7]

Finally, over the last decade, the sensitivity of color (power) Doppler imaging systems has dramatically increased, thus allowing not only detection of the mere presence of Doppler signals within or around an indeterminate mass but also providing detailed mapping of the tumor-associated vascularity. This now makes it possible to distinguish benign from malignant types of vascularity, thereby facilitating differentiation between benign and malignant breast masses (Figure 10–4).[8] The use of contrast agents with harmonic imaging has also shown promising results,[9,10] but ultrasound contrast agents remain investigational in the United States and their cost effectiveness is not yet proven.[11]

SONOGRAPHIC EXAMINATION TECHNIQUE

In the United States, except in very young patients, US of the breast is usually performed to characterize a lesion detected mammographically. Therefore, the mammograms must be reviewed before sonographic examination is undertaken. In addition, it is good practice to perform a targeted physical examination before starting a sonographic study.

Scans should be obtained longitudinally, transversely, and also radially around the nipple along the orientation of the ducts. Scans must be carefully labeled; labeling includes, but is not restricted to, the

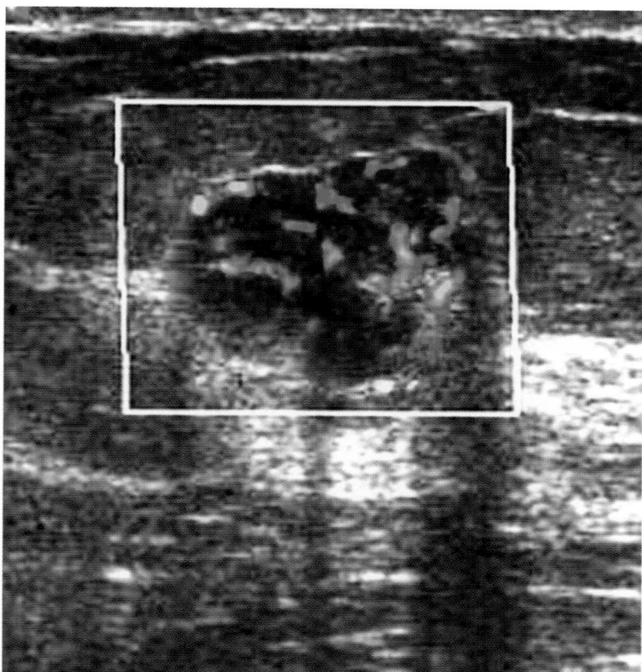

Figure 10–4. Power Doppler sonogram of an infiltrating ductal carcinoma shows intense internal vascularity with tortuous vessels, which are typical of malignancy.

patient's demographic information, the location of the area examined, and the orientation of the scan.

Altering the amount of compression applied to the breast with the transducer is a key step in real-time sonographic examination. This maneuver clears or confirms the presence of artifacts and demonstrates both the compressibility of a lesion and its mobility in relation to the surrounding tissues, features that can be assessed only with real-time US.

Whenever a mass is demonstrated on US, conventional color and power Doppler imaging should be used to assess its vasçularity.

The concordance between sonographic and mammographic findings must be a priority for the sonologist. The size, shape, and location (ie, clock position, distance from the nipple, and depth) of the lesion and the appearance of the surrounding tissues (fatty or glandular) must correlate perfectly between sonograms and mammograms, although minimal differences between the two modalities in size (< 10%) resulting from mammographic magnification and slight differences in clock location (about 1 hour) caused by differences in breast positioning and compression are acceptable.

When evaluating a patient with a history of breast cancer, whether it is suspected, already diagnosed, or being followed up, the sonographic examination should systematically include the entire breast, the axilla, and the internal mammary lymphatic chains.

ROLE OF US IN DIAGNOSIS OF BREAST CANCER

Carcinomas, even those less than 1 cm in diameter, are routinely identified on US with the use of state-of-the-art sonographic equipment.

Infiltrating Ductal Carcinomas

Infiltrating ductal carcinomas account for most invasive cancers of the breast. Most of these tumors have no special features and fall into the category of "not otherwise specified." The majority of invasive carcinomas are stellate (or spiculated) carcinomas, but some are circumscribed.

Stellate Carcinomas

Stellate or spiculated carcinomas contain a large amount of fibrosis, which accounts for the firmness of these scirrhous (hard) tumors. The sonographic appearance of these carcinomas parallels their mammographic appearance. The hypoechoic solid mass has a markedly irregular, angular, or spiculated margin, disrupting the architecture of the breast (Figure 10–5). Unlike fibroadenomas and other benign masses, invasive carcinomas, especially when small, may exhibit a taller-than-wide shape, with the tumor's longest diameter perpendicular to the skin (length-to-anteroposterior-diameter ratio of < 1) (Figure 10–6). This shape is highly characteristic of carcinoma, although carcinomas, especially when they are large, may also have an elongated shape. An echogenic rim reflecting the desmoplastic reaction around the tumor is often present (Figure 10–7). Large tumors often exhibit echotexture heterogeneity, although they rarely have cystic necrotic areas. As a rule, the presence of cystic areas within a solid mass is most likely associated with a benign mass rather than with a malignancy.

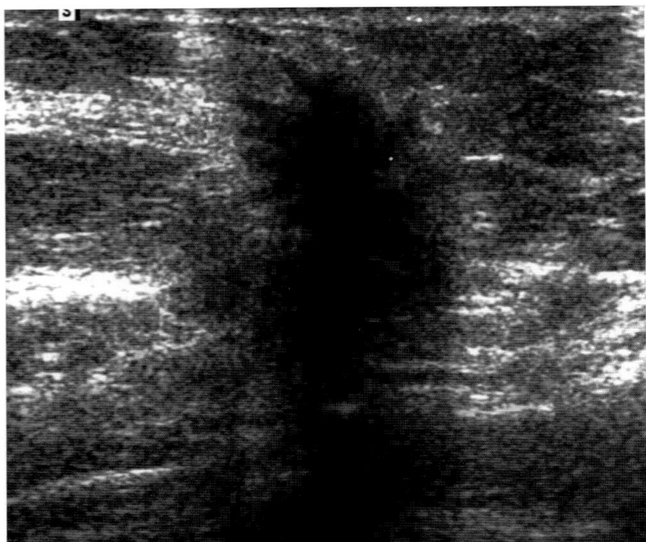

Figure 10–5. Sonogram of a spiculated infiltrating ductal carcinoma shows the spicules around the markedly hypoechoic tumor. Note the marked acoustic shadow.

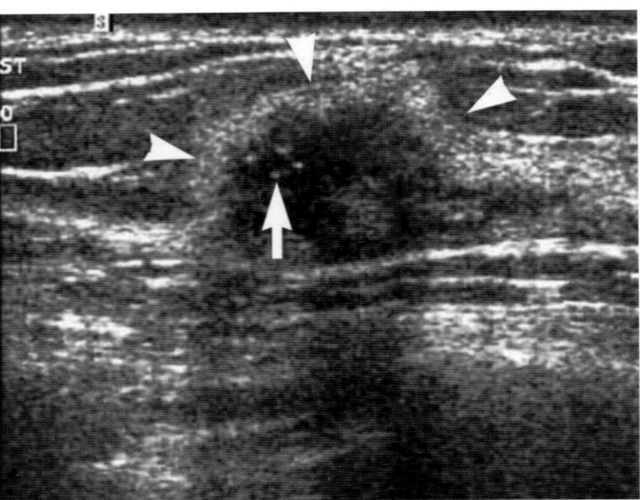

Figure 10–7. Sonogram shows an echogenic rim representing the desmoplastic reaction (arrowheads) around an irregular infiltrating ductal carcinoma. Note the presence of microcalcifications (arrow) within the tumor.

With state-of-the-art transducers, bright dot echoes are frequently seen within the tumor, correlating with microcalcifications seen on mammography (Figure 10–8). Their visualization in a mass is another clue to the diagnosis of malignancy, although the limitation of US—the inability to appreciate the size, shape, number, density, and distribution (ductal versus lobular) of the microcalcifications like mammography does—must always be kept in mind. Suspicious clusters of microcalcifications without other mammographic abnormalities are infrequently visualized on sonograms, but when they are, they are more likely to be associated with an invasive malignancy.[12]

Because of the dense fibrosis present, infiltrating ductal carcinomas are often associated with massive acoustic shadowing (see Figure 10–5). On real-time scanning, there is obvious attraction (pulling) of the adjacent tissues toward the tumor's core. The

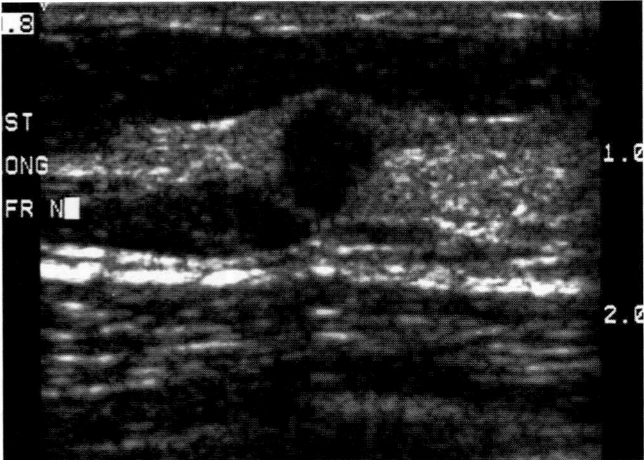

Figure 10–6. Sonogram shows the typical taller-than-wide shape of a small (0.7 cm) infiltrating ductal carcinoma.

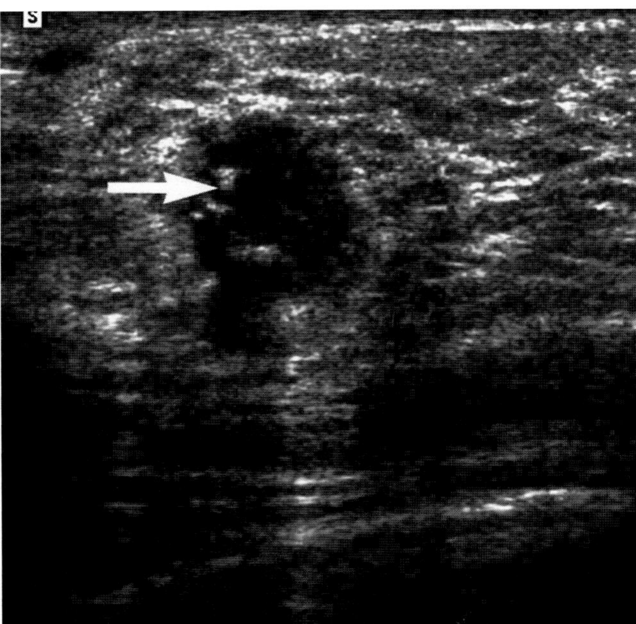

Figure 10–8. Sonogram shows a typical infiltrating ductal carcinoma with irregular margins, taller-than-wide shape, and internal bright dot echoes representing microcalcifications (arrow).

lack of compressibility and adherence of the tumor to the surrounding tissues when compression with the transducer over the mass is increased are very suggestive of malignancy. Invasion into the overlying skin, when present, is readily demonstrated by high-frequency US. On occasion, US can demonstrate associated ductal carcinoma in situ (DCIS) extending into the adjacent ducts (Figure 10–9).

In malignant tumors, newly formed vessels are typically tortuous and disorganized, and they penetrate the tumor at a 90-degree angle (see Figure 10–4); in contrast, the vessels associated with fibroadenomas are usually straight or curvilinear, often draping smoothly over the lesion or coursing along septa.[8] However, the flow-mapping features of carcinomas and fibroadenomas (especially fast-growing fibroadenomas) overlap. The degree of differentiation of the carcinoma appears to correlate with the amount of internal vascularity on color Doppler imaging: the poorer the differentiation, the greater the vascularity. There also seems to be a trend toward decreased echogenicity of the tumor with increasing tumor grade.

Circumscribed Carcinomas

Circumscribed carcinomas include medullary, mucinous (or colloid), and papillary carcinomas. Medullary carcinomas are packed with cells (including the characteristic lymphocytic infiltrate), which explains their marked hypoechogenicity and sound through-transmission that may mimic a cyst (Figure 10–10).

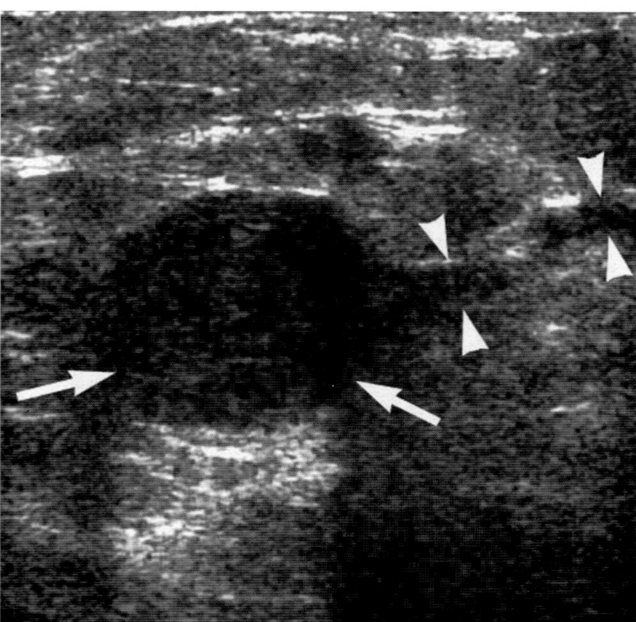

Figure 10–9. Sonogram shows a duct distended by DCIS (arrowheads) associated with an infiltrating ductal carcinoma (arrows).

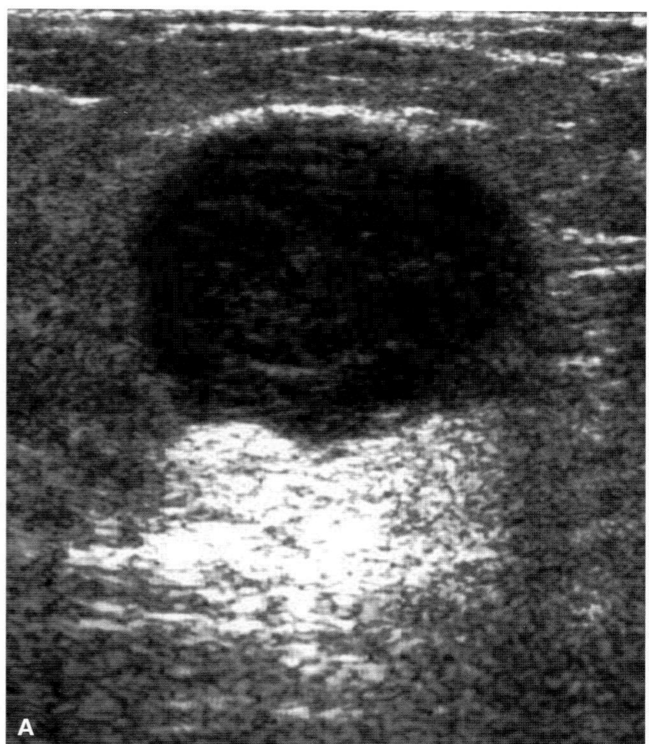

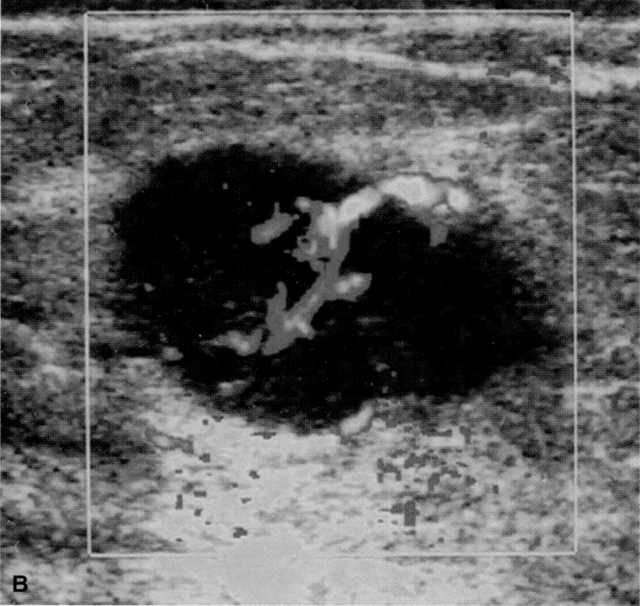

Figure 10–10. *A,* Gray-scale sonogram of a medullary cancer shows a relatively well-circumscribed mass with distal sound enhancement and a pseudocystic appearance. *B,* Power Doppler sonogram of the same lesion shows significant internal vascularity, which rules out a fluid collection.

On closer inspection, however, the margins are irregular, and low-level internal echoes are present. The use of power Doppler imaging is pivotal in the diagnosis of such circumscribed pseudocystic carcinomas. If vascularity is demonstrated within the markedly hypoechoic mass, the diagnosis of a cyst or any other fluid collection is excluded and the suspicion for malignancy increases.[13]

Mucinous carcinomas are also well circumscribed, and are rounded or lobulated (Figure 10–11). Those of the pure type are often homogeneous, markedly hypoechoic, and associated with a degree of distal sound enhancement, thus potentially mimicking a cyst.[14]

Papillary carcinomas arise in cysts or ducts. Intracystic papillary carcinomas have a nodular appearance and often infiltrate through the wall of the cyst into the adjacent pericystic parenchyma (Figure 10–12). Except for their intracystic location, they have no specific features on US.

Other Breast Carcinomas with Special Features

Tubular carcinomas are very small spiculated masses with no distinctive sonographic features.

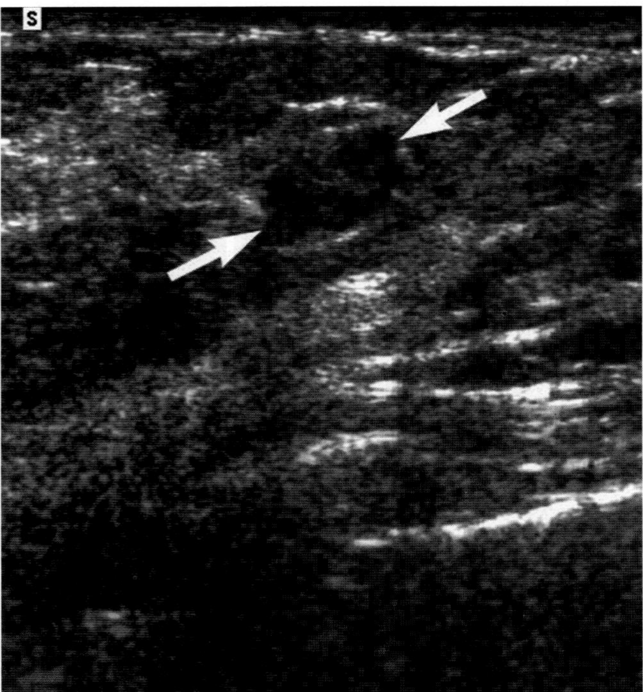

Figure 10–11. Sonogram of a mucinous cancer shows a small, mostly well-circumscribed hypoechoic mass (arrows) with some distal sound enhancement.

Invasive lobular carcinomas are difficult to identify on US, just as they are on mammography. The substantial distortion and fibrosis seen on mammograms appears on sonograms as areas of marked shadowing without a well-defined mass (Figure 10–13). Recent studies have shown the superiority of US to mammography in the diagnosis of infiltrating lobular carcinoma.[15] Color Doppler imaging may reveal moderate but often very suspicious vascularity at the periphery of the lesion (Figure 10–14). Extensive biopsy sampling throughout the area of shadowing is required for a definite diagnosis. Very rarely will an invasive lobular carcinoma appear as a small well-defined mass.

Ductal Carcinoma In Situ

Typically, DCIS is nonpalpable and is detected as microcalcifications on mammography. At this early stage, the volume of the intraductal lesion is usually too small to allow its clear depiction on US. However, as the tumor expands within a duct, the duct, which becomes distended and filled with hypoechoic tumor and calcifications, may become visible on US (Figure 10–15).[16] In addition, color Doppler US may demonstrate vascularity associated with the intraductal tumor.

Carcinoma of the Male Breast

The sonographic appearances of carcinoma of the breast in men does not differ from those in women (Figure 10–16).

Inflammatory Breast Cancer

Like mammography, US provides limited information about inflammatory breast cancer. However, US shows a mass more frequently than mammography does and has the advantage of revealing frequent axillary involvement. The architecture of the breast is diffusely disorganized with significant skin thickening (up to 1 cm) (Figure 10–17A).[17] Power Doppler US shows some vascularity in the thickened dermis and the absence of flow in the multiple subdermal communicating tubular structures, which represent lymphatic vessels distended with tumor (Figure 10–17B).

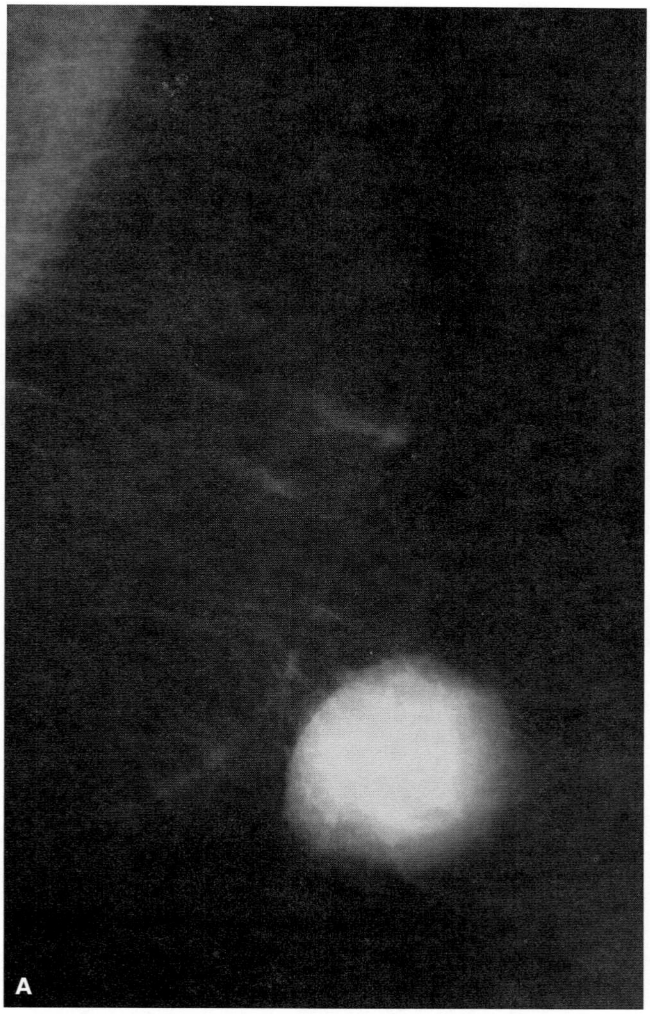

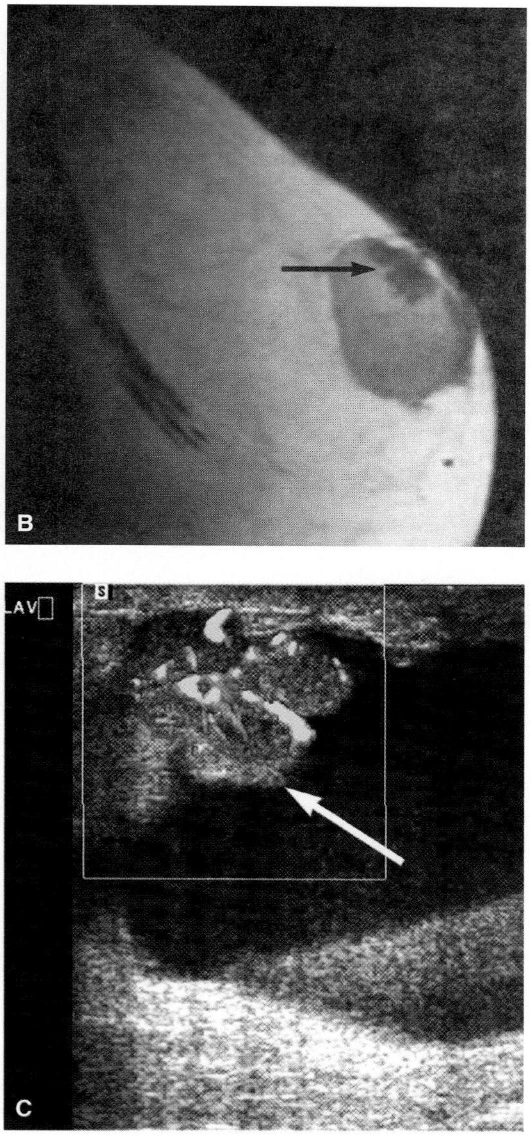

Figure 10–12. Intracystic papillary cancer in a male patient. *A,* Mammogram shows a well-circumscribed density. *B,* MRI shows a tumor (arrow) developing inside the mass. *C,* Power Doppler sonogram shows a solid nodule (arrow) with marked hypervascularity.

Metastases to the Breast from Extramammary Primary Cancers

Metastases to the breast from extramammary primary cancers are rare. When they occur, they usually derive from melanoma or pulmonary carcinoma or, more rarely, from renal cell carcinoma, gastrointestinal tract malignancies, or other primary tumors. These metastases usually have a benign, rounded appearance on mammograms, but rapid growth should raise the possibility of a metastasis, especially if the patient has a history of an extramammary malignancy. On sonograms, these metastases in the breast appear as round, solid, hypoechoic masses, occasionally with a hypervascular echogenic rim (Figure 10–18).

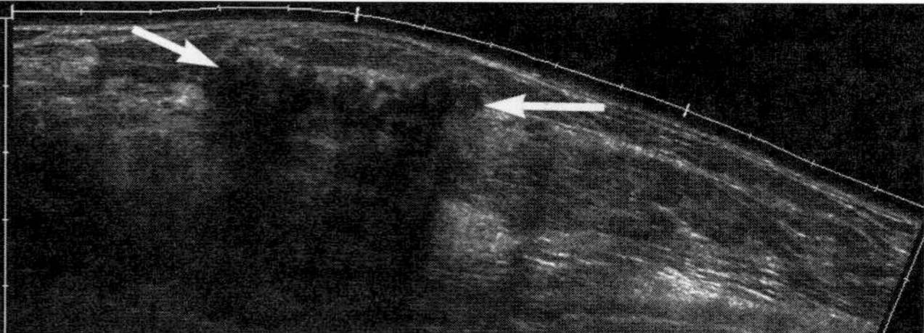

Figure 10–13. Extended-field-of-view sonogram provides a global view of the breast and demonstrates better than conventional US the abnormal area of shadowing (arrows) in contrast with the adjacent normal breast in a case of invasive lobular carcinoma.

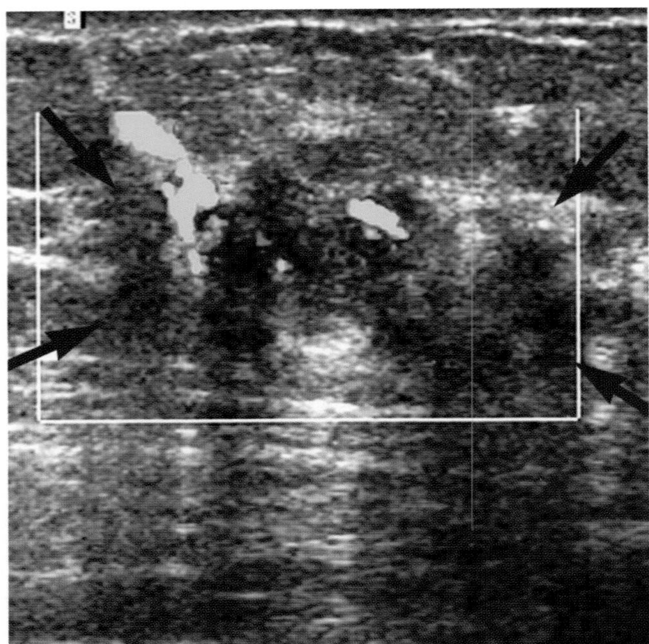

Figure 10–14. Power Doppler sonogram of an invasive lobular carcinoma shows scanty but suspicious vascularity feeding a poorly-defined mass (arrows) associated with shadowing.

Secondary involvement of the breast with lymphoma is not uncommon and is probably less rare than involvement with leukemia. Any new mass in the breast of a patient with a history of lymphoma or leukemia should be considered to possibly represent secondary involvement of the breast, especially if

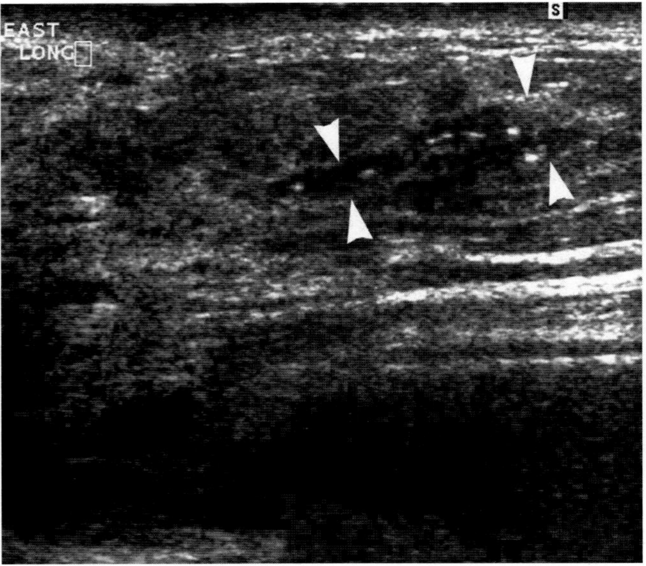

Figure 10–15. Sonogram shows DCIS with microcalcifications filling a duct (arrowheads). DCIS = ductal carcinoma in situ.

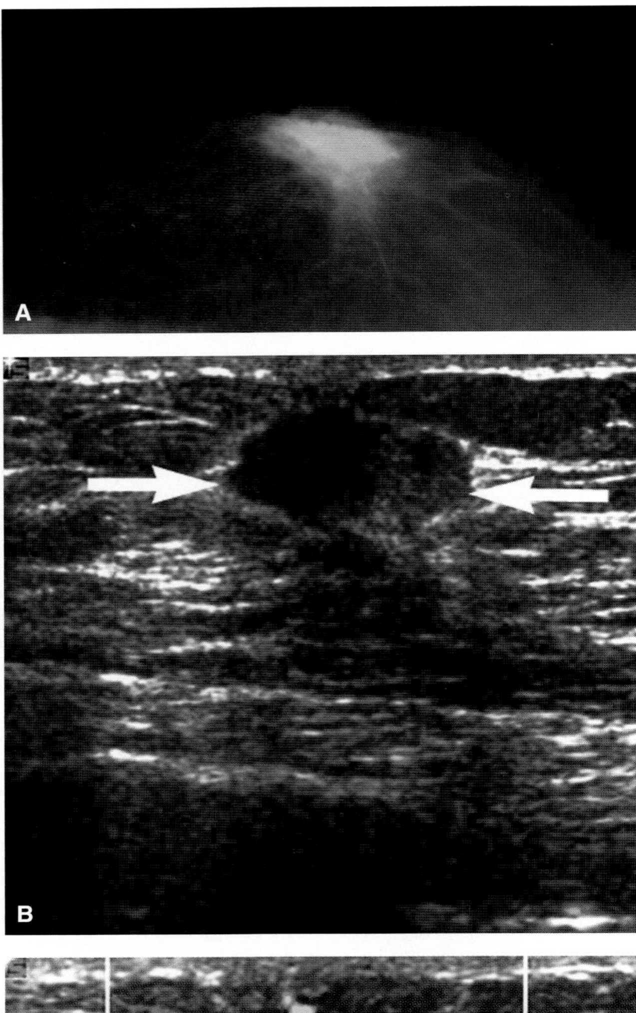

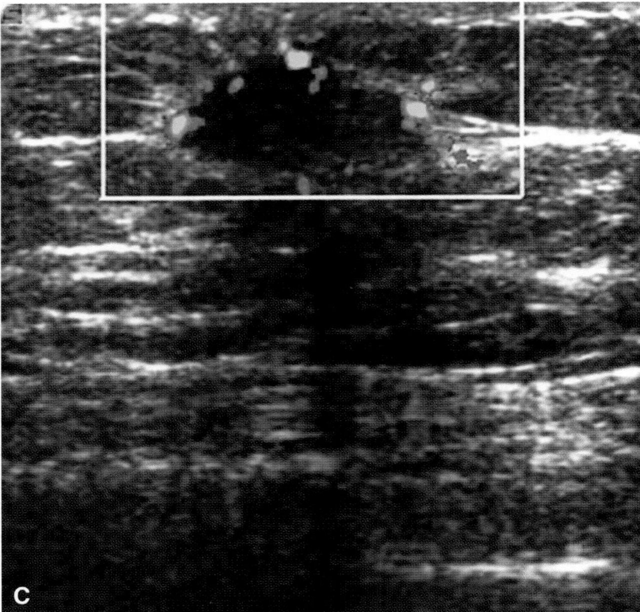

Figure 10–16. Male breast cancer. *A,* Mammogram shows a suspicious ill-defined, irregular mass in the retroareolar area. *B,* Sonogram shows the markedly irregular tumor (arrows). *C,* Power Doppler sonogram shows a high level of vascularity, with multiple vascular poles at the periphery of the tumor.

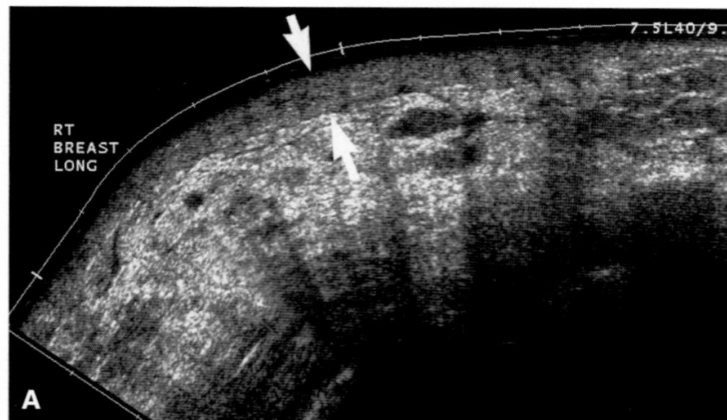

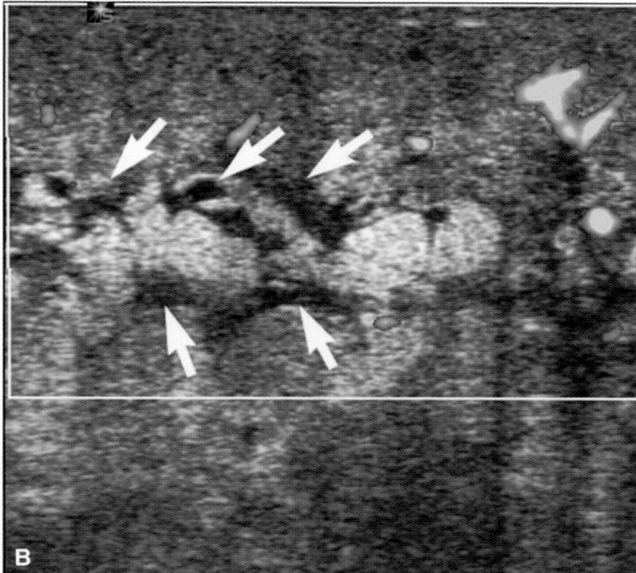

Figure 10–17. Inflammatory breast cancer. *A,* Extended-field-of-view sonogram shows diffuse disorganization of the breast's echotexture without a discrete focal tumor and significant skin thickening (arrows) with prominent subdermal lymphatic channels. *B,* Power Doppler sonogram shows scant vascularity within the thickened dermis and subdermis and numerous flow-void, tumor-filled distended lymphatic vessels (arrows).

the mass is relatively circumscribed and growing rapidly. Lymphomatous masses are markedly hypoechoic, lobulated, and hypervascular on color Doppler US (Figure 10–19).

The Breast Imaging Reporting and Data System for US

The Breast Imaging Reporting and Data System, or BI-RADS, which was initially developed by the American College of Radiology for mammography, now includes a lexicon for breast US.[18] When US is performed as an adjunct to mammography, one final

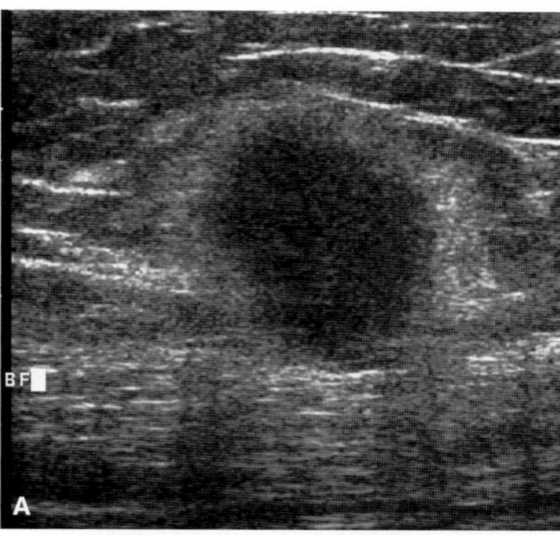

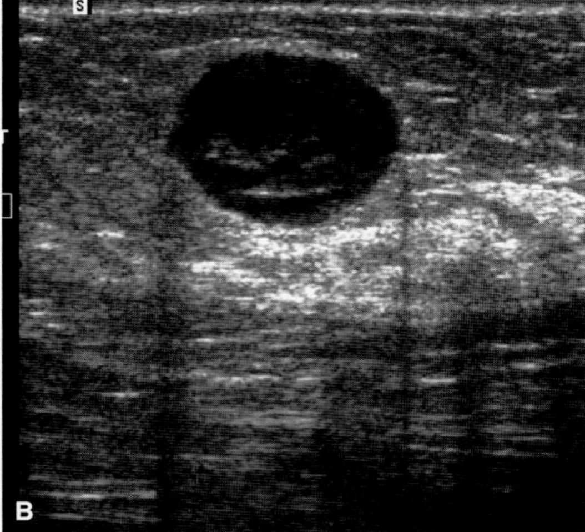

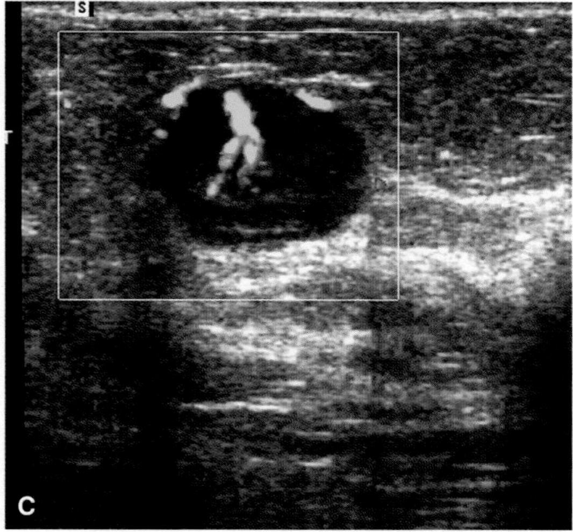

Figure 10–18. Metastases to the breast from extramammary primary cancers. *A,* Sonogram of a metastasis from lung cancer shows a rounded hypoechoic mass surrounded by an echogenic rim. *B,* Gray-scale sonogram of a metastasis from an abdominal leiomyosarcoma shows a well-circumscribed cystic-like mass with distal sound enhancement. *C,* Power Doppler sonogram of the lesion shown in B shows internal vascularity with suspicious branching, tortuous vessels.

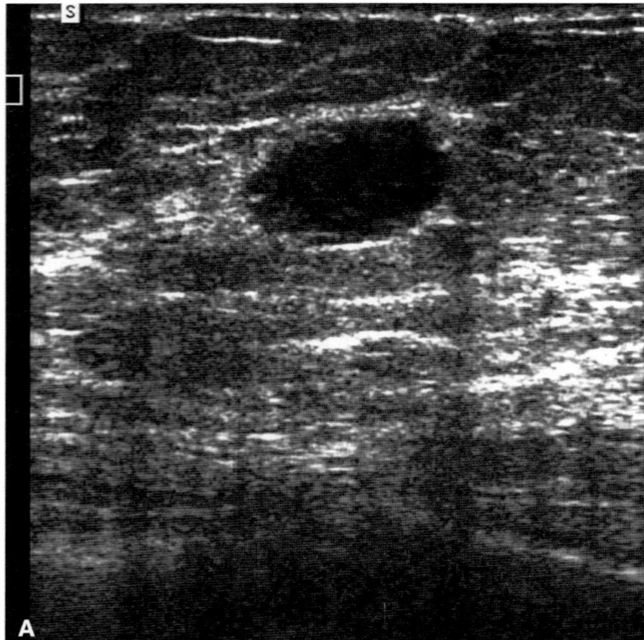

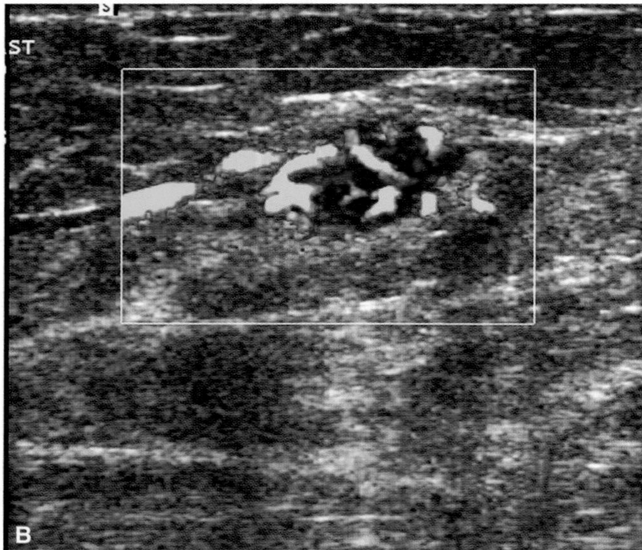

Figure 10–19. Lymphoma of the breast. *A,* Gray-scale sonogram shows a markedly hypoechoic mass mimicking a cyst. *B,* Power Doppler sonogram confirms the solid nature of the mass by demonstrating intense internal vascularity.

BI-RADS assessment and recommendation category should be specified that reflects the combined mammographic and sonographic findings and is determined by the most suspicious finding. This final BI-RADS category indicates the relative diagnostic likelihood of normal, benign, or malignant tissue, so proper recommendations (routine screening, short-interval follow-up, or biopsy) can be made. The BI-RADS categories and recommendations for US are as follows:

0. Assessment is incomplete. Additional imaging evaluation is needed before the final assessment can be made.
1. Negative. The sonograms show no lesion; only routine follow-up for age is recommended.
2. Benign finding(s). There is no malignancy. This category includes simple cysts, intramammary lymph nodes, implants, stable postsurgical changes, and probable fibroadenomas with no change over successive sonographic examinations; only routine follow-up for age or necessary clinical management is recommended.
3. Probably benign finding. This category includes probable fibroadenomas, complicated cysts, and clustered microcysts; initial short-interval follow-up is recommended.
4. Suspicious abnormality. Biopsy should be considered.
5. Highly suggestive of malignancy (almost certainly malignant). Appropriate action should be taken (most often needle biopsy).
6. Known biopsy-proven cancer (prior to initiation of therapy).

Screening Sonography

The use of screening mammography is severely limited in the evaluation of patients with dense breasts and patients with breast implants. Although it can detect microcalcifications, it is widely accepted that mammography can miss even fairly large masses in such breasts.[19,20] The capability of US to detect nonpalpable breast carcinomas not seen on mammograms is becoming recognized, but its cost effectiveness for breast cancer screening remains to be evaluated, especially in the United States, where the cost of US is higher than it is in the rest of the world. Also, the increasing use of US results in the detection of a large number of nonpalpable, mammographically occult, benign-appearing solid masses in dense breasts, leading to additional tests required to confirm their benign nature.

In Asian countries, however, where the average size of the female breast is smaller than in the

United States and Europe, thus making US easier and mammography more difficult to perform, and where the charges for the sonographic examination are nearly 10 times less than they are in the United States, US has shown promise for detecting invasive carcinoma. However, US cannot replace screening mammography for this purpose because it cannot detect DCIS, the earliest and most curable form of breast cancer. Therefore, screening US should be offered as a supplement to mammography to a subset of high-risk patients, including those with a previous history of breast cancer.

ROLE OF SONOGRAPHY IN STAGING BREAST CANCER

US can play an important role in both local and regional staging of breast cancer. In patients with a suspected or known cancer, sonographic examination of the breast must include a survey of the ipsilateral node-bearing areas, including the axilla, the infraclavicular region, and the internal mammary chains.

Local Staging

US is useful clinically for determining a primary tumor's true size—a major prognostic factor—although this depends on the type of cancer. For example, some cancers, such as invasive lobular carcinomas, are so poorly defined on US that accurate measurements cannot be obtained.

US is also helpful because it can detect additional foci of carcinoma, which are not always demonstrated by mammography, particularly in dense breasts, and the identification of such foci may have a crucial effect on the treatment plan if breast-conserving therapy is being considered.[21] US permits precise mapping of the lesions and accurate measurement of the distances between lesions, allowing differentiation between multifocal disease (ie, multiple foci in the same quadrant within a distance of 3 cm) (Figure 10–20) and multicentric disease (ie, multiple foci in different quadrants or more than 3 cm apart, thus precluding segmentectomy) (Figure 10–21).

Sonography can demonstrate the involvement of the skin or of the pectoralis muscle by the tumor.

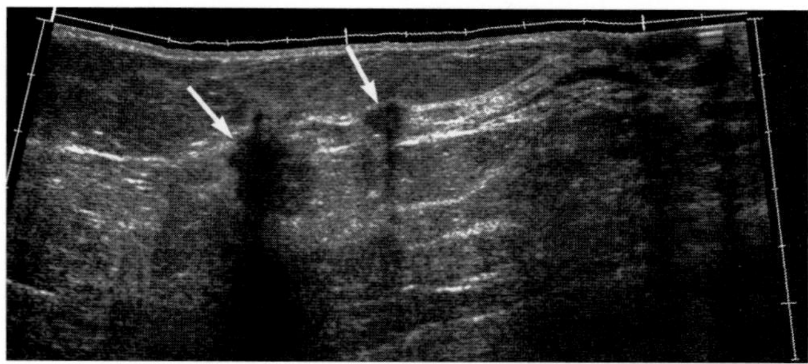

Figure 10–20. Sonogram of a bifocal infiltrating ductal carcinoma shows the two small malignant lesions (arrows) separated by less than 2 cm.

Regional Staging

For the last 15 years at M.D. Anderson, we have included the ipsilateral axilla and the internal mammary nodal chains in sonographic examinations of the breast in patients who have or have had breast cancer. If suspicious nodes are demonstrated in the axilla, the examination is extended to include the supraclavicular fossa and the low neck.

In normal adults, axillary lymph nodes appear as ovoid or elongated structures containing fat. Most often, the central fat is markedly echogenic (Figure 10–22). Normal internal mammary nodes are not usually visible on US, but tiny fat-containing oval nodes are occasionally seen in the supraclavicular fossa and, more commonly, in the low neck.

The sonographic diagnosis of lymph node metastases is based on nodal enlargement, deformity, and a marked decrease in echogenicity of intranodal tumor deposits (Figure 10–23). Metastatic foci as small as a few millimeters can be detected readily if present at the periphery of a totally

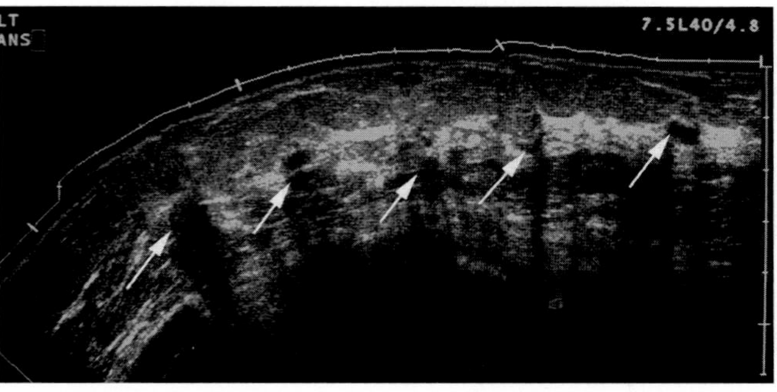

Figure 10–21. Extended-field-of-view sonogram of a multicentric carcinoma shows multiple lesions (arrows) extending across two quadrants.

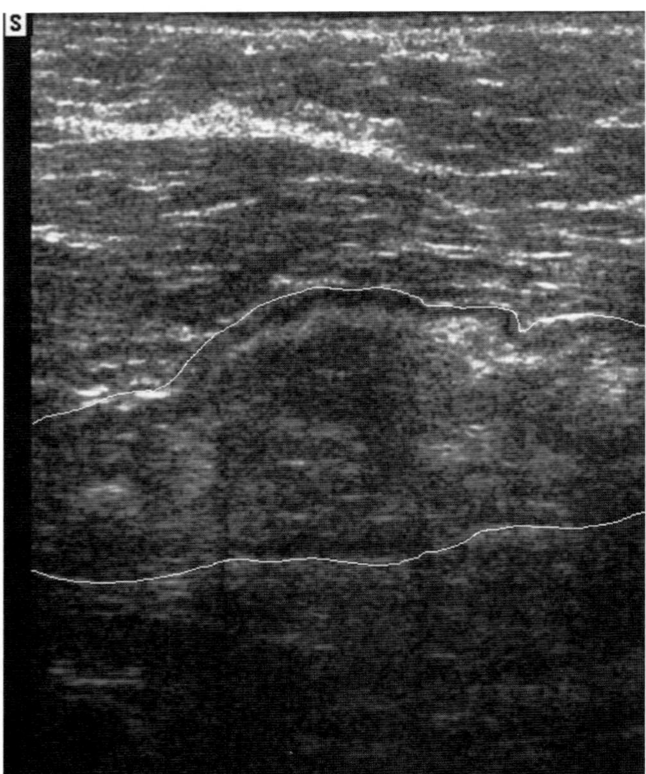

Figure 10–22. Sonogram shows a large normal axillary node that is completely replaced by mildly echogenic fat. Note the presence of only a very thin residual cortex, which helps delineate the node (white line).

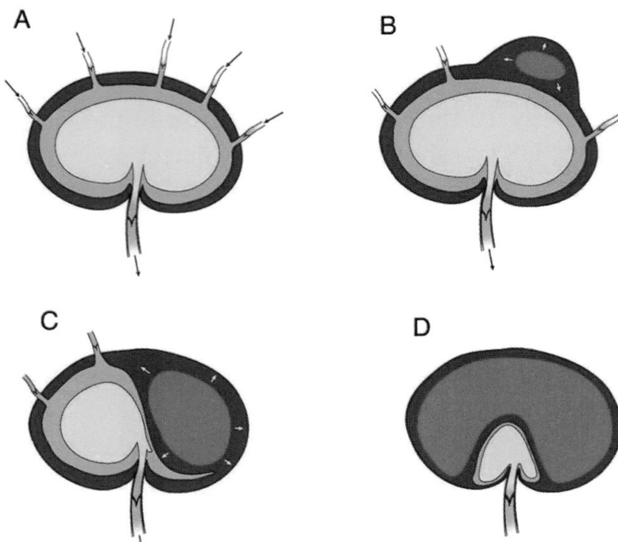

Figure 10–23. Diagram shows the progressive replacement of a normal lymph node (A) by tumor (B through D) as metastatic involvement progresses. The metastatic deposit is represented in red, the central fat in yellow.

echogenic node or if they produce a focal hypoechoic bulge on the surface of the node (Figure 10–24). Even when the central fat is not echogenic, metastatic deposits appear darker than the hypoechoic nodal background. Lymph nodes that are massively involved with metastatic tumor are easily recognized on US as rounded (when small) or irregularly shaped (when large) masses with little or no residual central echogenic fat (Figure 10–25). The presence of internal microcalcifications, especially if present within the primary tumor, is highly suggestive of metastatic involvement.

Color Doppler signals associated with metastatic lymph nodes range from absent to numerous and typically malignant. In enlarged nodes that are not significantly deformed, color Doppler US does not discriminate between benign reactive hyperplasia and metastasis, although the demonstration of dense harmonious vascularization in the thickened cortex of a node is more suggestive of benign hyperplasia than of metastasis.

Although state-of-the-art US can accurately detect lymph node metastases larger than 7 or 8 mm, it cannot, like other "nonfunctional" imaging modalities, demonstrate metastases that are smaller than a few millimeters.

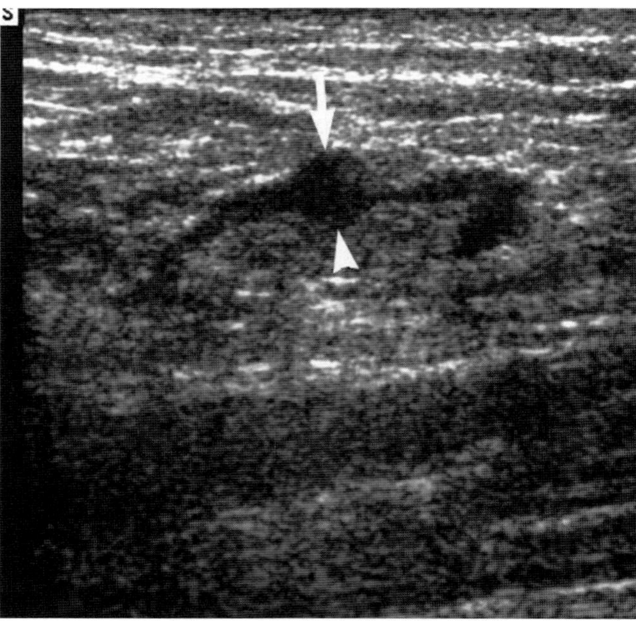

Figure 10–24. Sonogram of an early lymph node metastasis shows a small bulge (arrow) at the surface of an otherwise normal lymph node. The metastatic deposit is also responsible for indentation of the central fat (arrowhead).

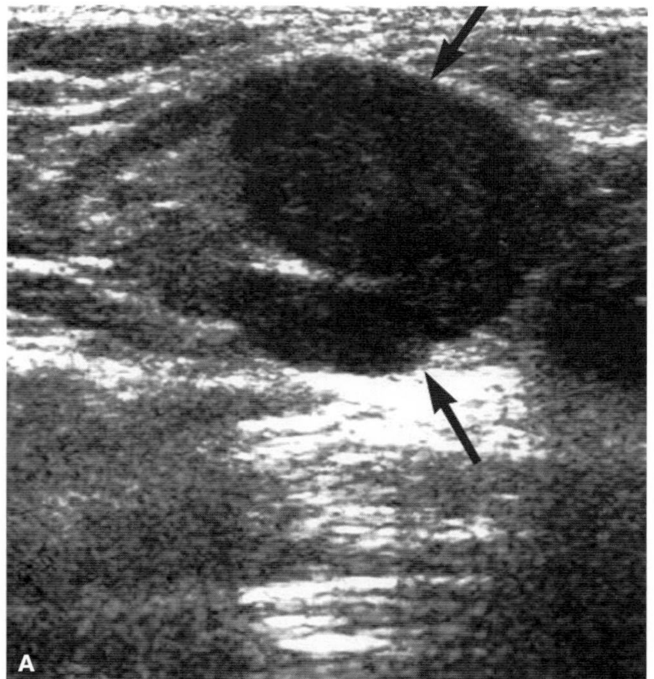

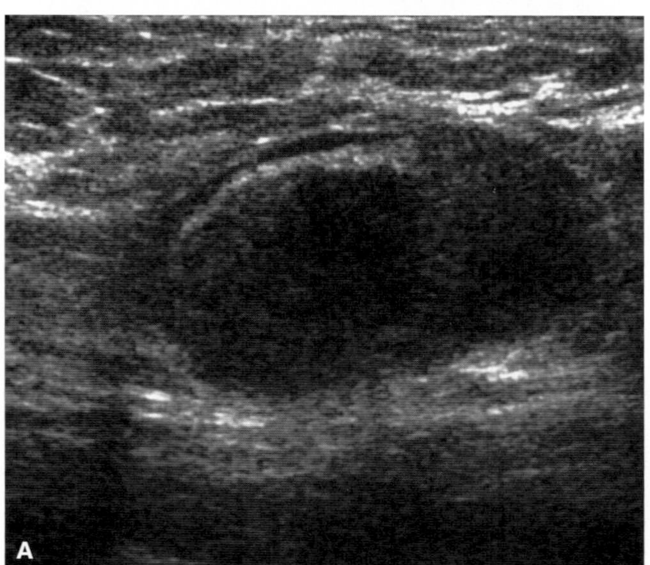

Figure 10–25. Lymph node metastases. *A,* Sonogram shows markedly hypoechoic tumor (arrows) involving more than half of the fat replaced node. *B,* Sonogram in a different patient shows massive replacement of the enlarged node by tumor.

At a time when efforts are being made to reduce unnecessary axillary lymph node dissections, sonographic detection of a nonpalpable metastasis in an axillary node (confirmed with ultrasound-guided fine-needle aspiration biopsy [FNAB]) has a substantial effect because it prevents the need for sentinel lymph node mapping and biopsy in 14 to 17% of patients.[22,23]

As indicated, we also routinely examine the internal mammary chains, which constitute alternate pathway for lymphatic drainage of the breast, particularly for medial quadrant lesions. Sonographic examination of the parasternal region is an expeditious and effective method of detecting internal mammary lymphatic involvement. Any hypoechoic node along the internal mammary chains in a patient with breast cancer should be viewed as a potential metastasis (Figure 10–26). Demonstration of lymph node metastases in the internal mammary chains (in the absence of metastases in the axillary nodes) results in staging the disease as stage IIIA, regardless of how small the primary tumor is.[24,25]

Metastases to the supraclavicular nodes make the disease stage IIIC, whereas the demonstration of a metastatic cervical or contralateral internal mammary node would make the disease stage IV. Because of such finding's effect on the staging of the disease, any suspicious supraclavicular or cervical node on US should be verified by ultrasound-guided FNAB.

Other unusual metastases can be incidentally found during sonographic examination of the breast, such as metastases to the thyroid, which will have the same sonographic appearance as a primary thyroid cancer (Figure 10–27). On other occasions, US will demonstrate the metastatic involvement of a regional bone—a rib, the clavicle, or the sternum—

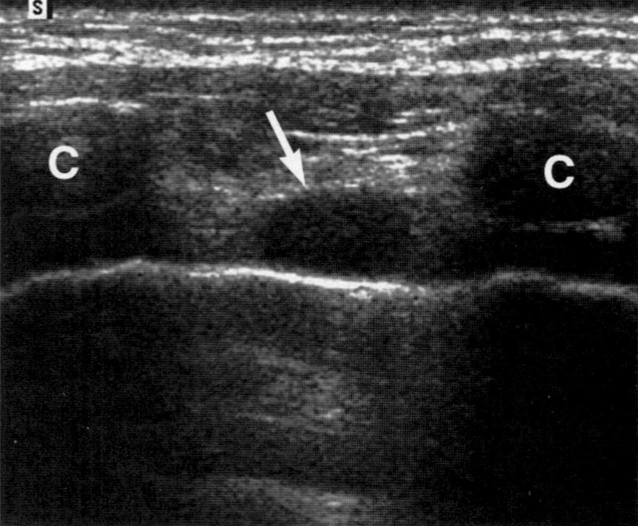

Figure 10–26. Longitudinal sonogram obtained along the internal mammary vessels shows an abnormal hypoechoic mass representing a metastasis to an internal mammary lymph node (arrow). C = sternocostal cartilage.

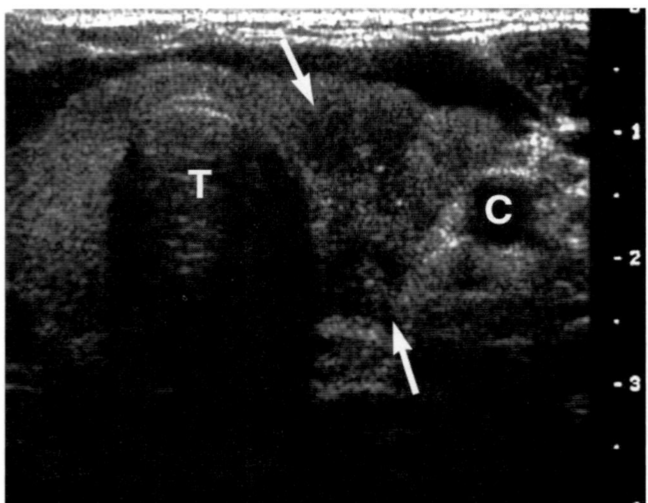

Figure 10–27. Transverse sonogram of the thyroid shows a metastasis of breast cancer to the thyroid detected incidentally during a staging sonographic examination of a patient with recently diagnosed breast cancer. Note the irregular mass (arrows) in the left lobe of the thyroid that contains calcifications. Diagnosis was confirmed by ultrasound-guided FNAB. C = common carotid artery; T = trachea.

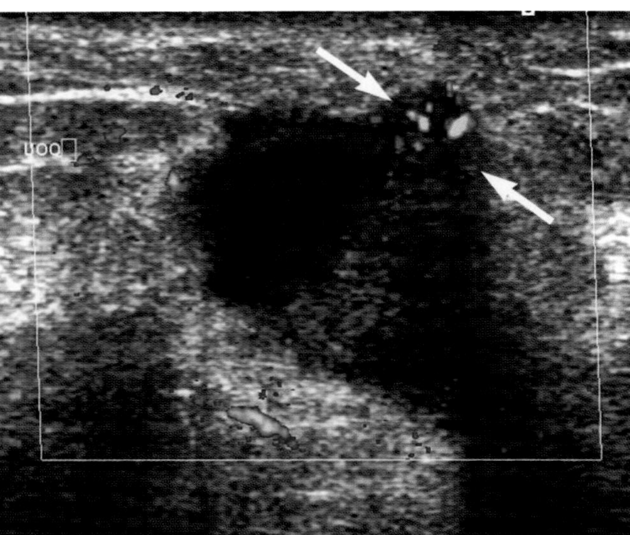

Figure 10–28. Power Doppler sonogram shows residual tumor at the periphery of the postoperative cavity after lumpectomy for infiltrating ductal carcinoma as represented by the cluster of color Doppler signals in a small hypoechoic mass (arrows) at the edge of the cavity.

with destruction of its cortex. If clinically indicated, an US-guided FNAB can readily confirm any suspicious metastasis, including osseous metastases.

ROLE OF SONOGRAPHY IN EXAMINING THE TREATED BREAST

For several weeks after the performance of a lumpectomy for cancer, a serohematoma fills the surgical cavity. This collection often has a complex sonographic appearance, typically with numerous fine internal septa and echogenic clots. Any mass detected at the edge of this cavity should be considered to represent residual or recurrent disease until proven otherwise, especially if color Doppler US shows the presence of vessels within that mass (Figure 10–28). Resorption of the serohematoma may result in scarring that may lie at some distance from the cutaneous scar and may extend over a long distance, depending on the surgical technique and approach used. These scars are often associated with shadowing and may have irregular margins, although they are usually concave in contrast to the convex margins of an expanding neoplasm (Figure 10–29); it is important to examine them dynamically by changing the transducer compression. Scars will usually deform along with adjacent tissues more readily than recurrent disease. Scars are usually hypovascular on color Doppler US. Correlation of postoperative sonograms with mammograms and previous imaging studies is of paramount importance for detecting any interval changes in a scar. On rare occasions, extensive biopsy of a scar will be necessary to rule out a recurrence.

Sonography demonstrates the skin thickening that occurs after radiation therapy as a homogenous, mildly echogemic dermal stripe.

Local recurrences after breast conservation therapy are not rare. Sonography is capable of demonstrating local recurrences that appear as small masses and is superior to mammography in dense breasts or breasts with implants. The sonographic appearance of local recurrences is not different from that of primary tumors.

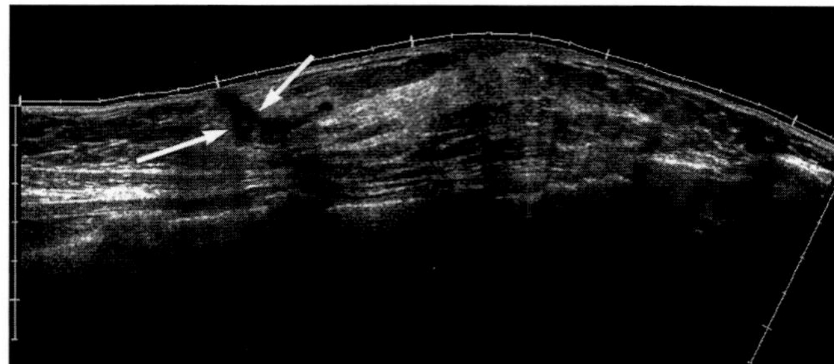

Figure 10–29. Extended-field-of-view sonogram of a lumpectomy scar shows the thin scar with concave margins (arrows).

After mastectomy and reconstructive surgery, US can be used to assess the condition of the soft tissues surrounding the expander or implant. Mammography is not usually performed on breasts reconstructed with a transverse rectus abdominis myocutaneous (TRAM) flap because of the low risk of local recurrence. The most common mass that develops after TRAM reconstruction is fat necrosis, which appears on US as an ill-defined area of variable echogenicity often associated with calcifications. Variable degrees of vascularity are seen on power Doppler US. The presence of a small oil cyst within the solid mass is typical. However, because local recurrence is not exceptional in TRAM-reconstructed breasts, it is prudent to confirm the diagnosis of any indeterminate solid mass with an ultrasound-guided needle biopsy.[26]

At M.D. Anderson Cancer Center, US is used to quantify the response of breast cancer to preoperative chemotherapy by measuring the volumes of both the primary tumor in the breast and the metastatic nodes before, during, and after the treatment. The formula for calculating the volume of a prolate ellipsoid (0.52 times the product of the three longest diameters) is used to obtain the volumes of the primary tumor and the metastatic nodes. These can then be compared with the volumes calculated on previous studies (Figure 10–30). This allows the breast imager to provide the clinician with a per-

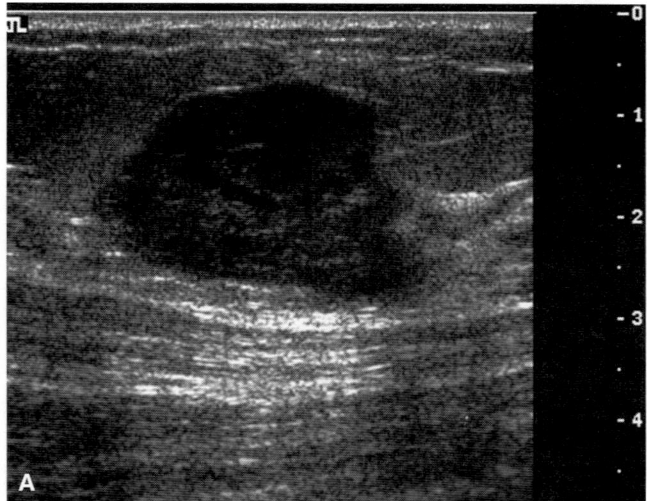

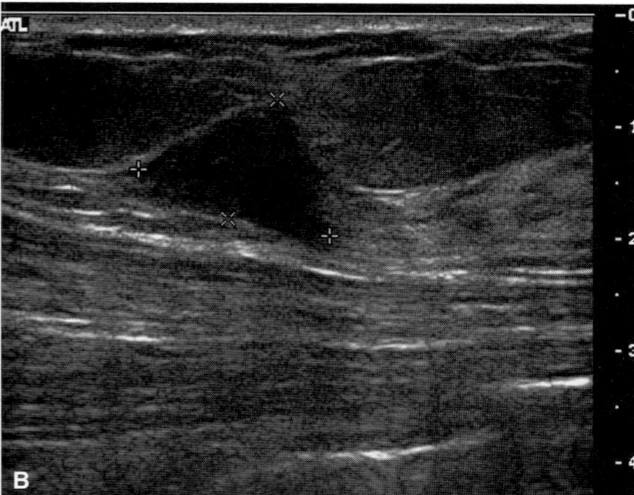

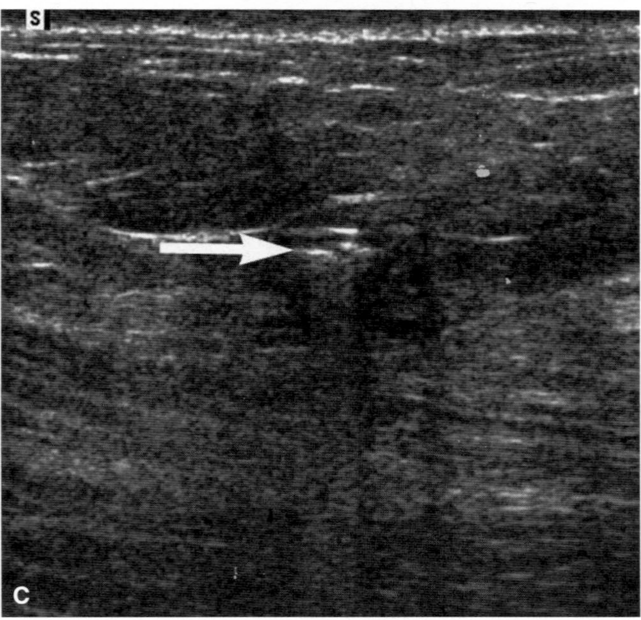

Figure 10–30. Sonograms obtained at different stages of therapy depict the response of the cancer to preoperative chemotherapy. *A,* Baseline sonogram shows a hypoechoic mass measuring 3.2 × 3.1 × 2.0 cm. *B,* Sonogram obtained during chemotherapy shows the tumor, which now measures 1.7 × 1.5 × 1.1 cm, reflecting an 85% decrease in its volume. *C,* Sonogram obtained at the end of chemotherapy shows only a vague area of distortion around the hyperechoic metallic markers (arrow) that were inserted to tag the tumor bed. Histopathologic examination revealed no residual tumor in the surgical specimen.

centage decrease in volume that accurately reflects the response of the tumor to chemotherapy. Nodal metastases usually regress faster and resume a normal appearance sooner than the primary tumor.

INTERVENTIONAL SONOGRAPHY

Because it is currently the only real-time cross-sectional imaging modality, US has emerged as the optimal guidance technique for percutaneous interventional procedures involving nonpalpable breast masses. Ultrasound-guided procedures range from aspiration of a cyst to percutaneous ablation of tumors.

Ultrasound-Guided Percutaneous Needle Biopsies

Percutaneous needle biopsies should be performed only after completing all evaluations including the physical examination and all imaging (ie, additional mammographic views, magnetic resonance imaging, positron-emission tomographic scanning, etc) procedures in order to avoid the risk of misinterpreting a postbiopsy hematoma on examination or subsequently obtained images.[27] Both FNAB and core-needle biopsy (CNB) techniques are performed with real-time sonographic guidance.[28,29] Optimal sonographic visualization of the needle and its tip requires insertion from one end of the transducer and alignment with the scanning plane (Figure 10–31).

Fine-Needle Aspiration Biopsy

For several decades, FNAB has been used routinely in the workup of palpable breast masses. Ultrasound-guided FNAB of nonpalpable breast masses was first reported in the mid-1980s.[30]

At M.D. Anderson, we use a standard 20-gauge 3.8 cm–long or a 21-gauge 5 cm–long hypodermic needle. No local anesthesia is needed. The freehand technique allows reorientation of the needle at different angles and therefore permits sampling of a larger volume (Figure 10–31). FNAB of infiltrating ductal carcinomas usually yields highly cellular cytologic aspirates, and in most cases, the diagnosis is established with a single pass.[31] The hormonal receptor status of carcinomas and proliferation markers (eg, *HER2/neu*) may also be determined using these aspi-

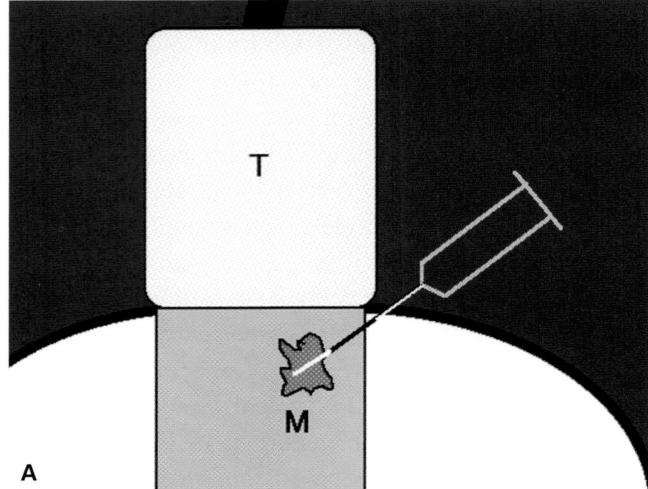

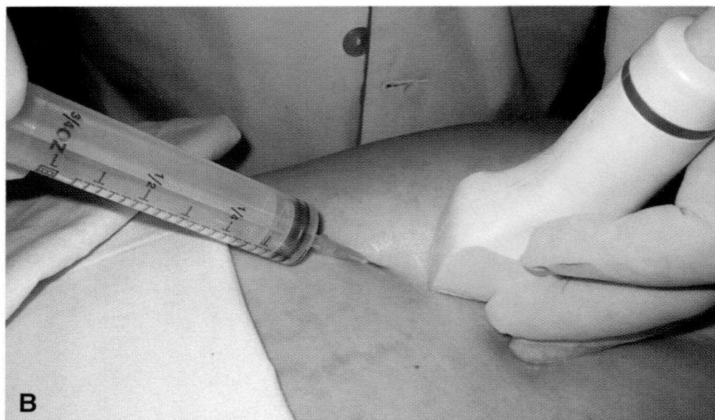

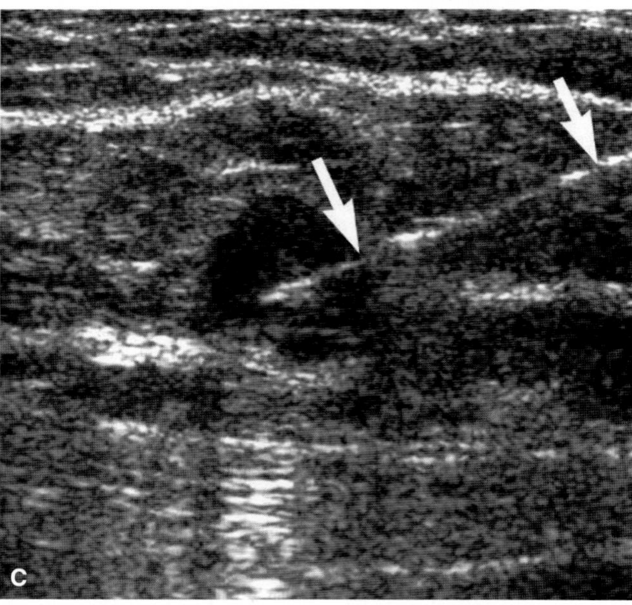

Figure 10–31. Technique of sonographically guided FNAB. *A,* Diagram shows the fine needle inserted obliquely from one end of the linear-array transducer (T) into the targeted mass (M). *B,* Photograph shows the relative positions of the needle and transducer during the procedure. *C,* Sonogram obtained during the procedure shows the echogenic needle (arrows), the tip of which has reached the center of a small carcinoma.

rates if necessary, but most will be determined using a specimen obtained during CNB or surgery.

Ultrasound-guided FNAB readily allows sampling of enlarged lymph nodes in any of the nodal basins, including the internal mammary chains (Figure 10–32).[32] FNAB of lymph nodes is easy to perform because of their rich cellularity. As a rule, a single pass is sufficient for obtaining an adequate specimen from a lymph node.

Core-Needle Biopsy

CNB is performed with cutting needles with a fixed throw and a sampling notch of a little less than 2 cm and automated spring-loaded biopsy devices. Although the standard needle used for CNB has been 14 gauge, needles as fine as 18 gauge yield cores of diagnostic quality. The golden rule is that the pathologist must be comfortable with the amount of material submitted.

Because of the throw of the needle, the cutting biopsy needle must be inserted as nearly parallel to the chest wall as possible to avoid injury to the chest wall (Figure 10–33). Under sonographic guidance and using the freehand technique, the tip of the needle is brought into contact with the mass, the perfect alignment of the needle with the scan plane is verified, the mechanism is fired, and a postfiring sonogram showing the needle traversing the target is printed. To ensure that the needle is actually traversing a minute lesion, the transducer is swiveled 90 degrees, and a transverse sonogram is obtained to show the cross section of the needle inside the target (see Figure 10–33F).[33]

What constitutes an optimal number of cores is debatable. In our experience, when transfixion of the target has been clearly documented with US and cores appear to be of satisfactory size, no more than three or four cores obtained with an 18-gauge needle are needed for diagnosis.[34]

A recent trend has been toward the use of new larger-gauge, vacuum-assisted biopsy devices such as the Mammotome (Ethicon Endosurgery, Cincinnati, OH). The advantages of these devices over CNB include the need for only a single insertion, convenient automatic core retrieval, the ability to obtain multiple large contiguous samples, and the potential for complete removal of small masses.[35] Disadvantages of the Mammotome include its large size (and thus greater associated trauma) and cost. Such vacuum-assisted core biopsy devices and the large volume of the cores they yield are well adapted for stereotactically guided biopsy of microcalcifications, but they are not necessary for the tissue diagnosis of breast masses.

Comparison of Fine-Needle Aspiration and Core-Needle Biopsy Techniques

The major advantages of ultrasound-guided FNAB include its pinpoint accuracy, its excellent tolerance by patients, and the ability to aspirate or inject fluid or air. Also, results can be obtained within minutes. Its disadvantages include its absolute requirement for an expert cytopathologist, its failure to yield adequate material in cases of fibrous tumors, and the inability to differentiate between invasive and noninvasive breast carcinomas.

The advantages of CNB, on the other hand, include a nearly 100% tissue recovery rate (even in fibrous masses), the ability to assess the invasiveness of the cancer, and the fact that tissue cores can be readily

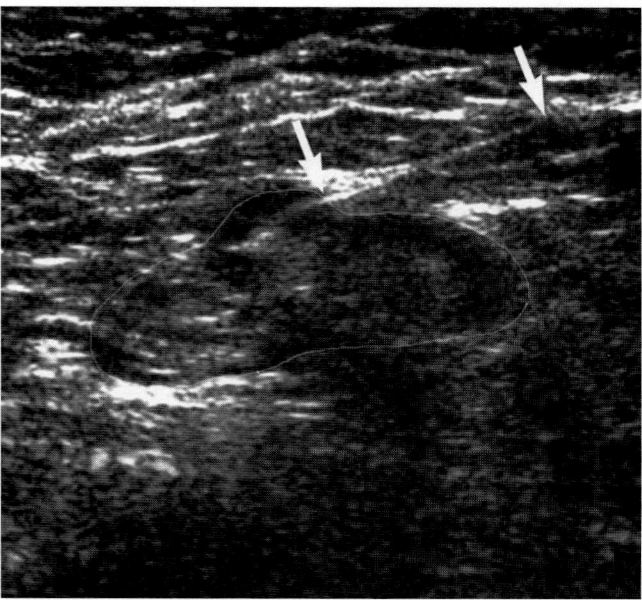

Figure 10–32. Sonographically guided fine-needle aspiration biopsy of a nonpalpable axillary lymph node metastasis in a patient with known breast cancer. Sonogram obtained during the aspiration shows the echogenic needle (arrows) whose tip has been placed within a suspicious 5 mm hypoechoic focal bulge in the cortex of an otherwise normal node (white outline).

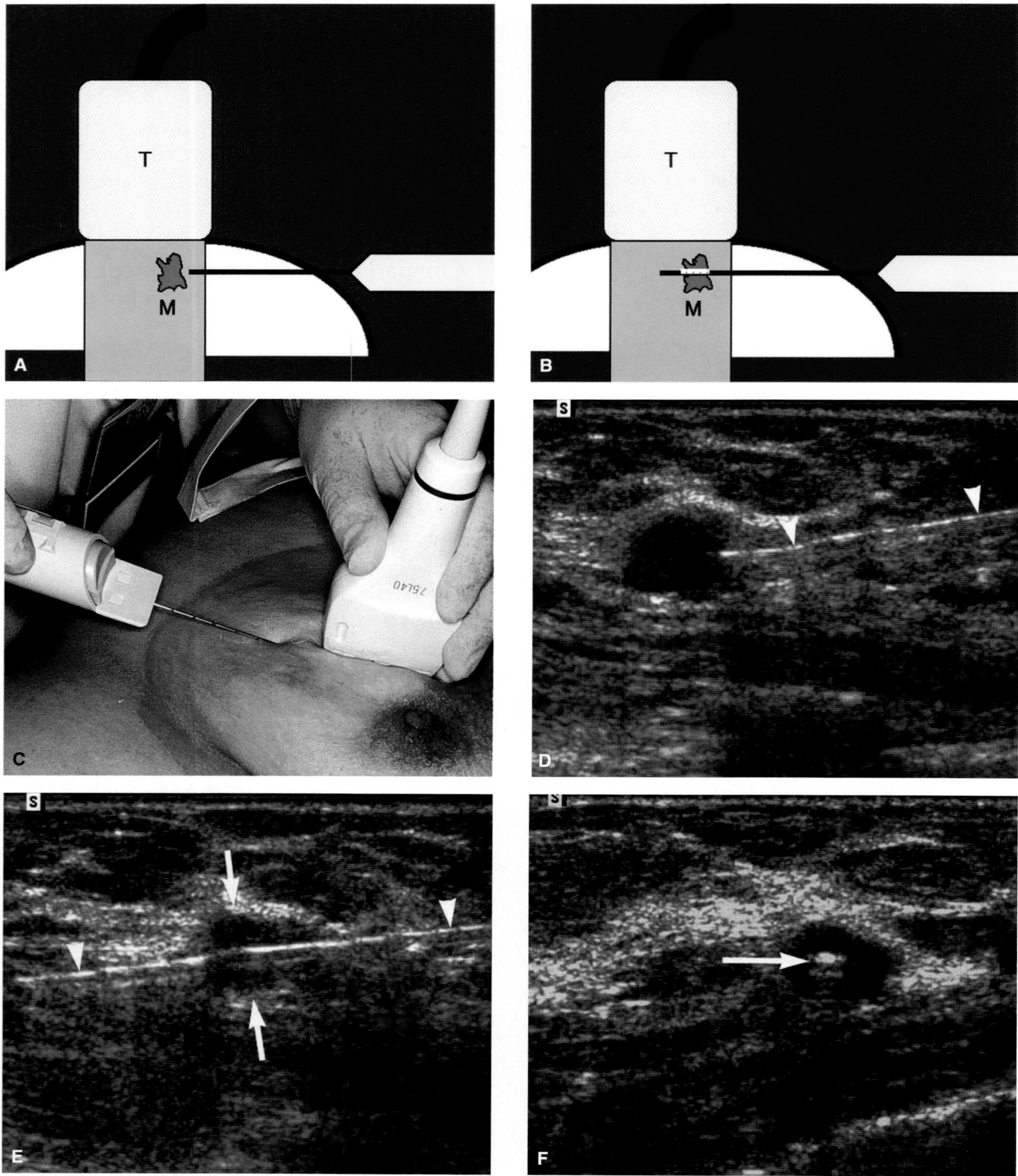

Figure 10–33. Technique of ultrasound-guided CNB of breast masses using an automated cutting-needle biopsy device. *A,* Diagram shows the prefiring position of the cutting needle, which is inserted parallel to the chest wall. M = mass, T = transducer. *B,* Diagram shows the post-firing position of the needle, which has traversed the mass. *C,* Photograph shows the relative positions of the needle and transducer during the procedure. *D,* Prefiring sonogram shows the echogenic needle (arrowheads) in contact with the small hypoechoic mass. *E,* Postfiring sonogram shows that the echogenic needle (arrowheads) has traversed the tumor (arrows). *F,* Postfiring sonogram obtained after swiveling the transducer 90 degrees shows the cross section of the needle (arrow) in the center of the mass.

interpreted by any pathologist. However, compared with FNAB, CNB is more invasive, has a higher rate of bleeding complications, and may be associated with a higher risk for malignant seeding along the needle track (reported with the use of 14-gauge needles).[36]

Thus, FNAB and CNB are two complementary facets of the same procedure, percutaneous needle biopsy of the breast. In institutions in which an expert cytopathologist is available, the radiologist should be expert in both techniques and must determine for each patient whether the lesion should be sampled with FNAB or CNB.[33] Whenever there is the possibility that the lesion might be fluid filled, FNAB should be performed first. Although some benign masses like fibroadenomas, fat necrosis, or intramammary nodes can easily be diagnosed via FNAB by an experienced cytopathologist provided with an adequate specimen, some solid benign masses, such as hyalinized fibroadenomas or fibrous masses, cannot be adequately diagnosed with FNAB. In addition, because of the risk of false-negative results in invasive lobular carcinoma, FNAB should not be attempted in these cases. Failure to obtain an adequate specimen with a repeat FNAB pass should prompt a CNB. Because CNB can determine invasiveness, which FNAB cannot, CNB is required to diagnose breast cancer before treatment planning begins. However, FNAB is ideal for the diagnosis of metastatic lymph nodes and can be used for diagnosing a recurrence. The goal to be kept in mind is that at the end of the biopsy procedure, a definitive tissue diagnosis must be available so that decisions can be made about patient care.

Ultrasound-guided needle biopsy of nonpalpable breast lesions requires teamwork and ongoing communication between the radiologist, the pathologist, the surgeon, and the medical oncologist. Ultrasound-guided interventional procedures require excellent eye-hand coordination and considerable practice before the required 100% accuracy level in hitting the target can be reached. Practicing with easily made phantoms shortens a beginner's learning curve.[37] Similarly, making a cytologic diagnosis requires considerable experience. Implementation of this procedure in the general medical community may be associated with substantial difficulties if these prerequisites cannot be met.

The golden rule of breast biopsy remains concordance between the biopsy results and the imaging and clinical findings. Any discrepancy, such as a negative result of the needle biopsy in the face of a single suspicious finding—physical, mammographic, or sonographic—should not delay surgical excision.

Other Ultrasound-Guided Interventional Procedures

Insertion of Metallic Markers to Localize Tumors that Respond to Preoperative Chemotherapy

A growing number of patients with breast carcinomas are receiving preoperative chemotherapy, and a growing number of complete responses are being observed.[38] To allow the surgeon to locate and excise the tumor bed in the event of a complete response, metallic markers are first implanted intratumorally under ultrasound guidance.[39]

At M.D. Anderson, we currently use commercially available platinum embolization coils (MCE-35P-1-2-VA coil; Cook Group, Inc, Bloomington, IN) that are well visualized on US (Figure 10–34). Smaller metallic clips, such as the UltraClip (Inrad, Inc, Kentwood, MI), are more difficult to visualize sonographically but can be used if subsequent localization will be done using mammography or if the purpose is to help the pathologist identify multiple malignant foci within a mastectomy specimen.

These markers are implanted in tumors that have responded significantly after two courses of chemotherapy or, if the tumor is small, at the time of diagnosis. After completion of preoperative chemotherapy, the breast is reassessed, and if the metallic markers can be identified sonographically by their distinctive comet-tail artifact, the tumor bed can be localized using US. If the markers cannot be seen on US, however, they can still be localized preoperatively using mammography.

Injection of Radiotracer and Dye for Sentinel Lymph Node Mapping and Biopsy

Injections of technetium-labeled sulfur colloid and isosulfan blue at the periphery of nonpalpable carcinomas are accurately performed with real-time sono-

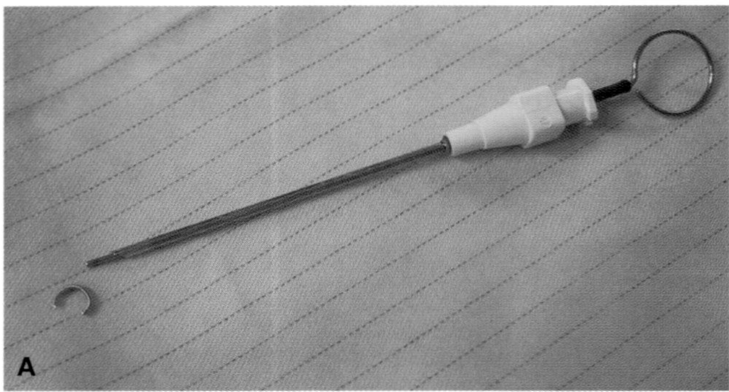

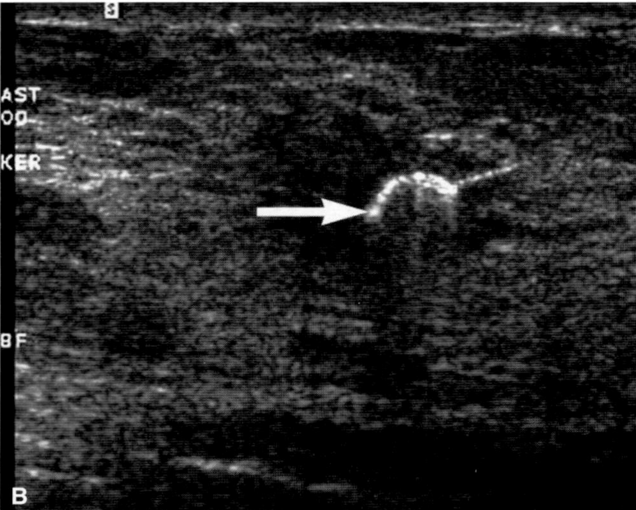

Figure 10–34. Technique of ultrasound-guided insertion of metallic markers in tumors that are responding to preoperative chemotherapy. *A*, Photograph shows a C-shaped platinum microembolization coil and the needle and blunt stylet used for its percutaneous placement in a tumor. *B*, Sonogram obtained after placement of a coil in a residual tumor that is responding to chemotherapy shows the C-shaped echogenic microembolization coil (arrow).

graphic guidance, although the need for this level of accuracy is probably not justified. In fact, intradermal injections of technetium sulfur colloid are more accurate than peritumoral injections in identifying the sentinel lymph node in some series.[40,41]

Localization of Nonpalpable Masses

Localization of nonpalpable masses that are visualized sonographically can be achieved with either preoperative or intraoperative US. The same localizing devices used for mammographic guidance can be inserted preoperatively with sonographic guidance. The device, usually a hookwire, is inserted through the mass and helps anchor the needle in place. US has the advantage of identifying the shortest distance from the entry site of the localizer to the mass, which is advantageous for the surgeon. US can be used when mammography cannot, such as when the breast is very small, the mass is very close to the chest wall or an implant, or the lesion is not clearly visualized on mammography. Obviously, masses detected only sonographically must be localized with US. In general, when a nonpalpable tumor has been visualized on both mammography and US, ultrasound-guided localization is preferable because it is faster and therefore better tolerated by the patient than mammographically guided techniques.

For the last 13 years, we at M.D. Anderson have been localizing nonpalpable breast masses with US in the operating room.[42] Intraoperative ultrasound-guided localizations are done with the patient anesthetized and positioned for surgery, decreasing the risk of the needle dislodgment during skin preparation or positioning and without the added stress of a separate localization procedure in a different department. In the vast majority of cases, a simple skin marking is made over the lesion, with the depth of the lesion being measured and communicated to the surgeon (Figure 10–35).[43] Our successful experience with intraoperative US has been confirmed recently in several studies at other institutions, and interest in this procedure is growing in the surgical community.[44–46]

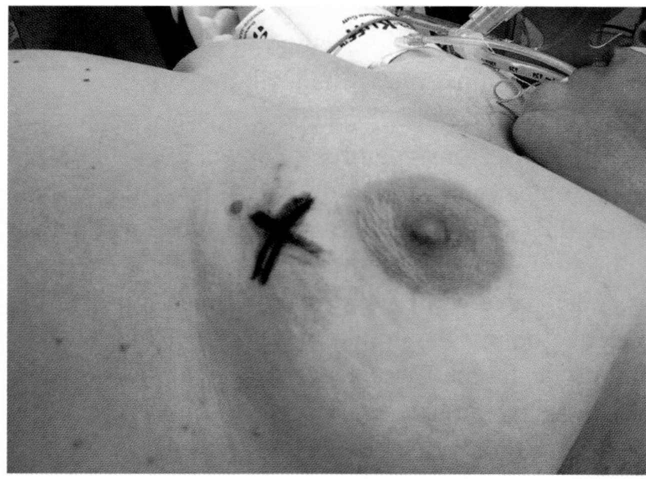

Figure 10–35. Photograph illustrates the intraoperative localization of a nonpalpable carcinoma. The patient is placed in the operative position, and after the tumor is visualized, its projection is marked on the skin and its depth is indicated to the surgeon.

Sonographic confirmation of the excised lesion detected sonographically, but not mammographically (and for which radiography of the specimen is therefore irrelevant) can be obtained by scanning the freshly excised specimen in a saline-filled container. If the mass is not seen within the specimen, then the radiologist must scan the wound to identify the residual mass and further guide the surgeon.[42] Alternatively, surgeons may want to use continuous intraoperative US to monitor their progress toward the lesion and to ensure the adequacy of the excision margins.[44–46]

Placement of the MammoSite System

The MammoSite radiation therapy system (Proxima Therapeutics, Inc, Alpharetta, GA) is a new minimally invasive method of delivering internal radiation therapy (brachytherapy) after a lumpectomy for breast cancer. This system consists of a small balloon catheter that is inserted into the postoperative cavity and then inflated with saline and a contrast agent to fit the edges of the cavity. Insertion of this device into the lumpectomy cavity can be done using real-time sonographic monitoring (Figure 10–36), although CT is usually used for confirming proper positioning of the device and for treatment planning. In 10 fractions administered twice daily over 5 days, the radioactivity source (^{192}Ir) is loaded through the catheter into the center of the balloon to deliver the prescribed dose (about 34 Gy in total) directly to the tissues surrounding the initial tumor (which are the most likely to harbor residual viable tumor cells).[47]

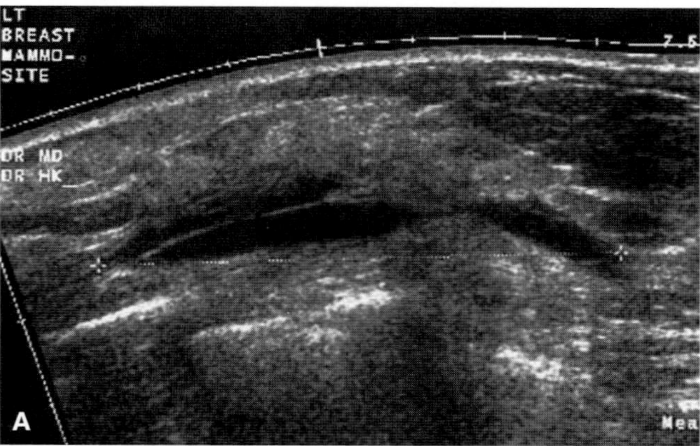

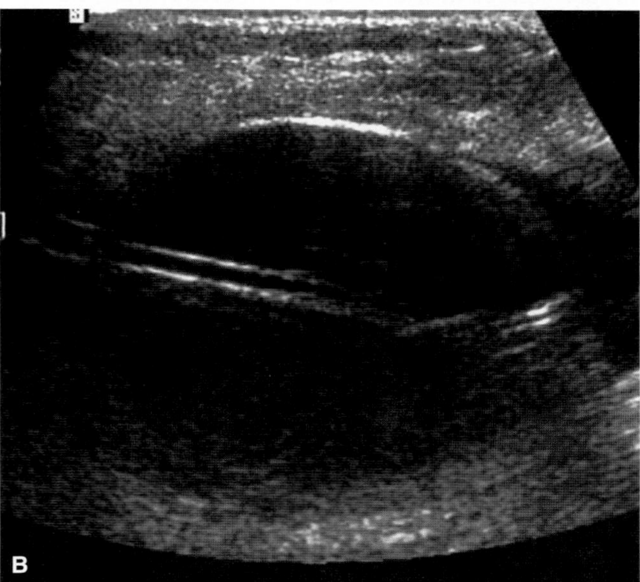

Figure 10–36. *A,* Extended-field-of-view sonogram obtained before ultrasound-guided placement of the MammoSite device in the postoperative cavity after lumpectomy for breast cancer shows the flat postoperative cavity (calipers). *B,* Sonogram obtained after placement of the MammoSite device shows the device's fluid-filled balloon that fills the post-lumpectomy cavity.

Percutaneous Ablation of Breast Tumors

In the context of using less-invasive local therapy for small breast cancers, interest has emerged in nonsurgical ablative procedures to treat the primary tumor. Image-guided ablation techniques include thermotherapy (hyperthermia induced by application of radiofrequency current, laser irradiation, or microwave irradiation), insonation with high-intensity focused ultrasound waves, and cryotherapy.

Until now, percutaneous ablation (eg, radiofrequency ablation [RFA] or cryotherapy) has been used only for palliation in patients with advanced or metastatic disease for whom conventional surgical procedures are impractical or associated with increased morbidity. The ethical issue with percutaneous ablation of small breast cancers is that patients who are eligible for such treatment options already have an excellent prognosis. Therefore, if percutaneous ablation fails, such patients may have compromised their best chance for a cure. The major technical issue with these forms of treatment is their inability to assess the margins of the ablated volume pathologically and thereby confirm the success of the treatment.

In RFA, local hyperthermia is produced by applying high-frequency alternating electrical current that flows through an uninsulated multi-pronged needle-electrode. Frictional heating is generated when the ions in the tissues around the needle-electrode attempt to follow the rapidly changing direction of the alternating current. The tissue heats resistively in the area that contacts the electrode tip, and the heat is transferred conductively to more distant tissues. Thus, RFA produces a lethal thermal zone that encompasses the primary breast cancer and a margin of surrounding normal tissue, allowing destruction of peripheral microscopic disease.

At M.D. Anderson, we investigated the feasibility and safety of ultrasound-guided RFA in the local treatment of small (T1) invasive breast carcinomas.[48] In this pilot study, we performed RFA of the small invasive carcinoma immediately before lumpectomy or mastectomy. After the multi-array needle-electrode had been inserted percutaneously into contact with the lesion, its prongs were deployed through the mass over a distance of 3 cm (Figure 10–37). The RFA generator was then set to reach a temperature of 95°C at the tip of the electrodes and maintain it for 15 minutes.

During this procedure, no specific changes were evident in the sonographic appearance of the tumor that would reliably reflect the pathologic changes induced by RFA or contribute to determining the extent of the thermal lesion. After the procedure, however, color Doppler US showed complete extinction of any preexisting vascularity in and around the tumor.

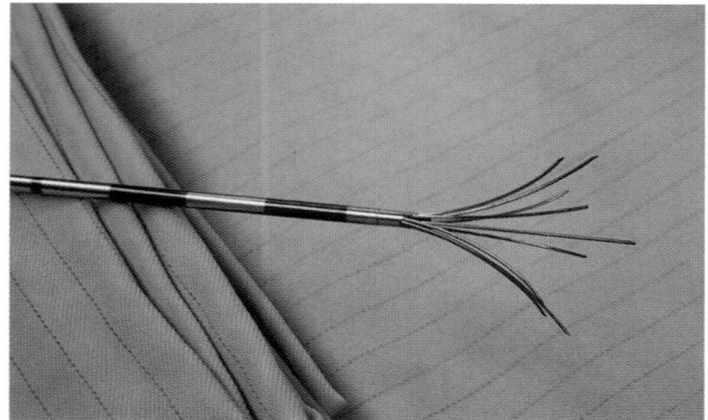

Figure 10–37. Photograph shows the multi-array needle-electrode (prongs deployed) used for RFA of breast cancer.

In our study, the lesion targeted for RFA was completely ablated in all cases (Figure 10–38).[48] However, in the case of one tumor that had been downstaged preoperatively by neoadjuvant chemotherapy from a T2 tumor to a small residual tumor of about 1 cm, RFA successfully ablated the minute tumor residue, but histopathologic specimens revealed extensive residual invasive and in situ carcinoma surrounding the residual visible tumor. Consequently, we believe that RFA should not be attempted in patients who have undergone preoperative chemotherapy.

The most important end point for future trials designed to evaluate RFA as an alternative to lumpectomy will be long-term local control. It is unknown whether RFA-induced hyperthermia producing coagulative necrosis of the tumor and a surrounding rim of tissue will be as effective in ablating the carcinoma as surgical excision is and will provide similar long-term local control. Because the expected 5-year recurrence rate is low, large-scale studies are needed to detect any statistically significant difference between conventional surgery and RFA.

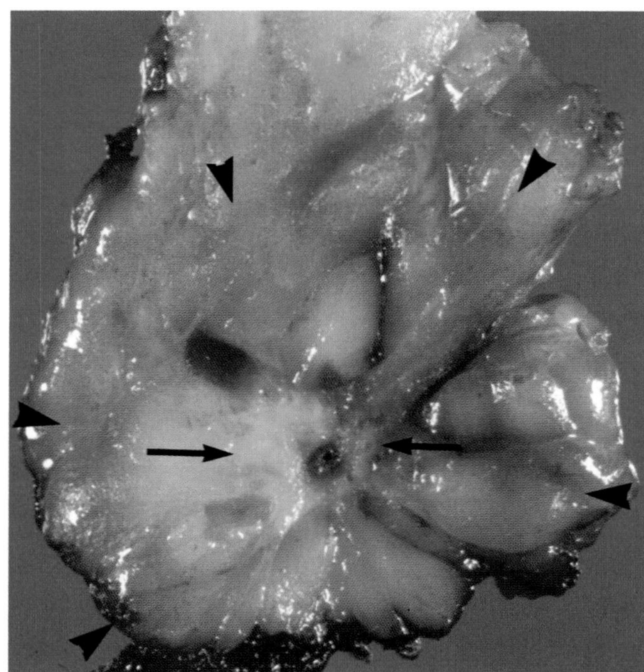

Figure 10–38. Photograph of a breast tissue specimen excised after completion of radiofrequency ablation shows a hyperemic ring (arrowheads) at the periphery of the ablated area. The small carcinoma (arrows) is seen in the center of the ring. Note the track of the needle and of the prongs.

Finally, which patients will benefit from and should be offered RFA as an alternative therapy for breast cancer is still unknown. Until RFA proves to be equivalent to breast-conserving surgery, only selected patients, such as elderly patients with small, slow-growing tumors, should be offered RFA, preferably as participants in a clinical trial. Selected patients with local recurrence could also be considered for RFA. RFA of the tumor before surgical or percutaneous excision may also be considered to minimize dissemination of tumor cells during dissection.

Cryoablation is well suited for use under sonographic guidance because of the sharp hyperechoic interface of the advancing ice ball.[49] Thus, the extent of freezing can be visualized and controlled in real time, which is not possible with RFA. As a result, cryoablation is easily tailored to the size of the lesion. If the lesion lies close to the skin, sterile saline can be injected under sonographic guidance between the advancing ice ball and the overlying skin to protect it from frostbite.

In a study of 16 breast cancers with a mean size of 2.1 cm treated with a 3 mm cryoprobe with two freeze–thaw cycles, the mean diameter of the ice ball after the second freezing cycle was 2.8 ± 0.3 cm. Five tumors smaller than 1.6 cm showed no residual invasive cancer after treatment, but two of them had DCIS in the surrounding tissues. Tumors 2.3 cm or larger, however, showed incomplete necrosis.[50]

Although the use of cryotherapy for breast cancer is subject to the same ethical and technical problems as RFA, its use for fibroadenomas is not, and this latter application is gaining popularity as an office-based procedure.[51]

SUMMARY

Sonographic examination is routinely used in breast imaging centers as an essential complement to physical and mammographic examinations for evaluating breast masses. US not only differentiates cystic from solid masses but also aids in discriminating between benign and malignant solid masses. In patients with known breast cancer, US of lymph node–bearing areas with ultrasound-guided FNAB of suspicious nodes can reveal findings that greatly alter the pretherapeutic staging.

Although US can detect nonpalpable carcinomas missed by mammography, it cannot replace mammography for routine cancer screening as it cannot demonstrate microcalcifications and its success is highly operator dependent. The efficacy of US in its application as a supplement to mammography remains to be measured.

Because of its unique real-time capability, however, US has become the standard method for guiding needle biopsies of nonpalpable breast masses and for preoperative or intraoperative localization of such lesions. An exciting new field of investigation is the use of US to guide and monitor percutaneous ablation of small nonpalpable breast cancers.

REFERENCES

1. Fornage BD, Atkinson EN, Nock LF, et al. US with extended field of view: phantom-tested accuracy of distance measurements. Radiology 2000;214:579–84.
2. Ghate SV, Soo MS, Mengoni PM. Extended field-of-view two-dimensional ultrasonography of the breast: improvement in lesion documentation. J Ultrasound Med 1999; 18:597–601.
3. Fornage BD. Recent advances in breast sonography. J Belge Radiol 2000;83:75–80.
4. Rosen EL, Soo MS. Tissue harmonic imaging sonography of breast lesions: improved margin analysis, conspicuity, and image quality compared to conventional ultrasound. Clin Imaging 2001;25:379–84.
5. Chen WM, Chang RF, Moon WK, et al. Breast cancer diagnosis using three-dimensional ultrasound and pixel relation analysis. Ultrasound Med Biol 2003;29:1027–35.
6. Fenster A, Surry KJ, Mills GR, et al. 3D ultrasound guided breast biopsy system. Ultrasonics 2004;42:769–74.
7. Konofagou EE. Quo vadis elasticity imaging? Ultrasonics 2004;42:331–6.
8. Lee SW, Choi HY, Baek SY, et al. Role of color and power Doppler imaging in differentiating between malignant and benign solid breast masses. J Clin Ultrasound 2002;30: 459–64.
9. Fornage BD, Brown C, Edeiken BS, et al. Contrast-enhanced breast sonography: preliminary results with gray-scale and contrast harmonic imaging of breast carcinoma. J Ultrasound Med 2000;19(Suppl):85A.
10. Forsberg F, Goldberg BB, Merritt CR, et al. Diagnosing breast lesions with contrast-enhanced 3-dimensional power Doppler imaging. J Ultrasound Med 2004;23:173–82.
11. Zdemir A, Kilic K, Ozdemir H, et al. Contrast-enhanced power Doppler sonography in breast lesions: effect on differential diagnosis after mammography and gray scale sonography. J Ultrasound Med 2004;23:183–95.
12. Soo MS, Baker JA, Rosen EL. Sonographic detection and sonographically guided biopsy of breast microcalcifications. AJR Am J Roentgenol 2003;180:941–8.

13. Fornage BD. Role of color Doppler imaging in differentiating between pseudocystic malignant tumors and fluid collections. J Ultrasound Med 1995;14:125–8.
14. Lam WW, Chu WC, Tse GM, et al. Sonographic appearance of mucinous carcinoma of the breast. AJR Am J Roentgenol 2004;182:1069–74.
15. Selinko VL, Middleton LP, Dempsey PJ. Role of sonography in diagnosing and staging invasive lobular carcinoma. J Clin Ultrasound 2004;32:323–32.
16. Chen SC, Cheung YC, Lo YF, et al. Sonographic differentiation of invasive and intraductal carcinomas of the breast. Br J Radiol 2003;76:600–4.
17. Gunhan-Bilgen I, Ustun EE, Memis A. Inflammatory breast carcinoma: mammographic, ultrasonographic, clinical, and pathologic findings in 142 cases. Radiology 2002; 223:829–38.
18. Mendelson EB, Berg WA, Merritt CR. Toward a standardized breast ultrasound lexicon, BI-RADS: ultrasound. Semin Roentgenol 2001;36:217–25.
19. Gordon PB, Goldenberg SL. Malignant breast masses detected only by ultrasound. A retrospective review. Cancer 1995;76:626–30.
20. Kolb TM, Lichy J, Newhouse JH. Occult cancer in women with dense breasts: detection with screening US—diagnostic yield and tumor characteristics. Radiology 1998; 207:191–9.
21. Berg WA, Gutierrez L, NessAiver MS, et al. Diagnostic accuracy of mammography, clinical examination, US, and MR imaging in preoperative assessment of breast cancer. Radiology 2004;233:830–49.
22. Deurloo EE, Tanis PJ, Gilhuijs KG, et al. Reduction in the number of sentinel lymph node procedures by preoperative ultrasonography of the axilla in breast cancer. Eur J Cancer 2003;39:1068–73.
23. De Kanter AY, van Eijck CH, van Geel AN, et al. Multicentre study of ultrasonographically guided axillary node biopsy in patients with breast cancer. Br J Surg 1999; 86:1459–62.
24. Sobin LH, Wittekind C, editors. International Union Against Cancer: TNM classification of malignant tumours. 6th ed. New York: Wiley; 2002. p. 131–41.
25. Greene FL, Page DL, Fleming ID, et al, editors. AJCC cancer staging manual. 6th ed. New York: Springer-Verlag; 2002. p. 223–40.
26. Edeiken BS, Fornage BD, Bedi DG, et al. Recurrence in autogenous myocutaneous flap reconstruction after mastectomy for primary breast cancer: US diagnosis. Radiology 2003;227:542–8.
27. Svensson WE, Tohno E, Cosgrove DO, et al. Effects of fine-needle aspiration on the US appearance of the breast. Radiology 1992;185:709–11.
28. Fornage BD, Sneige N, Faroux MJ, et al. Sonographic appearance and ultrasound-guided fine-needle aspiration biopsy of breast carcinomas smaller than 1 cm^3. J Ultrasound Med 1990;9:559–68.
29. Parker SH, Jobe WE, Dennis MA, et al. US-guided automated large-core breast biopsy. Radiology 1993;187:507–11.
30. Fornage BD, Faroux MJ, Simatos A. Breast masses: US-guided fine-needle aspiration biopsy. Radiology 1987;147:409–14.
31. Boerner S, Fornage B, Singletary S, et al. Ultrasound-guided fine-needle aspiration of nonpalpable breast lesions: a review of 1,885 FNA cases using the NCI-supported recommendations on the uniform approach to breast fine-needle aspiration. Cancer Cytopathol 1999;87:19–24.
32. Fornage BD, Coan JD, David CL. Ultrasound-guided needle biopsy of the breast and other interventional procedures. Radiol Clin North Am 1992;30:167–85.
33. Fornage BD, Sneige N, Edeiken BS. Interventional breast sonography. Eur J Radiol 2002;42:17–31.
34. Sauer G, Deissler H, Strunz K, et al. Ultrasound-guided large-core needle biopsies of breast lesions: analysis of 962 cases to determine the number of samples for reliable tumour classification. Br J Cancer 2005;92:231–5.
35. Johnson AT, Henry-Tillman RS, Smith LF, et al. Percutaneous excisional breast biopsy. Am J Surg 2002;184:550–4.
36. Stolier A, Skinner J, Levine EA. A prospective study of seeding of the skin after core biopsy of the breast. Am J Surg 2000;180:104–7.
37. Fornage BD. A simple phantom for training in ultrasound-guided needle biopsy using the freehand technique. J Ultrasound Med 1989;8:701–3.
38. Valero V, Buzdar AU, McNeese M, et al. Primary chemotherapy in the treatment of breast cancer: The University of Texas M.D. Anderson Cancer Center experience. Clin Breast Cancer 2002;3(Suppl 2):S63–8.
39. Edeiken BS, Fornage BD, Bedi DG, et al. US-guided implantation of metallic markers for permanent localization of the tumor bed in patients with breast cancer who undergo preoperative chemotherapy. Radiology 1999; 213:895–900.
40. Lin KM, Patel TH, Ray A, et al. Intradermal radioisotope is superior to peritumoral blue dye or radioisotope in identifying breast cancer sentinel nodes. J Am Coll Surg 2004; 199:561–6.
41. Fleming FJ, Hill AD, Kavanagh D, et al. Intradermal radioisotope injection optimises sentinel lymph node identification in breast cancer. Eur J Surg Oncol 2004;30:708–9.
42. Fornage BD, Ross MI, Singletary SE, et al. Localization of impalpable breast masses: value of sonography in the operating room and scanning of excised specimens. AJR Am J Roentgenol 1994;163:569–73.
43. Fornage BD. Intraoperative sonography of the breast. In: Kane RA, editor. Intraoperative, laparoscopic, and endoluminal ultrasound. New York: Churchill Livingstone; 1998. p. 142–7.
44. Moore MM, Whitney LA, Cerilli L, et al. Intraoperative ultrasound is associated with clear lumpectomy margins for palpable infiltrating ductal breast cancer. Ann Surg 2001;233:761–8.
45. Rahusen FD, Taets van Amerongen AHM, van Diest PJ, et al. Ultrasound-guided lumpectomy of nonpalpable breast cancers: a feasibility study looking at the accuracy of obtained margins. J Surg Oncol 1999;72:72–6.
46. Smith LF, Rubio IT, Henry-Tillman R, et al. Intraoperative ultrasound-guided breast biopsy. Am J Surg 2000;180: 419–23.
47. Zannis VJ, Walker LC, Barclay-White B, et al. Postoperative ultrasound-guided percutaneous placement of a new

breast brachytherapy balloon catheter. Am J Surg 2003; 186:383–5.
48. Fornage BD, Sneige N, Ross MI, et al. Small (≤ 2-cm) breast cancer treated with US-guided radiofrequency ablation: feasibility study. Radiology 2004;231:215–24.
49. Roubidoux MA, Sabel MS, Bailey JE, et al. Small (< 2.0-cm) breast cancers: mammographic and US findings at US-guided cryoablation. Initial experience. Radiology 2004;233:857–67.
50. Pfleiderer SO, Freesmeyer MG, Marx C, et al. Cryotherapy of breast cancer under ultrasound guidance: initial results and limitations. Eur Radiol 2002;12:3009–14.
51. Littrup PJ, Freeman-Gibb L, Andea A, et al. Cryotherapy for breast fibroadenomas. Radiology 2005;234:63–72.

11

Magnetic Resonance Imaging

MITCHELL SCHNALL

Imaging plays a central role in the fight against breast cancer. In particular, imaging is important for detection through screening; the characterization of breast findings, its role in breast cancer extent, and the response to treatment. Traditionally, film screen x-ray mammography has been the mainstay of breast imaging. Although this remains the case, concerns over poor sensitivity in the radiographically dense breast and low specificity have led to the application of newer technologies for breast cancer detection and characterization. The introduction of digital mammography with its associated image processing and tomosynthesis promises to improve mammographic performance. Sonography is routinely employed in the diagnostic setting and is supported for screening by some investigators. Although positron emission tomography is gaining more widespread use in the evaluation of therapeutic response, it appears limited by low spatial resolution in the evaluation of disease in the breast. Among the most exciting new technologies for breast imaging is magnetic resonance imaging (MRI).

The initial attempts to apply MRI for the detection of breast cancer in the mid-1980s were not successful.[1,2] Although it was clear that high-quality images of the breast could be obtained with MRI, the natural contrast available in MRI was not sufficient for breast cancer detection. In 1989, Heywang and colleagues and Kaiser and Zeitler independently reported on the use of intravenous contrast enhancement to detect breast cancer.[3,4] Importantly, they demonstrated that MRI was capable of imaging mammography occult breast cancers. These observations led to extensive investigation of contrast-enhanced MRI as a tool for the detection, diagnosis, and characterization of breast cancer. Today, although still controversial, the clinical use of breast MRI is gaining wide acceptance among the radiologists, medical oncologists, surgeons, and radiation oncologists who are involved in breast cancer care.

TECHNOLOGY AND TECHNIQUE

MRI relies on the detection of the nuclear magnetic resonance (NMR) signal from protons within the water and fat content of tissue in order to develop anatomic images. Central to the MRI instrument is the magnet. The MRI magnet provides the magnetic field that slightly magnetizes the protons in the body so that they can create an NMR signal. The signal is stronger with stronger magnetic fields. Clinical MRI magnets vary from 0.2 to 3 Tesla in field strength. Most breast MRIs are performed at 1.5 Tesla (the most common clinical magnet field strength); however, there are reports of breast MRI being performed from 0.5 to 4 Tesla.[5,6] The NMR signal is detected by an antenna placed around the breast. This antenna is referred to as a coil (Figure 11–1). Typically, the patient lies prone on the breast coil. Most breast coils offer the option for gentle compression in order to orient and reshape the breast. Although early in the history of breast MRI, there were limited options, causing investigators to often construct their own breast coils, there are many high-quality coils currently available. This has had a large impact on the dissemination of breast MRI as a clinical tool. Most current breast coils provide access to the breast, so that in conjunction with

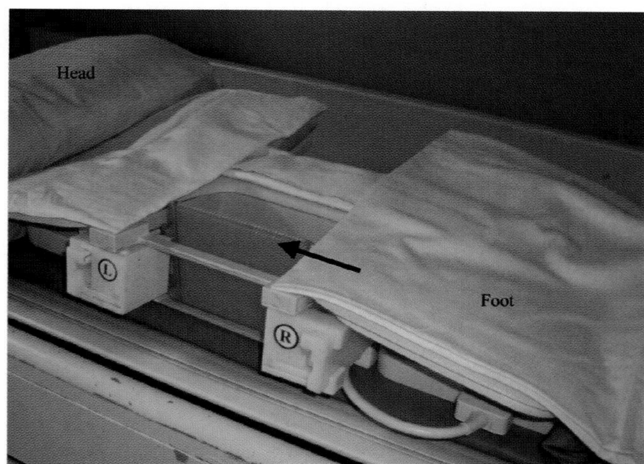

Figure 11–1. Typical breast coil. The patient lies prone with the breasts dependent, gently compressed by the lateral compression plate (arrow). The lateral compression plate also serves as a biopsy guidance grid.

guidance appliances, MRI-guided biopsy is possible. There are a number of options for MRI-guided breast biopsy, ranging from needle localization to vacuum-assisted core biopsy.[7,8]

As discussed above, MRI relies on the observation of contrast enhancement in order to image a breast cancer. The contrast enhancement serves as a loose surrogate for vascularity and vascular permeability. Thus, breast MRI can be considered a "functional imaging" modality, targeting tumor angiogenesis. Current clinical practice uses low molecular weight gadolinium (Gd) chelates as contrast agents. These agents diffuse relatively freely throughout the capillary membrane and into the extracellular space. They do not enter the intracellular compartment. A typical breast MRI examination will acquire precontrast and several postcontrast images over approximately 5 to 7 minutes in order to sample aspects of the pharmacokinetics of the contrast agents. The pharmacokinetics of contrast agents are predominantly governed by flow, vascular permeability, and available extracellular space for the contrast diffusion. The product of the flow and permeability (PS product) governs the exchange constant (Ktr) between the vascular and intracellular space, and can be estimated by modeling of the kinetic response of tumor enhancement to an injection of contrast media.[9] Tissue with high perfusion and permeability and relatively low extracellular space will experience rapid increases in Gd concentrations after an intravenous bolus, and a relatively rapid (over 5 minutes) washout of Gd as the vascular concentration decreases. This tends to be the case for vascular and cellular cancers. Tissue with relatively low perfusion and permeability and an extensive extracellular space will demonstrate slower increases in Gd concentration after an intravenous injection, due to a large space in which contrast can pool. There is a continual increase in the Gd concentration for over 5 to 10 minutes after injection. Rapid contrast enhancement and an associated washout within 5 minutes are considered a sign of malignancy.[10]

The quantitative analysis of the enhancement is complicated by the mechanism of signal enhancement caused by Gd. Gadolinium affects the MRI signal by interacting with the protons in water and shortening their T1 relaxation times. Imaging techniques that weight the signal according to T1 relaxation times will demonstrate increased signal (referred to as signal enhancement) in areas of high Gd concentration. The relationship between signal and Gd concentration is nonlinear and technique dependent. Thus, relating the quantitative signal enhancement between different acquisition techniques is not valid. This issue has complicated the quantitative analysis of the pharmacokinetic response of tumors to the Gd bolus. Thus, current clinical practice typically involves the identification of enhancement and the pharmacokinetics of the uptake and washout pattern. The architecture of the enhancing foci is also an important consideration for interpretation.

Breast MRI can be performed as a single or dual examination. Newer techniques employing parallel imaging with multiple receiver channels allow both breasts to be examined simultaneously without sacrificing image resolution.[11] Images are most often acquired in a three-dimensional (3D) acquisition and, in principal, can be displayed in any imaging plane. However, most techniques do not acquire images with equal resolution in all dimensions and, therefore, have preferred orientations for image display. All three planes are used in clinical practice, and their use depends on the technology available and user preference. In addition, 3D reconstructions of the entire breast can be generated.

An additional issue related to MRI technique is the suppression of signals from fat. Fat tissue has intrinsically short T1 relaxation times and will also be bright on T1-weighted images. The presence of fat within the breast can make it difficult to detect enhancement. Subtraction of post-injection from pre-injection images can be helpful in this regard, but may be difficult to interpret because of patient motion. Thus, the use of adjunct techniques that selectively suppress fat signals based on its chemical shift is common in breast MRI. An example of fat-suppressed, pre- and postcontrast breast, T1-weighted MRI images demonstrating a breast cancer is illustrated in Figure 11–2. The associated enhancement curve demonstrating rapid enhancement and washout is also shown.

The use of ^{1}H-NMR spectroscopy as an adjunct to imaging in the evaluation of cancer has been proposed. This is based on the association of high choline levels on ^{1}H-NMR spectroscopy with cancer in general and breast cancer specifically. There have been reports of a positive association of the presence of choline and cancer on MR spectroscopy studies. However, the routine implementation of ^{1}H-NMR spectroscopy in the breast is challenging. This is due to the fact that the breast often contains large amounts of lipid tissue, which when combined with the water, create large background signals.[6,12] Strategies to extract the choline signal from this background are under development. Thus currently, spectroscopy is limited to lesions > 1 cm in the smallest dimension. An example of a breast MRI spectrum of a cancer demonstrating choline is included in Figure 11–3.

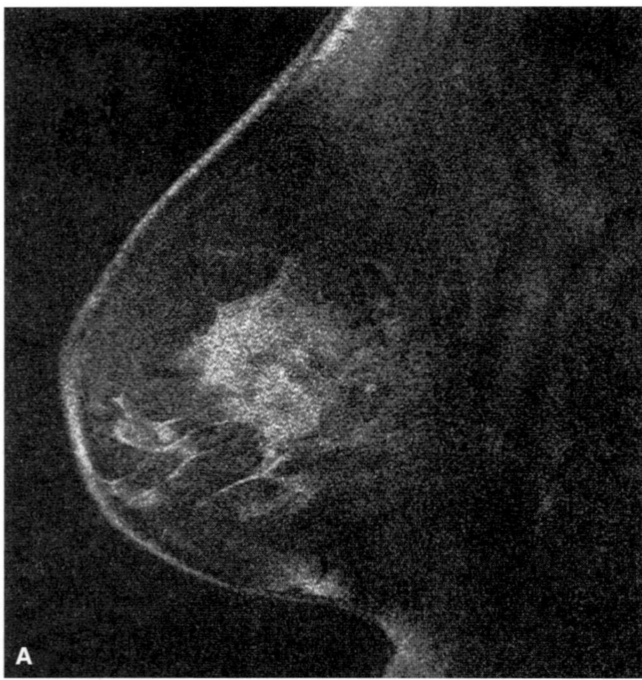

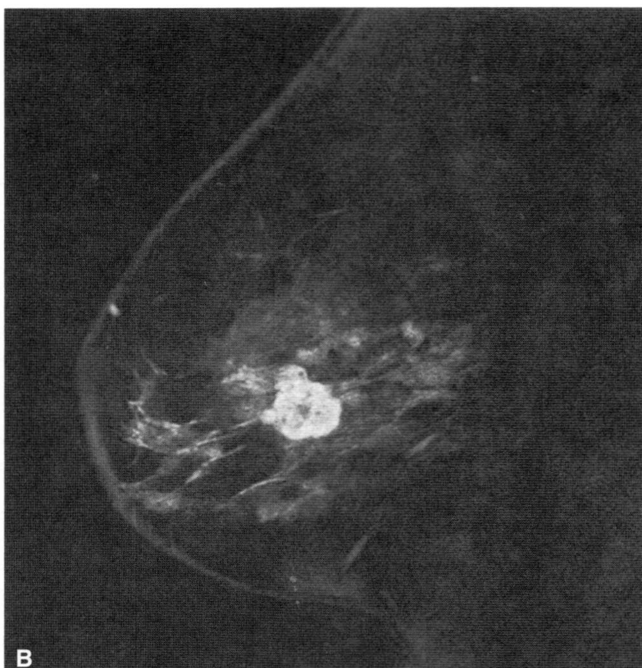

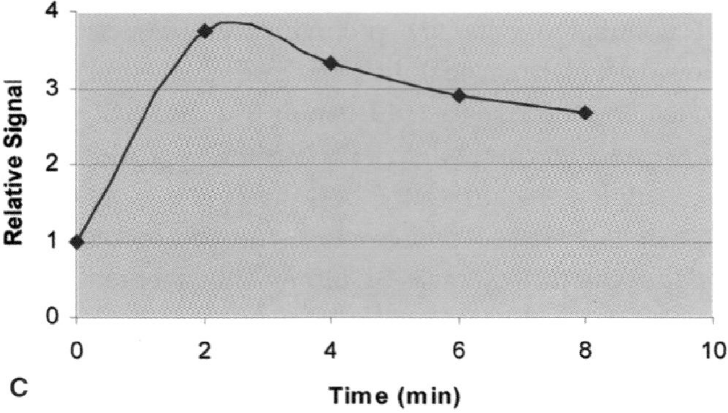

Figure 11–2. Pre- *A*, and post- *B*, contrast sagittal images demonstrate an irregular enhancing mass that represents a biopsy proven invasive ductal carcinoma. *C*, illustrates the dynamic signal intensity curve demonstrating rapid enhancement and washout that is often associated with cancer.

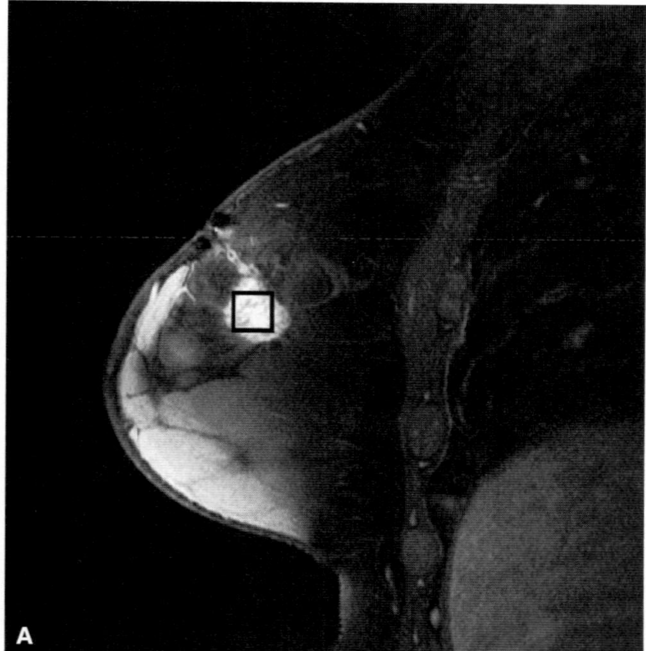

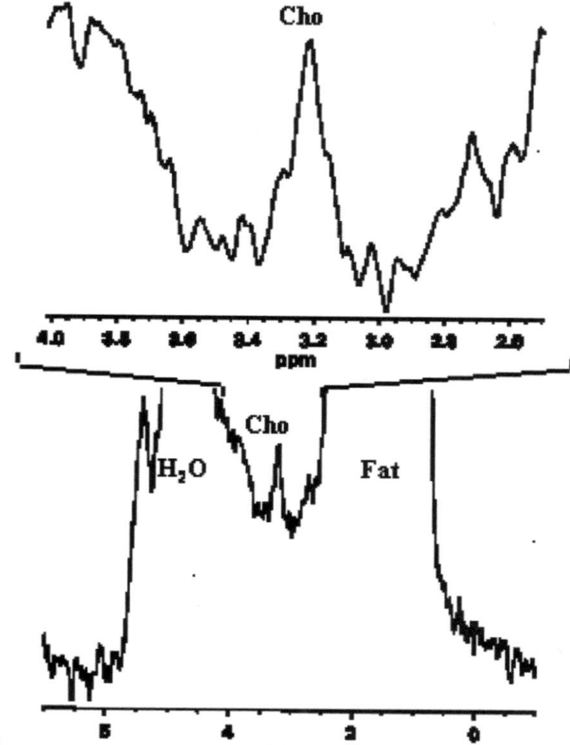

Figure 11–3. *A*, Image demonstrating an enhancing lesion and a box illustrating the location of spectral localization; *B*, spectrum from a breast cancer demonstrating choline between the large fat and water signals. A spectrum with an expanded scale is shown on top.

PRACTICE AND REPORTING STANDARDS FOR BREAST MRI

Breast imaging is among the most regulated of medical practices. The Mammogram Quality Standards Act (MQSA) imposes federal regulation of the practice of mammography and requires periodic audits of mammography practices. Although breast MRI is not governed by MQSA, the American College of Radiology has published standards for breast MRI reporting.[13] These standards are an extension of the Breast Imaging Reporting and Data System (BIRADS) originally developed for mammography. As in mammography, they mandate comparison to prior breast imaging and correlation with clinical history. Thus, patients presenting for breast MRI should make sure that prior imaging studies are available to the interpreting radiologist.

In addition to describing the technical details that should be included in a breast MRI report, the BIRADS standards include a lexicon for describing findings that include a final assessment of 0 to 6, similar to mammography, where

0 indicates an incomplete examination or workup (the prior images are not available for comparison, there was a technical failure, etc),

1 indicates "no abnormal enhancement,"

2 indicates "benign,"

3 indicates "probably benign" and is associated with a recommendation for follow-up,

4 indicates "suspicious" and is associated with a biopsy recommendation,

5 indicates "highly suspicious," and

6 refers to cases with a known diagnosis of cancer.

Adherence to this standard removes any ambiguity over the significance and recommendation relative to a finding on breast MRI.

The lexicon for describing findings on breast MRI prescribes a description that includes architectural and "dynamic" (pharmacokinetic) features of each area of abnormal enhancement. Architecturally, enhancement on breast MRI is broadly classified as mass or nonmass enhancement. Mass enhancement is described by border features and other morphologic criteria. Some particular mass features that are unique to MRI include enhancement preferentially around the rim of a lesion (rim enhancement), and the presence of dark septation within a smooth-bordered mass (internal septation). Rim enhancement has a strong association with cancer, whereas internal septation has a strong association with a diagnosis of fibroadenoma.

Nonmass-like enhancement is typically described by its distribution and form. The distribution is described on a classification including ductal, segmental, regional, patchy, and diffuse, similar to the description used for the distribution of microcalcifications. The more that enhancement conforms to a duct or segmental distribution, the more likely it is to be malignant. The form of nonmass-like enhancement is described based on the size of the individual "cells" that make up the enhancing area. Small cells that seem to correspond to individual breast lobules are described as stippled enhancement. Larger cells are referred to as clumped enhancement. Larger areas of denser enhancement are referred to as confluent, heterogeneous, or reticular, depending on the texture of the enhancement. The larger the cells that comprise the enhancement, the more likely it is to be malignant.

The standards for describing the dynamics of breast MRI enhancement prescribe a qualitative assessment of the time signal intensity curve. The time signal intensity curve is divided into an initial phase (first 2 minutes after enhancement) and a delayed phase (2 to 7 minutes after enhancement). The rate of enhancement is rated during the initial phase as fast, medium, or slow. This rating is in general made by assessing the level of enhancement achieved in the first 1 to 2 minutes. The delayed phase is described as demonstrating a persistent increase of signal, plateau of signal, or washout of signal. Rapid enhancement in the initial phase and washout in the delayed phase are associated with the highest likelihood of cancer. In order to satisfy the requirements for reporting the dynamic features, at least three time points must be acquired during a breast MRI examination (precontrast, 2 minutes postcontrast, and 5 minutes postcontrast). Many centers use this three–time-point approach in conjunction with software tools that will provide color overlays to the MRI image, indicating dynamic classification of the delayed phase. It is understood that the dynamic response of a lesion to contrast is heterogeneous. Thus, the standard prescribes that the most suspicious area of the lesion be used to assign a dynamic classification. Examples of several types of lesions and their associated lexicon descriptions are included in Figure 11–4.

BREAST MRI AS A DIAGNOSTIC TOOL

One of the initial applications envisioned for breast MRI was as an adjunctive diagnostic test, to further evaluate clinical and mammographic findings in an effort to improve the yields from breast biopsy without sacrificing the sensitivity of breast cancer detection. As a diagnostic tool, the goal of breast MRI is to classify an already identified finding as benign or malignant. Although initially it was thought that the presence of signal enhancement after contrast injection would be a sensitive and specific sign for malignancy, it is clear that enhancement alone is not specific for cancer. Harms and colleagues performed careful correlation between breast MRI and mastectomy specimens.[14] They observed that approximately 40% of enhancing foci represented cancer. Given the high pretest probability of this particular patient population, this could be considered an upper limit for the positive predictive value of contrast enhancement on breast MRI. Strategies to reduce false-positive results include assessing the intensity of enhancement, the kinetics of enhancement, and the architecture of enhancement.

Among the initial efforts to develop criteria for distinguishing benign from malignant breast lesions was the recursive partitioning interpretation scheme developed by Nunes and colleagues.[15] This scheme incorporated only architectural features. However, in a diagnostic population, they were able to achieve 96% sensitivity and 79% specificity for cancer. Others have advocated the use of contrast enhancement kinetics for distinguishing cancer from benign conditions. Unfortunately, scan protocols and interpretation criteria vary widely among investigators. For example, Boetes and colleagues

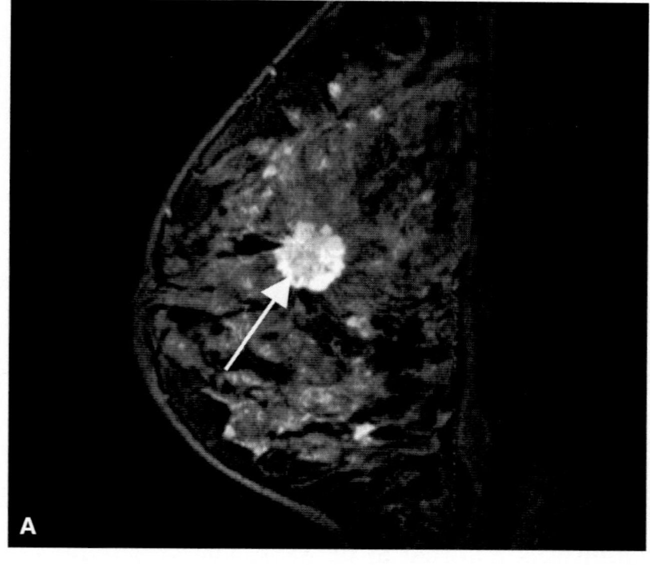

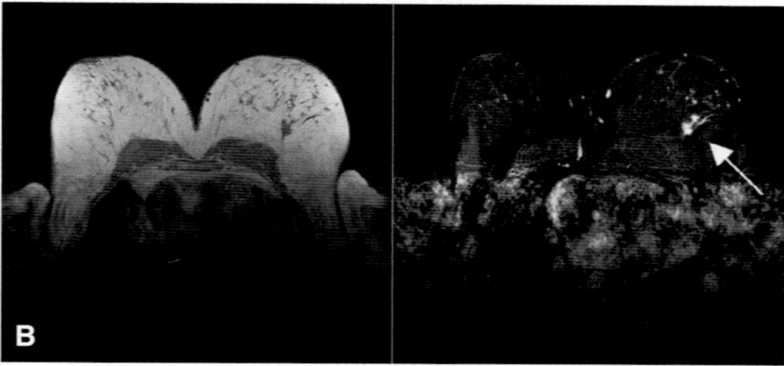

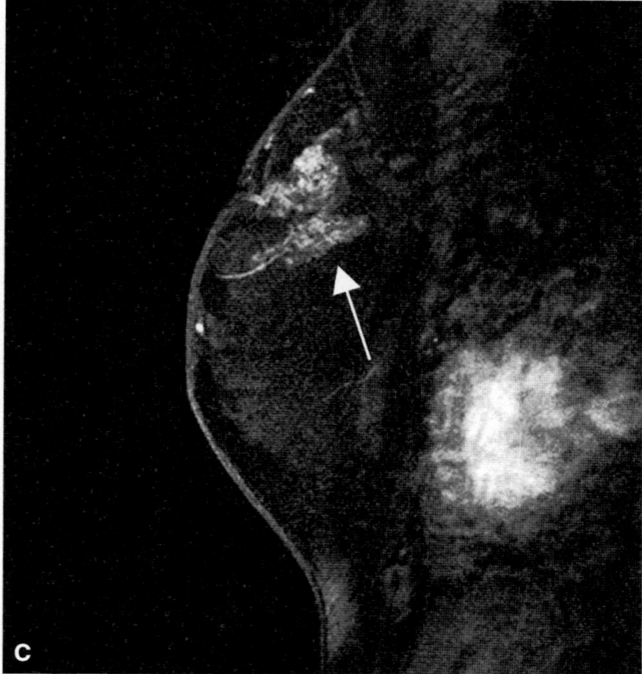

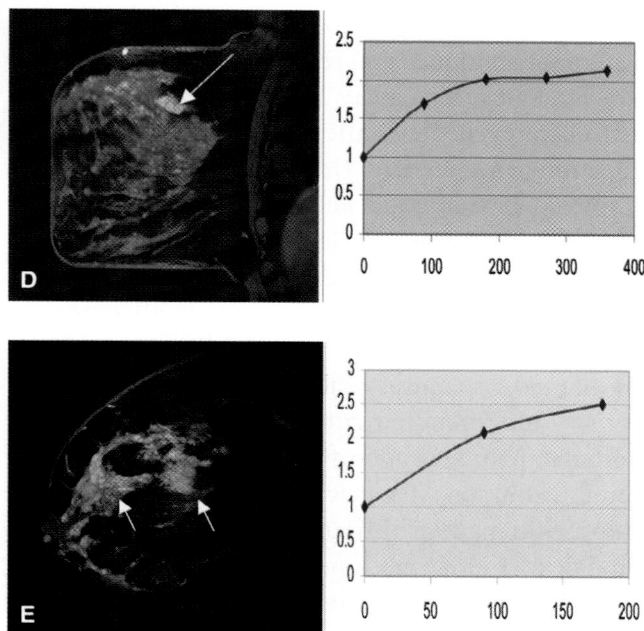

Figure 11–4 *A*, Fat suppressed postcontrast sagittal image demonstrates focal mass enhancement with irregular margins and rim enhancement pattern (arrow). Diagnosis was invasive ductal carcinoma. *B*, Precontrast (left, not fat suppressed) and postcontrast subtraction (right) axial images of both breasts demonstrate a spiculated enhancing mass in the left breast (arrow). Diagnosis was invasive cancer. *C*, Postcontrast fat suppressed sagital image of the breast demonstrates an oval focal mass with smooth borders and non enhancing internal septations. The dynamic curve (right) demonstrated persistent enhancement. The diagnosis was fibroadenoma. *D*, Fat suppressed sagittal postcontrast scan demonstrates clumped enhancement in a segmental distribution (arrow). Diagnosis was ductal carcinoma in situ. *E*, Fat suppressed sagittal postcontrast scan demonstrates diffuse stippled enhancement in a diffuse distribution (arrows). The dynamic enhancement curve (right) demonstrates persistent enhancement. This is a typical benign pattern of enhancement and no specific pathologic diagnosis is available.

placed a premium on high time resolution.[16] Their protocol consisted of single-slice nonfat-suppressed gradient echo images with 2.6 × 1.3 mM in plane spatial resolution (10 mM slice) at 2.3 second time intervals. They use a criterion that any lesion with visible enhancement < 11.5 seconds after arterial enhancement was suspicious for cancer. This criterion resulted in 95% sensitivity and 86% specificity for a cancer diagnosis in a limited population. Citing problems in determining the proper location on the precontrast images to perform a single-slice dynamic examination, and the need to detect other lesions within the breast, other investigators have recommended a multislice technique that records dynamic data from the entire breast after the injection of contrast.[17] These investigators have used multislice two-dimensional gradient echo, 3D gradient echo, and echo-planar techniques with time resolution varying from 12 seconds to 1 minute and widely distributed spatial resolution and section thickness. Criteria used to differentiate benign from malignant lesions have also varied widely among investigators. Criteria as simple as percent enhancement at 2 minutes, to more complex physiologic models that take into account the initial T1 of the lesion to estimate Gd concentration as a function of time in order to extract pharmacokinetic parameters, have been reported.[16–18] However, the most popular approach clinically has been the qualitative classification of enhancement curves demonstrating persistent, plateau, or washout enhancement.[10] This approach has gained popularity, since it is largely independent of imaging technique and technology. The accuracies cited by these investigators for interpretation based on contrast enhancement kinetics for differentiating benign from malignant lesions varies from 66 to 93%. Despite the many different techniques and results, it is clear that there is a tendency for cancer to enhance more rapidly than benign lesions after the bolus intravenous injection of Gd chelate. However, it is also clear that despite any technique and interpretation criterion used, there is some overlap in the dynamic curves between cancer and benign lesions. This has resulted in false-negative diagnoses in all series.

Much of the controversy in the literature regarding the use of contrast enhancement kinetics as the primary interpretation criteria for breast MRI stems from the inherent trade-off between spatial and temporal resolution. The technology available in the mid-1990s made it difficult to acquire images fast enough to follow the kinetic of enhancement with enough spatial resolution to observe the subtle architecture of enhancing lesions. More recently, technology has advanced, and combined approaches have been shown to offer the best results.[18–20] Today, most experts agree that breast MRI interpretation should be based on both the morphologic appearance of findings and contrast enhancement kinetics. Nunes and colleagues demonstrated a significant improvement in the diagnostic accuracy of breast MRI after integrating kinetic data into the architectural model.[15] In addition, Kuhl and colleagues have advocated a combined approach to interpretation of breast MRI.[10]

The generalized diagnostic performance of breast MRI can be best assessed by the results of the multi-institutional trial conducted by the International Breast MRI Consortium (IBMC). In a study of 1,004 women with suspicious mammograms or clinical findings, this study found that the overall diagnostic performance of MRI as it is performed in most clinical centers was not sufficient to avoid biopsy.[21] Although the IBMC study showed a higher positive predictive value for MRI compared with mammography in this setting (72.4% versus 52.8%), the sensitivity was not sufficient to reliably exclude cancer. The overall sensitivity in this population was reported to be 88%. The sensitivity for invasive cancer was 90.9%, whereas that for ductal carcinoma in situ was 73%. A significant finding was that the sensitivity for cancer in patients who presented with microcalcifications was lower than those who presented with other findings (83.5% versus 90.3%), although the overall accuracy of breast MRI was not significantly different in these populations. A more detailed evaluation of the imaging features that guide the interpretation of these examinations indicates that some cancers show no enhancement at all. In fact, the negative predictive value for enhancement of any type was 88%. However, most of the cancers reported as non-enhancing were ductal carcinoma in situ or lesions with mixed histology and small invasive components. Most presented with microcalcifications. Thus, the lack of enhancement in the setting of microcalcifications does not exclude cancer. The data from the IBMC study also support the use of combined architectural and kinetic data. The ROC area for kinetic curve classification was 0.66, whereas the ROC area for the best performing multivariate model including architectural and kinetic features was 0.88.[22]

Although the diagnostic performance of breast MRI will continue to improve with experience and improvements in technology, its current performance is not sufficient to routinely triage women with suspicious mammographic or clinical findings to biopsy or follow-up. This is particularly true for those presenting for microcalcifications.

MRI EVALUATION OF WOMEN WITH BREAST CANCER

There are several clinical scenarios for which breast MRI may be considered in women with a diagnosis of breast cancer. These include the evaluation of the extent of disease in the affected breast (including the detection of chest wall invasion), the detection of cancer in the contralateral breast, and the detection of response to preoperative neoadjuvant therapy. Although controversial, the use of MRI in the setting of a new breast cancer diagnosis is growing.

Evaluation of Cancer Extent

In women with a new diagnosis of breast cancer, the extent of the disease within the breast can have a significant impact on the available treatment options. This is likely to be a more significant factor in the future with the evolution of more conservative treatments of breast cancer, such as partial-breast irradiation and ablative techniques. The elegant pathologic studies reported by Holland and colleagues have clearly shown that the extent of breast cancer is often underestimated by mammography and physical examination, with 16% of women having invasive foci > 2 cm from the index cancer.[23] Although the use of radiation therapy has a significant impact on local control after lumpectomy, the recurrence rates after breast conservation therapy vary widely and are reported to be as high as 19% at 10 years.[24] In addition, the finding of increased recurrence rates in women with close or positive surgical margins indicate that incomplete excision of disease is associated with a higher risk of local recurrence.[24] Thus, it would appear as though an accurate technique to map the extent of breast cancer would be valuable to inform decisions about therapeutic approach.

In women with posterior lesions, it is often difficult to accurately detect superficial invasion into the pectoralis muscle. This may impact the treatment approach, particularly with respect to neoadjuvant chemotherapy. MRI has been shown to accurately assess chest wall invasion. Morris and colleagues have reported 100% accuracy in detecting chest wall invasion by observing enhancement within the pectoralis muscle.[25]

There have been a number of studies that have demonstrated that MRI can detect multifocal and multicentric cancer, occult to mammography and clinical findings. An initial report by Harms and colleagues revealed mammographically occult foci of carcinoma detected by MRI in 37% of women undergoing mastectomy.[14] MRI-detected multifocal/multicentric carcinoma varies from 12 to 88%.[26–30] This includes the detection of disease distant from the index lesion that would not likely be detected by the surgical margin status in many cases. The wide range of results may reflect small and potentially biased patient populations. In addition, the definition of multicentric disease and the characterization of the MRI-detected disease are inconsistent. However, the body of evidence clearly points to the fact that MRI is more sensitive than mammography in cancer detection. There have been fewer comparisons of the relative yield of MRI and sonography for detecting additional cancer foci in women with known breast cancer. Berg and colleagues demonstrated that MRI detected cancer foci that were not demonstrated by sonography in 4 of 72 breasts presenting with a known index cancer.[31] Chaudry and colleagues detected multicentric cancer (defined as > 2 cm from the index lesion) in 17% of 86 women as compared with 10% for sonography.[32]

These data were confirmed by a multi-institutional study conducted by the IBMC.[33] In a population of 428 women presenting with newly diagnosed breast cancer, the multicentricity rate (defined by a separation from the index cancer of > 2 cm) detected by MRI was 17% compared with 7% for mammography. The IBMC also reported that MRI-detected multicentric disease was invasive in 78% of cases (compared with 80% for cases detected by mammography) and had a median size of 1.1 cm (compared with 1.2 cm for cases detected by mammography). Thus, the characteristics of multicentric disease detected by MRI did not appear to be different than that detected by mammography. Figure 11–5 illustrates a case of MRI-detected multicentric disease.

Although the finding of mammographically detected multicentric disease has been associated with a high local recurrence rate and is considered a contraindication to breast conservation therapy, the

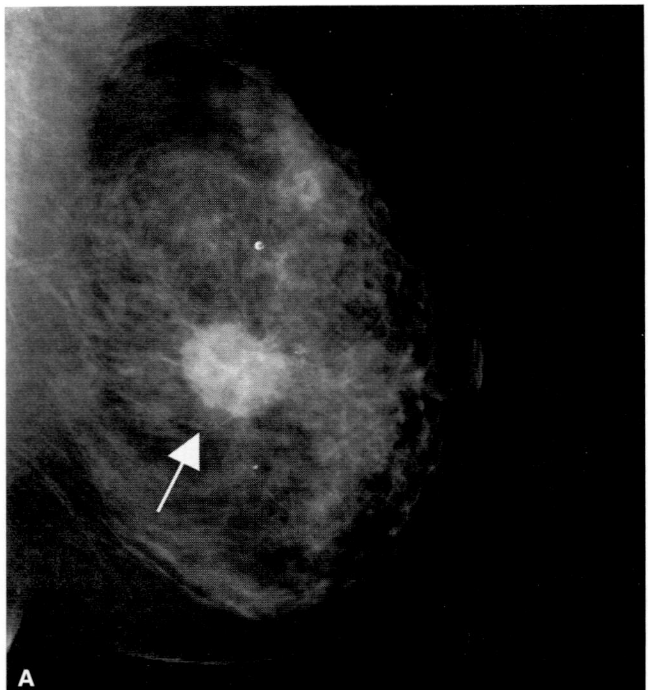

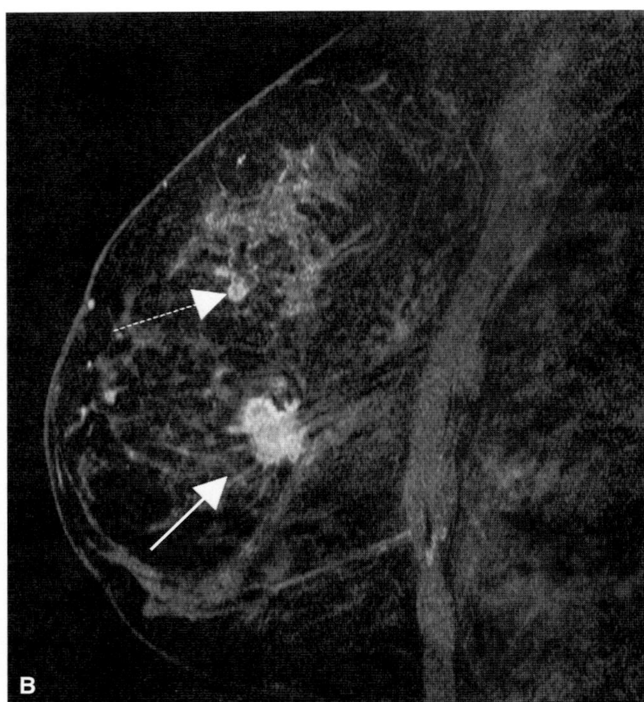

Figure 11–5. *A*, MLO mammogram demonstrates an index cancer. *B*, Sagittal fat suppressed postcontrast MRI demonstrates the main cancer (solid arrow) and a second 5 mm rim enhancing focal mass (dashed arrow) which represented multicentric invasive cancer.

integration of MRI information into the clinical decision-making relative to the initial treatment approach for breast cancer remains controversial. Bedrosian and colleagues examined the impact of breast MRI on the initial management of 267 women with a new diagnosis of breast cancer.[34] They reported that the MRI findings changed the initial management in 26% of women, including converting 16% (44 women) from lumpectomy to mastectomy, prompting wider excision due to multifocal disease in 4%, and prompting additional biopsies in 5%. Of these changes in management, 20 (7% of the population) were caused by false-positive results, including the conversion of 2 women to mastectomy. Although MRI-compatible vacuum-assisted core needle biopsy may provide a diagnosis for MRI-detected findings, there is still concern that false-positive MRI results will lead to more procedures and treatment delays. In addition, concerns are raised regarding the potential for true-positive MRI results to impact patient outcome. Although it may be presumed that the detection of this additional multicentric and multifocal disease should reduce re-excision rates and improve local control for breast conservation therapy, there are no data to support this. Breast MRI is a new technology and follow-up studies to address the impact on patient outcome are lacking. There is a single publication reporting on the follow-up of women treated for breast cancer after being evaluated by preoperative MRI.[35] With a 20-month follow-up, they reported a local recurrence rate of 1.2% in a population of 121 women evaluated preoperatively with MRI versus 6.5% for a control group of 225 women not evaluated with MRI. Although this result seems significant, there appears to be a considerable bias between the MRI and non-MRI populations, as evidenced by differences in tumor stage (20.4% T3 or T4 for the non-MRI group versus 7.4% T3 or T4 for the MRI group) and node status (45.8% positive nodes for the non-MRI group versus 38.8% positive nodes for the MRI group). Although a randomized trial would be best to address this question, the widespread availability of breast MRI would make a randomized study difficult. It is expected over time that there will be many other retrospective reports, with less biased populations that will help address the issue of long-term patient benefit from breast MRI.

Evaluation of the Contralateral Breast

Women diagnosed with breast cancer are known to be at risk for synchronous and metachronous cancer in the contralateral breast. Therefore, evaluation of the contralateral breast is an important component of the initial evaluation of a woman with a new diagnosis of breast cancer. The incidence of synchronous contralateral cancer detected by traditional methods (mammography and physical examination) is approximately 2%.[36] On continued follow-up, there is a 1% per-year risk of metachronous cancer, resulting in a cumulative risk of 10% at 10 years.[36] In women who carry a breast cancer susceptibility gene, the cumulative 10-year risk is much larger and can approach 30%.[37] The 10-year cumulative risk of developing contralateral cancer has stimulated interest in investigating the role of MRI in earlier detection of contralateral cancer. A good estimate of the true incidence of cancer in the contralateral breast at the time of presentation with primary breast cancer is available through the pathology evaluation of women choosing prophylactic contralateral mastectomy. On pathologic examination, Goldflam and colleagues reported occult contralateral cancer in 4.6% of 239 cases.[38]

There have been a number of single institutional studies reporting on the MRI detection of mammographically and clinically occult contralateral breast.[39–42] The IBMC performed a pilot multicenter study to estimate the incremental yield of MRI over mammography and physical examination in the detection of contralateral cancer in 100 women with a new diagnosis of breast cancer. Consistent with single institutional studies, this study reported a 4% incremental yield of MRI in detecting contralateral cancer in the women with a recent diagnosis of breast cancer. The call-back rate based on MRI was 12% and the biopsy rate was 9%. However, because of the small sample size in this pilot, the confidence intervals are quite high.[43] The American College of Radiology Imaging Network, a National Cancer Institute-funded cooperative group, has just finished accrual of 1,000 women into a study aimed at establishing the incremental yield of MRI in detecting occult contralateral breast cancer. However, based on available single institutional and pilot multi-institutional data, it is expected that this yield with be in the 4 to 5% range. An improvement in the detection of contralateral disease at the time of initial diagnosis will have several potential clinical implications. In addition to supporting better decisions regarding the treatment options for managing a woman's cancer, there is some evidence that early detection of contralateral disease may improve outcome.[44]

MRI in the Neoadjuvant Setting

Evaluating the extent of disease in patients with locally advanced breast cancer undergoing neoadjuvant chemotherapy is important to assessing the prognosis and planning the therapy. Several groups have investigated the use of MRI to determine therapy response. Overall, MRI has been found to be more accurate than mammography in assessing the extent of residual tumor after neoadjuvant therapy.[45] In addition, the difference in tumor volume between pre- and post-therapy scans was a strong predictor of recurrence.[46] Figure 11–6 demonstrates the response of a locally advanced cancer to neoadjuvant chemotherapy.

In addition to detecting response, there has been interest in predicting histologic response based on early functional response. Several investigators have studied changes in the dynamic enhancement curve early in a treatment cycle, in an effort to predict anatomic response. Different approaches to quantitating the dynamic enhancement curve have been employed, including the calculation of the early enhancement ratio (ECU), the ratio of delayed to early contrast uptake (SER), and formal physiologic modeling to calculate the extraction flow product (EFP).[47,48] In a study of 30 women undergoing neoadjuvant therapy for breast cancer, Martincich and colleagues have reported that the decrease in ECU observed after 2 cycles of an anthracycline- and taxane-based regimen significantly predicted a major histopathologic response.[47] In addition to functional assessment, Esserman and colleagues have leveraged the exquisite visualization of the tumor anatomy by MRI to develop a classification of the tumor phenotype.[49] This phenotype is based on the compactness of the tumor. Well-circumscribed tumors are on one end of the spectrum, whereas infiltrative tumors are at the other end. Esserman and

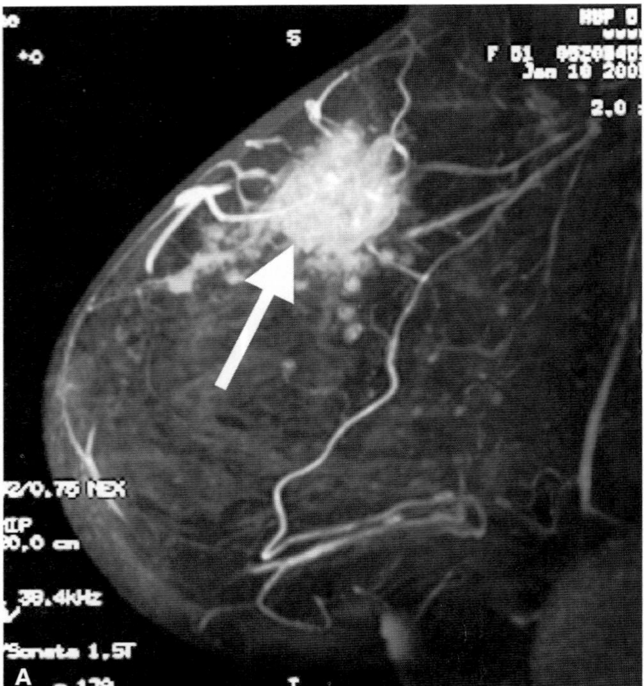
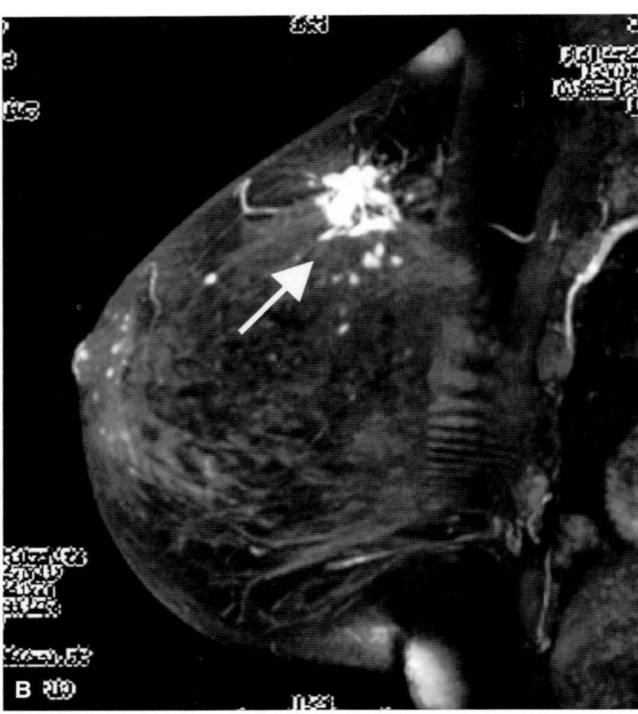

Figure 11–6. Three-dimensional projection from before (A) and after (B) neoadjuvant chemotherapy demonstrating marked decrease in the extent of enhancement (arrow) consistent with a partial response.

colleagues reported that the MRI phenotype was able to predict response to a regimen of doxorubicin and cyclophosphamide. Well-circumscribed lesions were the best responders with a 77% response rate, whereas extensively infiltrating lesions had a 25% response rate. Although these small pilots demonstrate the potential of MRI to play an important role in the neoadjuvant setting, reproducibility in a multicenter setting is required before the MRI markers of response get widespread acceptance.

HIGH-RISK SCREENING

Mammography is the primary screening modality for breast cancer. Multiple randomized studies have been performed to investigate the effect of mammographic screening on breast cancer mortality. Most leaders in the field agree that these studies demonstrate an 18 to 30% reduction in breast cancer mortality.[50–53] The recent decline in the breast cancer death rate and decrease in the size of detected cancers likely reflects dissemination of mammographic screening.[54]

Although mammography has clearly become the "gold standard" in the detection of early clinically occult breast cancer, it has limitations. For example, not all cancers are detected mammographically; some cancers present as interval palpable lesions that do not produce changes in the breast that are detected by conventional film-screen techniques. Variations in the composition of the breast led to the wide range of resultant mammographic appearances. The volume of glandular or radiographically "dense" tissue in the breast has a significant impact on the ability to detect small lesions mammographically. It is more difficult to diagnose a breast cancer in a radiographically dense breast, and the dense breast is considered to be a major factor in the false-negative mammographic interpretation.[55–57] The sensitivity of film-screen mammography is estimated at approximately 78% overall and is as low as 69% in women with radiographically dense breasts. However, these estimates are optimistic since there are no good techniques to estimate the true cancer incidence in the population. Thus, not all false negatives are detected. More recent data from multimodality screening studies would suggest that the sensitivity of film-screen mammography is significantly less than initial perceptions.[58–62]

A strong asset of mammography as a screening examination is its relatively low cost and wide availability. Although MRI has a reported high sensitivity for cancer, it would be difficult to consider total population screening with MRI in its current form. However, with the recent advances in risk stratification, focusing MRI screening on populations at high risk would be feasible. There have been multiple studies aimed at estimating the yield of mammography in the detection of cancer in women at high risk. Different investigators have defined high risk differently. Examples include testing positive for a breast cancer susceptibility gene, a 20% lifetime risk by the Gail or Clause models, or having one first-degree relative diagnosed with breast cancer prior to the age of 40 years.[50–52] Several smaller studies have all shown that the sensitivity of MRI is superior to that of mammography.[58–60] The Dutch high-risk screening study was the largest and included 1,909 women.[62] This study estimated the sensitivity of mammography at 40%, clinical breast examination at 17.8%, and MRI at 73.1%. Although it had the highest sensitivity, MRI also had the highest false-positive rate. Using an assessment of "suspicious" or "highly suspicious" as a cut-off, the positive predictive value for clinical breast examination, mammography, and MRI were 50, 47, and 32%, respectively. In addition 8.1% of all MRI examinations resulted in some finding requiring additional work-up (follow-up in 275 and biopsy in 65). Another large multicenter study performed in the United Kingdom (MARIBS) reported similar results.[61] They reported sensitivities for MRI and mammography at 77 and 40%, respectively. They also reported lower PPV for MRI. Figure 11–7 demonstrates an MRI-detected mammogram-occult cancer in a high-risk patient.

It is noteworthy that there were 14 cancers missed by MRI, but detected by mammography, in these 2 series combined. These represent 18% of all cancers detected. Therefore, despite the high sensitivity of MRI, mammography does offer the unique ability to detect microcalcifications associated with cancer. Mammographic microcalcifications can be thought of as an imaging biomarker of cancer, and as such, can signal changes at a microscopic level prior to being visible by MRI. Therefore, MRI should not be used as a screening test on its own, but in combination with mammography. This combination will provide the high sensitivity of MRI for macroscopic cancers, and the detection of mammographic microcalcifications indicative of in situ disease.

CONCLUSION

There has been tremendous progress over the last 15 years in the development and implementation of breast MRI. Although early in its history, this technique suffered from a lack of commercial support; there has been a rapid evolution of high-quality coils, visualization workstations, and biopsy devices. In addition to a demonstrated effectiveness in breast cancer detection, diagnosis, and staging through multiple clinical series, there are now well-controlled multicenter studies to confirm these findings. In addition, there are standards developed by the American College of Radiology that govern the technique and reporting of breast MRI examinations. There is a growing consensus on the use of a combination of MRI and mammography for screening women at high risk for breast cancer. Although still controver-

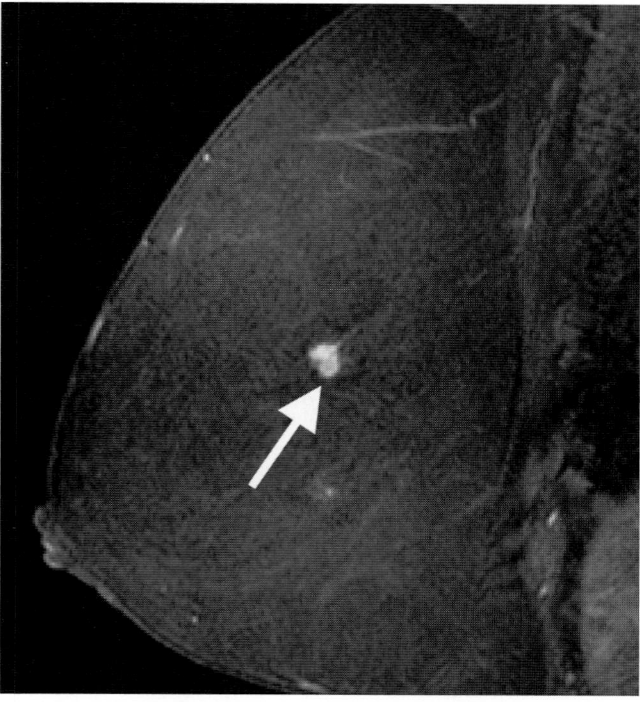

Figure 11–7. Sagittal postcontrast fat suppressed MRI scan performed under a high-risk screening protocol demonstrates an 8 mm spiculated focal mass (arrow). This patient had a negative mammogram. The pathologic diagnosis was invasive cancer.

sial because of lack of follow-up data, the use of MRI in the preoperative assessment of breast cancer is continuing to grow. Although MRI is not recommended for routine diagnostic evaluation of suspicious mammograms, it can provide important input in complex or difficult cases. In addition, MRI promises to play an important role in evaluating and predicting response in the neoadjuvant setting.

REFERENCES

1. Stelling CB, Wang PC, Lieber A, et al. Prototype coil for magnetic resonance imaging of the female breast. Radiology 1985;154:457–62.
2. Dash N, Lupetin AR, Daffner RH, et al. Magnetic resonance imaging in the diagnosis of breast disease. AJR Am J Roentgenol 1986;146:119–25.
3. Heywang SH, Wolf A, Pruss E, et al. MR imaging of the breast with Gd-DTPA: use and limitations. Radiology 1989;171:95–103.
4. Kaiser WA, Zeitler E. MR imaging of the breast: fast imaging sequences with and without Gd-DTPA. Radiology 1989;170:681–6.
5. Kuhl CK, Kreft BP, Hauswirth A, et al. MR mammography at 0.5 tesla. iII. The capacity to differentiate malignant and benign lesions in MR mammography at 0.5 and 1.5 T. Rofo 1995;162:482–91.
6. Meisamy S, Bolan PJ, Baker EH, et al. Neoadjuvant chemotherapy of locally advanced breast cancer: predicting response with in vivo (1)H MR spectroscopy—a pilot study at 4 T. Radiology 2004;233:424–31.
7. Orel SG, Schnall MD, Newman RW, et al. MR imaging-guided localization and biopsy of breast lesions: initial experience. Radiology 1994;193:97–102.
8. Lehman CD, Deperi ER, Peacock S, et al. Clinical experience with MRI-guided vacuum-assisted breast biopsy. AJR Am J Roentgenol 2005;184:1782–7.
9. Tofts PS, Berkowitz B, Schnall MD. Quantitative analysis of dynamic Gd-DTPA enhancement in breast tumors using a permeability model. Magn Reson Med 1995;33:564–8.
10. Kuhl CK, Mielcareck P, Klaschik S, et al. Dynamic breast MR imaging: are signal intensity time course data useful for differential diagnosis of enhancing lesions? Radiology 1999;211:101–10.
11. Friedman PD, Swaminathan SV, Smith R. SENSE imaging of the breast. AJR Am J Roentgenol 2005;184:448–51.
12. Cecil KM, Schnall MD, Siegelman ES, Lenkinski RE. The evaluation of human breast lesions with magnetic resonance imaging and proton magnetic resonance spectroscopy. Breast Cancer Res Treat 2001;68:45–54.
13. Ikeda D, Hylton N, Kuhl C, et al. Breast imaging and reporting data system-magnetic resonance imaging in ACR BI-RADS-magnetic resonance. In: ACR breast imaging and reporting data system, breast imaging atlas. Reston (VA): American College of Radiology; 2003.
14. Harms SE, Flamig DP, Hesley KL, et al. MR imaging of the breast with rotating delivery of excitation off resonance: clinical experience with pathologic correlation. Radiology 1993;187:493–501.
15. Nunes LW, Schnall MD, Orel SG, et al. Breast MR imaging: interpretation model. Radiology 1997;202:833–41.
16. Boetes C, Barentsz JO, Mus RD, et al. MR characterization of suspicious breast lesions with a gadolinium-enhanced turboFLASH subtraction technique. Radiology 1994;193: 777–81.
17. Hulka CA, Smith BL, Sgroi DC, et al. Benign and malignant breast lesions: differentiation with echo-planar MR imaging. Radiology 1995;197:33–8.
18. Daniel BL, Yen YF, Glover GH, et al. Breast disease: dynamic spiral MR imaging. Radiology 1998;209:499–509.
19. Song HK, Dougherty L, Schnall MD. Simultaneous acquisition of multiple resolution images for dynamic contrast enhanced imaging of the breast. Magn Reson Med 2001; 46:503–9.
20. Schnall MD, Rosten S, Englander S, et al. A combined architectural and kinetic interpretation model for breast MR images. Acad Radiol 2001;8:591–7.
21. Bluemke DA, Gatsonis CA, Chen MH, et al. Magnetic resonance imaging of the breast prior to biopsy. JAMA 2004;292:2735–42.
22. Schnall MD, Blume J, Bluemke D, et al. A multicenter study of diagnostic architectural and dynamic features in breast MRI. Radiology. [In press.]
23. Holland R, Veling SH, Mravunac M, Hendriks JH. Histologic multifocality of Tis, T1-2 breast carcinomas. Implications for clinical trials of breast-conserving surgery. Cancer 1985;56:979–90.
24. Morrow M, Strom EA, Bassett LW, et al; American College of Radiology; American College of Surgeons; Society of Surgical Oncology; College of American Pathology. Standard for breast conservation therapy in the management of invasive breast carcinoma. CA Cancer J Clin 2002; 52:277–300.
25. Morris EA, Schwartz LH, Drotman MB, et al. Evaluation of pectoralis major muscle in patients with posterior breast tumors on breast MR images: early experience. Radiology 2000;214:67–72.
26. Orel S, Schnall M, Powell C, et al. Staging of suspected breast cancer: effect of MR imaging and MR guided biopsy. Radiology 1995;196:115–22.
27. Fischer U, Kopka L, Grabbe E. Breast carcinoma: effect of preoperative contrast enhanced MR imaging on the therapeutic approach. Radiology 1999;213:881–8.
28. Boetes C, Mus RD, Holland R, et al. Breast tumors: comparative accuracy of MR imaging relative to mammography and US for demonstrating extent. Radiology 1995;197:743–7.
29. Mumtaz H, Hall-Craggs MA, Davidson T, et al. Staging of symptomatic primary breast cancer with MR imaging. AJR Am J Roentgenol 1997;169:417–24.
30. Kramer S, Schulz-Wendtland R, Hagedorn K, et al. Magnetic resonance imaging and its role in the diagnosis of multicentric breast cancer. Anticancer Res 1998;18:2163–4.
31. Berg WA, Gutierrez L, NessAiver MS, et al. Diagnostic accuracy of mammography, clinical examination, US, and MR imaging in preoperative assessment of breast cancer. Radiology 2004;233:830–49.
32. Chaudhry M, Schnall M, Alavi A, Putt M. Multimodality

detection of multicentric breast cancer [abstract]. ASCO Annual Meeting. 2005 May. Abtract 624.

33. Schnall MD, Blume J, Bluemke D, et al, International Breast MRI Consortium. MRI detection of multi focal breast carcinoma: report from the International Breast MRI Consortium [abstract]. ASCO Annual Meeting. 2004 June. Abstract 504.
34. Bedrosian I, Mick R, Orel SG, et al. Changes in the surgical management of patients with breast carcinoma based on preoperative magnetic resonance imaging. Cancer 2003;98:468–73.
35. Fischer U, Zachariae O, Baum F, et al. The influence of preoperative MRI of the breasts on recurrence rate in patients with breast cancer. Eur Radiol 2004;14:1725–31.
36. Polednak AP. Bilateral synchronous breast cancer: a population-based study of characteristics, method of detection, and survival. Surgery 2003;133:383–9.
37. Metcalfe K, Lynch HT, Ghadirian P, et al. Contralateral breast cancer in BRCA1 and BRCA2 mutation carriers. J Clin Oncol 2004;22:2328–35.
38. Goldflam K, Hunt KK, Gershenwald JE, et al. Contralateral prophylactic mastectomy. Predictors of significant histologic findings. Cancer 2004;101:1977–86.
39. Slanetz PJ, Edmister WB, Yeh ED, et al. Occult contralateral breast carcinoma incidentally detected by breast magnetic resonance imaging. Breast J 2002;8:145–8.
40. Liberman L, Morris EA, Kim CM, et al. MR imaging findings in the contralateral breast of women with recently diagnosed breast cancer. AJR Am J Roentgenol 2003;180:333–41.
41. Lee SG, Orel SG, Woo IJ, et al. MR imaging screening of the contralateral breast in patients with newly diagnosed breast cancer: preliminary results. Radiology 2002;226:773–8.
42. Viehweg P, Rotter K, Laniado M, et al. MR imaging of the contralateral breast in patients after breast conserving therapy. Eur Radiol 2004;14:402–8.
43. Lehman CD, Blume JD, Thickman D, et al. The added cancer yield of MRI in screening the contralateral breast of women recently diagnosed with breast cancer: results from the International Breast Magnetic Resonance Consortium (IBMC) trial. J Surg Onocol [In press].
44. Ciatto S, Guido M, Marco Z. Prognostic impact of the early detection of metachronous contralateral breast cancer. Eur J Cancer 2004;40:1496–501.
45. Partridge SC, Gibbs JE, Lu Y, et al. Accuracy of MR imaging for revealing residual breast cancer in patients who have undergone neoadjuvant chemotherapy. AJR Am J Roentgenol 2002;179:1193–9.
46. Partridge SC, Gibbs JE, Lu Y, et al. MRI measurements of breast tumor volume predict response to neoadjuvant chemotherapy and recurrence-free survival. AJR Am J Roentgenol 2005;184:1774–81.
47. Martincich L, Montemurro F, De Rosa G, et al. Monitoring response to primary chemotherapy in breast cancer using dynamic contrast-enhanced magnetic resonance imaging. Breast Cancer Res Treat 2004;83:67–76.
48. Delille JP, Slanetz PJ, Yeh ED, et al. Invasive ductal breast carcinoma response to neoadjuvant chemotherapy: noninvasive monitoring with functional MR imaging—pilot study. Radiology 2003;228:63–9.
49. Esserman L, Hylton N, George T, Weidner N. Contrast-enhanced magnetic resonance imaging to assess tumor histopatholgy and angiogenesis in breast carcinoma. Breast J 1999;5:13–21.
50. Nystrom L, Rutqvist LE, Wall S, et al. Breast cancer screening with mammography: overview of Swedish randomized trials. Lancet 1993;342:973–8.
51. Hendrick RE, Smith RA, Rutledge JH, Smart CR. Benefit of screening mammography in women ages 40–49: a new meta-analysis of randomized controlled trials. J Natl Cancer Inst Monogr 1997;22:87–92.
52. Smart CR, Byrne C, Smith RA, et al. Twenty-year follow-up of the breast cancers diagnosed during the Breast Cancer Detection Demonstration Project. CA Cancer J Clin 1997;47:134–49.
53. Tabar L, Vitak B, Chen HH, et al. The Swedish Two-County Trial twenty years later. Updated mortality results and new insights from long-term follow-up. Radiol Clin North Am 2000;38:625–51.
54. Letton AH, Mason EM, Rainshaw BJ. Twenty-year review of a breast cancer-screening project. Ninety-five percent survival of patients with nonpalpable breast cancers. Cancer 1996;77:104–6.
55. Baker LH. Breast cancer detection demonstration project: five-year summary report. Cancer 1982;32:194–225.
56. Bird RE, Wallace TW, Yankaskas BC. Analysis of cancers missed at screening mammography. Radiology 1992;184: 613–7.
57. Dershaw DD. The false-negative mammogram. Appl Radiol 1994;23:27–9.
58. Lehman CD, Blume JD, Weatherall P, et al; International Breast MRI Consortium Working Group. Screening women at high risk for breast cancer with mammography and magnetic resonance imaging. Cancer 2005;103:1898–905.
59. Kuhl CK, Schmutzler RK, Leutner CC, et al. Breast MR imaging screening in 192 women proved or suspected to be carriers of a breast cancer susceptibility gene: preliminary results. Radiology 2000;215:267–79.
60. Warner E, Plewes DB, Hill KA, et al. Surveillance of BRCA1 and BRCA2 mutation carriers with magnetic resonance imaging, ultrasound, mammography, and clinical breast examination. JAMA 2004;292:1317–25.
61. Leach MO, Boggis CR, Dixon AK, et al; MARIBS study group. Screening with magnetic resonance imaging and mammography of a UK population at high familial risk of breast cancer: a prospective multicenter cohort study (MARIBS). Lancet 2005;365:1769–78.
62. Kriege M, Brekelmans CT, Boetes C, et al. Efficacy of MRI and mammography for breast-cancer screening in women with a familial or genetic predisposition. N Engl J Med 2004;351:427–37.

12

Diagnostic Techniques

RICHARD FINE

The increase in detection of non-palpable breast abnormalities requiring further evaluation is thought to be the direct result of more favorable participation in mammography screening. Appropriate diagnostic work-up has led to a relative increase in lesions that are of sufficient risk to warrant a biopsy. In fact, it has been estimated that approximately 1.4 million breast biopsies are performed per year in the United States. Unfortunately, an average positive predictive value for mammography of 20% (range 15 to 35%) will yield a significant number of biopsies performed for benign disease.[1–4] If five women are identified with a mammogram lesion requiring biopsy, based on this relatively low predictive value, only one of these five women has a breast cancer. Therefore, if traditional methods for histologic confirmation are utilized, all five women would proceed to the operating room for an open surgical biopsy after first having a wire localization procedure in the radiology suite. An effective alternative, image-guided percutaneous breast biopsy has essentially eliminated open surgical biopsy for diagnostic purposes for most mammographically detected abnormalities. Image-guided percutaneous breast biopsy provides a secondary level of screening for these five women in a less invasive, cost-effective manner which provides histologic diagnosis without sacrificing accuracy.[5–9] The patient with breast cancer may then proceed to definitive surgical management, and the other four women with a benign diagnosis may be placed into an appropriate follow-up protocol. It is with this concept in mind that we review the state of the art in image-guided breast biopsy.

IMAGE-GUIDED BREAST BIOPSY

Physicians have overcome many of the concerns about instituting an image-guided breast biopsy program experienced by the early pioneers of this technology, such as patient acceptance (sampling rather than excision), accuracy (false-negative rate), overutilization (ie, Will the proper indications be maintained?) and qualifications (Should image-guided breast biopsy be performed by radiologists or surgeons?). At the same time physicians have dealt with these concerns, the patient has been exposed to media headlines, such as "The Needle Replaces the Knife." It did not take a very sophisticated patient consumer to understand that a needle biopsy is less invasive than a knife (scalpel) for open surgical breast biopsy. In addition to the media deluge, patients have also been exposed to corporate-driven advertisement of new breast biopsy devices. Acceptance of a new technology, in the face of physician reluctance, has been spawned by outside sources. The use of minimally invasive image-guided percutaneous breast biopsy has become the first line intervention for both palpable and non-palpable image detected abnormalities.

Imaging Modalities

Percutaneous breast biopsy for non-palpable disease requires imaging. The two most common imaging modalities are stereotaxis and ultrasonography. These modalities are complementary, and, therefore, knowledge of both is required to provide the physician with the full range of options. The decision of which modality is best suited for a particular biopsy is based on both the characteristics of the patient's breast and the type of lesion requiring biopsy. A large fatty replaced breast will be amenable to stereotaxis because of the breast size and the ease of visualizing the relatively greater density of breast masses. Masses tend to be more easily visualized with ultrasonography in a small breast with dense parenchyma. The small breast size can limit the ability to perform a biopsy between the compression paddles of a stereotactic unit when the breast is compressed to a minimum thickness. However, with the exception of high-resolution units, microcalcifications are not visualized by ultrasonography and, therefore, represent the most common indication for a stereotactic breast biopsy in women with breasts of any size.

Stereotactic Breast Biopsy

Equipment

Stereotactic breast biopsy is performed using stereotaxis mammography equipment. The equipment obtains stereo mammogram images of a lesion within the breast and then relies on computerized triangulation of the targeted lesion to calculate the three-dimensional position of this lesion.[5,10] There are two categories of stereotactic equipment; upright, add-on units and dedicated prone tables.[11–13] Add-on stereotactic equipment utilizes standard up-right mammography with an attachable platform to perform targeting and biopsy. Add-on stereotactic units provide the advantage of maximizing the use of equipment with dual capabilities, screening or diagnostic mammography, and stereotactic breast biopsy (Figure 12–1). This provides considerable cost savings by avoiding not only dedicated equipment but also dedicated space within a breast diagnostic facility. Despite these potential advantages, add-on stereotactic breast biopsy units have traditionally been less popular than dedicated prone stereotactic tables. Because of the upright patient position and patient visualization of the procedure, there is an increased potential for syncopal episodes.[5,14] In addition, upright units provide minimal workspace and limited access to the breast. Dedicated prone stereotactic tables are more costly and require dedicated space. However, the prone position allows gravity to aid the technologist in reaching more posterior lesions and a greatly enhanced workspace beneath the table that remains out of the patient's view, which allows for more advanced breast biopsy devices.

There are two dedicated prone systems available: the MammoTest Select™ Breast Biopsy System™ (Fischer Imaging, Denver, CO) and the Hologic Lorad MultiCare™ Platinum Stereotactic System (Hologic Inc, Bedford, MA) (Figure 12–2). The Fischer MammoTest™ is a single-direction patient-positioning table, with the aperture for the patient's breast located at one end of the table. The Hologic stereotactic table is a bi-directional patient positioning table with the aperture for the breast in the center of the table and a foot extension on either end.

Initial experience with stereotactic breast biopsy was based on film screen technology until 1993, when the charged coupled device camera replaced the film cassette image receptor. This allowed for digital re-creation of the breast lesion on a computer monitor. Several advantages were imme-

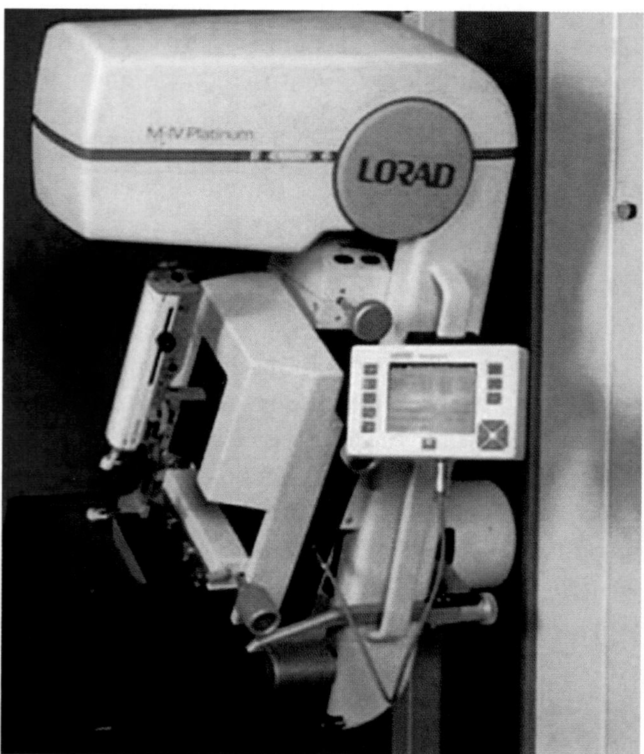

Figure 12–1. Hologic Lorad StereoLoc™ II is the upright add-on stereotactic guidance system used with the Lorad ™ mammography unit.

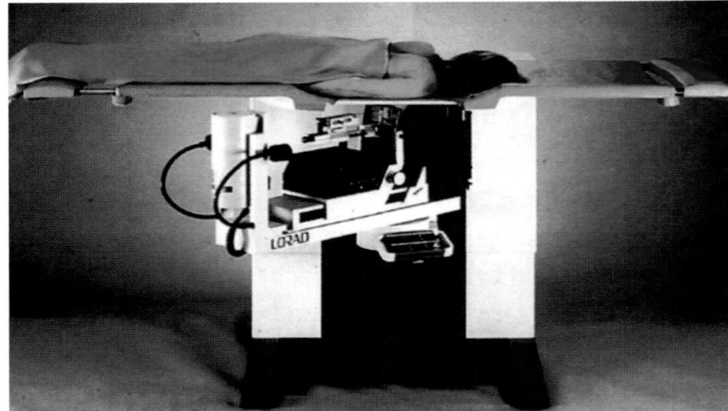

Figure 12–2. Hologic Lorad MultiCare™ Stereotactic System.

diately recognized for digital image acquisition, including reduced procedure time, post processing of the image (allowing lesion magnification and enhancement) and lower radiation exposure owing to a narrower field of view. Digital imaging for stereotactic biopsy is not full field (ie, the entire breast is not imaged). The area of the breast imaged is limited to a 5 cm square area. In fact, the true learning curve in performing stereotactic breast biopsy revolves around this narrow field of view. The physician must recognize and transfer the appearance of the lesion identified on a high-quality, screening or diagnostic film mammogram (imaging the entire breast) to a digital image which may be magnified and where the lesion is not seen in relation to the remainder of the breast.

Stereotactic Breast Biopsy Principles

After review of the mammogram, the general approach to the breast is chosen. The shortest skin to lesion distance and the ability to clearly visualize the lesion are both factors in choosing the optimal approach.[15] The mammography technologist is responsible for positioning the patient for the desired approach. Other responsibilities of the technologist include calibration and maintenance of the equipment and quality assurance.

The first digital image to be taken is the zero degree scout image. A set of stereo images is obtained by rotating the mammography tube head to a + 15 and –15 to yield an arc of separation between the two stereo images of 30 degrees (Figure 12–3A and B). With the appropriate targets entered, the computer software determines the horizontal, parallax shift of the lesion from stereo image number one to stereo image number two. The system software then calculates the horizontal, vertical, and depth coordinates of the lesion within the breast.

With the three-dimensional coordinates of the lesion calculated, the puncture device or stage, which houses the biopsy instrumentation, is driven to the calculated horizontal and vertical position. The biopsy device is advanced towards the skin, and the site for insertion is identified. After local anesthetic is injected and the skin incised, the biopsy device is advanced into the breast to the calculated depth of the lesion. Once imaging confirms the position of the biopsy device in the breast, depending on which type of device is used, the tissue acquisition portion of the device is advanced forward to achieve the most complete lesion sampling.

Specimen Acquisition Devices

Technologic advancements of the tools used in the performance of image-guided breast biopsy closely parallels the evolution and acceptance of both stereotactic and ultrasound minimally invasive procedures for diagnosis and potential therapy. Fine-needle aspiration using stereotactic guidance was the first minimally invasive biopsy technique used for non-palpable lesions and is still preferred by some to this day. In 1989, *The Lancet* published a landmark article from the Karolinski Institute which evaluated the stereotactic fine-needle biopsy of

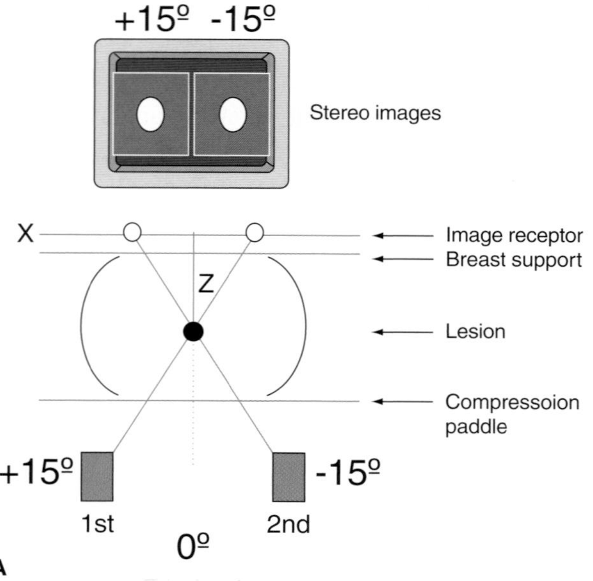

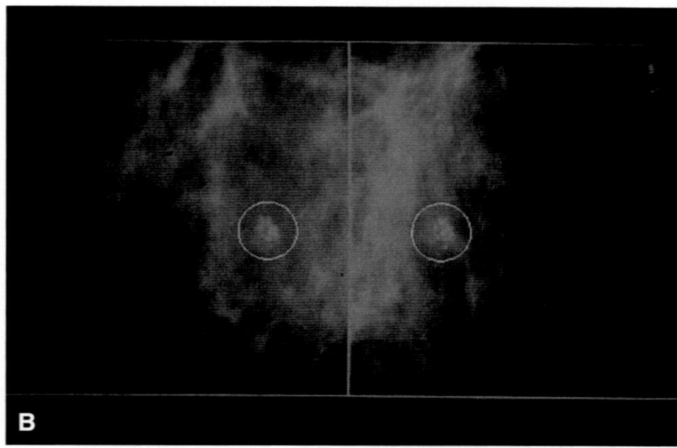

Figure 12–3. *A,* Viewing the stereotactic table from above. The diagram illustrates the movement of the tube head for acquiring stereo images (Fischer MammoTest table) and the resultant z-value determination. *B,* Stereotactic digital images.

2,594 mammographically detected, non-palpable lesions from 1983 to 1987.[16] Of 2,005 (77.3%) cases judged to be benign, only 1 turned out to be cancer 14 months later. Of the 576 cases (21.9%) selected for needle localization followed by open breast biopsy based on cytology and/or mammographic interpretation, cancer was identified in 429 (75.7%). Dr. Kambiz Dowlat Shahi, a surgeon performing some of the first stereotactic work in this country, published 528 cases of stereotactic fine-needle aspiration, in corroboration with the University of Kiel from the Federal Republic of Germany.[17] Dowlat Shahi and colleagues demonstrated stereotactic guidance with 23-gauge fine-needle aspiration to have a sensitivity of 95% and accuracy of 92%. Furthermore, this article confirmed the accuracy of stereotactic localization by imaging the tip of the needle within 2 mm of the center of the lesion in 96% of the cases.

Acceptance of fine-needle aspiration as a standard technique for performance of stereotactic biopsy had limited success, especially in the United States. Fine-needle aspiration has long been recognized to have several potential pitfalls. This includes insufficient sampling that has been recorded as high as 38% in some series, with the sensitivity ranging between 68 and 93% and the specificity between 88 and 100%.[18] The broad range of sensitivity and specificity is dependent not only on availability of expert cytopathology but also by the fine-needle aspiration technique and the type of lesion sampled. Also, many community physicians participating in managed care have limited access to expert cytopathology. Finally, cytology rarely provides a specific benign diagnosis.

Automated Tru-cut™ Type Biopsy. In the late 1980s, Parker and colleagues began working with the automated Tru-cut Biopsy™ instrument (Bard Urologic, Covington, GA) developed for biopsy of the prostate. He combined this technology on the prone Fischer stereotactic table for performing large core stereotactic breast biopsy. In 1991, Dr. Parker published a series of 102 patients where every patient had a stereotactic-guided large core needle biopsy followed by traditional surgical excision of the lesion.[5] There was agreement in histology in 98 cases (96%). One cancer missed with core was determined to be a very difficult lesion to localize because of its posterior position. Parker set the standards for performing stereotactic procedures still relied upon today. In addition to prone stereotactic tables, another principle identified to increase the accuracy was the routine utilization of pre- and post-fire stereotactic imaging. Pre-fire stereo images assess the appropriate alignment of the needle to the lesion, and post-fire stereo images document penetration of the needle through the lesion. Parker also advocated the use of "long throw" biopsy needle devices. The longer excursion of the inner and outer sheath of the needle provided a consistently larger tissue sample. Parker and colleagues demonstrated that stereotactic localization with the Tru-cut™ core biopsy with stereotactic localization proved to be a less invasive, cost-effective procedure with reduced patient anxiety. It has a lower false-negative rate when compared to fine-needle aspiration.[5–8] Furthermore, the need for expertise in cytology interpretation was avoided, which was important in the community setting where availability of an expert cytopathologist was limited. The standard use of the 14-gauge needle essentially eliminated the risk of insufficient sampling. Several different gauge needles for automated Tru-cut™ biopsy have been evaluated. The lower rate of insufficient sampling and increased sensitivity, without increased complications, has led to the 14-gauge size as the standard (Figure 12–4).[19,20]

Lieberman and colleagues have addressed the number of core biopsy specimens that were needed for a needle core biopsy.[21] Biopsies were performed on 145 lesions; 92 were nodular densities and 53 were microcalcifications. Five cores with a 14-gauge automated Tru-cut™ needle yielded diagnosis in 99% of the biopsies for masses. A biopsy for microcalcifications requires greater sampling. Five cores yielded a diagnosis in only 87% of the microcalcifications cases, and more than 6 cores yielded a diagnosis in 92% of the cases. At The Breast Center, Marietta, GA, the average number of core samples was between 9 and 12 for the usual cluster of indeterminate microcalcifications.[10,22] Even in open biopsy, pathologic assessment has diagnosed atypical hyperplasia and ductal carcinoma in situ at a "distance" from the targeted microcalcifications.[23] Post-procedure digital images are acquired to document the removal of the microcalcifications and at the same time to verify the presence of residual calcifications. In addition, a digital specimen radiograph of the tissue samples was required, as accuracy is improved when calcifications are documented within the core samples.[24,25] Many stereotactic breast biopsies showed limited removal of targeted microcalcifications despite the added sampling. Frequently, only a few calcifications were evident on specimen radiography (Figure 12–5A and B). Increasingly the literature has begun to support concern over insufficient sampling of core biopsy for microcalcifications. The Breast Center demonstrated the accuracy of core biopsy in 500 consecutive cases with a sensitivity of 97.8% and a false-negative rate of 1.5%. However, upgrading of diagnosis on open surgical excision was evident in 33% of the cases where atypical ductal hyperplasia was diagnosed on core biopsy and ductal carcinoma in situ was identified on excision. The presentation for the upgrading of diagnosis was microcalcifications.[22] Not surprisingly, atypical ductal hyperplasia diagnosed at stereotactic core biopsy has been called an indication for open surgical biopsy.[26–28] Consistent with the reporting of others, Liberman and colleagues reported a series of 25 cases of atypical ductal hyperplasia identified on stereotactic core biopsy, with significant upgrading (52%) to carcinoma on open surgical excision.[27]

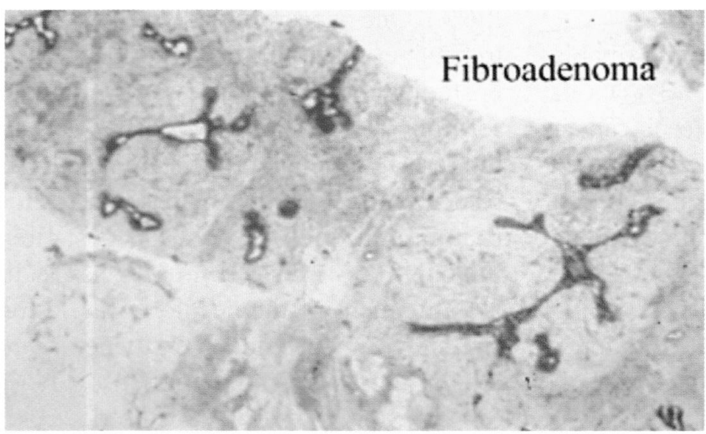

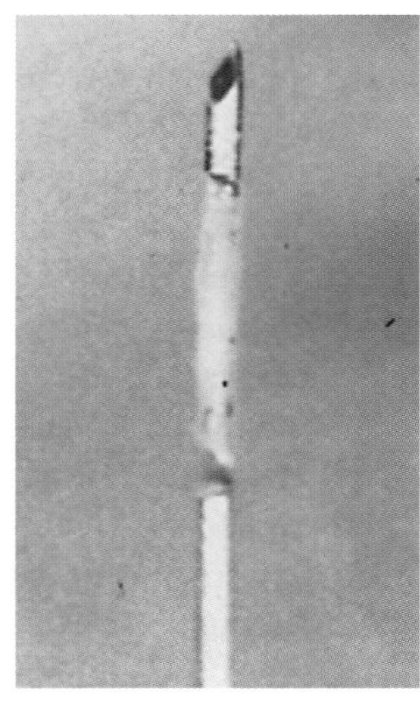

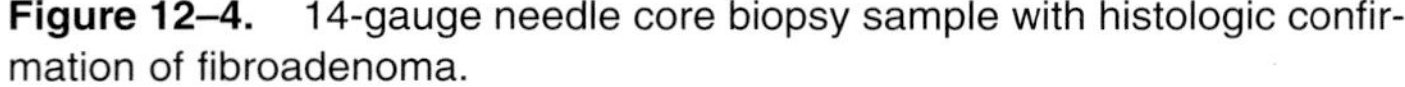
Figure 12–4. 14-gauge needle core biopsy sample with histologic confirmation of fibroadenoma.

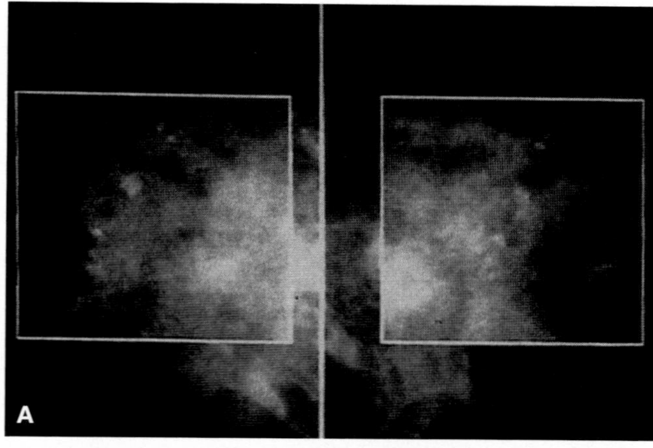

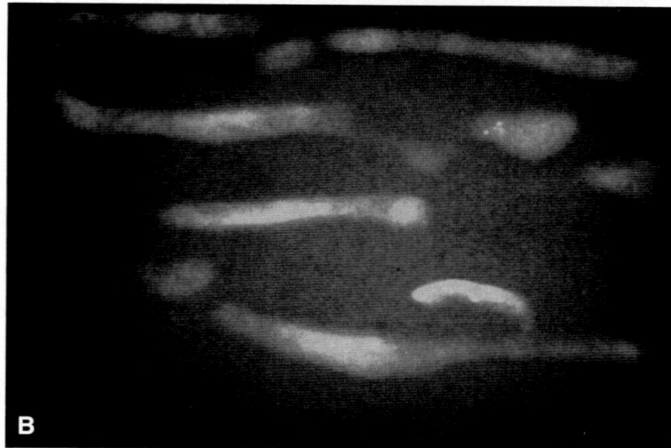

Figure 12–5. *A,* Post-procedure images after 9 to 12 samples with a 14-gauge Tru-cut™ biopsy needle illustrating the presence of residual microcalcifications. *B,* Specimen radiograph reveals only a few calcifications in the specimens.

Vacuum-Assisted Biopsy Devices. One solution addressing the diagnostic upgrading has been increased tissue sampling. Tissue sampling can be improved by increasing the number of samples taken, increasing the size of the tissue sample, or the manner in which the samples are obtained. The vacuum-assisted biopsy (VAB) device satisfied these requirements.[29,30] Not only was the sample size larger, but also the samples could be taken in a circumferential, contiguous manner. The first of the VAB devices, consists of a biopsy probe within a driver that has a sampling notch with several holes that are connected to a vacuum. A rotating cutter lumen within the probe moves forward to cut the tissue from the breast that is vacuumed into the sampling notch. The cutter lumen, attached to a rear vacuum, is automatically retracted, pulling the tissue sample outside the breast to the collection chamber, while the biopsy probe remains in the breast aligned with the targeted lesion (Figure 12–6). The vacuum-assisted biopsy system was ideally suited for performing an image-guided biopsy of microcalcifications under stereotactic guidance. Once the calcifications are stereotactically imaged, they are targeted on the computer monitor. Pre-fire stereo images assess the alignment of the probe tip with the microcalcifications. The driver has a spring-loaded mechanism to allow for automated advancement of the probe through the breast tissue. The sampling notch may be positioned with the lesion by the automated forward movement of the probe, or it can be manually aligned with the lesion by taking the driver to the appropriate depth with the probe already in its full excursion. After stereo images confirm the alignment of the sampling notch with the lesion, samples are obtained. (Figure 12–7A and B). By changing the position of the sampling notch with rotation, multiple tissue samples can be obtained. The size of the lesion, the volume of tissue desired, and the goal of removing the entire mammographic evidence of the lesion determine the number of samples harvested.

Today, there are three VAB devices (Mammotome®, Ethicon Endosurgery Inc, Cincinnati, OH; ATEC® [Automated Tissue and Collection], Suros Surgical Systems Inc, Indianapolis, IN; and EnCor™, SenoRx Inc, Aliso Viejo, CA) that function in a very similar manner and are able to accomplish the same goal. The vacuum assistance reduces the need for pinpoint accuracy required with automated Tru-cut™ biopsy instruments and allows for removal of multiple tissue samples without removal of the

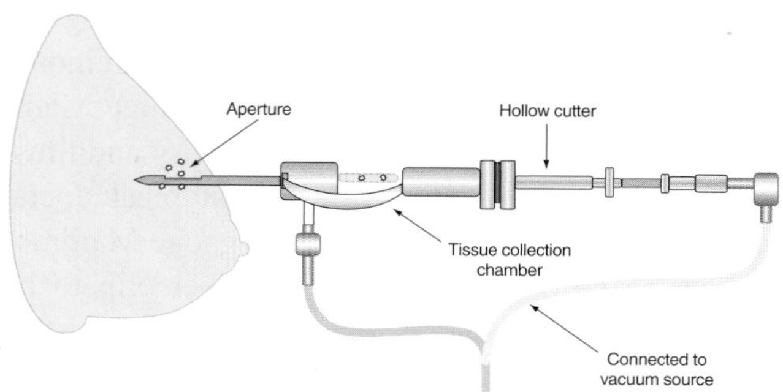

Figure 12–6. Vacuum-assisted core needle biopsy: tissue is captured with vacuum, cut, transported, and retrieved.

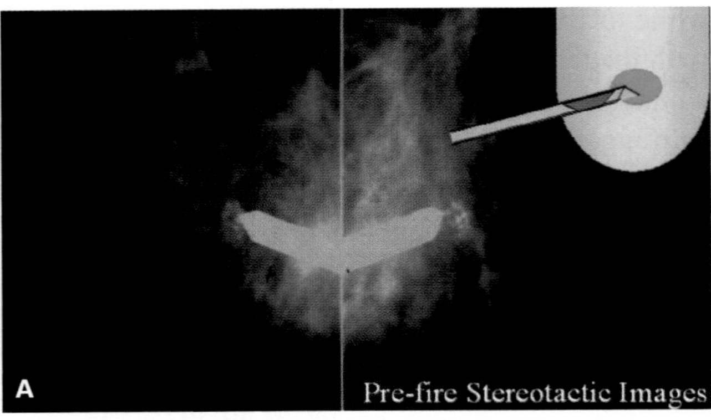

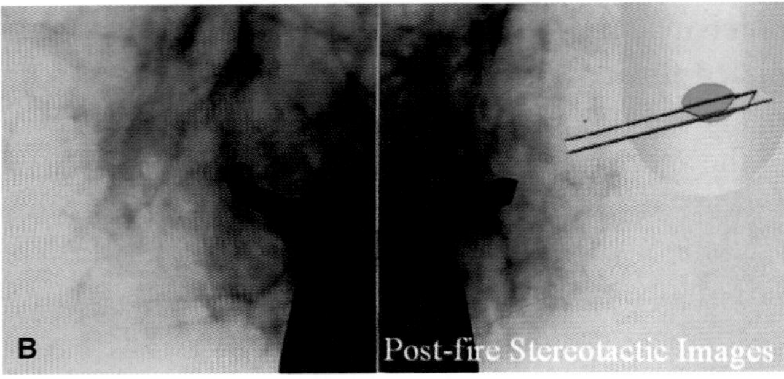

Figure 12–7. *A*, Pre-fire alignment; the relationship of the tip of the biopsy device to the lesion must be symmetrical. *B*, Post-fire alignment; the relationship of the sampling area to the lesion must be symmetrical.

biopsy probe.[29] In addition, the notch can be positioned for specific directional sampling based on the alignment of the probe notch with the lesion. The larger tissue samples provide a greater chance of removing image evidence of the lesion and a greater percentage of positive specimen radiographs (Figure 12–8). Burbank and Jackman demonstrated that the improved accuracy with the directional vacuum-assisted biopsy device lowered the rate of diagnosis upgrading seen with conventional needle core biopsy technology.[31,32] Burbank demonstrated that the 14-gauge Mammotome™ provided no upgrading of atypical ductal hyperplasia to carcinoma or upgrading of ductal carcinoma in situ to invasive carcinoma at open biopsy. Jackman compared 14-gauge Mammotome™ to 14-gauge needle core biopsy and illustrated a reduction of upgrading of atypical ductal hyperplasia from 48 to 18%. The 11-gauge Mammotome™ probe also allows for a marker clip to be placed in the wall of the biopsy cavity to assist in future localizations for lesions that are no longer mammographically evident.[33] The marker clip or residual cavity may be localized using the same stereotactic equipment if the diagnosis requires further surgical management.

Difficulties in Stereotactic Breast Biopsies

It is important for the physician to anticipate that some patients and lesions will be difficult to biopsy. Certain lesion characteristics such as low-density nodules, faint or non-clustered microcalcifications, or vague asymmetric densities may be difficult to visualize with digital imaging despite post-processing features. The position of certain lesions, such as those that are very superficial, adjacent to the chest wall, or in the axillary tail, may require innovative positioning by the experienced technologist (Figure 12–9A and B). However, some lesions may be inaccessible. It is essential that the physician be able to recognize and correct for targeting errors. Certain patient characteristics will interfere with the success of a stereotactic breast biopsy. Patients with neurological or musculoskeletal conditions may not tolerate positioning on the stereotactic table. Patients who are coughing because of an acute or chronic respiratory condition will cause breast and lesion movement, interfering with accurate targeting. Patients with a high level of anxiety, especially those suffering from claustrophobia or agoraphobia, may require sedation. As any biopsy has the potential for bleeding complications, those patients with a history of bleeding abnormalities or those taking anticoagulants will require correction prior to biopsy. The small or ptotic breast creates one of the most common difficulties in stereotactic breast

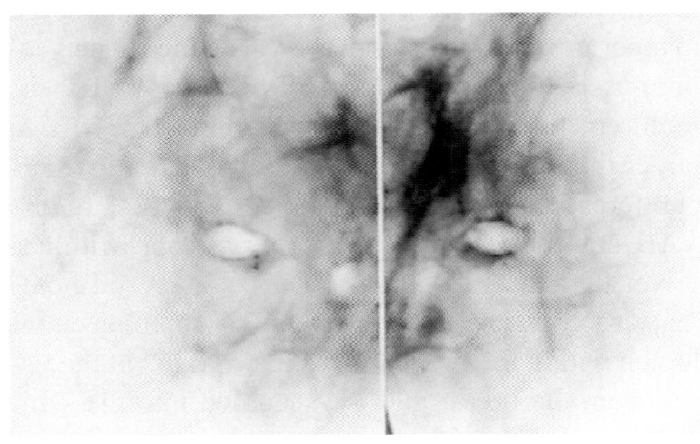

Figure 12–8. Post-procedure images after 6 samples with the vacuum-assisted device illustrated the air-contrast cavity and the majority of calcifications removed.

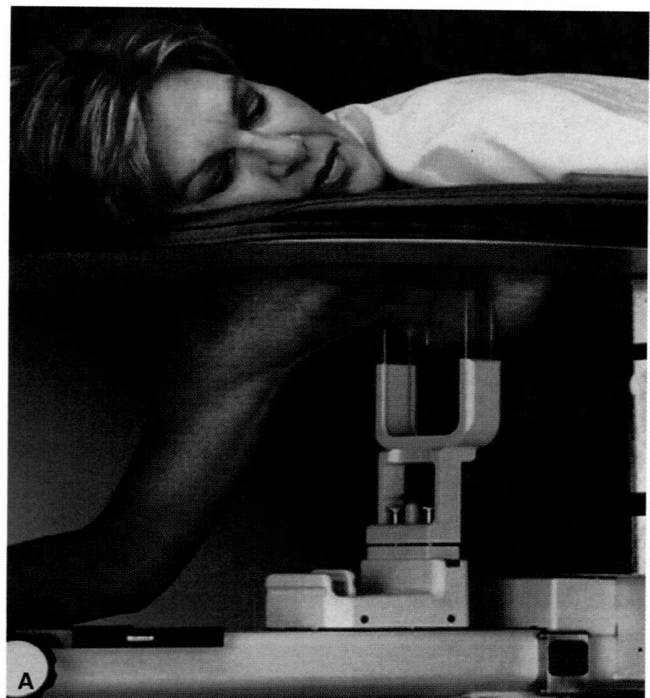

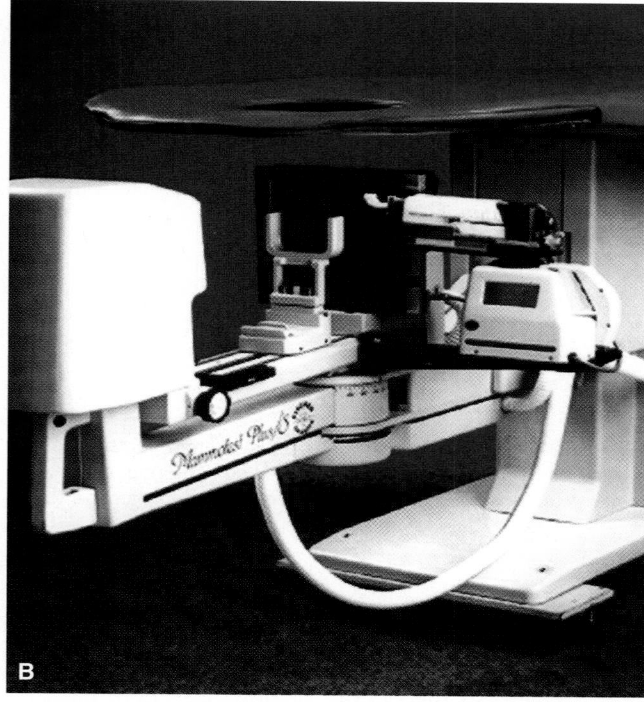

Figure 12–9. *A,* Innovative positioning on Fischer MammoTest Select™ for a lesion located in the tail of the breast. *B,* The Fischer MammoTest Select™ lateral approach biopsy system for orthogonal access to compressed breast.

biopsy. A breast that flattens to a marginal thickness in compression may lead to "stroke margin problems." The stroke margin is defined as the distance from the post-fired biopsy needle/probe to the back of the breast or the rear image receptor (Figure 12–10). When a patient's breast is very thin or when the lesion is in a more posterior position, a negative stroke margin may be encountered. This situation will result in the biopsy needle or probe striking the rear image receptor and piercing the back of the patient's breast skin. The most commonly employed solution is pulling back the pre-fire position of the needle/probe until the calculated stroke margin is adequate. Other methods for dealing with difficult stroke margins include, but are not limited to, taking a different approach to the breast lesion, using a shorter "throw" biopsy instrument, manual insertion of the vacuum-assisted biopsy probe instead of utilizing the "firing mechanism," using the lateral approach biopsy system (Fischer MammoTest™ Select only) for orthogonal access to the compressed breast (see Figure 12–9B) and using a double paddle technique, which separates the breast from the rear image receptor with a second compression paddle placed behind the breast.

Breast Ultrasonography Intervention

Technique

In order to have consistent success in ultrasound-guided interventional procedures, positioning and scanning must be optimized. The patient is positioned supine with the ipsilateral arm raised above the head. A pillow placed under the shoulder assists with access to lateral lesions. Proper placement of the equipment and the physician enhances visualization and comfort.[34] The ultrasound scan is optimized with appropriate gain and focal zone settings.[35] The target lesion is then identified, compared with the original diagnostic images, and documented with measurements and demographics.

Once the breast skin is antiseptically prepped, the ultrasound transducer is positioned to demonstrate the lesion's greatest diameter, and then the lesion is positioned on the ultrasound monitor for minimal skin-to-lesion distance. Local anesthetic is injected under direct ultrasound visualization. The biopsy device is inserted through a small skin incision and guided along the long axis of the trans-

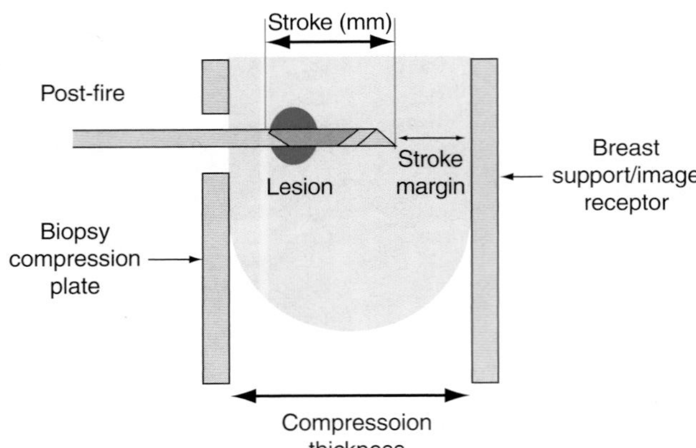

Figure 12–10. With an adequate stroke margin, the back of the breast and image receptor are protected. Ignoring a negative stroke margin will result in patient discomfort and damage to the image receptor.

ducer. By propping the patient with a pillow laterally and by gently pushing the far end of the transducer into the breast, the needle or device is kept parallel to the transducer face, allowing better visualization of the advancing device and monitoring as it is positioned for intervention.[34] (Figure 12-11).

Indications

A symptomatic or enlarging cyst, whether palpable or non-palpable, is a common indication for intervention. Typically, a symptomatic, palpable cyst is aspirated by inserting a needle under palpation guidance and withdrawing fluid until the lesion is no longer palpable. However, direct visualization of the procedure with ultrasound accurately positions the needle in the lesion, especially when dealing with a thick-walled cyst, ensures complete collapse of the cyst, and provides documentation of the procedure.[34] Ultrasound guidance, of course, allows access to nonpalpable cysts. Aspiration is performed with a 25- to 20-gauge, 1.5-inch needle, using either a syringe-holder system or a Vacutainer (BD, Franklin Lakes, NJ).

Indeterminate lesions not meeting criteria for a simple cyst require aspiration. A lesion with a mixed internal echo pattern with posterior enhancement suggests the presence of fluid versus a solid lesion, and aspiration may be attempted prior to a core biopsy.[36] The aspiration of thick, paste-like material, frequently found with mammary duct ectasia, might require local anesthetic and the use of a larger gauge (18- to 14-gauge) needle. Aspirated fluid is sent for cytology if the fluid is bloody or the cyst does not resolve.

The presence of a nonpalpable, solid lesion is an indication for an ultrasound-guided needle core biopsy (US-NCB) to obtain a histologic diagnosis.[37] These non-cystic lesions can be categorized based on their risk of malignancy.[38,39] For the solid hypoechoic lesion with smooth margins, a homogeneous internal echo pattern, and ellipsoid shape, ultrasound-guided biopsy can confirm a benign diagnosis, and the lesion may be safely monitored.[34] "Indeterminate-risk" lesions often have heterogeneous interiors, indistinct yet smooth margins, and a lateral/anteroposterior dimension ratio greater than

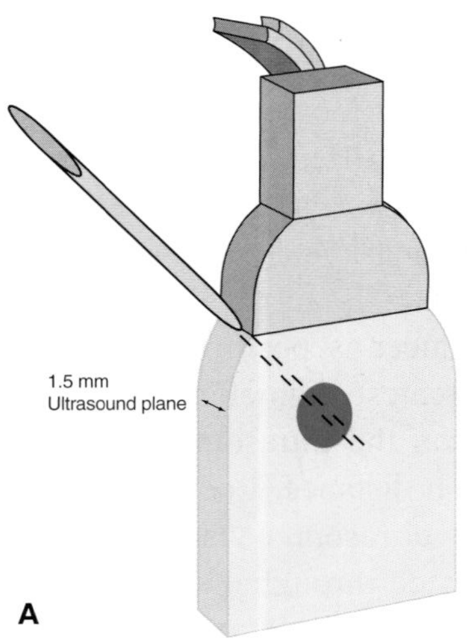

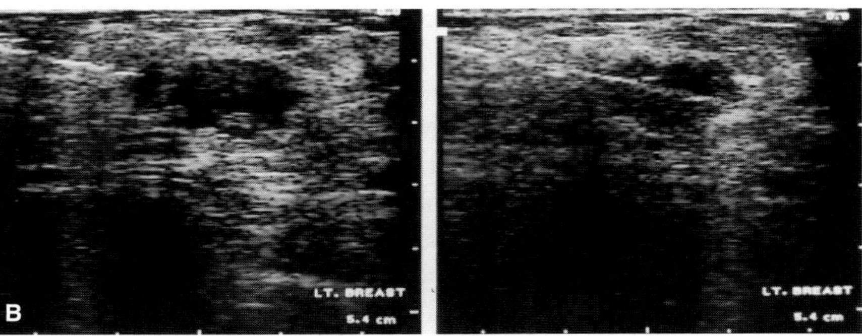

Figure 12–11. *A,* With the ultrasound transducer and breast stabilized with the non-dominant hand, the biopsy instrument is advanced forward through a small skin incision maintaining orientation of the needle in the long axis of the transducer. *B,* Documenting alignment and penetration under real-time ultrasound guidance.

one. A 10 to 15% risk of malignancy requires diagnosis with histologic sampling.[40,41] Only resolution of a complex cyst or a specific benign diagnosis will avoid surgical excision. For the more suspicious, high-risk lesions with irregular edges, non-homogeneous internal echo pattern and irregular shadowing, ultrasound-guided biopsy is a cost-effective, efficient procedure that may be used in the office setting to provide a diagnosis.[34,37]

Specimen Acquisition Devices

Fine Needle-Aspiration Biopsy. Confirmation of malignancy with cytology or histology is the minimum requirement for ultrasound-guided biopsy of "indeterminate" or "high-risk" solid lesions. Despite the criticism, especially in the United States, related to the degree of insufficient sampling and the need for expert cytopathology, fine-needle aspiration biopsy is a quick, inexpensive technique to assist in several areas of breast care management.[42] Despite the limitations, in experienced hands ultrasound-guided fine-needle aspiration can delineate benign from malignant solid breast masses. Fornage and colleagues evaluated 355 breast masses with ultrasound-guided fine-needle aspiration biopsy and demonstrated a sensitivity of 97% and a specificity of 91%.[43] Gordon and colleagues confirmed the diagnosis of malignancy with ultrasound-guided fine-needle aspiration in 213 of 225 cases, yielding a 95% sensitivity and a 92% specificity.[44] Six of 12 of false-negative cases in this series were lobular carcinoma. Lobular carcinoma does not shed cells well at aspiration and therefore limits the usefulness of fine-needle aspiration in these cases.[45] In addition to confirmation of malignancy of a "high-risk" lesion with cytology, ultrasound-guided fine-needle aspiration is frequently used to evaluate lesions in areas where more invasive biopsy devices may be difficult or dangerous, such as the axilla or adjacent to a breast implant.[46] The diagnosis of lymph node metastasis by fine-needle aspiration can assist with preoperative staging in consideration of neoadjuvant chemotherapy[47] or eliminate sentinel lymph node biopsy for pathologically involved lymph nodes. Hormone receptor status can be determined from fine-needle aspiration.[48]

Automated Tru-cut™ Biopsy. Ultrasound-guided automated large-core needle biopsy eliminates the problems with fine-needle aspiration, especially for "high risk" lesions.[49,50] As in stereotactic guidance, histologic type and grade of a diagnosed cancer can be adequately determined with core histology.[51,52] Staren reduced the initial false-negative rate obtained with ultrasound-guided fine-needle aspiration from 20 to 3.6% using ultrasound-guided 14-gauge core biopsy in 210 patients with non- palpable mammographically detected lesions. There were no false positives. No cancers were detected in a median follow-up of 18 months in the patients with a benign diagnosis.[53]

The automated Tru-cut™ needles used to perform ultrasound-guided biopsy are available in a variety of lengths, gauges (12 to 16), and forward throw (1 cm to 2.3 cm). The mechanism of tissue acquisition is similar with the automated forward movement of an inner cannula with a sampling notch, followed immediately by an outer sheath that transects the specimen. Recently, several advanced coring devices have been developed which utilize either vacuum, coring rotation, or both in an attempt to obtain larger tissue samples with greater consistency. The SenoCor 360™ (SenoRx Inc, Aliso Viejo, CA), the Cassi™ Rotational Core Biopsy Device (Sanarus Medical, Pleasanton, CA), and the Vacora™ (CR Bard Inc, Murray Hill, NJ) are distinguished from the traditional vacuum-assisted devices because these all require reinsertion into the breast for each sample obtained. There have been no data to substantiate additional value for these devices over the traditional automated Tru-cut™ devices.

Ultrasound-guided large core biopsy for histologic diagnosis requires more planning than cyst aspiration or fine-needle aspiration biopsy but is still quick, minimally invasive, cost effective, and can often be performed on the initial patient evaluation.[37] Another advantage of ultrasound-guidance compared to stereotaxis, besides the patient comfort in the supine position, is the ability to inject more local, under real-time ultrasound imaging and therefore provide a pain-free procedure without altering the ability to visualize the lesion. When adequate sampling is achieved, the procedure is terminated, manual compression is applied for hemostasis, and the incision is appropriately dressed without suturing using Steri-strips™ (3M Health Care, St. Paul, MN) and Tegaderm™ (3M Health Care, St. Paul, MN) (Figure 12–12). The core samples are sent in formalin for permanent histology.

The accuracy of ultrasound-guided needle core biopsy (US-NCB) has been widely documented. Parker found no subsequent cancers in 132 lesions with a benign diagnosis on US-NCB.[51] Eventually, an updated report of a larger, multicenter, image-guided biopsy series (stereotactic and ultrasound-guided) showed 15 false-negatives in 280 benign lesions diagnosed by core biopsy, with most representing biopsy of microcalcifications.[54] The false-negative rate for US-NCB of solid masses was 1.4%.

A concordant, specific benign diagnosis such as a fibroadenoma does not require further intervention. The patient is usually followed up in 6 months with mammography and/or ultrasonography.[51] A diagnosis of cancer allows the physician to plan definitive therapy. With a known diagnosis of breast carcinoma, a surgeon may take more tissue at lumpectomy to improve the chances that clear pathologic margins will be obtained at the initial surgical setting, prioritizing the cancer surgery above the cosmetic outcome. When the initial lumpectomy followed an image-guided biopsy diagnosis, Whitten and colleagues achieved a tumor-free margin rate of 71% compared with only a 35% tumor-free margin rate when the initial diagnostic procedure was an open surgical excision.[55] Excision of a lesion will follow a US-NCB for cytologic atypia because of the significant number of cancers that are identified in association with these pathologic changes,[56] or if medical judgment dictates because sample quality was poor, or there is discordant pathology.

Ultrasound-guided aspiration and/or biopsy will assist in the management of postoperative complications such as seromas or hematomas. With the increasing use of breast conservation therapy, the architectural distortion identified at the lumpectomy site may be ideally suited for further evaluation with image-guided breast biopsy. With image-guided aspiration and drainage frequently a part of the surgical management of intracavitary abscesses, a more conservative approach applies for a breast abscess.

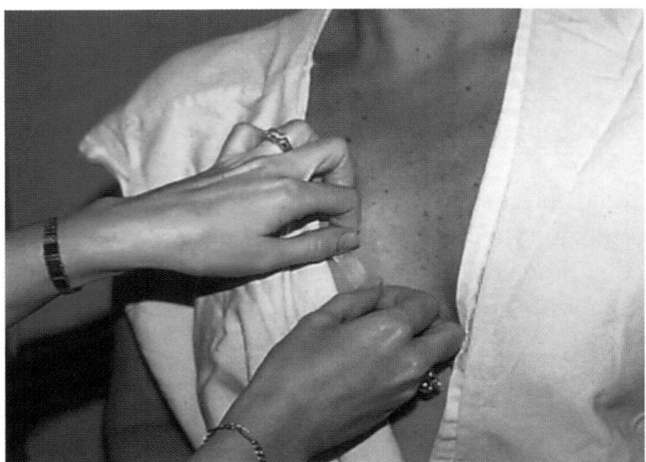

Figure 12–12. The skin incision is reapproximated using a Steri-strip™ after manual compression had been applied for hemostasis. A dressing may then be applied.

Ultrasound guidance is advantageous for aspiration of an abscess, insertion of a catheter for drainage, and monitoring of the resolving abscess cavity.

Ultrasound-Guided Vacuum-Assisted Biopsy (US-VAB). Vacuum-assisted technology was adapted for ultrasound-guided biopsy procedures with the goal of reducing physician error associated with multiple reinsertions and repositioning of the core biopsy needle.[45] The indications for ultrasound-guided vacuum-assisted biopsy are similar to those for needle core biopsies, including any indeterminate ultrasound visible, palpable or non-palpable solid mass. Smaller solid masses (less than 1 cm) with a non-specific benign diagnosis with needle core biopsy may be well suited to diagnosis with the vacuum-assisted device.[34] By removing larger tissue samples and perhaps ablating the image evidence of the lesion, the follow-up dilemma of this mildly discordant pathology is resolved.

When performing a US-VAB procedure, the biopsy probe must be guided beneath the lesion along the long axis of the ultrasound transducer. The artifact created by the device may eliminate the visualization of any portion of the lesion below the biopsy probe. Positioning in the lateral decubitus position, injection of local anesthetic posterior to the lesion for a lifting effect, and applying downward torque on the biopsy device handle as the probe approaches the underside of the lesion may provide a shallower angle of insertion and easier access, especially when the lesion is in a posterior position.[34] Tissue acquisition is achieved through the same mechanism of action described previously for the stereotactic vacuum-assisted biopsy device. Following a vacuum-assisted biopsy procedure, manual compression is applied for hemostasis, and the incision (4 to 6 mm) is reapproximated with a Steri-strip™ and covered with a Tegaderm™ dressing. The patient may also be sent home wrapped with a binder around the chest for patient comfort and continued pressure for hemostasis.

The success of US-VAB is enhanced by focused attention of the technical aspects of the procedure, including positioning of the patient, equipment, and physician, and the relationship of the biopsy probe to the lesion (Figure 12–13A and B). False-negative rates with US-VAB range from 0 to 2.7%.[57,58] The sensitivity ranges from 95 to 97% and the specificity from 98 to 100%, with a reported complication rate of 2 to 8% (hematoma and infection).[57,59]

Low- to intermediate-risk lesions can be adequately addressed with the use of ultrasound-guided aspiration to resolve complex cysts, and US-NCB or US-VAB for diagnosing solid masses. The majority of low- and often many intermediate-risk solid masses will turn out to be fibroadenomas or benign fibrous nodules. If concordant and the patient desires, these do not require further intervention or removal.[39] The natural history of such lesions should be addressed with the patient. Carty and colleagues[60] reported on the long-term, conservative, follow-up of 70 women with 87 fibroadenomas using the triple test for diagnosis (cytology, ultrasonography, and clinical breast examination). Fifty-three underwent excision showing a sensitivity of 84% with cytology and 98% with ultrasound. Thirty-four fibroadenomas reassessed at 5 years showed that 52% decreased in size, 16% remained the same, and 32% increased in size. No cancers were found. Another series of follow-ups of 201 presumed fibroadenomas resulted in resolution in 31%, regression in 12%, and further enlargement in 32%. One-quarter initially chose non-operative management, but another quarter requested subsequent excision.[61] Only 27% of women under 25 years of age opted for observation.[62] The reasons for preferring excision were fear of cancer, fear of the later development of cancer, and not wishing to have a palpable lump.

Breast cancer risk associated with fibroadenomas in retrospective studies is 1.3 to 2.1%.[63–65] "Complex fibroadenomas" (with elements of sclerosing adenosis, epithelial calcifications, or papillary apocrine metaplasia) show a 3.1% increased risk. The relative risk rises to 3.7% and 3.8% with family history and proliferative changes respectively.[66] The incidence of carcinoma arising in a fibroadenoma is reported to be 0.0002 to 0.0125% (primarily non-invasive).[67,68] A study of 105 women with carcinoma in a fibroadenoma showed a mean higher age (44 versus 23 years). In situ carcinoma comprised 95% of malignant cases and there were no axillary metastasis detected.[69]

Non-operative therapy is being evaluated to address the concerns that women have regarding

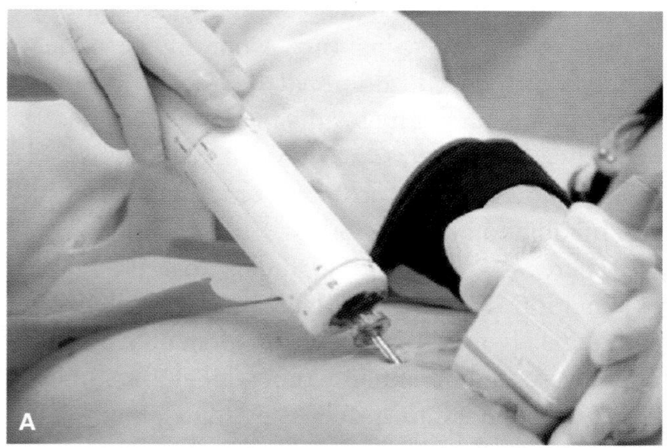

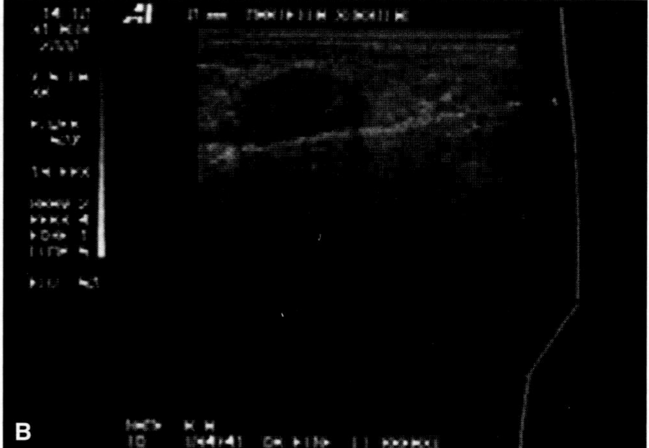

Figure 12–13. *A,* The vacuum-assisted biopsy probe inserted with ultrasound guidance directed beneath the lesion. *B,* Ultrasound documentation of the sampling portion of biopsy probe under the lesion.

observation of a benign lesion. Image and palpability ablation and more extensive sampling are reasons that non-operative therapy is being considered.[70] Several studies have indicated the ability of vacuum-assisted biopsy with stereotactic or ultrasound guidance to provide complete lesion removal in addition to an accurate diagnosis.[71–73] Fine and colleagues reported on the use of a vacuum-assisted handheld device with ultrasound guidance to remove low-risk palpable breast masses.[72,73] This was a multicenter, non-randomized study using both the 11-gauge and 8-gauge HandHeld Mammotome® (Ethicon Endo-surgery, Cincinnati, OH) for removal of benign masses up to 3 cm in size. The initial report of 124 patients showed complete removal of the imaged lesion in 99% of patients with the 8-gauge device and 96% with the 11-gauge device.[72] Subsequently, with 216 patients entered into the study and 99 available for evaluation at 6 months, 73% had no ultrasound evidence of the original mass and 98% had no remaining palpability. None of the patients needed to undergo additional diagnostic or therapeutic procedures. The results of this series and others indicate that ultrasound-guided vacuum-assisted biopsy allows for diagnostic accuracy as well as successful ablation of palpability.[73]

There are no specific studies that provide an explanation for the residual image evidence at 6 months. It may be related to difficulty of accurately assessing complete removal at the time of biopsy secondary to tissue, fluid, and blood in the biopsy cavity. In addition, as the removal of the mass proceeds in a "piecemeal" fashion and becomes smaller, the remainder of the mass becomes more difficult to visualize with real-time ultrasound. Another theory suggests there may be regrowth of these lesions from the residual tissue left behind.[34]

Advancing Technology; Large Intact Sample Devices. The complete removal of an imaged abnormality with large core and vacuum-assisted biopsy devices may be more efficacious and provide a more complete diagnosis in some patients. However, removing an abnormality in numerous pieces does not allow for optimal pathologic assessment, especially in size and margin status, and does not allow for specimen orientation.[34] Newer technology is evaluating the potential therapeutic effect of large, intact sampling devices (En-bloc™, Neothermia, Natick, MA; EnCapsule™, Rubicor Medical, Redwood City, CA). The Enbloc™ and EnCapsule™ are both radio-frequency devices. The Enbloc™ is inserted under ultrasound or stereotactic-guidance and advanced up to the front of the lesion. When activated, an expanding metallic basket advances forward with a leading radio-frequency loop for cutting. The loop of the basket then automatically contracts, closing the basket around the lesion. The EnCapsule™ device is also inserted underneath or adjacent to the lesion in a fashion similar to the vacuum-assisted biopsy probe. A radio-frequency–assisted cutting loop with an attached silicone bag is advanced out and rotated around the lesion. This is followed by retraction of the loop to complete the cutting and trapping of the lesion within the bag. The biopsy action of the EnCapsule™ can be monitored real-time with ultrasound but is also amenable to stereotactic guidance (Figure 12–14A, B, and C). The device and enclosed specimen is withdrawn through a small (less than 1 cm) incision. A recent series of EnCapsule™ biopsy procedures showed that complete pathologic analysis was achieved in all specimens, including prognostic markers with minimal (less than 1 mm) radio-frequency artifact. The single, intact sample was easily assessed for size (average 2 cm) and margin.[74] The technology of large, intact sample devices with ultrasound-guidance is promising, both for facilitating biopsy of breast lesions and for percutaneous removal of benign lesions. Such success brings into question the role of such technology in the treatment of small, malignant breast lesions.

IMAGE-DIRECTED SURGICAL EXCISION/LUMPECTOMY

The "gold standard" to which image-guided percutaneous breast biopsy is compared is the needle or wire localization open surgical breast biopsy. However, this traditional management of a suspicious non-palpable breast abnormality is not without its own error rate. The inability to successfully remove the appropriate lesion ranges from 0.5 to 17%.[75–80] Some of the reasons given for unsuccessful biopsies include: (1) poor radiologic placement of the localization

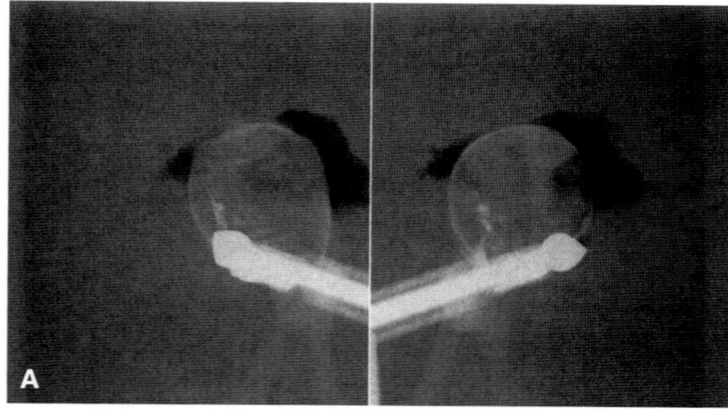

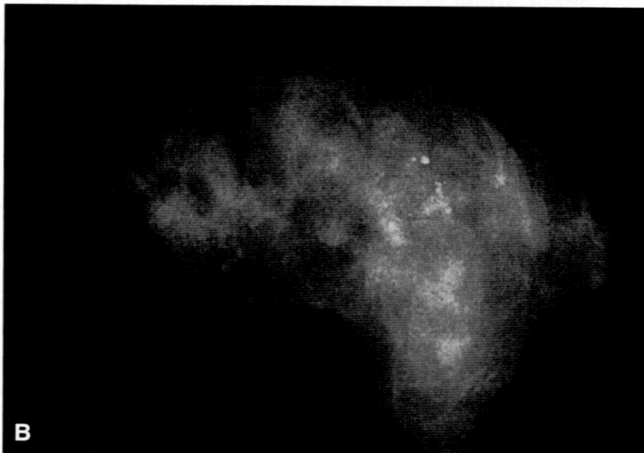

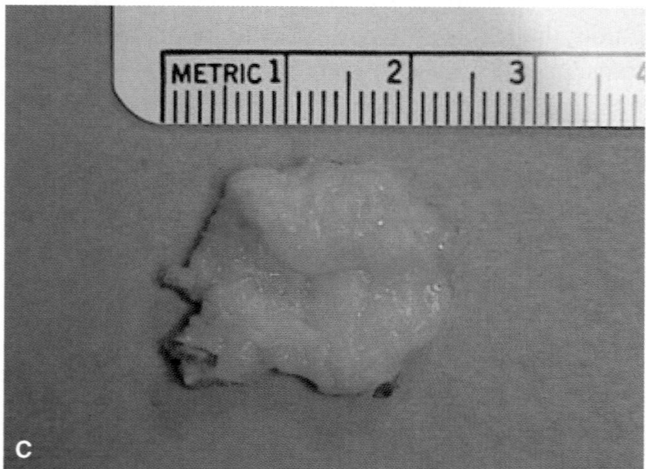

Figure 12–14. *A*, Phantom representation of the Rubicor EnCapsule™ with stereotactic guidance. *B*, Large intact biopsy specimen. *C*, Complete removal of mammographic microcalcifications.

wire, (2) preoperative and intraoperative dislodgment of the wire, (3) surgical inaccuracy and inadequacy in excising the appropriate tissue, (4) failure to obtain a specimen radiograph, and (5) the pathologist missing the focus of disease when searching through a larger tissue sample provided by the surgeon.

The needle localization/open surgical breast biopsy is typically more invasive. Whereas a surgeon may discount the importance of a scar on the breast, women frequently have a great concern over even a one- to two-inch scar, especially placed on the superior aspect of the breast. The possibility of altered breast shape associated with tissue removal is also important. This fear is thought to be responsible for women failing to participate in recommended screening because it might lead to a subsequent surgical biopsy.

In addition to cutaneous scarring, parenchymal scarring may complicate future mammographic screening.[6] Kopans and colleagues have suggested that significant parenchymal scarring is rarely associated with a properly performed needle localization breast biopsy.[81] However, surgeons are frequently faced with mammogram reports indicating architectural distortion in the site of a prior biopsy that might mimic the changes associated with a malignancy.

Despite the potential advantages of image-guided percutaneous breast biopsy, there are still reasons why a standard open needle localization surgical biopsy may be chosen for histologic diagnosis. Some patients desire complete surgical removal of a breast abnormality and will not be satisfied with a "sampling procedure." Certain facilities and insurance plans do not provide access to facilities where image-guided procedures (ie, stereotaxis) are performed. There are also certain lesion characteristics, patient characteristics, and potential pathologic entities where image-guided breast biopsy may be difficult or inappropriate.

The essentials for a properly performed wire localization breast biopsy include accurate localization, a comfortable, confident patient, and appropriate surgical planning and technique.[75] The radiologist often localizes the lesion with orthogonal mammography.[82] Increasingly, stereotaxis and ultrasound are used to identify the location of a non-palpable lesion.[10,83] Whatever technique is used, it is important to have the wire within 1 cm of the lesion for the localization to be considered accurate and to limit the potential for error.[84]

Direct involvement with interventional breast ultrasonography has naturally led to an ever-increasing role for the adjunct use of ultrasound in the operating room.[34] Intraoperative ultrasound is a useful technology for localization of non-palpable lesions, with and without localization devices. With the patient awake and usually upright, episodes of syncope are reported in 9 to 20% of prebiopsy needle localization procedures.[85] Because the patient must be scheduled in the radiology department, a surgeon has less flexibility with scheduling early morning operations and may experience delays in the schedule as a result of a difficult localization. Other disadvantages are wire transection and dislodgement.[85,86] Clip migration after a stereotactic image-guided breast biopsy may also lead to an increased miss rate at the time of definitive surgical management. Clip migration after stereotactic breast biopsy has been reported to average 1 cm and be greater than 2 cm from the biopsy site approximately 20% of the time.[87] These disadvantages have led to replacing mammographically guided wire localization with intraoperative ultrasound localization. Several authors have reported their experience with preoperative ultrasound localization by placing marks on the skin and providing the surgeon with the depth of the lesion. In these studies, the surgeon did not use ultrasound intraoperatively.[83,88,89]

The technique of performing intraoperative ultrasound for both localization and excision has been extensively described.[88,90–92] The localization may be performed with and without localization devices. Traditional localization wires (Hawkins™ (Boston Scientific, Watertown, MA), Bard™ (CR Bard, Inc, Covington, GA), Kopans™ (Cook, Bloomington, IN) formerly used only for mammographic or stereotactic localizations, are easily inserted under direct ultrasound-guidance in the operating room after the patient is in position and sedated. This may be done immediately before surgery by the operating surgeon, thereby eliminating a trip to radiology and the resultant lack of scheduling control. The patient is on the operating table supine, which allows wire placement in accordance with the location and direction of the planned incision. The wire/needle combination is guided into and through the lesion under direct ultrasound visualization. The needle is then withdrawn, allowing the barb or hook of the wire to engage the tissue just beyond the far edge of the lesion so as to minimize the chance it will become dislodged during dissection. The ability to inject local anesthesia under direct visualization without the concern of obscuring the lesion is another advantage of ultrasound-guided wire localizations over mammographically guided needle localization.

Ultrasound excision without a localization device is performed using a high-frequency linear array transducer placed in a sterile transducer sleeve (Figure 12–15A and B). The lesion is visualized and centered on the monitor, and the skin is marked at each end of the long axis of the transducer. After rotating 90 degrees and maintaining center, the skin is again marked at the ends of the transducer. The marks are connected, and where they cross is the position of the lesion. The depth of the lesion is noted on the ultrasound monitor. The incision is placed appropriately close to the lesion with a greater chance for improved cosmetic results.[91,93] Depending on the ultrasound equipment and its length, the transducer is placed inside the incision to re-visualize the lesion. The adequacy of the deep margin is determined by placing the ultrasound transducer perpendicular to the lesion parallel to the chest wall.[45] Even if the transducer cannot be placed within the incision, it can be manipulated to guide the excision. With the lesion centered, the transducer is guided to mark the inferior and superior margins. The transducer is then rotated 90 degrees, and a similar movement of the transducer perpendicular to the long axis is used to mark the medial and lateral margins. The specimen, once removed, is examined with ultrasound ex vivo to determine margin width and provide immediate documentation of lesion removal (Figure 12–16).

Several studies have reported on the use of intraoperative ultrasound and found its use in localizing breast masses both accurate and effective for surgical excision. Snider found equal success (100%) in excising 44 cancers using intraoperative ultrasound versus preoperative wire localization.[90] Both groups had a similar mean margin width and pathologically free margins, but the intraoperative ultrasound localization technique yielded a significantly smaller mean volume of excised tissue. Paramo and colleagues similarly found the two techniques to have equal accuracy without any significant difference in operative time or volume of excision.[91] Smaller excised volumes and adequate margins have been consistently observed

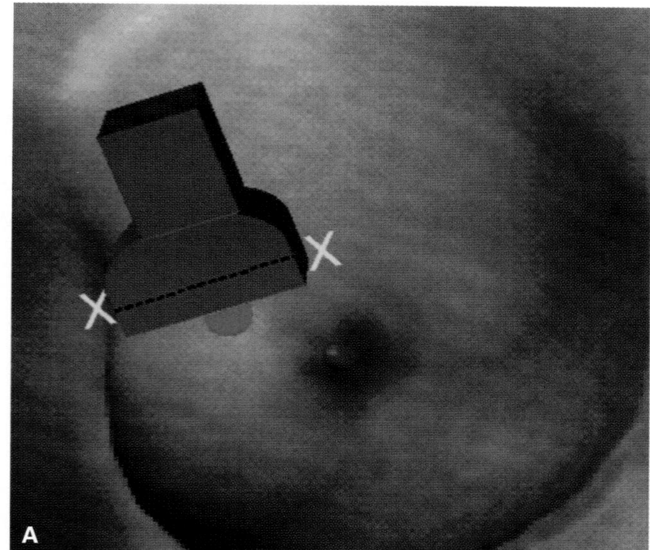

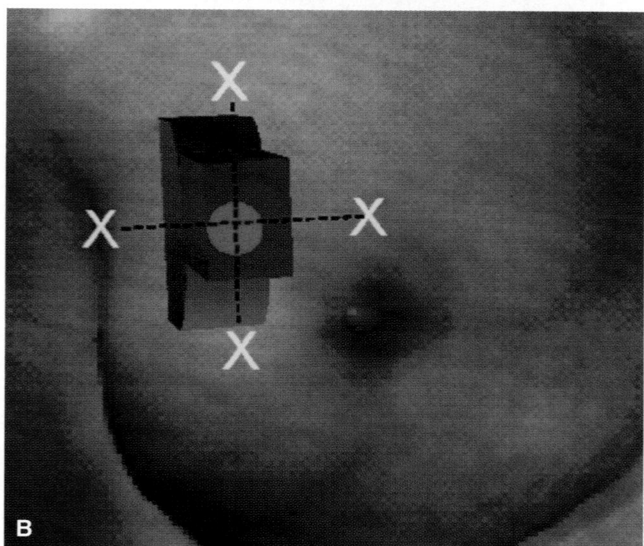

Figure 12–15. *A,* Ultrasound-guided localization of a nonpalpable breast lesion without use of a wire for guidance. *B,* After placing marks on the skin with perpendicular ultrasound transducer orientation and the lesion centered, the surgeon can confidently know the lesion is directly beneath, at a depth determined by ultrasound.

with intraoperative ultrasound-guided localization and excision for both palpable and non-palpable lesions.[88,91,93,94] Positive margins in most of these studies are related to ductal carcinoma in situ.[90,93] Harlow and colleagues recommend performing specimen mammography on those lesions where the initial mammogram indicates microcalcifications or spiculations that extend beyond the mass.[92]

Localization can be performed on any ultrasound visible lesion requiring further evaluation or definitive management. The advantages of avoiding preoperative wire localization have recently been expanded to lesions that are traditionally considered ultrasound invisible by converting these lesions into ultrasound visible status. An ultrasound visible marker can be placed at the time of a stereotactic-guided breast biopsy for microcalcifications.[95,96] Several ultrasound visible markers have become available which contain absorbable, echogenic material plus a metallic marker.[97] The absorbable material may be similar to Vicryl or contain a collagen-like substance that allows ultrasound visibility for several weeks. Intraoperative ultrasound localization and excision can also be performed after a stereotactic biopsy by visualizing the vacuum-assisted, hematoma-filled biopsy cavity.[34] In both techniques, it is important to perform preoperative ultrasonography in the office 2 to 3 days before surgery to confirm visualization of the target. Smith and colleagues reported successful removal of the hematoma as long as 56 days after the biopsy.[95] Ultrasound localization of lesions detected only by magnetic resonance imaging may be accomplished by creating iatrogenic breast hematomas with injection of 2 to 5 mL of the patient's own blood.[98] Ultrasound-guided wire localization can then be performed immediately before surgery in the operating room.

In an effort to obtain adequate margins during surgery and to perhaps create a more uniform

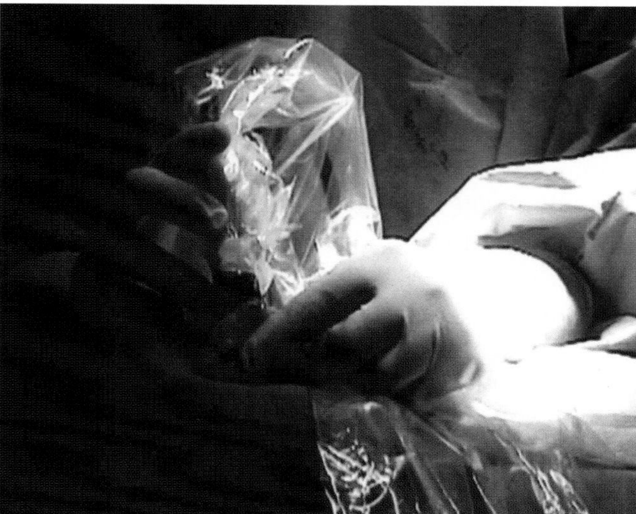

Figure 12–16. Intraoperative ultrasound assessment of the lumpectomy specimen for adequate margins.

lumpectomy cavity, several localization devices have been developed.[34] The Anchor Guide™ (SenoRx, Aliso Viejo, CA) is a radio-frequency–assisted localization device that causes a non-palpable lesion to be palpable (Figure 12–17A, B and C). This monopolar instrument consists of a calibrated shaft with a radio-frequency cutting tip. Within the device is a set of fixation wires that can be deployed in a radial fashion. When fully extended, the wires mark a 3 cm palpable area around the shaft of the device. The Anchor Guide™ can be placed using either stereotactic or ultrasound guidance that is directed through the tumor. Israel and colleagues reported on 114 patients assigned to either traditional needle localization (n = 62) or Anchor Guide™ (n = 52) procedures.[99] The device placement success within 1 cm of the lesion center was 96% for the Anchor Guide™ and 98% for traditional localization. Target lesion removal and concordant histological diagnosis was 100% in both groups. There was a significant difference in procedure enhancement perceived by the investigators; usefulness as a palpable guide was noted to be 94% for the Anchor Guide™ versus 16% for control cases. Use as a retractor was noted in 98% of Anchor Guide™ cases versus 3% for the control cases. The need for re-excision secondary to involved margins was reduced from 30% in the control group to 10% in the treatment group. However, the Anchor Guide™ group had a greater proportion of masses than the control (54 versus 34%) and fewer calcifications (50 versus 33%). Such differences may impact on the ability to achieve clear margins.

Cryoprobe-assisted lumpectomy (CAL) is another strategy that may assist the surgeon with intraoperative localization and excision of sonographically detectable, non-palpable breast cancers.[100] As with cryoablation techniques, once the probe is positioned in the lesion's center, Argon gas is used to generate an ice ball that is easily visualized on ultrasound. The growth of the ice ball is observed with real-time ultrasound to encompass the tumor and a margin of normal tissue. The formation of the ice ball also creates a palpable lesion from one that was initially non-palpable. Surgical resection is facilitated by the palpation of the ice ball and manipulation and traction of the cryoprobe (a ball-on-a-stick effect).

In a pilot study, 24 CAL procedures were performed; all were successfully localized. In these patients with a frozen margin 6 mm or more beyond the sonographic edge of the lesion, the margin re-

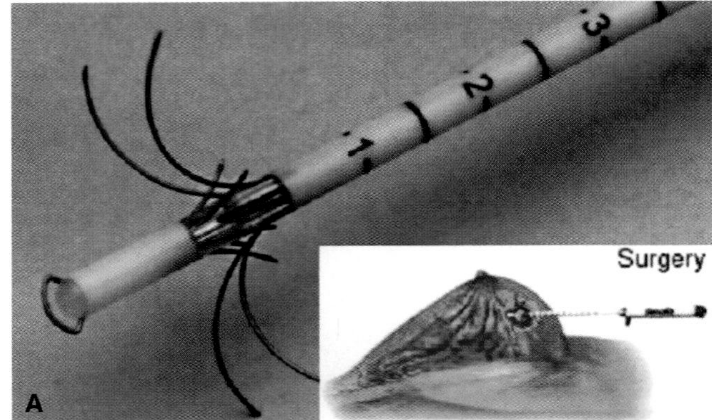

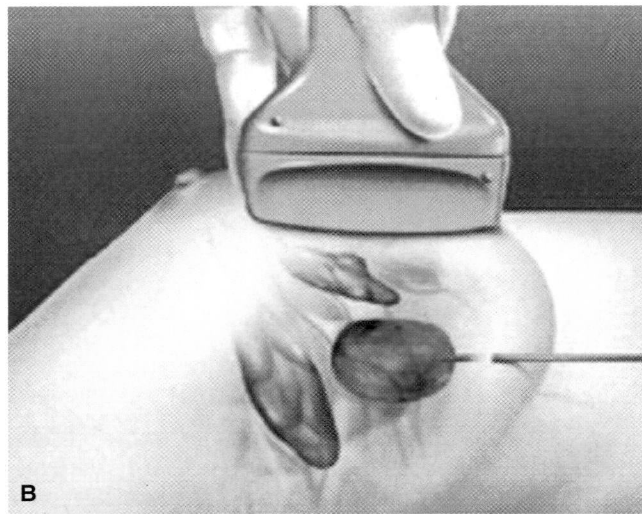

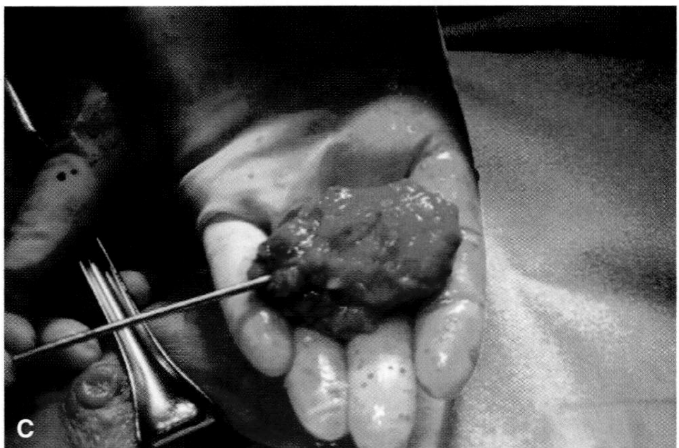

Figure 12–17. *A*, The Anchor Guide™ uses radio-frequency prongs to convert a non-palpable lesion to a palpable target. *B*, The Visica™ cryoprobe creates a palpable ice ball. *C*, These localization tools provide a method for traction while performing the excision.

excision rate was only 5.6%. Although margins were adequately evaluated pathologically, there was some difficulty obtaining accurate tumor markers (ER, PR, *HER2/neu*). Therefore, although CAL clearly demonstrates benefits of avoiding traditional mammographically guided wire localization, further clinical trials are needed.

Regardless of the localization method, planning the incision site should take into consideration cosmesis without ignoring cancer surgery principles.[83] If a lesion has a relativity low probability of malignancy and is within a reasonable distance from the nipple areolar complex, a circumareolar incision should be considered. When a wire is placed with mammographic guidance, regardless of the wire insertion site, the localization mammograms should be utilized to estimate the location of the lesion within the breast.[101] There is no need for a biopsy incision to extend from the wire insertion site to the location of the lesion to be removed. In addition to the mammograms, familiarity with the localization wire lengths and inherent markings may aid in more accurate estimation of lesion location (Figure 12–18A and B).[101,102]

Once the lesion location is determined, the incision is planned to avoid tunneling of a suspicious lesion through benign breast tissue.[103] The incision is carried through the subcutaneous layer without the development of any flaps until the body of the wire is encountered and delivered within the confines of the biopsy cavity. This may avoid potential indentation. Based on the relationship of the lesion to the tip of the wire, the excision is completed.

If the needle localization biopsy is being performed for follow-up to an abnormal image-guided percutaneous breast biopsy or potential malignancy, it is then performed as an image-directed lumpectomy.[104] Margin assessment becomes crucial to the success of the procedure. A technique of assisting the pathologist with margin assessment involves intraoperative inking of the margins by the surgeon using the Davidson™ multicolor inking system (Figure 12–19). The anterior, 12, 3, 6, and 9 o'clock positions as well as the deep margins may be marked with corresponding colors (red, green, blue, black, yellow, and orange) using a cotton-tipped applicator (see Figure 12–19). The specimen is then dipped into 3% acetic acid (vinegar) to set the colors. Subsequently, the specimen is sent to radiology for a specimen radiograph and then to pathology. The specimen is sent dry so as to allow further stabilization of the ink prior to pathology sectioning.

After hemostasis is obtained, the wound is closed. Closure consists only of reapproximating the subcuticular and dermal layers. There is neither draining nor reconstruction of the deep aspect of the biopsy cavity. If postoperative radiation therapy is a probability for the patient, small hemoclips are placed in the walls and base of the cavity. This will assist the radiation oncologist in planning therapy (especially if boost therapy is required for close margins or if partial breast radiotherapy is given). However, if the patient is a candidate for accelerated partial breast

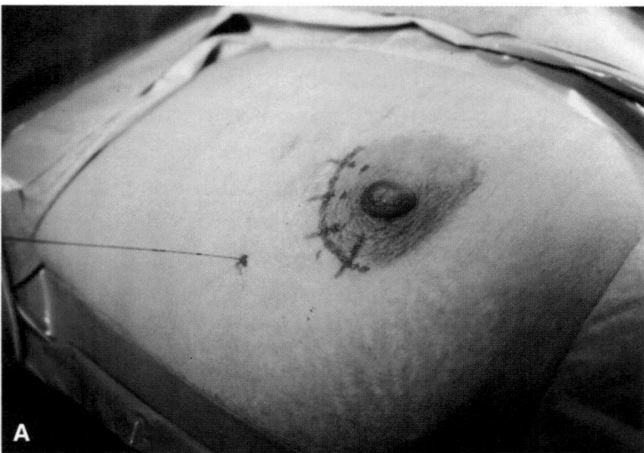

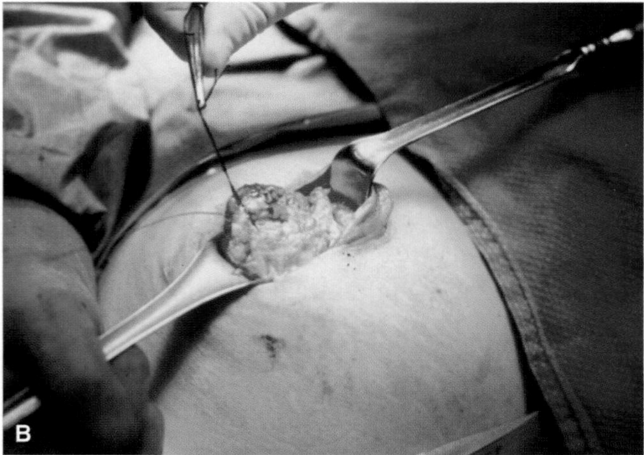

Figure 12–18. *A,* Based on the wire length, angle of insertion, and the localization mammograms, the position of the wire tip and lesion are determined and the incision planned. *B,* The incision is carried down through subcutaneous tissue, the wire is brought into the confines of the cavity, a 2-0 silk suture is used for traction, and dissection is carried out around the course and tip of the wire.

irradiation with the MammoSite (Cytyc Corp, Boxborough, MA) catheter, clips are not used and care is taken to preserve an appropriate skin-to-balloon distance. A clear, waterproof Tegaderm™ dressing is applied; this allows the patient to shower or bathe in the immediate post-operative period.

The patient returns to the office during the following week for wound assessment, to discuss pathology, and to plan future follow-up. A baseline mammogram of the breast is obtained in 6 months to look for any parenchymal scarring and to evaluate for appropriate and adequate biopsy.

SUMMARY

When patients are referred with mammographic abnormalities requiring further evaluation, the mammogram lesion is evaluated to determine if the workup is complete. When the abnormality is determined to require a biopsy, options are presented to the patient. The options presented should include traditional, open surgical biopsy, and percutaneous, image-guided breast biopsy. The option of image-guided breast biopsy must include a discussion of monitoring and follow-up. If this type of breast biopsy is acceptable, then the physician must choose the most appropriate method of imaging to guide the biopsy.

Microcalcifications unable to be visualized with current ultrasound technology may require stereotactic guidance. Certain nodular densities, architectural distortions, and asymmetric densities without ultrasound findings will also be more amenable to stereotactic biopsy.[31,36,37] When both mammogram and ultrasound visualize a lesion such as a solid nodular density, ultrasound is the preferable method for image guidance.[36,37,43] The real-time nature of ultrasound imaging provides increased accuracy and is more cost effective. In addition, ultrasound-guided biopsies are more comfortable for the patient. The patient may lay supine, and local anesthetic may be injected under direct visualization. This contrasts with stereotactic breast biopsy, where the patient lies prone with the breast in compression and the neck hyperextended for the entire procedure. Also, the ability to guide injection under direct visualization deals with the concerns associated with liberal use of local anesthetic and the potential for obscuring or moving a lesion undergoing stereotactic needle core biopsy.

The vast majority of non-palpable lesions recommended for biopsy are evaluated with percutaneous image-guided breast biopsy. If a benign diagnosis is obtained, no further work-up is recommended, and the patient is placed in a follow-up protocol. A specific benign diagnosis (fibroadenoma) requires only a return to routine screening. With microcalcifications or nodular densities with a less specific benign diagnosis, a short-term mammogram in 4 to 6 months is recommended.[10]

The obvious indication to proceed with open surgical excision is an image-guided biopsy pathology of malignancy or atypical hyperplasia. Medical judgment or lack of pathologic and radiologic diagnostic concordance would also be sufficient cause for further intervention. The issue of pathologic concordance with a suspicious mammogram lesion has fueled a debate over the indication to perform an image-guided breast biopsy on a highly suspicious lesion. Histologic confirmation assists in patient planning and allows wider excision for clear margins at the first surgical setting. Image-guided breast biopsy of a suspicious lesion may bypass open biopsy altogether for those patients requiring a mastectomy and who are not candidates for breast conservation. Histologic confirmation of an obvious cancer with image-guided technology leaves a tumor in situ to aid in the successful performance of the

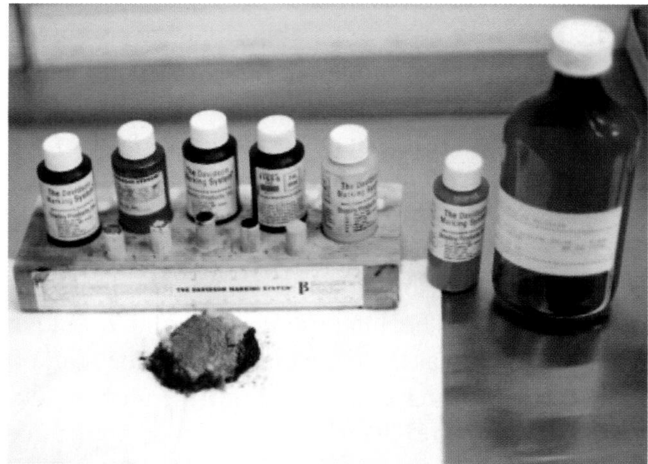

Figure 12–19. The Davidson™ multicolor inking system is used to identify margins of resection.

sentinel lymph node biopsy procedure. Concerns over potential added cost of using image-guided biopsy for highly suspicious lesions (that would require excision regardless of a benign diagnosis) are over-scored.

As technology advances and the approach to breast cancer treatment evolves, additional indications for image-guided biopsy of suspicious lesions will emerge. For many, image-guided percutaneous breast biopsy has permanently altered the management of non-palpable breast disease. Image-guided percutaneous breast biopsy will provide the stage for achieving non-operative histologic diagnosis and the potential for future therapeutic modalities.

REFERENCES

1. Kopans DB. The positive predictive value of mammography. AJR 1992;158:521–6.
2. Sailors DM, Crabtree JD, Land RL, et al. Needle localization for non-palpable breast lesions. Am Surg 1994;60:186.
3. Wilhelm NC, DeParedes ES, Pope RT. The changing mammogram: a primary indication for needle localization biopsy. Arch Surg 1986;121:1311.
4. Miller ES, Adelman RW, Espinosa MH. The early detection of non-palpable breast carcinoma with needle localization. Experience with 500 patients in a community hospital. Am Surg 1992;58:195.
5. Parker SH, Lovin JD, Jobe WE, et al. Nonpalpable breast lesions: stereotactic automated large-core biopsies. Radiology 1991;180:403–7.
6. Elvecrog EL, Lechner MC, Nelson MT. Nonpalpable breast lesions: correlation of stereotaxic large-core needle biopsy and surgical biopsy results. Radiology 1993;188:453–5.
7. Parker SH, Burbank F, Jackman RJ et al. Percutaneous large-core breast biopsy: a multi-institutional study. Radiology 1994;193:359–64.
8. Dershaw DD, Morris EA, Liberman L, et al. Nondiagnostic stereotaxic core breast biopsy: results of rebiopsy. Radiology 1996;198:323–5.
9. Liberman LL, Fahs MC, Dershaw DD, et al. Impact of stereotaxis core breast biopsy on cost of diagnosis. Radiology 1995;195:633–7.
10. Fine RE, Boyd BA. Stereotactic breast biopsy: a practical approach. Am Surg 1996;62:96–102.
11. Lovin JD, Parker SH, Leuthke JM, Hopper KD. Stereotactic percutaneous breast core biopsy, technical adaptation, and initial experience. Breast Dis 1990;176:741–7.
12. Parker SH, Lovin JD, Jobe WE, et al. Stereotactic breast biopsy with a biopsy gun. Radiology 1990;176:741–7.
13. Caines JS, McPhee MD, Konak GP, Wright BA. Stereotactic needle core biopsies of breast lesions using a regular mammographic table with an adaptable stereotaxic device. AJR 1994;163:317–21.
14. Parker SH, Burbank F. State of the art: A practical approach to minimally invasive breast biopsy. Radiology 1996; 200:11–20.
15. Soo MS. Imaging-guided core biopsies in the breast. South Med J 1998;91:994–1000.
16. Azavedo E, Svane G, Auer G. Stereotactic fine-needle biopsy in 2594 mammographically detected non-palpable breast lesions. Lancet 1989;171:373–6.
17. Dowlatshahi K, Gent HJ, Schmidt R, et al. Nonpalpable breast tumors: diagnosis with stereotaxic localization and fine-needle aspiration. Radiology 1989;170:427–33.
18. Schmidt RA. Stereotactic breast biopsy. Cancer J Clin 1994; 44:172–91.
19. Parker SH. When is a core really a core? Radiology 1992; 185:641–2.
20. Dowlatshahi K, Yaremko ML, Kluskens LF, et al. Nonpalpable breast lesions: findings of stereotactic needle-core biopsy and fine-needle aspiration cytology. Radiology 1991;181:745–50.
21. Liberman LL, Derwhaw DD, Rosen PR, et al. Stereotactic 14-gauge breast biopsy: how many core biopsy specimens are needed? Radiology 1994;192:793–5.
22. Israel PZ, Fine RE. Stereotactic needle core biopsy for occult breast lesions: a minimally invasive alternative. Am Surg 1995;61:87–91.
23. Tocino I, Gaargia B, Carter D. Surgical biopsy findings in patients with atypical hyperplasia diagnosed by stereotactic core needle biopsy. Ann Surg Oncol 1996 3;483–8.
24. Liberman LL, Evans WP, Dershaw DD, et al. Radiography of microcalcifications in stereotaxic mammary core biopsy specimens. Radiology 1994;190:223–5.
25. Meyer JE, Lester SC, Grenna TH, White FV. Occult breast calcifications sampled with large-core biopsy: confirmation with radiography of the specimen. Radiology 1993;188:581–2.
26. Jackman RJ, Nowels KWW, Shepard MJ, et al. Stereotaxic large-core needle biopsy of 450 non-palpable breast lesions with surgical correlation in lesions with cancer or atypical hyperplasia. Radiology 1994;193:91–5.
27. Liberman L, Cohen MA, Dershaw DD, et al. Atypical ductal hyperplasia diagnosed at stereotaxic core biopsy of breast lesions: an indication for surgical biopsy. AJR 1995;164: 1111–13.
28. Liberman L, Dershaw DD, Rosen PP, et al. Stereotaxic core biopsy of breast carcinoma: accuracy of predicting invasion. Radiology 1995;194:379–81.
29. Burbank F, Parker SH, Fogerty TJ. Stereotactic breast biopsy: improved tissue harvesting with the Mammotome. Am Surg 1996;62:738–44.
30. Berg WA, Kerbs TL, Campassi C, et al. Evaluation of 14 and 11-gauge directional vacuum-assisted biopsy probes and 14-gauge biopsy guns in a breast parenchymal model. Radiology 1997;205:203–8.
31. Burbank F. Stereotactic breast biopsy of atypical ductal hyperplasia and ductal carcinoma in situ lesions: improved accuracy with directional vacuum-assisted biopsy. Radiology 1997;202:843–7.
32. Jackman RJ, Burbank SH, Parker SH, et al. Atypical ductal hyperplasia diagnosed at stereotactic breast biopsy: Improved reliability with 14-gauge, directional vacuum-assisted biopsy. Radiology 1997;204:485–8.

33. Burbank F, Forcier N. Tissue marking clip for stereotactic breast biopsy: initial placement accuracy, long-term stability and usefulness as a guide for wire localization. Radiology 1997;205:407–15.
34. Fine RE, Staren ED. Updates in breast ultrasound. Surg Clin North Am 2004:84:1001–34.
35. Staren ED. Physics and principles of breast ultrasound. Am Surg 1996;62:69.
36. Jackson VP. The role of ultrasound in breast imaging. Radiology 1990;177:305.
37. Parker SH, Stavros AT. Interventional breast ultrasound. In: Parker SH, Jobe WE, editors. Percutaneous breast biopsy. New York: Raven; 1993. p. 129.
38. Staren E, Fine R. Breast ultrasound. Prob Gen Surg. 1997;14(1):46–53.
39. Staren ED, O'Neill TP. Surgeon-performed US: breast US. Surg Clin North Am 1998;78:219–35.
40. Stavros AT, Dennis MA. An introduction to breast ultrasound. In: Parker SH, Jobe WE, editors. Percutaneous breast biopsy. New York: Raven Press; 1993. p. 95.
41. Khattar S, Staren ED. Diagnostic breast ultrasound. In: Staren ED, Arrugui ME, editors. Ultrasound for the surgeon. Philadelphia: Lippincott-Raven; 1997. p. 85.
42. Kopans DB. Fine-needle aspiration of clinically occult breast lesions. Radiology 1989;170:313–4.
43. Fornage BD, Coan JD, David CL. Ultrasound-guided needle biopsy of the breast and other interventional procedures. Radiol Clin North Am 1992;30:167–85.
44. Gordon PB, Goldenberg SL, Chan NH. Solid breast lesions: diagnosis with US-guided fine-needle aspiration biopsy. Radiology 1993;189:573–80.
45. Rubio, IT, Henry-Tillman R, Klimberg S. Surgical use of breast ultrasound. Surg Clin North Am 2003;83:771–88.
46. Fornage BD, Sneige N, Singletary SE. Masses in breast with implants: diagnosis with US-guided fine-needle aspiration biopsy. Radiology 1994;191:339–42.
47. Vlastos G, Fornage BD, Mirza NQ, et al. The correlation of axillary ultrasonography with histologic breast cancer downstaging after induction chemotherapy. Am J Surg 2000;179:446–52.
48. Lundy J, Lozowski M, Sadri T, et al. The use of fine-needle aspirates of breast cancers to evaluate hormone-receptor status. Arch Surg 1990;125:174.
49. Staren ED. Surgical–office-based ultrasound of the breast. Am Surg 1995;61:619–27.
50. Roe SM, Sumida MP, Burns RP, et al. Bringing core biopsy into a surgical practice. Am Surg 1996;62:113–6.
51. Parker, SH, Jobe WE, Dennis MA, et al. Ultrasound-guided automated large core breast biopsy. Radiology 1993;187: 507.
52. Parker SH, Stavros T, Dennis MA. Needle biopsy techniques. Radiol Clin North Am 1995;33:1171–86.
53. Staren ED. Ultrasound-guided biopsy of nonpalpable breast masses by surgeons. Ann Surg Oncol 1996;3:476.
54. Parker SH, Burbank F, Jackman RJ, et al. Percutaneous large-core breast biopsy: a multi-institutional study. Radiology 1994;193:359–64.
55. Whitten TM, Wallace TW, Bird RE, et al. Image-guided core biopsy has advantages over needle localization biopsy for the diagnosis of nonpalpable breast cancer. Am Surg 1997;63:1072–7.
56. Bassett L, Winchester DP, Caplan RB, et al. Stereotactic core-needle biopsy of the breast: a report of the joint task of the American College of Radiology, American College of Surgeons and College of American Pathologists. CA Cancer J Clin 1997;47:171–90.
57. Meloni GB, Dessole DS, Becchere MP, et al. Ultrasound-guided Mammotome vacuum biopsy for the diagnosis of impalpable breast lesions. Ultrasound Obstet Gynecol 2001;18:520–4.
58. Parker SH, Klaus AJ, McWey PJ, et al. Sonographically-guided directional vacuum assisted breast biopsy using a handheld device. AJR 2001;177:405–8.
59. Simon JR, Kalbhen CL, Cooper RA, et al. Accuracy and complications rates of US-guided vacuum-assisted core breast biopsy: initial results. Radiology 2000;215:694–7.
60. Carty N, Carter C, Rubin C, et al. Management of fibroadenoma of the breast. Ann R Coll Surg Engl 1995;77:127–30.
61. Dent D, Cant P. Fibroadenoma. World J Surg 1989;13: 706–10.
62. Cant P, Madden M, Close P, et al. Case for conservative management of selected fibro-adenoma of the breast. Br J Surg 1987;74:857.
63. Dupont W, Page D, Park F. Long-term risk for breast cancer in women with fibroadenoma. N Engl J Med 1994;331:10–5.
64. Dupont W, Parl F, Hartmen W. Breast cancer associated with proliferative breast disease. Cancer 1993;71:125–30.
65. McDivitt R, Stevens J, Lee M, Wingo P. Histologic types of benign breast disease and the risk for breast cancer. Cancer 1992;69:1408–14.
66. Haagensen C. Disease of the breast. 3rd ed. Philadelphia: WB Saunders; 1996. p. 267–83.
67. Deschenes L. Jacob S. Fobia J. Christen A. Beware of the breast fibroadenoma in middle aged women. Can J Surg 1985;28:372–3.
68. Bazanowski-Konarky K, Harrison E, Payne W. Lobular carcinoma arising fibroadenoma of the breast. Cancer 1975;35:450–6.
69. Diaz N, Palmer J, McDivitt R. Carcinoma arising within fibroadenoma of the breast: a clinicopathological study of 105 patients. Am J Clin Pathol 1991;95:614–22.
70. Morris E, Liberman L, Trevisan S, et al. Histologic heterogeneity of masses at percutaneous breast biopsy. Breast J 2002;8:187–91.
71. Fine RE, Israel PZ, Walker LC, et al. A prospective study of the removal rate of imaged breast lesions by an 11-gauge vacuum-assisted biopsy probe system. Am J Surg 2001; 182:335–400.
72. Fine R, Boyd B, Whitworth P, et al. Percutaneous removal of benign breast masses using a vacuum-assisted hand-held device with ultrasound-guidance. Am J Surg 2002;184: 332–6.
73. Fine R, Whitworth P, Kim J, et al. Low risk palpable breast masses removed using a vacuum-assisted hand-held device. Am J Surg 2003;186:362–7.
74. Bloom K, Fine R, Lerner A, et al. Intact specimen capture and collection of image detected breast lesions via percutaneous radiofrequency device. In: Programs and

abstracts of the 5th Annual American Society of Breast Surgeons Annual Meeting. Las Vegas: 2004.

75. Tinnemans JGM, Wobbes T, Hendricks JHCL, et al. Localization and excision of nonpalpable breast lesions: a surgical evaluation of three methods. Arch Surg 1987; 122:802.
76. Norton LW, Zeligman BE, Pearlman MD. Accuracy and cost of needle localization breast biopsy. Arch Surg 1988; 123:947–50.
77. Kopans DB, Meyer JE, Lindfors KK, McCarthy KA. Spring-hookwire breast lesion localizer: use with rigid compression mammographic systems. Radiology 1985;157:537–38.
78. Bigelow R, Smith R. Goodman PA, Wilson GS. Needle localization of non-palpable breast lesions. Arch Surg 1985;120:565–9.
79. Landercasper J, Gunderson SB, Gunderson AL, et al. Needle localization and biopsy of non palpable lesions of the breast. Surg Gynecol Obst 1987;164:477–81.
80. Homer MJ, Smith TJ, Marchant DJ. Outpatient needle localization and biopsy for nonpalpable breast lesions. JAMA 1984;252:2452–4.
81. Kopans DB, Meyer JE, Lindfors KK, McCarthy KA. Spring-hookwire breast lesion localizer: use with rigid compression mammographic systems. Radiology 1985;157:537–8.
82. Feig SA. Localization of clinically occult breast lesions. Radiol Clin North Am 1983;21:155.
83. Schwartz GF, Goldberg BB, Riften MD, D'Orazio SE. Ultrasonography: an alternative to x-ray guided needle localization of non-palpable breast masses. Surgery 1988;104: 870.
84. Kopans DB. Breast Imaging. Philadelphia, PA: Lippincott-Raven; 1998.
85. Homer MJ, Smith TJ, Safaii H. Prebiopsy needle localization: methods, problems, and expected results. Radiol Clin North Am 1992;30:139–53.
86. Rinassen TJ, Makarainen SI, Mattilla AI, et al. Wire localized biopsy of breast lesions: a review of 425 cases found in screening or clinical mammography. Clin Radiol 1993; 47:14–22.
87. Kass R, Kumar G, Klimberg VS, et al. Clip migration. Am J Surg 2002;184:325–31.
88. Wilson M, Boggis CR, Mansel RE, et al. Non-invasive ultrasound localization of impalpable breast lesions. Clin Radiol 1993;47:337–8.
89. Rahusen FD, Taets Van Amerongen AH, Van Diest PJ, et al. Ultrasound-guided lumpectomy of nonpalpable breast cancers: a feasibility study looking at the accuracy of obtained margins. J Surg Oncol 1999;72:72–6.
90. Snider HC Jr, Morrison DG. Intraoperative ultrasound localization of nonpalpable breast lesions. Ann Surg Oncol 1999;6:308–14.
91. Paramo JC, Landeros M, McPhee MD, et al. Intraoperative ultrasound-guided excision of nonpalpable breast lesions. Breast J 1999;5:389–94.
92. Harlow SP, Krag DN, Ames S, et al. Intraoperative ultrasound localization to guide surgical excision of nonpalpable breast carcinoma. J Am Coll Surg 1999;189:241–6.
93. Smith LF, Rubio IT, Henry-Tillman R, et al. Intraoperative ultrasound-guided breast biopsy. Am J Surg 2000;180:419–23.
94. Henry-Tillman R, Johnson AT, Smith LF, et al. Intraoperative ultrasound and other techniques to achieve negative margins. Semin Surg Oncol 2001;20:206–13.
95. Smith LF, Henry-Tillman R, Rubio IT, et al. Intraoperative localization after stereotactic breast biopsy without a needle. Am J Surg 2001;182:584–9.
96. Whaley D, Adamczyk D, Jensen E. Sonographically guided needle localization after stereotactic breast biopsy. AJR Am J Roentgenol 2003;180:352–4.
97. Lechner M, Day D, Kusnick C, et al. Ultrasound visibility of a new breast biopsy marker on serial evaluation. Radiology 2002:223(Suppl):115.
98. Smith LF, Henry-Tillman RS, Harms S, et al. Hematoma-directed ultrasound-guided breast biopsy. Ann Surg 2000; 180:434–8.
99. Israel P, Gittleman M, Fenoglio M, et al. A prospective, randomized, multicenter clinical trial to evaluate the safety and effectiveness of a new lesion localization device. Am J Surg 2002;184:318–21.
100. Tafra L, Smith S, Woodward J, et al. Pilot trial of cryoprobe-assisted breast-conserving surgery for small ultrasound-visible cancers. Ann Surg Oncol 2003;10:1018–24.
101. Swann CA, Kopans DB, McCarthy KA, et al. Practical solutions to problems of triangulation and preoperative localization of breast lesions. Radiology 1987;163:577–9.
102. Wilhelm, MC, Wanebo HJ. Technique and guidelines for needle localization biopsy of nonpalpable lesions of the breast. Surg Gynecol Obstet 1988;176:439–41.
103. Leeming R, Madden M, Levy L. An improved technique for needle localization biopsies of the breast. Surg Gynecol Obstet 1993;177:85–7.
104. Fisher B. Reappraisal of breast biopsy prompted by the use of lumpectomy. JAMA 1985;253:3585–8.

13

Pathology of Invasive Breast Cancer

AYSEGUL A. SAHIN

Invasive breast cancer is the most common cancer in women and represents a heterogeneous group of tumors.[1,2] It is characterized by the proliferation of malignant epithelial cells with invasion into adjacent breast parenchyma and has the potential to metastasize to distant sites. The great majority of breast carcinomas are adenocarcinomas that derive from the mammary glandular epithelial cells, most commonly cells from terminal ductal lobular units.[3–6] Breast cancer is characterized by a wide range of morphologic features that are commonly used for classification. Most classification systems use morphologic features, including growth pattern, infiltration pattern, and cytologic features, and do not imply the cell of the origin.

Approximately two-thirds of invasive breast cancers are classified as invasive ductal carcinoma or not otherwise specified (NOS).[7] This diagnosis is based on the exclusion of special types of breast cancer and, therefore, represents a heterogenous group of neoplasms with different morphologic patterns. Approximately one-third of invasive breast cancers is classified as special types of breast cancer and show distinctive growth patterns and cytologic features.[3–6,8,9] Because of their distinctive histopathologic features, these special types are important for pathologists to recognize as a special entity, but, more importantly, many of these special types have a unique clinical presentation and behavior. Table 13–1 shows the major special types of breast cancers grouped according to their prognosis. Recent molecular and cytogenetic studies demonstrate significant differences in their gene expression patterns that are most likely linked to their clinical behavior and response to therapy.[10–17]

Although some clinical and imaging features may suggest a special type of invasive breast cancer, considerable overlap exists, and a specific diagnosis requires histopathologic evaluation.

Breast cancers can be accurately classified on limited tissue samples, such as core-needle biopsy or fine-needle aspiration.[18–21] However, it should always be remembered that these techniques provide only partial sampling. Breast cancers frequently show mixed morphologic patterns, and, depending on the size of the tumor and amount of sampling, there may be significant discordance between the tumor classification on biopsy and the final excision. Similarly, fine-needle aspiration may define the cytomorphologic features of a tumor to reach a diagnosis of carcinoma. However, evaluation of stromal invasion requires core biopsy or excision to assess the interaction of tumor

Table 13–1. CATEGORIZATION OF SPECIAL TYPES OF INVASIVE CARCINOMAS OF THE BREAST BASED ON PROGNOSIS

Favorable	Intermediate	Unfavorable
Tubular	Medullary	High-grade metaplastic
Cribriform	Secretory	Micropapillary
Mucinous	Invasive lobular (Classic type)	Signet ring cell
Adenoid cystic		Centrally necrotic carcinoma
		Inflammatory carcinoma

and stroma. Certain types of breast cancers can be recognized on limited tissue sampling, although the majority of the special types of breast cancers require evaluation of architectural features for their classification that are established only with surgically excised tissue samples. For example, medullary carcinoma is characterized by high-grade carcinoma cells forming a well-circumscribed mass. Although fine-needle aspiration or core biopsy can establish the diagnosis of carcinoma on the basis of the cytologic features, the solid growth pattern and circumscription of the tumor seen only on excisional biopsy is necessary to confirm the diagnosis of a medullary carcinoma.

The frequency of histologic types of invasive breast cancer varies among different patient populations.[22,23] Widespread use of breast cancer screening methods has resulted in increased detection of special types of breast cancers, such as tubular carcinoma and invasive cribriform carcinoma (Figure 13–1). Depending upon the proportion of patients with screen-detected carcinomas included in a given study, variations may exist in the distribution of different histologic types.[24–32]

A variety of classification systems and criteria are used to categorize invasive breast cancer.[3–6] Classification schemes of invasive breast carcinoma have evolved over long periods of time and have included different parameters, including architectural patterns, cytologic features, stromal characteristics, and pattern of spread. Use of these diverse criteria has resulted in considerable confusion and a lack of universal agreement on all types of invasive breast cancer. However, a high degree of reproducibility can be accomplished with a large number of pathologists using the same classification system and criteria.[33] Most invasive breast cancers are associated with an in situ carcinoma component. Multiple studies have shown that both in situ and invasive carcinoma components of a given tumor have similar morphologic, immunophenotypic, and molecular characteristics. However, the classification of an invasive carcinoma should be based on its own characteristics and not on the basis of the in situ carcinoma component.

INVASIVE DUCTAL CARCINOMA (INVASIVE CARCINOMA NOS)

Invasive ductal carcinoma is the most common type of invasive carcinoma of the breast. It is a heterogenous group of tumors that do not demonstrate morphologic features of any special type of breast cancer.[3–6] Therefore, the diagnosis is primarily based on exclusion of all other special types. Invasive ductal carcinomas have no special macroscopic appearance. Most commonly, they form stellate or spiculated firm masses with irregular, ill-defined margins. This consistency is usually due to a desmoplastic reaction elicited by invading tumor cells. Some invasive ductal carcinomas are not associated with marked stromal response; therefore, they tend to be less firm on

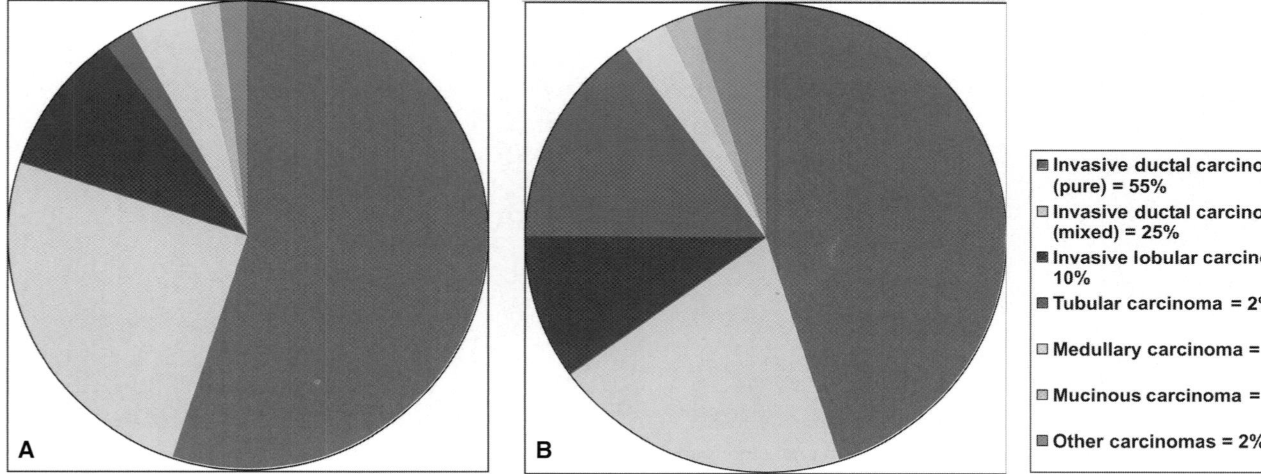

Figure 13–1. *A,* Histologic types of invasive breast cancer among patients in general population without mammographic screening. *B,* Histologic types of invasive breast cancer among mammographically screened populations.

palpation. The cut surface is usually gray-white with yellow streaks, Areas of necrosis and hemorrhage are common (Figure 13–2).

Microscopic features of invasive ductal carcinoma vary considerably from case to case. Tumor cells can grow in diffuse sheets, well-formed nests, cords, or as individual cells. Gland/tubule differentiation may be extensive, focal, or absent. The tumor cells vary in size and shape but, by definition, are larger and significantly more pleomorphic than normal duct epithelium. The cytoplasm is often abundant and eosinophilic. Areas of necrosis can be seen. Poorly differentiated, high-grade carcinomas may display extensive necrosis. The amount of stroma is also very variable. Some tumors have abundant dense stroma with a minor component of tumor cells whereas others infiltrate into breast parenchyma without any stromal response. Mitotic activity can range from imperceptible to abundant. The stroma associated with invasive breast cancer is formed by fibroblasts and myofibroblasts. Calcifications can be seen in approximately half of the cases, either as fine or coarse granules or, rarely, as psammoma-type calcifications.[34]

Invasive ductal carcinomas show immunoreactivity for low-molecular-weight keratins, particularly for keratin 7, 8, 18, and 19, and for epithelial membrane antigen.[35] Some invasive ductal carcinomas can be positive for high-molecular-weight keratins. In general, breast cancers are negative for keratin 20, and this feature can be used in the differential diagnosis of gastrointestinal tract can-

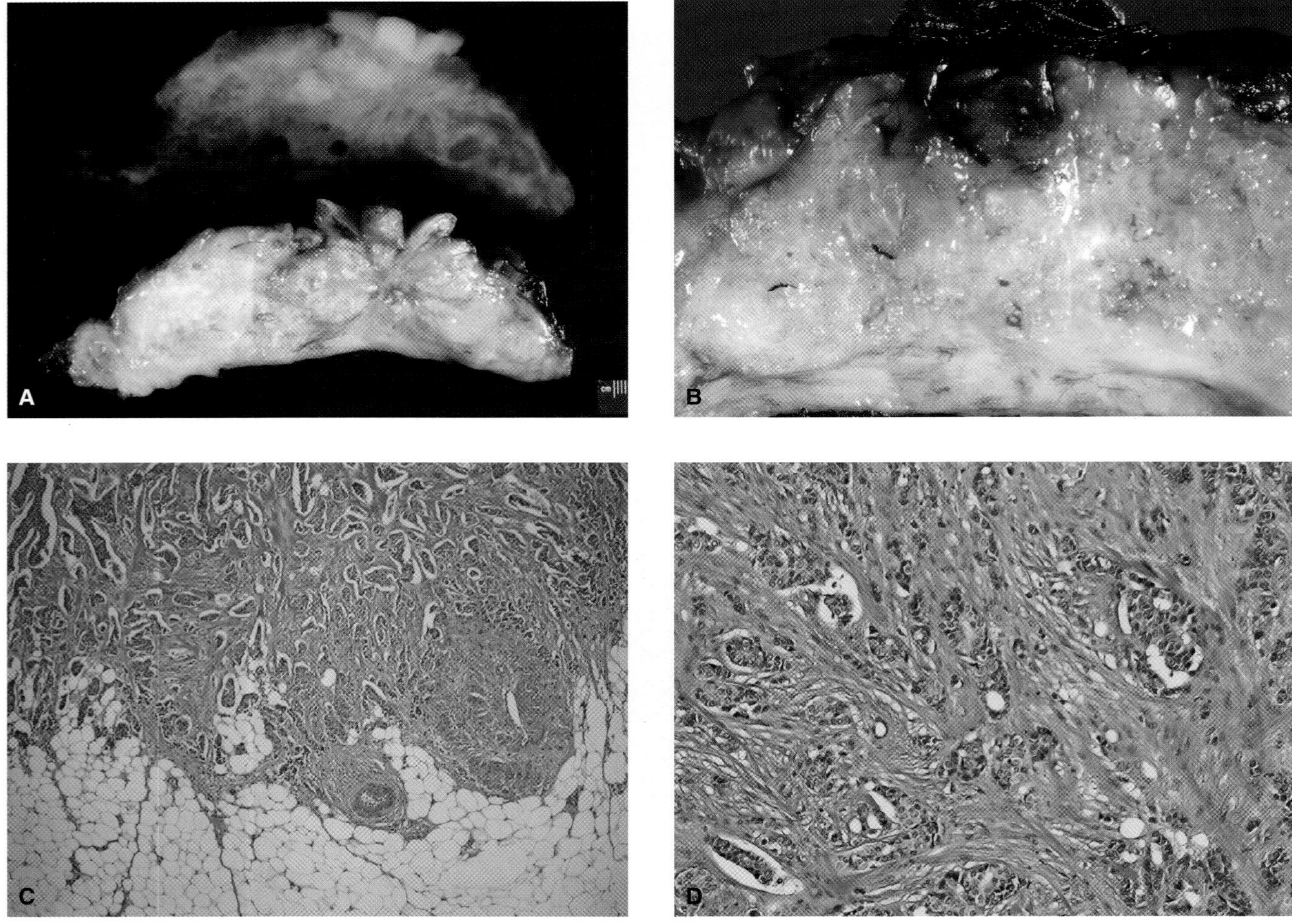

Figure 13–2. *A,* Invasive ductal carcinoma, (carcinoma not otherwise specified). The tumor forms an irregular, gray-white mass with irregular infiltration into parenchyma. Note the extension into skin with dimpling and retraction of skin. *B,* Closer view shows variegated cut surface with areas of hemorrhage and necrosis. *C,* Histologically, the tumor shows diffuse infiltration of invasive carcinoma cells into adjacent parenchyma and is associated with marked desmoplasia. *D,* Higher magnification view shows pleomorphic cells with varying nuclear size and shape.

cers. Immunohistochemical markers for basement membrane components and myoepithelial cells show discontinuous patterns or absence in invasive cancers. This feature is commonly used in the differential diagnosis of in situ and invasive ductal carcinomas.[36,37] Breast cancers may show immunoreactivity for vimentin, and some studies showed prognostic significance of co-expression of keratin and vimentin.[38] One-third of breast carcinomas may express S-100 protein.[39]

INVASIVE LOBULAR CARCINOMA

Invasive lobular carcinoma is the second most common type of breast cancer and represents 5 to 15% of all invasive breast cancers.[9,40,41] An increase in its incidence has been reported in postmenopausal women, which may be due to increased use of hormone replacement therapy.[42–44] The mean age of patients with invasive lobular carcinoma is a few years older than that of patients with invasive ductal carcinoma. As with invasive ductal carcinomas, invasive lobular carcinoma may present as a palpable mass or a mammographic finding that, most frequently, is architectural distortion.[45–49] Although microcalcifications can be seen, they are less common in invasive lobular carcinomas than in invasive ductal carcinomas. Because of the diffuse invasive growth pattern, invasive lobular carcinomas may form ill-defined lesions, and both primary tumors and metastases may be difficult to detect, either by physical examination or by imaging studies. More frequently, they metastasize to cerebrospinal fluid, serosal surfaces, the retroperitoneum, ovaries, and bone marrow, as compared to other types of invasive breast carcinomas. Invasive lobular carcinomas tend to be bilateral far more frequently than other histologic types.[45,47,49] The likelihood of this type of cancer in the contralateral breast is approximately 20%.[40–45] They also tend to be multicentric within the same breast.[40–49]

On histologic examination, classic invasive lobular carcinoma is characterized by the proliferation of small and relatively uniform tumor cells arranged in single-file cords that invade fibrous stroma. The tumor cells frequently encircle existing structures or lobular carcinoma in situ, and their growth pattern is described as target-like. Tubule formation is not a feature of invasive lobular carcinoma. Usually the tumor cells invade the surrounding breast parenchyma without evoking a significant stromal response. This infiltration pattern accounts for the difficulty of determining the extent of the tumor on clinical examination, imaging, and palpation of the specimen. The individual tumor cells typically lack cohesion, which is related to the decrease or absence of the adhesion molecule, E (epithelial)-cadherin expression.[50–52] The *E-cadherin* gene is located on chromosome 16q22, and its protein is implicated in the maintenance of epithelial coherence.[53] The loss of protein expression is most commonly associated with gene mutations and the inactivation of the wild-type allele. Mutation analysis or protein expression analysis of *E-cadherin* is commonly used in the differential diagnosis of lobular carcinomas from other breast cancers (both invasive and in situ). An in situ lobular carcinoma component is found in the great majority of the cases. Approximately 80 to 90% of lobular carcinoma cases are positive for estrogen and progesterone receptors.[54] The tumor proliferation rate is usually low, and *HER2/neu* gene amplification and protein expression rates are significantly lower than those reported for invasive ductal carcinoma.[55–57] In addition to the classic pattern described above, other subtypes of invasive lobular carcinoma have been recognized.[58] These special types include alveolar, solid, tubulolobular, and pleomorphic types, and they differ with regard to their growth pattern and cytologic features. The alveolar pattern is characterized by typical lobular carcinoma cells arranged in round clusters, in contrast to the classic single cell infiltration. The solid variant is also composed of classic lobular carcinoma cells, but they form solid nests, rather than single cords. In the tubulolobular carcinoma, the tumor cells form microtubular structures. Pleomorphic lobular carcinoma, on the other hand, shows the growth pattern of classic invasive lobular carcinoma but exhibits significant cytologic atypia and is frequently associated with apocrine differentiation.[59–62] A diffuse solid growth pattern of invasive lobular carcinoma has recently been reported to be associated with an aggressive clinical behavior.[63] Although signet ring cells can be found in both ductal and lobular carcinoma, they are common in lobular carcinomas, and some authors consider signet ring cell carcinoma as a subtype of invasive lobular carcinoma.[64,65] Signet ring cell morphology is most likely related to α-catenin deficiency, most commonly due to mutations.[66] The incidence of these subtypes is difficult to assess because the diagnostic criteria for each subtype is not clearly defined, and many cases appear as a mixture of these patterns. Consequently, the prognostic significance of these subtypes is difficult to assess. Several studies have suggested that the classic type of invasive lobular carcinoma has a better prognosis than that for subtypes such as the solid variant. Pleomorphic invasive lobular carcinoma and signet ring cell carcinoma, on the other hand, appear to be associated with a poorer clinical outcome. Although cumulative data in the literature suggests that invasive lobular carcinoma is associated with a more favorable overall outcome than that of invasive ductal carcinoma, this prognostic advantage appears to be more significant in early (stage I) breast cancer patients. Treatment of invasive lobular carcinoma should be based on the stage of the tumor, and despite higher incidence of multicentricity, invasive lobular carcinoma can be adequately treated by breast conservation therapy.[67] Local recurrence rates after breast-conserving therapy are not significantly different for patients with invasive lobular carcinoma, as compared to patients with invasive ductal carcinoma.

TUBULAR CARCINOMA

Tubular carcinoma is a special type of invasive breast cancer that is typically associated with limited metastatic potential and an excellent prognosis.[9,68–76] Pure tubular carcinomas account for fewer than 5% of all invasive carcinomas in historic published series. They represent 9 to 30% of carcinomas in mammographically screened populations.[22,26,27] When compared to invasive ductal carcinoma, tubular carcinoma is more likely to occur in older patients. Association with family history of breast cancer is reported by some, but not confirmed by others.[77] The majority of the patients present with a mammographic abnormality that is most commonly a spiculated mass.[78] In the great majority of the cases, tubular carcinoma measures less than 1 cm; it is very unusual to have a case of tubular carcinoma that is larger than 2 cm. Mammographic and macroscopic features of tubular carcinoma are indistinguishable from those of invasive ductal carcinoma. Histologically, tubular carcinoma is characterized by haphazard proliferation of small angulated, round glands that are lined by a single layer of bland epithelial cells. Because of the well-differentiated nature of the glands and low-grade appearance of the cells, tubular carcinoma can be confused with benign small glandular proliferations, such as adenosis or radical scar. The stroma of tubular carcinoma is usually desmoplastic and cellular, and this feature should be helpful in the differential diagnosis of these benign conditions. In the majority of tubular carcinomas and in situ ductal carcinoma component, usually low-grade cribriform or micropapillary ductal carcinoma in situ, lobular neoplasia, and other intraductal epithelial proliferations, such as flat epithelial atypia, coexist.[79,80] Focal tubular carcinoma differentiation is common in many invasive carcinomas. Although there is no consensus concerning the proportion of tubular carcinoma component that is required for the diagnosis of tubular carcinoma, most pathologists require that the majority of the tumor (90%) should have tubular growth pattern. Tumors showing 50 to 90% tubular carcinoma component are usually classified as mixed tubular carcinoma, and if the tubular carcinoma component is less than 50%, the tumor should be regarded as invasive carcinoma NOS. The separation between pure tubular carcinoma and others is clinically important since pure tubular carcinomas are associated with excellent clinical outcome.[70–76] It should be emphasized that this diagnosis can be established on core biopsy, but owing to limited sampling, discrepancies between core and excision can occur. Before a lesion is considered to be a tubular carcinoma, extensive histologic sampling should be confirmed. Incidence of axillary lymph node metastasis of pure tubular carcinoma is approximately 10%, which is significantly lower than that of invasive ductal carcinoma.[70–76] When tubular carcinoma has an axillary node metastasis, usually only a few lymph nodes in the level I axilla are involved.[81] Metastatic foci frequently show a tubular growth pattern similar to primary tumor. Tubular carcinomas are almost always positive for estrogen and progesterone receptors.[82]

INVASIVE CRIBRIFORM CARCINOMA

Invasive cribriform carcinoma is a rare form of breast cancer closely related to tubular carcinoma.[83,84] Similar to tubular carcinoma, it is a well-differentiated cancer with a favorable clinical outcome. Invasive cribriform carcinoma accounts for approximately 2 to 3% of all breast cancers. The tumor may present as a clinically apparent mass, but a significant proportion of cases have been reported to be mammographically occult. Invasive cribriform carcinomas are characterized by nests and aggregates of neoplastic cells showing a prominent cribriform pattern similar to that seen in cribriform in situ ductal carcinoma. In contrast to in situ cribriform carcinoma, invasive cribriform carcinoma has a haphazard distribution of tumor nests. The tumor cells are small and show a low degree of nuclear atypia. Mitoses are rare. Invasive cribriform carcinomas have remarkably favorable clinical outcome: the 10-year survival rate is reported to be 90 to 100%.[85]

MUCINOUS CARCINOMA

Mucinous carcinoma, also known as mucoid, colloid, or gelatinous carcinoma, usually occurs in older women and grows slowly during the course of many years.[86–88] The mean reported age in most studies is in the seventh decade. Characteristically, a tumor is extremely soft and has the consistency and appearance of grayish blue gelatin (Figure 13–3). The tumor usually appears as a well-circumscribed lobulated mass that may mimic benign lesions on physical examination and mammographic evaluation. The tumor size ranges from less than 1 cm to over 20 cm, with an average size of 3 cm. The histologic hallmark of the mucinous carcinoma is the abundant extracellular accumulation of mucin, in which small clusters of tumor cells float (see Figure 13–3B). The number of carcinoma cells is variable. Occasionally, the tumor consists almost entirely of mucin, and the evaluation of multiple levels is required to identify sparse tumor cells within a large amount of mucin. Delicate fibrous septae divide the mucus lakes into compartments. The tumor cells usually form small clusters and may exhibit acinar or papillary arrangement. Cytologic atypia and mitoses are uncommon. A recognizable in situ carcinoma component is absent in most cases. Invasive ductal carcinoma with focal extracellular mucin accumulation is a common histologic finding and does not have any clinical significance. It is generally accepted that diagnosis of mucinous carcinoma requires that virtually the entire tumor has a mucinous pattern.[88–90] When another pattern is evident, the tumor should be classified as a mixed tumor, and the most common pattern is a mixed mucinous and ordinary invasive ductal carcinoma. Typically, mucinous carcinomas are positive for estrogen receptor. Almost

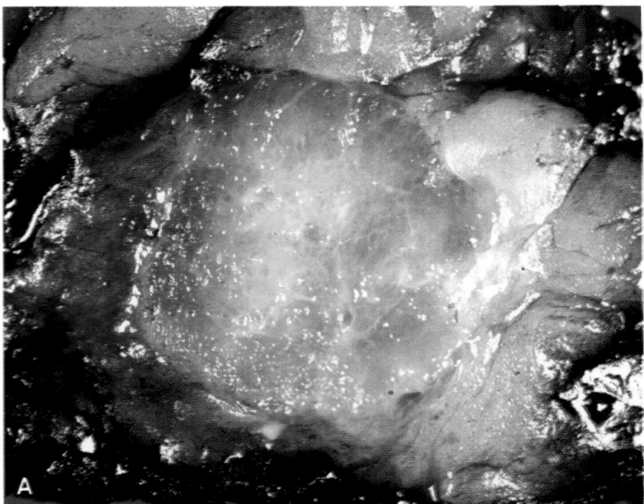

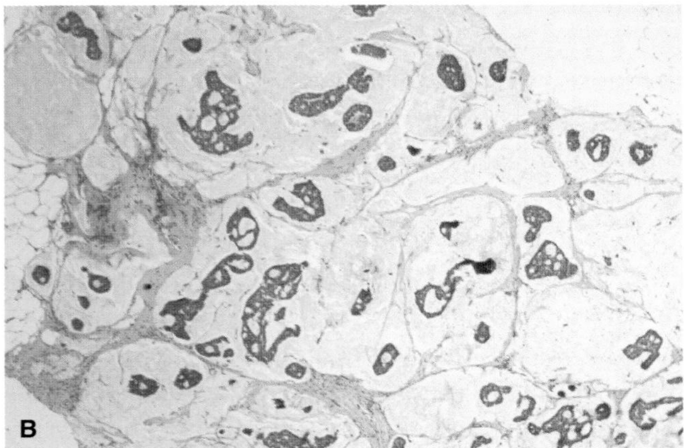

Figure 13–3. *A*, Mucinous carcinoma with grayish white gelatinous appearance. (Partial dense blue discoloration is due to intratumoral injection of blue dye for sentinel lymph node identification.) *B*, Histological hallmark of mucinous carcinoma is abundant extracellular mucin production.

all pure mucinous carcinomas are diploid. Approximately one-third of mucinous carcinomas show endocrine differentiation that can be demonstrated by histochemical, immunohistochemical or ultrastructural examination.

Pure mucinous carcinomas are associated with an excellent prognosis. In general, the incidence of axillary lymph node metastases is quite low. Late (up to 30 years after the initial diagnosis) distant metastases have been observed in some series.[89,90] Rare case reports with mucin embolism and pseudomyxoma peritonea in association with mucinous carcinoma of the breast exist.[91,92]

BREAST CANCERS WITH PAPILLARY FEATURES

Papillary Carcinoma

Invasive carcinomas with papillary architecture are rare and represent fewer than 1% of all invasive cancers. Papillary architecture is more commonly observed in ductal carcinoma in situ lesions. The clinical presentation of invasive papillary carcinoma is similar to that of carcinomas of no special type. In the reported series, invasive papillary carcinomas were more frequent in postmenopausal patients.[93] In the majority of cases, the tumor forms a circumscribed mass grossly.[94] Histologically, the tumors are characterized by a proliferation of cells organized around fibrovascular cores. Although the data on the prognostic significance of invasive papillary carcinoma are scant, most studies report a favorable prognosis, even with axillary lymph node metastases.[93] The papillary growth pattern is usually preserved in metastatic foci.

Micropapillary Carcinoma

Invasive micropapillary carcinoma is a rare variant of invasive carcinoma comprising approximately 2 to 3% of all breast cancers.[95–97] Unlike invasive papillary carcinoma, invasive micropapillary carcinoma is associated with a relatively aggressive clinical behavior.[96–98] The presentation, mammographic findings, and gross appearance of the tumor are very similar to those of the ordinary invasive breast cancer (Figure 13–4). Small clusters of cells arranged in micropapillae characterize the histology of invasive micropapillary carcinoma.[99] These tumor clusters appear to be encased within small spaces. These micropapillary

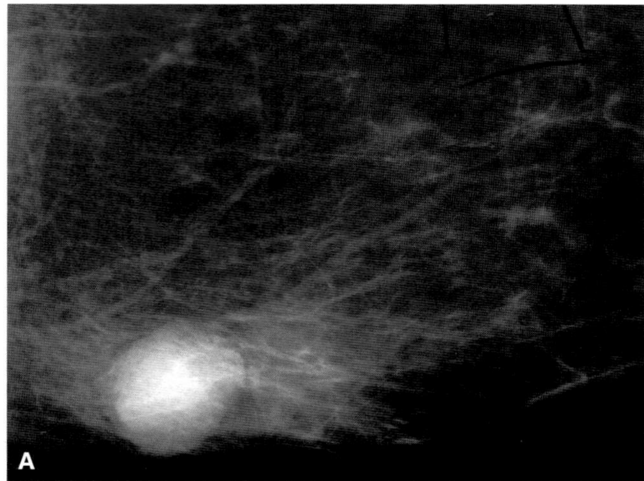

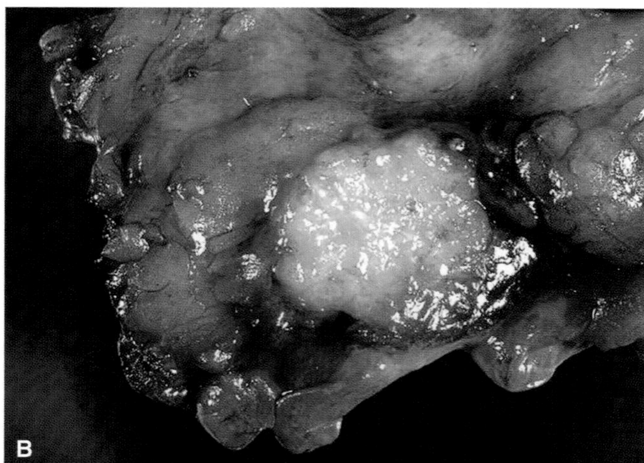

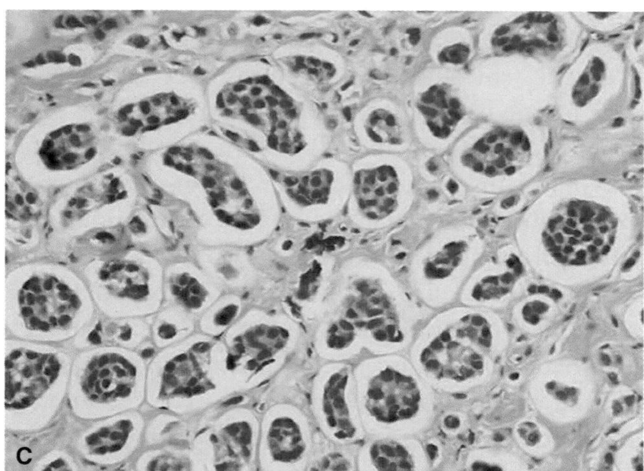

Figure 13–4. *A*, Mammogram showing a well-circumscribed mass. *B*, The tumor forms a well-circumscribed mass with a bulging surface. *C*, Invasive micropapillary carcinoma of the breast characterized by small clusters of tumor proliferating within empty stromal spaces.

clusters, unlike papillary carcinomas, lack fibrovascular cores. The histologic features of invasive cribriform carcinoma mimic ovarian serous papillary carcinoma, with some authors using the term "serous carcinoma-like pattern" to describe invasive micropapillary carcinoma of the breast. Microcalcifications, commonly psammoma body type laminar microcalcifications, are often observed. Tumor cells usually have low- to intermediate-grade nuclei. Lymphatic invasion is seen in the great majority of cases. Axillary lymph node metastases are commonly found at the time of diagnosis. Most patients have lymph node metastases at presentation, usually involving a large number of nodes.[100] Distinction from metastatic carcinomas from other sites, particularly from serous carcinoma of the female genital tract, is very important and may be very difficult on histology alone.

MEDULLARY CARCINOMA

Medullary carcinoma accounts for 2 to 5% of all breast cancers and occurs in patients younger than 50 years of age.[101–103] It is a frequent phenotype of hereditary breast cancer, specifically in women with *BRCA1* germline mutations in which medullary carcinoma accounts for 13% of all breast cancers.[104–106] Grossly, medullary carcinoma is well circumscribed and may be mistaken clinically for benign tumors. Microscopic features include solid, syncytium-like sheets of large cells with pleomorphic nuclei and marked lymphoplasmacytic infiltrate surrounding and within the tumor with pushing, non-infiltrative margins. Most of the lymphocytes are of the peripheral T-cell type.[107,108] The syncytial growth pattern and pushing borders may reflect retention and overexpression of adhesion molecules that could potentially play a role in limiting metastatic potential. The prognostic significance of medullary carcinoma has received considerable attention in the literature since it was first described. Medullary carcinoma was first established as a separate entity because of its apparently favorable outcome. Although some subsequent studies have supported this view, others have failed to demonstrate any prognostic significance.[105–109] Several reproducibility studies have yielded significant intra- and inter-observer variability in the histologic diagnosis of medullary carcinoma.[102] Tumors bearing some, but not all, of the features of medullary carcinoma are designated as atypical medullary carcinoma. Since the histologic boundaries of atypical medullary carcinoma are not well defined, currently this entity is over-diagnosed among pathologists. When strict histologic guidelines are followed, early stage medullary carcinoma predicts a good prognosis, whereas atypical medullary carcinoma has a behavior characteristic of ductal carcinoma.

METAPLASTIC CARCINOMA

Metaplastic carcinoma is a general term describing a heterogeneous group of cancers that display metaplastic squamous or spindle cells with an admixture of epithelial and mesenchymal differentiation.[110–115] Different terms have been used to describe these lesions, with the World Health Organization (WHO) classification categorizing them into broad subtypes according to the phenotypic appearance of the cells, as shown in Table 13–2.[6] Metaplastic carcinomas are rare, constituting fewer than 1% of all invasive cancers. In general, clinical presentation is not significantly different from invasive ductal carcinoma. Most are well circumscribed with pushing borders. They tend to be larger than invasive ductal carcinomas, with an average size greater than 3 cm. When osteocartilaginous differentiation presents, this may be evident on mammogram or macroscopic evaluation.

Since the histologic features of metaplastic carcinoma are quite diverse and designation of each category is imprecise, the term should not be used without a qualifier. The most frequent metaplastic elements are high-grade pleomorphic spindle cells. Osteosarcomatous, chondrosarcomatous, leiomyosarcomatous, rhabdomyosarcomatous, or angiosarcomatous components may be present. The epithelial nature of these spindle cells can be demonstrated by immunohistochemical staining for epithelial

Table 13–2. CLASSIFICATION OF METAPLASTIC CARCINOMAS

Pure Epithelial	Mixed (Epithelial/Mesenchymal)
Squamous	Carcinoma with chondroid or osseous metaplasia
Spindle	Matrix Producing
Adenosquamous	Sarcomatoid carcinoma (carcinosarcoma)

markers, such as cytokeratin. If the epithelial differentiation is evident by light microscopy and the tumor shows the biphasic appearance of epithelial and mesenchymal cells, some authors use the term "carcinosarcoma" or malignant mixed tumor. The term "spindle cell carcinoma" has been used to describe tumors composed predominantly of uniform spindle cells with a relatively bland appearance.[116] These tumors frequently show areas of squamous differentiation. The term "matrix-producing carcinoma" is reserved for those tumors showing abrupt differentiation from carcinoma to osseous or cartilaginous matrix without an intervening spindle cell component. In general, extensive sampling of metaplastic carcinomas is essential to identify different components of the tumor and to distinguish them from true sarcomas. It is difficult to assess the prognostic significance of metaplastic carcinomas because of their relative rarity and histologic diversity. In general, tumors with a biphasic morphology behave as invasive ductal carcinomas and are associated with lymphatic spread. Metastatic foci may show a carcinomatous or sarcomatous phenotype. Pure spindle cell tumors may have tendency for hematogenous rather than lymphatic spread.

CARCINOMAS WITH NEUROENDOCRINE DIFFERENTIATION

Carcinomas with neuroendocrine differentiation can occur in the breast.[117–120] Depending on the definition of neuroendocrine differentiation and methods used to identify this differentiation, the incidence of neuroendocrine carcinomas of the breast varies from 1 to 5%. Although rare, immunohistochemical and ultrastructural features of neuroendocrine differentiation can be demonstrated in many types of breast cancers. A higher proportion of mucinous and lobular carcinomas show immunohistochemical and ultrastructural features of neuroendocrine differentiation.[91] In rare cases, ectopic hormonal production is observed. There are no notable clinical or mammographic features of neuroendocrine carcinomas. Histologically, they range from a typical carcinoid to small cell neuroendocrine carcinoma (oat cell carcinoma).[117,118] Although these tumors do not appear to be associated with any clinical characteristics or outcome, it is important to recognize these lesions and establish their primary versus metastatic nature. Gastrointestinal and lung neuroendocrine tumors may metastasize to the breast as the presenting symptom. Diagnostic evaluation may be required to exclude other primaries.

ADENOID CYSTIC CARCINOMA

Adenoid cystic carcinoma is a rare and morphologically distinct type of breast cancer that represents fewer than 1% of all breast cancers.[121,122] It is histologically identical to its counterparts in the salivary glands. However, it is associated with an excellent prognosis in the breast. The majority of cases are located within the subareolar region. As observed in the salivary glands, adenoid cystic carcinoma of the breast may display cribriform, tubular, or solid patterns of growth. The tumor consists of a proliferation of two cell types: basaloid cells with scant cytoplasm and monomorphic nuclei and larger cells with abundant cytoplasm. The distinction between adenoid cystic and invasive cribriform carcinoma can be made by recognition of these two cell types in adenoid cystic carcinoma and only a single cell type in invasive cribriform carcinoma.[122] Adenoid cystic carcinoma is a low-grade malignancy with infrequent lymph node metastases, recurrences, and distant metastases.

SECRETORY (JUVENILE) CARCINOMA

Secretory carcinoma is a rare but histologically distinct type of breast cancer seen primarily in children and occasionally in adults.[123–126] Secretory carcinoma typically forms a well-circumscribed mass. The histologic hallmark is proliferation of low-grade cells forming glandular structures and microcystic spaces filled with eosinophilic secretions. Despite the prominent secretory features, there is no association with hormonal status, pregnancy, or lactation. Rare cases have been reported in males. The paucity of reported cases with a long follow-up precludes a definite determination of clinical behavior, but, in general, secretory carcinoma is regarded as an indolent tumor. Axillary lymph node metastases and local recurrences have been reported in rare cases.

OTHER RARE TYPES OF INVASIVE BREAST CANCERS WITH SPECIAL HISTOLOGIC PATTERNS

Carcinomas with Myoepithelial Differentiation

In normal ductal lobular units, myoepithelial cells are located between the luminal epithelial cells and basal lamina. These cells co-express epithelial and muscular markers. Rare breast tumors may show myoepithelial differentiation at the morphologic, immunohistochemical, or ultrastructural level.[127] Morphologically, these tumors show a spectrum of changes, including low-grade biphasic tumors to high-grade carcinomas indistinguishable from invasive ductal carcinomas. These high-grade tumors can be recognized only on the basis of the immunohistochemical profile of the tumors. Many metaplastic carcinomas show a myoepithelial immunohistochemical profile. The histologic criteria for their distinction are not well characterized in the literature. Recently, DNA microarray technology has been used to study molecular differences in different histologic types of breast cancers.[128] A novel molecular classification based on gene expression profile is proposed. Tumors expressing myoepithelial cell type genes are classified as basal-like carcinomas.[11] Preliminary data indicates that these tumors may have a distinct clinical behavior pattern.[11,12,16] These tumors tend to be negative for both estrogen and progesterone receptors and *HER2/neu* amplification. Further studies are necessary to understand the biologic behavior of these tumors.

Invasive Carcinomas with Particular Cytologic Features

Apocrine differentiation is characterized by abundant eosinophilic cytoplasm.[129–131] Lipid-rich and glycogen-rich carcinomas display clear vacuolated cytoplasm with abundant accumulation of lipids[132] and glycogen,[133] respectively. Although focal changes may be observed in ductal carcinomas, they rarely show a predominance of these cytologic findings. When present, there is no evidence to suggest that these cytologic changes are associated with a unique biologic behavior.

Invasive Carcinomas with Particular Stromal Features

Many different histologic changes can be seen in the stroma of an invasive cancer. Abundant osteoclast-like giant cells or marked granulamotous reactions may occur in the stroma. Although these are distinctive histologic changes, no prognostic significance is associated with these features. Tumors with marked central necrosis have been described recently and referred to as "centrally necrotic breast cancer."[134] It has been suggested that this morphology is frequently associated with a high incidence of lung and brain metastases.[134]

Invasive Carcinoma with Choriocarcinomatous Features

Choriocarcinoma differentiation characterized by trophoblastic cells and immunohistochemical evidence of human chorionic gonadotropin production by the tumor cells is rarely reported in breast cancer.[135] Clinical exclusion of metastatic choriocarcinoma is very important in establishing the diagnosis.

CARCINOMAS WITH UNIQUE CLINICAL MANIFESTATIONS

Inflammatory Breast Cancer

Inflammatory breast cancer is one of the most aggressive forms of breast cancer. It represents 1 to 3% of all breast cancers.[136,137] The diagnosis of inflammatory breast cancer is not based upon histologic features. This entity is diagnosed on clinical grounds, based on the presence of diffuse inflammatory changes of erythema and skin thickening, without a well-defined tumor (Figure 13–5A). Histologically, the underlying carcinoma is usually of ductal carcinoma NOS, and most tumors show extensive lymphatic permeation, particularly in the dermis (Figure 13–5B). However, dermal lymphatic invasion is not a necessary component of the diagnosis of inflammatory breast cancer. Most inflammatory breast cancers are negative for estrogen and progesterone receptors and show frequent *p53* gene mutations and amplifications of *HER2/neu* gene.[138,139]

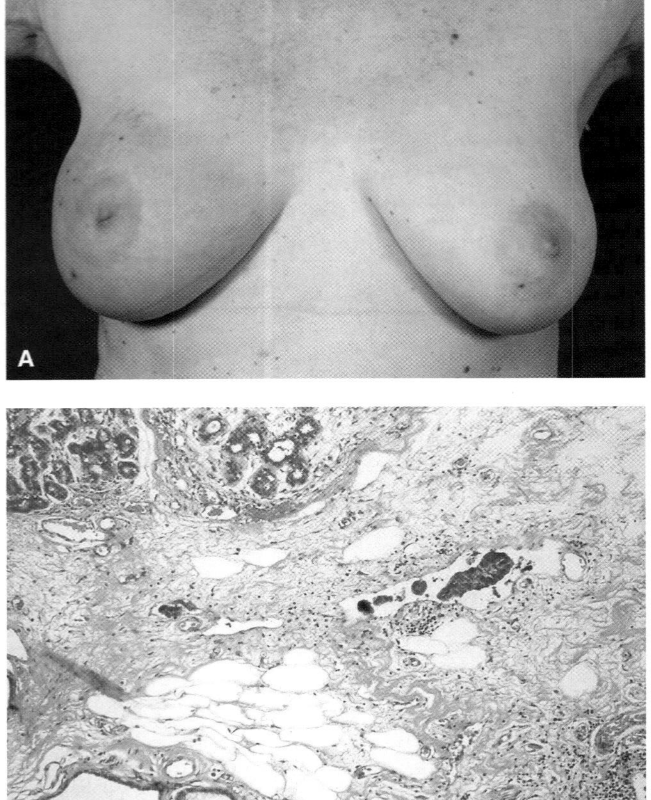

Figure 13–5. *A*, Inflammatory breast cancer is typically characterized by diffuse redness of the skin. *B*, Tumor emboli in dilated parenchymal and dermal lymphatics.

Paget's Disease of the Nipple

Paget's disease of the nipple is characterized by an eczematous change in the nipple and surrounding skin (Figure 13–6). In most cases, it is accompanied by an underlying in situ ductal carcinoma with or without associated stromal invasion.[140–142] Histologically, large clear cells with atypical nuclear features are present within the epidermis, usually concentrated along the basal layer. The cells can be isolated or in small clusters, sometimes forming small glandular structures. The origin of Paget's cells has been the subject of discussion since Sir James Paget first recognized the lesion in 1874. It is now generally accepted that most cases of Paget's disease represent colonization of tumor cells from the underlying breast cancer. In some cases, an underlying breast

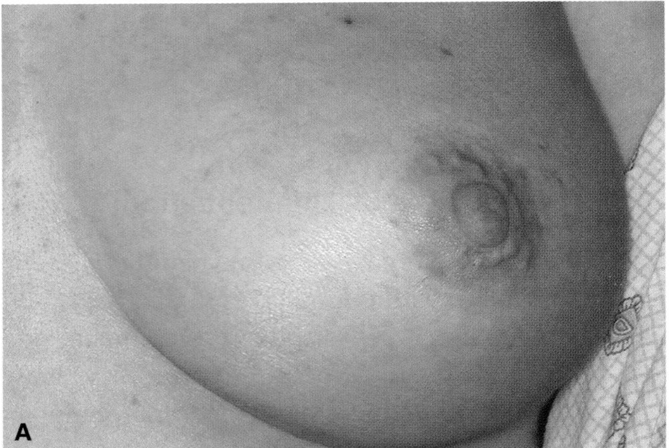

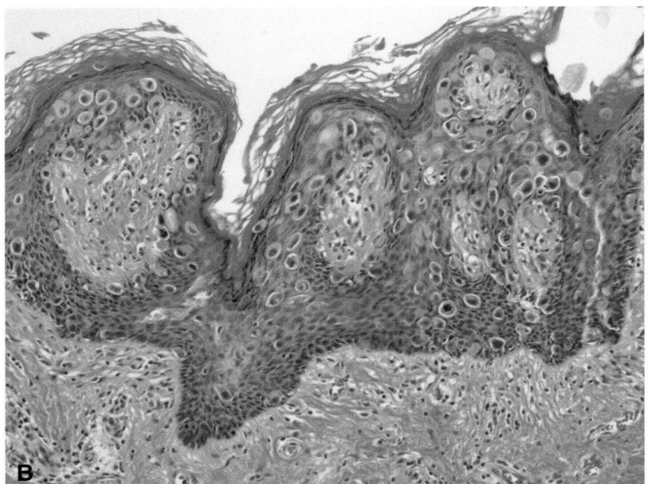

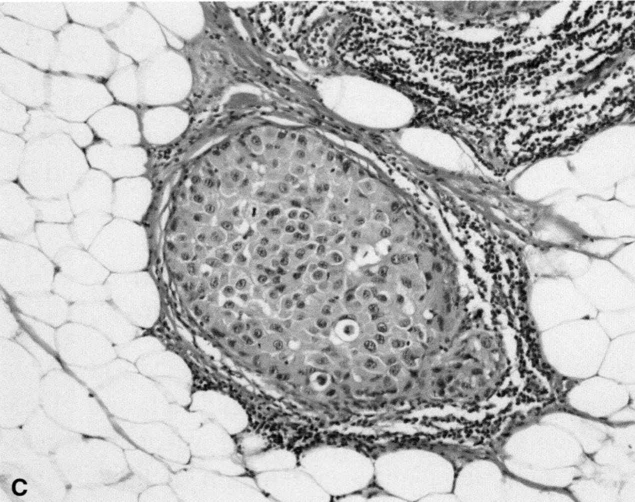

Figure 13–6. *A*, Paget's disease of the nipple. Nipple and surrounding skin show eczematous change. *B*, Skin biopsy shows clusters of Paget's cells aggregating in deep dermis and scattering in epidermis. The cells have large nuclei and pale cytoplasm. *C*, In situ ductal carcinoma with solid pattern is identified in the underlying breast tissue. Note the cytologic similarities between in situ carcinoma and Paget's cells.

cancer is not demonstrated. It has been proposed that intraepidermal malignant cells may arise from Toker cells, which are intraepidermal cells.[143,144] Paget's cells can be distinguished from the surrounding keratinocytes using immunohistochemical staining for low-molecular weight cytokeratins. Amplification of *HER2/neu* gene is observed in over 90% of cases. The management and prognosis depend predominantly on the in situ versus invasive nature of the underlying carcinoma, rather than the presence and extent of the intraepithelial component.

Occult Breast Cancer

Breast cancer may present with metastatic adenocarcinoma in axillary lymph nodes. The histologic features suggest a breast cancer primary, but no primary breast tumor is demonstrated by clinical evaluation or imaging findings. If there is no clinicoradiographic evidence of tumor elsewhere, ipsilateral mastectomy is recommended.[145] With extensive tissue sampling, the primary tumor is identified in up to 75% of cases. Occasional occult breast carcinomas may be identified on histologic evaluation of tissue samples removed during reduction mammaplasty. The majority of these lesions are low-grade carcinomas.

Bilateral Breast Cancer

It is well recognized that a previous history of breast cancer is a risk marker for subsequent development of breast cancer. Approximately 10% of patients with breast cancer will develop contralateral breast cancer.[146–148] If the contralateral breast cancer is detected within 2 months of the initial diagnosis, by convention, they are designated as synchronous breast cancers.[147] Approximately 1% of all breast carcinomas are synchronous bilateral breast cancer. An increased incidence of synchronous bilateral breast cancers has been observed in centers using bilateral mammography for clinical evaluation of patients with breast cancer. A higher percentage of invasive lobular carcinoma is identified in patients with synchronous bilateral breast cancer compared to patients with unilateral breast cancer.[149] The prognostic significance of synchronous bilateral breast cancer is controversial, with reports of equivalent or decreased survival for patients with bilateral breast cancer as compared to patients with unilateral breast cancer.

Hereditary Breast Cancer

Heredity is one of the most important risk factors that is known to influence a woman's risk of breast cancer development. Approximately 20 to 25% of women with breast cancer have at least one relative with breast cancer, and 5 to 10% have a recognized hereditary predisposition to breast cancer.[5,6] The majority of recognizable hereditary breast cancers are due to mutations of *BRCA1* and *BRCA2*. Rare syndromes that account for fewer than 1% of all breast cancers include Li-Fraumeni syndrome, Cowden disease, Peutz-Jeghers syndrome, Muir-Torre syndrome, and ataxia-telangiectasia heterozygosity.

The histopathologic features of hereditary breast cancers have been studied in the literature.[105,106] Patients with *BRCA1*-related cancers have a disproportionately high percentage of medullary and atypical medullary carcinomas, as compared to patients with sporadic breast cancers. Invasive ductal carcinomas in patients with *BRCA1* mutations tend to be poorly differentiated, with a high mitotic rate and a dense lymphocytic infiltrate.[105,150] Although these tumors have a higher frequency of aneuploidy, *p53* expression, high S-phase fraction, and infrequent estrogen receptor positivity, the clinical outcome of these patients does not appear to be significantly different from patients with sporadic breast cancer. The histologic features of *BRCA2* related carcinomas are controversial, with inconsistent reporting of tubular and tubulo-lobular carcinomas.[4–6,105]

Extramammary Carcinomas Metastatic to Breast

The great majority of the cancers in the breast are primary breast cancers. Occasionally, however, metastases from other primary sites can occur in the breast.[4–6,151] Metastasis from extramammary carcinomas represent approximately 1% of all breast malignancies and may pose a diagnostic difficulty. A full knowledge of the clinical history is essential before rendering a diagnosis, particularly with a limited tissue sample. The distinction is crucial for appropriate clinical management. A wide variety of tumors has been reported to metastasize to the breast, with malignant melanoma, lung, and ovarian cancers accounting for the majority. In children, rhabdomyosarcoma is the most common type of malignancy that metastasizes to the breast. Generally, metastatic lesions consist of well-circumscribed nodules. The presence of in situ carcinoma should be helpful to confirm the primary nature of the tumor. Unfortunately, not all invasive carcinomas have an in situ carcinoma component, and, furthermore, rounded outline of small metastatic tumor nodules may mimic in situ carcinoma.

METASTATIC PATTERN OF BREAST CANCER

Invasive breast cancer spreads primarily through the lymphatics to the regional lymph nodes, including axillary, internal mammary, and supraclavicular nodes, via hematogenous routes to distant organs within the breast ducts or by direct extension to adjacent structures. Lymph nodes metastases are present in approximately 30% of cases, depending upon the patient population and time of diagnosis. The probability of lymph node metastases is directly related to the size of the primary breast cancer. The pattern of nodal spread is also influenced by the location of the tumor. Distant metastases through hematogenous spread may affect virtually any organ in the body. Most common sites of metastases are lungs, liver, bones, adrenals, and brain. Direct extension into skin or deep fascia may cause fixation of the tumor, skin dimpling, and retraction, which are important criteria for staging.

PROGNOSTIC FACTORS OF BREAST CANCER

It is now well recognized that the prognosis of breast cancer is related to a large variety of clinical and pathologic factors.[3–6,152,153] Predicting outcomes for patients with breast cancer, especially those whose carcinoma is confined to breast without axillary lymph node involvement, is very important.[153,154] Although considerable research has focused on the identification of molecular, biologic, and genetic markers that may identify different prognostic categories, significant prognostic information can be obtained from routine histopathologic evaluation of invasive breast cancer.[154] Clinical follow-up studies have repeatedly demonstrated that routine histopathologic studies should be the gold standard against which any new prognostic marker or test is measured. Table 13–3 lists these histopathologic markers, which should be evaluated in all newly diagnosed breast cancers.

Tumor Size

Tumor size is one of the most important prognostic markers of invasive breast cancer. Many studies have shown a linear correlation with tumor size and presence of lymph node metastases and clinical outcome. The clinical evaluation of tumor size is inaccurate with concordance of clinical and pathologic measurements in only half of all cases. Radiographic assessment may be more precise, with ultrasonography being the most reliable technique for the preoperative determination of tumor size. Tumor size should be determined on the macroscopic evaluation of the specimen in the fresh state. The invasive nature of the tumor and size of the invasive cancer should be confirmed by microscopic evaluation.[4–6]

Lymph Node Status

Lymph node status provides the most powerful prognostic factor in breast cancer. Although lymph node metastasis is a time-dependent factor, it is also a significant predictor of aggressive biologic behavior. Numerous studies have shown that patients with axillary lymph node positive breast cancer have significantly poorer outcomes than those patients without nodal involvement. The greater the number of nodes involved, the poorer the prognosis. With each

Table 13–3. MORPHOLOGIC PROGNOSTIC FACTORS OF BREAST CARCINOMAS
Tumor size
Lymph node stage
Tumor grade
Tumor type
Vascular/lymphatic invasion

additional node positivity there is a stepwise decrease in survival. The clinical significance of micrometastases and isolated tumor cells found by immunohistochemistry is a controversial subject.

Histologic Type

As described above, specific breast cancers subtypes are associated with an improved good prognosis (Figure 13–7). These include tubular carcinoma, invasive cribriform, mucinous carcinoma, and adenoid cystic carcinoma.

Histologic Grade

Histologic grading has been repeatedly shown to predict overall and disease-free survival in patients with invasive breast cancer. Grading is recommended for all invasive carcinomas, regardless of the histologic type, to provide an estimation of differentiation. WHO endorses a histologic grading system based on criteria established by Bloom and Richardson and Elston and Ellis.[155] This grading system evaluates three parameters, including tubule formation, degree of nuclear pleomorphism, and number of mitotic figures identified on histologic sections. Nuclear grading is the cytologic assessment of tumor cells. Because nuclear grading does not assess the growth pattern of the tumor, it is more versatile to apply to all types of invasive and in situ carcinomas. Black and Speer introduced the most commonly used nuclear grading system[156] (Figure 13–8). The histological and nuclear grades of invasive breast cancers coincide in many cases. The reproducibility of histologic grading systems has been scrutinized.[154–160] However, several studies have demonstrated the reproducibility of grading systems if objective criteria are used with care.[157,158]

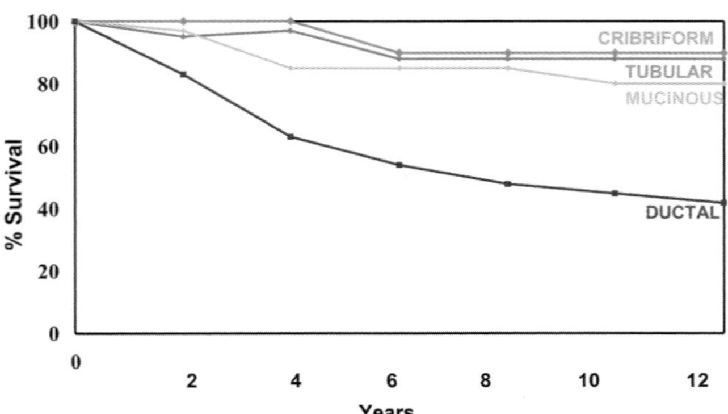

Figure 13–7. Patients with tubular, cribriform, and mucinous carcinoma of the breast have significantly longer disease-free survival compared to patients with invasive ductal carcinoma.

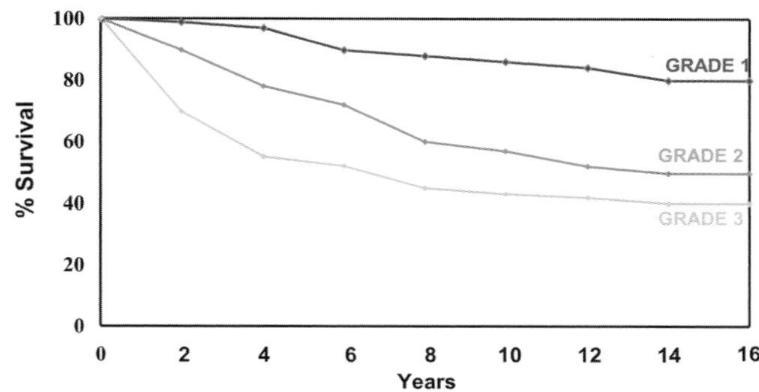

Figure 13–8. Grading of invasive breast cancer provides clear stratification of patients into three distinct categories.

Vascular/Lymphatic Invasion

The presence of tumor emboli in vascular spaces of breast parenchyma is an unfavorable prognostic factor. It is not possible to distinguish blood vessels from lymphatic spaces accurately. Evaluation of vascular/lymphatic invasion is particularly important in T1 lesions without nodal involvement since it can identify patients with high risk for recurrence. Vascular/lymphatic invasion should be distinguished from tumor clusters within artifactual tissue spaces.

Tumor Necrosis

In most studies, the presence of tumor necrosis has been associated with poor clinical outcome. However, independent prognostic significance of this histologic feature is not established in the literature. Furthermore, quantification of necrosis has not been standardized.

Molecular Markers and Gene Expression Patterns

A large number of genetic alterations have been recognized in breast cancers. Many of these factors play an important role in initiation and progression of breast cancer and development of metastases. Some provide important information on clinical outcome; others identify important predictive markers in response to different therapy options. Detailed discussion of these markers is included in Chapter 6. There is a great hope that new technologies, such as gene expression profiling, will allow sharper separation of prognostic groups than currently is available.

REFERENCES

1. Ries LAG, Kosarry CL, Hankey BF, et al, editors. SEER Cancer Statistics Review, 1973-1996. Bethesda, MD: National Cancer Institute; 1999.
2. Sondik EJ. Breast cancer trends. Incidence, mortality, and survival. Cancer 1994;74:995–9.
3. Rosen PP. Rosen's Breast Pathology. 2nd ed.: Lippincott Williams and Wilkins; 2001.
4. Ellis IO, Pinder SE, Lee AHS, Elston CW. Tumors of the breast: diagnostic histopathology of tumors. Vol 1. 2nd ed.. Fletcher CDM, editor. 2000.
5. Tavassoli FA. Pathology of the Breast. 2nd ed.: Appleton-Lange; 1999.
6. Tavassoli FA, Devilee P, editors. World Health Organization classification of tumors. Pathology and genetics of tumors of the breast and female genital organs. Lyon: IARC Press; 2003.
7. Fisher B, Redmond C, Fisher ER, et al. The contributions of recent NSABP clinical trails of primary breast cancer therapy to an understanding of tumor biology: An overview of findings. Cancer 1980;46:1009–25.
8. Rosen PP. The pathological classification of human mammary carcinoma: past, present, and future. Ann Clin Lab Sci 1979;9:144–56.
9. Page DL. Special types of invasive breast cancer, with clinical implications. Am J Surg Pathol 2003;27:832–5.
10. Allemani C, Sant M, Berrino F, et al. Prognostic value of morphology and hormone receptor status in breast cancer—a population based study. Br J. Cancer 2004;91: 1263–8.
11. Perou CM, Sorlie T, Eisen MB, et al. Moleculear portraits of human breast tumors. Nature 2000;406:747–52.
12. Sorlie T, Perou CM, Tibshirani R, et al. Gene expression patterns of breast carcinomas distinguish tumor subclasses with clinical implications. Proc Natl Acad Sci U S A 2001;98:10869–74.
13. Lakhani SR, Ashworth A. Microarray and histopathological analysis of tumours: the future and the past? Nat Rev Cancer 2001;1:151–7.
14. Paik S, Shak S, Tang G, et al. A multigene assay to predict recurrence of tamoxifen-treated, node-negative breast cancer. New Eng J Med 2004;351:2817–26.
15. Berucci F, Nasser V, Granjeaud S, et al. Gene expression profiles of poor-prognosis primary breast cancer correlate with survival. Hum Mol Genet 2002;11:863–72.
16. Loo LW, Grove DI, Williams EM, et al. Array comparative genomic hybridization analysis of genomic alterations in breast cancer subtypes. Cancer Res 2004;64:8541–9.
17. Wang Y, Klijn JG, Zhang Y, et al. Gene-expression profiles to predict distant metastasis of lymph-node-negative primary breast cancer. Lancet 2005;365:671–9.
18. Collins LC, Connolly JL, Page DL, et al. Diagnostic agreement in the evaluation of image guided breast core needle biopsies: results from a randomized controlled trial. Am J Surg Pathol 2004;28:126–131.
19. Deshpande A, Garud T, Holt SD. Core biopsy as a tool in planning the management of invasive breast cancer. World J Surg Oncol. 2005;3:1–4.
20. Sauer G, Deissler H, Strunz K, et al. Utlrasound-guided large-core needle biopsies of breast lesions: Analysis of 962 cases to determine the number of samples for reliable tumor classification. Br J Cancer 2005;92:231–5.
21. Willis SL, Ramzy I. Analysis of false results in a series of 835 fine needle aspirates of breast lesions. Acta Cytol 1999;39:858–64.
22. Gibbs NM. Comparative study of the histopathology of breast cancer in a screened and unscreened population investigated by mammography. Histopathol 1985;9:1307–18.
23. Tabar L, Duffy SW, Krusemo UB. Detection method, tumour size, and node metastases in breast cancers diagnosed during a trial of breast cancer screening. Eur J Cancer Clin Oncol 1987;23:959–62.
24. Rosenberg J, Chia YL, Plevritis S. The effect of age, race, tumor size, tumor grade, and disease stage on invasive ductal breast cancer survival in the US SEER database. Breast Cancer Res Treat 2005;89:47–54.
25. Patchefsky AS, Shaber GS, Schwartz GF, et al. The pathology of breast cancer detected by mass population screening. Cancer 1977;40:1659–70.
26. Rajakariar R, Walker RA. Pathological and biological features of mammographically detected invasive breast carcinomas. Br J Cancer 1995;71:150–54.
27. O'Regan, R. Do tumors detected by mammography screening have a favorable prognosis? JAMA 2004;292;1062–3.
28. Porter PL, El-Bastawissi AY, Mandelson MT, et al. Breast tumor characteristics as predictors of mammographic detection. J Natl Cancer Inst 1999;91:2020–8.
29. Fisher B, Dignam J, Tan-Chiu E, et al. Prognosis and treatment of patients with breast tumors of one centimeter or less and negative axillary lymph nodes. J Natl Cancer Inst 2001;93:112–20.
30. Porter GJ, Evans AJ, Pinder SE, et al. Patterns of metastatic breast carcinoma: influence of tumor histological grade. Clin Radiol 2004;59:1094–8.
31. Stalsberg H, Thomas DB. Age distribution of histologic types of breast carcinoma. Int J Cancer 1993;54:1–7.
32. Anderson TJ, Lamb J, Donnan P, et al. Comparative pathology of breast cancer in a randomized trial of screening. Br J Cancer 1991;64:108–13.
33. Sloane JP. National Coordinating Group for Breast Cancer Screening Pathology. Consistency of histopathologic reporting of breast lesions detected by screening: findings of the UK National External Quality Assessment Scheme. Eur J Cancer 1994;30A:1414–9.
34. Jarasch E-D, Nagle RB, Kaufmann M, et al. Differential diagnosis of benign epithelial proliferations and carcinomas of the breast using antibodies to cytokeratins. Hum Pathol 1998;19:376–89.
35. Tot T. The role of cytokeratins 20 and 7 and estrogen receptor analysis in separation of metastatic carcinoma of the

breast and metastatic signet ring cell carcinoma of the gastrointestinal tract. APMIS 2000;108:467–72.

36. Werling RW, Hwang H, Yazjii H, Gawn AM. Immunohistochemical distinction of invasive from non-invasive breast lesions: A comparative study of p63 versus calponin and smooth muscle myosin heavy chain. Am J Surg Pathol 2003;27:82–90.
37. Lerwill MF. Current practical application of diagnostic immunohistochemistry in breast pathology. Am J Surg Pathol 2004;28:1076–91.
38. Thomas PA, Kirschmann DA, Cerhan JR, et al. Association between keratin and vimentin expression, malignant phenotype, and survival in postmenopausal breast cancer patients. Clin Cancer Res 1999;5:2698–703.
39. Cross SS, Hamdy FC, Deloulme JC, Rehman I. Expression of S100 proteins in normal human tissues and common cancers using tissue microarrays: S100A6, S100A8, S100A9 and S100A11 are all overexpressed in common cancers. Histopathology 2005;46:256–69.
40. Martinez V, Azzopardi JG. Invasive lobular carcinoma of the breast: Incidence and variants. Histopathology 1979;3: 467–88.
41. Ashikari R, Huvos AG, Urban JA, et al. Infiltrating lobular carcinoma of the breast. Cancer 1973;31:110–16.
42. Li CI, Anderson BO, Daling JR, Mor RE. Trends in incidence rates of invasive lobular and ductal breast carcinoma. JAMA 2003;289:1421–4.
43. Invasive lobular carcinoma incidence increasing. CA Cancer J Clin 2003;53:137.
44. Li CI, Weiss NS, Stanford JL, Daling JR. Hormone replacement therapy in relation to risk of lobular and ductal breast carcinoma in middle-aged women. Cancer 2000; 88:2570–7.
45. Arpino G, Bardou VJ, Clark GM, Elledge RM. Infiltrating lobular carcinoma of the breast: Tumor characteristics and clinical outcome. Breast Cancer Res 2004;6:R149–56.
46. Korhonen T, Huhtala H, Holli K. A comparison of the biological and clinical features of invasive lobular and ductal carcinomas of the breast. Breast Cancer Res Treat 2004; 85:23–9.
47. Winchester DJ, Chang HR, Graves TA, et al. A comparative analysis of lobular and ductal carcinoma of the breast: Presentation, treatment, and outcomes. J Am Coll Surg 1998;186:416–22.
48. Moreno-Elola A, Aguilar A, Roman JM, et al. Prognostic factors in invasive lobular carcinoma of the breast: A multivariate analysis. A multicenter study after seventeen years of follow-up. Ann Chir Gynaecol 1999;88: 252–8.
49. Acs G, Lawton TJ, Rebbeck TR, et al. Differential expression of E-cadherin in lobular and ductal neoplasms of the breast and its biologic and diagnostic implications. Am J Clin Pathol 2001;115:85–98.
50. Lehr H-A, Folpe A, Yaziji H, et al. Cytokeratin 8 immunostaining pattern and E-cadherin expression distinguish lobular from ductal breast carcinoma. Am J Clin Pathol 2000;114:190–6.
51. De Leeuw WJ, Berx G, Voc CB. Simultaneous loss of E-cadherin and catenins in invasive lobular breast cancer and lobular carcinoma in situ. J Pathol 1997;183:404–11.
52. Vos CB, Clenton-Jansen AM, Berx G, et al. E-cadherin inactivation in lobular carcinoma in-situ of the breast: an early event in tumorigenesis. Br J Cancer 1997;76:1131–3.
53. Brinck U, Jacobs S, Neuss M, et al. Diffuse growth pattern affects E-cadherin expression in invasive breast cancer. Anticancer Res 2004;24:2237–42.
54. Sastre-Garau X, Jouve M, Asselain B, et al. Infiltrating lobular carcinoma of the breast. clinicopathologic analysis of 975 cases with reference to data on conservative therapy and metastatic patterns. Cancer 1996;77:113–20.
55. Nishizaki T, Chew K, Chu L, et al. Genetic alterations in lobular breast cancer by comparative genomic hybridization. Int J Cancer 1997;74:513–7.
56. Zhao H, Langerod A, Ji Y, Nowels KW, et al. Different gene expression patterns in invasive lobular and ductal carcinomas of the breast. Mol Biol Cell 2004;15:2523–36.
57. Korkola JE, DeVries S, Fridlyland J, et al. Differentiation of lobular versus ductal breast carcinomas by expression microarray analysis. Cancer Res 2003;63:7167–75.
58. Fechner RE. Histologic variants of infiltrating lobular carcinoma of the breast. Hum Pathol 1975;6:373–8.
59. Bentz JS, Yassa N, Clayton F. Pleomorphic lobular carcinoma of the breast: clinicopathologic features of 12 cases. Mod Pathol 1998;11:814–22.
60. Frolik D, Caduff R, Varga Z. Pleomorphic lobular carcinoma of the breast: its cell kinetics, expression of oncogenes and tumour suppressor genes compared with invasive ductal carcinoma and classical infiltrating lobular carcinomas. Histopathology 2001;39:503–13.
61. Sneige N, Wang J, Baker BA, et al. Clinical, histopathologic, and biologic features of pleomorphic lobular (ductal-lobular) carcinoma in-situ of the breast: a report of 24 cases. Mod Pathol 2002;15:1044–50.
62. Palacios J, Sarrio D, Garcia-Macias MC, et al. Frequent E-cadherin gene inactivation by loss of heterozygosity in pleomorphic lobular carcinoma of the breast. Mod Pathol 2003;16:674–8.
63. Tot T. The diffuse type of invasive lobular carcinoma of the breast: morphology and prognosis. Virchows Arch 2003;443:718–24.
64. Frost AR, Terahata S, Yeh IT, et al. The significance of signet ring cells in infiltrating lobular carcinoma of the breast. Arch Pathol Lab Med 119:64–8.
65. Eltorky M, Hall JC, Osborne PT, et al. Signet-ring cell variant of invasive lobular carcinoma of the breast: a clinicopathologic study of 11 cases. Arch Pathol Lab Med 1994; 118:245–8.
66. Maeno Y, Moroi S, Nagashima H, et al. α-catenin-deficient F9 cells differentiate into signet ring cells. Am J Pathol 1999;154:1323–8.
67. Stolier AJ, Barre G, Bolton JS, et al. Breast conservation therapy for invasive lobular carcinoma: the impact of lobular carcinoma in-situ in the surgical specimen on local recurrence and axillary node status. Am Surg 2004;70: 818–21.
68. Papadotos G, Rangan AM, Psarianos, et al. Probability of axillary node involvement in patients with tubular carcinoma of the breast. Br J Surg 2001;88:860–4.
69. Kader HA, Jackson J, Mates D, et al. Tubular carcinoma of the breast: a population-based study of nodal metastases at presentation and of patterns of relapse. Breast J 2001;7:8–13.
70. Diab SG, Clark GM, Osborne CK, et al. Tumor characteris-

tics and clinical outcome of tubular and mucinous breast carcinomas. J Clin Oncol 1999;17:1442–8.
71. Cooper HS, Patchefsky AS, Krall RA. Tubular carcinoma of the breast. Cancer 1978;42:2334–42.
72. Peters GN, Wolff M, Haagensen CD. Tubular carcinoma of the breast. Clinical pathologic correlations based on 100 cases. Ann Surg 1981;193:138–49.
73. Roses DF, Bell DA, Flotte TJ. Pathologic predictors of recurrence in stage 1 (T1N0M0) breast cancer. Am J Clin Pathol 1982;78:817–20.
74. McBoyle MF, Razek HA, Carter JL, Helmer SD. Tubular carcinoma of the breast: an institutional review. Am Surg 1997;636:639–44.
75. Livi L, Paiar F, Meldolesi E, et al. Tubular carcinoma of the breast: outcome and loco-regional recurrence in 307 patients. Eur J Surg Oncol 2005;31:9–12.
76. Winchester DJ, Sahin AA, Tucker SL, Singletary SE. Tubular carcinoma of the breast: predicting axillary nodal metastases and recurrence. Ann Surg 1996;223:342–7.
77. Lagios MD, Rose MR, Margolin FR. Tubular carcinoma of the breast. association with multicentricity, bilaterality, and family history of mammary carcinoma. Am J Clin Pathol 1980;73:25–30.
78. Vega A, Garijo F. Radial scar and tubular carcinoma. mammographic and sonographic findings. Acta Radiol 1993; 34:43–7.
79. Goldstein NS, O'Malley BA. Cancerization of small ectatic ducts of the breast by ductal carcinoma in-situ cells with apocrine snouts: a lesion associated with tubular carcinoma. Am J Clin Pathol 1997;107:561–6.
80. Fraser JL, Raza S, Chorny K, et al. Columnar alteration with prominent apical snouts and secretions: a spectrum of changes frequently present in breast biopsies performed for microcalcifications. Am J Surg Pathol 1998;22: 1521–7.
81. Papadatos G, Rangan AM, Psarianos T, et al. Probability of axillary node involvement in patients with tubular carcinoma of the breast. Br J Surg 2001;88:860–4.
82. Kader HA, Jackson J, Mates D, et al. Tubular carcinoma of the breast: a population-based study of nodal metastases at presentation and of patterns of relapse. Breast J 2001;7:8–13.
83. Page DL, Dixon JM, Anderson TJ, et al. Invasive cribriform carcinoma of the breast. Histopathology 1983;7:525–36.
84. Venable JG, Schwartz AM, Silverberg SG. Infiltrating cribriform carcinoma of the breast. A distinctive clinicopathologic entity. Hum Pathol 1990;21:333–8.
85. Page DL, Dixon JM, Anderson T, et al. Invasive cribriform carcinoma of the breast. Histopathology 1993;7:525–36.
86. Chinyama CN, Davies JD. Mammary mucinous lesions: prevalence and important pathological associations. Histopathology 1996;29:533–9.
87. Clayton F. Pure mucinous carcinomas of the breast. Morphologic features and prognostic correlates. Hum Pathol 11986;7:34–8.
88. Rasmussen BB, Rose C, Christensen IB. Prognostic factors in primary mucinous breast carcinoma. Am J Clin Pathol 1987;87:155–60.
89. Rosen PP, Wang T-Y. Colloid carcinoma of the breast. Analysis of 64 patients with long-term follow-up. Am J Clin Pathol 1980;73:304.
90. Toikkanen S, Kujari H. Pure and mixed mucinous carcinomas of the breast: a clinicopathologic analysis of 61 cases with long-term follow-up. Hum Pathol 1989;20:758–64.
91. Scopsi L, Andreola S, Pilotti S, et al. Mucinous carcinoma of the breast. A clinicopathologic, histochemical, and immunocytochemical study with special reference to neuroendocrine differentiation. Am J Surg Pathol 1994;18: 702–11.
92. Towfighi J, Simmonds MA, Davidson EA. Mucin and fat emboli in mucinous carcinomas. Cause of hemorrhagic cerebral infarcts. Arch Pathol Lab Med1983;107:646–9.
93. Fisher ER, Palekar AS, Redmond C, et al. Pathologic findings from the National Surgical Adjuvant Breast Project (protocol no. 4) VI. Invasive papillary cancer. Am J Clin Pathol 1980;73:313–22.
94. McCulloch GL, Evans AJ, Yeoman L, et al. Radiological features of papillary carcinoma of the breast. Clin Radiol 1997;52:865–8.
95. Luna-More S, Gonzalez B, Acedo C, et al. Invasive micropapillary carcinoma of the breast. A new special type of invasive mammary carcinoma. Pathol Res Pract 1994;190:668–74.
96. Paterakos M, Watkin WG, Edgerton SM, et al. Invasive micropapillary carcinoma of the breast: a prognostic study. Hum Pathol 1999;30:1459–63.
97. Nassar H, Wallis T, Andrea A, et al. Clinicopathologic analysis of invasive micropapillary differentiation in breast carcinoma. Mod Pathol 2001;14:836–41.
98. Walsh MM, Bleiweiss IJ. Invasive micropapillary carcinoma of the breast: eighty cases of an underrecognized entity. Hum Pathol 2001;32:583–9.
99. Peterse JL. Breast carcinoma with an unexpected inside-out growth pattern, rotation of polarisation associated with angioinvasion. Pathol Res Pract 1993;189:780.
100. Kuroda H, Skamoto G, Ohnisi K, Itoyama S. Clinical and pathologic features of invasive micropapillary carcinoma. Breast Cancer 2004;11:169–74.
101. Armes JE, Venter DJ. The pathology of inherited breast cancer. Pathology 2002;34:309–14.
102. Eichhorn JH. Medullary carcinoma, provocative now as then. Semin Diagn Pathol 2004;21:64–73.
103. Rapin V, Contesso G, Mouriesse H, et al. Medullary breast carcinoma. A re-evaluation of 95 cases of breast cancer with inflammatory stroma. Cancer 1988;61:2503–10.
104. Adem C, Reynolds C, Soderberg CL, et al. Pathologic characteristics of breast parenchyma in patients with hereditary breast carcinoma, including *BRCA1* and *BRCA2* mutation carriers. Cancer 2003;97:1–11.
105. Shousha S. Medullary carcinoma of the breast and *BRCA1* Mutation. Histopathology 2000;37:182–5.
106. Breast Cancer Linkage Consortium: Pathology of familial breast cancer differences between breast cancers of *BRCA1* or *BRCA2* mutations and sporadic cases. Lancet 1997;349:1505–10.
107. Yakirevich E, Ben Izhak O, Rennert G, et al. Cytotoxic phenotype of tumor infiltrating lymphocytes in medullary carcinoma of the breast. Mod Pathol 1999;12:1050–6.
108. Yazawa T, Kamma H, Ogata T. Frequent expression of HLA-DR antigen in medullary carcinoma of the breast. A possible reason for its prominent lymphcytic infiltration and

favorable prognosis. Appl Immunohistochem 1993;1: 289–96.

109. Ridolfi RL, Rosen PP, Port A, et al. Medullary carcinoma of the breast: a clinicopathologic study with 10-year follow-up. Cancer 1997;40:1365–85.
110. Kaufman MW, Marti JR, Gallaer HS, Hoehn JL. Carcinoma of the breast with pseudosarcomatous metaplasia. Cancer 1984;53:1908–17.
111. Oberman HA. Metaplastic carcinoma of the breast. Am J Surg Pathol 1987;11:918–29.
112. Wargotz ES, Deos PH, Norris HJ. Metaplastic carcinomas of the breast. II. Spindle cell carcinoma. Hum Pathol 1989;20:732–40.
113. Wargotz ES, Norris HJ. Metaplastic carcinomas of the breast. I. Matrix-producing carcinoma. Hum Pathol 1989;20: 628–35.
114. Wargotz ES, Norris HJ. Metaplastic carcinomas of the breast. IV. Squamous cell carcinoma of ductal origin. Cancer 1990;65:272–6.
115. Koker MM, Kleer CG. P63 expression in breast cancer: a highly sensitive and specific marker of metaplastic carcinoma. Am J Surg Pathol 2004;28:1506–12.
116. Gobbi H, Simpson JF, Borowsky A, et al. Metaplastic breast tumors with a dominant fibromatosis-like phenotype have a high risk of local recurrence. Cancer 1999;85:2170–82.
117. Sapino A, Righi L, Cassoni P, et al. Expression of apocrine differentiation markers in neuroendocrine breast carcinomas of aged women. Mod Pathol 2001;14:768–76.
118. Shin SJ, DeLellis RA, Ying L, et al. Small cell carcinoma of the breast: a clinicopathologic and immunohistochemical study of nine patients. Am J Surg Pathol 2000;24:1231–8.
119. Van Krimpen C, Elferink A, Broodman CA, et al. The prognostic influence of neuroendocrine differentiation in breast cancer: results of a long-term follow-up study. 2004;Breast 13:329–33.
120. Miremadi A, Pinder SE, Lee, A, et al. Neuroendocrine differentiation and prognosis in breast adenocarcinomas. Histopathology 2022;40:215–22.
121. Lamovec J, Us-Krasovec M, Zidar A, et al. Adenoid cystic carcinoma of the breast: a histologic, cytologic, and immunohistochemical study. Semin Diagn Pathol 1989;6:153–64.
122. Kasami M, Olson SJ, Simpson JF, Page DL. Maintenance of polarity and a dual cell population in adenoid cystic carcinoma of the breast: an immunohistochemical study. Histopathology 1998;32:232–8.
123. McDivitt RW, Stewart FW. Breast carcinoma in children. JAMA 1966;195:388–90.
124. Krausz T, Jenkins D, Grontoft O, et al. Secretory carcinomas of the breast in adults: emphasis on late recurrence and metastasis. Histopathology 1989;14:25–36.
125. Oberman HA. Secretory carcinomas of the breast in adults. Am J Surg Pathol 1980;4:465–70.
126. Costa NM, Rodrigues H, Pereira H, et al. Secretory breast carcinoma—case report and review of the medical literature. Breast 2004;13:353–5.
127. Mclaren BK, Smith J, Schuyler PA, et al. Adenomyoepithelioma: clinical, histologic, and immunohistologic evaluation of a series of related lesions. Am J Surg Pathol 2005; 209:1294.
128. Birnbaum D, Bertucci F, Ginestier C, et al. Basal and luminal breast cancers: basic or luminous? Int J Oncol 2004;25: 249–58.
129. Eusebi V, Betts C, Haagensen DE Jr, et al. Apocrine differentiation in lobular carcinoma of the breast. A morphologic, immunologic, and ultrastructural study. Hum Pathol 1984;15:134–40.
130. Eusebi V, Millis RR, Cattani MG, et al. Apocrine carcinoma of the breast. A morphologic and immunocytochemical study. Am J Pathol 1986;123:532–41.
131. Pagani A, Sapino A, Eusebi V, et al. PIP/GCDFP-15 gene expression and apocrine differentiation in carcinomas of the breast. Virchows Arch 1994;425:459–65.
132. Wrba F, Ellinger A, Reiner G, et al. Ultrastructural and immunohistochemical characteristics of lipid-rich carcinoma of the breast. Virchows Arch A Patholg Anat Histopathol 1988;413:381–5.
133. Fisher ER, Tavares J, Bulatao IS, et al. Glycogen-rich, clear cell breast cancer: with comments concerning other clear cell variants. Hum Pathol 1985;16:1085–90.
134. Tsuda H, Takarabe T, Hasegawa F, et al. Large, central acellular zones indicating myoepithelial tumor differentiation in high-grade invasive ductal carcinoma as markers of predisposition to lung and brain metastases. Am J Surg Pathol 2000;24:197–202.
135. Saigo PE, Rosen PP. Mammary carcinoma with choriocarcinomatous features. Am J Surg Pathol 1981;5:773–8.
136. Chang S, Parker SL, Pham T, et al. Inflammatory breast carcinoma incidence and survival: the surveillance, epidemiology, and end results program of the National Cancer Institute, 1975-1992. Cancer 1998;82:2366–72.
137. Fields JN, Kuske RR, Perez CA, et al. Prognostic factors in inflammatory breast cancer. Univariate and multivariate analysis. Cancer 1989;63:1225–32.
138. Panadea M, Olivotto IA, Speers CH, et al. Evolving treatment strategies for inflammatory breast cancer: a population-based survival analysis. J Clin Oncol 2005;23:1941–50.
139. Bieche I, Lerebours F, Tozlu S, et al. Molecular profiling of inflammatory breast cancer: identification of a poor-prognosis gene expression signature. Clin Cancer Res 2004; 10:6789–95.
140. Lloyd J, Flanagan AM. Mammary and extramammary Paget's disease. J Clin Pathol 2000;53:742–49.
141. Fu W, Mittel VK, Young SC. Paget disease of the breast: analysis of 41 patients. Am J Clin Oncol 2001;24:397–400.
142. Piekarski J, Jeziorski A, Baklinksa M, et al. Patients with Paget disease of nipple and with palpable mass in breast have unfavorable prognosis. J Exp Clin Cancer Res 2004; 23:33–7.
143. Morandi L, Pession A, Marucci GL, et al. Intraepidermal cells of Paget's carcinoma of the breast can be genetically different from those of the underlying carcinoma. Hum Pathol 2003;34:1321–30.
144. Marucci G, Betts CM, Golouth R, et al. Toker cells are probably precursors of Paget cell carcinoma: a morphological and ultrastructural description. Virchows Arch 2002; 441:117–23.
145. Blanchard DK, Farley DR. Retrospective study of women presenting with axillary metastases from occult breast carcinoma. World J Surg 2004;28:535–9.
146. Kollias J, Ellis IO, Elston CW, et al. Prognostic significance

of synchronous and metachronous bilateral breast cancer. World J Surg 2001;25:1117–24.

147. Fisher ER, Fisher B, Sass R, Wickerham L. Pathologic findings from the National Surgical Adjuvant Breast Project (protocol no. 4) XI. Bilateral breast cancer. Cancer 1984; 54:3002–11.
148. Holmberg L, Adami HO, Ekbom A, et al. Prognosis in bilateral breast cancers. Effects of time interval between first and second primary tumors. Br J Cancer 1988;58:191–4.
149. Kollias J, Ellis IO, Elston CW, Blamey RW. Clinical and histological predictors of contralateral breast cancer. Eur J Surg Oncol 2 1999;5:584–9.
150. Palacios J, Honrado E, Osorio A, et al. Phenotypic characterization of *BRCA1* and *BRCA2* tumors based in a tissue microarray study with 37 immunohistochemical markers. Breast Cancer Res Treat 2005;90:5–14.
151. Georgiannos SN, Chin Aleong J, Goode AW, et al. Secondary neoplasms of the breast: a survey of the 20th century. Cancer 2001;92:2259–66.
152. Tuma RS. Multiple gene signatures aim to qualify risk in breast cancer. Natl Cancer Inst 2005;97:332.
153. Cianfrocca M, Goldstein LJ. Prognostic and predictive factors in early-stage breast cancer. Oncologist 2004;9:606–16.
154. Walker RA. Prognostic and predictive factors in breast cancer: Martin Dunitz; 2003.
155. Elston CW, Ellis IO. Pathological prognostic factors in breast cancer. I. The value of histological grade in breast cancer: experience from a large study with long-term follow-up. Histopathology 1991;19:403–10.
156. Black MM, Speer FD. Nuclear structure in cancer tissues. Surg Gynecol Obstet 1957;105:97–105.
157. Meyer JS, Alvarez C, Milikowski C, et al. Breast carcinoma malignancy grading by Bloom-Richardson system vs proliferation index: reproducibility of grade and advantages of proliferation index. Mod Pathol 2005. [In press].
158. Italian Network for Quality Assurance of Tumour Biomarkers (INQAT) Group. Quality control for histological grading in breast cancer: an Italian experience. Pathologica 2005;97:1–6.
159. Hopton DS, Thorogood J, Clayden AD, et al. Observer variation in histological grading of breast cancer. Eur J Surg Oncol 1989b;15:21–3.
160. Thessig F, Kunze KD, Haroske G, et al. Histological grading of breast cancer—interobserver reproducibility and prognostic significance. Pathol Res Pract 1990;186:732–6.

14

Staging and Histologic Grading

DAVID P. WINCHESTER

THE HISTORY OF CANCER STAGING

The concept of classifying cancers by primary tumor, regional lymph nodes, and distant metastases dates back to the 1940s when Pierre Denoix in France first suggested the usefulness of a reproducible cancer staging system with anatomic components.[1] Soon thereafter, the International Union Against Cancer (UICC) embarked on the development of a formalized anatomic staging system for all sites.

The American Joint Committee on Cancer (AJCC) was first constituted as the American Joint Committee for Cancer Staging and End-results Reporting in 1959. The founding organizations of the AJCC were the American College of Surgeons, the American College of Radiology, the College of American Pathologists, the American College of Physicians, the American Cancer Society, and the National Cancer Institute.

The *AJCC Cancer Staging Manual* has been through six editions since 1977,[2] confirming the observation that cancer staging is a dynamic process. For the past 25 years, the AJCC and UICC have closely collaborated. As a result, for at least the past 15 years, the two organizations have agreed upon uniform and identical definitions in stage groupings of cancers for all anatomic sites.

PURPOSES OF BREAST CANCER STAGING

Staging of breast cancer patients places them into stage groupings based on the best current available evidence gained from clinical trials or observation studies. Many purposes are served with the utilization of breast cancer staging. The major disciplines of surgery, medical oncology, and radiation oncology rely heavily on a contemporary staging system to plan treatment. Uniform staging facilitates estimation of prognosis, evaluation of outcomes, and worldwide exchange of information. Staging is also an integral part of the continuing investigation of breast cancer, whether it be through basic science or clinical trials.

The value of breast cancer staging cannot be underestimated with respect to patient and family communication. Breast cancer patients are becoming progressively sophisticated in the knowledge of their disease. Clinicians must thoroughly understand staging to conduct an intelligent conversation about treatment planning and prognosis.

GENERAL RULES OF THE TNM SYSTEM FOR BREAST CANCER

In the TNM system, T defines the extent of the primary tumor, N defines the status of regional lymph node metastasis, and M defines the presence or absence of distance metastasis.[2] Numerical subsets then define the progressive extent of disease. Further letter subsets provide more precise anatomic and non-anatomic information.

Stage should be defined through the first course of surgery or 4 months, whichever is longer, and should have histologic confirmation. There are four classifications: clinical (c) TNM, pathologic (p) TNM, retreatment (r) TNM, and autopsy (a) TNM.

The clinical stage is derived from history and clinical breast examination, imaging studies, and biopsies. Clinical breast examination should focus on evaluation of the primary tumor if palpable, skin changes, and regional lymph node examination. The clinical assessment of metastatic disease is usually confined to good history-taking, focusing on symptoms associated with common metastatic sites. These would include dyspnea for pleural-based metastases, bone pain, abdominal complaints with weight loss, and central nervous system changes.

Imaging studies such as mammography, ultrasonography, and magnetic resonance imaging, in selected cases, further characterize the primary tumor.

Histologic or cytologic confirmation is best accomplished by core needle biopsy or fine needle aspiration, with or without image guidance.

The definition of chest wall invasion should be understood to include ribs, intercostal muscles, and serratus anterior muscle, but not the pectoralis major or minor muscles.

The clinical assessment of regional lymph nodes must include ipsilateral axillary nodes and interpectoral (Rotter's) nodes. Other regional nodes include the internal mammary nodes in the intercostal spaces along the sternum and supraclavicular nodes, previously designated as M1 disease. For a lymph node to be considered supraclavicular, it must be located in a triangle bound by the clavicle at the base, the internal jugular vein medially, and omohyoid muscle and tendon laterally and superiorly. Any nodes outside this triangle are categorized as cervical (M1).

Clinical staging provides information for initial treatment planning and estimation of prognosis, whereas pathologic staging includes additional information derived from pathologic examination of tissue and other tests. Pathologic staging may provide new, more precise information to guide the clinician in further treatment and explanation of prognosis.

If a breast cancer is incompletely resected with gross residual disease, it must be coded pTX.

Nodules of cancer cells found in the axillary fat without evidence of lymph node histology are classified as axillary regional lymph nodes. Intramammary lymph nodes are categorized as axillary lymph nodes for staging purposes.

A patient undergoing neoadjuvant therapy should be staged clinically at the time of diagnosis. After completion of preoperative therapy, the pathologic staging information derived from the surgery should include the prefix "y," for example, ypT2N1,M0.

BREAST CANCER STAGING

The 6th edition of the *AJCC Cancer Staging Manual*, published in 2002, contains several changes from the previous edition. The changes have been based on the validation of sentinel lymph node biopsy as an accurate method for staging regional lymph nodes, an improved understanding of the biologic significance of micrometastases and isolated tumor cells, and the prognostic significance of regional lymph nodes detected by lymphoscintigraphy or clinical examination.

Primary Tumor Classification (T)

Clinical tumor size may be best ascertained by direct measurement of a palpable tumor or mammographic/ultrasonographic measurement of palpable or occult primary tumors.[2]

Pathologic tumor size often requires a reconstructive estimate based on preoperative core needle biopsies and tumor dimensions following excision.

It is common to encounter a combination of invasive cancer and ductal carcinoma in situ. The measured invasive component supersedes the noninvasive component.

In the case of multiple, synchronous, ipsilateral primary tumors, the T designation is based on the largest measured invasive tumor.

Inflammatory carcinoma is clinically characterized as a relatively rapid onset of diffuse erythema, edema, and a heavy sensation described by the patient, often without a three-dimensional palpable mass. Biopsy is necessary to confirm breast cancer within the dermal lymphatics and/or breast. The failure to demonstrate dermal lymphatic tumor emboli does not exclude the diagnosis of inflammatory breast cancer. Locally advanced breast cancer with tumor necrosis may occasionally mimic inflammatory carcinoma.

Skin or nipple retraction may or may not be regarded as locally advanced breast cancer, depending on the presence or absence of edema and erythema.

Microinvasive primary breast cancers can be unifocal or multifocal. When multifocal, the largest measured area should be used, rather than adding all microinvasive areas. The AJCC defines microinvasion as tumor penetration of the basement membrane no greater than 0.1 cm in diameter (Figure 14–1).

The importance of accurate primary tumor size determination cannot be overemphasized. The decision to administer cytotoxic or hormonal adjuvant therapy may be based on as little as a 1-mm difference in tumor size.

Table 14–1 is the AJCC classification of primary tumor (T).

Regional Lymph Nodes (N)

In contrast to the T classification in which the clinical and pathologic parameters are identical, classification of regional lymph nodes includes both clinical and pathologic staging.[2]

Clinical Classification of Regional Lymph Nodes

"Clinically apparent" regional lymph nodes are defined by the AJCC as nodes detected by clinical examination, imaging studies (excluding lymphoscintigraphy), or grossly visible pathologic findings.

Table 14–2 summarizes the clinical classification of regional lymph nodes. Many of the changes in the 6th edition of the *AJCC Cancer Staging Manual* relate to regional lymph nodes. Variables responsible for these changes include tumor burden, method of detection, and relationship of positive or negative axillary, internal mammary, and supraclavicular nodal basins. Clinical or pathologic positive supraclavicular lymph nodes, formerly categorized

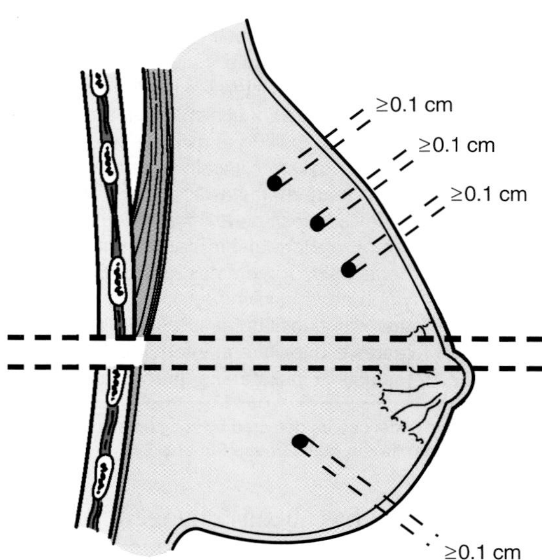

Figure 14–1. Microinvasion of primary tumor, unifocal or multifocal, none exceeding 0.1 cm. Reproduced with permission from AJCC Cancer Staging Manual, 6th ed.[2]

Table 14–1. PRIMARY TUMOR (T)	
TX	Primary tumor cannot be assessed
T0	No evidence of primary tumor
Tis	Carcinoma in situ
Tis (DCIS)	Ductal carcinoma in situ
Tis (LCIS)	Lobular carcinoma in situ
Tis (Paget's)*	Paget's disease of the nipple with no tumor
T1	Tumor 2 cm or less in greatest dimension
T1mic	Microinvasion 0.1 cm or less in greatest dimension
T1a	Tumor more than 0.1 cm but not more than 0.5 cm in greatest dimension
T1b	Tumor more than 0.5 cm but not more than 1 cm in greatest dimension
T1c	Tumor more than 1 cm but not more than 2 cm in greatest dimension
T2	Tumor more than 2 cm but not more than 5 cm in greatest dimension
T3	Tumor more than 5 cm in greatest dimension
T4	Tumor of any size with direct extension to (a) chest wall or (b) skin, only as described below
T4a	Extension to chest wall, not including pectoralis muscle
T4b	Edema (including peau d'orange) or ulceration of the skin of the breast, or satellite skin nodules confined to the same breast
T4c	Both T4a and T4b
T4d	Inflammatory carcinoma

*Paget's disease associated with a tumor is classified according to the size of the tumor.
Reproduced with permission from Greene FL, et al.[2]

Table 14–2. REGIONAL LYMPH NODES (N): CLINICAL	
NX	Regional lymph nodes cannot be assessed (eg, previously removed)
N0	No regional lymph node metastasis
N1	Metastasis to movable ipsilateral axillary lymph node(s)
N2	Metastases in ipsilateral axillary lymph nodes fixed or matted, or in clinically apparent* ipsilateral internal mammary nodes in the *absence* of clinically evident axillary lymph node metastasis
N2a	Metastasis in ipsilateral axillary lymph nodes fixed to one another (matted) or to other structures
N2b	Metastasis only in clinically apparent* ipsilateral internal mammary nodes and in the *absence* of clinically evident axillary lymph node metastasis
N3	Metastasis in ipsilateral infraclavicular lymph node(s) with or without axillary lymph node involvement, or in clinically apparent* ipsilateral internal mammary lymph node(s) and in the *presence* of clinically evident axillary lymph node metastasis; or metastasis in ipsilateral supraclavicular lymph node(s) with our without axillary or internal mammary lymph node involvement
N3a	Metastasis in ipsilateral infraclavicular lymph node(s)
N3b	Metastasis in ipsilateral internal mammary lymph node(s) and axillary lymph node(s)
N3c	Metastasis in ipsilateral supraclavicular lymph node(s)

*Clinically apparent is defined as detected by imaging studies (excluding lymphoscintigraphy) or by clinical examination or grossly visible pathologically.
Reproduced with permission from Greene FL, et al.[2]

as M1 disease, has been changed to the most advanced regional nodal disease (N3c) based on the report from Brito and colleagues,[3] demonstrating the stratification and improved prognosis in patients with supraclavicular disease treated more aggressively than historically versus those with distant metastatic disease (Figure 14–2).

Regional Lymph Nodes (pN)

The meticulous study of sentinel lymph nodes, including multiple histologic sections, immunohistochemistry (IHC), and reverse transcriptase/polymerase chain reaction (RT-PCRN), produced a body of literature that was examined by the AJCC and incorporated into the staging system.[4–13]

Table 14–3 represents the prevailing opinion that a small regional lymph node tumor burden detected by IHC and RT-PCRN should be regarded as N0 disease.

Table 14–4 is the AJCC pathologic classification for regional lymph nodes. It has been significantly expanded from the 5th edition of the *AJCC Cancer Staging Manual.*

The relationship between positive or negative axillary and internal mammary regional lymph nodes, as related to prognosis, has been reported by several investigators as summarized in Table 14–5. Based on this information, the AJCC now classifies patients with N2b and N3b disease on the basis of the relationship of these two nodal basins (Figures 14–3 and 14–4).

The present addition of the *AJCC Cancer Staging Manual* designates isolated tumor cells in regional lymph nodes as node negative but designates micrometastatic disease in regional lymph nodes as node positive (Figure 14–5). This is based on two factors. Micrometastases are more likely to demonstrate histologic proliferation or stromal reaction in contrast to isolated tumor cells. Patients with micrometastatic nodal disease detected by IHC

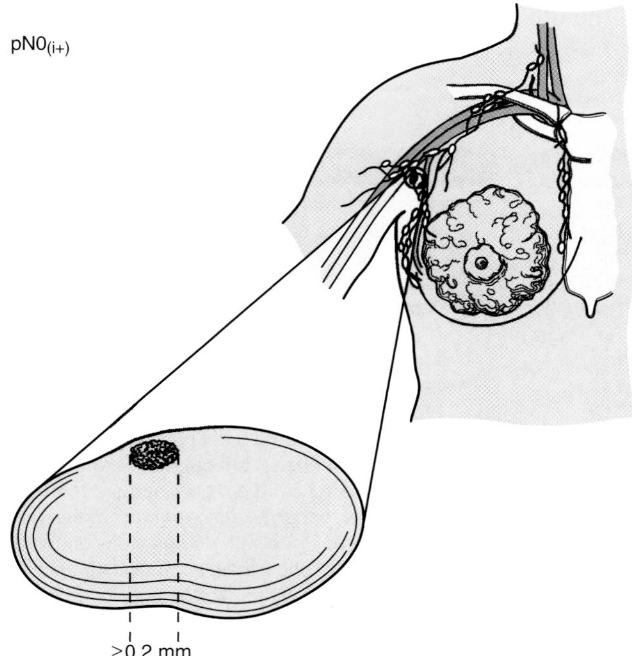

Figure 14–2. pN3c metastasis in ipsilateral supraclavicular lymph nodes. Reproduced with permission from AJCC Cancer Staging Manual, 6th ed.[2]

Table 14–3. REGIONAL LYMPH NODES: PATHOLOGIC (PN)[A]

pNX	Regional lymph nodes cannot be assessed (eg, previously removed or not removed for pathologic study)
pN0	No regional lymph node metastasis histologically, no additional examination for ITC
pN0(i –)	No regional lymph node metastasis histologically, negative IHC
pN0(i +)	No regional lymph node metastasis histologically, positive IHC, no IHC cluster greater than 0.2 mm (Figure 14–6)
pN0(mol –)	No regional lymph node metastasis histologically, negative molecular findings (RT-PCR)
pN0(mol +)	No regional lymph node metastasis histologically, positive molecular findings (RT-PCR)

Classification is based on axillary lymph node dissection with or without sentinel lymph node dissection. Classification based solely on sentinel node dissection without subsequent axillary lymph node dissection is designated (sn) for "sentinel node," for example, pN0(i+) (sn).
IHC = immunohistochemical; ITC = isolated tumor cells, defined as single tumor cells or small cell clusters not greater than 0.2 mm, usually detected only by IHC or molecular methods but which may be verified on H & E stains. ITC's do not usually show evidence of malignant activity (eg, proliferation or stromal reaction); RT-PCR = reverse transcriptase/polymerase chain reaction.
Reproduced with permission from Reproduced with permission from Greene FL, et al.[2]

Table 14–4. REGIONAL LYMPH NODES[2]: PATHOLOGIC (PN)

pN1	Metastasis in 1 to 3 axillary lymph nodes and/or in internal mammary nodes with microscopic disease detected by sentinel lymph node dissection but not clinically apparent**
pN1mi	Micrometastasis (greater than 0.2 mm, none greater than 2.0 mm) (Figure 14–5)
pN1a	Metastasis in 1 to 3 axillary nodes
pN1b	Metastasis in internal mammary nodes with microscopic disease detected by sentinel lymph node dissection but not clinically apparent** (Figure 14–7)
pN1c	Metastasis in 1 to 3 axillary lymph nodes and in internal mammary lymph nodes with microscopic disease detected by sentinel lymph node dissection but not clinically apparent.** (If associated with greater than 3 positive axillary lymph nodes, the internal mammary nodes are classified as pN3b to reflect increased tumor burden.) (Figure 14–8)
pN2	Metastasis in 4 to 9 axillary lymph nodes, or in clinically apparent* internal mammary lymph nodes in the *absence* of axillary lymph node metastasis
pN2a	Metastasis in 4 to 9 axillary lymph nodes (at least 1 tumor deposit greater than 2.0 mm)
pN2b	Metastasis in clinically apparent* internal mammary lymph nodes in the *absence* of axillary lymph node metastasis (Figure 14–3)
pN3	Metastasis in 10 or more axillary lymph nodes, or in infraclavicular lymph nodes, or in clinically apparent* ipsilateral internal mammary lymph nodes in the *presence* of 1 or more positive axillary lymph nodes; or in more than 3 axillary lymph nodes with clinically negative microscopic metastasis in internal mammary lymph nodes; or in ipsilateral supraclavicular lymph nodes
pN3a	Metastasis in 10 or more axillary lymph nodes (at least 1 tumor deposit greater than 2.0 mm) or metastasis to the infraclavicular lymph nodes
pN3b	Metastasis in clinically apparent* ipsilateral internal mammary lymph nodes in the presence of 1 or more positive axillary lymph nodes; or in more than 3 axillary lymph nodes and in internal mammary lymph nodes with microscopic disease detected by sentinel lymph node dissection but not clinically apparent**(Figures 14–4 and 14–9)
pN3c	Metastasis in ipsilateral supraclavicular lymph nodes (figure 14–2)

**Clinically apparent* is defined as detected by imaging studies (excluding lymphoscintigraphy) or by clinical examination.
***Not clinically apparent* is defined as not detected by imaging studies (excluding lymphoscintigraphy) or by clinical examination.
Reproduced with permission from Greene FL, et al.[2]

Table 14–5. 5-YEAR SURVIVAL RATES IN BREAST CANCER PATIENTS AS A FUNCTION OF NODAL STATUS IN THE AXILLARY AND INTERNAL MAMMARY LYMPH NODES

		% Survival		
Author	N	IM–/AX+	IM+/AX–	IM+/AX+
Bucalossi, et al, 1971[16]	610	56	79	28
Caceres, 1967[17]	425	52	56	24
Li and Shen, 1983[18]	1,242	60	73	38
Urban and Marjani, 1971[19]	500	68	64	54
Veronesi, et al, 1983[20]	995	72	88	56

AX = axillary lymph nodes; IM = internal mammary lymph node.
Reproduced with permission from Greene FL, et al.[2]

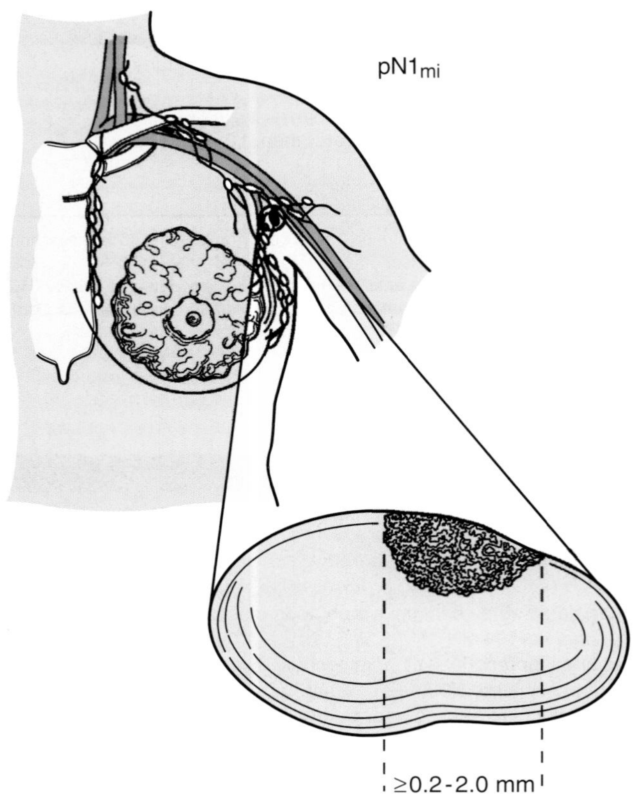

Figure 14–3. pN2b clinically apparent internal mammary lymph nodes without axillary lymph node involvement. Reproduced with permission from AJCC Cancer Staging Manual, 6th ed.[2]

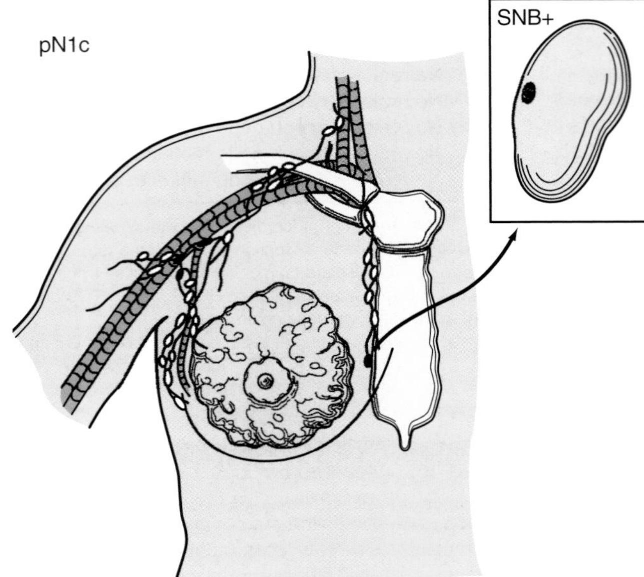

Figure 14–5. Lymph node micrometastasis (> 0.2 mm, none > 2.0 mm). Reproduced with permission from AJCC Cancer Staging Manual, 7th ed.[2]

experienced decreased survival rates ranging from 10 to 22%.[9–13] An unresolved issue is whether nodal micrometastases detected by IHC need to be verified by standard hematoxylin and eosin histology.

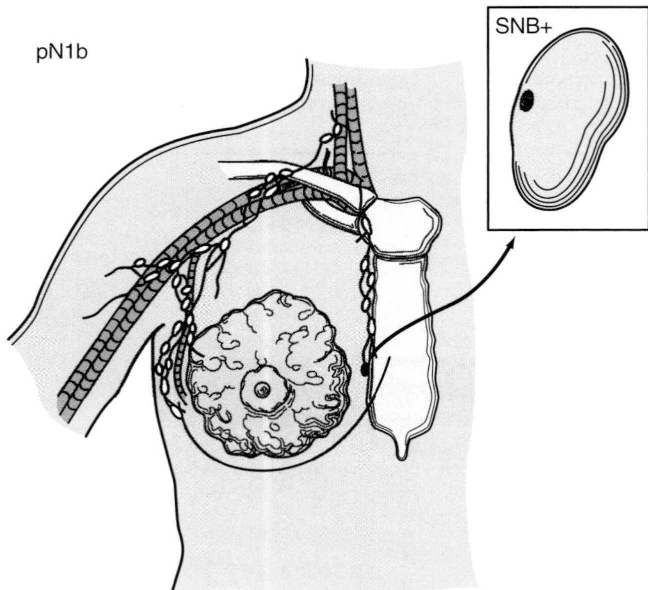

Figure 14–4. pN3b metastasis in clinically apparent internal mammary lymph nodes in the presence of 1 or more positive axillary lymph nodes. Reproduced with permission from AJCC Cancer Staging Manual, 6th ed.[2]

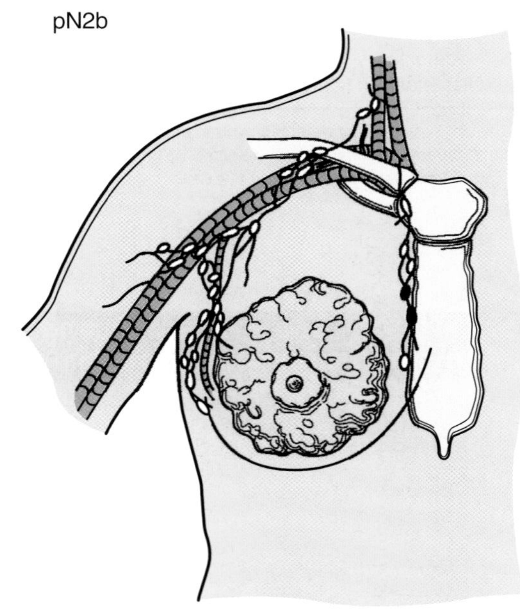

Figure 14–6. Isolated tumor cells ≤ 0.2 mm pN0(i+). Reproduced with permission from AJCC Cancer Staging Manual, 6th ed.[2]

Distant Metastasis (M)

Table 14–6 describes the classification for distant metastasis.[2] If the consulting pathologist is providing the final stage on the pathology report, the designation MX is frequently used because the pathologist is not in a position to assess distant metastasis. The final stage designated by the managing physician should change this to M0 when there is no clinical evidence of distant metastases. This does not necessarily require a systemic staging work-up.

Table 14–6. DISTANT METASTASIS (M)	
MX	Distant metastasis cannot be assessed
M0	No distant metastasis
M1	Distant metastasis

Reproduced with permission from Greene FL, et al.[2]

Summary Staging

Table 14–7 is a simplified and condensed stage grouping utilizing the major TNM categories without subsets or prefixes.[2] The combinations depicted, however, are derived and prognostically grouped on the basis of a more detailed description.

Histologic Grade (G)

The AJCC uses the Nottingham combined histologic grade (Elston-Ellis modification of Scarff-Bloom-Richardson grading system).[2,14,15] This grading system is more objective and quantitative than previous attempts at grading. It is based on the assignment of scores for percentage of tubule formation, degree of pleomorphism, and mitotic count.

The question of whether grading should be incorporated into the staging system for breast cancer is pertinent. Physicians have a large number of variables

Table 14–7. STAGE GROUPING			
Stage 0	Tis	N0	M0
Stage 1	T1*	N0	M0
Stage IIA	T0		
T1*			
T2	N1		
N1			
N0	M0		
M0			
M0			
Stage IIB	T2		
T3	N1		
N0	M0		
M0			
Stage IIIA	T0		
T1*			
T2			
T3			
T3	N2		
N2			
N2			
N1			
N2	M0		
M0			
M0			
M0			
M0			
Stage IIIB	T4		
T4			
T4	N0		
N1			
N2	M0		
M0			
M0			
Stage IIIC	Any T	N3	M0
Stage IV	Any T	Any N	M1

*T1 includes T1mic

Stage designation may be changed if post-surgical imaging studies reveal the presence of distance metastases, provided that the studies are carried out within 4 months of diagnosis in the absence of disease progression and provided that the patient has not received neoadjuvant therapy.

Reproduced with permission from Greene FL, et al.[2]

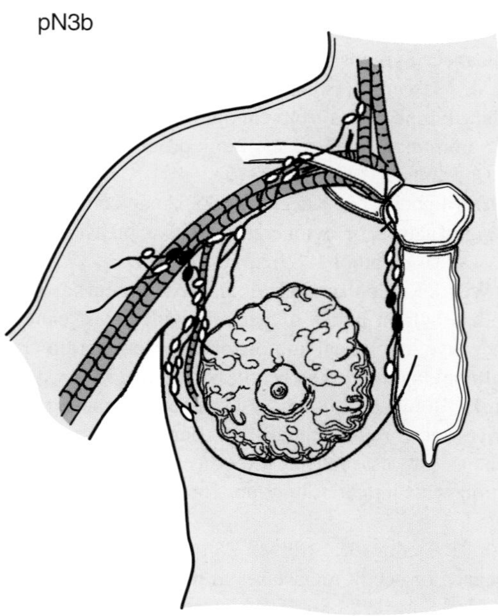

Figure 14–7. pN1b metastasis in internal mammary nodes with microscopic disease detected by sentinel lymph node biopsy but not clinically apparent. Reproduced with permission from AJCC Cancer Staging Manual, 6th ed.[2]

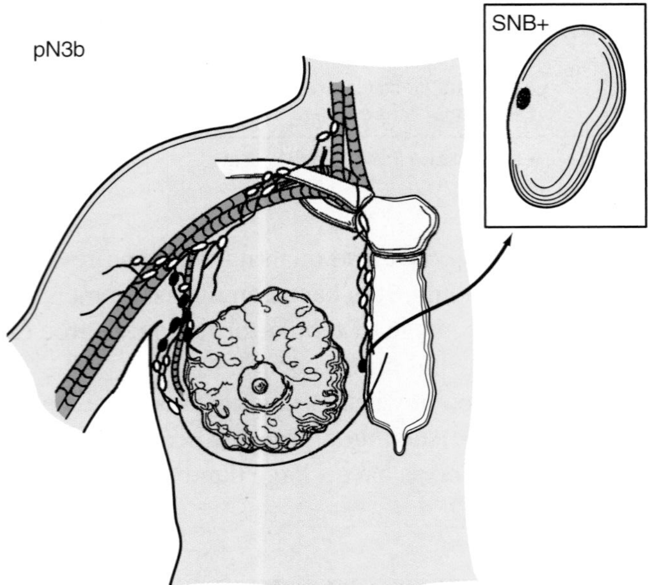

Figure 14–8. pN1c sentinel node positive internal mammary node with 1 to 3 involved axillary lymph nodes. Reproduced with permission from AJCC Cancer Staging Manual, 6th ed.[2]

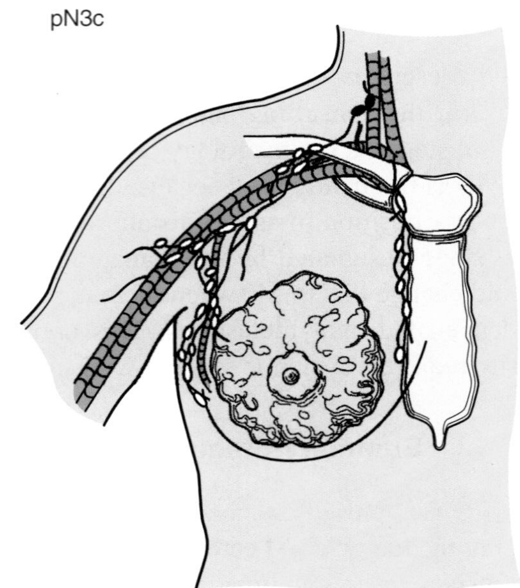

Figure 14–9. pN3b sentinel node positive internal mammary lymph node plus > 3 involved axillary lymph nodes. Reproduced with permission from AJCC Cancer Staging Manual, 6th ed.[2]

in their armamentarium for determining prognosis and selecting patients for adjuvant therapy. Histologic grade is one of those variables, but the potential flaws of observer variability, technique for fixation, and inconsistent outcomes studies in patients with small tumors stratified by grade led the AJCC to the conclusion that histologic grade has not reached sufficient data maturity and reliability to be incorporated into the staging system for breast cancer.

REFERENCES

1. Denois P. De l'importance d'une nomenclature uniflée dans Petude du cancer. Rev Med Franc 1947;28:130–2.
2. Greene FL, Page DL, Fleming ID, et al, editors. AJCC Cancer Staging Manual. 6th ed. Philadelphia: Springer–Verlag; 2002.
3. Brito RA, Valero VV, Buzdar UA, et al. Long-term results of combined-modality therapy for locally advanced breast cancer with ipsilateral supraclavicular metastases: The University of Texas M.D. Anderson Cancer Center experience. J Clin Oncol 2001;19:628–33.
4. Czerniecki BH, Schreff, AM, Callans, LS, et al. Immunohistochemistry with pancytokeratins improves the sensitivity of sentinel node biopsy in patients with breast carcinoma. Cancer 1999;85:1098–103.
5. Clare SE, Sener SF, Wilkens W, et al. Prognostic significance of occult lymph node metastases in node-negative breast cancer. Ann Surg Oncol 1997;4:447–51.
6. Hermanek P, Hutter RVP, Sobin LH, Wittekind C. Classification of isolated tumor cells and micrometastases. Cancer 1999;86:2668–73.
7. Huvos AG, Hutter RVP, Berg JW. Significance of axillary macrometastases and micrometastases in mammary cancer. Ann Surg 1971;173:44–6.
8. Verbanac KM, Fleming TP, Min CH, et al. RT-PCR increases detection of breast cancer sentinel lymph node micrometastases. Abstract 125. 22nd Annual San Antonio Breast Cancer Symposium, 1999.
9. Trojani M, de Mascarel I, Bonichon F, et al. Micrometastases to axillary lymph nodes from carcinoma of breast: detection by immunohistochemistry and prognostic significance. Br J Cancer 1987;55:303–6.
10. Senmak DD, Meineke TA, Knechtges DS, Anderson J. Prognostic significance of cytokeratin-positive breast cancer metastases. Mod Pathol 1989;2:516–20.
11. Chen ZL, Wen DR, Coulson WF, et al. Occult metastases in the axillary lymph nodes of patients with breast cancer node negative by clinical and histologic examination and conventional histology. Dis Markers 1991;9:238–48.
12. de Mascarel I, Bonichon F, Coindre JM, et al. Prognostic significance of breast cancer axillary lymph node micrometastases assessed by two special techniques: reevaluation with longer follow-up. Br J Cancer 1992;66: 523–7.
13. Hainsworth PI, Tjandra JJ, Stillwell RG, et al. Detection and significance of occult metastases in node-negative breast cancer. Br J Surg 1993;80:459–63.
14. Elston CW, Ellis IO. Pathologic prognostic factors in breast cancer. The value of histologic grade in breast cancer: experience from a large study with long-term follow-up. Histopathology 1991;19:403–10.
15. Fitzgibbons PL, Page DL, Weaver D, et al. Prognostic factors

in breast cancer. College of American Pathologists consensus statement 1999. Arch Pathol Lab Med 2000;124: 966–78.

16. Bucalossi P, Veronesi U, Zingo L, Cantu C. Enlarged mastectomy for breast cancer: review of 1,213 cases. Am J Roentgenol Radium Ther Nucl Med 1971;111:119–22.
17. Caceres E. An evaluation of radical mastectomy and extended radical mastectomy for cancer of the breast. Surg Gynecol Obstet 1967;123:337–41.
18. Li KYY, Shen Z-Z. An analysis of 1,242 cases of extended radical mastectomy. Breast. 1984;10:10–9.
19. Urban JA, Marjani MA. Significance of internal mammary lymph node metastases in breast cancer. Am J Roentgenol Radium Ther Nucl Med 1971;111:130–6.
20. Veronesi U, Cascinelli N, Bufalino R, et al. Risk of internal mammary lymph node metastases and its relevance on prognosis of breast cancer patients. Ann Surg 1983;198: 681–4.

15

Ductal Carcinoma In Situ

MELVIN J. SILVERSTEIN
HEATHER R. MACDONALD
HELEN C. MABRY
S. BRENDA MOORTHY

Ductal carcinoma in situ (DCIS) of the breast is a proliferation of malignant cells within the lumen of the mammary duct. The basement membrane appears intact by light microscopy, and if this is true for the entire lesion, in theory, there should be no possibility of metastatic disease. Most patients with DCIS should survive their disease. The only way to die from DCIS is for it to recur as an invasive lesion or if an invasive component was missed when the patient was originally treated (in which case, it was not purely DCIS).

DCIS is a heterogeneous group of lesions with diverse malignant potential and a wide range of treatment options. The architecture of these lesions may vary widely, and combinations of two or more architectures are common.

DCIS is the most rapidly growing subgroup within the breast cancer family of diseases. More than 57,000 new cases were diagnosed in the United States during 2004 (21% of all new cases of breast cancer).[1] Most new cases (> 90%) are nonpalpable and discovered mammographically.

Most of the molecular changes that characterize invasive breast cancer are already present in DCIS cells.[2] The ability for those cells to invade through the basement membrane lies in quantitative changes in the expression of genes that have already undergone malignant transformation. These genes may initiate or control invasion by affecting angiogenesis, adhesion, cell motility, the composition of extracellular-matrix, and more. To date, no gene that explicitly encodes for the ability to invade has been identified. DCIS is the precursor lesion for most invasive breast cancers, but not all DCIS lesions will become invasive breast cancer.

Treatment for DCIS ranges from excision of the lesion alone to various forms of wide excision (segmental resection, quadrant resection, oncoplastic resection, etc) to mastectomy. It is common practice to follow an excision with radiation therapy, but almost half of conservatively treated patients are treated with excision alone. When breast preservation is not feasible, total mastectomy, with or without immediate reconstruction, is generally performed.

Patient needs and preferences are an important factor influencing therapy selection. Since DCIS is a heterogeneous group of lesions rather than a single entity[3,4] and because patients have a wide range of personal needs that must be considered during treatment selection, it is clear that no single approach will be appropriate for all forms of the disease or for all patients.

THE CHANGING PRESENTATION OF DUCTAL CARCINOMA IN SITU

The presentation and diagnosis of DCIS has changed dramatically during the last 15 to 20 years and has led to changes in therapy and the patient's experience of the disease. Table 15–1 illustrates some of the changes that have occurred. Before mammography was a routine screening tool, DCIS

Table 15–1. CHANGING NATURE OF DCIS		
	Before 1990	After 1990
Frequency	Unusual	Common
Presentation	Palpable	Mammographic
Biopsy	Surgical	Needle
Molecular biology	Minimal understanding	Rapid knowledge growth
Treatment	Mastectomy	Breast conservation
Reconstruction	None/delayed	Immediate
Confusion	None	Great

DCIS = Ductal carcinoma in situ

was rare, representing less than 1% of all breast cancer.[5] Today, DCIS is common, representing 21%[6] of all newly diagnosed cases and as many as 30 to 50% of new breast cancers diagnosed by mammography.[7–10] In 2005, there will be more than 60,000 new cases of DCIS in the United States.

Historically, most patients with DCIS presented with clinical symptoms, such as a breast mass, bloody nipple discharge, or Paget's disease.[11] Today, most lesions are nonpalpable; they are clinically unapparent (the breast examination is within normal limits) and usually detected by mammography alone.

The widespread use of mammography changed the way DCIS was detected. In addition, it changed the nature of the disease detected by allowing entrance to the neoplastic continuum at an earlier time.

During the 1980s and early 1990s, biopsies for DCIS were generally wire-directed open surgical procedures. With the development of stereotactic breast biopsy, most biopsies today are done with vacuum-assisted or large gauge needles. During the 1980s, there was little knowledge of the molecular biology of DCIS. Today, the field is expanding rapidly.

Until approximately 15 years ago, the treatment for most patients with DCIS was mastectomy. Today, three-fourths of newly diagnosed patients with DCIS are treated with breast conservation.[12] In the past, when mastectomy was common, reconstruction was uncommon; if it was performed, it was done as a delayed procedure. Today, reconstruction for patients with DCIS is generally done immediately, at the conclusion of the mastectomy. In the past, when a mastectomy was performed, large amounts of skin were sacrificed. Today, it is acceptable to perform a skin-sparing mastectomy for DCIS. In the past, there was little confusion. All breast cancers were considered essentially the same, and mastectomy was the only treatment. Today, all breast cancers are different, and there is a range of acceptable treatments for every lesion. Physicians who care for patients with breast cancer are now able to consider patient preferences much more than the one diagnosis/one treatment algorithm of the past. For those who chose breast conservation, there continues to be debate as to whether radiation therapy is necessary in every case.

Major medical and social changes led to this evolution in the treatment of breast disease. This includes widespread use of screening mammography, acceptance of breast conservation for invasive disease, and political mobilization of women demanding earlier diagnosis and less disfiguring treatments.

The acceptance of breast conservation therapy (lumpectomy, axillary node dissection, and radiation therapy) for invasive breast cancer changed the way preinvasive disease was treated. Until 1980, the treatment for most patients with any form of breast cancer was generally mastectomy. Since that time, numerous prospective randomized trials have shown an equivalent rate of survival for patients with invasive breast cancer treated with breast conservation therapy.[13–16] Based on these results, it made little sense to continue treating less aggressive DCIS with mastectomy while treating more aggressive invasive breast cancer with breast preservation.

Current data suggest that many patients with DCIS can be successfully treated with breast conservation, with or without radiation therapy. The next two chapters ("Oncoplastic Surgery of the Breast" and "Evaluation and Surgical Management of Stage I and II Breast Cancer")will discuss two goals of conservative treatment: complete oncologic resection of the tumor and excellent postoperative cosmesis and how the two can be reconciled in the same patient.

PATHOLOGY

An understanding of pathology is critical to diagnosing and treating DCIS.

Classification

Although there is no universally accepted histopathologic classification, most pathologists divide DCIS into five architectural subtypes (papillary, micropapillary, cribriform, solid, and comedo), often comparing the first four (noncomedo) with comedo.[7,17] Comedo DCIS is frequently associated with high nuclear grade,[7,17] aneuploidy,[18] a higher proliferation rate,[19] *HER2/neu* gene amplification or protein overexpression,[20–25] and clinically more aggressive behavior.[26–29] Noncomedo lesions tend to be just the opposite.

However, the division by architecture alone, comedo versus noncomedo, is an oversimplification and does not always stratify patients into those with a high risk of local recurrence versus those with a low risk. High nuclear grade noncomedo lesions can express markers similar to those of high-grade comedo lesions and have a similar risk of local recurrence. Mixtures of various architectural subtypes within a single biopsy specimen are common. Seventy percent of all lesions have significant amounts of two or more architectural subtypes, making division into a predominant architectural subtype difficult.

Among pathologists, there is no uniform agreement of exactly how much comedo DCIS needs to be present to classify a lesion as comedo DCIS. Although it is clear that lesions exhibiting a predominant high-grade comedo DCIS pattern are generally more aggressive and more likely to recur if treated conservatively than low-grade noncomedo lesions, architectural subtyping alone does not reflect biologic diversity or clinical behavior.

Nuclear grade is a better biologic predictor than architecture, and, therefore, it has emerged as a key histopathologic factor for identifying aggressive behavior.[17,26,28,30–33] In 1995, the Van Nuys Group introduced a new pathologic DCIS classification [31] based on the presence or absence of high nuclear grade and comedo-type necrosis (the Van Nuys Classification).

The Van Nuys Group chose high nuclear grade as the most important factor in their classification because there was general agreement that patients with high nuclear grade lesions were more likely to recur at a higher rate and in a shorter time period after breast conservation than patients with low nuclear grade lesions.[17,26,31–34] Comedo-type necrosis was chosen because its presence also suggests a poorer prognosis,[7,28,29,35–37] and it is easy to recognize.[38]

The pathologist, using standardized criteria, first determines whether the lesion is high nuclear grade (nuclear grade 3) or non–high nuclear grade (nuclear grades 1 or 2). Then, the presence or absence of necrosis is assessed in the non–high-grade lesions. This results in three groups (Figure 15–1).

Nuclear grade is scored by previously described methods.[7] Essentially, low-grade nuclei (grade 1) are defined as nuclei 1 to 1.5 red blood cells in diameter with diffuse chromatin and unapparent nucleoli. Intermediate nuclei (grade 2) are defined as nuclei 1 to 2 red blood cells in diameter with coarse chromatin and infrequent nucleoli. High-grade nuclei (grade 3) are defined as nuclei with a diameter greater than two red blood cells, with vesicular chromatin, and one or more nucleoli.

In the Van Nuys classification, no requirement is made for a minimum or specific amount of high nuclear grade DCIS, nor is there any requirement for a minimum amount of comedo-type necrosis. Occasional desquamated or individually necrotic cells are ignored and are not scored as comedo-type necrosis.

The most difficult part of most classifications is nuclear grading, particularly the intermediate grade lesions. The subtleties of the intermediate grade lesion are not important to the Van Nuys classification; only nuclear grade 3 need be recognized. The cells must be large and pleomorphic, lack architectural differentiation and polarity, have prominent nucleoli and coarse-clumped chromatin, and generally show mitoses.[7,17,36]

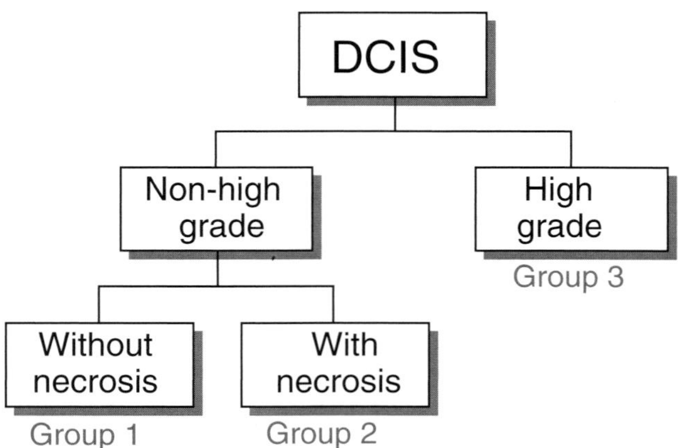

Figure 15–1. The Van Nuys pathologic classification. Ductal carcinoma in situ (DCIS) patients are separated into high nuclear grade and non–high nuclear grade. Non–high nuclear grade cases are then separated by the presence or absence of comedo-type necrosis. Lesions in group 3 (high nuclear grade) may or may not show comedo-type necrosis.

The Van Nuys classification is useful because it divides DCIS into three different biologic groups with different risks of local recurrence after breast conservation therapy (Figure 15–2). This pathologic classification, when combined with patient age, tumor size and margin status, is an integral part of the University of Southern California/Van Nuys Prognostic Index (USC/VNPI), a system that will be explained later.

Progression to Invasive Breast Cancer

Predicting which lesions will become invasive and the time frame in which that will happen are the most important issues in the DCIS field today. Currently, there is growing interest in molecular genetic study and developing knowledge regarding the progression of normal breast epithelium through hyperplastic and atypical hyperplastic changes to DCIS and then to invasive breast cancer.[2] Most of the genetic and epigenetic changes present in invasive breast cancer are already present in DCIS.[39–42] To date, no genes uniquely associated with invasive cancer have been identified.[2] As DCIS progresses to invasive breast cancer, quantitative changes in the expression of genes related to angiogenesis, adhesion, cell motility, and the composition of the extracellular-matrix may occur.[43–46] Using gene-array technology, researchers are attempting to identify high-risk patterns which will require more aggressive treatment.

Since most patients with DCIS have been treated with mastectomy, knowledge of the natural history of this disease is scant. In a study of 110 consecutive autopsies of young and middle-aged women between the ages of 20 and 54 years, 14% were found to have DCIS.[47] This suggests that the subclinical prevalence of DCIS is significantly higher than the clinical expression of the disease.

The studies of Page and colleagues[48] and Rosen and colleagues[49] enlighten us regarding untreated DCIS. In these studies, patients with noncomedo DCIS were initially misdiagnosed as having benign lesions and therefore went untreated. Subsequently, approximately 25 to 35% of these patients developed invasive breast cancer, generally within 10 to 15 years.[50] Had the lesions been high-grade comedo DCIS, the invasive breast cancer rate likely would have been higher than 35%, and the time period likely would have been shorter. With few exceptions, in both of these studies, the invasive breast carcinoma was of the ductal type and located at the site of the original DCIS. These findings and the fact that autopsy series have shown up to a 14% incidence of DCIS suggest that not all DCIS lesions progress to invasive breast cancer or become clinically significant[47,51] but that most invasive lesions are preceded by DCIS.

Page and colleagues followed 28 women with low-grade DCIS misdiagnosed as benign lesions and treated with biopsy between 1950 and 1968. Ten patients have recurred locally, nine with invasive breast cancer. This is a 42% actuarial local recurrence rate projected to 30 years of follow-up. Five of these patients have died of metastatic breast cancer, a 22% actuarial breast cancer specific fatality rate at 30 years. These recurrence and fatality rates, at first glance, seem alarming. However, they are only slightly higher than what can be expected with long-term follow-up of patients with lobular carcinoma in situ (LCIS), a disease that most clinicians are willing to treat with careful clinical follow-up. In addition, Page and colleagues' patients were treated with biopsy only. No attempt was ever made to excise these lesions with a clear surgical margin.

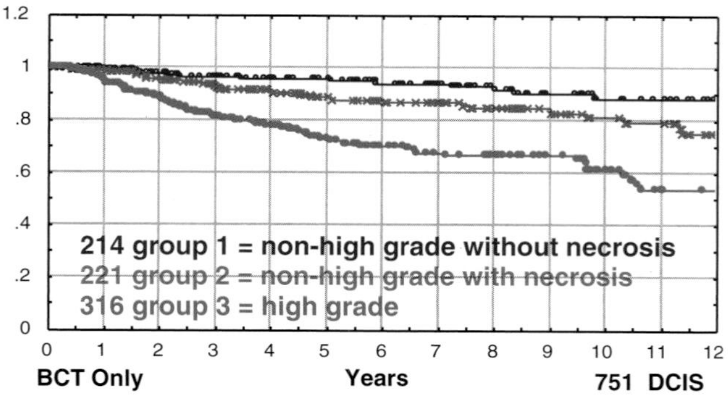

Figure 15–2. Probability of local recurrence-free survival for 751 breast conservation patients using Van Nuys ductal carcinoma in situ pathologic classification (both $p \leq .01$). BCT = breast conserving therapy; DCIS = ductal carcinoma in situ.

Microinvasion

The incidence of microinvasion within early series of DCIS is difficult to quantify because, until recently, there was no universally accepted definition of exactly what constitutes microinvasion. The 1997 edition of *The Manual for Cancer Staging* (5th edition) carried the first official definition of what is now classified as pT1mic and reads as follows: "Microinvasion is the extension of cancer cells beyond the basement membrane into adjacent tissues with no focus more than 1 mm in greatest dimension. When there are multiple foci of microinvasion the size of only the largest focus is used to classify the microinvasion (do not use the sum of all individual foci). The presence of multiple foci of microinvasion should be noted, as it is with multiple larger invasive carcinomas."[53]

The reported incidence of occult invasion (invasive disease at mastectomy in patients with a biopsy diagnosis of DCIS) varies greatly, ranging from as little as 2 to 20% or higher.[32,54] This issue was addressed by Lagios and Bellamy and colleagues.[26,37] They performed a meticulous serial subgross dissection of total mastectomy specimens correlated with specimen radiography. Occult invasion was found in 13 of 111 mastectomy specimens from patients who had initially undergone excisional biopsy of DCIS. All occult invasive cancers were associated with DCIS greater than 45 mm in diameter; the incidence of occult invasion approached 50% for DCIS greater than 55 mm.

Gump and colleagues found foci of occult invasion in 11% of patients with palpable DCIS but none in patients with clinically occult DCIS.[55] These results suggest a correlation between the size of the DCIS lesion and the incidence of occult invasion. Clearly, as the size of the DCIS lesion increases, microinvasion and occult invasion become more likely.

If even the smallest amount of invasion is found, the lesion should not be classified as DCIS. It is a T1mic (if the largest invasive component is 1 mm or less) with an extensive intraductal component (EIC). If the invasive component is 1.1 mm to 5 mm, it is a T1a lesion with EIC. If there is only a single focus of invasion, these patients do quite well. When there are many tiny foci of invasion, these patients have a poorer prognosis than expected.[56] Unfortunately, the TNM staging system does not have a T category that fully reflects their malignant potential since they are classified by their largest single focus of invasion.

Multicentricity and Multifocality of Ductal Carcinoma In Situ

Multicentricity is defined as DCIS in a quadrant other than the quadrant in which the original DCIS (index quadrant) was diagnosed. Normal breast tissue must separate the two foci. However, definitions of multicentricity vary among investigators. Hence, the reported incidence of multicentricity also varies. Rates from zero to 78%,[32,57–60] averaging about 30%, have been reported. The 30% rate of multicentricity has been used by surgeons as the rationale for mastectomy in patients with DCIS. It is, however, incorrect.

Holland and colleagues[61] evaluated 82 mastectomy specimens by taking a whole-organ section every 5 mm. Each section was radiographed. Paraffin blocks were made from every radiographically suspicious spot. In addition, an average of 25 blocks were taken from the quadrant containing the index cancer; random samples were taken from all other quadrants, the central subareolar area, and the nipple. The microscopic extension of each lesion was verified on the radiographs. This technique permitted a three-dimensional reconstruction of each lesion. This study demonstrated that most DCIS lesions were larger than expected (50% were greater than 50 mm), involved more than one quadrant by continuous extension (23%), but most importantly, were unicentric (98.8%). Only one of 82 mastectomy specimens (1.2%) had "true" multicentric distribution with a separate lesion in a different quadrant. This study suggests that complete excision of a DCIS lesion is possible because of its unicentric distribution but may be extremely difficult owing to larger than expected size. In a recent update, Holland reported whole-organ studies in 119 patients, 118 of whom had unicentric disease.[62,63] This information, when combined with the fact that most local recurrences are at or near the original DCIS, suggests that the problem of multicentricity per se is not important in the DCIS treatment decision-making process.

Multifocality is defined as separate foci of DCIS within the same ductal system. The studies of Holland and colleagues[61,62] and Noguchi and colleagues[64] suggest that a great deal of multifocality may be an artifact, resulting from looking at a three-dimensional arborizing entity in two dimensions on a glass slide. It would be analogous to saying that the branches of a tree were not connected if the branches were cut at one plane, placed separately on a slide, and viewed in cross-section. Multifocality may be due to small gaps of DCIS or skip areas within ducts as described by Faverly and colleagues and occurs in about 30% of patients with DCIS.[65]

DETECTION AND DIAGNOSIS

The importance of high-quality mammography cannot be overemphasized. During the past 5 years, 95% of new DCIS patients at the USC Norris Comprehensive Cancer Center presented with nonpalpable lesions detected by mammography or as a random unexpected finding within a benign breast biopsy (a few percent). The most common mammographic findings were microcalcifications, frequently clustered and generally without an associated soft-tissue abnormality. More than 80% of our DCIS patients exhibited microcalcifications on preoperative mammography. The patterns of these microcalcifications may be focal, diffuse, or ductal, with variable size and shape. Patients with comedo DCIS tend to have "casting calcifications." These are linear, branching, or bizarre and are almost pathognomonic for comedo DCIS.[66] (Figure 15–3). Almost all comedo lesions, 91% in our series, have calcifications that can be visualized on mammography.

Thirty-seven percent of noncomedo lesions in our series did not have mammographic calcifications, making them more difficult to find and the patients more difficult to follow if treated with breast conservation. When noncomedo lesions are calcified, they tend to have fine granular powdery calcifications.

Calcifications do not always map out the entire DCIS lesion, particularly those of the noncomedo type. Even with removal of all of the calcifications, noncalcified DCIS may be left behind. Conversely, in some patients, the majority of the calcifications are benign and map out a larger area than the true DCIS lesion. In other words, the DCIS lesion may be smaller, larger, or the same size as the calcifications that lead to its identification. Calcifications more accurately approximate the size of high-grade comedo lesions than low-grade noncomedo lesions.[61]

Before mammography was common or of good quality, most DCIS was usually clinically apparent, diagnosed by palpation or inspection; it was gross disease. Gump and colleagues[55] divided DCIS by method of diagnosis into gross and microscopic disease. Similarly, Schwartz and colleagues[29] divided DCIS into two groups: clinical and subclinical. Both researchers thought patients presenting with a palpable mass, nipple discharge, or Paget's disease of the nipple required more aggressive treatment. Schwartz believed that palpable DCIS should be treated as though it were an invasive lesion. He suggested that the pathologist simply has not found the area of invasion. Although it seems intuitive that the change from nonpalpable to palpable disease is a poor prognostic sign, our group has not been able to demonstrate this for DCIS. In our series, when equivalent patients (by size and nuclear grade) with palpable and nonpalpable DCIS were compared, they did not differ in the rate of local recurrence or fatality.

Microcalcifications are the most common mammographic abnormality, but a nonpalpable mass or a subtle architectural distortion is also possible. These findings require additional radiologic workup which generally includes compression mammography, magnification views, and ultrasonography. Magnetic resonance imaging is becoming increasingly popular as a tool to map out the size and shape of biopsy-proven DCIS or invasive breast cancer.

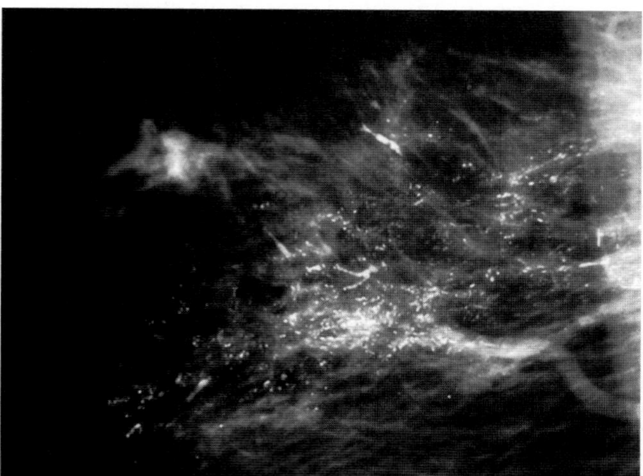

Figure 15–3. Mediolateral mammography in a 47-year-old woman shows irregular branching calcifications. Histopathology revealed high-grade comedo DCIS, Van Nuys group 3. DCIS = ductal carcinoma in situ.

Biopsy and Tissue Handling

If an occult lesion requires biopsy, there are three approaches: fine-needle aspiration biopsy (FNAB), stereotactic core biopsy (with various sizes and types of needles), and directed surgical biopsy using guide wires, radioactivity, or other guidance methods. FNA is generally of little help for nonpalpable DCIS. With FNA, it is possible to obtain neoplastic cells, but because there is no tissue, there is no architecture and the cytopathologist generally cannot determine whether the lesion is invasive. In addition, FNA of a nonpalpable lesion is more difficult to perform and must be done under mammographic or ultrasonic control.

Stereotactic core biopsy became available in the early 1990s, and it is now widely used. Dedicated digital tables make this a precise tool in experienced hands. Currently large gauge vacuum assisted needles are the tools of choice for diagnosing DCIS with a variety of new needles and tissue acquisition methods being introduced. Open surgical biopsy with guide wires should only be used if the lesion cannot be biopsied using minimally invasive techniques. Needle localization segmental resection should be a critical part of the treatment not the diagnosis.

When needle localization excision is done, intraoperative specimen radiography and correlation with the preoperative mammogram should be performed in every case. Margins should be inked or dyed (Figure 15–4) and specimens should be serially sectioned at 2 to 4 mm intervals (Figure 15–5), depending on the size of the excision. The tissue sections should be arranged and processed in sequence. Pathologic reporting should include a description of all architectural subtypes, a determination of nuclear grade, an assessment of the presence or absence of necrosis, the measured size on a single slide, and the estimated extent of the lesion over a series of blocks. The margin width should be determined for all margins.

Tumor size should be determined by direct measurement or ocular micrometry from stained slides for smaller lesions. For larger lesions, a combination of direct measurement and estimation, based on the distribution of the lesion in a sequential series of slides, should be used. The proximity of DCIS to an

Figure 15–4. The specimen is being color-coded.

inked margin should be determined by direct measurement or ocular micrometry. The closest single distance between any involved duct containing DCIS and an inked margin should be reported.

If the diagnosis is unproven, stereotactic or ultrasound-guided biopsy should be the first step. Once the diagnosis is made, if the patient is motivated for breast conservation, a multiple-wire–directed oncoplastic excision can be planned. This will give the patient her best chance to accomplish two opposing goals: clear margins and good cosmesis. The best chance of completely removing a large lesion is with a large initial excision. The best chance at good cosmesis is with a small initial excision. It is the surgeon's job to optimize these opposing goals. A large quadrant resection should not be performed unless there is cytologic or histologic proof of malignancy. This type of resection may lead to breast deformity and should the diagnosis prove to be benign, the patient will be quite unhappy.

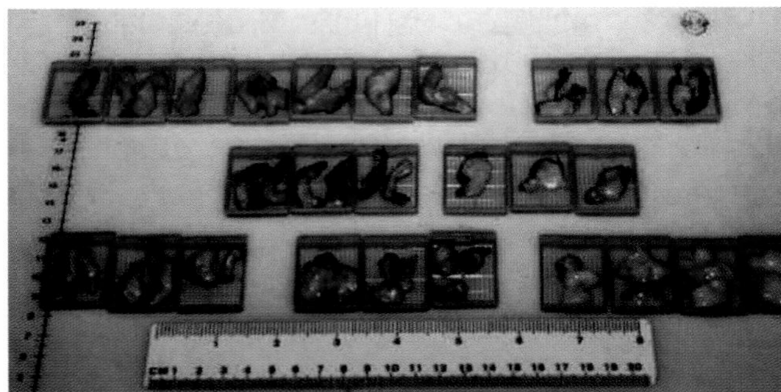

Figure 15–5. The specimen has been color-coded with dyes and serially sectioned and is in cassettes ready for processing.

Removal of nonpalpable lesions is best performed by an integrated team of surgeon, radiologist, and pathologist. The radiologist who places the wires must be experienced, as must the surgeon who removes the lesion and the pathologist who processes the tissue.

TREATMENT

For most patients with DCIS, there will be no single correct treatment. There will generally be a choice. The choices, although seemingly simple, are not. As the choices increase and become more complicated, frustration increases for both the patient and her physician.[27]

Counseling the Patient with Biopsy-Proven Ductal Carcinoma In Situ

It is never easy to tell a patient that she has breast cancer. But is DCIS really cancer? From a biologic point of view, DCIS is unequivocally cancer.[2] But when we think of cancer, we generally think of a disease that, if untreated, runs an inexorable course toward death. That is certainly not the case with DCIS. It must be emphasized to the patient that she has a borderline cancerous lesion (some prefer the term 'precancerous'), a preinvasive lesion, which at this time is not a threat to her life. In the USC/Van Nuys series of 1,162 patients with DCIS, the raw fatality rate from breast cancer is less than 1%. Numerous other DCIS series[7,11,67,68] confirm an equally extremely low fatality rate.

Patients often ask, "Why do any patients die if DCIS is truly a noninvasive lesion?" If DCIS recurs as an invasive lesion and the patient goes on to die from metastatic breast cancer, the source of the metastases is clear (the local invasive recurrence). But what about the patient who undergoes mastectomy and some time later develops metastatic disease or a patient who is treated with breast preservation who never develops a local invasive recurrence but still dies of metastatic breast cancer? These latter patients probably had an invasive focus with established metastases at the time of their original treatment but the invasive focus was not found during routine histopathologic evaluation. Even with thorough and careful examination, it is still a sampling process and a small invasive focus can be overlooked.

Patients diagnosed with cancer frequently fear that the cells have spread. The patient with DCIS can be assured that since no invasion was seen microscopically, the likelihood of systemic spread is minimal.

Patients need to be educated that the term "breast cancer" encompasses a multitude of lesions with a wide range of aggressiveness and lethal potential. The patient with DCIS needs to be reassured that she has a minimal lesion and that she is likely going to need additional treatment, which may include surgery, radiation therapy, an antiestrogen, or some combination. She will be relieved to hear that she will not need chemotherapy, that her hair will not fall out, and that it is highly unlikely that she will die from this lesion. She will, of course, need careful clinical follow-up.

End Points for Patients with DCIS

When evaluating the results of treatment for patients with breast cancer, a variety of end points must be considered. Important end points include local recurrence (both invasive and DCIS), regional recurrence, distant recurrence, breast cancer-specific survival, overall survival, and quality of life. The importance of each end point varies depending on whether the patient has DCIS or invasive breast cancer

When treating invasive cancer, the most important end points are distant recurrence and breast cancer-specific survival; in other words, living with or dying from breast cancer. For invasive breast cancer, a variety of different systemic treatments have been shown to significantly improve survival. These include a wide range of chemotherapeutic regimens, radiation therapy, and anti-estrogen drugs. Variations in local treatment do not affect survival.[69] They do, however, affect local recurrence.

DCIS is similar to invasive breast cancer in that variations in local treatment affect local recurrence, but no study to date has shown a significant difference in distant disease-free or breast cancer-specific survival, regardless of any treatment (systemic or local), and no study is likely to show a difference since there are so few breast cancer deaths in patients with pure DCIS. The most important outcome measure, breast cancer-specific survival, is essentially the same no matter what local or systemic treatment is given. Consequently, local recurrence has become the most important and commonly used end point when evaluating treatment for patients with DCIS.

It is important to prevent local recurrences in patients treated with DCIS. They are demoralizing. They often lead to mastectomy, and, if invasive, they upstage the patient and are theoretically a threat to life.

Following treatment for DCIS, 40 to 50% of local recurrences are invasive. About 10 to 20% of DCIS patients who develop local invasive recurrences develop distant metastases and die from breast cancer.[70–72]. Long term, this is likely to translate into a mortality rate of about 0 to 0.5% for patients treated with mastectomy, 1 to 2% for conservatively treated patients who receive radiation therapy, and 2 to 3% for patients treated with excision alone. In order to save their breasts, many patients are willing to accept this theoretical, and as of now statistically unproven, small absolute risk associated with breast conservation therapy.

Treatment Options

Mastectomy

Mastectomy is an extreme but highly effective treatment for DCIS if the goal is simply to prevent local recurrence. Most mastectomy series reveal local recurrence rates of approximately 1% with mortality rates close to zero.[73] But, mastectomy is an aggressive form of treatment for patients with DCIS. It clearly provides a local recurrence benefit but only a theoretical survival benefit. It is, therefore, often difficult to justify mastectomy, particularly for otherwise healthy women with image-detected DCIS, during an era of increasing use of breast conservation for invasive breast carcinoma. Mastectomy is indicated in cases of true multicentricity (multiquadrant disease) and when a unicentric DCIS is too large to excise with clear margins and an acceptable cosmetic result.

Patients who test positive for *BRCA 1* or *2* and who develop DCIS do not have an absolute contraindication for breast conservation but many of these patients will elect bilateral mastectomies.

Breast Conservation

The most recently available SEER data reveal that 72% of patients with DCIS are treated with breast conservation; 39% with excision plus radiation therapy, and 33% with excision alone.

Clinical trials have shown that local excision and radiation therapy in patients with negative margins can provide excellent rates of local control.[68,69,74–80] However, even radiation therapy may be overly aggressive since many cases of DCIS may not recur or progress to invasive carcinoma when treated by excision alone.[26,52,81–83] Conversely, there are patients with DCIS whose local recurrence rate with breast preservation is so high that mastectomy is clearly a more appropriate treatment. However, the majority of women with DCIS diagnosed currently are candidates for breast conservation.

Rationale for Excision Alone

There are three lines of reasoning that suggest that excision alone may be an acceptable treatment for selected patients with DCIS.

1. Anatomic: Evaluation of mastectomy specimens using the serial subgross tissue processing technique reveals that most DCIS is unicentric, involves a single breast segment and is radial in its distribution.[30,34,61–63,65] This means that, in many cases, it is possible to excise the entire lesion with a segment or quadrant resection. Since DCIS, by definition, is not invasive and has not metastasized, it can be thought of in Halstedian terms. Complete excision should cure the patient without any additional therapy.
2. Biologic: Some DCIS is simply not aggressive, for example, low-grade lesions bordering on atypical ductal hyperplasia. Lesions like this carry a low potential for development into an invasive lesion, about 1% per year at most.[48,50,52,84,85] This is only slightly more than lobular carcinoma in situ (LCIS), a lesion that is routinely treated with careful clinical follow-up.
3. Prospective Randomized Data: The prospective randomized trials show no difference in breast cancer-specific survival, regardless of treatment after excision.[69,79,80] If this is true, why not strive for the least aggressive treatment?

Prospective Randomized Trials

All of the prospective randomized trials have shown a significant reduction in local recurrence for patients treated with radiation therapy compared with excision alone, but no trial has reported a survival benefit, regardless of treatment.[68,69,74,75,77–80,86,87]

Only one trial has compared mastectomy with breast conservation for patients with DCIS, and the data were only incidentally accrued. The National Surgical Adjuvant Breast Project (NSABP) performed protocol B-06, a prospective randomized trial for patients with invasive breast cancer.[14,57] There were three treatment arms: total mastectomy, excision of the tumor plus radiation therapy, and excision alone. Axillary nodes were removed regardless of the treatment assignment.

During central slide review, a subgroup of 78 patients was confirmed to have pure DCIS without any evidence of invasion.[57] After 83 months of follow-up, the percentage of patients with local recurrences were as follows: 0 for mastectomy, 7% for excision plus radiation therapy, and 43% for excision alone.[88] In spite of these large differences in the rate of local recurrence for each different treatment, there was no difference among the three treatment groups in breast cancer-specific survival.

Contrary to the lack of trials comparing mastectomy with breast conservation, a number of prospective randomized trials comparing excision plus radiation therapy with excision alone for patients with DCIS are ongoing.[89] Three have been published: the NSABP (protocol B-17),[68] the European Organization for Research and Treatment of Cancer (EORTC), protocol 10853,[79] and the United Kingdom, Australia, New Zealand DCIS Trial (UK Trial).[78,80]

The results of NSABP B-17 were updated in 1995,[87] 1998,[75,76] 1999,[74] and 2001.[68] In this study, more than 800 patients with DCIS excised with clear surgical margins were randomized into two groups: excision alone versus excision plus radiation therapy. The main end point of the study was local recurrence, invasive, or noninvasive (DCIS). The definition of a clear margin was non-transection of the DCIS. In other words, if one fat or fibrous cell separated the DCIS from the inked margin, it was considered clear. Many margins, of course, were likely much wider.

After 12 years of follow-up, there was a 50% decrease in local recurrence of both DCIS and invasive breast cancer in patients treated with radiation therapy. The overall local recurrence rate for patients treated by excision alone was 32% at 12 years. For patients treated with excision plus breast irradiation, it was 16%, a relative benefit of 50%.[69] There was no difference in distant disease-free or overall survival in either arm. These updated data led the NSABP to confirm their 1993 position and to continue to recommend post-operative radiation therapy for all patients with DCIS who chose to save their breasts. This recommendation was clearly based primarily on the decreased local recurrence rate for those treated with radiation therapy and secondarily on the potential survival advantage it might confer, although none could be proven.

The early results of B-17, in favor of radiation therapy for patients with DCIS, led the NSABP to perform protocol B-24.[74] In this trial, more than 1,800 patients with DCIS were treated with excision and radiation therapy and then randomized to receive either tamoxifen or placebo. After 7 years of follow-up, 11% of patients treated with placebo had recurred locally, whereas only 8% of those treated with tamoxifen had recurred.[69] The difference, although small, was statistically significant for invasive local recurrence but not for noninvasive (DCIS) recurrence. Data presented at the 2002 San Antonio Breast Cancer Symposium suggested that the ipsilateral benefit was seen only in estrogen receptor positive patients.[90] Again, there was no difference in distant disease-free or overall survival in either arm of the B-24 Trial.

The EORTC results were published in 2000.[79] This study was essentially identical to B-17 in design and margin definition. Just over 1,000 patients were included. The data were updated at the EORTC DCIS Consensus Conference in 2002 (E. Rutgers, personal communication, June 2002). After 6 years of follow-up, 11% of patients treated with excision plus radiation therapy had recurred locally compared with 20% of patients treated with excision alone, results similar to those obtained by the NSABP at the same point in their trial. As in the B-17 Trial, there was no difference in distant disease-free or overall survival in either arm of the

EORTC Trial. In the initial report, there was a statistically significant increase in contralateral breast cancer in patients who were randomized to receive radiation therapy. This was not maintained when the data were updated in 2002.

The UK Trial was published in 2003.[80] This trial, which involved more than 1,600 patients, performed a two-by-two study in which patients could be randomized into two separate trials within a trial. The patients and their doctors chose whether to be randomized in one or both studies. After excision with clear margins (same non-transection definition as the NSABP), patients were randomized to receive radiotherapy (yes or no) and/or tamoxifen versus placebo. This yielded four subgroups: excision alone, excision plus radiation therapy, excision plus tamoxifen, and finally, excision plus radiation therapy plus tamoxifen. Those who received radiation therapy obtained a statistically significant decrease in ipsilateral breast tumor recurrence similar in magnitude to the ones shown by the NSABP and EORTC. Contrary to the findings of the NSABP, there was no significant benefit from tamoxifen.[77,78,80] As with the NSABP and the EORTC, there was no benefit in terms of survival in any arm of the UK DCIS study.

Overall, these trials support the same conclusions. They all show that radiation therapy decreases local recurrence by a relative 50% and they all show no survival benefit, regardless of treatment. The only difference is that the NSABP B-24 Trial shows a significant decrease in local recurrence attributable to tamoxifen although the UK Trial does not.

Limitations of the Prospective Randomized Trials

The randomized trials were designed to answer a single broad question: does radiation therapy decrease local recurrence? All have clearly shown that, overall, radiation therapy decreases local recurrence, but they cannot identify in which subgroups the benefit is so small that the patients can be safely treated with excision alone.

Many of the parameters currently considered important in predicting local recurrence (tumor size, margin width, nuclear grade, etc) were not routinely collected prospectively during the randomized DCIS trials. In addition, the trials did not specifically require the marking of margins or the measurement of margin width. The exact measurement of margin width was present in only 5% of the EORTC pathology reports.[86]

The NSABP did not require size measurements, and many of their pathologic data were determined by retrospective slide review. In the initial NSABP report, more than 40% of patients had no size measurement.[68] Unfortunately, if margins were not inked and tissues not completely sampled and sequentially submitted, then these predictive data can never be determined accurately by retrospective review.

The relative reduction in local recurrence seems to be the same in all three trials—about 50% for any given subgroup at any point in time. What does this relative reduction mean? If the absolute local recurrence rate is 30% at 10 years for a given subgroup of patients treated with excision alone, radiation therapy will reduce this rate by approximately 50%, leaving a group of patients with a 15% local recurrence rate at 10 years. Radiation therapy seems indicated for a subgroup with such a high local recurrence rate. But consider a more favorable subgroup, a group of patients with a 6% absolute recurrence rate at 10 years. These patients receive only a 3% absolute benefit. Here, we must ask whether the benefits are worth the risks and costs involved. Every attempt possible should be made to identify such low-risk subgroups.

Radiation therapy is expensive, time consuming, and is accompanied by significant side effects in a small percentage of patients (cardiac, pulmonary, etc)[91] Radiation fibrosis continues to occur, but it is less common with current techniques than it was during the 1980s. Radiation fibrosis changes the texture of the breast and skin, makes mammographic follow-up more difficult, and may result in delayed diagnosis if there is a local recurrence. The use of radiation therapy for DCIS precludes its use if an invasive recurrence develops at a later date. The use of radiation therapy with its accompanying skin and vascular changes make skin-sparing mastectomy, if needed in the future, more difficult to perform. Studies have also shown that radiation therapy given during the 1970s through the 1980s may result in late myocardial perfusion defects for patients treated for left-sided breast cancer.[92]

Most importantly, if we give radiation therapy for DCIS, we must assume all of these risks and costs without any proven distant disease-free or breast cancer specific survival benefits. The only proven benefit will be a decrease in local recurrence. It is important, therefore, to carefully examine the need for radiation therapy in all conservatively treated patients with DCIS. In 2001, the NSABP agreed that all patients with DCIS may not need postexcisional radiation therapy.[69] The problem is how to accurately identify those patients. If we can identify subgroups of patients with DCIS in which the probability of local recurrence after excision alone is low, they may be the patients where the costs, risks, and side effects of radiotherapy outweigh the benefits.

In spite of the randomized data, which suggest that all conservatively treated patients benefit from radiation therapy, physicians and patients have embraced the concept of excision alone. 1999 SEER data reveal that 72% of patients with DCIS were treated with breast conservation. Almost half of these conservatively treated patients were treated with excision alone. When all patients with DCIS are considered, 28% received mastectomy, 39% received excision plus radiation therapy, and 33% were treated with excision alone.[12]

PREDICTING LOCAL RECURRENCE IN CONSERVATIVELY TREATED PATIENTS WITH DCIS

There is now sufficient information that can aid clinicians in differentiating patients who significantly benefit from radiation therapy after excision from those who do not. These same data can point out patients who are better served by mastectomy because recurrence rates with breast conservation are unacceptably high, even with the addition of radiation therapy.

Our research[31,93,94] and the research of others[26,28,32,36,37,81,82,85,87,95] have shown that various combinations of nuclear grade, the presence of comedo-type necrosis, tumor size, margin width, and age are all important factors that can be used to predict the probability of local recurrence in conservatively treated patients with DCIS.

The Original Van Nuys Prognostic Index (VNPI) and its Updated Version, the USC/VNPI

In 1995, the Van Nuys DCIS pathologic classification, based on nuclear grade and the presence or absence of comedonecrosis, was developed[31] (see Figure 15–1). Nuclear grade and comedo-type necrosis reflect the biology of the lesion, but neither alone nor together are they adequate as the sole guidelines in the treatment decision-making process. Tumor size and margin width reflect the extent of disease, the adequacy of surgical treatment, and the likelihood of residual disease and are of paramount importance.

The challenge was to devise a system using these variables (all independently important by multivariate analysis) that would be clinically valid, therapeutically useful, and user-friendly. The original Van Nuys Prognostic Index (VNPI)[96,97] was devised in 1996 by combining tumor size, margin width, and pathologic classification (determined by nuclear grade and the presence or absence of comedo-type necrosis). All of these factors had been collected prospectively in a large series of DCIS patients who were selectively treated (nonrandomized).[98]

A score ranging from 1 for lesions with the best prognosis to 3 for lesions with the worst prognosis was given for each of the 3 prognostic predictors. The objective with all 3 predictors was to create 3 statistically different subgroups for each, using local recurrence as the marker of treatment failure. Cutoff points (for example, what size or margin width constitutes low, intermediate, or high risk of local recurrence) were determined statistically, using the log rank test with an optimum p-value approach.

Size Score

A score of 1 was given for small tumors 15 mm or less, 2 was given for intermediate-sized tumors 16 to 40 mm, and 3 was given for large tumors 41 mm or more in diameter. The determination of size required complete and sequential tissue processing along with mammographic/pathologic correlation. Size was determined over a series of sections rather than on a single section and is the most difficult parameter to reproduce. If a 3-centimeter specimen is cut into 10 blocks, each block is estimated to be 3 mm thick. If a lesion measuring 5 mm in maximum diameter on a single slide appears in seven sequential blocks, it is estimated to be 21 mm (3 mm × 7) in maximum size, not 5 mm as measured on a single slide. The maximum diameter on a single slide was the way size was measured for most of the patients in the prospective randomized trials.

Margin Score

A score of 1 was given for widely clear tumor-free margins of 10 mm or more. This was often achieved by re-excision with the finding of no residual DCIS or only focal residual DCIS in the wall of the biopsy cavity. A score of 2 was given for intermediate margins of 1 to 9 mm and a score of 3 for margins less than 1 mm (involved or close margins).

Pathologic Classification Score

A score of 3 was given for tumors classified as group 3 (high grade lesions), 2 for tumors classified as group 2 (non-high grade lesions with comedo-type necrosis), and a score of 1 for tumors classified as group 1 (non-high grade lesion without comedo-type necrosis).[31,99] The classification is diagrammed in Figure 15-1.

The final formula for the original VNPI became:

VNPI = pathologic classification score
+ margin score + size score

The University of Southern California/ Van Nuys Prognostic Index (USC/VNPI)

By early 2001, a multivariate analysis at USC revealed that age was also an independent prognostic factor in our database (Figure 15–6) and that it should be added to the VNPI with a weight equal to that of the other factors.

An analysis of our local recurrence data by age revealed that the most appropriate break points for our data were between ages 39 and 40 and between ages 60 and 61 (Figure 15–7). Based on this, a score of 3 was given to all patients 39 years of age or younger, a score of 2 was given to patients aged 40 to 60, and a score of 1 was given to patients aged 61

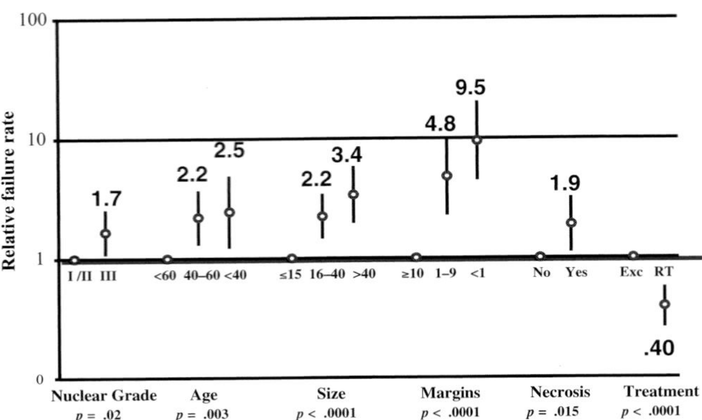

Figure 15–6. Cox multivariate analysis of factors affecting ductal carcinoma in situ recurrence-free survival (conservatively treated patients only). Exc = excision; RT = radiation therapy.

or older. The new scoring system for the USC/VNPI is shown in Table 15–2. The final formula for the USC/VNPI became:

USC/VNPI = pathologic classification score
+ margin score + size score + age score

Scores range from 4 to 12. The patients least likely to recur after conservative therapy had a score of 4 (small, low-grade, well-excised lesions in older women). The patients most likely to recur had a score of 12 (large, poorly excised, high-grade lesions in younger women). The probability of recurrence increased as the USC/VNPI score increased.

Updated Results Using the USC/VNPI

Through June 2004, our group treated 1,162 patients with pure DCIS; 411 patients were treated with mas-

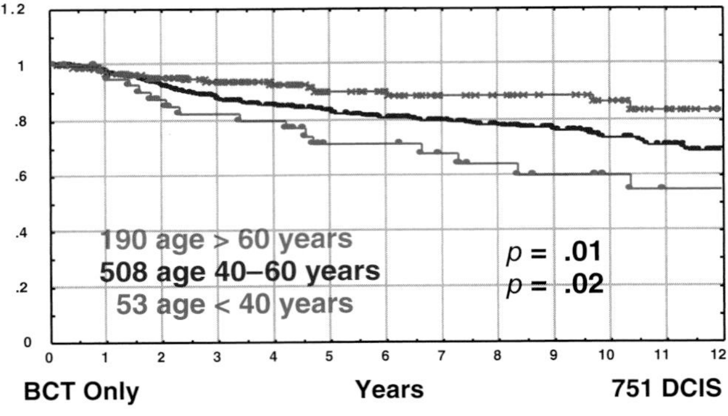

Figure 15–7. Probability of local recurrence-free survival by age group for 751 breast conservation patients (both $p = .02$). BCT = breast conserving therapy; DCIS = ductal carcinoma in situ.

Table 15-2. THE USC/VAN NUYS PROGNOSTIC INDEX SCORING SYSTEM

Score	1	2	3
Size (mm)	≤15	16–40	≥41
Margins (mm)	≥10	1–9	< 1
Pathologic classification	Non–high-grade without necrosis	Non–high-grade with necrosis	High-grade with or without necrosis
Age	> 60	40–60	< 40

One to three points are awarded for each of four different predictors of local breast recurrence (size, margins, pathologic classification, and age). Scores for each of the predictors are totaled to yield a VNPI score ranging from a low of 4 to a high of 12. USC = University of Southern California

tectomy and are not included in any analysis that uses local recurrence as the end point; 751 patients were treated with breast conservation (459 by excision alone and 292 by excision plus radiation therapy). The average follow-up for all patients was 85 months: 86 months for mastectomy, 108 months for excision plus radiation therapy, and 70 months for excision alone.

There were 135 local failures, 56 (41.5%) of which were invasive. The probability of local failure was reduced, overall, by 60% if radiation therapy was given, a result almost identical with the prospective randomized trials (See Figure 15–6). The local recurrence-free survival is shown by treatment in Figure 15–8. As expected, at any point in time, mastectomy had the lowest probability of local recurrence and excision alone had the highest.

Seven patients (2.5%) treated with radiation therapy developed local recurrences and distant metastases, six of whom have died from breast cancer. Three of these recurrences after radiation therapy were inflammatory breast cancer. This fact has always concerned us that a recurrence in a radiation field might have a worse prognosis than a recurrence in a non-radiated field.

One patient (0.2%) treated with excision alone developed a local invasive recurrence and metastatic disease and died from breast cancer. Two patients with mastectomy developed distant disease after developing local invasive recurrences. Neither has died from breast cancer. There is no statistical difference in breast cancer-specific survival when patients treated with excision alone, excision plus irradiation, or mastectomy are compared (Figure 15–9). There is no statistical difference in breast cancer-specific survival when patients are compared by USC/VNPI groupings (Figure 15–10). Sixty-six additional patients have died from other causes without evidence of recurrent breast cancer. The 12-year actuarial overall survival, including deaths from all causes, is 90%. It is virtually identical for all three treatment groups (Figure 15–11) and for all three USC/VNPI groups.

The local recurrence-free survival for all 751 breast conservation patients is shown by tumor size in Figure 15–12, by margin width in Figure 15–13, by pathologic classification in Figure 15–2 and by age in Figure 15–7. The differences between every local disease-free survival curve for each of the four predictors that make up the USC/VNPI are statistically significant.

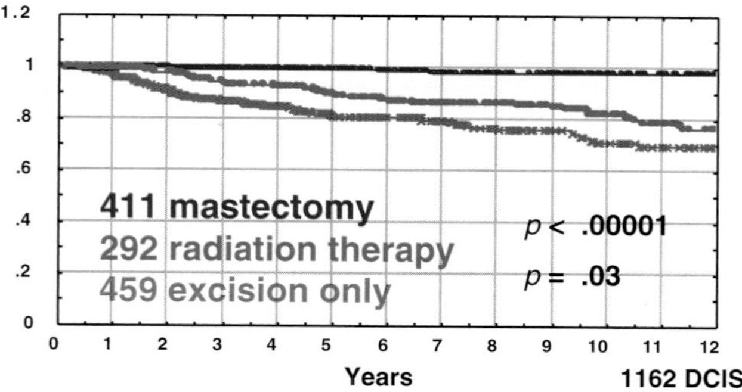

Figure 15–8. Probability of local recurrence-free survival by treatment for 1,162 patients with DCIS ($p \leq .03$). DCIS = ductal carcinoma in situ.

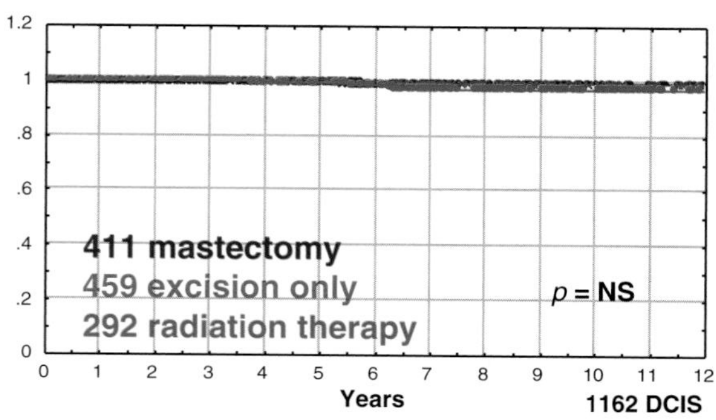

Figure 15–9. Probability of breast cancer specific survival by treatment for 1,162 patients with DCIS (p = NS). DCIS = ductal carcinoma in situ; NS = not significant.

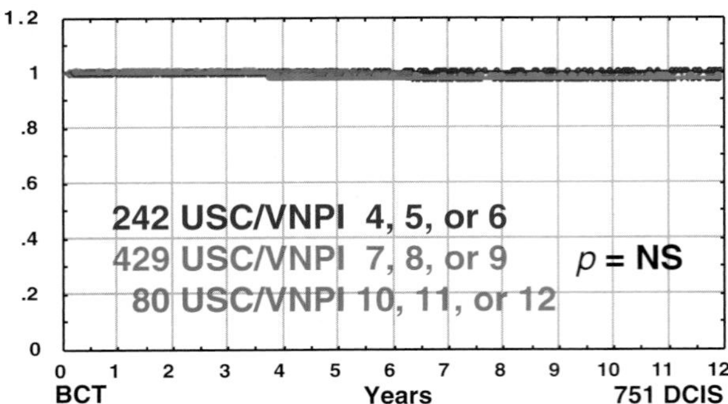

Figure 15–10. Probability of breast cancer specific survival survival for 751 breast conservation patients grouped by Modified USC/Van Nuys Prognostic Index score (4, 5, or 6 versus 7, 8, or 9 versus 10, 11, or 12) (p = NS). BCT = breast conserving therapy; DCIS = ductal carcinoma in situ; NS = not significant; VNPI = USC/Van Nuys Prognostic Index.

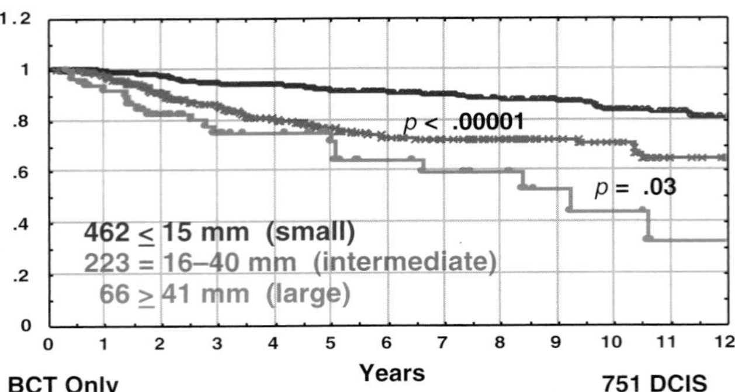

Figure 15–12. Probability of local recurrence-free survival by tumor size for 751 breast conservation patients (both $p \leq .01$). BCT = breast conserving therapy; DCIS = ductal carcinoma in situ.

Figure 15–14 shows all breast conservation patients by USC/VNPI score (4 to 12) and Figure 15–15 groups patients with low (USC/VNPI = 4, 5, or 6), intermediate (USC/VNPI = 7, 8, or 9), or high (USC/VNPI = 10, 11, or 12) risks of local recurrence together. Each of these three groups is statistically different from one another and leads to our suggestion for treatment (Table 15–3).

Patients with USC/VNPI scores of 4, 5, or 6 do not show a local recurrence-free survival benefit from breast irradiation (Figure 15–16) (p = NS). Patients with an intermediate rate of local recurrence, USC/VNPI = 7, 8, or 9, benefit from irradiation (Figure 15–17). There is a statistically significant decrease in the probability of local recurrence, averaging 12 to 15% throughout the curves, for irradiated patients with intermediate USC/VNPI scores compared to those treated by excision alone ($p = .02$). Figure 15–18 divides patients with a USC/VNPI of 10, 11, or 12 into those treated by excision plus irradiation and those treated by excision alone. Although, the difference between the two groups is highly significant ($p = .001$), conservatively treated DCIS patients with a USC/VNPI of 10, 11, or 12 recur at an extremely high rate even with radiation therapy.

Use of Margin Width as the Sole Predictor of Local Recurrence

Owing to the difficulty of estimating size, in 1997, we began evaluating the possibility of using margin width as the sole predictor of local recurrence as a surrogate for the USC/VNPI.[94] The rationale was based on the multivariate analysis (see Figure 15–6), where patients with margin widths less than 1 mm had a nearly 10-fold increase in the probability local recurrence compared with patients who had 10 mm

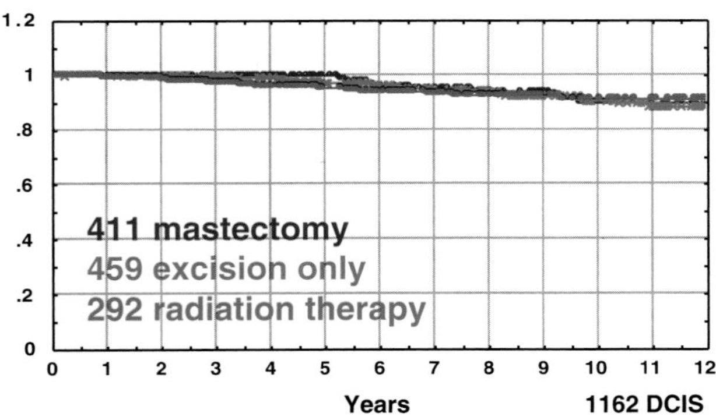

Figure 15–11. Probability of overall survival by treatment for 1,162 patients with DCIS (p = NS). DCIS = ductal carcinoma in situ.

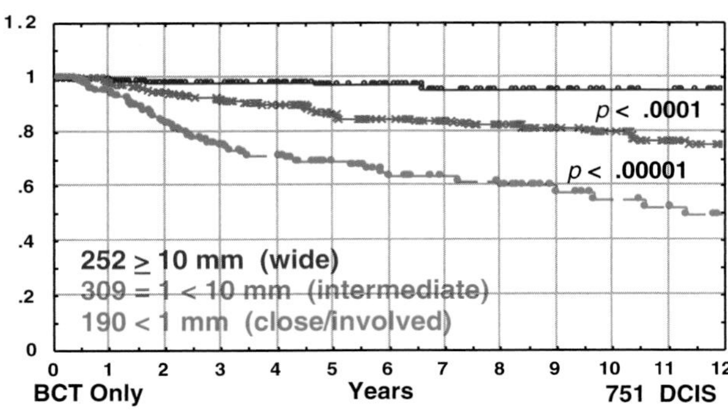

Figure 15–13. Probability of local recurrence-free survival by margin width for 751 breast conservation patients (both $p \leq .001$). BCT = breast conserving therapy; DCIS = ductal carcinoma in situ.

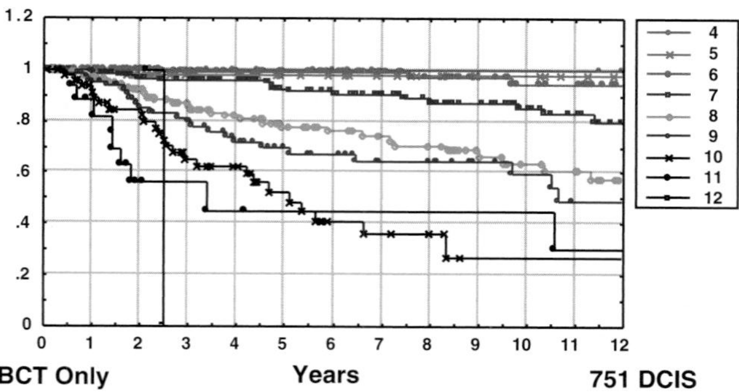

Figure 15–14. Probability of local recurrence-free survival for 751 breast conservation patients by USC/Van Nuys Prognostic Index score 4 to 12. BCT= breast conserving therapy; DCIS = ductal carcinoma in situ.

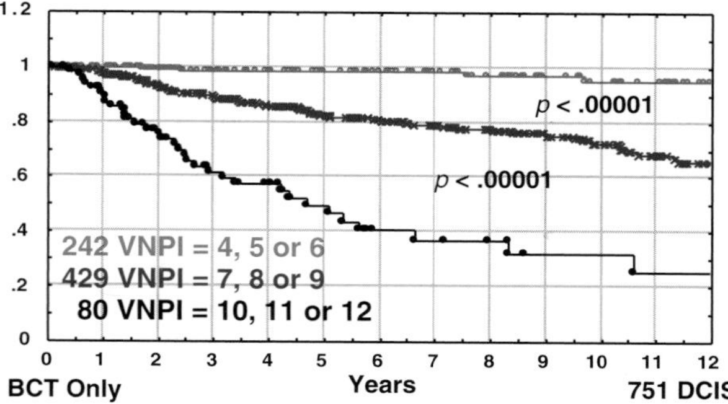

Figure 15–15. Probability of local recurrence-free survival for 751 breast conservation patients grouped by USC/Van Nuys Prognostic Index score (4, 5, or 6 versus 7, 8, or 9 versus 10, 11, or 12). (both $p < .00001$). BCT = breast conserving therapy; DCIS = ductal carcinoma in situ; VNPI = USC/Van Nuys Prognostic Index.

or more margin widths. Narrow margin width was the single most powerful predictor of local failure.

In the current data set presented here, there were 252 patients with margin widths of 10 mm or more, 11 of whom (4.4%) have developed a local recurrence. There was no statistically significant benefit for those who received post-excisional radiation therapy if margins were equal or greater than 10 mm (Figure 15–19).

There were 242 patients with USC/VNPI scores of 4, 5, or 6, four of whom (1.7%) have developed a local recurrence. The USC/VNPI is a better predictor of local recurrence than margin width alone (half as many recurrences), and it should be, since it is based on 5 predictive factors, including margin width. Nevertheless, there are so few recurrences among patients with widely clear margins that for all practical purposes, margin width can be used by itself as a surrogate for the USC/VNPI.

Figures 15–20 to 15–23 evaluate local recurrence by various parameters for patients with 10 mm or more margin widths. Figure 15–20 shows that if widely clear margins are obtained, the presence of comedonecrosis does not significantly increase the local recurrence rate. Figure 15–21 shows that if widely clear margins are obtained, high nuclear grade (grade 3) does not significantly increase the local recurrence rate. Figure 15–22 shows that if widely clear margins are obtained, young age does not significantly increase the local recurrence rate. Figure 15–23 shows that if widely clear margins are obtained, large size may continue to increase the local recurrence rate, although there are too few lesions greater than 40 mm with 10 mm or more margins ($n = 12$) to draw firm conclusions.

Table 15–3. TREATMENT GUIDELINES, USC/VAN NUYS PROGNOSTIC INDEX

USC/VNPI Score	Recommended Treatment
4, 5, or 6	Excision only
7, 8, or 9	Excision + radiation
10, 11, or 12	Mastectomy

USC = University of Southern California

TREATMENT OF THE AXILLA FOR PATIENTS WITH DCIS

In 1986, our group suggested that axillary lymph node dissection be abandoned for DCIS.[100,101] In 1987, the NSABP made axillary node dissection for

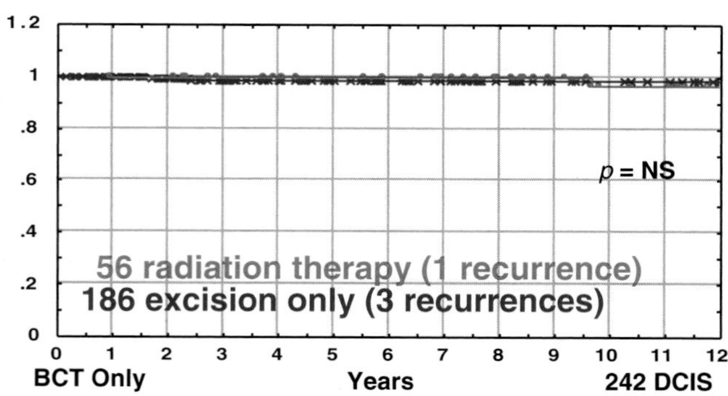

Figure 15–16. Probability of local recurrence-free survival by treatment for 242 breast conservation patients with USC/Van Nuys Prognostic Index scores of 4, 5, or 6 (p = NS). BCT = breast conserving therapy; DCIS = ductal carcinoma in situ; NS = not significant.

patients with DCIS optional, at the discretion of the surgeon. Since that time, we have published a series of papers that continue to show that axillary node dissection is not indicated for patients with DCIS.[8,35,93,102,103] To date, our group had performed a total of 524 node evaluations (310 level 1 and 2 dissections and 214 samplings of 9 nodes or less), 2 of which (0.5%) contained positive nodes by hematoxylin and eosin (H and E) staining. Both those patients were treated with adjuvant chemotherapy as

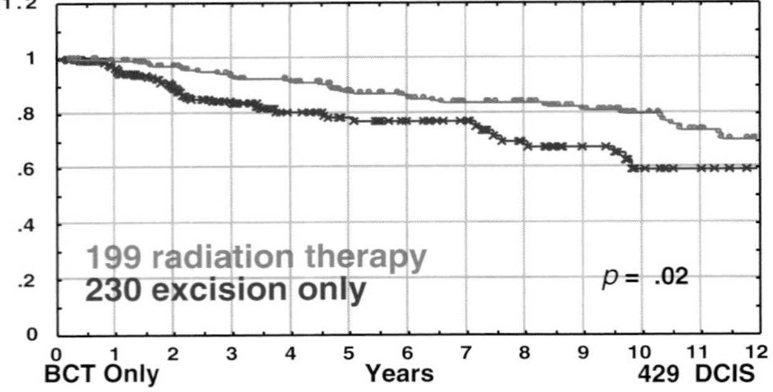

Figure 15–17. Probability of local recurrence-free survival by treatment for 429 breast conservation patients with USC/Van Nuys Prognostic Index scores of 7, 8, or 9 (p = .02). BCT = breast conserving therapy; DCIS = ductal carcinoma in situ.

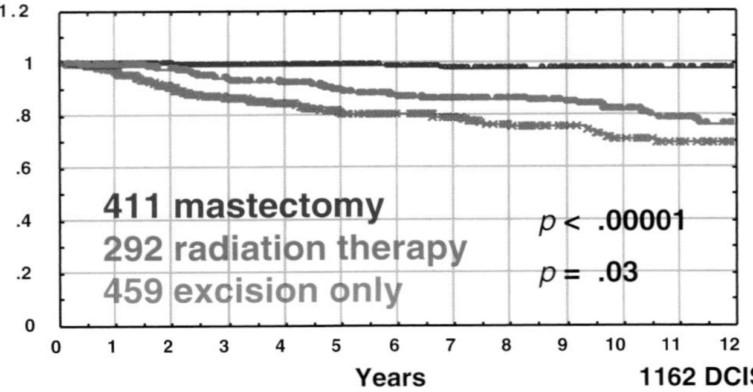

Figure 15–18. Probability of local recurrence-free survival by treatment for 80 breast conservation patients with Modified USC/Van Nuys Prognostic Index scores of 10, 11, or 12 (p = .001). BCT = breast conserving therapy; DCIS = ductal carcinoma in situ.

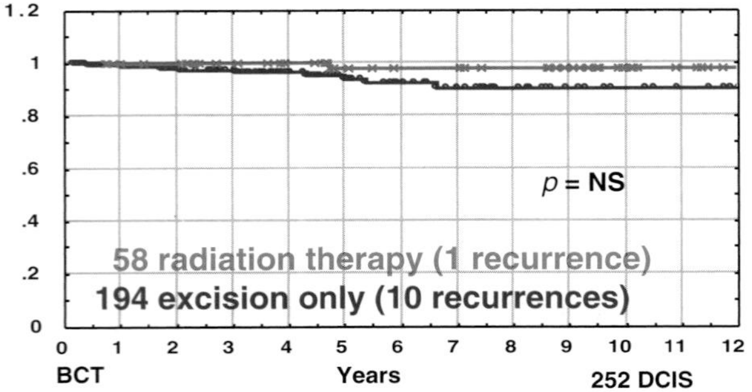

Figure 15–19. Probability of local recurrence-free survival by treatment for 252 breast conservation patients with margins widths ≥ 10 mm (p = NS). BCT = breast conserving therapy; DCIS = ductal carcinoma in situ; NS = not significant.

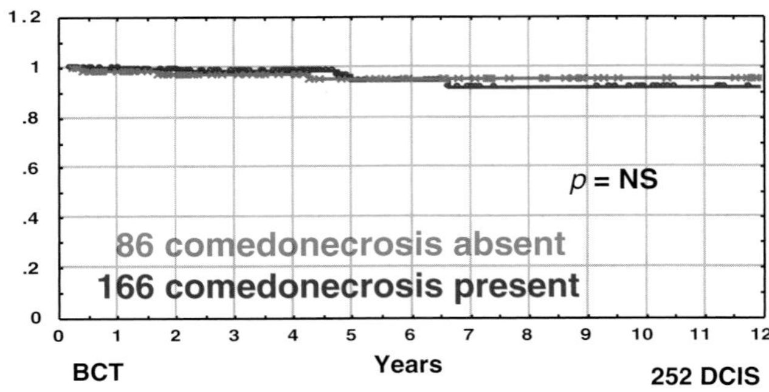

Figure 15–20. Probability of local recurrence-free survival by the presence or absence of comedonecrosis for 252 breast conservation patients with margins widths ≥ 10 mm (p = NS). BCT = breast conserving therapy; DCIS = ductal carcinoma in situ; NS = not significant.

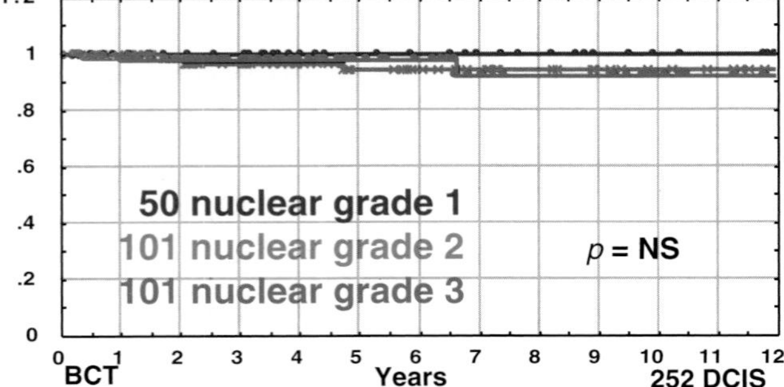

Figure 15–21. Probability of local recurrence-free survival by nuclear grade for 252 breast conservation patients with margins widths ≥ 10 mm (p = NS). BCT = breast conserving therapy; DCIS = ductal carcinoma in situ; NS = not significant.

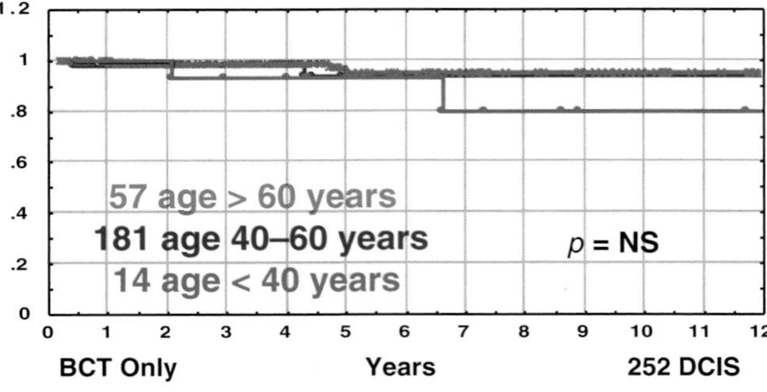

Figure 15–22. Probability of local recurrence-free survival by age 252 breast conservation patients with margins widths ≥ 10 mm (p = NS). BCT = breast conserving therapy; DCIS = ductal carcinoma in situ; NS = not significant.

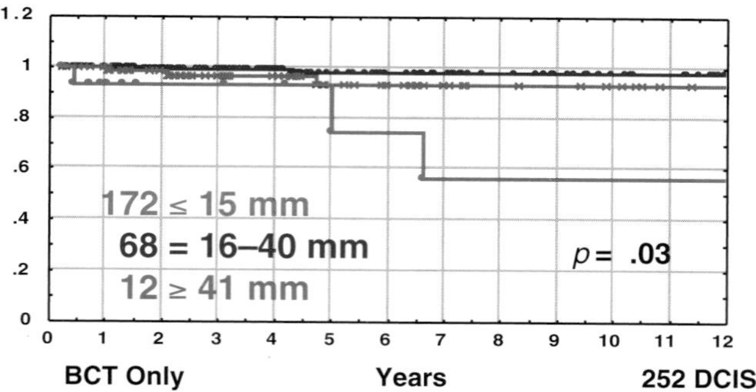

Figure 15–23. Probability of local recurrence-free survival by tumor size for 252 breast conservation patients with margins widths ≥ 10 mm ($p = .03$). BCT = breast conserving therapy; DCIS = ductal carcinoma in situ.

stage II disease. Both were alive and well without local or distant recurrence at 5 and 8 years after their initial surgery (both had mastectomies, and invasive cancer was likely missed during the serial sectioning of their specimens).

Frykberg and colleagues[104] compiled the data of nine studies with a total of 754 DCIS patients. The incidence of axillary lymph node metastasis for patients with DCIS was 1.7%.[104] Despite these low probabilities of nodal positivity, some authors continue to advocate removal of the axillary nodes in patients with palpable or extensive DCIS because of their belief that these patients have a higher risk of occult invasion and positive nodes.[29,55,105]

Sentinel Node Biopsy for DCIS

We have performed 145 sentinel node biopsies for patients with DCIS. All were negative by H and E; 9 (6%) were positive by immunohistochemistry (IHC). In every case, there were only a few positive cells, generally fewer than 10 to 15. In no cases were the patients upstaged to stage II nor were any treated with chemotherapy. All are alive and well without distant recurrence with follow-up ranging from 0.7 to 9 years (average 3.8 years). Not all IHC positive cells are cancer cells. Some may merely be cytokeratin positive debris. Their morphology must be looked at closely.

Our policy for sentinel node biopsy in patients with DCIS is as follows: We perform it in all patients with DCIS who are undergoing a mastectomy. We perform it if the DCIS is an upper outer quadrant lesion, and the sentinel node can be easily removed through the same incision. We also remove a sentinel node if the DCIS is palpable or large (> 4 cm on mammography).

SUMMARY

DCIS is now relatively common, and its frequency is increasing. This is due to an increased use of screening mammography and better detection.

DCIS is the precursor lesion for most invasive breast cancer. But not all microscopic DCIS will progress to invasive cancer. If a patient has DCIS and is not treated, she is more likely to develop an ipsilateral invasive breast cancer than is a woman without DCIS.

Most DCIS detected today will be nonpalpable. It will be detected by mammographic calcifications. It is not uncommon for DCIS to be larger than expected by mammography, to involve more than a quadrant of the breast, and to be unicentric in its distribution.

Preoperative evaluation should include film-screen mammography with magnification and ultrasonography. MRI is becoming increasingly more popular. The surgeon and the radiologist should plan the excision procedure carefully. The first attempt at excision is the best chance to get a complete excision with a good cosmetic result.

Reexcisions often yield poor cosmetic results and the overall plan should be to avoid them whenever possible. In light of this, the initial breast biopsy should be an image-guided biopsy, not an open surgical breast biopsy.

After the establishment of the diagnosis, the patient should be counseled. If she is motivated for breast conservation, the surgeon and radiologist should plan the procedure carefully, using multiple wires to map out the extent of the lesion

When considering the entire population of patients with DCIS without subset analyses, the prospective randomized trials have shown that postexcisional radiation therapy can reduce the relative risk of local recurrence by about 50% for conservatively treated patients. But in some low-risk DCIS patients, the costs may outweigh the potential benefits. In spite of a relative 50% reduction in the probability of local recurrence, the absolute reduction may be only a few percentage points. Although local recurrence is extremely important, breast cancer-specific survival is the most important end point for all patients with breast cancer, including patients with DCIS, and no DCIS trial has ever shown a survival benefit for radiation therapy when compared with excision alone. Additionally, radiation therapy is not without financial and physical cost. Therefore, in recent years, an increasing number of selected patients with DCIS have been treated with excision alone.

The USC/VNPI uses five independent predictors to predict the probability of local recurrence after conservative treatment for DCIS. These include tumor size, margin width, nuclear grade, age, and the presence or absence of comedonecrosis. In combination, they can be used as an aid to identify subgroups of patients with extremely low probabilities of local recurrence after excision alone, for example, patients who score 4, 5, or 6 using the USC/VNPI. If size cannot be accurately determined, margin width by itself can be used as a surrogate for the USC/VNPI, although it is not quite as good.

New oncoplastic techniques that allow for more extensive excisions can be used to achieve both acceptable cosmesis and widely clear margins, alleviating the need for radiation therapy in many cases.

The decision to use excision alone as treatment for DCIS should be made only if complete and sequential tissue processing has been used and the patient has been fully informed and has participated in the treatment decision-making process.

REFERENCES

1. Jemal AM, Taylor, Samuels A, et al. Cancer Statistics, 2003. CA Cancer J Clin 2003;53:5–26.
2. Burstein HJ, Polyak K, Wong JS, et al. Ductal carcinoma in situ of the breast. N Engl J Med 2004;350:1430–41.
3. Page D, Anderson T. Diagnostic histopathology of the breast. New York: Churchill Livingstone; 1987. p. 157–74.
4. Patchefsky A, Schwartz G, Finkelstein S, et al. Heterogeneity of intraductal carcinoma of the breast. Cancer 1989;63:731–41.
5. Nemoto T, Vana J, Bedwani R, et al. Management and survival of female breast cancer: results of a national survey by The American College of Surgeons. Cancer 1980;45:2917–24.
6. Jemal A, Tiwari R, Murray T, et al. Cancer Statistics, 2004. CA Cancer J Clin 2004;54:8–29.
7. Lagios MD. Duct carcinoma in situ: pathology and treatment. Surg Clin North Am 1990;70:853–71.
8. Silverstein MJ, Cohlan B, Gierson E, et al. Duct carcinoma in situ: 227 cases without microinvasion. Eur J Cancer 1992;28:630–4.
9. Duffy SW, Tabar L, Smith RA. Screening for breast cancer with mammography. Lancet 2001;358:2166; author reply 2167–8.
10. Tabar L, Smith RA, Vitak B, et al. Mammographic screening: a key factor in the control of breast cancer. Cancer J 2003;9:15–27.
11. Ashikari R, Hadju S, Robbins G. Intraductal carcinoma of the breast. Cancer 1971;28:1182–7.
12. Baxter N, Virnig B, Durham S, et al. Trends in the treatment of ductal carcinoma in situ of the breast. J Natl Cancer Inst 2004;96:443–48.
13. Veronesi U, Saccozzi R, Del Vecchio M, et al. Comparing radical mastectomy with quadrantectomy, axillary dissection and radiotherapy in patients with small cancers of the breast. N Engl J Med 1981;305:6–10.
14. Fisher B, Bauer M, Margolese R, et al. Five-year results of a randomized clinical trial comparing total mastectomy and lumpectomy with or without radiation therapy in the treatment of breast cancer. N Eng J Med 1985;312: 665–73.
15. Fisher B, Redmond C, Poisson R, et al. Eight-year results of a randomized clinical trial comparing total mastectomy and lumpectomy with or without radiation therapy in the treatment of breast cancer. N Eng J Med 1989;320:822–8.
16. Veronesi U, Banfi A, Salvadori B, et al. Breast conservation is the treatment of choice in small breast cancer: Long-term results of a randomized trial. Eur J Cancer 1990; 26:668–70.
17. Tavassoli F. Intraductal carcinoma. In: Tavassoli, FA, editor. Pathology of the breast. Norwalk, CT: Appleton and Lange; 1992. p. 229–61.
18. Aasmundstad T, Haugen O. DNA ploidy in intraductal breast carcinomas. Eur J Cancer 1992;26:956–9.
19. Meyer J. Cell kinetics in selection and stratification of patients for adjuvant therapy of breast carcinoma. Nat Cancer Inst Mono 1986;1:25–8.
20. Allred D, Clark G, Molina R, et al. Overexpression of HER-2/neu and its relationship with other prognostic factors change during the progression of in situ to invasive breast cancer. Hum Pathol 1992;23:974–9.
21. Liu E, Thor A, He M, et al. The HER2 (c-erbB-2) oncogene is frequently amplified in in situ carcinomas of the breast. Oncogene 1992;7:1027–32.
22. Barnes D, Meyer J, Gonzalez J, et al. Relationship between c-erbB-2 immunoreactivity and thymidine labelling index in breast carcinoma in situ. Breast Cancer Res Treat 1991;18:11–7.
23. Bartkova J, Barnes D, Millis R, et al. Immunhistochemical demonstration of c-erbB-2 protein in mammary ductal carcinoma in situ. Hum Pathol 1990;21:1164–7.
24. Bobrow L, Happerfield L, Gregory W, et al. The classification of ductal carcinoma in situ and its association with biological markers. Semi Diagn Pathol 1994;11:199–207.
25. van de Vijver M, Peterse J, Mooi WJ, et al. Neu-protein overexpression in breast cancer: association with comedo-

type ductal carcinoma in situ and limited prognostic value in stage II breast cancer. N Engl J Med 1988;319: 1239–45.

26. Lagios M, Margolin F, Westdahl P, et al. Mammographically detected duct carcinoma in situ. Frequency of local recurrence following tylectomy and prognostic effect of nuclear grade on local recurrence. Cancer 1989;63:619–24.
27. Silverstein MJ. Intraductal breast carcinoma: two decades of progress? Am J Clin Oncol 1991;14:534–7.
28. Solin L, Yeh I, Kurtz J, et al. Ductal carcinoma in situ (intraductal carcinoma) of the breast treated with breast-conserving surgery and definitive irradiation. Correlation of pathologic parameters with outcome of treatment. Cancer 1993;71:2532–42.
29. Schwartz G, Finkel G, Carcia J, et al. Subclinical ductal carcinoma in situ of the breast: treatment by local excision and surveillance alone. Cancer 1992;70:2468–74.
30. Holland R, Peterse J, Millis R, et al. Ductal carcinoma in situ: A proposal for a new classification. Semin Diag Pathol 1994;11:167–80.
31. Silverstein MJ, Poller D, Waisman J, et al. Prognostic classification of breast ductal carcinoma-in-situ. Lancet 1995;345:1154–7.
32. Lagios M, Westdahl P, Margolin F, et al. Duct carcinoma in situ: Relationship of extent of noninvasive disease to the frequency of occult invasion, multicentricity, lymph node metastases, and short-term treatment failures. Cancer 1982;50:1309–14.
33. Morrow M, Schnitt S, Harris J. Ductal carcinoma in situ. In: Harris J, Lippman ME, Morrow M et al, editors. Diseases of the breast. Philadelphia – New York: Lippincott-Raven; 1995. p. 355–68.
34. Holland R, Hendriks J. Microcalcifications associated with ductal carcinoma in situ: mammographic-pathologic correlation. Semin Diag Pathol 1994;11:181–92.
35. Silverstein MJ, Waisman J, Gierson E, et al. Radiation therapy for intraductal carcinoma: is it an equal alternative? Arch Surg 1991;126:424–8.
36. Poller D, Silverstein M, Galea M, et al. Ductal carcinoma in situ of the breast: a proposal for a new simplified histological classification association between cellular proliferation and c-erbB-2 protein expression. Mod Pathol 1994;7:257–62.
37. Bellamy C, McDonald C, Salter D, et al. Noninvasive ductal carcinoma of the breast: the relevance of histologic categorization. Hum Pathol 1993;24:16–23.
38. Sloane J, Ellman R, Anderson T, et al. Consistency of histopathological reporting of breast lesions detected by breast screening: Findings of the UK national external quality assessment (EQA) scheme. Eur J Cancer 1994; 10:1414–19.
39. Radford DM, Phillips NJ, Fair KL, et al. Allelic loss and the progression of breast cancer. Cancer Res 1995;55:5180–3.
40. Stratton M, Collins N, Lakhani S, et al. Loss of heterozygosity in ductal carcinoma in situ of the breast. J Pathol 1995;175:195–201.
41. O'Connell P, Pekkel V, Fuqua S, et al. Analysis of loss of heterozygosity in 399 premalignant breast lesions at 15 genetic loci. J Natl Cancer Inst 1998;90:697–703.
42. Farabegoli F, Champeme M, Bieche I, et al. Genetic pathways in the evolution of breast ductal carcinoma in situ. J Pathol 2002;196:280–6.
43. Damiani S, Ludvikova M, Tomasic G, et al. Myoepithelial cells and basal lamina in poorly differentiated in situ duct carcinoma of the breast: an immunocytochemical study. Virchows Arch 1999;434:227–34.
44. Guidi A, Schnitt S, Fischer L, et al. Vascular permeability factor (vascular endothelial growth factor) expression and angiogenesis in patients with ductal carcinoma in situ of the breast. Cancer 1997;80:1945–53.
45. Guidi A, Fischer L, Harris J, et al. Microvessel density and distribution of ductal carcinoma in situ of the breast. J Natl Cancer Inst 1994;86:614–9.
46. Allred D. Biologic characteristics of ductal carcinoma in situ. In: Silverstein, MJ, Lagios, M, Recht A, editors. Ductal carcinoma in situ of the breast. 2nd ed. Philadelphia: Lippincott Williams & Wilkins; 2002. p. 37–48.
47. Nielson M, Thomsen J, Primdahl S, et al. Breast cancer and atypia among young and middle-aged women; A study of 110 medicolegal autopsies. Br J Cancer 1987 1987;56: 814–9.
48. Page D, Dupont W, Roger L, et al. Intraductal carcinoma of the breast: Follow-up after biopsy only. Cancer 1982;49: 751–8.
49. Rosen P, Braun D, Kinne D. The clinical significance of pre-invasive breast carcinoma. Cancer 1980:46: 919–25.
50. Page D, Rogers L, Schuyler P, et al. The natural history of ductal carcinoma in situ of the breast. In: Silverstein MJ, Recht A, Lagios M, editors. Ductal Carcinoma in Situ of the Breast. Philadelphia: Lippincott, Williams and Wilkins; 2002. p. 17–21.
51. Alpers C, Wellings S. The prevalence of carcinoma in situ in normal and cancer-associated breast. Hum Pathol 1985;16:796–807.
52. Page D, Dupont W, Rogers L, et al. Continued local recurrence of carcinoma 15-25 years after a diagnosis of low grade ductal carcinoma in situ of the breast treated only by biopsy. Cancer 1995;76:1197–1200.
53. AJCC Cancer Staging Handbook 6th ed. American Joint Committee on Cancer. Chicago, Il: p. 257–81.
54. Schuh M, Nemoto T, Penetrante R, et al. Intraductal carcinoma: analysis of presentation, pathologic findings, and outcome of disease. Arch Surg 1986;121:1303–7.
55. Gump F, Jicha D, Ozzello L. Ductal carcinoma in situ (DCIS): A revised concept. Surgery 1987;102:190–5.
56. Tabar L, Chen HH, Duffy SW, et al. A novel method for prediction of long-term outcome of women with T1a, T1b, and 10-14 mm invasive breast cancers: a prospective study. Lancet 2000:355:429–33.
57. Fisher E, Sass R, Fisher B, et al. Pathologic findings from the National Surgical Adjuvant Breast Project (Protocol 6) Intraductal carcinoma (DCIS). Cancer 1986;57: 197–208.
58. Schwartz G, Patchefsky A, Finkelstein S, et al. Nonpalpable in situ ductal carcinoma of the breast. Arch Surg 1989; 124:29–32.
59. Rosen P, Senie R, Schottenfeld D, et al. Noninvasive breast carcinoma: Frequency of unsuspected invasion and implications for treatment. Ann Surg 1979;1989:377–82.

60. Simpson T, Thirlby R, Dail D. Surgical treatment of ductal carcinoma in situ of the breast: 10 to 20 year follow-up. Arch Surg 1992;127:468–72.
61. Holland R, Hendriks J, Verbeek A, et al. Extent, distribution, and mammographic/histological correlations of breast ductal carcinoma in situ. Lancet 1990;335:519–22.
62. Holland R, Faverly D. Whole organ studies. In: Silverstein M, editor. Ductal carcinoma in situ of the breast. Baltimore: Williams and Wilkins; 1997. p. 233–40.
63. Holland R, Faverly D. Whole organ studies. In: Silverstein MJ, Recht A, Malios M, editors. Ductal carcinoma in situ of the breast. Philadelphia: Lippincott, Williams and Wilkins; 2002. [In press].
64. Noguchi S, Aihara T, Koyama H, et al. Discrimination between multicentric and multifocal carcinomas of breast through clonal analysis. Cancer 1994;74:872–7.
65. Faverly D, Burgers L, Bult P, et al. Three dimensional imaging of mammary ductal carcinoma is situ: Clinical implications. Semin Diag Pathol 1994;11:193–8.
66. Tabar L, Dean P. Basic principles of mammographic diagnosis. Diagn Imag Clin Med 1985;54:146–57.
67. Fentiman I, Fagg N, Millis R, et al. In situ ductal carcinoma of the breast: Implications of disease pattern and treatment. Eur J Surg Oncol 1986;12:261–6.
68. Fisher B, Costantino J, Redmond C, et al. Lumpectomy compared with lumpectomy and radiation therapy for the treatment of intraductal breast cancer. N Engl J Med 1993;328:1581–6.
69. Fisher B, Land S, Mamounas E, et al. Prevention of invasive breast cancer in women with ductal carcinoma in situ: an update of the National Surgical Adjuvant Breast and Bowel Project Experience. Semin Oncol 2001;28:400–18.
70. Silverstein MJ, Lagios M, Martino S, et al. Outcome after local recurrence in patients with ductal carcinoma in situ of the breast. J Clin Oncol 1998;16:1367–73.
71. Silverstein MJ, Waisman J. Outcome after invasive local recurrence in patients with ductal carcinoma in situ of the breast. In: Silverstein MJ, Recht A, Lagios M, editors. Ductal carcinoma in situ of the breast. Philadelphia: Lippincott, Williams and Wilkins; 2002. p. 545–53.
72. Romero L, Klein L, Ye W, et al. Outcome after invasive recurrence in patients with ductal carcinoma in situ of the breast. Am J Surg 2004;188:371–6.
73. Swain S. Ductal carcinoma in situ—incidence, presentation and guidelines to treatment. Oncology 1989;3:25–42.
74. Fisher B, Dignam J, Wolmark N, et al. Tamoxifen in treatment of intraductal breast cancer: National Surgical Adjuvant Breast and Bowel Project B-24 randomized controlled trial. Lancet 1999;353:1993–2000.
75. Fisher B, Dignam J, Wolmark N, et al. Findings from National Surgical Adjuvant Breast and Bowel Project B-17. J Clin Oncol 1998;16:441–52.
76. Fisher B, Dignam J, Wolmark N, et al. Lumpectomy and radiation therapy for the treatment of intraductal breast cancer: findings from National Surgical Adjuvant Breast and Bowel Project B-17. J Clin Oncol 1998;16:441–52.
77. George W, Houghton J, Cuzick J, et al. Radiotherapy and tamoxifen following complete local excision (CLE) in the management of ductal carcinoma in situ (DCIS): preliminary results from the UK DCIS trial. Proc Am Soc Clin Oncol 2000;19:70A.
78. Houghton J, George W. Radiotherapy and tamoxifen following complete excision of ductal carcinoma in situ of the breast. In: Silverstein MJ, Recht A, Lagios M, editors. Ductal carcinoma in situ of the breast. Philadelphia: Lippincott, Williams and Wilkins; 2002. p. 453–8.
79. Julien J, Bijker N, Fentiman I, et al. Radiotherapy in breast conserving treatment for ductal carcinoma in situ: first results of EORTC randomized phase III trial 10853. Lancet 2000;355:528–33.
80. UK Coordinating Committee on Cancer Research (UKCCCR) Ductal Carcinoma in Situ (DCIS) Working Party, Radiotherapy and tamoxifen in women with completely excised ductal carcinoma in situ of the breast in the UK, Australia, and New Zealand: randomised controlled trial. Lancet 2003;362:95–102.
81. Zafrani B, Leroyer S, Fourquet S, et al. Mammographically detected ductal in situ carcinoma of the breast analyzed with a new classification. A study of 127 cases: correlation with estrogen and progesterone receptors, *p53* and c-erbB-2 proteins, and proliferative activity. Semin Diagn Pathol 1994;11:208–14.
82. Schwartz G. The role of excision and surveillance alone in subclinical DCIS of the breast. Oncology 1994;8:21–6.
83. Schwartz G. Treatment of subclinical ductal carcinoma in situ of the breast by local excision and surveillance: An updated personal experience. In: Silverstein MJ, Recht A, Lagios M, editors. Ductal carcinoma in situ of the breast. Philadelphia: Lippincott, Williams and Wilkins; 2002. p. 308–21.
84. Page D, Dupont W, Roger L, et al. Atypical hyperplastic lesions of the female breast. A long-term follow-up study. Cancer 1985;55:2698–708.
85. Lagios M. Controversies in diagnosis, biology, and treatment. Breast J 1995;1:68–78.
86. Bijker N, Peterse J, Duchateau L, et al. Risk factors for recurrence and metastasis after breast-conserving therapy for ductal carcinoma in situ: Analysis of European Organization for Research and Treatment of Cancer Trial 10853. J Clin Oncol 2001;19:2263–71.
87. Fisher E, Constantino J, Fisher B, et al. Pathologic findings from the National Surgical Adjuvant Breast Project (NSABP) Protocol B-17. Cancer 1995;75:1310–9.
88. Fisher E, Lemming R, Andersen S, et al. Conservative management of intraductal carcinoma (DCIS) of the breast. J Surg Oncol 1991;47:139–47.
89. Recht A. Randomized trial overview. In: Silverstein M, editor. Ductal carcinoma in situ of the breast. Baltimore: Williams and Wilkins; 1997. p. 463–7.
90. Allred D, Bryant J, Land S, et al. Estrogen receptor expression as a predictive marker of effectiveness of tamoxifen in the treatment of DCIS: Findings from NSABP Protocol B-24. Breast Cancer Res Treat 2003;76(suppl 1):36.
91. Recht A. Side effects of radiation therapy. In: Silverstein M, editor. Ductal carcinoma in situ of the breast. Baltimore: Williams and Wilkins; 1997. p. 347–52.
92. Adams M, Lipshultz S, Schwartz C, et al. Radiation-associated cardiovascular disease: manifestations and management. Semin Radiat Oncol 2003;13:346–56.

93. Silverstein MJ, Barth A, Poller D, et al. Ten-year results comparing mastectomy to excision and radiation therapy for ductal carcinoma in situ of the breast [abstract]. Eur J Cancer 1995;31:1425–7.
94. Silverstein MJ, Lagios M, Groshen S, et al. The influence of margin width on local control in patients with ductal carcinoma in situ (DCIS) of the breast. N Engl J Med 1999; 340:1455–61.
95. Ottesen G, Graversen H, Blichert-Toft M, et al. Ductal carcinoma in situ of the female breast. Short-term results of a prospective nationwide study. Am J Surg Pathol 1992; 16:1183–96.
96. Silverstein MJ, Lagios M, Craig P, et al. The Van Nuys Prognostic Index for Ductal Carcinoma in Situ. Breast J 1996; 2:38–40.
97. Silverstein MJ, Poller D, Craig P, et al. A prognostic index for ductal carcinoma in situ of the breast. Cancer 1996; 77:2267–74.
98. Silverstein MJ. The Van Nuys/USC experience by treatment. In: Silverstein MJ, Recht A, Lagios M, editors. Ductal carcinoma in situ of the breast. Philadelphia: Lippincott, Williams and Wilkins; 2002. p. 337–42.
99. Poller D, Silverstein MJ. The Van Nuys ductal carcinoma in situ: An update. In: Silverstein MJ, Recht A, Lagios M, editors. Ductal carcinoma in situ of the breast. 2002, Philadelphia: Lippincott, Williams and Wilkins; 2002. p. 222–33.
100. Silverstein MJ, Rosser R, Gierson E, et al. Axillary lymph node dissection for intraductal carcinoma—is it indicated? Cancer 1987;59:1819–24.
101. Silverstein MJ, Rosser R, Gierson E, et al. Axillary lymph node dissection for intraductal carcinoma—is it indicated? Proc Am Soc Clin Oncol 1986;5:265.
102. Silverstein MJ, Gierson E, Colburn W, et al. Can intraductal breast carcinoma be excised completely by local excision? Clinical and pathologic predictors. Cancer 1994; 73:2985–9.
103. Silverstein MJ. Noninvasive breast cancer: The dilemma of the 1990s. Obstet Gynecol Clin North Am 1994;21: 639–58.
104. Frykberg E, Masood S, Copeland E, et al. Duct carcinoma in situ of the breast. Surg Gynecol Obstet 1993;177:425–40.
105. Balch C, Singletary E, Bland K. Clinical decision-making in early breast cancer. Ann Surg 1993;217:207–22.

16

Oncoplastic Surgery of the Breast

NEAL HANDEL
MELVIN J. SILVERSTEIN

ONCOPLASTIC SURGERY

In recent years, there has been growing emphasis on minimizing the disfigurement associated with the treatment of breast cancer. This trend has manifested in three major areas: increased popularity of breast conservation therapy, development of techniques to reduce deformity following lumpectomy and segmentectomy, and major advances in post-mastectomy reconstruction. As a result of the emphasis on preserving a normal-appearing breast, the role of the plastic surgeon in treating breast cancer patients has greatly expanded. In fact, the emergence of a new discipline, where the interests of the oncologic surgeon and the plastic surgeon overlap, has evolved into what is now labeled "oncoplastic surgery." This term refers to application of the principles and techniques of plastic surgery to the challenges of treating cancer patients. This chapter will outline the role of oncoplastic surgery in the diagnosis and management of women with carcinoma of the breast. This approach, which generally requires coordination of the oncologic surgeon with a pathologist, a radiologist, and a plastic surgeon, is rapidly growing in popularity.

During the last 20 years, we have developed a comprehensive oncoplastic strategy for managing breast cancer.[1] With this approach, it is usually possible to widely excise tumors while maintaining good cosmetic results. Because larger cancers can be excised without deforming the breast, greater numbers of women can be treated with breast conservation surgery.[2] In individuals who require mastectomy, immediate breast reconstruction can be offered in nearly all cases. In our hands, these techniques evolved mainly from the treatment of women with ductal carcinoma in situ (DCIS), but the exact same principles apply to patients with invasive cancers.

Oncoplastic Considerations in Lumpectomy

DCIS generally involves a single breast segment and is distributed radially. Serial subgross whole organ sectioning suggests that when margin widths exceed 10 mm, the likelihood of residual disease is small.[3] With these facts in mind, the goal in cases of biopsy-proven DCIS is to widely excise the entire involved ductal unit in radial fashion and achieve the best possible cosmetic result. DCIS is the precursor lesion to invasive breast cancer, and most invasive cancers have a DCIS component that can be found by careful microscopic examination of the specimen. This is the rationale for our use of a similar approach for both invasive breast cancer and DCIS.

Oncoplastic resection is a therapeutic procedure, not a breast biopsy. It is performed on patients with a proven diagnosis of breast cancer. The goal is to perform a definitive procedure in one operation. Whenever possible, the initial breast biopsy should be made using a minimally invasive percutaneous technique. This usually provides ample tissue for diagnosis; the rate of upgrading of DCIS to invasive breast cancer is low (around 10 to 15%), and the core biopsy site so small that it can be closed simply with a Steri-strip (3M Corp. St. Paul, MN).

When excising either in situ or invasive tumors, the surgeon faces two conflicting goals: clear margins versus an acceptable cosmetic result. Oncologic principles dictate that the largest possible specimen should be removed to achieve the widest margins. From a cosmetic standpoint, it is desirable to remove the smallest amount of tissue. The initial attempt to resect a malignant lesion is critical as it offers the best chance to remove the entire lesion in one piece, evaluate its margins, and achieve a good cosmetic result. Since more than 90% of currently diagnosed DCIS lesions are nonpalpable and nonvisualizable, the surgeon is usually operating "blindly." Multiple hooked wires can help delineate the radiographic extent of the lesion (Figure 16–1). Using bracketing wires, the surgeon should make an attempt to excise the entire lesion within a single piece of tissue. This should include overlying skin as well as pectoral fascia (Figure 16–2). The excised specimen should be carefully oriented for the pathologist. To facilitate this, we routinely label the specimen with Margin Map (Figure 16–3) (Beekley Corporation, Boston, MA). If the specimen is removed piecemeal, it is difficult to accurately evaluate size and tumor margins.

Complete excision of DCIS or invasive cancer with a DCIS component should not be attempted using a single guide wire; this can lead to incomplete resection and necessitate re-excision of the biopsy cavity. Whereas the bracketing wire technique does not guarantee complete removal, it increases the likelihood. Incomplete excision is more likely when the mammographic abnormality does not correlate with the full dimensions of the lesion. This is more frequent with low-grade than high-grade tumors. Failure to perform specimen radiography in every wire-directed case may also lead to incomplete removal, since the surgeon lacks immediate feedback regarding the adequacy of resection.

The radial nature of DCIS should be kept in mind when planning the skin incision. A curvilinear incision in the natural lines of the breast, which is very popular, often does not work in these cases

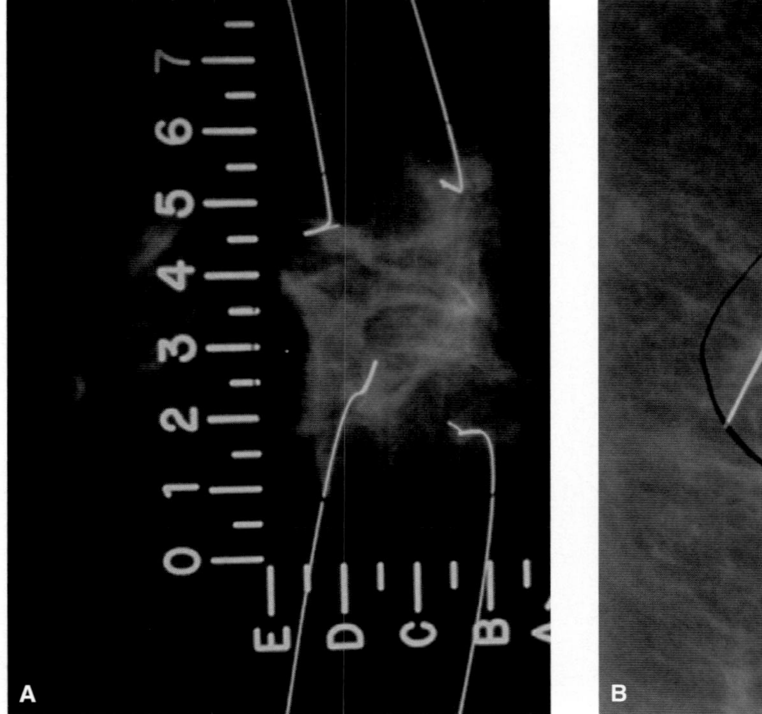

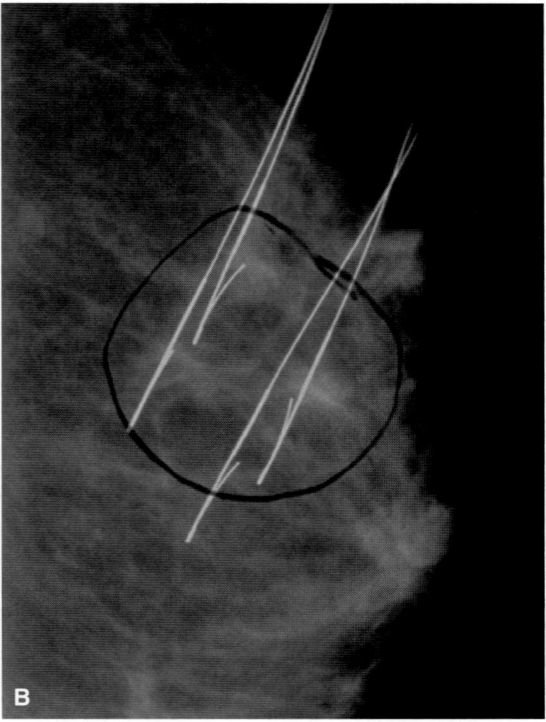

Figure 16–1. *A,* craniocaudal and *B,* mediolateral views of 4 hooked wires bracketing an area of architectural distortion; final pathology revealed low-grade micropapillary ductal carcinoma in situ.

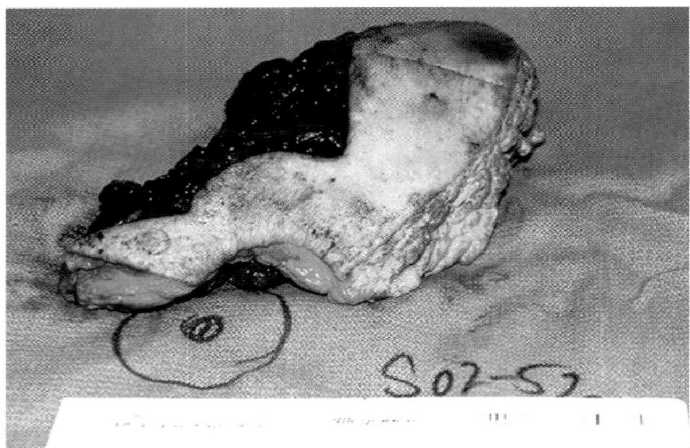

Figure 16–2. A color-coded specimen from a hemi-batwing excision; skin, full-thickness breast, and pectoral fascia have been removed in continuity.

because DCIS usually extends radially toward the nipple. A variety of oncoplastic excisions can be designed to take advantage of the radial distribution of DCIS (Figure 16–4).

All segmental resections should be closed in layers and drained for 24 to 48 hours. Wounds heal best when the least amount of serum and blood is present. During wound closure, the cosmetic result should be constantly monitored and reappraised. Whereas radial segmental resection may slightly alter the size and shape of the breast, good cosmetic results are generally achieved (Figure 16–5). A radial excision will not displace the nipple areola complex even though overlying skin is removed.

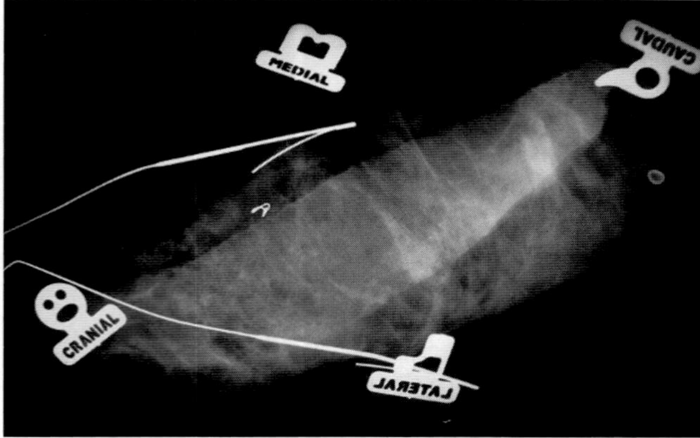

Figure 16–3. Specimen radiograph of a 2-wire directed excision. The microclip marking the area of the stereotactic biopsy can be seen. The specimen is oriented with the Margin Map (Beekley Corporation, Boston, MA). The medial, lateral, superior, and inferior margins are marked. A large piece of overlying skin has been removed and can be seen on the x-ray.

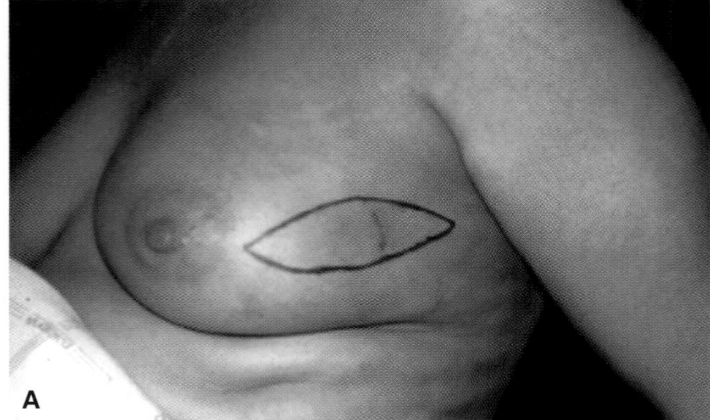

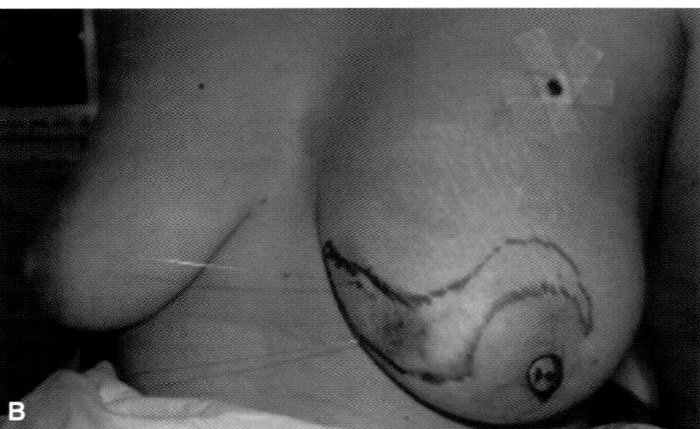

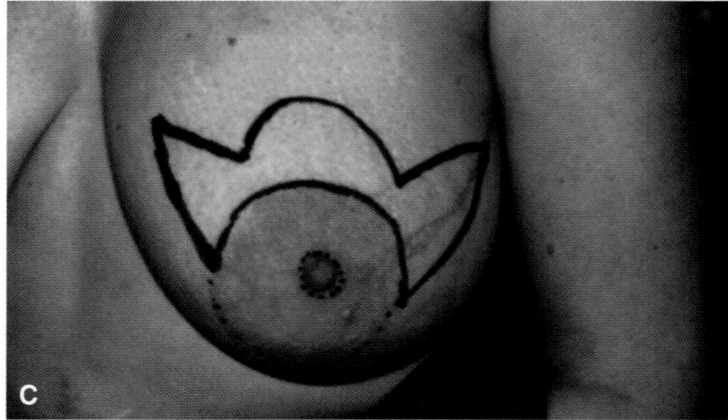

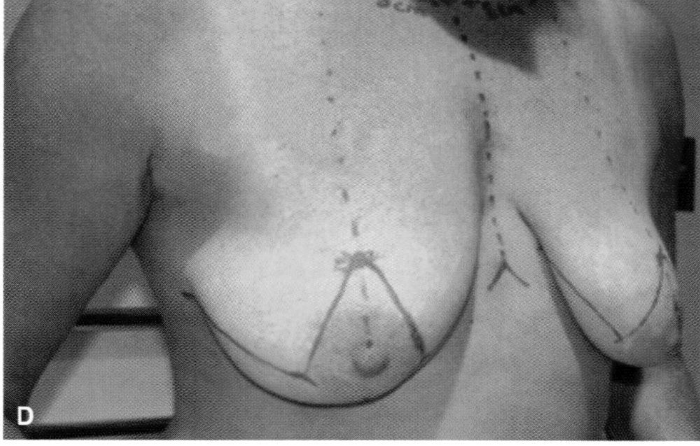

Figure 16–4. Four different oncoplastic incisions: *A,* radial; *B,* hemi-batwing; *C,* standard batwing; *D,* conventional reduction (Wise pattern).

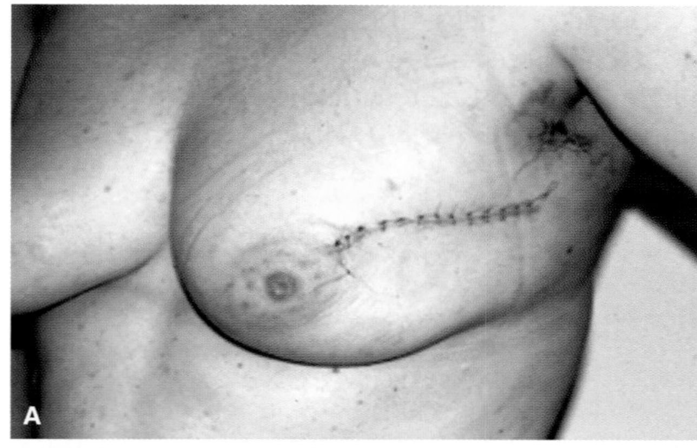

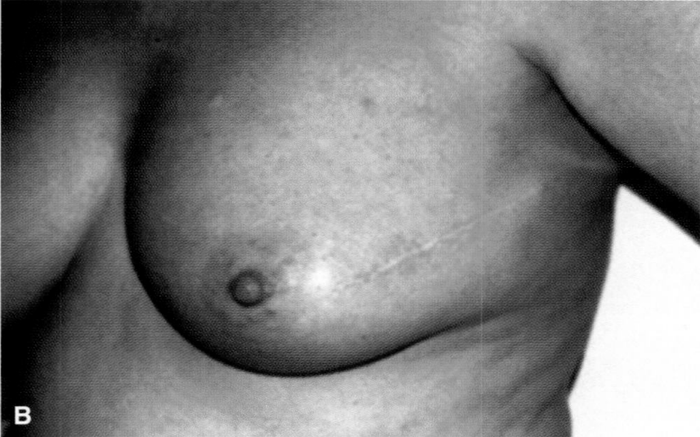

Figure 16–5. Typical results of radial excisions: *A,* a patient 3-days post radial excision and sentinel node biopsy; skin sutures still in place; *B,* a patient more than 1-year post radial excision of a breast lesion, scar is barely visible, no significant change in breast shape.

Segmentectomy Using Various Mammaplasty Incisions

By creatively employing the skin incisions used by plastic surgeons for mastopexy and breast reduction, it is possible in many cases to resect significant amounts of breast tissue while maintaining a desirable breast appearance.

For lesions in the lower hemisphere of the breast, a standard (Wise pattern or "keyhole") reduction incision can be used. This allows access to lesions of the inferior pole of the breast anywhere from the 3 o'clock to the 9 o'clock position. Large amounts of breast tissue can be removed with excellent cosmetic results; wide margins can generally be achieved.

If the lesion is in the upper pole of the breast, along the median axis, and not too far above the nipple, a crescent mastopexy skin incision can be used to resect the tumor, while preserving the appearance of the breast (Figure 16–6). This will elevate the nipple, so contralateral surgery may be indicated for symmetry.

For lesions in the upper hemisphere that are large or off the midline, batwing or hemi-batwing excisions can be used (Figure 16–7). Both of these patterns enable the lesion to be generously removed (specimens often weigh 200 grams or more), while allowing recontouring of the breast in a desirable fashion. When using batwing or hemi-batwing excisions, the nipple is raised. Often these patients present with some degree of breast ptosis, and raising the nipple actually improves the cosmetic appearance of the breast. Figure 16–8 shows a patient with bilateral DCIS that was excised using bilateral hemi-batwing excisions. Wide margins were obtained on

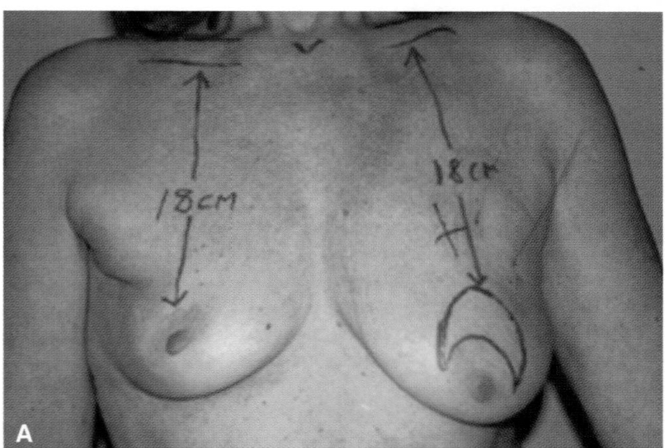

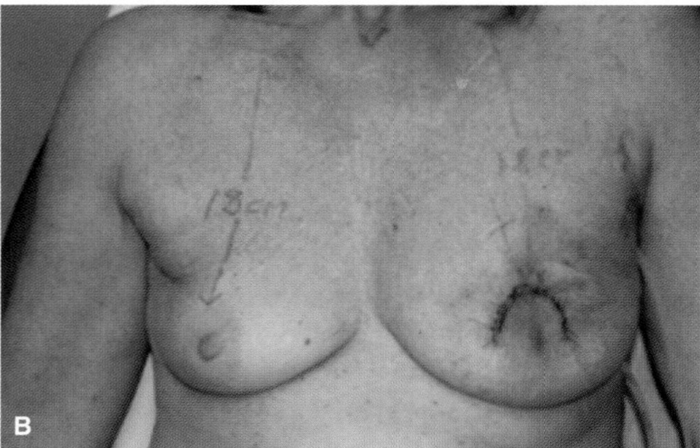

Figure 16–6. *A,* Preoperative crescent mastopexy excision plan for a patient with a lesion in the 12 o'clock position of the left breast. Two guide wires mark the lesion. This is an ideal approach for this patient because the right breast is smaller than the left side owing to previous conservation therapy for breast cancer. *B,* 1-day postoperative, the breasts are symmetrical and the cancer has been excised with clear margins.

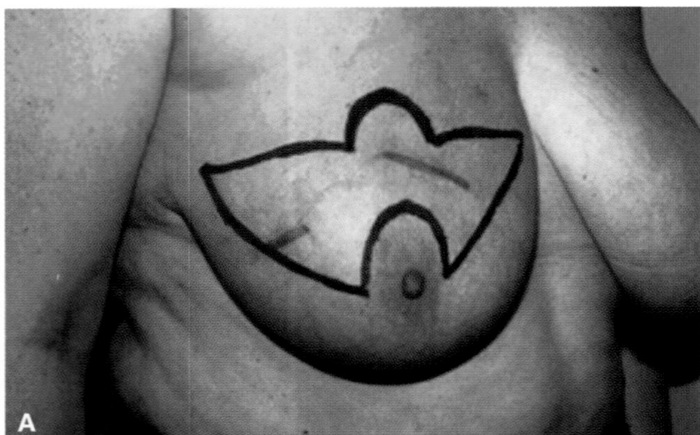

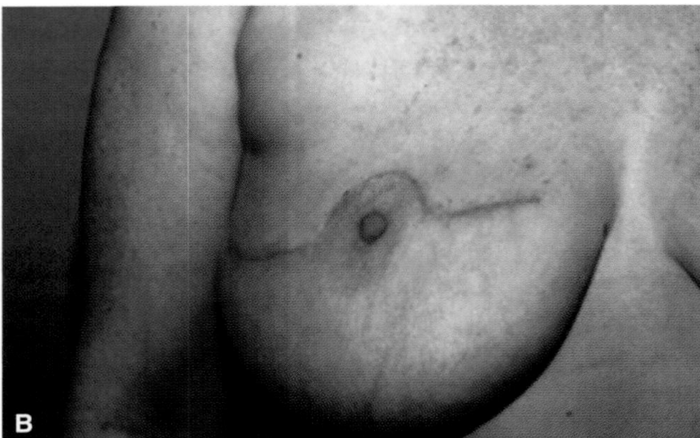

Figure 16–7. *A,* typical batwing excision plan. This skin pattern can be used in any patient with a medium- to large-sized breast. The wings of the excision are designed to allow removal of lesions anywhere from the 8 to 4 o-clock position (clockwise); *B,* result of batwing excision 1 month postoperatively.

both sides, and the shape of the breast was actually improved following tumor removal.

Another approach that can be adapted to resection of large lesions of the upper pole is the short-scar periareolar-inferior pedicle reduction (SPAIR) mammaplasty.[4] This technique relies on an inferior pedicle to provide blood supply to the nipple areola complex coupled with periareolar and vertical skin excision to reduce the skin envelope. Relatively large amounts of tissue can be resected from the upper half of the breast, and redundant tissue from the lower pole is transposed to fill the defect. Periareolar and vertical skin excision yield a pleasing contour with minimal scarring (Figures 16–9 to 16–12).

As a general rule, the contralateral breast should not be adjusted at the time of lumpectomy or segmentectomy. It is preferable to know the final pathology, particularly margin status, before altering the opposite breast. However, if the patient is willing to accept the risks of close or positive margins (which might require re-operation) yet still prefers a single operation, the contralateral side may be adjusted at the initial procedure.

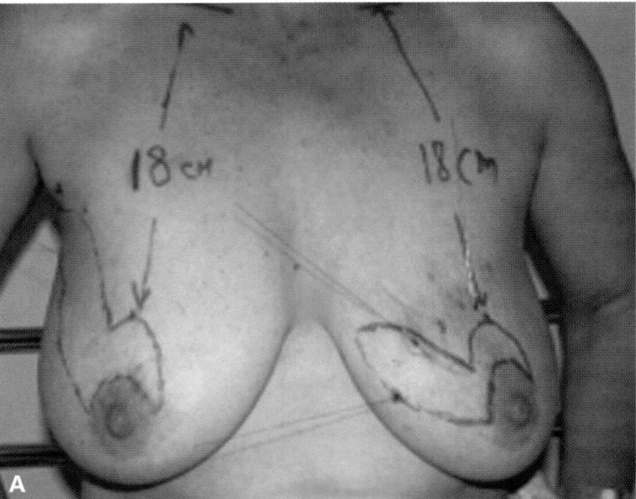

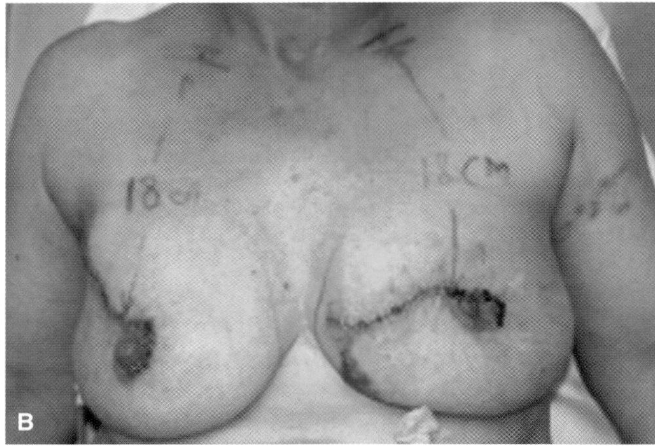

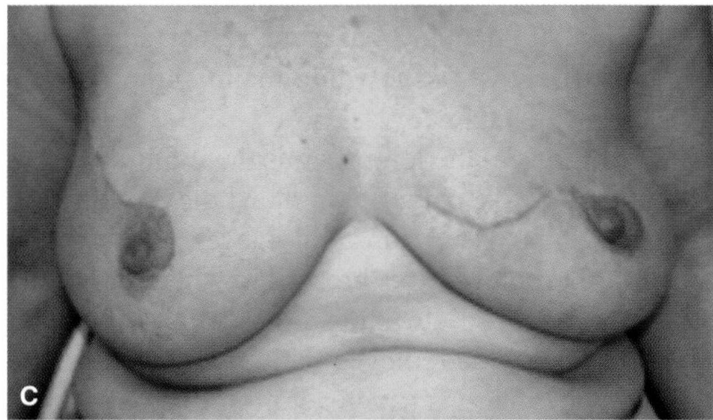

Figure 16–8. Bilateral hemi-batwing excisions: *A,* preoperative bilateral segmental excision plan, nipple to be raised to 18 cm below the midpoint of the clavicle on both sides; *B,* 1-day postoperative with drains in place; *C,* 3-weeks postoperative bilateral hemi-batwing excisions; the scars will continue to fade with time.

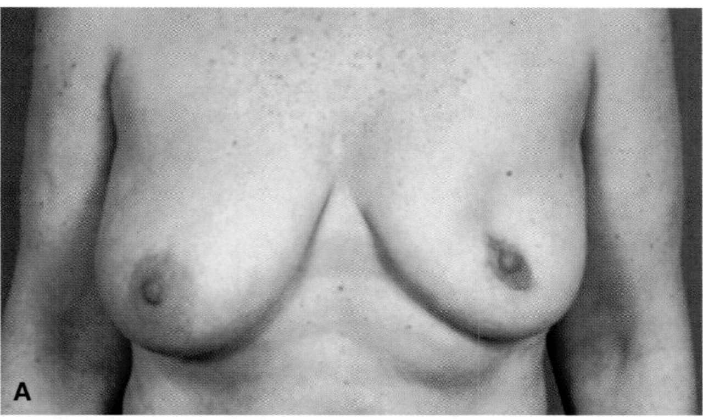

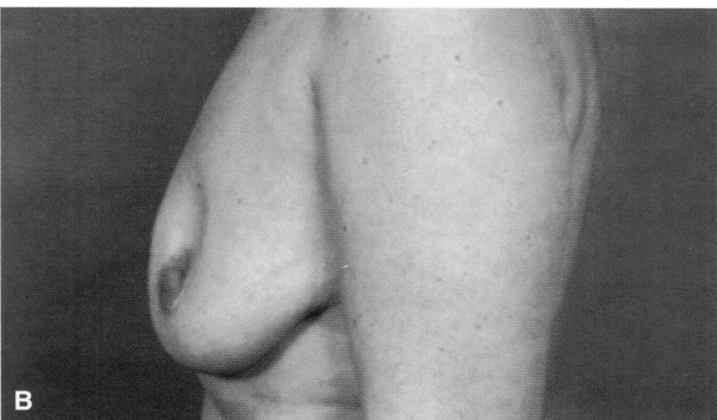

Figure 16–9. *A,* frontal and *B,* lateral views of a 43-year-old woman who previously underwent resection of a large tumor from the upper pole of the left breast resulting in asymmetry and left breast deformity. (Courtesy of Dennis Hammond, MD).

If the patient has only DCIS, the permanent microscopic sections reveal involved margins, and the residual breast is amenable to re-excision, the inflammatory response should be allowed to subside before re-excision. This may take as long as 3 to 4 months. There is little chance that residual DCIS, if present, will progress to invasive cancer within such a short period of time. The cosmetic results from re-

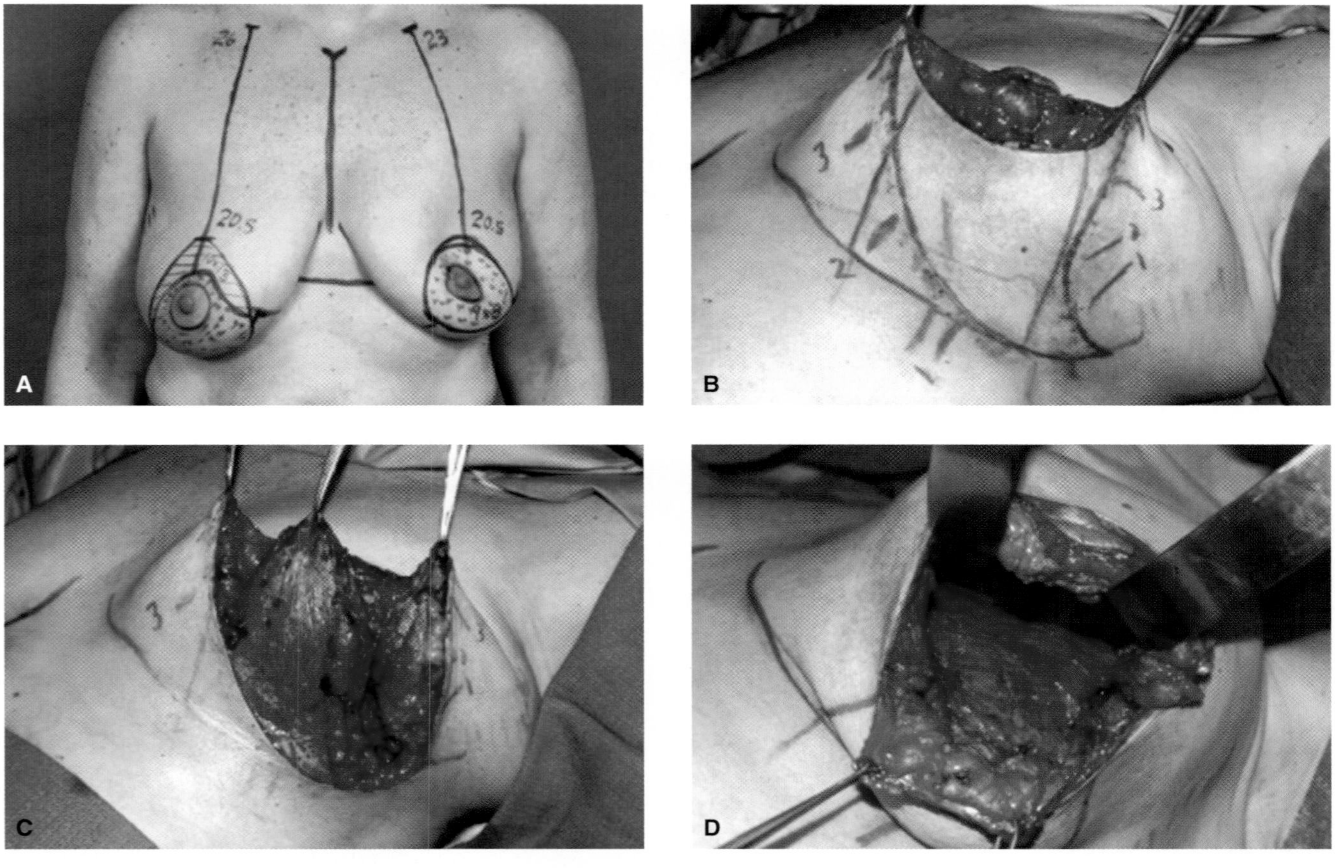

Figure 16–10. *A,* preoperative markings for bilateral breast reduction using SPAIR approach. The right breast will be reduced to match the left side and the redundant parenchyma from the inferior pole of the left breast will be redistributed to fill the deformity of the upper pole; *B,* skin markings indicate the area which will be de-epithelialized to create the inferior dermal pedicle; *C,* the inferior pedicle has been de-epithelialized; *D,* the upper pole defect is recreated to prepare for transfer of the pedicle flap. SPAIR = short-scar periareolar-inferior pedicle reduction. (Courtesy of Dennis Hammond, MD).

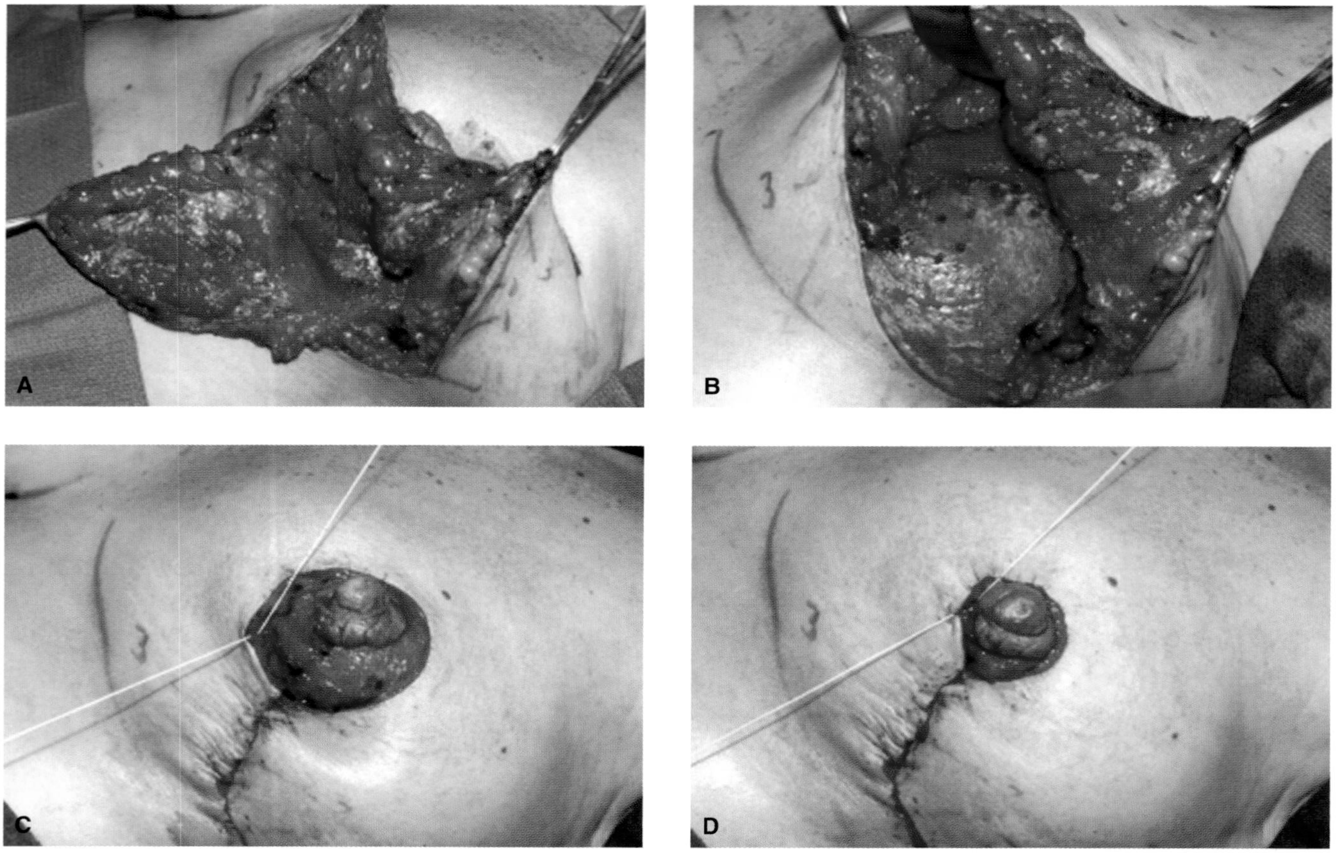

Figure 16–11. *A,* inferiorly based pedicle readied for transposition; *B,* pedicle flap rotated into the segmentectomy defect and sutured in place; *C,* periareolar Gore-Tex (W.L. Gore & Associates, Inc. Newark, DE) purse string suture placed around the periphery of the areola; *D,* periareolar purse string suture tightened to close skin defect. (Courtesy of Dennis Hammond, MD).

excision are better after an adequate period of wound healing and scar resolution. An example of the application of oncoplastic principles to segmentectomy in a patient with persistent DCIS, despite two prior excisions, is illustrated in Figure 16–13.

If a patient has invasive breast cancer with positive margins and wishes to pursue breast conservation therapy, we generally allow the medical oncologist to treat first with chemotherapy if indicated. We proceed with re-excision at the conclusion of

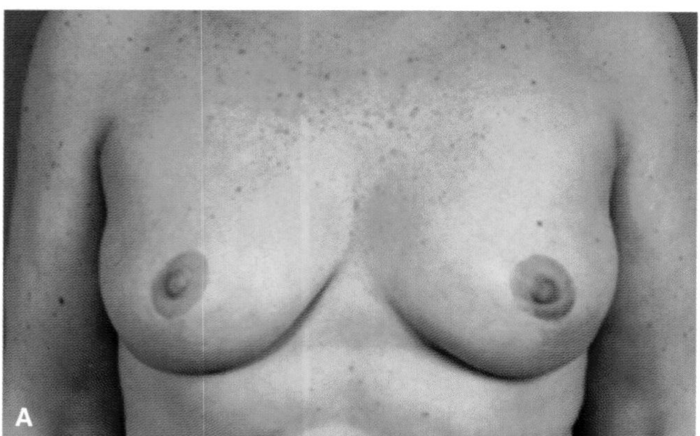

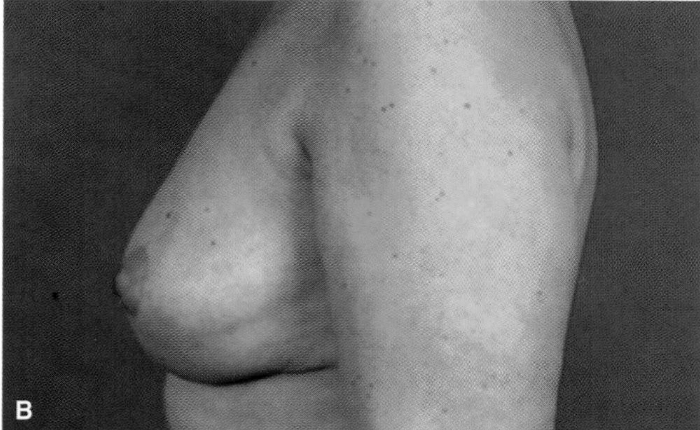

Figure 16–12. *A,* frontal and *B,* lateral views of final appearance of the breasts showing restoration of upper pole fullness, correction of ptosis, and good symmetry. (Courtesy of Dennis Hammond, MD).

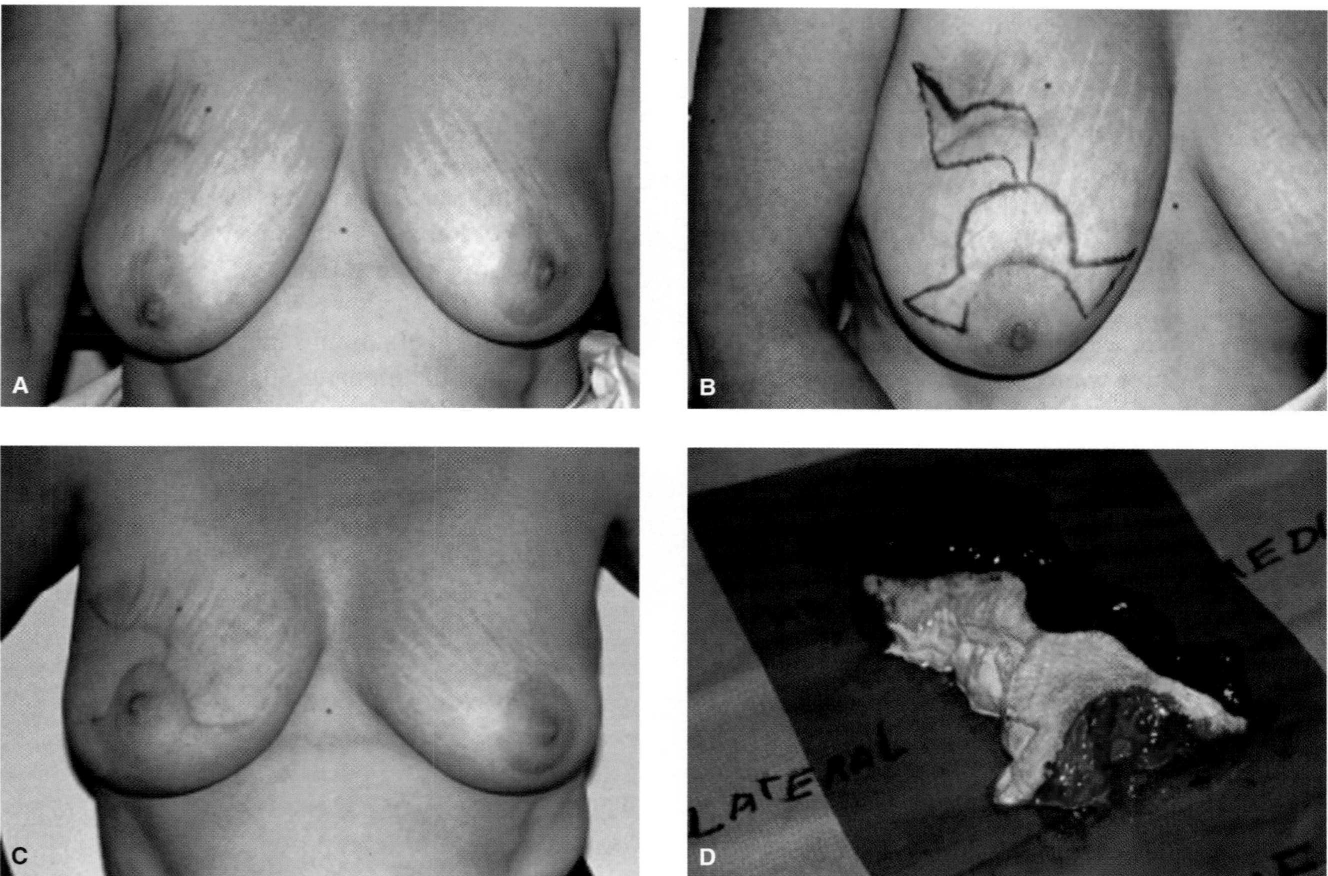

Figure 16–13. *A,* a patient who has undergone two previous excisions elsewhere for a large DCIS through a transverse upper central incision (no skin was removed). The margins were persistently positive inferiorly, toward the nipple. *B,* excision plan: batwing with re-excision of previous biopsy site. This will elevate the nipple areola complex and reduce the right breast in size. Fortunately the right breast is a bit larger than the left. This excision will convert the upper transverse excision into a radial resection; *C,* 1-month postoperative, symmetry is good, shape is excellent, scars will continue to improve and lighten; *D,* the color-coded excision specimen. DCIS = ductal carcinoma in situ.

chemotherapy. If the patient decides to proceed with mastectomy, it may be performed right away. Immediate reconstruction is appropriate if the likelihood of postoperative radiation therapy is small. If it is clear that radiation therapy will be required (patients with a T3 tumor or 4 or more positive axillary lymph nodes), autologous immediate reconstruction is not recommended. Numerous studies have documented that breasts reconstructed with autologous tissues do not tolerate radiation well, often with serious deterioration of the results.[5,6] Although immediate autologous reconstruction is not recommended in patients who will be irradiated, insertion of an implant or a tissue expander is acceptable. There is a relatively high incidence of radiation-induced capsulitis and contracture around implants and expanders,[7,8] but the prosthetic device may serve as a "spacer" which facilitates later completion of the reconstruction. If a patient wishes to proceed with autologous reconstruction, it is best to begin after the acute inflammatory response secondary to radiation therapy has resolved, usually at about 6 months.

MASTECTOMY AND BREAST RECONSTRUCTION

In patients with lesions too large to yield clear margins with an acceptable cosmetic result, skin-sparing mastectomy and breast reconstruction can be performed. Reconstruction may be done immediately following mastectomy, or as a delayed procedure, months, years, or even decades later. Women who have immediate reconstruction suffer less anxiety and depression than those who remain unreconstructed or have delayed reconstruction.[9,10] Immediate reconstruction does not significantly increase the rate of complications[11] and reduces the total number of operations, anesthetics, and hospitalizations.

Recent advances in plastic surgery allow successful reconstruction to be performed in nearly all mastectomy patients. Modern techniques yield cosmetic results greatly superior to those achieved in the past.[12,13] Post-mastectomy reconstruction may be divided into three component parts: reconstruction of the breast mound, reconstruction of the nipple areola complex, and treatment of the contralateral breast. New developments in each area will be discussed.

Breast Mound Reconstruction

A variety of techniques are currently available for breast mound reconstruction.[14] These are conveniently divided into methods requiring a silicone implant and methods in which only autogenous tissues are used.

Reconstruction with Silicone Implants

Under current FDA guidelines, breast reconstruction is permitted both with saline-filled and silicone gel-filled devices. In cases where there is adequate soft tissue present following mastectomy, it is possible to proceed with direct implantation of a prosthesis.[15–17] If insufficient skin is present, preliminary stretching of the soft tissue envelope may be accomplished with a tissue expander.[18–20] In some cases, a latissimus dorsi myocutaneous flap is used in conjunction with an implant.[21,22] The common thread in all implant reconstructions is that the overlying cover of the breast comprises the patient's own skin, whereas the required volume replacement is achieved with a prosthetic implant.

Direct Implant Reconstruction. When radical mastectomy was standard treatment for breast cancer, there rarely remained adequate soft tissue for direct placement of a silicone prosthesis.[23,24] With popularization of the modified radical mastectomy, more skin was preserved, and the pectoral muscles were spared. This greatly facilitated implant reconstruction. In recent years, with a trend toward earlier mammographic diagnosis of breast cancer and growing acceptance of skin-sparing mastectomy, increasing numbers of patients are candidates for reconstruction with implants. The ideal case for implant reconstruction is when the contralateral breast is small and non-ptotic and the mastectomy flaps can be draped over the prosthesis and closed without tension (Figure 16–14).

When reconstruction is performed at the time of the mastectomy, a sub-muscular pocket is created for insertion of the implant. Superiorly, the pocket is in between the pectoralis major and pectoralis minor muscles. Inferiorly, it is deep to the rectus abdominis and serratus anterior muscles.[25,26] It is ideal to achieve complete muscle coverage over the implant. This not only reduces the risk of implant exposure in the event of delayed wound healing but also reduces the risk of capsular contracture around the prosthesis. When delayed reconstruction is performed, the mastectomy scar is re-incised and the sub-muscular pocket is created as described above. In some cases, when there is a particularly thick and robust skin flap, partial or even complete subcutaneous placement of the prosthesis is acceptable.

Currently a wide variety of prosthetic implants are available for reconstruction. All modern implants consist of a silicone elastomer shell filled either with silicone gel or saline. Silicone gel-filled implants have physical characteristics that more closely mimic breast tissue and thus may give a more natural result. However, there have been concerns about silicone gel bleed and the possibility of rupture with leakage of the gel;[27] for these reasons some surgeons (and some patients) are more comfortable with saline-filled devices. Implants come in a variety of shapes (round, anatomical) with various degrees of projection (low, moderate, and high profile) and in a range of sizes. The wide variety of implants available gives the surgeon great latitude in selecting a prosthesis that will give the best result. Breast implants do not increase the risk of local recurrence or adversely impact prognosis. Nipple areolar reconstruction is generally carried out secondarily 3 to 6 months after completion of breast mound reconstruction. This allows the reconstructed breast to soften, settle, and take on its final shape. In patients who have undergone uni-

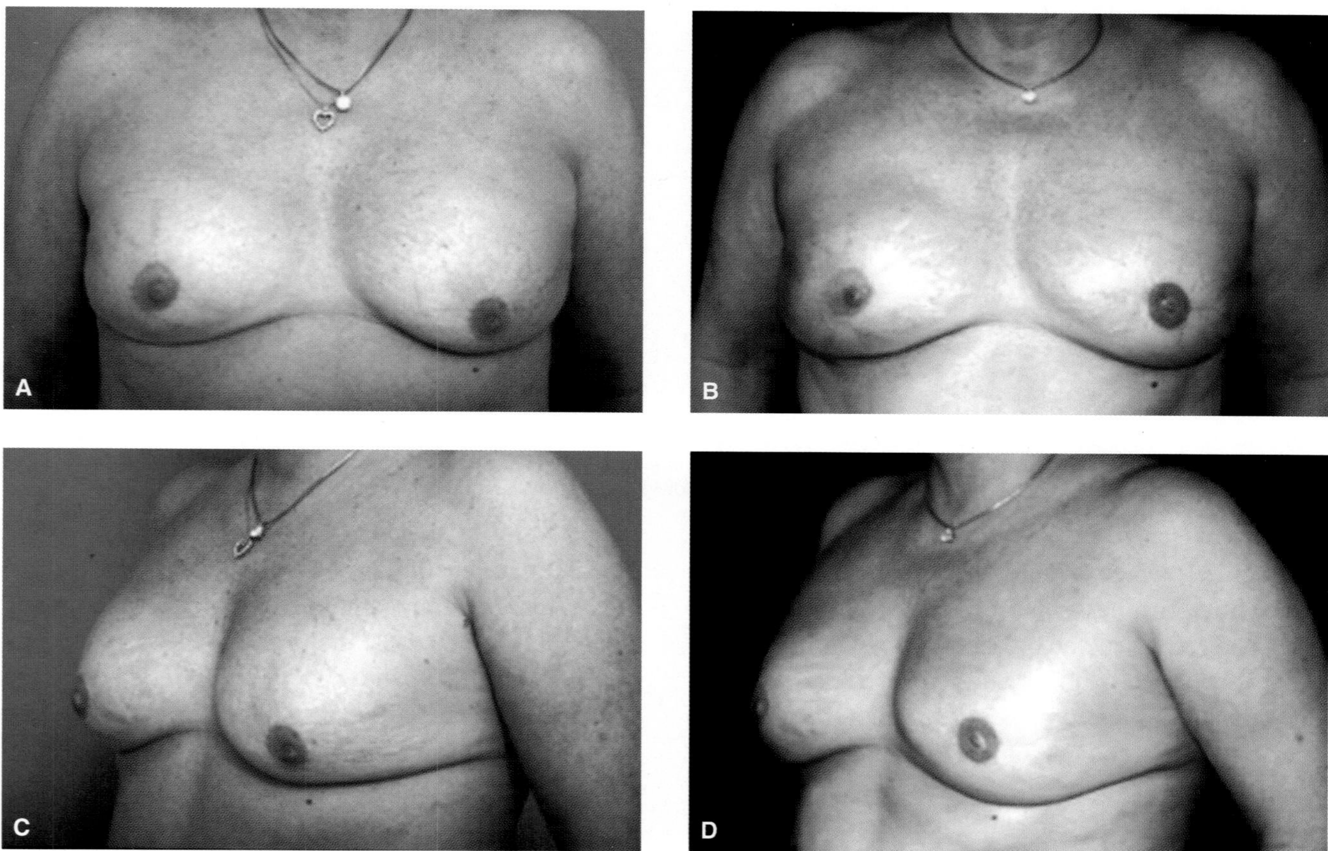

Figure 16–14. *A, B,* preoperative and *C, D,* postoperative views of a patient with a small infiltrating ductal cancer of the left breast. Left mastectomy performed through a small transverse ellipse including removal of nipple and areola; patient had immediate submuscular reconstruction with silicone implant; 6 months later, the nipple was reconstructed with a local flap and the areola reconstructed with a full thickness skin graft from the upper inner thigh.

lateral implant reconstruction, there is a tendency for the contralateral breast to become progressively more ptotic with time, leading to asymmetry. Patients who have had bilateral reconstruction often have better long-term results (Figure 16–15).

Complications following reconstruction with implants include hematomas, infections, flap necrosis, and capsular contracture.[28,29] Hematomas are unusual and can be treated by surgical drainage without compromising the final result. Infections are relatively rare, considering a large foreign body is placed in a relatively superficial location; infections occur in fewer than 5% of silicone implant reconstructions.[30–32] Infections can be successfully treated with antibiotics in most cases. If the process involves the periprosthetic space and contaminates the implant surface, it may be difficult or impossible to salvage the prosthesis. In these cases, it is usually necessary to remove the implant and wait several months before replacing it.[33,34] Flap necrosis is a serious complication because it may portend wound dehiscence and implant extrusion. In cases where only a small margin of skin is involved, the necrotic area can be excised and the wound closed with salvage of the prosthesis. If flap necrosis is more extensive, nonviable tissue must be debrided and the prosthesis removed. After the area has healed, further efforts at reconstruction may be undertaken. In cases where substantial skin has been lost, tissue expansion or distant flaps may be required to successfully complete reconstruction.

The most common complication after implant reconstruction with implants is capsular contracture.[35,36] A scar tissue capsule invariably forms around the silicone prosthesis. In most patients, this capsule remains thin and pliable, and the reconstructed breast is soft and mobile. However, in a considerable number of cases, the scar tissue capsule undergoes progressive

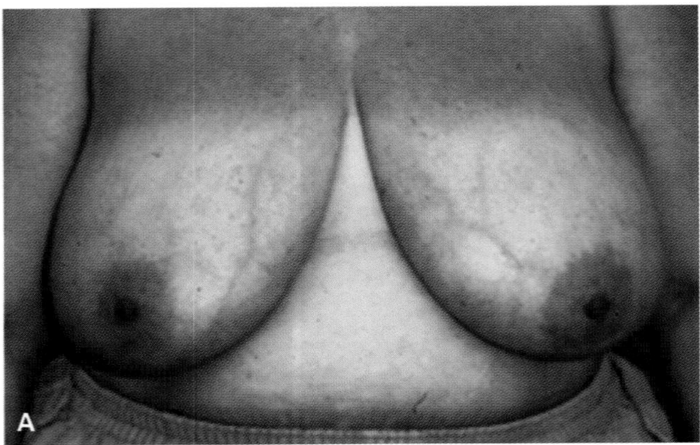

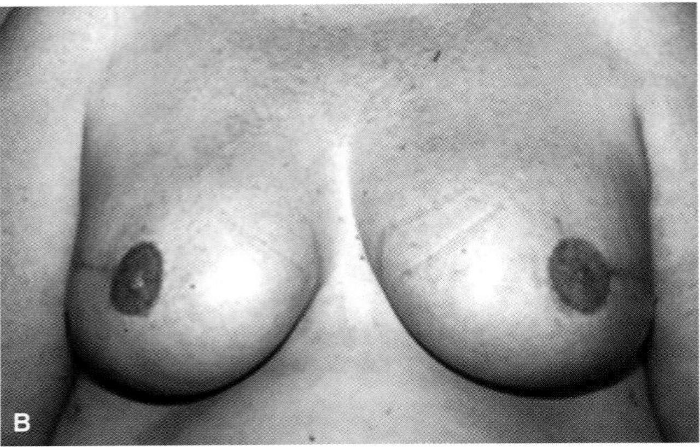

Figure 16–15. *A,* this patient presented with infiltrating carcinoma of the right breast and a positive family history; she elected to undergo bilateral mastectomy with immediate implant reconstruction; nipple areola reconstruction and tattooing were performed as delayed procedures 6 months later. *B,* the postoperative views were obtained 9 years following reconstruction and reveal excellent symmetry.

contracture, which results in spherical deformity, undesirable firmness, and rigidity.[37,38] In advanced cases, the reconstructed breast may be extremely hard, cold to the touch, painful, and tender. Treatment usually consists of periprosthetic capsulotomy or capsulectomy, enlargement of the implant pocket, and, often, replacement of the prosthesis. Occasionally, implant reconstruction may be abandoned, and autologous reconstruction pursued (Figure 16–16).

Soft Tissue Expansion Combined with an Implant. Preliminary soft tissue expansion has proven useful in situations where there is inadequate skin to proceed with direct placement of a prosthesis.[18,19] This is particularly appropriate in patients where additional skin coverage is needed to accommodate a larger implant or to give the reconstructed breast a ptotic appearance to match the opposite side.[39,40] In such cases, the preliminary step is insertion of a tissue expander. Several varieties of tissue expander are currently available. The most widely used devices have a mechanically textured surface, are anatomically shaped, and have integrated filling ports for injection of saline by percutaneous needle puncture. The purpose of surface texturing is to reduce the likelihood of capsular contracture, pacilitating expansion and resulting in more pliable flaps. The textured surface also prevents displacement or rotation of the expander.

Ordinarily, the expander is partially inflated at the time of insertion. Several weeks are allowed for the

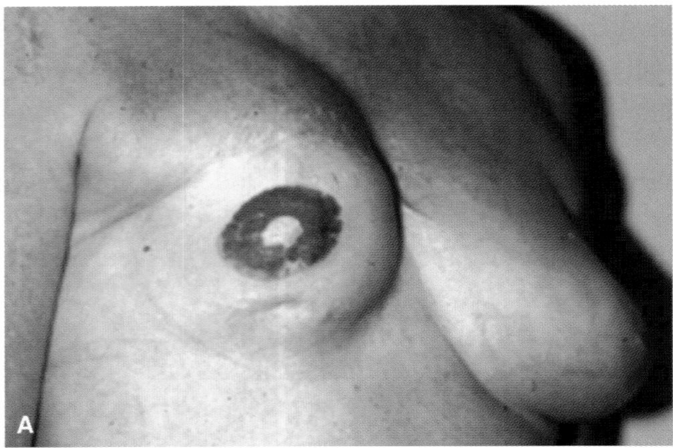

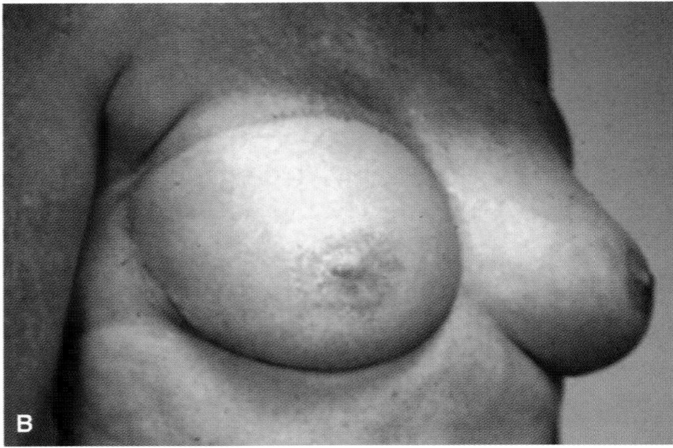

Figure 16–16. A patient with an unsatisfactory result from implant reconstruction. *A,* owing to capsular contracture, the breast mound is firm and distorted, areolar graft is excessively pigmented, nipple has lost projection; *B,* implant reconstruction was discarded and replaced with autologous tissue using a TRAM flap, nipple was reconstructed with skate flap and areola with a full thickness graft from contralateral breast. TRAM = transverse rectus abdominis myocutaneous.

operative incision to heal prior to initiation of expansion. Sequential inflations are done as outpatient (office) procedures and do not require anesthesia. The device is generally inflated to a capacity of about one and a half times the volume of the intended permanent implant. Overexpansion promotes softness of the final breast and contributes to a more natural (ptotic) appearance. A minimum of 6 to 8 weeks elapses between the final inflation and replacement with the permanent prosthesis. Allowing the flaps to remain maximally expanded during this interval reduces the risk of subsequent contracture, which could result in undesirable firmness and loss of desired ptosis. Nipple areolar reconstruction is ordinarily delayed until the reconstructed mound has taken on its final configuration. Because breast reconstruction using tissue expansion consists of a series of small steps, it may be accomplished entirely as an outpatient procedure without great disruption of a woman's normal routine.

Complications specific to reconstruction with tissue expanders include mechanical failure of the device and capsular contracture precluding further expansion.[41] Mechanical problems, such as inability to inflate the expander, were more common with older style expanders that had distant injection ports. The connecting tube between the injection port and the expander could become kinked or twisted, in which case surgical exploration was necessary to re-establish flow. This complication is uncommon in expanders with an integrated injection port. Deflation of an expander is unusual but may occur spontaneously or secondary to trauma or accidental needle puncture. Deflation requires surgical exploration and replacement of the device. Capsular contracture can occur around an expander, just as with any prosthetic implant; in the case of the tissue expander, however, contracture can make continued expansion painful or even impossible. If symptoms are severe enough, surgical capsulotomy is warranted.[42,43]

Latissimus Dorsi Myocutaneous Flap and Implant. The latissimus dorsi myocutaneous flap is a useful adjunct when there is insufficient or poor quality skin at the mastectomy site, when radiation therapy has (or will be) administered, and in cases where it is desirable to reconstruct a larger or more ptotic breast to match the opposite side. The latissimus dorsi flap recruits additional healthy tissue needed for reconstruction in conjunction with an implant. With this approach, an ellipse of skin from the upper back and varying amounts of the underlying latissimus dorsi muscle (as needed) are transposed to the mastectomy defect[44–46] (Figure 16–17). The tissues maintain their viability through the intact thoracodorsal blood vessels, which course within the muscle pedicle[47,48]; sensory innervation is sacrificed. The donor defect is closed directly. An ellipse of skin measuring up to 10 cm in width and 20 cm in length can routinely be added to the mastectomy defect. In addition, well-vascularized latissimus muscle is available to provide lining beneath the mastectomy flaps and, if needed, to fill the infraclavicular hollow and recreate the anterior axillary fold (particularly useful in cases of radical mastectomy)[49,50] (Figure 16–18). With popularization of soft tissue expansion and the advent of effective techniques for autologous breast reconstruction, there has been diminished use of the latissimus flap. However, this procedure remains useful in the radical mastectomy patient in whom a skin graft was used to close the defect, in individuals with a history of chest wall radiation, and in patients who are not candidates for autologous reconstruction.

Among the complications and side effects specifically related to the latissimus flap are a noticeable scar on the back and loss of the posterior axillary fold. There is also a frequent incidence of seromas at the latissimus donor site; these generally can be managed conservatively. Most patients do not notice any functional deficit attributable to sacrifice of the muscle (an adductor and internal rotator of the humerus). Other muscles with the same function usually compensate for the missing latissimus. Complications such as wound breakdown and flap necrosis are rare because of the vigorous blood supply that characterizes this flap.

Autologous Breast Reconstruction

For many years, virtually all breast reconstructions relied on the use of an alloplastic implant. Despite advances in implant technology, there have always been limitations associated with the use of prosthetic devices. These include infections, capsular contracture, and mechanical implant failure. Even in cases

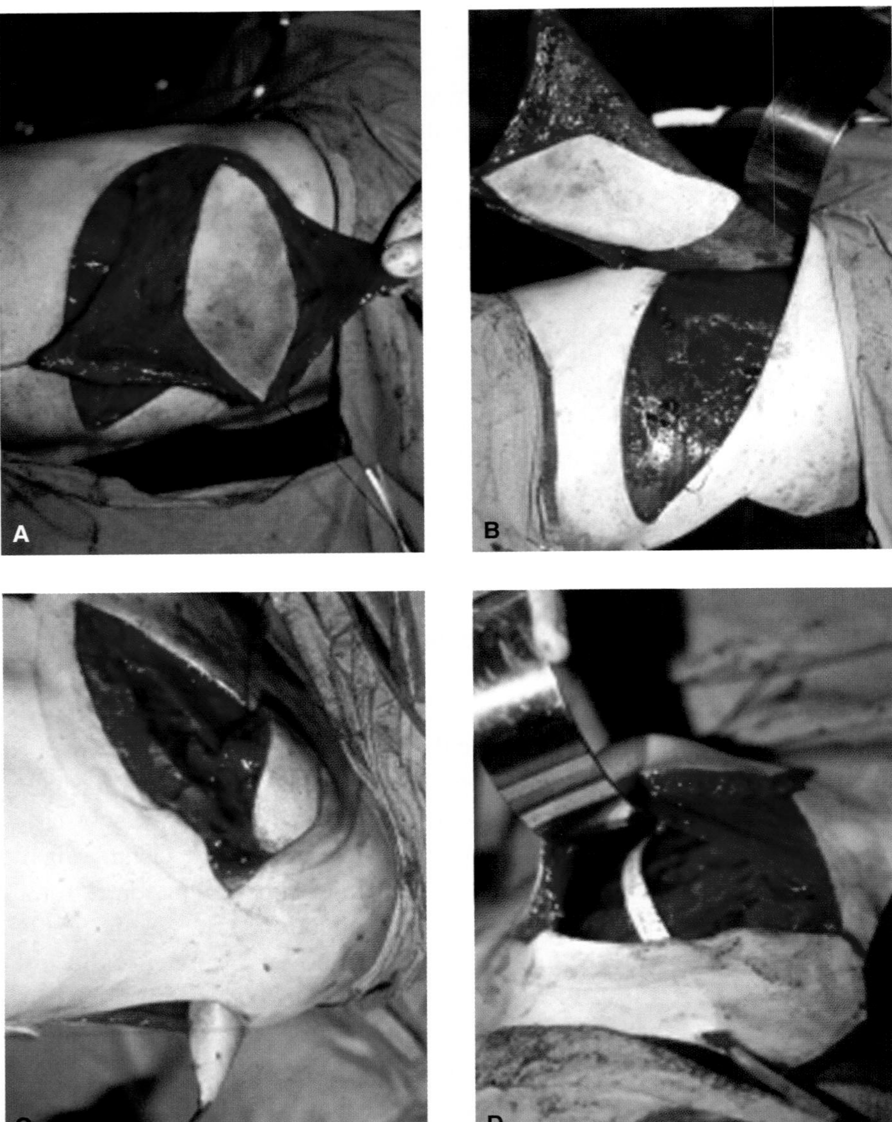

Figure 16–17. Latissimus dorsi flap. *A,* latissimus muscle and adjacent skin paddle have been dissected from surrounding structures; *B,* musculocutaneous flap isolated on dominant blood supply (thoracodorsal artery) traversing the muscle insertion; *C,* flap being tunneled subcutaneously from the back to the mastectomy defect; *D,* flap inset into mastectomy defect and ready for insertion of prosthesis.

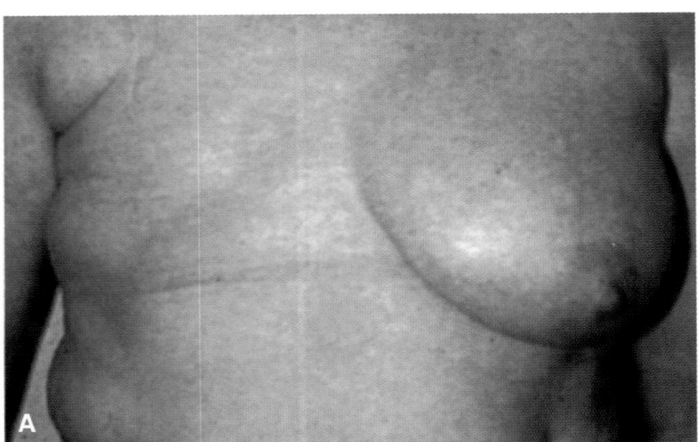

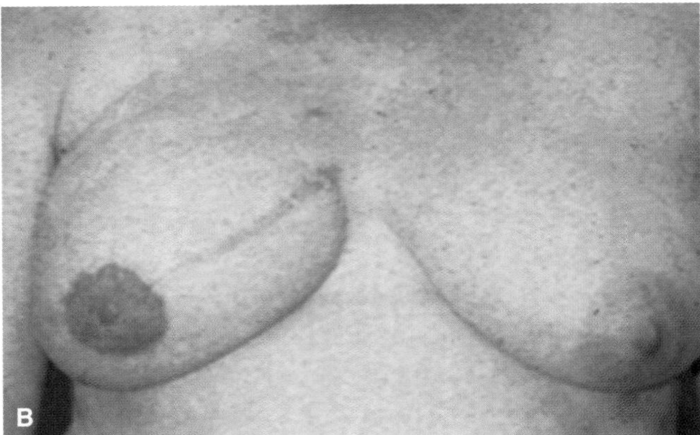

Figure 16–18. *A,* a patient with a right modified radical mastectomy and a ptotic contralateral breast; *B,* following breast mound reconstruction with latissimus dorsi myocutaneous flap in conjunction with a breast implant; areola reconstructed from post auricular skin (still erythematous) and nipple reconstructed with composite graft from contralateral breast.

where the initial result is good, implant reconstructions tend to deteriorate over time. Typically the contralateral natural breast becomes larger and more ptotic as the patient ages, whereas the reconstructed breast remains the same size and takes on an increasingly spherical configuration (owing to scar tissue contracture). This leads to progressively worsening asymmetry. Multiple "touch up" operations may be necessary if the patient wants to maintain the best possible result. Because of these shortcomings, the development of reliable techniques for autologous reconstruction represents a milestone in reconstructive breast surgery.[51]

Autologous Reconstruction with Pedicle Flaps. The most commonly used method of autologous breast reconstruction is the transverse rectus abdominis myocutaneous (TRAM) flap. With this technique, a large ellipse of skin and subcutaneous tissue, measuring up to 14 cm in width and 30 cm in length, can reliably be harvested from the lower abdomen and transposed to the mastectomy defect. The soft tissue remains attached to one or both of the paired rectus abdominis muscles. The rectus muscles contain the epigastric artery and vein, which, through a series of periumbilical perforator vessels, provide blood supply to the skin and subcutaneous tissues of the flap (Figure 16–19). This living tissue may be folded, trimmed, and inset to create the desired breast mound[52,53] (Figure 16–20). The abdominal wall donor defect can be closed by muscle approximation, with or without synthetic mesh; the skin is readily closed by direct approximation. The resulting transverse scar of the lower abdomen is cosmetically acceptable to most patients (Figure 16–21). In fact, there is often improvement in the contour of the abdomen as a result of removal of lax skin and tight-

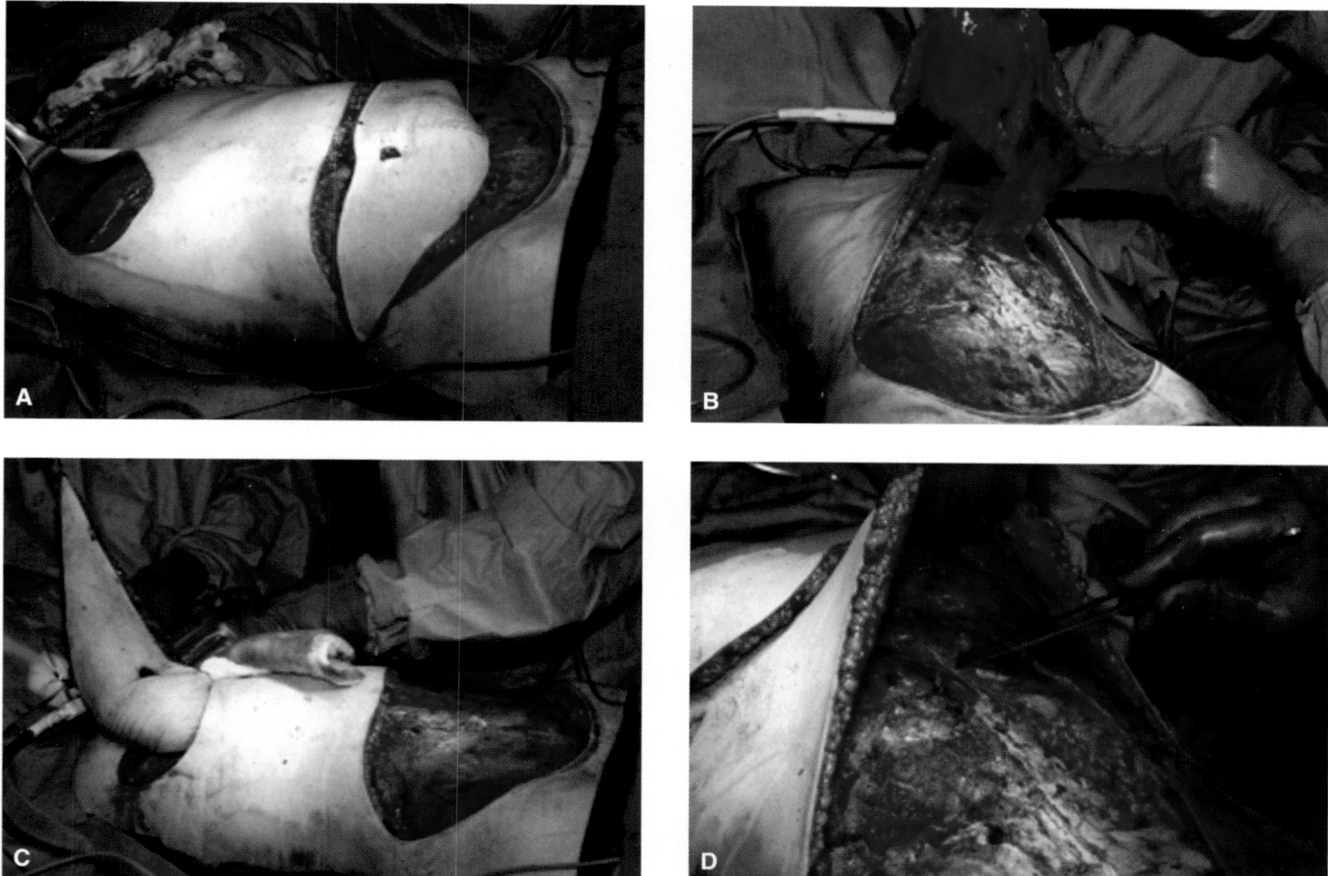

Figure 16–19. Pedicle TRAM flap. *A*, the mastectomy defect has been created and the transverse skin island on the lower abdomen incised; *B*, the skin paddle has been elevated on the left rectus abdominis muscle, which carries the vascular pedicle; *C*, the flap tunneled subcutaneously and brought to the mastectomy defect; *D*, the abdominal fascial defect has been closed, forceps indicate the location of the superior epigastric artery which provides blood supply to the transposed flap. TRAM = transverse rectus abdominis myocutaneous.

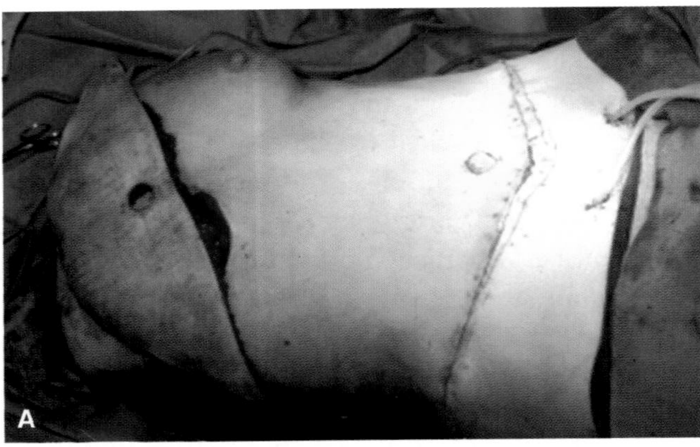

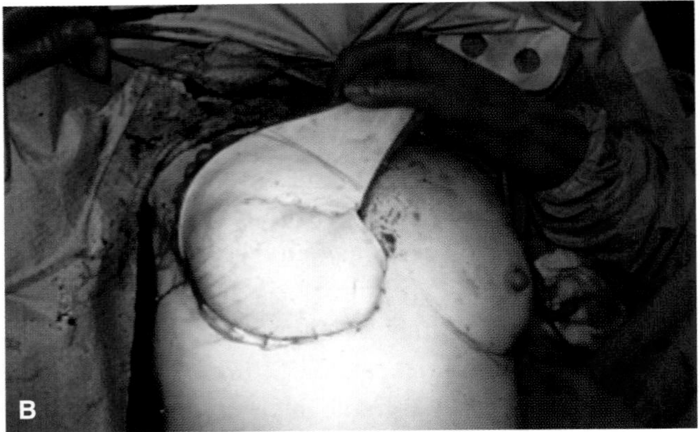

Figure 16–20. Pedicle TRAM flap. A, the flap transposed to the mastectomy defect, abdominal donor site closed; B, flap being rotated, trimmed and inset to recreate the breast mound. TRAM = transverse rectus abdominis myocutaneous.

ening of the underlying muscles (similar to a cosmetic abdominoplasty).

In most cases, the TRAM flap provides more than enough skin and subcutaneous tissue to recreate a breast mound that matches the opposite side (Figure 16–22). It is generally possible to simulate the desired degree of ptosis by proper trimming and insetting of the flap. When necessary, it is usually feasible to carry out bilateral breast reconstruction with the TRAM flap (Figure 16–23), although breast size is more limited owing to the fact the only one-half of the abdominal tissue is available for reconstruction on each side.

There are many potential advantages associated with autologous reconstruction. Because the reconstructed breast consists of viable tissue with its own intrinsic blood supply, wound healing problems involving the mastectomy flaps (necrosis, slough, wound separation) are well tolerated and generally do not lead to the adverse consequences that may occur with an alloplastic implant. The growing acceptance of skin-sparing mastectomy further enables creative approaches to reconstruction. The incisions used for mastopexy or reduction mammaplasty can be adapted to mastectomy, and when the absent breast is replaced with autologous tissue, the mastectomy flaps can be reconfigured and closed to achieve a pleasing shape in a one-stage operation (Figure 16–24).

Another advantage of autologous reconstruction is that over time the reconstructed breast behaves much like the opposite breast. Therefore, as the patient ages, ptosis occurs to a similar degree on both sides. If the patient gains or loses weight, the changes are reflected equally in both breasts. And, of course, implant-related complications, such as contracture, deflation, or rupture, are completely elimi-

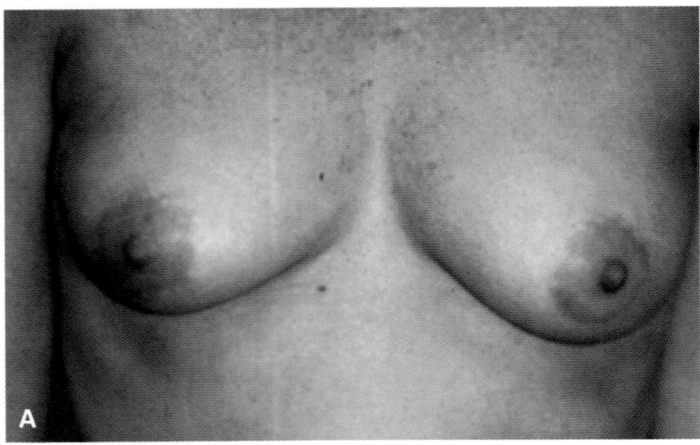

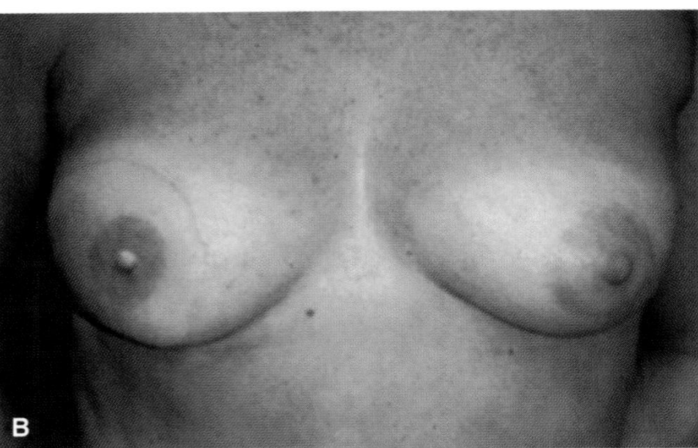

Figure 16–21. Immediate reconstruction with a TRAM flap; *A,* pre-op view of patient with biopsy proven infiltrating ductal cancer right breast; *B,* following immediate breast mound reconstruction with pedicle TRAM flap, nipple areola reconstructed 3 months later. TRAM = transverse rectus abdominis myocutaneous.

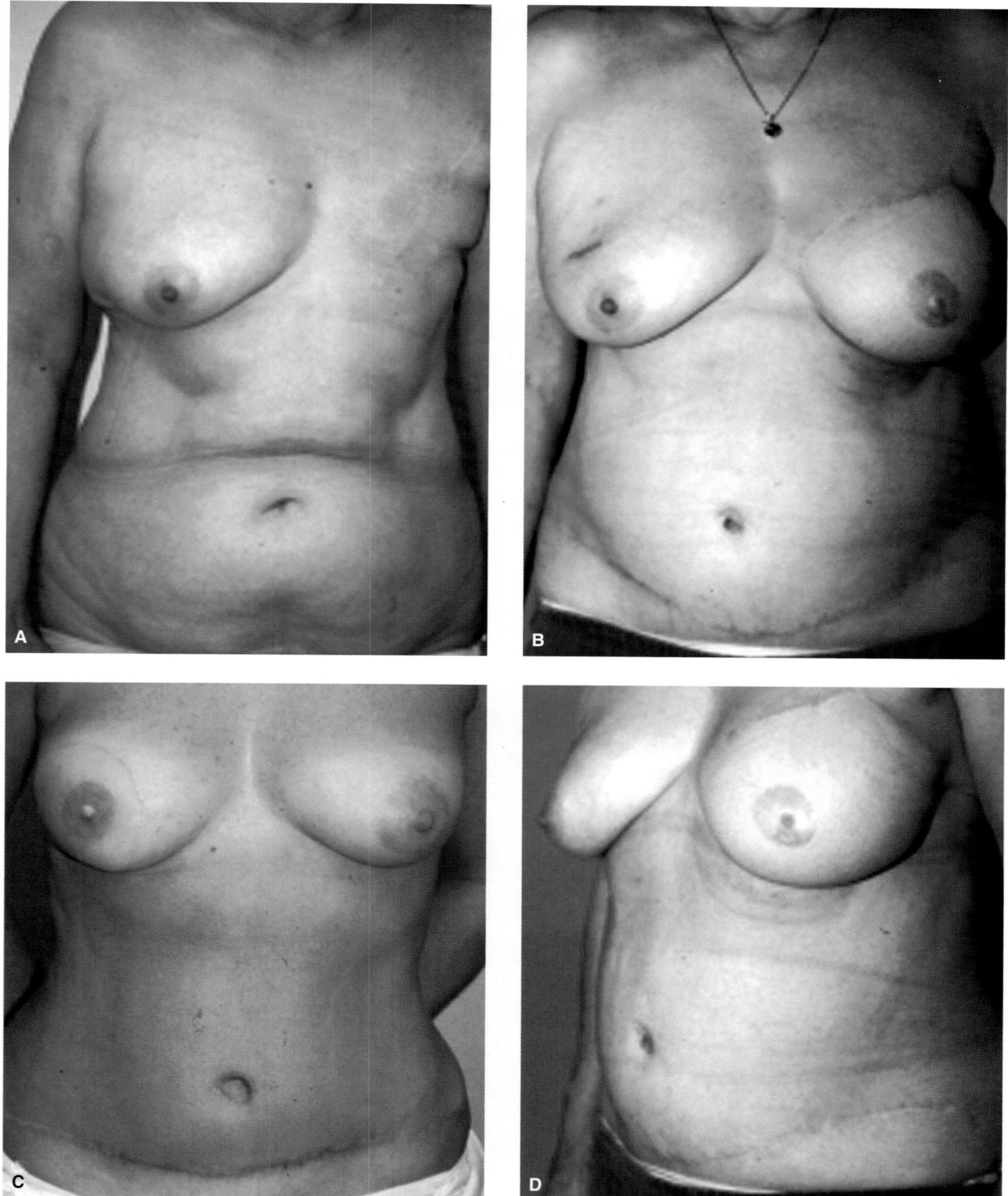

Figure 16–22. *A, B,* preoperative and postoperative frontal views and *C, D,* preoperative and postoperative oblique views of a modified radical mastectomy patient reconstructed with a unipedicle TRAM flap; nipple reconstructed with a skate flap, areola with full thickness skin from upper inner thigh; with autologous reconstruction it is possible to match the remaining ptotic breast obviating the need of surgery on the contralateral side; the abdominal contour is improved after harvesting of TRAM flap. TRAM = transverse rectus abdominis myocutaneous.

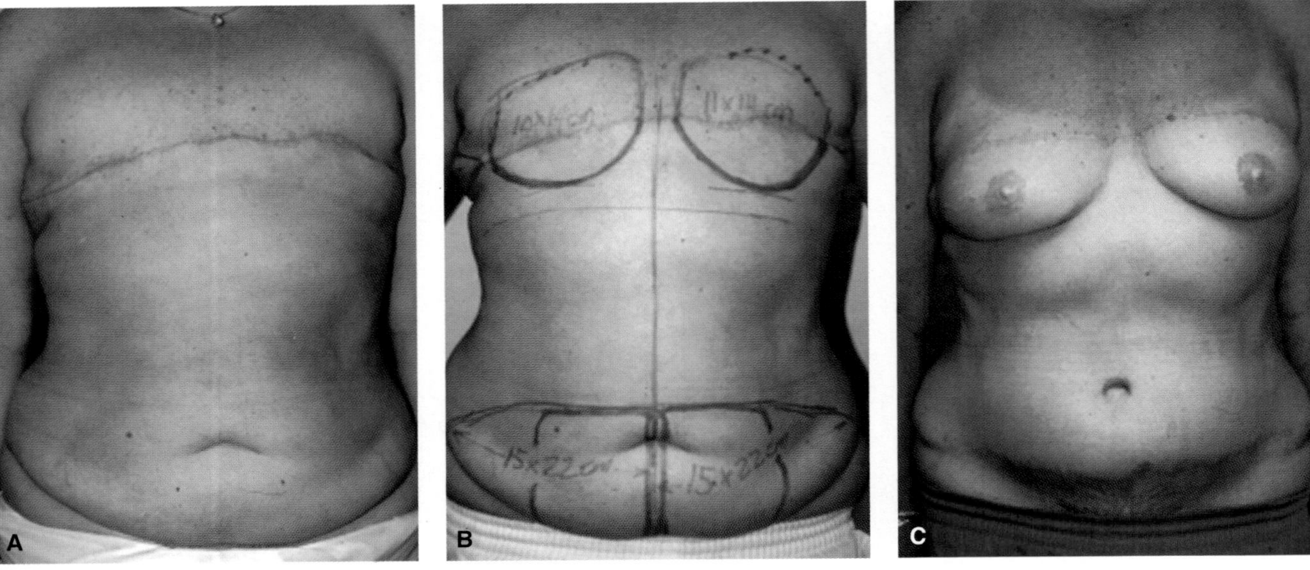

Figure 16–23. *A,* patient following bilateral modified radical mastectomies; *B,* the plan for bilateral pedicle TRAM flaps, one-half of the redundant abdominal tissue to be transposed to the mastectomy defect on each side; *C,* the completed reconstruction. TRAM = transverse rectus abdominis myocutaneous.

nated. Therefore, patients with successful autologous reconstruction have a greatly reduced need for secondary revisions.

The most common serious complication in TRAM flap reconstruction is fat and skin necrosis secondary to ischemia. Certain risk factors predis-

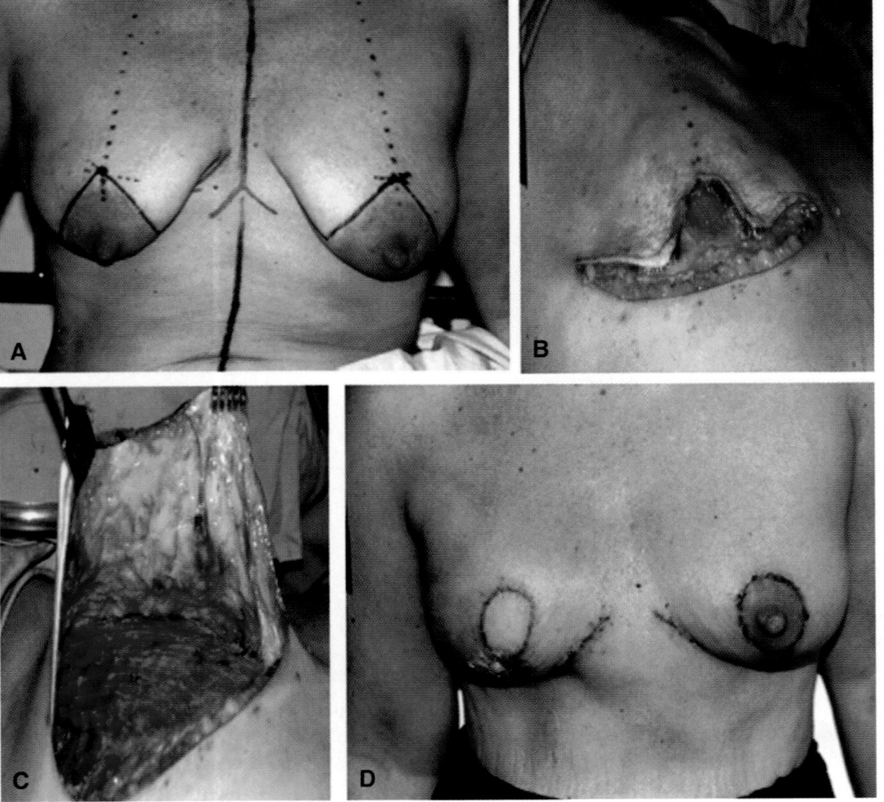

Figure 16–24. Skin-sparing mastectomy and immediate reconstruction with autologous tissue. This patient had a 70 mm right-sided DCIS; owing to the large size of lesion and relatively small breast size, she was not a candidate for breast conservation. *A,* a right mastectomy with sentinel node biopsy will be performed through a standard (Wise pattern) reduction incision, which has been drawn. On the right side the nipple-areola complex will be removed and on the left side a mastopexy will be performed. *B,* the right mastectomy has been performed through a reduction mammaplasty incision. The nipple-areola complex has been removed. *C,* Isosulfan blue, which has turned green, was used to find the sentinel lymph node and can be seen in lymphatics of the superior mastectomy flap. The skin flaps are thin but viable, and the pectoralis major muscle fascia has been removed with the mastectomy specimen. *D,* the patient 1-week post immediate reconstruction with a pedicle TRAM flap. The right nipple areola will be reconstructed with a local flap and tattooed approximately 3 to 4 months after surgery. DCIS = ductal carcinoma in situ; TRAM = transverse rectus abdominis myocutaneous.

pose to flap ischemia and necrosis. These include obesity,[54] previous abdominal scars, radiation therapy, and cigarette smoking.[55] In the ideal candidate, tissue from the lower abdomen usually can be safely transferred on a single (unpaired) rectus muscle. In higher-risk patients, there are alternatives to increase flap safety.[56] One option is to use both rectus muscles.[57] This doubles the blood supply to the flap but at the expense of potentially causing more abdominal wall morbidity. Another option is to surgically delay the flap. A variety of delay procedures have been described that significantly enhance the blood supply and increase the chance of successful flap transfer.[58–60] The major disadvantage of a delay procedure is that it necessitates an additional operation with increased expenses and additional recovery. Another option for improving the reliability of the TRAM procedure is to "supercharge" the flap.[61] The blood supply coming through the non-dominant superior epigastric vessels is enhanced by anastomosing the cut end of the inferior epigastric artery and vein (dominant vessels) to appropriate recipient vessels.

Autologous Reconstruction with Free Flaps. The pedicled TRAM flap was the first widely used technique for autologous reconstruction and still remains popular. However, in recent years there has been growing use of "free flaps" for breast reconstruction (Figure 16–25).[62–64] Free flap technology enables transfer of a composite block of tissue from one area of the body to another. A mass of soft tissue (skin, subcutaneous fat, and variable amounts of muscle) is isolated on the dominant vascular pedicle, resected, and transplanted to a new location. Blood supply is re-established by anastomosing the flap vessels to an appropriate recipient artery and vein (usually with microvascular technique). The donor site ordinarily can be closed by direct approximation.[65]

The most common donor site for free flap breast reconstruction is the lower abdomen, with the inferior epigastric vessels serving as the vascular pedicle (see Figure 16–25). The epigastric vessels may be anastomosed to either the thoracodorsal artery and vein in the axilla or to the internal mammary vessels. The advantages of using abdominal tissue as a free flap (instead of a musculocutaneous pedicle flap) include greater flexibility in orientation of the flap at the recipient site, more reliable

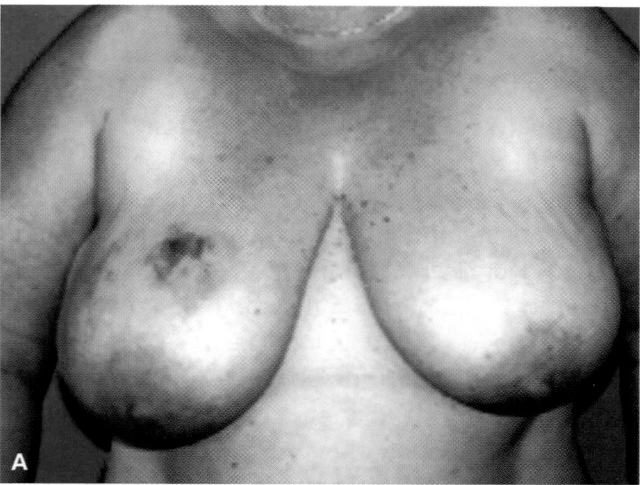

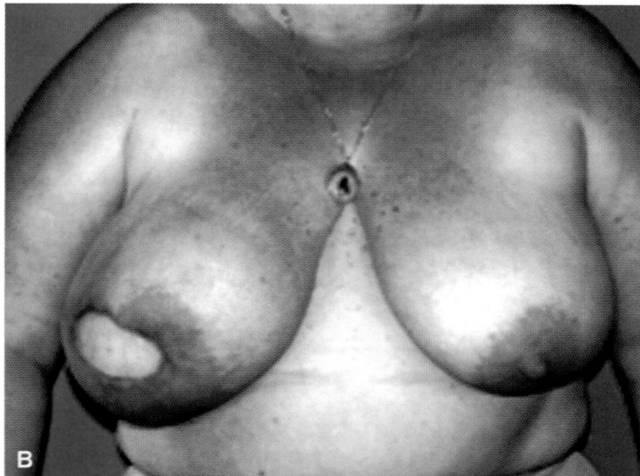

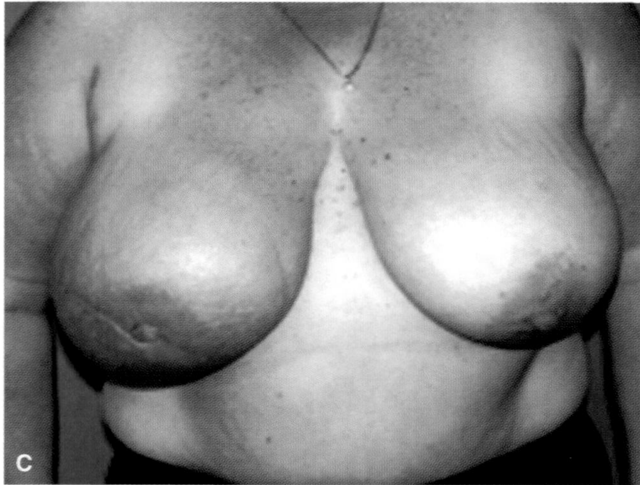

Figure 16–25. Immediate reconstruction with free TRAM flap. *A,* a patient with biopsy-proven ductal carcinoma in situ; *B,* the breast has been removed along with the entire nipple and part of the areola, reconstruction performed with a free TRAM flap, part of which remains exposed providing a "window" to monitor flap viability; *C,* 4 months later, residual flap skin is removed, the areola reconfigured, and the nipple reconstructed with a local flap. TRAM = transverse rectus abdominis myocutaneous. (Courtesy of J. Arthur Jensen, MD).

perfusion, and greater integrity of the abdominal wall (because of preservation of the rectus muscle and fascia). Breast reconstruction with lower abdominal skin and subcutaneous tissue may also be performed using deep inferior epigastric artery perforator (DIEP) flaps.[66] This permits sacrifice of less rectus abdominis muscle and anterior fascia to further decrease abdominal donor-site weakness, discomfort, and postoperative complications.[67,68]

The superficial inferior epigastric artery flap has also been described for breast reconstruction and permits transfer of abdominal skin and fat without sacrifice of any abdominal muscles or incision of the rectus fascia.[69] This approach is technically more challenging and is not applicable in all cases. As an alternative to free abdominal flaps, the gluteal tissues have also been transposed based on the superior gluteal artery and vein.[70,71] This donor site has the disadvantage of deforming the buttock and necessitating changes in the position of the patient while under anesthesia. The gluteal free flap also requires the use of vein grafts, which prolongs the surgery, is associated with greater technical difficulty, and increases the risk of thrombosis. Other free flap donor sites have been described but are used less frequently.[72–74] Skin-sparing mastectomy coupled with immediate free flap reconstruction enables design of a unique treatment plan to meet the specific needs of each patient (Figure 16–26).

Autogenous breast reconstruction is a major undertaking and is associated with potential complications that are not encountered with implant reconstruction.[75,76] The pedicled TRAM flap necessitates sacrifice of one or both rectus muscles. This violates the integrity of the abdominal wall and may lead to ventral hernias or areas of abdominal wall

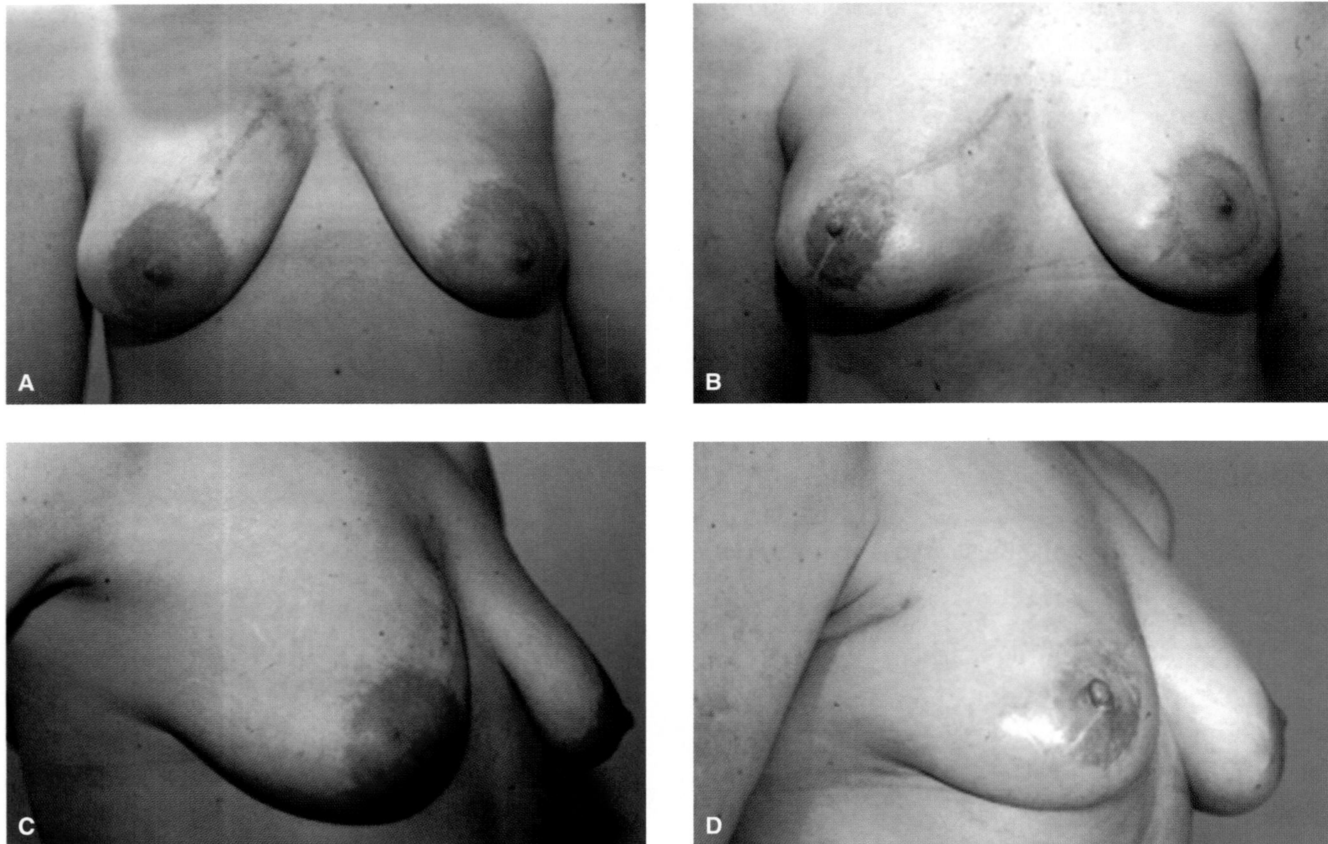

Figure 16–26. Skin-sparing mastectomy and immediate free TRAM flap reconstruction. *A, B,* preoperative and postoperative frontal views and *C, D,* preoperative and postoperative oblique views of a patient who had mastectomy with preservation of the nipple and areola. During surgery, frozen sections of tissue excised from beneath the nipple revealed no evidence of disease; immediate reconstruction performed with de-epithelialized free TRAM flap; periareolar mastopexy performed on contralateral side to correct ptosis and achieve symmetry. TRAM = transverse rectus abdominis myocutaneous. (Courtesy of J. Arthur Jensen, MD).

weakness and bulging without frank hernia. The reported incidence of hernia after TRAM flap reconstruction is less than 5%. Other complications at the donor site, including hematomas, infection, and fat necrosis with prolonged drainage, may delay wound healing.[77] Because the blood supply to tissues transposed on a narrow muscle pedicle may be marginal, there can be significant areas of skin and/or fat necrosis. If skin necrosis occurs, immediate debridement and closure is usually indicated to facilitate primary healing. Fat necrosis causes indurated, tender areas to form within the reconstructed breast. Sometimes these resolve spontaneously; on other occasions, delayed surgical excision is warranted. When autogenous reconstruction is performed using free flaps, complications may occur related to the microsurgical vascular anastomosis.[78] The free flap must be closely monitored during the early postoperative period; if thrombosis or kinking of the anastomosis threatens flap viability, immediate surgical re-exploration is mandatory. Free flap surgery also tends to require a longer operative session, a longer time under general anesthesia, a longer hospitalization, and greater costs than pedicle flap or implant reconstruction.

Reconstruction of the Nipple and Areola

Nipple areola reconstruction is desirable to recreate the most natural appearing breast. Not all patients are motivated to undergo the additional procedures necessary for nipple reconstruction; however, women who have the nipple reconstructed enjoy significant psychological benefit.[79] Excellent techniques are now available for reconstruction of a realistic appearing nipple and areola.[80,81]

The goal of nipple reconstruction is to create a papilla that permanently maintains its shape and projection.[82] One method is a composite graft from another part of the body. If the opposite nipple is large enough, it makes an ideal donor site. Composite grafts from the nipple almost always heal successfully,[83] and the color and texture match are excellent.[84] Other donor sites for composite grafting, such as the earlobe and pulp of the toe, have been used,[85,86] but these areas do not heal as reliably as the contralateral nipple and do not provide as exact a color match.

A more common method for recreating a projecting nipple is with a local flap. Many different configurations have been used.[87–89] Most techniques rely upon folding small skin flaps, like the petals of a flower, to create a bud-like nipple. A very popular method is the "skate flap," in which a pedicled flap of tissue with attached wing-like projections of skin is raised at the appropriate location on the reconstructed mound. The "wings" of the flap are wrapped around the central projecting pedicle of skin and subcutaneous tissue to create the conical, projecting nipple.[90]

A pigmented areola can be simulated using one of several techniques. Skin grafts from the labia, once popular,[91] have largely been abandoned because they are generally much darker than the contralateral areola. However, they may still have a role in darkly pigmented patients. Thin split-thickness grafts from the intact areola have been used, but these often shrink and undergo depigmentation during healing. Full thickness skin grafts from the intact contralateral areola (when it is large enough) make an excellent choice; such grafts usually heal well and provide very good color and texture match.

There are some patients in whom the contralateral areola is too small to permit harvesting of a graft; others are reluctant to have surgery on the sole remaining sensate nipple. In these cases, pigmented skin from other parts of the body may be used. Skin cephalic to the clavicle has a ruddy color and makes a contrasting areola when grafted onto the paler chest skin. The post-auricular area is a convenient donor site; a full thickness graft up to 3 cm in diameter may be harvested and the donor defect closed directly. Post-auricular skin can be quite erythematous, resulting in an areola that is redder than the opposite side (see Figure 16–18). The upper inner thigh is another popular donor site.[92] It is easy to harvest an adequate-sized full thickness graft from this area (even for bilateral areolar reconstruction) and still close the donor defect directly, leaving an inconspicuous scar. The graft usually heals with a pleasing brown or tan color, matching the contralateral areola nicely.[93] Unfortunately, grafts from the upper inner thigh have a tendency to fade; what initially looks like an excellent result may deteriorate over several years as the pigmentation of the grafted skin disappears.

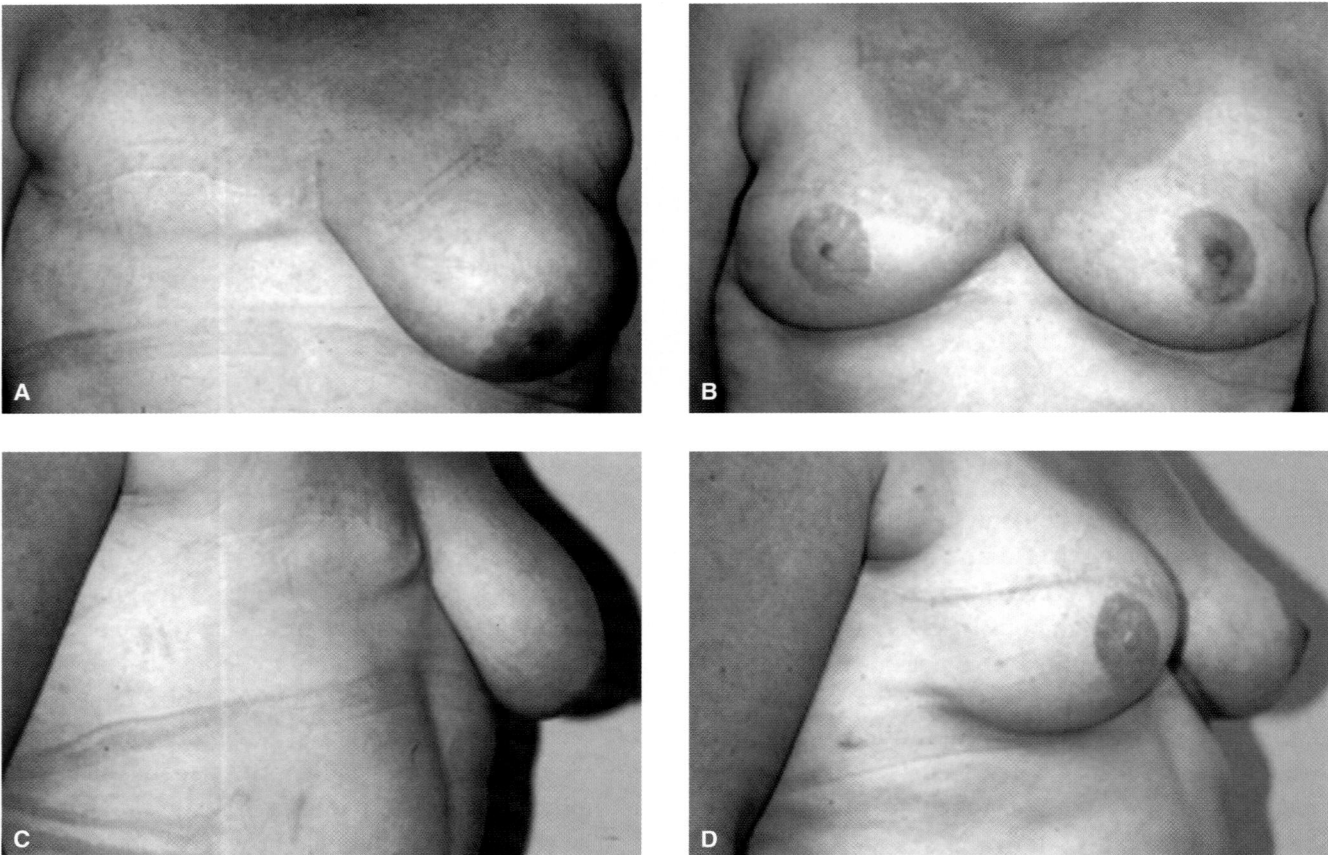

Figure 16–27. *A, B,* preoperative and postoperative frontal views and *C, D,* preoperative and postoperative oblique views of a patient with modified radical mastectomy reconstructed with an implant; because the opposite side was larger and more ptotic than the reconstructed breast, contralateral reduction mammaplasty was performed. Following the advent of techniques for autologous reconstruction, the need for contralateral symmetry operations was greatly diminished.

Tattooing is a valuable adjunct in nipple reconstruction.[94,95] Equipment specifically designed for medical tattooing is now marketed along with sterile, nontoxic pigments in shades suitable for nipple areolar reconstruction.[96] Tattooing is used to color the reconstructed nipple when it is made of local non-pigmented flaps. Tattooing is especially helpful in creating a pigmented areola and can be used independently or in conjunction with a graft.

Complications associated with nipple areolar reconstruction include failure to achieve or maintain adequate projection of the papilla, graft slough, and late loss of pigmentation.

Treatment of the Opposite Breast

The approach to the opposite breast in mastectomy patients has changed dramatically in recent years.[97,98] Prior to the advent of tissue expansion and flap reconstruction, it was often difficult or impossible to recreate a natural appearing, ptotic breast. It could also be difficult to reconstruct a breast large enough to match the opposite side. To achieve symmetry, the majority of patients underwent contralateral mastopexy or breast reduction (Figure 16–27). This inevitably caused scarring of the remaining breast and had the potential of interfering with sensation. Less radical ablative surgery, with preservation of more skin, the development of tissue expansion, and the introduction of various flaps, enabled reconstruction of larger more ptotic breasts. This dramatically reduced the need for contralateral surgery. At the present time, the aesthetic goal in most patients is to reconstruct a breast that closely matches the opposite side. Sometimes, in women with small, non-ptotic breasts, contralateral augmentation is indicated to help facilitate symmetry. Likewise, in women who have pre-existing macromastia, a smaller breast may be reconstructed in conjunction with reduction of the remaining intact breast.

Great progress has been made in breast reconstruction during the past several decades. It is now possible to offer reconstruction to virtually every mastectomy patient. Thanks to modern techniques, excellent results can be achieved in most cases. Breast reconstruction improves self-image, restores self-esteem, and helps women to put the experience of breast cancer behind them. Reconstruction also has practical benefits: it eliminates the need for cumbersome external prostheses, makes it easier to wear a wide variety of clothing styles, and allows a woman to freely pursue athletic activities. Surgeons should educate breast cancer patients about reconstructive options and make this alternative available to as many women as possible.

REFERENCES

1. Silverstein MJ, Larsen L, Soni R, et al. Breast biopsy and oncoplastic surgery for the patient with ductal carcinoma in situ: Surgical, pathologic and radiologic issues. In: Silverstein MJ, Recht A, Lagios M, editors. Ductal carcinoma in situ of the breast. Philadelphia: Lippincott, Williams and Wilkins; 2002. p. 185–206.
2. Clough K, Lewis JS, Couturaud B, et al. Oncoplastic techniques allow extensive resections for breast conserving therapy of breast carcinomas. Ann Surg 2003;237:26–34.
3. Holland R, Faverly D. Whole organ studies. In: Silverstein MJ, Recht A, Lagios M, editors. Ductal carcinoma in situ of the breast. Philadelphia: Lippincott, Williams and Wilkins; 2002. p. 240–8.
4. Hammond, DC. Short-scar periareolar-inferior pedicle reduction (SPAIR) mammaplasty. Oper Tech Plast Reconstr Surg 1999;6:106–18.
5. Kronowitz SJ, Robb GL Breast reconstruction with postmastectomy radiation therapy: current issues. Plast Reconstr Surg 2004;114:950–60.
6. Spear S L, Ducic I, Low M, Cuoco F. The effect of radiation on pedicled TRAM flap breast reconstruction: Outcomes and implications. Plast Reconstr Surg 2005;115:84–95.
7. Handel N, Lewinsky B, Silverstein, MJ, et al. Conservation therapy for breast cancer following augmentation mammaplasty. Plast Reconstr Surg 1991;87:873–8.
8. Handel N, Lewinsky B, Jensen JA, Silverstein MJ. Breast conservation therapy after augmentation mammaplasty: is it appropriate? Plast Reconstr Surg 1996;98:1216–24.
9. Wellisch DK, Schaine WS, Noone RB, Little JW. Psychosocial correlates of immediate versus delayed reconstruction of the breast. Plast Reconstr Surg 1985;76:713–8.
10. Stevens LA, McGrath MH, Druss RG, et al. The psychological impact of immediate breast reconstruction for women with early breast cancer. Plast Reconstr Surg 1984;73: 619–28.
11. Georgiade G, Georgiade N, McCarty KS Jr, Seigler HF. Rationale for immediate reconstruction of the breast following modified radical mastectomy. Ann Plast Surg 1981;8:20–4.
12. Bostwick J. Aesthetic and reconstructive breast surgery. St. Louis: The C.V. Mosby Company; 1983.
13. Goldwyn R. Breast reconstruction after mastectomy. N Engl J Med 1987;318:1711–4.
14. Handel N. Breast reconstruction in patients with DCIS. In: Silverstein MJ, editor. Ductal carcinoma in-situ of the breast. Baltimore: Williams & Wilkins; 1997. p. 505–19.
15. Apfelberg DB, Laub DR, Maser MR, Lash H. Submuscular breast reconstruction—indications and techniques. Ann Plast Surg 1981;7:213–21.
16. Snyderman RK. Reconstruction of the breast after surgery for malignancy. In: Goldwyn RM, editor. Plastic and reconstructive surgery of the breast. Boston: Little, Brown and Company; 1976.
17. Fee-Fulkerson K, Conaway MR, Winer EP, et al. Factors contributing to patient satisfaction with breast reconstruction using silicone gel implants. Plast Reconstr Surg 1996;97: 1420–6.
18. Radovan C. Breast reconstruction after mastectomy using a temporary expander. Plast Reconstr Surg 1982;69: 195–208.
19. Schuster R, Rotter S, Boonn W, Efron G. The use of tissue expanders in immediate breast reconstruction following mastectomy for cancer. Br J Plast Surg 1990;43:413–8.
20. Spear SL, Spittler CJ. Breast reconstruction with implants and expanders. Plast Reconstr Surg 2001;107:177–87.
21. Bostwick J III, Nahai F, Wallace JG, Vasconez LO. Sixty latissimus dorsi flaps. Plast Reconstr Surg 1979;63:31–41.
22. Gerber BD, Krause A, Reimer T, et al. Breast reconstruction with latissimus dorsi flap: Improved aesthetic results after transection of its humeral insertion. Plast Reconstr Surg 1999;103:1876–81.
23. Birnbaum L. Breast reconstruction utilizing custom implant and dermal grafting. In: Gant TD, Vasconez LO, editors. Post-mastectomy reconstruction. Baltimore: The Williams and Wilkins Company; 1981.
24. Bostwick JL, Vasconez LO, Jurkiewicz MJ, Breast reconstruction following radical mastectomy. Plast Reconstr Surg 1978;61:682–93.
25. Gruber RP, Kahn RA, Lash H, et al. Breast reconstruction following mastectomy: A comparison of submuscular and subcutaneous techniques. Plast Reconstr Surg 1981; 67:312–7.
26. Freeman BS, Hueston JT. Reconstruction after mastectomy: Simple. In: Chang, WH, Petry, JJ, editors. The breast—an atlas of reconstruction. Baltimore: The Williams and Wilkins Company; 1984.
27. Beekman WH., van Straalen WR, Hage JJ, et al. Imaging signs and radiologists' jargon of ruptured breast implants. Plast Reconstr Surg 1998;102:1281–9.
28. Guthrie RH. The untoward result in breast reconstruction. In: Goldwyn RM, editor. The unfavorable result in plastic

surgery—avoidance and treatment. Boston: Little, Brown and Company; 1984.

29. van Heerden JA, Jackson I, Martin JK, Fisher J. Surgical technique and pitfalls of breast reconstruction immediately after mastectomy for carcinoma: initial experience. Mayo Clin Proc 1987;62:185–91.
30. Armstrong RW, Berkowitz RL, Bolding F. Infection following breast reconstruction. Ann Plast Surg 1989;23:284–8.
31. de Cholnky T. Augmentation mammoplasty: a survey of complications in 10,941 patients by 265 surgeons. Plast Reconstr Surg 1970;45:573–7.
32. Nahabedian MY, Tsangaris T, Momen B, Manson PN. Infectious complications following breast reconstruction with expanders and implants. Plast Reconstr Surg 2003; 112:467–76.
33. Courtiss EH, Goldwyn RM, Anastasi GP. The fate of breast implants with infections around them. Plast Reconstr Surg 1979;63:812–6.
34. Handel N. Managing local implant-related problems. In: Spear SL, editor. Surgery of the breast: principles and art. Philadelphia: Lippincott-Raven; 1998. p. 953–68.
35. Freeman BS. Successful treatment of some fibrous envelope contractures around breast implants. Plast Reconstr Surg 1972;50:107–13.
36. Hetter GP. Satisfactions and dissatisfactions of patients with augmentation mammaplasty. Plast Reconstr Surg 1979; 64:151–5.
37. Woods JE, Irons GB Jr, Arnold PG. The case for submuscular implantation of prostheses in reconstructive breast surgery. Ann Plast Surg 1980;5:115–22.
38. Gylbert L, Asplund O, Jurell G. Capsular contracture after breast reconstruction with silicone-gel and saline-filled implants: a 6-year follow-up. Plast Reconstr Surg 1990; 85:373–7.
39. Gibney J. Use of a permanent tissue expander for breast reconstruction. Plast Reconstr Surg 1989;84:607–17.
40. Argenta LC. Tissue expansion revisited. Adv Opthalmic Plast Reconstr Surg 1987;4:113–8.
41. Russell IS, Collins JP, Holmes AD, Smith JA. The use of soft tissue expansion for immediate breast reconstruction after mastectomy. Med J Aust 1990;152:632–5.
42. Slavin SA, Colen SR. Sixty consecutive breast reconstructions with the inflatable expander: a critical appraisal. Plast Reconstr Surg 1990;86:910–9.
43. Rosen PB, Jabs AD, Kistere SJ, Hugo NE. Clinical experience with immediate breast reconstruction using tissue expansion or transverse rectus abdominis musculocutaneous flaps. Ann Plast Surg 1990;25:249–57.
44. Bostwick J III, Scheflan M. The latissimus dorsi musculotaneous flap: a one stage breast reconstruction. Clin Plast Surg 1980;7:71–8.
45. Biggs TM, Cronin ED. Technical aspects of the latissumus dorsi myocutaneous flap in breast reconstruction. Ann Plast Surg 1981;6:381–8.
46. Hokin JAB, Silfverskiold K. Breast reconstruction without an implant: results and complications using an extended latissimus dorsi flap. Plast Reconstr Surg 1987;79: 58–66.
47. Mathes S, Nahai F. Clinical atlas of muscle and musculocutaneous flaps. St. Louis: The CV Mosby Company; 1979.
48. McCraw J, Dibbell D. Experimental definitions of independent myocutaneous vascular territories. Plast Reconstr Surg 1977;60:212–20.
49. Schneider WJ, Hill HL, Brown RG. Latissimus dorsi myocutaneous flap for breast reconstruction. Br J Plast Surg 1977;30:277–81.
50. Maxwell GP, Goldwyn RM, Vasconez LO. Reconstruction after mastectomy with latissimus dorsi musculocutaneous flap. In Chang WH, Petry JJ, editors. The breast—an atlas of reconstruction. Baltimore: The Williams and Wilkins Company; 1984.
51. Kroll SS, Baldwin B. A comparison of outcomes using three different methods of breast reconstruction. Plast Reconstr Surg 1992;90:455–62.
52. Hartrampf CR, Scheflan M, Black PW. Breast reconstruction with the transverse abdominal island flap. Plast Reconstr Surg 1982;69:216–25.
53. Maxwell GP. Technical alternatives in transverse rectus abdominis breast reconstruction, Persp Plast Surg 1987;1:1.
54. Chang DW, Wang B, Robb GL, et al. Effect of obesity on flap and donor-site complications in free transverse rectus abdominis myocutaneous flap breast reconstruction. Plast Reconstr Surg 2000;105:1640–8.
55. Chang DW, Reece GP, Wang B, et al. Effect of smoking on complications in patients undergoing free TRAM flap breast reconstruction. Plast Reconstr Surg 2000;105: 2374–80.
56. Kroll SS, Schusterman, MA, Reece GP, et al. Breast reconstruction with myocutaneous flaps in previously irradiated patients. Plast Reconstr Surg 1994;93:460–9.
57. Ishii CH Jr, Bostwick J III, Raine TJ, et al. Double-pedicle transverse rectus abdominis musculocutaneous flap for unilateral breast and chest-wall reconstruction. Plast Reconstr Surg 1985;76:901–7.
58. Jensen JA, Handel N, Silverstein MJ, et al. Extended skin island delay of the unipedicle TRAM flap: Experience in 35 patients. Plast Reconstr Surg 1995;96:1341–5.
59. Hudson DA. The surgically delayed unipedicled TRAM flap for breast reconstruction. Ann Plast Surg 1996;36: 238–42.
60. Restifo RJ, Ward BA, Scoutt LM. Timing, magnitude, and utility of surgical delay in the TRAM flap: II. Clinical studies. Plast Reconstr Surg 1997;99:1217–23.
61. Harashina T, Sone K, Inoue T, et al. Augmentation of circulation of pedicled transverse rectus abdominis musculocutaneous flaps by microvascular surgery. Br J Plast Surg 1987;40:367–70.
62. Fujino T, Harashina T, Aoyagi F. Reconstruction for aplasia of the breast and pectoral region by microvascular transfer of a free flap from the buttock. Plast Reconstr Surg 1975;56:178–81.
63. Gant TD, Serafin D, Buncke H. Free flap reconstruction of the breast. In: Gant TD, Vasconez LO editors. Post-mastectomy reconstruction. Baltimore: The Williams and Wilkins Company; 1981.
64. Beckenstein MS, Grotting JC. Breast reconstruction with free-tissue transfer. Plast Reconstr Surg 2001;108: 1345–54.
65. Schusterman MA, Kroll SS, Miller MJ, et al. The free transverse rectus abdominis musculocutaneous flap for breast

reconstruction: one center's experience with 211 consecutive cases. Ann Plast Surg 1994;32:234–41.

66. Allen RJ, Treece P. Deep inferior epigastric perforator flap for breast reconstruction. Ann Plast Surg 1994;32:32–8.
67. Futter C, Webster M, Hagen S, Mitchell S. A retrospective comparison of abdominal muscle strength following breast reconstruction with a free TRAM or DIEP flap. Br J Plast Surg 2000;53:578–83.
68. Kroll S, Sharma S, Koutz C, et al. Postoperative morphine requirements of free TRAM and DIEP flaps. Plast Reconstr Surg 2001;107:338–41.
69. Chevray PM. Breast reconstruction with superficial inferior epigastric artery flaps: a prospective comparison with TRAM and DIEP flaps. Plast Reconstr Surg 2004;114: 1077–83.
70. Shaw WW. Breast reconstruction by superior gluteal microvascular free flaps without silicone implants. Plast Reconstr Surg 1983;72:490–501.
71. Paletta CE, Bostwick J III, Nahai F. The inferior gluteal free flap in breast reconstruction. Plast Reconstr Surg 1989;84:875–83.
72. Elliott LF. Lateral transverse thigh flap for autogenous tissue breast reconstruction. Perspect Plast Surg 1989;3:80.
73. Hartrampf CR Jr, Noel RT, Drazan L, et al. Rubens fat pad for breast reconstruction: A peri-iliac soft-tissue free flap. Plast Reconstr Surg 1994;93:402–7.
74. Elliott LF, Beegle PH, Hartrampf CR Jr, et al. The lateral transverse thigh free flap: An alternative for autogenous tissue breast reconstruction. Plast Reconstr Surg 1990; 85:169–78.
75. Kroll SS, Gherardini G, Martin JE. Fat necrosis in free and pedicled TRAM flaps. Plast Reconstr Surg 1998;102: 1502–7.
76. Kroll SS, Schusterman MA, Reece GP, et al. Abdominal wall strength, bulging and hernia after TRAM flap breast reconstruction. Plast Reconstr Surg 1995;96:616–9.
77. Hartrampf CR Jr, Bennett KG. Autogenous tissue reconstruction in the mastectomy patient: a critical review of 300 patients. Ann Surg 1987;205:508–19.
78. Shaw WW. Microvascular free flap breast reconstruction. In: Scheflan M, editor. Clin Plast Surg 11:333, 1984. Philadelphia: W. B. Saunders Company; 1984, p. 333–41.
79. Wellisch DK, Schain WS, Noone B, Little JW. The psychological contribution of nipple addition in breast reconstruction. Plast Reconstr Surg 1987;80:699–704.
80. Shestak KC, Gabriel A, Landecker A, et al. Assessment of long-term nipple projection: a comparison of three techniques. Plast Reconstr Surg 2002;110:780–86.
81. Kroll SS, Reece GP, Miller MJ, et al. Comparison of nipple projection with the modified double-opposing tab and star flaps. Plast Reconstr Surg 1997;99:1602–5.
82. Few JW, Marcus JR, Casas LA, et al. Long-term predicatable nipple projection following reconstruction. Plast Reconstr Surg 1999;104:1321–4.
83. Mendelson BC. Results of nipple areola reconstruction. Aust NZ J Surg 1983;53:63–6.
84. Adams WM. Free composite grafts of the nipples in mammaplasty. South Surg 1947;13:715–33.
85. Brent B, Bostwick J III. Nipple-areola reconstruction with auricular tissues. Plast Reconstr Surg 1977;60:353–61.
86. Klatsky SA, Manson PN. Toe pulp free grafts in nipple reconstruction. Plast Reconstr Surg 1981;68:245–8.
87. Kroll SS, Hamilton S. Nipple reconstruction with the double-opposing-tab flap. Plast Reconstr Surg 1989;84:520–5.
88. Losken A, Mackay GJ, Bostwick J. Nipple reconstruction using the C-V flap technique: a long-term evaluation. Plast Reconstr Surg 2001;108:361–9.
89. Di Benedetto G, Sperti V, Pierangeli M, Bertani A. A simple and reliable method of nipple reconstruction using a spiral flap made of residual scar tissue. Plast Reconstr Surg 2004;114:158–61.
90. Little JW, Spear SL. The finishing touches in nipple-areolar reconstruction. Plast Surg 1988;2:1.
91. Adams WM. Labial transplant for correction of loss of the nipple. Plast Reconstr Surg 1949;4:295–8.
92. Broadbent TR, Metz PS, Woolf RM. Restoring the mammary areola by a skin graft from the upper inner thigh. Br J Plast Surg 1977;30:220–2.
93. Asplund O. Nipple and areola reconstruction. Scand J Plast Reconstr Surg 1983;17:233–40.
94. O'Donoghue JM, Clough KB, Sarfati I. Solving the problem of color mismatch in nipple-areola reconstruction. Plast Reconstr Surg 1999;104:1936.
95. Becker H. The use of intradermal tattoo to enchance the final result of nipple-areola reconstruction. Plast Reconstr Surg 1986;77:673–6.
96. Spear SL, Convit R., Little JW III. Intradermal tattoo as an adjunct to nipple-areola reconstruction. Plast Reconstr Surg 1989;83:907–11.
97. Labandter HP, Dowden RV. Surgical considerations in managing the remaining breast during postmastectomy breast reconstruction. In: Scheflan M editor. Clin Plast Surg 11:365 Philadelphia: W.B. Saunders Company; 1984. p. 365–8.
98. Losken A, Carlson GW, Bostwick J, et al. Trends in unilateral breast reconstruction and management of the contralateral breast: the Emory experience. Plast Reconstr Surg 2002;110:89–97.

17

Evaluation and Surgical Management of Stage I and II Breast Cancer

DAVID J. WINCHESTER
TIMOTHY KENNEDY

The management of patients with breast cancer has undergone significant evolution over the past two decades as a result of a better understanding of the biologic behavior of breast cancer, advances in adjuvant chemotherapy and hormonal therapy, advances in radiographic detection of early-stage breast cancer, and the implementation of breast conservation therapy and sentinel lymph node biopsy. The vast majority of breast cancers diagnosed today are early stage. The use of routine screening mammography and increased breast cancer awareness are primarily responsible for the trend towards earlier diagnosis. Although radical and modified radical mastectomies have been the mainstay treatment for early-stage breast cancer for decades, breast-conserving therapy has become the preferred method of treatment for appropriate patients with early-stage breast cancer. As a result, disfiguring outcomes have become less common (Figures 17–1 and 17–2).

DIAGNOSTIC EVALUATION

Although most patients with a breast abnormality or a diagnosis of breast cancer will be referred for further evaluation, the diagnosis will be suspected initially by the primary care provider. Therefore, it is imperative that physicians be familiar with the key issues relevant to the initial evaluation of women with suspected breast cancer.

Screening for breast cancer should include monthly breast examinations, annual clinical breast examinations, and mammography beginning at age 40 years. Patients with a genetic predisposition or other major risk factors may benefit from earlier screening. When an abnormality is detected on screening examination, additional diagnostic studies may include compression or magnification views, ultrasonography, and magnetic resonance imaging (MRI).

Most patients with early-stage breast cancer will present with a mass discovered on routine physical examination or a suspicious finding on mammogram or ultrasound. Prior to obtaining a histologic or cytologic diagnosis, a complete history, physical examination, and radiographic evaluation should be performed. If the lesion is palpable, a surgical consultation should be considered. A breast biopsy per-

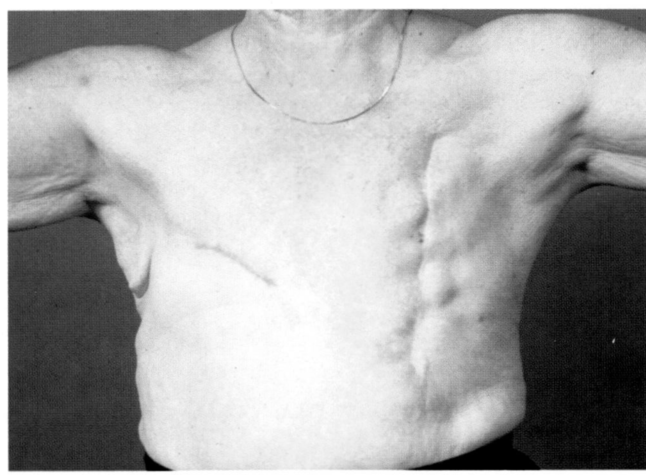

Figure 17–1. Metachronous bilateral breast cancers treated with radical mastectomy (left) and modified radical mastectomy (right).

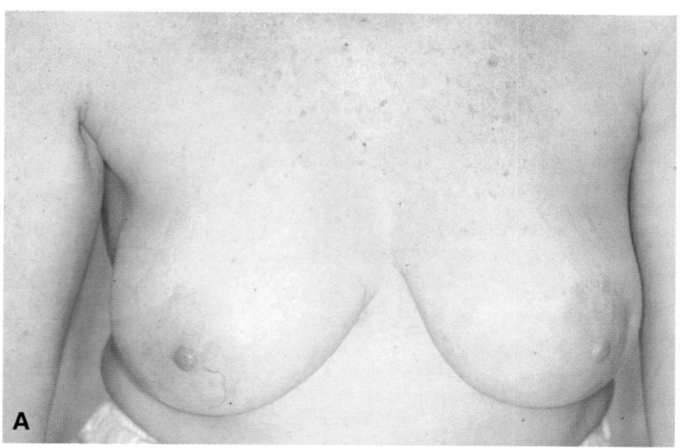

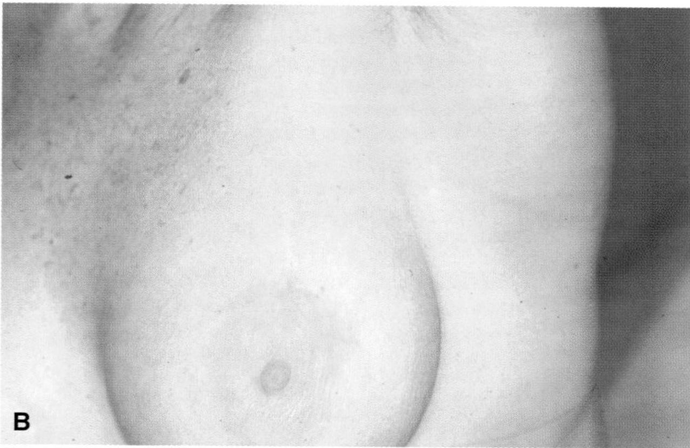

Figure 17–2. *A* and *B*. Excellent cosmetic outcome from breast-conserving surgery (left breast).

formed prior to this evaluation can obscure physical findings in the event that a hematoma develops with a diagnostic procedure.

Physical examination of a patient with a breast cancer should begin with inspection of the breasts. Any asymmetry of the breasts, skin or nipple changes, or masses should be noted. The axillary and supraclavicular nodal basins should be palpated for the presence of nodal disease. The breast parenchyma should be systematically evaluated in the upright and supine positions. Any palpable masses should be characterized by the location, size, shape, mobility, and proximity to skin or chest wall. Skin, nipple, or breast parenchyma retraction are not necessarily signs of a locally advanced breast cancer and do not represent contraindications to breast conservation therapy but raise suspicion for more advanced disease.

A mammographic examination within 3 months of a planned biopsy or definitive surgery is important in establishing whether a patient is a candidate for breast conservation therapy. The mammogram will help to define the size and extent of the patient's disease, assist in detecting multicentric disease, and evaluate the contralateral breast. The features most commonly associated with malignant breast lesions are masses, microcalcifications, architectural distortion, or a combination of these findings. Ultrasonography is frequently used to further characterize lesions according to their benign or malignant characteristics. MRI may serve as a useful adjunct to mammography and ultrasonography for the identification of multicentric disease. However, the precise role in evaluation of the breast cancer patient and in the screening of high-risk women remains under investigation.[1–4]

After the physical examination and radiographic studies, a cytologic or histologic diagnosis is required prior to any therapeutic procedure (Figure 17–3). If the lesion can be appreciated on physical examination, an office-based aspiration or core biopsy is cost effective, expeditious, and may avoid a subsequent localization of the malignancy. Establishing a diagnosis with a core biopsy provides histologic confirmation with the ability to distinguish between invasive and in situ carcinoma. This approach requires a local anesthetic and has greater potential for hematoma formation. Compared with core biopsy, fine-needle aspiration (FNA) cytology is a less invasive technique but requires expertise in the interpretation of cytologic preparations. It has very limited capabilities in distinguishing invasive from in situ tumors, although there may be suggestive features in certain tumor types.[5] Hormone receptor assays and immunohistochemical stains for prognostic markers such as *HER2/neu* and *p53* can be determined from both core samples and cytology preparations. The false-negative and false-positive rates for core biopsy and FNA cytology are comparable.[6–8]

SURGICAL MANAGEMENT

The treatment of breast cancer has evolved over the past several decades and involves a multi-disciplinary team to provide the patient with optimal therapy. To define the optimal local, regional, and systemic therapies of breast cancer, the patient needs to

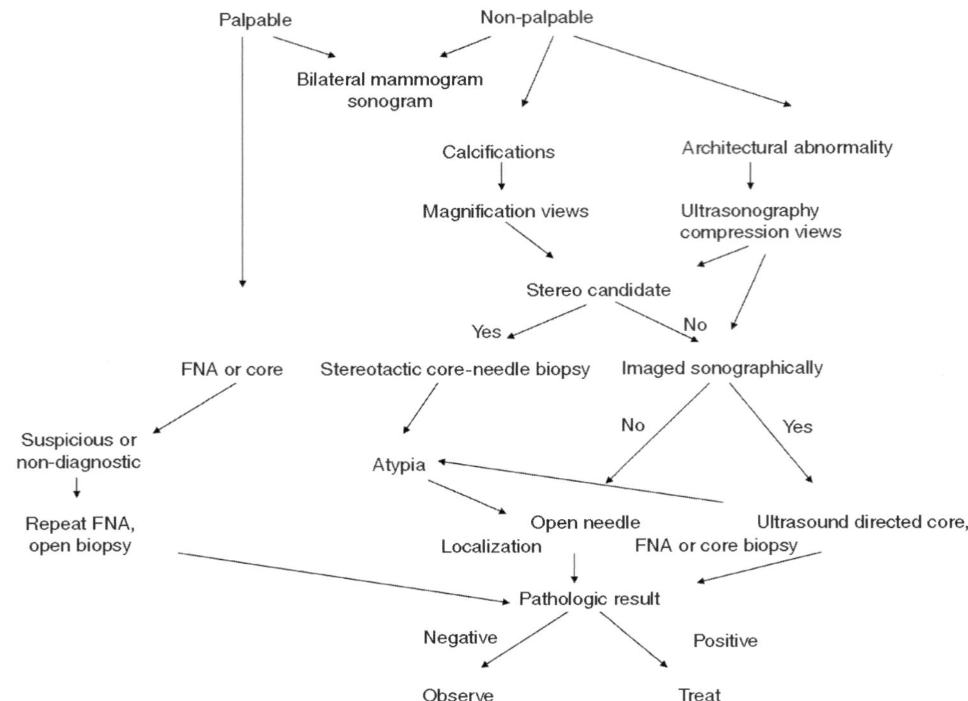

Figure 17–3. Diagnostic algorithm for early breast cancer.

be staged according to the tumor-nodes-metastasis (TNM) staging system. The American Joint Committee on Cancer, in cooperation with the TNM Committee and the International Union Against Cancer, has developed a revised staging schema based on tumor size, nodal status, and the presence or absence of distant metastases[9] (see Chapter 7 "Breast Cancer Risk Assessment and Management"). For most patients with early-stage breast cancer, surgical intervention serves as the first phase of treatment. This step also moves beyond clinical staging to pathologic staging to provide important prognostic information to direct adjuvant therapy decisions.

Breast Conservation Therapy

Most patients who are diagnosed with breast cancer are candidates for breast conservation therapy. Six prospective randomized trials have compared the efficacy of breast conservation therapy (BCT) to mastectomy for stage I and II breast cancer. There are no differences in overall survival rates when comparing the two treatments in all six of these trials[10–15] (Table 17–1). A nonrandomized comparison,[16] as well as a meta-analysis of randomized trials,[17] has shown equivalent survival rates between these two approaches.

Furthermore, 20-year follow-up data from the National Surgical Adjuvant Breast and Bowel Project (NSABP) B-06 clinical trial and the Milan trials have shown similar long-term survival for BCT compared to mastectomy. In the NSABP B-06 trial, 2,105 patients with stage I or II tumors were randomized to one of three treatment groups: total mastectomy, BCT alone, or BCT with breast irradiation. No significant difference was observed between these three groups with respect to distant disease-free survival and overall survival. The Milan trial studied 701 patients with stage I breast cancer and randomized them to quadrantectomy with breast irradiation or radical mastectomy. There was no significant difference between the groups in the rate of distant metastases, overall mortality, or breast cancer–specific mortality. Based upon abundant data, BCT is appropriate and the treatment of choice for most women with early-stage breast cancer. However, acceptance of this treatment approach has been gradual and dependent upon regional preferences and availability of radiation therapy facilities.[18]

Table 17–1. EFFICACY OF BREAST CONSERVATION THERAPY TO MASTECTOMY FOR STAGE I AND II BREAST CANCER

Author	Trial	Median Follow-Up (yr)	No. of Patients	Size of Tumor	No. of Treatment Groups	Mastectomy Local Recurrence (%)	BCT Local Recurrence (%)	Mastectomy Overall Survival (%)	BCT Overall Survival (%)
Veronesi et al	Milan	20	701	< 2 cm	2	2.3	8.8	58.8	58.3
Fisher et al	NSABP- B06	20	1,851	< 4 cm	3	10.2	39 (lump) 14 (lump + XRT)	47	46 (lump) 47 (lump + XRT)
Arriagada et al	Institut Gustave-Roussy Breast Cancer Group	14	179	< 2 cm	2	4	NR	79	78
Van Dongen et al	EORTC 10801 trial	10	868	< 5 cm	2	20	12	66	65
Poggi et al	NCI	18	237	< 5 cm	2	22	0	58	54
Blichert-Toft et al	Danish Breast Cancer Cooperative Group	6	905	< 5 cm	2	NR	NR	82	79

BCT = breast-conserving therapy, EORTC = European Organisation for Research and Treatment of Cancer, NCI = National Cancer Institute, NR = Not reported, NSABP = National Surgical Adjuvant Breast and Bowel project, XRT = radiation therapy.

Improvements in surgery and radiation therapy have minimized the poor results seen initially (Figures 17–4 and 17–5). The selection process for BCT is based upon surgical margins, cosmetic outcome, ability to undergo breast irradiation, and patient preference. Extensive, suspicious mammographic microcalcifications, multicentricity, persistent involvement of surgical margins, and a large tumor-to-breast volume ratio are reasons to consider a total mastectomy. A subset of patients who are not candidates for breast irradiation (early pregnancy, previous breast irradiation, connective tissue diseases) may be treated more appropriately with total mastectomy. Centrally located lesions, including Paget's disease, (Figure 17–6) were at one time considered a relative contraindication to BCT. However, this and other centrally located tumors may be approached with a central lumpectomy and excision of the nipple–areolar complex with an acceptable cosmetic outcome (Figure 17–7). This treatment has

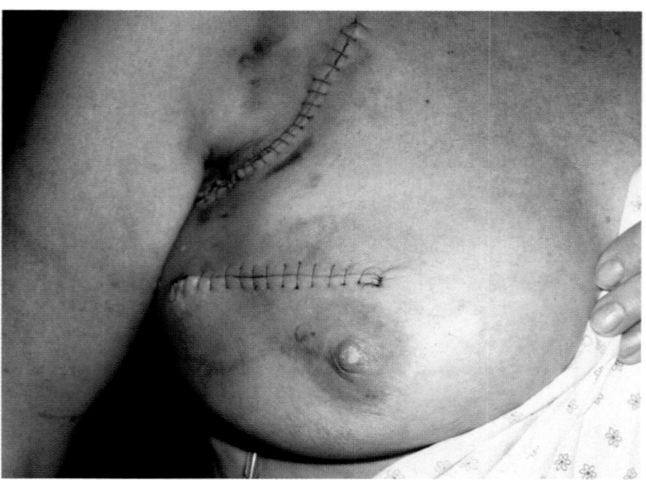

Figure 17–4. Poor cosmetic outcome resulting from poor incision placement, incision size, and hematoma formation.

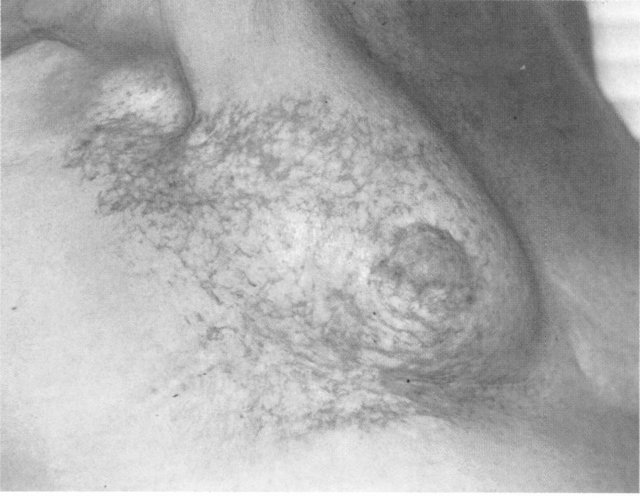

Figure 17–5. Poor cosmetic outcome resulting from radiation injury.

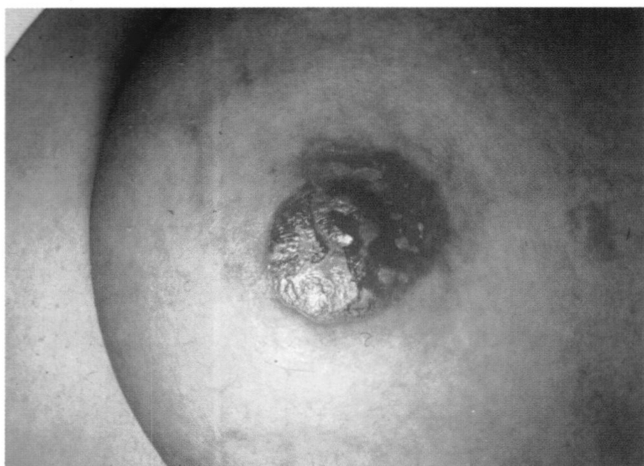

Figure 17–6. Paget's disease.

the distinct advantage of maintaining the breast mound and a sensate breast.

For patients with large T2 tumors or those with a large tumor-to-breast volume ratio, neoadjuvant chemotherapy may downsize the tumor and allow subsequent breast conservation. The NSABP B-18 trial used preoperative chemotherapy and demonstrated an increase in breast conservation surgery without compromising survival.[19] Other studies have confirmed these results, leading to an increased interest in patients desiring BCT.[20,21]

When a patient has been deemed a candidate for BCT, the goal of surgery is the removal of all known malignant disease with a minimal cosmetic deformity. Placement of the incision is important to create a good cosmetic result and to allow for additional surgery in the event of margin involvement. This bears greater importance for patients requiring mastectomy for extensive margin involvement. Optimal cosmesis usually involves an incision placed within skin folds or in a curvilinear fashion around the nipple (Figure 17–8). However, in the lower breast, a radial incision may provide better results, particularly if skin removal is necessary. Incisions should be placed directly over the primary to avoid tunneling and to limit the deformity and extent of dissection in the breast. With the exception of superficial lesions, resection of skin or subcutaneous tissue is usually not required and is undesirable as it may alter the position of the nipple or the inframammary crease. Although an adequate margin is important, a more extensive resection needs to be balanced with the cosmetic and functional aspects of the operation. In most instances, resection of the pectoralis fascia with the lumpectomy specimen will avoid concerns about posterior extension. Without muscle involvement, inclusion of the pectoralis fascia with the lumpectomy specimen should assist in good local control, even with a close margin.

The breast tumor should be removed with a margin of normal breast tissue while avoiding excessive sacrifice of normal breast tissue. Meticulous hemostasis is important to minimize the recovery period. Postoperative hematomas may complicate the timing and delivery of adjuvant therapy and obscure future physical examinations and mammograms. Breast tissue should not be reapproximated. The skin incision is usually closed with an absorbable subcuticular closure.

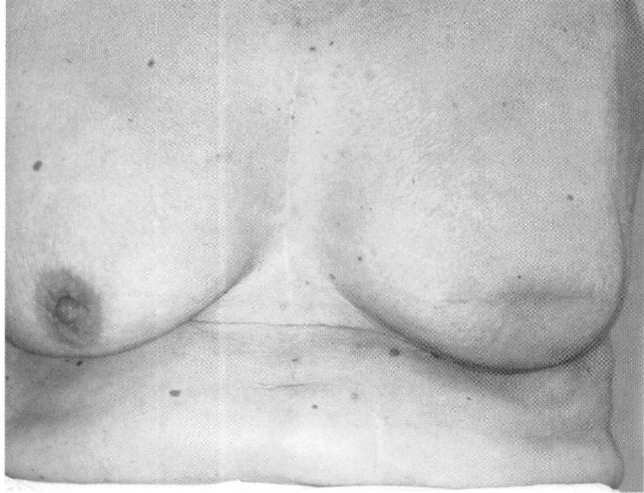

Figure 17–7. Central lumpectomy.

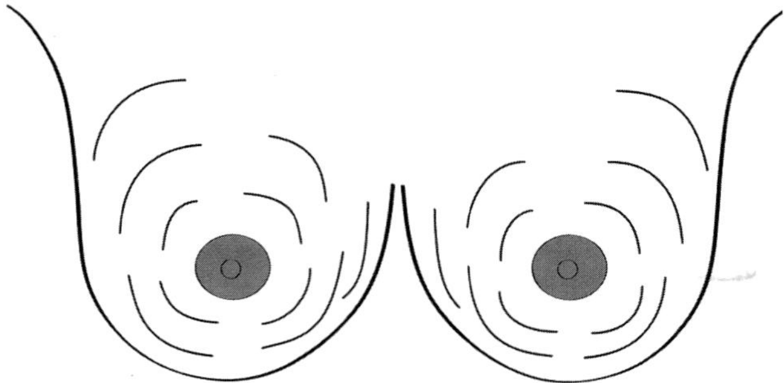

Figure 17–8. Incision placement for lumpectomy.

Specimen orientation by the surgeon, preferably with a multicolored ink approach, provides essential information for the pathologist and the surgeon if re-excision is necessary. Lumpectomy cavities are optimally defined for the radiotherapist with placement of radiopaque clips along the borders of the cavity. This may help facilitate the delivery of a radiation therapy boost to the lumpectomy site.

If a patient has a breast cancer that is nonpalpable and diagnosed by image-guided biopsy, breast-conserving surgery should be conducted with preoperative guide wire localization or intraoperative ultrasonography. Others have reported successful localization with technetium sulfur colloid, while also providing identification of the sentinel lymph node.[22] If the lesion is localized in the radiology suite, close collaboration between the radiologist and surgeon is important to determine the positioning, depth, and angle of placement to ensure an accurate excision. Following excision, the specimen should be submitted for radiographic analysis to confirm complete removal of the mammographic abnormality. Communication between the pathologist and surgeon will minimize errors in the margin analysis.

Risk of Local Recurrence

A number of demographic, pathologic, and treatment factors have been identified as predictors for local recurrence after BCT. These factors include age,[23,24] histologic type and grade,[25,26] the presence or absence of tumor necrosis,[27] vascular or lymphatic invasion,[28,29] presence of an extensive intraductal component,[30,31] margins of resection,[32] pathologic nodal status,[33] and use of adjuvant therapy.[34,35] The only variable to predict local recurrence from the analysis of NSABP B-06 was age under 45 years.[36] Trials by Albain and colleagues and Nixon and colleagues have demonstrated a worse prognosis for patients younger than 35 years of age, even after adjustment for other prognostic factors.[23,24] Others have shown an increased risk of local recurrence with tumor necrosis, high-grade tumors, or vascular or lymphatic invasion.[37,38]

Although the histologic subtype of the invasive breast cancer does not appear to have an impact on the local recurrence rate, the issue is somewhat controversial. In addition to ductal carcinoma in situ (DCIS), which may extend great distances in the breast without any mammographic or physical findings, invasive lobular carcinoma may have a pervasive presentation. For patients with DCIS, preoperative magnification views may help identify extensive pleomorphic calcifications extending beyond the index lesion. All suspicious calcifications should be included with the excision. Invasive lobular carcinoma has a more indolent presentation with a less defined mass and indistinct borders. Mammographic findings are subtle[39,40] and more likely to underestimate tumor dimensions, compared with other invasive cancers.[41] These characteristics account for the greater likelihood of re-excision. The histologic evaluation of the lumpectomy and regional lymph nodes is more difficult because of the frequency of single malignant lobular cells that can extend into the breast parenchyma. Cytokeratin stains may facilitate the identification of lobular cells within the breast and lymph nodes but have uncertain prognostic information in axillary staging with individual tumor cells and micrometastases.[9,42]

Randomized clinical trials addressing breast preservation therapy have not been specifically designed to address the therapy of lobular carcinomas, but most have included patients with this histologic category. Several non-randomized studies have found no difference in the local recurrence rates or disease-free survival rates between breast preservation patients with lobular carcinoma and those with ductal carcinoma.[43–45] However, patients with lobular carcinomas are more likely to have positive margins at attempted BCT and higher rates of mastectomy.[44,46] Other studies have found an increased incidence of local recurrence in patients with lobular carcinoma treated with BCT and with clear margins.[47] Analysis of the National Cancer Data Base did not identify any significant differences in size, stage, or survival according to histology.[48] It would appear that there are not any specific histologic categories that should exclude consideration of BCT. The same principles of a careful preoperative assessment and microscopic evaluation of lumpectomy margins should lead to successful BCT for all histologic variants.

Extensive intraductal component (EIC) refers to a breast cancer comprised of at least 25% of DCIS within the surrounding normal tissue or DCIS with focal areas of invasion. Approximately 20% of patients with early-stage breast cancer undergoing BCT for invasive ductal carcinoma have EIC. Although some have found an increased risk of local recurrence in EIC positive tumors, others have noted that this risk is diminished with a negative margin of resection.[49] Although EIC may be indicative of more extensive disease, it does not appear to be an independent risk factor for local recurrence when margin status is taken into consideration.

Margin involvement is a strong predictor of local recurrence,[32] and identification of an involved margin should prompt consideration for re-excision. Positive margins have also been found to be an independent predictor of decreased breast cancer specific survival.[50] However, the impact of close surgical margins on local recurrence risk is more controversial. Singletary reviewed the literature addressing local recurrence rates and margins of resection. Outcomes ranged from no difference in the risk of recurrence to an increased risk.[51] Although this issue remains controversial, attempting to achieve widely negative margins may offer an improvement in local control and overall survival.

Despite the usefulness of a microscopic margin assessment, clear surgical margins under the most stringent conditions do not ensure local control rates that are equivalent to those achieved with the addition of radiotherapy. The Uppsala Swedish trial included patients with tumors less than 20 mm in size. Each patient underwent a sector resection consisting of removal of a portion of the skin and pectoralis fascia. Each margin was assessed twice. Any microscopic margin involvement or lymph node involvement was an exclusion criterion. Patients were randomized to observation or radiotherapy after sector resection. Despite these favorable conditions and careful analysis of margins, local recurrence was significantly more common in the observation arm of the study.[52] As an anatomic correlation to explain this outcome, serial sectioning of mastectomy specimens of patients who would have been lumpectomy candidates has shown that microscopic foci of cancer are identified beyond 2 cm of the primary tumor in 41% of patients.[53]

The use of adjuvant systemic therapy in addition to BCT has been shown to be associated with a decreased ipsilateral breast recurrence rate. Several randomized clinical trials have shown benefits to both chemotherapy and hormonal therapy. In NSABP B-13, node-negative, hormone receptor negative patients were randomized to either chemotherapy or observation. The control group had an 8-year local recurrence rate of 13.4% compared to 2.6% for those treated with chemotherapy.[54] In NSABP B-14, node-negative, hormone receptor positive patients were randomized to either tamoxifen or placebo. The 10-year ipsilateral breast recurrence rate was 14.7% for those treated without tamoxifen and 4.3% with tamoxifen.[34] These results were substantiated by the Stockholm Breast Cancer Study Group with similar local recurrence rates.[55]

An ipsilateral breast recurrence after BCT may be difficult to distinguish from a second primary tumor. Although this may not be an important distinction to define the surgical management, the distinction between a recurrence and a new primary may be indicated by the location of the second lesion relative to the initial primary tumor, the histologic features, and the disease-free interval. Proximity to a previous lumpectomy site increases the likelihood of the tumor being a recurrence. In the absence of any previous history of in situ carcinoma, an in situ component is suggestive of a new primary lesion. Local recurrences are most likely to occur within the first 3 years of initial treatment, whereas a long disease-free interval is more suggestive of a second primary tumor. In a retrospective analysis, Huang and colleagues designated an ipsilateral breast recurrence as a tumor with an identical histologic subtype within 3 cm of the original primary tumor. Of 126 ipsilateral tumors following initial therapy, 62% were classified as true recurrences and 38% as new primaries. True recurrences developed at a shorter time interval and had a worse 10-year breast cancer specific survival than those patients with second primaries.[56]

In addition to providing prognostic significance, the distinction between a new primary and a recurrent breast cancer is important in understanding the biology of the disease and the efficacy of the treatment selected. For the surgical intervention, an ipsilateral event is managed in a similar fashion with either scenario. Without the ability to deliver additional radiotherapy in most patients, most are treated with a completion mastectomy. An ipsilateral event should also lead to a metastatic evaluation as recurrences are commonly the harbinger of metastatic disease.[57] In patients previously treated with mastectomy, a chest wall recurrence should be managed with a margin-free resection. In unusual circumstances, this may necessitate resection of the pectoralis muscle, ribs, or sternum. In patients who have undergone previous radiation treatments, a more extensive resection may represent the only therapeutic option to achieve local control. Closure of the chest wall defect may be facilitated by a myocutaneous flap closure. Hormonal and cytotoxic chemotherapy should also be considered at the time of a local recurrence.

Total Mastectomy

Total mastectomy remains a sound choice for many patients with breast cancer. A clear advantage of mastectomy is the avoidance of radiation therapy for patients without large tumors or multiple involved lymph nodes. This has more appeal for patients who are less concerned with the cosmetic outcome of surgery. Older, more sedentary patients may find this preferable to the alternative of lumpectomy and radiation therapy. Total mastectomy is indicated for multicentric disease or tumors with extensive DCIS, where achieving a clear surgical margin may be difficult with a segmental mastectomy. It is also indicated for individuals who are not radiation therapy candidates, including those with scleroderma, a history of prior radiotherapy, ataxia-telangiectasia, and early pregnancy.

Excellent cosmetic results can be achieved with a variety of reconstructive options, which can occur either simultaneously or as a delayed procedure. If a patient is contemplating reconstruction, a skin-sparing mastectomy should be performed. This operation involves the removal of the nipple-areolar complex and breast tissue but differs from a standard incision in preserving as much of the skin over the breast as possible (Figure 17–9). Most patients with early-stage breast cancer can undergo immediate reconstruction. This has the advantage of limiting the surgical intervention to a single-stage procedure and providing the patient with the psychological benefit of an immediately reconstructed breast. Immediate reconstruction also best preserves the elasticity of the elevated flaps and helps maintain the natural contour of the breast, including the inframammary fold, which may be affected with a delayed reconstruction. Considerations for delayed reconstruction include the urgency to address adjuvant systemic treatment, a patient who remains undecided regarding reconstruction options, or a patient who is likely to receive chest wall radiation therapy. Although radiation therapy can be successfully delivered after autogenous reconstruction with good cosmetic results, the incidence of capsular contraction after radiation therapy is prohibitive in those patients undergoing implant reconstruction.[58]

For patients with a strong familial history of breast cancer, a decision may be made to combine a therapeutic operation with a prophylactic operation. The identification of breast cancer susceptibility genes has fostered this concept. However, in practical terms, it is very difficult to assess risk and screen for a genetic mutation in a timely fashion before embarking on a therapeutic operation for a diagnosis that led to the genetic evaluation. Counseling these patients can be very difficult as they have to cope with both a diagnosis of cancer and an emotional decision as to whether or not to undergo a bilateral mastectomy. For those patients who might have greater difficulty in reaching a comfortable decision regarding a bilateral operation, a safe approach is to proceed with breast conserving surgery in conjunction with genetic testing. With this approach, the more important delivery of systemic therapy would not be delayed and would allow for the more time-consuming process of genetic test-

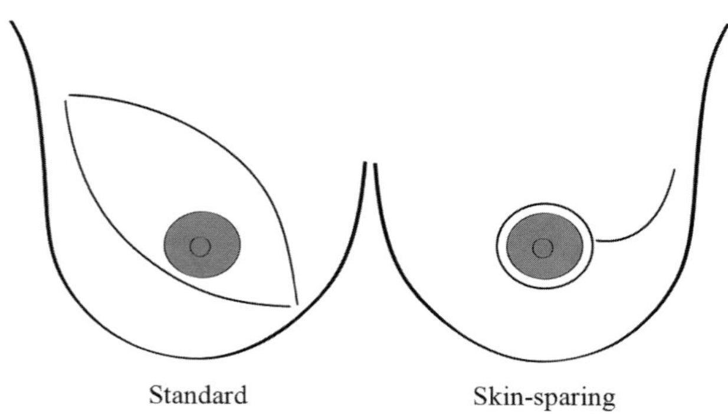

Figure 17–9. Incision placement for mastectomy.

ing if indicated. If the patient is found not to carry a genetic mutation, radiation therapy serves as the last step of the treatment plan. For those patients with an identified mutation, a completion mastectomy and contralateral mastectomy with or without reconstruction may be performed. If elected, compartmentalizing treatment and prophylaxis may help to ease the burden of complex decisions that a patient may face at the time of diagnosis.

Radical Mastectomy

In the context of early breast cancer, there is virtually no need to resect the pectoralis muscles and axillary tissue. Occasionally, tumors located posteriorly along the chest wall may focally invade the pectoralis muscle. Invasion of the pectoralis muscle does not constitute chest wall invasion and is staged according to the size of the primary tumor. Small breast cancers that present with muscle involvement are usually located peripherally or posteriorly, and extension, in part, reflects proximity to the muscle. This scenario can be safely managed with resection of a portion of the muscle as part of either a lumpectomy or a total mastectomy. With either surgical approach, radiation therapy should be considered.

Management of the Axilla

Axillary dissection was the standard treatment for surgical management of the axilla for breast cancer patients until recently. However within the past decade, extensive efforts have focused on attempts to reduce the extent of axillary surgery and the associated morbidity. Sentinel lymph node (SLN) biopsy has emerged as the standard of care for early breast cancer. Introduced by Morton and colleagues in 1992 for the treatment of melanoma,[59] this technique was quickly applied to breast cancer.[60–62] Like lymphatic mapping for other disease sites, the sentinel lymph node is identified through the constant anatomic relationship between a tumor and draining lymphatics. Conceptually, each specific area in the breast drains to a sentinel lymph node that may be located anywhere within the axilla, supraclavicular fossa, or internal mammary chain (Figure 17–10). Larger tumors may have more than one draining lymphatic vessel (Figure 17–11). The SLN biopsy continues to be refined and defined for patients with early breast cancer; in several studies, it has been demonstrated to yield reliable correlation to an axillary dissection.[60–66]

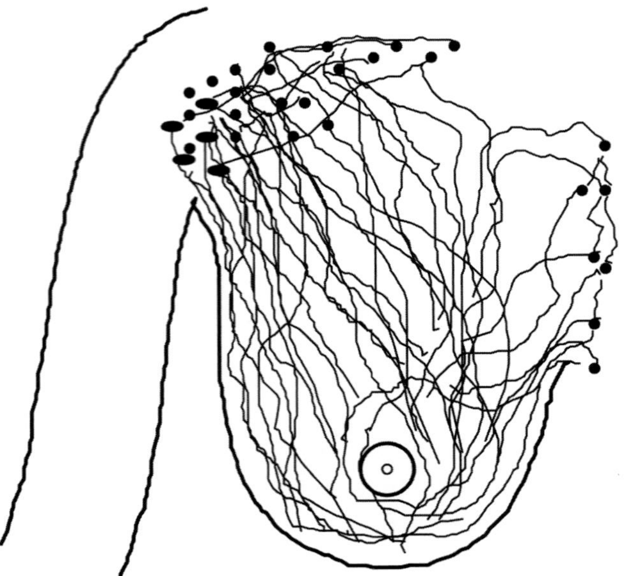

Figure 17–10. Breast lymphatic drainage patterns.

Axillary dissection has been recognized as an excellent procedure for staging and for providing regional control. Lymph node involvement represents the most important variable, aside from

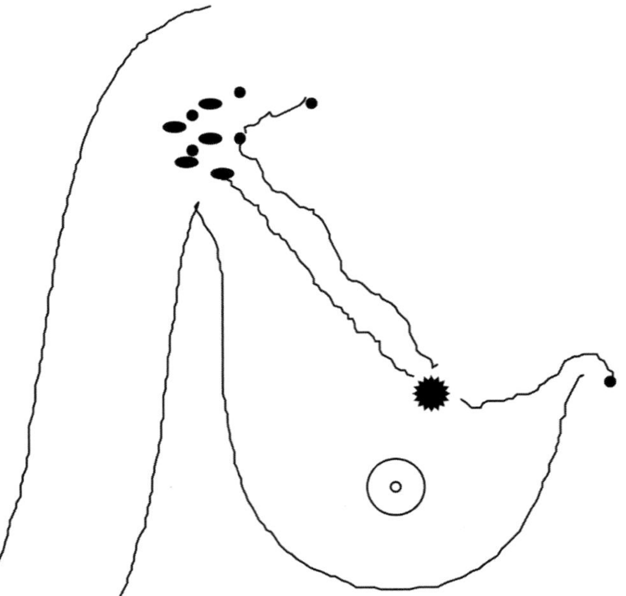

Figure 17–11. Lymphatic drainage pattern of an upper inner quadrant breast tumor.

metastatic disease, to predict outcome.[67] This information is important in defining the prognosis and in tailoring the adjuvant therapy of patients with breast cancer. Axillary staging remains a critical variable in defining the prognosis of patients presenting with early breast cancer. In the context of early detection and screening mammography, nodal involvement is, at times, the only prognosticator that leads to the clear recommendation of adjuvant therapy.

Aside from providing important prognostic information, axillary dissection represents the most effective means of controlling regional disease.[68] The yield of an axillary dissection has been well established with multiple studies analyzing the presence of metastatic disease within anatomically defined levels I, II, and III nodal basins.[69–71] Although anatomically defined by the relationship of the node to the pectoralis minor, this definition serves as an arbitrary division. On average, there is a 1% chance of metastatic disease in level III lymph nodes that would not be detected in levels I and II but a 10% chance of disease in level II or III nodes in the absence of disease in level I. Mathiesen and colleagues demonstrated that the potential for identifying micrometastases increased until 10 lymph nodes were removed from the axilla.[72] Unless extensive axillary involvement is recognized at the time of surgery, a level I/II node dissection should encompass axillary disease in 99% of patients.

For the majority of patients with early breast cancer, an axillary dissection does not confer any therapeutic benefit. The greatest concern, particularly for younger, active patients, is the risk of lymphedema. This risk is directly related to the extent of the axillary dissection and is further increased with the addition of radiation therapy.[73] This risk remains indefinitely for the life of the patient. Other potential side effects include paresthesias, loss of mobility, and cosmetic deformity. Avoiding the side effects of an axillary dissection in a substantial number of patients who do not achieve any therapeutic benefit has been a major impetus in identifying an alternative means of staging the axilla. Other methods that have been evaluated to replace axillary dissection include ultrasonography, computed tomography, and scintigraphy. All of these techniques have had the same major limitation of an unacceptably high false-negative rate.[74–76] Positron emission tomographic (PET) scanning has emerged as a more sensitive test that relies on the metabolic differences of tumors rather than on anatomic changes. To date, this test shows promise but is still not sensitive enough to exclude the presence of axillary disease.[77–80]

It is unlikely that any imaging technology will compare with the sensitivity of a microscopic examination, which has the potential to identify single metastatic cells. The shortcoming of a standard axillary dissection is that pathologists are incapable of reviewing every cell of every lymph node. The ability to detect micrometastases is directly related to the intensity with which a lymph node is analyzed. Serial sectioning studies have identified a higher incidence of true nodal positivity and mortality in those with unrecognized micrometastases.[42,81] Outside of investigational studies, serial sectioning of axillary dissection specimens is impractical.

Sentinel lymphadenectomy has several conceptual advantages over standard axillary dissection. Most significant to the patient is that avoiding an extensive axillary dissection significantly reduces the risk of long-term complications. Recovery is much shorter, and for most, BCT, under these circumstances, can be accomplished as an outpatient procedure. Compared to a standard axillary incision, the sentinel lymph node can be removed through a smaller incision with transcutaneous localization of the node with a handheld gamma probe. In addition to the reduction in morbidity, sentinel lymphadenectomy provides the pathologist with the opportunity to perform a much more comprehensive analysis of the specimen, given the more limited material to analyze. Techniques such as serial sectioning and immunohistochemistry using cytokeratin antibodies can be performed more readily on a limited number of nodes. Several studies have found that sentinel node lymphadenectomy with multiple sectioning and immunohistochemical staining increases the accuracy of axillary staging; these techniques can identify significantly more patients with lymph nodes metastases, especially micrometastases, than can axillary dissection with routine histopathologic processing of lymph nodes.[82–84]

Although a strong correlation between sentinel node biopsy and axillary dissection has been established to identify microscopic disease, a more important end point is the impact on regional recurrence and breast cancer–specific mortality. Although the follow-up for these end points is relatively limited, it appears that these two operations have similar outcomes. In a retrospective review of 916 patients, the risk of regional recurrence was equivalent for patients having a sentinel node biopsy with or without involved nodes to those having a standard axillary dissection.[85] Other studies have reached similar conclusions[86–88] and have questioned the utility of an axillary dissection in patients with a positive sentinel lymph node. Randomized clinical trial data from the American College of Surgeons Oncology Group Z0011 and from the NSABP B-32 remain under investigation to help define any survival differences or regional recurrence risk between these two surgical approaches.

The introduction of radiocolloid for this technique greatly enhanced this procedure by providing a nonvisual means of localizing a sentinel node using a handheld gamma probe (Figure 17–12). This has simplified the procedure by obviating the lymphatic mapping required to identify the blue lymph node. Additionally, technetium-labeled sulfur colloid binds to lymphatic tissue and provides a much greater window of opportunity to localize sentinel lymph nodes. The intraparenchymal and intradermal routes of administration of radiocolloid and blue dye have been well described. A large multi-institutional study involving 1,585 patients compared intradermal radiocolloid injection to intraparenchymal radiocolloid injection.[89] A complete axillary dissection was performed on all patients following sentinel lymph node mapping and biopsy. The study found an increased intraoperative sentinel node localization rate (98 versus 90%) in patients undergoing intradermal injection with no effect on the false-negative rate. This finding is supported by several smaller retrospective studies[90,91]; hence the intradermal injection route for radiocolloid has gained popularity.

Another area of controversy in the sentinel node debate is the detection and clinical significance of sentinel nodes found outside the axilla. Lymphoscintigraphy done prior to the surgical procedure can assist in confirming the migration and location of radiocolloid, allowing localization of internal mammary nodes (Figure 17–13).[66] The frequency of detection of extra-axillary sentinel lymph nodes by preoperative lymphoscintigraphy varies widely in the literature, and therefore the utility of this technique is controversial. Several studies have demonstrated no benefit to preoperative lymphoscintigraphy owing to a low frequency of extra-axillary localization.[92,93] However, others have shown that about 20% of patients with breast cancer have internal mammary sentinel lymph nodes, and 5% will have isolated internal mammary sentinel nodes with the absence of axillary sentinel lymph nodes.[94–96] Conceptually, the use of radiocolloid may also identify lymph nodes

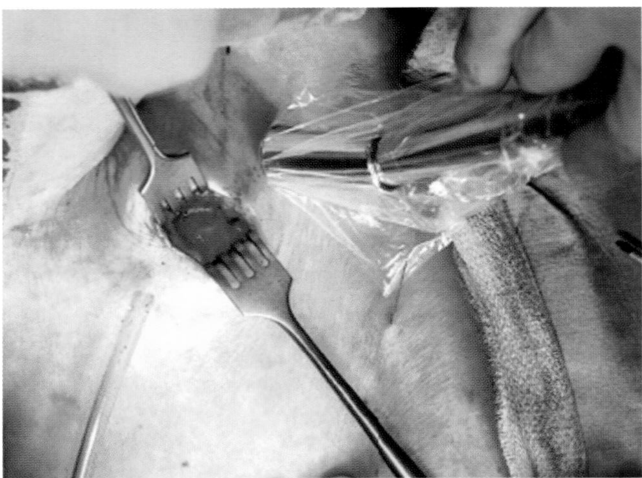

Figure 17–12. Transcutaneous localization of axillary sentinel nodes.

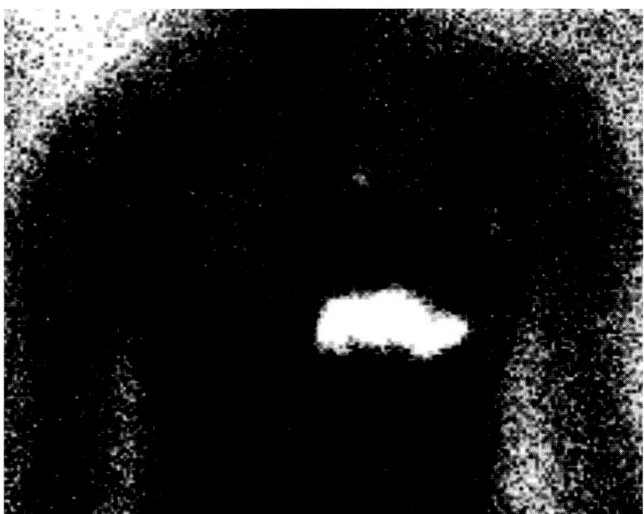

Figure 17–13. Lymphoscintigram of breast primary with migration to axillary and internal mammary sentinel nodes.

that are present in the contralateral nodal basins (Figures 17–14 and 17–15). Although controversial, sentinel node biopsy may also be attempted in patients with a history of prior BCT with either recurrent or new primary tumors (see Figure 17–14).

Four-node axillary sampling is an alternative to sentinel node biopsy subject to randomized studies with evaluation of long-term outcomes. This technique was pioneered in the Edinburgh breast unit and is based on the theory that involved axillary nodes are the ones most likely to be palpable intraoperatively. The procedure involves mobilizing the lower axilla and excising four individual nodes. Two studies have been conducted comparing the technique to axillary dissection and have shown decreased morbidity and similar recurrence and mortality rates.[97,98] A more recent study by Macmillan and colleagues comparing four node axillary sampling to sentinel node biopsy found no difference in the sensitivity of axillary node staging between the two techniques,[99]

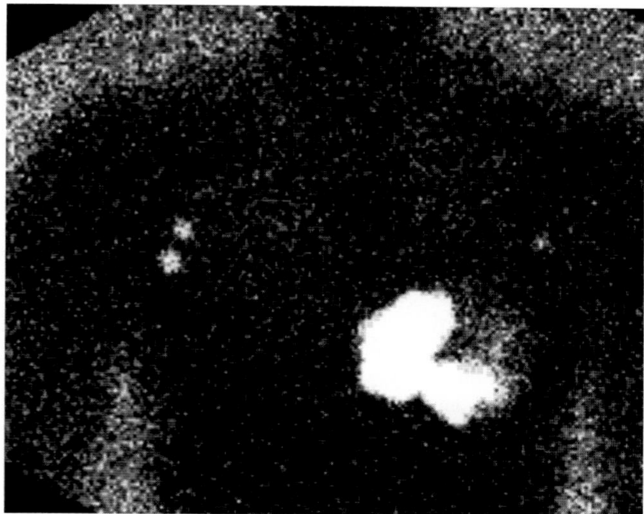

Figure 17–15. Lymphoscintigram of a breast primary in a 42-year-old woman with a 2 cm left breast cancer with migration to two ipsilateral and two contralateral axillary sentinel nodes, all four containing metastatic disease.

CONCLUSIONS

Local and regional surgical treatment of early breast cancer continues to evolve toward a more limited and tailored approach. The diagnostic evaluation also continues to improve in defining the extent of the disease and in providing accurate staging information to guide resection and adjuvant therapy. With these strategies, the treatment of breast cancer has become more precise and effective.

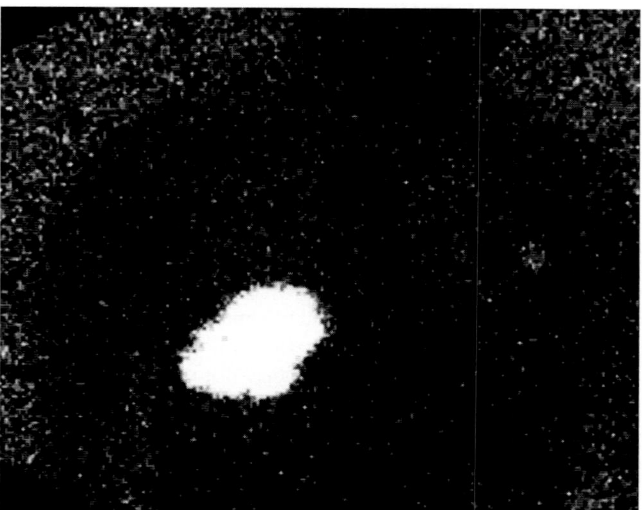

Figure 17–14. Lymphoscintigram of a breast primary in an 84-year-old woman, 6 months following a median sternotomy for cardiac surgery and 13 years following a right lumpectomy and radiation therapy for ductal carcinoma in situ. Eighteen hours after injection, there is migration to a contralateral (left) axillary lymph node that was histologically normal.

REFERENCES

1. Gilles R, Meunier M, Lucidarme O, et al. Clustered breast microcalcifications: evaluation by dynamic contrast-enhanced subtraction MRI. J Comput Assist Tomogr 1996;20:9–14.
2. Nakahara H, Namba K, Fukami A, et al. Three-dimensional MR imaging of mammographically detected suspicious microcalcifications. Breast Cancer 2001;8:116–24.
3. Trecate G, Tess JD, Vergnaghi D, et al. Breast microcalcifications studied with 3D contrast-enhanced high-field magnetic resonance imaging: more accuracy in the diagnosis of breast cancer. Tumori 2002;88:224–33.
4. Westerhof JP, Fischer U, Moritz JD, Oestmann JW. MR imaging of mammographically detected clustered microcalcifications: is there any value? Radiology 1998;207: 675–81.
5. Shin HJ, Sneige N. Is a diagnosis of infiltrating versus in situ ductal carcinoma of the breast possible in fine-needle aspiration specimens? Cancer 1998;84:186–91.
6. Ariga R, Bloom K, Reddy VB, et al. Fine-needle aspiration of clinically suspicious palpable breast masses with histopathologic correlation. Am J Surg 2002;184:410–3.
7. Ballo MS, Sneige N. Can core needle biopsy replace fine-needle aspiration cytology in the diagnosis of palpable breast carcinoma. A comparative study of 124 women. Cancer 1996;78:773–7.
8. Oyama T, Koibuchi Y, McKee G. Core needle biopsy (CNB)

as a diagnostic method for breast lesions: comparison with fine needle aspiration cytology (FNA). Breast Cancer 2004;11:339–42.

9. Singletary SE, Allred C, Ashley P, et al. Revision of the American Joint Committee on Cancer staging system for breast cancer. J Clin Oncol 2002;20:3628–36.
10. Arriagada R, Le MG, Rochard F, Contesso G. Conservative treatment versus mastectomy in early breast cancer: patterns of failure with 15 years of follow-up data. Institut Gustave-Roussy Breast Cancer Group. J Clin Oncol 1996;14:1558–64.
11. Blichert-Toft M, Rose C, Andersen JA, et al. Danish randomized trial comparing breast conservation therapy with mastectomy: six years of life-table analysis. Danish Breast Cancer Cooperative Group. J Natl Cancer Inst Monogr 1992:19–25.
12. Fisher B, Anderson S, Bryant J, et al. Twenty-year follow-up of a randomized trial comparing total mastectomy, lumpectomy, and lumpectomy plus irradiation for the treatment of invasive breast cancer. N Engl J Med 2002; 347:1233–41.
13. Poggi MM, Danforth DN, Sciuto LC, et al. Eighteen-year results in the treatment of early breast carcinoma with mastectomy versus breast conservation therapy: the National Cancer Institute Randomized Trial. Cancer 2003;98:697–702.
14. van Dongen JA, Voogd AC, Fentiman IS, et al. Long-term results of a randomized trial comparing breast-conserving therapy with mastectomy: European Organization for Research and Treatment of Cancer 10801 trial. J Natl Cancer Inst 2000;92:1143–50.
15. Veronesi U, Cascinelli N, Mariani L, et al. Twenty-year follow-up of a randomized study comparing breast-conserving surgery with radical mastectomy for early breast cancer. N Engl J Med 2002;347:1227–32.
16. Winchester DJ, Menck HR, Winchester DP. The National Cancer Data Base report on the results of a large nonrandomized comparison of breast preservation and modified radical mastectomy. Cancer 1997;80:162–7.
17. Effects of radiotherapy and surgery in early breast cancer. An overview of the randomized trials. Early Breast Cancer Trialists' Collaborative Group. N Engl J Med 1995;333: 1444–55.
18. Winchester DJ, Menck HR, Winchester DP. National treatment trends for ductal carcinoma in situ of the breast. Arch Surg 1997;132:660–5.
19. Wolmark N, Wang J, Mamounas E, et al. Preoperative chemotherapy in patients with operable breast cancer: nine-year results from National Surgical Adjuvant Breast and Bowel Project B-18. J Natl Cancer Inst Monogr 2001:96–102.
20. Cance WG, Carey LA, Calvo BF, et al. Long-term outcome of neoadjuvant therapy for locally advanced breast carcinoma: effective clinical downstaging allows breast preservation and predicts outstanding local control and survival. Ann Surg 2002;236:295–302.
21. McIntosh SA, Ogston KN, Payne S, et al. Local recurrence in patients with large and locally advanced breast cancer treated with primary chemotherapy. Am J Surg 2003; 185:525–31.
22. Cox CE, Furman B, Dupont EL, et al. Novel techniques in sentinel lymph node mapping and localization of nonpalpable breast lesions: the Moffitt experience. Ann Surg Oncol 2004;11(3 Suppl):222S–6S.
23. Albain KS, Allred DC, Clark GM. Breast cancer outcome and predictors of outcome: are there age differentials? J Natl Cancer Inst Monogr 1994:35–42.
24. Nixon AJ, Neuberg D, Hayes DF, et al. Relationship of patient age to pathologic features of the tumor and prognosis for patients with stage I or II breast cancer. J Clin Oncol 1994;12:888–94.
25. Le Doussal V, Tubiana-Hulin M, Friedman S, et al. Prognostic value of histologic grade nuclear components of Scarff-Bloom-Richardson (SBR). An improved score modification based on a multivariate analysis of 1,262 invasive ductal breast carcinomas. Cancer 1989;64:1914–21.
26. Sasson AR, Fowble B, Hanlon AL, et al. Lobular carcinoma in situ increases the risk of local recurrence in selected patients with stages I and II breast carcinoma treated with conservative surgery and radiation. Cancer 2001;91:1862–9.
27. Cornfield DB, Palazzo JP, Schwartz GF, et al. The prognostic significance of multiple morphologic features and biologic markers in ductal carcinoma in situ of the breast: a study of a large cohort of patients treated with surgery alone. Cancer 2004;100:2317–27.
28. Neville AM, Bettelheim R, Gelber RD, et al. Factors predicting treatment responsiveness and prognosis in node-negative breast cancer. The International (Ludwig) Breast Cancer Study Group. J Clin Oncol 1992;10:696–705.
29. Rosen PP, Groshen S, Saigo PE, et al. Pathological prognostic factors in stage I (T1N0M0) and stage II (T1N1M0) breast carcinoma: a study of 644 patients with median follow-up of 18 years. J Clin Oncol 1989;7:1239–51.
30. Holland R, Connolly JL, Gelman R, et al. The presence of an extensive intraductal component following a limited excision correlates with prominent residual disease in the remainder of the breast. J Clin Oncol 1990;8:113–8.
31. Schnitt SJ, Connolly JL, Harris JR, et al. Pathologic predictors of early local recurrence in Stage I and II breast cancer treated by primary radiation therapy. Cancer 1984; 53:1049–57.
32. Spivack B, Khanna MM, Tafra L, et al. Margin status and local recurrence after breast-conserving surgery. Arch Surg 1994;129:952–6.
33. Fisher B, Bauer M, Wickerham DL, et al. Relation of number of positive axillary nodes to the prognosis of patients with primary breast cancer. An NSABP update. Cancer 1983; 52:1551–7.
34. Fisher B, Dignam J, Bryant J, Wolmark N. Five versus more than five years of tamoxifen for lymph node-negative breast cancer: updated findings from the National Surgical Adjuvant Breast and Bowel Project B-14 randomized trial. J Natl Cancer Inst 2001;93:684–90.
35. Fisher B, Dignam J, Mamounas EP, et al. Sequential methotrexate and fluorouracil for the treatment of node-negative breast cancer patients with estrogen receptor-negative tumors: eight-year results from National Surgical Adjuvant Breast and Bowel Project (NSABP) B-13 and first report of findings from NSABP B-19 comparing methotrexate and fluorouracil with conventional cyclophosphamide, methotrexate, and fluorouracil. J Clin Oncol 1996;14:1982–92.

36. Fisher ER, Sass R, Fisher B, et al. Pathologic findings from the National Surgical Adjuvant Breast Project (protocol 6). II. Relation of local breast recurrence to multicentricity. Cancer 1986;57:1717–24.
37. Kurtz JM, Jacquemier J, Amalric R, et al. Risk factors for breast recurrence in premenopausal and postmenopausal patients with ductal cancers treated by conservation therapy. Cancer 1990;65:1867–78.
38. Mate TP, Carter D, Fischer DB, et al. A clinical and histopathologic analysis of the results of conservation surgery and radiation therapy in stage I and II breast carcinoma. Cancer 1986;58:1995–2002.
39. Krecke KN, Gisvold JJ. Invasive lobular carcinoma of the breast: mammographic findings and extent of disease at diagnosis in 184 patients. AJR Am J Roentgenol 1993; 161:957–60.
40. Le Gal M, Ollivier L, Asselain B, et al. Mammographic features of 455 invasive lobular carcinomas. Radiology 1992;185:705–8.
41. Yeatman TJ, Cantor AB, Smith TJ, et al. Tumor biology of infiltrating lobular carcinoma. Implications for management. Ann Surg 1995;222:549–59.
42. Clare SE, Sener SF, Wilkens W, et al. Prognostic significance of occult lymph node metastases in node-negative breast cancer. Ann Surg Oncol 1997;4:447–51.
43. Chung MA, Cole B, Wanebo HJ, et al. Optimal surgical treatment of invasive lobular carcinoma of the breast. Ann Surg Oncol 1997;4:545–50.
44. Molland JG, Donnellan M, Janu NC, et al. Infiltrating lobular carcinoma—a comparison of diagnosis, management and outcome with infiltrating duct carcinoma. Breast 2004;13:389–96.
45. Santiago RJ, Harris EE, Qin L, et al. Similar long-term results of breast-conservation treatment for Stage I and II invasive lobular carcinoma compared with invasive ductal carcinoma of the breast. Cancer 2005;103: 2447–54.
46. Moore MM, Borossa G, Imbrie JZ, et al. Association of infiltrating lobular carcinoma with positive surgical margins after breast-conservation therapy. Ann Surg 2000;231: 877–82.
47. Hussien M, Lioe TF, Finnegan J, Spence RA. Surgical treatment for invasive lobular carcinoma of the breast. Breast 2003;12:23–35.
48. Winchester DJ, Chang HR, Graves TA, et al. A comparative analysis of lobular and ductal carcinoma of the breast: presentation, treatment, and outcomes. J Am Coll Surg 1998;186:416–22.
49. Gage I, Schnitt SJ, Nixon AJ, et al. Pathologic margin involvement and the risk of recurrence in patients treated with breast-conserving therapy. Cancer 1996;78:1921–8.
50. Meric F, Mirza NQ, Vlastos G, et al. Positive surgical margins and ipsilateral breast tumor recurrence predict disease-specific survival after breast-conserving therapy. Cancer 2003;97:926–33.
51. Singletary SE. Surgical margins in patients with early-stage breast cancer treated with breast conservation therapy. Am J Surg 2002;184:383–93.
52. Liljegren G, Holmberg L, Adami HO, et al. Sector resection with or without postoperative radiotherapy for stage I breast cancer: five-year results of a randomized trial. Uppsala-Orebro Breast Cancer Study Group. J Natl Cancer Inst 1994;86:717–22.
53. Holland R, Veling SH, Mravunac M, Hendriks JH. Histologic multifocality of Tis, T1-2 breast carcinomas. Implications for clinical trials of breast-conserving surgery. Cancer 1985;56:979–90.
54. Fisher ER, Costantino J, Fisher B, et al. Pathologic findings from the National Surgical Adjuvant Breast Project (NSABP) Protocol B-17. Five-year observations concerning lobular carcinoma in situ. Cancer 1996;78:1403–16.
55. Dalberg K, Johansson H, Johansson U, Rutqvist LE. A randomized trial of long term adjuvant tamoxifen plus postoperative radiation therapy versus radiation therapy alone for patients with early stage breast carcinoma treated with breast-conserving surgery. Stockholm Breast Cancer Study Group. Cancer 1998;82:2204–11.
56. Huang E, Buchholz TA, Meric F, et al. Classifying local disease recurrences after breast conservation therapy based on location and histology: new primary tumors have more favorable outcomes than true local disease recurrences. Cancer 2002;95:2059–67.
57. Bedwinek JM, Fineberg B, Lee J, Ocwieza M. Analysis of failures following local treatment of isolated local-regional recurrence of breast cancer. Int J Radiat Oncol Biol Phys 1981;7:581–5.
58. Schuster RH, Kuske RR, Young VL, Fineberg B. Breast reconstruction in women treated with radiation therapy for breast cancer: cosmesis, complications, and tumor control. Plast Reconstr Surg 1992;90:445–52.
59. Morton DL, Wen DR, Wong JH, et al. Technical details of intraoperative lymphatic mapping for early stage melanoma. Arch Surg 1992;127:392–9.
60. Krag DN, Weaver DL, Alex JC, Fairbank JT. Surgical resection and radiolocalization of the sentinel lymph node in breast cancer using a gamma probe. Surg Oncol 1993; 2:335–9.
61. Albertini JJ, Lyman GH, Cox C, et al. Lymphatic mapping and sentinel node biopsy in the patient with breast cancer. JAMA 1996;276:1818–22.
62. Giuliano AE, Kirgan DM, Guenther JM, Morton DL. Lymphatic mapping and sentinel lymphadenectomy for breast cancer. Ann Surg 1994;220:391–8.
63. Giuliano AE, Jones RC, Brennan M, Statman R. Sentinel lymphadenectomy in breast cancer. J Clin Oncol 1997; 15:2345–50.
64. Krag D, Weaver D, Ashikaga T, et al. The sentinel node in breast cancer—a multicenter validation study. N Engl J Med 1998;339:941–6.
65. Veronesi U, Paganelli G, Galimberti V, et al. Sentinel-node biopsy to avoid axillary dissection in breast cancer with clinically negative lymph-nodes. Lancet 1997;349:1864–7.
66. Winchester DJ, Sener SF, Winchester DP, et al. Sentinel lymphadenectomy for breast cancer: experience with 180 consecutive patients: efficacy of filtered technetium 99m sulphur colloid with overnight migration time. J Am Coll Surg 1999;188:597–603.
67. Ciatto S, Cecchini S, Iossa A, Grazzini G. "T" category and operable breast cancer prognosis. Tumori 1989;75: 18–22.
68. Fisher B, Redmond C, Fisher ER, et al. Ten-year results of a randomized clinical trial comparing radical mastectomy

and total mastectomy with or without radiation. N Engl J Med 1985;312:674–81.
69. Boova RS, Bonanni R, Rosato FE. Patterns of axillary nodal involvement in breast cancer. Predictability of level one dissection. Ann Surg 1982;196:642–4.
70. Rosen PP, Lesser ML, Kinne DW, Beattie EJ. Discontinuous or "skip" metastases in breast carcinoma. Analysis of 1,228 axillary dissections. Ann Surg 1983;197:276–83.
71. Veronesi U, Rilke F, Luini A, et al. Distribution of axillary node metastases by level of invasion. An analysis of 539 cases. Cancer 1987;59:682–7.
72. Mathiesen O, Carl J, Bonderup O, Panduro J. Axillary sampling and the risk of erroneous staging of breast cancer. An analysis of 960 consecutive patients. Acta Oncol 1990;29:721–5.
73. Larson D, Weinstein M, Goldberg I, et al. Edema of the arm as a function of the extent of axillary surgery in patients with stage I-II carcinoma of the breast treated with primary radiotherapy. Int J Radiat Oncol Biol Phys 1986; 12:1575–82.
74. Kao CH, Wang SJ, Yeh SH. Tc-99m MIBI uptake in breast carcinoma and axillary lymph node metastases. Clin Nucl Med 1994;19:898–900.
75. March DE, Wechsler RJ, Kurtz AB, et al. CT-pathologic correlation of axillary lymph nodes in breast carcinoma. J Comput Assist Tomogr 1991;15:440–4.
76. Tate JJ, Lewis V, Archer T, et al. Ultrasound detection of axillary lymph node metastases in breast cancer. Eur J Surg Oncol 1989;15:139–41.
77. Zornoza G, Garcia-Velloso MJ, Sola J, et al. 18F-FDG PET complemented with sentinel lymph node biopsy in the detection of axillary involvement in breast cancer. Eur J Surg Oncol 2004;30:15–9.
78. Barranger E, Grahek D, Antoine M, et al. Evaluation of fluorodeoxyglucose positron emission tomography in the detection of axillary lymph node metastases in patients with early-stage breast cancer. Ann Surg Oncol 2003; 10:622–7.
79. Fehr MK, Hornung R, Varga Z, et al. Axillary staging using positron emission tomography in breast cancer patients qualifying for sentinel lymph node biopsy. Breast J 2004;10:89–93.
80. Greco M, Crippa F, Agresti R, et al. Axillary lymph node staging in breast cancer by 2-fluoro-2-deoxy-D-glucose-positron emission tomography: clinical evaluation and alternative management. J Natl Cancer Inst 2001;93:630–5.
81. Prognostic importance of occult axillary lymph node micrometastases from breast cancers. International (Ludwig) Breast Cancer Study Group. Lancet 1990; 335:1565–8.
82. Giuliano AE, Dale PS, Turner RR, et al. Improved axillary staging of breast cancer with sentinel lymphadenectomy. Ann Surg 1995;222:394–9.
83. Wong SL, Abell TD, Chao C, et al. Optimal use of sentinel lymph node biopsy versus axillary lymph node dissection in patients with breast carcinoma: a decision analysis. Cancer 2002;95:478–87.
84. Jani AB, Basu A, Heimann R, Hellman S. Sentinel lymph node versus axillary lymph node dissection for early-stage breast carcinoma: a comparison using a utility-adjusted number needed to treat analysis. Cancer 2003;97:359–66.
85. Jeruss JS, Winchester DJ, Sener SF, et al. Axillary recurrence after sentinel node biopsy. Ann Surg Oncol 2005;12: 34–40.
86. Naik AM, Fey J, Gemignani M, et al. The risk of axillary relapse after sentinel lymph node biopsy for breast cancer is comparable with that of axillary lymph node dissection: a follow-up study of 4,008 procedures. Ann Surg 2004; 240:462–8.
87. Fant JS, Grant MD, Knox SM, et al. Preliminary outcome analysis in patients with breast cancer and a positive sentinel lymph node who declined axillary dissection. Ann Surg Oncol 2003;10:126–30.
88. Guenther JM, Hansen NM, DiFronzo LA, et al. Axillary dissection is not required for all patients with breast cancer and positive sentinel nodes. Arch Surg 2003;138:52–6.
89. McMasters KM, Wong SL, Martin RC Jr, et al. Dermal injection of radioactive colloid is superior to peritumoral injection for breast cancer sentinel lymph node biopsy: results of a multiinstitutional study. Ann Surg 2001;233: 676–87.
90. Martin RC, Derossis AM, Fey J, et al. Intradermal isotope injection is superior to intramammary in sentinel node biopsy for breast cancer. Surgery 2001;130:432–8.
91. Povoski SP, Dauway EL, Ducatman BS. Sentinel lymph node mapping and biopsy for breast cancer at a rural-based university medical center: initial experience with intraparenchymal and intradermal injection routes. Breast Cancer 2002;9:134–44.
92. Burak WE Jr, Walker MJ, Yee LD, et al. Routine preoperative lymphoscintigraphy is not necessary prior to sentinel node biopsy for breast cancer. Am J Surg 1999;177:445–9.
93. McMasters KM, Wong SL, Tuttle TM, et al. Preoperative lymphoscintigraphy for breast cancer does not improve the ability to identify axillary sentinel lymph nodes. Ann Surg 2000;231:724–31.
94. Birdwell RL, Smith KL, Betts BJ, et al. Breast cancer: variables affecting sentinel lymph node visualization at preoperative lymphoscintigraphy. Radiology 2001;220: 47–53.
95. Sugg SL, Ferguson DJ, Posner MC, Heimann R. Should internal mammary nodes be sampled in the sentinel lymph node era? Ann Surg Oncol 2000;7:188–92.
96. Uren RF, Howman-Giles R, Thompson JF. Metastatic disease in the internal mammary lymph nodes has an adverse effect on patient prognosis and survival, regardless of axillary node status. Ann Surg Oncol 2000;7:790.
97. Chetty U, Jack W, Prescott RJ, et al. Management of the axilla in operable breast cancer treated by breast conservation: a randomized clinical trial. Edinburgh Breast Unit. Br J Surg 2000;87:163–9.
98. Forrest AP, Everington D, McDonald CC, et al. The Edinburgh randomized trial of axillary sampling or clearance after mastectomy. Br J Surg 1995;82:1504–8.
99. Macmillan RD, Barbera D, Hadjiminas DJ, et al. Sentinel node biopsy for breast cancer may have little to offer four-node-samplers. Results of a prospective comparison study. Eur J Cancer 2001;37:1076–80.

18

Locally Advanced Breast Cancer

LISA A. NEWMAN

Screening mammography programs implemented over the past 20 years have resulted in a welcome shift toward an earlier-stage distribution and improved outcomes for breast cancers diagnosed in the United States.[1] Locally advanced breast cancer (LABC), nonetheless, continues to account for a substantial fraction of the breast cancer burden. LABC is generally characterized by bulky primary chest wall tumors and/or extensive adenopathy. The American Joint Commission on Cancer (AJCC) 5th and 6th editions staging systems classify these lesions as T3 tumors (> 5 cm), T4 tumors (associated with chest wall fixation or skin ulceration and/or satellitosis), and N2/N3 disease (matted axillary and/or internal mammary metastases).[2] The AJCC 5th edition staging system defined supraclavicular nodal involvement as a stage IV disease; however, recent studies have demonstrated that prolonged disease-free survival can be achieved in patients with metastatic disease limited to this nodal basin when an aggressive multidisciplinary treatment approach is offered.[3,4] As a result, the 6th edition of the AJCC staging system now includes isolated supraclavicular metastases in the stage III/LABC disease category.[2] According to the American College of Surgeons National Cancer Database, approximately 6% of breast cancers in the United States present as stage III disease.[5] Five-year survival for stage III breast cancer is approximately 50%, compared to 87% for stage I disease. The extent to which LABC represents neglected disease and a delayed diagnosis versus inherently aggressive tumor biology is poorly understood. Public health efforts to promote breast health awareness and early detection programs are therefore of vital importance.

EVOLUTION OF TREATMENT OPTIONS IN LOCALLY ADVANCED BREAST CANCER

Surgeons have historically been at the forefront with investigations of LABC outcomes based on different treatment strategies. The Columbia University breast group, led by Haagensen and Stout, provided early data regarding the dismal results of radical mastectomy alone as treatment for LABC more than six decades ago, reporting 5-year local recurrence and survival rates of 46% and 6%, respectively.[6] This experience led to the stratification of LABC as inoperable when any of the following were present: extensive breast skin edema or satellitosis, intercostal/parasternal nodules, arm edema, supraclavicular metastases, and inflammatory breast cancer. In contrast, several "grave local signs" of LABC were defined as very poor prognostic features but not necessarily indicators of unresectability; these include ulceration, limited skin edema, fixation to the pectoralis muscle, and bulky axillary adenopathy.

Attempts to control LABC with primary therapeutic doses of chest wall radiation were similarly inadequate. Studies reported during the 1970s and 1980s by the Joint Center for Radiation Therapy, Guy's Hospital, and the Mallinckrodt Institute of Radiology all revealed excessively high failure rates, with 5-year local recurrence rates ranging from 46 to 72%, and survival only 16 to 30%.[7–9] Combined modality treatment with irradiation and surgery was also explored during this era, but yielded no significant improvement in rates of disease control.[10–12]

Implementation of preoperative chemotherapy protocols (also commonly referred to as neoadjuvant or induction chemotherapy) revolutionized the management of LABC cases, and this approach is now considered the standard of care for patients with bulky breast and/or axillary disease. Early skepticism regarding this treatment sequence was based on concerns that preoperative chemotherapy would exert an adverse effect on (1) surgical complication rates, (2) the prognostic value of the axillary nodal status, and (3) overall survival, as a consequence of delayed surgery. Clinical investigations reported during the 1980s and 1990s addressed and alleviated these concerns.

Broadwater and colleagues demonstrated comparable operative morbidity among nearly 200 LABC patients treated with mastectomy, approximately half of whom received preoperative doxorubicin-based chemotherapy.[13] The induction chemotherapy patients in fact had a lower rate of postoperative seroma formation. Danforth and colleagues similarly reported that preoperative chemotherapy had no adverse effect on surgical complication rates and did not result in delayed delivery of any postoperative cancer care.[14] Most patients are ready to undergo surgery approximately 3 weeks after the last chemotherapy treatment, when the absolute neutrophil and platelet counts have normalized (> 1,500 and 100,000, respectively).

McCready and colleagues confirmed that the axillary nodal status retains its prognostic value in the neoadjuvant chemotherapy setting.[15] Their study of 136 LABC patients undergoing modified radical mastectomy following induction chemotherapy revealed that patients with no axillary metastases in the postchemotherapy mastectomy specimen had an excellent outcome, with nearly 80% surviving 5 years. In contrast, fewer than 10% of patients with 10 or more positive nodes survived 5 years, and patients with an intermediate number of residual metastatic nodes had an intermediate survival rate.

The third issue regarding induction chemotherapy and its relative impact on breast cancer survival in comparison with conventional postoperative adjuvant therapy remains controversial. It is clear, however, that preoperative treatment and deferral of surgery do not increase rates of unresectability. On the contrary, approximately 80% of patients will have at least 50% shrinkage of the primary tumor mass, and only 2 to 3% will have signs of progressive disease.[16–18] Fears that the surgeon will lose a "window of opportunity" to resect chest wall disease are therefore unfounded, and preoperatively-treated patients are likely to be rendered improved operative candidates. A surgical resection is essential in accurately documenting chemotherapy response and in achieving durable locoregional control of disease, as the clinical assessment of response will overestimate the actual pathologic extent by two-to-threefold.[19,20]

Table 18–1 summarizes the results of different combinations and sequences for LABC treatment that have been investigated over the past several decades. Optimal control is achieved with preoperative chemotherapy, followed by surgery and then radiation therapy for consolidation of local therapy. A clinical trial reported by Olson and colleagues revealed acceptable outcomes when patients with resectable LABC had undergone surgery as the first step, followed by postoperative chemotherapy and irradiation.[21] Patients with clinically occult LABC can therefore be salvaged with postoperative multimodality therapy. The neoadjuvant therapy benefits of tumor downstaging and the ability to rapidly identify chemoresistant disease by in vivo observation have motivated expanded applications of this treatment to the setting of early-stage disease. Accordingly, the outcomes from prospective clinical trials have now been reported, where preoperative chemotherapy has been compared directly with postoperative chemotherapy in women with LABC as well as early-stage disease. Some of these phase III clinical trial results are shown in Table 18–2.[22–29] All have demonstrated overall survival equivalence for the two treatment sequences, confirming the oncologic safety of the neoadjuvant approach.

Subset analyses of the phase III studies, however, reveal that patients found to have a complete pathologic response (pCR) do have a statistically significant survival benefit, substantiating the concept that primary breast tumor response is a reliable surrogate for chemo-effect on micrometastases. In the NSABP B-18 trial, patients with stages I to III breast cancers, who were randomized to receive four cycles of doxorubicin and cyclophosphamide (Cytoxain) preoperatively and who experienced a pCR, had a 5-year overall survival of 86%, which was statistically superior to the outcome seen in all other study participants.[29] Sim-

Table 18–1. LOCALLY ADVANCED BREAST CANCER OUTCOME BASED ON TREATMENT DELIVERED AND SEQUENCE OF MULTIMODALITY THERAPY

Treatment Approach	Components and Sequence of Treatment	Study	Sample Size	5-Year Local Recurrence Rate (%)	5-Year Survival (%)
Single modality	Surgery only	Haagensen and Stout, 1943[6]	35	46	6
		Arnold and Lesnick, 1979[11]	50	50	33
	XRT only	Rubens et al, 1977[9]	184	72	18
		Harris et al, 1983[7]	137	46	30
Dual modality	Preop XRT, Surgery	Arnold and Lesnick, 1979[11]	54	70	30
		Townsend et al, 19845[10]	53	11	47
	Surgery, Postop XRT	Arnold and Lesnick, 1979[11]	122	70	32
		Montague and Fletcher, 1985[12]	132	13	43 (at 10 years)
	Preop CTX, Surgery	Valagussa et al, 1983[81]	205	18	49
		Perloff et al, 1988[17]	43	19	Median survival 39 months
	Preop CTX, XRT	Valagussa et al, 1983[81]	198	36	35
		Perloff et al, 1988[17]	44	27	Median survival 39 months
	Surgery, CTX	Olson et al, 1997[21]	148	20	65 (estimated from graph)
Triple modality	Preop CTX, Surgery, XRT	Kuerer et al, 1999[30]	372		
			pCR; $n = 43$	5	89
			< pCR; $n = 329$	9	64
		Cance et al, 2002[82]	62	14	76
	Surgery, CTX, XRT	Olson et al, 1997[21]	164	9	66 (estimated from graph)

CTX = chemotherapy; pCR = complete pathologic response; Preop = preoperative; Postop = postoperative; XRT = irradiation.

ilarly, the University of Texas M.D. Anderson Cancer Center reported an overall survival rate of 89% for pCR patients treated on preoperative chemotherapy protocols designed specifically for LABC, and this outcome also represented a statistically significant benefit compared with patients who had a lesser response.[30] Unfortunately, both studies found that only 12 to 13% of patients will experience a pCR when treated with a doxorubicin-based regimen, and this proportion is simply insufficient in yielding a survival benefit for the entire pool of preoperatively-treated patients. Predictors of a pCR include relatively smaller primary breast tumors, estrogen receptor negativity, and high-grade lesions.[30] The latter two features probably characterize rapidly cycling tumors that may be particularly sensitive to chemotherapy effects.

DIAGNOSTIC AND THERAPEUTIC MANAGEMENT SEQUENCE

Establishing a definitive tissue diagnosis is the initial priority when a locally advanced breast cancer is encountered. This can usually be accomplished by performing a freehand direct core needle biopsy of the breast mass. Ultrasound guidance for these percutaneous biopsies can optimize the diagnostic yield. Core needle biopsy is preferred over fine-needle aspiration biopsies (FNAB) of the breast, because cytology will not be adequate to confirm the presence of invasive breast cancer. Furthermore, multiple cores should be extracted so that the predominant invasive nature of a lesion can be confirmed. This is a critical point, because bulky palpable ductal carcinoma in situ (DCIS) is a rare but well-known occurrence, and induction chemotherapy would clearly be inappropriate for large masses that comprise DCIS with microinvasion. Alternatively, some cases characterized by direct skin involvement may be amenable to a punch biopsy of the affected skin. When matted, fixed axillary, or supraclavicular adenopathy is present, an FNAB of the nodal disease may be offered for staging purposes. A final comment regarding percutaneous needle biopsy is that an adequate amount of tissue must be retrieved so that hormone receptor status and *HER2/neu* expression can be addressed. Should the needle biopsy return as negative or nondiagnostic in the setting of a clinically suspicious examination, it would be incumbent upon the surgeon to further investigate this discordant picture by performing an open biopsy of the breast or nodal basin.

Prompt bilateral breast imaging with mammography in this setting is essential, regardless of the

Table 18-2. RANDOMIZED STUDIES OF NEOADJUVANT VERSUS ADJUVANT CHEMOTHERAPY FOR BREAST CANCER

Study	*n*	Stages	Treatment	Median F/U	BCT Rate		Local Recurrence after BCT		Overall Survival at Median F/U	
					Preop CTX	Postop CTX	Preop CTX	Postop CTX	Preop CTX	Postop CTX
Institut Bergonie[22,23]	272	II–IIIa (T > 3 cm)	N+/ER-: MRM→EVM × 3→MTV × 3 N-/ER+: MRM versus EVM × 3→MTV × 3→S and/or XRT	124 months	63.1%	0%	XRT: 34% L/ALND/XRT: 23%	NA	55%*	55%*
Institut Curie[83,84]	414	IIa–IIIa	FAC × 4→XRT ± S versus XRT ± S→FAC × 4 (S reserved for incomplete responders)	66 months	82%	77%	24%	18%	86%	78%
Royal Marsden[26,27]	309	I–IIIb	Tam + MM ± M × 4→S→Tam + MM ± M × 4 versus S→MM ± M × 8 + Tam	48 months	89%	78%	3%†	4%†	80%*	80%*
NSABP[28,29]	1,523	I–IIIa	AC × 4→S versus S→AC × 4	72 months	68%	60%	7.9%	5.8%	80%‡	80%‡

ALND = axillary lymph node dissection; BCT = breast cancer treatment; CTX = chemotherapy; ER+ = estrogen receptor-positive; ER- = estrogen receptor-negative; EVM = epirubicin, vincristine, methotrexate; FAC = 5-fluorouracil, doxorubicin, cyclophosphamide; F/U = follow-up; L = lumpectomy; MM ± M = mitoxantrone, methotrexate, with or without mitomycin C; MRM = modified radical mastectomy; MTV = mitomycin C, thiotepa, vindesine; N+ = node positive; N- = node negative; NA = not applicable; NSABP = NSABP B-18 trial; Preop = preoperative; Postop = postoperative; S = surgery; T = tumor; Tam = tamoxifen; XRT = irradiation.

*Rate estimated from graph.

†Local recurrence rates reported for lumpectomy and mastectomy patients combined.

‡Overall survival rate at 5 years.

patient's age and date of her most recent study. The baseline mammogram should be carefully scrutinized for evidence of multicentric disease that would contraindicate eventual breast preservation. Diffuse and suspicious-appearing microcalcifications and satellite lesions in different quadrants of the breast are difficult to follow for evidence of response, and patients with these findings should be informed that they will require mastectomy regardless of their degree of response to induction chemotherapy.[31]

Breast and axillary ultrasound for the affected side will frequently yield valuable information regarding the extent of disease. In particular, ultrasound evaluation of the axilla can be useful for image-guided needle biopsies, and ultrasound detection of apical axillary/infraclavicular nodal metastases has been shown to provide important prognostic information.[32–34] Unfortunately, this imaging modality has a false-negative rate approximating 20%, because it will generally not be able to identify metastases smaller than 5 mm in size.

Once a tissue diagnosis is established, LABC patients should receive a baseline assessment that is multidisciplinary in nature prior to any treatment, so that a consensus opinion is reached regarding the stage of the disease. It is appropriate for these patients to undergo a radiographic work-up, looking for evidence of distant metastases to the liver, lungs, and/or bones. Directed x-rays to any sites of new bone pain, or a head computed tomography scan to evaluate new neurologic symptoms, might also be appropriate in select cases. Although the yield of a metastatic work-up for early-stage breast cancer in an asymptomatic patient is low (approximately 2 to 3%), this risk rises to 30% in the setting of LABC.[35]

The multidisciplinary team should assess patients receiving preoperative chemotherapy after one or two cycles of treatment, and again at the completion of therapy to document response and to decide on subsequent treatment options. Repeat imaging with breast ultrasound and/or mammography can be useful in this regard. If minimal or no response is observed after the first couple of cycles, a decision should be made to either proceed with surgery and confirm the pathologic status of disease at that time, or to cross the patient over to a different systemic therapy regimen. Continued treatment with a clinically ineffective regimen will not improve lumpectomy eligibility, and places the patient at risk for cumulative toxicity. If the decision is made to proceed with surgery for a nonresponder, then the multidisciplinary team may choose to evaluate the tumor for pathologic evidence of response, facilitating decisions regarding the selection of an appropriate postoperative systemic therapy regimen. If the decision is made to switch to an alternative chemotherapy regimen, then the response evaluation should be repeated after two cycles of the crossover regimen.

CONTROVERSIES IN THE MANAGEMENT OF LOCALLY ADVANCED BREAST CANCER PATIENTS

Controversies persist regarding optimal management of LABC patients, and they are primarily related to the patient's locoregional management.

Breast Conservation Therapy Versus Mastectomy

The magnitude of the clinical response to neoadjuvant chemotherapy in many LABC cases has motivated investigations into the feasibility of breast-conserving approaches for selected patients. However, uncertainty regarding the pathologic correlate to this response made this approach appear risky. Initially, it was unclear whether the observed clinical response correlated with concentric diminution in the malignant tumor mass, or whether the primary tumor mass might actually decrease in extent while leaving multiple foci of ductal carcinoma in situ or satellitosis in the surrounding parenchyma.

Singletary and colleagues therefore conducted a feasibility study to evaluate the pathologic extent of residual disease in 136 LABC patients treated with induction chemotherapy.[36] Careful and extensive scrutiny of the postchemotherapy mastectomy specimens from these patients revealed that in approximately 25% of these cases, the volume of residual disease in the breast would have been amenable to lumpectomy.

From this and other studies, the following criteria for breast conservation therapy in LABC following induction chemotherapy (which are similar to those for primary surgery in early-stage disease) have been widely adopted:

1. Patient desire for breast preservation
2. Absence of multicentric disease (tumors in separate quadrants of the breast) at time of presentation or preoperatively
3. Absence of diffuse microcalcifications on mammogram
4. Absence of skin involvement consistent with inflammatory breast cancer
5. Residual tumor mass amenable to a margin-negative lumpectomy resection

As shown in Table 18–1, local recurrence rates are comparable in breast conservation therapy patients treated with preoperative versus postoperative chemotherapy. The NSABP B-18 investigators did note, however, that there was a trend toward higher local recurrence rates among patients who required preoperative treatment in order to become eligible for the lumpectomy approach (15% versus 7%).[29] This would be expected, since local recurrence following lumpectomy is largely a manifestation of underlying disease biology, and larger tumors are likely to demonstrate a more aggressive nature, whether treated by lumpectomy or mastectomy. Postmastectomy radiation is recommended for patients with T3 tumors because of this concept.[37] Furthermore, the NSABP B-18 trial did not require a lumpectomy boost dose, and tamoxifen was only offered to patients over the age of 50 years; both of these modalities may contribute to decreased local recurrence rates. Lastly, the NSABP defines a negative lumpectomy margin as the absence of any tumor cells at the cut, inked specimen margin. A more aggressive approach to margin status is preferable for patients receiving induction chemotherapy for primary tumor downstaging.

Optimal Preoperative Systemic Therapy Regimen

Doxorubicin-based neoadjuvant chemotherapy is the regimen for which the most data have been published, and this highly effective agent will result in at least 50% tumor shrinkage (pCR and/or cCR) in more than 75% of cases. Unfortunately, very few patients will achieve the complete pathologic response that predicts long-term disease-free survival. Numerous investigators have therefore explored alternative neoadjuvant chemotherapy regimens, in the hope of identifying a non–cross-resistant strategy for use in cases where response to the initial regimen is suboptimal. Hopefully, these crossover regimens will enlarge the proportion of patients experiencing a pCR.

The NSABP B-27 protocol randomized patients with resectable breast cancer to one of three different neoadjuvant treatment arms: (1) doxorubicin and cyclophosphamide alone; (2) doxorubicin, cyclophosphamide, and docetaxel; or (3) doxorubicin with cyclophosphamide preoperatively followed by docetaxel postoperatively. Preliminary data have revealed a pCR rate of 26.1% with the addition of docetaxel to the preoperative regimen compared with 13.7% for patients receiving doxorubicin and cyclophosphamide only ($p < .001$).[38,39] Furthermore, a larger proportion of patients receiving docetaxel preoperatively were node-negative (58.2% versus 50.8%; $p < .001$). Similarly, the M.D. Anderson Cancer Center has reported a pCR rate of nearly 30% in patients treated with preoperative doxorubicin, cyclophosphamide, 5-fluorouracil, and weekly paclitaxel.[40] Further maturation of these studies is necessary before the impact of these response rates on survival can be assessed. Early reports from the NSABP B-27 study, however, revealed outcome benefit limited to the endpoint of time to relapse. Despite continued outcome superiority in the pCR subset, survival rates were not significantly different for the docetaxel-containing arm of this trial.[41]

Scotland's Aberdeen trial addressed the question of whether the number of delivered chemotherapy cycles is the stronger predictor of tumor response compared with the type of chemotherapy.[42,43] This group evaluated 162 patients with primary breast tumors (at least 3 cm in size) by delivering four cycles of doxorubicin-based chemotherapy; if there were evidence of at least partial response, patients were then randomized to treatment with an additional four cycles of doxorubicin, or to be crossed over to four cycles of docetaxel. Nonresponders to doxorubicin were directly crossed over to docetaxel. With this trial design, all patients received a total of eight preoperative cycles of chemotherapy. Among the responders, the pCR rate for the doxorubicin-only group was 16%, compared with 34% for the responders who were randomized to the crossover docetaxel regimen ($p = .04$), thereby indicating that the nature of the chemotherapy is more important than the quantity of chemotherapy. This study also showed that poor responders may be salvaged by crossover to an alternative chemotherapy regimen, and may be transformed into complete responders. Among the 55 doxorubicin nonresponders, 33% experienced a complete response to docetaxel. Furthermore, short-term survival analyses at 3 years in the Aberdeen study suggested improved outcome for patients receiving docetaxel in addition to doxorubicin.[43]

Neoadjuvant endocrine therapy for estrogen receptor-positive LABC is also being explored more aggressively, and holds great promise related to the targeted nature of this treatment, as reviewed by Dixon and colleagues.[44] When hormonally active agents are delivered as induction therapy, 3 months of treatment is the preferred duration for adequate assessment of response. Preliminary studies suggest that aromatase inhibitors such as letrozole are more effective than tamoxifen.[44,45] Other novel neoadjuvant regimens currently being evaluated include trastuzumab, vinorelbine, capecitabine, and gemcitabine.

Monitoring Response to Neoadjuvant Chemotherapy

As discussed above, a significant response to the primary chemotherapy regimen is observed in approximately 80% of cases, however, an accurate prediction of a complete pathologic response is challenging. Conventional modalities for assessing chemotherapy response, including clinical examination, mammography, and breast ultrasonography, will be incorrect in identifying pCR patients in nearly half of cases.[31] Standard breast imaging is clearly more useful than physical examination alone.[31,46] Other imaging modalities, such as breast magnetic resonance imaging, positron emission tomography, and nuclear medicine scanning for sestamibi uptake, have all been reported to be potential alternative monitoring strategies with encouraging results, but in limited numbers of patients.[47–51] Microarray technology holds great promise to individualize the optimal chemotherapy regimen based on primary tumor genetic composition.[52]

IMMEDIATE BREAST RECONSTRUCTION

LABC has traditionally been perceived as a contraindication to immediate breast reconstruction (IBR), because of concerns that prolonged surgery would contribute to delays in delivering postoperative treatment, as well as concerns regarding the effect of postmastectomy radiation therapy to the reconstructed breast. Several investigators have evaluated outcome in this setting, with encouraging results.

Newman and colleagues studied 50 patients from the M.D. Anderson Cancer Center with stages IIb to IIIa breast cancer (24% treated with preoperative chemotherapy) who underwent mastectomy with IBR, and found no adverse effect on surgical complication rates in comparison with 72 patients with LABC undergoing mastectomy without IBR.[53] There was a slight increase in the interval for postoperative delivery of chemotherapy among the reconstructed patients (35 days versus 21 days; $p = .05$); however, this did not affect the local or distant recurrence rates (10% versus 12.5%, and 32% versus 36%, respectively). The implant IBRs, however, did have higher rates of radiation-related complications; nearly half of the irradiated implants developed contractures or recurrent infections that ultimately necessitated implant revision. Patients undergoing autogenous tissue (68% transverse rectus abdominis myocutaneous flaps, 2% latissimus dorsi flaps) reconstruction had better postoperative outcomes. Other investigators have reported similarly favorable results when LABC patients were managed with mastectomy and IBR.[54]

Recent studies have demonstrated high cosmetic complications rates following irradiation of autogenous tissue reconstructions, but occurring in a delayed fashion. Irradiation of implant reconstructions has also yielded consistently high failure rates. The decision to proceed with IBR in patients with known LABC should be made cautiously, and implant reconstructions should be avoided prior to delivery of postmastectomy irradiation.

Occasionally, LABC patients will require plastic surgery at the time of mastectomy, purely for soft tissue coverage of an extensive chest wall defect. In these cases, the latissimus dorsi flap is the most frequently used approach, as this flap is a relatively straightforward procedure and it provides durable and radiation-tolerant chest wall coverage.

LOCOREGIONAL IRRADIATION FOR LABC PATIENTS TREATED WITH NEOADJUVANT CHEMOTHERAPY

In the adjuvant setting, the American Society of Clinical Oncology recommends postmastectomy locoregional irradiation for all patients found to have four or more metastatic axillary lymph nodes. It should also be considered for patients with operable locally advanced cancer or T3 tumors associated with axillary metastases.[37] Since preoperative chemotherapy is quite effective for disease downstaging, the precise pathologic tumor and nodal information at the time of presentation may be difficult to assess at the time of surgery. Since postmastectomy locoregional irradiation appears to provide an outcome advantage to patients presenting with high-risk disease that is documented pathologically (via primary surgery), a valid question arises regarding the possibility that neoadjuvant chemotherapy might impair the ability to identify some of these patients.

Patients with at least four metastatic lymph nodes, or at least 5 cm of residual disease in the breast following chemotherapy, will clearly benefit from locoregional irradiation. Lumpectomy patients require at least breast irradiation. A very conservative approach might be to recommend consolidation therapy with locoregional chest wall irradiation to all LABC patients, regardless of chemotherapy response. However, patients with little or no residual disease in the breast and no axillary metastases after chemotherapy may not derive a substantial benefit from regional nodal irradiation. Data from the M.D. Anderson Cancer Center suggest that locoregional irradiation should also be considered for patients with postchemotherapy findings that include 1 to 3 metastatic axillary nodes, or axillary metastases associated with extracapsular extension.[55,56] Mamounas and colleagues reported patterns of locoregional failure among participants of the NSABP B-18 protocol, where stages I to III breast cancer patients were randomized to preoperative versus postoperative chemotherapy, and none received adjuvant irradiation.[57] This study revealed that the 10-year rates of locoregional failure were reasonably low and were similar in both arms of the study: 14% in the preoperative chemotherapy arm versus 12% in the postoperative arm. Furthermore, predictors of locoregional failure were the same in both arms, with four or more metastatic axillary nodes identifying high-risk patients who might benefit from chest wall irradiation regardless of neoadjuvant chemotherapy effect.

INTEGRATION OF LYMPHATIC MAPPING/SENTINEL LYMPH NODE BIOPSY INTO NEOADJUVANT CHEMOTHERAPY PROTOCOLS

Lymphatic mapping and sentinel lymph node biopsy has achieved rapid acceptance over the past 10 years in the oncology community for axillary staging in early breast cancer, and as a means of avoiding the morbidity of a standard axillary lymph node dissection. Application of this technology in cases of LABC has been approached more cautiously, because of concerns that tumor embolization from a bulky lesion in the breast might obstruct and alter lymphatic drainage pathways. This could contribute to identification of an incorrect sentinel node, or to a failed mapping procedure altogether. Findings by Bedrosian and colleagues and Chung and colleagues, however, are quite reassuring.[58,59] These investigators reported excellent sentinel node identification rates (99% and 100%, respectively), and very low false-negative rates (3% for both studies) in their respective series of 104 patients with tumors at least 3 cm in size and 41 patients with T3 tumors of the breast.

Another issue to be resolved is the question of whether the mapping procedure should be performed prior to or following delivery of the neoadjuvant chemotherapy. The earliest studies of sentinel lymph node biopsy in LABC have involved the postchemotherapy sequence, at the time of definitive breast surgery. Table 18–3 tabulates the findings of multiple studies reported to date, where the sentinel lymph node biopsy was performed with a concomitant axillary lymph node dissection (ALND)

Table 18–3. STUDIES OF SENTINEL LYMPH NODE BIOPSY PERFORMED AFTER NEOADJUVANT CHEMOTHERAPY

Study	T Status	Sample Size	Sentinel Node Identification Rate	False-Negative Rate	Metastases Limited to Sentinel Node(s)
Breslin et al, 2000[60]	2,3	51	85% (42/51)	12% (3/25)	40% (10/25)
Nason et al, 2000[61]	2,3	15	87% (13/15)	33% (3/9)	≥ 11%* (≥ 1/9)
Haid et al, 2001[62]	1–3	33	88% (29/33)	0% (0/22)	50% (11/22)
Fernandez et al, 2001[63]	1–4	40	90% (36/40)	20% (4/20)	20% (4/20)
Tafra et al, 2001[85]	1,2	29	93% (27/29)	0% (0/15)	NR
Stearns et al, 2002[65]	3,4	T4d (inflammatory), 8	75% (6/8)	40% (2/5)	24% (5/21)
		Noninflammatory, 26	88% (23/26)	6% (1/16)	
Julian et al, 2002[86]	1–3	34	91% (31/34)	0% (0/12)	42% (5/12)
Miller et al, 2002[67]	1–3	35	86% (30/35)	0% (0/9)	44% (4/9)
Brady, 2002[87]	1–3	14	93% (13/14)	0% (0/10)	60% (6/10)
Piato et al, 2003[88]	1,2	42	98% (41/42)	17% (3/18)	0% (0/18)
Balch et al, 2003[89]	2–4	32	97% (31/32)	5% (1/19)	56% (10/18)
Schwartz et al, 2003[70]	1–3	21	100% (21/21)	9% (1/11)	64% (7/11)
Reitsamer et al, 2003[90]	2,3	30	87% (26/30)	7% (1/15)	53% (8/15)
Mamounas at al, 2002[91] (abstract)	1–3	428	85% (363/428)	11% (15/140)	50% (70/140)

NR = no record.

after neoadjuvant chemotherapy.[60–71] The first report, by Breslin and colleagues from the M.D. Anderson Cancer Center, revealed the presence of a significant learning curve, reflecting the additional technical difficulty of lymphatic mapping related to the chemotherapy effect on the soft tissue in the axilla.[60] A parallel learning curve is reflected in Table 18–3; false-negative rates of as high as 33% are seen in some of the earlier studies with smaller sample sizes, compared with more recent studies reporting no false-negative cases. The largest-volume experience was reported by the NSABP B-27 study, where more than 400 patients underwent lymphatic mapping with concomitant axillary lymph node biopsy following preoperative doxorubicin and Taxotere treatment. The sentinel lymph node identification rate was 85%, and the false-negative rate was 11% in this multicenter study.

Because of ongoing uncertainty regarding the accuracy of lymphatic mapping procedures when performed after neoadjuvant chemotherapy, several surgical groups have adopted the practice of axillary staging with a sentinel lymph node biopsy prior to the delivery of induction chemotherapy. Table 18–4 summarizes the results of selected reported studies. Although this sequence subjects the patient to an additional surgical procedure, it does provide more definitive information for stratifying the extent of disease at presentation. This may be useful to medical oncologists in planning chemotherapy regimens, and to radiation oncologists in defining benefit from regional irradiation. Although this approach is technically feasible, accepted practice standards mandate that the prechemotherapy sentinel node-positive patients undergo a completion ALND after delivery of the neoadjuvant chemotherapy. A significant proportion of these completion ALNDs will be completely negative, since the preoperative chemotherapy can sterilize axillary metastases in approximately 25% of cases, and because metastatic disease is limited to the sentinel node(s) in 30 to 50%. It can therefore be argued that this approach results in many unnecessary ALNDs. Table 18–5 lists the advantages and disadvantages of sentinel lymph node biopsy performed prior to delivery of neoadjuvant chemotherapy versus after this treatment.

MANAGEMENT OF LOCOREGIONAL RECURRENCES

Chest wall recurrence following mastectomy, or any bulky recurrence following lumpectomy requiring chest wall resection, have historically been perceived as grave events, indicating a particularly aggressive underlying tumor biology. Downey and colleagues

Table 18–4. RESULTS OF SENTINEL LYMPH NODE BIOPSY PERFORMED PRIOR TO DELIVERY OF NEOADJUVANT CHEMOTHERAPY

		Pre-NeoCTX SLN Biopsy Results		Post-NeoCTX Status	
Study	Sample Size	SLN ID Rate (%)	SLN-Pos (%)	Management Strategy	No. Post-NeoCTX ALNDs Negative for Residual Metastases (%)
Zirngibl et al, 2002[92]	15	14/15 (93)	6/14 (43)	Completion of ALND in SLN-pos patients only	6/6 (100)
Sabel et al, 2003[93]	24	24/24 (100)	10/24 (42)	Completion of ALND in SLN-pos patients only	3/10 (30)
Olilla et al, 2003[94]	22	22/22 (100)	10/22 (45)	Completion of ALND in all patients	12 SLN-neg patients: 12/12 (100) 10 SLN-pos patients: 6/10 (60)

ALND = axillary lymph node dissection; ID = identification; neg = negative; NeoCTX = neoadjuvant chemotherapy; pos = positive for metastatis disease; SLN = sentinel lymph node.

and Chagpar and colleagues have recently reviewed the experiences of Memorial Sloan-Kettering and M.D. Anderson Cancer Center, respectively, in managing this pattern of relapse.[72,73] These investigators reported that prolonged survival can be achieved in a subset of these patients, when aggressively managed by surgical resection of the local recurrence. The 5-year overall survival rate was 35% in the Memorial Sloan-Kettering series and median survival was 83% in the M.D. Anderson series for cases where the chest wall recurrence was the isolated site of disease failure. Additional chest wall recurrences occurred in 37 and 22% of patients, respectively. Factors predictive of improved survival include a disease-free interval from initial diagnosis of at least 2 years and node-negative disease in the M.D. Anderson series, and a recurrence size < 4 cm in the Memorial Sloan-Kettering series. Morbidity associated with surgical resection of the recurrence was acceptably low. Extent of resection included sternectomy in 6 of 72 resections from the M.D. Anderson series, and in 1 of 38 patients from the Memorial Sloan-Kettering series; an additional 15 and 22 patients from Memorial Sloan-Kettering had ribs or ribs plus sternum resected. Assistance from the reconstructive team was required in many cases, and induction chemotherapy to downsize the site of recurrence was also delivered for many patients.

Table 18–5. ADVANTAGES AND DISADVANTAGES OF SENTINEL LYMPH NODE BIOPSY PERFORMED PRIOR TO VERSUS DELIVERY OF NEOADJUVANT CHEMOTHERAPY

	SLN Biopsy Performed After Delivery of Neoadjuvant Chemotherapy	SLN Biopsy Performed Prior to Delivery of Neoadjuvant Chemotherapy
Advantages	Among neoadjuvant chemotherapy patients, there is more widespread experience with lymphatic mapping performed after chemotherapy, since breast and axillary surgeries have typically been performed concomitantly upon completion of preoperative chemotherapy; Surgical sequence consistent with conventional neoadjuvant chemotherapy regimens	Significance of nodal status is better understood when axillary staging is performed at presentation; Preferred by many medical and radiation oncologists, who may modify their treatment recommendations on the basis of pretreatment nodal status; Most surgeons are already experienced with lymphatic mapping technology in the prechemotherapy setting
Disadvantages	False-negative rates not yet optimized; range, 0 to 40%; Significant learning curve	Commits some patients to unnecessary ALND; metastatic disease limited to the previously excised SLN in 30 to 50%; chemotherapy downstages 25 to 30% of patients to node-negativity; Requires an additional surgical procedure

ALND = axillary lymph node dissection; SLN = sentinel lymph node.

INFLAMMATORY BREAST CANCER

Inflammatory breast cancer (IBC) is categorized as a specific form of breast cancer that is distinctly different from typical patterns of LABC and long-standing neglected LABC with secondary inflammatory changes. Primary IBC is characterized by the rapid onset (usually reported by the patient as having evolved within a period of a few weeks to a few months) of an enlarged, edematous, and inflamed-appearing breast. The classic findings of the orange-peel breast skin (peau d'orange) however are not always present, and some of the more subtle presentations of IBC may include a faint patch of edematous breast localized to the central periareolar skin. Pathologically, the skin edema is caused by invasion and obstruction of dermal lymphatics by tumor cells, and an underlying tumor mass may or may not be present. Approximately one-third of cases will have clinical axillary lymph node involvement, and a similar proportion of IBC patients will have distant metastases at the time of diagnosis.[74,75] Dermal lymphatic involvement on skin biopsy is present in approximately 75% of cases, but the diagnosis of IBC can be made on clinical assessment only, regardless of whether histopathology offers supporting evidence.[76] Conversely, dermal lymphatic cancer involvement can be identified incidentally in cases of noninflammatory breast cancer.[75,77]

IBC is an uncommon pattern of breast cancer, accounting for < 5% of all cases in most series.[75,78] Worldwide, IBC has been identified with increased incidence in the mideast and northern Africa. Median age at diagnosis for IBC cases tends to be slightly younger than for non-IBC cases.[78] There are no known breast cancer risk factors that are specific for IBC. Prognostically, IBC is a more aggressive pattern of disease than other forms of breast cancer, with 3-year survival rates of approximately 40% and 5-year survival rates of only 15%.[74,78] This rather dismal outcome has motivated studies that have tried to define distinct genetic profiles to explain this aggressive breast cancer phenotype.[79] Cases of primary IBC are defined by the AJCC staging system as T4d (stage IIIc) breast cancer.[2] Similar treatment strategies are offered to patients with LABC and IBC, generally consisting of neoadjuvant chemotherapy, breast/axillary surgery, and irradiation. However, the excessive failure rates seen in cases of IBC have prompted a specialized and particularly aggressive approach in selected aspects of care; many treatment protocols for LABC will specifically exclude cases of IBC. Mastectomy offers superior locoregional control for IBC, even in cases of excellent response to neoadjuvant chemotherapy, and is therefore routinely preferred over any attempt at breast conservation. As shown by Stearns and colleagues, sentinel lymphadenectomy is inaccurate for cases of IBC, and mastectomy must therefore be performed as a modified radical procedure to insure inclusion of the standard ALND.[65] Chest wall irradiation, frequently with extended fields that treat the nonsurgical nodal basins (eg, supraclavicular and internal mammary), is also recommended. The usual treatment sequence is chemotherapy followed by modified radical mastectomy and postmastectomy irradiation, and several years of endocrine therapy for cases of hormone receptor-positive disease.

In one of the largest IBC studies to date, Panades and colleagues reported the population-based IBC experience from British Columbia between 1980 and 2000, involving 485 patients and representing 1.5% of the total breast cancer patient population during this time frame.[80] Median follow-up among survivors was 6.5 years, and the median breast cancer specific survival was 3.2 years for patients presenting with IBC but no evidence of distant metastases at diagnosis. These investigators also documented the superiority of mastectomy over breast preservation in management for IBC. The locoregional relapse-free survival hazard was 2.21 (95% CI, 0.96–5.11) for the comparison of mastectomy performed prior to chemotherapy versus no mastectomy, and 2.19 (95% CI, 1.17–4.08) for the comparison of mastectomy performed after neoadjuvant chemotherapy compared with no mastectomy. Estrogen receptor positivity, premenopausal status, and extent of pathologic response to neoadjuvant chemotherapy were all factors that correlated with a relatively better outcome.

SUMMARY

In summary, locally advanced breast cancer is defined as bulky T3 and T4 tumors of the breast, or breast cancer associated with matted axillary or supraclavicular adenopathy; inflammatory breast cancer is defined as T4d disease. Screening mammography and early detection programs have reduced the incidence of this category of disease. Overall outcome and local control rates have improved markedly with the use of multimodality therapy, including neoadjuvant chemotherapy followed by definitive surgery and locoregional radiation therapy to consolidate treatment. Additional uses of postoperative chemotherapy and postradiation hormonal therapy are determined by the extent of residual disease at the time of surgery and by hormone receptor status, respectively. Breast-conservation therapy may be offered to select cases of locally advanced breast cancer following adequate tumor downstaging by the neoadjuvant chemotherapy. Improved survival is seen for those patients, who experience a complete pathologic response. Ongoing studies are underway that seek to define the optimal induction chemotherapy regimen for maximizing response rates. Incorporation of lymphatic mapping into neoadjuvant chemotherapy protocols requires further study. Inflammatory breast cancer is a distinctly different and aggressive breast cancer phenotype that is best managed by neoadjuvant chemotherapy, modified radical mastectomy, postmastectomy irradiation, and endocrine therapy for hormone receptor-positive cases.

REFERENCES

1. Weir HK, Thun MJ, Hankey BF, et al. Annual report to the nation on the status of cancer, 1975–2000, featuring the uses of surveillance data for cancer prevention and control. J Natl Cancer Inst 2003;95:1276–99.
2. Singletary SE, Allred C, Ashley P, et al. Revision of the American Joint Committee on Cancer staging system for breast cancer. J Clin Oncol 2002;20:3628–36.
3. Olivotto IA, Chua B, Allan SJ, et al. Long-term survival of patients with supraclavicular metastases at diagnosis of breast cancer. J Clin Oncol 2003;21:851–4.
4. Brito RA, Valero V, Buzdar AU, et al. Long-term results of combined-modality therapy for locally advanced breast cancer with ipsilateral supraclavicular metastases: the University of Texas M.D. Anderson Cancer Center experience. J Clin Oncol 2001;19:628–33.
5. National Cancer Database. Available at http://www.pacs.org/cancer/ncdb (Accessed September 2005).
6. Haagensen C, Stout A. Carcinoma of the breast II. Criteria of operability. Ann Surg 1943;118:859.
7. Harris JR, Sawicka J, Gelman R, Hellman S. Management of locally advanced carcinoma of the breast by primary radiation therapy. Int J Radiat Oncol Biol Phys 1983;9:345–9.
8. Rao DV, Bedwinek J, Perez C, et al. Prognostic indicators in stage III and localized stage IV breast cancer. Cancer 1982;50:2037–43.
9. Rubens RD, Armitage P, Winter PJ, et al. Prognosis in inoperable stage III carcinoma of the breast. Eur J Cancer 1977;13:805–11.
10. Townsend CM Jr, Abston S, Fish JC. Surgical adjuvant treatment of locally advanced breast cancer. Ann Surg 1985;201:604–10.
11. Arnold DJ, Lesnick GJ. Survival following mastectomy for stage III breast cancer. Am J Surg 1979;137:362–6.
12. Montague ED, Fletcher GH. Local regional effectiveness of surgery and radiation therapy in the treatment of breast cancer. Cancer 1985;55:2266–72.
13. Broadwater JR, Edwards MJ, Kuglen C, et al. Mastectomy following preoperative chemotherapy. Strict operative criteria control operative morbidity. Ann Surg 1991;213:126–9.
14. Danforth DN Jr, Lippman ME, McDonald H, et al. Effect of preoperative chemotherapy on mastectomy for locally advanced breast cancer. Am Surg 1990;56:6–11.
15. McCready DR, Hortobagyi GN, Kau SW, et al. The prognostic significance of lymph node metastases after preoperative chemotherapy for locally advanced breast cancer. Arch Surg 1989;124:21–5.
16. De Lena M, Varini M, Zucali R, et al. Multimodal treatment for locally advanced breast cancer. Result of chemotherapy-radiotherapy versus chemotherapy-surgery. Cancer Clin Trials 1981;4:229–36.
17. Perloff M, Lesnick GJ, Korzun A, et al. Combination chemotherapy with mastectomy or radiotherapy for stage III breast carcinoma: a Cancer and Leukemia Group B study. J Clin Oncol 1988;6:261–9.
18. Papaioannou A, Lissaios B, Vasilaros S, et al. Pre- and postoperative chemoendocrine treatment with or without postoperative radiotherapy for locally advanced breast cancer. Cancer 1983;51:1284–90.
19. Hortobagyi GN, Ames FC, Buzdar AU, et al. Management of stage III primary breast cancer with primary chemotherapy, surgery, and radiation therapy. Cancer 1988;62:2507–16.
20. Lippman ME, Sorace RA, Bagley CS, et al. Treatment of locally advanced breast cancer using primary induction chemotherapy with hormonal synchronization followed by radiation therapy with or without debulking surgery. NCI Monogr 1986:153–9.
21. Olson JE, Neuberg D, Pandya KJ, et al. The role of radiotherapy in the management of operable locally advanced breast carcinoma: results of a randomized trial by the Eastern Cooperative Oncology Group. Cancer 1997;79:1138–49.
22. Mauriac L, Durand M, Avril A, Dilhuydy JM. Effects of primary chemotherapy in conservative treatment of breast cancer patients with operable tumors larger than 3 cm. Results of a randomized trial in a single centre. Ann Oncol 1991;2:347–54.
23. Mauriac L, MacGrogan G, Avril A, et al. Neoadjuvant chemotherapy for operable breast carcinoma larger than 3 cm: a unicentre randomized trial with a 124-month

median follow-up. Institut Bergonie Bordeaux Groupe Sein (IBBGS). Ann Oncol 1999;10:47–52.

24. Schwartz GF, Birchansky CA, Komarnicky LT, et al. Induction chemotherapy followed by breast conservation for locally advanced carcinoma of the breast. Cancer 1994;73:362–9.
25. Schwartz GF, Lange AK, Topham AK. Breast conservation following induction chemotherapy for locally advanced carcinoma of the breast (stages IIB and III). A surgical perspective. Surg Oncol Clin N Am 1995;4:657–69.
26. Powles TJ, Hickish TF, Makris A, et al. Randomized trial of chemoendocrine therapy started before or after surgery for treatment of primary breast cancer. J Clin Oncol 1995;13:547–52.
27. Makris A, Powles TJ, Ashley SE, et al. A reduction in the requirements for mastectomy in a randomized trial of neoadjuvant chemoendocrine therapy in primary breast cancer. Ann Oncol 1998;9:1179–84.
28. Fisher B, Brown A, Mamounas E, et al. Effect of preoperative chemotherapy on local-regional disease in women with operable breast cancer: findings from National Surgical Adjuvant Breast and Bowel Project B-18. J Clin Oncol 1997;15:2483–93.
29. Fisher B, Bryant J, Wolmark N, et al. Effect of preoperative chemotherapy on the outcome of women with operable breast cancer. J Clin Oncol 1998;16:2672–85.
30. Kuerer HM, Newman LA, Smith TL, et al. Clinical course of breast cancer patients with complete pathologic primary tumor and axillary lymph node response to doxorubicin-based neoadjuvant chemotherapy. J Clin Oncol 1999; 17:460–9.
31. Newman LA, Buzdar AU, Singletary SE, et al. A prospective trial of preoperative chemotherapy in resectable breast cancer: predictors of breast-conservation therapy feasibility. Ann Surg Oncol 2002;9:228–34.
32. Bedrosian I, Bedi D, Kuerer HM, et al. Impact of clinicopathological factors on sensitivity of axillary ultrasonography in the detection of axillary nodal metastases in patients with breast cancer. Ann Surg Oncol 2003;10:1025–30.
33. Krishnamurthy S, Sneige N, Bedi DG, et al. Role of ultrasound-guided fine-needle aspiration of indeterminate and suspicious axillary lymph nodes in the initial staging of breast carcinoma. Cancer 2002;95:982–8.
34. Newman LA, Kuerer HM, Fornage B, et al. Adverse prognostic significance of infraclavicular lymph nodes detected by ultrasonography in patients with locally advanced breast cancer. Am J Surg 2001;181:313–8.
35. Samant R, Ganguly P. Staging investigations in patients with breast cancer: the role of bone scans and liver imaging. Arch Surg 1999;134:551–3; discussion 554.
36. Singletary SE, McNeese MD, Hortobagyi GN. Feasibility of breast-conservation surgery after induction chemotherapy for locally advanced breast carcinoma. Cancer 1992;69: 2849–52.
37. Recht A, Edge SB, Solin LJ, et al. Postmastectomy radiotherapy: clinical practice guidelines of the American Society of Clinical Oncology. J Clin Oncol 2001;19:1539–69.
38. Mamounas E. Preliminary results of the NSABP B-27 Trial. San Antonio Breast Cancer Symposium; Dec 2001; San Antonio, Texas.
39. Bear HD, Anderson S, Brown A, et al. The effect on tumor response of adding sequential preoperative docetaxel to preoperative doxorubicin and cyclophosphamide: preliminary results from National Surgical Adjuvant Breast and Bowel Project B-27. J Clin Oncol 2003;21:4165–74.
40. Green M, Buzdar AU, Smith T, et al. Weekly paclitaxel improves pathologic complete remission in operable breast cancer when compared with paclitaxel once every 3 weeks. J Clin Oncol 2005;23:5983–92.
41. Bear HD, Anderson S, Smith RE et al. A randomized trial comparing preoperative (preop) doxorubicin/cyclophos phamise (AC) to preop AC followed by preop docetaxel (T) to preop AC followed by postoperative (postop) T in patients with operable carcinoma of the breast: results of NSABP B-27. San Antonio Breast Cancer Symposium. December 2004 Abstract 26. San Antonio, Texas.
42. Smith IC, Heys SD, Hutcheon AW, et al. Neoadjuvant chemotherapy in breast cancer: significantly enhanced response with docetaxel. J Clin Oncol 2002;20:1456–66.
43. Heys SD, Hutcheon AW, Sarkar TK, et al. Neoadjuvant docetaxel in breast cancer: 3-year survival results from the Aberdeen trial. Clin Breast Cancer 2002;3 Suppl 2:S69–74.
44. Dixon JM, Anderson TJ, Miller WR. Neoadjuvant endocrine therapy of breast cancer: a surgical perspective. Eur J Cancer 2002;38:2214–21.
45. Ellis M, Coop A, Singh B, et al. Letrozole is a more effective neoadjuvant endocrine therapy than tamoxifen for ErbB-1 and/or ErbB-2-positive, estrogen receptor-positive primary breast cancer: evidence from a phase III randomized trial. J Clin Oncol 2001;19:3808–16.
46. Helvie MA, Joynt LK, Cody RL, et al. Locally advanced breast carcinoma: accuracy of mammography versus clinical examination in the prediction of residual disease after chemotherapy. Radiology 1996;198:327–32.
47. Delille JP, Slanetz PJ, Yeh ED, et al. Invasive ductal breast carcinoma response to neoadjuvant chemotherapy: noninvasive monitoring with functional MR imaging pilot study. Radiology 2003;228:63–9.
48. Abraham D, Jones R, Jones S, et al. Evaluation of neoadjuvant chemotherapeutic response of locally advanced breast cancer by magnetic resonance imaging. Cancer 1996;78:91–100.
49. Wahl R, Zasadny K, Helvie M. Metabolic monitoring of breast cancer chemohormonal therapy using positron emission tomography: initial evaluation. J Clin Oncol 1993;11:2101–11.
50. Mezi S, Primi F, Capoccetti F, et al. In vivo detection of resistance to anthracycline based neoadjuvant chemotherapy in locally advanced and inflammatory breast cancer with technetium-99m sestamibi scintimammography. Int J Oncol 2003;22:1233–40.
51. Wilczek B, von Schoultz E, Bergh J, et al. Early assessment of neoadjuvant chemotherapy by FEC-courses of locally advanced breast cancer using 99mTc-MIBI. Acta Radiol 2003;44:284–7.
52. Pusztai L, Ayers M, Stec J, Hortobagyi GN. Clinical application of cDNA microarrays in oncology. Oncologist 2003;8:252–8.
53. Newman LA, Kuerer HM, Hunt KK, et al. Feasibility of immediate breast reconstruction for locally advanced breast cancer. Ann Surg Oncol 1999;6:671–5.

54. Styblo T, Lewis M, Carlson G, et al. Immediate breast reconstruction for stage III breast cancer using transverse rectus abdominis musculotaneous (TRAM) flap. Ann Surg Oncol 1996;3:375–80.
55. Buchholz TA, Strom EA, Perkins GH, McNeese MD. Controversies regarding the use of radiation after mastectomy in breast cancer. Oncologist 2002;7:539–46.
56. Woodward W, Strom E, Tucker S, et al. Locoregional recurrence after doxorubicin-based chemotherapy and postmastectomy: implications for breast cancer patients with early-stage disease and predictors for recurrence after postmastectomy radiation. Int J Radiat Oncol Biol Phys 2003;57:336–44.
57. Mamounas E, Wang J, Bryant J, et al. Patterns of locoregional failure in patients receiving neoadjuvant chemotherapy: results from NSABP B-18. 26th Annual San Antonio Breast Cancer Symposium; 2003 Dec 3–6; San Antonio, Texas.
58. Bedrosian I, Reynolds C, Mick R, et al. Accuracy of sentinel lymph node biopsy in patients with large primary breast tumors. Cancer 2000;88:2540–5.
59. Chung M, Ye W, Giuliano A. Role for sentinel lymph node dissection in the management of large (> or + 5 cm) invasive breast cancer. Ann Surg Oncol 2001;8:688–92.
60. Breslin TM, Cohen L, Sahin A, et al. Sentinel lymph node biopsy is accurate after neoadjuvant chemotherapy for breast cancer. J Clin Oncol 2000;18:3480–6.
61. Nason KS, Anderson BO, Byrd DR, et al. Increased false negative sentinel node biopsy rates after preoperative chemotherapy for invasive breast carcinoma. Cancer 2000;89:2187–94.
62. Haid A, Tausch C, Lang A, et al. Is sentinel lymph node biopsy reliable and indicated after preoperative chemotherapy in patients with breast carcinoma? Cancer 2001;92:1080–4.
63. Fernandez A, Cortes M, Benito E, et al. Gamma probe sentinel node localization and biopsy in breast cancer patients treated with a neoadjuvant chemotherapy scheme. Nucl Med Commun 2001;22:361–6.
64. Tafra L, Verbanac K, Lannin D. Preoperative chemotherapy and sentinel lymphadenectomy for breast cancer. Am J Surg 2001;182:312–5.
65. Stearns V, Ewing CA, Slack R, et al. Sentinel lymphadenectomy after neoadjuvant chemotherapy for breast cancer may reliably represent the axilla except for inflammatory breast cancer. Ann Surg Oncol 2002;9:235–42.
66. Julian TB, Dusi D, Wolmark N. Sentinel node biopsy after neoadjuvant chemotherapy for breast cancer. Am J Surg 2002;184:315–7.
67. Miller AR, Thomason VE, Yeh IT, et al. Analysis of sentinel lymph node mapping with immediate pathologic review in patients receiving preoperative chemotherapy for breast carcinoma. Ann Surg Oncol 2002;9:243–7.
68. Brady E. Sentinel lymph node mapping following neoadjuvant chemotherapy for breast cancer. Breast J 2002;8:97–100.
69. Piato J, Barros A, Pincerato K, et al. Sentinel lymph node biopsy in breast cancer after neoadjuvant chemotherapy. A pilot study. Eur J Surg Oncol 2002;29:118–20.
70. Schwartz GF, Meltzer AJ. Accuracy of axillary sentinel lymph node biopsy following neoadjuvant (induction) chemotherapy for carcinoma of the breast. Breast J 2003;9:374–9.
71. Mamounas E. Accuracy of sentinel node biopsy after neoadjuvant chemotherapy in breast cancer: updated results from NSABP B-27. Program Proceedings of the 38th Annual Meeting of the American Society of Clinical Oncology; 2002 May 18–21; Orlando, Florida. Vol. 21.
72. Downey R, Rusch V, Hsu F, et al. Chest wall resection for locally recurrent breast cancer: is it worthwhile? J Thorac Cardiovasc Surg 2000;119:420–8.
73. Chagpar A, Meric-Bernstam F, Hunt K, et al. Chest wall recurrence after mastectomy does not always portend a dismal outcome. Ann Surg Oncol 2003;10:628–34.
74. Jaiysemi I, Buzdar A, Hortobagyi GN. Inflammatory breast cancer: a review. J Clin Oncol 1992;10:1014–24.
75. Lerebours F, Bieche I, Lidereau R. Update on inflammatory breast cancer. Breast Cancer Res 2005;7:52–8.
76. Bonnier P, Charpin C, Lejeune C, et al. Inflammatory carcinomas of the breast: a clinical, pathological, or a clinical and pathological definition? Int J Cancer 1995;62:382–5.
77. Amparo R, Angel C, Ana L, et al. Inflammatory breast carcinoma: a pathological or clinical entity? Breast Cancer Res Treat 2000;64:269–73.
78. Chang S, Parker S, Pham T, et al. Inflammatory breast carcinoma incidence and survival: the Surveillance, Epidemiology and End Results Program of the National Cancer Institute. Cancer 1998;82:2366–72.
79. Bertucci F, Finetti P, Rougemont J, et al. Gene expression profiling identifies molecular subtypes of inflammatory breast cancer. Cancer Res 2005;2005:2170–8.
80. Panades M, Olivotto IA, Speers CH, et al. Evolving treatment strategies for inflammatory breast cancer: a population-based survival analysis. J Clin Oncol 2005;23:1941–50.
81. Valagussa P, Zambetti M, Bignami P, et al. T3b-T4 breast cancer: factors affecting results in combined modality treatments. Clin Exp Metastasis 1983;1:191–202.
82. Cance WG, Carey LA, Calvo BF, et al. Long-term outcome of neoadjuvant therapy for locally advanced breast carcinoma: effective clinical downstaging allows breast preservation and predicts outstanding local control and survival. Ann Surg 2002;236:295–302; discussion 302–3.
83. Scholl SM, Fourquet A, Asselain B, et al. Neoadjuvant versus adjuvant chemotherapy in premenopausal patients with tumours considered too large for breast conserving surgery: preliminary results of a randomised trial: S6. Eur J Cancer 1994;30A:645–52.
84. Scholl SM, Pierga JY, Asselain B, et al. Breast tumour response to primary chemotherapy predicts local and distant control as well as survival. Eur J Cancer 1995;31A: 1969–75.
85. Tafra L, Verbanac KM, Lannin DR. Preoperative chemotherapy and sentinel lymphadenectomy for breast cancer. Am J Surg 2001;182:312–5.
86. Julian TB, Dusi D, Wolmark N. Sentinel node biopsy after neoadjuvant chemotherapy for breast cancer. Am J Surg 2002;184:315–7.
87. Brady EW. Sentinel lymph node mapping following neoadjuvant chemotherapy for breast cancer. Breast J 2002; 8:97–100.
88. Piato JR, Barros AC, Pincerato KM, et al. Sentinel lymph node biopsy in breast cancer after neoadjuvant chemotherapy. A pilot study. Eur J Surg Oncol 2003;29:118–20.

89. Balch GC, Mithani SK, Richards KR, et al. Lymphatic mapping and sentinel lymphadenectomy after preoperative therapy for stage II and III breast cancer. Ann Surg Oncol 2003;10:616–21.
90. Reitsamer R, Peintinger F, Rettenbacher L, Prokop E. Sentinel lymph node biopsy in breast cancer patients after neoadjuvant chemotherapy. J Surg Oncol 2003;84:63–7.
91. Mamounas EP, Brown A, Anderson S, et al. Sentinel node biopsy after neoadjuvant chemotherapy in breast cancer: results from National Surgical Adjuvant Breast and Bowel Project Protocol B-27. J Clin Oncol 2005;23:2694–702.
92. Zirngibl C, Steinfeld-Birg D, Vogt H, et al. Sentinel lymph node biopsy before neoadjuvant chemotherapy: conservation of breast and axilla. Abstract #516, San Antonio Breast Cancer Symposium; 2002 December 13; San Antonio, Texas.
93. Sabel MS, Schott AF, Kleer CG, et al. Sentinel node biopsy prior to neoadjuvant chemotherapy. Am J Surg 2003;186: 102–5.
94. Ollila D, Neuman H, Dees E, et al. Lymphatic mapping and sentinel lymphadenectomy prior to neoadjuvant chemotherapy in locally advanced breast cancer patients. 26th Annual San Antonio Breast Cancer Symposium; 2003 Dec 3–6; San Antonio, Texas.

19

Axillary Staging and Therapeutics

JACOBO NURKO
JOHN RALPH BROADWATER
MICHAEL J. EDWARDS

Staging is a term that refers to the process of grouping patients according to the extent and/or severity of their disease. By estimating prognosis, staging classifies patients into groups so that treatment may be prescribed according to the severity of the malignancy. Staging also allows for the comparison of outcomes for different treatments for specific groups of patients, and is therefore a critical consideration for clinical trial design. Staging of malignant tumors is based on specific clinical and pathologic findings. Among the first clinical staging systems used in the United States was the Columbia Clinical Classification of 1942 for patients with breast cancer. The current most commonly used staging classification is that provided by the American Joint Committee on Cancer. This is a clinical and pathologic system based on tumor size (T), the extent of lymph node involvement (N), and the presence of tumor metastasis (M), the so-called "TNM staging" system.

Axillary lymph node staging for breast cancer requires a clinical and pathologic assessment of the presence and extent of breast cancer in the regional lymph nodes. In the absence of distant metastasis, axillary lymph node status is the most accurate predictor of survival. Axillary lymph node staging is a vital prerequisite to prescribing adjuvant hormonal therapy, cytotoxic drug, irradiation, and surgical therapy to achieve the therapeutic goals of local, regional, and systemic disease control.

Both breast cancer staging and therapy have changed and evolved over time. Staging was formerly based solely on clinical findings and usually followed by extensive surgery. Staging is now more precise and accurate, and less invasive. For example, consider the following transitions; in recent years, we have advanced from (1) open surgical biopsy to image-guided biopsy for diagnosis, (2) modified radical mastectomy to breast conserving surgery, and (3) complete axillary lymph node dissection to sentinel lymph node staging for accurate axillary lymph node staging. These collective surgical advances have provided our breast cancer patients with improved diagnostic and therapeutic efficacies; all represent more precise and less morbid approaches.

HISTORIC PERSPECTIVES

Axillary dissection for the staging and therapy of breast cancer was first clinically applied in the nineteenth century by Lorenz Heister.[1] In 1875, Von Volkmann reported the communication of breast lymphatics with axillary nodes and advocated removal of the breast and all axillary nodes for patients with locally and regionally advanced breast cancer.[2,3] Banks advocated removal of axillary nodes even when there were no signs of clinical metastasis.[4] Moore also recognized the occult involvement of axillary nodes and suggested that "the cure of breast carcinoma" was only possible when the "disease glands" were removed with the breast.[5,6] Halsted endorsed Moore's ideas and outlined principles that were ultimately proven valid in achieving local and regional disease control for breast cancer. He described the technique for radical mastectomy in specific detail and established the surgical principles for local and regional control of breast cancer that remained in place for nearly half a century.[7–9]

In the 1930s, Gray performed breast lymphography by injecting colloidal thorium dioxide in surgical breast specimens. His findings corroborated earlier theories that the mode of spread of cancer to lymphatic glands was likely due to lymphatic emboli.[10] Cabanas went on to perform meticulous lymphography studies in patients with penile cancer.[11] His data led him to suggest that a specific lymph node, the so-called "sentinel lymph node," served as the primary initial site of metastasis from a specific anatomic site of origin. His studies were reported in 1976 at the Society of Surgical Oncology meeting, where he made the first controversial recommendation for sentinel lymph node staging in the management of an epithelial malignancy. Cabanas' hypothesis was revolutionary. The concept that a primary tumor would reliably, and repeatedly, spread to a specific lymph node, and that by knowing the status of disease involvement in the specific lymph node, the presence or absence of metastatic disease for that entire region could be inferred, was a concept that was difficult to accept. His concept was so revolutionary and controversial that it was not adopted by the leading surgeons of the time.

MINIMIZING THE MORBIDITY OF AXILLARY NODAL STAGING

The presence of tumor cells in axillary lymph nodes is the most important prognostic factor for patients with breast cancer without evidence of distant metastasis. Axillary nodal staging may be crucial for deciding the appropriate management for a specific patient. However, axillary dissection for nodal staging has significant morbidity. The likelihood of postoperative lymphedema correlates with the extent of surgery. Lymphedema also represents the operative complication most likely to cause permanent disability with chronic pain and is often associated with recurrent episodes of cellulitis (Figure 19–1).[6] Other complications associated with axillary lymph node dissection include postoperative seromas, decreased range of shoulder motion, and thrombophlebitis.

Most surgeons have adopted the level I/II axillary dissection over the level I/II and III dissection for staging purposes for two primary reasons. A level I, II, and III axillary dissection involves a more extensive operation associated with a significantly greater risk of lymphedema. Little staging efficacy is lost with the elimination of the level III dissection. A level I dissection understages approximately 15% of patients, whereas a level I/II node dissection identifies 97 to 98% of all node-positive patients as compared with a dissection that includes level III. A 2 to 3% false-negative rate with this approach has the advantage of a reduction in postoperative morbidity.[12–16.]

Surgeons have tried to identify a subset of patients with breast cancer who do not benefit from axillary staging. This issue has increasingly become clinically irrelevant, since the morbidity of sentinel lymphadenectomy as the current staging method, is minimal. Nevertheless, important information has been learned from these studies and will be discussed in the following paragraphs.

Noting that small primary tumors have a lower risk of lymph node metastasis, these patients have been targeted for primary treatment without axillary dissection.[17,18] Silverstein and colleagues found no risk of nodal positivity for ductal carcinoma in situ, and T1a lesions had a 3% risk for nodal metastasis.[19] Unfortunately, such small primary lesions are a very small subgroup of all patients diagnosed with breast cancer (even in this, the modern era of mammographic screening). Once the tumor size exceeds 5 mm, the risk of axillary metastasis increases to 17%

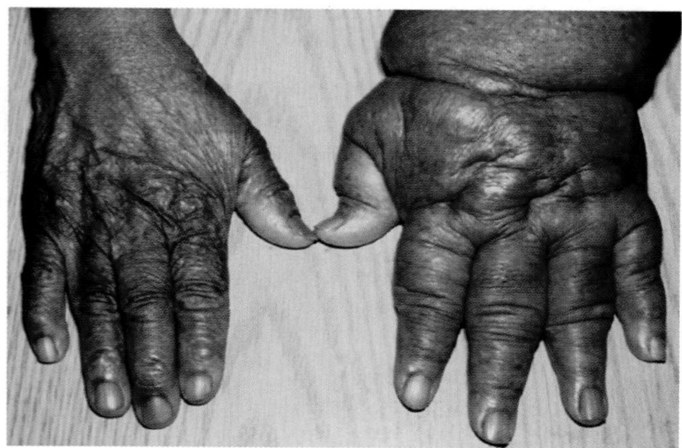

Figure 19–1. Breast cancer patient with lymphedema in the left hand after a modified radical mastectomy.

or greater.[19] Thus, omitting an axillary dissection may potentially understage this subset of patients.

Based on the National Surgical Adjuvant Breast and Bowel Project (NSABP-B04), axillary dissection does not lead to a survival benefit.[20] Thus, if adjuvant chemotherapy decisions could be made based on the features on the primary lesion alone, then axillary dissection might be reasonably omitted for certain patients. The size of the primary tumor is related to the risk for relapse. Comparing patients with tumors of the same size, the long-term risk for relapse is significantly greater with node involvement. In addition, adjuvant therapy decisions today have become more complex, often involving multiple treatment modalities based upon a rigorous discussion and consideration of staging criteria. Patients are no longer distinguished as requiring "no adjuvant therapy," "hormonal therapy," or "chemotherapy." Rather, decisions involve combinations of chemotherapy, a number of hormonal therapies, and the extent of adjuvant radiation treatment. All of these decisions are influenced by the number of metastatic axillary lymph nodes.

The above arguments, related to the prevalence of nodal disease in small tumors and the potential lack of therapeutic efficacy of axillary nodal dissection, have become largely irrelevant in the era of sentinel lymph node staging. Sentinel lymph node staging involves the removal of, on average, two lymph nodes.[21,22] Consequently, the risk of associated lymphedema, decreased shoulder motion, and intercostal brachial nerve related paresthesias is greatly minimized, diminishing interest in a selective approach to axillary staging.[21]

THERAPEUTIC ROLE OF AXILLARY DISSECTION

Whereas the staging value of axillary lymph node histology is widely recognized, the therapeutic value of axillary dissection in terms of survival is poorly defined and remarkably controversial.

Halsted demonstrated that a proper surgical operation unequivocally provided superior local disease control for breast cancer.[7–9] However, in spite of this seminal achievement, local control did not significantly impact survival time or likelihood of cure. This prompted an interest in extended nodal dissections including mediastinal, internal mammary, and supraclavicular nodes; however, none of these more aggressive approaches influenced the likelihood of being cured or yielded an enhancement of survival duration.

The results of the NSABP-B04 trial are often quoted as the definitive source of information in regard to the efficacy of therapeutic axillary dissection. In fact, these results seemingly indicate a lack of therapeutic efficacy for axillary dissection. In this study, patients with clinically negative axillary lymph nodes were randomized to three treatment modalities: radical mastectomy, total mastectomy alone, and total mastectomy with adjuvant radiation therapy; only the radical mastectomy group was intended to have axillary dissection. In spite of the axillary lymphadenectomy, no survival advantage was seen; the survival curves were virtually identical for all three treatment groups, suggesting a lack of therapeutic efficacy for axillary dissection (Table 19–1).[20] However, this study was not intended to determine the therapeutic impact of axillary lymphadenectomy. It did not have

Table 19–1. RESULTS OF NSABP-B04 SHOWING THE IMPACT OF AXILLARY DISSECTION ON AXILLARY RECURRENCE AND OVERALL SURVIVAL

Treatment Modality	Regional Recurrence at 10-Year Follow-Up (%)	10-Year Overall Survival (%)
Node-Negative		
Modified radical	2.5	58 ± 2.6
Total mastectomy + XRT	3.4	59 ± 2.7
Total mastectomy	4.1	54 ± 2.7
Node-Positive		
Modified radical	7.5	38 ± 2.9
Total mastectomy + XRT	11.9	39 ± 2.9

Adapted from Fisher B et al.[20]
NSABP-B04 = National Surgical Adjuvant Breast and Bowel Project B04; XRT = irradiation.

the power to detect a reasonable difference in survival outcome. As an example, if NSABP-B04 were designed to determine the therapeutic efficacy of axillary lymphadenectomy, then the trial might have been designed with a 90% power to detect a 7% (or less) difference between treatment arms. This would have required approximately 2,000 patients for randomization. In fact, just over half that number was evaluated. Recognizing such, it is possible that a smaller (< 10%) survival benefit was overlooked with axillary lymph node dissection in NSABP-B04. The magnitude of any potential survival benefit of the axillary dissection remains unknown.

AXILLARY DISSECTION FOR LOCAL DISEASE CONTROL

With regard to local control, convincing scientific data have confirmed the therapeutic efficacy of axillary dissection. Axillary lymphadenectomy minimizes the probability of axillary recurrence in surgically treated patients.[20,23–26] In a patient with a 2 cm primary breast cancer, axillary dissection of levels I and II reduces the probability for regional recurrence from approximately 20 to 3%. However, there are problems with the interpretation of this benefit in the context of current adjuvant therapy. One should consider that the data defining this magnitude of risk reduction in local recurrence were generated when adjuvant systemic therapy was not commonly prescribed. Hormonal therapy and chemotherapy improve locoregional control.[24] The degree to which these treatments improve the therapeutic impact of axillary lymph node dissection remains undefined. Therefore, the exact magnitude of reduction in local recurrence by axillary dissection with adjuvant therapy remains unknown.

In the final analysis, axillary dissection provides accurate lymph node staging, effective regional control, and may offer an unclear, but probably small, survival advantage.[25,27]

EVOLUTION OF SENTINEL NODE STAGING

Clinically applied sentinel lymph node staging for breast cancer had its origin in the pioneering work of Morton and colleagues. They devised a lymphatic mapping technique with Lymphazurin blue dye to identify the first draining node within a given regional nodal basin.[28] Morton and his colleagues were the first to systematically design a series of clinical studies to conclusively and convincingly determine the efficacy and reliability of the sentinel lymph node staging concept. In 1992, using intraoperative lymphatic mapping in 500 patients, they first successfully implemented sentinel lymph node staging for patients with melanoma. With confirmatory data from clinical follow-up and nodal dissection histology, Morton and others confirmed that the first draining lymph node, or "sentinel lymph node," was also the node most likely to harbor a metastasis in a regional nodal basin. Most importantly, perhaps, with long-term follow-up and the histologic assessment of the remaining nodes, he and others found that if the sentinel lymph node did not harbor a metastasis, other nodes were unlikely to have, or eventually develop, metastatic involvement.[28–32]

With the demonstrated success of sentinel lymph node staging for patients with melanoma, interest expanded to other malignancies, including breast cancer. The transition to sentinel lymph node staging from conventional level I/II axillary dissection required confirmation of equivalent staging efficacy.

In 1994, Giuliano and colleagues, working with Morton, proposed the application of sentinel lymph node biopsy as a means to stage the axilla in patients with breast cancer and thus identify women with negative nodes who might be spared the morbidity of an axillary dissection.[30] Giuliano and colleagues first reported the clinical application of the blue dye technique in patients with breast cancer.[30] Subsequently, multiple investigators have confirmed the diagnostic efficacy of sentinel lymph node staging.[27,28,30–35] A sentinel lymph node identification rate > 95% is the rule, with accuracy rates exceeding 95% and false-negative rates ranging up to 10%, or even higher in unusual reports.[36,37] A high false-negative rate may understage women with breast cancer. A well-trained multidisciplinary team must be systematically assembled to ensure the success of the procedure.

LYMPHATIC MAPPING TECHNIQUES

Isosulfan blue (Lymphazurin) and methylene blue are two dyes that have been used for lymphatic mapping.

The dye may be injected in the peritumoral location or in subareolar or dermal locations. This is done 5 to 10 minutes before the surgical procedure. The breast may be massaged to facilitate lymphatic uptake. A transverse axillary incision is made and carried through the axillary fascia. A blue afferent lymphatic can often be identified and traced to a blue lymph node (Figure 19–2). With this technique, the sentinel node is identified as any node partially or completely stained by blue dye, or any unstained node connected to a blue-stained afferent lymphatic channel.[28–30,32,34,38] All such nodes should be removed, since staining indicates a direct lymphatic pathway from the tumor to that particular node. These "sentinel nodes" are removed along with any palpably suspicious nodes.

The surgeon and anesthesiologist should be aware that Lymphazurin blue dye has a low sporadic incidence of hypersensitivity reactions (including anaphylaxis).[39] This may be recognized by the appearance of hives, hypotension, increasing peak inspiratory pressures, laryngospasm, or vasomotor collapse. It should be emergently treated as for any anaphylactic drug reaction. The surgical and anesthetic teams should also be aware that immediately following the injection of isosulfan blue dye, the pulse oximeter may report a spurious decrease in oxygen saturation; this phenomenon is a false-positive reading of the monitor and is not related to the hypersensitivity response.

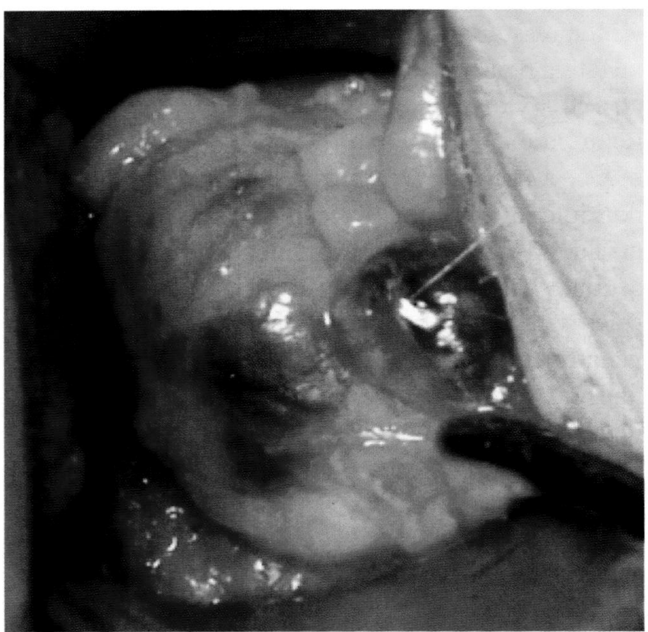

Figure 19–2. Identification of blue staining within a lymph node after subareolar injection of blue dye.

The blue dye technique has been proven successful in reliably identifying the sentinel lymph node in the John Wayne experience.[17,30,40] This has not been readily duplicated by others; in fact, the cumulative experience suggests the contrary. The learning curve for the identification of the sentinel lymph node using blue dye is difficult to achieve. In the first half of Giuliano's initial series, the sentinel lymph node could only be identified successfully in 55% of patients; there were also four false-negative cases. In the second half of the initial series, the sentinel node was identified in 75% , with two false-negative cases. It is important to keep in mind that this learning curve was generated at the time when the procedure was being defined. Nevertheless, others have not achieved the same success rate using blue dye alone.[41]

Krag and colleagues reported a series of patients with breast cancer, where the sentinel lymph node was identified using the intraparenchymal injection of technetium sulfur colloid.[35,38–42] The status of the sentinel lymph node predicted the status of the axillary lymph nodes with excellent results, similar to that previously reported by Giuliano. Initially, controversy arose regarding the optimum technique for identifying the sentinel lymph node; some argued that the blue dye technique was preferable because of its simplicity and accuracy; others argued that the isotope technique offered specific advantages, including a smaller incision, a less extensive axillary dissection, and no risk of blue dye tattooing.

Technically, the gamma probe is first used to percutaneously identify areas of increased radioactivity (Figure 19–3). Once the radiolabeled node is identified, a small transverse incision is made near the "hot spot." Localization continues within the dissection, using the gamma probe to direct the operative approach. Defining a transition in audible pitch and the detection of high radioactive counts are the goals of percutaneous and intraoperative "gamma-guided" dissection. A peak ex vivo radioactivity count is then taken after the first sentinel node is excised. Any residual axillary tissue that yields a persistent count of 10% or more of the ex vivo count of the excised sentinel node should be dissected, although this threshold

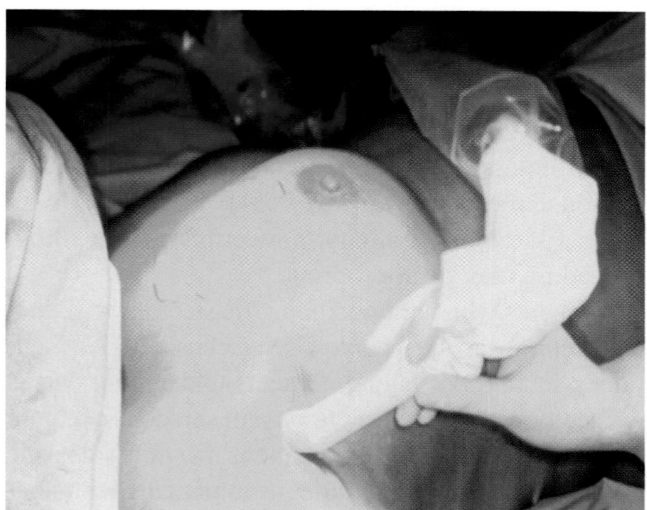

Figure 19–3. Technique for percutaneous identification of an area with increased radioactivity with the gamma probe.

serves as an arbitrarily defined guideline. This helps to minimize the false-negative rate (Figure 19–4). The "hottest" node contains metastatic disease in 88.5% of patients with nodal involvement.[43] However, this leaves a significant number of patients who would remain understaged without removing other sentinel nodes. This has obvious implications for the false-negative rate of sentinel lymph node staging. Any suspicious palpable nodes should be removed as well.

Using this localization technique, the internal mammary and supraclavicular nodes may also be evaluated. Suspected nodes in the internal mammary chain may occasionally be identified, and some highly experienced centers advocate pursuing internal mammary biopsy to support treatment planning. Internal mammary nodes are not routinely removed at most centers, since sentinel lymph node staging is usually employed as a replacement for axillary nodal staging.[44]

Intradermal and subareolar injections of the radiolabeled colloid have certain advantages over peritumoral injection. These techniques allow a shorter interval between the time of injection and the node biopsy, allow a better discrimination of sentinel lymph node radioactivity from the injection site at or near the primary tumor, yield "hotter" sentinel lymph nodes, induce less radioactivity in the excised breast specimen, and yield superior identification rates in the hands of less experienced surgeons.[44–46] Data from the University of Louisville Breast Cancer Sentinel Lymph Node Study indicate that the dermal injection of radioactive colloid significantly improves both the sentinel node identification rate and the false-negative rate.[47] The improved technical features of an intradermal injection make it an attractive approach for many surgeons. The large zone of radioactive diffusion seen with a peritumoral injection may be problematic for upper outer-quadrant breast cancers, and minimized with a dermal or subareolar injection. Another advantage of subareolar and intradermal injections is simplicity. These techniques do not require localization prior to surgery. The routine use of lymphoscintigraphy is not necessary or helpful in sentinel lymph node staging.[45]

Significant controversy exists over the optimal technique for locating the sentinel lymph node; using blue dye, sulfur colloid, or a combination. A combination of the blue dye and technetium provides a complementary approach, using both visual and auditory clues for node identification. Combining the two agents may also accelerate the learning curve. Tafra and colleagues organized a multi-institutional trial that compared the use of technetium, blue dye, and the combination, revealing a superior identification

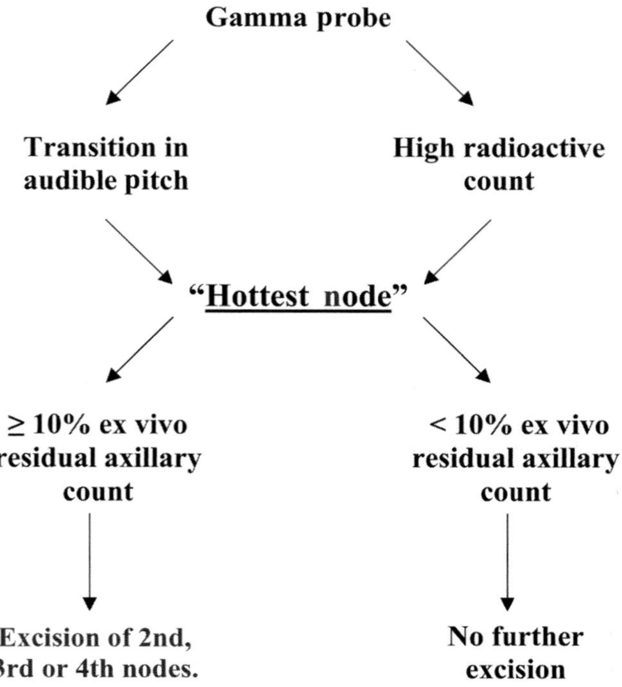

Figure 19–4. Gamma-guided dissection technique to decrease the false-negative rate.

rate with the combination approach.[41] Most importantly, the false-negative rate with the combined agent technique differed by only 2% between experienced and less experienced surgeons.[41] McMasters and colleagues, in a prospective multi-institutional study, found that the use of dual agents provided more accurate nodal staging than the use of either agent alone and also accelerated the learning curve.[48] The optimal technique for most is a combination of blue dye and technetium sulfur colloid.

Failure to identify the sentinel node may indicate the presence of extensive nodal disease. In a series of 1,094 consecutive patients, the risk of nonmapping was 40.9% for patients with 10 or more involved nodes as compared with 5.3% for node-negative patients.[49] In the event that a sentinel node is not identified, suspicion for extensive nodal disease should be raised. In most situations, an axillary dissection should be performed.

PATIENT SELECTION FOR SENTINEL LYMPH NODE STAGING

Patients undergoing sentinel lymph node staging should have no evidence of clinically suspicious nodes by palpation. If there is palpable involvement of the axillary lymph nodes, then sentinel lymph node biopsy is unlikely to be helpful, and may be misleading. If the sentinel lymph node is completely replaced by tumor, then the mapping agent may bypass the sentinel node and flow to an unaffected second echelon node, resulting in a false-negative study. For this reason, it is important that the surgeon palpate the axillary contents. This is especially important in patients with generous adipose tissue or a deep axilla, where the clinical examination of the axilla can be unreliable.[14] Several institutions have supplemented the preoperative palpation-guided physical examination with axillary ultrasonography and fine-needle aspiration cytology to enhance the staging evaluation.[50,51] This approach requires the expertise of skilled ultrasonographers, but allows for axillary dissection without sentinel lymph node biopsy in patients with cytologic evidence of metastatic disease.

Patients with T1 or T2 tumors without palpable nodal metastases should be preferentially staged by sentinel lymph node biopsy. Patients with larger breast cancers may be staged by either sentinel lymph node biopsy or by a level I/II axillary lymph node dissection. It is important to recognize that sentinel lymph node biopsy has been validated for larger tumors.[52] However, given the high prevalence of nodal metastasis (up to 75%), in patients with large T3 tumors, axillary dissection as the initial procedure may be appropriate.[53,54]

Patients who are undergoing mastectomy for ductal carcinoma in situ should also be considered for sentinel lymph node staging. Patients undergoing partial mastectomy for ductal carcinoma in situ do not require axillary staging. The implications of micrometastic disease or individual tumor cells in patients with ductal carcinoma in situ has unknown significance and may lead to systemic therapy in individuals who have a high cure rate with local therapy alone.

CLINICAL IMPLICATIONS OF SENTINEL LYMPH NODE STAGING

Sentinel lymph node staging is more sensitive in detecting lymph node metastasis than a standard axillary lymph node dissection.[21] The number of lymph nodes removed in a routine axillary lymph node dissection varies according to the dissection, the patient's anatomy, and the pathologic evaluation. This infers that the conventional histologic examination of an axillary dissection has an intrinsic false-negative rate created by sampling errors of both the surgeon and the pathologist. This also relates to the standard practice to submit only a fraction of each node for histologic examination. Sentinel lymph node staging provides a cost-effective alternative, allowing for serial sectioning of nodal tissue.

Sentinel lymph node staging allows for a more focused histologic evaluation with multiple sections on a small number of lymph nodes that are more likely to harbor micrometastasis. By optimizing the likelihood that the most valuable lymph nodes are histologically examined, sentinel lymph node staging minimizes sampling variation. A higher rate of nodal metastasis is detected in patients who are staged with the sentinel lymph node technique compared with patients staged with axillary dissection.[40]

If the sentinel lymph node is found to contain metastasis on histopathologic evaluation, then a complete axillary dissection is indicated. Chu and colleagues studied patients with micrometastases that then underwent axillary lymph node dissection.[22] They found nonsentinel node involvement in 6% of patients, regardless of the primary tumor size.[22] If the sentinel node contained macrometastases, however, the incidence of nonsentinel node metastases increased to 48%. However, there is no consensus with regard to the clinical importance of micrometastic nodal disease.

Is there any significance of this enhanced histologic yield? Clinically important metastases may be found with sentinel lymph node staging that might otherwise go undetected with standard axillary staging; but exactly what extent or number of malignant cells constitutes a clinically relevant parameter has yet to be defined. The Ludwig trial, reported in 1990 with 921 patients, and the DeMascarel trial, reported in 1992 with 905 patients, both demonstrated a significant difference in survival for patients who were node-negative on standard pathologic evaluation, but who were divided into true-negative and occult-positive by intensive pathologic examination of the axillary lymph nodes.[55,56] Five-year overall survival in the Ludwig trial for true-negative patients was 88%, as opposed to 79% for patients who had occult-positive lymph nodes. Eleven-year overall survival in the DeMascarel trial was 75% for patients with true-negative lymph nodes and 58% for patients with occult-positive lymph nodes. These two studies suggest that the presence of occult nodal micrometastasis is significant and correlates with decreased disease-free and overall survival.[55,56] However, the routine use of immunohistochemistry for the detection of micrometastasis remains controversial. Recently, the American Collage of Pathology issued recommendations to discontinue the use of routine immunohistochemical staining for sentinel nodes until more conclusive data are available.

The enhanced diagnostic efficacy afforded by sentinel lymph node biopsy may have important long-term staging implications relating to the prognosis of sentinel node-negative patients.

In all likelihood, sentinel lymph node staging identifies populations of node-negative patients who may not benefit, or benefit very little, from adjuvant therapy. The challenge that lies ahead is not only to more accurately identify those women with micrometastatic nodal disease who need additional therapy, but also to determine subsets of women who can safely avoid adjuvant therapy. This "staging shift," the so-called "Will Rogers phenomenon," confounds what is known and can be inferred about node-negative patients defined by sentinel lymph node biopsy (Figure 19–5). Only with the passage of time will the magnitude of the predictive value of the negative sentinel lymph node biopsy result be understood. The inference is that in this era of sentinel lymph node staging, fewer women may benefit from adjuvant chemotherapy. With time, this phenomenon will likely be more precisely defined, and the quality of life for such breast cancer patients should be enhanced by the avoidance of unnecessary adjuvant therapy.

QUALITY OF LIFE ADVANTAGES WITH SENTINEL LYMPH NODE STAGING

On balance, sentinel lymph node staging has enhanced the quality of life for patients with breast cancer. Patients staged by sentinel lymphadenectomy have less wound morbidity, since the extent of axillary dissection is dramatically less than that required by axillary dissection. Although lymphedema may rarely occur in patients with a sentinel lymph node

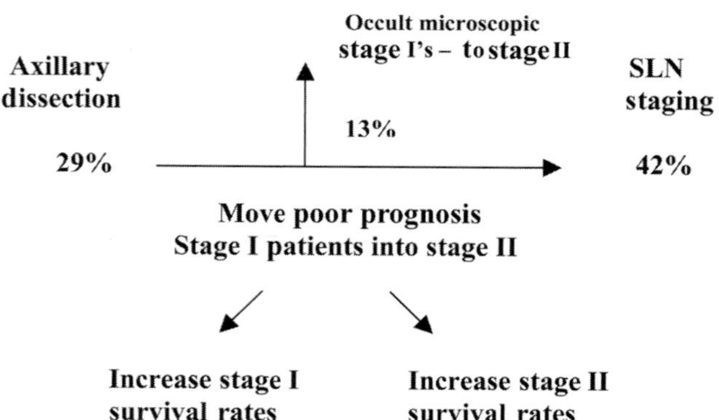

Figure 19–5. "Will Rogers Phenomenon." Axillary dissection will identify 29 patients with nodal involvement out of 100 patients, whereas sentinel lymph node (SLN) staging will identify 42 patients out of a 100 patients.[40] This phenomenon will increase survival rates in stage I (group of patients with negative nodes) and will also increase survival rates in stage II (group of patients with microscopic nodal disease detected only by SLN, otherwise undetected by axillary dissection and still considered stage I).

biopsy, the rate of such an occurrence is low.[57] In addition, patients undergoing sentinel lymph node biopsy experience fewer major paresthesias compared with patients who have their intercostobrachial nerve branches manipulated or transected during axillary dissection. Finally, patients should also have less postoperative pain with sentinel lymph node biopsy; patients having breast conservation therapy have a procedure that amounts to little more than a combined breast and lymph node biopsy.

There are, however, at least two situations in which sentinel lymph node staging does not represent an improvement over the historic standard. Patients who undergo sentinel lymph node biopsy and are subsequently found to have a positive sentinel lymph node may require a return to the operating room for a completion axillary; this adds a procedure where one would not have been necessary if axillary dissection had been initially prescribed. A false-negative sentinel lymph node biopsy may also present with an axillary recurrence. Initial studies suggest that this risk is $< 1\%$.[58,59]

SUMMARY

Axillary staging remains an important consideration in treatment planning for patients with breast cancer. Remarkable changes in the diagnostic efficacy and treatment morbidity have occurred with the advent of sentinel lymph node staging. Recognizing the "Will Rogers phenomenon," assessing the regional control of the sentinel lymph node procedure, and defining the clinical significance of micrometastasis are areas of evolving knowledge with regard to this technique.

REFERENCES

1. Meyer KK, Beck WC. Mastectomy performed by Lorenz Heister in the eighteenth century. Surg Gynecol Obstet 1984;159:391–4.
2. Thorek M. Surgery of the breast. In: Modern surgical technic. 2nd ed. Philadelphia: J.B Lippincott; 1949. p. 25–87.
3. Volkman R. Beitrage zur Churgie. Leipzig: Breitkopf & Hartel; 1985. p. 320–38.
4. Banks WM. On free removal of mammary cancer with extirpation of the axillary glands as a necessary accompaniment. BMJ 1882;2:1138–41.
5. Moore C. On the influence of inadequate operations on the theory of cancer. R Med Chir Soc London 1867;1:244–80.
6. Taneja C, Garden B. Therapeutic value of axillary lymph node dissection for breast cancer. In: Bland KI, Copeland EM, editors. The breast. Comprehensive management of benign and malignant disease. Vol 2. 2nd ed. Philadelphia: W.B. Saunders; 1998. p. 320–38.
7. Halsted WS. The results of operations for the cure of cancer of the breast performed at the Johns Hopkins from June 1889 to January 1894. Arch Surg 1894;20:447–55.
8. Halsted WS. A clinical and histological study of certain adenocarcinoma of the breast. Ann Surg 1898;28:557–76.
9. Halsted WS. The results of radical operations for the cure of carcinoma of the breast. Ann Surg 1907;46:1–19.
10. Gray JH. The relation of lymphatic vessels to the spread of cancer. Br J Surg 1938;26:462–95.
11. Cabanas RM. An approach for the treatment of penile carcinoma. Cancer 1977;39:456–66.
12. Rosen PP, Martin LL, Kinne DW, et al. Discontinuous or skip metastasis in breast carcinoma: analysis of 1228 axillary dissections. Ann Surg 1983;197:276–83.
13. Pigott J, Nichols R, Maddox WA, et al. Metastasis of the upper levels of the axillary nodes in carcinoma of the breast and its implications for nodal sampling procedures. Surg Gynecol Obstet 1984;158:255–9.
14. Boova RS, Roseann B, Rosato F. Patterns of axillary nodal involvement in breast cancer. Predictability of level-one dissection. Ann Surg 1982;196:642–4.
15. Hill ADK, Tran KN, Akhurst T, et al. Lessons learned from 500 cases of lymphatic mapping for breast cancer. Ann Surg 1999;229:528–35.
16. Veronesi U, Rilke F, Luine A, et al. Distribution of axillary metastases by level of invasion. Cancer 1987;59:682–7.
17. Giuliano AE, Barth AM, Spivack B, et al. Incidence and predictors of axillary metastasis in T1 carcinoma of the breast. J Am Coll Surg 1996;183:185–9.
18. Cady B. The need to re-examine axillary lymph node dissection in invasive breast cancer. Cancer 1994;73:505–8.
19. Silverstein MJ, Gierson ED, Waisman JR, et al. Axillary lymph node dissection for T1a breast carcinoma. Cancer 1994;73:664–7.
20. Fisher B, Fisher ER, Bauer M, et al. Ten year results of a randomized clinical trial comparing radical mastectomy and total mastectomy with or without radiation. N Engl J Med 1985;14:674–81.
21. Whitworth P, McMasters KM, Tafra L, Edwards MJ. State of-the-art lymph node staging for breast cancer in the year 2000. Am J Surg 2000;180:262–7.
22. Chu KU, Turner RR, Hansen NM, et al. Do all patients with sentinel node metastasis from breast carcinoma need complete axillary node dissection? Ann Surg 1999;229:536–41.
23. Moore P, Kinne DW. Axillary lymphadenectomy: a diagnostic and therapeutic procedure. J Surg Oncol 1997;66:2–6.
24. Fisher B, Redmond C. Systemic therapy in node negative patients: updated findings from NSABP clinical trials. National Surgical Adjuvant Breast and Bowel Project. J Natl Cancer Inst Monogr 1992;127:392–9.
25. Cabanes PA, Salomon RJ, Vilcoq JR, et al. Value of axillary dissection in addition to lumpectomy and radiotherapy in early breast cancer. Lancet 1992;339:1244–8.
26. Lucci A, Kelemen PR, Miller CM, et al. National practice patterns of sentinel lymph node dissection for breast carcinoma. J Am Coll Surg 2001;192:453–8.

27. Sosa JA, Diener-West M, Gusev Y, et al. Association between extent of axillary lymph node dissection and survival in patients with stage I breast cancer. Ann Surg Oncol 1998;5:140–9.

28. Morton DL, Wen DR, Wong JH, et al. Technical details of intraoperative lymphatic mapping for early-stage melanoma. Arch Surg 1992;127:392–9.

29. Krag DN, Meijer SJ, Weaver DL, et al. Minimal-access surgery for staging malignant melanoma. Arch Surg 1995;130:654–60.

30. Giuliano AE, Kirgan DM, Guenther JM, et al. Lymphatic mapping and sentinel lymphadenectomy for breast cancer. Ann Surg 1994;220:391–8.

31. Morton DL, Wen DR, Cochran A. Management of early stage melanoma by intraoperative lymphatic mapping and selective lymphadenectomy: an alternative to routine elective lymphadenectomy or "watch and wait." Surg Oncol Clin N Am 1992;1:246–59.

32. Albertini JJ, Cruse C, Wayne M, et al. Intraoperative radiolymphoscintigraphy improves sentinel lymph node identification for patients with melanoma. Ann Surg 1996; 223:217–24.

33. Mudun A, Murray DR, Herda S, et al. Early stage melanoma lymphoscintigraphy, reproducibility of sentinel lymph node detection, and effectiveness of the intraoperative gamma probe. Radiology 1996;199:171–5.

34. Kapteijn BAE, Nieweg OE, Olmos RAV, et al. Reproducibility of lymphoscintigraphy for lymphatic mapping in cutaneous melanoma. J Nucl Med 1996;37:972–5.

35. Krag DN, Weaver DL, Alex JL, et al. Surgical resection and radiolocalization of the sentinel lymph node in breast cancer using a gamma probe. Surg Oncol 1993;2:335–40.

36. Tafra L, McMasters KM, Whitworth P, Edwards MJ. Credentialing issues with sentinel lymph node staging for breast cancer. Am J Surg 2000;180:268–73.

37. Edwards MJ, Whitworth P, Tafra L, McMasters KM. The details of successful sentinel lymph node staging for breast cancer. Am J Surg 2000;180:257–61.

38. Kern KA. Sentinel lymph node mapping in breast cancer using subareolar injection of blue dye. J Am Coll Surg 1999;189:539–45.

39. Woltsche-Kahr I, Komericki P, Kranke B, et al. Anaphylactic shock following peritumoral injection of patent blue in sentinel lymph node biopsy procedure. Eur J Surg Oncol. 2000;26:313–4.

40. Giuliano AE, Dale PS, Turner RR, et al. Improved axillary staging of breast cancer with sentinel lymphadenectomy. Ann Surg 1995;222:394–401.

41. Tafra L, Lanin DR, Melvin SS, et al. Multicenter trial of sentinel node biopsy for breast cancer using both technetium sulfur colloid and isosulfan blue dye. Ann Surg 2001; 233:51–9.

42. Krag DN, Ashikaga T, Harlow SP, et al. Development of sentinel lymph node targeting technique in breast cancer patients. Breast 1998;4:67–74.

43. Wong SL, Edwards MJ, Tuttle TM, et al. Sentinel lymph node biopsy for breast cancer: impact of the number of sentinel nodes removed on the false negative rate. Surgery 2000; 128:139–44.

44. Klimberg VS, Rubio IT, Henry R, et al. Subareolar versus peritumoral injection for location of the sentinel lymph node. Ann Surg 1999;229:860–5.

45. McMasters KM, Wong SL, Tuttle TM, et al. Preoperative lymphoscintigraphy for breast cancer does not improve the ability to accurately identify axillary sentinel lymph nodes. Ann Surg 2000;231:724–31.

46. Martin RCG, Edwards MJ, Wong SL, et al. Practical guidelines for optimal gamma probe detection of sentinel lymph nodes in breast cancer: results of a multi-institutional study. Surgery 2000;128:139–44.

47. McMasters KM, Wong SL, Martin RCG, et al. Dermal injection of radioactive colloid is superior to peritumoral injection for breast cancer sentinel node biopsy: results of a multi-institutional study. Ann Surg 2001;233:676–87.

48. McMasters KM, Tuttle TM, Carlson DJ, et al. Sentinel lymph node biopsy for breast cancer: a suitable alternative to routine axillary dissection in multi-institutional practice when optimal technique is used. J Clin Oncol 2000;18: 2560–6.

49. Sener SF, Winchester DJ, Brinkmann E, et al. Failure of sentinel lymph node mapping in patients with breast cancer. J Am Coll Surg 2004;198:732–6.

50. Newman LA, Kuerer HM, Fornage B, et al. Adverse prognostic significance of infraclavicular lymph nodes detected by ultrasonography in patients with locally advanced breast cancer. Am J Surg 2001;181:313–8.

51. Krishnamurthy S, Sneige N, Bedi DG, et al. Role of ultrasound-guided fine-needle aspiration of indeterminate and suspicious axillary lymph nodes in the staging of breast carcinoma. Cancer 2002;95:982–8.

52. Wong SL, Chao C, Edwards MJ, et al. Accuracy of sentinel lymph node biopsy for patients with T2 and T3 breast cancer [published erratum appears in Am Surg 2002;68:503]. Am Surg 2001;67:522–6; discussion 527–8.

53. Silverstein MJ, Gierson ED, Waisman JR, et al. Predicting axillary node positivity in patients with invasive carcinoma of the breast by using a combination of T category and palpability. J Am Coll Surg 1995;180:700–4.

54. Wong SL, Edwards MJ, Chao C, et al. Predicting the status of the nonsentinel axillary nodes: a multicenter study. Arch Surg 2001;136:563–8.

55. International (Ludwig) Breast Cancer Study Group. Prognostic importance of occult axillary node micrometastases from breast cancer. Lancet 1990;335:1565–8.

56. DeMascarel I, Bonichon F, Coindre JM, Trojani M. Prognostic significance of breast cancer axillary lymph node micrometastases by two special techniques: reevaluation with longer follow-up. Br J Cancer 1992;66:523–7.

57. Sener SF, Winchester DJ, Martz CH, et al. Lymphedema after sentinel lymphadenectomy for breast carcinoma. Cancer 2001;92:748–52.

58. Jeruss JS, Winchester DJ, Sener SF, et al. Axillary recurrence after sentinel node biopsy. Ann Surg Oncol 2005;12:34–40.

59. Naik AM, Fey J, Gemignani M, et al. The risk of axillary relapse after sentinel lymph node biopsy for breast cancer is comparable with that of axillary lymph node dissection: a follow-up study of 4008 procedures. Ann Surg 2004; 240:462–8.

20

Adjuvant Chemotherapy

BRYAN T. HENNESSY
VICENTE VALERO

Historically, breast cancer relapse occurred in more than 70% of women undergoing radical breast surgery alone.[1] Along with earlier detection methods, adjuvant systemic chemotherapy reduces the risk of recurrence and death from breast cancer. This was initially demonstrated in animal models several decades ago.[2] The mechanism by which cytotoxic chemotherapy reduces such risks is through eradication of micrometastatic disease, which is not detectable with conventional radiologic techniques at the time of diagnosis. Since the risk of having micrometastatic disease at diagnosis of breast cancer is dependent on the stage of disease, the absolute benefit of adjuvant systemic chemotherapy is related to tumor size and the axillary lymph node status, in addition to other factors, such as the age of the patient, the tumor grade, and the hormone receptor status. The Early Breast Cancer Trialists' Collaborative Group (EBCTCG or Oxford Overview) analyzes many randomized trials of adjuvant chemotherapy in women with early-stage breast cancer and provides an accurate estimate of the absolute and relative benefits associated with adjuvant breast cancer chemotherapy. The most recently published overview involved about 30,000 women in 69 clinical trials.[3] Since Bonadonna and colleagues first reported the efficacy of adjuvant systemic chemotherapy in early-stage breast cancer, many trials have been performed and published to improve upon adjuvant chemotherapy, both in terms of delivering higher efficacy with less toxicity and less inconvenience to the patient.[4] Adjuvant chemotherapy is generally considered for women with stages II and III breast cancer and for women who have stage I disease and a high risk of relapse. However, there is still much debate as to the most appropriate chemotherapy regimen to use for women with the different stages of breast cancer. Clinical trials continue in an effort to resolve these issues and to establish new agents with efficacy in the adjuvant setting. In addition, breast cancer is a heterogenous disease, and new technologies such as transcriptional profiling are being applied to breast cancer in an attempt to allow us to determine the specific biology of breast cancers with different clinical features, including those which benefit from adjuvant systemic chemotherapy, and to identify the genes and proteins in resistant cancers that explain the clinical behavior of these tumors and that may constitute targets for new agents with potential activity in the metastatic and adjuvant setting.[5]

THE EBCTCG POLYCHEMOTHERAPY (OXFORD) OVERVIEW

The EBCTCG last met in 2000, and the results have recently been published (Table 20–1).[6,7] This group has met approximately every 5 years since the mid-1980s, and in 2000 used data on 53,353 women from 102 available clinical trials to perform a meta-analysis to estimate the absolute and relative benefits associated with adjuvant breast cancer systemic chemotherapy and hormonal therapy.[3] Of these, 28,000 patients from 56 clinical trials were randomized to either polychemotherapy or to no chemotherapy, and

Table 20–1. SUMMARY OF THE RESULTS OF THE 2000 OXFORD OVERVIEW

	Reduction in Annual Odds (Standard Error)		
	Breast Cancer Recurrence (%)	Breast Cancer Mortality (%)	Any Death (%)
Chemotherapy vs not:			
Single agents	14 ± 4	5 ± 5	3 ± 5
CMF regimens	24 ± 2	16 ± 3	15 ± 3
Anthracyclines	24 ± 3	20 ± 4	17 ± 4
Other	21 ± 5	14 ± 5	13 ± 5
OVERALL	22 ± 2	15 ± 2	13 ± 2
Longer vs shorter chemotherapy:			
< 6 months vs longer	6 ± 5	8 ± 5	6 ± 6
6 months vs longer	3 ± 6	–4 ± 6	–2 ± 6
Anthracyclines vs CMF	11 ± 3	16 ± 3	15 ± 3
Polychemotherapy vs not by age:			
< 35	32 ± 12	18 ± 16	11 ± 15
35–39	47 ± 7	32 ± 9	31 ± 9
40–44	36 ± 7	26 ± 8	23 ± 8
45–49	37 ± 5	31 ± 7	28 ± 6
50–54	23 ± 5	15 ± 6	13 ± 6
55–59	24 ± 4	17 ± 5	17 ± 5
60–64	16 ± 4	11 ± 5	8 ± 5
65–69	8 ± 5	3 ± 6	4 ± 6
70 +	18 ± 11	21 ± 13	16 ± 11
OVERALL	24 ± 2	17 ± 2	17 ± 2
Polychemotherapy vs not by menopausal status and age:			
Age < 50			
Pre/perimenopausal	35 ± 4	18 ± 8	26 ± 4
Postmenopausal	40 ± 10	31 ± 12	28 ± 12
Age 50–59			
Pre/perimenopausal	23 ± 7	18 ± 8	17 ± 7
Postmenopausal	18 ± 2	12 ± 3	11 ± 3
ER status and tamoxifen			
Age < 50			
Polychemotherapy + tamoxifen vs tamoxifen:			
ER-poor	Not analyzed	Not analyzed	Not analyzed
ER-positive	36 ± 8	35 ± 10	32 ± 10
ER unknown	28 ± 16	25 ± 19	21 ± 18
Polychemotherapy alone vs nothing:			
ER-poor	39 ± 7	32 ± 8	30 ± 8
ER-positive	44 ± 7	31 ± 10	27 ± 10
ER unknown	29 ± 6	24 ± 7	22 ± 6
Age 50–59			
Polychemotherapy + tamoxifen vs tamoxifen:			
ER-poor	25 ± 6	14 ± 7	11 ± 7
ER-positive	15 ± 4	11 ± 4	10 ± 4
ER unknown	14 ± 7	12 ± 8	13 ± 7
Polychemotherapy alone vs nothing:			
ER-poor	33 ± 7	26 ± 8	25 ± 8
ER-positive	16 ± 7	5 ± 8	1 ± 8
ER unknown	19 ± 6	12 ± 6	10 ± 6
Lymph nodes (polychemotherapy):			
Age < 50			
Negative	36 ± 5	29 ± 6	26 ± 6
Positive	37 ± 5	30 ± 5	28 ± 5
Age 50–59			
Negative	22 ± 5	23 ± 6	20 ± 6
Positive	17 ± 3	10 ± 3	9 ± 3

(continued)

Table 20–1. CONTINUED

	Reduction in Annual Odds (Standard Error)		
	Breast Cancer Recurrence (%)	Breast Cancer Mortality (%)	Any Death (%)
Tumor size (polychemotherapy):			
Age < 50			
< 2 cm	38 ± 8	35 ± 12	31 ± 12
2–5 cm	43 ± 7	34 ± 10	31 ± 10
> 5 cm	59 ± 27	64 ± 28	55 ± 28
Unknown	24 ± 9	12 ± 12	12 ± 12
Age 50–59			
< 2 cm	20 ± 8	26 ± 10	22 ± 9
2–6 cm	27 ± 8	16 ± 10	13 ± 10
> 5 cm	38 ± 22	34 ± 25	Not analyzed
Unknown	14 ± 11	26 ± 12	25 ± 11
Tumor differentiation (polychemotherapy):			
Age < 50			
Good	44 ± 15	21 ± 22	Not analyzed
Moderate	38 ± 8	32 ± 9	29 ± 9
Poor	43 ± 9	42 ± 11	41 ± 11
Unknown	34 ± 4	28 ± 5	26 ± 5
Age 50–59			
Good	8 ± 10	9 ± 11	11 ± 10
Moderate	10 ± 5	4 ± 6	4 ± 5
Poor	22 ± 5	12 ± 7	13 ± 7
Unknown	22 ± 3	15 ± 3	13 ± 3

Adapted from Early Breast Cancer Trialists' Collaborative Group[6] and Stearns V and Davidson NE.[7]

14,000 patients were included in 15 trials of anthracycline-based versus nonanthracycline-based therapy. This overview has established that the use of systemic chemotherapy in the adjuvant treatment of breast cancer reduces the annual odds of disease recurrence by 23.9%, the annual odds of breast cancer mortality by 15%, and the annual odds of all-cause mortality by 14.9%, with polychemotherapy regimens superior to single-agent-based therapy, although the differences were not statistically significant. Women who received adjuvant anthracycline-based regimens had outcomes that were superior to those who were treated with cyclophosphamide, methotrexate and 5-fluorouracil (CMF)-based regimens, with an additional reduction in the annual odds of breast cancer recurrence of 10.8% and in any death of 15.7%. The absolute differences were 3.5 and 4.6%, respectively. Outcomes were not improved by using regimens given over a 6-month period or longer, compared with regimens administered for less than 6 months.

The benefits associated with cytotoxic chemotherapy were greater in premenopausal women, and there was an inverse correlation between chemotherapy benefits and age. Systemic polychemotherapy led to absolute improvements in the 15-year risk of recurrence and breast cancer mortality of 12 and 10%, respectively, compared with no chemotherapy, in women under the age of 50 years. In women aged 50 to 59 years, the 15-year absolute benefits were more modest (4.1% and 3%, respectively). Women aged 65 to 69 years had the lowest benefits. Whereas the improvements in outcome with cytotoxic chemotherapy were greater in women aged 50 to 59 years who had estrogen receptor (ER)-poor tumors compared to those in this age group with ER-positive tumors, these differences were not seen in women under the age of 50 years. In addition, women aged less than 50 years benefited equally regardless of their menopausal status (although only 10% of this group were postmenopausal), as did those aged 50 to 59 years. Thus, although it has been suggested that the greater benefits seen with cytotoxic chemotherapy in younger women are associated with ovarian ablation, it is very likely that other factors also contribute to these differences. For example, breast cancer in younger women is significantly more likely to be hormone-receptor negative, *HER2/neu* positive, and of higher nuclear grade, all of which are associated with greater responsiveness to chemotherapy.[8] Older women are significantly underrepresented in many of the clinical trials used in the Oxford overview. Finally, the overview suggests women with node-negative breast cancer derive similar proportional benefit from chemotherapy as do women with node-positive disease; the same is true for tumors of different sizes, although the absolute benefits are greater in women with node-positive tumors and in women with larger tumors.

COMPUTER PROGRAMS AS AN AID TO ADJUVANT THERAPY DECISIONS

Recently, a number of computer programs have become available that can give physicians an accurate estimate of the risks of recurrence and of death from breast cancer and of the absolute benefits to be gained with adjuvant systemic chemotherapy and hormonal treatment. These programs use information known to influence the risk of relapse, including age, the size of the tumor, the number of metastatic lymph nodes, the hormone receptor status, and the grade of the tumor. These programs have become very helpful in doctor-patient discussions regarding the benefits of adjuvant therapy. One such program is Adjuvant! (Adjuvant! Inc.), and this and other software can play practical and educational roles in clinical settings.[9] Actuarial analysis was used in the creation of Adjuvant! to project the outcomes of patients, with and without adjuvant therapy, based on prognosis estimates derived mainly from Surveillance, Epidemiology, and End Results data, and from estimates of the benefits of adjuvant therapy based on the 1998 Oxford Overview.[3] These estimates are refined using a Prognostic Factor Impact Calculator, which uses a Bayesian method to make adjustments based on the relative risks conferred and the prevalence of positive test results. From the entry of patient data (age, menopausal status, and estimates of comorbidity) and tumor characteristics (tumor size, the number of positive axillary nodes, and the ER status), baseline prognostic estimates are made. Estimates for the efficacy of endocrine therapy (tamoxifen for 5 years) and of systemic chemotherapy (CMF-like regimens, anthracycline-based regimens, or treatment with both an anthracycline and a taxane) can then be used to project outcomes, which are presented in both numerical and graphical forms. Additional speculative estimates of the number of years of remaining life expectancy and long-term survival curves can also be produced. Help files give general information about breast cancer. The program's Internet links supply national treatment guidelines, cooperative group trial options, and other related information. Other computer programs have been developed to similarly facilitate a better understanding among physicians and patients of the absolute magnitude of benefits from available systemic adjuvant therapies in women with primary breast cancer.[10]

PROGNOSTIC AND PREDICTIVE FACTORS

Prognostic factors in breast cancer, which reflect the underlying biology of the cancer and thus influence an individual patient's risk of relapse, can be subdivided into those that are patient related (age, race, and comorbidities) and those that are tumor related (tumor size, axillary lymph-node status, tumor grade and mitotic rate, histologic tumor type, lymphovascular invasion, hormone receptor, and HER2/neu status).[11] In addition, many of these are predictive factors of the magnitude of benefit from the available adjuvant therapies. Many other factors have been, and are currently being, investigated for their role as potential prognostic and predictive factors, but none are widely used. As mentioned, the Oxford Overview suggests women with both lymph node-positive and lymph node-negative breast cancer derive some benefit from adjuvant systemic chemotherapy, and that it is also effective in both premenopausal and postmenopausal women. However, the decision as to whether or not to administer adjuvant systemic chemotherapy must take into account the individual patient's risk of relapse, the absolute benefits associated with chemotherapy, its potential toxicities, and the patient's comorbidities. Since endocrine therapy is generally considered to have a favorable risk-benefit ratio, it is offered to most women in the adjuvant treatment of hormone receptor-positive breast cancer.

Adjuvant systemic chemotherapy is usually recommended to women with axillary lymph node-positive breast cancer and to those women with high-risk stage I tumors despite having negative lymph nodes, because the risk-benefit ratio is considered to favor its use.[11,12] Mucinous and tubular carcinomas are an exception; they are associated with a particularly good prognosis, and adjuvant chemotherapy is generally not offered to patients with tumors under 3 cm in size.[7] In women with stage I breast cancer, the decision regarding adjuvant systemic chemotherapy is more difficult and is sometimes controversial. Table 20–2 shows the 5- and 10-year relapse-free survivals in a recently published population-based cohort of stage I, lymphovascular invasion-negative early-stage breast cancers in patients who did not receive adjuvant systemic therapy.[13] Those with grade 3 tumors of 1 to 2 cm had a high likelihood of recurrence. The National Institutes of Health (NIH) Consensus Conference and the St. Gallen International Consensus panel have published guidelines that assist in the decision-making process for systemic chemotherapy in stage I breast cancer.[11,12] The St. Gallen International Consensus panel defines risk categories for patients with node-negative breast cancer (Table 20–3). For patients with minimal risk, the panel recommends only adjuvant hormonal therapy with tamoxifen or an aromatase inhibitor (the latter only if postmenopausal) or no adjuvant treatment. For patients with node-negative hormone receptor-negative disease (regarded as average risk), chemotherapy is the recommendation, whether pre- or post-menopausal. For patients with hormone receptor-positive average risk tumors, the panel recommendations depend on menopausal status. If post-menopausal, it recommends chemotherapy followed by tamoxifen (or an aromatase inhibitor), or hormonal therapy alone. If pre-menopausal, the panel recommends one of the following:

1. ovarian ablation (eg, a gonadotrophin-releasing hormone analogue) plus tamoxifen (± chemotherapy), or
2. chemotherapy followed by tamoxifen (± ovarian ablation), or
3. tamoxifen alone, or
4. ovarian ablation alone.

In these patients, the threshold for considering the addition of chemotherapy to endocrine therapy may depend on the level of confidence in hormone responsiveness. The panel stated that considerations about a low relative risk, age, toxic effects, socioeconomic factors, and information on the patient's preference might justify the use of endocrine therapy alone.

The NIH guidelines suggest that use of a 1 cm tumor size cutoff is appropriate, since a group of women with tumors less than 1 cm in size who have a poor prognosis has not been identified in large datasets.[14] They recommend increased recognition of the extremely favorable outcome and the corresponding lack of a major benefit from chemotherapy in women with grade I breast cancers 1 to 2 cm in size and for those with node-negative tubular and mucinous cancers up to 3 cm in size. In women with ER-positive, lymph node-negative breast cancer, the benefit of adding chemotherapy to endocrine therapy is small and often outweighed by added toxicity. Improved definition of prognostic subsets and stratification of outcomes based on comorbidities are required to better define therapeutic recommendations in this subset of women. In women with lymph node-negative breast cancer aged over 70 years, deaths from causes other than breast cancer are significant. A survival advantage for chemotherapy has not been clearly demonstrated in these women and is likely to be small. Treatment should be reserved for

Table 20–2. FIVE- AND 10-YEAR RELAPSE-FREE SURVIVAL RATES

	COHORT 1 (0–1 cm)			COHORT 2 (1–2 cm)		
	Grade 1	Grade 2	Grade 3	Grade 1	Grade 2	Grade 3
Patient number	105	210	115	72	284	151
5-year RFS (%)	90	89	86	92	87	81
10-year RFS (%)	88	84	74	89	74	71

Five- and 10-year relapse-free survivals in a recently published population-based cohort of stage I, lymphovascular invasion-negative early-stage breast cancer patients who did not receive adjuvant systemic therapy. RFS = relapse-free survival. Reproduced with permission from Chia SK, et al.[13]

Table 20–3. DEFINITION OF RISK CATEGORIES FOR PATIENTS WITH NODE-NEGATIVE BREAST CANCER

Risk Category	ER/PR-Positive Tumors	ER/PR-Negative Tumors
Minimal risk*	pT < or = 2 cm *and* grade 1 *and* age > or = 35 years	None
Average risk	*At least one of:* pT > 2 cm *or* grade 2/3 *or* age < 35	Any node-negative tumor

*Some panel members recognize lymphatic and/or vascular invasion as a factor indicating greater risk than minimal; pure tubular or mucinous histologic types are associated with low risk of relapse. ER = estrogen receptor; PR = progesterone receptor; pT = pathologic tumor size. Note that all node-positive tumors are regarded as high risk.
Reproduced with permission from Goldhirsch A, et al.[12]

those elderly women who have a high risk of relapse from breast cancer and no major comorbidities. Ultimately the decision to have chemotherapy is made by an individual patient after a discussion with the oncologist of her individual risks and benefits. For some patients, an absolute improvement of 1 to 2% in survival is meaningful, and these women may opt for systemic chemotherapy, even if they belong to a favorable prognostic group.

It is clear that breast cancer is a heterogenous disease. Clinicopathologic criteria are always used to guide adjuvant therapy. However, there are a number of inherent problems with this approach. First, it does not define tumor biology, and tumors of the same grade and stage often behave very differently. Second, and as a result, a large percentage of patients treated with adjuvant chemotherapy are not destined to relapse and are thus over-treated. Third, a significant proportion of treated patients do relapse. We need a better understanding of the molecular mechanisms underlying this wide variation in breast cancer behavior; this will also reveal potential therapeutic targets in those tumors not benefiting from current adjuvant systemic therapy. Transcriptional profiling is beginning to take us in this direction.[5] A 70 gene-expression profile has been found to be a more powerful predictor of the outcome of young women with breast cancer than standard systems based on clinical and histologic criteria (Figure 20–1).[15] This is now being taken to clinical trial by the European Organization for the Research and Treatment of Cancer that plans to randomize 5,000 premenopausal women with lymph node-negative breast cancer into two groups. One group will have an adjuvant chemotherapy decision made based on standard clinicopathologic criteria. In this group, 85% will receive adjuvant systemic chemotherapy. The other study arm will have an adjuvant chemotherapy decision made based on the 70 gene-expression profile; in this group, 40% are expected to possess the favorable profile and thus will not receive chemotherapy. The primary end point of this trial will be survival.

EARLY TRIALS

By the 1970s, it was clear that more extensive surgery, such as a Halsted mastectomy, was not more effective than limited resection for curing breast cancer because of the presence of systemic micrometastases. Fisher and colleagues reported that only 25% of women with lymph node-positive breast cancer treated with radical mastectomy were alive at 10 years.[16] Adjuvant chemotherapy for breast cancer was thus first tested in patients with positive lymph nodes. Initial studies tested single agents such as L-phenylalanine mustard, or thiotepa, and showed that these can improve both the disease-free and overall survivals.[16,17] Combination chemotherapy was subsequently explored in an attempt to increase its efficacy. Women with node-positive breast cancer at the Istituto Nazionale Tumori in Milan were randomized to receive either surgery alone or surgery followed by 12 months of conventional CMF chemotherapy.[18] Treatment was given every 4 weeks, with cyclophosphamide 100 mg/m^2 orally on days 1 to 14, plus methotrexate 40 mg/m^2 and 5-fluorouracil 600 mg/m^2 intravenously on days 1 and 8. The disease-free and overall survival rates were improved in patients who received adjuvant chemotherapy (Figure 20–2A and B). With the exception of postmenopausal women, a benefit from adjuvant chemotherapy was evident in all subgroups. This lack of benefit in postmenopausal women may have been because of an insufficient patient number to detect the smaller absolute benefits seen in these women or

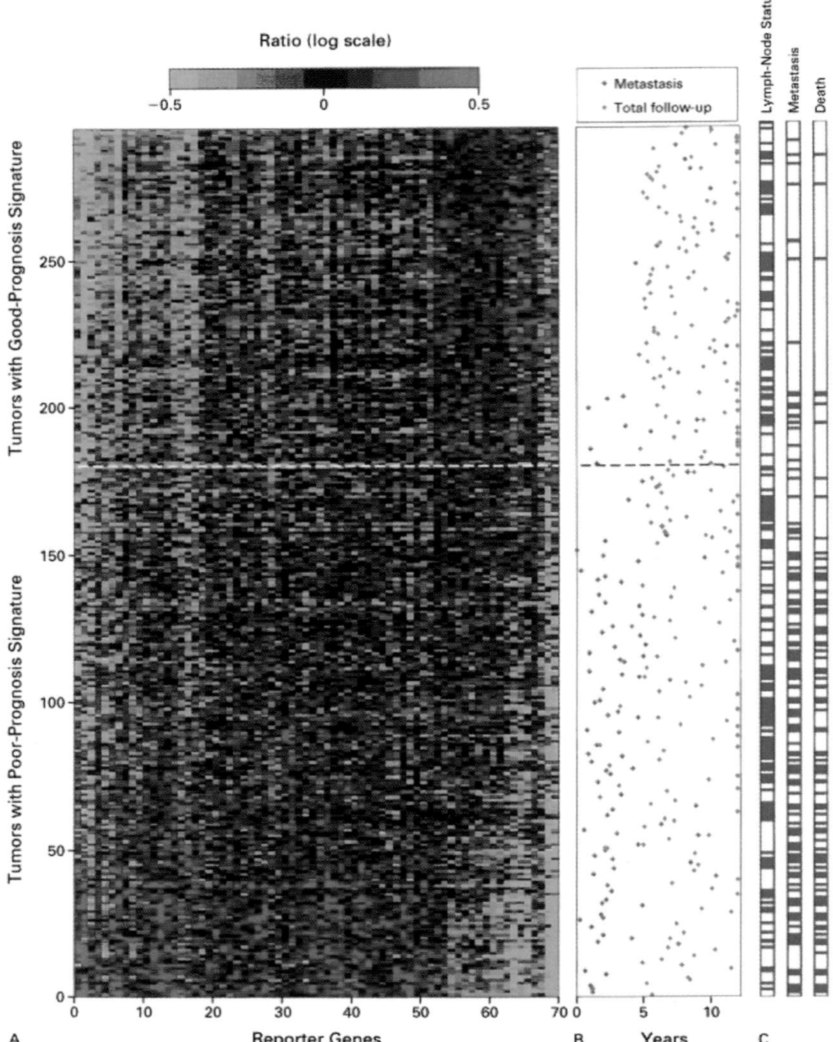

Figure 20–1. A gene-expression signature as a predictor of survival in breast cancer. The broken white line indicates the division between the favorable (above) and the unfavorable (below) gene profiles. The favorable profile was clearly associated with fewer metastases and deaths, although there was not a significant difference in lymph node positivity at diagnosis. Reproduced with permission from van de Vijver MJ, He YD, van't Veer LJ, et al.[15]

because the chemotherapy doses were routinely reduced in patients older than 60 years.

Other studies subsequently evaluated the role of anthracyclines in the adjuvant treatment of breast cancer. Misset and colleagues randomized 245 patients with lymph node-positive breast cancer, recruited from eight French cancer centers, to receive 12 monthly cycles of adjuvant CMF or doxorubicin, vincristine, cyclophosphamide, and fluorouracil (AVCF).[19] No grade IV toxicity was seen. In the AVCF arm, 88% of the planned treatments were given; in the CMF arm, 75% were administered. With a median follow-up of 16 years, the disease-free (53 versus 36%; $p = .006$) and overall survival (56 versus 41%; $p = .01$) rates were significantly better in the AVCF arm. When analyzed according to menopausal status, the differences remained significant only in pre-menopausal women. The National Surgical Adjuvant Breast and Bowel Project (NSABP) protocol B-15 compared four cycles (administered at 3-week intervals) of doxorubicin 60 mg/m^2 and cyclophosphamide 600 mg/m^2 (AC) with 6 months of conventional CMF in 2,194 patients with tamoxifen-nonresponsive (ER-negative) lymph

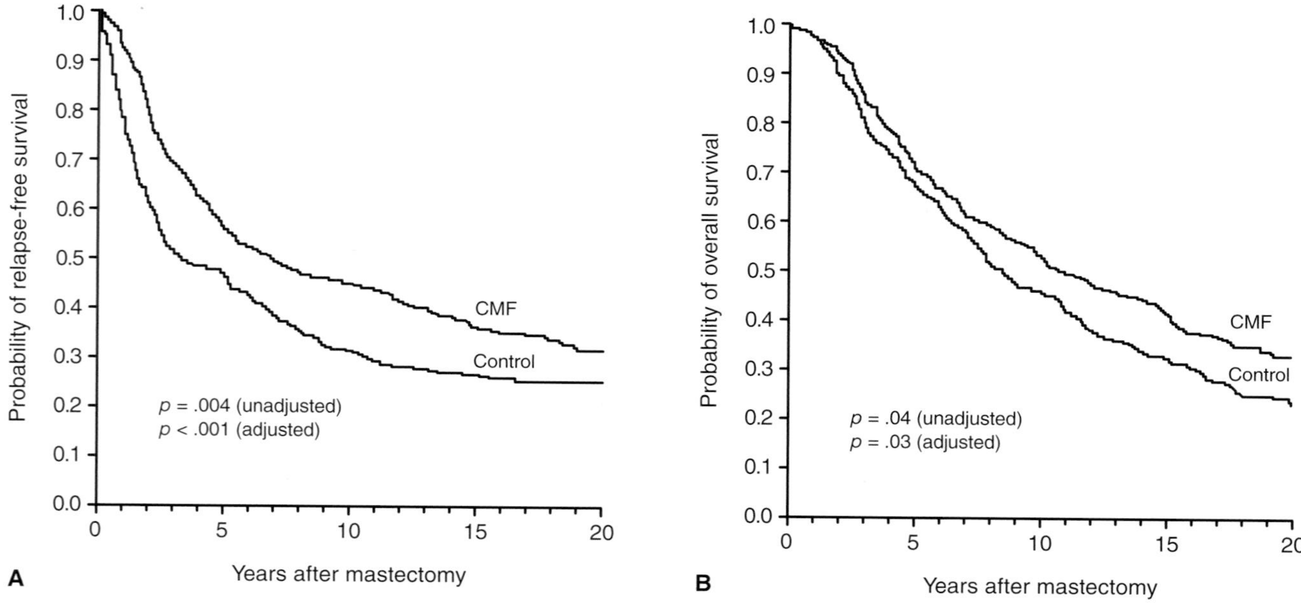

Figure 20–2. Significantly improved disease-free (A) and overall survival (B) rates in patients treated with adjuvant cyclophosphamide, methotrexate, and 5-fluorouracil (CMF) chemotherapy after mastectomy, in comparison with observation. Reproduced with permission from Bonadonna G, Valagussa P, Moliterni A, et al.[18]

node-positive breast cancer, with a second aim to determine whether AC followed in 6 months by reinduction with intravenous CMF was more effective than AC alone.[20] With 3 years of follow-up, there was no significant difference in disease-free survival, distant disease-free survival, or overall survival among the three groups. The study authors concluded that AC was preferable because there was a shorter duration of treatment with fewer antiemetic requirements. Alopecia was observed with AC in almost all patients and in 71% of the CMF-treated patients; in 41% of the patients given CMF, hair loss was greater than 50%. The intergroup INT 0102 trial randomized 2,691 women with node-negative breast cancer to CMF or CAF (cyclophosphamide, doxorubicin, and 5-fluorouracil) chemotherapy and found CAF to be significantly superior to CMF in disease-free and overall survivals ($p = .03$ for both).[21] Table 20–4 shows this and other trials that have compared adjuvant CMF chemotherapy with anthracycline-based treatment. Although the results are mixed, the Oxford Overview used these and other studies to determine an absolute superiority of 3.2% in recurrence-free survival for anthracycline-based regimens compared with CMF.[3] In addition, many physicians also believe, based on inference from these trials, that six cycles of a CAF/FAC or 5-fluorouracil, epirubicin, and cyclophosphamide (FEC)-type regimen are superior to four cycles of AC or EC, although these regimens have not been directly compared in a prospective randomized trial. Currently ongoing trials are investigating this; for example, the NSABP B-36 trial randomizes patients with lymph node-negative breast cancer to receive four cycles of AC or six cycles of FEC-100 (epirubicin 100 mg/m^2 every 3 weeks).

Other studies have demonstrated the benefits of adjuvant chemotherapy in postmenopausal women. The NSABP B-16 trial randomized 1,124 postmenopausal women with lymph node-positive breast cancer to receive tamoxifen, tamoxifen with AC, or tamoxifen with melphalan, doxorubicin and 5-fluorouracil (PAFT; initially this arm was opened as PFT but later modified).[27] Initial results at a median follow-up of 3 years showed that patients treated with the combination of AC and tamoxifen did significantly better than those treated with tamoxifen alone in terms of disease-free (84 versus 67%; $p = .0004$) and overall survival (93 versus 85%; $p = .04$) rates. The disease-free survival rates of PFT- and PAFT-treated patients were also significantly better than those in women given tamoxifen alone (81%, $p = .07$,

Table 20–4. TRIALS COMPARING ADJUVANT CMF CHEMOTHERAPY TO AN ANTHRACYCLINE-BASED REGIMEN

Trial	Patient Number	Anthracycline Regimen × Cycles	Number of CMF Cycles	Follow-Up (yr)	RFS Anthracycline vs. CMF	*p*	OS Anthracycline vs CMF	*p*
INT 0102[21]	2,691	CAF × 6	6	–	85 vs 82%	.03	92 vs 90%	.03
NSABP B-23[22]	2,008	AC × 4	6	–	87 vs 87%	NS	90 vs 89%	NS
Coombes et al[23]	759	FEC 50 × 6	6	4.5	65 vs 64%	NS	82 vs 79%	NS
Levine et al[24]	710	CEF 120 × 6*	6	5	63 vs 53%	.009	77 vs 70%	.03
Piccart et al[25]	510	EC 100 × 8	6	3	80 vs 78%	NS	92 vs 91%	NS
Bang et al[26]	124	AC 40 × 6†	6	5	64 vs 78%	NS	90 vs 86%	NS

A = doxorubicin; C = cyclophosphamide; E = epirubicin; F = 5 fluorouracil; M = methotrexate; NS = not significant ; OS = overall survival; RFS = relapse-free survival.
*Epirubicin given intravenously at 60 mg/m² on days 1 and 8 every 4 weeks.
†Doxorubicin administered at 40 mg/m² on day 1 every 3 weeks.

and 83%, p = .0002, respectively), although overall survival was not significantly superior in these arms. Thus, chemotherapy was found to benefit lymph node-positive postmenopausal women. In the Southwest Oncology Group (SWOG) 8814 (INT-0100) trial, 1,477 postmenopausal women with ER-positive, node-positive breast cancer were randomized to receive tamoxifen alone, six cycles of CAF chemotherapy combined with tamoxifen (CAFT) or CAF, followed by tamoxifen (CAF-T); 58% of women had 1 to 3 positive lymph nodes, 7% had a primary tumor larger than 5 cm, and 21% had a progesterone receptor-negative tumor.[28,29] Chemotherapy resulted in significant improvements in the 5-year disease-free (76 versus 67%; p = .0001) and overall survival (84 versus 79%; p = .007) rates in the chemotherapy arms compared to the tamoxifen-treated group. The 10-year disease-free survival estimates were 48% for tamoxifen, 53% for CAFT, and 60% for CAF-T. For overall survival, the 10-year estimates were 60, 62, and 68%, respectively. CAFT was worse than CAF-T in terms of disease-free and overall survival rates, with adjusted risk ratios (RR) of 1.20 and 1.12, respectively. After a median follow-up of 4 years, the incidence of congestive heart failure in anthracycline-treated patients was 2%. Adverse prognostic factors in this study were *HER2/neu* positivity (p = .005), high mitotic grade (p = .0002), and *p53* positivity (p = .022). Exploratory biomarker analyses showed no CAF benefit if the tumor had a high ER score, a low or intermediate nuclear grade, or if the tumor was *HER2/neu*-negative in patients with 1 to 3 positive lymph nodes.

Studies have also evaluated adjuvant chemotherapy in women with node-negative breast cancer. The NSABP B-13 study randomized 760 pre- and postmenopausal patients with ER-negative, node-negative breast cancer to sequential methotrexate/5-fluorouracil (MF) chemotherapy or to observation. Cyclophosphamide was omitted because of a fear of secondary leukemia in these relatively low-risk patients. At 8 years, there was a significant improvement in the disease-free (74 versus 59%; p < .001) survival rate in chemotherapy-treated patients; a significant overall survival advantage was seen only in patients aged over 50 years (89 versus 80%; p = .03).[30] In the NSABP B-19 trial, which randomized similar patients to adjuvant CMF or MF chemotherapy, at 5 years there was a disease-free survival improvement (82 versus 73%; p < .001) and a borderline overall survival improvement (88 versus 85%; p = .06) with adjuvant CMF. In contrast, the survival benefits seen in this trial were more marked in women aged less than 50 years (84 versus 72%; p < .001 and 89 versus 84%; p = 0.04, respectively).[30] Grade 3 toxicity was higher in CMF-treated patients. NSABP B-20 randomized 2,306 patients with ER-positive, node-negative breast cancer to tamoxifen, MF with tamoxifen (MFT), or CMF with tamoxifen (CMFT).[31] At 5 years, patients receiving chemotherapy with tamoxifen had improvements in disease-free (90% for MFT versus 85% for tamoxifen, p = .01, and 89% for CMFT versus 85% for tamoxifen, p = .001) and overall survival (97 for MFT versus 94% for tamoxifen, p = .05, and 96% for CMFT versus 94% for tamoxifen, p = .03) rates. All subgroups of patients evaluated in this study benefited from chemotherapy, although the benefit was greatest in women aged less than 50 years.

Findings from these and other studies, in addition to the Oxford Overview, make it clear that almost all patients with breast cancer, regardless of age, lymph node status, tumor size, or ER status, derive benefit from adjuvant chemotherapy. As discussed earlier, a decision to administer adjuvant chemotherapy must be made after consideration of the risks and benefits of treatment, in conjunction with a detailed discussion with the individual patient. At present, available evidence supports the use of an anthracycline- or CMF-based regimen alone in patients with node-negative breast cancer in whom a decision has been made to proceed with adjuvant chemotherapy. As discussed above, an anthracycline-based regimen is slightly superior, and six cycles of a CAF- or FEC-type regimen may be superior to four cycles of AC or EC, although prospective randomized evidence of this superiority is not available. The optimal dose of epirubicin in FEC chemotherapy is 100 mg/m^2 (FEC-100), which is associated with disease-free and overall survival benefits and an improved risk-benefit ratio when compared to six cycles of the same chemotherapy administered every 3 weeks with 50 mg/m^2 epirubicin (FEC-50).[32] An indirect comparison between two older trials, one which found six cycles of FEC-50 to be equivalent to six cycles of CMF and one which found six cycles of CEF-120 to be superior to six cycles of CMF, had previously suggested this (see Table 20–4).[23,24]

TAXANES

The taxanes (paclitaxel and docetaxel) are among the most active agents in metastatic breast cancer.[33,34] Therefore, they have been extensively studied in the adjuvant treatment of early-stage breast cancer. Currently, data are available from 13 of 25 trials that assess the addition or substitution of taxanes into primary or adjuvant breast cancer therapy, including more than 15,000 women. A recent systematic review of these trials reiterated the benefit obtained with the addition of taxanes to adjuvant chemotherapy in women with early-stage breast cancer and involved lymph nodes.[35] This benefit is independent of hormone-receptor status; evidence does not support restricting taxanes to women with hormone-receptor negative tumors. Available data at present support the addition of four cycles of paclitaxel to four cycles of AC, the substitution of six cycles of FAC with six cycles of docetaxel, doxorubicin, and cyclophosphamide (TAC), or the use of three cycles of FEC followed by three cycles of docetaxel in patients with lymph node-positive breast cancer.

Results are currently available from eight trials of adjuvant chemotherapy that have compared taxane-containing treatment with a non-taxane regimen (Table 20–5), including 15,517 women, 3,618 relapses, and 2,121 deaths.[35] Four of these eight trials enrolled only women with lymph node-positive breast cancer. The largest of these eight trials is the Cancer and Leukemia Group B (CALGB) 9344 trial.[36] This trial showed that the addition of four cycles of paclitaxel after the completion of a standard course of AC improves the disease-free and overall survivals of patients with node-positive early breast cancer. After surgical treatment, 3,121 women with operable breast cancer and positive lymph nodes were randomly assigned to receive a combination of cyclophosphamide, 600 mg/m^2, with one of three doses of doxorubicin, 60, 75, or 90 mg/m^2, for four cycles followed by no further therapy or four cycles of paclitaxel at 175 mg/m^2 every 3 weeks. There was no evidence of a doxorubicin dose effect. The hazard reductions from adding paclitaxel to AC were 17% for recurrence (p = .0023) and 18% for death (p = .0064). At 5 years, the disease-free survivals were 65 and 70%, and overall survival rates were 77 and 80% after AC alone versus AC plus paclitaxel, respectively. The effects of adding paclitaxel were not significantly different in subsets defined by the protocol, but in an unplanned subset analysis, the RR of AC plus paclitaxel versus AC alone was 0.72 (95% CI, 0.59 to 0.86) for those with ER-negative tumors and only 0.91 (95% CI, 0.78 to 1.07) for patients with ER-positive tumors. The additional toxicity from four added cycles of paclitaxel was modest.

The second of the eight trials is NSABP B-28, with 3,060 node-positive patients randomized to treatment with or without four cycles of adjuvant paclitaxel (225 mg/m^2 every 3 weeks as a 3-hour infusion) following four cycles of standard AC.[37] All patients aged over 50 years and those under 50 years with ER- or PR-positive tumors also received tamoxifen 20 mg daily for 5 years, starting with AC. Patient and tumor characteristics were well balanced between the treatment groups. This trial showed a statistically significant improvement in relapse-free survival after a median follow-up of 64 months with the addition of paclitaxel (RR, 0.83 with 95% CI, 0.73 to 0.95; $p = .008$). Overall survival was not significantly different between the two groups; the RR was 0.94 with the addition of paclitaxel (95% CI, 0.78 to 1.12, $p = .46$). In this trial, the addition of paclitaxel was equally effective in women with ER-positive and ER-negative tumors. A grade 3 or 4 toxicity occurred in 28% of the patients during AC and in 34% during paclitaxel; the latter toxicities included neurotoxicity in 19%, arthralgia/myalgia in 11%, febrile neutropenia in 2%, infection in 2%, thromboembolic events in 2%, and hypersensitivity reactions in 1%.

The results of a planned second interim analysis of the Breast Cancer International Research Group (BCIRG) 001 trial have been reported in abstract form.[38] In this trial, 1,491 women with node-positive breast cancer were randomized to six cycles of postoperative TAC at 75/50/500 mg/m^2 (745 women) versus six cycles of FAC (746 women); 62% had 1 to 3 positive lymph nodes. This trial showed significant improvements in the relapse-free and overall survival rates in the TAC arm. After a median follow-up of 55 months, the RR was 0.72 ($p = .001$) for relapse-free survival and 0.70 ($p = .008$) for overall survival. The use of docetaxel was equally effective in women with ER-positive tumors as in those with ER-negative tumors in a prospectively defined subset analysis. TAC was superior to FAC in patients with *HER2/neu*-amplified tumors (RR, 0.61; 95% CI, 0.42 to 0.90; $p = .0118$) and also in patients whose tumors had a normal *HER2/neu* gene copy number (RR, 0.76; 95% CI, 0.58 to 0.99; $p = .0380$). To date, this trial is associated with the greatest absolute benefit for a taxane-containing adjuvant chemotherapy (see Table 20–5). In a prospectively defined subset analysis, TAC was shown to be associated with significant benefits only in those with 1 to 3 positive nodes (RR, 0.61; 95% CI, 0.46 to 0.82; $p = .0009$). Febrile neutropenia (24 versus 2%) and grade 3 or 4 infection (2.8 versus 1.3%) were more common with TAC chemotherapy, necessitating the routine use of growth factor support in TAC-treated patients. The rates of congestive heart failure were 1.2% with TAC and 0.1% with FAC chemotherapies.

The University of Texas M.D. Anderson Cancer Center (MDACC 94-002) reported on 524 women with stage T1–3, N0–1 breast cancer who were randomized to four cycles of paclitaxel followed by four cycles of FAC ($n = 265$), or to eight cycles of FAC chemotherapy ($n = 259$).[39] Of note only this trial,

Table 20–5. ADJUVANT CHEMOTHERAPY TRIALS INVESTIGATING TAXANE-BASED VERSUS NON-TAXANE-BASED CHEMOTHERAPY IN BREAST CANCER

Study	Patients	Median Follow-up (mo)	Eligibility by lymph node (LN) status	Trial Arms	5 year OS: Control Arm	5 year OS: Taxane Arm	*p* Value	5 year RFS: Control Arm	5 year RFS: Taxane Arm	*p* value
CALGB 9344[36]	3,121	69	All LN positive	AC vs AC ≥ P	77	80	.001	65	70	.006
NSABP B28[37]	3,060	64	All LN positive	AC vs AC ≥ P	85	85	.46	72	76	.008
BCIRG 001[38]	1,491	55	All LN positive	FAC vs TAC	81	87	.008	68	75	.001
MDACC 94-002[39]	524	60	†	FAC vs P ≥ FAC	–	–	–	79	83	.09
US Oncology 9735[40]	1,015	43	53% LN positive	AC vs TC	94*	95*	NS	90*	92*	NS
PACS01[41]	1,999	60	All LN positive	FEC vs FEC ≥ T	86.7	90.7	.013	73.2	78.3	.012
E2197[42‡]	2,952	53	35% LN positive	AC vs AT	94	94	.49	87	87	.7
ECTO[43§]	1,355	43	46% LN positive (clinical)	A ≥ CMF vs AP ≥ CMF	87	91	.16	80	86	.012

With the exception of E2197, these phase III trials enrolled only patients with lymph node-positive breast cancer. CMF = cyclophosphamide, methotrexate, and 5-fluorouracil; (F)AC = (5-fluorouracil), doxorubicin and cyclophosphamide; NS = not significant; OS = overall survival; P = paclitaxel; RFS = relapse-free survival; T = docetaxel.

*3-year results.

†In this trial, 62% of patients treated with neoadjuvant chemotherapy were clinically node positive, and 72% of patients treated with adjuvant chemotherapy were node positive at surgery.

‡4-year disease-free and overall survivals.

§Results shown in the RFS column are representative of freedom from progression at a median follow-up of 43 months; the overall surviral rates are 5-year estimates. The comparison shown includes only the 2 adjuvant arms in the ECTO trial but not the 3rd primary therapy arm (see text).

BCIRG 001, and the recently reported PACS01 trial have tested the benefit of adding a taxane to anthracycline-containing chemotherapy while maintaining the overall number of cycles administered. In this trial, 174 patients were treated preoperatively with four cycles of chemotherapy, and these were reported with the other patients. After a median follow-up of 60 months, the RR was 0.70 (95% CI, 0.47 to 1.07, $p = .09$) for relapse-free survival and was not reported for overall survival. There was a non-significant trend suggesting that the addition of paclitaxel was more beneficial in women with ER-negative tumors.

The fifth reported adjuvant taxane trial, US Oncology 9735, randomized 1,015 women after resection of stage I to III invasive breast cancer to four postoperative cycles of docetaxel and cyclophosphamide (75/600 mgs/m^2; n = 506) or to four postoperative cycles of standard AC (n = 510).[40] After a median follow-up of 43 months, there were no significant differences in the disease-free survival or overall survival rates. No subgroup analyses have yet been reported. The French group reported the results of a very well-designed trial of adjuvant taxane-based versus non–taxane-based chemotherapy in 1,999 patients with lymph node-positive breast cancer, PACS01.[41] In this trial, 62% of patients had 1 to 3 involved lymph nodes. Table 20–5 shows the significant 5-year absolute benefits reported for patients treated with three cycles of FEC-100 (5-fluorouracil, epirubicin, and cyclophosphamide at 500/100/500 mg/m^2, respectively, every 3 weeks) followed by three cycles of docetaxel 100 mg/m^2 every 3 weeks in comparison to patients given six cycles of FEC-100 alone. The most recently presented phase III trial of adjuvant taxanes in breast cancer was E2197, a trial comparing 4 cycles of AT (doxorubicin 60 mg/m^2 and docetaxel 60 mg/m^2) and 4 cycles of AC in the adjuvant treatment of node-positive and high-risk node-negative breast cancer.[42] At 59 months median follow-up, there is no difference in disease-free or overall survivals between the arms, although there are fewer events in the AT arm (see Table 20–5). A subgroup analysis of this trial suggests progesterone receptor-negative tumors may derive more benefit from AT. In the eighth trial (ECTO), 1,355 women with operable breast cancer (tumor size > 2 cm) were randomized to adjuvant doxorubicin (75 mg/m^2 every 21 days × 4) followed by intravenous CMF (day 1 and 8 every 28 days × 4), or to adjuvant doxorubicin (60 mg/m^2) with paclitaxel (200 mg/m^2 over 3 hours every 21 days × 4) followed by CMF (AT→CMF), or to AT→CMF as primary systemic therapy.[43] Table 20–5 shows the results of the comparison between the two adjuvant arms. Adjuvant AT ≥ CMF was superior to adjuvant A ≥ CMF in freedom from progression at a median follow up of 43 months without leading to increased cardiac toxicity. No difference between the adjuvant or primary administration of AT→CMF has been observed so far, although longer follow-up is needed for conclusive consideration of overall survival.

In summary, therefore, available data support the addition of four cycles of paclitaxel to four cycles of standard AC, the substitution of six cycles of FAC with six cycles of TAC, or the use of three cycles of FEC-100 followed by three cycles of docetaxel in patients with lymph node-positive breast cancer. At present, taxanes are therefore part of the standard of care for the adjuvant treatment of women with lymph node-positive breast cancer, but their role in the adjuvant treatment of women with node-negative disease is still controversial, owing to the lack of clinical trial information. The relative benefit associated with the use of taxanes in node-negative breast cancer is probably equivalent to that in node-positive disease, although this will obviously translate into a smaller absolute benefit which will therefore be more difficult to detect in clinical trials. This situation is analogous to the controversy surrounding the use of adjuvant chemotherapy in stage II colorectal cancer. In our opinion, it is appropriate to use taxanes in the adjuvant treatment of women with high-risk node-negative breast cancer. Ongoing trials will help to further define the role of taxanes in the adjuvant setting for patients with operable breast cancer, including those with node-negative disease.

PACLITAXEL VERSUS DOCETAXEL

Paclitaxel was introduced to the treatment of metastatic breast cancer as a drug given at 3-weekly intervals. At 3-weekly intervals in metastatic breast cancer, it is inferior to docetaxel administered every 3 weeks.[44] This trial confirmed previous indirect evidence of the superiority of docetaxel.[33,45] Paclitaxel is a schedule-dependent drug and has recently been shown to be significantly more effective in metastatic breast cancer when administered every week than when given at 3-weekly intervals.[46] The weekly paclitaxel arm of CALGB 9840 was associated with a median time to progression of 9 months in comparison to 5 months with paclitaxel given every 3 weeks (p = .0008) to patients with metastatic breast cancer; there was more neurotoxicity and less myelosuppression in the former arm. In CALGB 9741, a trial of adjuvant dose-dense chemotherapy in breast cancer discussed in more detail in the next section, paclitaxel was given at 2-weekly intervals in the treatment arms associated with significantly improved outcome, and at 3-weekly intervals in the inferior treatment arms, although there were also other differences between the study arms.[47] Weekly paclitaxel has not been compared to docetaxel in metastatic breast cancer. At MDACC, we currently have a prospective trial (MDACC 01-580) in which women with node-positive or high-risk node-negative breast cancer are randomized to weekly paclitaxel alone or docetaxel administered every 3 weeks in combination with capecitabine, followed by four cycles of FEC chemotherapy administered at 3-weekly intervals.

DOSE-DENSE CHEMOTHERAPY

It is hypothesized that the more frequent administration of cytotoxic therapy may be a more effective way of minimizing residual tumor burden in adjuvant cancer treatment than dose escalation.[48] Dose-density refers to the administration of drugs with a shortened inter-treatment interval. The concept is based on observations in experimental models that a given chemotherapy dose kills a certain fraction, rather than a certain number, of exponentially growing cancer cells, and tumor regrowth is felt to be particularly rapid when the number of viable cells is at its lowest with a Gompertzian shape to the growth curve.[49] Treatment resulting in a fixed cell kill over a shorter period of time would thus have a greater impact because of a shorter time in which the cells can regrow. Initial evidence of a benefit to dose density in the adjuvant treatment of breast cancer came from a randomized trial in women with three or more positive axillary lymph nodes.[50] This trial showed that sequential chemotherapy with doxorubicin followed by CMF yields superior results to the alternating administration of these regimens. The sequential arm has a higher dose density of doxorubicin and CMF than the arm in which they were alternated. Theoretically, subpopulations of cells sensitive to individual drugs are more effectively eradicated when the time intervals between treatments to which the cells are sensitive are shorter.

Since the publication of CALGB 9741, dose-dense chemotherapy is accepted as having an important role in the adjuvant treatment of lymph node-positive breast cancer.[47] This is the first trial to demonstrate a benefit for the administration of adjuvant chemotherapy to breast cancer patients in a dose-dense schedule in comparison to a standard schedule.[51] However, we do not have conclusive evidence that the efficacy of anthracyclines alone in the adjuvant treatment of breast cancer patients is increased when they are administered in a dose-dense schedule. It has been shown in locally advanced breast cancer that dose-dense FEC chemotherapy given every 2 weeks does not result in significant improvements in clinical or pathologic response rates or in disease-free survival, compared to the same treatment administered at standard 3-weekly intervals.[52] In this trial, FEC was administered alone for three cycles before surgery, but it was alternated with CMF chemotherapy after surgery.

CALGB 9741 used a 2 × 2 factorial design in 2,005 women with axillary node-positive breast cancer, randomizing them to sequential doxorubicin, paclitaxel, and cyclophosphamide (four doses of each drug) every 2 or 3 weeks, or to AC for four cycles followed by paclitaxel for four cycles every 2 or 3 weeks.[47] The doxorubicin dose used was 60 mg/m^2, the cyclophosphamide dose was 600 mg/m^2, and the paclitaxel dose was 175 mg/m^2 in all treatment arms. Filgrastim was required in the dose-dense arms. Approximately 60% of women in each of the four treatment arms had 1 to 3 involved lymph nodes. At a median follow-up of 36 months, dose-dense treatment significantly improved the disease-free survival (risk ratio [RR] = 0.74; p = .01) and overall survival (RR = 0.69; p = .013) rates. The 4-year disease-free survival rates were 82% for the dose-dense regimens and 75% for the standard-schedule regimens. However, an update of this trial was presented at the 2005 American Society of Clinical Oncology (ASCO) meeting. Whereas disease-free survival remains significantly improved in the dose-dense arms (p = .02), the difference in overall survival between the dose-dense and standard-dose arms is somewhat less marked (p = .06) and further follow-up is required. A subset analysis revealed the benefit of dose-dense chemotherapy to be restricted to ER-negative tumors. There were no differences in the disease-free or overall survival rates between the concurrent and sequential schedules. Severe neutropenia was less frequent in patients who received the dose-dense regimens because of the routine use of filgrastim, although a subset of only 25% of the patients was used to determine toxicities. This trial provides preliminary evidence that dose density improves clinical outcomes significantly in node-positive breast cancer.

Further evidence of the efficacy of adjuvant dose-dense anthracycline- and paclitaxel-containing adjuvant chemotherapy in node-positive breast cancer was presented at the 2004 annual meeting of ASCO; this trial also employed higher doses of epirubicin and cyclophosphamide in the dose-dense arm.[53] This was a multicenter phase III trial of the German "Arbeitsgemeinschaft fuer Gynaekologische Onkologie" (AGO) group that prospectively randomized 1,284 patients to three courses each of epirubicin (150 mg/m^2), paclitaxel (225 mg/m^2), and cyclophosphamide (2500 mg/m^2) at 2-weekly intervals (ETC) with filgrastim support, or to four courses of epirubicin/cyclophosphamide (EC-90/600 mg/m^2), followed by four courses of paclitaxel (175 mg/m^2), each administered every three weeks. Patients under 65 years of age were eligible if they had at least four involved axillary lymph nodes. Risk factors were well balanced between both treatment arms. Fifty-nine percent of patients had 4 to 9 involved nodes. The median number of involved lymph nodes was 8. Hematologic toxicity and febrile neutropenia were more frequent in the ETC arm ($p < .0001$); the incidence was highest during treatment with cyclophosphamide and lowest during treatment with paclitaxel. The number of dose reductions was 6.5% in the ETC arm and 2% in the standard arm. At a median follow-up of 28 months, the dose-dense treatment significantly improved the relapse-free survival (RR = 0.64; p = .0009) and overall survival (RR = 0.65; p = .03) rates. The estimated 3-year relapse-free survivals were 80% in the ETC arm and 70% in the standard arm. The overall survival rates were 90% in the ETC arm and 87% in the standard arm.

Thus, dose-dense chemotherapy containing an anthracycline and a taxane is a potent and acceptable adjuvant treatment for women with lymph node-positive breast cancer. Recent evidence also suggests the administration of a dose-dense epirubicin- and paclitaxel-containing regimen with filgrastim support is feasible in elderly patients with four or more positive lymph nodes, with a tolerable safety profile.[54] However, the efficacy of adjuvant anthracycline- and paclitaxel-containing chemotherapy in comparison to adjuvant TAC has not been determined. We do not know if dose-dense anthracycline- and docetaxel-containing chemotherapy is better than this treatment administered in a standard fashion. Some ongoing trials will help to answer this question. For example, the closed Eastern Cooperative Oncology Group (ECOG) 1199 trial treated lymph node-positive and high-risk node-negative breast cancer patients with four cycles of standard AC chemotherapy and then randomized them to one of four arms:

1. Paclitaxel weekly × 12 doses
2. Paclitaxel every 3 weeks × 4 doses
3. Docetaxel weekly × 12 doses
4. Docetaxel every 3 weeks × 4 doses

DOSE-INTENSE–HIGH-DOSE CHEMOTHERAPY

Two large prospective clinical trials have established that increasing the total dose of doxorubicin or cyclophosphamide above standard doses currently used does not significantly improve either the disease-free or overall survival rates in the adjuvant treatment of breast cancer (CALGB 9344 and NSABP B-22).[36,55] However, high-dose chemotherapy was the subject of intense scrutiny and study in breast cancer for several years. Initial non-randomized trials were encouraging, but the early randomized prospective trials evaluating this approach were uniformly negative,[56,57] although recent studies, including a meta-analysis, have reported a benefit for high-dose chemotherapy in patients with early high-risk breast cancer.[58,59] However, the lack of dramatic benefits associated with significantly increased toxicity have resulted in a significant decline in the use of high-dose chemotherapy in breast cancer to the point where it is now rarely used. Currently, high-dose chemotherapy is being investigated only in women with very high-risk early receptor-negative breast cancer.

TRASTUZUMAB

Trastuzumab (Herceptin®, Genentech, Inc., San Francisco, CA) is a humanized monoclonal antibody with high affinity for HER2/neu, a member of the epidermal growth factor receptor family of proteins. Overexpression of the HER2/neu protein is measured by immunohistochemistry, and gene amplification of HER2 is measured by fluorescent in situ hybridization (FISH). It is essential that the level of expression and/or amplification is accurately assessed in each individual. Immunohistochemistry is a reliable measure of expression for tumors that strongly or weakly express HER2/neu (3+ or 0–1+). It is important that positive and negative controls be used routinely with each assay. FISH may be a more objective assessment relative to immunohistochemistry in assessing HER2/neu positivity. However, immunohistochemistry is a simpler and more economical assay. Excellent concordance (97%) between these two assays is noted for 0, 1+, or 3+ staining. However, 2+ immunohistochemical staining has a 75% discordance rate with FISH and should lead to routine FISH analysis.[60]

The pivotal trial demonstrated that trastuzumab, in combination with AC or paclitaxel, is associated with significantly higher response rates and longer progression-free and overall survival rates in metastatic breast cancer overexpressing HER2/neu, although a high rate of clinically significant cardiotoxicity was seen in the patient group treated with concurrent trastuzumab and AC.[61] Trastuzumab is thus the first novel targeted therapy to demonstrate clinical efficacy in breast cancer since the introduction of tamoxifen. Several small phase II trials and one phase III study provide evidence that trastuzumab has significant activity when combined with primary chemotherapy in the treatment of HER2-overexpressing breast cancer.[62–64]

The early results of three prospective adjuvant trials of trastuzumab added to HER2/neu-positive breast cancer chemotherapy were presented at the 2005 ASCO meeting. The results were presented at a special education session. The results of two large US trials (NSABP B-31 and N9831) were combined. In these trials, AC was administered alone for four cycles and then paclitaxel was administered at weekly or 3-weekly intervals alone or combined with weekly trastuzumab. After chemotherapy, trastuzumab treatment continued for a total of 1 year in those randomized to receive it. Lymph node involvement was an eligibility requirement in the NSABP B-31 trial; N9831 also allowed patients with high-risk node negative disease. At a median follow-up of approximately 2 years, the 4-year disease-free survival was 67% in the chemotherapy-alone arms (1,679 women combined from the two trials) and 85% in the trastuzumab arms combined from the two trials (1,672 women; RR = 0.48; $p = 3 \times 10^{-12}$). Subgroup analyses did not reveal any difference in benefit for patients with tumors of different T stages or hormone receptor status. There were not enough node-negative patients to determine benefit. In N9831, a third arm, omitted from the previous analysis, treated patients with trastuzumab for 1 year following, but not concurrent with, paclitaxel chemotherapy. In this arm, the RR for disease-free survival was 0.87 compared to the chemotherapy-alone arm (p = .29). These results are still very early, and more follow-up is awaited. Congestive heart failure was more common in patients treated with trastuzumab (4.1 versus 0.7% [NSABP B-31] and ≈3 versus 0% [N9831]). Of concern, the rate of congestive heart failure in those older than 55 years with an ejection fraction after completing AC under 55% treated with concurrent trastuzumab and paclitaxel in NSABP-31 was 19%.

The other presented adjuvant trial at this ASCO meeting was the HERA trial. This multinational trial randomized 3,387 (> 5,000 in entire trial; this number excludes those randomized to 2 years of trastuzumab) node-positive and high-risk node-negative HER2/neu-positive breast cancer patients to 1 year of trastuzumab following, but not concurrent with, chemotherapy or to adjuvant chemotherapy alone. The chemotherapy regimen used was at the discretion of the treating physician. Disease-free survival at 2 years was superior in trastuzumab-treated patients (85.8 versus 77.4%, $p < .0001$). The rate of congestive heart failure was only 0.5% in the trastuzumab arm of this trial, possibly owing to its sequential administration after chemotherapy.

In summary, the addition of trastuzumab produces a major reduction in risk of recurrence for patients with HER2/neu-positive breast cancer. This effect appears at least as large as the effect of tamoxifen in ER-positive tumors. Although the sequential administration of trastuzumab after chemotherapy appears also to be effective, longer follow-up will be needed to determine whether simultaneous and sequential administration are equally effective or not. Although trastuzumab is well tolerated, these data suggest that about 3% of patients will experience transient or permanent heart failure as a result of treatment, possibly related to the proximity of antibody administration to anthracycline administration. This risk is also likely to be higher in older patients and those with pre-existing cardiac risk factors. Careful patient selection will be important to minimize cardiac toxicity. In addition, the results of the other large adjuvant trastuzumab trial, BCIRG006, are eagerly awaited, particularly since one arm in this trial did not contain an anthracycline (concurrent taxane, carboplatin, trastuzumab for 6 cycles). Nonetheless, these data strongly support the use of trastuzumab in the adjuvant setting for women with HER-2 positive tumors.

FUTURE DIRECTIONS

Currently, the approaches used to advance adjuvant chemotherapy in breast cancer include bringing from the metastatic setting drugs with proven efficacy against breast cancer. Such drugs include capecitabine, vinorelbine, and gemcitabine. As mentioned earlier, we, along with US Oncology, are evaluating capecitabine in combination with docetaxel in a prospective phase III trial. Gemcitabine has demonstrated significant antitumor activity in patients with advanced breast cancer, and several ongoing and planned adjuvant trials are incorporating it (sequentially or in combination) into anthracycline/taxane regimens.[65]

Significant progress has been made in the last 30 years in adjuvant breast cancer chemotherapy. However, current adjuvant therapy regimens are nonspecific and not individualized because of our inability to predict accurately who will benefit from this treatment. We are also unable to predict which patients will relapse in spite of receiving adjuvant chemotherapy. Breast cancer is a molecularly heterogenous disease, and recently developed technologies such as transcriptional and protein profiling are beginning to help us to understand this.[66,67] As proof of the potential that these technologies possess, transcriptional profiling identified HER2-amplified breast cancer as one of six major different subtypes after trastuzumab had been developed and found to have clinical benefit in patients with HER2-overexpressing breast cancer. A multigene polymerase chain reaction-based assay has recently been validated as capable of quantifying the likelihood of distant recurrence in tamoxifen-treated patients with node-negative, ER-positive breast cancer.[68] We need to further characterize the molecular heterogeneity of breast cancers and determine the specific genes and proteins driving the growth of distinct subtypes. These can then be used as potential targets in the future to achieve the goal of truly individualized therapy, either alone or in combination with cytotoxic chemotherapy in specific tumors.

REFERENCES

1. Halsted WS. The results of operations for the cure of cancer of the breast performed at the Johns Hopkins Hospital from June, 1889, to January, 1894. Johns Hopkins Hospital Reports 1894/1895;iv:297–350.
2. Shapiro DM, Fungmann RA. A role of chemotherapy as an adjunct to surgery. Cancer Res 1957;17:1098.
3. Polychemotherapy for early breast cancer: an overview of the randomized trials. Early Breast Cancer Trialists' Collaborative Group. Lancet 1998;352:930–42.
4. Bonadonna G, Brusamolino E, Valagussa P, et al. Combination chemotherapy as an adjuvant treatment in operable breast cancer. N Engl J Med 1976;294:405–10.
5. Sorlie T, Perou CM, Tibshirani R, et al. Gene expression pat-

terns of breast carcinomas distinguish tumor subclasses with clinical implications. Proc Natl Acad Sci U S A 2001;98:10869–74.

6. Early Breast Cancer Trialists' Collaborative Group (EBCTCG). Effects of chemotherapy and hormonal therapy for early breast cancer on recurrence and 15-year survival: an overview of the randomised trials. Lancet 2005;365:1687–717.
7. Stearns V, Davidson NE. Adjuvant chemotherapy and chemoendocrine therapy. In: Harris JR, Lippman ME, Morrow M, Osborne CK, editors. Diseases of the breast. 3rd ed. Philadelphia: Lippincott Williams and Wilkins; 2004.
8. Kuerer HM, Sahin AA, Hunt KK, et al. Incidence and impact of documented eradication of breast cancer axillary lymph node metastases before surgery in patients treated with neoadjuvant chemotherapy. Ann Surg 1999;230:72–8.
9. Ravdin PM, Siminoff LA, Davis GA, et al. Computer program to assist in making decisions about adjuvant therapy for women with early breast cancer. J Clin Oncol 2001; 19:980–91.
10. Loprinzi CL, Thome SD. Understanding the utility of adjuvant systemic therapy for primary breast cancer. J Clin Oncol 2001;19:972–9.
11. The National Institutes of Health Consensus Development Conference: Adjuvant therapy for breast cancer. Bethesda, MD. Proceedings; 2000 Nov 1-3. J Natl Cancer Inst Monogr 2001;30:1–152.
12. Goldhirsch A, Wood WC, Gelber RD, et al. Meeting highlights: updated international expert consensus on the primary therapy of early breast cancer. J Clin Oncol 2003;21:3357–65.
13. Chia SK, Speers CH, Bryce CJ, et al. Ten-year outcomes in a population-based cohort of node-negative, lymphatic, and vascular invasion-negative early breast cancers without adjuvant systemic therapies. J Clin Oncol 2004;22: 1630–37.
14. Morrow M, Krontiras H. Who should not receive chemotherapy? Data from American databases and trials. J Natl Cancer Inst Monog 2001;30:109–13.
15. van de Vijver MJ, He YD, van't Veer LJ, et al. A gene-expression signature as a predictor of survival in breast cancer. N Engl J Med 2002;347:1999–2009.
16. Fisher B, Slack N, Katrych D, Wolmark N. Ten year follow-up results of patients with carcinoma of the breast in a co-operative clinical trial evaluating surgical adjuvant chemotherapy. Surg Gynecol Obstet 1975;140:528–34.
17. Fisher B, Fisher ER, Redmond C.Ten-year results from the national surgical adjuvant breast and bowel project (NSABP) clinical trial evaluating the use of L-phenylalanine mustard in the management of primary breast cancer. J Clin Oncol 1986;4:929–41.
18. Bonadonna G, Valagussa P, Moliterni A, et al. Adjuvant cyclophosphamide, methotrexate, and flurouracil in node-positive breast cancer. N Engl J Med 1995;332:901–6.
19. Misset JL, di Palma M, Delgado M, et al. Adjuvant treatment of node positive breast cancer with cyclophosphamide, doxorubicin, fluorouracil and vincristine versus cyclophosphamide, methotrexate, and fluorouracil: final report after a 16-year median follow-up duration. J Clin Oncol 1996;14:1136–45.
20. Fisher B, Brown AM, Dimitrov NV, et al. Two months of doxorubicin-cyclophosphamide with and without interval reinduction therapy compared with 6 months of cyclophosphamide, methotrexate, and fluorouracil in positive-node breast cancer patients with tamoxifen-nonresponsive tumors: results from the National Surgical Adjuvant Breast and Bowel Project B-15. J Clin Oncol 1990;8: 1483–96.
21. Hutchins L, Green S, Ravdin P, et al. CMF versus CAF with and without Tamoxifen in high-risk node-negative breast cancer patients and a natural history follow-up study in low-risk node negative patients: first results of intergroup trial INT 0102. Abstract. Proc Am Soc Clin Oncol 1998;17:1.
22. Fisher B, Anderson S, Tan-Chiu E, et al. Tamoxifen and chemotherapy for axillary node-negative, estrogen receptor negative breast cancer: findings from National Surgical Adjuvant Breast and Bowel Project B-23. J Clin Oncol 2001;19:931–42.
23. Coombes RC, Bliss JM, Wils J, et al. Adjuvant cyclophosphamide, methotrexate and fluorouracil versus fluorouracil, epirubicin and cyclophosphamide chemotherapy in premenopausal women with axillary node-positive operable breast cancer: results of a randomized trial. The International Collaborative Cancer Group. J Clin Oncol 1996;14:35–45.
24. Levine MN, Bramwell VH, Pritchard KI, et al. Randomized trial of intensive cyclophosphamide, epirubicin and fluorouracil chemotherapy compared with cyclophosphamide, methotrexate and fluorouracil in premenopausal women with node-positive breast cancer. National Cancer Institute of Canada Clinical Trials Group. J Clin Oncol 1998;16:2651–8.
25. Piccart MJ, DiLeo A, Beauduin M, et al. Phase III trial comparing two dose levels of epirubicin compared with cyclophosphamide with cyclophosphamide, methotrexate, and fluorouracil in node-positive breast cancer. J Clin Oncol 2001;19:3103–10.
26. Bang SM, Heo DS, Lee KH, et al. Adjuvant doxorubicin and cyclophosphamide versus cyclophosphamide, methotrexate and 5-fluorouracil chemotherapy in premenopausal women with axillary lymph node positive breast cancer. Cancer 2000;89:2521–6.
27. Fisher B, Redmond C, Legault-Poisson S, et al. Postoperative chemotherapy and tamoxifen compared with tamoxifen alone in the treatment of positive-node breast cancer patients aged 50 years and older with tumors responsive to tamoxifen: results from the national surgical adjuvant breast and bowel project B-16. J Clin Oncol 1990;8:1005–18.
28. Albain K, Green S, Osborne K, et al. Tamoxifen (T) versus cyclophosphamide, Adriamycin and 5-FU plus either concurrent or sequential T in postmenopausal, receptor (+), node (+) breast cancer: a Southwest Oncology Group phase III intergroup trial [abstract]. Proc Am Soc Clin Oncol 1997:450.
29. Albain K, Barlow W, O'Malley F, et al. Concurrent (CAFT) versus sequential (CAF-T) chemohormonal therapy (cyclophosphamide, doxorubicin, 5-fluorouracil, tamoxifen) versus T alone for postmenopausal , node-positive, estrogen (ER) and/or progesterone (PgR) receptor-positive breast cancer: mature outcomes and new bio-

logic correlates on phase III intergroup trial 0100 (SWOG-8814). Abstract. San Antonio Breast Cancer Conference 2004:37.

30. Fisher B, Dignam J, Mamounas EP, et al. Sequential methotrexate and fluorouracil for the treatment of node-negative breast cancer patients with estrogen receptor negative tumors: eight-year results from national surgical adjuvant breast and bowel project (NSABP) B-13 and first report of findings from NSABP B-19 comparing methotrexate and fluorouracil with conventional cyclophosphamide, and fluorouracil. J Clin Oncol 1996;14:1971–3.
31. Fisher B, Dignam J, Wolmark N, et al. Tamoxifen and chemotherapy for lymph node-negative, estrogen receptor-positive breast cancer. J Natl Cancer Inst 1997;89:1673–82.
32. Bonneterre J, Roche H, Kerbrat P, et al. Long-term cardiac follow-up in relapse-free patients after six courses of fluorouracil, epirubicin, and cyclophosphamide, with either 50 or 100 mg of epirubicin, as adjuvant therapy for node-positive breast cancer: French adjuvant study group. J Clin Oncol 2004;22:3070–9.
33. Chan S, Friedrichs K, Noel D, et al, . Prospective randomized trial of docetaxel versus doxorubicin in patients with metastatic breast cancer. J Clin Oncol 1999;17:2341–54.
34. Abrams JS, Vena DA, Baltz J, et al. Paclitaxel activity in heavily pretreated breast cancer: a National Cancer Institute Treatment Referral Center trial. J Clin Oncol 1995; 13:2056–65.
35. Nowak AK, Wilcken NR, Stockler MR, et al. Systematic review of taxane-containing versus non-taxane–containing regimens for adjuvant and neoadjuvant treatment of early breast cancer. Lancet Oncol 2004;5:372–80.
36. Henderson IC, Berry DA, Demetri GD, et al. Improved outcomes from adding sequential Paclitaxel but not from escalating Doxorubicin dose in an adjuvant chemotherapy regimen for patients with node-positive primary breast cancer. J Clin Oncol 2003;21:976–83.
37. Mamounas EP, Bryant J, Lembersky BC, et al. Paclitaxel following doxorubicin/cyclophosphamide as adjuvant chemotherapy for node-positive breast cancer [abstract]. Proc Am Soc Clin Oncol 2003;22:12.
38. Martin M, Pienkowski T, Mackey J, et al. Adjuvant docetaxel for node-positive breast cancer. N Engl J Med 2005; 352:2302–13.
39. Buzdar AU, Singletary SE, Valero V, et al. Evaluation of paclitaxel in adjuvant chemotherapy for patients with operable breast cancer: preliminary data of a prospective randomized trial. Clin Cancer Res 2002;8:1073–9.
40. Jones SE, Savin MA, Asmar L, et al. Three-year results of a prospective randomized trial of adjuvant chemotherapy for patients with stage I–III operable, invasive breast cancer comparing four courses of doxorubicin/cyclophosphamide to four courses of docetaxel/cyclophosphamide [abstract]. Proc Am Soc Clin Oncol 2003;22:59.
41. Roche H, Fumoleau P, Spielmann M, et al. Five year analysis of the PACS01 trial: 6 cycles of FEC100 vs. 3 cycles of FEC100 followed by 3 cycles of docetaxel (D) for the adjuvant treatment of node positive breast cancer [abstract]. San Antonio Breast Cancer Symposium 2004:27.
42. Goldstein L, O'Neill A, Sparano J, et al. E2197: Phase III AT (doxorubicin/docetaxel) vs. AC (doxorubicin/cyclophosphamide) in the adjuvant treatment of node positive and high risk node negative breast cancer [abstract]. Annual meeting of American Society of Clinical Oncology 2005:512.
43. Gianni L, Baselga J, Eiermann W, et al. European Cooperative Trial in Operable Breast Cancer (ECTO): Improved freedom from progression (FFP) from adding paclitaxel (T) to doxorubicin (A) followed by cyclophosphamide methotrexate and fluorouracil (CMF) [abstract]. Annual meeting of American Society of Clinical Oncology 2005:513.
44. Jones S, Erban J, Overmoyer B, et al. Randomized trial comparing docetaxel and paclitaxel in patients with metastatic breast cancer [abstract]. San Antonio Breast Cancer Symposium 2003:10.
45. Paridaens R, Biganzoli L, Bruning P, et al. Paclitaxel versus doxorubicin as first-line single-agent chemotherapy for metastatic breast cancer: a European Organization for Research and Treatment of Cancer Randomized Study with cross-over. J Clin Oncol 2000;18:724–33.
46. Seidman AD, Berry D, Cirrincione C, et al. CALGB 9840: Phase III study of weekly (W) paclitaxel (P) via 1-hour(h) infusion versus standard (S) 3h infusion every third week in the treatment of metastatic breast cancer (MBC), with trastuzumab (T) for HER2 positive MBC and randomized for T in HER2 normal MBC [abstract]. Proc Am Soc Clin Oncol 2004;22:512.
47. Citron ML, Berry DA, Cirrincione C, et al. Randomized trial of dose-dense versus conventionally scheduled and sequential versus concurrent combination chemotherapy as postoperative adjuvant treatment of node-positive primary breast cancer: first report of Intergroup Trial C9741/Cancer and Leukemia Group B Trial 9741. J Clin Oncol 2003;21:1431–9.
48. Norton L. Theoretical concepts and the emerging role of taxanes in adjuvant therapy. Oncologist 2001;3(Suppl):30–5.
49. Skipper HE. Laboratory models: Some historical perspectives. Cancer Treat Rep 1986;70:3–7.
50. Bonadonna G, Zambetti M, Valagussa P. Sequential or alternating doxorubicin and CMF regimens in breast cancer with more than three positive nodes. Ten-year results. JAMA 1995;273:542–7.
51. Hudis C. Dose-dense chemotherapy for breast cancer: the story so far. Br J Cancer 2000;82:1897–9.
52. Baldini E, Gardin G, Giannessi PG, et al. Accelerated versus standard cyclophosphamide, epirubicin and 5-fluorouracil or cyclophosphamide, methotrexate and 5-fluorouracil: a randomized phase III trial in locally advanced breast cancer. Ann Oncol 2003;14:227–32.
53. Möbus VJ, Untch M, Du Bois A, et al. Dose-dense sequential chemotherapy with epirubicin(E), paclitaxel (T) and cyclophosphamide (C) (ETC) is superior to conventional dosed chemotherapy in high-risk breast cancer patients (≥ 4 +LN). First results of an AGO-trial [abstract]. J Clin Oncol 2004;22(14S):513.
54. Kuemmel S, Krocker J, Kohls A, et al. A phase III randomized trial comparing the tolerability of dose-dense chemotherapy in older to that in younger breast cancer patients with four or more positive lymph nodes [abstract]. J Clin Oncol 2004;22(14S):589.

55. Fisher B, Anderson S, Wickerham DL, et al. Increased intensification and total dose of cyclophosphamide in a doxorubicin-cyclophosphamide regimen for the treatment of primary breast cancer: findings from National Surgical Adjuvant Breast and Bowel Project B-22. J Clin Oncol 1997;15:1858–69.
56. Hortobagyi GN. What is the role of high-dose chemotherapy in the era of targeted therapies. J Clin Oncol 2004;22: 2263–6.
57. Crown J. Smart bombs versus blunderbusses: high-dose chemotherapy for breast cancer. Lancet 2004;364: 1299–1300.
58. Nitz UA, Frick M, Mohrmann S, et al. Tandem high dose chemotherapy versus dose-dense conventional chemotherapy for patients with high risk breast cancer: interim results from a multi-centre phase III trial [abstract]. Proc Am Soc Clin Oncol 2003;22:832a.
59. Farquhar C, Basser R, Marjoribanks J, Lethaby A. High dose chemotherapy and autologous bone marrow or stem cell transplantation versus conventional chemotherapy for women with early poor prognosis breast cancer. In: The Cochrane Library, Issue 1, 2003, Oxford Update Software.
60. Lal P, Salazar PA, Hudis CA, et al. HER-2 testing in breast cancer using immunohistochemical analysis and fluorescence in situ hybridization: a single-institution experience of 2,279 cases and comparison of dual-color and single-color scoring. Am J Clin Pathol 2004;121:631–6.
61. Slamon DJ, Leyland-Jones B, Shak S, et al. Use of chemotherapy plus a monoclonal antibody against HER2 for metastatic breast cancer that overexpresses HER2. N Engl J Med 2001;344:783–92.
62. Buzdar AU, Hunt K, Smith T, et al. Significantly higher pathological complete remission (PCR) rate following neoadjuvant therapy with trastuzumab (H), paclitaxel (P), and anthracycline-containing chemotherapy (CT): Initial results of a randomized trial in operable breast cancer (BC) with HER/2 positive disease. J Clin Oncol Proceedings of the ASCO Annual Meeting (Post-Meeting Edition) 2004;22(14S):520.
63. Burstein HJ, Harris LN, Gelman R, et al. Preoperative therapy with trastuzumab and paclitaxel followed by sequential adjuvant doxorubicin/cyclophosphamide for HER2 overexpressing stage II or III breast cancer: a pilot study. J Clin Oncol 2003;21:46–53.
64. Van Pelt AE, Mohsin S, Elledge RM, et al. Neoadjuvant trastuzumab and docetaxel in breast cancer: preliminary results. Clin Breast Cancer 2003;4:348–53.
65. Mamounas EP, Geyer CE Jr, Swain SM. Rationale and clinical trial design for evaluating gemcitabine as neoadjuvant and adjuvant therapy for breast cancer. Clin Breast Cancer 2004;(4 Suppl 3):S121–6.
66. Sorlie T, Perou CM, Tibshirani R, et al. Gene expression patterns of breast carcinomas distinguish tumor subclasses with clinical implications. Proc Natl Acad Sci U S A 2001;98:10869–74.
67. Charboneau L, Scott H, Chen T, et al. Utility of reverse phase protein arrays: applications to signaling pathways and human body arrays. Brief Funct Genomic Proteomic 2002;1:305–15.
68. Paik S, Shak S, Tang G, et al. A multigene assay to predict recurrence of tamoxifen-treated, node-negative breast cancer. N Engl J Med 2004;351:2817–26.

21

Endocrine Therapy of Early and Advanced Breast Cancer

AMAN U. BUZDAR

Over 100 years ago, Beatson made the link between the endocrine system and breast cancer.[1] Fifty years later, Huggins and colleagues first described the surgical adrenalectomy as second-line endocrine therapy.[2] At that time, there was little understanding of the biological basis underlying the responses, but substantial research has accumulated to describe mechanisms to form a rational foundation of therapy for greater clinical benefit.

Hormone-sensitive breast cancer can be effectively treated with agents that reduce the stimulation of tumor cells by estrogen. For the past 25 years, the estrogen antagonist tamoxifen has been the established as the first-line treatment of hormone-sensitive metastatic breast cancer, and as adjuvant therapy for early breast cancer in patients with hormone receptor-positive tumors. Although an effective treatment, there are limitations to its use due to its partial agonist activity in some tissues; this partial activity results in an increased incidence of endometrial cancer and thromboembolic disease and may be involved in the development of resistance to tamoxifen.[3,4] More than 80% of breast cancer cases occur in women over the age of 50 years, and for such women, one of the new alternatives to tamoxifen is the use of a third-generation aromatase inhibitor (AI) to suppress the concentration of endogenous estrogens to extremely low levels, thus preventing estrogen from reaching the tumor. Approximately 75% of postmenopausal patients have hormone receptor-positive tumors that undergo estrogen-dependent proliferation.[5] Several therapeutic strategies have been developed to deprive the tumor of estrogen stimulation, either by modulating the estrogen receptor (ER)-signaling pathway or by lowering serum or tumor concentrations of estradiol.[6] In postmenopausal women, ovarian estrogen production diminishes with age, and low levels of circulating estrogens are derived by aromatization of androgens in peripheral tissues including skin, adipose tissue, and breast tissue (including malignant breast tumors)[7] (Figure 21–1). Stromal cells in breast adipose tissue produce estrogen that is biologically active in both a paracrine and autocrine manner, and there is increasing evidence that breast tumor cells themselves produce estrogens that may play a major role in tumor proliferation.[8–10] AIs inhibit the cytochrome P-450 enzyme complex aromatase that catalyzes the final step in estrogen synthesis, the conversion of androstenedione and testosterone into estrone and estradiol, respectively.[10,11] In postmenopausal women, AIs act to suppress estrogen synthesis, thereby reducing local and distant estrogen levels.[8,12,13] AIs are indicated for the treatment of breast cancer in women whose ovarian function has ceased either due to the menopause or oophorectomy. The first-generation AI aminoglutethimide became available in the late 1970s, but despite proven efficacy, its widespread use was limited by its overall toxicity and lack of selectivity for the aromatase enzyme, necessitating concomitant corticosteroid supplementation.[14] Formestane, an

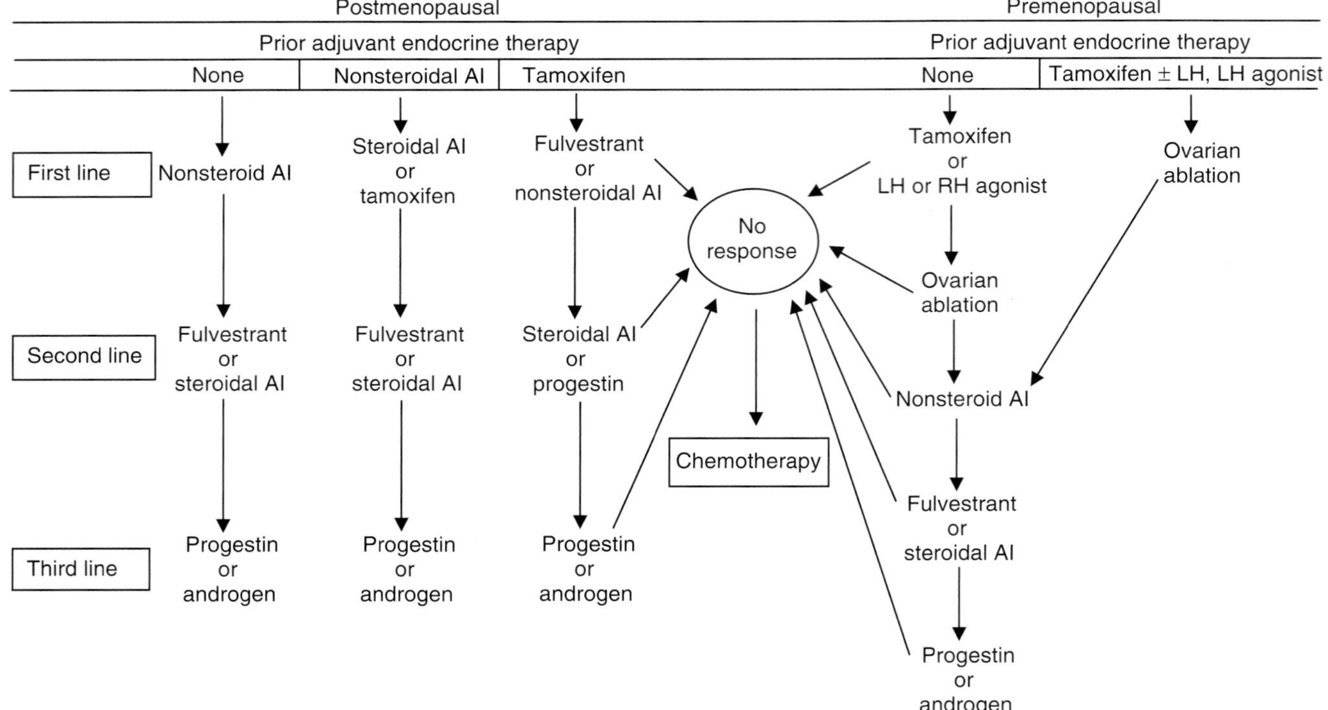

Figure 21–1. Steroid hormone synthesis. Reproduced with permission from Singletary SE, Robb GI, Hortobagyi G, editors. Advanced Therapy of Breast Disease, 2nd edition, BC Decker, Hamilton, Ontario. 2004.

effective and more specific aromatase inhibitor, became available in 1993. Due to its specificity, formestane has fewer side effects than aminoglutethimide. However, it does not provide complete and consistent suppression of estrogen synthesis because of extensive first-pass metabolism.[15] The third-generation AIs can be divided into two classes: nonsteroidal drugs such as anastrozole and letrozole, and steroidal drugs such as exemestane. Whereas aminoglutethimide and second-generation compounds inhibit aromatase by 85 to 90%, anastrozole, letrozole, and exemestane are highly selective for the enzyme and effectively inhibit aromatase by 97 to 99% in postmenopausal women.[12,13,16,17] Preliminary data have indicated that letrozole and anastrozole may exert different potencies with respect to aromatase inhibition and estrogen suppression. Letrozole has been shown to lower aromatase activity, and to lower plasma estrone and estrone sulfate levels to a greater extent than anastrozole; however, the effects on plasma concentrations of estradiol are similar for both agents.[13] In a recent open-label trial, there was no significant difference between letrozole and anastrozole for the primary efficacy endpoint of time to progression (TTP). Of the secondary end points (objective response [OR] rate, duration of response rate, rate and duration of overall clinical benefit [CB], time to treatment failure [TTF], and overall survival [OS]), only the OR rate was significantly different between treatments (19.1% versus 12.3% for letrozole and anastrozole, respectively; $p = .013$). However, when patients with confirmed hormone receptor-positive tumors only were evaluated, the two treatment groups had similar OR rates (letrozole 17.3% versus anastrozole 16.8%).[18] Small changes in potency between anastrozole and letrozole do not appear to be associated with clinically relevant differences in efficacy, suggesting the existence of a threshold of aromatase inhibition, above which no further improvements in clinical efficacy may be gained. However, this does not preclude differences in side-effect profiles between agents. The three third-generation AIs (anastrozole, letrozole, and exemestane) and one second-generation AI (fadrozole, only available in Japan) are available for the treatment of breast cancer.

METASTATIC BREAST CANCER ENDOCRINE THERAPY

The treatment schema for the management of metastatic breast cancer with various endocrine therapies as used at M.D. Anderson is shown in Figure 21–2.

Ovarian Ablation

Ovarian function can be ablated by surgical intervention, irradiation, or by pharmacologic intervention. Although each treatment modality results in a similar response rate, surgical ablation is the fastest means of removing the source of estrogen.[6] It does require a procedure that may be accomplished laparoscopically. One of its disadvantages is that it is an irreversible procedure. Radiation ablation is a somewhat slower process and some of the scatter from the irradiation may cause gastrointestinal and bone marrow disturbances.

Lutinizing Hormone-Releasing Hormone (LHRH) Agonists

These agents, also known as gonadotropin-releasing hormone agonists, result in a suppression of ovarian function that is comparable to surgical ablation. LHRH agonists reduce the estrogen release by providing a constant high level of pituitary-releasing hormone and shutting down the gonadotropin production. Several different forms of LHRH agonists are available, but only goserelin acetate is approved for treatment of metastatic disease in premenopausal women. There are very limited data that LHRH inhibitors have activity in postmenopausal women. It may be due to a direct antitumor effect, as some tumors have LHRH receptors.[6]

LHRH agonist administration may cause an initial rise in gonadotropin levels and may be associated with tumor flare. Chronic administration of the drug is associated with serum levels of estrogen and progesterone that are comparable to those detected in postmenopausal and oophorectomized women. LHRH agonists are now available in a slow-release format that may be injected at 1- to 3-month intervals. OR rates are comparable to ablative surgical procedures.

Progestins

Progestins are synthetic derivatives of progesterone with a progesterone agonist effect. Progestins such as megestrol acetate and medroxyprogesterone acetate are effective in treatment of metastatic disease. Their exact mechanism of action is unknown.[6] They have

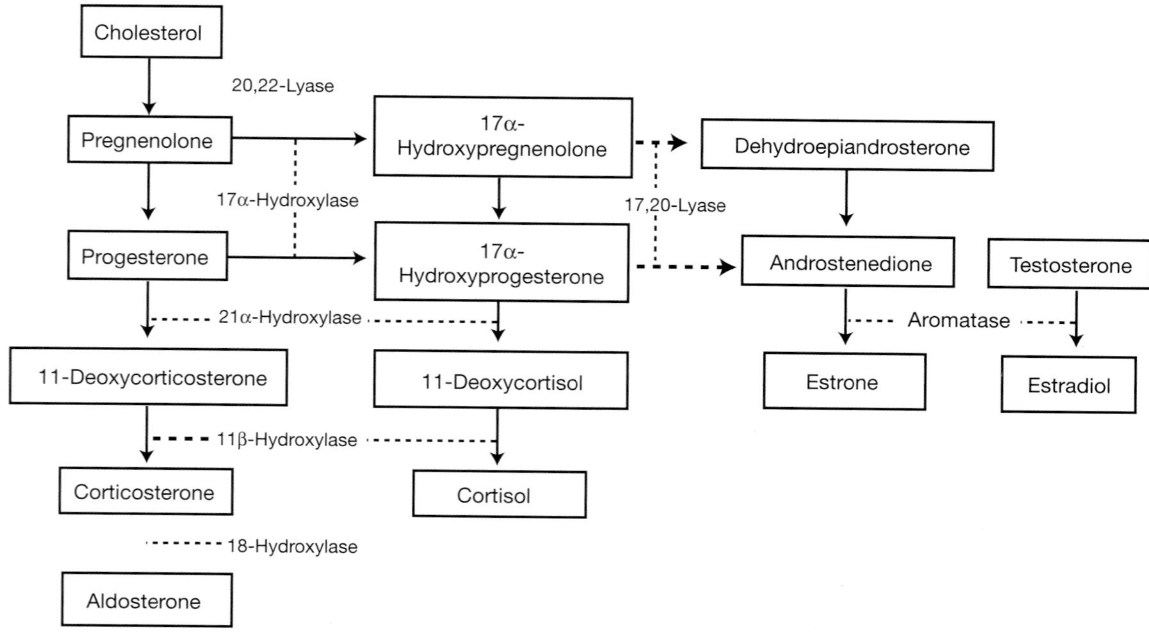

Figure 21–2. Sequence of treatment for patients with metastatic disease.

antiestrogenic properties and may result in interruption of the pituitary-ovarian axis. It has also been suggested that increased levels of progestin may mimic pregnancy. Invitro progestins have direct cytotoxic effects. Progestins were extensively evaluated and used as a second-line therapy, but were associated with a number of side effects, including dyspnea, vaginal bleeding, nausea, fluid retention, hot flashes, skin rashes, and thromboembolic complications. Megestrol acetate is the only Food and Drug Administration approved progestin for the treatment of advanced breast cancer. These agents may be used as a second-line therapy for palliation of metastatic disease. With the availability of aromatase inhibitors, progestins have been moved down in the sequential therapy of this disease (see Figure 21–2).

Androgens have been evaluated and are still used as a fourth-line therapy in patients with metastatic breast cancer.

Second-Line Therapy of Metastatic Disease

Third-generation AIs were initially shown to be effective in several studies conducted in postmenopausal women with advanced breast cancer, who had progressed on tamoxifen or other antiestrogens (Table 21–1). Based on a combined analysis of two large multicenter phase III studies, treatment with anastrozole 1 mg resulted in a statistically significant advantage over the progestin megestrol acetate in terms of OS at a median follow-up of 31 months.[19–21] Letrozole 2.5 mg was superior to aminoglutethimide for TTP, TTF, and OS[22]; however, when compared with megestrol acetate, there were some inconsistencies in study results. Data from one US study did not replicate the previously observed statistical superiority of letrozole 2.5 mg versus megestrol acetate for OR or TTF that was demonstrated in a European study.[23,24] In both studies, there was no significant difference between letrozole 2.5 mg and megestrol acetate in terms of OS, although a trend was noted at the nonclinical dose of letrozole 0.5 mg (hazard ratio (HR), 0.79; 95% CI, 0.62–1.00; p = .053). There are no mature survival data available for exemestane. However, initial analysis at a median follow-up of 11.3 months demonstrated a significant increase in TTP and a survival advantage for exemestane compared with megestrol acetate.[25] In all of these trials, anastrozole, letrozole, and exemestane were well tolerated and showed a significant advantage over conventional treatment in at least one tolerability parameter. Of particular note is that weight gain was more common in patients who received megestrol acetate compared with those who received an AI.

Another alternative endocrine treatment available for patients who had been treated with tamoxifen is fulvestrant. This drug is an estrogen receptor antagonist, which downregulates estrogen and progesterone receptors, and has no known agonist activity. Fulvestrant has been shown to be as efficacious as anastrozole in patients progressing on tamoxifen, and it has been approved in the United States for the treatment of postmenopausal women with hormone receptor-positive metastatic breast cancer following progression on antiestrogen therapy.[26–28]

First-Line Therapy for Metastatic Breast Cancer

Based on the use of AIs as second-line therapy, several randomized trials have been conducted to assess their effectiveness, compared with tamoxifen, for the first-line treatment of hormone-sensitive advanced breast cancer in postmenopausal women (Table 21–2, page 344). Anastrozole was the first AI to be studied in this setting in a prospectively planned combined analysis of the North American and Tamoxifen or Arimidex Randomized Group Efficacy and Tolerability (TARGET) trials.[29,30] Results showed that in the overall population, anastrozole was equivalent to tamoxifen in terms of TTP, OR, CB, TTF, and OS (see Table 21–2).[31,32] However, when the clinically relevant population was considered in a retrospective subgroup analysis of patients with ER- and/or progesterone receptor (PgR)-positive tumors, anastrozole was significantly superior to tamoxifen with respect to TTP (median values of 10.7 and 6.4 months for anastrozole and tamoxifen, respectively; two-sided p = .022).[31] Both treatments were well tolerated, with anastrozole leading to significantly fewer venous thromboembolic events (3.6% versus 6.5% for anastrozole and tamoxifen, respectively; p = .043), and fewer reports of vaginal

Table 21–1. SUMMARY OF KEY EFFICACY RESULTS FROM TRIALS OF AROMATASE INHIBITORS VERSUS MEGESTROL ACETATE OR AMINOGLUTETHIMIDE IN SECOND-LINE THERAPY OF ADVANCED BREAST CANCER

	Anastrozole			Letrozole									Exemestane		
	Combined Analysis of European* and North American† Trials[21]			International Trial[22]			European Trial[24]			US Trial[23]			International Trial[25]		
Study Arm	Anastrozole 1 mg (n = 263)	Megestrol Acetate (n = 253)	p Value	Letrozole 2.5 mg (n = 185)	Amino-glutethimide (n = 178)	p Value	Letrozole 2.5 mg (n = 174)	Megestrol Acetate (n = 189)	p Value	Letrozole 2.5 mg (n = 199)	Megestrol Acetate (n = 201)	p Value	Exemestane 25 mg (n = 366)	Megestrol Acetate (n = 403)	p Value
Median follow-up (months)	31			20			33			37			11		
ORR (CR+PR) (%)	12.5	12.2	N/A	19.5	12.4	N/A	24	16	.04	16	15	.75	15.0	12.4	N/S
Median TTP (months)	4.8	4.6	.49	3.4	3.2	.008	5.6	5.5	.07	3	3	.906	4.7	3.8	.037
Median TTF (months)	N/A	N/A	N/A	N/A	N/A	N/A	5.1	3.9	.04	3	3	.689	3.8	3.6	.042
Median OS (months)	26.7	22.5	< .025	28	20	.002	25.3	21.5	N/A	29	26	.492	NR	28.5	.039

CR = complete response; N/A = not available; NR = not reached; NS = not significant; ORR = objective response rate; OS = overall survival; PR = partial response; TTF = time to treatment failure; TTP = time to progression.

*European trial.[19]

†North American trial.[20]

bleeding compared with tamoxifen (1.0% versus 2.2% for anastrozole and tamoxifen, respectively).[31] An initial survival analysis at a median of 43.7 months follow-up showed that anastrozole was non-inferior to tamoxifen in terms of OS in both the overall population (56.0% and 56.1% patients in the anastrozole and tamoxifen groups had died, respectively; HR, 1.00; lower 95% CI, 0.84) and the ER- and/or PgR-positive subgroups (55.1% and 55.9% patients in the anastrozole and tamoxifen groups had died, respectively; HR, 1.00; lower 95% CI, 0.83).[32] Taken together, the favorable profile of anastrozole with respect to TTP and tolerability supports the use of anastrozole as a first-line therapy in postmenopausal women with hormone-sensitive advanced breast cancer.[32,33] Recently, an efficacy update of a phase III trial with letrozole has confirmed the superiority of letrozole over tamoxifen for TTP (Figure 21–3), TTF, overall OR rate, and overall CB, although OS was not significantly higher with letrozole compared with tamoxifen (see Table 21–2).[34,35] In the primary analysis (overall median duration of study, 18 months), the frequency of adverse events suspected to be related to the study drug were similar between treatments (38% for letrozole and 37% for tamoxifen).[35] Based on their excellent activity as first- and second-line therapies in the metastatic disease setting, the third-generation AIs have been under evaluation in the adjuvant setting.

In a randomized trial, there was no significant difference in TTP between the group administered fulvestrant (250 mg intramuscular injection, once monthly) as a first-line therapy and the tamoxifen (20 mg daily) group (median, 6.8 versus 8.3 months; HR, 1.18; 95% CI, 0.98–1.44; $p = .088$). In patients with ER-positive and/or PgR-positive tumors, there was no significant difference in TTP (median TTP, fulvestrant versus tamoxifen, 8.2 versus 8.3 months; HR, 1.10; 95% CI, 0.89–1.36; $p = .388$), CB (fulvestrant versus tamoxifen, 57.1% versus 62.7%; $p = .218$), and OR (fulvestrant versus tamoxifen, 33.2% versus 31.1%; $p = .637$) between the fulvestrant and tamoxifen groups.[36] Further evaluation is necessary to define the most appropriate patient population for this drug in the first-line setting.

Preoperative Hormonal Therapy

In the adjuvant setting, endocrine therapy has been shown to significantly reduce the risk of breast cancer and death in patients with early disease.[37] Studies comparing endocrine therapy with chemotherapy alone have shown that endocrine therapy is a better choice in the adjuvant setting, resulting in improved

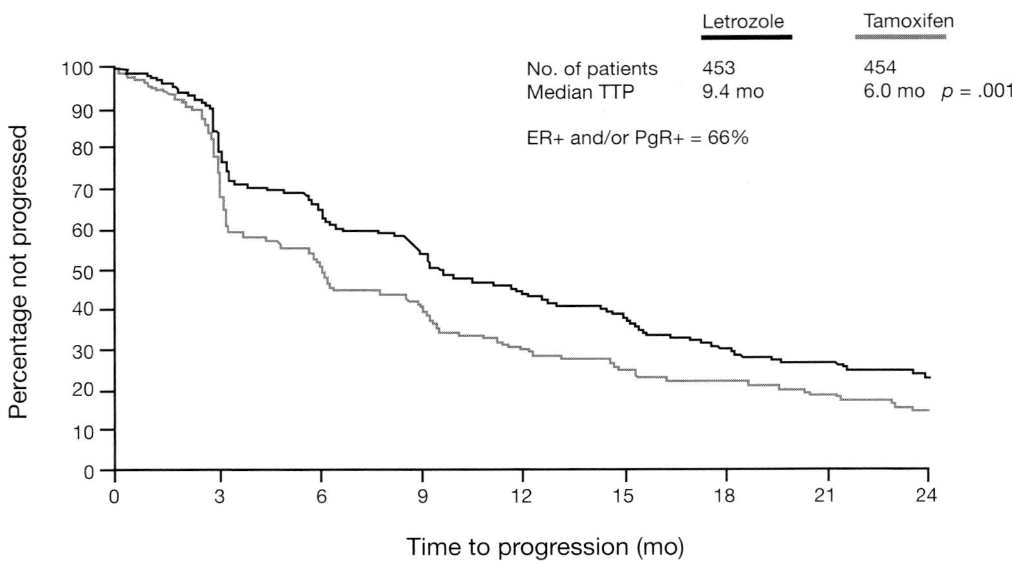

Figure 21–3. Kaplan-Meir curve of the probability of time to progression (TTP) in patients receiving letrozole or tamoxifen once daily. ER+ = estrogen receptor positive; PgR+ = progesterone receptor positive. Reproduced with permission from Mouridsen H et al.[35]

disease-free and overall survival.[38–40] Tamoxifen has been the established endocrine treatment for postmenopausal women with hormone-sensitive early breast cancer for more than 20 years. As a consequence, tamoxifen has been investigated as an alternative to initial surgery in elderly patients with locally advanced or operable breast cancer in several phase III randomized trials. Two studies compared surgery without tamoxifen versus tamoxifen without initial surgery.[41,42] Two additional studies compared tamoxifen versus immediate surgery followed by adjuvant tamoxifen.[43–45] These studies have shown that immediate surgery confers improved local control over tamoxifen, whereas patients treated with tamoxifen had fewer metastatic relapses and an equivalent survival.[41–45] To date, relatively few well-controlled clinical trials have investigated the option of using endocrine therapy prior to, rather than in place of, surgery. The IMmediate Preoperative 'Arimidex,' tamoxifen, or Combined with Tamoxifen (IMPACT) trial has been conducted to compare anastrozole with tamoxifen, or a combination of both anastrozole and tamoxifen, as preoperative treatment of ER-positive operable breast cancer (including locally advanced tumors) in postmenopausal women.[46] A total of 330 ER-positive postmenopausal patients were randomized among the three treatment arms. All patients received 3 months of preoperative therapy with anastrozole, tamoxifen, or both. Results from this trial indicated that for those patients requiring mastectomy at study entry, treatment with preoperative anastrozole was more likely to downstage tumors, thereby enabling more patients to have breast-conserving surgery, compared with tamoxifen alone. The efficacy of preoperative anastrozole therapy has been confirmed in the PReOperative Arimidex Compared with Tamoxifen (PROACT) trial.[47] In this study, significant improvements in actual surgery were observed in 262 postmenopausal women with large, operable, or potentially operable locally advanced hormone receptor-positive tumors, who were treated with anastrozole therapy alone (no additional preoperative chemotherapy) compared with tamoxifen. In a prospectively planned combined analysis of the IMPACT and PROACT trials ($n = 535$), significantly more patients treated with preoperative anastrozole therapy experienced improvement in both feasible and actual surgery, confirming that anastrozole is more effective than tamoxifen in the preoperative setting.[48] Several clinical trials have also investigated the use of other third-generation AIs as preoperative therapy. An ongoing clinical trial has compared 3 months of preoperative exemestane with tamoxifen in 73 postmenopausal patients with hormone receptor-positive breast cancer. A preliminary report has shown that exemestane is effective and well tolerated when used as preoperative therapy in hormone receptor-positive breast cancer.[49] A randomized, double-blind, multicenter study compared 4 months of preoperative letrozole therapy with tamoxifen in 337 postmenopausal women with ER- and/or PgR-positive primary breast cancer.[50] Patients treated with letrozole were more likely to have breast-conserving surgery than those treated with tamoxifen.[50] These results were comparable with the breast conservation rates in the IMPACT and PROACT trials.[46,47] Letrozole has also been shown to inhibit tumor proliferation to a greater extent than tamoxifen, with the tumor response to letrozole shown to be related to the ER and PgR status of the tumor.[51,52] Overall, these trials show that the use of preoperative AI therapy is emerging as a valuable option for the treatment of postmenopausal women with hormone receptor-positive tumors.

The presence of hormone receptor-positive tumors is predictive of a good response to endocrine therapy, and this variable is important in the selection of preoperative endocrine therapy in postmenopausal patients.[53] Although chemotherapy has been used irrespective of ER status, the influence of ER status on response to chemotherapy remains unclear. Recently, a retrospective analysis of complete pathologic remission (pCR) rates with respect to tumor ER status in 1,292 patients treated with preoperative chemotherapy was performed. pCR rates after preoperative anthracycline therapy, with or without taxanes, were higher in patients with ER-negative tumors compared with those with ER-positive disease.[54] Tumor ER status may therefore alter the efficacy of preoperative endocrine therapy or chemotherapy, although randomized studies are needed to define their relative efficacy. Preoperative endocrine therapy appears to be effective in downstaging breast tumors. In addition, this treatment approach has the potential to provide predictive markers for adjuvant endocrine therapy outcomes, and offers an attractive alternative to preoperative chemotherapy. Studies in the preoperative setting have shown that response rates may be higher in postmenopausal patients treated with AIs compared with tamoxifen.[46–50,55] In the preoperative setting, improved selection and administration of therapy regimens, optimal sequencing and scheduling of endocrine therapy with or without chemotherapy, and the appropriate use of patient and tumor characteristics may increase the therapeutic advantage with currently available treatments. Appropriate prospective studies are needed to define appropriate therapeutic candidates for either preoperative endocrine, chemotherapy, or combination therapy, and to identify which patients will benefit from these therapies.

OVARIAN ABLATION AS ADJUVANT THERAPY

Ovarian ablation, through surgical oophorectomy or ovarian irradiation, is an effective treatment for premenopausal women with early breast cancer. In a meta-analysis conducted by the Early Breast Cancer Trialists' Collaborative Group (EBCTCG), women less than 50 years of age had a significant disease-free survival (DFS) and OS advantage with ovarian ablation compared with women receiving no adjuvant treatment.[56] These results were comparable to those found in a similar analysis of patients who received adjuvant chemotherapy.[57] The major disadvantage of oophorectomy or ovarian irradiation for premenopausal patients is the morbidity and mortality associated with these procedures and their irreversibility. Therefore, the LHRH agonists, which produce medical ovarian ablation, have been developed for the treatment of breast cancer in premenopausal women, avoiding the potential complications associated with surgery and radiation. This therapy allows patients to maintain their ovarian function after completion of their LHRH agonist adjuvant therapy. The most extensively studied LHRH agonist in both the advanced and early breast cancer setting is goserelin acetate, a decapeptide analogue of LHRH. Other LHRH agonists (leuprolide and triptorelin) are available in the United States and are currently undergoing trials in many diseases including breast cancer. Several phase III trials have been conducted and are summarized below.

Goserelin as an Alternative to Chemotherapy

The Zoladex Early Breast Cancer Research Association (ZEBRA) trial investigated the effect of goserelin in pre/perimenopausal women with early breast cancer (n = 1,640). Patients were randomized to receive either goserelin for 2 years or CMF (cyclophosphamide, methotrexate, 5-fluorouracil) for 6 cycles.[58]

In the ER-positive patients, DFS was not better with goserelin compared with CMF (p = .597), whereas for ER-negative patients, DFS demonstrated goserelin to be inferior to CMF (p = .0001). At the time of the updated analysis, 28% of the patients had died. Overall survival for the entire population illustrated no difference with goserelin compared with CMF (p = .137). ER-positive patients showed noninferiority of goserelin compared with CMF (p = .622), whereas ER-negative patients continued to demonstrate significantly better OS with CMF compared with goserelin (p = .009), thus confirming the lack of efficacy of hormonal treatment for such tumors.

Three years after treatment, menses returned in the majority of women randomized to goserelin (compared with only 23% who remained amenorrheic). Seventy-seven percent of patients treated with CMF maintained amenorrhea, suggesting permanent ovarian ablation. Return of menses did not impact the recurrence rate or OS in this patient population. This trial established goserelin as an effective alternative for the treatment of early breast cancer in premenopausal, node-positive, and ER-positive patients.

Goserelin Plus Tamoxifen as an Alternative to Chemotherapy

Australian Breast Cancer Study Group (ABCSG) Trial

The ABCSG 05 trial was set up to compare DFS and OS among premenopausal women with hormone receptor-positive or -negative, node-positive or -negative early breast cancer.[59] Patients received

CMF for 6 cycles or goserelin for 3 years plus tamoxifen for 5 years. At a median follow-up of 5 years, only 9% of patients had died from breast cancer, and survival differences between the two treatments were not significant (p = .19). Overall survival was not significantly different between the endocrine arm and the chemotherapy group (p = .195). The authors concluded that goserelin plus tamoxifen is more effective and better tolerated than CMF as adjuvant therapy in premenopausal women with hormone-sensitive breast cancer.

GROCTA 02 Trial

The Gruppo di Recerca in Oncoloia Clinica E Terapioe Associate (GROCTA) 02 Trial was a randomized study comparing chemotherapy (CMF) with ovarian suppression (either with goserelin for 2 years, or ovarian irradiation) plus tamoxifen (20 mg orally daily) in premenopausal women for 5 years.[60] A total of 120 patients were randomized to CMF and 124 patients were randomized to goserelin plus tamoxifen. This trial demonstrated that the combination of hormonal therapy plus ovarian suppression was safe and effective in ER-positive patients with early breast cancer.

Ovarian Suppression in Women Who Maintained Ovarian Function after Chemotherapy

Zoladex in Premenopausal Patients (ZIPP) Trial

The ZIPP analysis involved a combination of data from randomized trials initiated by four international collaborative groups. Premenopausal patients were randomized to one of four groups: goserelin for 2 years, tamoxifen for 2 years, goserelin for 2 years plus tamoxifen for 2 years, or no further endocrine therapy. Results to date have only been published in abstract form. With a median follow-up of 4.3 years, initial results show that patients who receive goserelin in addition to standard chemotherapy compared with no goserelin had a significant decrease in the risk of recurrence (20% versus 25%, respectively; p < .001).[61] A benefit in OS was not demonstrated to be statistically significant (11% versus 12%, respectively; p = .12).

INT-0101

Intergroup trial (INT)-0101 was designed to investigate the effect of adjuvant chemohormonal therapy in patients with hormone receptor-positive (ER- and/or PgR-positive), node-positive breast tumors.[62] Patients were randomized to chemotherapy (cyclophosphamide, doxorubicin, and 5-fluorouracil), chemotherapy plus goserelin for 5 years, or chemotherapy plus goserelin for 5 years plus tamoxifen for 5 years. After 6 years of median follow-up, results showed significant benefit in 5-year DFS for only the triplet arm compared with the other groups. Patients treated with chemotherapy plus goserelin had similar DFS compared with patients receiving chemotherapy alone, thus the value of goserelin alone in this study remains unclear. Overall survival was similar among all three groups. In patients < 40 years of age, the relative benefit in DFS with triplet therapy was particularly marked (72% versus 65% for chemotherapy plus goserelin versus 54% with chemotherapy alone), although this may be due in part to the fact that a high fraction of this subset of women maintained ovarian function in spite of chemotherapy. One limitation of the study was that a chemotherapy plus tamoxifen alone arm was not included, which would be considered standard of care.

International Breast Cancer Study Group (IBCSG) Trial

The IBCSG VIII trial randomized 1,063 premenopausal women with node-negative, hormone receptor-positive or -negative breast cancer, to one of four treatment arms.[63] Following surgery, patients were randomized to either chemotherapy (CMF for 6 cycles), goserelin alone for 2 years, CMF for 6 cycles plus goserelin for 18 months, or no adjuvant systemic treatment. During the course of this trial, the control arm (no treatment) was dropped because of results from other ongoing trials. Results have recently been published with a median follow-up of 7 years. No differences among the three treatment arms were observed for DFS. Five-year DFS for 6 cycles of CMF was 82% (95% CI, 78–86%). With 6 cycles of CMF followed by goserelin for 18 months, DFS was 87% (95% CI, 83–91%). With goserelin alone, DFS was 79% (95% CI, 75–84%). In patients with ER-positive disease, those treated with either 6 cycles of CMF or with goserelin had equivalent 5-year DFS (81%: 95% CI, 76–87%; 81%: 95% CI, 76–87%, respectively). With the sequential administration of CMF followed by goserelin, the 5-year DFS was 86% (95% CI, 82–91%). Cumulative data of the three treatment arms resulted in a significantly longer DFS compared with the no-treatment arm (77% versus 60%; $p = .02$). One limitation of the study was that none of the arms included tamoxifen, because at the time of the study conception, it was suggested that tamoxifen would not be beneficial in women less than 50 years of age.[64] More detailed results and other studies need to be compared to better understand if triplet therapy (chemotherapy plus ovarian suppression plus other endocrine agents) is better than either chemotherapy alone or chemotherapy combined with tamoxifen.

A number of ongoing trials will help us to better understand treatment options. In summary, these trials demonstrate that ovarian suppression is an effective means of reducing risk of recurrence in ER-positive patients. The results of these studies support the point that ovarian suppression may be used as an alternative to chemotherapy in this subset of patients. It should be emphasized that, unfortunately, many of the trials included ER-negative patients, and in many of the trials, tamoxifen was not included. Whenever tamoxifen was added, it was not in the chemotherapy arm but generally added to the ovarian suppression arm.

Mam-1 GOCSI Trial

This study ($n = 446$) randomized node-positive, premenopausal women to CMF (Group A), doxorubicin followed by CMF (Group B), CMF followed by goserelin plus tamoxifen (Group C), and doxorubicin followed by CMF followed by goserelin plus tamoxifen (Group D). Planned comparisons for the rate of relapse were Groups A and C versus Groups B and D, and Groups A and B versus Groups C and D. After a median follow-up of 5 years and adjusting for tumor size, number of lymph nodes, and hormone receptor status, there was no difference in DFS between the anthracycline-containing arms compared with the non–anthracycline-containing arms (HR, 0.86; $p = .42$). There was, however, a significant difference in DFS between the goserelin plus tamoxifen-containing arms versus the chemotherapy-alone arms (HR, 0.71; $p = .04$). No differences were demonstrated in OS with the anthracycline-containing arms versus the non—anthracycline-containing arms (HR, 0.79; $p = .31$) and goserelin plus tamoxifen-containing arms versus the chemotherapy-alone arms (HR, 0.86; $p = .52$).[65] From this limited data, it can be concluded that DFS is superior for patients receiving chemoendocrine treatment compared with chemotherapy alone in premenopausal patients with breast cancer. No report on OS was published.

Selective Estrogen Receptor Modulators as Adjuvant Therapy

Tamoxifen as Monotherapy

In 1986, tamoxifen was approved as monotherapy for the treatment of early breast cancer in node-positive postmenopausal women. The Nolvadex Adjuvant Trial Organisation (NATO) conducted one of the earliest trials identifying tamoxifen's benefit in delaying recurrence.[66] Patients were randomized to tamoxifen 10 mg twice daily for 2 years ($n = 559$) versus no further therapy ($n = 565$) after definitive surgery (total mastectomy with either axillary nodal clearance or sampling). The mean follow-up was 21 months. Significantly fewer events defined as first recurrence of breast cancer, including contralateral disease, or death without confirmed recurrence, occurred in the tamoxifen group compared with the no-treatment arm (14.2% versus 20.5%, respectively; $p = .01$). At that time, many questions surfaced regarding tamoxifen. Does tamoxifen work in both node-negative and -positive diseases? Does tamoxifen work in ER-positive and -negative diseases? Does tamoxifen work in both pre- and postmenopausal patients? How long should one treat with tamoxifen? These questions were answered in subsequent trials.

The Stockholm trial was designed for patients to receive either no adjuvant hormonal therapy or tamoxifen 40 mg/day for 2 years in node-negative postmenopausal patients.[67] During the course of the study, the question was raised as to what the appropriate length of tamoxifen therapy should be. This sparked a new trial in which patients who were disease free at 2 years were randomized to either discontinue therapy or continue with tamoxifen for a total of 5 years. After a median follow-up of 7 years, tamoxifen exhibited significant prolongation of DFS compared with the control arm ($p < .01$) and fewer deaths ($p = .02$). Survival (when analyzing all causes of death) was not statistically significantly better with tamoxifen ($p = .11$). Tamoxifen benefit was documented in only ER-positive patients.

In a further follow-up of 5 years, the event-free survival and OS were statistically significant for the 5-year tamoxifen group ($p = .03$ versus $p = .009$, respectively). Benefit was shown regardless of lymph node status.[67]

The Scottish trialists group conducted two tamoxifen trials. The first study consisted of 1,312 patients being randomized to tamoxifen for 5 years versus tamoxifen for the treatment until first relapse (control arm).[68] At a median follow-up of 47 months, 157 patients (24%) in the tamoxifen arm and 250 patients (38%) in the control arm had developed recurrent disease. The delay in recurrence rate was evident regardless of nodal status. DFS and OS were statistically significant in the tamoxifen arm compared with the control arm ($p < .0001$ versus $p = .002$, respectively).

Another question that the investigators wanted to answer was the optimal duration of therapy. Patients who received tamoxifen for 5 years were allowed randomization to stop therapy ($n = 169$) or to continue tamoxifen until relapse ($n = 173$). Fifteen-year follow-up results have now been published.[69] The median duration of tamoxifen for the 5-year group was 60 months (range, 56–205) and in the continuation arm it was 163 months (range, 58–205). Overall survival was statistically significantly better in patients taking tamoxifen for 5 years compared with those allocated to continue tamoxifen until recurrence (HR, 0.78; $p = .006$). This trial clearly defined the benefit of tamoxifen when given for 5 years.

The NSABP B-14 trial evaluated ER-positive, node-negative patients given either 5 years or > 5 years of tamoxifen.[3] During the first randomization of tamoxifen versus placebo for 5 years, distant disease-free survival (DDFS) was 76% for tamoxifen compared with 67% for placebo ($p < .0001$). Overall survival was significantly improved for the 5-year tamoxifen arm ($p = .02$) during the 5 to 10 years of follow-up. Disease-free survival regardless of age (< 50 years or > 50 years) was statistically significant.

The duration question was tested when patients who had received 5 years of tamoxifen were randomized to 5 more years of tamoxifen (total 10 years; $n = 583$) or placebo (total 5 years; $n = 570$). With a 4-year follow-up, DFS was significantly longer for those who were switched from tamoxifen to placebo (92% versus 86%, respectively) in those patients who continued tamoxifen for 10 years ($p = .003$). Patients treated with 5 years of tamoxifen experienced fewer recurrences compared with those assigned to the longer-treatment arm. Safety profiles were also more favorable in those patients treated with 5 years of tamoxifen compared with those receiving 10 years of treatment.

The EBCTCG evaluated the largest comparison of tamoxifen with no tamoxifen in a meta-analysis of randomized trials.[56] Women were identified from trials of tamoxifen for early breast cancer prior to 1990. In women with ER-positive disease in the trials with 5 years of planned tamoxifen therapy, the annual recurrence rate was almost halved (recurrence rate ratio, 0.59; SE, 0.03) and the breast cancer mortality rate was reduced by a third (death rate ratio, 0.66; SE, 0.04). The proportional risk reductions produced by tamoxifen were independent of age, nodal status, and use of chemotherapy.

Other studies are continually evaluating the duration question. The Adjuvant Tamoxifen-Longer Against Shorter (ATLAS) and the adjuvant Tamoxifen Treatment offers more (aTTom) trials plan to recruit over 20,000 patients to further answer this question.[70,71]

Tamoxifen versus Toremifene

Toremifene, a triphenylethylene antiestrogen, was developed with the premise to demonstrate similar efficacy to tamoxifen but with fewer side effects.[72–74] Tamoxifen has been compared with toremifene in postmenopausal patients with node-positive breast cancer in the adjuvant setting.[75] Patients were randomized to receive tamoxifen 20 mg daily ($n = 440$) or toremifene 40 mg daily

($n = 459$) for 3 years. At the time of the analysis, the median follow-up was 3.4 years. Recurrence rates, OS, and side-effect profiles were not statistically significantly different between the groups.[75] The authors concluded that toremifene had similar efficacy and toxicity to tamoxifen in postmenopausal node-positive early breast cancer patients.

The IBCSG conducted two randomized trials of toremifene compared with tamoxifen for 5 years in a similar population of patients.[76] The IBCSG trials 12-93 and 14-93 randomized 1,035 patients. Seventy-nine percent of patients had ER-positive breast cancer. At 4.9 years of median follow-up, the results were not statistically significantly different, and toremifene was considered equivalent to tamoxifen in this setting.[76] Toremifene is not approved in the adjuvant setting.

Tamoxifen plus Chemotherapy

The addition of chemotherapy in the adjuvant setting requires the evaluation of many factors. The EBCTCG has conducted a meta-analysis of randomized trials to evaluate the treatment of breast cancer. In the latest published update, polychemotherapy plus tamoxifen continued to demonstrate a beneficial reduction of recurrence in ER-positive patients, regardless of age or menopausal status. Contralateral breast cancer and survival were also improved with combination therapy, irrespective of age and menopausal status.[56] Optimal sequences of treatment modalities have recently been evaluated, and patients offered antiestrogen therapy after completion of chemotherapy experienced fewer risks of recurrence compared with concomitant administration of the two modalities.[77]

AROMATASE INHIBITORS AS ADJUVANT THERAPY FOR EARLY BREAST CANCER

Studies of Aromatase Inhibitors versus Tamoxifen

'Arimidex,' Tamoxifen, Alone or in Combination (ATAC) Trial

The ongoing ATAC trial is the largest adjuvant breast cancer study in women with early disease to provide data on a third-generation AI versus tamoxifen in this setting.[78–80] A total of 9,366 postmenopausal women with early disease were enrolled in this prospective, double-blind trial and were randomized to receive anastrozole 1 mg alone, tamoxifen 20 mg alone, or a combination of anastrozole and tamoxifen.

The first analysis of the ATAC trial was performed at a median follow-up of 33 months.[79] In the overall population and in the known hormone receptor-positive group (defined as positive for ER or PgR), representing 84% of the total population, anastrozole was superior to tamoxifen with regard to DFS and TTR (Figures 21–4 and 21–5). Overall, anastrozole significantly reduced the incidence of contralateral breast cancer (CLBC) compared with tamoxifen (Figure 21–6). Efficacy data at a median follow-up of 68 months that have recently been reported from the ATAC trial reveal a significant benefit in favor of anastrozole over tamoxifen in terms of DFS (HR, 0.87; 95% CI, 0.78–0.97; $p = .01$), the incidence of CLBC (HR, 0.58; 95% CI, 0.38–0.88; $p = .01$), and the time-to-distant recurrence (HR, 0.86; 95% CI, 0.74–0.99; $p = .04$).[78,80] For patients with hormone receptor-positive disease, the hazard ratios were 0.83 (95% CI, 0.73–0.94; $p = .005$) for DFS, 0.47 (95% CI, 0.29–0.75; $p = .001$) for the CLBC, and 0.84 (95% CI, 0.70–1.00; $p = .06$) for the time-to-distant recurrence. A total of 831 women died: 500 (60%) after recurrence of breast cancer, and 331 (40%) without

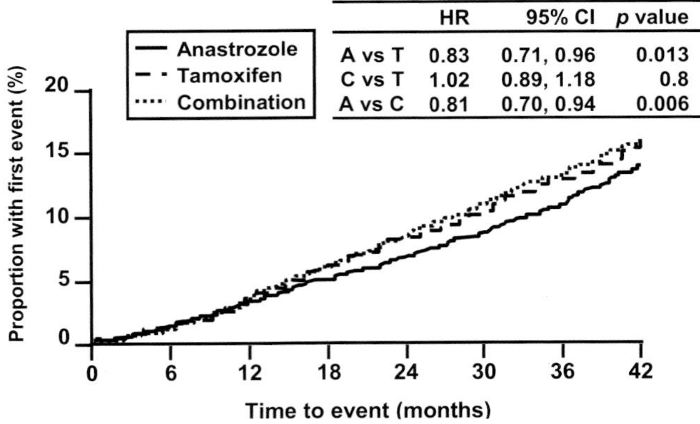

Figure 21–4. Probability of first even in the intention-to-treat population in the anastrozole, tamoxifen, and combination arms of the Arimidex (anastrozole), Tamoxifen, Alone or in Combination (ATAC) trial. A = anastrozole; C = combined anastrozole and tamoxifen; T = tamoxifen. Reproduced with permission from Baum M et al Lancet 2002;359:2131–9.

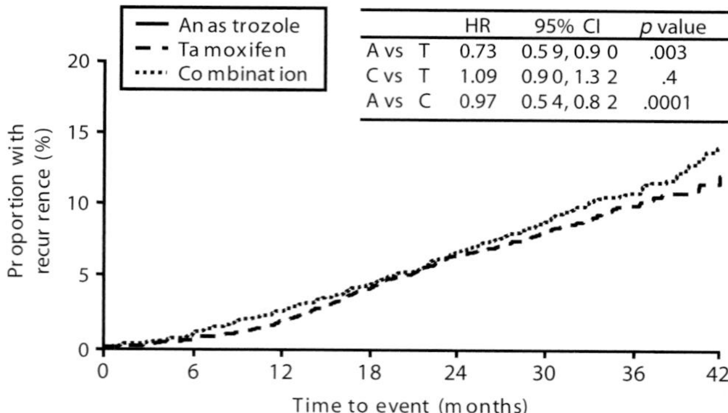

Figure 21–5. Probability of recurrence in the hormone-receptor-positive population in the anastrozole, tamoxifen, and combination arms of the Arimidex (anastrozole), Tamoxifen, Alone or in Combination (ATAC) trial. A = anastrozole; C = combined anastrozole and tamoxifen; T = tamoxifen. Reproduced with permission from Baum M et al Lancet 2002;359:2131–9.

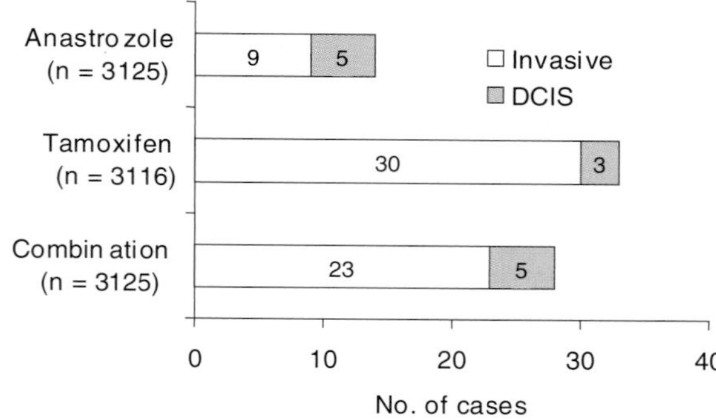

Anastrozole versus tamoxifen OR 0.42; 95% CI 0.22, 0.79; $p = .007$
Combination versus tamoxifen OR 0.84; 95% CI 0.51, 1.40; $p = .51$

DCIS = ductal carcinoma in situ; OR = odds ratio; CI = confidence interval

Figure 21–6. Incidence of new (contralateral) breast primaries in the intention-to-treat population in the anastrozole, tamoxifen, and combination arms of the Arimidex (anastrozole), Tamoxifen, Alone or in Combination (ATAC) trial. DCIS = ductal carcinoma in situ; OR = odds ratio. Reproduced with permission from Baum M et al Lancet 2002;359:2131–9.

recurrences and due to other causes. Of those patients that died without recurrences and due to other causes, 176 were in the anastrozole-treated group and 155 in the tamoxifen-treated group. The number of deaths due to cardiovascular events was similar between the two groups (49 for the anastrozole group and 46 for the tamoxifen group).[81] These long-term data, with the median duration of treatment exposure being a full 60 months, also confirm the safety and tolerability of anastrozole over tamoxifen that were reported in earlier analyses. The incidence of several of the predefined side effects was significantly lower in the anastrozole group compared with the tamoxifen group (endometrial cancer [0.2% versus 0.8%; $p = .02$], vaginal bleeding [5.4% versus 10.2%; $p < .0001$], ischemic cerebrovascular events [2.0% versus 2.8%; $p = .03$], venous thromboembolic events [2.8% versus 4.5%; $p = .0004$], and deep venous thromboembolic events [1.6% versus 2.4%; $p = .02$]). The increased gynecologic adverse events observed in the tamoxifen group ultimately resulted in a fourfold increase in the number of hysterectomies (1.35% in the anastrozole group versus 5.14% in the tamoxifen group; OR, 0.25; 95% CI, 0.17–0.38; $p < .0001$). Drug-related serious adverse events occurred significantly less frequently in the anastrozole group compared with the tamoxifen group (4.7% versus 9.0%; $p < .0001$). Withdrawals due to adverse events were also significantly less frequent in anastrozole patients compared with tamoxifen patients (11.1% versus 14.3%; $p = .0002$).

Fractures were less common in the tamoxifen group compared with the anastrozole group (11% versus 7.7%; $p < .0001$); however, the relative risk of fracture stayed constant throughout treatment. In addition, the rates of hip fracture were not significantly different between the groups (1.0% versus 1.2%; $p = .5$).[78,80]

Breast International Group (BIG) 1-98 Trial

The BIG 1-98 trial randomized 8,028 postmenopausal women with newly diagnosed hormone receptor-positive breast cancer and included two primary adjuvant arms comparing 5 years of letrozole with 5 years of tamoxifen and two sequential treatment arms (2 years of letrozole followed by 3 years of tamoxifen, and 2 years of tamoxifen followed by 3 years of letrozole). Patients from all four arms were included in the primary core analysis, but events in the sequential arms were only counted up to the time of the treatment switch plus 30 days. At a median follow-up of 25.8 months, a significant benefit was seen in favor of letrozole over tamoxifen in terms of DFS (HR, 0.81; 95% CI, 0.70–0.93; $p = .003$). There was a significantly greater incidence of bone fractures in the letrozole patients compared with the tamoxifen patients (OR, 1.44; $p = .0006$). Patients in the tamoxifen group had significantly more grades 3 to 5 thromboembolic events than patients in the

Table 21–2. SUMMARY OF KEY PUBLISHED EFFICACY RESULTS FROM PHASE III TRIALS OF AROMATASE INHIBITORS VERSUS TAMOXIFEN IN FIRST-LINE THERAPY OF ADVANCED BREAST CANCER

	Anastrozole						Letrozole		
	Combined Analysis of TARGET* and North American† Trials[31,32]			Single-Center Study[117]			International Trial[34]		
Study Arm	Anastrozole 1 mg (n = 511)	Tamoxifen (n = 510)	p Value	Anastrozole 1 mg (n = 121)	Tamoxifen (n = 117)	p Value	Letrozole 2.5 mg (n = 453)	Tamoxifen (n = 454)	p Value
Proportion of patients HR+ tumors (%)	60			100			65	67	
Median follow-up (months)	18			13			32		
ORR (CR + PR) (%)	29.0	27.1	NS	36	26	.172	32	21	.0002
CB (CR + PR + SD for 6 months)	57.1	52.0	.1129	83	56	.001	50	38	.0004
Median TTP (months)	8.5	7.0	.103	18.0	7.0	.01	9.4	6.0	< .0001
Median TTF (months)	N/A	N/A	N/A	N/A	N/A	N/A	9.0	5.7	< .0001
Median OS (months)	39.2‡	40.1‡	NS	17.4	16.0	.003	34	30	.53

CB = clinical benefit; CR = complete response; HR+ = hormone receptor-positive; N/A = not available; NR = not reached; NS = not significant; ORR = objective response rate; OS = overall survival; PR = partial response; TTF = time-to-treatment failure; TTP = time to progression.
*Tamoxifen or Arimidex Randomized Group Efficacy and Tolerability (TARGET) trial.[30]
†North American trial.[29]
‡Data reported after an extended median follow-up of 43.7 months.

letrozole group (OR, 0.38; $p < .0001$). The overall incidence of adverse events was similar in the two treatment groups. Fifty-five patients on letrozole and 38 patients on tamoxifen died without recurrence ($p = .08$); there were more cerebrovascular and cardiac deaths in patients receiving letrozole compared with those receiving tamoxifen (7 versus 1 and 26 versus 13, respectively).[82]

Studies of Adjuvant Aromatase Inhibitor Switching

Breast International Group (BIG) 97-02 Trial

Efficacy analysis. Recently, the results of the second planned interim analysis of the double-blind BIG 97-02 trial were reported.[83] This study enrolled 4,742 postmenopausal women with primary breast cancer, of which 2,362 patients were randomly assigned to switch to exemestane 25 mg after 2 to 3 years of tamoxifen therapy and 2,380 patients were to continue on tamoxifen 20 mg. At a median follow-up of 30.6 months, exemestane was shown to be superior to tamoxifen with regard to DFS, both in the overall study population and in patients with ER-positive tumors. The absolute difference in DFS in favor of exemestane was 4.7% (95% CI, 2.6–6.8) at 3 years. Exemestane significantly reduced the risk of CLBC (HR, 0.44; 95% CI, 0.20–0.98; $p = .04$), but was not associated with a survival benefit at this stage.

Safety analysis. Exemestane was associated with a slightly higher rate of discontinuation of treatment, and a higher incidence of arthralgia and diarrhea than tamoxifen.[83] There was also a suggestion of an increased incidence of osteoporosis and visual disturbances with exemestane and a trend toward increased fractures (3.1% versus 2.3% for exemestane versus tamoxifen, respectively; $p = .08$). However, gynecologic symptoms, vaginal bleeding, muscle cramps, and thromboembolic events were more common with tamoxifen. No significant differences between the exemestane and tamoxifen groups were observed in the incidence of hot flashes (42.0% versus 39.6%, respectively), endometrial cancer (data not available), and cardiovascular disease (42.6% versus 39.2%, respectively), although data for the incidence of myocardial infarction were not included in this analysis.[83]

Intergruppo Tamoxifen Anastrozole (ITA) Trial

Efficacy analysis. The ITA trial randomized 448 postmenopausal women with breast cancer, who had already received 2 to 3 years of tamoxifen therapy, to receive a further 2 to 3 years of tamoxifen (n = 225) or switch therapy to 2 to 3 years of anastrozole (n = 223), for a total of 5 years.[84] Hormone receptor status was unknown for 8% of those who switched to anastrozole and for 14% who continued on tamoxifen. At a median follow-up of 36 months, there was a significant difference in event-free survival (17 events in the anastrozole group and 45 in the tamoxifen group; $p = .0002$) and recurrence-free survival ($p = .001$), which favored the anastrozole treatment group. There was no significant difference in mortality between the treatment groups, probably due to the small number of deaths observed to date (4 in the anastrozole group and 10 in the tamoxifen group).

Safety analysis. Switching to anastrozole resulted in a significant reduction in the incidence of gynecologic changes, including endometrial cancer (0.9% for anastrozole versus 7.1% for tamoxifen).[84] No significant differences were evident in the incidence of joint/bone disorders (7.2% for anastrozole versus 5.8% for tamoxifen; $p = .5$) or bone fractures (0.9% for anastrozole versus 0.9% for tamoxifen; $p = .9$). However, compared with tamoxifen, switching to anastrozole was associated with raised cholesterol levels (8.1% for anastrozole versus 2.7% for tamoxifen; $p = .01$) and gastrointestinal symptoms (6.3% for anastrozole versus 1.3% for tamoxifen; $p = .006$). These latter differences have been attributed, at least in part, to a group of patients who had hiatal hernias at baseline. These preliminary data were based on a small number of events following tamoxifen therapy, and a longer follow-up is needed to observe differences between treatments.

Study of Aromatase Inhibitors in the Extended Adjuvant Setting: National Cancer Institute of Canada (NCIC) MA.17 Trial

The double-blind, placebo-controlled NCIC MA.17 trial investigated whether extended adjuvant therapy with letrozole after 5 years of tamoxifen offered a clinical advantage compared with no further drug therapy (placebo) in postmenopausal women with early breast cancer.[85] A total of 5,187 patients who had received 4.5 to 6.0 years of adjuvant tamoxifen were randomized to receive an anticipated 5 years of letrozole 2.5 mg or placebo. Tamoxifen was not continued in the control arm of this study, as more than 5 years of tamoxifen treatment has been related to worse outcomes compared with 5 years of therapy.

Efficacy analysis. At the first planned interim analysis (median follow-up of 29 months), sequential treatment with 5 years of tamoxifen followed by letrozole reduced the risk of local or distant recurrence or new CLBC by 43% compared with 5 years of tamoxifen alone (letrozole: 75 new breast cancer events; placebo: 132 such events; HR, 0.57; 95% CI, 0.43–0.75; $p \leq .001$). With < 0.5% of the enrolled patients (20 patients still at risk) having reached 50 months of follow-up without recurrence or new CLBC, the estimated 4-year survival rate was 93% in the letrozole group and 87% in the placebo group, equating to an estimated difference in DFS between treatment groups of 6% (95% CI, 2.0–10.1). However, survival analysis demonstrated no difference in OS between the two treatment groups ($p = .25$). Early curtailment of this trial rendered it impossible to determine the potential benefit of letrozole with respect to DFS, because of uncertainty about the interval for which the treatment benefit may persist, and precluded a mature analysis of MA.17.

Safety analysis. At the time of the first interim analysis, limited safety data were available for the first 4,299 women enrolled in the study, with a median follow-up of < 2 years. Hot flashes, arthritis, arthralgia, and myalgia were more frequent in the letrozole group compared with the placebo group ($p < .05$).[85] Vaginal bleeding was less common in the letrozole group compared with the placebo group (4.3% versus 6.0 %, respectively; $p = .01$). Slightly more patients in the letrozole group compared with the placebo group experienced cardiovascular events (4.1% versus 3.6%, respectively) or bone fractures (3.6% versus 2.9%, respectively), and there was a trend for newly diagnosed osteoporosis to be increased with letrozole (5.8% for letrozole versus 4.5% for placebo; $p = .07$).[85] Owing to the premature curtailment of this trial, only approximately one-quarter of patients were followed for ≥ 30 months for the efficacy analysis and the follow-up for AEs was even shorter.[86,87] Although a recent efficacy and safety update of the MA.17 trial has been reported at a median follow-up of 2.5 years, only 22% of patients were followed for ≤ 40 months.[88,89] Overall, mortality rates were similar in the letrozole and placebo groups ($p = .30$), whereas women with node-positive breast cancer on letrozole had a reduced risk of death (HR, 0.61; 95% CI, 0.38–0.98; $p = .04$) and a reduced risk of distant recurrence (HR, 0.53; 95% CI, 0.36–0.78; $p = .001$) compared with those on placebo. Safety data were consistent with the initial analysis; in addition, newly diagnosed osteoporosis was higher in the letrozole group compared with the placebo group ($p = .003$), although the incidence of bone fractures was similar for both groups ($p = .2$). More patients in the letrozole group experienced a reduced quality of life compared with the placebo group, in the following domains: short form general health survey (SF36) physical functioning ($p < .001$), SF36 bodily pain ($p = .001$), SF36 vitality ($p = .005$), menopause-specific quality-of-life (MSQL) vasomotor ($p < .001$), MSQL physical functioning ($p = .004$), and MSQL sexual functioning ($p = .02$).[90]

We look forward to the full publication of these data, which will require careful interpretation because of the limitations imposed by their preliminary nature.[91] Indeed, early termination of the MA.17 trial has meant that overall long-term safety results and data relating to fractures, osteoporosis, and cardiovascular events will not be available. Hence, the long-term risk-benefit profile of letrozole will not be determined from available data.

Safety and Tolerability of Aromatase Inhibitors

There are many differences between AIs in terms of pharmacokinetics, effects on lipid profiles, and bone turnover that may influence their long-term safety profiles.[92] In the majority of trials, anastrozole does not appear to have a detrimental effect on lipid profiles.[93–95] In the ITA trial, switching from adjuvant tamoxifen to anastrozole was associated with raised cholesterol levels[84]; however, these results may have been due to the effects of discontinuing tamoxifen, which is known to have a beneficial effect on the lipid profile. Conflicting results have been reported for the effects of exemestane on plasma lipids, whereas data are available to show that letrozole may have an unfavorable effect on the serum lipid profile.[96–101] However, it is not yet clear whether letrozole-induced changes in lipid profiles correlate with an increased risk of cardiovascular morbidity and mortality. Data from the extended adjuvant MA.17 trial showed that the rate of cardiovascular events was slightly higher in the letrozole group compared with the placebo group. Longer follow-up is needed to rule out the possibility that letrozole is associated with adverse cardiovascular events[85]; however, the unblinding of the MA.17 trial has meant that a meaningful risk-benefit analysis cannot be performed.

Several studies have shown that letrozole and anastrozole may increase bone resorption markers.[102,103] In a subprotocol of the ATAC study, 1 year of primary adjuvant anastrozole was associated with a decrease in spine and hip bone mineral density (BMD) and an increase in bone resorption and bone formation markers.[104] The rate of bone loss remained constant over 2 years of treatment, although further assessment of the clinically relevant end point of fractures showed that the fracture rates stabilized after this time.[105,106] Exemestane increased bone turnover in healthy volunteers and caused a slight but nonsignificant increase in the rate of osteoporosis and reported fractures compared with tamoxifen in the BIG 97-02 study.[83,107] A substudy of this trial has been planned to determine the degree of bone mineral loss in patients who have been switched from tamoxifen, although these results have not yet been reported. Preliminary data from a small, randomized, double-blind study of exemestane ($n = 73$) versus placebo ($n = 74$) on bone metabolism in postmenopausal women with early breast cancer have recently been presented. Exemestane increased both bone resorption and formation markers, indicating an increase in bone remodeling, which corresponded to a significant increase in the annual rate of BMD loss in the femoral neck but not in the lumbar spine.[108,109] These data highlight the need for long-term studies for each AI in the appropriate adjuvant setting, to ascertain whether their differential pharmacologic effects transform into diverse tolerability profiles.

IMPLICATIONS FOR CLINICAL PRACTICE

There is now considerable experience gained with adjuvant anastrozole in postmenopausal women with early breast cancer, showing that anastrozole is superior to tamoxifen and that 5 years of tamoxifen monotherapy after surgery may be suboptimal.[78,80] However, despite these promising results, a technology assessment of the ATAC trial by the American Society of Clinical Oncology (ASCO) concluded that, in the absence of a difference in survival, the updated ATAC results were preliminary, with few data available for long-term (> 5 years) analysis.[110] The ASCO Technology Panel therefore recommended that tamoxifen should remain the standard adjuvant endocrine therapy for the treatment of hormone-sensitive breast cancer and that anastrozole should be considered for the treatment of postmenopausal women with hormone receptor-positive tumors who have an absolute or relative contraindication to the use of tamoxifen.[110] Although longer follow-up is necessary to assess the overall impact on survival and to determine the long-term effects of estrogen suppression, the most recent ATAC efficacy data indicate that benefits with anastrozole are likely to improve over time.[111] The early improvement in DFS observed with anastrozole in the ATAC trial is likely to correlate closely with survival, as in previous studies of adjuvant tamoxifen therapy where early improvements in DFS have been translated into later benefits in all-cause and cause-specific mortality.[112]

Both the BIG 97-02 and ITA trials show the benefit of AI treatment following tamoxifen, compared with tamoxifen alone, in postmenopausal women with early breast cancer.[83,84] However, both studies are limited by the immaturity of data in terms of OS and safety, but should provide long-term assessment of survival in years to come. Data from the BIG 97-02 and ITA trials provide guidance on appropriate treatment for patients who are currently receiving adjuvant tamoxifen. However, the data from switching trials do not support the sequential use of tamoxifen followed by an AI in endocrine-naïve patients. Based on the current published data, 5 years of adjuvant anastrozole offers the best chance of preventing breast cancer recurrence in these patients.[78,80] Data from the MA.17 trial show that letrozole is an option for patients who are currently finishing 5 years of tamoxifen therapy.[85] Although letrozole is the first AI shown to achieve a significant DFS benefit in the extended adjuvant setting to date, this trial does not provide information on the best choice of adjuvant therapy in the first 5 years following surgery, when most breast cancer recurrences occur.[113] These results are therefore only relevant to women who have successfully completed or are about to complete 5 years of tamoxifen therapy. On the basis of the DFS results of the MA.17 trial, the data and safety monitoring committee recommended that, in the interest of patient care, the study be discontinued early.[86] Although some clinicians advocate the early disclosure of trial results for efficacy reasons, as occurred in the MA.17 trial, this approach precludes any meaningful determination of optimal duration of therapy, the long-term impact on OS, and potential long-term toxicities associated with treatment.[85] A more realistic approach is to use distant relapse as a predictor of OS in adjuvant trials.[114] Indeed, patients with locoregional recurrence usually have a better prognosis than those with distant recurrence, probably because local recurrence may reflect a failure in surgery, rather than a failure of adjuvant treatment.[115,116]

CONCLUSIONS

Trials reported to date with the third-generation AIs have cast doubt on the future role of tamoxifen as the standard choice in the management of early breast cancer in the adjuvant setting. In postmenopausal women with advanced disease, anastrozole and letrozole offer benefits over tamoxifen for a first-line therapy. Although small differences in potency have been reported between anastrozole and letrozole, these do not translate into improvements in clinical efficacy, but may impact on the long-term tolerability profiles of these two AIs.

As the risk of breast cancer recurrence is highest during the first 5 years of adjuvant treatment post surgery, it may be important that the most effective drug be used to treat the patient in the adjuvant setting, but long term overall health impact will need to be considered. Clinical trials directly comparing adjuvant tamoxifen and AI therapies, as well as studies comparing the AIs to another will play a critical role in assessing the effectiveness of these therapies as do studies evaluating later implementation of the AIs in postmenopausal women with newly diagnosed early disease. Anastrozole is the only endocrine agent with efficacy and safety data to support its use as an alternative primary adjuvant therapy to tamoxifen for hormone-responsive breast cancer in postmenopausal women with newly diagnosed early disease. To date, anastrozole is the only AI that has been approved for this indication. Since there are differences in pharmacologic profiles between AIs, efficacy and tolerability data for anastrozole as a primary adjuvant therapy should not be extrapolated to other AIs. The results of ongoing studies are required to more precisely define the optimal use of these agents.

For patients who are currently receiving tamoxifen, results from the ITA and BIG 97-02 studies have demonstrated the benefits of switching to anastrozole or exemestane, if they switch after 2 to 3 years of tamoxifen treatment. Data from the MA.17 trial indicate that patients who have completed 5 years of tamoxifen therapy may benefit from extended adjuvant therapy with letrozole. However, the early curtailment of the MA.17 trial means that long-term efficacy and tolerability data for letrozole will not be available.

In conclusion, data from large well-controlled studies are needed to determine whether sequencing of adjuvant endocrine therapy is appropriate, and what the most appropriate agent for use in the first-line adjuvant setting is. Efficacy and safety data derived with each AI should not be extrapolated to other Ais, and current treatment decisions should be based on available trial data for each agent.

REFERENCES

1. Beatson GT. On the treatment of inoperable cases of carcinoma of the mamma: suggestions for a new method of treatment, with illustrative cases. Lancet 1896;ii:104–7.
2. Huggins C, Bergenstal DM. Inhibition of human mammary and prostatic cancer by adrenalectomy. Cancer Res 1952; 12:134–41.
3. Fisher B, Dignam J, Bryant J, et al. Five versus more than five years of tamoxifen therapy for breast cancer patients with negative lymph nodes and estrogen receptor-positive tumors. J Natl Cancer Inst 1996;88:1529–42.
4. Jaiyesimi IA, Buzdar AU, Decker DA, et al. Use of tamoxifen for breast cancer: twenty-eight years later. J Clin Oncol 1995;13:513–29.
5. Chen S. Aromatase and breast cancer. Front Biosci 1998;3: d922–33.
6. Buzdar AU, Hortobagyi G. Update on endocrine therapy for breast cancer. Clin Cancer Res 1998;4:527–34.
7. Simpson ER, Zhao Y, Agarwal VR, et al. Aromatase expression in health and disease. Recent Prog Horm Res 1997; 52:185–213.
8. Miller WR. Biology of aromatase inhibitors: pharmacology/endocrinology within the breast. Endocr Relat Cancer 1999;6:187–95.
9. Tekmal RR, Ramachandra N, Gubba S, et al. Overexpression of int-5/aromatase in mammary glands of transgenic mice results in the induction of hyperplasia and nuclear abnormalities. Cancer Res 1996;56:3180–5.
10. Gruber CJ, Tschugguel W, Schneeberger C, et al. Production and actions of estrogens. N Engl J Med 2002;346:340–52.
11. Simpson ER, Dowsett M. Aromatase and its inhibitors: significance for breast cancer therapy. Recent Prog Horm Res 2002;57:317–38.
12. Geisler J, King N, Anker G, et al. In vivo inhibition of aromatization by exemestane, a novel irreversible aromatase inhibitor, in postmenopausal breast cancer patients. Clin Cancer Res 1998;4:2089–93.
13. Geisler J, Haynes B, Anker G, et al. Influence of letrozole and anastrozole on total body aromatization and plasma estrogen levels in postmenopausal breast cancer patients evaluated in a randomized, cross-over study. J Clin Oncol 2002;20:751–7.
14. Wells SA Jr, Santen RJ, Lipton A, et al. Medical adrenalectomy with aminoglutethimide: clinical studies in postmenopausal patients with metastatic breast carcinoma. Ann Surg 1978;187:475–84.
15. Goss PE, Powles TJ, Dowsett M, et al. Treatment of advanced postmenopausal breast cancer with an aromatase inhibitor, 4-hydroxyandrostenedione: phase II report. Cancer Res 1986;46:4823–6.
16. Jones AL, MacNeill F, Jacobs S, et al. The influence of intramuscular 4-hydroxyandrostenedione on peripheral aromatisation in breast cancer patients. Eur J Cancer 1992; 28A:1712–6.
17. MacNeill FA, Jones AL, Jacobs S, et al. The influence of aminoglutethimide and its analogue rogletimide on peripheral aromatisation in breast cancer. Br J Cancer 1992;66:692–7.
18. Rose C, Vtoraya O, Pluzanska A, et al. An open randomised trial of second-line endocrine therapy in advanced breast cancer: comparison of the aromatase inhibitors letrozole and anastrozole. Eur J Cancer 2003;39:2318–27.
19. Jonat W, Howell A, Blomqvist C, et al. A randomised trial comparing two doses of the new selective aromatase

inhibitor anastrozole (Arimidex) with megestrol acetate in postmenopausal patients with advanced breast cancer. Eur J Cancer 1996;32A:404–12.

20. Buzdar AU, Jones SE, Vogel CL, et al. A phase III trial comparing anastrozole (1 and 10 milligrams), a potent and selective aromatase inhibitor, with megestrol acetate in postmenopausal women with advanced breast carcinoma. Arimidex Study Group. Cancer 1997;79:730–9.
21. Buzdar AU, Jonat W, Howell A, et al. Anastrozole versus megestrol acetate in the treatment of postmenopausal women with advanced breast carcinoma: results of a survival update based on a combined analysis of data from two mature phase III trials. Arimidex Study Group. Cancer 1998;83:1142–52.
22. Gershanovich M, Chaudri HA, Campos D, et al. Letrozole, a new oral aromatase inhibitor: randomised trial comparing 2.5 mg daily, 0.5 mg daily and aminoglutethimide in postmenopausal women with advanced breast cancer. Letrozole International Trial Group (AR/BC3). Ann Oncol 1998;9:639–45.
23. Buzdar A, Douma J, Davidson N, et al. Phase III, multicenter, double-blind, randomized study of letrozole, an aromatase inhibitor, for advanced breast cancer versus megestrol acetate. J Clin Oncol 2001;19:3357–66.
24. Dombernowsky P, Smith I, Falkson G, et al. Letrozole, a new oral aromatase inhibitor for advanced breast cancer: double-blind randomized trial showing a dose effect and improved efficacy and tolerability compared with megestrol acetate. J Clin Oncol 1998;16:453–61.
25. Kaufmann M, Bajetta E, Dirix LY, et al. Exemestane is superior to megestrol acetate after tamoxifen failure in postmenopausal women with advanced breast cancer: results of a phase III randomized double-blind trial. The Exemestane Study Group. J Clin Oncol 2000;18:1399–411.
26. Howell A, Robertson JF, Quaresma AJ, et al. Fulvestrant, formerly ICI 182,780, is as effective as anastrozole in postmenopausal women with advanced breast cancer progressing after prior endocrine treatment. J Clin Oncol 2002;20:3396–403.
27. Howell A, Osborne CK, Robertson JF, et al. ICI 182,780 (Faslodex™) versus anastrozole (Arimidex™) for the treatment of advanced breast cancer in postmenopausal women: prospective combined analysis of two multicenter trials. Eur J Cancer 2001;37 Suppl 6:151
28. Osborne CK, Pippen J, Jones SE, et al. Double-blind, randomized trial comparing the efficacy and tolerability of fulvestrant versus anastrozole in postmenopausal women with advanced breast cancer progressing on prior endocrine therapy: results of a North American trial. J Clin Oncol 2002;20:3386–95.
29. Nabholtz JM, Buzdar A, Pollak M, et al. Anastrozole is superior to tamoxifen as first-line therapy for advanced breast cancer in postmenopausal women: results of a North American multicenter randomized trial. Arimidex Study Group. J Clin Oncol 2000;18:3758–67.
30. Bonneterre J, Thurlimann B, Robertson JF, et al. Anastrozole versus tamoxifen as first-line therapy for advanced breast cancer in 668 postmenopausal women: results of the Tamoxifen or Arimidex Randomized Group Efficacy and Tolerability study. J Clin Oncol 2000;18:3748–57.
31. Bonneterre J, Buzdar A, Nabholtz JM, et al. Anastrozole is superior to tamoxifen as first-line therapy in hormone receptor positive advanced breast carcinoma. Cancer 2001;92:2247–58.
32. Nabholtz JM, Bonneterre J, Buzdar A, et al. Anastrozole (Arimidex) versus tamoxifen as first-line therapy for advanced breast cancer in postmenopausal women: survival analysis and updated safety results. Eur J Cancer 2003;39:1684–9.
33. Nabholtz JM. Advanced breast cancer updates on anastrozole versus tamoxifen. J Steroid Biochem Mol Biol 2003;86: 321–5.
34. Mouridsen H, Gershanovich M, Sun Y, et al. Phase III study of letrozole versus tamoxifen as first-line therapy of advanced breast cancer in postmenopausal women: analysis of survival and update of efficacy from the International Letrozole Breast Cancer Group. J Clin Oncol 2003;21:2101–9.
35. Mouridsen H, Gershanovich M, Sun Y, et al. Superior efficacy of letrozole versus tamoxifen as first-line therapy for postmenopausal women with advanced breast cancer: results of a phase III study of the International Letrozole Breast Cancer Group. J Clin Oncol 2001;19:2596–606.
36. Howell A, Robertson JF, Abram P, et al. Comparison of fulvestrant versus tamoxifen for the treatment of advanced breast cancer in postmenopausal women previously untreated with endocrine therapy: a multinational, double-blind, randomized trial. J Clin Oncol 2004;22: 1605–13.
37. Early Breast Cancer Trialists' Collaborative Group. Tamoxifen for early breast cancer (Cochrane Review). The Cochrane Library. Vol 1. Chichester (UK): John Wiley & Sons, Ltd; 2004. p. 1–38.
38. Assikis V, Buzdar A, Yang Y, et al. A phase III trial of sequential adjuvant chemotherapy for operable breast carcinoma: final analysis with 10-year follow-up. Cancer 2003;97:2716–23.
39. Boccardo F, Rubagotti A, Amoroso D, et al. Chemotherapy versus tamoxifen versus chemotherapy plus tamoxifen in node-positive, oestrogen-receptor positive breast cancer patients. An update at 7 years of the 1st GROCTA (Breast Cancer Adjuvant Chemo-Hormone Therapy Cooperative Group) trial. Eur J Cancer 1992;28:673–80.
40. Hubay CA, Pearson OH, Marshall JS, et al. Adjuvant therapy of stage II breast cancer: 48-month follow-up of a prospective randomized clinical trial. Breast Cancer Res Treat 1981;1:77–82.
41. Gazet JC, Markopoulos C, Ford HT, et al. Prospective randomised trial of tamoxifen versus surgery in elderly patients with breast cancer. Lancet 1988;1:679–81.
42. Robertson JF, Ellis IO, Elston CW, et al. Mastectomy or tamoxifen as initial therapy for operable breast cancer in elderly patients: 5-year follow-up. Eur J Cancer 1992; 28A:908–10.
43. Bates T, Riley DL, Houghton J, et al. Breast cancer in elderly women: a Cancer Research Campaign trial comparing treatment with tamoxifen and optimal surgery with tamoxifen alone. The Elderly Breast Cancer Working Party. Br J Surg 1991;78:591–4.
44. Mustacchi G, Ceccherini R, Milani S, et al. Tamoxifen alone versus adjuvant tamoxifen for operable breast cancer of the elderly: long-term results of the phase III randomized

controlled multicenter GRETA trial. Ann Oncol 2003; 14:414–20.

45. Mustacchi G, Milani S, Pluchinotta A, et al. Tamoxifen or surgery plus tamoxifen as primary treatment for elderly patients with operable breast cancer: the G.R.E.T.A. Trial. Group for Research on Endocrine Therapy in the Elderly. Anticancer Res 1994;14:2197–200.
46. Smith I, Dowsett M, on behalf of the IMPACT Trialists. Comparison of anastrozole vs. tamoxifen alone and in combination as neoadjuvant treatment of estrogen receptor-positive (ER+) operable breast cancer in postmenopausal women: the IMPACT trial. Breast Cancer Res Treat 2003;82 Suppl 1:6.
47. Cataliotti L, Buzdar A, Noguchi S, et al. Efficacy of PReOperative Arimidex (anastrozole) Compared with Tamoxifen (PROACT) as neoadjuvant therapy in postmenopausal women with hormone receptor-positive breast cancer. Eur J Cancer 2004;2 Suppl:69.
48. Smith I, Cataliotti L. Anastrozole versus tamoxifen as neoadjuvant therapy for oestrogen receptor-positive breast cancer in postmenopausal women: the IMPACT and PROACT trials. Eur J Cancer 2004;2 Suppl:69.
49. Semiglazov VF, Semiglazov VV, Ivanov VG, et al. Neoadjuvant endocrine therapy: exemestane (E) vs. tamoxifen (T) in postmenopausal ER+ breast cancer patients (T1-4N1-2MO). Breast Cancer Res Treat 2003;82 Suppl 1:22.
50. Eiermann W, Paepke S, Appfelstaedt J, et al. Preoperative treatment of postmenopausal breast cancer patients with letrozole: a randomized double-blind multicenter study. Ann Oncol 2001;12:1527–32.
51. Ellis MJ, Coop A, Singh B, et al. Letrozole inhibits tumor proliferation more effectively than tamoxifen independent of HER1/2 expression status. Cancer Res 2003;63:6523–31.
52. Ellis MJ, Coop A, Singh B, et al. Letrozole is a more effective neoadjuvant endocrine therapy than tamoxifen for ErbB-1- and/or ErbB-2-positive, estrogen receptor-positive primary breast cancer: evidence from a phase III randomized trial. J Clin Oncol 2001;19:3808–16.
53. Dixon JM, Jackson J, Renshaw L, et al. Neoadjuvant tamoxifen and aromatase inhibitors: comparisons and clinical outcomes. J Steroid Biochem Mol Biol 2003;86:295–9.
54. Buzdar AU, Valero V, Theriault R, et al. Pathological complete response to chemotherapy is related to hormone receptor status. Breast Cancer Res Treat 2003;82:69.
55. Semiglazov V, Semiglazov VV, Ivanov VG, et al. Anastrozole (A) vs. tamoxifen (T) vs. combine (A+T) as neoadjuvant endocrine therapy of postmenopausal breast cancer patients. Proc Am Soc Clin Oncol 2003;22:880.
56. Early Breast Cancer Trialists' Collaborative Group. Effects of chemotherapy and hormonal therapy for early breast cancer on recurrence and 15-year survival: an overview of the randomised trials. Lancet 2005;365:1687–717.
57. Early Breast Cancer Trialists' Collaborative Group. Ovarian ablation in early breast cancer: overview of the randomised trials. Lancet 1996;348:1189–96.
58. Jonat W, Kaufmann M, Sauerbrei W, et al. Goserelin versus cyclophosphamide, methotrexate, and fluorouracil as adjuvant therapy in premenopausal patients with node-positive breast cancer: the Zoladex Early Breast Cancer Research Association Study. J Clin Oncol 2002;20:4628–35.
59. Jakesz R, Hausmaninger H, Kubista E, et al. Randomized adjuvant trial of tamoxifen and goserelin versus cyclophosphamide, methotrexate, and fluorouracil: evidence for the superiority of treatment with endocrine blockade in premenopausal patients with hormone-responsive breast cancer. The Austrian Breast and Colorectal Cancer Study Group Trial 5. J Clin Oncol 2002;20:4621–7.
60. Boccardo F, Rubagotti A, Amoroso D, et al. Cyclophosphamide, methotrexate, and fluorouracil versus tamoxifen plus ovarian suppression as adjuvant treatment of estrogen receptor-positive pre-/perimenopausal breast cancer patients: results of the Italian Breast Cancer Adjuvant Study Group 02 randomized trial. J Clin Oncol 2000;18:2718–27.
61. Rutqvist L. Zoladex and tamoxifen as adjuvant therapy in premenopausal breast cancer: a randomized trial by the Cancer Research Campaign (C.R.C.) Breast Cancer Trials Group, Stockholm Breast Cancer Study Group, The South-East Sweden Breast Cancer Group & The Gruppo Interdisciplinare Valutazione Interventi in Oncologia (G.I.V.I.O.) [abstract]. Proc Am Soc Clin Oncol 1999;18:67.
62. Davidson N, O'Neill A, Vukov A. Effect of chemohormonal therapy in premenopausal, node (+), receptor (+) breast cancer: an Eastern Cooperative Oncology Group Phase III Intergroup Trial (E5188, INT-0101) [abstract]. Proc Am Soc Clin Oncol 1999;18:67.
63. Castiglione-Gertsch M, O'Neill A, Gelber RD. Is the addition of adjuvant chemotherapy always necessary in node-negative (N-) pre/perimenopausal breast cancer patients (pts) who receive goserelin [abstract]? Proc Am Soc Clin Oncol 2002;21:38.
64. Early Breast Cancer Trialists' Collaborative Group. Systemic treatment of early breast cancer by hormonal, cytotoxic, or immune therapy: 133 randomised trials involving 31,000 recurrences and 24,000 deaths among 75,000 women. Lancet 1992;339:1–15.
65. Bianco A, Costanzo R, Di Lorenzo G. The Mam-1 GOCSI Trial: a randomised trial with factorial design of chemo-endocrine adjuvant treatment in node-positive (N+) early breast cancer (EBC) [abstract]. Proc Am Soc Clin Oncol 2001;20:27.
66. NATO (Nolvadex Adjuvant Trial Organisation). Controlled trial of tamoxifen as adjuvant agent in management of early breast cancer. interim analysis at four years by Nolvadex Adjuvant Trial Organisation. Lancet 1983;1:257–61.
67. Rutqvist LE, Cedermark B, Glas U, et al. Randomized trial of adjuvant tamoxifen in node negative postmenopausal breast cancer. Stockholm Breast Cancer Study Group. Acta Oncol 1992;31:265–70.
68. Breast Cancer Trials Committee & Scottish Cancer Trials Office. Adjuvant tamoxifen in the management of operable breast cancer: the Scottish Trial. Report from the Breast Cancer Trials Committee, Scottish Cancer Trials Office (MRC), Edinburgh. Lancet 1987;2:171–5.
69. Stewart HJ, Prescott RJ, Forrest AP. Scottish adjuvant tamoxifen trial: a randomized study updated to 15 years. J Natl Cancer Inst 2001;93:456–62.
70. Gray R, Milligan K, Padmore L, and Study Group. Tamoxifen: assessment of the balance of benefits and risks for long-term treatment. Br J Cancer 1997;76 Suppl 1:24.
71. Davies C, Monoghan H, Peto R. Early breast cancer: how long

should tamoxifen continue? Eur J Cancer 1998;34 Suppl:43.

72. Wiseman LR, Goa KL. Toremifene. A review of its pharmacological properties and clinical efficacy in the management of advanced breast cancer. Drugs 1997;54:141–60.
73. Tomas E, Kauppila A, Blanco G, et al. Comparison between the effects of tamoxifen and toremifene on the uterus in postmenopausal breast cancer patients. Gynecol Oncol 1995;59:261–6.
74. Marttunen MB, Hietanen P, Tiitinen A, et al. Comparison of effects of tamoxifen and toremifene on bone biochemistry and bone mineral density in postmenopausal breast cancer patients. J Clin Endocrinol Metab 1998;83:1158–62.
75. Holli K, Valavaara R, Blanco G, et al. Safety and efficacy results of a randomized trial comparing adjuvant toremifene and tamoxifen in postmenopausal patients with node-positive breast cancer. Finnish Breast Cancer Group. J Clin Oncol 2000;18:3487–94.
76. Pagani O, Gelber S, Simoncini E. Randomized comparison of adjuvant toremifene (Tor) versus tamoxifen (Tam) for postmenopausal women with node-positive (N+), estrogen receptor-positive (ER+) early stage breast cancer. Proc Am Soc Clin Oncol 2003;22:20.
77. Albain KS, Green SJ, Ravdin PM, et al. Adjuvant chemohormonal therapy for primary breast cancer should be sequential instead of concurrent: initial results from intergroup trial 0100 (SWOG-8814) [abstract]. Proc Am Soc Clin Oncol 2002;21:37.
78. Howell A, Cuzick J, Baum M, et al. Results of the ATAC (Arimidex, Tamoxifen, Alone or in Combination) trial after completion of 5 years' adjuvant treatment for breast cancer. Lancet 2005;365:60–2.
79. The ATAC ('Arimidex', Tamoxifen, Alone or in Combination) Trialists Group: Anastrozole alone or in combination with tamoxifen versus tamoxifen alone for adjuvant treatment of postmenopausal women with early breast cancer: first results of the ATAC randomised trial. Lancet 2002;359:2131–9.
80. The ATAC ('Arimidex', Tamoxifen, Alone or in Combination) Trialists Group: Anastrozole alone or in combination with tamoxifen versus tamoxifen alone for adjuvant treatment of postmenopausal women with early breast cancer: first results of the ATAC randomised trial. Cancer 2003;98:1802–10.
81. The ATAC ('Arimidex', Tamoxifen, Alone or in Combination) Trialists Group: ATAC Trial Update. Lancet 2005;365:1225.
82. Thurlimann B. Letrozole vs. tamoxifen as adjuvant endocrine therapy for postmenopausal women with receptor-positive breast cancer. BIG 1-98: a prospective randomized double-blind phase III study. St. Gallen Breast Cancer Conference; 2005. St. Gallen, Switzerland.
83. Coombes RC, Hall E, Gibson LJ, et al. A randomized trial of exemestane after two to three years of tamoxifen therapy in postmenopausal women with primary breast cancer. N Engl J Med 2004;350:1081–92.
84. Boccardo F, Rubagotti A, Amoroso D, et al. Anastrozole appears to be superior to tamoxifen in women already receiving adjuvant tamoxifen treatment. Breast Cancer Res Treat 2003;82 Suppl 1:6–7.
85. Goss PE, Ingle JN, Martino S, et al. A randomized trial of letrozole in postmenopausal women after five years of tamoxifen therapy for early-stage breast cancer. N Engl J Med 2003;349:1793–802.
86. Bryant J, Wolmark N. Letrozole after tamoxifen for breast cancer: what is the price of success? N Engl J Med 2003; 349:1855–7.
87. Burstein HJ. Beyond tamoxifen: extending endocrine treatment for early-stage breast cancer. N Engl J Med 2003; 349:1857–9.
88. Goss PE, Ingle JN, Martino S, et al. Updated analysis of the NCIC CTG MA17 randomized placebo (P) controlled trial of letrozole (L) after 5 years of tamoxifen in postmenopausal women with early stage breast cancer. Proc Am Soc Clin Oncol 2004;23:87.
89. Goss PE, Ingle JN, Martino S, et al. Updated analysis of the NCIC CTG MA.17 randomized placebo (P) controlled trial of letrozole (l) after five years of tamoxifen in postmenopausal women with early stage breast cancer. J Clin Onc 2004;22(14 Suppl):88.
90. Whelen T, Goss P, Ingle J, et al. Assessment of quality of life (QOL) in MA.17, a randomized placebo-controlled trial of letrozole in postmenopausal women following five years of tamoxifen. Proc Am Soc Clin Oncol 2004;23:6.
91. Buzdar AU. Letrozole in breast cancer. N Engl J Med 2004; 350:727–30.
92. Buzdar AU, Robertson JF, Eiermann W, et al. An overview of the pharmacology and pharmacokinetics of the newer generation aromatase inhibitors anastrozole, letrozole, and exemestane. Cancer 2002;95:2006–16.
93. Sawada S, Sato K. Effect of anastrozole and tamoxifen on serum lipid levels in Japanese postmenopausal women with early breast cancer. Breast Cancer Res Treat 2003;82 Suppl 1:31–2.
94. Wojtacki J, Les'niewski-Kmak K, Pawlak W, Nowicka E. Anastrozole therapy and lipid profile: an update. Eur J Cancer 2004;2 Suppl:142.
95. Wojtacki J, Les'niewski-Kmak K, Kruszewski WJ. Anastrozole therapy does not compromise lipid metabolism in breast cancer patients previously treated with tamoxifen. Breast Cancer Res Treat 2002;76 Suppl 1:75.
96. Atalay G, Dirix L, Biganzoli L, et al. The effect of exemestane on serum lipid profile in postmenopausal women with metastatic breast cancer: a companion study to EORTC Trial 10951, 'Randomized phase II study in first line hormonal treatment for metastatic breast cancer with exemestane or tamoxifen in postmenopausal patients'. Ann Oncol 2004;15:211–7.
97. Engan T, Krane J, Johannessen DC, et al. Plasma changes in breast cancer patients during endocrine therapy: lipid measurements and nuclear magnetic resonance (NMR) spectroscopy. Breast Cancer Res Treat 1995;36:287–97.
98. Krag LE, Geisler J, Lonning PE, et al. Lipid and coagulation profile in postmenopausal women with early breast cancer at low risk treated with exemestane: a randomized, placebo-controlled study. Proc Am Soc Clin Oncol 2004; 23:39.
99. Lohrisch C, Paridaens R, Dirix LY, et al. No adverse impact on serum lipids of the irreversible aromatase inactivator Aromasin [Exemestane (E)] in first-line treatment of

metastatic breast cancer (MBC): companion study to a European Organization of Research and Treatment of Cancer (Breast Group) Trial with Pharmacia Upjohn [abstract]. Proc Am Soc Clin Oncol 2001;20:43.

100. Markopoulos C, Polychronis A, Farfarelos C, et al. The effect of exemestane on the lipidemic profile of breast cancer patients: Preliminary results of the TEAM trial Greek sub-study. Proc Am Soc Clin Oncol 2004;23:76.
101. Elisaf MS, Bairaktari E, Nicolaides C, et al. Effect of letrozole on the lipid in postmenopausal women with breast cancer. Eur J Cancer 2001;37:1510–3.
102. Bajetta E, Martinetti A, Zilembo N, et al. Biological activity of anastrozole in postmenopausal patients with advanced breast cancer: effects on estrogens and bone metabolism. Ann Oncol 2002;13:1059–66.
103. Heshmati HM, Khosla S, Robins SP, et al. Role of low levels of endogenous estrogen in regulation of bone resorption in late postmenopausal women. J Bone Miner Res 2002;17:172–8.
104. Eastell R, Adams J. Results of the 'Arimidex' (anastrozole, A), Tamoxifen (T), Alone or in Combination (C) (ATAC) trial: effects on bone mineral density (BMD) and bone turnover (ATAC Trialists Group). Ann Oncol 2002;13 Suppl 5:32.
105. Howell A. Effect of anastrozole on bone mineral density: 2-year results of the 'Arimidex' (anastrozole), Tamoxifen, Alone or in Combination (ATAC) trial. Breast Cancer Res Treat 2003;82 Suppl 1:27.
106. Locker GY, Eastell R. The time course of bone fractures observed in the ATAC ('Arimidex', Tamoxifen, Alone or in Combination) trial. Proc Am Soc Clin Oncol 2003;22:25.
107. Goss PE, Thomsen T, Banke-Bochita J, Hadji P. Effects of steroidal and nonsteroidal aromatase inhibitors on markers of bone turnover and lipid metabolism in healthy volunteers. Breast Cancer Res Treat 2003;82 Suppl 1:101.
108. Geisler J, Lonning P, Krag LE, et al. Estrogens and bone metabolism in postmenopausal women with early breast cancer at low risk treated with exemestane. A randomized placebo-controlled study. Proc Am Soc Clin Oncol 2004; 23:98.
109. Lonning P, Geisler J, Krag LE, et al. Effect of exemestane on bone: a randomized placebo controlled study in postmenopausal women with early breast cancer at low risk. Proc Am Assoc Cancer Res 2004;23:6.
110. Winer EP, Hudis C, Burstein HJ, et al. American Society of Clinical Oncology technology assessment working group update: use of aromatase inhibitors in the adjuvant setting. J Clin Oncol 2003;21:2597–9.
111. Early Breast Cancer Trialists' Collaborative Group: Tamoxifen for early breast cancer: an overview of the randomized trials. Lancet 1998;351:1451–67.
112. Current Trials Working Party of the Cancer Research Campaign Breast Cancer Trials Group. Preliminary results from the cancer research campaign trial evaluating tamoxifen duration in women aged fifty years or older with breast cancer. J Natl Cancer Inst 1996;88:1834–9.
113. Saphner T, Tormey DC, Gray R. Annual hazard rates of recurrence for breast cancer after primary therapy. J Clin Oncol 1996;14:2738–46.
114. Piccart-Gebhart MJ. New stars in the sky of treatment for early breast cancer. N Engl J Med 2004;350:1140–2.
115. Sainsbury JR, Anderson TJ, Morgan DA. ABC of breast diseases: breast cancer. BMJ 2000;321:745–50.
116. Donegan WL. Tumor-related prognostic factors for breast cancer. CA Cancer J Clin 1997;47:28–51.
117. Milla-Santos A, Milla L, Portella J, et al. Anastrozole versus tamoxifen as first-line therapy in postmenopausal patients with hormone-dependent advanced breast cancer: a prospective, randomized, phase III study. Am J Clin Oncol 2003;26:317–22.

22

Radiation Therapy in Early and Advanced Breast Cancer

SABIN B. MOTWANI
ERIC A. STROM

Radiation therapy has a long history of use in the care of the breast cancer patient. Both roentgen rays and radium applications were used shortly after their discoveries in the late nineteenth century, to treat breast cancer patients. Despite the acknowledged advances in surgical and medical therapies, the role of radiotherapy continues to remain important for nearly all stages of breast cancer. Radiation therapy, too, has undergone profound evolution in its basic scientific foundation and the technical advances in its application. This chapter will begin with a brief discussion of the scientific principles underlying the clinical use of radiotherapy, followed by a focused review of the clinical literature, emphasizing important concepts in early-stage invasive cancer and ductal carcinoma in situ (DCIS). It will then focus on the techniques of breast irradiation including prone breast irradiation and partial-breast irradiation. The chapter will then shift to the postmastectomy setting, and end with a discussion on radiation therapy for palliation and the adverse reactions associated with breast radiation therapy.

KEY PRINCIPLES OF RADIATION BIOLOGY AND PHYSICS

Interaction of Ionizing Radiation with Matter

The category of ionizing radiation includes that segment of the electromagnetic spectrum that is sufficiently energetic to result in ejection of orbital electrons when it passes through or collides with some material. The loss of this electron results in a positive charge in the affected atom and can result in a chemical change in the irradiated material. The loss of an electron is called ionization and a charged atom is called an ion.

Categories of ionizing radiation include photons, such as x-rays and gamma rays, as well as particles, such as electrons (beta particles), neutrons, protons, and nuclear fragments (alpha particles and heavy ions). The distinction between x-rays and gamma rays is somewhat arbitrary and is based solely on whether the photon is produced by a nuclear process (such as a cobalt-60 gamma ray, 1.25 MV) or an extranuclear process (such as an x-ray produced from a linear accelerator).

Ionizing radiation is measured in terms of the energy of the radiation, the strength or radioactivity of the radiation source, and the radiation dose or the amount of radiation energy absorbed. The frequency of ionizing radiation is very high and begins in the million gigahertz (GHz) range, compared with FM radio stations that transmit at frequencies of around 100 MHz (megahertz) or 0.1 GHz. Since these numbers are so large, it becomes more useful to describe the energy required to produce a particular beam. Typical x-rays used in diagnostic radiology are produced by vacuum tubes with an electric potential of 60 to 120 kV (kilovolt), whereas those used for external-beam radiation therapy are produced in a linear accelerator and are typically in the 6 to 18 MV (megavolt) range. Electron beams that are produced by a linear accelerator and beams in the 4 to 20 MeV (mega electronvolt) range are also commonly employed in clinical use. Fast neutrons, produced in a few regional centers, require beams of 40 to 70 MeV for clinical use. Proton beam therapy, currently undergoing rapid development, uses cyclotrons to produce beams of 70 to 250 MeV for patient care.

Radioactive sources may also be used for direct application in cancer care. This form of radiotherapy, called brachytherapy (brachy = short), may use a variety of radionuclides including radium-226 (no longer in standard use), iridium-192, iodine-125, gold-198, palladium-103, cesium-131, strontium-90, and yttrium-90. The strength of a radioactive source is a function of the number of radiation emissions per unit time. This is measured using the becquerel (1 Bq = 1 radiation emission per second) or the curie (1 Ci = activity of 1 gram of radium-226 or 3.7×10^{10} disintegrations per second). The intensity of these sources diminishes with time as more and more radioactive atoms decay and become stable atoms. Thus, they are also characterized by their half-life, which is the time after which the radiation intensity is reduced by one-half its original value. Half-lives differ widely from one radioactive substance to another and range from a fraction of a second to millions of years.

When ionizing radiation interacts with the human body, it imparts its energy to the tissue that it encounters. The amount of energy absorbed per unit mass of tissue is called absorbed dose and is expressed in units of gray (Gy). One gray is equivalent to 1 joule of radiation energy absorbed per kilogram of tissue (One joule of *heat* energy absorbed per kilogram is about 4 food calories!). Rad is the old and still used unit of absorbed dose. One gray is equivalent to 100 rads. Equal doses of all types of ionizing radiation are not equally harmful. Alpha particles and neutrons produce greater harm than do beta particles, gamma rays, and x-rays for a given absorbed dose. To account for this difference, radiation dose is expressed as *equivalent dose* in units of sievert (Sv). The dose in Sv is equal to *absorbed dose* multiplied by a *radiation weighting factor*, and is commonly employed in radiation safety evaluations.

Radiochemistry and Biology

The primary impact of ionizing radiation on living systems is the development of deoxyribonucleic acid (DNA) damage. Whereas radiation can directly cause single-strand and double-strand DNA breakage, the primary impact is indirect. Since water is the most common molecule in the human body, the most common radiochemical effect is the development of the ionized water molecule: H_2O^+. The lost electron in the outer shell gives the molecule an electric charge and this *free radical* is highly chemically reactive. Ultimately, this can diffuse short distances, and if it comes into contact with a DNA molecule, it can indirectly result in a single-strand break. It is estimated that two-thirds of the DNA change to mammalian cells is the result of these free-radical effects. All of this happens in the lifetime of a free radical, estimated at 10^{-5} seconds.

Since these DNA effects can be extensively repaired, especially in normal tissues, not all radiation damage results in cell death. Cell survival curves, plotting radiation dose versus cell survivorship, show that radiation effects are not linear, especially at low doses. This results in a complicated dose-response relationship, since multiple small doses (1 Gy × 8 fractions) of radiation do not have the same cell killing effect as a single large dose (8 Gy × 1 fraction). Radiotherapy functions as an effective local treatment primarily by giving many small treatments that the normal tissues can repair, but that tumor cells cannot.

The probability of tumor eradication is primarily a function of the dose delivered. Higher doses generally result in better local tumor control, assuming that the entire residual tumor is located in the target volume. Normal tissue complications are also a function of total dose, as well as dose per fraction, type of tissue, and volume treated. Hence, treatment programs have been developed that result in reasonable therapeutic indices for the disease treated. For any treatment plan developed, the radiation oncologist chooses a presumed probability of success (measured by tumor control) and, *at the same time*, chooses a probability of harm (measured by normal tissue complication). In breast cancer care, a plan for a locally advanced breast cancer may be inappropriate for someone who only has DCIS.

RADIATION THERAPY FOR EARLY-STAGE INVASIVE CANCER: REVIEW OF THE LITERATURE

The treatment of early-stage breast cancer demonstrates the full spectrum of therapeutic development from investigational concept to standard of care. Up until the 1970s, mastectomy (radical and modified) was the preferred and perhaps only accepted method of treatment of stages I and II breast cancers. It continues to be the treatment of choice in select subgroups of patients. However, breast conservation therapy (BCT) with wide local excision (also called lumpectomy, tylectomy, or segmental mastectomy), followed by whole-breast irradiation, has become the more common method of treatment. Numerous prospective and retrospective studies have shown the equivalence of mastectomy and breast conservation treatment with respect to disease-specific end points and the superiority of breast conservation with respect to quality of life measures.

Six prospective, randomized trials have compared mastectomy with breast conservative surgery and radiation for stages I and II breast cancers (Figures 22–1 and 22–2).[1–7] The whole breast was irradiated with doses of 45 to 50 Gy in all the trials, and a boost to the primary site was employed in all the trials except in the National Surgical Adjuvant Breast and Bowel Project (NSABP) B-06 trial. In the remaining trials, the total dose in the region of the primary site was ≥ 60 Gy. There was no significant

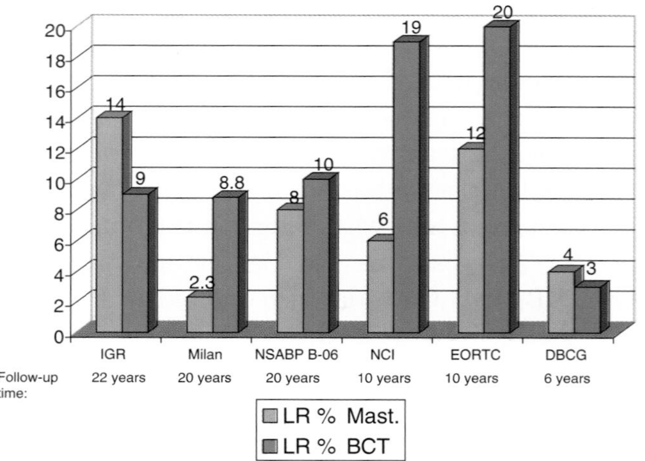

Figure 22–1. Local recurrence (LR) comparisons for breast conservation therapy versus mastectomy in prospective randomized trials.

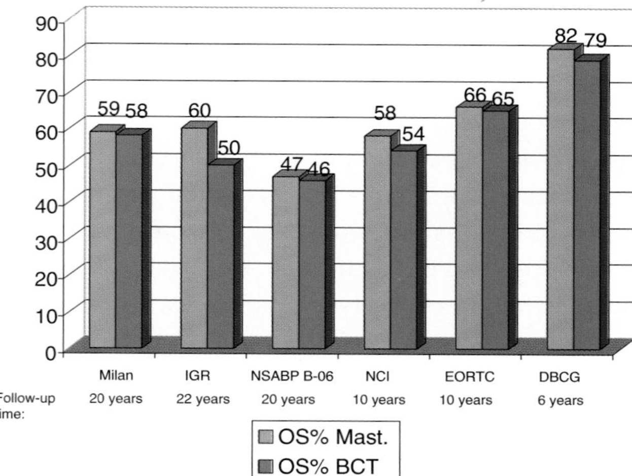

Figure 22–2. Overall survival (OS) comparisons for breast conservation therapy versus mastectomy in prospective randomized trials.

difference in overall survival or disease-free survival when comparing the two treatment arms of any of the trials (see Figure 22–2). Even node-positive patients in the NSABP B-06 and Milan trials treated with chemotherapy did not have better outcomes when treated with mastectomy.[1,3]

In 4 of the 6 clinical trials, there was no significant difference in ipsilateral recurrence in the treated breast or chest wall following mastectomy. The National Cancer Institute (NCI) trial had a higher local failure rate in the breast conservation group than other trials, which may be attributable to the fact that only gross tumor was removed for study entry. In the European Organization for Research and Treatment of Cancer (EORTC) trial, 81% of patients in breast-conserving surgery had T2 tumors, and 48% of patients had microscopically positive margins.[6]

Local recurrence after breast preservation may be attributed to faulty patient selection, inadequate surgery or radiation therapy, or biologically aggressive disease. In the NCI trial and EORTC trials, the risk of breast recurrence may have been high due to a lack of understanding of the importance of tumor-free margins. The absolute risk of local recurrence is highly dependent on follow-up interval, and ranges from 3 to 20% based on these trials (see Figure 22–1). Under more favorable conditions, the hazard rate for local recurrence is approximately 0.5% per year, and the majority of in-breast failures can be salvaged by mastectomy.

The fear of a local recurrence should not be a criterion to encourage a patient, who otherwise is a good candidate for breast conservation, to choose mastectomy. Both procedures are associated with an equal risk of local failure in appropriately selected and treated women. A meta-analysis of nine prospective, randomized trials comparing conservative surgery and radiation to mastectomy has demonstrated no survival differences. Local recurrence was reported at 6.2% in the mastectomy patients and in 5.9% of the patients treated with breast conservation.[8] The randomized trials also addressed the issue of a second malignancy related to radiation, finding no difference in the incidence of contralateral breast cancer or a second non-breast cancer malignancy.[8]

Multiple randomized trials have compared breast conservation (excision and radiation) with surgery alone. Seven of those trials results are found in Figures 22–3 and 22–4.[3,9–14] The trials vary substantially with regard to patient selection, extent of surgery and radiotherapy, and the use of systemic therapy. Quadrantectomy was employed in the Milan and Swedish trials. Adjuvant chemo and/or tamoxifen were used in the NSABP, Milan, British, Scottish, and West Midland trials. Despite these differences, all of the trials demonstrated a reduction in the rate of recurrence in the breast in the irradiated group (mean, 84%; range, 73–97%). The absolute magnitude of this benefit varied between these trials, primarily due to differences in the operative procedure (quadrant resections have lower local recurrence rates than wide local excision) and the number of years of available follow-up. Since quadrant resection usually results in a highly compromised cosmetic outcome, these reports have less impact to usual practice in North America. A recent meta-analysis of 10 randomized trials comparing conservative surgery to surgery and radiation reported an absolute reduction in breast recurrence rates of 17% for axillary node-negative women (25% versus 8%) and 19% for axillary node-positive women (35% versus 16%).[8] The absolute benefit from radiation for any recurrence was 16% for the node-negative group (44% versus 28%; $p < .00001$) and 8% for the node-positive group (58% versus 50%; $p = .002$).[8]

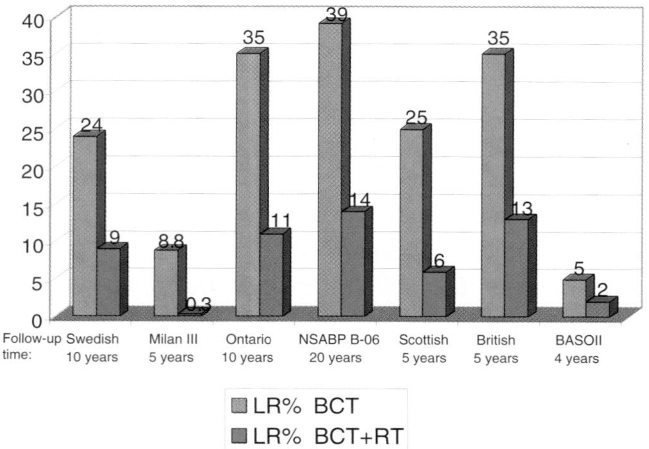

Figure 22–3. Local recurrence in prospective randomized trials comparing breast conservation with and without radiation therapy.

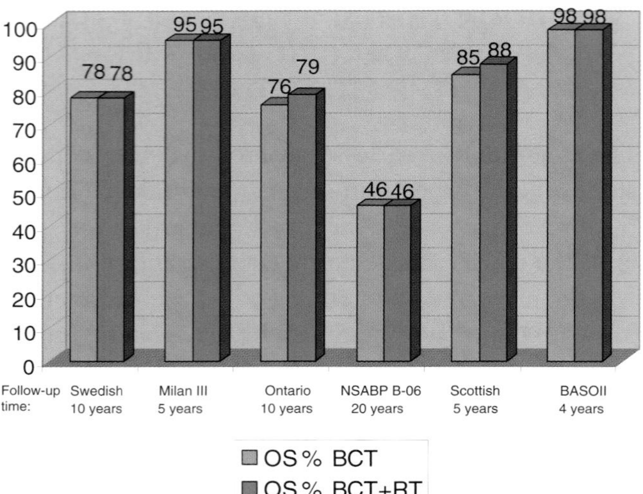

Figure 22–4. Overall survival in prospective randomized trials comparing breast conservation with and without radiation therapy.

Subset analyses within these trials have shown women older than 55 years, with small primary infiltrating ductal tumors (< 2 cm) and negative axillary nodes that lack an extensive intraductal component (EIC) or lymphatic invasion, as having the lowest risk of breast recurrence when radiation is omitted.[10,11,15] Further analysis from the Cancer and Leukemia Group B (CALGB) trial also showed that women over the age of 70 years, treated with tamoxifen and radiation therapy, had a lower 5-year local recurrence rate compared with those who were treated with tamoxifen alone (4% versus 1%; $p < .001$), but the magnitude of this benefit was small.[16] However, there were no significant differences between the two groups with regard to rates of mastectomy for local recurrence, distant metastases, or 5-year rates of overall survival. The CALGB trial concluded that lumpectomy plus adjuvant tamoxifen alone was an appropriate treatment for women over the age of 70 years who have early-stage, estrogen receptor-positive (ER+) disease. Despite these conclusions, even in the lowest risk groups from the Swedish and CALGB trials, radiation reduced the risk of a breast recurrence.

Nonrandomized retrospective studies further support the effectiveness of breast conservation treatment in appropriately selected patients. At 10 years, overall survival has ranged from 67 to 88% depending on the stage of the disease (Table 22–1). These series have demonstrated long-term control within the treated breast with primary tumors of ≤ 5 cm in diameter. At 10 years, local recurrence rates range from 8 to 20% (Table 22–2). For patients with negative margins of resection, the 10-year actuarial risk of breast recurrence is 10% or less. Overall survival and local control rates in the breast reported by these retrospective series are comparable to results from the six prospective, randomized trials.

RADIATION THERAPY FOR DUCTAL CARCINOMA IN SITU: REVIEW OF THE LITERATURE

With the advent of screening mammography, the incidence of DCIS has increased dramatically. Before 1980, DCIS was rarely diagnosed, but current reports have suggested that 22% of all breast neoplasms in the United States are DCIS.[17,18] Approximately 1 in 1,300 screening mammographic examinations have led to the diagnosis of DCIS.[19]

Some of the early data defining the role of radiation therapy for DCIS were derived from the NSABP B-06 trial. Although this trial intended to treat women having early-stage invasive breast cancer with mastectomy or lumpectomy and radiation, 76 patients were subsequently found to have pure DCIS without invasion. After a median follow-up of 83 months, the local recurrence rate was 7% for patients treated with lumpectomy and radiation compared with 43% treated with lumpectomy alone ($p = .01$).[20] In 1985, the NSABP began a trial to specifically define the role of radiation in the treatment of DCIS. Subsequently, the EORTC and a cooperative effort from the United Kingdom, Australia, and New Zealand designed similar randomized trials to assess the benefit of irradiation in breast conservation of DCIS. In all these trials, radiation added to lumpectomy reduced ipsilateral breast recurrences, both in invasive and noninvasive events for unselected patients with DCIS.[21–23]

While the benefit of radiation was clearly shown in the NSABP B-17 trial and subsequent prospective trials, the routine use of irradiation for DCIS has not been incorporated into standard clinical practice in

Table 22–1. NONRANDOMIZED TRIALS: 10-YEAR SURVIVAL RESULTS FOLLOWING BREAST CONSERVATION AND RADIATION THERAPY

Study	No. of Patients	Stage	10-Year Survival (%)
Dewar et al	757	I	79
Veronesi et al	1,232	I	78
Perez et al	520	I	85
Zafrani et al	434	I	86
Kini	281	I	88
Fowble et al	697	I, II	83
Haffty et al	278	I, II	67
Leung et al	493	I, II	68
Mansfield et al	1,070	I, II	80
Spitalier et al	1,133	I, II	80
Stotter et al	490	I, II	74
Kin et al	400	I, II	74

Reprinted with permission from Morrow M et al.[130]

Table 22–2. NONRANDOMIZED TRIALS: 10-YEAR RECURRENCE RATES IN IPSILATERAL BREAST AFTER BREAST CONSERVATION AND RADIATION THERAPY

Study	No. of Patients	Maximum Primary Tumor Size (cm)	Breast Recurrence Rate at 10 Years (%)
Gage et al	1,628	5	13
Kurtz et al	1,593	5	14
Meric-Bernstam et al	1,236	5	10
Veronesi et al	1,232	2	8
Clark et al	1,130	5	16
Mansfield et al	1,070	5	14
Dewar et al	757	3	8
Fowble et al	697	5	18
Fourquet et al	518	5	11
Halverson et al	511	5	14
Leung et al	493	5	10
Haffty et al	433	5	19
Kini et al	390	5	10

Reprinted with permission from Morrow M et al.[130]

the United States. The lack of use of irradiation can be attributable to the small number of deaths of patients from these trials for patients who did not receive irradiation, and the recognition that certain subgroups of DCIS have a low risk of local recurrence when treated with surgery alone. Silverstein and colleagues developed the Van Nuys Prognostic Index in attempt to classify subgroups of DCIS based on clinical and pathologic characteristics. The index took into account tumor grade and the presence or absence of necrosis (one category), tumor size, and margin status.[24] A recent update has added age to the formula.[25] Although most investigators support the concept of risk stratification in DCIS, these conclusions have been based on a small number of patients, and so the use and application of the index to patients with DCIS continues to be an area of ongoing clinical research.

FACTORS AFFECTING THE OUTCOME OF BREAST CONSERVATION THERAPY

Several factors can affect the outcome of BCT and have been found to influence the local recurrence rate. The most widely validated of these factors are multicentricity, surgical margins, extensive intraductal component (EIC), age, family history, systemic therapy, race, and boost treatment.

Multicentricity and Extensive Microcalcifications

The most important set of features associated with an increased risk after BCT is the presence of clinically apparent multicentric disease or extensive malignant-appearing microcalcifications. Both features imply that there is extensive tumor through a large portion of the breast and make it unlikely that complete removal of the disease can be accomplished with an acceptable cosmetic result. There are limited data regarding the success of BCT in patients with multicentric disease, because mastectomy has been the preferred treatment for women who present with disease that would require separate surgical incisions. One of the largest studies done by Kurtz and colleagues reported a recurrence rate of 25% in 61 patients compared with an 11% rate (n = 525) with unifocal disease.[26] However, there was no increased risk of recurrence if the disease was found on microscopic examination of the specimen, nor was an increased risk evident in 22 patients in whom the margin was negative.[26] For women with multifocal disease within a sphere of 4 cm that can be resected with a single segmental mastectomy, the option of BCT is offered, provided that negative surgical margins can be achieved, along with clearance of the mammographic abnormality.

Surgical Margins

Surgical margins have a critical influence on the local control rate after breast-conserving surgery and radiation therapy. Numerous series have demonstrated that positive margins of resection are associated with an increased risk of breast recurrence, but there has been considerable variability in the magnitude of this effect (Table 22–3).[27] The variability may stem from the extent of the surgical resection from the primary tumor, the presence or absence of an EIC, the definition of a positive margin, the number of margins that are positive, and the extent of margin positivity. Achieving negative surgical margins should be a goal for breast conservation surgery, since radiotherapy may not completely compensate for the excess tumor burden.

Extensive Intraductal Component

A histopathologic feature that appeared to be associated with a high risk of breast cancer recurrence following conservative surgery and irradiation is the presence of an EIC. By definition, an EIC consists of a simultaneous presence of DCIS compromising 25% or more of the primary invasive tumor and DCIS in the surrounding normal breast tissue. The definition also includes DCIS with focal areas of invasion. Approximately 20% of women with early-stage breast cancer undergoing conservative surgery and irradiation for invasive ductal carcinoma have an EIC. Several studies have reported an increased risk of breast recurrence in women with EIC-positive tumors.[28] The risk at 10 years has ranged from 22 to 32%. The increased risk for breast recurrence in EIC-positive tumors appears to be related to the presence of a significant residual tumor burden following

Table 22–3. LOCAL RECURRENCE RATE AS A FUNCTION OF MARGIN STATUS IN PATIENTS WITH INVASIVE BREAST CARCINOMA TREATED WITH BREAST CONSERVATION THERAPY

Margin Assessment	Author	No. of Patients	Follow-Up (months)	Local Recurrence (%) Negative Margin	Local Recurrence (%) Positive Margin
Positive versus negative*	Cooke et al, 1995	44	50	3	13
	Pierce et al, 1997	396	60	3	10
	Heimann et al, 1996	869	60	2	11
	Burke et al, 1995	306	60	2	15
	Slotman et al, 1994	514	68	3	10
	LeBorgne et al, 1995	817	75	9	6
	Veronesi et al, 1995	289	79	9	17
	Van Dongen et al, 1992	431	96	9	20
	Fourquet et al, 1989	518	103	8	29
	Clarke et al, 1985	436	120	4	10
	DiBiase et al, 1998	453	120	13	31
	Mansfield et al, 1995	704	120	8	16
Negative > 1 mm	Assersohn et al, 1999	184	57	0	3
	Recht et al, 1996	134	58	3	22
	Schnitt et al, 1994	181	60	0	21
	Gage et al, 1996	343	109	3	16†
	Park et al, 2000	533	127	7	19‡
Negative > 2 mm	Hallahan et al, 1989	219	36	5	9
	Solin et al, 1991	697	60	3	0
	Markiewicz et al, 1998	210	72	10	4
	Petersen et al, 1999	1,021	73	8	10
	Freedman et al, 1999	480	76	7	12
	Wazer et al, 1999	509	86	4	16
	Touboul et al, 1999	528	84	6	8
	Smitt et al, 1995	303	120	2	22
	Dewar et al, 1995	663	120	6	14
	Obedien et al, 1999	984	120	2	18
	Kini et al, 1998	400	120	6	17
Negative > 3 mm	Pittinger et al, 1994	183	54	3	25
Negative > 5 mm	Iloriguchi et al, 1999	161	47	1	11
	Schmidt-Ulrich et al, 1989	108	60	0	0
Microscopic	Spivack et al, 1994§	258	48	4	18
	Borger et al, 1994?	723	66	2	16
	Bartelink et al, 1988?	585	72	2	9

Positive margins are defined as tumor cells appearing at the cut edge of the excised specimen.
*Negative margins not defined quantitatively.
†Local recurrence: 9% with focally positive margin, 28% with extensively positive margin.
‡Local recurrence: 14% with focally positive margin, 27% with extensively positive margin.
§Negative margin defined as no microscopic foci of tumor cells at inked margins.
?Negative margins defined as greater than one microscopic field.
Reprinted with permission from Singletary SE.[27]

gross excision. However, a number of recent studies have reported that negative surgical margins diminish the risk of breast cancer recurrence in EIC-positive tumors.[29,30] Although the presence of an EIC is a pathologic indicator for possibly more extensive disease, it does not appear to be an independent risk factor for local recurrence when the margin status is taken into consideration. Patients with EIC-positive tumors, in whom the initial margins of resection are positive, should undergo re-excision. If the re-excision margins are negative, then these patients would be excellent candidates for breast conservation surgery and irradiation. If re-excision or margins remain positive and further re-excision is not possible, then mastectomy is the preferred treatment.

Age

Local and distant recurrence rates are strongly influenced by patient age. Several retrospective studies have reported that young patient age, defined as < 35 years old or 40 years, is associated with increased risk of distant metastases and reduced disease-specific survival. The higher recurrence rate found in younger patients can be attributable to the more aggressive nature of disease, a higher incidence of lymphovascular invasion, high nuclear grade, tumor necrosis, and the frequent presence of an EIC. Since these patients also have a higher risk of local recurrence after mastectomy, a young age should not be used to exclude breast conservation therapy.

Conversely, it has been perceived by some that breast cancer in the elderly is so indolent as to permit less rigorous treatment. Solin and colleagues have shown that the 10-year outcomes of BCT in women of at least 65 years of age and women 50 to 65 years of age had equivalent risks of in-breast recurrence (as determined by stage and prognostic factors) and equivalent breast cancer deaths.[31]

Family History/Biologic Tumor Markers

Family history and genetic disposition for breast cancer may play a role on the outcome of BCT. One study from the Joint Center for Radiation Therapy (JCRT) compared local control rates in 29 women age 36 years or less, who had a first-degree relative with breast cancer before age 50 years as well as a family history of ovarian carcinoma, and172 women aged 36 years or less, who did not have these family history criteria.[32] The 5-year crude rate was 3% in patients with a positive family history and 14% in patients who did not have a family history. The study also showed that those patients with a positive family history had a 5.7-fold increase of developing contralateral breast cancer compared with those with a negative family history. A similar study conducted at the University of Pennsylvania showed no difference in local control based on family history of breast cancer in young patients. For patients under 40 years of age, 5-year local failure results were 8% for those with first-degree relatives with breast cancer, 2% for those with a non–first-degree relative with breast cancer, and 12% for those with a negative family history.[33]

An area of active research is the effect of germline mutations on the outcome of BCT. Turner and colleagues from Yale University reported that 15% of the patients (n = 52) who had *BRCA1* and *BRCA2* mutations developed an ipsilateral recurrence after BCT.[34] Surprisingly, those who developed a recurrence, and who had a germline mutation, recurred at a median interval of 7.8 years compared with 4.7 years for those who did not.[34] Pierce and colleagues reported a 5-year local failure-free survival rate of 98% in 71 women with *BRCA1* and *BRCA2* mutations and 96% in 213 matched controls with sporadic breast cancer.[35] No additional complications from radiation therapy were found in women with these germline mutations. In another study, 329 women of Ashkenazi Jewish heritage were found to have the same recurrence rate in the ipsilateral breast as in the contralateral breast. Although their reported rates of 5- and 10-year ipsilateral breast tumor recurrence were 15 and 22%, respectively, these rates were not statistically differentiable from non-*BRCA* carriers.[36]

Expression of various biologic markers and their relation to the risk of local recurrence continue to be an area of ongoing study. Overexpression of the HER2/neu oncoprotein, insulin-like growth factor, and accumulation of the *p53* protein have all been reported to be associated with an increased local recurrence rate, following conservative surgery and radiotherapy.[37] However, the results have not been established and should not be considered guidelines. Additional studies are warranted to make recommendations regarding local therapy on the results of such biologic marker studies.

From these studies, BCT may be considered an appropriate treatment for women with a positive family history or a genetic predisposition to breast cancer. It is likely that these patients have an increased risk of secondary tumor development in the ipsilateral and contralateral breast.

Adjuvant Systemic Therapy

The use of adjuvant systemic therapy has been shown to be an important factor associated with a reduced risk of recurrence in the ipsilateral breast when used in conjunction with surgery and radiation therapy. Illustrative of these findings is the NSABP B-13 trial, where the 8-year rates of recurrence in the ipsilateral breast were 13.4% without chemotherapy and 2.6%

with chemotherapy.[38] When adjuvant tamoxifen was added, similar results were seen. In the NSABP B-14 trial of 1,062 node-negative, ER-positive patients treated with lumpectomy and irradiation, the 10-year rates of recurrence in the ipsilateral breast were 14.7% without tamoxifen and 4.3% with tamoxifen.[39] Similar results were seen in the Stockholm Breast Cancer Study Group study, in which patients were randomized to tamoxifen or to a placebo.[40] The 10-year rates of recurrence among 432 patients treated with lumpectomy and radiation therapy in the ipsilateral breast were 12% without tamoxifen and 3% with tamoxifen.[40] In the absence of complete local therapy, this effect is not seen, and chemotherapy does not appear to take the place of adequate surgery or radiotherapy.

Race

Race may be an independent predictor of outcome. Although some minorities may appear to have a higher death rate from breast cancer, this appears to be completely accounted for by disparities in health care access.[41] The data that exist for race are primarily for African American women. From multiple cancer surveillance sources, African American women have lower overall incidence rates of breast cancer compared with Caucasian women, but are diagnosed with later stage disease, shorter survival, and among the highest rate of breast cancer mortality of all racial-ethnic groups.[42] Despite these trends, cancer surveillance programs, such as Surveillance, Epidemiology, and End Results (SEER), were designed to monitor geographically defined populations, not racially or ethnically defined populations. The SEER breast cancer database for African American women reflects a highly urban African American population, particularly in the Western and Midwestern regions, which may overestimate the incidence of the African American women population at large, but may also underestimate the incidence since there is no information from Southern or rural African American communities.[43] Surveillance data regarding race need to continue to improve data quality, to render the data more readily available, and to enumerate accurately the population at risk.

Boost Treatment

The use of a tumor bed boost after irradiation has an important influence in decreasing the risk of local recurrence. The Lyon Group investigated the use of a 10 Gy boost after 50 Gy of breast irradiation. The use of a boost led to a small but statistically significant reduction in the 5-year local recurrence rate (3.6% versus 4.5%).[44] The EORTC subsequently conducted a much larger randomized clinical trial that validated the earlier results from France. Findings showed that a 16 Gy boost reduced the 5-year rate of local recurrence from 6.8 to 4.3% ($p < .0001$).[45] Since boosts are ideally delivered to the region of the tumor, delineation of the operative bed with clips is desired in most cases, and this can also assist with radiotherapy planning of the primary fields.

INTEGRATION OF RADIATION THERAPY AND CHEMOTHERAPY

The use of systemic therapy is continuing to increase in patients with early-stage breast cancer, and its integration with surgery and radiation therapy remains an important clinical question. Retrospective reviews suggest that increased rates of local regional recurrence may occur when radiation therapy is delayed after surgery.[46] Delaying chemotherapy in order to give radiation therapy may increase the risk of distant metastasis and ultimately impact survival.[47] Based on these studies, the JCRT conducted a randomized, prospective clinical trial, randomly assigning four cycles of doxorubicin-based combination chemotherapy followed by radiation therapy, or radiation therapy followed by four cycles of the same chemotherapy. Among the entire cohort of breast cancer patients treated with conservative surgery, there was no advantage to giving radiation therapy before adjuvant chemotherapy.[48] Subgroup analysis pointed out that this equivalence may not persist in patients with positive margins of resection. Several investigators have shown in case-control studies that long intervals between surgery and radiotherapy, without any intervening treatment, result in impaired locoregional control.[49]

BREAST CONSERVATION RADIATION THERAPY

The primary objective of radiation therapy in breast conservation therapy is to eradicate microscopic residual disease adjacent to the original site of tumor and to eliminate any evidence of microscopic multicentric disease. A significant majority of the early failures in this patient group are in the same quadrant as the original primary, and therefore, achieving adequate coverage in that area is imperative. The risk of failure in other quadrants of the breast appears relatively low, even in patients who receive no radiotherapy at all. It is this fact that has led some investigators to consider less-than-whole-breast treatment in selected patients (see Partial Breast Irradiation below). Computed tomography (CT) permits the easy evaluation of the operative bed (especially if clips or a seroma is present) and identification of the majority of the remaining breast tissue as well as adjacent avoidance structures such as the heart and lung. CT-based planning is highly preferred over fluoroscopic planning and is rapidly becoming a standard of care.

Treatment to Breast Only

Radiation therapy is administered to the breast alone in all patients who have excision ("lumpectomy" or segmental resection) of early-stage invasive carcinomas. Current standards also recommend the use of postexcision irradiation for most patients with DCIS, although selective avoidance is considered in a subset of patients with "favorable" DCIS; that is, those with very small low-grade lesions with excessive wide-to-clear margins. Lymph node-negative patients with an adequate axillary assessment do not need to have their regional lymphatics treated, nor is it generally useful in patients with early-stage disease. If regional nodal irradiation is considered, then its intent must be integrated into the original planning sessions. Schlembach and colleagues reported the possibility of using opposing pairs of "high tangents" to treat the level I and level II axillary nodes in patients with incompletely assessed axillae or with microscopic involvement of the sentinel nodes.[50] Tumors located at the extreme edges of the breast are particularly at risk for a geographic miss of the peritumoral tissue. Tumor beds are easily contoured in patients with recent lumpectomies. The placement of surgical clips remains useful for the radiation oncologist when planning radiation treatment fields. If long time intervals pass from surgery to irradiation planning, as is common for adjuvant chemotherapy, there may be almost no visible operative bed to guide radiotherapy planning.

The basic technique for supine breast tangential treatment is surprisingly variable. Subtle differences in target delineation, immobilization techniques, dose specification, and missing tissue compensation suggest that there is no such thing as a single "standard" breast treatment. From the CT data set (Figure 22–5) and prior to beginning the final development of the tangential field set, contouring of the incision site and operative bed is performed; any adjacent avoidance structures may also be contoured. The development of a tangent pair with a non-coplanar posterior edge is determined to obtain optimum coverage of the tumor bed and the majority of the breast mound, while at the same time minimizing the exposure of adjacent structures not at risk (Figure 22–6, A and B). Generally, no cardiac structure should be included within the tangent fields and it is usually possible to minimize the amount of adjacent lung to 1.5 to 2 cm (Figure 22–7)

The dose is specified at the pectoral surface and with appropriate compensation for missing tissue or lung heterogeneity. Typically, 50 Gy in 25 fractions

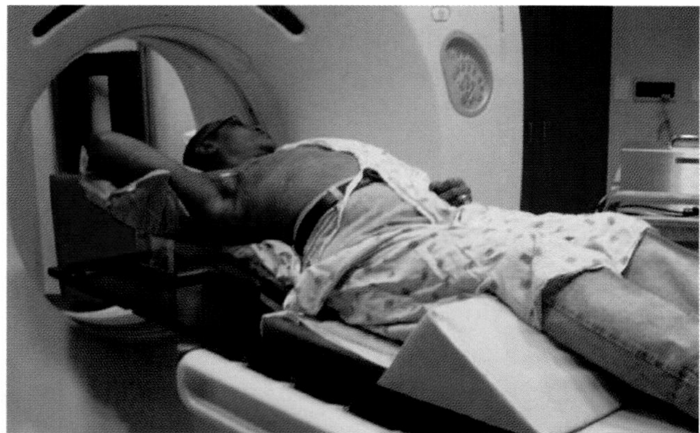

Figure 22–5. Computed tomography simulation with slant board and cradle, with the arm highly abducted. These ensure proper immobilization of the body and arm as well as daily reproducibility of the patient's treatment position.

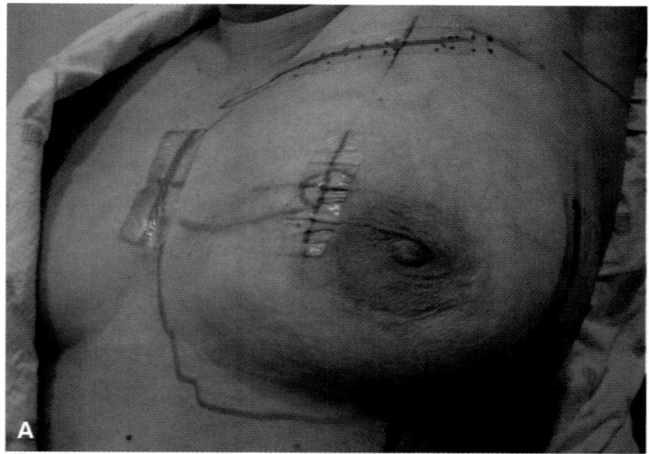

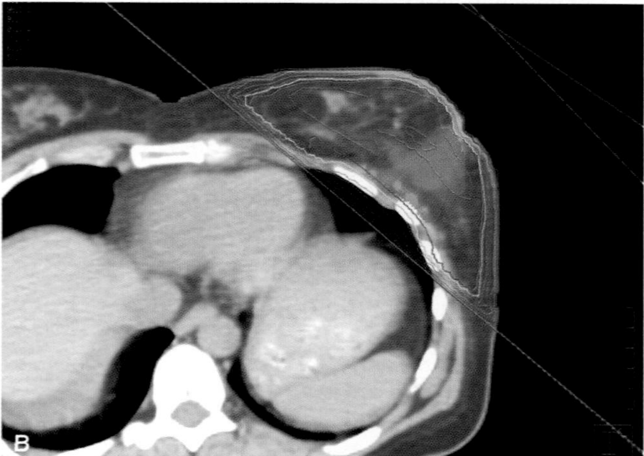

Figure 22–6. *A,* Treatment fields drawn on an intact breast. The lines in *red* represent the primary field and central axis. The lines in blue represent the set-up lasers. *B,* Computed tomography plan of tangent fields with tumor bed contour.

is prescribed at the dose specification isodose. Intensity modulation with a field-in-field "step and shoot" technique results in better homogeneity of the dose within the target volume than with classic wedge-filtered fields. Additional advantages include the need for fewer monitoring units than comparable wedged plans, and hence enhanced treatment times, as well as decreased dose to distant normal tissue such as the opposite breast.[51] Radiation treatment for BCT is relatively well tolerated. The treatment is targeted to the entire ipsilateral breast. Generally, 45 to 50 Gy is delivered in 25 to 28 fractions over a 5-week period. Many institutions add a boost to the region of the tumor bed, delivering an additional 10 to 16 Gy in 5 to 8 fractions. Therefore, the therapy lasts approximately 6 to 7 weeks.

Each treatment only lasts a few minutes, and during the course of treatment, most patients can continue to work and maintain a near-normal functional status. Patients sometimes can experience fatigue and mild irritation over the ipsilateral breast. Symptoms usually subside after the treatment is completed. Long-term breast esthetics are very good to excellent with this approach.

Prone Position Breast Conservation Radiation Therapy

Large pendulous breasts have been a historic contraindication for BCT. If these women are treated in the standard supine position, an excessive amount of lung and heart irradiation may ensue. The consequences of tissue folds and large separations may result in excessive skin reaction and late fibrosis. Treating these patients in the prone position minimizes breast separation and dose inhomogeneity within the treatment field and removes most skin folds (Figure 22–8). In addition, it is frequently possible to reduce irradiation to the heart, lung, and contralateral breast when the patient is placed prone, since the tumor bed moves away from these structures.[52]

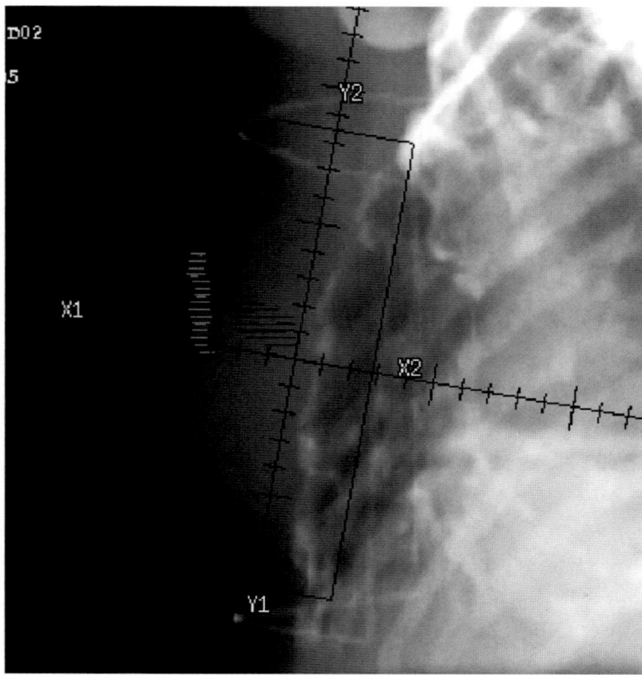

Figure 22–7. Right medial tangent digital reconstructed radiograph with contouring of the tumor bed.

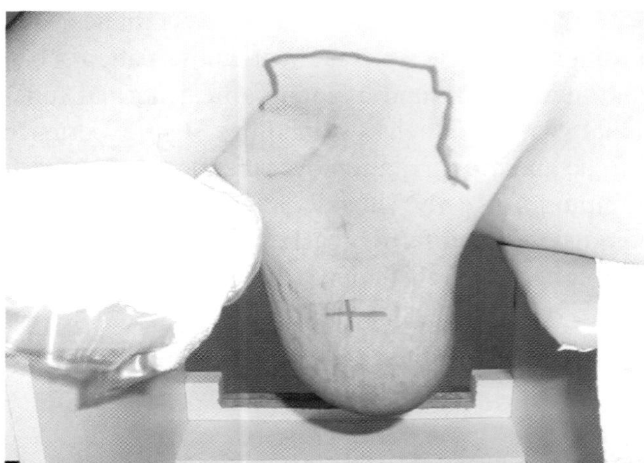

Figure 22–8. Set-up for prone breast irradiation.

CONSIDERATIONS FOR RADIATION THERAPY IN BREAST CONSERVATION THERAPY

Although most patients with early-stage breast cancer may be considered for BCT with excision and irradiation, there are several absolute contraindications and special considerations from the radiation oncologist's point of view.

Contraindications

Pregnancy

Women who are pregnant are generally advised against radiation therapy. Early in the course of pregnancy, internal radiation scatter from radiation of the intact breast can reach teratogenic dose levels, which cannot be eliminated by increasing external shielding.[53,54] As an alternative, it may be possible to perform breast conserving surgery and/or chemotherapy during the pregnancy and treat the patient with radiation after delivery.

Collagen Vascular Disease

A history of certain autoimmune or collagen vascular diseases, particularly systemic lupus erythematosus, mixed connective tissue disorder, or scleroderma (progressive systemic sclerosis), is an important contraindication to elective radiation treatment. Those who undergo radiation therapy tolerate it poorly.[55,56] Most radiation oncologists will not treat a patient who has active lupus or scleroderma. Women with such connective tissue disorders are at increased risk for significant late radiation complications, including breast fibrosis, pain, chest wall necrosis, and brachial plexopathy. Patients with rheumatoid arthritis and other rheumatologic illness may tolerate radiation much better.[57]

Multicentricity or Multifocality

Women with diffuse suspicious microcalcifications should be advised to have a mastectomy rather than BCT. Women with two or more primary tumors in separate quadrants of the breast are also a contraindication (see "Multicentricity and Extensive Microcalcifications," above).

Previous History of Radiation Therapy

History of prior therapeutic radiation to the breast region is another contraindication to BCT because it would require additional treatment to an excessively high cumulative radiation dose.

Special Issues

Persistent Positive Margins

Persistent positive margins after reasonable surgical attempts is a relative contradiction. The importance of a single focally positive microscopic margin needs further study and may not be an absolute contraindication (see "Surgical Margins," above).

Central Breast Cancers

Patients whose breast cancer directly involves the nipple or areola (including those with Paget's disease of the nipple), are usually excluded from BCT and continue to be treated with mastectomy.[58] Breast-conserving surgery for this group of patients requires resection of some or all of the nipple-areolar complex (NAC) for complete tumor excision. Resection has been rejected because of a purported higher incidence of multicentricity associated with central breast cancers.[59] Many also feel that resection of the NAC will lead to an unacceptable cosmesis.[60] Since several authors have shown successful results of BCT for patients with central tumors, in the absence of demonstrated multicentricity, patients should be the primary arbiters of the cosmetic outcome of this procedure.[58]

Breast Size

The size of the breast in relation to mass size is an important issue in achieving complete neoplasm removal and maintaining adequate cosmesis. In a small-breasted patient, wide local excision with negative margins can result in a significant deformity of the breast. This difficulty can be overcome by using local rotational flaps to fill the defect left after the tumor removal.[61] Using this technique can achieve excellent cosmesis and yet still maintain low rates of local recurrence. On the other end of the spectrum, women with large pendulous breasts have different challenges. After excision the delivery of homogeneous doses of radiation to a pendulous breast is difficult, and thus incurs more radiation-induced adverse effects. This challenge can be overcome by performing additional reduction mammoplasty contemporaneously with the lumpectomy.[62] As long as the surgeon and patient are committed to the approach, small-breasted or large-breasted women should not be used as exclusion criteria for BCT.

Prosthesis

Previous breast augmentation with saline or silicone can develop unfavorable consequences in some patients treated with radiotherapy. Although the dosimetry and acute side effects of treatment are no different than those for other patients groups, the development of excessive capsular fibrosis and contracture can be significant. Skin thickness and texture may remain excellent, but fibrosis can lead to chronic pain and fixation of the implant. Unfavorable long-term cosmesis occurs in as many as 40% of patients. Since it appears that patients may be more tolerant of capsular contracture than physicians we do not routinely recommend their removal prior to BCT.[63,64]

ADVANCED PRESENTATIONS DOWN-STAGED BY CHEMOTHERAPY

Primary breast tumors that are > 4 to 5 cm or are associated with signs of advanced disease are not candidates for primary breast conservation. Those patients with T3 or T4 primaries or with advanced nodal disease are considered to have locally advanced breast cancer (LABC) and are typically treated with initial chemotherapy. It is estimated that approximately 80% of patients will have some objective response with the use of anthracyclines and/or taxane chemotherapy. An initial feasibility study, of 143 patients with LABC who had responded to initial chemotherapy, showed the following factors associated with clinically unsuspected tumor in other quadrants of the breast: (1) persistent skin edema, (2) residual tumor > 5 cm, (3) extensive lymphatic invasion in initial biopsy, or (4) mammographic evidence of multicentric lesions or diffuse microcalcification.[65] The absence of these features is the primary selection criterion for patients who are to be offered breast conservation after initial chemotherapy.

Pretreatment evaluation is particularly important since initial chemotherapy may obscure the results of subsequent evaluations. Ambiguous lesions in other quadrants of the breast should be characterized by ultrasonography, magnetic resonance imaging, or biopsy, if needed. The extent and distribution of nodal metastasis should be clearly defined. Ideally, these patients are seen by a multidisciplinary team, including the radiation oncologist, prior to beginning therapy.

Assuming the successful down-staging of an advanced primary tumor and subsequent complete surgical excision and lymph node assessment, radiotherapy planning for these patients is feasible but can be challenging. It combines the extended volumes usually encountered in the postmastectomy setting, with the desire for cosmetically superior outcomes. Inclusion of nodal basins involves the use of multiple adjacent treatment portals, which must be precisely matched to avoid the consequences of junctional overlap or geographic miss. The treatment fields are based on the *original* extent of disease. This results in treating the ipsilateral supraclavicular fossa, internal mammary nodes, and possibly the axilla in addition to the glandular breast, depending on the original disease stage and tumor distribution. All targeted areas are treated to a minimum of 50 Gy, with a 10 Gy boost to the region of the primary tumor.

Nodal sites known to contain tumor at presentation, but that are not resected (ie, infraclavicular or internal mammary nodes), are boosted with an additional 10 to 16 Gy, depending on the response.

PARTIAL-BREAST IRRADIATION

General Concepts

Partial-breast irradiation can be delivered with brachytherapy, hypofractionated conformal external-beam radiation therapy, or intraoperatively using either electrons or a linear accelerator. Each technique has its advantages and limitations. Reports of patients in phase I and II studies treated with accelerated partial-breast irradiation after breast-conserving surgery have suggested favorable early results; however, there is limited long-term follow-up.[66] The major potential benefit of partial-breast irradiation is the ability to complete the local therapy in a much shorter period of time than classic whole-breast treatment. Typical dose schedules complete the treatment in the span of days to a week. Although large-dose per fraction radiation treatment, called *hypofractionation*, typically results in increased radiation late effects, it is thought that the reduced treatment volume of partial-breast irradiation may result in acceptable toxicity rates. It is also theorized that the reduced treatment volumes may permit a second course of BCT to be administered, should the need arise. This potential has not been assessed.

Multiplane, Multineedle Implant

When contemplating definitive partial-breast irradiation with a needle- or catheter-based approach, a larger volume implant is usually required. Definitive catheter-based brachytherapy, although the most validated of the partial-breast techniques, is also technically challenging.[67] Typically, a minimum of two planes are required, with more if the surgical volume is extensive. The deep plane is located at the level of and parallel to the posterior aspect of the excision cavity. The superficial plane is at the level of the superficial border of the cavity. Within a given plane, catheters are separated between 1.0 to 1.5 cm and extend at least 2 cm beyond the edge of the cavity and 1 cm or more beyond the edge of the target. As with all planar implants, the catheters are parallel and as straight as possible. Although multineedle brachytherapy has historically been delivered using low-dose-rate radiation sources, high-dose-rate (HDR) treatments have become increasingly popular and can be delivered on an outpatient basis. A typical HDR dose of 34 Gy is delivered twice daily, in fractions of 3.4 Gy over a total of 5 days.

MammoSite

The MammoSite applicator is a completely different kind of brachytherapy method that combines a balloon-like device with a point source of ^{192}Ir.[68–71] While it may be placed during the local excision or a few weeks after the surgical procedure, catheters may need to be removed, owing to unexpected pathology or unacceptable implant geometry. Applicators should be selected to conform to the seroma cavity without large air or fluid collections (Figure 22–9). Ideally, the applicator is 1 cm or more from the skin surface, as focal skin necrosis has been noted with < 7 mm separation. After verifying that no significant distortion of the applicator has occurred and that the source travels to the geometric center of the applicator, 34 Gy is prescribed at 1 cm distance from the balloon surface and is delivered in 2 fractions per day, separated by at least 6 hours, for a total of 10 fractions of 3.4 Gy each. It has been argued that the volume of peritumoral tissue treated with the MammoSite® and the dose gradient within the treated volume permit only limited extrapolation of outcomes from other brachytherapy series.

Conformal External Beam

Three to 5 non-coplanar photon beams have also been used to achieve partial-breast irradiation.[72–74] The clinical target volume (CTV) is defined by uniformly expanding the excision cavity volume by 10 to 15 mm. The CTV is limited to at least 5 mm from the skin surface and lung–chest wall interface. The CTV is further expanded an additional 10 mm (less, if breathing motion studies have been performed) to generate a planning target volume. A total of 38.5 Gy is prescribed to the isocenter, in 10 fractions

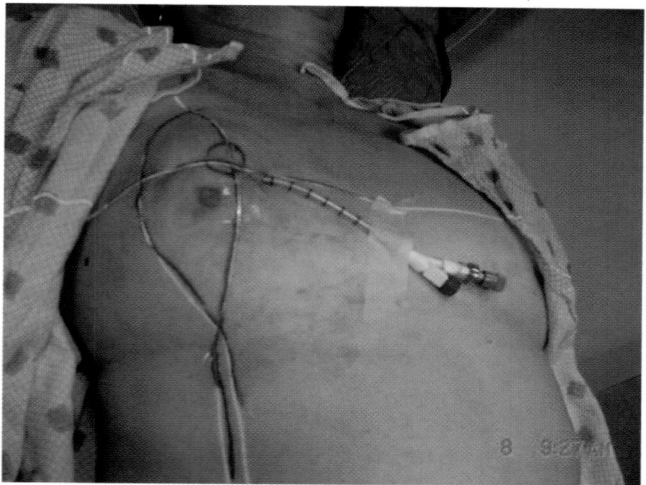

Figure 22–9. MammoSite applicator.

of 3.85 Gy delivered twice, daily, with at least a 6-hour interfraction interval. Ideally, < 25% of the whole breast receives the prescribed dose, and < 50% of the whole breast receives ≥ 50% of the prescribed dose. The heart, contralateral lung, and contralateral breast should receive < 5% of the dose.

BOOST TREATMENT

Although there has been controversy regarding whether or not a boost is required for treatment, recent clinical trials have substantiated its usefulness.[75] Among these trials, the EORTC has reported the favorable impact of boosts on local recurrent rates.[76] Boost treatment is clearly indicated for patients with focally positive or close margins of resection. The total dose to the primary tumor site is increased to approximately 60 to 66 Gy (Figure 22–10). Selection of the boost dose and volume is based on the patient's surgical and pathologic information. A boost may not be required for those patients with more favorable tumors, whose margins are clearly negative as long as the whole breast is treated to at least 50 Gy.[77]

If margins are close or unknown, then re-excision should be considered to ensure the lowest failure rate and avoid the consequences of higher doses of irradiation provided that the amount of breast tissue is sufficient.[78] With most invasive carcinomas, especially with an extensive or multifocal intraductal component, lymphatic invasion, or high nuclear grade, or in any patient who has irradiation deferred until after chemotherapy, the field is reduced after 50 Gy. An additional 10 Gy of electrons in 5 fractions is delivered to include the lumpectomy and incision sites. The choice of energy depends on the thickness of the breast in treatment position. Appropriate electron energy is selected to allow the 90% isodose line to encompass the target volume. We currently use a 2 cm radial expansion of the combined operative bed and incision site to set the field borders. If the tumor bed is > 4 to 5 cm deep within the breast, then an interstitial implant may be preferable, because of the decreased skin dose with the implant compared with the dose that would be delivered by electrons. Use of a staggered double-plane technique is usually best, because of the possibility of a geographic miss with a single-plane implant. For patients with tumors deep in the breast, additional external irradiation may be delivered by means of a compression technique or by turning the patient into the lateral decubitus position for lateral tumors. Higher doses (typically 14 to 16 Gy) may be used if the margins are close or focally positive, or if the breast tangent dose is reduced to < 50 Gy.

REGIONAL NODES

When regional nodal irradiation is combined with breast tangent fields, additional complexities are

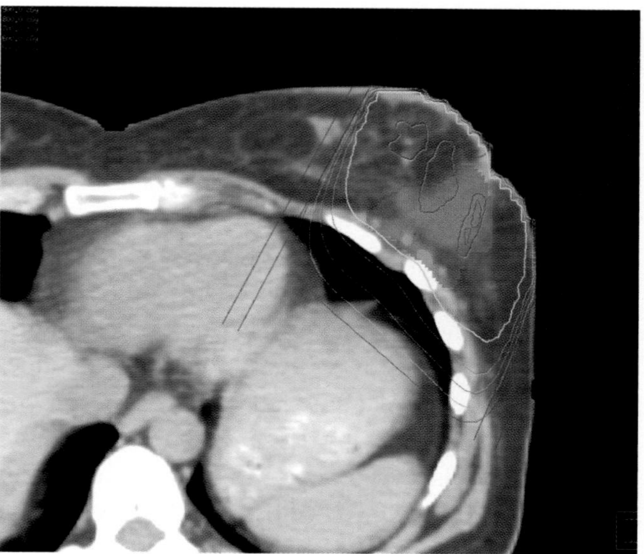

Figure 22–10. Contouring of the tumor bed incision site on a three-dimensional treatment boost plan.

involved. Junctional variation, always an area of dosimetric uncertainty, should be minimized through standardized techniques and superior immobilization. Breast field planning with nondivergent field edges is required at field abutments. The techniques used to treat the supraclavicular, axillary, and internal mammary nodes are identical to those described below for the postmastectomy setting.

COSMETIC OUTCOME

Ever since the climate had changed toward minimally invasive surgical procedures for the management of breast cancer, cosmetic outcome has become an even more important goal in addition to local tumor control. Variation in the type of breast-conserving surgery can influence cosmetic outcome, with quadrantectomy recognized as giving a worse cosmetic outcome than lumpectomy.[79] Breast size, location of tumor, extent of surgery, number of surgical procedures, surgical scar length, and radiation therapy are other factors that can influence the cosmetic outcome in patients with early-stage breast cancer.[80] Even though radiation therapy may negatively impact cosmesis, a majority of these patients still have good to excellent cosmetic outcomes judged by themselves and their surgeons.[81]

POSTMASTECTOMY RADIATION THERAPY

Postmastectomy radiation continues to be an important component of therapy for patients with more advanced cancers. After the publication in 1987 of a meta-analysis by Cuzick and colleagues that reported increased mortality in women who had received postmastectomy radiation therapy, the use of postmastectomy irradiation was intensely challenged.[82] This meta-analysis and subsequent studies were strongly influenced by the results of several early trials that were hampered by poor radiation technique, improper patient selection, and infrequent use of adjuvant systemic therapy. Recent reports from large prospective trials have reversed this former judgment against postmastectomy radiation therapy. These trials have shown excellent locoregional control, disease-free survival, and improved overall survival with the use of radiation therapy after mastectomy. The best overall results are seen with combined modality therapy including systemic therapy. In the Early Breast Cancer Trialists Group study that combined the results of multiple randomized trials, radiotherapy following surgery reduced the risk of breast cancer mortality with an odds ratio of 0.91 (99% CI 0.87–0.95, $p = 0.001$).[83] Trials performed by the Danish Breast Cancer Cooperative Group and in British Columbia have shown a survival increase resulting from chest wall irradiation for premenopausal, node-positive disease.[84,85] A separate report from the Danish Breast Cancer Cooperative Group demonstrated that postmenopausal women with node-positive breast cancer also benefited from radiation therapy after mastectomy and adjuvant tamoxifen.[86]

Although initial surgery with a detailed pathology report can provide similar information about the extent of disease in early- and intermediate-stage breast cancers, these data are unavailable when neoadjuvant chemotherapy is used. For more advanced tumors, thorough initial imaging is mandatory and includes full characterization of the primary and regional nodal tumor burden. After beginning chemotherapy, periodic imaging assessment of the tumor response at every 6 to 8 weeks is key to confirming the appropriateness of the current intervention and determining the operability of the tumor. Patients with persistent extensive lymph node disease may need to be switched to alternative chemotherapy regimens or offered investigational therapy.

Local treatment planning is informed by this more detailed regional nodal information. For example, when patients present with disease in the infraclavicular region (anatomically, the level II/III axilla and interpectoral space), radiotherapy planning should specifically address this finding. Using complete initial staging information, the radiation oncologist can specifically target the region using clinically, sonographically, or CT-defined parameters for boosting. Similarly, disease initially identified in the internal mammary or supraclavicular regions, which is rarely resected, can be addressed at radiotherapy planning.

Indications

Postmastectomy radiation continues to be an important therapy for patients with more advanced cancers.

It substantially reduces locoregional recurrence rates and contributes to improved disease-specific survival. It is indicated in the following subset of patients[87]:

1. Four or more axillary lymph nodes
2. T3 or T4 tumors with positive axillary nodes and patients with operable stage III tumors
3. Positive margins or gross (> 2 mm) extranodal extension
4. Advanced regional nodal disease (N_2 or N_3)

In addition, postmastectomy radiation therapy may be indicated for selected patients with several or some of the following features:

1. Inner quadrant tumors associated with positive axillary nodes
2. Extensive lymphatic vascular space invasion[88]
3. One to 3 axillary lymph nodes containing macrometastasis[89]
4. > 20% lymph nodes containing tumor[90]
5. Estrogen receptor-negative[91]
6. Young age[91]

Regional Nodal Targets

Since most of the recurrences in patients with high-risk breast cancer involve the supraclavicular fossa–axillary apex and/or chest wall, these are the two obligate targets for postmastectomy radiation therapy. Factors predictive of locoregional recurrence in the supraclavicular fossa–axillary apex parallel those for the chest wall and include the presence of four or more axillary lymph nodes, or > 20% involved axillary nodes.[92] These patients have a 15 to 20% risk of failure in the supraclavicular fossa–axillary apex and should therefore be offered adjuvant radiation therapy to this region as well as to the chest wall.[90] There is no consensus about the role of specific irradiation of the internal mammary chain (IMC) lymphatics, nor of the completely dissected low (lateral) axilla. However, those trials that demonstrate a survival benefit for radiotherapy did include the IMC in the treated volume.

Internal Mammary Chain

Treatment of the IMC, in the context of postmastectomy radiation therapy continues to be a controversial topic.[93,94] Although IMC recurrences rarely happen and are rarely detected, women with LABC have rates of IMC lymph node involvement of up to 50%.[95] Whereas it may not be useful to treat the IMC in the majority of early-stage breast cancer patients, it should be considered for patients with advanced presentations, inner or central tumors, axillary node-positive disease, or early-stage disease with primary drainage to the IMC on lymphoscintigraphy. Historically, two-dimensional fluoroscopic simulations did not allow direct visualization of the IMC. Conversely, with the advent of three-dimensional CT simulation, accurate localization of these nodal regions is possible while minimizing cardiac toxicity.

With CT-based planning, the ipsilateral IMC can be contoured on the CT data set by visualizing the patient's anatomy in axial, coronal, and sagittal views. Coverage can be accomplished by either extending the deep tangent field border to cover the IMC or by creating a separate appositional IMC electron field that is matched to the edge of the medial tangent field (Figure 22–11). Treatment to the ipsilateral IMC nodes is given with electron beam irradiation to avoid underlying cardiac and mediastinal tissues.

When using electrons, 50 Gy is given over 5 weeks, at 5 fractions per week, and 2 Gy per fraction. It may not be possible to give the entire dosage with electrons since skin doses vary according to the accelerator being used. As an alternative, a combination of electrons and photons may be necessary to achieve a lower dose to the skin. CT planning or ultrasonography is highly desirable to measure the depth to the pleural interface.

Axilla

Specific radiation treatment of the axilla is rarely required since failure in this area is rare after axillary dissection and chemotherapy. At M.D. Anderson Cancer Center, 1,031 patients treated with mastectomy, including an axillary dissection, and doxorubicin-based systemic therapy without radiation were studied for regional nodal failure patterns. Failure in the low-mid axilla was an uncommon occurrence (3% at 10 years), and supplemental radiotherapy is probably not warranted for most patients.[90] The risk

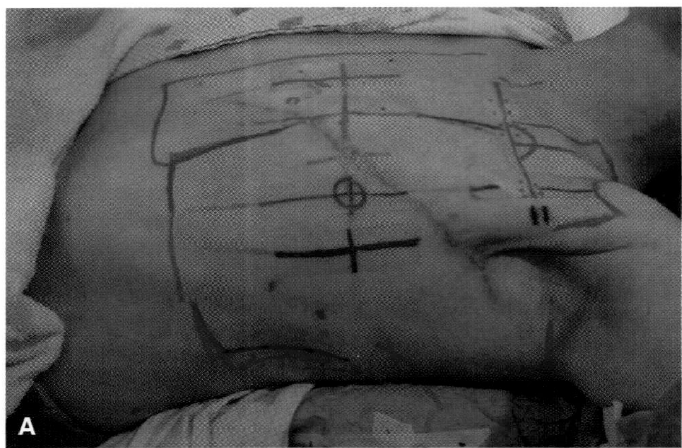

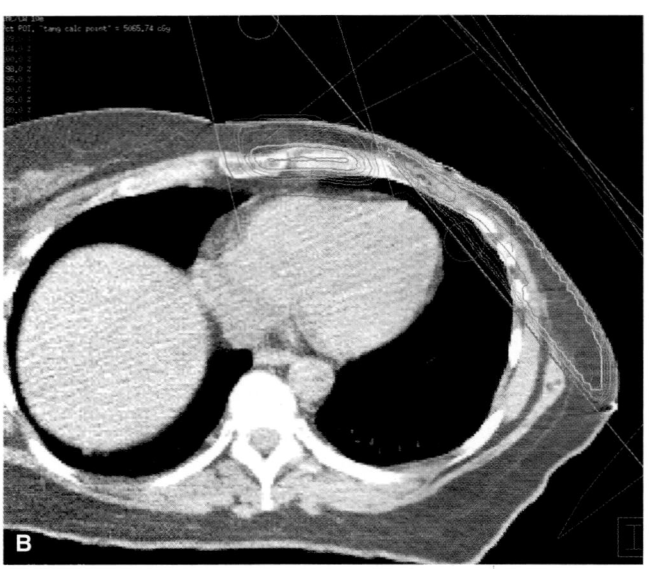

Figure 22–11. *A,* Internal mammary chain and medial tangent field arrangement for postmastectomy irradiation. *B,* Left-sided tumor, showing minimal irradiation of the heart and lung in the tangential fields.

of failure was not higher for patients with an increased number of axillary lymph nodes, increasing percentage of involved axillary lymph nodes, larger nodal size, or gross extranodal extension than for patients who did not have these features.

Irradiation of the dissected axilla should be considered under the following circumstances: (1) after simple or segmental mastectomy without axillary dissection, (2) for preoperative treatment (eg, inoperable N_2 patients), or (3) in patients who require axillary irradiation because of inadequate axillary dissection (only a few nodes are recovered and are positive). It may be considered for gross (> 2 mm) extranodal axillary disease, or matted or fixed axillary nodes (N_2 disease) at presentation.

The posterior axillary portal supplements the dose from the anterior portal to deliver the dose to the thickest part of the axilla. Because axillary recurrences are rare after levels I and II axillary dissection, and radiotherapy can increase the risk of lymphedema, the dose contribution from the anteroposterior and posteroanterior fields should not exceed 2.0 Gy per fraction at midplane.

For preoperative treatment (designed to reduce matted or fixed nodes to facilitate axillary dissection), a midplane dose of 50 Gy is necessary. For postoperative patients in whom extranodal extension in the axilla is found, but no gross residual disease remains, the midaxillary dose is reduced to 40 to 45 Gy in an attempt to decrease the risk of lymphedema.

Postmastectomy Boost

The targets for boost in the postmastectomy setting are the central operative flaps. Rigid conformation to the incision site (the effect of sometimes naming this a "scar" boost) is in fact not desired. Generous coverage of the central portion of the operative flaps with attention to the skin overlying the original tumor will prevent a geographic miss. Boosts of 10 to 16 Gy are typically done in the postmastectomy setting using low-energy electrons, so that the distal 90% isodose line encompasses the flaps and underlying pectoralis musculature (Figure 22–12).

POSTMASTECTOMY IRRADIATION AND RECONSTRUCTION

The increasing use of postmastectomy radiation therapy for early-stage disease has offered new challenges for reconstructive surgeons. Immediate breast reconstruction gives better cosmetic outcomes if postmastectomy radiation therapy is not required; however, if postmastectomy radiation therapy is necessary, then delayed reconstruction is recommended to avoid potential esthetic and radiation delivery problems.[96] Unfortunately, the need for postmastectomy radiation therapy usually cannot be reliably determined until after histologic evaluation of the mastectomy specimen.

There are two potential problems with a patient who undergoes immediate breast reconstruction if they ultimately need postmastectomy radiation therapy. The first problem, which is widely reported, is that postmastectomy radiation therapy can negatively impact the cosmetic outcome of an immediate reconstruction. The second and less-recognized problem is that immediate breast reconstruction can interfere with the delivery of postmastectomy radiation therapy. At the University of Texas, M.D. Anderson Cancer Center, a scoring system was developed to evaluate if the objectives of postmastectomy radiation therapy (breadth of chest wall coverage, treatment of the IMC, minimization of lung exposure, and avoidance of any heart irradiation) were being achieved in women who had undergone immediate breast reconstruction after mastectomy.[97] Reconstruction significantly compromised the delivery of radiation therapy.

Recently, at the M.D. Anderson Cancer Center, a delayed-immediate reconstruction approach was developed.[98] The first stage consists of a skin-sparing mastectomy followed by placement of a tissue expander. After reviewing the tissue specimens, those patients who did not require postmastectomy radiation therapy underwent immediate breast reconstruction. Those patients that required postmastectomy radiation therapy had their expanders fully deflated to minimize radiation delivery problems. After irradiation was completed, the tissue expander was inflated back to the pre-radiation therapy volume, followed by delayed breast reconstruction. Several aspects of delayed-immediate breast reconstruction will require further clinical investigation to define the long-term outcome.

INFLAMMATORY BREAST CANCER

Inflammatory breast cancer has long been recognized as a disease that requires effective systemic therapy to achieve an improvement in survival. However, the importance of locoregional control should not be overlooked. Barker and colleagues reported that the addition of chemotherapy to radiation treatment (without surgery) in 31 patients improved 5-year survival rates (30 to 40%), but the locoregional failure rate decreased by only 1%, from 27 to 26%.[99] Liao and colleagues concluded that twice-daily postmastectomy radiation to a total of 66 Gy for patients with inflammatory breast cancer resulted in improved locoregional control, disease-free survival, and overall survival.[100] Accelerated fractionation schedules are used to treat most patients unless the patient cannot comply with the twice-daily schedule.

RADIATION THERAPY FOR UNKNOWN PRIMARY TUMORS

Adenocarcinoma presenting in the axillary lymph nodes without an identifiable primary tumor site is a clinical entity. The presentation is usually the result of an occult primary breast tumor, although carcinomas of the thyroid, lung, stomach, and colorectum may also metastasize to the axillary nodes. Incidence of this phenomenon is rare. Reports indicate that it accounts for 0.3% of the 1% of breast cancer cases.[101]

Halsted observed that patients with an unknown primary tumor subsequently manifested with an overt breast primary.[102] Classic treatment was ipsilateral mastectomy. Today, locoregional therapy for most patients with an unknown primary tumor consists of surgical excision of gross disease, followed by radiation therapy to the breast and regional lymphatics. In most cases, surgical removal of the apparently normal breast has no therapeutic advantage, because comprehensive radiation will be required. Definitive irradiation of the breast at the same time as adjuvant irradiation of the regional nodes is a logical combination.

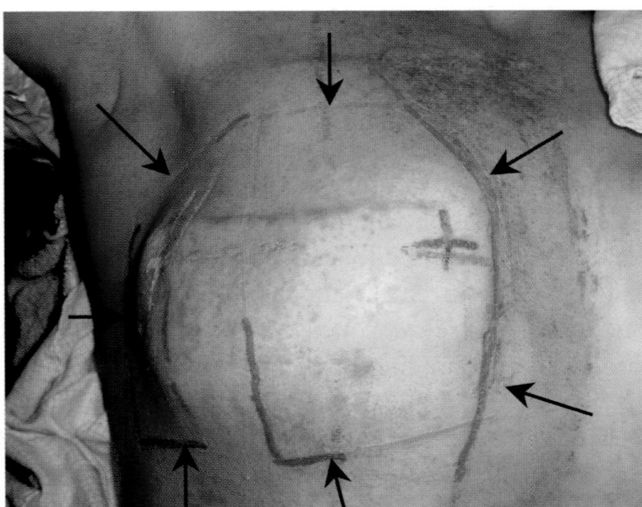

Figure 22–12. Electron boost field drawn on the chest wall flaps. Acute dermatitis to the chest wall is also seen.

Whillis and colleagues treated 12 patients with radiation therapy to the breast and lymphatics, and reported no local recurrences with follow-up times from 4 to 89 months.[103] Campana and colleagues also used conservative treatment[104]; in their series of 30 patients, 8 locoregional recurrences were evident, 4 in the breast and 4 in the axilla, with a 71% survival rate. The median time to recurrence was 112 months in the breast and 23 months in the axilla.[104] Long follow-up times are necessary to determine the true local control rates, because many relapses may not occur until several years after treatment. Studies from M.D. Anderson Cancer Center show similar results. In a recent analysis of 27 patients with adenocarcinoma in axillary nodes with an unknown primary tumor treated with BCT, high rates of local and regional control were achieved. The 5-year actuarial local control rate in the breast was 100% and the regional control rate at 5 years was 92.6%.[105]

The ipsilateral breast is treated with tangential fields of megavoltage photons to a dose of 50 Gy in 25 fractions. The supraclavicular fossa and axillary apex are also treated to 50 Gy in 25 fractions, and because most patients have N_2 disease, the midaxilla is often supplemented using a posterior field to a dose of 40 to 50 Gy, depending on the pathologic extent of disease.

LOCOREGIONAL RECURRENCE

Locoregional recurrences span a large spectrum of disease, from the very curable single nodule to the very symptomatic and extensive chest wall disease. When possible, patients without distant metastasis should be treated similarly to a locally advanced primary tumor with intent to cure. After achieving maximum response to initial systemic agents, consideration for resection and/or radiotherapy should be entertained. Recent pilot studies of radiation therapy delivered concurrently with chemosensitizing agents such as paclitaxel, docetaxel, and capecitabine have produced encouraging response rates.[106–108] Continued research is necessary before this regimen becomes standard of care.

Extensive tumor recurrence in the regional nodes, chest wall, or brachial plexus often require multimodal therapy, including intensive radiation therapy to minimize pain, neuropathy, and wound-care problems. Irradiation may provide substantial palliation when disease is unresectable or unresponsive to systemic agents. Large tumor volumes require higher doses to achieve the desired effect. The region is treated to 45 Gy in 15 fractions, with vigorous use of bolus doses over cutaneous nodules. A treatment break is usually required, because confluent moist desquamation and exfoliation of thin layers of normal skin overlying bulk tumor occur. After this break, an additional 15 to 20 Gy can be delivered to any residual tumor, provided that no dose-limiting structures are located in the boost volume.

RADIATION FOR PALLIATION

Objectives

Radiation therapy is an effective treatment for patients with symptomatic breast cancer. The two main functions for palliative therapy are (1) relief from symptoms such as pain, and (2) control of local tumor growth to prevent structural complications or complications arising from increasing pressure.

Palliation is achieved by balancing the potential benefits of relieving symptoms with the side effects, the cost, and any inconvenience that the patient must bear. If the patient has a good long-term outlook, then higher cumulative doses and smaller fractions are used. Faster schedules are preferred in patients with rapidly evolving disease.

Bone Metastasis

Breast cancer often metastasizes to bone and radiation therapy is helpful for patients with bone metastasis. Relief of pain can happen during the course of treatment, but more commonly occurs after treatment has finished. Restoration of bone can be expected after treatment commences. Breast cancer patients with bone disease can live for years, even decades. Treatment must be designed to minimize late effects and to anticipate future courses of radiation therapy (Figure 22–13). Typically, 30 Gy in 10 fractions over 2 weeks is given, although higher doses can be appropriate for patients with dormant disease. Several clinical trials have shown that the effectiveness of 8 Gy as a single fraction can also be used for short-term symptom relief, if the patient has a short life expectancy.[109]

Brain Metastasis

Brain metastases usually represent a more ominous phase of metastatic breast cancer. Whenever possible, symptomatic brain lesions should be removed to achieve a more rapid response. Whole-brain radiation therapy (WBRT) is effective against microscopic and small-volume macroscopic disease, but consideration must be made for potential late morbid effects on normal brain parenchyma. Fraction sizes of 2 or 2.5 Gy are preferable to larger doses, reducing the incidence of functional impairment. Doses of 30 to 35 Gy are commonly delivered to the whole brain, with boost doses targeted at individual tumor nodules using reduced fields or with a stereotactic approach. Stereotactic radiosurgery (SRS) for multiple brain metastases from breast carcinoma may become a future treatment for some patients. Muacevic and colleagues showed that the local brain tumor control rate was 94% in 151 patients who received stereotactic radiosurgery.[110] Even though 30% of the patients also received WBRT, there was no difference in local tumor control or survival. Future randomized clinical trials comparing SRS/WBRT versus SRS alone are warranted.

RADIATION THERAPY COMPLICATIONS

Arm edema

The most frequent complication associated with this treatment is arm edema, with between 5 and 20% of patients having this complication.[111] The incidence of arm edema is clearly related to the extent of axillary dissection and to the use of axillary irradiation.[112] One randomized trial from the NCI showed that the incidence of arm edema was found to be equal in each follow-up visit, regardless of whether the patient had mastectomy as opposed to lumpectomy and irradiation.[113] Full-course radiotherapy to an already dissected axilla increases the risk of arm edema to 40%. Recent clinical research has shown that adjunctive intermittent pneumatic compression, in conjunction with decongestive lymphatic therapy, reduces mean volume edema, compared with decongestive lymphatic therapy alone (45% versus 26%).[114]

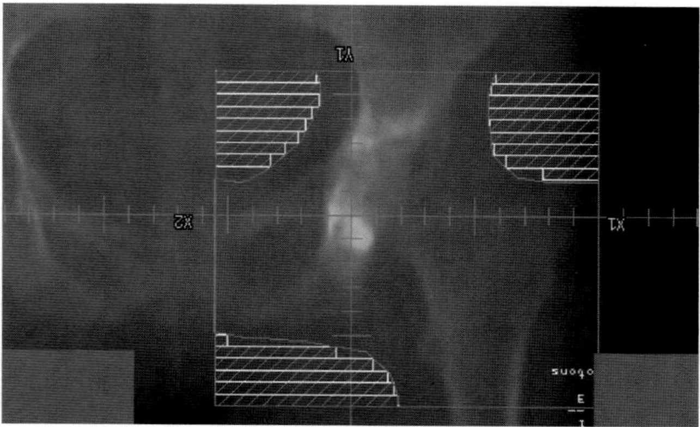

Figure 22–13. Bone metastasis in the left hip.

Radiation Pneumonitis

Radiation pneumonitis is now a rare complication of breast radiation treatment, occurring in 1 to 2% of treated patients.[115] Characterized by a nonproductive cough, along with a geographic lung infiltrate that conforms to the irradiated volume, the risk of developing symptomatic radiation pneumonitis is increased if the patient is treated with chemotherapy or if the supraclavicular nodes and apex of the lung are treated.[116] Patients who develop symptomatic pneumonitis usually have mild symptoms that resolve either spontaneously or after a short course of steroids, since the typical affected lung volumes are small.

Cardiac Toxicity

Radiation-induced cardiac damage was initially noted in the postmastectomy setting.[117] Excess cardiac deaths were seen in long-term survivors who had undergone mastectomy plus chest wall irradiation, compared with those treated with mastectomy alone. However, much of this excess cardiac mortality comes from older trials that treated the heart along with the internal mammary lymph nodes with photons. Two of these techniques, the direct photon "hockey-stick" and the "deep-tangent" approach, have been abandoned because of this toxicity. Cardiac consequences of breast irradiation have long latencies, estimated to begin 15 years after delivery of radiation therapy. Current approaches to the treatment of the IMC include either electrons or protons with three-dimensional CT planning to minimize cardiac toxicity. Recent series do not show an increase in cardiac events, for women treated with lumpectomy and irradiation, since the 1980s.[118–119]

Rib Fractures

Rib fractures are occasionally seen after breast or chest wall irradiation, with an incidence of approximately 2 to 5% after conventionally fractionated treatment used in older series, many using Co-60 radiation.[120] The use of higher energy photons and improved dose calculation algorithms have largely eliminated this complication. Many of these fractures are asymptomatic and are serendipitously found on bone scans or chest x-rays, requiring no further intervention.

Brachial Plexus Injury

A rare treatment complication is a brachial plexus injury, especially if large daily fractions of radiation are used.[121] The threshold dose is thought to be 60 Gy, but technique and neurotoxic chemotherapy may also impact the risk. Classic radiation plexopathy is primarily a motor neuron effect with a minor sensory component. In severe cases, it can progress to a flail arm.

Acute Radiation Dermatitis

The majority of patients treated with radiotherapy develop minor and reversible skin changes. After radiation therapy, acute treatment changes usually occur and resolve within 90 days. Generalized erythema, sometimes undetectable without special instrumentation, may occur hours after radiation exposure, and fades within hours to days.[122] A second phase consisting of more sustained erythematous changes are apparent 10 to 14 days after dosing, and are characterized by a blanchable reactive pink color, without other epidermal changes, and are most likely mediated by cytokines.[123]

Grade 1 changes, usually seen in the fourth or fifth week of therapy, include follicular or generalized erythema, and dry desquamation. Other changes include pruritus, epilation, scaling, and dyspigmentation (see Figure 22–13). Grade 2 changes, consisting of persistent, tender, or edematous erythema, may progress to focal loss of the epidermis and moist desquamation in skin folds. This usually occurs after 4 to 5 weeks of therapy, with radiation doses to the skin of ≥ 40 Gy.[124] Confluent moist desquamation outside of skin folds is typical of grade 3 dermatitis, whereas the formation of ulcers, hemorrhage, and necrosis heralds grade 4 toxicity. These problems may become chronic or late complications after the acute dermatitis has healed.

The effectiveness of nonsteroid topical agents for the prevention of acute dermatitis during adjuvant radiotherapy for breast carcinoma has not been demonstrated. Pommier and colleagues found that the occurrence of acute dermatitis of grade 2 or higher was significantly lower (41% versus 63%; $p < .001$) with the use of *Calendula officinalis*.[125] Patients also had less frequent interruption of radiotherapy and significantly reduced radiation-induced pain. Treatment is largely symptomatic and highly variable, due in part to a relative paucity of compelling clinical trials.

Late Radiation Skin Changes

The skin may appear relatively normal for a varying length of time after radiation therapy, and chronic changes may not develop for months to years after exposure. These changes may be transient, like the edematous peau d'orange appearance that appears in the postirradiated breast, usually resolving in the first year. Postinflammatory hypo- and hyperpigmentation is commonly seen after any disruption of the dermal–epidermal junction, and depending on the severity of the initial reaction and skin type of the patient, this may persist or slowly normalize. Patchy telangiectasia is occasionally seen, especially in areas where the surface radiation dose is increased, such as boost fields or in skin folds.

Radiation Necrosis

Radiation necrosis is an uncommon late or consequential injury associated with high-dose radiation therapy. Although it can occur in poorly vascularized flaps as acute dermatitis and resultant dermal ischemia, it is more likely to be seen many years after completion of radiotherapy.[126] It is particularly difficult to manage, as healing is impaired and superinfection is common in tissues rendered relatively avascular. These problems are exacerbated by peripheral vascular disease, diabetes, hypertension, and connective tissue disease. Suspected radiation necrosis should not undergo surgical biopsy, since this is likely to exacerbate the condition. Needle-aspiration biopsy can rule out underlying tumor, if suspected. Any surgical intervention should anticipate the need for a tissue flap transfer from an adjacent nonradiated area for closure.

SECOND MALIGNANT NEOPLASMS

The development of a second malignant neoplasm after breast radiotherapy is a very rare event. The Early Breast Cancer Collaborative Group was unable to detect clinically significant increases in lung cancers, leukemias, or other solid tumors in a cohort of nearly 20,000 patients, who participated in randomized trials of surgery alone versus surgery plus radiotherapy.[127] In a Swedish registry study of 13,490 patients, Karlsson and colleagues identified an increase of 10 sarcomas more than expected in patients who were irradiated for breast cancer and followed for a cumulative interval of 113,686 person-years.[128] This concurs with a separate data set from the Institut Gustave-Roussy that observed an excess of 9.92 sarcomas in a cohort of irradiated breast cancer patients per 100,000 person-years at risk.[129]

FOLLOW-UP CARE

Radiation oncologists should participate in the follow-up of patients who have been treated with radiation therapy. The outcome of therapy, including results of tumor control and survival as well as consequences of treatment, should be monitored, especially for patients treated with curative intent. When radiation consequences are suspected, the radiation oncologist should be contacted to provide useful information on treatment techniques and volumes treated. It is axiomatic that radiation consequences can only occur in areas that have been treated. Since some conformal and intensity modulated treatments can give low doses of radiation to large areas away from the region of interest, review of the patient's specific treatment plan is obligatory.

REFERENCES

1. Veronesi U, Cascinelli N, Mariani L, et al. Twenty-year follow-up of a randomized study comparing breast-conserving surgery with radical mastectomy for early breast cancer. N Engl J Med 2002;347:1227–32.
2. Arriagada R, Le MG, Guinebretiere JM, et al. Late local recurrences in a randomised trial comparing conservative treatment with total mastectomy in early breast cancer patients. Ann Oncol 2003;14:1617–22.
3. Fisher B, Anderson S, Bryant J, et al. Twenty-year follow-up of a randomized trial comparing total mastectomy, lumpectomy, and lumpectomy plus irradiation for the treatment of invasive breast cancer. N Engl J Med 2002; 347:1233–41.
4. Jacobson JA, Danforth DN, Cowan KH, et al. Ten-year results of a comparison of conservation with mastectomy in the treatment of stage I and II breast cancer. N Engl J Med 1995;332:907–11.
5. Poggi MM, Danforth DN, Sciuto LC, et al. Eighteen-year results in the treatment of early breast carcinoma with mastectomy versus breast conservation therapy: the National Cancer Institute Randomized Trial. Cancer 2003;98:697–702.
6. van Dongen JA, Voogd AC, Fentiman IS, et al. Long-term results of a randomized trial comparing breast-conserving therapy with mastectomy: European Organization for Research and Treatment of Cancer 10801 trial. J Natl Cancer Inst 2000;92:1143–50.
7. Blichert-Toft M, Rose C, Andersen JA, et al. Danish randomized trial comparing breast conservation therapy with mastectomy: six years of life-table analysis. Danish Breast Cancer Cooperative Group. J Natl Cancer Inst Monogr 1992:19–25.
8. Effects of radiotherapy and surgery in early breast cancer. An overview of the randomized trials. Early Breast Cancer Trialists' Collaborative Group. N Engl J Med 1995;333: 1444–55.
9. Veronesi U, Luini A, Del Vecchio M, et al. Radiotherapy after breast-preserving surgery in women with localized cancer of the breast. N Engl J Med 1993;328:1587–91.
10. Liljegren G, Holmberg L, Bergh J, et al. Ten-year results after sector resection with or without postoperative radiotherapy for stage I breast cancer: a randomized trial. J Clin Oncol 1999;17:2326–33.
11. Clark RM, Whelan T, Levine M, et al. Randomized clinical trial of breast irradiation following lumpectomy and axillary dissection for node-negative breast cancer: an update. Ontario Clinical Oncology Group. J Natl Cancer Inst 1996;88:1659–64.
12. Forrest AP, Stewart HJ, Everington D, et al. Randomised controlled trial of conservation therapy for breast cancer: 6-year analysis of the Scottish trial. Scottish Cancer Trials Breast Group. Lancet 1996;348:708–13.

13. Renton SC, Gazet JC, Ford HT, et al. The importance of the resection margin in conservative surgery for breast cancer. Eur J Surg Oncol 1996;22:17–22.
14. Blamey RW. The British Association of Surgical Oncology Guidelines for surgeons in the management of symptomatic breast disease in the UK (1998 revision). BASO Breast Specialty Group. Eur J Surg Oncol 1998;24:464–76.
15. Veronesi U, Luini A, Galimberti V, et al. Conservation approaches for the management of stage I/II carcinoma of the breast: Milan Cancer Institute trials. World J Surg 1994;18:70–5.
16. Hughes KS, Schnaper LA, Berry D, et al. Lumpectomy plus tamoxifen with or without irradiation in women 70 years of age or older with early breast cancer. N Engl J Med 2004;351:971–7.
17. Rosner D, Bedwani RN, Vana J, et al. Noninvasive breast carcinoma: results of a national survey by the American College of Surgeons. Ann Surg 1980;192:139–47.
18. Jemal A, Murray T, Ward E, et al. Cancer statistics, 2005. CA Cancer J Clin 2005;55:10–30.
19. Ernster VL, Ballard-Barbash R, Barlow WE, et al. Detection of ductal carcinoma in situ in women undergoing screening mammography. J Natl Cancer Inst 2002;94:1546–54.
20. Fisher ER, Leeming R, Anderson S, et al. Conservative management of intraductal carcinoma (DCIS) of the breast. Collaborating NSABP investigators. J Surg Oncol 1991; 47:139–47.
21. Fisher B, Dignam J, Wolmark N, et al. Lumpectomy and radiation therapy for the treatment of intraductal breast cancer: findings from National Surgical Adjuvant Breast and Bowel Project B-17. J Clin Oncol 1998;16:441–52.
22. Julien JP, Bijker N, Fentiman IS, et al. Radiotherapy in breast-conserving treatment for ductal carcinoma in situ: first results of the EORTC randomised phase III trial 10853. EORTC Breast Cancer Cooperative Group and EORTC Radiotherapy Group. Lancet 2000;355:528–33.
23. Houghton J, George WD, Cuzick J, et al. Radiotherapy and tamoxifen in women with completely excised ductal carcinoma in situ of the breast in the UK, Australia, and New Zealand: randomised controlled trial. Lancet 2003;362: 95–102.
24. Silverstein MJ, Lagios MD, Groshen S, et al. The influence of margin width on local control of ductal carcinoma in situ of the breast. N Engl J Med 1999;340:1455–61.
25. Silverstein MJ. The University of Southern California/Van Nuys prognostic index for ductal carcinoma in situ of the breast. Am J Surg 2003;186:337–43.
26. Kurtz JM, Jacquemier J, Amalric R, et al. Breast-conserving therapy for macroscopically multiple cancers. Ann Surg 1990;212:38–44.
27. Singletary SE. Surgical margins in patients with early-stage breast cancer treated with breast conservation therapy. Am J Surg 2002;184:383–93.
28. Boyages J, Recht A, Connolly JL, et al. Early breast cancer: predictors of breast recurrence for patients treated with conservative surgery and radiation therapy. Radiother Oncol 1990;19:29–41.
29. Dewar JA, Arriagada R, Benhamou S, et al. Local relapse and contralateral tumor rates in patients with breast cancer treated with conservative surgery and radiotherapy (Institut Gustave Roussy 1970–1982). IGR Breast Cancer Group. Cancer 1995;76:2260–5.
30. Gage I, Schnitt SJ, Nixon AJ, et al. Pathologic margin involvement and the risk of recurrence in patients treated with breast-conserving therapy. Cancer 1996;78:1921–8.
31. Solin LJ, Schultz DJ, Fowble BL. Ten-year results of the treatment of early-stage breast carcinoma in elderly women using breast-conserving surgery and definitive breast irradiation. Int J Radiat Oncol Biol Phys 1995;33:45–51.
32. Chabner E, Nixon A, Gelman R, et al. Family history and treatment outcome in young women after breast-conserving surgery and radiation therapy for early-stage breast cancer. J Clin Oncol 1998;16:2045–51.
33. Haas JA, Schultz DJ, Peterson ME, et al. An analysis of age and family history on outcome after breast-conservation treatment: the University of Pennsylvania experience. Cancer J Sci Am 1998;4:308–15.
34. Turner BC, Harrold E, Matloff E, et al. BRCA1/BRCA2 germline mutations in locally recurrent breast cancer patients after lumpectomy and radiation therapy: implications for breast-conserving management in patients with BRCA1/BRCA2 mutations. J Clin Oncol 1999;17:3017–24.
35. Pierce LJ, Strawderman M, Narod SA, et al. Effect of radiotherapy after breast-conserving treatment in women with breast cancer and germline BRCA1/2 mutations. J Clin Oncol 2000;18:3360–9.
36. Robson M, Levin D, Federici M, et al. Breast conservation therapy for invasive breast cancer in Ashkenazi women with BRCA gene founder mutations. J Natl Cancer Inst 1999;91:2112–7.
37. Freedman G, Fowble B, Hanlon A, et al. Patients with early stage invasive cancer with close or positive margins treated with conservative surgery and radiation have an increased risk of breast recurrence that is delayed by adjuvant systemic therapy. Int J Radiat Oncol Biol Phys 1999;44:1005–15.
38. Fisher B, Dignam J, Mamounas EP, et al. Sequential methotrexate and fluorouracil for the treatment of node-negative breast cancer patients with estrogen receptor-negative tumors: eight-year results from National Surgical Adjuvant Breast and Bowel Project (NSABP) B-13 and first report of findings from NSABP B-19 comparing methotrexate and fluorouracil with conventional cyclophosphamide, methotrexate, and fluorouracil. J Clin Oncol 1996;14:1982–92.
39. Fisher B, Dignam J, Bryant J, et al. Five versus more than five years of tamoxifen therapy for breast cancer patients with negative lymph nodes and estrogen receptor-positive tumors. J Natl Cancer Inst 1996;88:1529–42.
40. Dalberg K, Johansson H, Johansson U, et al. A randomized trial of long term adjuvant tamoxifen plus postoperative radiation therapy versus radiation therapy alone for patients with early stage breast carcinoma treated with breast-conserving surgery. Stockholm Breast Cancer Study Group. Cancer 1998;82:2204–11.
41. Newman LA, Mason J, Cote D, et al. African-American ethnicity, socioeconomic status, and breast cancer survival: a meta-analysis of 14 studies involving over 10,000 African-American and 40,000 White American patients with carcinoma of the breast. Cancer 2002;94:2844–54.

42. Jemal A, Clegg LX, Ward E, et al. Annual report to the nation on the status of cancer, 1975–2001, with a special feature regarding survival. Cancer 2004;101:3–27.
43. Clarke CA, West DW, Edwards BK, et al. Existing data on breast cancer in African-American women: what we know and what we need to know. Cancer 2003;97:211–21.
44. Romestaing P, Lehingue Y, Carrie C, et al. Role of a 10-Gy boost in the conservative treatment of early breast cancer: results of a randomized clinical trial in Lyon, France. J Clin Oncol 1997;15:963–8.
45. Vrieling C, Collette L, Fourquet A, et al. Can patient-, treatment- and pathology-related characteristics explain the high local recurrence rate following breast-conserving therapy in young patients? Eur J Cancer 2003;39:932–44.
46. Huang J, Barbera L, Brouwers M, et al. Does delay in starting treatment affect the outcomes of radiotherapy? A systematic review. J Clin Oncol 2003;21:555–63.
47. Buzdar AU, Kau SW, Smith TL, et al. The order of administration of chemotherapy and radiation and its effect on the local control of operable breast cancer. Cancer 1993; 71:3680–4.
48. Bellon JR, Come SE, Gelman RS, et al. Sequencing of chemotherapy and radiation therapy in early-stage breast cancer: updated results of a prospective randomized trial. J Clin Oncol 2005;23:1934–40.
49. Buchholz TA, Hunt KK, Amosson CM, et al. Sequencing of chemotherapy and radiation in lymph node-negative breast cancer. Cancer J Sci Am 1999;5:159–64.
50. Schlembach PJ, Buchholz TA, Ross MI, et al. Relationship of sentinel and axillary level I–II lymph nodes to tangential fields used in breast irradiation. Int J Radiat Oncol Biol Phys 2001;51:671–8.
51. Hong L, Hunt M, Chui C, et al. Intensity-modulated tangential beam irradiation of the intact breast. Int J Radiat Oncol Biol Phys 1999;44:1155–64.
52. Grann A, McCormick B, Chabner ES, et al. Prone breast radiotherapy in early-stage breast cancer: a preliminary analysis. Int J Radiat Oncol Biol Phys 2000;47:319–25.
53. Stovall M, Blackwell CR, Cundiff J, et al. Fetal dose from radiotherapy with photon beams: report of AAPM Radiation Therapy Committee Task Group No. 36. Med Phys 1995;22:63–82.
54. Mayr NA, Wen BC, Saw CB. Radiation therapy during pregnancy. Obstet Gynecol Clin North Am 1998;25:301–21.
55. Robertson JM, Clarke DH, Pevzner MM, et al. Breast conservation therapy. Severe breast fibrosis after radiation therapy in patients with collagen vascular disease. Cancer 1991;68:502–8.
56. Fleck R, McNeese MD, Ellerbroek NA, et al. Consequences of breast irradiation in patients with pre-existing collagen vascular diseases. Int J Radiat Oncol Biol Phys 1989; 17:829–33.
57. De Naeyer B, De Meerleer G, Braems S, et al. Collagen vascular diseases and radiation therapy: a critical review. Int J Radiat Oncol Biol Phys 1999;44:975–80.
58. Pezzi CM, Kukora JS, Audet IM, et al. Breast conservation surgery using nipple-areolar resection for central breast cancers. Arch Surg 2004;139:32–37; discussion 38.
59. Vyas JJ, Chinoy RF, Vaidya JS. Prediction of nipple and areola involvement in breast cancer. Eur J Surg Oncol 1998; 24:15–6.
60. Danoff BF, Pajak TF, Solin LJ, et al. Excisional biopsy, axillary node dissection and definitive radiotherapy for stages I and II breast cancer. Int J Radiat Oncol Biol Phys 1985;11:479–83.
61. Bold RJ, Kroll SS, Baldwin BJ, et al. Local rotational flaps for breast conservation therapy as an alternative to mastectomy. Ann Surg Oncol 1997;4:540–4.
62. Smith ML, Evans GR, Gurlek A, et al. Reduction mammaplasty: its role in breast conservation surgery for early-stage breast cancer. Ann Plast Surg 1998;41:234–9.
63. Krueger EA, Wilkins EG, Strawderman M, et al. Complications and patient satisfaction following expander/implant breast reconstruction with and without radiotherapy. Int J Radiat Oncol Biol Phys 2001;49:713–21.
64. Senkus-Konefka E, Welnicka-Jaskiewicz M, Jaskiewicz J, et al. Radiotherapy for breast cancer in patients undergoing breast reconstruction or augmentation. Cancer Treat Rev 2004;30:671–82.
65. Singletary SE, McNeese MD, Hortobagyi GN. Feasibility of breast-conservation surgery after induction chemotherapy for locally advanced breast carcinoma. Cancer 1992;69: 2849–52.
66. Kuerer HM, Julian TB, Strom EA, et al. Accelerated partial breast irradiation after conservative surgery for breast cancer. Ann Surg 2004;239:338–51.
67. Arthur DW, Vicini FA. Accelerated partial breast irradiation as a part of breast conservation therapy. J Clin Oncol 2005;23:1726–35.
68. Arthur DW, Vicini FA. MammoSite RTS: the reporting of initial experiences and how to interpret. Ann Surg Oncol 2004;11:723–4.
69. Keisch M, Vicini F, Kuske RR, et al. Initial clinical experience with the MammoSite breast brachytherapy applicator in women with early-stage breast cancer treated with breast-conserving therapy. Int J Radiat Oncol Biol Phys 2003;55:289–93.
70. Dowlatshahi K, Snider HC, Gittleman MA, et al. Early experience with balloon brachytherapy for breast cancer. Arch Surg 2004;139:603–7; discussion 607–8.
71. Richards GM, Berson AM, Rescigno J, et al. Acute toxicity of high-dose-rate intracavitary brachytherapy with the MammoSite applicator in patients with early-stage breast cancer. Ann Surg Oncol 2004;11:739–46.
72. Baglan KL, Sharpe MB, Jaffray D, et al. Accelerated partial breast irradiation using 3D conformal radiation therapy (3D-CRT). Int J Radiat Oncol Biol Phys 2003;55:302–11.
73. Vicini FA, Remouchamps V, Wallace M, et al. Ongoing clinical experience utilizing 3D conformal external beam radiotherapy to deliver partial-breast irradiation in patients with early-stage breast cancer treated with breast-conserving therapy. Int J Radiat Oncol Biol Phys 2003; 57:1247–53.
74. Formenti SC, Truong MT, Goldberg JD, et al. Prone accelerated partial breast irradiation after breast-conserving surgery: preliminary clinical results and dose-volume histogram analysis. Int J Radiat Oncol Biol Phys 2004;60: 493–504.
75. Bartelink H, Horiot JC, Poortmans P, et al. Recurrence rates after treatment of breast cancer with standard radiotherapy with or without additional radiation. N Engl J Med 2001;345:1378–87.

76. Vrieling C, Collette L, Fourquet A, et al. The influence of the boost in breast-conserving therapy on cosmetic outcome in the EORTC "boost versus no boost" trial. EORTC Radiotherapy and Breast Cancer Cooperative Groups. European Organization for Research and Treatment of Cancer. Int J Radiat Oncol Biol Phys 1999;45:677–85.
77. Kurtz JM. Which patients don't need a tumor-bed boost after whole-breast radiotherapy? Strahlenther Onkol 2001;177: 33–6.
78. Schnitt SJ, Abner A, Gelman R, et al. The relationship between microscopic margins of resection and the risk of local recurrence in patients with breast cancer treated with breast-conserving surgery and radiation therapy. Cancer 1994;74:1746–51.
79. Sacchini V, Luini A, Tana S, et al. Quantitative and qualitative cosmetic evaluation after conservative treatment for breast cancer. Eur J Cancer 1991;27:1395–400.
80. Al-Ghazal SK, Blamey RW, Stewart J, et al. The cosmetic outcome in early breast cancer treated with breast conservation. Eur J Surg Oncol 1999;25:566–70.
81. Liljegren G, Holmberg L, Westman G. The cosmetic outcome in early breast cancer treated with sector resection with or without radiotherapy. Uppsala-Orebro Breast Cancer Study Group. Eur J Cancer 1993;29A:2083–9.
82. Cuzick J, Stewart H, Peto R, et al. Overview of randomized trials of postoperative adjuvant radiotherapy in breast cancer. Cancer Treat Rep 1987;71:15–29.
83. Early Breast Cancer Trialists' Cooperative Group. Radiotherapy for early breast cancer. Cochrane Rev. Issue 4. Cochrane Library; 2003.
84. Overgaard M, Hansen PS, Overgaard J, et al. Postoperative radiotherapy in high-risk premenopausal women with breast cancer who receive adjuvant chemotherapy. Danish Breast Cancer Cooperative Group 82b Trial. N Engl J Med 1997;337:949–55.
85. Ragaz J, Jackson SM, Le N, et al. Adjuvant radiotherapy and chemotherapy in node-positive premenopausal women with breast cancer. N Engl J Med 1997;337:956–62.
86. Overgaard M. Overview of randomized trials in high risk breast cancer patients treated with adjuvant systemic therapy with or without postmastectomy irradiation. Semin Radiat Oncol 1999;9:292–9.
87. Recht A, Edge SB, Solin LJ, et al. Postmastectomy radiotherapy: clinical practice guidelines of the American Society of Clinical Oncology. J Clin Oncol 2001;19:1539–69.
88. White J, Moughan J, Pierce LJ, et al. Status of postmastectomy radiotherapy in the United States: a patterns of care study. Int J Radiat Oncol Biol Phys 2004;60:77–85.
89. Marks LB, Prosnitz LR. "One to three" or "four or more"? Selecting patients for postmastectomy radiation therapy. Cancer 1997;79:668–70.
90. Strom EA, Woodward WA, Katz A, et al. Regional nodal failure patterns in breast cancer patients treated with mastectomy without radiotherapy. Int J Radiat Oncol Biol Phys 2005.[In press]
91. Truong PT, Olivotto IA, Kader HA, et al. Selecting breast cancer patients with T1-T2 tumors and one to three positive axillary nodes at high postmastectomy locoregional recurrence risk for adjuvant radiotherapy. Int J Radiat Oncol Biol Phys 2005;61:1337–47.
92. Grills IS, Kestin LL, Goldstein N, et al. Risk factors for regional nodal failure after breast-conserving therapy: regional nodal irradiation reduces rate of axillary failure in patients with four or more positive lymph nodes. Int J Radiat Oncol Biol Phys 2003;56:658–70.
93. Freedman GM, Fowble BL, Nicolaou N, et al. Should internal mammary lymph nodes in breast cancer be a target for the radiation oncologist? Int J Radiat Oncol Biol Phys 2000;46:805–14.
94. Buchholz TA. Internal mammary lymph nodes: to treat or not to treat? Int J Radiat Oncol Biol Phys 2000;46:801–3.
95. Urban JA, Marjani MA. Significance of internal mammary lymph node metastases in breast cancer. Am J Roentgenol Radium Ther Nucl Med 1971;111:130–6.
96. Kronowitz SJ, Robb GL. Breast reconstruction with postmastectomy radiation therapy: current issues. Plast Reconstr Surg 2004;114:950–60.
97. Schechter NR, Strom EA, Perkins GH, et al. Immediate breast reconstruction can impact postmastectomy irradiation. J Clin Oncol 2005.[In press]
98. Kronowitz SJ, Hunt KK, Kuerer HM, et al. Delayed-immediate breast reconstruction. Plast Reconstr Surg 2004;113: 1617–28.
99. Barker JL, Montague ED, Peters LJ. Clinical experience with irradiation of inflammatory carcinoma of the breast with and without elective chemotherapy. Cancer 1980;45:625–9.
100. Liao Z, Strom EA, Buzdar AU, et al. Locoregional irradiation for inflammatory breast cancer: effectiveness of dose escalation in decreasing recurrence. Int J Radiat Oncol Biol Phys 2000;47:1191–200.
101. Knapper WH. Management of occult breast cancer presenting as an axillary metastasis. Semin Surg Oncol 1991;7: 311–3.
102. Halsted WS. The results of radical operations for the cure of carcinoma of the breast. Ann Surg 1907;46:1–19.
103. Whillis D, Brown PW, Rodger A. Adenocarcinoma from an unknown primary presenting in women with an axillary mass. Clin Oncol (R Coll Radiol) 1990;2:189–92.
104. Campana F, Fourquet A, Ashby MA, et al. Presentation of axillary lymphadenopathy without detectable breast primary (T0 N1b breast cancer): experience at Institut Curie. Radiother Oncol 1989;15:321–5.
105. Read NE, Strom EA, McNeese MD. Carcinoma in axillary nodes in women with unknown primary site-results of breast-conserving therapy. Breast J 1996;2:403–9.
106. Kao J, Conzen SD, Jaskowiak NT, et al. Concomitant radiation therapy and paclitaxel for unresectable locally advanced breast cancer: results from two consecutive phase I/II trials. Int J Radiat Oncol Biol Phys 2005;61:1045–53.
107. Karasawa K, Katsui K, Seki K, et al. Radiotherapy with concurrent docetaxel for advanced and recurrent breast cancer. Breast Cancer 2003;10:268–74.
108. Miller KD, Chap LI, Holmes FA, et al. Randomized phase III trial of capecitabine compared with bevacizumab plus capecitabine in patients with previously treated metastatic breast cancer. J Clin Oncol 2005;23:792–9.
109. Wai MS, Mike S, Ines H, et al. Palliation of metastatic bone pain: single fraction versus multifraction radiotherapy. A systematic review of the randomised trials. Cochrane Database Syst Rev 2004:CD004721.

110. Muacevic A, Kreth FW, Tonn JC, et al. Stereotactic radiosurgery for multiple brain metastases from breast carcinoma. Cancer 2004;100:1705–11.
111. Larson D, Weinstein M, Goldberg I, et al. Edema of the arm as a function of the extent of axillary surgery in patients with stage I–II carcinoma of the breast treated with primary radiotherapy. Int J Radiat Oncol Biol Phys 1986;12: 1575–82.
112. Liljegren G, Holmberg L. Arm morbidity after sector resection and axillary dissection with or without postoperative radiotherapy in breast cancer stage I. Results from a randomised trial. Uppsala-Orebro Breast Cancer Study Group. Eur J Cancer 1997;33:193–9.
113. Lichter AS, Lippman ME, Danforth DN Jr, et al. Mastectomy versus breast-conserving therapy in the treatment of stage I and II carcinoma of the breast: a randomized trial at the National Cancer Institute. J Clin Oncol 1992;10:976–83.
114. Szuba A, Achalu R, Rockson SG. Decongestive lymphatic therapy for patients with breast carcinoma-associated lymphedema. A randomized, prospective study of a role for adjunctive intermittent pneumatic compression. Cancer 2002;95:2260–7.
115. Lingos TI, Recht A, Vicini F, et al. Radiation pneumonitis in breast cancer patients treated with conservative surgery and radiation therapy. Int J Radiat Oncol Biol Phys 1991; 21:355–60.
116. Lind PA, Marks LB, Hardenbergh PH, et al. Technical factors associated with radiation pneumonitis after local +/- regional radiation therapy for breast cancer. Int J Radiat Oncol Biol Phys 2002;52:137–43.
117. Gyenes G, Fornander T, Carlens P, et al. Morbidity of ischemic heart disease in early breast cancer 15–20 years after adjuvant radiotherapy. Int J Radiat Oncol Biol Phys 1994;28:1235–41.
118. Vallis KA, Pintilie M, Chong N, et al. Assessment of coronary heart disease morbidity and mortality after radiation therapy for early breast cancer. J Clin Oncol 2002;20:1036–42.
119. Giordano SH, Kuo YF, Freeman JL, et al. Risk of cardiac death after adjuvant radiotherapy for breast cancer. J Natl Cancer Inst 2005;97:419–24.
120. Pierce SM, Recht A, Lingos TI, et al. Long-term radiation complications following conservative surgery (CS) and radiation therapy (RT) in patients with early stage breast cancer. Int J Radiat Oncol Biol Phys 1992;23:915–23.
121. Olsen NK, Pfeiffer P, Johannsen L, et al. Radiation-induced brachial plexopathy: neurological follow-up in 161 recurrence-free breast cancer patients. Int J Radiat Oncol Biol Phys 1993;26:43–9.
122. Schmuth M, Sztankay A, Weinlich G, et al. Permeability barrier function of skin exposed to ionizing radiation. Arch Dermatol 2001;137:1019–23.
123. Kupper TS. The activated keratinocyte: a model for inducible cytokine production by non-bone marrow-derived cells in cutaneous inflammatory and immune responses. J Invest Dermatol 1990;94 Suppl:146–50.
124. Mendelsohn FA, Divino CM, Reis ED, et al. Wound care after radiation therapy. Adv Skin Wound Care 2002;15:216–24.
125. Pommier P, Gomez F, Sunyach MP, et al. Phase III randomized trial of Calendula officinalis compared with trolamine for the prevention of acute dermatitis during irradiation for breast cancer. J Clin Oncol 2004;22:1447–53.
126. Hopewell JW. The skin: its structure and response to ionizing radiation. Int J Radiat Biol 1990;57:751–73.
127. Marchal C, Weber B, de Lafontan B, et al. Nine breast angiosarcomas after conservative treatment for breast carcinoma: a survey from French comprehensive Cancer Centers. Int J Radiat Oncol Biol Phys 1999;44:113–9.
128. Karlsson P, Holmberg E, Johansson KA, et al. Soft tissue sarcoma after treatment for breast cancer. Radiother Oncol 1996;38:25–31.
129. Taghian A, de Vathaire F, Terrier P, et al. Long-term risk of sarcoma following radiation treatment for breast cancer. Int J Radiat Oncol Biol Phys 1991;21:361–7.
130. Morrow M, Strom EA, Bassett LW, et al. Standard for breast conservation therapy in the management of invasive breast carcinoma. CA Cancer J Clin 2002;52:277–300.

23

Evolution in Breast Reconstruction

GEOFFREY C. FENNER
THOMAS A. MUSTOE

Techniques in breast reconstruction have continued to evolve to provide breast cancer patients options with less donor morbidity and more durable implantable devices. Over the past decade, practice patterns have gradually trended towards more immediate reconstructions for non-irradiated patients owing to superior esthetic outcome, a more facilitating recovery, and the ability to maintain an equivalent oncologic outcome. Current techniques and materials may provide all patients, regardless of age, stage, or previous treatment, outcomes that simulate the patient's expectations and desires.

Breast cancer detection has paralleled improved techniques and availability of screening mammography, an increase in the aging female population, and the impact of changes in the age of childbearing, menarche, and menopause. The recognition of high-risk groups through genetics and, in some cases, greater reluctance to risk contralateral disease have spawned an increased interest in prophylactic treatment through both hormonal and surgical choices. Surgical options remain available for patients with proportionately large breast lesions and those choosing breast conservation and/or completion mastectomy. Younger women, through improved early detection, also seek alternatives for breast restoration.

The female breast is intimately associated with a woman's self-esteem, sexuality, and interpersonal relations. The response to the impact of breast cancer varies widely among women. Breast cancer therapies present myriad emotional and physical implications. Although breast reconstruction may be viewed as a positive alternative to breast loss, it represents only one facet that newly diagnosed cancer patients must face. Patients uphold an individual, often rigid, esthetic standard, persona, and anatomy that guide them towards a specific reconstructive technique. It remains the plastic surgeon's responsibility to inform and educate the patient and to work with the breast surgeon.

IMMEDIATE RECONSTRUCTION

Immediate reconstruction provides inherent advantages for the newly diagnosed breast cancer patient (Table 23–1). General acceptance of immediate post-mastectomy reconstruction is based upon a greater understanding of tumor response to treatment modalities and timing, and the establishment of less morbid, transparent reconstructive options. Immediate reconstruction does not affect the incidence of recurrence or delay the detection of chest wall recurrences.[1] It has proven to be more cost effective and has contributed to comparative improvements in self-esteem, interpersonal relations, and psychosocial interactions.

Historically, delayed reconstructions were more often performed owing to a heightened fear of recur-

Table 23–1. ADVANTAGES OF IMMEDIATE RECONSTRUCTION
Diminished psychologic trauma
Facilitates coverage of radical defects
Eases recipient pedicle dissection
Superior esthetic results
Incorporates skin-sparing mastectomy
Minimizes anesthesia and improves cost

rence, concerns that immediate reconstruction would mask detection of a recurrence, and the possibility that immediate reconstruction would hinder the initiation of adjuvant therapy. It was also felt that patients would be more appreciative of reconstruction if they were required to live for a time with the postmastectomy defect. For many patients, these ideas have been rendered obsolete by the need to consider the emotional impact of mastectomy and by technical and therapeutic advances.

Patients undergoing immediate reconstruction tend to incorporate the new breast into their body image, thereby maintaining greater self-esteem, personal sexuality, and confidence in interpersonal relationships.[2] They tend to have lower "cancer anxiety," less recall, and greater freedom in choosing clothing.[3] Patients undergoing mastectomy and immediate reconstruction demonstrate a similar psychosocial outcome to that of breast conservation patients who have had a lumpectomy, with or without radiation.[4] Body image of patients with mastectomies may be adversely affected owing to greater breast and donor site scarring compared to patients who have been treated with breast conservation. Overall, psychologic morbidity is similar and clearly favorable compared with that of patients having delayed reconstruction.[5]

The opportunity to attain optimal esthetic results is enhanced with immediate reconstruction. The newly raised mastectomy skin flaps tend to preserve the shape of the natural breast, providing a structural template that determines the shape of the underlying volume with either implant or flap reconstruction. Skin flap fibrosis associated with delayed reconstruction may require either greater tissue expansion or greater skin replacement with autologous reconstruction. Fibrosis of the mastectomy skin flaps is an impediment to achieving a natural breast shape. Skin-sparing mastectomy with immediate reconstruction can further increase the ability to attain a symmetric result, limit scarring, and minimize the need for contralateral procedures such as reductions and mastopexies.[6–10]

Administration of adjuvant therapy is not delayed in patients undergoing immediate breast reconstruction nor is the rate of complications higher.[11,12] The usual 3- to 4-week interval prior to the initiation of adjuvant chemotherapy is ample time for uncomplicated, post-reconstructive wound healing and patient recovery. Only 1 to 2% of patients have their chemotherapy delayed beyond 3 to 4 weeks owing to complications from immediate reconstruction, such as delayed healing.[13]

Although neoadjuvant and adjuvant chemotherapy have no relative impact upon immediate reconstruction, adjuvant radiation is known to unequivocally detract from the esthetic result and increase the local complication rate. Historically, radiation exaggerated the extent of fibrous capsular contracture, to some extent, in all expander/implant reconstructions.[14–16] The rate of poor cosmetic results in early series ranged from 18 to 40%, with a failure rate of up to 40%.[17] In 2005, Spear and colleagues reported that although there was no statistically significant difference in the rate of partial or total flap failure in pre– and post–transverse rectus abdominis myocutaneous (TRAM) flap radiation patients, the radiation did affect the esthetic appearance, symmetry, contracture rate, and degree of hyperpigmentation.[18] Investigators at M.D. Anderson Cancer Center (University of Texas) compared immediate autologous reconstruction patients requiring postoperative radiation to those without radiation. Overall, the studies indicate that autologous tissue is preferable for breast reconstruction patients who have received radiation, and that breast reconstruction ought to be delayed in patients who are known preoperatively to require postmastectomy radiation.[19]

Immediate postmastectomy reconstruction for locally advanced disease has been reported as encouraging. Sultan reported on 22 patients with stage IIB or III disease who had undergone neoadjuvant chemotherapy and completion chemotherapy 3 weeks subsequent to surgery. Perioperative morbidity was 14%. Delay in resumption of chemotherapy occurred in no instances, and patients expressed appreciation for having been offered this option.[20,21] Styblo and colleagues reported on 21 patients with stage III disease who had undergone immediate TRAM reconstruction. There were no delays in reinstitution of adjuvant treatment and no increase in local relapse.[22] Langstein and colleagues confirmed that immediate reconstruction does not delay the detection of either subcutaneous or deep chest wall recurrences. There were no differences in recurrence rates among those having had immediate TRAM, expander/implant, or latissimus dorsi reconstructions.[23]

Immediate reconstruction also has economic advantages. Ablation and reconstruction combined in one procedure limits anesthetic risk and the time committed to postoperative recovery. Patients welcome the opportunity for a single procedure with less impact on occupational and domestic responsibilities. Avoidance of a staged second surgery and hospitalization in delayed reconstruction has obvious cost advantages.

SKIN-SPARING MASTECTOMY

Toth and Lappert first described skin-sparing mastectomy (SSM) in 1991.[6] This technique is indicated for patients with early stage (I and II) breast cancer, patients managed with prophylactic mastectomy, and in attempts to facilitate a highly esthetic outcome through maximal skin preservation (Figure 23–1). Incisions are planned that will remove the breast, nipple-areolar complex, adjacent biopsy scars, and the skin over more superficial tumors.

Local recurrence is dependent upon tumor size and loco-regional nodal involvement. Despite variations in mastectomy technique, including SSM, the rate of local recurrence has remained stable. SSM is more challenging for the oncologic surgeon, more time consuming, and requires delicate handling of the skin flaps to avoid ischemic complications.

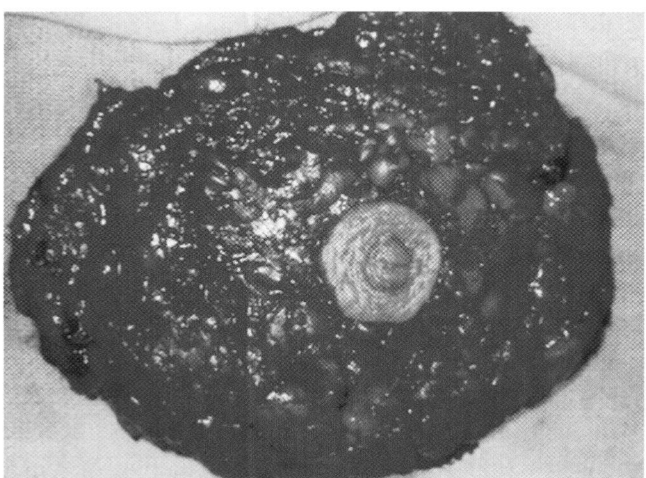

Figure 23–1. Skin-sparing mastectomy.

These efforts to preserve the skin envelope and inframammary fold (IMF) are much appreciated by the patient and result in greater symmetry, often diminishing the need for a contralateral procedure. Subsequent areolar tattooing may completely camouflage the central incisions.

In 1999, Kroll and colleagues compared 114 patients undergoing SSM and immediate reconstruction to 40 non-SSM control patients with TI or TII lesions in a 6-year follow-up. The local recurrence rate was 7.0% for the SSM group and 7.5% for the non-SSM group.[24] Ninety-six percent of these recurrences presented as palpable skin flap masses.[8] Hidalgo reported on 28 patients who underwent immediate reconstruction (92% receiving TRAM flaps) after SSM, with a mean follow-up of 27 months. Complications at the reconstructive site were limited to cellulitis and marginal periareolar skin loss. Esthetic results were judged as excellent in 75% of patients.[9] Because local recurrence after SSM is low and the likelihood of local control and survival are high, SSM with immediate reconstruction is an acceptable treatment for breast cancer.

BREAST IMPLANTS

The number of women with breast implants ranges between 1.5 and 2 million. Contents of single chamber implants consist of either silicone gel, which is factory sealed and nonadjustable, or saline, which may be adjusted intra- and/or perioperatively. Dual chamber implants were devised to provide the benefits and camouflage of silicone texture (outer lumen), along with postoperative saline adjustability (inner lumen). All implants consist of a silicone elastomer shell that may be single or double lumen, with a smooth or textured surface.

Silicone is ubiquitous in our environment. Individual exposure occurs through contact with needles, syringes, medications (insulins, simethicone), lipstick, creams, cosmetics, and implantable devices, such as pacemakers, joint replacements, defibrillators, shunts, stents, and implants.[25] Silicone gel found in implants is composed of an amorphous matrix consisting of silicone oils of various sizes and weights. Recent advances have led to the availability of a more "cohesive" grade silicone, which is less likely to diffuse through the implant shell or migrate if freely ruptured from acute trauma. Previously, smaller caliber oils were known to diffuse through the elastomer shell (silicone gel "bleed") and become incorporated into the fibrous capsule. Extensive research since the Food and Drug Administration (FDA)-directed silicone breast implant moratorium in 1992 has confirmed that implantable medical grade silicone is among the least bioreactive, most inert substance available for implantation.[26] It has been estimated that the daily silicone metabolite exposure from silicone implant gel diffusion is 10,000-fold less than exposure to the above-mentioned daily domestic items. Studies have failed to show a link between connective tissue disease and silicone gel implants. Collective data from multiple independent studies, including over 34,000 patients, have concluded that there is not just a lack of association of silicone breast implants with connective tissue disorders, but that patients with silicone implants actually represent a lower percentage of patients with connective tissue diseases than the population at large. The silicone elastomer shell and gel of breast implants, however, like all implanted devices, will trigger a foreign body inflammatory cell response, with giant cell formation and eventual scarring. The extent and impact of this fibrotic capsular response upon the fluid and the physical characteristics of breast implants are dependent upon capsular density, implant-tissue incorporation, the presence of myofibroblasts, and/or the presence of intracapsular silicone or sepsis.[26–28]

Silicone implants, available since 1962, are now in their third generation. They have undergone a multitude of mechanical and material improvements and are now of a "low bleed" variety composed of a multi-layer shell and more viscous gel media. Reduction in rates of intra- and extracapsular rupture, capsular contracture, and inflammatory response, while preserving the esthetic and tactile advantages of silicone implants, has been the goal. Intra-capsular rupture, usually imperceptible, is caused by cyclic fatigue or a gradual attenuation of the elastomer shell leading to gel "bleed." This occurs in up to 63% of patients after 12 years, as documented during surgery in patients having implants removed.[29–32] Abrupt or premature rupture may be prompted by capsular contracture; implant shell folding, thus leading to accelerated stress fractures; and trauma. Once a gel implant shell ruptures from longevity or trauma, the contents are usually contained within the surrounding fibrous capsule. This is likely to remain undetected and has demonstrated no systemic effects.

The extracapsular rupture rates of these third generation implants have improved to 0.8%, compared to 13.5% and 17.7% for second and first generation implants, respectively. These earlier extracapsular ruptures were largely caused by closed capsulotomies, a technique to release contractures through aggressive manual compression. The goal was to "pop" the surrounding constricting capsule, leading to a softer breast. Today, the rupture-free rate has been shown to be 98% at 5 years, and between 83 and 85% at 10 years.

Capsular contracture represents the most common complication of breast implants. It consists of progressive fibrous constriction around the breast implant and is unpredictable and variable. Significant contracture may cause implant deformation, migration, and rupture (Figure 23–2) and may, on occasion, become calcified and detour from effective mammography. It may be objectively graded according to a scale developed by Baker[33] (Table 23–2) and ranges from visually imperceptible (class I), to stone hard and painful (class IV). Capsular contracture is not in itself a health risk. Twenty to 50% of reconstruction patients who develop contractures require operative intervention (Figure 23–3). It may occur immediately or years after implantation. There is a

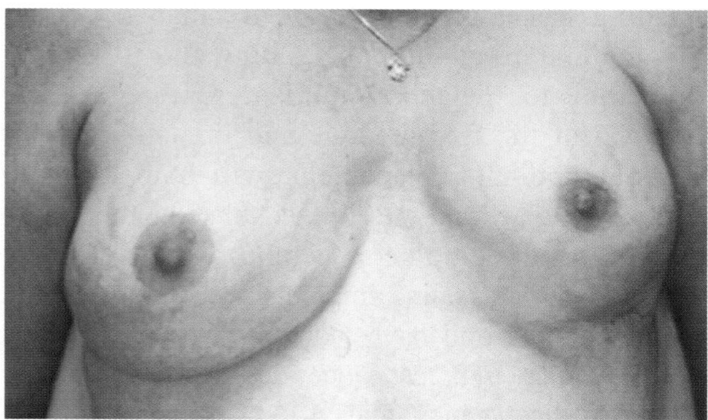

Figure 23–2. Left breast class III capsule contracture.

Table 23–2. BAKER'S CLASSIFICATION OF CAPSULE CONTRACTURE	
Class I	Augmented breast feels as soft as an unoperated-upon breast.
Class II	Minimal; less soft, the implant can be palpated but is not visible.
Class III	Moderate; more firm, the implant can be easily palpated and is visible.
Class IV	Severe; the breast is hard, tender, painful, cold, and distorted.

Reproduced with permission from Little G, Baker JL. Results of closed compression capsulotomy for treatment of contracted breast implant capsules. Plast Reconstr Surg 1980;65:30.

greater incidence associated with smooth silicone implants and with sub-glandular placement in cosmetic augmentation. Some theories suggest local contamination with *Staphylococcus epidermidis* as one inciting cause. The powder from gloves and inflammation from even limited hematomas may play a role in some cases. Mentor Corporation, during the recent April 13, 2005, FDA hearings on silicone implants, confirmed long-term data indicating a capsular contracture rate of 8.2% for augmentation patients and 8.8% for postmastectomy implant reconstructive patients using third generation implants.

Perception of posttraumatic implant changes includes herniation, deflation, malposition, or deformation and may manifest extracapsular extravasation. When this occurs, free gel may infiltrate breast parenchyma and tissue planes, and/or elicit a granulomatous foreign body reaction. This may lead to regional silicone migration, silicone mastitis, and formation of irregular nodules that may, on physical examination and mammography, simulate a malignancy.[34] Suspected implant rupture warrants evaluation. Magnetic resonance imaging has a greater sensitivity than do either mammography or ultrasonography and is the test of choice for detecting implant rupture.[35] Early removal of the free silicone and implant, with or without implant replacement, will help to avoid these sequelae and minimize subsequent confusion in mammographic screening.

Silicone and saline implants are radiopaque on mammography and have led to concerns regarding potential delay in breast cancer detection.[36,37] Implant characteristics, which may affect the sensitivity of standard mammography, include implant size, the proportion of overlying breast tissue, implant placement (subglandular versus submuscular), and the presence and immobility of capsular contracture.[38,39] As recommended by the American Cancer Society and the American Society of Plastic and Reconstructive Surgeons, women with breast implants should maintain the same schedule of mammography as other women. They should secure a certified facility that has sufficient experience with breast implants and confirm the availability of displacement mammography and ultrasonography.[40] Patients with postmastectomy implant reconstruction are typically followed by physical examination only. One major epidemiologic study has confirmed that the stage at breast cancer detection in women with implants is identical or better than it is in the general population.[41] In addition, there is no evidence that silicone is carcinogenic in humans. In fact, in two large studies women with implants exhibit 10 to 30% less breast cancer than would be statistically expected when matched with the general population; the results, however, did not show statistical significance[42–45]

In 1992, a series of poorly documented case reports and the subsequent intense media scrutiny, combined with a temporary suspension of silicone gel implant usage by the FDA, led to lawsuits and an eventual multibillion dollar settlement with the major implant manufacturers. Two US implant companies (Mentor Corporation and Inamed Corporation) were allowed to provide gel implants for reconstruction patients, with specific and rigid criteria on a highly monitored, investigational basis. There were a plethora of syndromes, autoimmune diseases, and

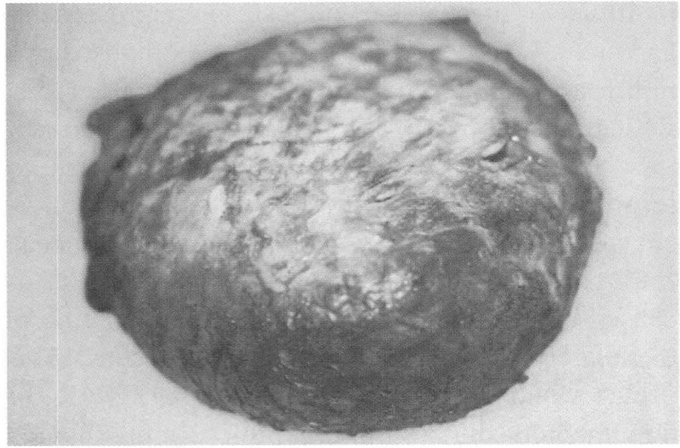

Figure 23–3. Excised implant and enveloping capsule contracture.

symptoms associated with silicone breast implants, and intense litigation followed. Many of these proposed associations, such as rheumatoid arthritis, were, in fact, shown in subsequent, large retrospective studies to occur in a lesser percentage of augmented patients than in the general population. Scleroderma-like syndromes were not shown to be associated with breast implants. On October 22, 1995, the American College of Rheumatology issued the following statement based on accumulated data: "Studies provide compelling evidence that silicone implants expose patients to no demonstrable additional risk for connective tissue or rheumatologic disease." None of the postulated syndromes have withstood the scrutiny of prospective epidemiologic testing.[46–48] Results from a large National Cancer Institute study are still pending.

Based on the data presented at the April 13, 2005, FDA hearings for silicone breast implants, one of the two US manufacturers has been recommended to proceed with pre-market approval applications for providing silicone implants with the caveat of continued surveillance of patients.

PRIMARY IMPLANT RECONSTRUCTION

One-stage primary implant reconstruction, the workhorse of breast reconstruction in the 1980s, has become less frequently used owing to improved outcome with expander or autologous reconstruction. Postmastectomy skin flaps are inherently vascularly compromised and prone to complications from added pressure such as that experienced in an expanded primary implant reconstruction. Candidates for one-stage implant reconstruction include patients with A- to B-sized breasts, having limited ptosis and sufficiently redundant skin flaps, who wish to expedite and simplify their approach to breast restoration. Patients may remain candidates for either immediate or delayed single-staged implant reconstruction.

Inherent to mastectomy are resection of the nipple-areolar complex, inclusion of adjacent biopsy incisions, and a resultant, variable, ipsilateral skin deficiency. Immediate reconstruction requires an initial assessment of skin flap vascularity, trauma, and tension. Only the healthiest skin flaps should signify proceeding with immediate implant reconstruction. Questionable vascularity, or marginal necrosis, warrants reappraisal and the choice of an alternative option, such as an immediate expander or autologous flap reconstruction, or delayed reconstruction. Compromised flaps and/or insertion of a large implant under tension risks dehiscence and implant exposure.

Delayed implant reconstruction is a safer and more popular option. The well-healed skin flaps are elevated in the sub-pectoral plane and may be stretched, thickened, and scored to provide improved projection and ptosis without regard to vascular compromise. The final outcome may be similarly improved by a symmetry procedure.

One-stage implant reconstruction is an option ideally suited to the rare patient with small- to moderate-sized nonptotic breasts who possesses sufficient soft tissue coverage and who desires the simplest reconstructive option. Despite an initial desire to avoid a secondary procedure, many patients require future implant adjustments or symmetry procedures. This technique has been largely supplanted by adjustable and permanent expanders/implants and the popular, time-tested, two-stage expander technique.

ADJUSTABLE IMPLANT RECONSTRUCTION

Adjustable implants, or permanent expander/implants, represent an option intermediate to the single-stage implant reconstruction and the more conventional two-stage technique (Figure 23–4). Postoperatively, adjustable implants enable precision in symmetry and the ability to attain a softer, often larger reconstruction with greater ptosis. The technique offers protection against tension-related wound complications and is generally considered preferable to primary implant reconstruction. It offers an excellent alternative to patients with limited skin deficits, A- to B-sized contralateral breasts, and/or those patients who require only limited expansion. In addition, a second-stage implant exchange can be avoided.

Poor candidates for implant reconstruction are those with large, pendulous breasts. These women, often obese, represent a challenge with any technique and are unlikely to achieve satisfactory symmetry without a contralateral reduction or mastopexy. Prior radiation treatment is a strong relative contraindication. The fibrotic and relatively

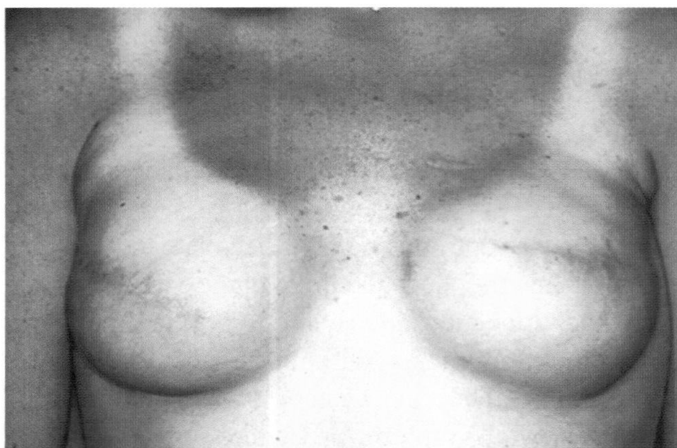

Figure 23–4. Bilateral reconstruction with adjustable expander/prosthesis.

ischemic nature of radiated skin flaps resists expansion and tolerates an underlying implant poorly, with a tendency towards cutaneous erosion and exposure. These patients are better served with either an autologous or composite reconstruction.

There are two types of adjustable prostheses currently available. One is a round anatomic, textured or smooth, postoperatively adjustable, saline implant. The implants are successively expanded with saline by percutaneous injection through a remote or integral subcutaneous injection port. Alternatively, Becker expander/prostheses are composed of a dual chamber system. The inner lumen, like the Mentor implant (Mentor Corp. Santa Barbara, CA), is filled and expanded with saline through a self-sealing, removable injection port. The outer lumen is factory sealed with silicone gel. It provides patients with the tangible advantages and surface camouflage of silicone and the postoperative adjustability of a saline implant.

Expansion is usually initiated 7 to 14 days postoperatively, following confirmation of skin flap viability. The frequency and extent of each expansion is dependent upon wound healing, skin sufficiency, and the patient's tolerance and comfort level. Typically, saline is injected to the point of tolerable skin tension, without blanching, on a weekly basis. Maintenance of the implant at maximum volume for a minimum of 3 months allows for capsule maturation. The implant may then be adjusted, within a narrow range, prior to port removal, to optimize consistency, shape, and ptosis.

IMMEDIATE TWO-STAGE BREAST RECONSTRUCTION

Tissue expansion in breast reconstruction was pioneered through the efforts of Chadomer Radovan and initially reported in 1976.[49] The postmastectomy defect lacks both skin for coverage and the underlying breast mound. To be reconstructed, the skin envelope must have adequate laxity to allow the breast mound to project sufficiently, achieve symmetric ptosis, and remain soft in consistency. These goals often require the recruitment of substantial adjacent skin through temporary overexpansion. Expanders, presently available for immediate breast reconstruction, enable focused expansion and simulation of a realistic IMF, without the physiologic donor site and rehabilitative demands of autologous reconstruction. Second-stage exchange, with either saline or silicone implants, is a simple, outpatient procedure. Tissue expanders remain the most popular method of immediate breast reconstruction.

Although all patients who undergo a mastectomy may be considered candidates for expander reconstruction, preferred patients are those with smaller, minimally ptotic breasts. The two-staged approach is a reliable, predictable reconstruction and has the ability to incorporate maximal adjacent skin, achieve greater volumes and preferential lower pole ptosis, and enable patient-directed modifications. Final refinements, including fold adjustments and capsulotomy, are facilitated at the time of implants exchange, optimizing the esthetic result. Conversely, patients with large or pendulous breasts require greater, more prolonged expansion and a contralateral symmetry procedure to achieve an acceptable result.

Complications of expander reconstruction parallel those of primary and adjustable implant reconstruction[50–54] (Table 23–3). Advantages and their ranges are illustrated in Table 23–1. Capsular contracture remains the single most troublesome complication and is reported in 10 to 25% of patients.[55,56] Progressive contracture may lead to asymmetry, deformation, and pain and require intervention, such as capsulotomy, in 20% of cases.

In 2001, Spear and Spittler reported the George Washington University Hospital experi-

Table 23–3. IMPLANT COMPLICATIONS		
	No XRT (%)	XRT (%)
Implant loss/extrusion	3.4–18	4–10
Deflation	3–4	—
Infection	1.2–8	10
Capsule contracture	2.9–31	20
Skin necrosis	10–24	3–7
Satisfaction	80–98	49–55

XRT = external radiation beam therapy.

ence with expander/implant reconstruction in 171 consecutive cases using textured expanders with integrated valves. They reported a capsular contracture rate of 3%, an infection rate of 1.2%, a spontaneous deflation rate of 0.6%, a 1.8% overall deflation rate, and no valve dysfunctions. Most of the expanders were electively replaced with permanent implants within one year.[57] This compares to a capsular contracture rate of between 8 and 15% reported by Francel and colleagues.[52] Slavin and Colen, reporting on 60 consecutive cases of expanders with remote valves, recorded valvular dysfunction in 5%, an infection rate of 6.7%, and a 5% incidence of incidental deflation.[58]

Prior or anticipated chest-wall radiation after breast conservation or mastectomy remains a strong relative contraindication to immediate expander reconstruction. Cutaneous radiation fibrosis resists effective expansion, limits ultimate projection, and increases the risk of capsular contracture, skin flap necrosis, implant exposure, infection, and chest wall pain. If radiation is deemed necessary subsequent to expander placement, full, pre-radiation expansion, with 15 to 20% overcompensation, helps resist the fibrotic contracture associated with radiation. Spear and Ontewu compared 40 immediate saline implant reconstruction patients requiring post-reconstruction radiation with 40 saline implant control patients from 1990 to 1997. Of the irradiated patients, 32% had symptomatic capsular contractures. Implant extrusion occurred in 5% and the infection rate was 12.5%. Of the irradiated patients, 47% required further flap reconstruction to correct contour and soft tissue deficits.[59]

Simulating the contralateral base width and the height of maximal projection are the key elements in attaining optimal cosmetic outcome. The goal is to accomplish the major surgical steps at the first procedure, which requires careful analysis of the contralateral breast. Simulation of minimal ptosis can be accomplished through overexpansion of the skin envelope and subsequent deflation or secondary replacement with an implant of lower vertical profile. Moderate ptosis can be simulated through the use of overexpansion and anatomic expanders, and by lowering of the IMF. Moderate to severe ptosis cannot be accurately matched and necessitates either a contralateral reduction, mastopexy, or composite reconstruction using the latissimus dorsi myocutaneous flap. Contralateral procedures are usually more precise when based upon the quality and extent of expansion achieved and are, therefore, preferentially performed during the second stage. This end point of the expansion process occurs when adequate projection is achieved in relation to the contralateral breast, rather than the ultimate volume being attained.

Patients and their reconstructions are not adversely affected if concurrent expansion and adjuvant chemotherapy are superimposed, pending wound stability at initiation. When implemented, completion of a chemotherapeutic regimen and granulocyte recovery is usually required prior to the second stage.

The advantages of prosthetic breast reconstruction include the ability to attain a reasonably good esthetic result utilizing adjacent tissue of similar color, texture, and sensation while eliminating distant donor site morbidity and minimizing scarring and post-operative recovery. Prosthetic reconstruction remains appealing for bilateral cases in which symmetry is less of a problem and where bilateral autologous reconstruction would impose substantial demands on the patient and surgeon. Similarly, in patients with smaller breasts, in older patients, and in those less motivated, expander or implant reconstruction remains a desirable option.

ADVANTAGES OF AUTOLOGOUS RECONSTRUCTION

As described, prosthetic reconstruction is safe and expeditious, with a limited recovery period. It is suited to the patients desiring a simple approach toward breast restoration. Candidates include those who wish to avoid external prosthesis, those with limited expectations, those with smaller breasts and limited to no ptosis, those with existing medical risk factors, and anxious patients who have difficulty comprehending more technical procedures. Expander/implant reconstruction may also pacify younger patients who wish to ultimately convert to autologous reconstruction following anticipated pregnancies.

Implant-based breast reconstruction, however, has many disadvantages. The implant, which is clad only by a thin layer of skin and muscle, is often poorly camouflaged and leads to a round, "mechanical," unnaturally aptotic, and asymmetric replacement. Periimplant capsule contractures may impose further distortion, migration, asymmetry, and discomfort. Capsular fibrosis limits the fluidity of both saline and silicone implants. It is noticeable upon palpation and for its inability to react naturally to positional changes. This is especially apparent when lying supine, when the reconstructed breast remains fixed and projecting while the native breast falls naturally to the side. This represents the most common adverse postoperative development, occurring in 20 to 40% of all mastectomy patients, requiring operative intervention in up to 20% of cases.[55,56] Implant-based reconstruction may, therefore, be a less strategic option for younger patients. Kroll and Balwin reported on 325 postmastectomy patients who had undergone either expander or autologous reconstruction. Complications occurred in 23% of expander patients and 9 and 3% in latissimus and TRAM flap reconstructions, respectively.[60]

Implants are devices and are thus susceptible to device failure. It has been well demonstrated that the silicone elastomer shell of both silicone and saline implants fatigue over time. This may manifest itself as either a silicone or saline bleed and/or a leak. An intracapsular silicone implant rupture is likely to remain undetected until an adverse event occurs. Most commonly, this may involve an increased tendency toward progressive capsular contracture. Blunt trauma resulting from a car, bicycle, or rollerblade incident, or even an overzealous mammogram, may convert a contained rupture into an extracapsular rupture. Patients typically notice a change in the shape and/or volume of the implant. This scenario warrants either mammographic, ultrasonographic, or magnetic resonance imaging (MRI) to rule out rupture.[35] Conversely, rupture of saline implants leads to implant deflation and a flat breast. In either case, implant replacement is warranted.

In contrast, autologous tissue has the warmth, consistency, feel, and reactive mobility of the patient's own tissues. It is a malleable, conformable, permanent medium that does not elicit a foreign body fibrotic response and is more tolerant of adjuvant therapy, trauma, and infection (Table 23–4). In contrast to the greater contracture and rupture rates of implants, autologous tissue softens and ages commensurate with adjacent structures and is, therefore, an ideal option for younger patients. An autologous flap may be contoured to match a contralateral breast of almost any size and shape. Although the initial overall cost of the flap reconstruction is greater, the long-term costs of autologous reconstruction have been shown to be less than those of prosthetic reconstruction owing to subsequent secondary capsulotomies, revisions, and implant exchanges required with the latter procedure.

Autologous reconstruction is inherently more complex from both a technical and an artistic standpoint. The functional and esthetic outcome of the initial procedure, which lasts from 4 to 5 hours, largely depends upon the surgeon's experience and microsurgical expertise. Although the initial procedure requires a longer hospitalization (3 to 4 days) and postoperative recovery, the result is permanent and rarely requires a secondary adjunctive procedure. The TRAM flap, or variant thereof, is overwhelmingly the flap of choice when available. Alternatives include the latissimus dorsi, Rubens or peri-iliac, lateral thigh, gluteal, and perforator flaps.

Table 23–4. ADVANTAGES OF AUTOLOGOUS RECONSTRUCTION
Soft
Warm
Pliable
Permanent
Enables wide resection
No foreign body response
Natural consistency and appearance
Tolerates adjuvant therapy well
Decreases need for symmetry procedure
More economic in the long term

CONVENTIONAL TRAM FLAP

The TRAM flap is the most frequently used method for autogenous breast reconstruction, whether conventional or free, and is one of the most ingenious techniques in plastic surgery. It is successful, safe, and reproducible, and presents the reconstructive surgeon with the opportunity to create a breast of unsurpassed esthetic beauty, simulate the opposite breast, and secondarily improve the contour of the lower abdomen. Attaining consistently good results requires careful planning and technical proficiency. The lower abdomen consistently provides exceptional and sufficient tissue for unilateral and, in the majority of patients, bilateral breast reconstruction. The procedure is versatile and reliable when performed within its recognized vascular and volumetric constraints. Hartrampf and colleagues' landmark introduction of the TRAM flap in 1982, still the "gold standard" for autologous breast reconstruction, provided the foundation for the modern era of breast reconstruction.[61]

The conventional, unipedicled TRAM flap, as originally described, consists of a transverse ellipse of skin and fat based on one rectus muscle and its intrinsic musculocutaneous perforators from the deep superior epigastric pedicle. The pedicle branches as it transgresses through the substance of the ipsilateral rectus through a network of "choke" vessels, which reconstitute in the mid-abdomen.[61–65] This inflow communicates with the periumbilical, myocutaneous perforators that supply the suprafacial and subcutaneous plexus. Perfusion has been graded and is depicted as a sequence of zones, with zone VI, the most distal tissue, representing strictly random perfusion (Figure 23–5). Flow in the conventional TRAM is, therefore, secondary and unpredictable beyond the midline. Patient selection is critical and is limited, among experienced surgeons, to those patients who have tissue requirements met by the ipsilateral "hemi-TRAM."

In the uncomplicated case, the flap extends from the umbilicus to a point superior to the pubis. The incisions are beveled to incorporate additional periumbilical perforators and subcutaneous fat. The flap is elevated at the supra-fascial level toward the medial and lateral row of ipsilateral musculocutaneous perforators. The fascia is incised adjacent to the perforators, and the underlying rectus is mobilized.

Most commonly, a full width muscle harvest is performed. The rectus muscle is elevated beneath the superior abdominal skin flap to the costal margin. The superior epigastric pedicle is easily identified, enabling transection of the lateral rectus fibers and intercostal nerves. This facilitates muscle atrophy and, thereby, minimizes the central xiphoid bulge, common early after this procedure. This flap is transposed through the medial IMF and is inset into the breast defect. Zones IV and II may be discarded prior to transposition to facilitate passage.

In an effort to preserve abdominal wall integrity, an alternative "split-muscle" harvest has been advocated.[66–68] Pedicle (muscle) width is based upon the laterality of the medial and lateral row of perforators. It is usually possible to preserve a substantial (one-third) width of the lateral rectus and often a slip of infraumbilical medial rectus. Although the muscle is,

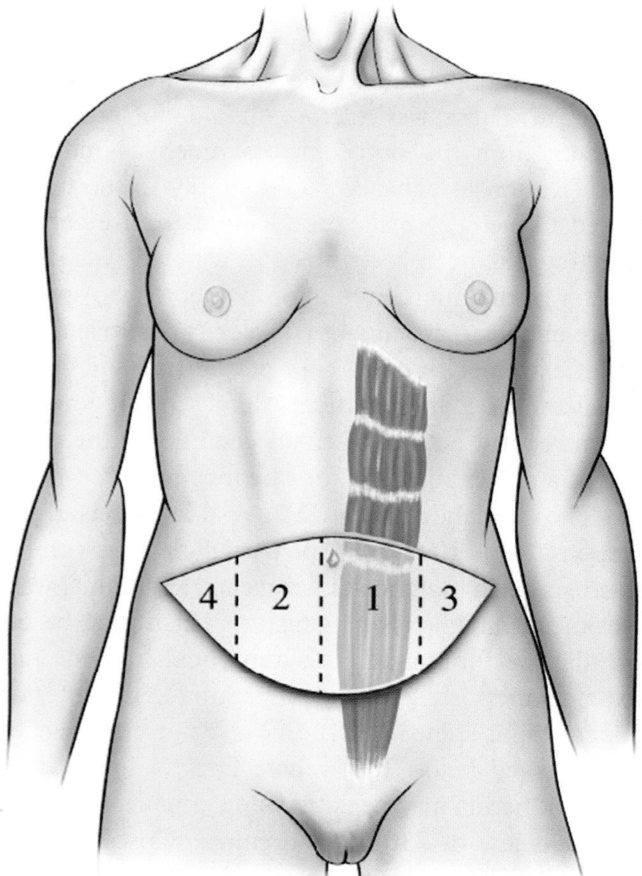

Figure 23–5. TRAM flap zones.

in most cases, denervated, it is thought to uphold the muscular interface of the semi-lunar line and adds fibrous stability in the perioperative period.

It is common practice to include a segment of skeletonized inferior epigastric pedicle in the event additional perfusion is necessary to sustain the flap.[69,70] This "lifeboat" enables supplementary perfusion through a "super-charged" microvascular anastomosis, usually to the thoracodorsal pedicle, if intrinsic vascular insufficiency is noted. Fascial donor site closure is achieved with either interrupted figure-of-eight sutures or a running, heavy, braided synthetic. The patient is then flexed to 45 degrees to facilitate abdominal closure and ascertain breast symmetry. Postoperative flap monitoring is institution-specific and may encompass temperature probes, ultrasonography or laser Doppler, and clinical surveillance.

Use of the superiorly based unipedicled TRAM flap requires strict adherence to patient selection criteria. It has been clearly demonstrated that patients who smoke, are obese, have significant abdominal scarring, or have had previous radiation have an increased risk of complications, including fat necrosis, partial flap failure, and donor site complications.[71–75] These risk factors should not eliminate patients from the procedure so much as indicate modification to enhance blood supply to the transferred tissue. For instance, nicotine from cigarette smoking has been recognized as a potent vasoconstrictor of the microcirculation. Patients who smoke or are unable to abstain 4 to 6 weeks prior to surgery are at extremely high risk for partial flap and donor site necrosis.[76] These patients, likely to fail conventional reconstruction, often succeed under the preface of a delay, bipedicle, or free technique.

The midabdominal TRAM was devised in response to a 20 to 60% of partial flap loss or fat necrosis and a high rate of hernia and abdominal wall weakness in high-risk patients.[77,78] This flap is based on the perforator-rich periumbilical region and extends inferiorly to a tangent parallel to the anterior superior iliac spine (ASIS). Because muscle integrity is preserved below the arcuate lines, a lower incidence of hernia may be anticipated. Slavin and Goldwyn's review of 236 midabdominal flaps showed a 2% rate of partial flap necrosis and a 1% incidence of fat necrosis.[77] The primary disadvantages are an occasionally displeasing high or midabdominal scar and the lack of the abdominoplasty effect inherent in conventional TRAM reconstruction.

Although largely supplanted by microsurgical advances, preoperative surgical delay of a conventional TRAM is another technique for augmenting reliable flap dimensions.[79–82] In 1995, Codner and colleagues demonstrated improved inflow and diminished congestion after surgical delay.[82] Zones II and III proved more vigorous and reliable, especially in the high-risk patient, and lessened the need for a bipedicled approach. In 1997, Restifo documented greater pedicle caliber (1.3 versus 1.8 mm) and flow rates (7.5 versus 18.2 ml/min) compared to controls after surgical delay.[83] Staged interruption of the inferior epigastric pedicle, on a physiologic basis, is highly effective in augmenting vascularity and is beneficial in the high-risk patient.

Operative assessment of the contralateral breast helps in formulating a reconstructive strategy in optimizing symmetry. The location and breadth of the IMF is a critical landmark and serves as the basis for building a symmetric breast. Attention to the condition and volume of retained skin (mastectomy skin flap), the size, shape, base width, and ptosis of the contralateral breast and how it relates to the IMF is necessary if symmetry is to be optimized. Patients with preexisting macromastia may elect to undergo concurrent or delayed contralateral breast reduction, both to alleviate objective symptoms (shoulder pain and grooving, intertrigo, lower back pain) and improve the ultimate esthetic outcome. Patients with substantial glandular ptosis may elect to undergo mastopexy for similar reasons. It is our preference to perform these contralateral procedures as a second stage. Improved accuracy of a symmetry procedure may be attained after resolution of flap edema, muscle atrophy, and skin retraction. Staging also enables concurrent refinements (suction-assisted lipectomy, IMF revision) on the recently restored breast.

FREE TRAM FLAP

The main disadvantage of TRAM flap reconstruction is the potential for weakening the abdominal wall. Questions remain as to the best technique of abdominal closure and, historically, the impact of free versus pedicled flap reconstruction on the abdominal wall. Despite all of the advantages of the TRAM, it is a major surgical procedure and carries the risk of abdominal weakness, bulging, and hernia formation. True hernias resulting from the procedure are rare (< 3% of cases). Abdominal wall bulges, indicating a separation and attenuation of the internal and external oblique muscles, occur frequently (3 to 12% of cases).[84–86]

Several studies have obtained objective measures of abdominal muscle strength. Trunk muscle strength, as measured by an isokinetic dynamometer, demonstrated postoperative recovery of 92, 96 and 98% at 3, 6, and 12 months, respectively, for unilateral free TRAM flap patients.[87] Kind and colleagues compared the recovery after pedicled and free TRAM reconstruction. Flexion torque, as measured by dynamometer, was 58 and 89% at 6 weeks and 6 months, respectively. The investigators concluded that the pedicled TRAM caused a significantly greater insult to the abdominal wall in the early postoperative period, but that the two techniques equilibrated to over 90% of preoperative levels at 12 months. It was also determined that early muscle splitting techniques appeared to offer no functional advantage.[88]

Over the past decade, there has been an evolution in breast reconstruction using muscle sparing abdominal flaps prompted by aspirations to minimize abdominal morbidity. Minimizing the amount of muscle removed may reduce the morbidity of the abdominal wall, as it relates to strength and contour, and lead to a more expeditious, functional recovery. (Figure 23–6). The volume of rectus muscle harvested may be limited to a small cuff of fibers surrounding all or a small group of perforators transgressing through the rectus muscles. Thus, a medial and/or lateral strip of rectus muscle may be preserved, designated a muscle-sparing free TRAM, which benefits young, active patients or those desiring future pregnancies. Alternatively, one or two individual perforators may be dissected through the rectus muscle to the deep inferior epigastric pedicle, completely sparing injury to all rectus fibers and its inherent nerve supply (deep inferior epigastric perforator [DIEP] flap). This aggressive, technically demanding, often challenging approach towards greater muscle preservation stems from aspirations to minimize abdominal wall morbidity, to preserve function, and to diminish recovery, postoperative pain and cost.[89–92] An inherent risk of these muscle sparing and perforator flap techniques is that perfusion to the fascio-cutaneous component of the flap may be compromised. As the collateral vessels and perforators are ligated, there is an alteration in perfusion that may result in venous congestion or arterial insufficiency.

All variants of the free TRAM are based on the dominant inferior epigastric pedicle and require a microvascular anastomosis. They represent a reliable, versatile, highly esthetic option for both immediate and delayed reconstruction (see Figure 23–5). Complications associated with conventional TRAM reconstruction, occurring in up to 25% of reported cases, are partial flap loss and fat necrosis and are

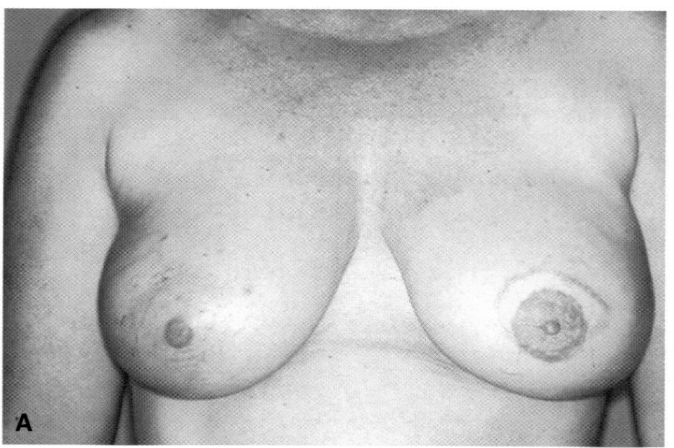

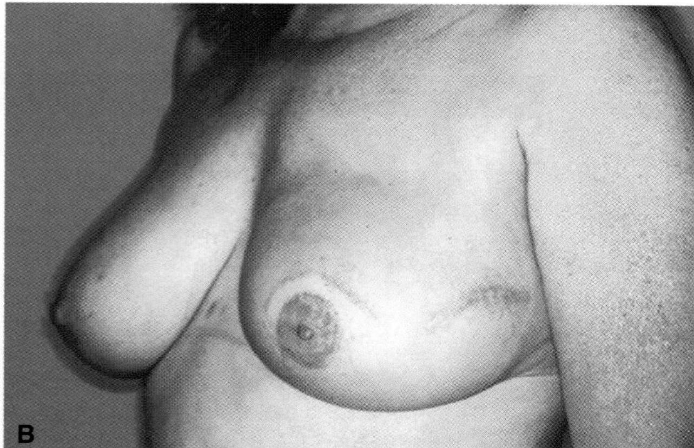

Figure 23–6. *A*, Free TRAM reconstruction; *B*, 9 months postoperative.

inherent to the procedure's secondary blood supply and volume constraints.[54,66,73–76,83–85] Kroll and colleagues reported in 1998 on the incidence of fat necrosis among patients who had had conventional versus free TRAM reconstruction. Of the 49 free TRAM patients, 8.2% exhibited clinical fat necrosis. Of the 67 pedicled TRAM patients, 27% demonstrated fat necrosis on examination and 9 patients on mammogram.[93] These complications may impose prolonged wound healing and considerable delay in the therapeutic sequence. Although the free TRAM procedure requires greater technical proficiency and a slightly longer operating time, the flap has unparalleled vascular reliability and versatility, a lower complication rate, and is the flap of choice in high-risk patients. These include obese patients, smokers, and those patients with prohibitive scars or who have had prior radiation treatment.[73–76]

Fascial, and resultantly, muscle-sparing variants are dependent upon analysis of the location, caliber, and proximity of the perforating vessels. The DIEP flap represents complete preservation of the rectus abdominis muscle and anterior rectus sheath as the single or limited number of perforators are dissected free of the encompassing rectus muscle fibers. The muscle and overlying fascia are only incised, not excised, in the flap harvest. Various studies have attempted to discern whether the physiologic abdominal wall benefits warrant the greater demands with regard to microsurgical expertise, operative times, and potential perfusion related complications. In 2005, Nahabedian and colleagues reported a 2 and 5% failure rate for unilateral and bilateral DIEP flaps compared to a 3 and 0% failure rate for unilateral and bilateral muscle-sparing free TRAM flaps, respectively. The rate of fat necrosis was 9, 5, 11, and 2% for unilateral DIEP, bilateral DIEP, unilateral free TRAM, and bilateral free TRAM flaps, respectively. The bulge rate was 2 and 5% for unilateral and bilateral DIEP flaps, compared to a 5 and 21% rate for unilateral and bilateral free TRAM flaps. The ability to perform a sit-up was 100 and 95% after unilateral and bilateral DIEP flaps, and 97 and 83% after unilateral and bilateral free "muscle-sparing" TRAM flaps.[94] This compares favorably with previous reports of "non–muscle-sparing" free and conventional TRAM flaps, where percentages of patients able to perform sit-ups were 63, 57, 46 and 27% for single free and conventional TRAM flaps and bilateral free and conventional TRAM flaps, respectively.[89] Fitoussi and colleagues reported that 47% of single pedicle TRAM and 0% of bipedicle TRAM patients could perform sit-ups postoperatively and concluded that, although the hernia rate did not vary between the two groups, functional sequelae were statistically significant.[90] Complication rates among various groups are compared in Table 23–5.

Whether to use a free TRAM or DIEP flap is decided on the basis of the physical characteristics of the patient and the anatomic characteristics of the flap. A free TRAM can be used for breast reconstructions of almost any volume, however, it is especially indicated when the tissue requirements exceed 1,000 cc. In general, the DIEP is useful for breast reconstructions that do not exceed 1,000 cc. The rationale for using the DIEP flap is that the perforating vessels are of sufficient caliber to adequately perfuse the fascio-cutaneous component, and that

Table 23–5. STATISTICS FOR FREE FLAP BREAST RECONSTRUCTION

		#	Fat Necrosis	Partial Loss	Total Loss	Hernia
Ped TRAM	Watterson[118]	729	11	5	0	9
Free TRAM	Kroll[119]	279	12.9	2.2	0.4	—
Free TRAM	Nahabedian[120]	143	9.8	0	3.5	—
Free TRAM	Fenner*	420	3	1	0.1	—
DIEP	Blondeel[121]	100	6	7	0	9
DIEP	Hamdi[108]	50	6	6	2	0
DIEP	Kroll[119]	23	17.4	8.7	0	—
DIEP	Keller	148	6.8	—	0.7	1.4
DIEP	Nahabedian[120]	20	10	0	5	0
DIEP	Allen[122]	758	12.9	2.5	0.5	0.6

*Unpublished data.

these perforators can be adequately separated from the rectus abdominis muscle. Perforator calibers of greater than 1.5 mm, a palpable pulse in the perforator, a diminutive superficial inferior epigastric artery (SIEA) pedicle, and adjacent perforators along a parallel musculocutaneous perforator have all been described as characteristics necessary in sustaining a successful DIEP flap. The final decision to proceed with a DIEP flap must be made intraoperatively after all of the perforators have been visualized. Statistics for pedicled TRAM, free TRAM, and DIEP flaps are shown in Table 23–5 (see Figure 23–6).

Supra-fascial elevation is identical to that employed in the pedicled TRAM procedure. Widely dispersed perforators may be omitted owing to the dominant inflow, thereby limiting the fascial harvest. The lateral edge of the rectus muscle is elevated to discern the path of the epigastric pedicle. This determines whether a medial and/or lateral muscular strip may be preserved in the muscle-sparing free TRAM varieties. Alternatively, individual or tandem perforators in DIEP flaps are dissected through the breadth of the rectus muscle to the DIEP pedicle. The pedicle is ligated at the external iliac origin. Axillary and/or internal mammary recipient vessels are normally reliable, even if prior radiation therapy has been implemented. An interrupted or running arterial microvascular anastomosis is typically performed with 9.0 nylon suture. Venous anastomosis may be similarly performed, or one may use an anastomotic coupling device (3M, St. Paul, MN) for added speed. The occluding clamps are removed, and the quality of flap perfusion is confirmed both clinically and with the use of an intraoperative Doppler.

Use of free flaps in breast reconstruction enables preservation of the inframammary fold, does not compromise the marginal perfusion of the freshly elevated mastectomy skin flaps, and optimizes the esthetic outcome. Freedom upon insetting, owing to the absence of the conventional muscular "leash," facilitates a quick, easy, and highly cosmetic and symmetric reconstruction (Figure 23–7). The improved blood supply may expedite wound healing and initiation of adjuvant therapy, which may also be better tolerated than in the conventional TRAM flap procedure.

The only absolute contraindications to free TRAM reconstruction include prohibitive scarring, violation of the inferior epigastric blood supply from previous abdominoplasty, suction lipectomy, an extended Pfannenstiel incision, or a previous TRAM procedure. Pre-existing medical conditions may limit the patient's ability to tolerate 4 to 6 hours combined anesthesia time. This should be addressed preoperatively.

In a series of 211 free TRAM flaps, Schusterman and colleagues reported a flap thrombosis rate of 3.3% and a flap loss rate of 1.4%.[86] One study compared outcome among conventional and free TRAM reconstruction. It was demonstrated that despite a higher percentage of high-risk patients

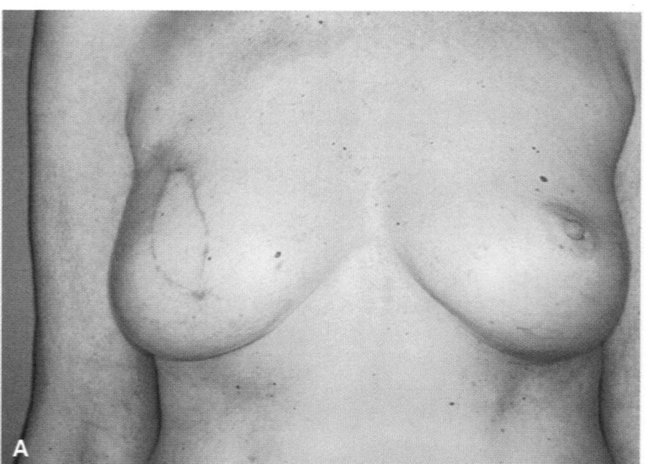

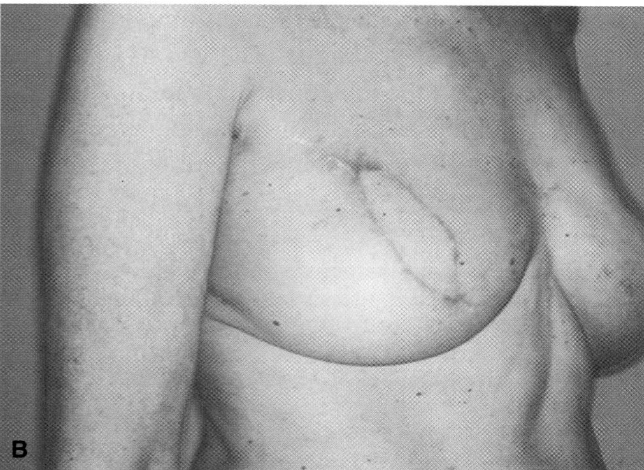

Figure 23–7. *A* and *B*, Right free TRAM reconstruction prior to nipple/areolar reconstruction.

(63 versus 28%), the free TRAM group had fewer complications (9 versus 28%) than the conventional TRAM group. The advantages of the free TRAM procedure are outlined in Table 23–6.

BIPEDICLED TRAM FLAP

An unipedicled conventional TRAM will reliably perfuse all of zone I, 20% of zone II, and 80% of zone III (see Figure 23–5).[95] An alternative technique or flap choice is warranted if tissue requirements exceed these specifications. Indications for a bipedicled TRAM include those patients who insist on autogenous reconstruction, who require additional volume, and for whom microsurgical reconstruction is not possible owing to an absence of reasonable recipient axillary vessels. The indications parallel those for surgical vascular delay.

The lower abdominal pannus is isolated on the medial and lateral row of perforators, bilaterally. Once the upper abdominal apron is elevated, each superior epigastric pedicle is isolated with the assistance of Doppler mapping, and a split bipedicle muscle harvest is performed. The flap is transposed and inset in much the same way as for a unipedicled TRAM flap.

Multiple reports have investigated the long- and short-term impact of bilateral rectus harvest. Hartrampf[91] reported that 64% of patients could not perform a single sit-up after bipedicled reconstruction, compared with 17% in the unipedicled group. Petit and colleagues reported a 20% incidence of subsequent severe back pain in bipedicled patients.[96]

The bipedicled flap has reduced the incidence of partial flap loss and fat necrosis in much the same manner as the free technique. The use of mesh has markedly reduced the incidence of abdominal hernia formation and bulging. Although these patients have objective loss of abdominal function, subjective interference with daily activity is rare.

Table 23–6. ADVANTAGES OF FREE TRAM
Primary and dominant blood supply
Greater available volume
Less muscle harvest/abdominal dissection
More comfortable recovery
More reliable in high-risk patients
Greater freedom in insetting
Good tolerance to adjuvant therapy

Use of the bipedicled TRAM for unilateral reconstruction has invoked substantial controversy in the plastic surgery literature. Antagonists claim the morbidity from bilateral muscle harvest, including abdominal wall weakness and the propensity toward future back pain, "can no longer be defended" in the current realm of reliable microsurgical capability and surgical delay.[97] Conversely, proponents claim that the split muscle technique and addition of mesh reinforcement limit functional morbidity and that the resultant abdominal wall integrity is dependent upon the closure technique used.[98] They adhere to its use as a reliable alternative in high-risk patients.

LATISSIMUS DORSI

The latissimus dorsi myocutaneous flap was originally described by Tansini in 1906 and used to cover radical mastectomy defects.[99] It has since demonstrated remarkable versatility and is useful in providing purely autogenous, composite implant, and partial mastectomy reconstruction (Figure 23–8). The straightforward anatomy, easy elevation, relative lack of donor morbidity, and ability to provide an additional "curtain" of conforming tissue have made it a reasonable adjunct to breast reconstruction, most commonly in healthy patients considering expander reconstruction.

The indications for latissimus reconstruction vary widely and depend upon the preferences and capabilities of the surgeon. Several subsets exist, all governed by the assumption that a TRAM flap has

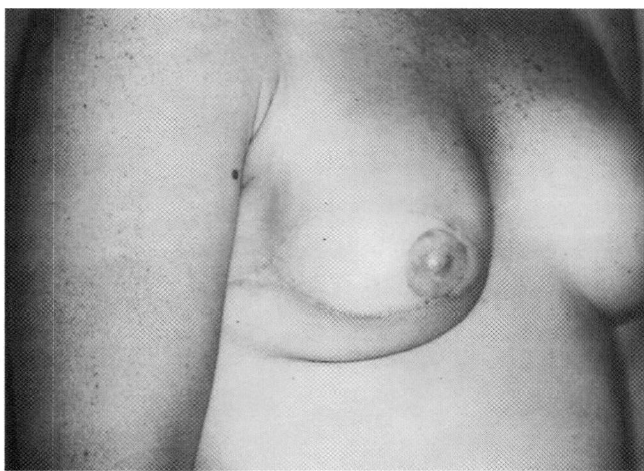

Figure 23–8. Latissimus dorsi myocutaneous flap reconstruction.

been ruled out for medical, anatomic, or personal reasons. The first set includes those patients who are otherwise appropriate candidates for expander reconstruction but for whom less than optimal coverage is predicted. This may include patients who have had a prior radical mastectomy and lack a pectoralis, those who have thin mastectomy skin flaps, or those who require a large skin resection owing to inclusive resection of a remote biopsy site or to prior radiation.

The second set includes those patients amenable to expander reconstruction who have sufficient coverage and high esthetic expectations. The challenge in unilateral postmastectomy expander reconstruction is to provide a breast form that simulates the contralateral side. Prosthetic reconstruction provides a round, firm, relatively immobile breast form, which is ideally suited for patients with small- to intermediate-sized breast and limited to no ptosis. Patients who are moderate or large in size and develop some degree of ptosis with age and childbirth will demonstrate variable asymmetry with unilateral prosthetic reconstruction. These non-TRAM candidates may elect to undergo either contralateral mastopexy and/or composite latissimus-expander reconstruction for improved symmetry. The flap provides supplemental muscle and fat, which helps camouflage the underlying prosthesis and replaces the resected skin, leading to a more natural ptotic breast form.

The third category includes those patients who prefer an autogenous restoration but lack flap alternatives owing to medical or surgical reasons. Most patients have a breast volume in excess of their available flank tissue and require supplemental volume in the form of an implant. The resultant satisfaction in esthetic outcome, greater projection, and natural ptosis allay most patients' preoperative reluctance toward a supplemental implant. The fourth and fifth sets involve autogenous latissimus reconstruction without supplemental prosthesis and apply to two patient extremes where the available flank tissue volume simulates breast volume. Solely autogenous latissimus reconstruction is routinely possible in heavier patients having substantial upper flank tissue. These patients typically have redundant flank skin and additional subcutaneous bulk that may be incorporated into the flap to provide necessary volume and ptosis. Conversely, patients with marked breast hypoplasia may also attain sufficient volume, contour, and symmetry from a purely autogenous latissimus myocutaneous flap.

The flap has an extremely reliable blood supply and is versatile even in smokers and diabetics. Partial flap necrosis has been reported in up to 7% of patients.[100] The most common complication is the persistence of seromas, which often require prolonged drainage or aspiration. Implant-related complications include implant slippage and capsule contracture. Use of textured, saline expanders and implants has reduced these complications.

The latissimus dorsi flap represents a popular, extremely reliable option for the mastectomy patient. The results are outstanding when used in conjunction with textured, anatomic saline expanders and implants, typically better than those achieved with expanders alone.

RUBENS FLAP

Peter Paul Rubens was known for his portraits of voluptuous, full-figured females with particular fullness in the supra-iliac region. The skin and subcutaneous tissue in the region may be sustained by the deep circumflex iliac artery, as originally described by Taylor and colleagues.[101] Hartrampf coined this peri-iliac fat pad the "Rubens flap."[102]

It is with some bewilderment that occasional patients complain of a greater lower abdominal circumference, not a reduction, and have greater difficulty wearing their previously well-fitting clothing after undergoing a TRAM flap breast reconstruction. Closing the anterior TRAM donor site leads to accentuation of the peri-iliac tissue and can cause an increase in the peri-iliac circumference. This redundancy represents the tissue available for free tissue transfer after a previous TRAM flap. The predominant indication for use of the Rubens flap is therefore a prior TRAM harvest or abdominoplasty. Other indications for use of the Rubens flap include thin patients and prohibitive anterior abdominals scars.

Flap dissection requires a precise knowledge and familiarity with the intrinsic support of the abdominal wall. The primary disadvantage of the flap is the occurrence of an occasional flank hernia. Compulsive closure of the donor site is paramount to the success of this procedure and requires a dedicated surgeon. Other potential morbidity includes longstanding seromas that require prolonged drainage and compression garments. There may be prolonged postoperative discomfort and the necessity for extended physical therapy.

The flap is oriented parallel to the iliac crest, with two-thirds of the skin paddle above and one-third below the crest (Figure 23–9A). An inguinal incision lateral to the femoral pulse and through the intrinsic muscles will expose the underlying deep circumflex iliac vessels upon which the flap is based. The inferior skin flap is elevated above the tensor of fascia lata to the iliac crest. Sub-periosteal dissection will ensure the integrity of both the deep circumflex iliac artery (DCIA) pedicle and perforators. The lateral femoral cutaneous nerve runs inferiorly, within 1 cm of the anterior superior iliac spine, and may lie either above or below the DCIA. This nerve should be preserved.

Donor site closure is initiated by approximation of the transversalis fascia to the iliopsoas fascia. The remaining flank muscles are secured to the iliac crest through drill holes and heavy suture or wire.

Deep circumflex iliac artery pedicle length facilitates anastomosis to the preferred thoracodorsal vessels in the majority of cases. This flap tends to be less robust than the TRAM and may exhibit a weak Doppler signal, at best. The flap provides excellent projection (Figure 23–9B) and is an ideal option for bilateral reconstruction, which may be performed simultaneously, concurrent with mastectomy.

SUPERIOR GLUTEAL FLAP

The superior gluteal flap was the first free flap described for breast reconstruction.[103] Microsurgical expertise is essential for success owing to a tedious flap dissection, an inherently short vascular pedicle, the presence of a large disproportionate thin-walled vein, and because the micro-anastomoses are most commonly performed to the delicate and variable internal mammary vessels.[104]

Candidates include patients who fail qualification for implants owing to prior chest-wall irradiation or "implant anxiety" or who have abdominal scars precluding TRAM reconstruction. Such scars may have resulted from laparotomies, enterotomies, previous abdominoplasties, liposuction, or TRAM harvests. This flap may represent the only autogenous option in thin patients who lack sufficient abdominal or lateral thigh tissue for unilateral or bilateral reconstruction.

Like the TRAM, the gluteal flap offers a permanent, soft, warm, and natural reconstruction. It has a denser fat-septal network, providing an intermediate size reconstruction with excellent projection. It may be the flap of choice for patients who have had a previous TRAM and require a staged contralateral mastectomy. It also offers an inconspicuous donor site.

Flap dimensions typically extend from the lateral mid-sacrum to within 5 cm of the ASIS. The vertical height of the flap depends on the tissue needed but may vary from 10 to 15 cm. Flap dissection necessitates identification of the fragile supe-

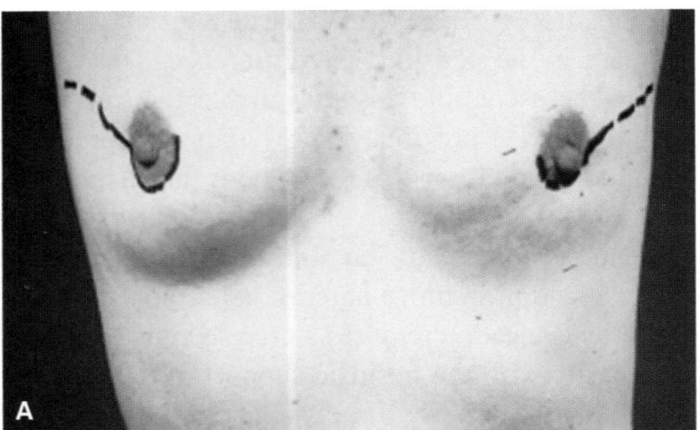

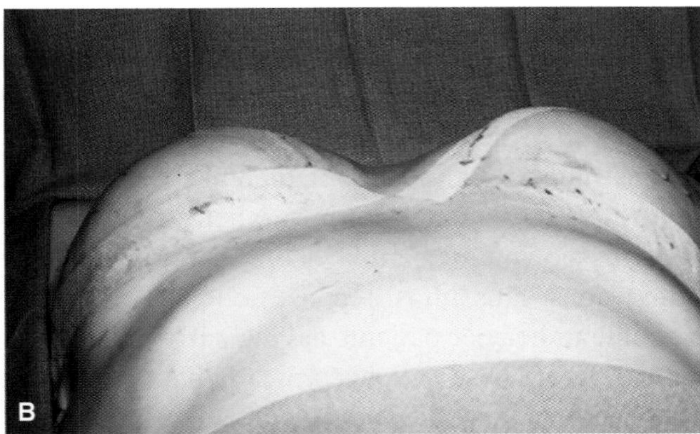

Figure 23–9. Ruben's flap. *A*, Bilateral flap design; *B*, Immediate postoperative projection demonstrated. Reproduced with permission from William W. Shaw, MD, Division of Plastic Surgery, UCLA.

rior gluteal vessels deep to the gluteus muscle. This pedicle emerges from the greater sciatic foramen amidst numerous branches and provides 1.5 to 2.0 cm of pedicle length. The internal mammary vessels are exposed and mobilized through a third peri-sternal rib resection.

Like its counterpart, the inferior gluteal flap is indicated in rare patients who refuse prosthetic reconstruction and who are not candidates for TRAM, lateral thigh, or latissimus flaps. Although the length of the donor inferior gluteal vessels enable anastomosis to the more forgiving thoracodorsal pedicle and the donor site scar is the least conspicuous of any autogenous option, harvest necessitates sacrifice of the gluteal motor nerve, occasional sacrifice of the posterior cutaneous nerve, and close dissection to the sciatic nerve, all of which may lead to transient pain syndromes and weakness with ambulation; prolonged rehabilitation may be required. For these reasons, the gluteal flap is generally the least favored flap in the breast reconstruction algorithm.

LATERAL THIGH FLAP

The lateral transverse thigh flap and tensor of fascia lata flap are two reconstructive variants that are based upon the lateral femoral circumflex vessels and make use of the lateral "riding breeches" or "saddle bags."[105] The pedicle transgresses through and requires the sacrifice of the modest tensor muscle. Preservation of adjacent fascia lata helps to ensure lateral knee stability without functional compromise. More imposing, and representing the primary disadvantage, is the often-disfiguring lateral thigh scars, which are long and remain poorly camouflaged.

Preoperative design requires experience and precision. An excessive subcutaneous harvest will result in objectionable lateral thigh contour deficits. These are difficult to correct but do benefit from delayed suction lipectomy. Patients may require prolonged drainage and garment compression to limit the tendency toward seroma formation. Advantages include a 7 to 8 cm vascular pedicle, excellent flap projection, and the ability to perform concurrent bilateral simultaneous harvests and reconstruction.

BILATERAL BREAST RECONSTRUCTION

A patient testing positive for either the *BRCA1* or *BRCA2* gene has a 50 to 80% risk of developing breast cancer by the age of 65. Prophylactic mastectomies in these patients provide a risk reduction between 90 to 100%. Life expectancy is increased from 2.9 to 5.3 years.[106,107] The psychological benefits include a 70% rate of satisfaction and a decrease in emotional concern of developing breast cancer in 74% of women who undergo prophylactic mastectomies for *BRCA1* and *BRCA2* gene positivity.[108] Other indications for contralateral prophylactic mastectomy include a strong family history of breast cancer, lobular carcinoma in situ (LCIS), cancer anxiety, and equivocal or progressively difficult clinical and/or radiographic examinations.

With improvements in breast cancer screening, a greater number of early breast cancers are being detected in young, premenopausal patients, many of whom have some degree of familial cancer history. Patients with young families present with the intent to absolve breast cancer risk for the benefit of their young ones and represent a new indication for either prophylactic or bilateral mastectomy. Breast cancer awareness has elevated the level of sophistication of all patients. Prosthetic and autologous reconstruction is a known entity that continues to become more reliable, safe, and esthetically satisfying. As this awareness becomes more apparent and outcomes improve, it is not surprising that an increasing number of susceptible women are at least questioning the option of bilateral ablation and immediate reconstruction.

Esthetic outcome is often better in bilateral reconstruction than in unilateral reconstruction owing to the symmetry achieved. Macromastia and pseudoptosis are not compounding factors since skin redundancy may be addressed symmetrically. Bilateral implants and/or permanent expander implants, postmastectomy, usually provide exceptional results, in contrast to unilateral procedures, which exaggerate implant characteristics. Postoperative adjustability ensures a symmetric result. This is ideal for the older patient or the patient with marginal reserves who desires to avoid an external prosthesis and could not tolerate a long operative procedure. Metcalfe and colleagues reported in 2004 that

68% of patients having autologous reconstruction and 74% of those having had implant reconstruction after bilateral prophylactic mastectomies were satisfied with their cosmetic result.[108]

The TRAM flap, once again, is the flap of choice, providing reliability and minimal morbidity in bilateral autologous reconstruction (Figure 23–10). Sufficient tissue is present for bilateral reconstruction in 75 to 80% of patients. The majority of patients, when advised of the ability to perform an immediate, single-stage, highly esthetic and symmetric, permanent, bilateral autogenous reconstruction and simultaneously rid themselves of an often pervasive lower abdominal pannus, are most often highly grateful and not overly concerned about the possibility of having slightly smaller breasts if less than profound amounts of tissue are available. Advantages of bilateral TRAM reconstruction include the ability to perform a simultaneous harvest in the supine position.

Either bilateral conventional or free TRAMs may be performed. The vascular reliability of bilateral "hemi-TRAM" flaps is normally adequate because cross perfusion across the midline is not necessary, depending on an absence of excessive scarring, obesity, prior radiation, and history of smoking. Use of the conventional flaps is usually faster and technically simpler than free TRAM reconstruction but requires inherent sacrifice of both rectus muscles, which may lead to objective and subjective abdominal wall weakness in the majority of more active patients. Extensive superior abdominal dissection and tunneling is required and may prolong postoperative discomfort and recovery. Transposition of bilateral flaps may lead to an upper abdominal bulge and violate some aspect of both inframammary folds, compromising final cosmesis.

The advantages of bilateral free TRAM or DIEP flap reconstruction include limited to no muscle harvest, limited upper abdominal dissection (which minimizes discomfort and expedites recovery), and unparalleled esthetic outcome. Lateral extension of these free "hemi-flaps" may be incorporated to boost tissue volume in thin patients and is made possible by the exceptional blood supply. The incidence of abdominal wall bulging and hernia formation is similar for free and conventional bilateral reconstruction and has been outlined for free TRAM versus DIEP flaps. The potential to exclude medial, diminutive, or outlying perforators in bilateral free reconstruction facilitates fascial closure without the use of mesh in free TRAM patients. Although it is reported that mesh may be avoided in 60 to 80% of patients having bilateral TRAM reconstruction, the use of a more relaxed closure using mesh may facilitate postoperative comfort, recovery, and return of bowel motility. Prolene mesh is currently the authors' preferred choice for reinforcement. Closure may be facilitated by a preoperative bowel prep, the appropriate use of relaxing agents, avoidance of nitrous oxide (which can lead to bowel dilatation), and the use of lateral external oblique relaxing incisions. The incidence of true hernias is rare. Lower abdominal attenuation or abdominal wall bulging occurs in 4.4 to 20% of cases.[109]

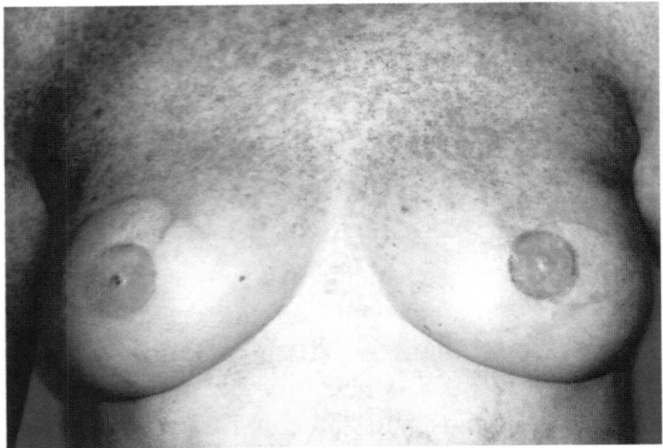

Figure 23–10. Bilateral free TRAM reconstruction.

RECONSTRUCTION OF THE PARTIAL MASTECTOMY DEFECT

Breast conserving surgery combined with adjuvant radiation has been accepted as a regime equivalent to modified radical mastectomy for early stage (I and II) breast cancer. The technique is popular owing to its ability to eradiate breast cancer while preserving a maximal volume of breast tissue.

Skin incisions are designed directly over the lesion, and skin and subcutaneous tissues are preserved unless involved by the lesion. Closure involves subcuticular closure only and the avoidance of drains. The resulting deformity after lumpectomy or quadrantectomy depends on initial breast size, tumor size and location, radiation dose, surgical technique, and adjuvant chemotherapy. The relative excision in proportion to breast size is perhaps the most important factor. Patients with large, pendulous breasts may easily accommodate a 4 cm lumpectomy. The same resection in a smaller-breasted woman may lead to an unacceptable cosmetic result. Radiation therapy exaggerates the tissue deficit in the form of ischemic fibrous contracture.

The treated breast is subject to edema, retraction, fibrosis, calcification, hyperpigmentation, depigmentation, telangiectasia formation, and atrophy. It is not until 24 to 36 months post radiation that radiation-induced changes stabilize. Initial edema camouflages the initial deficit and is replaced with fibrosis and contracture that tend to worsen with time. Deficits within the lower pole tend to retract upward. Deficits along the supero-medial aspect of the breast are difficult to camouflage owing to the paucity of available adjacent tissue and are, unfortunately, socially conspicuous. Centrally located lesions are more forgiving unless resection involves a portion of the nipple-areolar complex.

An assessment of the patient's overall oncologic risk for recurrence should be considered prior to any attempt at partial mastectomy reconstruction. Breast cancer history, the nature of the inciting lesion, and the patient's family history should be review prior to an additional procedure that may further affect subsequent screening examinations. In any event, stabilization of the breast appearance is a prerequisite and occurs 1 to 3 years post radiation.

Investigators have attempted to classify the spectrum of partial mastectomy deficits and relate them to specific treatment options. Classification is based upon the localized deficit of skin and glandular tissue, malposition and/or distortion of the areola, and the extent of fibrous contracture of the breast.[110] Local flap transposition is recommended for mild deformities, whereas myocutaneous flaps are reserved for more extensive defects.

Approximately 15% of patients treated with breast conservation therapy (BCT) are not content with the esthetic outcome.[111] These patients often seek consultation to improve self-esteem and body image. Careful assessment of the actual and apparent tissue deficits is crucial in the selection of the appropriate reconstructive strategy. Contour deficits signify substantial parenchymal loss, whereas radiation contracture represents extensive cutaneous deficits. Nipple-areolar distortion necessitates a substantial increase in cutaneous replacement as central areolar support requires dermal rather than subcutaneous support.

The majority of patients are poor candidates for implant reconstruction. Cutaneous fibrosis responds poorly to implant displacement, and implant radiopacity impairs an already complex screening examination. Autologous tissues, conversely, are reliable, versatile, and provide all the components necessary for partial restoration. The inherent vascularity may actually improve the quality of the relatively ischemic and radiated recipient tissue. Large central excisions involving the nipple-areolar complex and primary closure take on a flat, attenuated appearance, lacking projection. These defects may be reconstructed in one of two ways. It may be possible to mobilize a skin glandular flap based on inferolateral perforators from the underlying pectoral fascia, which is then mobilized into the defect. The curvilinear incision extends from the inferomedial aspect of the previous areola to the central inframammary fold. All but a central skin paddle, rotated into the areolar defect, is de-epithelialized. Undermining at the parenchymal interface facilitates primary akin closure. The second technique parallels conventional mastopexy and enables superior advancement of an inferior dermo-glandular pedicle. It is performed through a Wise or keyhole pattern incision.[110,112,113]

Upper outer quadrant excisions are the most frequent and, fortunately, the most forgiving.[110,112,113] The great majority of these excisions do not require reconstruction. Occasionally, delayed augmentation, scar lengthening via Z-plasty, and areolar transposition are indicated. If a discrepancy between the medial and lateral breast quadrant is recognized owing to a substantial superolateral resection, immediate centralization of the nipple-areolar complex over the point of maximal projection is warranted. This involves simple areolar transposition after release of the dermal attachments. Wide excisions may require transfer of regional or distant tissue. The latissimus dorsi myocutaneous flap represents the ideal choice for these defects (Figure

23–11).

Partial inferior defects may be corrected on an immediate or delayed basis. The occasional patient lacking significant radiation change may benefit from delayed insertion of a small round or custom (one-third) implant for volume replacement. Most defects, however, benefit from a procedure that parallels a standard superior pedicle reduction mammoplasty.[112,113] The resection and reconstruction are facilitated through a standard keyhole pattern. Medial and lateral parenchymal flaps are mobilized from the pectoralis fascial and inframammary fold and mobilized into the inferior defect, whether it is lateral, central, or medial.

Supra-areolar defects are socially conspicuous and necessitate local reconstruction owing to the paucity of available adjacent tissue and the tendency to develop a visible and depressed scar. These defects are corrected by superior advancement of the areolar complex, based on an inferior pedicle, in a procedure similar to an inferior pedicle reduction mammoplasty.[110,112,113]

The latissimus dorsi myocutaneous flap represents the flap of choice for the majority of partial mastectomy defects. Its regional location, malleability, ease of dissection, and lack of donor site morbidity are ideally suited for this indication. All breast conservation defects should be reconstructed by overcorrecting the skin and soft tissue deficits. In general, twice the apparent tissue loss should be inset to compensate for normal wound contracture, continued retraction of the post radiation fibrosis, and anticipated muscle atrophy inherent in raising muscle flaps. The muscle may be folded and contoured to accommodate the most irregular defects. Although small skin paddles may be harvested to precisely accommodate the apparent skin deficit, a typical 4 by 6 cm skin paddle facilitates flap harvest and replacement of compromised or contracted radiated skin.

Although partial latissimus harvests are possible, the majority of partial mastectomy defects warrant total flap elevation. Preservation of the thoracodorsal nerve will maintain greater muscle bulk but will lead to early postoperative contractions. Compulsive fixation at the recipient site is necessary to avoid disruption. Transection or resection of the muscular insertion will help avoid the typical bulges within the anterior axilla. Finally, supporting the radiated native breast skin with a de-epithelialized portion of the transposed skin paddle will improve ultimate wound contour.

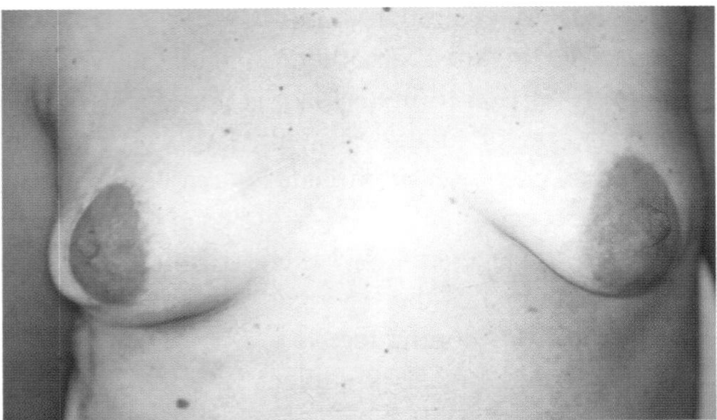

Figure 23–11. Reconstruction of the partial mastectomy defect. Superolateral reconstruction with latissimus dorsi myocutaneous flap.

The TRAM flap represents a flap of substantial bulk, typically incurring greater donor site morbidity and a longer recovery. It would appear less desirable in restoration of limited tissue defects. It is indicated for the reconstruction of large inferior pole deficits in large-breasted women.

Continued surveillance for recurrent cancer after partial reconstruction should proceed unimpeded. Studies comparing pre- and postoperative mammograms after partial reconstruction have confirmed the radiolucency of these flaps. The development of new microcalcifications, fat necrosis, and new lesions are easily discernible. Some reports, interestingly, have noted improved mammographic visualization and resolution of breast density and fibrosis as a result of improved local vascularity.

Immediate reconstruction of partial mastectomy defects is gaining popularity. The demand for these techniques has evolved owing to a tendency toward more aggressive resection in BCT and an accumulated experience with unfavorable tumors. Petit and colleagues reported that immediate reconstruction of the partial mastectomy defect was performed in 25% of cases. They advocated close preoperative collaboration to optimize cosmetic results and enable "improved radicality" of the surgical breast conservation.[114] Thus, this potential for immediate partial mastectomy reconstruction facilitates a more aggressive resection or marginal clearance in BCT and may lessen the need and/or frequency of re-excision. Also, it may lessen the need for staged reconstruction following radiation-induced exaggeration of the defect.

NIPPLE-AREOLAR RECONSTRUCTION

Nipple-areolar reconstruction is a critical stage in breast reconstruction and may add remarkable realism to the new breast mound (Figure 23–12). Areolar tattooing facilitates symmetry in color, may camouflage minor discrepancies and scars, and lacks the morbidity associated with skin grafts. Nipple reconstruction is typically performed at a second stage, at the time of port removal or breast mound revision. Although single-stage reconstruction may be performed, attaining symmetry of nipple-areolar position is crucial to esthetic outcome and is most accurately attained at a second stage, when dermal edema and skin elasticity have normalized.

The insensate, adynamic nipple remains static in size, contour, and projection and will likely by visualized through undergarments, swimsuits, and clothing. The patient's final assessment and perception may closely parallel the quality and symmetry of the newly constructed nipple. Consideration of a symmetry procedure should, therefore, be entertained prior to final nipple reconstruction and should encompass whether the patient prefers support (bra) and to what extent. Simulation in a bra or sheer blouse preoperatively may help the patient's understanding of these issues.

Various techniques of nipple reconstruction are available and provide a range of caliber potential projection. Modification, reduction, or composite grafting of the contralateral nipple may be considered as an option in the patient with redundant nipples. Although this represents the most realistic reconstruction, it necessitates a procedure on the remaining intact nipple and is sensitive perioperatively.

Local flaps are the technique of choice for nipple reconstruction, most of which are variants of the original skate flap. The skate flap has proven to be a reliable workhorse, with the potential for a long projectile nipple if needed. The donor site does require a skin graft, most commonly harvested from the groin, inner thigh, or axilla. Precise demarcation of the central nipple complex is critical and serves as a basis for dermal flap elevation. The lateral dermal wings are elevated, preserving the central nipple core and an inferior extension of fat. These components are elevated, preserving the subcutaneous perforators, and then surfaced by the lateral wings. The circular de-epithelialized harvest site is then covered with a full-thickness skin graft.

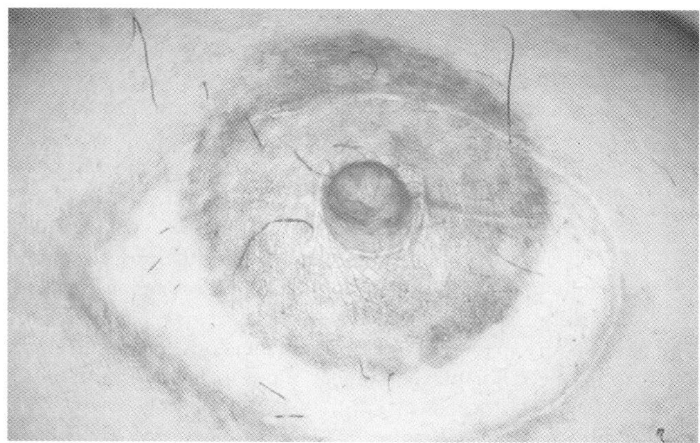

Figure 11–12. Completed nipple-areolar reconstruction.

The Star flap, C-V flap, fishtail flap, and double opposing tab flap are additional flap options, most of which are modifications of the skate flap.[115–117] Although they provide less nipple projection than does the skate flap, they avoid the need for a skin graft. These are excellent alternatives for the majority of patients with small- to moderate-sized contralateral nipples.

Intradermal areolar tattoo has greatly simplified the final phase of restoration and adds abrupt and striking realism to the physical breast form. It remains an artistic challenge among surgeons to simulate contralateral areolar pigments. This final phase enables the surgeon one additional opportunity to optimize symmetry. Nipple-areolar reconstruction may enhance the focus of the reconstructed breast and improve overall patient incorporation of the reconstructed breast, both physically and psychologically.

REFERENCES

1. Georgiade G, Georgiade N, Mckarty K Jr et al. Rationale for immediate reconstruction of the breast following modified radical mastectomy. Ann Plast Surg 1982;8;20–8.
2. Rosenqvist S, Sandelin K, Wickman M. Patients' psychological and cosmetic experience after immediate breast reconstruction. Eur J Surg Oncol 1996;22:262–6.

3. Wellisch DK, SchainWS, Noone RB, et al. Psychological correlates of immediate vs delayed reconstruction of the breast. Plast Reconst Surg 1985;76:713–8.
4. Shover LR, Yetman RJ, Tuason LJ, et al. Partial mastectomy and breast reconstruction. A comparison of their effects on psychological adjustment, body image and sexuality. Cancer 1995;75:54–64.
5. Noguchi M, Kitagawa H, Kinoshita K, et al. Psychologic and self assessments of breast conserving therapy compared with mastectomy and immediate breast reconstruction. J Surg Oncol 1993;54:260–6.
6. Toth BA, Lappert P. Modified skin incisions for mastectomy: the need for plastic surgery input in pre-operative planning. Plast Reconstr Surg 1991;87:1048–53.
7. Kroll SS, Ames F, Singletary SE, et al. The oncologic risks of skin preservation at mastectomy when combined with immediate reconstruction of the breast. Surg Gynecol Obstet 1991;172:17–20.
8. Newman LA, Keurer HM, Hunt KK, et al. Presentation, treatment and outcome of local recurrence after skin sparing mastectomy and immediate breast reconstruction. Ann Surg Oncol 1998;5:620–6.
9. Hidalgo DA. Aesthetic refinement in breast reconstruction: complete skin sparing mastectomy with autologous tissue transfer. Plast Reconstr Surg 1998;102:63–70.
10. Carlson GW, Bostwick J, Styblo TM, et al. Skin sparing mastectomy: oncologic and reconstructive considerations. Ann Surg 1997;225:570–5.
11. Yule Gj, Concannon MJ, Croll G, et al. Is there liability with chemotherapy following immediate breast reconstruction? Plast Reconstr Surg 1996;97:969–73.
12. Grotting JC, Urist MM, Maddow WA, Vasconez LO. Conventional TRAM flap vs free microsurgical TRAM flap reconstruction for immediate reconstruction. Plast Reconstr Surg 1989;84:1005–6.
13. Elliott LF, Eskanazi L, Beegle PH Jr, et al. Immediate TRAM flap breast reconstruction: 128 consecutive cases. Plast Reconstr Surg 1993;92:217–27.
14. Schuster RH, Kuske RB, Young VL, Fineberg B. Breast reconstruction in women treated with radiation therapy for breast cancer: cosmesis, complications, and tumor control. Plast Reconstr Surg 1992;90:445–52.
15. Evans GR, Schusterman MA, Kroll SS, et al. Reconstruction and the radiated breast: is there a role for implants? Plast Reconstr Surg 1995;96:1111–5.
16. Spear S, Majidan A. Immediate breast reconstruction in 2 stages using textured integrated-valve tissue expanders and breast implants: a retrospective review of 171 consecutive breast reconstructions from 1989–1996. Plast Reconstr Surg 1998;101:53–63.
17. Jackson WB, Goldson AL, Staud C. Post-operative radiation following immediate breast reconstruction using a temporary tissue expander. J Natl Med Assoc 1994;86: 538–42.
18. Spear S, Ducic I, Low M, Cuoco F. The effects of radiation on pedicle TRAM flap breast reconstruction: outcomes and implications. Plast Reconstr Surg 2005;115:84–95.
19. Tran NV, Chang DW, Gupta A, et al. Comparison of immediate and delayed free TRAM breast reconstruction in patients receiving post-mastectomy radiation therapy. Plast Reconstr Surg 2001;108:78–82.
20. Jacobson GM, Sause WT, Thompson JW, Plenk HP. Breast irradiation following silicone gel implants. Int J Radiat Oncol Biol Phys 1986;12:835–8.
21. Sultan MR, Smith ML, Estabrook A, et al. Immediate breast reconstruction in patients with locally advanced disease. Ann Plast Surg 1997;38:345–9.
22. Styblo TM, Lewis MM, Carlson GW, et al. Immediate breast reconstruction for stage III breast cancer using TRAM flaps. Ann Surg Oncol 1998;3:375–80.
23. Langstein HN, Cheng MH, Singletary SE, et al. Breast cancer recurrence after immediate reconstruction: patterns and significance. Plast Reconstr Surg 2003;111:721–2.
24. Kroll SS, Khoo A, Singletary SE, et al. Local recurrence risk after skin sparing and conventional mastectomies: a 6 year follow-up. Plast Reconstr Surg 1999;104:421–5.
25. Brody GS. Safety and effectiveness of breast implants. In: Spear S, editor. The breast: principles and art. Philadelphia: Lippincott-Raven; 1998. p. 336–46.
26. Peters W, Keystone E, Snow K, et al. Is there a relationship between autoantibodies and silicone gel implants? Ann Plast Surg 1994;32:1–5.
27. Kossovsky N, Heggers JP, Robson MC. Experimental demonstration of the immunogenicity of silicone protein complexes. J Biomed Mater Res 1987;21:1125–33.
28. Heggers JP, Kossovsky N, Parsons RW, et al. Biocompatability of silicone implants. Ann Plast Surg 1983;11:38–45.
29. Decamara DI, Sheridam SM, Kammer BA. Rupture and aging of saline breast implants. Plast Reconstr Surg 1993; 91:828–34.
30. Greenwald WB, Randolph M, May JW. Mechanical analysis of explanted silicone breast implants. Plast Reconstr Surg 1996;98:269–72.
31. Phillips JW, Decamara DL, Lockwood MD, et al. Strength of silicone breast implants. Plast Reconstr Surg 1996;97: 1215–25.
32. Robinson OG, Bradley EL, Wilson DS. Analysis of explanted silicone implants: a report of 300 patients. Ann Plast Surg 1995;34:1–6.
33. Baker JL, Bartels RJ, Douglas WM. Closed compressin technique for rupturing a contracted capsule around breast implants. Plast Reconstr Surg 1976;58:137
34. Ahn CY, Shaw WW. Regional silicone gel migration in patients with ruptured implants. Ann Plast Surg 1994;33:201–8.
35. Ahn CY, DeBruhl ND, Gorczyca DP, et al. Comparative silicone breast implant evaluation using mammography, sonography, and MRI: experience with 59 implants. Plast Reconstr Surg 1994;94:620–7.
36. Leibman AL, Kruse BD. Imaging of breast cancer after augmentation mammoplasty. Ann Plast Surg 1993;30:111–5.
37. Silverstein MJ, Gamagami P, Handel N. Missed breast cancer in an augmented woman using implant displacement mammography. Ann Plast Surg 1990;25:210–3.
38. Carlson GW, Curley SA, Martin FE, et al. The detection of breast cancer after augmentation mammoplasty. Plast Reconstr Surg 1993;91:837–40.
39. Gumico CA, Pin P, Young VL, et al. The effect of breast implants on the radiographic detection of microcalcifications and the soft tissue masses. Plast Reconstr Surg 1989;84:772–8.
40. Eklund GW, Cardenosa G. The art of mammographic positioning. Radiol Clin North Am 1992;30(1):21–53.

41. Birdsell DC, Jenkins H, Berkel H. Breast cancer diagnosis and survival in women with and without breast implants. Plast Reconstr Surg 1993;92:795–800.
42. Deapon DM, Berstein L, Brody GS. Are breast implants anticarcinogenic? A 14 year follow-up of the Los Angeles study. Plast Reconstr Surg 1997;99:1346–53.
43. Deapon DM, Pike MC, Casagrande JT, Brody GS. The relationship between breast cancer and augmentation mammoplasty: an epidemiologic study. Plast Reconstr Surg 1986;77:361–7.
44. Engel A, Lamm SH. Risk of sarcomas of the breast among women with breast augmentation. Plast Reconstr Surg 1992;89:571–2.
45. Su CW, Dreyfuss DA, Krizek TJ, et al. Silicone implants and the inhibition of cancer. Plast Reconstr Surg 1995;96: 513–8.
46. Brody GS, Conway DP, Deapon DM, et al. Consensus statement on the relationship of the breast implants to connective tissue disorders. Plast Reconstr Surg 1992;90:1102–5.
47. Gabriel SE, O'Faflon WM, Kurland LT, et al. Risk of connective tissue diseases and other disorders after breast implantation. N Engl J Med 1994;330:1697–702.
48. Giltay EJ, Moens HJB, Riley AH, et al. Silicone breast prostheses and rheumatic symptoms: a retrospective follow-up study. Ann Rheum Dis 1994;53:194–6.
49. Radovan C. Breast reconstruction after mastectomy using the temporary expander. Plast Reconstr Surg 1982;69:195–208.
50. Forman DL, Chui J, Restifo RJ, et al. Breast reconstruction in previously irradiated patients using tissue expanders and implants: a potentially unfavorable result. Ann Plast Surg 1998;40:360–3.
51. Mandrekas AD, Zambacos GJ, Katsantoni PN. Immediate and delayed breast reconstruction with permanent tissue expanders. Br J Plast Surg 1995;48:572–8.
52. Francel TJ, Ryan JJ, Manson PM. Breast reconstruction utilizing implants: a local experience and comparison of three techniques. Plast Reconstr Surg 1993;92:786–94.
53. Yeh KA, Lyle G, Wei JP, et al. Immediate breast reconstruction in breast cancer: morbidity and outcome. Am J Surg 64:1195–9.
54. Wickman M, Jurell G, Sandelin K. Techical aspects of immediate breast reconstruction: 2 year follow-up of 100 patients treated conservatively. Scand J Plast Reconstr Surg 1998; 32:265–73.
55. Caffee HH. Textured silicone and capsule contracture. Ann Plast Surg 1990;24:197–9.
56. Pakium AI, Young CS. Submuscular breast reconstruction: a one stage method of tissue expansion. Ann Plast Surg 1987;19:312–7.
57. Spear SL, Spittler CJ. Breast reconstruction with implants and expanders. Plast Reconstr Surg 2001;107:177–87.
58. Slavin SA, Colen SR. Sixty consecutive breast reconstructions with inflatable expanders: a critical appraisal. Plast Reconstr Surg 1990;86:910–9.
59. Spear SL, Ontewu C. Staged breast reconstruction with saline filled implants in the irradiated breast: recent trends and therapeutic implications. Plast Reconstr Surg 2000;105:930–42.
60. Kroll SS, Balwin B. A comparison of outcome using three different methods of breast reconstruction. Plast Reconstr Surg 1992;90:455–62.
61. Hartrampf CR, Schelan M, Black PW. Breast reconstruction with a transverse abdominal island flap. Plast Reconstr Surg 1982;69:216–9.
62. Boyd JB, Taylor GI, Corlett R. The vascular territories of the superior and deep inferior epigastric systems. Plast Reconstr Surg 1984;73:1–16.
63. Moon HK, Taylor GI. The vascular anatomy of the TRAM flap based on the deep superior epigastric system. Plast Reconstr Surg 1988;82:815–32.
64. Bostwick J. Plastic and reconstructive breast surgery. St Louis: Quality Medical Publishing; 1990.
65. Watterson PA, Bostwick J, Hester TR, et al. TRAM flap anatomy correlated with a 10 year clinical experience with 556 patients. Plast Reconstr Surg 1995;95:1185–94.
66. Hartrampf CR, Bennett GK. Autologous tissue reconstruction in the mastectomy patient: a critical review of 300 patients. Ann Plast Surg 1987;205:508–19.
67. Hartrampf CR, Michelow BJ. Breast reconstruction with living tissue. Norfolk (VA): Hampton Press; 1991.
68. Little JW. Breast reconstruction by the unipedicle TRAM operation: muscle splitting technique. In: Spear S, editor. The breast: principles and art. Phildelphia: Lippincott-Raven; 1998. p. 521–34.
69. Takayanagi S. Extended TRAM flap. Plast Reconstr Surg 1993;92:757–8.
70. Yamamota Y, Nohira K, Sugihara T, et al. Superiority of the microvascularly augmented flap: analysis of 50 TRAM flaps for breast reconstruction. Plast Reconstr Surg 1996;97:79–83.
71. Paige KT, Bostwick J, Bried JT, Jones G. A comparison of morbidity from bilateral, unipedicled and unilateral, unipedicled TRAM flap breast reconstructions. Plast Reconstr Surg 1998;101:1819–27.
72. Williams JK, Bostwick J III, Bried JY, et al. TRAM flap breast reconstruction after radiation treatment. Ann Surg 1995;221:756–64.
73. Jacobson WM, Meland NB, Woods JE. Autologous breast reconstruction with use of TRAM flap: Mayo clinic experience with 147 cases. Mayo Clin Proc 1994;69:635–40.
74. Berrino P, Campora E, Leone S, et al. The TRAM flap for breast reconstruction in obese patients. Ann Plast Surg 1991;27:221–31.
75. Takeishi M, Shaw WW, Ahn CY, et al. TRAM flaps in patients with abdominal scars. Plast Reconstr Surg 1997; 99:713–22.
76. Kroll SS, Gheradini G, Martin JE, et al. Fat necrosis in free and pedicled TRAM flaps. Plast Reconstr Surg 1998; 102:1502–7.
77. Slavin SA, Goldwyn RM. The midabdominal TRAM flap: review of 236 flaps. Plast Reconstr Surg 1988;81:189–97.
78. Slavin SA, Hein KD. The mid abdominal TRAM flap. In: Spear S, editor. The breast: principles and art. Philadelphia: Lippincott-Raven: 1998. p. 565–76.
79. Callegari PR, Taylor GI, Caddy CM, et al. An anatomic review of the delay phenomenon. I. Experimental studies. Plast Reconstr Surg 1992;89:397–407.
80. Morris SF, Taylor GI. The time sequence of the delay phenomenon: when is a surgical delay effective? An experimental study. Plast Reconstr Surg 1995;95:526–33.
81. Taylor GI. The surgically delayed unipedicled TRAM flap for breast reconstruction. Ann Plast Surg 1996;36:242–5.

82. Codner MA, Bostwick J, Nahai F, et al. TRAM flap vascular delay for high risk breast reconstruction. Plast Reconstr Surg 1995;96:1615–22.
83. Restifo RJ et al. Surgical delay in TRAM flap breast reconstructon: a comparison of 7 & 14 day delay periods. Ann Plast Surg 38:330–3.
84. Schusterman MA, Kroll SS, Weldon ME. Immediate breast reconstruction: why the free TRAM over the conventional TRAM flap. Plast Reconstr Surg 1992;90:255–61.
85. Kroll SS, Netscher DT. Complications of the TRAM flap breast reconstruction in obese patients. Plast Reconstr Surg 1989;84:866.
86. Schusterman MA, Kroll SS, Miller MJ, et al. The free TRAM flap for breast reconstruction: one center's experience with 211 consecutive cases. Ann Plast Surg 1994;32:234–41.
87. Suominien S, Asko-Seljavaara S, Kinnunen J, et al. Abdominal wall competence after free TRAM flap harvest: a prospective study. Ann Plast Surg 39;299–34.
88. Kind GM, Rademaker AW, Mustoe TA. Abdominal wall recovery following TRAM flap: a functional outcome study. Plast Reconstr Surg 1997;99:417–28.
89. Kroll SS, Schusterman MA, Reece GP, et al. Abdominal wall strength, bulging, and hernia after TRAM flap breast reconstruction. Plast Reconstr Surg 1995;96:616–9.
90. Fitoussi A, Le Taillandier M, Biffaud JC, et al. Functional evaluation of the abdominal wall after raising a rectus abdominus myocutaneous flap. Ann Chir Plast Esthet 1997;42:138–46.
91. Hartrampf CR, Bried JT. General considerations in TRAM flap surgery. In: Hartrampf CR, editor. Breast reconstruction with living tissue. New York: Raven Press; 1991. p. 33–70.
92. Kroll SS, Marchi M. Comparison of strategies for preventing abdominal wall weakness after TRAM flap breast reconstruction. Plast Reconstr Surg 1992;89:1045–51.
93. Kroll SS, Gherardini G, Martin JE, et al. Fat necrosis in free and pedicled TRAM flaps. Plast Reconstr Surg 1998;102: 1502–7.
94. Nahabedian MY, Tsangaris T, Momen B. Breast reconstruction with the DIEP flap or the muscle sparing (MS-2) free TRAM flaps: Is there a difference? Plast Reconstr Surg 2005;115:436–46.
95. Shestak KC. Bipedicle TRAM flap reconstruction. In: Spear S, editor. The breast: principles and art. Philadelphia: Lippincott-Raven; 1998. p.535–46.
96. Petit JY, Rietjens M, Ferreira MA, et al. Abdominal sequellae after pedicled TRAM flap breast reconstruction. Plast Reconstr Surg 1997;99:723–9.
97. Jensen JA. Is double pedicle TRAM flap reconstruction of a single breast within the standard of care? Plast Reconstr Surg 1989;102:586–7.
98. Spear S, Hartrampf CR Jr. The double pedicle TRAM flap and the standard of care. Plast Reconstr Surg 1998;100: 1592–3.
99. Maxwell GP. Iginino Tasini and the origin of the latissimus dorsi myocutaneous flap. Plast Reconstr Surg 1980;65: 686–92.
100. Hammond DC, Fisher J. Lastissimus dorsi musculocutaneous flap breast reconstruction. In: Spear S, editor. The breast: principles and art. Philadelphia: Lippincott-Raven; 1998. p. 477–90.
101. Taylor GI, Townsend P, Corlett R. Superiority of the deep circumflex iliac vessels as the supply for free groin flaps. Clinical work. Plast Reconstr Surg 1979;64:745–59.
102. Elliott LF, Hartrampf CR Jr. The Rubens flap. The deep circumflex iliac artery flap. Clin Plast Surg 1998;25:283–91.
103. Fugino T, Harashina T, Endomoto K. Primary breast reconstruction after a standard radical mastectomy by a free flap transfer. Plast Reconstr Surg 1976;58:372–4.
104. Shaw WW. Superior gluteal free flap breast reconstruction. Clin Plast Surg 1998;25:267–74.
105. Elliott LF, Beegle PH, Hartrampf CR Jr. The lateral transverse thigh free flap: an alternative for autologous-tissue breast reconstruction. Plast Reconstr Surg 1990;85:169–78.
106. Meijers-Heijboer M, et al: Breast cancer after prophylactic mastectomy in women with *BRCA-1* or *BRCA-2* mutation. N Engl J Med 2001;345:158.
107. Ford D. Risks of cancer in *BRCA-1* mutation carriers. Lancet 1994;343:692.
108. Metcalfe KA, et al. Satisfaction with breast reconstruction in women with bilateral prophylactic mastectomy in *BRCA-1* positive patients. Plast Reconstr Surg 2004;114:360–6.
109. Hamdi M, et al. Deep inferior epigastric perforator flap in breast reconstruction: experience in 1st 50 flaps. Plast Reconstr Surg 1999;103:86–95.
110. Slavin SA. Reconstruction of the breast conservation patient. In: Spear S, editor. The breast: principles and art. Philadelphia: Lippincott-Raven; 1998. p. 221–38.
111. Beadle F, Silver B, Botnick L, et al. Cosmetic results following primary radiation therapy for early breast cancer. Cancer 1984;54:2911–8.
112. Kroll SS, Singletary SE. Repair of partial mastectomy defects. Clin Plast Surg 1998;25:303–10.
113. Grisotti A. Immediate reconstruction after partial mastectomy. Oper Tech Plast Reconstr Surg 1994;1:1–12.
114. Petit JY, Rietjens M, Garusi C, et al. Integration of plastic surgery in the course of breast conserving surgery for cancer to improve cosmetic results and radicality of tumor excision. Recent Results. Cancer Res 1998;152:202–11.
115. Bostwick J III. Creating a nipple. In: Berger K, Bostwick J III, editors. A woman's decision. St Louis: Quality Medical Publishing; 1994.
116. Staggers WR, et al. Nipple reconstruction with skate flap and modifications. Strauch B, et al, editors. In: Grabb's encyclopedia of flaps. 2nd ed. Lippincott-Raven: Philadelphia; 1998. p.1363.
117. Kroll SS, Hamilton S. Nipple reconstruction with double opposing tab flap. Plast Reconst Surg 1989;84:520.
118. Watterson PA, Bostwick J III, Hester TR, et al. TRAM flap anatomy correlated with a 10 year clinical experience with 556 patients. Plast Reconstr Surg 1995;95:1185–94.
119. Kroll SS. Fat necrosis in free TRAM and DIEP flaps. Plast Reconstr Surg 2000;106:576–83.
120. Nahabedian MY, Momen B, Galdino G, et al. Breast reconstruction with the free TRAM or DIEP flap: patient selection, choice of flap, and outcome. Plast Reconstr Surg 2002;110:466–75.
121. Blondeel PN. One hundred free DIEP flap breast reconstructions. Br J Plast Surg 1999;52:104–11.
122. Gill PS, Hunt NP, Guerra AB, et al. A 10 year retrospective review of 758 DIEP flaps for breast reconstruction. Plast Reconstr Surg 2004;113:1153–60.

24

Unusual Breast Histology

DAVID R. BRENIN, MD
KRISTEN A. ATKINS

This chapter reviews breast malignancies rarely encountered in the course of a typical breast surgery practice. The majority of the data presented in this chapter was obtained from small studies of specific tumor subtypes, or had been gleaned from larger studies that included several types of more common breast cancers. Unfortunately, there is often insufficient information available to draw absolute conclusions regarding therapy and prognosis.

Much of the data cited was collected prior to the widespread use of breast conservation therapy. For this reason, the vast majority of patients studied were treated using mastectomy. The reliance on mastectomy has resulted in a lack of information regarding the natural history and radiosensitivity of many of the tumors presented. Therefore, the risk of local recurrence for patients with rare breast malignancies opting for breast conservation is unclear. There is, however, no reason to suspect a significant difference in the risk of local recurrence in this group of patients when compared with patients with more common types of breast cancer. Except where specifically indicated, the clinically appropriate use of breast conservation should be considered in the informed treatment of patients with rare breast malignancies (Table 24–1).

PAPILLARY CARCINOMA

Papillary carcinoma accounts for 1 to 2% of newly diagnosed breast cancers in women, and a slightly higher proportion in men.[1–3] It occurs in both an invasive and noninvasive form. The World Health Organization (WHO) has defined papillary carcinoma as follows: "A rare carcinoma whose invasive pattern is predominantly in the form of papillary structures. The same architecture is usually displayed in the metastases. Frequently, foci of intraductal papillary growth are recognizable."[4] Furthermore, the WHO classification states that "papillary carcinoma arising, and limited to a mammary cyst, is [to be] referred to as noninvasive intracystic carcinoma."[4] Invasive carcinoma, however, may be associated with an intracystic carcinoma.[5]

Papillary carcinoma occurs most frequently in the central portion of the breast, and is associated with a malignant nipple discharge in 22 to 34% of patients.[1,6] The mean age of diagnosis for papillary carcinoma, 63 to 67 years, is older when compared with the more common types of breast cancer.[1,2,7] The tumors tend to grow slowly, frequently being present for more than 1 year prior to patients seeking treatment. On physical examination, papillary carcinomas are well circumscribed and often lobulated. The average clinical size is 2 to 3 cm.[3] Clinically, enlarged axillary lymph nodes are not uncommon in patients with larger tumors, containing areas of hemorrhagic necrosis. Mammographically, papillary carcinomas typically have sharp margins and are rounded or lobulated. Breast ultrasound may reveal a solid component in an otherwise benign-appearing cyst.

The appearance of the gross tumor varies with the proportion of the cystic component. Some

Table 24–1. TREATMENT AND PROGNOSIS					
	Appropriate for Breast Conservation	Risk of Axillary Metastasis*	Radiation Sensitive	Adjuvant Chemo/Hormonal Therapy	Prognosis
Papillary carcinoma	Yes	++	Yes	Yes	Good
Metaplastic mammary carcinoma	See text	+	Insufficient data	Insufficient data	Poor
Apocrine carcinoma	Yes	++	Yes	Yes	Typical for stage
Adenoid cystic carcinoma	Yes	+	Insufficient data	Yes	Good
Squamous carcinoma	Yes	++	Insufficient data	Insufficient data	Typical for stage
Secretory carcinoma	Yes	++	Insufficient data	Yes	Good
Carcinoma of the breast with endocrine differentiation	Yes	++	Yes	Yes	Typical for stage
Phyllodes tumor	Yes	–	No	No	Varies; see text
Primary breast lymphoma	Yes	–	Yes	Yes	Varies; see text
Breast sarcoma	Yes	–	Yes	Yes	Varies; see text
Postradiotherapy angiosarcoma	See text	–	Insufficient data	Insufficient data	Varies; see text

*- = axillary metastasis rare, axillary staging not indicated.
+ = axillary metastasis less common, axillary staging indicated.
++ = axillary metastasis rates similar to more common cancers, axillary staging indicated.

fibrosis may be present. The cut surface of the tumor is typically described as tan or gray, and areas of focal hemorrhage and necrosis are common.[3] Larger tumors may form a large cyst, containing partially clotted blood and tumor fragments. Microscopically, the tumors form a predominately frond-like pattern (Figure 24–1). Cystic areas may be present, but are not a prerequisite for diagnosis. Distinguishing between benign and malignant papillary tumors can be challenging. Rosen, Lefkowitz and colleagues, and Kraus and Neubecker have attempted to delineate guidelines for diagnosis.[3,7,8] Various immunohistochemical markers have been evaluated, but have proved to be of little help. Analysis of DNA content, however, has demonstrated significant differences between papillary carcinoma and benign lesions.[9,10]

Papillary carcinoma has a favorable prognosis. Noninvasive papillary carcinoma is a variant of ductal carcinoma in situ (DCIS), and is associated with a < 1% rate of axillary metastasis.[3,7] To date, there is no significant body of data addressing the use of radiation therapy in the treatment of this lesion. As is the case with DCIS, there are no prospective trials comparing mastectomy to breast preservation with whole-breast irradiation in patients with noninvasive papillary carcinoma. The use of breast conservation, however, appears reasonable for these patients, as there is no reason to suspect a significant difference in the risk of local recurrence when compared with patients with more common types of noninvasive breast cancer. The low rate of axillary metastasis observed makes elimination of axillary dissection appropriate in patients with noninvasive papillary carcinoma and a clinically negative axilla.

Even less data exist to aid in treatment selection for patients with invasive papillary carcinoma. Fisher and colleagues reported on 35 patients with invasive papillary cancer.[2] Of the 22 patients who underwent axillary dissection, 32% were found to have axillary metastases. Of the patients with axillary metastases, only 2 women (9%) had 4 or more lymph nodes involved. Life-table plots calculated by Fisher and colleagues showed a favorable prognosis, comparable to patients with tubular cancers. At 5-year follow-up, only one patient had died of papillary carcinoma. Recurrences, when they do occur, are typically "late," occurring more than 5 years after the initial diagnosis.[3] The majority of reports concerning the treatment of invasive papillary carcinoma have addressed patients whose primary therapy consisted of mastectomy with or without axillary dissection. Again, there is no reason to suspect a significant difference in the risk of local recurrence in patients with invasive papillary carcinoma when compared with patients with more common types of breast cancer. When clinically appropriate, the use of breast conservation, irradiation, and axillary dissection or sentinel node biopsy is a reasonable option.

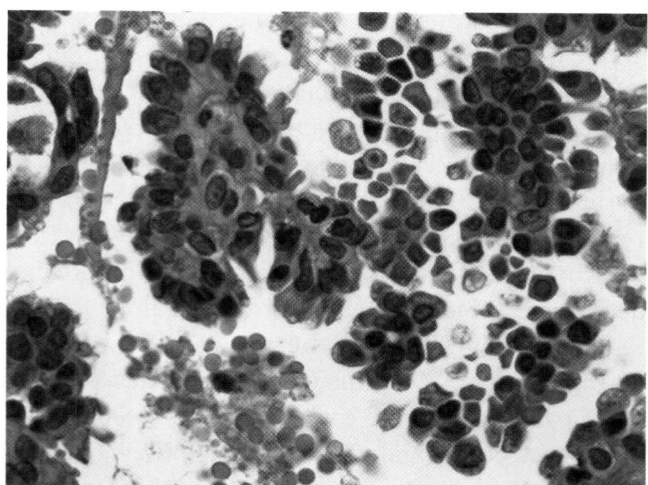

Figure 24–1. Papillary carcinoma demonstrating delicate papillae lined by high-grade cells. (Hematoxylin-eosin [H+E]; × 400 original magnification)

METAPLASTIC MAMMARY CARCINOMA

Metaplastic mammary carcinoma refers to a classic breast carcinoma containing a variable component exhibiting a nonglandular growth pattern. These tumors constitute < 1% of breast cancers.[11,12] The metaplastic changes typically manifest as squamous cells, spindle cells, and/or as areas of heterologous mesenchymal growth showing cartilaginous or osseous differentiation. The histologic diversity observed in metaplastic mammary carcinoma has led to various subdesignations, including spindle cell carcinoma, carcinoma with osseous metaplasia, carcinoma with pseudosarcomatous metaplasia, squamous cell carcinoma with pseudosarcomatous stroma, and carcinosarcoma. The histogenesis of these carcinomas is assumed to be of ductal origin. Results derived from ultrastructural and immunohistochemical studies suggest that metaplastic mammary carcinomas originate from undifferentiated multipotential cells.[13] Tavassolli suggested that myoepithelial cells are the cells of origin.[11] Although the number of reported cases is small, all of the subtypes appear to have a similar prognosis and will be presented as a single group in this chapter.[14]

Metaplastic mammary carcinoma typically presents as a mass. Skin changes and fixation to underlying tissues have been reported.[15] The gross appearance of the tumor varies with subtype, but most are described as hard with well-circumscribed borders. Cystic degeneration may occur when there is an extensive squamous metaplastic component.[14]

Histologically, metaplastic carcinoma is divided broadly into tumors showing squamous and/or heterologous (cartilaginous or osseus) or pseudosarcomatous differentiation (Figure 24–2). Although the former seems to occur more frequently, mixed and transition forms are common. The extent and degree of differentiation varies widely. The histology of carcinoma at metastatic sites may not be predicted by the extent and subtype seen in the breast.

The number of reported patients with metaplastic mammary carcinomas is insufficient to draw accurate conclusions concerning therapy and prognosis. The majority of the data has been obtained from small studies of specific tumor subtypes. Most patients underwent mastectomy. Rosen and Ernsberger reported that in 4 of 7 patients treated with excisional biopsy alone, tumor recurred locally between 1 and 3.5 years after diagnosis.[16] There is no information regarding the responsiveness of metaplastic carcinoma to irradiation or chemotherapy.[15] When compared with the more common histologies, metaplastic mammary carcinoma has a low rate of axillary lymph node involvement.[17–19] Distant failure is common, however, with the overall 5-year survival rate reported to be 44%.[13] Given the low rate of axillary metastasis sentinel lymph node biopsy may be appropriate.

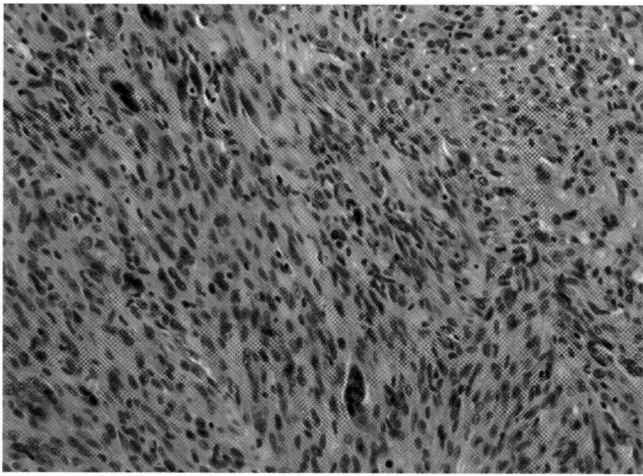

Figure 24–2. Metaplastic carcinoma with smooth muscle differentiation. (Hematoxylin-eosin [H+E]; × 400 original magnification)

APOCRINE CARCINOMA

Apocrine carcinoma of the breast accounts for 0.4% of new mammary malignancies.[20,21] This tumor derives its name from the apocrine glands normally present in skin. Apocrine carcinomas of the breast, however, do not originate from apocrine glands of the skin, but appear to arise from the apocrine metaplasia commonly found in excised breast tissue.[3] The histologic similarity of such breast tissue apocrine metaplasias to rare carcinomas with apocrine differentiation and to apocrine glands of the skin is due to their common embryologic derivation from the epidermis.

Apocrine carcinoma presents in a fashion similar to other more common breast cancers. The age range of affected patients is between 19 to 86 years.[22–25] A majority of patients with infiltrating apocrine carcinoma of the breast present with a palpable mass.[24,25] Abati and colleagues found that approximately one-third of both the intraductal and invasive lesions were detected mammographically.[24] Infiltrating apocrine carcinomas are hard on palpation. Grossly, the lesions are typically gray to white, with infiltrating borders.[3] Some tumors are cystic or have a medullary appearance.[3] Microscopically, the cytoplasm is markedly eosinophilic and may be granular or homogeneous (Figure 24–3). The cellular architecture of both intraductal and invasive apocrine carcinomas is similar to that seen with more common mammary carcinomas. The distinction between atypical apocrine hyperplasia and apocrine intraductal carcinoma can be difficult.[26–28]

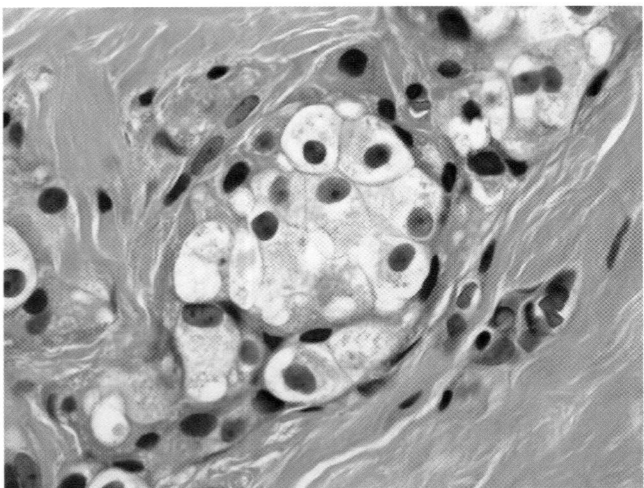

Figure 24–3. Apocrine carcinoma showing granular eosinophilic cytoplasm, large round nuclei, and prominent nucleoli. (Hematoxylin-eosin [H+E]; × 400 original magnification)

The prognosis for patients with apocrine carcinoma is generally considered to be analogous to patients with similarly staged ductal carcinomas.[23–25] Abati and colleagues identified a 15% local recurrence rate in 20 patients with intraductal apocrine carcinomas treated by biopsy alone, but no recurrences in 2 patients treated with lumpectomy and irradiation.[24] The majority of reported patients with invasive apocrine carcinoma have been treated with mastectomy and some form of axillary dissection. The radiosensitivity of these lesions has yet to be determined, but the use of breast-conserving therapy should be appropriate.

ADENOID CYSTIC CARCINOMA

Tumors that commonly occur in the salivary gland rarely arise in the breast. Adenoid cystic carcinoma of the breast is the most frequent of this subset but accounts for < 0.1% of mammary carcinomas.[15,29] First described in the breast by Geschickter in 1945, and then again by Foote and Stewart in 1946, its characteristic histopathologic appearance is identical to like-named tumors arising from the salivary glands, although primary breast adenoid cystic carcinomas have a more favorable prognosis.[30,31]

Adenoid cystic carcinomas typically present in the sixth or seventh decade of life. The characteristic presentation is that of a 2 to 3 cm movable tumor, which may be tender or painful.[32] The lesions tend to be centrally located in the breast, and may exhibit skin changes when superficial.[33] These tumors have a gray to pale-yellow cut surface with well-defined margins. Larger lesions have been found to undergo cystic degeneration.[32,34] Adenoid cystic carcinomas have marked histologic heterogeneity, making diagnosis by needle biopsy problematic. Classic histologic features include nests of epithelial and myoepithelial cells with cystic spaces filled with hyaluronidase-sensitive and periodic acid–Schiff (PAS)-negative mucin (Figure 24–4). The pattern is reminiscent of cribriform carcinoma; however, cribriform carcinoma is devoid of myoepithelial cells and contains PAS-positive luminal mucin. Examina-

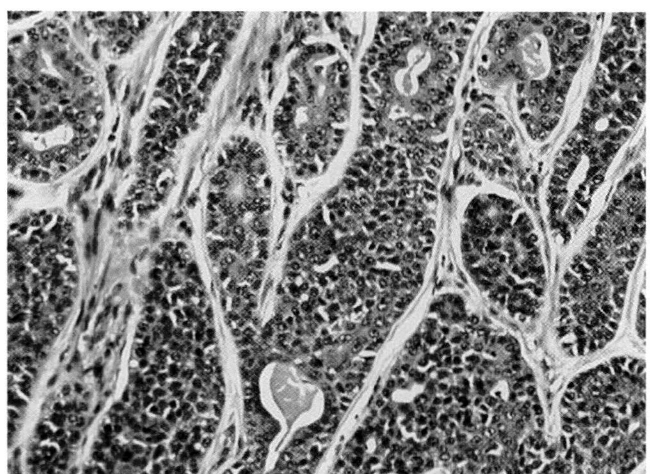

Figure 24–4. Adenoid cystic carcinoma characterized by solid uniform cells with punched out spaces filled with basement membrane material. (Hematoxylin-eosin [H+E]; × 400 original magnification)

tion of many microscopic fields may be required before the classic cylindromatous and/or cribriform growth pattern is identified. Ro and colleagues divided adenoid cystic carcinomas of the breast into three histologic grades based on the proportion of solid growth to the overall tumor size.[35] Tumors with no solid component are classified as grade I, those with < 30% solid component are grade II, and those of > 30% solid component are grade III. Ro noted that tumors with a solid component were more likely to be larger, to recur, or to metastasize.

Adenoid cystic carcinoma of the breast is associated with an excellent prognosis. The rate of axillary metastasis is < 1% and distant metastasis is rare.[32,35] When systemic recurrence occurs, it is typically pulmonary, although metastases to bone, liver, brain, and kidney have been reported.[35–37] All reported distant metastases occurred in patients who had negative axillary dissections, demonstrating a propensity for hematogenous spread similar to salivary gland adenoid cystic carcinomas.[32] There is no prospective data to support one therapeutic modality over another in the treatment of this disease. Reported data on prognosis have been gathered mostly from patients treated with modified radical or radical mastectomy. The use of breast conservation, however, appears reasonable for these patients, as there is no reason to suspect a significant difference in the risk of local recurrence when compared with patients with more common types of breast cancer.[38] The low rate of axillary metastasis observed, combined with a lack of prognostic information gained from axillary staging, suggests that observation of a clinically negative axilla is appropriate, although sentinel node biopsy should be considered.

SQUAMOUS CARCINOMA

Squamous carcinoma of the breast is an extremely rare form of metaplastic carcinoma consisting of a lesion entirely, or nearly entirely, composed of keratinizing squamous carcinoma. Typically, lesions composed of over 90% keratinizing squamous carcinoma have been placed in this group. One must be careful to exclude a metastatic squamous cell carcinoma or skin carcinoma involving the breast prior to accepting squamous cell carcinoma as a primary breast tumor. The precursor of this cancer is thought to be squamous metaplasia, which occurs in a wide variety of settings including fibroadenomas, cystic lesions, phyllodes tumors, gynecomastia, mammary duct hyperplasia, papillomatosis, subareolar abscesses, and inflammation.[3] An alternative hypothesis is that squamous carcinoma represents a variant of metaplastic carcinoma in which the adenocarcinomatous component has been overgrown by the squamous component.[15]

The mean age at diagnosis of patients with squamous carcinoma of the breast is similar to that seen with more common breast cancers.[39,40] The lesions are usually palpable, and fixation to the chest wall, as well as skin involvement, has been observed. Calcifications may be seen on mammography.[41] Grossly, the tumors frequently undergo cystic degeneration producing a cavity filled with necrotic squamous debris. Microscopically, squamous carcinomas resemble similar tumors arising in other sites (Figure 24–5). Keratin pearls and keratohyaline granules may be present.[3]

As squamous carcinoma is a very rare lesion, information on prognosis and treatment is limited. The majority of patients reported in the literature have been treated by mastectomy with axillary dissection. Radiosensitivity of this tumor has not been defined. Overall, the prognosis does not appear to be appreciably different from that of more commonly occurring types of breast cancers.

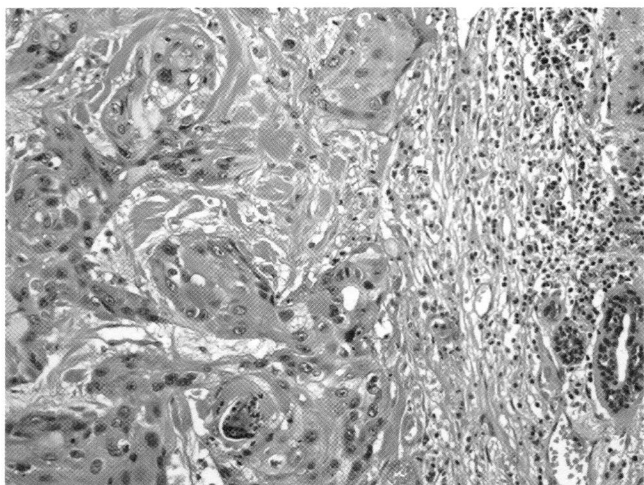

Figure 24–5. Squamous cell carcinoma characterized by sheet of cells demonstrating keratinization. Note the normal duct on the right side. (Hematoxylin-eosin [H+E]; × 200 original magnification)

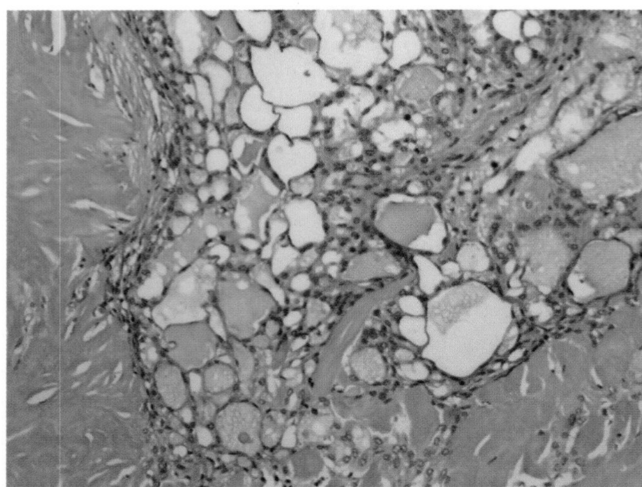

Figure 24–6. Secretory carcinoma. Note the abundant secretions within the ducts. (Hematoxylin-eosin [H+E]; × 200 original magnification)

SECRETORY CARCINOMA

Secretory carcinoma is a rare tumor affecting both adults and children. In 1966, McDivitt and Stewart described a series of 7 young patients with this tumor, referring to it as juvenile carcinoma.[42] It soon became apparent, however, that the majority of patients found to have this tumor were not juveniles. Tavassoli and Norris, reporting on a series of 19 patients, found a median age at the time of diagnosis to be 25 years, with 6 patients being 30 years of age or older.[43] As it became obvious that the majority of patients with "juvenile carcinoma of the breast" were adults, it was re-designated secretory carcinoma.

Secretory carcinoma has been described in patients from the first to the eighth decade of life. Typically, these lesions are palpable and present as painless and well-circumscribed masses. Grossly, secretory carcinomas are white to gray or tan to yellow in color and may be lobulated.[3] The margins are usually well circumscribed and are rarely infiltrative. Microscopically, the cells are filled with secretory material that is pale-pink or amphophilic when stained with hematoxylin-eosin (Figures 24–6 and 24–7).[3,42,43]

Secretory carcinoma is considered a low-grade carcinoma with an excellent prognosis. Axillary metastasis has been identified in approximately 20% of cases; however, very few patients have been reported to have distant metastasis.[43–45] There is, however a risk of late local recurrence.[43,46] Wide local excision is preferred in children, with an attempt to preserve the breast bud. In adults, breast conservation is appropriate. Axillary lymphadenectomy should be performed selectively based upon physical examination or with the identification of metastases on sentinel node biopsy. Radiosensitivity of this tumor has not been defined, and the majority of reported patients treated using breast conservation have not received postoperative radiation therapy.[46]

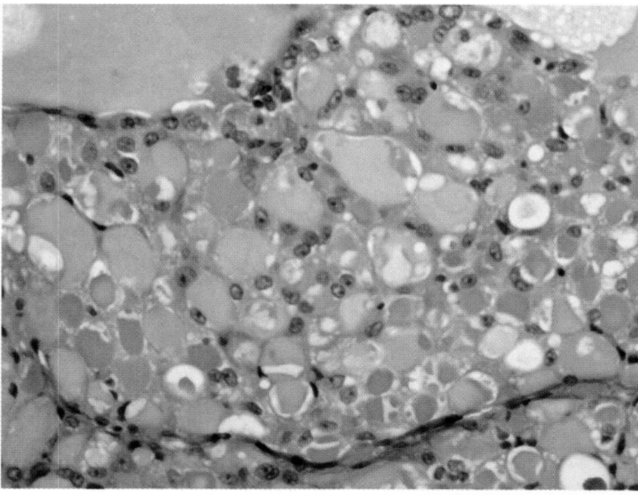

Figure 24–7. Eosinophilic material within the lumens of secretory carcinoma. (Hematoxylin-eosin [H+E]; × 400 original magnification)

CARCINOMA OF THE BREAST WITH ENDOCRINE DIFFERENTIATION

Rarely, tumors of the breast may undergo endocrine metaplasia and produce ectopic hormones such as human chorionic gonadotropin (hCG), calcitonin, adrenocorticotropin, and epinephrine. Endocrine differentiation may arise in the setting of ductal carcinoma in situ, small cell undifferentiated carcinoma, mucinous carcinoma, lobular carcinoma, and infiltrating ductal carcinoma.[3,47] Rarely, the microscopic architecture of a breast cancer with endocrine differentiation may mimic the histologic structure of nonmammary tissue that contains the ectopic hormone being produced.

The clinical presentation of patients with carcinomas of the breast with endocrine differentiation is similar to patients with more common mammary neoplasms. Systemic symptoms attributable to the ectopic hormone produced are absent in nearly all cases. However, rare reports of systemic manifestations ascribed to ectopic hormones do exist.[48–50]

The majority of tumors are palpable.[3] Grossly, there are no features that are specifically associated with endocrine differentiation. Microscopically, carcinomas of the breast with endocrine differentiation vary from small cell carcinoma to carcinoid tumors to large cell neuroendocrine tumors. Many are composed of basaloid cells that contain argyrophilic cytoplasmic granules (Figures 24–8 and 24–9). The tumor cells will often demonstrate some positivity for neuroendocrine immunohistochemical stains such as synaptophysin or chromogranin (Figure 24–10). Rarely, choriocarcinomatous differentiation may occur, resulting in tumors that are microscopically similar to syncytiotrophoblasts and cytotrophoblasts and are strongly reactive for hCG.[3]

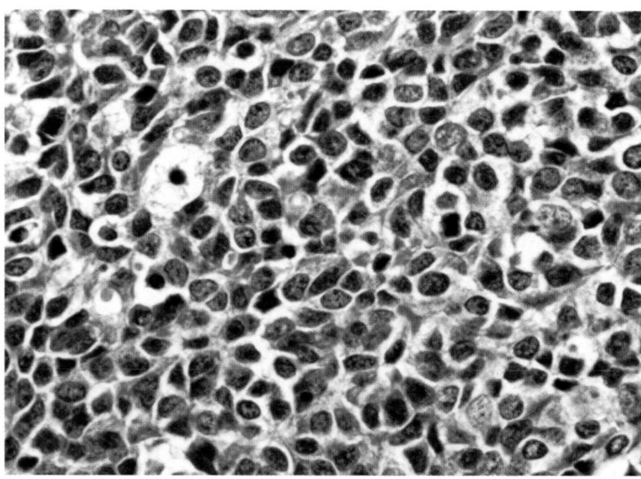

Figure 24–9. Nuclear molding and stippled chromatin characteristic of neuroendocrine carcinomas. (Hematoxylin-eosin [H+E]; × 400 original magnification)

There is general agreement that patients with carcinomas of the breast with endocrine differentiation have a similar prognosis to those with like-staged more common mammary cancers.[3,47] Treatment selection should be based on conventional clinical and pathologic criteria.

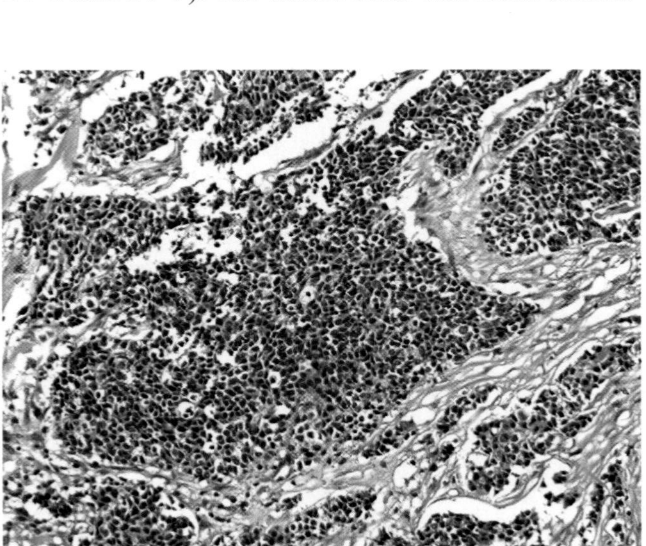

Figure 24–8. Basaloid appearance of neuroendocrine carcinoma. (Hematoxylin-eosin [H+E]; × 100 original magnification)

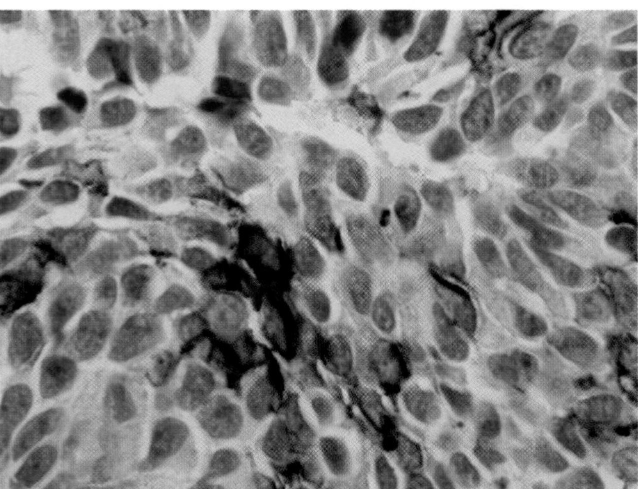

Figure 24–10. Positive chromogranin by immunohistochemistry confirming neuroendocrine differentiation. (× 400 original magnification)

PHYLLODES TUMOR

First characterized by Müller in 1838, phyllodes tumors (cystosarcoma phyllodes) are fibroepithelial neoplasms accounting for approximately 0.3 to 0.5% of breast tumors in women.[51–53] These tumors are primarily locally aggressive, with minimal capability for metastasis. Phyllodes tumors have been the subject of many reports, but their optimal management has yet to be clearly defined.

Patients typically present with firm, discrete, and mobile masses that are grossly indistinguishable from fibroadenomas. Palpable axillary lymph nodes may be present in as many as 20% of patients; however, they are infrequently involved by tumor.[3,54] Phyllodes tumors are common in younger women. The median age at presentation in the majority of published series is in the fourth or fifth decade, with a range of 10 to 86 years.[3,54,55] It is important to note, however, that the mean age of presentation for patients with fibroadenoma, approximately 30 years, is significantly lower than that of phyllodes tumors.[56] The occurrence of phyllodes tumors in patients under the age of 30 years is rare.[3] Berstein and colleagues identified race-specific differences in the incidence and mean age of diagnosis of patients in Los Angeles County with phyllodes tumors.[57] The average annual age-adjusted incidence rate for all racial-ethnic groups combined was 2.1 per 1 million women in the population. Latin American whites had the highest incidence rate (2.8 per 1 million) followed by non-Latin American whites, Asians, and African Americans, respectively.[57] Berstein and colleagues found that the mean age of diagnosis was 53.7 years for non-Latin American whites, 45.8 years for Latin American whites, 48.7 years for African Americans, and 32.9 years for Asians. Clinically, tumors that exhibit rapid growth, those that are > 4 cm in size, or previously stable tumors that suddenly increase in size should arouse suspicion. Mammographically, these lesions are smooth and lobulated. With locally invasive disease, margin irregularity may be present. Ultrasound typically reveals a solid mass with no posterior shadowing. Cysts may be present within the lesion.

Grossly, phyllodes tumors are well circumscribed and firm. On sectioning, the tumors are gray to tan and bulging. Focal cystic necrosis may be present. Microscopically, phyllodes tumors can be difficult to differentiate from benign cellular fibroadenomas. Typically, an increased cellularity of the stromal component is present. Long epithelial-lined clefts (intracanalicular pattern) are a prominent feature and may help to differentiate these tumors from fibroadenomas (Figure 24–11). Myxoid changes may be present. Some degree of epithelial hyperplasia is common, with as many as 10% of tumors containing squamous metaplasia.[58] Historically, these tumors have been divided into three histologic groups: benign, low-grade malignant (borderline), or high-grade malignant (Table 24–2). Benign phyllodes tumors are characterized by having < 1 mitosis per 10 high-power fields (HPF). The stromal expansion is uniform throughout the lesion, and the cellularity is modest in extent with mild cellular atypia. Low-grade malignant tumors typically have microscopically invasive borders, moderate heterogeneously distributed stromal expansion, and < 5 mitoses per 10 HPF. High-grade malignant phyllodes tumors have marked hypercellular stromal overgrowth (Figure 24–12). Cellular pleomorphism is common, and typically, there are > 5 mitoses per 10 HPF.[3] Although the proportion of patients with clinically enlarged axillary lymph nodes approaches 20%, the rate of pathologically confirmed axillary metastasis is well under 5%.[3,54,59,60] Since all phyllodes tumors have the capacity to recur and dedif-

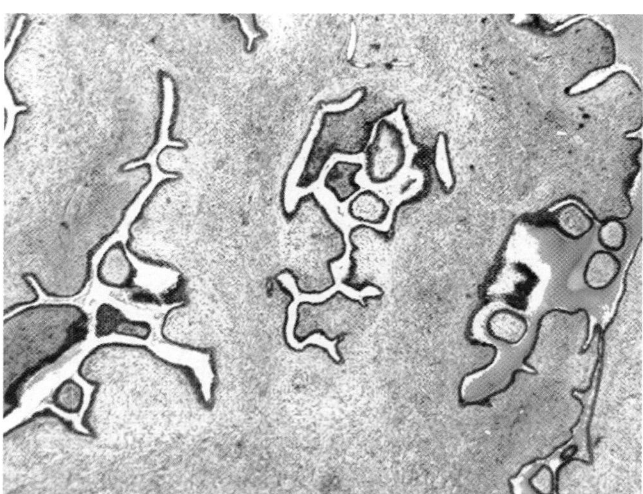

Figure 24–11. Low-grade phyllodes tumor highlighting the characteristic leaf-like pattern. (Hematoxylin-eosin [H+E]; × 200 original magnification)

Table 24–2. DIFFERENTIATION OF BENIGN, BORDERLINE, AND MALIGNANT PHYLLODES TUMORS

	Benign	Borderline	Malignant
Borders	Pushing	Mostly pushing	Infiltrating
Atypia	Slight	Moderate	Marked
Mitoses / HPF	0–4	5–9	≥10
Stromal overgrowth	Rare	Occasional	Frequent

HPF = high-power fields.

ferentiate, and the reproducibility of the three-tier system has come under scrutiny, some have advocated a two-tiered system of "low-grade" and "high-grade" phyllodes tumors and have discarded the term "benign phyllodes tumor." Low grade encompasses the benign and borderline group from the previous system and high grade correlates to the malignant group. Regardless of the classification system used, complete excision is essential to ensure that a high-grade lesion is not missed.[61,62]

The likelihood that a phyllodes tumor will metastasize and/or recur locally is dependent on its histologic classification. Histologically, benign lesions have a local recurrence rate of 6 to 10%, and minimal risk of systemic metastasis.[3,55,63–65] Low-grade malignant phyllodes tumors recur locally in 25 to 32% of cases and have a reported incidence of distant metastasis of < 5%.[3,58] Tumors with a malignant histologic classification have a high rate of local recurrence and a 25% risk of systemic metastasis.[3,58,65]

Primary therapy of phyllodes tumors is aimed at reducing the risk of local recurrence. These tumors must be excised to clear surgical margins. The magnitude of the negative margin must be dictated by the histologic features of the tumor and the size of the breast. Excision with negative margins up to 2 cm has been suggested by some authors.[3,15,54,55,65] Mastectomy may be indicated if the lesion cannot be completely excised in a cosmetically acceptable wide local excision. Axillary dissection is not required. Clinically suspicious nodes are invariably hyperplastic and should be individually biopsied. Locally recurrent phyllodes tumor does not mandate mastectomy. Complete excision to wide negative margins is acceptable.[15]

The role of radiotherapy in the treatment of patients with phyllodes tumor remains unclear. There are multiple reports of insensitivity to radiation when used for palliation.[66–68] Two investigators, however, describe the use of postoperative whole-breast irradiation following breast-preserving surgery for phyllodes tumor.[69,70] Local recurrence rates were not reported in those studies.

PRIMARY BREAST LYMPHOMA

Primary lymphoma of the breast is a rare disease accounting for < 1.0% of all breast malignancies.[71–73] The origin of this tumor remains unclear. Several investigators have suggested that mucosa-associated lymphoid tissue (MALT) may play a role in its development.[74–76] In 1972, Wiseman and Liao defined the lesion, creating the following criteria: (1) a close association between breast tissue and the infiltrating lymphoma, (2) no history of extramammary lymphoma, and (3) the breast must be the primary clinical site.[77]

Patients with primary breast lymphoma typically present with a palpable, sometimes tender, breast mass.[78–80] Rapid growth of the tumor is common.[79,80] Diffuse infiltration, skin changes, and clinically palpable axillary nodes have been described.[79–81] Lymphoma "B" type symptoms are rare.[3,78–80,82] Bilateral involvement has been reported in up to 25% of patients.[77,78,82] Although the majority of patients present in their sixth decade of life, a bimodal age distribution with peaks in the mid-30s and mid-60s has been reported.[3,78–83] Mammography and ultrasonography of patients with primary breast lymphoma demonstrate a solitary mass in the majority of cases.

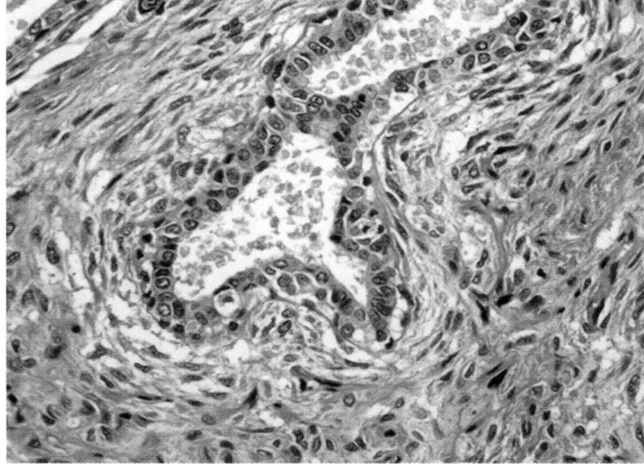

Figure 24–12. High-grade phyllodes tumor with anaplastic mitotically active cells. (Hematoxylin-eosin [H+E]; × 400 original magnification)

The imaging characteristics of this lesion are non-pathognomonic.[84]

Grossly, these tumors have a gray-white cut surface, are well circumscribed and fleshy, and may be nodular.[3] The majority of primary breast lymphomas are classified as B-cell diffuse, mixed, or large cell (Figure 24–13).[3,79–82] T-cell tumors are rare.[78,82] In some cases, the linear arrangement of lymphoma cells in the stroma may mimic invasive lobular carcinoma. Immunohistochemical stains for epithelial and lymphoid markers (such as cytokeratins, leukocyte common antigen, CD 20 and CD 3) may be required in order to differentiate between the two.[3]

Patients with primary breast lymphoma must be staged in a manner similar to other lymphoma patients. Local excision followed by radiation therapy provides excellent local control.[73,79,85,86] Negative margins are not required. The majority of patients who fail therapy will recur at distant sites or in the opposite breast.[3] As primary therapy appears to have little impact on survival, radical surgery is rarely required in the treatment of patients with primary breast lymphoma. Patients with stage I disease and those with histologically low-grade tumors have the most favorable prognosis.[72] Systemic therapy should be considered in all cases.[3]

BREAST SARCOMA

First described in 1828 by Chelius, breast sarcoma accounts for < 1% of all breast malignancies, with an annual incidence of approximately 17.5 new cases per 1 million women in the United States.[87–90] The rarity of this lesion has resulted in reports on breast sarcoma typically addressing a heterogeneous group of tumors, including malignant phyllodes tumors. Mammary sarcomas should be limited to tumors arising from interlobular mesenchymal elements comprising the supporting stroma.[3] These tumors include liposarcoma (Figure 24–14), leiomyosarcoma, osteogenic sarcoma, chondrosarcoma, malignant fibrous histiocytoma, fibrosarcoma, rhabdomyosarcoma, primary angiosarcoma, and hemangiopericytoma. Also included in this category, but discussed separately in this review, are postradiotherapy angiosarcomas. Phyllodes tumors, which arise from intralobular and periductal stroma, should be excluded.

Typically, breast sarcomas present as painless, mobile, and well-circumscribed breast masses.[3,15,91,92] A history of rapid growth in a preexisting mass is common.[15,92] Skin involvement and nipple changes have been reported, but are infrequent.[91,93] Axillary lymph node involvement is exceedingly uncommon.[3] Gutman and colleagues identified axillary nodal metastases only in the context of disseminated disease.[92] The mean age at the time of presentation in three recent reports ranged from 44 to 55 years old (range, 16–87 years).[92–94] Mammographically, these lesions typically appear as well-circumscribed, dense masses. Rarely, the presence of osseous trabeculae within an osteogenic sarcoma may be noted.[95]

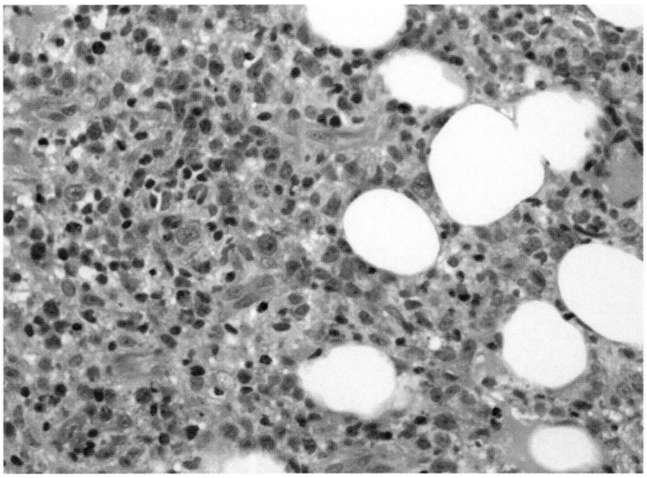

Figure 24–13. Large B-cell lymphoma infiltrating the normal breast adipose tissue. (Hematoxylin-eosin [H+E]; × 200 original magnification).

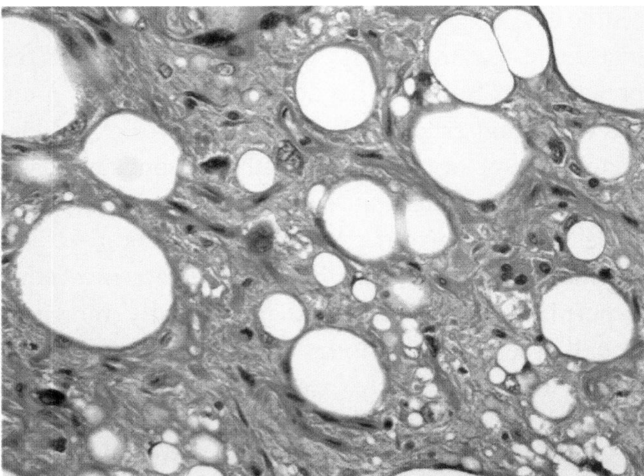

Figure 24–14. High-grade liposarcoma. (Hematoxylin-eosin [H+E]; × 400 original magnification).

Grossly, the majority of breast sarcomas are well circumscribed. The tumors usually grow as expansile masses, compressing surrounding tissue as they enlarge. The margin of a liposarcoma may be multinodular and infiltrative. The cut surface is typically yellow, gray, or white in color. A whorled texture as well as areas of necrosis may be present. Gelatinous areas are frequently noted in liposarcomas. Histologically, sarcomas of the breast are similar to their more common counterparts occurring in other areas of the body. In the breast, however, metaplastic carcinoma must be excluded prior to establishing a diagnosis of mammary sarcoma.[3] The lesion requires extensive sampling in order to rule out the presence of in situ or invasive carcinoma. Immunohistochemical studies for epithelial markers may be useful in difficult cases.

Breast sarcomas should be treated in a similar fashion to sarcomas occurring elsewhere in the body. Surgery is the mainstay of treatment. Wide local excision with histologically negative margins is required.[15,92,96] Mastectomy may be necessary in order to assure complete excision of larger tumors. Neoadjuvant chemoradiation should be considered in patients with large tumors. No staging, nor a therapeutic role, has been demonstrated for axillary lymphadenectomy.[92] Axillary lymph node dissection need be preformed only if required for complete excision of the tumor.

Gutman and colleagues, reporting 60 cases, found a median disease-free survival of 17.7 months and median overall survival of 67 months (median follow-up of 120 months).[92] Local failure was reported in 19 patients. Those suffering local failure typically did so within the first 24 months. Patients with sarcomas $<$ 5 cm in size were found to have a significantly better prognosis.[92] Pollard and colleagues identified an overall 5-year mortality of 64% with a local recurrence rate of 44% in the 25 patients in their series.[93] The role of adjuvant radiotherapy has yet to be defined.[92]

POSTRADIOTHERAPY ANGIOSARCOMA

The occurrence of sarcoma following radiotherapy has been well described.[97,98] The widespread acceptance of breast preservation in the treatment of breast cancer may have an unforeseen secondary result: an increase in the number of patients at risk to develop postirradiation sarcoma. Postradiotherapy sarcoma was defined by Cahan and colleagues in 1948 as sarcoma developing in a previously irradiated field after a latency period of several years.[99] Angiosarcoma, osteosarcoma, malignant fibrous histiocytoma, and fibrosarcoma have all been reported in the irradiated breast. Angiosarcoma has been the topic of many recent reports.[100–103] The rarity of these tumors makes the true incidence of postradiotherapy angiosarcoma of the breast difficult to determine. The estimated risk of patients treated with whole-breast irradiation ranges from 0.06 to 0.4%.[100,103–105] Strobbe and colleagues, reporting on 21 patients with postradiotherapy angiosarcomas of the breast collected from the Netherlands cancer registry, cite a potential incidence as high as 1.59% when a median latency period of 74 months is considered.[100]

The median interval between breast-preserving therapy and the occurrence of angiosarcoma of the breast has been reported to be between 6 and 11 years (range, 2–44 years).[98, 100,101,103] Patients typically present with skin changes reminiscent of a hematoma. These changes may be present over a broad area within the radiation field. An underlying breast mass may be present. Reddish-purple skin patches as well as vesicles have also been reported.[100] Findings on mammography, ultrasound, and magnetic resonance imaging are nonspecific.[106]

Grossly, the tumors may be friable, firm, or spongy. Areas of cystic hemorrhagic necrosis are common in high-grade lesions.[3] Histologically, the postirradiated angiosarcoma of the chest wall primarily occurs in the skin with occasional extension to underlying subcutaneous tissue or breast. It shows a wide spectrum of degree of differentiation but is commonly high grade. Well-formed interanastomosing vascular channels corresponding to low-grade angiosarcoma frequently merge with high-grade solid, epithelioid, or spindle cell-containing regions (Figures 24–15 and 24–16). Distinction from irradiation-related benign vascular changes including vascular or lymphatic ectasia and the so-called “atypical vascular lesions” in addition to hemangiomas is mandatory, albeit often chal-

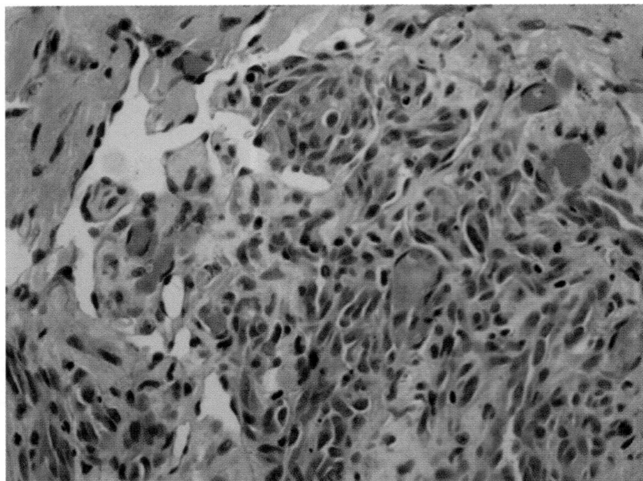

Figure 24–15. Angiosarcoma with spindled cells and vascular spaces. (Hematoxylin-eosin [H+E]; × 400 original magnification)

lenging, sometimes requiring complete excision for comprehensive evaluation.[107] Axillary lymph node involvement is uncommon. Gutman and colleagues, reporting on 17 patients with angiosarcoma, identified axillary nodal metastases only in the context of disseminated disease.[92]

Surgical treatment of postradiotherapy angiosarcoma should consist of complete resection with wide negative margins. Salvage mastectomy with en-bloc resection of involved skin and adjacent structures is often required.[100,108] Reconstruction of the resulting defect may require musculocutaneous flaps and/or skin grafts. Rarely, patients with small lesions may be adequately treated with a partial mastectomy.[108]

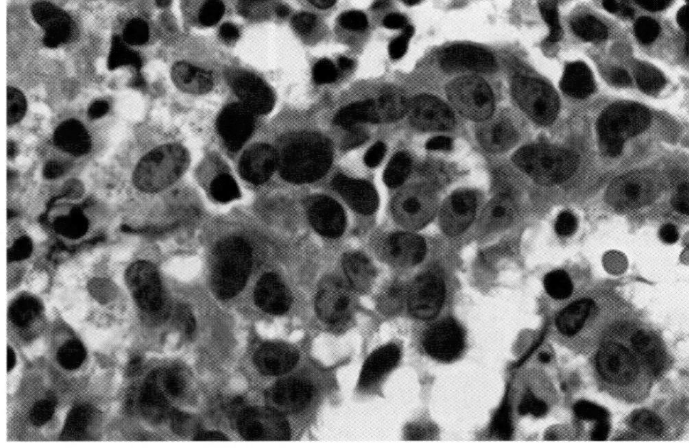

Figure 24–16. Epithelioid angiosarcoma, a tumor that can be mistaken for an epithelial malignancy (Hematoxylin-eosin [H+E]; × 400 original magnification)

Axillary dissection need be preformed only if required for complete excision of the tumor.[108,109]

The prognosis of primary angiosarcoma of the breast appears to depend on the grade of the tumor.[110] The prognosis for postradiotherapy angiosarcomas, however, remains unclear. The number of reported patients with postradiotherapy angiosarcomas is insufficient to draw accurate conclusions regarding prognosis. High-grade lesions are aggressive and tend to recur locally.[101,111] Low-grade tumors appear to have a more favorable prognosis.[3,101,112]

REFERENCES

1. Haagensen CD, editor. Diseases of the breast. 2nd ed. Philadelphia: WB Saunders; 1971.
2. Fisher ER, Palekar AS, Redmond C, et al. Pathologic findings from the National Surgical Adjuvant Breast Project (Protocol No. 4). VI. Invasive papillary cancer. Am J Clin Pathol 1980;73:313–20.
3. Rosen PP, editor. Rosen's breast pathology. Philadelphia: Lippincott-Raven Publishers; 1997.
4. World Health Organization. Histological typing of breast tumours. International histological classification of tumours. Vol 2. 2nd ed. Genova: World Health Organization; 1981.
5. Foote FW, Stewart FW. A histologic classification of carcinoma of the breast. Surgery 1946:74–99.
6. Carter D. Intraductal papillary tumors of the breast. A study of 76 cases. Cancer 1977;39:1689–92.
7. Lefkowitz M, Lefkowitz W, Wargotz ES. Intraductal (intracystic) papillary carcinoma of the breast and its variants: a clinicopathological study of 77 cases. Hum Pathol 1994;25:802–9.
8. Kraus FT, Neubecker RD. The differential diagnosis of papillary tumors of the breast. Cancer 1962;15:444–5.
9. Tsuda H, Uei Y, Fukutami T, Hirohashi S. Different incidence of loss of heterozygosity on chromosome 16q between intraductal papilloma and intracystic papillary carcinoma of the breast. Jpn J Cancer Res 1994;85:992–6.
10. Tsuda H, Takarabe T, Susumu N, et al. Detection of numerical and structural alterations and fusions of chromosomes 16 and 1 in low-grade papillary breast carcinoma by fluorescence in situ hybridization. Am J Pathol 1997;151:1027–34.
11. Tavassolli FA. Classification of metaplastic carcinoma of the breast. Pathol Annu 1992;27:89–119.
12. Rottino A, Wilson K. Osseous, cartilaginous and mixed tumors of the human breast: a review of the literature. Arch Surg 1945;50:184–93.
13. Kaufman MW, Marti JR, Gallager HS, Hoehn JL. Carcinoma of the breast with pseudosarcomatous metaplasia. Cancer 1984;53:1908–17.
14. Oberman HA. Metaplastic carcinoma of the breast: a clinicopathologic study of 29 patients. Am J Surg Pathol 1987; aa:918–29.
15. Harris JR, Lippman ME, Morrow M, Hellman S, editors.

Diseases of the breast. Philadelphia: Lippincott-Raven Publishers; 1996.
16. Rosen PP, Ernsberger D. Low-grade adenosquamous carcinoma: a variant of metaplastic mammary carcinoma. Am J Surg Pathol 1987;11:351–8.
17. Bauer TW, Rostock RA, Eggleston JC, Baral E. Spindle cell carcinoma of the breast. Hum Pathol 1984;15:148–52.
18. Gersell DJ, Katzenstein AA. Spindle cell carcinoma of the breast. Hum Pathol 1981;12:550–60.
19. Huvos AG, Lucas JC, Foote FW. Metaplastic breast carcinoma. NY State J Med 1973;73:1078–81.
20. Mossler JA, Barton TK, Brinkhous AD, et al. Apocrine differentiation in human mammary carcinoma. Cancer 1980; 46:2463–71.
21. Azzopardi JG. Problems in breast pathology. London: W.B. Saunders; 1979.
22. Eusebi V, Betts C, Haagensen DE, et al. Apocrine differentiation in lobular carcinoma of the breast: a morphologic, immunologic and ultrastructural study. Hum Pathol 1984;15:134–40.
23. Lee BJ, Pack GT, Scharnagel I. Sweat gland cancer of the breast. Surg Gynecol Obstet 1933;54:975–96.
24. Abati AD, Kimmel M, Rosen PP. Apocrine mammary carcinoma: a clinicopathologic study of 72 cases. Am J Clin Pathol 1990;94:371–7.
25. d'Amore ESG, Terrier-Lacombe MJ, Travagli JP, et al. Invasive apocrine carcinoma of the breast: a long term follow-up study of 34 cases. Breast Cancer Res Treat 1988;12:37–44.
26. O'Malley FP, Page DL, Nelson EH, Dupont WD. Ductal carcinoma in situ of the breast with apocrine cytology: definition of a borderline category. Hum Pathol 1994;25:164–8.
27. Tavossoli FA, Norris HJ. Intraductal apocrine carcinoma: a clinicopathologic study of 37 cases. Mod Pathol 1994;7:813–8.
28. Carter D, Rosen PP. Atypical apocrine metaplasia in sclerosing lesions of the breast: a study of 51 patients. Mod Pathol 1991;4:1–5.
29. Cavanzo FJ, Taylor HB. Adenoid cystic carcinoma of the breast. Cancer 1969;24:740–5.
30. Geschickter CF, editor. Diseases of the breast. Philadelphia: JB Lippincott; 1945.
31. Foote FW Jr, Stewart FW. A histologic classification of carcinoma of the breast. Surgery 1946;19:74–99.
32. Peters GN, Wolff M. Adenoid cystic carcinoma of the breast. Report of 11 new cases: review of the literature and discussion of biological behavior. Cancer 1982;52:680–6.
33. Qizilbash AH, Patterson MC, Oliveira KF. Adenoid cystic carcinoma of the breast. Arch Pathol Lab Med 1977;101; 302–6.
34. Rosen PP. Adenoid cystic carcinoma of the breast: a morphologically heterogeneous neoplasm. Pathol Annu 1989;24:237–54.
35. Ro JY, Silva EG, Callager HS. Adenoid cystic carcinoma of the breast. Hum Pathol 1987;18:1276–81.
36. Orenstein JM, Dardick I, van Nostrand AW. Ultrastructural similarities of adenoid cystic carcinoma and pleomorphic adenoma. Histopathology 1985;9:623–38.
37. Herzberg AJ, Bossen EH, Walther PJ. Adenoid cystic carcinoma of the breast metastatic to the kidney. A clinically symptomatic lesion requiring surgical management. Cancer 1991;68:1015–20.
38. Leeming R, Jenkins M, Mendelsohn G. Adenoid cystic carcinoma of the breast. Arch Surg 1992;127:233–5.
39. Rostock RA, Bauer TW, Eggleston JC. Primary squamous carcinoma of the breast: a review. Breast 1984;10:27–31.
40. Shousha S, James AH, Ferandez MD, Bull TB. Squamous cell carcinoma of the breast. Arch Pathol Lab Med 1984; 108:893–6.
41. Tashjian J, Kuni CC, Bohn LE. Primary squamous cell carcinoma of the breast; mammographic findings. J Can Assoc Radiol 1989;40:228–9.
42. McDivitt RW, Stewart FW. Breast carcinoma in children. JAMA 1966;195:388–90.
43. Tavassoli FA, Norris HJ. Secretory carcinoma of the breast. Cancer 1980;45:2404–13.
44. Akhtar M, Robinson C, Ali MA, Godwin JT. Secretory carcinoma of the breast in adults. Light and electron microscopic study of three cases with review of the literature. Cancer 1983;51:2245–54.
45. Rosen PP, Cranor ML. Secretory carcinoma of the breast. Arch Pathol Lab Med 1991;115:141–4.
46. Krausz T, Jenkins D, Grontoft O, et al. Secretory carcinoma of the breast in adults: emphasis on late recurrence and metastasis. Histopathology 1989;14:25–36.
47. Maluf HM, Koerner FC. Carcinomas of the breast with endocrine differentiation: a review. Virchows Arch 1994;425:449–57.
48. Coombes RC, Easty GC, Detre SI, et al. Secretion of immunoreactive calcitonin by human breast carcinomas. BMJ 1975;4:197–9.
49. Woodard BH, Eisenbarth G, Wallace NR, et al. Adrenocorticotropin production by a mammary carcinoma. Cancer 1981;47:1823–7.
50. Kaneko H, Hojo H, Ishikowa S, et al. Norepinephrine-producing tumors of bilateral breasts. A case report. Cancer 1978;41:2002–7.
51. Müller J. Uber den fein eran Bau and die Forman der Krakhaften Geschwilste. Berlin: G. Reiver; 1838.
52. Oberman HA. Cystosarcoma phyllodes. A clinicopathologic study of hypercellular periductal stromal neoplasms of the breast. Cancer 1965;18:697–710.
53. Rowell MD, Perry RR, Hsiu JG, Barranco SC. Phyllodes tumors. Am J Surg 1993;165:376–9.
54. Reinfuss M, Mitus J, Krzysztof D, et al. The treatment and prognosis of patients with phyllodes tumor of the breast an analysis of 170 cases. Cancer 1996;77:910–6.
55. Rajan PB, Cranor ML, Rosen PP. Cystosarcoma phyllodes in adolescent girls and young women: a study of 45 patients. Am J Surg Pathol 1998;22:64–9.
56. Foster ME, Garrahan N, Williams S. Fibroadenoma of the breast: a clinical and pathological study. J R Coll Surg Edin 1988;33:16–9.
57. Bernstein L, Deapen D, Ross RK. The descriptive epidemiology of malignant cystosarcoma phyllodes tumors of the breast. Cancer 1993;71:3020–4.
58. Grimes MM. Cystosarcoma phyllodes of the breast: histologic features, flow cytometry analysis and clinical correlations. Mod Pathol 1992;5:232–9.
59. Palmer ML, De Risi DC, Pelikan A, et al. Treatment options and recurrence potential for cystosarcoma phyllodes. Surg Gynecol Obstet 1990;170:193–6.

60. Norris HJ, Taylor HB. Relationship of histologic features to behavior of cystosarcoma phyllodes: analysis of ninety-four cases. Cancer 1967;20:2090–9.
61. Kapur K. Spindle cell tumors of the breast [correspondence]. Histopathology 2000;36:472–3.
62. Dacic S, Kounelis S, Kouri E, Jones MW. Immunohistochemical profile of cystosarcoma phyllodes of the breast: a study of 23 cases. Breast J 2002;8:376–81.
63. Ciatto S, Bonardi R, Cataliotti L, Cardona G, and members of the Coordinating Center and Writing Committee of FONCAM. Phyllodes tumor of the breast: a multicenter series of 59 cases. Eur J Surg Oncol 1992;18:545–9.
64. Zurrida S, Bartoli C, Galimberti V, et al. Which therapy for unexpected phyllode tumour of the breast? Eur J Cancer 1992;28:654–7.
65. Hines JR, Marad TM, Beal JM. Prognostic indicators in cystosarcoma phyllodes. Am J Surg 1987;153:276–80.
66. Sheen-Chen S, Chou F, Chen W. Cystosarcoma phyllodes of the breast: a review of clinical, pathological and therapeutic options in 18 cases. Int Surg 1991;76:101–4.
67. Al-Jurf A, Hawk WA, Crile G. Cystosarcoma phyllodes. Surg Gynecol Obstet 1978;146:358–64.
68. Blichert-Toft M, Hansen JPH, Hansen OH, Schiodt T. Clinical course of cystosarcoma phyllodes related to histologic appearance. Surg Gynecol Obstet 1975;140:929–31.
69. Cohn-Cedermark G, Rutqvist L, Rosendahl I, Silfversward C. Prognostic factors in cystosarcoma phyllodes: a clinicopathologic study of 77 patients. Cancer 1991;68:2017–22.
70. Hopkins ML, McGowan TS, Rawlings G, et al. Phylloides tumor of the breast: a report of 14 cases. J Surg Oncol 1994;56:108–12.
71. Fischer MG, Chideckel NJ. "Primary" lymphoma of the breast. Breast 1984;10:7–9.
72. Giardini R, Piccolo C, Rilke F. Primary non-Hodgkin's lymphomas of the female breast. Cancer 1992;69:725–35.
73. Anania G, Baccarani U, Risaliti A, et al. Primary non-Hodgkin's T-cell lymphoma of the breast. Eur J Surg 1997;163:633–5.
74. Mattia AR, Ferry JA, Harris NL. Breast lymphoma. A B-cell spectrum including the low grade B-cell lymphoma of mucosa associated lymphoid tissue. Am J Surg Pathol 1993;17:574–87.
75. Isaacson PG. Lymphomas of mucosa-associated lymphoid tissue (MALT). Histopathology 1990;16:617–9.
76. Lamovec J, Jancar J. Primary malignant lymphoma of the breast. Lymphoma of the mucosa-associated lymphoid tissue. Cancer 1987;60:3033–41.
77. Wiseman C, Liao KT. Primary lymphoma of the breast. Cancer 1972;29:1705–12.
78. Arber DA, Simpson JF, Weiss LM, Rappaport H. Non-Hodgkin's lymphoma involving the breast. Am J Surg Pathol 1994;18:288–95.
79. El-Ghazaway IMH, Singletary SE. Surgical management of primary lymphoma of the breast. Ann Surg 1991;214:724–6.
80. Misra A, Kapur BML, Rath GK. Primary breast lymphoma. J Surg Oncol 1991;47:265–70.
81. Hugh JC, Jackson FI, Hanson J, Poppema S. Primary breast lymphoma. An immunohistologic study of 20 new cases. Cancer 1990;66:2602–17.
82. Jeon HJ, Akagi T, Hoshida Y, et al. Primary non-Hodgkin's malignant lymphoma of the breast. An immunohistochemical study of seven patients with breast lymphoma in Japan. Cancer 1992;70:2451–9.
83. Adair FE, Hermann JB. Primary lymphosarcoma of the breast. Surgery 1944;16:836–53.
84. Liberman L, Giess CS, Dershaw DD, et al. Non-Hodgkin's lymphoma of the breast: imaging characteristics and correlation with histopathologic findings. Radiology 1994;192:157–60.
85. DeBlasio D, McCormick B, Straus D, et al. Definitive irradiation for localized non-Hodgkin's lymphoma of the breast. Int J Radiat Oncol Biol Phys 1989;17:843–6.
86. Smith MR, Brustein S, Straus DJ. Localized non-Hodgkin's lymphoma of the breast. Cancer 1987;59:351–4.
87. Chelius MJ. Teleangiektasie. Heidelberger Klin Ann 1828;499–517.
88. Oberman HA. Sarcomas of the breast. Cancer 1965;10:1233–43.
89. Callery CD, Rosen PP, Kinne DW. Sarcomas of the breast. A study of 32 patients with reappraisal of classification and therapy. Ann Surg 1985;201:527–32.
90. May DS, Stroup NE. The incidence of sarcomas of the breast among women in the U.S. 1973–1986. Plast Reconstr Surg 1991;87:193–4.
91. Moore MP, Kinne DW. Breast sarcoma. Surg Clin North Am 1996;76:383–92.
92. Gutman H, Pollock RE, Ross MI, et al. Sarcoma of the breast: implications for extent of therapy. The M.D. Anderson experience. Surgery 1994;116:505–9.
93. Pollard SG, Marks PV, Temple LN, Thompson HH. Breast sarcoma: a clinicopathologic review of 25 cases. Cancer 1990;66:941–4.
94. Terrier MJ, Terrier-Lacombe H, Mourisees S, et al. Primary breast sarcoma: a review of 33 cases with immunohistochemistry and prognostic factors. Breast Cancer Res Treat 1989;13:39–48.
95. Elson BC, Ikeda DM, Andersson I, Wattsgard C. Fibrosarcoma of the breast: mammographic findings in five cases. AJM Am J Roentgenol 1992;158:993–5.
96. Mies C. Mammary sarcoma and lymphoma. In: Bland, KI, Copeland EM, editors. The breast. Philadelphia: W.B. Saunders; 1998.
97. Laskin WB, Silverman TA, Enzinger FM. Postradiation soft tissue sarcomas: an analysis of 53 cases. Cancer 1988;62:2330–40.
98. Brady MS, Gaynor JJ, Brennan MF. Radiation-associated sarcoma of bone and soft tissue. Arch Surg 1992;127:1379–85.
99. Cahan WG, Woodard HW, Higinbotham NL, et al. Sarcoma arising in irradiated bone: report of 11 cases. Cancer 1948;1:3–29.
100. Strobbe LJA, Peterse HL, van Tinteren H, et al. Angiosarcoma of the breast after conservation therapy for invasive cancer, the incidence and outcome. An unforeseen sequela. Breast Cancer Res Treat 1998;47:101–9.
101. Bolin DJ, Lukas G. Low-grade dermal angiosarcoma of the breast following radiotherapy. Am Surg 1996;62:668–71.
102. Del Mastro L, Garrone O, Guenzi M, et al. Angiosarcoma of the residual breast after conservative surgery and radiotherapy for primary carcinoma. Ann Oncol 1994;5:163–5.

103. Slotman BJ, van Hattum AH, Meyer S, et al. Angiosarcoma of the breast following conserving treatment for breast cancer. Eur J Cancer 1994;30:416–7.
104. Wijnmaalen A, van Ooijen B, van Geel BN, et al. Angiosarcoma of the breast following lumpectomy, axillary lymph node dissection, and radiotherapy for primary breast cancer: three case reports and a review of the literature. Int J Radiat Oncol Biol Phys 1993;26:135–9.
105. Zuccali R, Merson M, Placucci M, et al. Soft tissue sarcoma of the breast after conservative surgery and irradiation for early mammary cancer. Radiother Oncol 1994;30:271–3.
106. Schnarkowski P, Kessler M, Arnholdt H, Helmberger T. Angiosarcoma of the breast: mammographic, sonographic, and pathological findings. Euro J Radiol 1997; 24:54–6.
107. Fineberg S, Rosen PP. Cutaneous angiosarcoma and atypical vascular lesions of the skin and breast after radiation therapy for breast carcinoma. Am J Clin Pathol 1994;102: 757–63.
108. Rosen PP, Kimel M, Ernsberger D. Mammary angiosarcoma. Cancer 1988;62:2145–51.
109. Jardines L. Other cancers in the breast. In: Harris JR, Hellman S, Harris JR, et al, editors. Diseases of the breast. Philadelphia: Lippincott-Raven Publishers; 1996.
110. Rosen PP, Kimmel M, Ernsberger D. Mammary angiosarcoma. The prognostic significance of tumor differentiation. Cancer 1988;62:2145–51.
111. Naka N, Ohsawa M, Tomita Y, et al. Prognostic factors in angiosarcoma: a multivariate analysis of 55 cases. J Surg Oncol 1996;61:170–6.
112. Donnell RM, Rosen PP, Lieberman PH, et al. Angiosarcoma and other vascular tumors of the breast. Pathologic analysis as a guide to prognosis. Am J Surg Pathol 1981;5: 629–42.

25

Multifocal, Multicentric, and Bilateral Breast Cancer

MALCOLM R. KELL
MONICA MORROW

Breast cancer usually presents as a focal abnormality within the breast. Multiple breast carcinomas, especially when occurring in an ipsilateral breast, are a challenge for both pathologists and clinicians in terms of identification of the cellular origins and the best therapeutic management of the cancer. There is much debate surrounding the prevalence of multicentric breast carcinoma (MCBC) with the reported incidence ranging from 4 to 65% of cases.[1–3] Likewise, multifocal breast carcinoma (MFBC) may occur in as many as 60% of cases of breast cancer. In addition to this, 4 to 5% of patients with breast cancer will have bilateral disease at the time of presentation.[4] The shift in breast cancer therapy towards breast-conserving surgery has meant that the management of these cancers is a problem of particular clinical interest. This chapter reviews the biologic and clinical data relevant to the management of these entities.

MULTIFOCAL AND MULTICENTRIC CANCER

Definition

The definition of MCBC has historically been two or more cancers arising in separate quadrants of the breast. However, this has been a source of debate, and other possible definitions have been suggested. Cheatle and colleagues described MCBC as two or more cancers separated by normal breast tissue,[1] and a definition of two or more cancers separated by greater than 5 cm of normal breast tissue has also been used.[3] In contrast, MFBC refers to two areas of breast cancer arising within the same quadrant of the breast.

These definitions are problematic since the "quadrants" of the breast are arbitrary external designations, as no internal boundaries exist. In addition, these definitions may result in similar lesions being classified differently, based on their location in the breast or the size of a patient's breast. For example, two lesions 2 cm apart at 10 o'clock and 1 o'clock could be classified as multicentric because they occur in the upper outer and upper inner quadrants, whereas two lesions at 1 o'clock and 3 o'clock could be classified as multifocal.

The original classification of carcinoma as multicentric or multifocal was based on the assumption that cancers arising in one quadrant of the breast were more likely to arise from the same ductal structures than those occurring in separate areas of the breast. The application of molecular biology techniques to this problem has provided some clarification of these issues. Whether multicentric carcinoma is due to the spread of a single carcinoma throughout the breast or is due to multiple different carcinomas arising simultaneously has been a matter of debate. Molecular studies suggest that most, but not all, multicentric carcinomas arise from the same cells. Noguchi and colleagues[5] performed a clonal analysis of the intraductal component of 7 predominantly intraductal carcinomas, including 3 involving widely separated areas of the breast. All of the tumors were monoclonal, and different areas of the tumor shared methylation of the same phosphoglycerokinase gene, suggesting a single carcinoma which had spread throughout the ducts. Volante and colleagues[6] studied 12 patients with multicentric ductal carcinoma in situ (DCIS) and examined loss of heterozygosity to determine if they originated from single- or multiple-cell clones. All 5 cases of high-grade (comedo) DCIS were found to be monoclonal, as were 5 of 7 cases of low-grade DCIS. In the other two low-grade tumors, the molecular profiles suggested different cells of origin. Studies of histologic and immunohistochemical features of multiple tumors have also been used to address this problem. Dawson and colleagues[7] looked at a range of immunohistochemical and histologic markers in multifocal/centric breast cancers. Using this analysis, they found features indicating a common clonality in 17 of 24 cases. Middleton and colleagues[8] found that in 31 of 32 patients with multicentric carcinoma, both tumors were of the same histology and grade, and 72% of patients had in situ carcinoma in both tumors. Immunohistochemical stains for hormone receptors, *HER2/neu* and *Ki-67*, were concordant in 11 of the 14 cases for which these data were available. Interestingly, in the single patient with 2 histologically distinct lesions (infiltrating lobular and infiltrating ductal carcinomas), the immunohistochemical results were concordant. As a group, these studies indicate that the majority of multicentric carcinomas arise from the same cells, and that the terms multicentric and multifocal do not indicate two biologically distinct processes. In general, the term multifocality indicates lesions in closer proximity than those designated as multicentric, but the therapeutic considerations for both groups are similar.

Incidence

The incidence of multicentric and multifocal cancer varies dramatically depending upon the definition used, the extent of pathologic sampling of the breast tissue, and whether in situ disease is considered evidence of multicentricity.

Multicentric carcinoma is a relatively infrequent clinical finding. Koida and colleagues[9] found that only 5% of 1,334 patients seen in a 25-year time period had multicentric carcinoma. Morrow and colleagues[10] observed multifocal or multicentric carcinoma in 39 of 432 consecutive patients (9%) treated between 1988 and 1993. Pathology studies using standard clinical techniques of examining breast tissue, which include gross inspection of the specimen and a limited number of random sections of grossly normal breast, have also identified multicentric carcinoma in fewer than 10% of cases.[11,12] In a study of 904 mastectomy specimens from the National Surgical Adjuvant Breast Project (NSABP) B04 protocol, 121 (13.4%) multicentric cancers were observed.[2]

In contrast, pathology studies that have examined multiple sections of the breast tissue or used serial sub-gross sectioning with radiologic correlation have reported substantially higher rates of multifocal/centric cancer. In 1957, Qualheim and Gall[13] reported that of 157 mastectomy specimens examined, 54% contained multiple foci of carcinoma. In 17% of cases, the multiple lesions were contained in the same quadrant of the breast as the index lesion, and in 37% they were located in other quadrants. Subsequently, other studies using serial sectioning have documented multifocal or multicentric foci of cancer in 21 to 63% of patients with invasive cancer (Table 25–1).[13–20] One of the most detailed studies of the distribution of the additional tumor foci was performed by Holland and colleagues,[20] who examined mastectomy specimens from 282 patients with T1 or T2 invasive carcinomas which were clinically and radiographically unicentric. Only 37% of patients had no additional tumor foci identified. Additional tumor was present within 2 cm of the reference cancer in 20% of cases; and in the remaining 121 patients (43%), at a greater distance. The multicentric foci were both invasive and intraductal carcinomas, and their presence was not related to the size of the primary lesion. In another study of 214 mastectomy specimens, Holland and colleagues[21] demonstrated that invasive carcinomas with an associated intraductal component (EIC) were significantly more likely to have multifocal/centric disease than those which were EIC negative (74 versus 42%; $p = .00001$).

Although studies in patients with an invasive index tumor have consistently identified multicentric tumor foci, findings in ductal carcinoma in situ have

Table 25–1. PATHOLOGIC STUDIES OF MULTIFOCALITY/MULTICENTRICITY

Author	# Cases	Population	% Multifocal/Centric
Qualheim and Gall[13]	157	Not stated	54
Rosen et al[14]	203	Invasive carcinoma	33
Lagios[15]	85	Not stated	21
Egan[16]	118	Not stated	60
Schwartz et al[17]	43	Non-palpable cancer	44
Vaidya et al[18]	30	Invasive carcinoma	63
Anastassiades et al[19]	366	Invasive ≤ 7 cm, noninvasive	49
Holland et al[20]	282	Clinically unicentric invasive cancer < 5 cm	63

been less uniform. Gump and colleagues[22] reported that 81% of patients with DCIS had multifocal or multicentric disease, and Schwartz and colleagues observed a 45% incidence of multicentricity.[17] Because cross sections of the same duct may appear as separate tumor foci on a microscopic slide, these studies may overestimate the incidence of multicentricity in DCIS. To overcome this problem, Faverly and colleagues[23] performed a three-dimensional analysis of involvement of the ductal system in 60 cases of DCIS treated by mastectomy. Although discontinuous tumor growth was present in 50% of cases, only five (8%) showed discontinuous growth with gaps wider than 10 mm. Discontinuous growth was more frequent in well-differentiated DCIS (70%) than in poorly differentiated DCIS (10%). These findings suggest that true multicentricity is uncommon in DCIS, but multifocal growth within a ductal system is common in low-grade lesions.

At the time when mastectomy was the only surgical treatment option for breast cancer, the existence of microscopic multifocal or multicentric tumor was of academic interest only. Many of the studies discussed above were used to argue that complete breast removal was the only appropriate management strategy for breast cancer. Subsequently, randomized trials have demonstrated that the majority of these subclinical tumor foci are controlled with radiotherapy,[24,25] and the terms multifocal and multicentric disease have been reserved for patients with evidence of multiple tumors on clinical exam, breast imaging with mammography or ultrasound, and routine pathologic examination. The increasing use of magnetic resonance imaging (MRI) has caused renewed clinical interest in multifocal/centric breast cancer. Table 25–2 summarizes a number of studies of MRI scans in patients with breast cancers thought to be unicentric by clinical exam and mammography.[26–35] These studies suggest that MRI detects approximately one-third to one-half of the multifocal or multicentric carcinoma that is found with a detailed pathology exam. The clinical implications of the ability to identify subclinical disease with MRI are unclear and are discussed in detail in the section on surgical therapy.

There is no agreement on factors that are associated with the development of multicentric carcinoma. Fukutomi and colleagues[36] compared the incidence of multicentricity in 469 patients with familial breast cancer and 3,334 with sporadic breast cancer treated during the same time period. No difference in the overall incidence of multicentricity was observed, although a non-significant trend for a higher incidence of multicentric carcinoma in premenopausal women with a family history of carcinoma was noted. Studies examining the pathologic features of cancers occurring in women with *BRCA1* or *2* mutations have not reported an increased incidence of multicentric disease.[37,38] Histologic subtype of invasive carcinoma does not appear to be predictive of multicentricity. Older studies have sug-

Table 25–2. DETECTION OF MULTIFOCAL/CENTRIC CANCER BY MAGNETIC RESONANCE IMAGING

Author	Year	*n*	% Additional Cancer
Harms et al[26]	1993	29	54
Boetes et al[27]	1995	61	15
Mumtaz et al[28]	1997	92	11
Fischer et al[29]	1999	336	16
Drew et al[30]	1999	178	23
Esserman et al[31]	1999	58	10
Liberman et al[32]	2003	70	19
Furman et al[33]	2003	76	13
Bedrosian et al[34]	2003	267	15
Schnall et al[35]	2004	426	24

gested that infiltrating lobular carcinoma is more likely to be a multicentric process, but when lobular carcinoma in situ is excluded from consideration, multicentricity is not more frequent with invasive lobular carcinoma.[39–41] In contrast, several small studies suggest that multicentricity is more frequent in micropapillary DCIS than in other histologic types of intraductal carcinoma.[42–44]

Staging

Multicentric invasive cancers are staged using the largest primary carcinoma to designate the T stage.[45] Tumor sizes are not added together, and a designation to identify the carcinoma as multicentric is added to allow for separate analysis of this group of tumors. There is some evidence to suggest that this staging system may not accurately reflect outcomes in multicentric carcinoma. Andea and colleagues[46] examined the incidence of axillary nodal metastases in 101 invasive breast cancer patients with multiple macroscopic tumors compared to 469 patients with unicentric tumors. When the diameter of the largest of the multicentric tumors was used to determine tumor size, patients with multicentric tumors had significantly more nodal metastases for T1 and T2 tumors than those with unicentric cancers. When the combined diameters of the multicentric tumors were used to estimate tumor size, no significant differences in the incidence of nodal metastases by T stage was observed. This suggests that, regardless of the stage designation, total tumor burden in the breast should be considered when making decisions about the need for adjuvant therapy in node-negative patients.

Surgery for Multicentric Carcinoma

The presence of clinically or mammographically evident multicentric carcinoma is considered a contraindication to the use of breast-conserving therapy (BCT).[47] The rationale for this recommendation is based on both studies of mastectomy specimens from patients with multicentric disease and clinical experience. Fowble and colleagues demonstrated, using routine pathologic examination, that 23 of 51 patients with multifocal or multicentric disease had residual invasive and intraductal tumor in multiple quadrants of the breast after removal of the grossly apparent tumors.[48] Leopold and colleagues[49] and Kurtz and colleagues[50] also observed that patients with gross multicentric disease were more likely to have an associated extensive intraductal component than patients with unicentric tumors. Early attempts at BCT for multicentric disease were associated with high rates of local recurrence. Between 1968 and 1981, Leopold and colleagues[49] treated 10 patients with multicentric cancer with excision to grossly negative margins and radiotherapy. After a median follow-up of 64 months, the local recurrence rate was 40% compared to 11% in patients with unifocal disease treated during the same time period. Kurtz and colleagues[50] treated 61 patients with multiple tumors with BCT, 22 of whom had clinically evident multifocal or centric disease and 39 who had multiple tumors identified on gross pathologic exam. The overall rate of local failure at a median follow-up of 71 months was 25% compared to 11% in 525 patients with unicentric cancer ($p < .005$). Local failure was more frequent in patients with 3 or more tumor foci (35%) than in those with 2 tumor foci (16%). In addition, local failures which occurred in patients with multiple tumors were more likely to be diffuse and to involve the skin than those occurring in patients with unicentric tumors. A 25% incidence of local failure was reported by Wilson and colleagues[51] in 13 patients with multicentric disease treated with BCT. All of these studies reported patients treated prior to 1988 and included patients with positive or unknown margins. More recent reports of BCT in patients with multicentric cancer indicate better rates of local control. Kaplan and colleagues observed 1 local failure in 36 patients observed for a mean of 45 months when clear margins were obtained, and Cho and colleagues reported no local failures in 15 patients followed for 76 months after excision to clear margins.[52,53] Studies of BCT in multicentric cancer are summarized in Table 25–3.[49–54] Although the more recent results are encouraging, it is important to recognize that they are representative of a very highly selected group of patients, some with multifocal rather than multicentric disease. Tumor multicentricity was the only tumor factor associated with a significant increase in the risk of local recurrence in a

Table 25–3. BREAST-CONSERVING THERAPY FOR MULTICENTRIC CARCINOMA

Author	# Patients	Years of Treatment	Margin Status	Median Follow-up (months)	# Local Recurrences
Leopold et al[49]	10	1968–81	Grossly negative	64*	4 (40%)
Kurtz et al[50]	61	1975–83	Not assessed	71	15 (25%)
Wilson et al[51]	13	Prior to 1988	Not assessed	71	3 (23%)
Hartsell et al[54]	27	1979–89	Grossly negative	53	1 (3.7%)
Cho et al[53]	15	1989–97	Negative, > 2 mm	76	0
Kaplan et al[52]	36	1989–2002	Negative	45*	1 (3%)

*Mean follow-up.

case-control study reported by Fredriksson and colleagues[55] with a relative risk (RR) of 1.6. In addition, in a study of factors predictive of poor prognosis after local recurrence in the preserved breast, Marret and colleagues[56] found that patients with multifocal/centric tumors had a 4.08 times greater risk of developing inflammatory or cutaneous local recurrences than those with unicentric disease ($p < .0004$), and this type of recurrence was associated with a significantly greater likelihood of metastases and death. In contrast, the treatment of multicentric cancer with mastectomy is not associated with a higher risk of local or distant recurrence than is seen for unicentric cancers of the same stage.[48,52] Based on the limited data available, BCT cannot be considered a standard approach to patients with multicentric cancer. Criteria for its use in highly selected patients should include the ability to remove all clinically and radiographically evident cancers with an acceptable cosmetic result, clear margins of resection, and the absence of an extensive intraductal component in association with the tumors. In addition, patients must be informed that this approach carries with it a higher risk of local recurrence than is seen with conventional breast-conserving therapy.

In contrast to the high rates of local failure seen with BCT for clinically or radiographically apparent multicentric carcinoma, the occult multifocality/centricity reported in pathology studies (see Table 25–1) does not appear to represent a contraindication to BCT. Local failure is observed in fewer than 10% of patients excised to negative margins in recent studies,[57–59] in spite of the presence of subclinical multifocal/centric disease in 21 to 63% of cases selected using conventional imaging. The ability to identify some of this disease with MRI (see Table 25–2) is leading to mastectomies which may not be necessary. Bedrosian and colleagues[34] reported that surgical management was altered by MRI in 69 of 267 patients thought to have unicentric disease by routine evaluation. The most common change was conversion from BCT to mastectomy, which occurred in 44 patients (16.5% of total population, 64% of those with MRI abnormalities). At present, there is no data to indicate whether or not selection of patients for BCT using MRI results in a decreased rate of local recurrence. Until such data are available, it is important to recognize that extensive clinical experience indicates that clinically or mammographically evident multicentricity is a contraindication to BCT, whereas occult disease is not.

The accuracy of sentinel lymph node biopsy in patients with multifocal/centric breast cancer has been another area of controversy. The pathologic status of the axillary lymph nodes remains the key prognostic indicator in breast cancer. The technique of sentinel lymph node biopsy (SLNB) has revolutionized the management of the axilla. Randomized trials have shown that SLNB reduces morbidity, while still providing accurate staging information.[60]

Initially SLNB was thought to be contraindicated in patients with MFBC and MCBC, based on the hypothesis that each tumor has a unique lymphatic drainage pathway, and multiple pathways could render lymphatic mapping inaccurate. Embryologically, the breast develops entirely within the superficial fascia of the skin, so the breast and its overlying skin can be regarded as a single functional lymphatic unit.[61] Injection studies provide good evidence to support this observation and indicate that the lymphatic drainage of the entire breast passes through common channels, regardless of the quadrant of the breast in which the primary tumor is located.[62] This observation eliminates the rationale for avoiding SLNB in multifocal and centric breast cancer. A number of small studies have examined the accuracy of SLNB in multifocal/centric carcinoma and are summarized in Table 25–4.[62–68] In the 237 reported cases, a sentinel node was identified in 95.4% with a sensitivity for the detection of metastases of 96.9%. Sentinel node biopsy in multicentric breast carcinoma can be performed using a subareolar injection of the mapping agent or multiple peritumoral injections.

Prognosis

There is no clear evidence that patients with multifocal/centric breast cancer have a worse clinical outcome than those with unicentric breast cancer who have been treated in a similar fashion. Fowble and colleagues[48] observed no difference in the actuarial 5-year risk of relapse-free or overall survival, freedom from distant metastases, or incidence of contralateral breast cancer among 88 stage I and II patients with multicentric cancer and 1,295 patients with unicentric disease. Vlastos and colleagues[69] examined the outcome of 284 patients with T1-2, N0-1, M0 breast cancer treated by modified radical mastectomy and doxorubicin-based adjuvant chemotherapy. After a median follow-up of 8 years, no differences in locoregional recurrence, contralateral breast cancer, distant metastases, or survival were noted between the 60 patients with multicentric disease and their counterparts with unicentric tumors.[69] These findings suggest that multicentricity alone is not an indication for postmastectomy radiotherapy, nor should it alter recommendations for adjuvant systemic therapy.

BILATERAL BREAST CANCER

Definition

Bilateral breast cancer (BBC) occurs when separate primary breast cancers arise in each breast. This is described as synchronous when the tumors are diagnosed within 6 months of each other, and metachronous if they are diagnosed with an interval greater than 6 months between occurrences.

When bilateral cancer occurs, one question which may arise is whether two primary lesions are present or a single primary tumor which has metastasized to the contralateral breast. Criteria used to distinguish primary from metastatic tumors include the presence of in situ change in the contralateral lesion, different histologies, differences in differentiation between lesions, and the absence of other evidence of local or systemic spread from the primary lesion.[70] Using these criteria, metastatic lesions to the contralateral breast are uncommon unless widespread metastatic disease or locally advanced breast cancer is present. Molecular studies support the observation that most bilateral breast cancers are independent tumors. Teixeira and colleagues[71] used comparative genomic hybridization to examine 7 bilateral breast carcinoma pairs and determined that 6 of the 7 were independent tumors. Similar findings were reported by Agelopoulos and colleagues in 16 patients with bilateral synchronous breast cancer,[72] and a study of allelic imbalances in 28 bilateral breast cancer tumor pairs excluded common clonality in 27 of the 28 cases.[73] Janschek and colleagues examined mutations in *p53* in 13 paired bilateral breast cancer specimens. Using this technique, 11 of 13 cases were demonstrated to be sepa-

Table 25–4. SENTINEL NODE BIOPSY FOR MULTICENTRIC CARCINOMA

Author	Number of Cases	Year of Study	% SLN Identified	Sensitivity (%)
Kumar et al[63]	10	2004	100	100
Tousimis et al[64]	70	2003	96	92
Kumar et al[65]	59	2003	93	100
Ozmen et al[66]	21	2002	86	89
Fernandez et al[67]	53	2002	98	100
Jin Kim et al[62]	5	2002	100	100
Schrenk et al[68]	19	2001	100	100
Total	237		95.4	96.9

rate tumors, whereas 2 shared the same *p53* mutation.[74] However, molecular techniques have failed to identify a distinct genetic alteration associated with bilateral breast cancer.[72]

The use of both adjuvant endocrine therapy and chemotherapy for the treatment of an initial cancer significantly reduces the risk of a metachronous contralateral breast cancer. The Oxford Overview Analysis[75] demonstrates that 5 years of tamoxifen treatment reduces the risk of contralateral breast cancers by 47% compared to placebo, and this risk reduction persists for 10 years after the treatment is discontinued. An even greater reduction in contralateral breast cancer incidence was seen in the prospective randomized trial comparing treatment with the aromatase inhibitor anastrozole alone to treatment with tamoxifen alone or the combination of the two drugs.[76] In the initial study report with a median follow-up of 33 months,[76] the odds ratio for contralateral breast cancer after treatment with anastrozole alone was 0.42 (95% confidence interval [CI] 0.22 to 0.79) compared to treatment with tamoxifen alone. This benefit persisted after a median follow-up of 68 months, with a 53% reduction above that seen with tamoxifen observed in hormone receptor positive patients.[77] Of the 3,092 women in the anastrozole arm of the study, only 35 have developed contralateral breast cancer, a remarkably low figure.

Cytotoxic chemotherapy also reduces the risk of contralateral breast cancer, although to a lesser extent than is seen with endocrine therapy. In the Oxford Overview,[78] a 20% reduction in contralateral cancer was seen in women receiving chemotherapy, and this benefit was observed in women both over and under age 50 years. These findings have significant implications since the overwhelming majority of women with unilateral breast carcinoma will receive endocrine therapy, chemotherapy, or both as part of their initial treatment. The risk reduction that will be obtained from treatment should be considered when estimating the risk of contralateral breast cancer and discussing management strategies.

Incidence

The incidence of synchronous disease has been reported to range from 0.3% to as high as 12%.[79–81] This wide range of reported incidence rates is probably due to the use of definitions of synchronous disease ranging from both breast carcinomas being diagnosed within 1 year, 6 months, or simultaneously.[82–84] A second primary breast cancer is responsible for approximately one-half of the second malignancies occurring in women with a diagnosis of unilateral breast cancer.[85] In a population-based study of 134,501 patients with DCIS or localized invasive breast cancer in the Surveillance, Epidemiology and End Results (SEER) database, a 4.2% rate of metachronous contralateral cancer was reported.[86] The 5-, 10-, and 20-year actuarial incidence rates of contralateral cancer were 3, 6.1, and 12%, respectively, and the median time to development was 4.5 years (range 4 months to 24 years). In a population-based case control study from Sweden, Adami and colleagues[81] observed a 5.1% incidence of bilateral disease. In Robbins and Berg's study[87] of bilateral breast cancer in the pre-adjuvant therapy era, the risk of developing a contralateral cancer was 0.7% per year of follow-up. As a group, these studies indicate that, although women with unilateral breast cancer have an increased risk of developing a new contralateral cancer compared to the general population, the absolute magnitude of this risk is relatively low. For many women, the risk of death from the initial cancer is greater than the risk of occurrence of a new primary cancer, particularly when adjuvant systemic chemotherapy or endocrine therapy are part of the initial treatment.

Risk Factors

Multiple clinical and pathologic features have been recognized as risk factors for bilateral breast cancer (Table 25–5). Mutations in *BRCA1* or *BRCA2* are strongly associated with the development of bilateral breast cancer. In the Breast Cancer Linkage Consortium report, *BRCA1* mutation carriers had a 65% risk of a second breast cancer by age 70, a risk of 2.6% per year.[88] For carriers of *BRCA2* mutations, these figures were 52.3% and 1.8% per year respectively.[89] These risk estimates are derived from families with large numbers of affected relatives and may represent the upper end of a spectrum of risk. However, Robson and colleagues[90] observed a 14.8% incidence of

Table 25–5. SIGNIFICANT RISK FACTORS FOR BILATERAL BREAST CANCER
BRCA1 or *BRCA2* mutations
Young age at time of diagnosis of unilateral breast cancer
Previous chest radiation in childhood or adolescence

second breast cancers at 5 years which increased to 27% at 10 years in a group of unselected Ashkenazi Jewish *BRCA1/2* mutation carriers. Although mutations in *BRCA1/2* are strongly associated with the development of bilateral breast cancer, the majority of women with bilateral breast cancer are not mutation carriers. Steinmann and colleagues[91] examined the frequency of *BRCA1/2* mutations in a group of 75 consecutive patients with synchronous bilateral breast cancer, unselected for age or family history. No increase in the frequency of mutations between this group and 75 patients with unilateral cancer, matched for age and family history, was noted. In a Danish cohort of 59 patients with bilateral breast cancer diagnosed before age 46 years, a 22% incidence of *BRCA1/2* mutations was observed, which did not differ from that seen in women in the same age group with unilateral, multifocal disease.[92]

Young age at diagnosis of the initial carcinoma has been identified as a risk factor for the development of bilateral disease in most studies. Hankey and colleagues[93] using population-based data for 27,175 cases from the Connecticut Tumor Registry, observed a RR of second cancers of 5.7 for women diagnosed initially before age 45 years compared to 2.4 for those diagnosed after age 54 years. Adami and colleagues reported a RR of 9.9 for those diagnosed prior to age 50 years compared to 1.9 for those diagnosed at older ages.[81] In contrast, in a multivariate analysis including histologic tumor type, race, age, and the use of radiotherapy, an analysis of SEER data[86] reported a RR of 1.15 for women diagnosed after age 55 years (95% CI 1.08 to 1.22, $p = .0001$) compared to those diagnosed at younger ages. A trend toward increased risk in those younger than 45 years was observed, but this was not statistically significant. Some of the variability in the effect of age on risk may be due to relatively small numbers of women in the younger age groups and a higher proportion of *BRCA1/2* mutation carriers in the younger age groups in the studies cited.

An increased risk of bilateral breast cancer is also seen in young women receiving mantle irradiation for Hodgkin's lymphoma.[94] This increased risk is observed in women radiated before 30 years of age and is greatest after 15 years of follow-up.[95] Yahalom and colleagues[94] reported that 22% of patients developing breast cancer after radiotherapy for Hodgkin's disease in their series had bilateral disease, half synchronous and half metachronous. In contrast, radiotherapy given as part of breast cancer treatment has not been associated with an increased risk of contralateral cancers.[86,93]

Lobular histology of the tumor has often been associated with an increased risk of bilateral breast cancer. Many of these reports are confounded by the inclusion of lobular carcinoma in situ as evidence of bilaterality. In the large, population-based study of Gao and colleagues,[86] the incidence of contralateral breast cancer for 8,686 patients with infiltrating lobular carcinoma was 4.5%, compared to 4.2% for those with infiltrating ductal carcinoma. In a study of patients treated at the Institut Curie, Broet and colleagues[96] found that lobular histology significantly increased the risk of contralateral cancer from 4.0% for those with other histologies to 5.3% in the lobular group ($p = .03$). A case control study of 70 patients with bilateral breast carcinoma, matched by age and length of survival to a control population, also found no increase in the frequency of lobular carcinoma.[97] In aggregate, the data on the incidence of bilateral invasive carcinoma in patients with an initial diagnosis of infiltrating lobular carcinoma do not support the routine use of contralateral prophylactic mastectomy in this population.

Surgery for Bilateral Cancer

Considerable debate exists regarding the surgical management of patients with bilateral breast cancer. Historically, clinicians have approached bilateral disease more aggressively than unilateral disease, and studies have shown a disproportionately higher incidence of bilateral mastectomies performed in patients with bilateral cancer.[98] A number of studies have demonstrated that bilateral breast conservation treatment is feasible and is not associated with an increased risk of complications or poor cosmetic outcome.[99–101] In a review of 63 patients with metachronous cancers, Heaton and colleagues reported that BCT was performed on 87% of patients. Recurrence rates did not differ from those of patients undergoing BCT for an initial cancer. In a study of 24 patients with synchronous bilateral breast carcinoma treated with BCT and compared to 1,314 patients with unilateral carcinoma treated in the same time period, Gollamudi and colleagues[101] observed no differences in site of first failure, disease-free survival, or cosmetic outcome. Similar results were reported by Lee and colleagues[102] for a mixed group of synchronous and metachronous bilateral cancers. The findings indicate that decisions regarding local therapy in patients with bilateral carcinoma, either synchronous or metachronous, should be made using the same criteria as are used in patients with unilateral carcinoma.[47] Synchronous bilateral disease, even in *BRCA1/2* mutation carriers, is not associated with a higher risk of true local recurrence. However, patients with a genetic mutation are at a significantly increased risk for the development of new primary cancers, and this should be considered in the decision-making process.[103,104] Bilateral sentinel node biopsy can be performed for patients with bilateral carcinoma.

Prognosis

Survival for patients with bilateral breast carcinoma is similar to that of patients with unilateral disease. The NSABP B04 protocol provides information on the outcome of bilateral breast cancer patients.[84] At 10-year follow-up, 66 of the 1,578 patients enrolled in the study of surgical therapy alone had developed a contralateral cancer. Analysis of the BBC patients showed that the tumors were smaller by an average of 1 cm than those of patients with unilateral cancer. However, no difference was seen between the nodal status of BBC patients and unilateral breast cancer patients, and no differences in 10-year survival were seen between groups.

Other single institution studies have found that patients with bilateral breast carcinoma have a worse prognosis than their counterparts with unilateral disease. Healey and colleagues[105] reported in a multivariate analysis of women treated with bilateral BCT that those with bilateral cancer had a significantly higher likelihood of developing distant metastases (RR = 2.17, 95% CI 1.28 to 3.69). Kollias and colleagues[106] found contralateral breast cancer to be a prognostic factor in a multivariate Cox model using tumor size, grade, nodal status, and bilaterality. This study included 3,104 women with unilateral cancer, 26 with synchronous bilateral disease, and 80 with metachronous disease. Survival at 16 years was 53.8, 42.4, and 60.1%, respectively, for these groups. Heron and colleagues[100] also found a significantly increased rate of distant metastases in patients with bilateral disease or metachronous cancers, whereas Carmichael and colleagues[107] reported a poorer survival in patients with synchronous bilateral cancer in univariate analysis, but this was not an independent risk factor in multivariate analysis. This variability in results is not surprising since most studies of prognosis in breast cancer have included fewer than 150 patients with bilateral disease, both synchronous and metachronous. After adjustment for known prognostic factors and variations in treatment, they have limited power to prove or disprove the presence of a survival difference.

REFERENCES

1. Cheatle GL, Cutler M. Tumours of the breast, their pathology, symptoms, diagnosis and treatment. London: E Arnold & Co; 1931. p. 483.
2. Fisher ER, Gregorio R, Redmond C, et al. Pathologic findings from the National Surgical Adjuvant Breast Project (protocol no. 4). I. Observations concerning the multicentricity of mammary cancer. Cancer 1975;35:247–54.
3. Lagios MD, Westdahl PR, Rose MR. The concept and implications of multicentricity in breast carcinoma. Pathol Annu 1981;16:83–102.
4. Skowronek J, Piotrowski T. Bilateral breast cancer. Neoplasma 2002;49:49–54.
5. Noguchi S, Motomura K, Inaji H, et al. Clonal analysis of predominantly intraductal carcinoma and precancerous lesions of the breast by means of polymerase chain reaction. Cancer Res 1994;54:1849–53.
6. Volante M, Sapino A, Croce S, Bussolati G. Heterogeneous versus homogeneous genetic nature of multiple foci of in situ carcinoma of the breast. Hum Pathol 2003;34:1163–9.
7. Dawson PJ, Baekey PA, Clark RA. Mechanisms of multifocal breast cancer: an immunocytochemical study. Hum Pathol 1995;26:965–9.
8. Middleton LP, Vlastos G, Mirza NQ, et al. Multicentric mammary carcinoma: evidence of monoclonal proliferation. Cancer 2002;94:1910–6.

9. Koida T, Kimura M, Yanagita Y, et al. Clinicopathological study of unilateral multiple breast cancer. Breast Cancer 2001;8:202–5.
10. Morrow M, Bucci C, Rademaker A. Medical contraindications are not a major factor in the underutilization of breast conserving therapy. J Am Coll Surg 1998;186:269–74.
11. Stratton RL. Multicentricity in cancer of the breast. J Kans Med Soc 1973;74:48–52.
12. Kern WH, Brooks RN. Atypical epithelial hyperplasia associated with breast cancer and fibrocystic disease. Cancer 1969;24:668–75.
13. Qualheim RE, Gall EA. Breast carcinoma with multiple sites of origin. Cancer 1957;10:460–8.
14. Rosen PP, Fracchia AA, Urban JA, et al. "Residual" mammary carcinoma following simulated partial mastectomy. Cancer 1975;35:739–47.
15. Lagios MD. Multicentricity of breast carcinoma demonstrated by routine correlated serial subgross and radiographic examination. Cancer 1977;40:1726–34.
16. Egan RL. Multicentric breast carcinomas: clinical-radiographic-pathologic whole organ studies and 10-year survival. Cancer 1982;49:1123–30.
17. Schwartz GF, Patchesfsky AS, Feig SA, et al. Multicentricity of non-palpable breast cancer. Cancer 1980;45:2913–6.
18. Vaidya JS, Vyas JJ, Chinoy RF, et al. Multicentricity of breast cancer: whole-organ analysis and clinical implications. Br J Cancer 1996;74:820–4.
19. Anastassiades O, Iakovou E, Stavridou N, et al. Multicentricity in breast cancer. A study of 366 cases. Am J Clin Pathol 1993;99:238–43.
20. Holland R, Veling SH, Mravunac M, Hendriks JH. Histologic multifocality of Tis, T1-2 breast carcinomas. Implications for clinical trials of breast-conserving surgery. Cancer 1985;56:979–90.
21. Holland R, Connolly JL, Gelman R, et al. The presence of an extensive intraductal component following a limited excision correlates with prominent residual disease in the remainder of the breast. J Clin Oncol 1990;8: 113–8.
22. Gump FE, Shikora S, Habif DV, et al. The extent and distribution of cancer in breasts with palpable primary tumors. Ann Surg 1986;204:384–90.
23. Faverly DR, Burgers L, Bult P, Holland R. Three dimensional imaging of mammary ductal carcinoma in situ: clinical implications. Semin Diagn Pathol 1994;11:193–8.
24. van Dongen JA, Voogd AC, Fentiman IS, et al. Long-term results of a randomized trial comparing breast-conserving therapy with mastectomy: European Organization for Research and Treatment of Cancer 10801 trial. J Natl Cancer Inst 2000;92:1143–50.
25. Veronesi U, Cascinelli N, Mariani L, et al. Twenty-year follow-up of a randomized study comparing breast-conserving surgery with radical mastectomy for early breast cancer. N Engl J Med 2002;347:1227–32.
26. Harms SE, Flamig DP, Hesley KL, et al. MR imaging of the breast with rotating delivery of excitation off resonance: clinical experience with pathologic correlation. Radiology 1993;187:493–501.
27. Boetes C, Mus RD, Holland R, et al. Breast tumors: comparative accuracy of MR imaging relative to mammography and US for demonstrating extent. Radiology 1995;197: 743–7.
28. Mumtaz H, Hall-Craggs MA, Davidson T, et al. Staging of symptomatic primary breast cancer with MR imaging. AJR Am J Roentgenol 1997;169:417–24.
29. Fischer U, Kopka L, Grabbe E. Breast carcinoma: Effect of preoperative contrast-enhanced MR Imaging on the therapeutic approach. Radiology 1999;213:881–8.
30. Drew PJ, Turnbull LW, Chatterjee S, et al. Prospective comparison of standard triple assessment and dynamic magnetic resonance imaging of the breast for the evaluation of symptomatic breast lesions. Ann Surg 1999;230: 680–5.
31. Esserman L, Hylton N, Yassa L, et al. Utility of magnetic resonance imaging in the management of breast cancer: evidence for improved preoperative staging. J Clin Oncol 1999;17:110–9.
32. Liberman L, Morris EA, Dershaw DD, et al. MR imaging of the ipsilateral breast in women with percutaneously proven breast cancer. AJR Am J Roentgenol 2003;180:901–10.
33. Furman B, Gardner MS, Romilly P, et al. Effect of 0.5 Tesla magnetic resonance imaging on the surgical management of breast cancer patients. Am J Surg 2003;186:344–7.
34. Bedrosian I, Mick R, Orel SG, et al. Changes in the surgical management of patients with breast carcinoma based on preoperative magnetic resonance imaging. Cancer 2003; 98:468–73.
35. Schnall M, Blume, J, Bluemke D, et al. MRI detection of multifocal breast carcinoma: Report from the International Breast MRI Consortium. Abstract 504. J Clin Oncol 2004;22:4s.
36. Fukutomi T, Akashi-Tanaka S, Nanasawa T, et al. Multicentricity and histopathological background features of familial breast cancers stratified by menopausal status. Int J Clin Oncol 2001;6:80–3.
37. Marcus JN, Watson P, Page DL, et al. Hereditary breast cancer: Pathobiology, prognosis, and *BRCA1* and *BRCA2* gene linkage. Cancer 1996;77:697–709.
38. de Bock GH, Tollenaar RA, Papelard H, et al. Clinical and pathological features of *BRCA1* associated carcinomas in a hospital-based sample of Dutch breast cancer patients. Br J Cancer 2001;85:1347–50.
39. Lesser ML, Rosen PP, Kinne DW. Multicentricity and bilaterality in invasive breast carcinoma. Surgery 1982;91: 234–40.
40. Molland JG, Donnellan M, Janu NC, et al. Infiltrating lobular carcinoma—a comparison of diagnosis, management and outcome with infiltrating duct carcinoma. Breast 2004;13:389–96.
41. Sastre-Garau X, Jouve M, Asselain B, et al. Infiltrating lobular carcinoma of the breast: Clinicopathologic analysis of 975 cases with reference to data on conservative therapy and metastatic patterns. Cancer 1996;77:113–20.
42. Patchefsky AS, Schwartz GF, Finkelstein SD, et al. Heterogeneity of intraductal carcinoma of the breast. Cancer 1989;63:731–41.
43. Bellamy CO, McDonald C, Salter DM, et al. Noninvasive ductal carcinoma of the breast: the relevance of histologic categorization. Hum Pathol 1993;24:16–23.
44. Ajisaka H, Tsugawa K, Noguch M, et al. Histological sub-

types of ductal carcinoma in situ of the breast. Breast Cancer 2002;9:55–61.

45. Breast. In: Green FL, Page DL, Fleming ID, et al, editors. AJCC Staging Manual. New York: Springer-Verlag; 2002. p. 223–40.
46. Andea AA, Wallis T, Newman LA, et al. Pathologic analysis of tumor size and lymph node status in multifocal/multicentric breast carcinoma. Cancer 2002;94:1383–90.
47. Morrow M, Strom EA, Bassett LW, et al. Standard for breast conservation therapy in the management of invasive breast carcinoma. CA Cancer J Clin 2002;52:277–300.
48. Fowble B, Yeh IT, Schultz DJ, et al. The role of mastectomy in patients with stage I–II breast cancer presenting with gross multifocal or multicentric disease or diffuse microcalcifications. Int J Radiat Oncol Biol Phys 1993;27:567–73.
49. Leopold KA, Recht A, Schnitt SJ, et al. Results of conservative surgery and radiation therapy for multiple synchronous cancers of one breast. Int J Radiat Oncol Biol Phys 1989;16:11–6.
50. Kurtz JM, Jacquemier J, Amalric R, et al. Breast-conserving therapy for macroscopically multiple cancers. Ann Surg 1990;212:38–44.
51. Wilson LD, Beinfield M, McKhann CF, Haffty BG. Conservative surgery and radiation in the treatment of synchronous ipsilateral breast cancers. Cancer 1993;72:137–42.
52. Kaplan J, Giron G, Tartter PI, et al. Breast conservation in patients with multiple ipsilateral synchronous cancers. J Am Coll Surg 2003;197:726–9.
53. Cho LC, Senzer N, Peters GN. Conservative surgery and radiation therapy for macroscopically multiple ipsilateral invasive breast cancers. Am J Surg 2002;183:650–4.
54. Hartsell WF, Recine DC, Griem KL, et al. Should multicentric disease be an absolute contraindication to the use of breast-conserving therapy? Int J Radiat Oncol Biol Phys 1994;30:49–53.
55. Fredriksson I, Liljegren G, Palm-Sjovall M, et al. Risk factors for local recurrence after breast-conserving surgery. Br J Surg 2003;90:1093–102.
56. Marret H, Perrotin F, Bougnoux P, et al. Histologic multifocality is predictive of skin recurrences after conserving treatment of stage I and II breast cancers. Breast Cancer Res Treat 2001;68:1–8.
57. Freedman G, Fowble B, Hanlon A, et al. Patients with early stage invasive cancer with close or positive margins treated with conservative surgery and radiation have an increased risk of breast recurrence that is delayed by adjuvant systemic therapy. Int J Radiat Oncol Biol Phys 1999;44:1005–15.
58. Park CC, Mitsumori M, Nixon A, et al. Outcome at 8 years after breast-conserving surgery and radiation therapy for invasive breast cancer: influence of margin status and systemic therapy on local recurrence. J Clin Oncol 2000;18:1668–75.
59. Dewar JA, Arriagada R, Benhamou S, et al. Local relapse and contralateral tumor rates in patients with breast cancer treated with conservative surgery and radiotherapy (Institut Gustave Roussy 1970–1982). IGR Breast Cancer Group. Cancer 1995;76:2260–5.
60. Veronesi U, Paganelli G, Viale G, et al. A randomized comparison of sentinel-node biopsy with routine axillary dissection in breast cancer. N Engl J Med 2003;349:546–53.
61. Hughes ESR. The development of the mammary gland. Ann R Coll Surg Engl 1950;6:99–119.
62. Jin Kim H, Heerdt AS, Cody HS, Van Zee KJ. Sentinel lymph node drainage in multicentric breast cancers. Breast 2002;8:356–61.
63. Kumar R, Jana S, Heiba SI, et al. Retrospective analysis of sentinel node localization in multifocal, multicentric, palpable, or nonpalpable breast cancer. J Nucl Med 2003;44:7–10.
64. Tousimis E, Van Zee KJ, Fey JV, et al. The accuracy of sentinel lymph node biopsy in multicentric and multifocal invasive breast cancers. J Am Coll Surg 2003;197:529–35.
65. Kumar R, Potenta S, Alavi A. Sentinel lymph node biopsy in multifocal and multicentric breast cancer. J Am Coll Surg 2004;198:674–6.
66. Ozmen V, Muslumanoglu M, Cabioglu N, et al. Increased false negative rates in sentinel lymph node biopsies in patients with multi-focal breast cancer. Breast Cancer Res Treat 2002;76:237–44.
67. Fernandez K, Swanson M, Verbanac K, et al. Is SLNB accurate in multifocal and multicentric breast cancer. Ann Surg Oncol 2002;9:16–7.
68. Schrenk P, Wayand W. Sentinel-node biopsy in axillary lymph-node staging for patients with multicentric breast cancer. Lancet 2001;357:122.
69. Vlastos G, Rubio IT, Mirza NQ, et al. Impact of multicentricity on clinical outcome in patients with T1-2, N0-1, M0 breast cancer. Ann Surg Oncol 2000;7:581–7.
70. Chaudary MA, Millis RR, Hoskins EO, et al. Bilateral primary breast cancer: a prospective study of disease incidence. Br J Surg 1984;71:711–4.
71. Teixeira MR, Ribeiro FR, Torres L, et al. Assessment of clonal relationships in ipsilateral and bilateral multiple breast carcinomas by comparative genomic hybridisation and hierarchical clustering analysis. Br J Cancer 2004;91:775–82.
72. Agelopoulos K, Tidow N, Korsching E, et al. Molecular cytogenetic investigations of synchronous bilateral breast cancer. J Clin Pathol 2003;56:660–5.
73. Imyanitov EN, Suspitsin EN, Grigoriev MY, et al. Concordance of allelic imbalance profiles in synchronous and metachronous bilateral breast carcinomas. Int J Cancer 2002;100:557–64.
74. Janschek E, Kandioler-Eckersberger D, Ludwig C, et al. Contralateral breast cancer: molecular differentiation between metastasis and second primary cancer. Breast Cancer Res Treat 2001;67:1–8.
75. Tamoxifen for early breast cancer: an overview of the randomised trials. Early Breast Cancer Trialists' Collaborative Group. Lancet 1998;351:1451–67.
76. Baum M, Budzar AU, Cuzick J, et al. Anastrozole alone or in combination with tamoxifen versus tamoxifen alone for adjuvant treatment of postmenopausal women with early breast cancer: first results of the ATAC randomised trial. Lancet 2002;359:2131–9.
77. Howell A, Cuzick J, Baum M, et al. Results of the ATAC (Arimidex, Tamoxifen, Alone or in Combination) trial

after completion of 5 years' adjuvant treatment for breast cancer. Lancet 2005;365:60–2.

78. Polychemotherapy for early breast cancer: an overview of the randomised trials. Early Breast Cancer Trialists' Collaborative Group. Lancet 1998;352:930–42.
79. Al-Jurf AS, Jochimsen PR, Urdantea LF, Scott DH. Factors influencing survival in bilateral breast cancer. J Surg Oncol 1961;16:343–47.
80. Pomerantz RA, Murad T, Hines JR. Bilateral breast cancer. Am Surg 1989;55:441–4.
81. Adami HO, Bergstrom R, Hansen J. Age at first primary as a determinant of the incidence of bilateral breast cancer. Cumulative and relative risks in a population-based case-control study. Cancer 1985;55:643–7.
82. Rosselli Del Turco J, Ciatto S, Perigli G, et al. Bilateral cancer of the breast. Tumori 1982;68:155–60.
83. Mueller CB, Ames F. Bilateral carcinoma of the breast: frequency and mortality. Can J Surg 1978;21:459–65.
84. Fisher ER, Fisher B, Sass R, Wickerham L. Pathologic findings from the National Surgical Adjuvant Breast Project (Protocol No. 4). XI. Bilateral breast cancer. Cancer 1984;54:3002–11.
85. Harvey EB, Brinton LA. Second cancer following cancer of the breast in Connecticut, 1935-82. Natl Cancer Inst Monogr 1985;68:99–112.
86. Gao X, Fisher SG, Emami B. Risk of second primary cancer in the contralateral breast in women treated for early-stage breast cancer: a population-based study. Int J Radiat Oncol Biol Phys 2003;56:1038–45.
87. Robbins GF, Berg JW. Bilateral primary breast cancer; a prospective clinicopathological study. Cancer 1964;17:1501–27.
88. Ford D, Easton DF, Bishop DT, et al. Risks of cancer in *BRCA1*-mutation carriers. Breast Cancer Linkage Consortium. Lancet 1994;343:692–5.
89. Cancer risks in *BRCA2* mutation carriers. The Breast Cancer Linkage Consortium. J Natl Cancer Inst 1999;91:1310–6.
90. Robson M, Levin D, Federici M, et al. Breast conservation therapy for invasive breast cancer in Ashkenazi women with *BRCA* gene founder mutations. J Natl Cancer Inst 1999;91:2112–7.
91. Steinmann D, Bremer M, Rades D, et al. Mutations of the *BRCA1* and *BRCA2* genes in patients with bilateral breast cancer. Br J Cancer 2001;85:850–8.
92. Bergthorsson JT, Ejlertsen B, Olsen JH, et al. *BRCA1* and *BRCA2* mutation status and cancer family history of Danish women affected with multifocal or bilateral breast cancer at a young age. J Med Genet 2001;38:361–8.
93. Hankey BF, Curtis RE, Naughton MD, et al. A retrospective cohort analysis of second breast cancer risk for primary breast cancer patients with an assessment of the effect of radiation therapy. J Natl Cancer Inst 1983;70:797–804.
94. Yahalom J, Petrek JA, Biddinger PW, et al. Breast cancer in patients irradiated for Hodgkin's disease: a clinical and pathologic analysis of 45 events in 37 patients. J Clin Oncol 1992;10:1674–81.
95. Hancock SL, Tucker MA, Hoppe RT. Breast cancer after treatment of Hodgkin's disease. J Natl Cancer Inst 1993;85:25–31.
96. Broet P, de la Rochefordiere A, Scholl SM, et al. Contralateral breast cancer: annual incidence and risk parameters. J Clin Oncol 1995;13:1578–83.
97. Newman LA, Sahin AA, Cunningham JE, et al. A case-control study of unilateral and bilateral breast carcinoma patients. Cancer 2001;91:1845–53.
98. Slanetz PJ, Edmister WB, Yeh ED, et al. Occult contralateral breast carcinoma incidentally detected by breast magnetic resonance imaging. Breast J 2002;8:145–8.
99. Heaton KM, Peoples GE, Singletary SE, et al. Feasibility of breast conservation therapy in metachronous or synchronous bilateral breast cancer. Ann Surg Oncol 1999;6:102–8.
100. Heron DE, Komarnicky LT, Hyslop T, et al. Bilateral breast carcinoma: risk factors and outcomes for patients with synchronous and metachronous disease. Cancer 2000;88:2739–50.
101. Gollamudi SV, Gelman RS, Peiro G, et al. Breast-conserving therapy for stage I–II synchronous bilateral breast carcinoma. Cancer 1997;79:1362–9.
102. Lee MM, Heimann R, Powers C, et al. Efficacy of breast conservation therapy in early stage bilateral breast cancer. Breast J 1999;5:36–41.
103. Pierce LJ, Strawderman M, Narod SA, et al. Effect of radiotherapy after breast-conserving treatment in women with breast cancer and germline *BRCA1/2* mutations. J Clin Oncol 2000;18:3360–9.
104. Haffty BG, Harrold E, Khan AJ, et al. Outcome of conservatively managed early-onset breast cancer by *BRCA1/2* status. Lancet 2002;359:1471–7.
105. Healey EA, Cook EF, Orav EJ, et al. Contralateral breast cancer: clinical characteristics and impact on prognosis. J Clin Oncol 1993;11:1545–52.
106. Kollias J, Ellis IO, Elston CW, Blamey RW. Prognostic significance of synchronous and metachronous bilateral breast cancer. World J Surg 2001;25:1117–24.
107. Carmichael AR, Bendall S, Lockerbie L, et al. The long-term outcome of synchronous bilateral breast cancer is worse than metachronous or unilateral tumours. Eur J Surg Oncol 2002;28:388–91.

26

Breast Cancer in the Previously Augmented Breast

COLLEEN MCCARTHY
ANDREA PUSIC
HIRAM S. CODY III
BABAK MEHRARA

According to the American Cancer Society, more than 200,000 women in the United States will be diagnosed with invasive breast cancer this year. Approximately 77% of these breast cancer cases will occur in women over 50 years.[1] Concomitantly, cosmetic breast augmentation has become one of the most commonly performed surgical procedures. According to the American Society of Plastic Surgeons, more than 250,000 women had cosmetic breast augmentation in 2004.[2] In total, it is estimated that more than two-million women have undergone augmentation mammaplasty in the United States.

As the population of women with breast augmentation matures into the range at risk for breast cancer, an increasing number of breast cancer cases among previously augmented women can be anticipated. Surprisingly, there are few reports of the management of breast cancer patients who have undergone prior breast augmentation. Breast cancer in a previously augmented breast raises questions regarding surgical and adjuvant therapies, reconstructive outcomes, management of the contralateral breast and continued breast cancer surveillance. The following is an overview of these issues pertaining to breast cancer in patients who have undergone prior cosmetic breast augmentation.

ISSUES OF HEALTH AND SAFETY WITH BREAST IMPLANTS

Over time, questions have arisen regarding breast implants and their impact on women's health. Evidence clearly shows that breast implants do *not* cause breast cancer.[3] In addition, there is no definitive evidence linking either saline or silicone implants to immunologic, neurologic, or other systemic diseases.[4,5] If anything, evidence, although limited, suggests that women with breast implants have fewer new cancers than their cohorts.[3,6]

In a series of studies, Deapen and colleagues described the association with breast cancer in a cohort of breast implant patients in the Los Angeles area over a 14-year period.[3,7,8] The 1997 study evaluated 3,182 patients from private practices in Los Angeles who had breast implants between 1953 and 1980.[3] Data on breast cancer were obtained from the Los Angeles County Cancer Surveillance Program through 1991. The average follow-up was 14.4 years, and the median interval from implant to diagnosis of breast cancer was 10.3 years. The standardized incidence ratio was 0.63 (95% CI, 0.42 to 0.89), indicating a significant decrease in breast cancer in the women with breast implants.

In a meta-analysis of four cohort studies, Lamm and colleagues reported a standardized incidence ratio for breast cancer that was significantly less than one (0.70; 95% CI, 0.55 to 0.87), suggesting that breast implants were associated with a decreased risk of this disease.[9] More recently, Brinton and colleagues performed a retrospective cohort study of 13,488 women receiving cosmetic implants and reached the same conclusion.[10]

The explanation for this, however, is not clear. More studies must be conducted to determine what role potential confounders may have had on the validity of these observations. It is reasonable to extract from this data, however, that patients who have breast implants are not at increased risk of breast cancer.

BREAST CANCER DETECTION AND DIAGNOSIS

Detection of Breast Cancer in the Augmented Breast

The augmented breast presents unique challenges with respect to imaging. Routine mammographic views consist of craniocaudal (CC) and medial-lateral oblique (MLO) projections. Breast implants, however, obscure a variable part of native breast tissue and make these routine examinations less reliable. In addition, the physical presence of a breast implant compresses fat and glandular tissues, creating a more homogenous, radiodense image. The resulting image may lack the contrast needed to detect subtle early features associated with breast cancer.

In 1988, Eklund and colleagues described a modified compression technique in order to permit a more effective imaging of breasts with implants.[11] Using this technique, a prosthesis is displaced posteriorly and superiorly against the chest wall, while the breast tissue is gently pulled anteriorly onto the image receptor and held in place by the compression device. The maneuver, used for both the CC and MLO views, are termed implant-displaced views. To date, the current standard for mammography of women with implants is four views per breast, which includes the CC and MLO views in both the implant-displaced and the standard modes.

Despite these advances in breast imaging, it is clear that breast implants still interfere with screening mammography. Silverstein and colleagues calculated the area of mammographically visualized breast tissue before and after augmentation mammaplasty using a transparent grid to measure surface area. Women whose implants were placed in a subglandular position had a mean decrease in measurable tissue of 49% with nondisplaced mammography and 39% with implant-displaced views. In patients with subpectoral implants, the decrease in measurable tissue was 28 and 9% in nondisplaced and displaced views, respectively.[12] Thus, whereas implants do interfere with screening, it is clear that implants placed in a subpectoral position do not interfere with mammography to the same extent as subglandular implants.[13]

It is also clear that the presence of a firm capsule around a prosthesis may make an examination with proper compression of the breast more difficult and occasionally impossible.[14] Concerns have been raised that calcification in implant capsules can lead to false-positive diagnoses of malignancy and unnecessary diagnostic or even therapeutic interventions. Alternatively, false-negative assumptions that calcifications are capsular instead of malignant might be made. Evaluation of the density of calcification and the use of chronologic comparison with prior mammograms may help to differentiate capsular from cancer-associated calcifications.[15]

Several studies have specifically examined features of breast cancers detected in women with implants (Table 26–1). In eight studies that included a total of 211 cancers in augmented breasts, the cancer was identified by mammography in 62% (range, 33 to 38%) and was palpable at diagnosis in 86% (range, 55 to 95%).[16–23] Cancer histology was invasive in 89% (range, 73 to 92%), and axillary metastases were present in 37% (range, 18 to 50%) (see Table 26–1).

Recent investigations suggest that magnetic resonance imaging (MRI) of the breast can provide information that cannot be obtained with conventional imaging methods alone. At present, MRI is considered the "gold standard" for evaluation of breast implant integrity.[24,25] Its utility in the detection, diagnosis, and staging of breast cancer, however, remains in the investigational stage.[26,27]

Table 26–1. BREAST CANCER DIAGNOSIS IN THE AUGMENTED BREAST: A REVIEW OF PUBLISHED EXPERIENCE

Study	Publication Year	No. of Cancers	No. Seen by Mammography (%)	No. Palpable (%)
Leibman[16]	1990	119	98 (82)*	6 (55)
Grace[17]	1990	6	5 (83)†	5 (83)
Silverstein[18]	1992	42	27 (64)‡	40 (95)
Carlson[68]	1993	37	17/31 (55)§	35 (95)
Birdsell[20]	1993	41	ns†	34/36 (94)ǁ
Clark[21]	1993	33	23 (70)#	23 (70)
Fajardo[22]	1995	18	6 (33)**	16 (89)
Cahan[23]	1995	23	ns††	19 (83)

*Implant displaced views were performed in 2/11 (18%) cases.
†The number of cases in which implant displaced views were performed was not stated.
‡Implant displaced views were performed in 7/42 (17%) cases. Among these 7 cases, the cancer was identified by both implant displaced and standard views in 5, by neither in 1; and, only by standard views in 1.
§Mammography was performed in 31 cases using standard views only (xeromammography in 27 and film-screen mammography in 4).
ǁAmong 41 cases, the cancer was identified by routine mammography in 2, by physical examination by the physician in 4, and by the patient in 30. In 4 cases, there was no information available regarding the method of detection.
#Patients were accrued from 1982 to 1991; implant displaced views were used after 1988.
**Implant displaced views were used in 12/18 (67%) cases. Among these 12 cases, the cancer was identified on implant displaced views only in 3 and on both standard and implant displaced views in 1; in 2 patients, the cancer was identified only on tangential views to the palpable findings. Among the 6 patients who had standard views only, none of the cancers were seen by mammography.
††Four (17%) of 23 cancers presented as nonpalpable calcifications detected only by mammography.
Adapted from Morris EA, Liberman L. Breast MRI: Diagnosis and intervention. Springer, NY: 2005.

Although the current evidence does not support the use of MRI as a routine screening tool for breast cancer, MRI may play an important role in select patient groups, such as those with prior breast augmentations.[28] MR imaging may be a valuable tool, for example, in the evaluation of a woman with silicone breast implants who presents with a palpable mass either related to implant integrity or parenchymal pathology. Similarly, MRI may be used in the diagnosis of locoregional recurrence following breast conservation therapy and/or postmastectomy reconstruction. Although promising, MRI of the breast is currently in a development stage. Additional clinical studies that define indications, interpretation criteria, and imaging parameters are needed.

Breast Cancer Stage at Time of Detection

The key to the current success of screening mammography is the early detection of non-palpable lesions. Routine mammography has been shown to decrease the mortality from breast cancer.[29,30] It has been suggested that in women with breast implants, however, that because of the difficulty of imaging these patients, breast cancer may be discovered at a more advanced stage and thus have a poorer prognosis.

Previous authors have refuted these claims, demonstrating that there is no difference in detection, tumor size, or number of positive axillary nodes between women with or without breast implants.[31–35] Others have shown that women with implants had larger primary tumors, more positive axillary nodes, or a lower percentage of palpable tumors visible on mammography than comparison groups of women without breast implants.[19,36–38] Because of the relatively young age of the women in these studies, screening mammography may not have been performed routinely in this subgroup of patients. This may have introduced a bias against the cohort of augmented patients in these reports. In addition, women with implants placed primarily in the 1970s and 1980s formed the study population in most of these studies. Thus, in reviewing these outcomes, the effectiveness of mammography techniques used must also be taken into account. Standard mammographic techniques prior to 1988 did not include implant-displaced views and were thus inferior to modern mammography.

Further investigation is needed to determine whether, among women who routinely undergo screening mammography, there are differences in the stage of breast cancers diagnosed in women with and without breast implants. Patients desiring cosmetic breast augmentation should be informed with regard to the limitations of future breast cancer screening.

Sentinel Lymph Node Mapping

Many studies support sentinel lymph node (SLN) mapping and biopsy as an accurate, less invasive alternative to complete axillary lymph node dissection for breast cancer staging.[39,40] As surgeons have gained more experience with this technique, SLN biopsy has proven appropriate for virtually all patients with non-metastatic disease. At this time, however, only two centers have studied the effect of prior breast augmentation.

Gray and colleagues attempted to evaluate the use of SLN mapping techniques in the previously augmented breast.[41] Eleven patients underwent SLN biopsy with an identification rate of 100% and a false-negative rate of 0%. The implant type, augmentation incision (inframammary versus peri-areolar), and implant location (subglandular versus subpectoral) did not adversely affect the ability to identify the SLN in their series. Their study, despite having small power, concluded that prior implant augmentation through inframammary or peri-areolar incisions does not interfere with the accuracy of SLN mapping. It is important to note, however, that no patient within their study group had a transaxillary implant placement. It is hypothesized that transaxillary breast augmentation, by disrupting the normal lymphatic drainage of the breast to the axilla, might interfere with SLN mapping.

Similarly, Jakub and colleagues evaluated the effectiveness of lymphatic mapping and SLN biopsy in 49 breast cancer patients who had prior breast augmentation.[31] They, too, reported both an identification rate of 100% in identifying the sentinel lymph node and a false-negative rate of zero. No patient in their series had an axillary recurrence after a negative sentinel lymph node biopsy. However, since none of these procedures were validated by a planned "backup" axillary lymph node dissection, their false-negative rate is based solely on clinical follow-up and not pathologic confirmation. Although further study of SLN biopsy in this setting is required, especially following transaxillary placement, SLN biopsy, in general, appears to be both feasible and safe for the augmented patient.

TREATMENT OPTIONS

Early-stage breast cancer can be treated with breast conservation therapy (lumpectomy and radiotherapy) or with a skin-sparing or modified radical mastectomy. Seven randomized trials have compared breast conservation with mastectomy; two of them have recently reported 20-year follow-up,[42,43] and demonstrate equal rates of distant metastases, overall mortality, and breast cancer-specific mortality.

The surgical treatment of breast cancer in the previously augmented patient differs from that of patients without augmentation however, because of altered breast anatomic features, the presence of an implant, and patients' emphasis on appearance. The standard treatment choices of breast conservation therapy versus mastectomy must be evaluated with respect to these differences.

The following is a list of surgical options for the treatment of early-stage breast cancer in patients with augmented breasts:

- Breast conservation therapy with maintenance of the implant
- Breast conservation therapy with explantation of the implant ± mastopexy
- Skin-sparing mastectomy with implant exchange
- Modified radical mastectomy with autogenous tissue and/or two-stage tissue expander/implant reconstruction

RECONSTRUCTIVE OPTIONS: BREAST CONSERVATION THERAPY WITH MAINTENANCE OF THE IMPLANT

As a result of numerous trials, breast conservation therapy has become accepted as the therapeutic equal of mastectomy. Specific comparisons relating to distant metastases and long-term survival confirm the efficacy of breast conservation.[42,43] Not only are these outcomes equivalent to those of mastectomy, but also most patients are left with an intact, sensate breast that may not differ significantly in appearance or consistency from its pretreatment state.

Breast conservation therapy might not, however, be appropriate for all patients. The adequacy of tumor resections, the influence of irradiation on the augmented breast, and the accuracy of continued surveillance are important considerations in patients with breast implants who would otherwise be candidates for breast conservation therapy.

Achieving an Adequate Tumor Resection

Aesthetic contraindications to breast conservation therapy, in general, include a large tumor in a small breast or a lumpectomy that might result in significant breast deformity. Both aesthetic outcomes and the adequacy of cancer resection might, therefore, be different for previously augmented patients compared with nonaugmented patients. The majority of women who undergo breast augmentation have small native breast volumes. In addition, permanent implants cause thinning of the overlying breast tissue with time.

Karanas and colleagues demonstrated that at the time of cancer diagnosis in 58 women with breast implants, native breast tissue comprised less than 50% of the overall breast volume.[44] Their group suggested that these small breast tissue volumes were easily deformed by a lumpectomy, resulting in an unacceptable cosmetic outcome. In addition, obtaining tumor-free margins was more difficult. Seven of 28 breast conservation therapy patients in their series developed local recurrences, perhaps illustrating the difficulty of achieving an adequate resection in these patients.

Because breast conservation is predicated on achieving tumor-free margins, it is generally recommended that re-excision be performed if pathologically negative margins are not initially achieved. In the series reported by Karanas and colleagues, 4 out of 28 patients ultimately underwent mastectomy because the surgeons were unable to achieve negative margins without removing a large portion of the remaining breast tissue.[44]

Radiotherapy and Implants

Radiotherapy, a critical component of breast conservation treatment, has been shown to decrease local recurrence rates.[45] Controversy exists, however, regarding the role of breast-conserving surgery and radiation in patients with implants. Radiation efficacy does not appear to be of concern.[46] Postoperative radiotherapy has, however, been shown to adversely affect the rate of complications and the overall aesthetic results in the presence of a prosthesis.[47] Recent reports have demonstrated that patients who received radiotherapy following implant-based breast reconstruction had a significantly higher incidence of capsular contracture than controls (Figure 26–1). The risk of infection, implant exposure, and subsequent extrusion was similarly increased.

Whereas numerous reports have addressed the potentially negative effects of irradiation on implant-based breast reconstruction,[48–51] many of these studies are hindered by heterogeneous patient populations and variations in timing of irradiation. Few studies have specifically examined the cosmetic outcomes of breast augmentation and implant-based reconstruction after radiotherapy. Handel and colleagues retrospectively evaluated 26 previously augmented patients who underwent breast conservation surgery and whole-breast irradiation. The incidence of capsular contracture in their series was 65%. Thirty percent of patients required revisional surgery, and some required multiple attempts at capsulotomy and/or capsulectomy and reimplantation in order to achieve a satisfactory outcome.[14] Similarly, Mark and colleagues reported a 57% incidence of capsular contracture after breast-conserving surgery and radiotherapy among 21 patients with permanent implants. All of these patients were judged to have a "fair" or "poor" cosmetic result at a median follow-up of 22 months.[52]

Thus, for many, the presence of a permanent implant is considered a relative contraindication to breast conservation therapy. Patients with prior implant augmentation who elect to proceed with breast conserving therapy should be informed that the rate of implant-related complications is increased in the setting of postoperative radiotherapy and that revisional surgery and/or removal of the implant may be required.

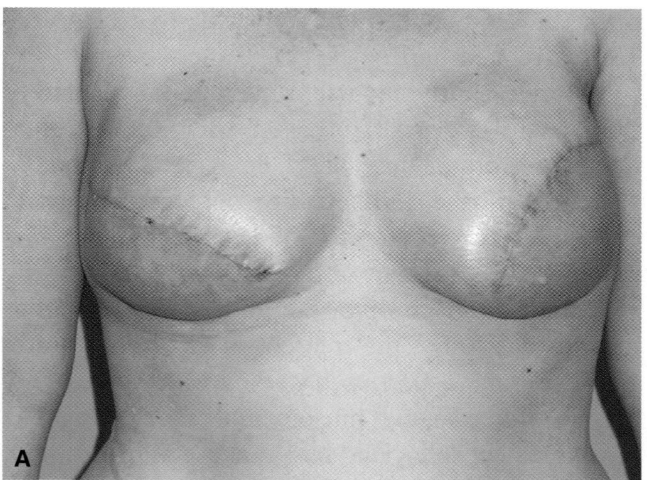

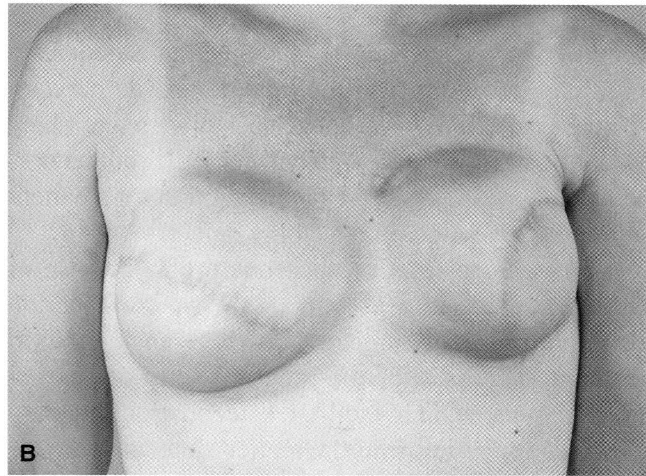

Figure 26–1. *A,* Post-operative view. Completed, bilateral tissue expander/implant breast reconstruction. *B,* Photo taken following unilateral, left adjuvant radiotherapy. Note presence of capsular contracture left breast with elevation of breast prothesis and resulting asymmetry.

Continued Breast Cancer Surveillance

Mammography and physical examination remain the main modalities for the diagnosis of local recurrences. Ipsilateral breast tumor recurrence, or true local recurrences, are cancer cells not removed surgically and not killed with radiation therapy. New primary tumors, which are new cases of cancer arising from the residual breast tissue, may also develop. The inability to mammographically detect local recurrences in patients who retain a permanent implant remains a concern. As ipsilateral breast cancer recurrences have been associated with worse breast cancer-specific survival, efforts should be made to minimize the risk of recurrence.[53] Patients who elect to keep their implants and undergo breast conservation therapy should be informed with regard to the current limitations of future breast cancer screening.

Reconstruction of the Lumpectomy Defect

As breast conservation is pushed further in terms of larger resections in smaller-breasted patients, increasing distortion of the breast is predictable. In addition, breast aesthetics may be adversely affected by radiation.[54] Although the theoretical benefit of breast conservation therapy is preservation of breast form, residual deformity and asymmetry is not uncommon. Thus, despite surgical conservatism in these patients, reconstruction of these defects may be considered.

Several controversies exist with regard to the appropriate management of a lumpectomy defect. A major concern is the timing of the reconstruction with respect to tumor resection. Other points of contention include the effectiveness of postoperative cancer surveillance and the management of a recurrence. For example, if reconstruction of the lumpectomy defect is performed immediately following the index cancer operation and tumor margins prove positive postoperatively, a potential reconstructive option may be lost. A muscle flap in contact with a positive tumor margin must be considered contaminated and a source for further tumor seeding if retained within the breast, even if a wider lumpectomy is subsequently performed. Alternatively, by using a staged approach to reconstruction of the lumpectomy defect, negative margins can be confirmed prior to initiation of reconstruction. Although this approach subjects a patient to multiple surgical procedures, it serves to satisfy oncologic principles.

Similarly, if a local cancer recurrence develops following reconstruction of a lumpectomy defect, a potential reconstructive option has already been used. For example, if the latissimus flap is used for a partial defect and a recurrence develops, the subsequent mastectomy defect must be reconstructed using the transverse rectus abdominis myocutaneous (TRAM) flap or tissues from other remaining donor sites. Critics suggest that the aesthetic outcome following postmastectomy reconstruction is similar, or even superior to, outcomes following reconstruction of the lumpectomy defect; and thus subjecting a patient to multiple procedures and multiple donor-site harvests increases morbidity without substantial gain. Many would, instead, elect to perform a completion mastectomy and postmastectomy reconstruction for a patient who presents with a lumpectomy defect.

Most reconstructive surgeons prefer the use of autogenous tissue over implants for reconstruction of the lumpectomy defect. This preference is based on many factors, including the pliability of autogenous tissues, which facilitates reconstruction of a focal contour deformity. Smaller defects, particularly those that are in the superolateral portion of the breast, are best treated with a pedicled latissimus dorsi myocutaneous flap. (Figure 26–2) Larger deformities, particularly those in the medial portion of the breast, may be more amenable to a TRAM or TRAM-related flap.

More recently, the use of a cutaneous island of the latissimus dorsi flap based solely on one cutaneous perforator has been described for reconstruction of the lumpectomy defect. The thoracodorsal artery perforator flap is a cutaneous flap that is based on perforators arising from a deep vascular system through the underlying latissimus muscle. Similarly, the intercostal artery perforator flap is a cutaneous flap based on a perforator that pierces the serratus muscle and runs above the latissimus muscle. Harvest of these flaps without sacrifice of either muscle or motor nerve is possible. In theory, this reduces donor site morbidity to a minimum. In practice, however, the use of these perforator flaps has not gained popularity because

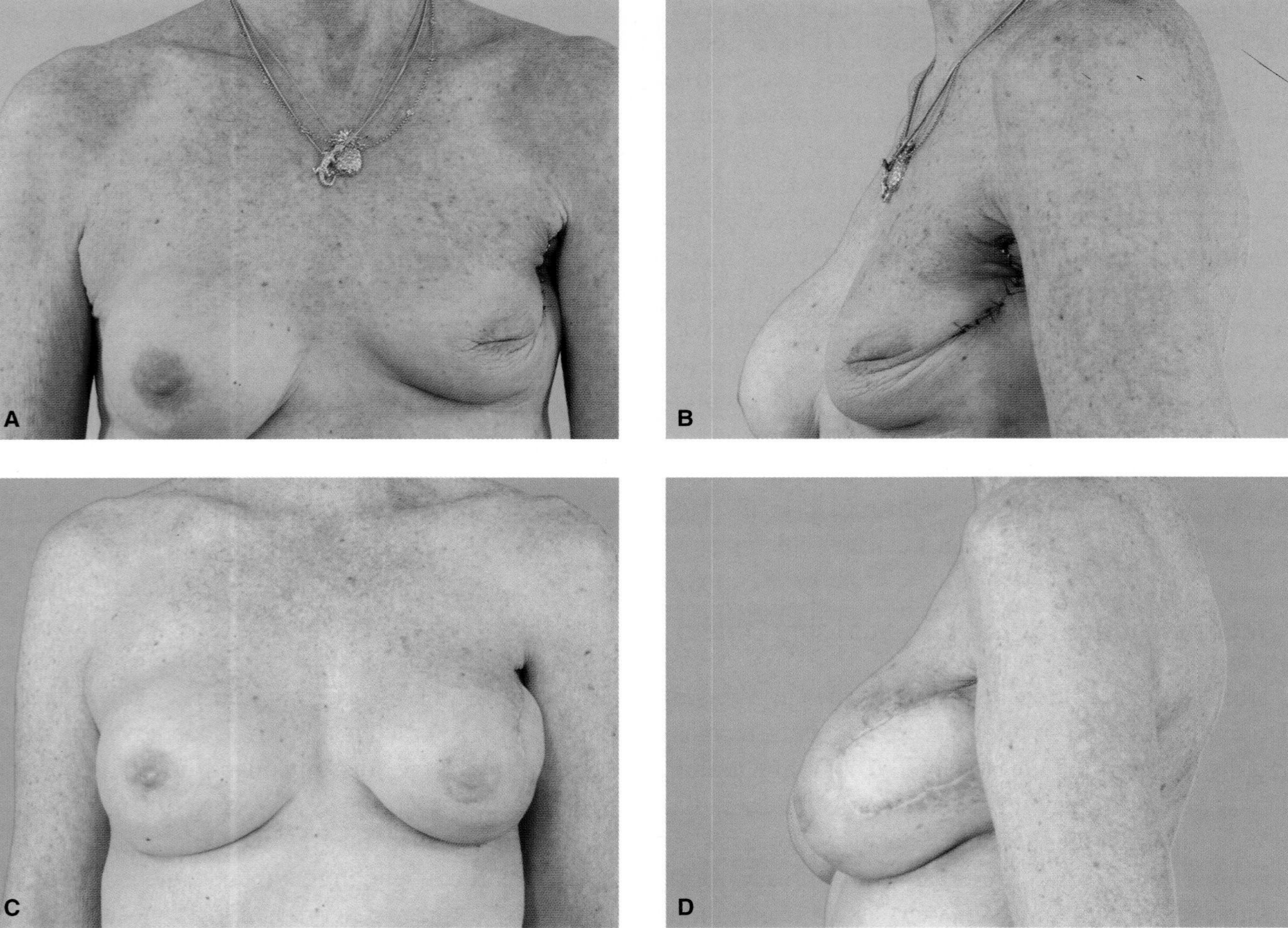

Figure 26–2. *A,* Left lumpectomy defect. Note concurrent loss of breast volume and symmetry. *B,* Lateral view: left lumpectomy defect. *C,* Left, combined latissimus dorsi flap/tissue expander-implant breast reconstruction. *D,* Lateral view; note skin-paddle pedicled, latissimus dorsi flap.

flap dissections are reported to be technically challenging and often unpredictable.[55]

RECONSTRUCTIVE OPTIONS: BREAST CONSERVATION THERAPY WITH EXPLANTATION OF THE IMPLANT ± MASTOPEXY

Continued surveillance for recurrent cancer is an integral part of the management of breast cancer patients. Any reconstructive procedure must not impede detection of a recurrent lesion. For some patients, this concern will lead to a request for permanent explantation of their implant(s).

Breast conservation therapy with explantation and mastopexy is appropriate for the rare patient with a large volume of native breast tissue. By removing the permanent implant and diminishing the breast volume, however, a quantity of excess skin remains. This discrepancy between the volume of native breast tissue and the surface area of the remaining skin envelope results in varying degrees of breast ptosis. Mastopexy, a surgical technique to reposition the nipple and reduce the surrounding skin envelope, can be employed in this setting.

The degree of ptosis will dictate the type of mastopexy. Where the ptosis is modest, a periareolar mastopexy may suffice. In this operation, circles of two different diameters are designed around the nipple. The skin between the two circles is resected, and the diameter of the larger circle is reduced using a purse-string suture. The outer circle is then sutured to the new border of the areola.

If the degree of ptosis is more substantial, the appropriate correction will require a vertical scar mastopexy or a classic, inverted-T scar pattern. A vertical scar technique provides for elevation of the nipple and a horizontal reduction of the skin envelope. The inverted-T scar technique consists of a full-thickness resection of appropriate areas of skin to allow reduction of the skin envelope in both the horizontal and vertical dimensions. In patients with advanced breast ptosis, this is the most effective treatment.

It is important to note that the combined procedure of lumpectomy, explantation, and mastopexy in the setting of insufficient breast tissue may create a situation where the blood supply to the nipple is compromised. Thus, it may be prudent to delay the mastopexy procedure.

RECONSTRUCTIVE OPTIONS: MASTECTOMY AND POSTMASTECTOMY RECONSTRUCTION

Although breast conservation therapy has been shown to have survival rates equal to that of mastectomy, many patients who develop breast cancer after augmentation mammaplasty are instead treated by total mastectomy.[56] This stems from concerns over the ability to achieve negative surgical margins, the adverse effect of radiotherapy on prosthetic reconstructions, and the perceived difficulty in achieving acceptable cosmesis with lumpectomy and radiation.

Schirber and colleagues described 9 patients who had developed cancer after breast augmentation; 5 of the 9 were treated by mastectomy.[57] Cahan and colleagues reported that, in their study, only 2 of 23 patients (13%) who had undergone prior breast augmentation were treated by breast conservation. In comparison, a control group of 611 non-augmented patients with similar tumor sizes and axillary node involvement had a breast conservation rate of 39%.[34] Clark and colleagues reported that 76% of breast cancers that developed in 33 patients after breast augmentation were treated by breast conservation.[58]

Mastectomy techniques have changed dramatically in the past 50 years. Today, it is understood that the skin envelope of the breast can safely be preserved in the absence of direct tumor invasion. Several long-term studies have shown equivalent local recurrence rates and disease-free survival for patient cohorts undergoing skin-sparing mastectomy or conventional mastectomy.[56,59,60]

A skin-sparing mastectomy includes resection of the breast tissue, the nipple areola complex, and the biopsy scar. In many cases, this can be achieved by performing the mastectomy through an elliptical incision that encompasses the nipple areola complex and the adjacent biopsy scar. Alternatively, if the diagnosis of cancer has been made by fine-needle aspiration or needle-core biopsy, the mastectomy can be accomplished through a periareolar incision in the breast. The largely intact mammary skin envelope preserves the contour of the native breast, once the immediate breast volume is restored. Restoration of breast symmetry is thus facilitated. The resulting periareolar scars are often well hidden after nipple reconstruction and areola tattooing are completed.

Reconstructive Options

Contemporary techniques provide numerous options for postmastectomy reconstruction. These options include: single-stage reconstruction with a standard or adjustable implant, tissue expansion followed by placement of a permanent implant, combined autologous tissue/implant reconstruction, or autogenous tissue reconstruction alone.

Procedure selection is based on a range of patient variables, including location and type of breast cancer, type of mastectomy performed (skin-sparing versus non–skin-sparing), availability of local, regional, and distant donor tissue, size and shape of the desired breast(s), surgical risk, and patient preference.

Prosthetic Reconstruction

Implant-based reconstruction has the distinct advantage of combining a lesser operative procedure with the capability of achieving excellent results. Donor-site morbidity is eliminated with the use of a prosthetic device; and, by using the patient's mastectomy incision to place the prosthesis, no new scars are introduced (Figure 26–3).

Prosthetic reconstruction techniques include: single-stage implant reconstruction with either a standard or an adjustable, permanent prosthesis, two-stage tissue expander/implant reconstruction, and combined implant/autogenous reconstruction.

Immediate single-stage breast reconstruction with a standard implant is best suited to the patient with adequate skin at the mastectomy site. In patients with previously augmented breasts who have undergone skin-sparing mastectomies, skin deficiency is likely to be minimal, and thus single-stage reconstruction is possible. In patients who have had previous subpectoral augmentations, single-stage reconstruction is further facilitated because the prosthetic pocket is already developed. In this setting, the reconstruction may simply involve an exchange to a larger-volume implant.

Although satisfactory results can be obtained with single-stage reconstruction, a far more reliable approach involves two-stage, tissue expander/implant reconstruction. Tissue expansion is used when there is insufficient tissue after mastectomy to create the desired size and shape of a breast in a single-stage. A tissue expander is placed under the skin and muscles of the chest wall at the primary procedure. Postoperatively, tissue expansion is performed over a period of weeks or months, stretching the soft tissues until the desired breast volume is achieved.

Exchange of the temporary expander for a permanent implant occurs at a subsequent operation. At

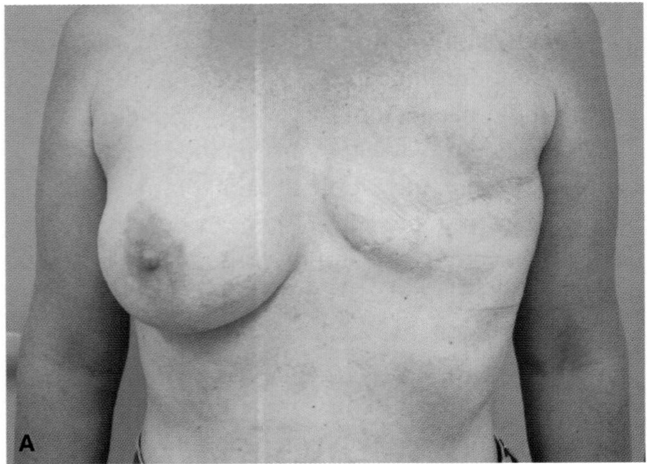

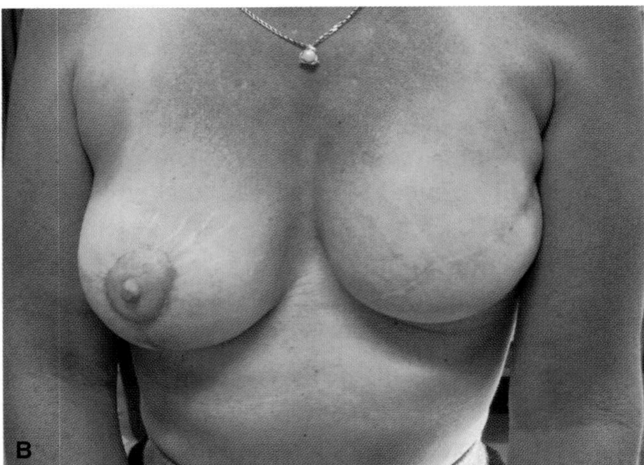

Figure 26–3. *A,* Preoperative photo: left mastectomy defect. *B,* Postoperative photo: Left, two-stage expander/implant reconstruction. Right, vertical scar pattern mastopexy.

the second procedure, access to the implant pocket enables adjustments to improve the final breast form. A capsulotomy is often performed at this second stage. By releasing the surrounding scar capsule, breast projection is increased. Similarly, precise positioning of the inframammary fold can be addressed.

Autogenous Tissue Reconstruction

For a patient who requests postmastectomy reconstruction without the use of a prosthesis, autologous tissue reconstruction is appropriate. The TRAM flap is the most frequently used method for autogenous breast reconstruction, whether pedicled or microsurgical techniques are chosen. In fact, the TRAM flap procedure now constitutes 25 to 50% of breast reconstructions performed in the United States and is generally considered the autogenous tissue of choice for postmastectomy reconstruction.[61]

One of the advantages of the TRAM flap procedure is the provision of adequate soft-tissue bulk to provide a breast reconstruction without the use of implants (Figure 26–4). There is characteristic infraumbilical fat deposit in the female that is ideally suited for reconstruction of the breast. The skin island of the TRAM flap is oriented transversely across the lower abdomen to camouflage the scar and doubles as an abdominoplasty.

Women who have had previous breast augmentation are, however, a unique group. In general, these women tend to place great importance on body image, and most maintain their ideal body weight. Thus, the availability of TRAM donor tissue may be an issue. Body habitus and a general acceptance of breast implants may instead make the latissimus flap the ideal reconstructive method.

The latissimus dorsi myocutaneous flap is advantageous in that it can provide additional vascularized skin and muscle to the breast mound in a single operative procedure. The skin island can be designed under the bra-line or along the lateral margin of the muscle, and the flap is tunneled anteriorly into the mastectomy defect. Although the latissimus dorsi myocutaneous flap is extremity reliable, the tissue bulk is often inadequate. In a patient who is accepting of a prosthesis, a permanent implant can be placed beneath the flap to provide adequate volume.

Further Options in Autologous Tissue Reconstruction

In a situation where a patient is an inappropriate TRAM flap candidate yet still desires a reconstruction without the use of implants, alternate flap options include the gluteal myocutaneous flaps and perforator flaps from the gluteal and lateral thigh donor sites. These free flaps are less commonly employed and have disadvantages when compared with flaps from the abdominal donor site.

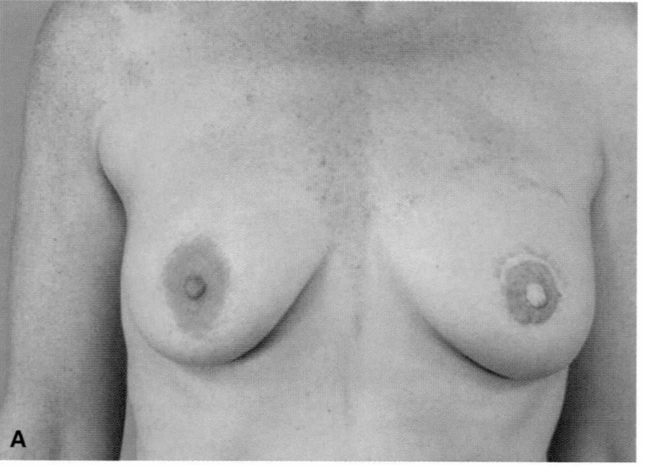

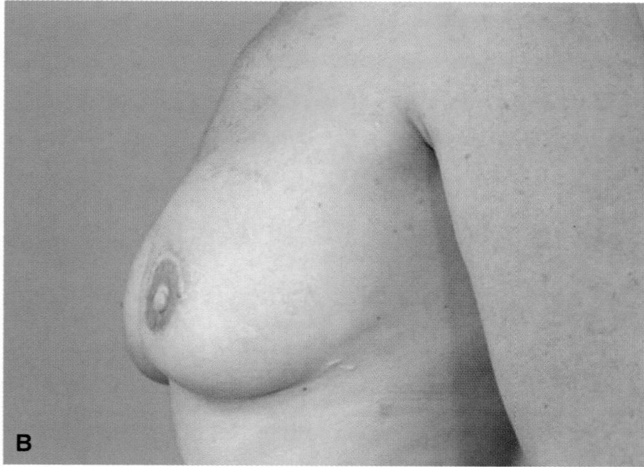

Figure 26–4. *A,* Unilateral, left free TRAM flap reconstruction. Nipple-areolar reconstruction and tattooing are completed. Note well-healed abdominal scar. TRAM = transverse rectus abdominis myocutaneous. *B,* Lateral view: left free TRAM flap. TRAM = transverse rectus abdominis myocutaneous.

The ample soft tissue of the gluteal region provides good soft tissue volume for creating a breast mound. There are two types of gluteal myocutaneous flaps: the superior and inferior.[62] The superior gluteal flap receives its blood supply from the superior gluteal vascular pedicle. The pedicle length is short, however, and flap dissection can be challenging. In addition, limited amounts of skin and soft tissue in some patients decrease the ability to match the contralateral breast.

The inferior gluteal flap is somewhat advantageous in that it provides tissue similar in volume and consistency to that of the superior gluteal flap; yet, the vascular pedicle is longer. A distinct disadvantage of the inferior gluteal donor site, however, is the exposure of the sciatic nerve during flap elevation. Sciatica is not uncommon following flap harvest and, thus, meticulous soft tissue coverage of the exposed nerve must be performed.

More recently, use of the superior gluteal artery perforator flap (SGAP) has supplanted both the superior and inferior gluteal musculocutaneous flaps.[63] This perforator flap is vascularized by a sole perforator from the superior gluteal artery and is harvested without the incorporation of gluteal muscle. Because of the low incidence of resultant donor site morbidity, the SGAP flap is often considered the second-line choice for autologous breast reconstruction if the TRAM or related flap is contraindicated.

The lateral transverse thigh flap overlies the tensor fasciae latae muscle and incorporates the subcutaneous fat from the greater trochanteric regions. Donor vessels, more specifically the lateral femoral circumflex artery and vein, are easily dissected. Perfusion to the flap is excellent, and there is a low incidence of fat necrosis. The major disadvantage of the flap is the resulting contour deformity and scar.[64]

MANAGEMENT OF THE CONTRALATERAL BREAST

The overriding goal of reconstructive breast surgery is to satisfy the patient with respect to her own self-image and expectations for the aesthetic result. Individualized selection of a reconstructive technique for each patient is a predominant factor in achieving a reconstructive success.

The presence of a contralateral, previously augmented breast, however, provides additional challenges for the reconstructive surgeon (Figure 26–5). Symmetry, with respect to the size and shape of the contralateral breast, is reconstructively ideal. In spite of ideals, the contralateral, previously augmented breast is likely to look different with respect to breast shape and projection when compared with the reconstructed breast mound. A good reconstructive outcome may be, in fact, one that provides symmetry in clothing, as it may not be possible to achieve exact symmetry with reconstruction.

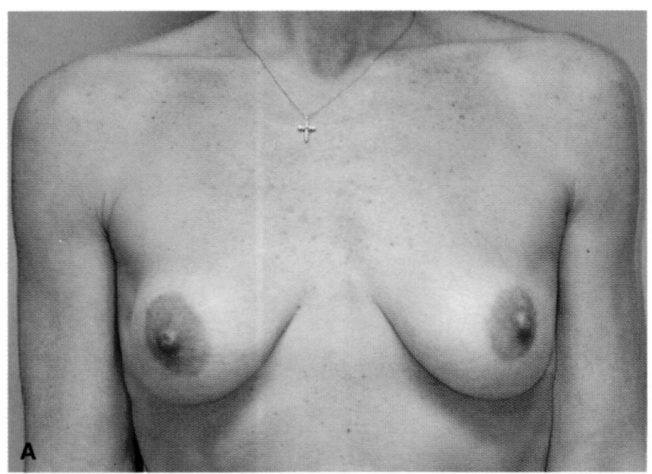

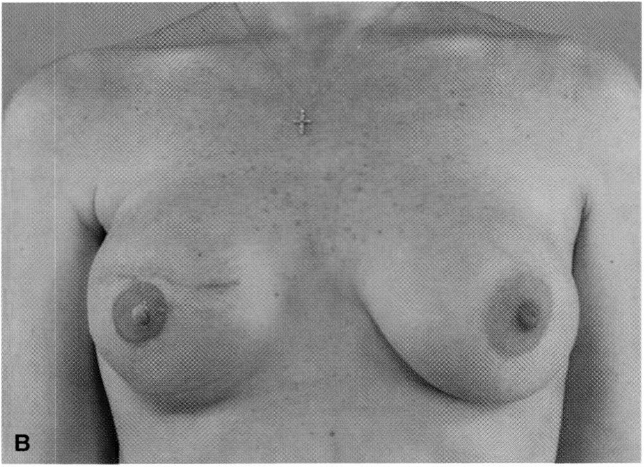

Figure 26–5. *A*, Preoperative photo: Patient has bilateral, subglandular breast implants. *B*, Unilateral, right postmastectomy tissue expander-implant reconstruction. Nipple-areolar reconstruction and tattooing are completed. The left subglandular implant has been exchanged for a larger-volume, submuscular implant to improve symmetry.

The breast mound achieved with implant reconstruction is generally more rounded and less projecting than the augmented breast. In order to decrease projection of the contralateral, augmented breast, a mastopexy can be performed using a periareolar approach. This technique tends to decrease projection, which is advantageous when the reconstructed breast also has limited projection. This approach is especially feasible in the patient who has existing periareolar scars.

Similarly, for a patient with a large-volume, contralateral augmentation, it remains difficult to achieve symmetry unless the permanent implant is exchanged for a smaller-volume prosthesis. In addition, exchange for a low-projection implant may provide better symmetry and superior results.

If a woman undergoes autogenous tissue reconstruction alone, she may request removal of her contralateral implant. Breast ptosis, a discrepancy between the volume of her native breast tissue and the surface area of the remaining skin envelope, is likely. A contralateral mastopexy repositions the nipple-areolar complex and reduces the excessive skin envelope. (See "Breast Conservation Therapy with Explantation of the Implant ± Mastopexy.")

It should be noted that if a subglandular implant is removed in a patient with minimal breast tissue, the simultaneous dissection required for a mastopexy may compromise the blood supply to the nipple. Thus, it is generally prudent to delay the mastopexy procedure. In addition, by simultaneously changing the volume of the breast, the complexity of the mastopexy increases. Whereas a mastopexy is designed to reposition the nipple and reduce the skin envelope, an explantation decreases the volume of the breast and the potential for malposition of the nipple is likewise aggravated. It is generally accepted that simultaneous explantation/mastopexy is a difficult and unpredictable procedure, and it is reasonable to stage the procedures on that basis alone.

AESTHETIC OUTCOMES: A COMPARISON OF RECONSTRUCTIVE TECHNIQUES

Previously augmented patients frequently have greater expectations with regard to aesthetic results, compared with nonaugmented patients. The self-esteem, attractiveness, and body image of these patients are frequently linked to the appearance of their breasts.[65–67]

Several studies have attempted to evaluate the aesthetic outcome of reconstructive techniques in patients whom have had previous implant breast augmentation. Gray and colleagues evaluated patients with permanent implants who had breast conservation surgery and postoperative radiotherapy. In nearly two-thirds of patients, the cosmetic result was deemed acceptable. With minor secondary revisional procedures, nearly 90% had acceptable cosmesis.[41] Spear and colleagues compared the cosmetic results of postmastectomy breast reconstructions in patients with and without cosmetic breast augmentations.[33] The aesthetic results of the previously augmented cohort were generally good to excellent, with a mean score by blinded observers of 3.35 of a possible 4.0. These results were comparable or better than those in the matched controls, who scored a mean of 3.0.

Although the results of reconstruction following either breast conservation therapy or mastectomy can be acceptable, patients must be counseled with regard to their expectations. In particular, they must understand that breast conservation therapy with retention of the implant does not provide the same results as cosmetic breast augmentation. Similarly, breast conservation therapy does not guarantee acceptable aesthetic results despite conservation of native breast tissue. Mastectomy with immediate reconstruction may yield superior aesthetic results. A contralateral, symmetry procedure may also improve overall aesthetics. Patients should be encouraged to compare the aesthetic outcomes of breast conservation therapy versus modified radical mastectomy with reconstruction before they choose a treatment plan.

CONCLUSION

With the aging of the population of women with breast implants, surgeons are increasingly likely to be faced with determining the proper oncologic and aesthetic treatment of breast cancer in the patient who has undergone a prior cosmetic breast augmentation.

Breast cancer surveillance in the previously augmented breast remains a concern. In addition, the effects of prior implant augmentation on SLN mapping and biopsy remain uncertain.

Breast conservation surgery and whole-breast radiotherapy can be used to treat breast cancer in patients who have undergone prior breast augmentation. Irradiation of the augmented breast can, however, increase breast fibrosis and capsular contracture. Adequate cancer resection, overall aesthetic outcomes, and continued surveillance are important considerations in the patients. Mastectomy and immediate reconstruction is an acceptable alternative.

For all patients who undergo treatment for breast cancer, the preservation of a normal breast form is important to their physical and mental quality of life. Individualized selection of both a therapeutic and reconstructive technique for patients is likely a predominant factor in achieving success.

REFERENCES

1. American Cancer Society. Estimated new cancer cases and deaths by sex for all sites, US, 2004. Available at: www.cancer.org. (accessed December 2004).
2. American Society of Plastic Surgeons. 2004 Quick Facts Cosmetic and Reconstructive Plastic Surgery Trends. Available at: www.plasticsurgery.org. (accessed December 2004).
3. Deapen DM, Bernstein L, Brody GS. Are breast implants anticarcinogenic? A 14-year follow-up of the Los Angeles Study. Plast Reconstr Surg 1997;99:1346–53.
4. Karlson EW, Hankinson SE, Liang MH, et al. Association of silicone breast implants with immunologic abnormalities: a prospective study. Am J Med 1999;106:11–9.
5. Ferguson JH. Silicone breast implants and neurologic disorders. Report of the Practice Committee of the American Academy of Neurology. Neurology 1997;48:1504–7.
6. Deapen DM, Brody GS. Augmentation mammaplasty and breast cancer: a 5-year update of the Los Angeles study. Plast Reconstr Surg 1992;89:660–5.
7. Deapen DM, Pike MC, Casagrande JT, Brody GS. The relationship between breast cancer and augmentation mammaplasty: an epidemiologic study. Plast Reconstr Surg 1986;77:361–8.
8. Deapen D, Hamilton A, Bernstein L, Brody GS. Breast cancer stage at diagnosis and survival among patients with prior breast implants. Plast Reconstr Surg 2000;105:535–40.
9. Lamm SH. Silicone breast implants and long-term health effects: when are data adequate? J Clin Epidemiol 1995; 48:507–11.
10. Brinton LA, Lubin JH, Burich MC, et al. Breast cancer following augmentation mammoplasty (United States). Cancer Causes Control 2000;11:819–27.
11. Eklund GW, Busby RC, Miller SH, Job JS. Improved imaging of the augmented breast. AJR Am J Roentgenol 1988; 151:469–73.
12. Silverstein MJ, Handel N, Gamagami P, et al. Mammographic measurements before and after augmentation mammaplasty. Plast Reconstr Surg 1990;86:1126–30.
13. Destouet JM, Monsees BS, Oser RF, et al. Screening mammography in 350 women with breast implants: prevalence and findings of implant complications. AJR Am J Roentgenol 1992;159:973–8.
14. Handel N, Silverstein MJ, Gamagami P, et al. Factors affecting mammographic visualization of the breast after augmentation mammaplasty. JAMA 1992;268:1913–7.
15. Raso DS, Greene WB, Kalasinsky VF, et al. Elemental analysis and clinical implications of calcification deposits associated with silicone breast implants. Ann Plast Surg 1999;42:117–23.
16. Leibman AJ, Kruse B. Breast cancer: mammographic and sonographic findings after augmentation mammoplasty. Radiology 1990;174:195–8.
17. Grace GT, Roberts C, Cohen IK. The role of mammography in detecting breast cancer in augmented breasts. Ann Plast Surg 1990;25:119–23.
18. Silverstein MJ, Handel N, Gamagami P, et al. Breast cancer diagnosis and prognosis in women following augmentation with silicone gel-filled prostheses. Eur J Cancer 1992;28:635–40.
19. Carlson GW, Curley SA, Martin JE, et al. The detection of breast cancer after augmentation mammaplasty. Plast Reconstr Surg 1993;91:837–40.
20. Birdsell DC, Jenkins H, Berkel H. Breast cancer diagnosis and survival in women with and without breast implants. Plast Reconstr Surg 1993;92:795–800.
21. Clark CP III, Peters GN, O'Brien KM. Cancer in the augmented breast. Diagnosis and prognosis. Cancer 1993;72: 2170–4.
22. Fajardo LL, Harvey JA, McAleese KA, et al. Breast cancer diagnosis in women with subglandular silicone gel-filled augmentation implants. Radiology 1995;194:859–62.
23. Cahan AC, Ashikari R, Pressman P, et al. Breast cancer after breast augmentation with silicone implants. Ann Surg Oncol 1995;2:121–5.
24. Ahn CY, DeBruhl ND, Gorczyca DP, et al. Comparative silicone breast implant evaluation using mammography, sonography, and magnetic resonance imaging: experience with 59 implants. Plast Reconstr Surg 1994;94:620–7.
25. Berg WA, Caskey CI, Hamper UM, et al. Single- and double-lumen silicone breast implant integrity: prospective evaluation of MR and US criteria. Radiology 1995;197:45–52.
26. Orel SG. MR imaging of the breast. Magn Reson Imaging Clin N Am 2001;9:273–88.
27. Hollingsworth AB, Stough RG. The emerging role of breast magnetic resonance imaging. J Okla State Med Assoc 2003;96:299–307.
28. Kvistad KA, Gribbestad IS, Haraldseth O, Nilsen G. [Diagnosis of breast diseases with magnetic resonance tomography]. Tidsskr Nor Laegeforen 2000;120:1451–8.
29. Kerlikowske K. Efficacy of screening mammography among women aged 40 to 49 years and 50 to 69 years: comparison of relative and absolute benefit. J Natl Cancer Inst Monogr 1997;79–86.
30. Smart CR, Hendrick RE, Rutledge JH III, Smith RA. Benefit of mammography screening in women ages 40 to 49

years. Current evidence from randomized controlled trials. Cancer 1995;75:1619–26.

31. Jakub JW, Ebert MD, Cantor A, et al. Breast cancer in patients with prior augmentation: presentation, stage, and lymphatic mapping. Plast Reconstr Surg 2004;114:1737–42.
32. Miglioretti DL, Rutter CM, Geller BM, et al. Effect of breast augmentation on the accuracy of mammography and cancer characteristics. JAMA 2004;291:442–50.
33. Spear SL, Slack C, Howard MA. Postmastectomy reconstruction of the previously augmented breast: diagnosis, staging, methodology, and outcome. Plast Reconstr Surg 2001;107:1167–76.
34. Cahan AC, Ashikari R, Pressman P, et al. Breast cancer after breast augmentation with silicone implants. Ann Surg Oncol 1995;2:121–5.
35. Leibman AJ, Kruse BD. Imaging of breast cancer after augmentation mammoplasty. Ann Plast Surg 1993;30:111–5.
36. Skinner KA, Silberman H, Dougherty W, et al. Breast cancer after augmentation mammoplasty. Ann Surg Oncol 2001;8:138–44.
37. Silverstein MJ, Handel N, Gamagami P, et al. Breast cancer in women after augmentation mammoplasty. Arch Surg 1988;123:681–5.
38. Reintgen D, Berman C, Cox C, et al. The anatomy of missed breast cancers. Surg Oncol 1993;2:65–75.
39. Pendas S, Giuliano R, Swor G, et al. Worldwide experience with lymphatic mapping for invasive breast cancer. Semin Oncol 2004;31:318–23.
40. Bold RJ, Schlieman M, Fahy BN. Sentinel lymph node biopsy for breast cancer. Cancer Biother Radiopharm 2001;16:347–57.
41. Gray RJ, Forstner-Barthell AW, Pockaj BA, et al. Breast-conserving therapy and sentinel lymph node biopsy are feasible in cancer patients with previous implant breast augmentation. Am J Surg 2004;188:122–5.
42. Fisher B, Anderson S, Bryant J, et al. Twenty-year follow-up of a randomized trial comparing total mastectomy, lumpectomy, and lumpectomy plus irradiation for the treatment of invasive breast cancer. N Engl J Med 2002; 347:1233–41.
43. Veronesi U, Cascinelli N, Mariani L, et al. Twenty-year follow-up of a randomized study comparing breast-conserving surgery with radical mastectomy for early breast cancer. N Engl J Med 2002;347:1227–32.
44. Karanas YL, Leong DS, Da Lio A, et al. Surgical treatment of breast cancer in previously augmented patients. Plast Reconstr Surg 2003;111:1078–83.
45. Morrow M, Strom EA, Bassett LW, et al. Standard for breast conservation therapy in the management of invasive breast carcinoma. CA Cancer J Clin 2002;52:277–300.
46. Ryu J, Yahalom J, Shank B, et al. Radiation therapy after breast augmentation or reconstruction in early or recurrent breast cancer. Cancer 1990;66:844–7.
47. Cordeiro PG, Pusic AL, Disa JJ, et al. Irradiation after immediate tissue expander/implant breast reconstruction: outcomes, complications, aesthetic results, and satisfaction among 156 patients. Plast Reconstr Surg 2004;113:877–81.
48. Kuske RR, Schuster R, Klein E, et al. Radiotherapy and breast reconstruction: clinical results and dosimetry. Int J Radiat Oncol Biol Phys 1991;21:339–46.
49. Chu FC, Kaufmann TP, Dawson GA, et al. Radiation therapy of cancer in prosthetically augmented or reconstructed breasts. Radiology 1992;185:429–33.
50. Krueger EA, Wilkins EG, Strawderman M, et al. Complications and patient satisfaction following expander/implant breast reconstruction with and without radiotherapy. Int J Radiat Oncol Biol Phys 2001;49:713–21.
51. Victor SJ, Brown DM, Horwitz EM, et al. Treatment outcome with radiation therapy after breast augmentation or reconstruction in patients with primary breast carcinoma. Cancer 1998;82:1303–9.
52. Mark RJ, Zimmerman RP, Greif JM. Capsular contracture after lumpectomy and radiation therapy in patients who have undergone uncomplicated bilateral augmentation mammoplasty. Radiology 1996;200:621–5.
53. Fredriksson I, Liljegren G, Arnesson LG, et al. Local recurrence in the breast after conservative surgery—a study of prognosis and prognostic factors in 391 women. Eur J Cancer 2002;38:1860–70.
54. Slavin SA, Love SM, Sadowsky NL. Reconstruction of the radiated partial mastectomy defect with autogenous tissues. Plast Reconstr Surg 1992;90:854–65.
55. Hamdi M, Van Landuyt K, Monstrey S, Blondeel P. Pedicled perforator flaps in breast reconstruction: a new concept. Br J Plast Surg 2004;57:531–9.
56. Carlson GW, Moore B, Thornton JF, et al. Breast cancer after augmentation mammaplasty: treatment by skin-sparing mastectomy and immediate reconstruction. Plast Reconstr Surg 2001;107:687–92.
57. Schirber S, Thomas WO, Finley JM, et al. Breast cancer after mammary augmentation. South Med J 1993;86:263–8.
58. Clark CP III, Peters GN, O'Brien KM. Cancer in the augmented breast. Diagnosis and prognosis. Cancer 1993; 72:2170–4.
59. Singletary SE, Robb GL. Oncologic safety of skin-sparing mastectomy. Ann Surg Oncol 2003;10:95–7.
60. Carlson GW, Styblo TM, Lyles RH, et al. The use of skin sparing mastectomy in the treatment of breast cancer: The Emory experience. Surg Oncol 2003;12:265–9.
61. Grotting JC, Beckenstein MS, Arkoulakis NS. The art and science of autologous breast reconstruction. Breast J 2003;9:350–60.
62. Shaw WW. Superior gluteal free flap breast reconstruction. Clin Plast Surg 1998;25:267–74.
63. Allen RJ. The superior gluteal artery perforator flap. Clin Plast Surg 1998;25:293–302.
64. Elliott LF, Beegle PH, Hartrampf CR Jr. The lateral transverse thigh free flap: an alternative for autogenous-tissue breast reconstruction. Plast Reconstr Surg 1990;85:169–78.
65. Young VL, Nemecek JR, Nemecek DA. The efficacy of breast augmentation: breast size increase, patient satisfaction, and psychological effects. Plast Reconstr Surg 1994;94:958–69.
66. Sarwer DB, Bartlett SP, Bucky LP, et al. Bigger is not always better: body image dissatisfaction in breast reduction and breast augmentation patients. Plast Reconstr Surg 1998; 101:1956–61.
67. Birtchnell S, Whitfield P, Lacey JH. Motivational factors in women requesting augmentation and reduction mammaplasty. J Psychosom Res 1990;34:509–14.
68. Carlson GW, Curley SA, Martin JE, et al. The detection of breast cancer after augmentation mammaplasty. Plast Reconstr Surg 1993;91:837–40.

27

Breast Cancer in the Irradiated Breast

WILLIAM D. BLOOMER
MICHAEL A. LACOMBE

The role of radiation therapy in the management of breast cancer continues to evolve. Historically, mastectomy was the treatment of choice. Radiation therapy was used as a supplement to surgical therapies when it was realized that simple, radical, and even extended radical mastectomies were all associated with unacceptable rates of local failures on the chest wall or in the axilla. Fletcher demonstrated the efficacy of radiation therapy in preventing local recurrence and reported a dose-response curve for control of regional adenopathy.[1]

The use of radiation therapy as an effective alternative to mastectomy arose from the pioneering studies of Baclesse and colleagues at the Fondation Curie in Paris in the 1930s, and was later popularized in North America by Crile at the Cleveland Clinic and by Peters in Toronto.[2–4] Subsequent rigorous sequential randomized trials by Fisher and the National Surgical Adjuvant Breast and Bowel Project cooperative group demonstrated the efficacy of lumpectomy and radiation as an equally effective alternative to mastectomy.[5]

Breast conservation therapy is now clearly established as the standard of care for early-stage breast cancer, and received National Institutes of Health endorsement in 1992.[6] It is possible that there may exist subsets of women whose risk of local recurrence in the breast after lumpectomy is low enough to preclude breast irradiation, but none has yet been identified. Although a recently reported study comparing tamoxifen to breast irradiation in elderly women with early breast cancer showed comparable overall survival, the relative risk of a locoregional recurrence was 6 to 8 times greater in unirradiated patients receiving only tamoxifen.[7]

BREAST CONSERVATION FAILURES

Rates of local recurrence after conservative surgery and radiotherapy range from 3 to 19%, depending on the reporting center and eligibility criteria.[5,8–13] Failure to require negative resection margins at the lumpectomy site, as in a National Cancer Institute study, leads to an unacceptably high local failure rate.[8] Local recurrences in mastectomy treated patients range from 4 to 14%. A meta-analysis of randomized trials demonstrated equivalent survival between mastectomy and limited surgery plus radiotherapy.[14] Furthermore, a threefold reduction in local recurrence was observed when radiation was added to lumpectomy.

Factors predicting the risk for local recurrence after conservative surgery and irradiation can be classified as patient related, tumor related, and/or treatment related. Age at diagnosis is a predictive indicator, with younger women being at higher risk, regardless of whether breast conservation therapy or mastectomy was the initial treatment.[15,16]

Multifocality in more than one quadrant of the breast is a contraindication to breast conservation because of a high local failure rate.[17,18] Multifocality is presumed to indicate a large subclinical tumor burden that is not controllable with the standard (4,500 to 5,000 cGy) dosage typically used in whole-breast irradiation. On the other hand, mastectomy for multifocal disease does not result in an increased risk of local recurrence.[19]

Historically, it was thought that extensive ductal carcinoma in situ within the lumpectomy specimen portended a high local recurrence rate.[20] However, when re-evaluated in association with negative resection margins for both invasive and in situ disease, no increase in local recurrence was observed.[21,22]

Lobular carcinoma in situ within the lumpectomy specimen does not affect local control.[23] Although invasive lobular carcinoma has different manifestations mammographically and histologically than infiltrating ductal carcinoma, it does not per se adversely affect local control.[24]

Although the definition of clear resection margins varies, adequacy of the lumpectomy resection margins is the single most important factor determining the risk of local recurrence after breast conservation therapy. Whereas the absence of tumor at the inked resection margins is defined by some authors as any negative margin, other authors use 1 to 3 mm of normal breast tissue to define and differentiate a negative margin from a close margin. These distinctions notwithstanding, there appears to be a consistently significant decrease in local control with anything less than negative margins.[25,26] The risk of residual tumor within the breast after local excision is a continuum based upon margin distance from the tumor.[27] Re-excision of questionable lumpectomy resection margins is more important than boost irradiation to the lumpectomy site after whole-breast irradiation.[28,29]

The question of whether a breast cancer developing years after lumpectomy and radiotherapy represents relapse or a new primary cancer can be difficult to resolve. Identifying a new cancer is straightforward, if it develops in a totally different quadrant of the breast and/or is of a different histopathologic type. Location of the recurrence in relation to the initial tumor, the time interval between events, and the presence or absence of diffuse disease in the surrounding stroma may help distinguish between recurrence and new tumor. Furthermore, differences in DNA ploidy detectable by flow cytometry are more likely in a second primary tumor than in a true recurrence.[30]

Although much attention is devoted to in-breast recurrences and/or new tumors after successful treatment of early breast cancer, women who experienced breast irradiation in childhood or as a young adult are also at increased risk of developing breast cancers later in life. One of the unintended consequences of successful cancer treatment is the risk of developing late treatment-related complications. Perhaps nowhere is this more of an issue than in cancers involving children and young adults, where increasingly successful therapies are leading to cures and otherwise normal life expectancies.

HODGKIN'S DISEASE AND SUBSEQUENT BREAST CANCER

Radiation therapy played a decisive role in establishing curative therapies for Hodgkin's disease. Especially in its early stages, Hodgkin's disease became a highly curative disease through the pioneering work of Kaplan, who adapted the linear accelerator to medical use and systematically used sequential clinical trials to stage and document the efficacy of radiation therapy and chemotherapy in curing this previously fatal disease, albeit one with an often long natural history.[31]

The mainstay of upper body radiation therapy for Hodgkin's disease is the field irradiation, using parallel-opposed anterior and posterior ports to treat peripheral and central lymph node bearing regions. One of the unintended consequences of such treatment, however, is substantial bilateral breast irradiation. Radiation carcinogenesis for the later development of breast cancer is inversely related to age of up to 30 to 35 years, beyond which there does not appear to be any increased age-related risk.[32–34] Age at irradiation is particularly relevant, because Hodgkin's disease is often a disease of adolescents and young adults, many of whom are women with mediastinal disease. The latent period for breast carcinogenesis is more than 15 years and easily as long as 20 to 30 years.

Although the use of radiation therapy in Hodgkin's disease has been waning in recent years, the cohort of women treated 20 to 30 years ago is now at an age where the natural incidence of breast cancer rises dramatically without accounting for any increased incidence associated with prior mantle field irradiation.[35,36] In one study of 3,817 women treated for Hodgkin's disease under the age of

30 years, between 1965 and 1994, 105 developed breast cancer.[37] The risk was lower, however, in women who had suffered ovarian damage from radiation or chemotherapy, indicating the role of hormonal milieu in breast cancer etiology.

Because of the heightened awareness and excellent therapeutic results of breast conservation therapy, women developing breast cancer after mantle field irradiation want to be spared the harsh emotional experience of a mastectomy.

ALTERNATIVES TO MASTECTOMY

Mastectomy has been the generally accepted treatment for a local or in-breast recurrence after previous lumpectomy and whole-breast irradiation.[38,39] Such recurrences develop at a rate of 1 to 2% per year of follow-up.[40,41] Recurrences developing within the first 3 to 5 years of initial treatment most likely represent failures of the initial therapy.[30] With longer disease-free intervals, the probability of the recurrence representing a new cancer rises significantly, and alternatives to mastectomy pose an interesting and fertile area for clinical investigation.

Re-irradiation for local recurrences in other body sites such as the brain, lung, and head and neck area are being reported with some frequency, often with acceptable toxicities for tumors at these sites. Unfortunately, the survival of patients with recurrences at these sites is usually limited, and long-term normal tissue effects cannot be assessed. This is in marked contrast to the long natural history of breast cancer after local recurrence.

The rationale for re-irradiation grew out of efforts to improve upon the results of re-excision only for in-breast tumor recurrences. In 1991, Kurtz reported on 55 women treated by re-excision only of locally recurrent breast cancer.[42] His reported local failure rate of 27% compared favorably with those reported after mastectomy in several contemporaneous reports.[38,43] In a more recent report from Milan, the local recurrence rate after mastectomy was much lower after mastectomy (4%) compared with re-excision (19%), but 5-year survival was better with re-excision (85%) than with mastectomy (70%).[44] Because of the small numbers of patients and lack of randomization, these differences are probably not clinically meaningful. Nonetheless, it is reasonable to say that repeat breast conservation may be an acceptable alternative to mastectomy in selected and motivated women desiring breast conservation. The selection criteria for breast re-irradiation after initial whole-breast radiation therapy are straightforward (Table 27–1). They include the time interval between initial therapy and recurrence, absence of late radiation changes, and disease parameters of the new lesion. Various radiation techniques have been proposed to improve local control and may become the subject of clinical trials.[45]

Re-irradiation Techniques

Breast re-irradiation can be accomplished using standard external-beam photons and/or electrons, catheter-based high-dose rate (HDR) or low-dose rate (LDR) brachytherapy, or intraoperative radiation therapy (IORT). Although IORT is under investigation with de novo breast cancer, it is unlikely to gain wide acceptance because of the need for a dedicated and expensive piece of equipment with low volume usage, as well as scheduling issues involving the operating room and specialists' time.[46] Skin and chest wall complications necessarily resulting from unidimensional application of the radiation with this equipment in the operating room may also limit its use.

Brachytherapy using linear tube catheters or a balloon catheter such as MammoSite are enjoying considerable attention, but in the authors' opinion, are unlikely to withstand the test of time.[47] Brachytherapy was used for many years to boost the radiation dose at the lumpectomy site in de novo breast cancer after whole-breast external-beam treatment, but has long since been replaced by electron beam therapy because of greater patient acceptance, ease of application, and consistently better cosmetic results.[48]

Conventional tangential external-beam irradiation using wedged or compensated ports has been the

Table 27–1. SELECTION FACTORS FOR BREAST RE-IRRADIATION
Interval from initial treatment (usually 3 years minimum)
Absence of late radiation changes in skin or breast tissue
Early T stage of new lesion (3 cm or less)
Absence of positive axillary lymph nodes with new lesion

mainstay of whole-breast re-irradiation. However, computed tomography simulation and sophisticated computer-based treatment planning systems, together with computer-driven collimation on linear accelerators, have made possible three-dimensional conformal radiation and intensity modulated radiation therapy (IMRT). IMRT is a noninvasive technology that permits individualized sculpting of the target tumor volume for either whole-breast or partial-breast irradiation. It represents a further extension of three-dimensional conformal technology, in that modulation of photon beam intensity allows even greater sparing of normal tissues without compromising dose to the target volume. For all these reasons, IMRT is likely to dominate breast re-irradiation techniques in the future.

Figure 27–1 illustrates the dosimetric differences between conventional tangents and IMRT radiation to the whole breast. The various isodose lines depict the distribution of dose delivered to the breast as percentages of the dose prescribed to the breast target volume. Simple visual inspection of the two graphic plans demonstrates greater sparing of dose to both the heart and the lung in a left-sided breast lesion using IMRT. The accompanying dose volume histograms quantify the magnitude of these substantial differences.

It is unusual for current conventional tangents to cause long-term normal-tissue damage in women with de novo breast cancer. In women with histories of prior breast irradiation using mantle field irradiation for Hodgkin's disease, however, it seems both

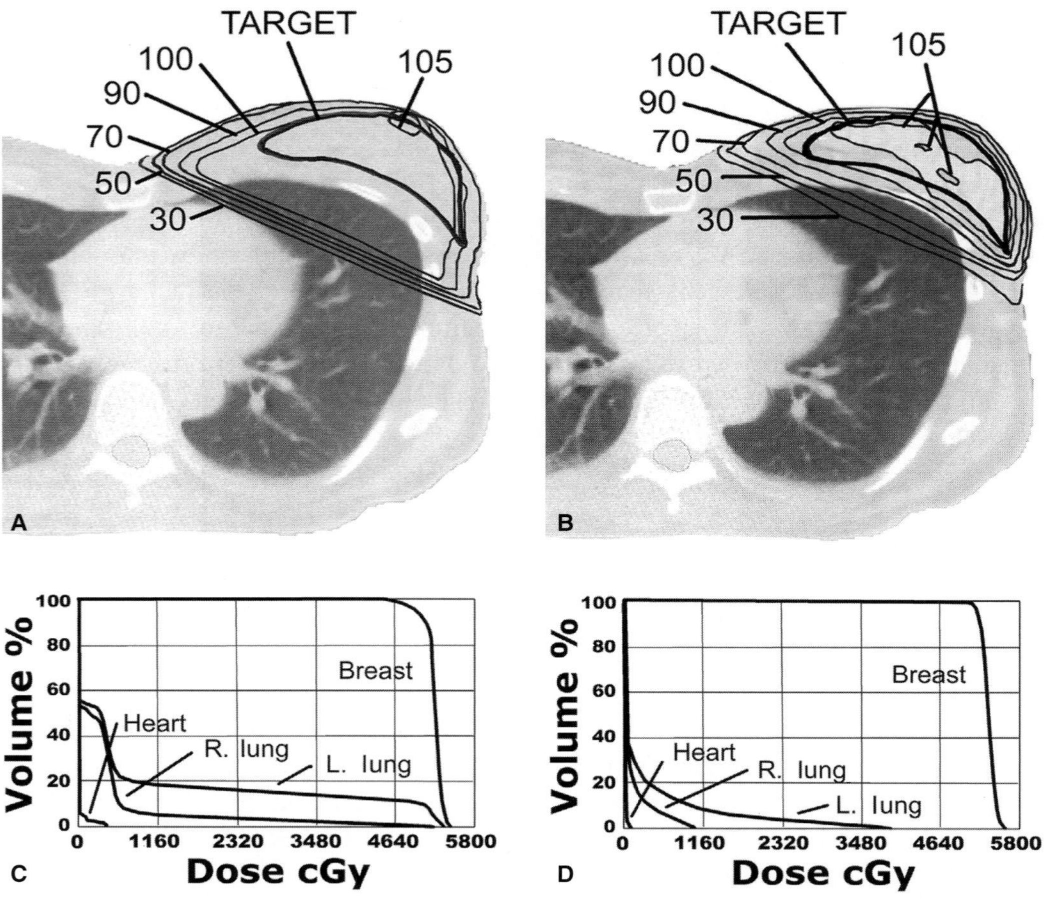

Figure 27–1. Comparison of whole-breast irradiation using conventional tangents *A*, *C*, or intensity modulated radiation therapy (IMRT; twice daily). The isodose lines depicted in *A* and *B*, are representations of percentages of the dose prescribed to the whole breast (target volume), as identified by computed tomography simulation. Dose volume histograms *C*, *D*, quantify the significant sparing of the dose to the underlying lung and heart, when IMRT is used.

prudent and justifiable to use IMRT, if significantly greater sparing of important normal tissue, such as the heart, results.

Accelerated Fractionation

Accelerated fractionation for de novo breast cancer has gained considerable press coverage in recent years, especially after approval from the Food and Drug Administration was granted for the MammoSite balloon catheter for interstitial brachytherapy. The motivation for accelerated fractionation is several-fold: more efficient use of existing equipment in resource-challenged countries, transportation difficulties for the elderly, and work-related issues for women whose careers require extensive travel. Many programs use twice-a-day fractionation, which benefits the concerns of women who travel but causes extra burdens for those dependent on outside sources of transportation, especially if travel times to the treatment facility are substantial. It is probably still too early to assess long-term cosmetic changes resulting from twice-a-day fractionation schemes. On the other hand, Whelan and colleagues have reported results in Canada of accelerated once-a-day fractionation for breast cancer.[49] Using 16 fractions of 265 cGy each to the whole breast without lumpectomy site boosts, they report excellent survival and cosmetic results with a median follow-up of almost 6 years. Our experience with IMRT and accelerated partial breast irradiation confirms the Canadian experience.[50]

RE-IRRADIATION RESULTS

A recent publication from several centers in France reported experience with brachytherapy, together with an excellent compilation of literature data on the subject.[51] No randomized trials exist. All the available data represent selected single or multi-institutional experiences. Based upon this compilation, the second local recurrence rates after mastectomy ranged between 5 and 48%. The local recurrence rates after some form of re-irradiation were in the same broad range of 5 to 44%. Five-year overall survivals, when reported, were not dissimilar, and ranged widely between 50 and 97%. It is difficult to draw conclusions from the brachytherapy experiences because of nonconformity in requiring clear resection margins after excision of the recurrence, as well as wide variations in time dose fractionation and technique. Nonetheless, there does appear to be the suggestion of a dose-response effect for local control with LDR brachytherapy, but at a significant risk of grades 3 to 4 toxicity.

The external-beam experience with partial-breast re-irradiation to the site of recurrence is much less heterogeneous. The initial experience at the University of Pittsburgh has been more recently updated by Deutsch.[52,53] A total of 39 women with in-breast recurrences were treated with repeat lumpectomies, with 34 women having achieved clear resection margins. The radiation treatment plan was 5,000 cGy in 25 fractions using 6 to 14 MV electrons just to the excision site. The median time to recurrence in the initial report was 2.9 years, but lengthened to 5.3 years in the updated report. There were no late sequelae to the radiation, and 30 women (78%) retained their breasts. With a median follow-up of 4.3 years, overall survival was 78% and disease-free survival was 69%.

Our evolving personal experience at Evanston Northwestern Healthcare with in-breast tumor recurrences supports the Pittsburgh experience. We require clear resection margins for eligibility. Although we use electron beam therapy for recurrences in the upper inner quadrant of the breast, we use IMRT to the lumpectomy site for recurrences elsewhere in the breast (Figure 27–2). Dose fractionation is usually 4,500 cGy, in 250 cGy fractions. While we have had no recurrences after this treatment, follow-up is short. Cosmetic results are uniformly good but somewhat better with IMRT than with electrons because of less skin hyperpigmentation. No late sequelae have been encountered to date.

Breast conservation therapy is not contraindicated in women developing breast cancer years after mantle irradiation for Hodgkin's disease or lymphoma.[54,55] Twelve patients treated at the University of Pittsburgh and Evanston Northwestern Healthcare, who received conventional whole-breast irradiation of 5,000 cGy and a 900 cGy boost to the lumpectomy site, had no unusual acute or late sequelae and experienced good to excellent cosmesis.

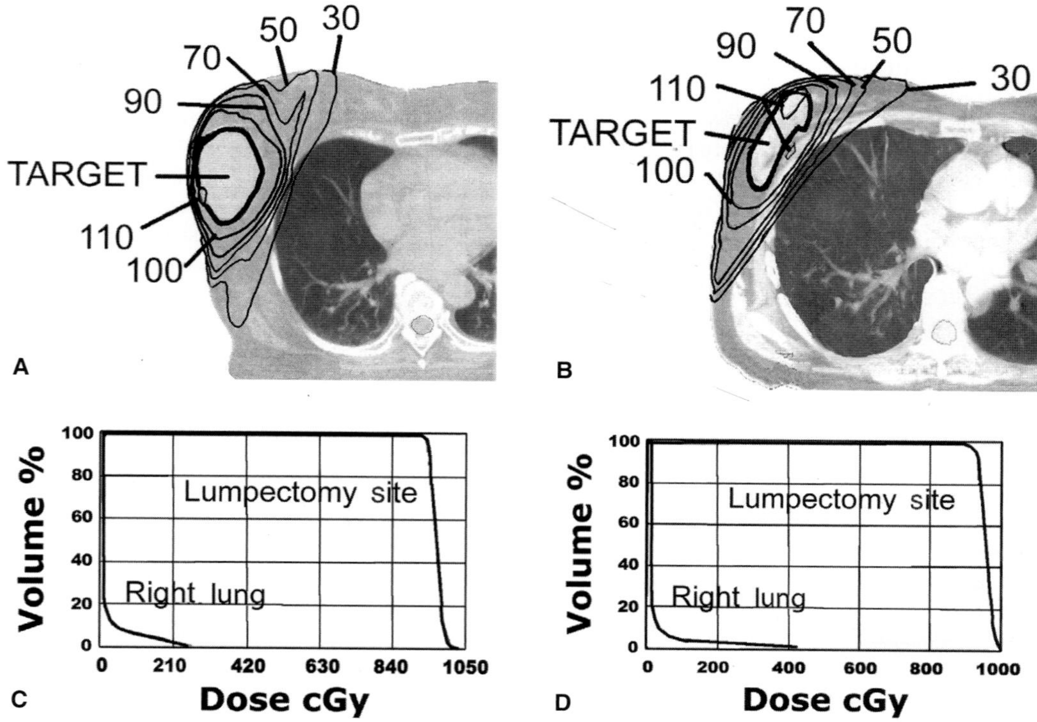

Figure 27–2. Representative isodose distributions using intensity modulated radiation therapy (IMRT) for partial-breast irradiation of two very differently shaped lumpectomy sites (target volume). Doses are expressed as percentages of the dose prescribed to the target volume. IMRT allows individualized sculpting of the dose to irregularly shaped target volumes.

Accelerated partial-breast irradiation using IMRT may also be appropriate in these cases.

The one case of soft tissue necrosis reported by Stanford University, 6 years after 4,560 cGy irradiation to the whole breast plus a 1,500 cGy boost to the lumpectomy site in the upper inner quadrant, suggests caution with inner quadrant lesions and attention to detailed dosimetry in this area where hot spots can occur from the overlap with initial mantle irradiation.[56] Intraoperative radiotherapy has been successfully reported from Milan.[57]

CONCLUSIONS

Breast conservation therapy is an attractive alternative to mastectomy for women with locally recurrent breast cancer after earlier lumpectomy and radiotherapy or prior mantle irradiation for Hodgkin's disease. Earlier concerns about excess normal-tissue damage can be allayed on the basis of the aggregated clinical experience and the promise of new technologies. IMRT or even less-sophisticated three-dimensional conformal radiation will likely supplant brachytherapy in these cases, because of greater patient acceptance and ease of application.

REFERENCES

1. Fletcher GH. Local results of irradiation in the primary management of localized breast cancer. Cancer 1972;29: 545–51.
2. Baclesse F, Gricouroff G, Talibefer A. Essai de roentgen therapie du cancer sein suivie d'operation large: resultats histologiques. Bull Cancer 1939;28:729–43.
3. Crile GC Jr. Management of breast cancer: limited mastectomy. Int J Radiat Oncol Biol Phys 1977;2:969–73.
4. Peters MV. Cutting the "Gordian Knot" in early breast cancer. Ann R Coll Phys Surg Can 1975;8:186–91.
5. Fisher B, Anderson S, Redmond CK. Reanalysis and results after 12 years of follow-up in a randomized clinical trial comparing total mastectomy with lumpectomy with or without irradiation in the treatment of breast cancer. N Engl J Med 1995;333:1456–61.
6. National Institutes of Health Consensus Development Panel. Consensus statement: treatment of early-stage breast cancer. J Natl Cancer Inst Monogr 1992;11:1–5.
7. Hughes KS, Schnaper LA, Berry D, et al. Lumpectomy plus tamoxifen with or without irradiation in women 70 years

of age or order with early breast cancer. N Engl J Med 2004;351:971–7.
8. Lichter AS, Lippmann ME, Danforth DN Jr, et al. Mastectomy versus breast conserving therapy in the treatment of stage I and II carcinoma of the breast: a randomized trial at the National Cancer Institute. J Clin Oncol 1992;10:976–83.
9. Jacobson JA, Danforth DN, Cowan KH, et al. Ten-year results of a comparison of conservation with mastectomy in the treatment of stage I and II breast cancer. N Engl J Med 1995;332:901–11.
10. Veronesi U, Luini A, Galimberti V, Zurrida S. Conservation approaches for the management of stage I/II carcinoma of the breast: Milan Cancer Institute Trials. World J Surg 1994;18:70–5.
11. Van Dongen JA, Bartelink H, Fentiman IS, et al. Randomized clinical trial to assess the value of breast-conserving therapy in stage I and II breast cancer: EORTC 10801 trial. J Natl Cancer Inst 1992;11:15–8.
12. Blichert-Toft M, Rose C, Anderson JA, et al. Danish randomized trial comparing breast conservation therapy with mastectomy: six years of life table analysis. J Natl Cancer Inst Monogr 1992;11:19–25.
13. Arriagada R, Le MG, Rochard F, Contesso G. Conservative treatment versus mastectomy in early breast cancer: patterns of failure with 15 years of follow-up data. Institut Gustave-Roussy Breast Cancer Group. J Clin Oncol 1996;14:1558–64.
14. Early Breast Cancer Trialists' Collaborative Group. Effects of radiotherapy and surgery in early breast cancer. N Engl J Med 1995;333:1444–55.
15. Fowble BL, Schultz DJ, Overmoyer B, et al. The influence of young age on outcome in early stage breast cancer. Int J Radiat Oncol Biol Phys 1994;30:23–33.
16. Donegan WL, Perez-Mesa CM, Watson FR. A biostatistical study of locally recurrent breast carcinoma. Surg Gyn Obstet 1966;122:529–40.
17. Fowble B. Radiotherapeutic considerations in the treatment of primary breast cancer. J Natl Cancer Inst Monogr 1992;11;49–58.
18. Recht A, Harris JR. Selection of patients with early stage breast cancer for conservative surgery and radiation. Oncology 1990;4:23–30.
19. Fowble B, Yeh I, Schultz DJ, et al. The role of mastectomy in patients with stage I-II breast cancer presenting with gross multifocal or multicentric disease or diffuse calcifications. Int J Radiat Oncol Biol Phys 1993;27:567–73.
20. Schnitt SJ, Connolly J, Khettry V, et al. Pathologic findings on reexcision of the primary site in breast cancer patients considered for treatment by primary radiation therapy. Cancer 1997;59:675–81.
21. Hurd TC, Sneige N, Allen PK, et al. Impact of extensive intraductal component on recurrence in patients with stage I or II breast cancer treated with breast conservation therapy. Ann Surg Oncol 1997;4:119–24.
22. Schnitt SJ, Abner A, Gelman R, et al. The relationship between microscopic margins of resection and the risk of local recurrence in patients with breast cancer treated with breast-conserving surgery and radiation therapy. Cancer 1994;74:1746–51.
23. Moran M, Haffty BG. Lobular carcinoma in situ as a component of breast cancer: the long-term outcome in patients treated with breast-conserving therapy. Int J Radiat Oncol Biol Phys 1998;40:353–8.
24. Schnitt SJ, Connolly JL, Recht A, et al. Influence of infiltrating lobular histology on local tumor control in breast cancer patients treated with conservative surgery and radiotherapy. Cancer 1989;64:448–54.
25. Anscher MS, Jones P, Prosnitz LR, et al. Local failure and margin status in early stage breast carcinoma treated with conservative surgery and radiation therapy. Ann Surg 1993;218:22–8.
26. Heimann R, Powers C, Halpern HJ, et al. Breast preservation in stage I and II carcinoma of the breast. The University of Chicago experience. Cancer 1996;78:1722–30.
27. Holland R, Veling SH, Mravunac M, Hendriks JH. Histologic multifocality of Tis, T1-2 breast carcinomas. Implications for clinical trials of breast conserving surgery. Cancer 1985;56:979–90.
28. Wazer DE, Schmidt-Ulrich RK, Ruthazer R, et al. Factors determining outcome for breast-conserving irradiation with margin-directed dose escalation to the tumor bed. Int J Radiat Oncol Biol Phys 1998;40:851–8.
29. Smitt MC, Nowels KW, Zdeblick MJ, et al. The importance of the lumpectomy surgical margin status in long-term results of breast conservation. Cancer 1995;76:259–67.
30. Smith TE, Lee D, Turner BC, et al. True recurrence vs. new primary ipsilateral breast tumor relapse: an analysis of clinical and pathologic differences and their implications in natural history, prognoses, and therapeutic management. Int J Radiat Oncol Biol Phys 2000;48:1281–9.
31. Kaplan HS. Hodgkin's disease. Cambridge: Harvard University Press; 1972.
32. Li FP, Corkery J, Vawter G, et al. Breast carcinoma after cancer therapy in childhood. Cancer 1983;51:521–3.
33. Waterhouse JAH, Prior MP. Breast cancer in young women. BMJ 1975;3:434.
34. Baral E, Larsson LE, Mattson B. Breast cancer following irradiation of the breast. Cancer 1977;40:2905–10.
35. Lipsztein R, Dalton JF, Bloomer WD. Sequelae of breast irradiation. JAMA 1985;253:3582–4.
36. Clemon M, Loijens L, Goss P. Breast cancer risk following irradiation for Hodgkin's disease. Cancer Treat Rev 2000;26:291–302.
37. Travis LB, Hill DA, Doves GM, et al. Breast cancer following radiotherapy and chemotherapy among young women with Hodgkin's disease. JAMA 2003;290:529–31.
38. Osborne MP, Borgen PI, Wong GY, et al. Salvage mastectomy for local and regional recurrence after breast-conserving operation and radiation therapy. Surg Gynecol Obstet 1992;174:189–94.
39. Abner AL, Recht A, Eberlein T, et al. Prognosis following salvage mastectomy for recurrence in the breast after conservative surgery and radiation therapy for early stage breast cancer. J Clin Oncol 1993;11:44–8.
40. Veronesi U, Cascinelli N, Mariani L, et al. Twenty-year follow-up of a randomized study comparing breast-conserving surgery with radical mastectomy for early breast cancer. N Engl J Med 2002;347:1227–32.
41. Fisher B, Anderson S, Bryant J, et al. Twenty-year follow-up of a randomized trial comparing total mastectomy,

lumpectomy, and lumpectomy plus irradiation for the treatment of invasive breast cancer. N Engl J Med 2002; 347:1233–41.

42. Kurtz JM, Jacquemier J, Amalric R, et al. Is breast conservation after local recurrence feasible? Eur J Cancer 1991;27:240–4.
43. Clarke DH, Le MG, Sarrozin D, et al. Analysis of local-regional relapses in patients with early breast cancer treated by excision and radiotherapy: experience of the Institut Gustave-Roussy. Int J Radiat Oncol Biol Phys 1985;11:137–45.
44. Salvador B, Marubini E, Miceli R, et al. Reoperation for locally recurrent breast cancer in patients previously treated with conservative surgery. Br J Surg 1999;86:84–7.
45. Kuerer HM, Arthur DW, Hoffty BG. Repeat breast-conserving surgery for in-breast local breast cancer recurrence. Cancer 2004;100:2269–80.
46. Veronesi U, Gott G, Luini A, et al. Full-dose intraoperative radiotherapy with electrons during breast-conserving surgery. Arch Surg 2003;138:1253–6.
47. Keisch M, Vicini F, Kuske RR, et al. Initial clinical experience with the Mammo Site breast brachytherapy applicator in women with early-stage breast cancer treated with breast-conserving therapy. Int J Radiat Oncol Biol Phys 2003;55:289–93.
48. Weber E, Hellman S. Radiation as primary treatment for local control of breast cancer. JAMA 1975;234:609–11.
49. Whelan T, Mackenzie R, Julian J, et al. Randomized trial of breast irradiation schedules after lumpectomy with lymph node negative breast cancer. J Natl Cancer Inst 2002; 94:1143–50.
50. LaCombe MA, Al-Najjar, McMahon J, et al. Accelerated partial breast irradiation using intensity modulated radiotherapy: dose-volume histogram comparison with standard breast irradiation [abstract]. Proceedings of the 2004 Annual Meeting of the American Society of Clinical Oncology. J Clin Oncol 2004;22:701.
51. Hannoun-Levi JM, Hounenaeghel G, Ellis S, et al. Partial breast irradiation as second conservative treatment for local breast cancer recurrence. Int J Radiat Oncol Biol Phys 2004;60:1385–92.
52. Mullen EE, Deutsch M, Bloomer WD. Salvage radiotherapy for local failures of lumpectomy and breast irradiation. Radiother Oncol 1997;42:25–9.
53. Deutsch M. Repeat high-dose external beam irradiation for in-breast tumor recurrence after previous lumpectomy and whole breast irradiation. Int J Radiat Oncol Biol Phys 2002;53:687–91.
54. Karasek K, Deutsch M. Lumpectomy and breast irradiation for breast cancer after radiotherapy for lymphoma. Am J Clin Oncol 1996;19:451–4.
55. Deutsch M, Gerszten K, Bloomer WD, Avisar E. Lumpectomy and breast irradiation for breast cancer arising after previous radiotherapy for Hodgkin's disease or lymphoma. Am J Clin Oncol 2001;24:33–4.
56. Wolden SL, Hancock SL, Carlson RW, et al. Management of breast cancer after Hodgkin's disease. J Clin Oncol 2000;18:765–72.
57. Intra M, Leonardi MC, Gotti G, et al. Intraoperative radiotherapy during breast conserving surgery in patients previously treated with radiotherapy for Hodgkin's disease. Tumori 2004;90:13–6.

28

Novel Radiation Therapy Techniques

RESHMA JAGSI
LORI PIERCE

ACCELERATED PARTIAL BREAST IRRADIATION

Rationale

Conventional radiation therapy to the breast following breast-conserving surgery results in high rates of local control for patients with early-stage breast cancer. Therefore, new radiation techniques for the treatment of these patients seek to minimize the cost, inconvenience, and/or toxicity associated with conventional therapy while still maintaining the high rates of local control that this therapy has allowed.

Conventional treatment has traditionally included radiation therapy to the whole breast with total doses of 45 to 50 Gy administered in 1.8 to 2 Gy daily fractions, followed in many centers by an additional 10 to 15 Gy boost dose to the tumor bed, for a total of 5 to 6 weeks of daily treatment.[1] Unfortunately, the cost and inconvenience of multiple weeks of radiation treatment may be a barrier to the utilization of breast-conserving therapy instead of mastectomy in some populations and may also partially explain the failure of some patients to receive the radiation therapy that is indicated following breast-conserving surgery.[2,3]

Hypo-fractionation is a strategy by which radiation dose is administered in fewer total fractions, with higher dose per fraction. Although a recent randomized trial suggests that hypo-fractionation allows similar rates of local control and cosmesis to that of conventional fractionation,[4] even the shorter schedule of hypo-fractionated irradiation of the whole breast involves 3 weeks of daily radiation treatments.

Investigators have explored the possibility of limiting the radiation field treated in breast cancer patients because it may be possible to administer even larger radiation fractions over a shorter time period with acceptable cosmesis if only a portion of the breast is treated. By shortening the treatment time, those developing these techniques of accelerated partial breast irradiation (APBI) hope that they may increase access to breast-conserving therapy for more women.[5] Moreover, some also hope that by decreasing the volume of irradiated tissue, these techniques may lead to a decrease in the already low rate of treatment-related toxicity that accompanies whole breast radiation with standard tangential fields. Furthermore, because chemotherapy is being used in increasing numbers of patients with earlier stage disease, the potential for using APBI so that neither radiation nor chemotherapy is delayed by the other is appealing.[6]

Data from several large studies have been taken by some to suggest that it may not be necessary to radiate the whole breast after lumpectomy in patients with early-stage disease as the majority of recurrences after breast-conserving therapy occur near the tumor bed, rather than elsewhere in the breast. In the Swedish trial of sector resection with or without adjuvant radiation, with nearly 10 years median follow-up, 67% of all local recurrences occurred in the surgical field.[7] The absolute rates of recurrence elsewhere in the breast are low not only among patients treated with radiation but also among those treated with conservative surgery alone. For example, after a median of 43 months of follow-up in the Canadian randomized trial assessing the effectiveness of whole breast irradiation after lumpectomy and axillary dissection, 108 of the 421 patients randomized to the control arm (no radiation) had experienced local breast relapses, of which 93 were at the site of initial surgery.[8] Among the 416 radiation-treated patients, 23 local breast relapses occurred, of which 19 were at the initial surgical site. Thus, the crude rate of failure outside the initial surgical site was 3.5% in the control arm and 0.9% in the radiation-treated arm. Therefore, whereas the addition of adjuvant radiation therapy in these and other large trials led to a significant reduction in the rate of local failure after breast-conserving surgery, some have speculated that it may not be necessary to treat the whole breast in selected patients, since most local failures occur near the tumor bed.

In a recent pathologic analysis of re-excision specimens from patients with early-stage breast cancer, Vicini and colleagues found residual disease in 38.2% of the 134 patients with negative margins (as defined as no tumor at the inked margin) on their initial excision specimen. In 90% of these cases, however, the residual disease did not extend beyond 10 mm from the initial lumpectomy cavity. The authors were able to predict all cases with extension beyond 10 mm by considering the maximum dimension ratio in addition to margin status of the invasive carcinoma, suggesting that it may be possible to identify the group of patients in whom partial breast irradiation might safely be administered.

Still, other data encourage caution regarding techniques in which only the region immediately surrounding the tumor bed is radiated. Prior pathologic analyses of mastectomy series have documented subclinical tumor deposits away from the tumor bed,[9–11] although their clinical relevance to the case of mammographically detected disease in the modern era is less clear. In any case, the results of the Milan III trial, in which patients with tumors less than 2.5 centimeters in size were randomized to quadrantectomy alone versus quadrantectomy and radiation, are sobering.[12] In that study, the rates of in-breast recurrence were significantly higher, with a crude cumulative incidence of 23.5% at 10 years, in the group of patients treated with quadrantectomy alone, as compared with only 5.8% in the radiation-treated arm. Because the surgical procedure was a full quadrantectomy, this suggests that failure to provide treatment outside the index quadrant can result in preventable recurrences, particularly in younger women. To the extent that partial breast irradiation provides a "radiation quadrantectomy" or even less, the results of the Milan III trial should temper the enthusiasm for partial breast irradiation until mature outcomes data are available regarding these techniques.

Thus, APBI is still an investigational technique, but one that has attracted a great deal of attention and interest. Those caring for patients with breast cancer should be acquainted with the various techniques by which partial breast irradiation (PBI) may be delivered as well as with the existing data exploring these techniques.

Techniques

Investigators have used a variety of methods by which to deliver partial breast irradiation, each with potential advantages and disadvantages. This section provides an overview of the preliminary results of various single institutional protocols and pilot collaborative studies that have been reported in the literature to date, closing with a discussion of the limited data available from Phase III studies.

Brachytherapy

Multi-catheter Implants. Prior to the widespread use and availability of electron beam therapy, multi-catheter interstitial brachytherapy was a common technique used to provide a boost dose of radiation to the tumor bed after external beam whole breast radiation. Investigators experienced in interstitial brachytherapy from this application initiated the first studies of partial breast irradiation. The majority of currently published studies of PBI have used this original technique.

Figure 28–1 shows a typical multi-catheter implant. Afterloading catheters are placed at the time of excision or as a separate procedure. After

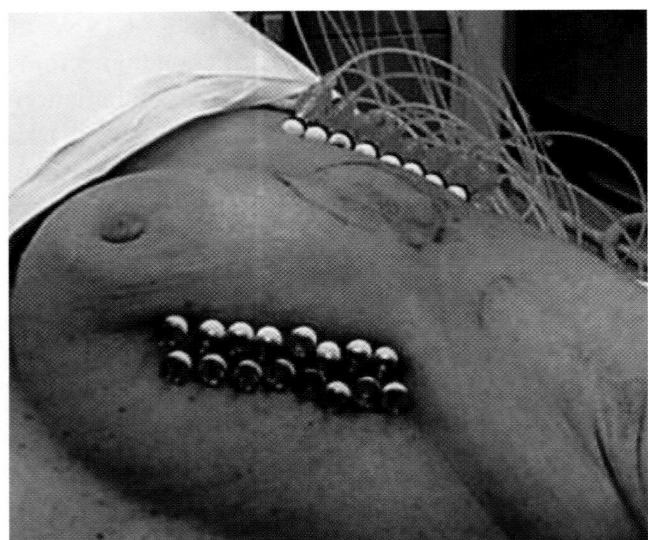

Figure 28–1. A typical multi-catheter brachytherapy implant.

confirming catheter positioning to be acceptable, radioactive sources are placed directly into the catheters, allowing for rapid dose fall-off in the surrounding tissues, as demonstrated in Figure 28–2. The radioactive sources may be selected to provide either a low-dose rate (LDR) of radiation, requiring several days of continuous exposure to achieve therapeutic dose, or high-dose rate (HDR) of radiation, allowing the full therapeutic dose to be administered in several short fractions administered periodically over several days.

To prevent the need for direct source handling in HDR brachytherapy, which would produce unacceptable levels of exposure to medical staff, a remotely controlled afterloading device is used, as pictured in Figure 28–3. This device automatically loads the source into the catheters on a cable, allows the source to dwell for a preprogrammed duration of time in different positions to achieve the optimal dose distribution, and then retracts the source back into a shielded safe. Thus, whereas HDR treatment must be administered in a shielded room, the treatment may be administered in several outpatient visits rather than the inpatient hospitalization that is necessary for LDR treatment.[13] Differences in dose rates lead to differences in radiobiologic effects owing to cellular repair mechanisms, such that the total iso-effective doses differ depending upon technique.[14]

An early series from Guy's Hospital, London,[15,16] reported a relatively high ipsilateral breast recurrence of 37% in patients treated with LDR brachytherapy alone after lumpectomy. The poor results in this series have been attributed to inadequate surgery, with positive margins in over half of the patients; improper patient selection; and poor technique, with small implant volume and inadequate dosimetry.

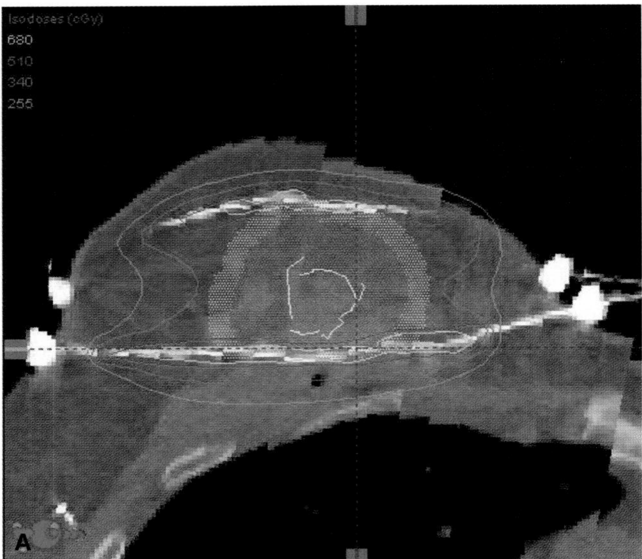

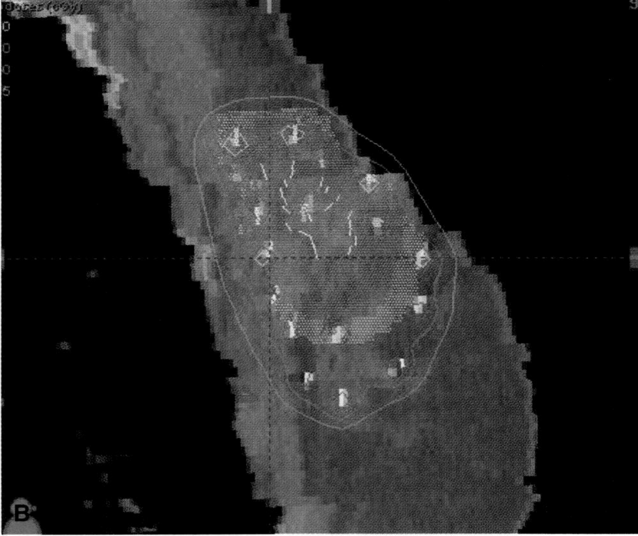

Figure 28–2. Dosimetry with a multi-catheter implant. The white line denotes the surgical resection cavity. The orange shading defines a clinical target volume including 1 cm of tissue around the cavity, and 100% of this volume receives 100% of the prescribed dose (340 cGy per fraction). The yellow shading denotes a volume extending to 1.5 cm beyond the surgical cavity, and 96% of this volume receives 100% of prescribed dose. Overall, 160 cc of tissue in this case received 100% of the prescribed dose; 30 cc received 150% of the prescribed dose; and 5 cc received 200% of the prescribed dose.

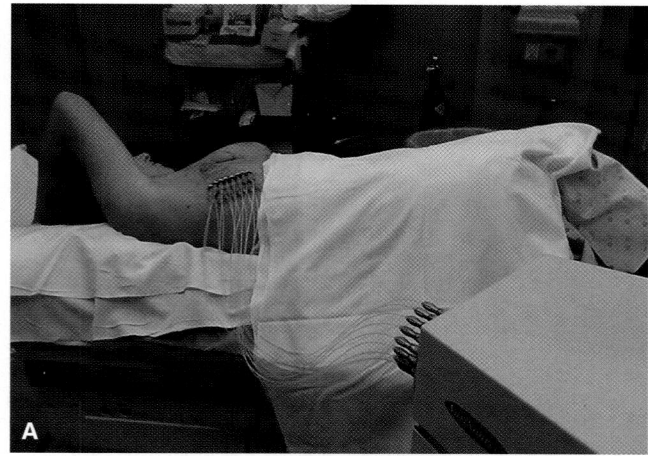

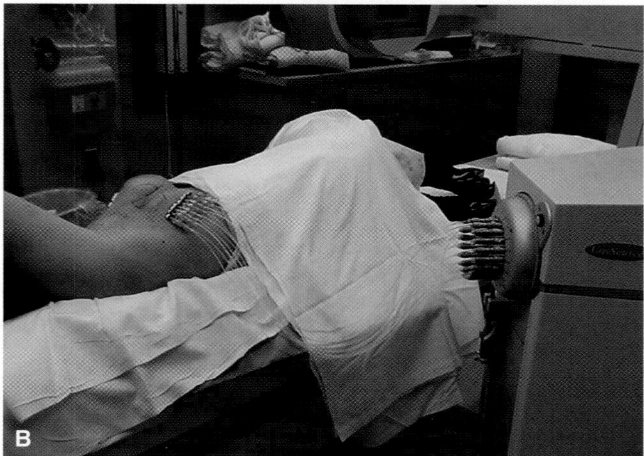

Figure 28–3. High-dose rate (HDR) afterloading device. Sources for HDR brachytherapy are loaded after connecting the catheters to the remote afterloading device.

More recent studies with proper patient selection and technique have not confirmed such high rates of local recurrence after brachytherapy.

The largest reported series of patients treated with multi-catheter brachytherapy to date is from the William Beaumont Hospital.[17–19] With a median follow-up of 65 months, there have been 5 local recurrences in this series of strictly selected patients, with a cumulative incidence of 1%. This rate of local recurrence was not statistically different from the rate of local recurrence found in a matched group of patients who received standard whole breast radiation. Infections were documented in 11% of patients, and fat necrosis in 21%, of which 78% were asymptomatic findings on mammography. Infection rates were higher with open (8.5%) versus closed (2.5%) cavity placement of the interstitial needles ($p = .005$).

A multi-institutional RTOG phase I/II study was initiated in 1995 to evaluate the outcomes of multi-catheter APBI administered via either HDR or LDR.[20] Patients were allowed to have 0 to 3 positive axillary nodes but no extracapsular extension. Preliminary results have been reported only in abstract form,[21,22] with an actuarial 4-year rate of breast recurrence of 3%. Breast failures occurred in 2 patients with T1N0 disease and in 1 with T1N1 disease, all treated with HDR. The 4-year nodal recurrence rate was also 3%. Nodal recurrences occurred in two patients with T1N0 disease, treated with HDR.

Several other institutions have also reported their experiences with brachytherapy, generally with similarly high rates of local control and cosmesis, with limited follow-up, as summarized in Table 28–1.[23–37] Ultimately, the quality of a multi-catheter implant depends upon the skill of the radiation oncologist placing the catheters. Because experience with interstitial brachytherapy of the breast has decreased in recent years as electron beam therapy has become the most common means by which to administer breast boost treatments, alternative, potentially more user friendly devices for brachytherapy have been developed.

MammoSite Device. The MammoSite device, approved by the FDA for safety in May 2002, is one such instrument. As pictured in Figure 28–4, it consists of a 6 mm diameter catheter with a balloon at its distal tip that can be inflated to either 4 to 5 cm or 5 to 6 cm in diameter. This balloon is placed in the tumor bed cavity at the time of the surgical procedure or as a separate procedure. The catheter exits either through the lumpectomy scar itself or at a single other exit site, thus avoiding the scar formation from multiple entry and exit sites that may mar cosmesis when multi-catheter implants are performed. Contrast may be used to fill the balloon and confirm positioning radiographically, and treatment is delivered with an afterloaded HDR source to the center of the balloon, delivering dose that is prescribed to a depth of 1 cm from the balloon surface.[38] Dosimetry with the MammoSite device is shown in Figure 28–5.

Investigators associated with the manufacturer of the MammoSite device have reported an 84% rate of good or excellent cosmesis, with two cases

Table 28–1. LARGE CLINICAL SERIES OF PATIENTS TREATED WITH MULTI-CATHETER INTERSTITIAL BRACHYTHERAPY FOR ACCELERATED PARTIAL BREAST IRRADIATION

Institution	Cases	Entry Criteria	F/U	Technique	Tumor Control	Complications and Cosmesis
Guy's Hospital[23,24]	27	< 70 yr old	72 mo	LDR (55 Gy over 5 days)	37% IBTR	No serious normal tissue effects; telangiectasia at site of superficially placed source in 1 case
Oschner Clinic[25]	51	Tumor < 4 cm; 0–3 LNs; negative inked margins	75 mo	LDR (45 Gy over 4 days: 25 cases) or HDR (32 Gy in 8 f bid: 26 cases)	8% LRF (1 IBTR & 3 regional nodal recurrences)	22% gr 1–2 complications, 8% gr 3 (including 2 cases fat necrosis); 75% excellent/good cosmesis at median f/u 20 mo
London Regional Cancer Clinic[26,27]	39	cT1–T2; cN0; no predominantly lobular histology	91 mo	HDR (37.2 Gy in 10 f, 5–7 days)	5-yr actuarial LR 16.2% (6 events)	10.3% fat necrosis; cosmesis at 12 months rated a mean of 78.5 on scale of 50 to 100
William Beaumont Hospital[28–30]	199	Tumor < 3 cm; age > 40; negative LNs; negative margins (≥ 2 mm); no EIC; no lobular histology; no DCIS; no significant LCIS	65 mo	LDR (50 Gy over 4 days: 120 cases) or HDR (32 Gy in 8 f or 34 Gy in 10 f bid: 79 cases)	Cumulative incidence of local recurrence 1% (5 cases of IBTR)	11% infections; 21% fat necrosis; good to excellent cosmesis in > 90%
RTOG[31,32]	99	Invasive, non-lobular carcinomas ≤ 3 cm; negative margins; 0–3 LNs; no ECE; no residual microcalcifications; no EIC	44 mo	LDR (45 Gy over 3.5–5 days: 33 cases) or HDR (34 Gy in 10 f bid: 66 cases)	4-yr actuarial IBTR 3%, 4-yr actuarial nodal recurrence 3%	10% gr 3–4 acute toxicity (at any f/u)
Tufts/Brown University[33]	33	T1–2; 0–3 LNs; no ECE; no lobular histology; negative margins; negative postexcision mammogram	33 mo	HDR (34 Gy in 10 f bid)	4-yr actuarial IBTR 3% (only one failure, appeared to be new primary)	33% gr 3–4 subcutaneous toxicity, including 8 cases clinically evident fat necrosis
National Institute of Oncology, Hungary[34]	45	pT1; negative margins; N0 or pN0–1a; grade < 3; no pure DCIS or LCIS; no lobular histology; no EIC	57 mo	HDR (30.3 Gy or 36.4 Gy in 7 f bid)	4.4% LF, 6.7% axillary failures; 5-yr LRFS 95.6%	Excellent cosmesis in 97.8%; 2.2% symptomatic fat necrosis
Massachusetts General Hospital[35]	48	cT1N0; no LVI; no EIC; negative sentinel node; negative margins	23 mo	LDR (50–60 Gy in 0.5 Gy/h)	No recurrences	Very good to excellent cosmesis in 91.8%
University of Kansas[36]	25	> 60 yrs; gr 1–2; pT1N0; no EIC; no DCIS; no LCIS; no nonclassical infiltrating lobular histology	47 mo	LDR (20 - 25 Gy in 1–2 days)	No recurrences	All very good to excellent cosmesis
Virginia Commonwealth University[37]	44	< 4 cm; negative inked margins; no EIC; 0–3 LNs (later restricted to N0)	42 mos	LDR (45 Gy in 90 h) or HDR (34 Gy in 10 f bid)	No local failures	79.6% good/excellent cosmesis

DCIS = ductal carcinoma in situ; ECE = extracapsular extension; EIC = extensive intraductal component; f = fraction; HDR = high-dose rate; IBTR = ipsilateral breast tumor recurrence; LCIS = lobular carcinoma in situ; LDR = low-dose rate; LF = local failure; LNs = lymph nodes; LRFS = local recurrence-free survival; LVI = lymphvascular invasion; LR = local recurrence.

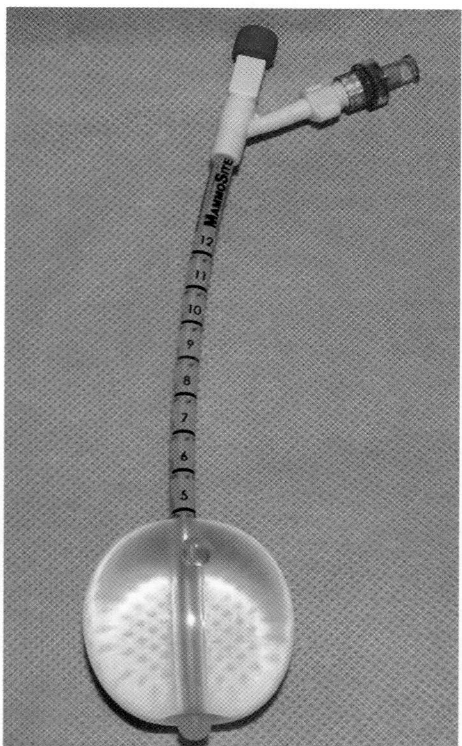

Figure 28–4. The MammoSite device consists of a balloon and catheter arrangement designed to simplify partial breast brachytherapy.

(4.9%) of fat necrosis after 29 months of follow-up in a series of 43 patients who received 34 Gy of HDR brachytherapy in 10 fractions with this device.[39] No ipsilateral breast failures have occurred. Other groups have reported similar results in small numbers of patients treated with this device with even shorter follow-up.[40] Still, concerns have been raised regarding whether the balloon can conform to the specific surgical cavity and deliver adequate dose to the desired tissue depth, the potential for fibrosis and tissue necrosis related to placement of the balloon (and source) too close to the skin, rupture of the balloon by surgical clips, and the absence of published clinical data suggesting efficacy beyond 2 years. Indeed, only 43 patients were reported in the series discussed above, even though 70 patients were enrolled in the study. Treatment could not be completed in the other patients for various reasons, including an overly large lumpectomy cavity size, inadequate skin spacing, and inability of the device to conform to the surgical cavity.[41] Further information regarding outcomes with the use of the MammoSite device are being gathered through a prospective registry trial.

Intraoperative Radiation Therapy

Selected institutions have access to facilities that allow for a single fraction of radiation therapy to be administered while the patient is still on the operating table, before the surgical wound is closed. Two European institutions have piloted such techniques to accomplish PBI.

Investigators at the European Institute of Oncology in Milan have used electron therapy (ELIOT) to deliver radiation to the target tissue. The skin is stretched out of the field to spare this tissue, and an aluminium-lead disc is placed between the breast and the pectoralis muscle to shield the thorax.[42,43] Veronesi and colleagues have reported on a series of 237 patients with T1 tumors treated with single-fraction doses of 17 to 21 Gy, using electron energies of 3 to 9 MeV administered with a portable linear accelerator.[44] With a median of 19 months of follow-up, only 4 patients had developed breast fibrosis (1 severe). Ipsilateral breast recurrence developed in 3 patients, contralateral breast cancer in 2, supraclavicular metastasis in 1, and distant metastases in 1.

Investigators at University College, London, have administered radiation using the INTRABEAM, a

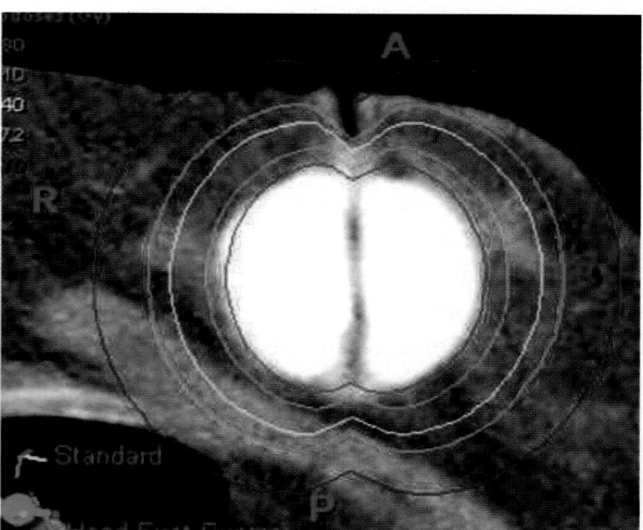

Figure 28–5. Dosimetry with MammoSite: The MammoSite device is designed to produce a roughly spherical dose distribution about the balloon, which conforms to the surgical cavity.

miniature electron-beam–driven source of low-energy x-rays (50 kV).[45] This allows delivery of 20 Gy to a depth of 2 mm and 5 Gy to a depth of 1.0 cm when the spherical applicator is inserted into the tumor bed. Tungsten-impregnated rubber shielding is used to protect the heart and lungs and to stop stray radiation. With only 2 years of follow-up, they have had no recurrences in their pilot series of 25 patients.[46] Still, the shallow coverage offered with this technique has raised concerns regarding rates of in-breast tumor recurrence with longer follow-up.

External Beam Partial Breast Irradiation

Improvements in target localization and dosimetric planning have led to an increasing interest in the possibility of accomplishing partial breast irradiation non-invasively, using external beam radiation therapy. Increased homogeneity of dose with external beam therapy might reduce complications from fat necrosis seen in brachytherapy series, but determining appropriate dose for tumor control by extrapolating from doses used in the brachytherapy studies has been difficult precisely because of these large differences in dose homogeneity between these techniques. Furthermore, ensuring appropriate targeting, including appropriate accounting for breathing motion[47,48] and set-up accuracy, has been a significant challenge with this approach.[49]

Formenti and colleagues at New York University have reported a series of 46 patients treated with three-dimensional conformal external beam APBI in the prone position.[50] They administered 30 Gy to the tumor bed plus a 1.5 to 2 cm margin in 5 fractions over 10 days. With a median of 18 months of follow-up, they report no local recurrences and modest acute toxicity, mainly Grade 1 to 2 erythema, with only one Grade 1 late toxicity.

Investigators at the William Beaumont Hospital performed a pilot study of three-dimensional conformal external beam APBI performed in the supine position, reporting results in 31 patients.[51] They defined the target volume to include the tumor cavity with a margin of 1 to 1.5 cm to account for possible subclinical disease, and an additional 1 cm expansion to allow for set-up uncertainty and organ motion. Dose used was 34 Gy in the first 6 patients and 38.5 Gy in the remainder, all in 10 fractions. With a median follow-up of only 10 months, only acute toxicities could be assessed, and these were minimal.

Figure 28–6 shows the dosimetry in a typical case treated with three-dimensional conformal PBI. Other external beam modalities are also under investigation. At the Massachusetts General Hospital in Boston,

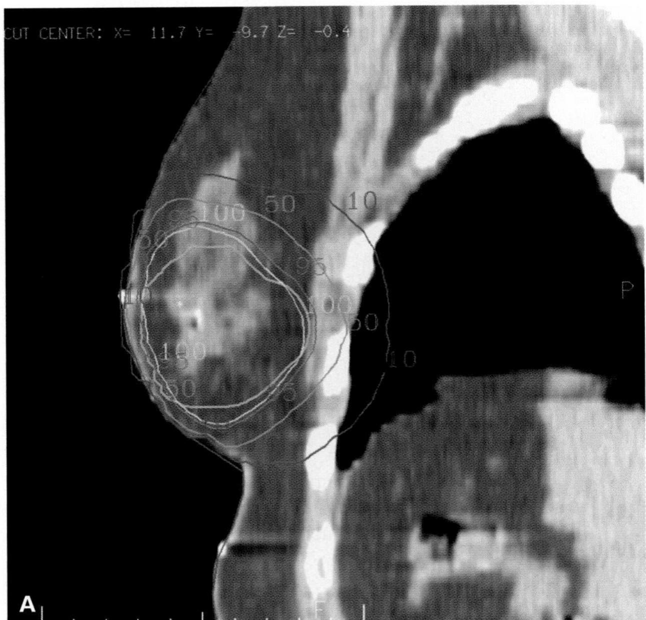

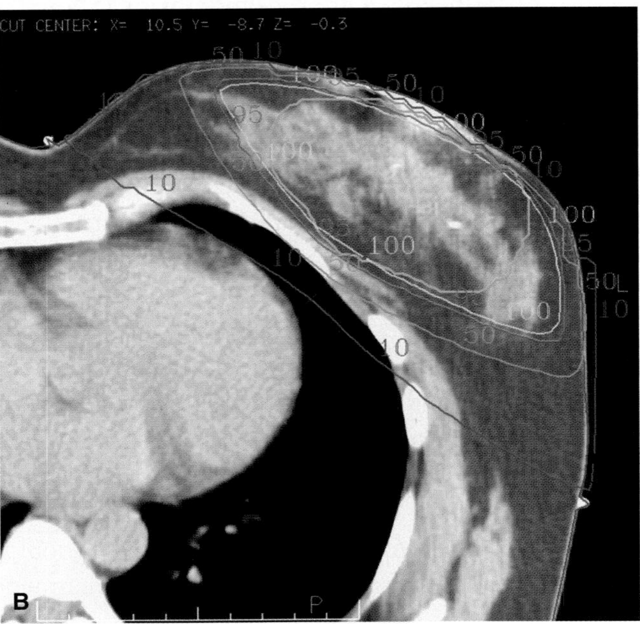

Figure 28–6. *A* and *B*, Dosimetry with three-dimensional conformal external beam partial breast treatment: A typical three-dimensional conformal external beam treatment plan for partial breast irradiation produces a more homogeneous dose distribution than that typically achieved with brachytherapy.

proton therapy is being investigated as a highly conformal means of treatment.[52] Other groups are investigating intensity modulated radiation therapy in the administration of partial breast irradiation.[53]

Phase III Studies

Because interest in APBI is relatively recent, few randomized trials have been completed that compare APBI to standard treatment. Preliminary results are available from a small Hungarian trial in which 126 patients were randomized to either 50 Gy of whole breast radiation or APBI. Selection criteria were identical to those used in the phase I/II study reported in Table 28–1. In this trial, APBI was accomplished with HDR brachytherapy (36.4 Gy in 7 fractions bid, 46 cases) or wide-field electron irradiation (50 Gy, 17 cases). With a median follow-up of only 30 months, the locoregional tumor control was 100% in both arms of this study, and no significant differences existed with regard to radiation-related side effects.[54]

Christie Hospital's Holt Radium Institute has also completed a randomized trial of APBI versus 40 Gy of whole breast radiation administered in 15 fractions.[55] They randomized 708 patients with breast cancers of 4 cm or less in diameter to limited-field versus wide-field radiation therapy. Limited-field radiation was administered using electrons of energies between 8 to 14 MeV, to a total dose of 40 to 42.5 Gy in 8 fractions over 10 days, with an average field size of 8×6 cm. Wide-field radiation was administered with 4 MeV photons, utilizing standard tangent fields matched to a single field treating the ipsilateral axilla, supraclavicular, and infraclavicular regions.

After a median of 65 months of follow-up,[56] overall survival was similar between the two groups. The 7-year actuarial rate of breast recurrence as a first event was 19.6% in the limited-field group, compared with 11.0% in the wide-field group ($p = .0008$). Histology was found to be important, and the differences in breast recurrence rates were greatest for patients with lobular histology (34% recurring after limited-field treatment compared with 8% after wide-field treatment). Still, even when patients with lobular histology or an extensive intraductal component were excluded, there was still a significant difference in breast recurrence rates for patients with infiltrating ductal carcinomas treated with limited- versus wide-field radiation: 15% vs 11% ($p = .01$). A larger percentage of patients treated with limited versus wide fields had marked telangiectasias (33 versus 12%) or marked fibrosis (14 versus 5%).

A number of other randomized studies have recently begun accruing patients or are soon to open. In North America, a collaborative effort of the NSABP and RTOG will soon lead to the opening of the NSABP B39–RTOG 0413 equivalence trial, which seeks to accrue 3,000 patients to provide a definitive answer regarding the relative efficacy of APBI compared with standard radiation treatment (50 to 50.4 Gy to the whole breast ± a 10 to 16 Gy boost). Permissible techniques for APBI on this upcoming American trial will include multi-catheter brachytherapy, MammoSite brachytherapy, and 3D conformal external beam radiation.

The National Institute of Oncology in Hungary continues to accrue further patients towards a target of 570 patients for a non-inferiority trial as described above. The European Brachytherapy Breast Center GEC-ESTRO Working Group has also recently activated a non-inferiority trial of APBI accomplished with HDR (32 Gy in 8 fractions or 30.3 in 7 fractions) or LDR (50 Gy) brachytherapy versus standard whole breast radiation followed by boost (50 to 50.4 Gy + 10 Gy boost). In addition, investigators at the European Institute of Oncology in Milan and at University College, London, are conducting equivalence trials to assess their unique methods of intraoperative single-fraction external beam APBI, which are described above. The target accrual of the Milan study is 824 patients and 1,600 patients for the London trial.

Conclusions

Growing numbers of radiation treatment facilities are beginning to offer partial breast irradiation to patients, and increasing media attention is leading many patients to inquire about this form of treatment. Therefore, it is important for all caregivers to understand the rationale for this strategy as well as the various techniques involved. It is also essential, however, for all those in the oncology community to recognize the still-investigational nature of this type of treatment.

At the present time, partial breast irradiation should only be offered to patients in the context of a clinical trial, or at the very least, only following detailed informed consent. Further follow-up and outcomes data is necessary to confirm the equivalence of this technique in terms of local control and to determine appropriate patient selection criteria, dose, technique, and fractionation. If a greater number of local failures occur with partial breast techniques, it is possible that there might also be an adverse impact on survival.[57] Randomized studies are necessary to offer definitive evidence regarding these important outcomes.

The American Brachytherapy Society[58] and American Society of Breast Surgeons[59] have outlined preliminary selection criteria for patients they feel may be considered for partial breast irradiation protocols. These include age older than 45 to 50 years, unifocal lesions smaller than 2 to 3 cm, negative margins of resection, and negative axillary lymph nodes. Both groups also recommend limiting the investigation of this technique to patients with ductal carcinoma. The ABS recommends the technique only for patients with invasive lesions, whereas the ASBS also approves it for patients with ductal carcinoma in situ.

In appropriately selected patients, APBI may indeed prove to be an effective technique. Still, continued study is necessary, as only after mature data from randomized trials have been analyzed can the safety and efficacy of this treatment strategy be determined.

INTENSITY MODULATED RADIOTHERAPY IN THE TREATMENT OF BREAST CANCER

Background

Standard two-dimensional radiation treatment planning to the whole breast for early stage breast cancer has historically used fixed medial and lateral tangential radiation fields of uniform intensity,[60,61] as shown in Figure 28–7. For this technique, dose distributions have generally been optimized with

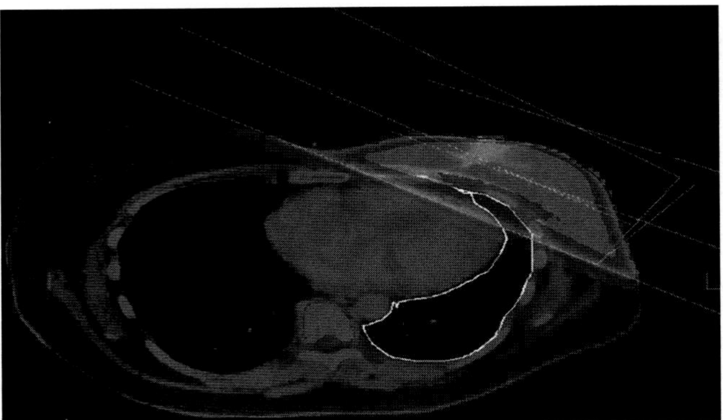

Figure 28–7. Standard medial and lateral tangential beams used to irradiate the intact breast.

wedges in a single plane. Although this approach has resulted in excellent rates of tumor control with minimal complications and has been associated with good-to-excellent cosmesis in the majority of patients treated with breast conservation,[62–65] recent emphasis has been placed on further technical improvements to reduce areas of dose inhomogeneity in the treated volume and the further reduction of treatment-related complications.

Conformal radiotherapy (RT) has been defined as the treatment of a high dose volume that conforms in three dimensions to the shape of the defined target while at the same time minimizing normal tissue dose.[66,67] The transition from two- to three-dimensional conformal RT allows the use of coplanar and non-coplanar beams. Computed tomography (CT)-based imaging systems provide serial two-dimensional images of the targets at risk, which are identified on each image and then summated to generate a three-dimensional representation of the target(s), as illustrated in Figure 28–8. With the improvement in dose distributions to the target as a result of multiple fields and the ability to further limit dose to close critical structures such as the heart for left-sided breast cancers as shown in Figure 28–9, three-dimensional treatment planning systems have become increasingly used in the treatment of breast cancer.[68]

Optimized target coverage with three-dimensional versus two-dimensional planning is particularly critical when regional nodes, specifically the internal mammary nodes (IMN), are included in the treatment volume. Using scans from patients treated

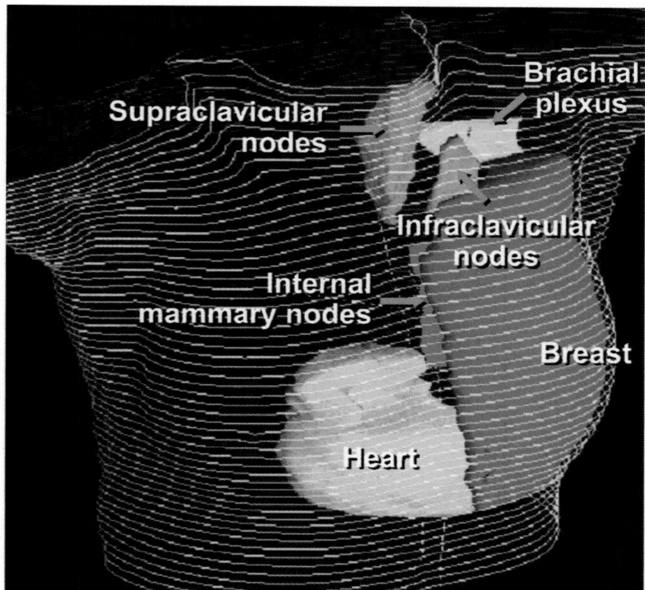

Figure 28–8. Three-dimensional representation of target volumes and normal tissues at risk for left-sided locoregional radiotherapy.

to the intact breast and IMN, a study by Arthur and colleagues from the Medical College of Virginia[69] of common treatment techniques demonstrated that although each of the four techniques studied resulted in acceptable dose distributions at central axis, the three-dimensional representation of the dose distributions revealed optimal coverage of the breast and IMN, reduced coverage of normal tissue, and high degree of reproducibility and dose homogeneity using the CT-planned technique. Pierce and colleagues from the University of Michigan[70] compared seven common techniques used in the treatment of the postmastectomy chest wall and regional lymph nodes using normal tissue complication probabilities (NTCP) and dose-volume metrics to assess target coverage to the chest wall, IMN, and normal tissue dose to heart and lungs. These plan comparisons also identified the CT-based three-dimensional technique partially wide tangent fields (PWTF) as the best compromise with respect to target coverage and normal tissue sparing when irradiating the chest wall and IMN. A recent study by Krueger and colleagues[71] of doses to the cardiac chambers and coronary arteries by radiotherapy technique also identified PWTF as the beam arrangement resulting in the least exposure to cardiac substructures of the common techniques studied. However, PWTF still resulted in low to moderate dose to the distal left anterior descending artery, suggesting the need for newer approaches to further minimize heart dose.

Although three-dimensional planning results in improved dose distributions over two-dimensional planning systems, further significant dose optimization can be achieved using intensity modulated radiotherapy (IMRT). The definition of IMRT is highly variable but essentially means the delivery of multiple fields of variable intensity patterns resulting in greater dose homogeneity and conformity than that obtained with flat radiation fields.[72–76] Thus, IMRT

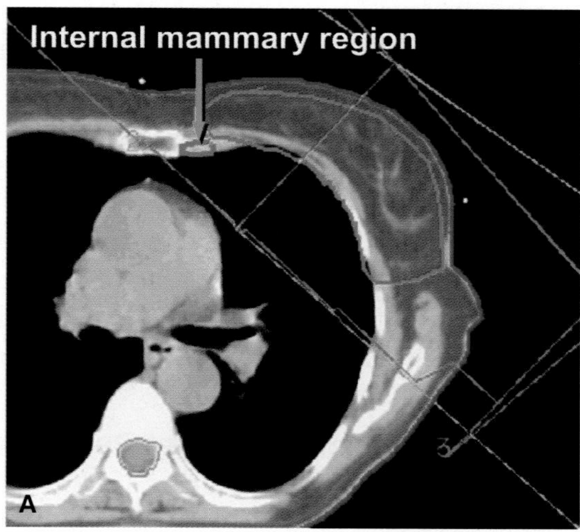

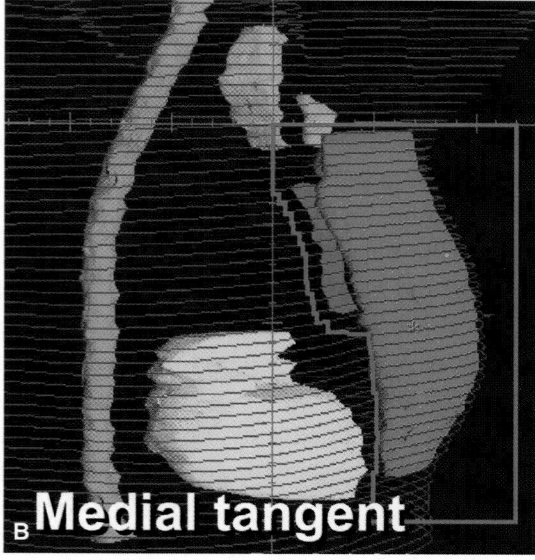

Figure 28–9. *A* and *B*, Three-dimensional planning in the treatment of the left breast and superior internal mammary nodes (IMN). The superior IMN (green volume) are included in the tangent fields. The lower tangents are blocked to exclude the heart from the radiotherapy field.

removes the usual reliance upon uniform intensity radiation fields and instead uses a variable intensity pattern (as shown in Figure 28–10) usually determined with a computerized optimization algorithm. Although IMRT is a form of three-dimensional radiotherapy, it provides more degrees of freedom for shaping dose to the target volumes. As discussed in the next section, IMRT plans can be either forward planned or inversely planned, where the parameters for an acceptable dose distribution are established first and then the isodose distributions and resultant beam arrangements are generated. The combination of IMRT delivery with planning algorithms is expected to achieve greater conformal dose distributions and improved dose homogeneity than two- or standard three-dimensional conformal radiation techniques, resulting in either improved local control owing to better target coverage, possible dose escalation for some tumor sites, and/or reduction of normal tissue dose while achieving the same tumor coverage. Use of IMRT requires precise target definitions and dose specifications as well as careful plan optimization and delivery. Each will be discussed below.

Planning Optimization/Target Definition

Although some IMRT dose distributions can be generated using forward planning, most are planned using inverse planning systems. With forward planning, the traditional method for radiotherapy planning, target volumes are initially defined and the treatment objectives, such as dose-volume constraints for the target and critical structures, are then defined. The dosimetrist then generates a plan that adheres to the planning directives. The plan is then reviewed by the radiation oncologist and amended as needed to conform to the desired clinical objectives. It is an iterative process, and for forward planned IMRT plans, beam weights can be varied and dose segments can be added until an acceptable plan is achieved. This contrasts with inverse planning, which uses automated optimization algorithms to generate the final plan. The treatment goals are stated initially, and the computer derives the optimized IMRT plan to achieve these goals while minimizing dose to normal tissues if normal tissue dose constraints are included in the treatment directives. Multiple mathematical optimization models have been used in inverse planning systems. These include simulated annealing and global optimization, multi-objective optimization, linear optimization (traditionally called linear programming), and mixed integer programming.[77] Although details of these optimization formulations are beyond the scope of this chapter, each approach can be used following designation of the objective (or cost) functions.

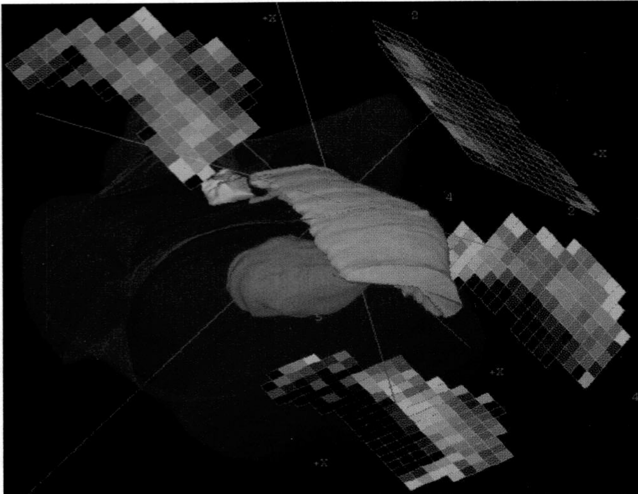

Figure 28–10. Intensity modulated fields consisting of 1 × 1 cm beamlets of non-uniform intensities.

With inverse planning, the target volumes and the critical tissues at risk must be carefully defined. Very specific dose constraints are generally placed on target and uninvolved tissues, and these objective constraints are compiled into a cost function which is used to measure how close the derived dose distributions are to the desired distribution.[78] Through repetitive computerized cycles, the plan is optimized such that beamlets (typically 1 × 1 cm segments of the beam) are configured that result in the desired fluence pattern allowing the minimum cost solution to be obtained. Once the desired solution is reached, the fluence pattern is shaped using multi-leaf collimators, which form individual beam segments in the head of the gantry.

IMRT is generally delivered using either a dynamic or a static delivery system. With a dynamic multi-leaf collimator IMRT delivery system, the leaves are in motion during the radiotherapy delivery and the fluence pattern is varied by the leaf trajectory and dose rate. With a static IMRT multi-leaf collimation delivery system (known as "step and shoot"), the leaves are stationary, and the fluence pattern is determined by the leaf position and the number of beamlets used. Using either system, the modulated dose can be effectively administered.

Important clinical and practical trade-offs must be considered for inverse-planned IMRT. As previously stated, the target volume must be completely defined as well as the tissues at risk. Unlike forward planned systems where the radiation oncologist and the dosimetrist are knowledgeable of normal tissue dose tolerances, computerized inverse planning systems require complete identification of all the tissues traversed by the beams as well as specification of dose constraints to all tissues at risk. This can add considerable time to the initial phases of the planning process for the radiation oncologist, depending upon the complexity of the plan and number of fields.

Given the variables that are possible with IMRT, including number of fields and beam segments, the plan complexity can vary greatly, which can affect both plan evaluation and time of treatment delivery. Evaluation of the plans will often involve not only assessment of maximum dose tolerances of whole organs (values that have been previously established) but also judgment of partial organ dose tolerances which, for some tissues, are not well defined. The time required to deliver the treatment varies as the levels of beam intensity increase. Thus the more complex the plan, the longer the treatment delivery will be, which can affect time on the accelerators, patient load per unit, and patient convenience. Thus, practical limitations must be considered when establishing optimization parameters for inverse planned IMRT, and, in general, reduction in the complexity of the plans is desirable to improve overall efficiency.

Adjustments for Respiratory Motion

To minimize rapid dose fall-off caused by sharp dose gradients that occur in IMRT-generated plans, adjustments are often critical to correct for organ motion secondary to breathing. This is especially a concern in that IMRT plans often include narrow margins around the target volume to allow dose escalation while limiting exposure to surrounding normal tissue. Thus, methods must be used that either incorporate or adjust for organ motion.

Although expansion of the target volume to allow for respiratory movement is one approach to account for motion, it can result in an excessive expansion of the target volume and considerable dose to uninvolved, and often critical, normal tissue. Therefore, two approaches have been used to adjust for organ motion associated with respiration: gating mechanisms, where radiation administration is synchronized with a part of a patient's respiratory cycle[79,80]; and breath-hold maneuvers,[81–83] where treatment is delivered only when breathing has been temporarily suspended. With gating and tracking systems, patients are allowed to breathe freely, and a respiration sensor detects the respiratory cycle, which then is translated into a signal to trigger radiation delivery at the pre-designated phase of the respiratory cycle. Commercial systems are available that capture patient respiratory motion by using markers placed on the abdomen or chest and record the resultant respiratory waveforms. In CT-based systems, scans are obtained at the phase of the respiratory cycle corresponding to the intended treatment respiratory phase, and the respiratory gating computer signals the linear accelerator to deliver treatment only during the designated gated interval. This sequence is repeated daily until the prescribed dose of radiation has been delivered. Respiratory-gated treatment is currently under study in clinical research protocols[80] and in some clinical settings.[79]

The alternate strategy to minimize respiratory variation is the use of breath-hold. The goal is to obtain the same point in the respiratory cycle during the treatment every day. To do so, the patient is asked to breathe through a tube which is connected to a flow-meter that records and displays lung volume. When the predetermined lung volume is reached, breath-hold is applied either using voluntary methods (generally deep inspiration breath-hold) or via mechanical active breathing control (ABC). The ABC device was developed by researchers at the William Beaumont Hospital, and its use allows patients to hold their breath at any phase of the respiratory cycle.[81–83] With ABC, a spirometer is connected to a balloon valve which, when closed, holds the patient's breath for a designated period of time.

As with gating and tracking systems, breath-hold methods also require simulation treatment–planning information at the same phase of the respiratory cycle as the intended phase during treatment. The reproducibility of breath-hold using the ABC device has been shown by multiple investigators.

Published reports have increased of the use of breath-hold maneuvers accomplished using the ABC device. In a detailed study by Moran and colleagues from the University of Michigan[84] of position and reproducibility of IMN under active breathing control, the average motion and reproducibility of the IMN position in all directions was approximately 2 mm with shallow breathing states (such as 20 and 40% vital capacity). Whereas the displacement from motion was much greater at end of exhalation and deep inspiration breath-hold, use of ABC resulted in a reproducibility of approximately 2 mm for these breathing states. This information will have obvious implications for IMRT optimization studies that include the IMN in the target volume. A recent dosimetric planning study by Remouchamps and colleagues from William Beaumont[85] presented results with moderate deep inspiration breath-hold using the ABC device in patients with breast cancer. Use of deep inspiration breath-hold significantly reduced cardiac exposure (for patients with left-sided breast cancers) and pulmonary exposure to radiotherapy when compared to standard planning techniques. Thus, the use of ABC appears promising, particularly in the treatment of women with left-sided breast cancers and in conjunction with IMRT.

IMRT in the Treatment of Breast Cancer

Multiple techniques have been used to modulate dose intensity in the breast. Simple solutions, such as mechanical compensators, have been designed based upon areas of inhomogeneity identified in the breast using three-dimensional planning tools.[86] Segmental multi-leaf collimators have also been used with forward planning to modulate dose in a more homogeneous distribution compared to standard tangents. In a paper by Vicini and colleagues,[87] static multi-leaf collimator (sMLC) segments were designed for breast cancer treatment based upon isodose surfaces from an open set of tangent fields, with each segment weight optimized using a computerized algorithm. This approach compensates well for the changing breast contour, which, in turn, may reduce areas of inhomogeneity and reduce acute and chronic skin toxicity. Preliminary results from Kestin and colleagues[88] in 10 patients with variable breast sizes suggested minimal or no acute skin reaction using this technique; a formal comparison of acute reactions using this technique versus standard tangents, however, was not performed. The follow-up study reported limited acute skin toxicity in an expanded series of 281 patients treated with this technique,[87] with 56% of patients experiencing Radiation Therapy Oncology Group Grade 0 or I acute skin toxicity, 43% Grade II toxicity, and 1% Grade III toxicity. Again, there was no comparison with patients treated with standard tangential fields.

Although dose distributions previously described in the treated breast appear to be improved using sMLC segments compared to standard fields, these optimization algorithms did not incorporate dose/volume constraints of normal tissues, such as lung and heart, into the optimization process. A comprehensive inverse planning IMRT study for breast cancer with objective optimization parameters, including normal tissue complication constraints, was reported by Hong and colleagues[89] from the Memorial Sloan-Kettering Cancer Center. The target volume was the breast only, and normal tissue constraints included dose to the ipsilateral lung, heart, contralateral breast, and surrounding soft tissue. The authors observed that intensity modulation using a standard tangential beam arrangement significantly reduced dose to the heart, ipsilateral lung, contralateral breast, and surrounding soft tissues compared to a standard-wedged plan; absolute dose reductions, however, were modest. Improved dose homogeneity was also observed in the superior and inferior regions above and below the central axis, regions not analyzed in standard breast plans.

Other groups have also shown improved dose distributions in the breast using IMRT compared to standard planning. Using phantoms, Chang and colleagues[90] from the University of North Carolina compared different intensity modulated techniques for tangential irradiation. Multi-leaf collimator-generated intensity modulated techniques were shown to reduce the contralateral breast dose by 50% when compared to the conventional two-wedge tangential technique. Li and colleagues[91] from Stanford compared the dose distributions to the breast using a combined electron and IMRT photon technique compared to standard tangential fields. The combined electron and IMRT plan showed better dose conformity to the target with significantly reduced dose to the ipsilateral lung and heart than the tangential fields. Hurkmans and colleagues[92] from the Netherlands Cancer Institute compared the NTCP for lung and heart using standard tangents with wedges, optimized wedges with conformal blocks, three-dimensional planning, and IMRT. A modest reduction in the estimated NTCP risk for pneumonitis was observed, with a risk of 0.5% with standard tangents, a 0.4% risk using conformal tangential fields, and a 0.3% risk using IMRT. The use of conformal three-dimensional tangential fields decreased the NTCP for late cardiac toxicity to 4.0% compared to 5.9% for standard fields, and tangential IMRT further reduced this to 2.0%. Thus, intensity modulation resulted in further improvement in the dose distribution over that obtained with three-dimensional planning.

All IMRT studies presented above have studied dose distributions in the breast/chest wall only, rather than the breast/chest wall and regional nodes. Whereas improved dose homogeneity in the breast only could result in decreased toxicity in some patients (such as large-breasted women) compared to standard tangential irradiation, the need for improved dose distribution with comprehensive locoregional RT is, in the authors' opinion, even more compelling. Randomized trials have shown a significant improvement in overall survival with the addition of comprehensive locoregional postmastectomy radiotherapy following systemic therapy, compared with postmastectomy systemic therapy alone.[93–95] Thus, a renewed interest in locoregional RT has been observed. Comprehensive RT can include treatment to the IMN, in addition to the breast/chest wall, and supraclavicular and infraclavicular lymph nodes. The proximity of the IMN to the heart increases the complexity of treatment planning, and survival can be compromised by radiation exposure to the heart.[96] Also, matching of standard RT fields can result in areas of over- and underdosing.[97] Thus, to maximize survival, comprehensive RT must be fully optimized. To this end, research into IMRT to the breast/chest wall and regional nodes is ongoing. With the innumerable degrees of freedom possible with IMRT, intensity modulated treatment could offer improved target coverage and less risk of cardiac exposure when compared to standard tangents and standard conformal three-dimensional CT-based planning. Cho and colleagues[98] compared IMRT and non-IMRT techniques in the treatment of the left breast and IMN and demonstrated superior breast and IMN target coverage using IMRT plans. Remouchamps and colleagues[85] observed improved dose homogeneity to the breast and IMN using IMRT-derived sMLC segments, with significant reductions in heart and lung dose using deep inspiration breath-hold with active breathing control and IMRT compared to a clinical 5-field technique, or deep tangents, without deep inspiration breath control. In a study by Smitt and colleagues[99] from Stanford comparing locoregional dose distributions derived using three-dimensional graphics and IMRT, IMRT plans resulted in better coverage of the whole breast as well as a reduction in the maximum cardiac dose. However, IMRT plans were associated with higher mean doses to the contralateral lung and heart. In a planning study of 10 patients, Krueger and colleagues[100] from the University of Michigan demonstrated more uniform chest wall coverage with a 9-field axial beamlet IMRT plan compared to the best three-dimensional conformal RT plan PWTF and a significant improvement in the minimum dose to the IMN region over a wide range of body habitus, while maintaining a low (less than 1%) NTCP for ischemic heart disease. Furthermore, the ipsilateral lung NTCP for pneumonitis was significantly less with IMRT compared to PWTF. However, a greater volume of the contralateral breast was exposed to radiation with IMRT, and the mean contralateral lung dose was greater compared to treatment with PWTF; the clinical significance of these low doses is unknown. Thus improvements in target coverage and sparing of heart and ipsilateral lung were offset by exposure of contralateral tissues to irradiation. It was concluded that additional planning studies were needed to either reduce the number of beamlet IMRT fields and/or further refine cost functions to limit the exposure of uninvolved tissues to low dose RT.

Final Considerations

Clearly IMRT results in more homogenous dose distributions than most standard RT plans, as shown in Figure 28–11A and B. Should IMRT be considered the new "gold standard" for treatment delivery? Although for some breast cancer patients the improved dose distributions achieved with IMRT could result in less treatment morbidity, in many patients these treatment goals can be accomplished using optimized CT-based forward planning. It is unclear whether IMRT represents a clinical advan-

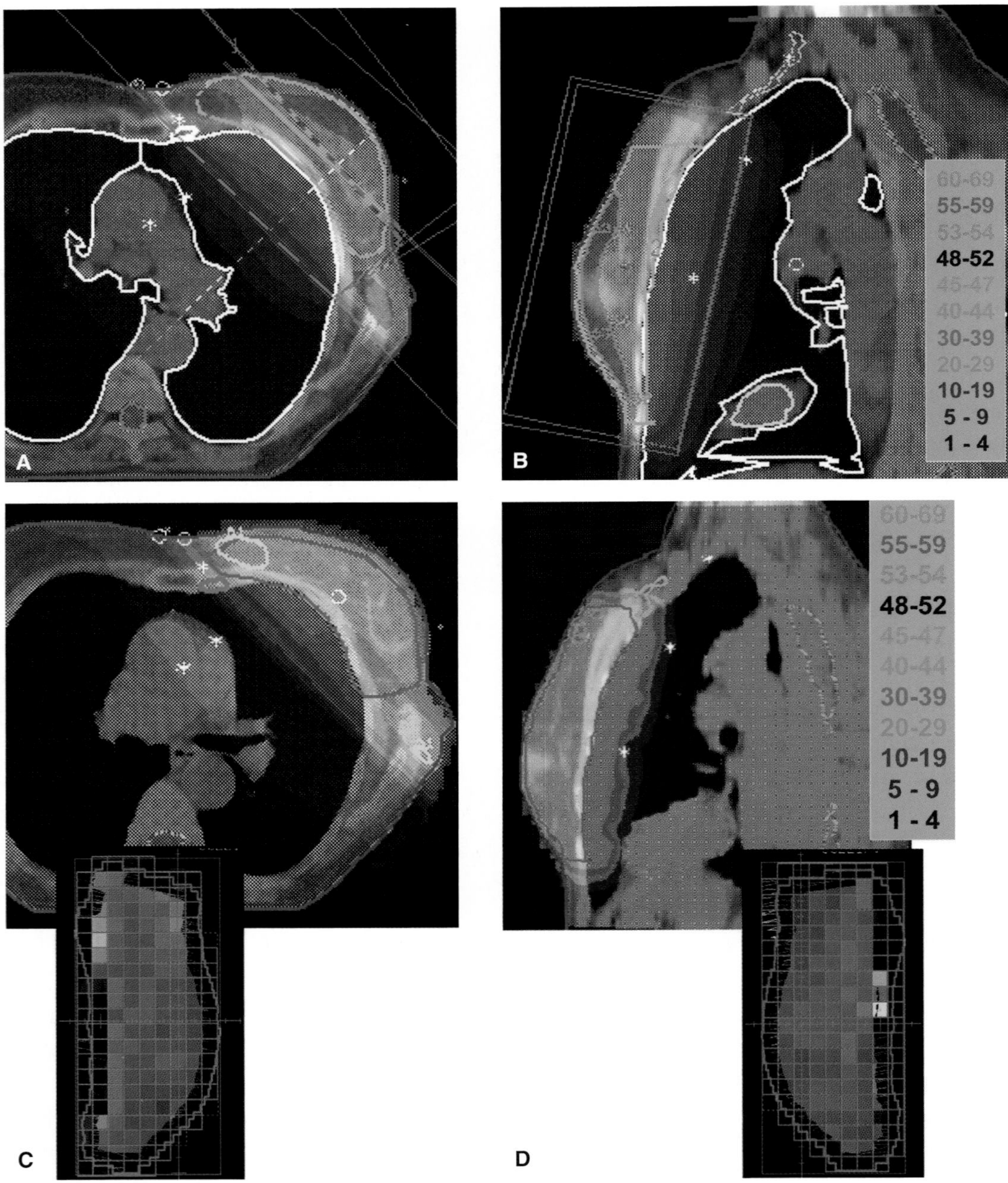

Figure 28–11. Areas of dose inhomogeneity in the irradiated breast treated with standard tangents *A* and *B*. Improved dose homogeneity in the irradiated breast using intensity modulated tangential fields. *C*, medial view; *D*, lateral view.

tage for most women treated to the breast only. Outcome studies are needed to compare the best standard treatment to IMRT for breast only and breast and nodal treatment to determine the patients who would derive an incremental benefit from IMRT. Practical issues could also affect the routine implementation of IMRT. With the variation in the approaches (and complexity) of IMRT, there is considerable range in the time needed to prepare an IMRT plan. Some centers are able to generate breast plans using IMRT in the same amount of time as standard plans, whereas more complicated plans require significantly more time and effort on the part of the physician, dosimetry and physics staff, and the radiation therapists delivering the treatment. As previously discussed, adjustments for motion are necessary to minimize rapid dose fall-off caused by sharp dose gradients observed with IMRT, and strategies must be incorporated into the treatment plan to account and correct for these variations. Furthermore, IMRT generally requires sophisticated computer-controlled delivery systems, and quality assurance standards are needed to verify their accuracy. Although some guidelines have been established, they must evolve as technologies change. And finally, theoretical concerns have been raised regarding exposure of uninvolved tissue to low dose irradiation possible with some forms of IMRT and risks of second malignancies.[101,102] Since many IMRT plans involve more fields and the potential for larger volume of tissue to be exposed to low doses of radiation, a theoretical risk exists for the development of second cancers; the actual risk is unknown. However, given the excellent prognosis of many patients with breast cancer, it is important that IMRT techniques minimize low-dose exposure and potential risk of second malignancies and that the true benefits of IMRT in the appropriate patients populations be established to justify its routine use. Clinical outcome studies are ongoing to address these end points.

REFERENCES

1. Ceilley E, Jagsi R, Goldberg SI, et al. Radiotherapy for invasive breast cancer in North America and Europe: results of survey. Int J Radiat Onol Biol Phys 2005;61:365–73.
2. Morrow M, White J, Moughan J, et al. Factors predicting the use of breast conserving therapy in stage I and II breast carcinoma. J Clin Oncol 2001;19:2254–62.
3. Nattinger AB, Veum J, Yahnke D, Goodwin JS. Geographic variation in the use of breast-conserving treatment of breast cancer. N Engl J Med 1992;326:1147–9.
4. Whelan T, MacKenzie R, Julian J, et al. Randomized trial of breast irradiation schedules after lumpectomy for women with lymph node-negative breast cancer. J Natl Cancer Inst 2002;94:1143–50.
5. Bankhead C. Accelerated partial breast irradiation: more data needed, researchers say. J Natl Cancer Inst 2003;95:259–61.
6. Bellon JR, Come SE, Gelman RS, et al. Sequencing of chemotherapy and radiation therapy for patients with early-stage breast cancer: updated results of a prospective randomized trial. Int J Radiat Oncol Biol Phys 2001; 51(3 Suppl 1):2–3.
7. Liljegren G, Holmberg L, Bergh A, et al. 10-year results after sector resection with or without postoperative radiotherapy for stage I breast cancer: a randomized trial. J Clin Oncol 1999;17:2326–33.
8. Clark RM, McCulloch PB, Levine MN, et al. Randomized clinical trial to assess the effectiveness of breast irradiation following lumpectomy and axillary dissection for node-negative breast cancer. J Natl Cancer Inst 1992;84:683–9.
9. Holland R, Veling S, Mravunac M, et al. Histologic multifocality of Tis, T1-2 breast carcinomas. Implications for clinical trials of breast conserving therapy. Cancer 1985; 56:979–90.
10. Vaidya JS, Vyas JJ, Chinoy RF, et al. Multicentricity of breast cancer: whole organ analysis and clinical implications. Br J Cancer, 1996;74:820–4.
11. Morimoto T, Okazaki K, Komaki K, et al. Cancerous residue in breast-conserving surgery. J Surg Oncol 1993;52:71–6.
12. Veronesi U, Marubini E, Mariani L, et al. Radiotherapy after breast-conserving surgery in small breast carcinoma: long-term results of a randomized trial. Ann Oncol 2001; 12(7):997–1003.
13. Khan FM. The physics of radiation therapy. Lippincott Williams & Wilkins, 2003.
14. Hall EJ. Radiobiology for the radiologist. Lippincott Williams & Wilkins, 2000.
15. Fentiman IS, Poole C, Tong D, et al. Iridium implant treatment without external radiotherapy for operable breast cancer: a pilot study. Eur J Cancer 1991;27:447–50.
16. Fentiman IS, Poole C, Tong D, et al. Inadequacy of iridium implant as sole radiation treatment for operable breast cancer. Eur J Cancer 1996;32A:608–11.
17. Vicini FA, Baglan KL, Kestin LL, et al. Accelerated treatment of breast cancer. J Clin Oncol 2001;19:1993–2001.
18. Vicini FA, Kestin L, Chen P, et al. Limited-field radiation therapy in the management of early-stage breast cancer. J Natl Cancer Inst 2003;95:1205–11.
19. Benitez PR, Chen PY, Vicini FA, et al. Partial breast irradiation in breast-conserving therapy by way of interstitial brachytherapy. Am J Surg 2004;188:355–64.
20. Kuske RR, Bolton JS. A phase I/II trial to evaluate brachytherapy as the sole method of radiation therapy for stage I and II breast carcinoma. Radiation Therapy Oncology Group Publication no. 1055. Philadelphia: Radiation Therapy Oncology Group: 1995.

21. Kuske RR, Winter K, Arthur D, et al. A phase I/II trial of brachytherapy alone following lumpectomy for select breast cancer: toxicity analysis of Radiation Therapy Oncology Group 95–17. Int J Radiat Oncol Biol Phys 2002;54(2 Suppl 1):87.
22. Kuske RR, Winter K, Arthur DW, et al. A phase II trial of brachytherapy alone following lumpectomy for stage I or II breast cancer: initial outcomes of RTOG 95-17. J Clin Oncol 2004;22(14 Suppl):565.
23. Fentiman IS, Poole C, Tong D, et al. Iridium implant treatment without external radiotherapy for operable breast cancer: a pilot study. Eur J Cancer 1991;27:447–50.
24. Fentiman IS, Poole C, Tong D, et al. Inadequacy of iridium implant as sole radiation treatment for operable breast cancer. Eur J Cancer 1996;32A:608–11.
25. King TA, Bolton JS, Kuske RR, et al. Long-term results of wide-field brachytherapy as the sole method of radiation therapy after segmental mastectomy for Tis,1,2 breast cancer. Am J Surg 2000;180:299–304.
26. Perera F, Engel J, Holliday R, et al. Local resection and brachytherapy confined to the lumpectomy site for early breast cancer: a pilot study. J Surg Oncol 1997;65:263–7.
27. Perera F, Yu E, Engel J, et al. Patterns of breast recurrence in a pilot study of brachytherapy confined to the lumpectomy site for early breast cancer with six years' minimum follow-up. Int J Radiat Oncol Biol Phys 2003;57:1239–46.
28. Vicini FA, Baglan KL, Kestin LL, et al. Accelerated treatment of breast cancer. J Clin Oncol 2001;19:1993–2001.
29. Vicini FA, Kestin L, Chen P, et al. Limited-field radiation therapy in the management of early-stage breast cancer. J Natl Cancer Inst 2003;95:1205–11.
30. Benitez PR, Chen PY, Vicini FA, et al. Partial breast irradiation in breast-conserving therapy by way of interstitial brachytherapy. Am J Surg 2004;188:355–64.
31. Kuske RR, Winter K, Arthur D, et al. A phase I/II trial of brachytherapy alone following lumpectomy for select breast cancer: toxicity analysis of Radiation Therapy Oncology Group 95–17. Int J Radiat Oncol Biol Phys 2002;54(2 Suppl 1):S87.
32. Kuske RR, Winter K, Arthur DW, et al. A phase II trial of brachtherapy alone following lumpectomy for stage I or II breast cancer: initial outcomes of RTOG 95-17. J Clin Oncol 2004;22(14 Suppl):565.
33. Wazer DE, Berle L, Graham R, et al. Preliminary results of a phase I/II study of HDR brachytherapy alone for T1/T2 breast cancer. Int J Radiat Oncol Biol Phys 2002;53: 889–97.
34. Polgar C, Sulyok Z, Fodor J, et al. Sole brachytherapy of the tumor bed after conservative surgery for T1 breast cancer: five-year results of a phase I-II study and initial findings of a randomized phase III trial. J Surg Oncol 2002;80:121–8.
35. Lawenda BD, Taghian AG, Kachnic LA, et al. Dose-volume analysis of radiotherapy for T1N0 invasive breast cancer treated by local excision and partial breast irradiation by low-dose rate interstitial implant. Int J Radiat Oncol Biol Phys 2003;56:671–80.
36. Krishnan L, Jewell WR, Tawfik OW, et al. Breast conservation therapy with tumor bed irradiation alone in a selected group of patients with stage I breast cancer. Breast J 2001; 7:91–6.
37. Arthur DW, Koo D, Zwicker RD, et al. Partial breast brachytherapy after lumpectomy: low dose rate and high dose rate experience. Int J Radiat Oncol Biol Phys 2003; 56:681–9.
38. Edmundson GK, Vicini FA, Chen PY, et al. Dosimetric characteristics of the mammosite RTS, a new breast brachytherapy applicator. Int J Radiat Oncol Biol Phys 2002;52: 1132–9.
39. Keisch M, Vicini F, Scroggins T, et al. Thirty month results with the MammoSite breast brachytherapy applicator: cosmesis, toxicity, and local control in partial breast irradiation. Int J Radiat Oncol Biol Phys 2004;60(1 Suppl 1):272.
40. Shah NM, Tenenholz T, Arthur D, et al. MammoSite and interstitial brachytherapy for accelerated partial breast irradiation: factors that affect toxicity and cosmesis. Cancer 2004;101:727–34.
41. Keisch M, Vicini F, Kuske R, et al. Initial clinical experience with the mammosite breast brachytherapy applicator in women with early stage breast cancer treated with breast conserving therapy. Int J Radiat Oncol Biol Phys 2003; 55:289–93.
42. Veronesi U, Orecchia R, Luini A, et al. A preliminary report of intraoperative radiotherapy (IORT) in limited-stage breast cancers that are conservatively treated. Eur J Cancer 2001;37:2178–83.
43. Orecchia R, Ciocca M, Lazzari R, et al. Intraoperative radiation therapy with electrons (ELIOT) in early-stage breast cancer. Breast 2003;12:483–90.
44. Veronesi U, Gatti G, Luini A, et al. Full-dose intraoperative radiotherapy with electrons during breast-conserving surgery. Arch Surg 2003;138:1253–6.
45. Vaidya JS, Baum M, Tobias JS, et al. The novel technique of delivering targeted intraoperative radiotherapy (Targit) for early breast cancer. Eur J Surg Oncol 2002;28:447–54.
46. Vaidya JS, Baum M, Tobias JS, et al. Targeted intra-operative radiotherapy (Targit): an innovative method of treatment for early breast cancer. Ann Oncol 2001;12:1075–80.
47. Baglan KL, Sharpe MB, Jaffray D, et al. Accelerated partial breast irradiation using 3-D conformal radiation therapy (3D-CRT). Int J Radiat Oncol Biol Phys 2003;55:302–11.
48. Frazier RC, Vicini F, Sharpe MB. The impact of respiration on whole breast radiotherapy: a dosimetric anslysis using active breathing control [abstract]. Int J Radiat Oncol Biol Phys 2000;48:200.
49. Weed DW, Yan D, Martinez AA, et al. The validity of surgical clips as a radiographic surrogate for the lumpectomy cavity in image-guided accelerated partial breast irradiation. Int J Radiat Oncol Biol Phys 2004;60:484–92.
50. Formenti SC, Rosenstein B, Skinner KA, et al. T1 stage breast cancer: adjuvant hypofractionated conformal radiation therapy to the tumor bed in selected postmenopausal breast cancer patients-pilot feasibility study. Radiology 2002;222:171–8.
51. Vicini FA, Remouchamps V, Wallace M, et al. Ongoing clinical experience utilizing 3D conformal external beam radiotherapy to deliver partial-breast irradiation in patients with early-stage breast cancer treated with breast-conserving therapy. Int J Radiat Oncol Biol Phys 2003;57:1247–53.
52. El-Ghamry MN, Doppke K, Gierga D, et al. Partial breast irradiation using external beams: a comparison of 3-D

conformal, IMRT and proton therapy treatment planning using dose-volume histogram analysis. [abstract]. Int J Radiat Oncol Biol Phys, 54(2 Supp):163.

53. Lacombe MA, McMahon J, Al-Najjar W, et al. Accelerated partial breast irradiation using intensity modulated radiotherapy. Int J Radiat Oncol Biol Phys 2004;60(1 Suppl 1): S237–4.
54. Polgar C, Sulyok Z, Fodor J, et al. Sole brachytherapy of the tumor bed after conservative surgery for T1 breast cancer: five-year results of a phase I-II study and initial findings of a randomized phase III trial. J Surg Oncol 2002;80:121–8.
55. Ribeiro GG, Dunn G, Swindell R, et al. Conservation of the breast using two different radiotherapy techniques: interim report of a clinical trial. Clin Oncol 1990;2:27–34.
56. Ribeiro GG, Magee B, Swindell R, et al;. The Christie Hospital breast conservation trial: an update at 8 years from inception. Clin Oncol 1993;5:278–83.
57. Wallner P, Arthur D, Bartelink H, et al. Workshop on partial breast irradiation: state of the art and the science, Bethesda, MD, December 8–10, 2002. J Natl Cancer Inst 2004;96(3):175–84.
58. Arthur D, Vicini F, Kuske RR, et al. Accelerated partial breast irradiation: an updated report of the American Brachytherapy Society. Brachytherapy 2002;1:184–90.
59. Arthur DW. Accelerated partial breast irradiation: a change in treatment paradigm for early stage breast cancer. J Surg Onc, 2003;84:185–91.
60. Lichter AS, Padikal TN. Treatment planning in the treatment of breast cancer. In: Bleehen N, Glastein E, editors. Radiation therapy treatment planning. London: Dekker; 1983. p. 639–662.
61. Svensson GK, Chin LM, Siddon RL, Harris JR. Breast treatment techniques at the Joint Center for Radiation Therapy. In: Harris JR, Hellman S, Silen W, editors. Conservative management of breast cancer. Philadelphia: JB Lippincott Co; 1983. p. 47–52.
62. Santiago R, Leester W, Harris E, et al. Fifteen-year results of breast-conserving surgery and definitive irradiation for stage I and II breast carcinoma: the University of Pennsylvania experience. Int J Radiat Oncol Biol Phys 2004; 58:233–40.
63. Pierce LJ, Strawderman M, Douglas K, et al. Conservative surgery and radiotherapy for early-stage breast cancer using a lung density correction: the University of Michigan experience. Int J Radiat Oncol Biol Phys 1997;39:921–8.
64. Heimann R, Powers C, Halpern H, et al. Breast preservation in stage I and II carcinoma of the breast: the University of Chicago experience. Cancer 1996;78:1722–30.
65. Gage I, Recht A, Gelman R, et al. Long-term outcome following breast-conserving surgery and radiation therapy. Int J Radiat Oncol Biol Phys 1995;33:245–51.
66. Fraass B, McShan DL, Ten Haken R, et al. 3-D treatment planning: VA fast 3-D photon calculation model, In: Bruinivis IAD, van der Giessen FH, van Kleffens HJ, et al, editors. The use of computers in radiation therapy. North-Holland: Elsevier Science Publishers; 1987. p. 521–5.
67. Fraass B, McShan D. 3-D treatment planning. I. Overview of a clinical planning system. In: Bruinivis IAD, editor. The use of computers in radiation therapy. North-Holland: Elsevier Science Publishers; 1987. p. 273–6.
68. Pierce LJ, Moughan J, White J, et al. 1998-1999 Patterns of Care Survey (PCS) update of national practice patterns using breast-conserving surgery (BCS) and radiotherapy (RT) in the management of stage I/II breast cancer [abstract]. Int J Radiat Oncol Biol Phys 2002;54:97.
69. Arthur DW, Arnfield MR, Warwicke LA, et al. Internal mammary node coverage: An investigation of presently accepted techniques. Int J Radiat Oncol Biol Phys 2000;48:139–46.
70. Pierce LJ, Butler J, Martel M, et al. Postmastectomy radiotherapy of the chest wall: dosimetric comparison of common techniques. Int J Radiat Oncol Biol Phys 2002;52:1220–30.
71. Krueger E, Schipper M, Koelling T, et al. Cardiac chamber and coronary artery doses associated with postmastectomy radiotherapy techniques to the chest wall and regional nodes. Int J Radiat Oncol Biol Phys 2004;60:1195–203.
72. Leibel S, Fuks Z, Zelefsky M, et al. Intensity-modulated radiotherapy. Cancer J 2002;8:164–76.
73. Verhey L. Issues in optimization for planning of intensity-modulated radiation therapy. Semin Radiat Oncol 2002; 12:210–8.
74. Low D. Quality assurance of intensity-modulated radiotherapy. Semin Radiat Oncol 2002;12:219–28.
75. Webb S. Historical perspective on IMRT. In: Palta J, Mackie T, editors. Intensity-modulated radiation therapy: the state of the art. Madison, WI: Medical Physics; 2003.
76. Langer M: What is different about IMRT? In: Palta J, Mackie T, editors. Intensity modulated radiation therapy: the state of the art. Madison, WI: Medical Physics; 2003.
77. Censor Y. Mathematical optimization for the inverse problem of intensity-modulated radiation therapy. In: Palta J, Mackie T, editors. Intensity modulated radiation therapy: the state of the art. Madison, WI: Medical Physics; 2003.
78. Bortfeld T. Optimized planning using physical objectives and constraints. Semin Radiat Oncol 1999;9:20–34.
79. Berson A, Emery R, Rodriguez L, et al. Clinical experience using respiratory gated radiation therapy: Comparison of free-breathing and breath-hold techniques. Int J Radiat Oncol Biol Phys 2004;60:419–26.
80. Wagman R, Yorke E, Ford E, et al. Respiratory gating for liver tumors: Use in dose escalation. Int J Radiat Oncol Biol Phys 2003;55:659–68.
81. Dawson L, Balter J. Interventions to reduce organ motion effects in radiation delivery. Semin Radiat Oncol 2004; 14:76–80.
82. Dawson L, Brock K, Kazanjian S, et al. The reproducibility of organ position using active breathing control (ABC) during liver radiotherapy. Int J Radiat Oncol Biol Phys 2001;51:1410–21.
83. Frazier R, Vicini F, Sharpe M, et al. Impact of breathing motion on whole breast radiotherapy: a dosimetric analysis using active breathing control. Int J Radiat Oncol Biol Phys 2004;58:1041–7.
84. Moran J, Ben-David M, March R, et al. The position and reproducibility of the internal mammary nodes under active breathing control [abstract]. Int J Radiat Oncol Biol Phys 2004;60:38.
85. Remouchamps V, Vicini F, Sharpe M, et al. Significant reductions in heart and lung doses using deep inspiration breath hold with active breathing control and intensity-modu-

lated radiation therapy for patients treated with locoregional breast irradiation. Int J Radiat Oncol Biol Phys 2003;55:392–406.

86. Aref A, Thornton D, Youssef E, et al. Dosimetric improvements following 3D planning of tangential breast irradiation. Int J Radiat Oncol Biol Phys 2000;48:1569–74.

87. Vicini F, Sharpe M, Kestin L, et al. Optimizing breast cancer treatment efficacy with intensity-modulated radiotherapy. Int J Radiat Oncol Biol Phys 2002;54:1336–44.

88. Kestin L, Sharpe M, Frazier R, et al. Intensity modulation to improve dose uniformity with tangential breast radiotherapy: Initial clinical experience. Int J Radiat Oncol Biol Phys 2000;48:1559–68.

89. Hong L, Hunt M, Chui C, et al. Intensity-modulated tangential beam irradiation of the intact breast. Int J Radiat Oncol 1999;44:1155–64.

90. Chang S, Deschesne K, Cullip T, et al. A comparison of different intensity modulation treatment techniques for tangential breast irradiation. Int J Radiat Oncol Biol Phys 1999;45:1305–14.

91. Li J, Williams S, Goffinet D, et al. Breast-conserving radiation therapy using combined electron and intensity-modulated radiotherapy technique. Radiotherapy and Oncology 2000;56:65–71.

92. Hurkmans C, Cho BC, Damen E, et al. Reduction of cardiac and lung complication probabilities after breast irradiation using conformal radiotherapy with or without intensity modulation. Radiother Oncol 2002;62:163–71.

93. Overgaard M, Hansen PS, Overgaard J, et al. Postoperative radiotherapy in high-risk premenopausal women with breast cancer who receive adjuvant chemotherapy: Danish Breast Cancer Cooperative Group 82b trial. N Engl J Med 1997;337:949–55.

94. Overgaard M, Jensen MB, Overgaard J, et al. Postoperative radiotherapy in high-risk postmenopausal breast-cancer patients given adjuvant tamoxifen: Danish Breast Cancer Cooperative Group DBCG 82c randomized trial. Lancet 1999;353:1641–8.

95. Ragaz J, Olivotto I, Spinelli J, et al. Locoregional radiation therapy in patients with high-risk breast cancer receiving adjuvant chemotherapy: 20-year results of the British Columbia Randomized Trial. J Natl Cancer Inst 2005;97:116–26.

96. Cuzick J. Stewart H, Rutqvist L, et al. Cause specific mortality in long-term survivors of breast cancer who participated in trials of radiotherapy. Clin Oncol 1994;12:447–53.

97. Lichter AS, Fraass B, Van de Geijn J, et al. A technique for field matching in primary breast irradiation. Int J Radiat Oncol Biol Phys 1983;9:263–70.

98. Cho BC, Hurkmans C, Damen E, et al. Intensity modulated versus non-intensity modulated radiotherapy in the treatment of the left breast and upper internal mammary lymph node chain: a comparative planning study. Radiother Oncol 2002;62:127–36.

99. Smitt M, Li S, Shostak C, et al. Breast-conserving radiation therapy: potential of inverse planning with intensity modulation. Radiology 1997;203:871–6.

100. Krueger E, Fraass B, McShan D, et al. Potential gains for irradiation of chest wall and regional nodes with intensity modulated radiotherapy. Int J Radiat Oncol Biol Phys 2003;56:1023–37.

101. Hall E, Wuu C. Radiation-induced second cancers: the impact of 3D-CRT and IMRT. Int J Radiat Oncol Biol Phys 2003;56:83–8.

102. Glatstein E. Intensity-modulated radiation therapy: the inverse, the converse, and the perverse. Semin Radiat Oncol 2002;12:272–81.

29

Pregnancy and Breast Cancer

EMER O. HANRAHAN
RICHARD L. THERIAULT

EPIDEMIOLOGY

The estimated incidence of breast cancer diagnosis during pregnancy is 1 in 3,000 to 3 in 10,000 pregnancies.[1–3] Approximately 10% of patients with breast cancer under the age of 40 years will be pregnant at the time of diagnosis.[4] Pregnancy-associated breast cancer (PABC) encompasses all diagnoses during pregnancy and within 12 months postpartum. PABC has been reported to represent 0.2 to 3.8% of all breast cancer diagnoses.[5] An analysis of 3,168,911 deliveries in California from 1992 to 1997 documented 423 cases of PABC.[6] This study found that 0.037 women per 1,000 live singleton births were diagnosed with breast cancer during pregnancy. Breast cancer was the most frequent tumor type per 10,000 live singleton births.

The average age of patients with PABC is 32 to 38 years.[7] A risk factor for breast cancer is increasing age, and breast cancer during pregnancy is expected to increase in incidence as women delay childbearing.[7–9] The birth rate for older women is rising in the United States.[10] The birth rate for women aged 35 to 39 years in 2002 was 41.4 per 1,000, a 31% increase in rate since 1990, and the highest level in more than three decades. For women aged 40 to 44 years, the birth rate in 2002 was 8.3 per 1,000, a 51% increase since 1990, and the highest level since 1969. Also, the number of births to women aged 45 to 49 and 50 to 54 years is rising.[10]

PRESENTATION AND DIAGNOSIS

Breast cancer in pregnancy usually presents as a painless mass or thickening.[11–13] It is occasionally associated with nipple discharge. In a Mayo Clinic (Rochester, MN) series, 60 of 63 women (95%) presented with a painless mass.[11] In a British series, 146 of 178 women (82%) also had a similar presentation.[13] Any breast mass in a pregnant or lactating patient must be fully evaluated using triple assessment: clinical examination, diagnostic imaging, and biopsy. Physiologic changes occurring in the breast during pregnancy result in increased density and nodularity of the breast tissue.[7,14] This can lead to delayed presentation and make findings on clinical palpation difficult to interpret, contributing to a later diagnosis. As breast cancer is relatively rare in young women, a physician's low level of suspicion of malignancy may also impede diagnosis. Delays in the diagnosis of PABC of up to 6 months were reported in older studies, but more recent studies report delays of about 1 to 2 months.[4] These delays may explain the more advanced stage at diagnosis in many patients with PABC.[15–19] It has been estimated that a 1-, 3- and 6-month delay in the diagnosis of an early stage breast cancer with a 130-day doubling time increases the risk of axillary lymph node metastases by 0.9, 2.6 and 5.1%, respectively.[20] With a more rapid doubling time of 65 days, the increases in risk are doubled.[20]

Diagnostic Imaging

Mammography with abdominal shielding is safe in pregnancy, but its efficacy is controversial.[21,22] Increased breast density during pregnancy and lactation may reduce the sensitivity of the test.[23,24] In a review of records of women aged 35 years or less diagnosed with breast cancer between 1970 and 1980 in Milwaukee, WI, 6 of 8 pregnant patients had normal mammograms.[25] Conversely, Liberman and colleagues reported that 18 of 23 mammograms in patients with PABC were abnormal, resulting in a sensitivity of 78%.[26] Samuels and colleagues reported that 5 of 8 mammograms performed on patients with PABC showed typical features of malignancy.[27] The most recent report of mammographic findings in PABC is by Ahn and colleagues.[23] They evaluated the mammograms of 15 patients with a diagnosis of PABC between 1998 and 2002. Even though all patients had dense breasts, 13 (86.7%) had abnormal mammographic findings. Eight patients had masses, but other abnormalities seen included calcifications, axillary lymphadenopathy, diffuse skin and trabecular thickening, and asymmetric densities. The authors concluded that, although mass lesions may not be seen on mammography in cases of PABC owing to increased radiodensity, other suspicious abnormalities can be seen.[23]

Ultrasonography (US) is safe and useful for evaluating breast masses during pregnancy and lactation, but available data are limited. Liberman and colleagues reported that breast US demonstrated a focal solid mass in 6 of 6 patients with PABC.[26] However, Samuels and colleagues reported that 2 of 4 patients with PABC had masses that appeared benign on US and advised that clinical, mammographic, and ultrasonographic findings should all be considered in conjunction for the most accurate interpretation of findings.[27] Most recently, Ahn and colleagues reported that US demonstrated a solid mass in 19 of 19 patients with PABC, and although the US findings differed somewhat from those seen in non-PABC cases, they concluded that US is a highly useful diagnostic imaging technique in PABC.

Although magnetic resonance imaging (MRI) of the breast can be helpful for evaluating lesions in nonpregnant patients, its routine use in assessing suspected cases of PABC cannot be advocated. The efficacy of breast MRI in these patients has not been defined in the context of clinical studies, and safety is unconfirmed in pregnancy. MRI has been used to evaluate fetal anomalies and appears to be safe in the second and third trimesters, but it is not recommended in the first trimester since effects on organogenesis are uncertain.[28] Also, the use of gadolinium-based intravenous contrast media is not recommended. It is known to cross the placenta and has been shown to cause developmental, skeletal, and visceral abnormalities in rats.[28,29] It may be appropriate to consider MRI of the breast in a pregnant patient if there is a high suspicion of malignancy and both mammography and US are unable to identify a lesion. However, a case report of MRI use in a 36-year-old lactating patient is of note.[30] This patient had a palpable breast mass with no mass visible on mammogram or US. On MRI, there was increased gadolinium uptake throughout the breasts, and in many areas the gadolinium uptake was similar to that seen in cases of breast cancer, but no focal abnormality corresponding to the palpable mass could be identified. The patient subsequently had an excisional biopsy performed, which showed benign changes consistent with lactation. The authors concluded that increased vascular permeability associated with lactation alters gadolinium uptake in a lactating breast and can cause interpretative difficulty or mimic malignancy. They recommended further study to define the role of MRI in evaluating suspicious masses in the lactating breast.[30]

Biopsy

Although 70 to 80% of breast mass biopsies performed during pregnancy are benign, any clinically suspicious mass or any mass persisting for 2 to 4 weeks warrants biopsy for complete evaluation.[31–33] A number of possible biopsy techniques are available. The diagnosis should be made with the least invasive method that gives a definitive answer. Fine-needle aspiration (FNA) will provide a sample for cytology. The accuracy of FNA in the diagnosis of PABC has been shown in a number of small studies, but a cytopathologist experienced in breast pathology and the normal changes consistent with pregnancy and lactation is essential.[34–36] Core biopsy has several advantages over FNA. It provides tissue for histologic study. This allows the diagnosis of invasive cancer to be made and prognostic markers (hormone receptor, *HER2/neu* status) to be assessed. There is one case report in the literature of a milk fistula occurring as a complication of a core biopsy.[37] If a diagnosis cannot be confirmed using FNA or core biopsy, an incisional or excisional biopsy will be necessary. This can be performed with relative safety in pregnancy.[38]

STAGING

Staging of breast cancer in pregnant women is important to decide on a treatment strategy and to provide prognostic information. Since PABC often presents with more advanced stage, nodal involvement or distant metastatic disease is more likely to be present.[15,16–19]

Clinical staging begins with a thorough physical examination of the patient, paying close attention to the nodal basin of the affected breast. If there is suspicion of involved lymph nodes, ultrasonography of the region in question and FNA, if possible, should be performed.

For discussion of the use of radiology in staging, it is important to consider the dose levels of radiation exposure thought to be acceptable in pregnancy. Much of what is known about the dangers of radiation is based on the experience of those exposed to radiation following the atomic bomb in Hiroshima-Nagasaki. The incidence of microcephaly and mental retardation in Japanese children exposed to 1 to 9 cGy air-dose during the first trimester of gestation as a consequence of the Hiroshima-Nagasaki atomic bomb is 11% compared to 4% in the general Japanese population (where 1 cGy is 1×10^{-2} Gy).[39] The National Commission on Radiation Protection (NCRP) recommends that a total radiation dose exposure during pregnancy of ≤ 5 cGy is acceptable with low likelihood of an adverse outcome; 5 to 10 cGy is low risk for a problem; 10 to 15 cGy is higher risk and consideration should be given to pregnancy termination; >15 cGy pregnancy termination is recommended.[40]

Chest radiography with abdominal shielding is considered safe in pregnancy. The dose to the fetus in the first trimester has been estimated to range between 0.002 and 0.43 mGy (where 1 mGy is 1×10^{-3} Gy), with little information about doses in the second and third trimesters.[41] Higher dose exposures in the second and third trimesters would be expected as the uterus rises out of the pelvis. Damilakis and colleagues estimated the conceptus radiation dose in all three trimesters.[41] For a posteroanterior (PA) chest x-ray, the dose in the first trimester ranged from 1.3 to 2.0×10^{-3} mGy. Estimated doses for the second and third trimesters, respectively, were 7.7×10^{-3} mGy and 13.8×10^{-3} mGy. They conclude that the dose to the conceptus from a chest x-ray can rarely exceed 0.1 mGy and that the radiation hazards to a conceptus associated with a chest radiograph should be considered negligible, but that all reasonable measures to reduce radiation dose should be taken. Interestingly, their study showed that the lead apron reduces radiation dose to the conceptus by only about 5%.[41] Nevertheless, abdominal shielding is easy to perform and is still advisable even for this small difference.

Assessment for liver metastases can be safely performed using liver ultrasonography, but fatty infiltration of the liver owing to pregnancy may make interpretation difficult. Computed tomography is not recommended because of the relatively high radiation doses to which the fetus would be exposed, estimated to be up to 43.6 mGy in the second and third trimesters.[42] MRI may be used if further assessment of the liver is needed, but the same safety issues discussed in relation to breast MRI must be considered.

Evaluation for possible bone metastases is more difficult. Serum alkaline phosphatase levels are not helpful, as they are always elevated two- to fourfold in pregnancy. Radionuclide bone scans result in only 1.94 mGy of radiation exposure to the fetus and can be performed safely during pregnancy, but adequate hydration and an indwelling catheter for 8 hours to prevent retention of radioisotope in the bladder are essential.[43,44] In view of these logistic difficulties with bone scanning and evidence of the efficacy of MRI of thoracic and lumbosacral spine to screen for bone metastases in non-pregnant patients, MRI may be the preferred method after the first trimester.[45–47] Many would consider it appropriate to perform diagnostic imaging only in those with symptoms or clinically advanced disease such as stage III disease.[4]

Pathologic Features

A number of studies have examined the pathologic features of PABC. Differences in study designs, study populations (some considering pregnant patients only, and others all PABC), and laboratory techniques make it difficult to draw any definite conclusions about comparisons between the pathologic characteristics of breast cancer in pregnant compared to non-pregnant women.[48] About 75 to 90% of tumors are ductal carcinomas in both groups.[4] Many studies have shown decreased estrogen and progesterone receptor (ER and PR) positivity in tumors of pregnant patients.[4] These findings in older studies have been questioned because the ligand binding assay (LBA) was used to determine ER status.[48] Immunohistochemistry (IHC) has been shown to be more sensitive in pregnant patients, possibly owing to receptor down-regulation in pregnancy leading to more negative results with LBA.[49] However, the three most recently published studies addressing the question of hormone receptor status have used immunohistochemistry and still show high rates of hormone receptor negativity.[50–52] One, a case control study, found 71% of cases of PABC ($n = 24$) were ER and PR negative compared with 42% in non-pregnant controls ($n = 315$).[50] Few studies have considered *HER2/neu* expression in PABC, and available results are conflicting.[49,50,53] Further studies, using modern techniques, of potential differences in prognostic and predictive tumor characteristics between pregnant and non-pregnant breast cancer patients are needed.

A large number of studies have found that women with PABC present with larger tumors and are more likely to have axillary node involvement, lymphovascular invasion, or metastatic disease. In their review of the literature, Woo and colleagues reported that up to 54% of non-pregnant women present with positive nodes at diagnosis, but this is up to 83% in pregnant patients.[4] Zemlickis and colleagues compared 118 pregnant women with breast cancer with 269 non-pregnant controls.[17] They found that pregnant women were 2.5 times more likely to have metastatic disease and had a significantly lower chance of having stage I disease ($p = .015$). It is not known if these differences are due to delays in diagnosis in pregnant women or tumor biology.

TREATMENT

Local Treatment

The need for anesthesia and surgery arises during 1.5 to 2% of pregnancies, and it is estimated that over 75,000 pregnant patients in the United States undergo non-obstetric surgery each year.[54] The safety of non-obstetric surgery and anesthesia in pregnancy has been well established, and breast and axillary surgery can be performed during pregnancy without significant risk to the developing fetus.[54–56] Duncan and colleagues compared the pregnancy outcomes in 2,565 pregnant women who had surgery with controls who did not and reported no increase in congenital anomalies.[56] However, they reported that there may be an increased risk of spontaneous abortion with general anesthetic in the first and second trimesters (risk ratio 1.54 for non-gynecologic procedures). Another report, by Mazze and colleagues, found a greater incidence of low and very low birth weight infants among women who underwent surgery during pregnancy, but the authors suggest that the underlying illness necessitating surgery may have negatively influenced the birth weights.[57]

In non-pregnant patients, breast-conserving surgery (BCS) (lumpectomy and axillary lymph node dissection) followed by radiotherapy has been shown to be as effective as mastectomy for local therapy. However, breast radiation therapy during pregnancy is relatively contraindicated as it may expose the fetus to an excessive radiation dose causing congenital abnormalities or an increased risk of malignancy in the child. A treatment course of 50 Gy to the breast with abdominal shielding results in estimated doses to the fetus of 2.1 to 7.6, 2.2 to 24.6 and 2.2 to 58.6 cGy in the first, second, and third trimesters, respectively.[58] Appreciating the earlier discussion of unsafe radiation doses in pregnancy, there is potential for exposure of the fetus to hazardous doses with breast irradiation. Although there are reports of normal children born to mothers who received supradiaphragmatic radiotherapy during pregnancy, mostly for Hodgkin's lymphoma, considering the possible risks and the alternative available local treatment options for breast cancer, breast radiotherapy is not recommended.[4,59]

Most pregnant women having surgery for breast cancer undergo modified radical mastectomy (MRM) with axillary lymph node dissection to avoid the need for radiotherapy. BCS can be considered in the case of patients who present in the third trimester, with radiotherapy being administered postpartum. Kuerer and colleagues reported a comparison between the outcomes of BCS and MRM in 22 patients with stage I–II PABC.[60] Two-thirds of the patients were pregnant, with a median gestational age of 7 months, at the time of diagnosis. Nine patients were treated with BCS, and 13 were treated with MRM. The authors found similar results for disease-free survival and overall survival for the two techniques. BCS may also be considered in patients who receive neoadjuvant chemotherapy during pregnancy, usually for locally advanced disease at presentation and complete this late in pregnancy or postpartum, when BCS, followed by radiotherapy within an appropriate time frame, may be feasible. Another report by Kuerer and colleagues detailed the cases of four patients who underwent BCS and chemotherapy for PABC between 1995 and 1997.[61] Three of the patients received neoadjuvant chemotherapy commenced during their pregnancy with definitive BCS in the postpartum period. The fourth patient underwent definitive BCS at gestational age 22 weeks, followed by adjuvant chemotherapy commenced at 26 weeks. At a median follow-up of 44 months, there were no local or systemic recurrences, and there was no evidence of developmental delay in the children. The authors suggest that mastectomy may not be necessary for pregnant women diagnosed with breast cancer if chemotherapy during pregnancy can be administered to control local and systemic disease and radiotherapy delayed until the postpartum period. The caveat is that chemotherapy is generally not advisable in the first trimester, as discussed later. Therefore, mastectomy may still be the best local treatment option for women presenting in early first trimester.

Sentinel lymph node biopsy (SLNB) is often performed in non-pregnant patients with early breast cancer. It can accurately stage the axilla and is associated with less morbidity than axillary dissection.[62] The use of SLNB has not been evaluated as an alternative to axillary lymph node dissection in pregnant patients. Isosulfan blue dye, radiocolloid, or both are used to identify the sentinel nodes in non-pregnant patients. Isosulfan blue dye has been associated with severe allergic reactions in non-pregnant patients. It should not be used in pregnant patients as its safety has not been assessed.[7] There is concern about the radiation dose to the fetus from radioisotope use for lymphoscintigraphy and SLNB. There is indirect evidence that the use of ^{99m}Tc for lymphoscintigraphy and SLNB may be safe in pregnancy.[22,63,64] Gentilini and colleagues reported on 26 premenopausal non-pregnant patients who underwent SLNB following a peritumoral injection of ^{99m}Tc.[64] They measured absorbed dose levels at the epigastrium, umbilicus, and hypogastrium to approximate the doses absorbed by the developing fetus in the first, second, and third trimesters, respectively. The absorbed dose measurements at all three levels were less than 10 μGy in 23 cases, and in the other 3 patients the dose ranges were 40 to 320, 120 to 250 and 30 to 140 μGy (where 1 μGy is 1×10^{-6} Gy). They concluded that lymphoscintigraphy and SLNB, using their described technique, can be performed safely during pregnancy as the dose of radiation to which the fetus would be exposed is very low. However, there are no cases or studies reported in the literature of lymphoscintigraphy and SLNB using ^{99m}Tc in pregnant breast cancer patients. SLNB using radiocolloid has been performed in pregnant patients with melanoma by Schwartz and colleagues, but the number of patients treated and fetal outcome is not reported.[65] The panel of the Consensus Conference on the role of SLNB in breast carcinoma in 2002 advised against SLNB in pregnant women until more data are available.[66] There is still insufficient evidence to recommend routine lymphoscintigraphy and SLNB as standard in pregnant patients with breast cancer.

Chemotherapy

The indications for systemic chemotherapy in pregnant patients are the same as those in non-pregnant patients.[67–69] A lot of confusion and controversy surrounds the use of cytotoxic chemotherapy during pregnancy because of potential teratogenic effects and poor understanding of possible altered pharmacokinetics in the pregnant patient.[70] No prospective studies of in utero amniotic fluid or fetal tissue concentrations of these agents have been performed.

Much of the available data on the use of cytotoxic agents in pregnancy comes from case reports or short case series and collected reviews. Ebert and colleagues reviewed 217 cases published between 1983 and 1995 of various cytotoxic agents used in pregnancy for malignancies or rheumatologic disorders.[71] Most adverse events were associated with first trimester use. Fourteen breast cancer patients were included in this review. There were eight live births with no congenital abnormalities, although one had intrauterine growth retardation. Two spontaneous abortions occurred, both in patients treated in the first trimester. One stillbirth with no physical abnormality occurred in a fetus exposed to vincristine, methotrexate, and doxorubicin from gestational week 25. Three infants had congenital abnormalities: one exposed to tamoxifen throughout pregnancy, one exposed to cyclophosphamide and radiation in the first trimester, and one following preconceptual use of methotrexate. The use of methotrexate during pregnancy is not recommended. It is a known abortifacient and can cause severe congenital abnormalities if given in the first trimester.[70,71] Another review of pregnant patients who received chemotherapy for various malignancies reported a 17% incidence of fetal abnormalities in 139 women treated in the first trimester, and an incidence of only 1.3% in 150 patients treated after the first trimester.[70] Clearly the timing of exposure to cytotoxic agents during pregnancy is critical. Most adverse outcomes occur following administration in the first trimester when organogenesis is occurring.

Many chemotherapy regimens used in the treatment of breast cancer contain an anthracycline, either doxorubicin or epirubicin. Although Grohard and colleagues reported that the transplacental passage of doxorubicin in vitro is low, there is an unusual case report of two pregnant women who both received anthracycline-containing chemotherapy regimens for lymphoproliferative disorders shortly before the birth of their children; one child was stillborn with measurable tissue levels of anthracycline, whereas the other child was born alive and well with no evidence of transplacental passage.[72,73] A case series of 28 pregnant patients treated with doxorubicin- or daunorubicin-based chemotherapy after the first trimester for various malignancies reported 24 normal infants, including a set of twins.[74] One pregnancy was terminated, two patients miscarried physically normal fetuses, and one neonate had transient marrow hypoplasia. Germann and colleagues collected information on 160 patients treated with anthracyclines during pregnancy from a review of the literature and their own experience.[75] Of these, 62% received doxorubicin, 31% received daunorubicin, 90% were treated with a combination regimen, and 31 patients received an anthracycline in the first trimester. Fetal outcome was normal in 73% of cases. Three of a total of five malformations followed treatment in the first trimester. Of 15 fetal deaths, 6 were associated with maternal death. Fetal deaths were more frequent after daunorubicin and in acute leukemia patients. In solid tumor patients, first trimester use of anthracyclines was significantly associated with more complications. The authors report a dose-dependent increase in the risk of fetal toxicity. They concluded that the risk to the fetus seems low, especially in the second and third trimesters and with doxorubicin doses less than 70 mg/m^2.[75]

There is less information available on epirubicin use in pregnant patients. Cardonick and Iacobucci describe reports of 13 patients treated with this agent during pregnancy, with 3 fetal deaths.[76] One of these deaths occurred in an 8-day old neonate exposed to third trimester treatment with 5-fluorouracil, epirubicin, and cyclophosphamide (FEC). Based on this 23% fetal mortality with epirubicin, Cardonick and Iacobucci recommend that doxorubicin should be the preferred anthracycline in pregnancy. In a letter to the editor, Peccatori and colleagues disagreed. They described 9 pregnant breast cancer patients treated with either weekly or 3-weekly epirubicin after 15 weeks of gestation.[77] No significant maternal or fetal complications occurred. Another 4 case reports describe 3 breast cancer patients and 1 lymphoma patient who received epirubicin-based treatment during pregnancy, one in the first trimester, with no adverse fetal outcomes.[78–81]

There is only one published prospective cohort of pregnant breast cancer patients treated with chemotherapy.[82] Twenty-four pregnant patients were treated in the second and/or third trimester for breast cancer with intravenous (IV) fluorouracil 500mg/m^2 days 1 and 4, doxorubicin 50 mg/m^2 by IV infusion over 72 hours, and cyclophosphamide 500 mg/m^2 IV day 1 repeated every 3 to 4 weeks. A median of four cycles of chemotherapy was administered. The only reported antepartum complications were hospitalization with diarrhoea and queried pyelonephritis in one patient, which resolved with symptomatic and supportive care, and a deep venous thrombosis in a patient with a prior history of same. There were three pre-term deliveries, two idiopathic cases and one owing to pre-eclampsia. The mean gestational age at delivery was 38 weeks, with birth weights, Apgar scores, and postpartum health reported normal in all infants with no congenital abnormalities.[82]

Taxanes are widely used in the treatment of node-positive breast cancer in non-pregnant patients. There are only a small number of case reports of their use in pregnancy, summarized in Table 29–1.[76,79,83–86] In all cases, the taxane was used after organogenesis with no adverse fetal outcomes.

Despite these few favorable case reports, there is inadequate information about the safety of taxanes in pregnancy to recommend their routine use. There is a significant body of evidence supporting the relative safety of anthracycline-containing chemotherapy regimens after the first trimester. Based on the only prospective study available, it would be reasonable to consider 5-fluorouracil, Adriamycin (doxorubicin), cyclophosphamide (FAC) used in the second and third trimesters the regimen of choice in pregnant patients.[82] If the diagnosis is made in the first trimester, appropriate surgery at that stage and institution of chemotherapy in the second trimester would be a reasonable option. For patients diagnosed late in the third trimester, initiation of chemotherapy may be deferred until postpartum.

Table 29–1. CASES OF TAXANE USE DURING PREGNANCY

Diagnosis	Chemotherapeutic Agents	Schedule	Timing	Fetal Outcome
Metastatic breast cancer[83]	Docetaxel 100 mg/m^2	3 weekly for 3 cycles	3rd trimester	Female infant, born 32 weeks, normal weight, no congenital abnormality
Ovarian cancer[84]	Paclitaxel 135 mg/m^2 + cisplatin 75 mg/m^2	3 weekly for 3 cycles	3rd trimester	Female infant, born 37 weeks, normal weight, no congenital abnormality, normal development at 30 months
Ovarian cancer[85]	Paclitaxel 175 mg/m^2 + carboplatin AUC 5	3 weekly for 6 cycles	2nd + 3rd trimester	Born at 35.5 weeks, birth weight 44th percentile (2,500 g), no congenital abnormality, normal development at 15 months
Breast cancer[79]	Epirubicin 120 mg/m^2 followed by paclitaxel 175 mg/m^2	Sequential, 3 weekly for 3 cycles each	2nd + 3rd trimester	Female infant, born 36 weeks, no congenital abnormality, normal development at 36 months
Bilateral breast cancer[86]	Paclitaxel 80 mg/m^2	Weekly for 12 weeks	2nd + 3rd trimester	Male infant, born 37 weeks, birth weight 5th–10th percentile, no congenital abnormality, normal development at 12 months
Not specified[76]	Paclitaxel	Not specified	Not specified	Twins, "no complications"
Not specified[76]	Paclitaxel	Not specified	Not specified	"No complications"

Endocrine Therapy

There are a number of case reports of tamoxifen use in pregnant breast cancer patients. One patient became pregnant while taking tamoxifen and continued it throughout her pregnancy.[87] She had a preterm delivery at 26 weeks of an infant with Goldenhar's syndrome (oculoauriculovertebral dysplasia). It must be noted that there was also a history of radiograph exposure and possible illicit drug use before and during pregnancy. Another report describes the case of a pregnant woman who took tamoxifen from the first trimester until delivery at 31 weeks and had a healthy male infant.[88] The infant had preauricular skin tags, but no other malformations, and development was normal at 24 months. Although this infant did not have Goldenhar's syndrome, preauricular skin tags are one of the features of this syndrome. A further case outlines the history of a woman who took tamoxifen until the 20th week of gestation.[89] Because of the mother's deteriorating condition, the infant was delivered at 29 weeks and was a female with ambiguous genitalia. Clark reported no fetal abnormalities in 85 women who became pregnant while taking tamoxifen for breast cancer prevention.[90] Information from female animal studies have shown metaplastic and dysplastic changes in the epithelium of the uterus and reproductive tract following in utero exposure to tamoxifen.[91–93] Tewari and colleagues advise close follow-up for all female infants exposed to tamoxifen in utero and the establishment of a registry of pregnancies and their outcomes similar to the registry developed for diethylstilbestrol.[89] Considering the available experimental data from animal studies and the limited clinical data, tamoxifen is not recommended as standard treatment for breast cancer in pregnant patients. Also, since most tumors are hormone receptor negative during pregnancy, it would not be warranted.

There is no information on the use of luteinizing hormone-releasing hormone (LHRH) analogues to treat breast cancer diagnosed during pregnancy, and they are not recommended. There is only one case report of fetal exposure to a LHRH analogue up to week 16 of gestation.[94]A healthy female infant with no anomalies was born at term.

Pregnancy Termination

Breast cancer is a hormone-sensitive disease, and it has been speculated that the altered hormonal environment in pregnant patients could stimulate more rapid growth of breast cancer. Many pregnant women diagnosed with breast cancer have been advised to have a termination. However, there is no convincing evidence that this will improve survival in these patients. In one early series, 24 pregnant patients with breast cancer underwent mastectomy, then half continued with the pregnancy and the other half had a termination.[95] There was no difference in cure rate between the two groups. There is some evidence from retrospective studies that termination of pregnancy may even worsen the prognosis of the patients.[96,97] There are no prospective studies assessing the effect of termination on the survival of these patients, and termination of pregnancy should not be recommended as a therapeutic option. Patients should be fully informed about all of their treatment options and the limited data pertaining to the question of termination. The decision to terminate a pregnancy should be considered in the context of the mother's prognosis, the possible effects of necessary treatment on the developing fetus, the potential consequences of fetal or maternal death, and the ability of the patient and her family to cope with an infant at this difficult time.[98]

MONITORING OF PREGNANCY, LABOR, AND DELIVERY

It is essential that an obstetrician or maternal/fetal health team follow pregnant women with breast cancer closely with regular prenatal examinations and serial fetal ultrasound. Ultrasonography can give important information about gestational age and expected date of delivery. This is central to treatment planning. Also, potential fetal consequences of treatment can be monitored for by ultrasound. In the prospective study of chemotherapy by Berry and colleagues, they reported that high-risk obstetric care was provided for all patients.[82] This comprised serial fetal growth ultrasound examinations every 3 to 4 weeks or as clinically indicated, fetal non-stress testing or biophysical profile, and amniocentesis for "standard obstetric indications." Close communication between the maternal/fetal health team and the involved medical and surgical oncologists should be maintained throughout the pregnancy and the postpartum period.

Attempts to avoid neutropenia when labor may be expected should be made. Cardonick and Iacobucci recommend that no chemotherapy be administered after 35 weeks.[76] There are few studies examining the complications that may arise during labor and delivery when the mother is being treated with chemotherapy. From available information, premature delivery appears to be common. In the study by Berry and colleagues, the median gestational age at delivery was 38 weeks.[82] There were three premature deliveries. One was at 33 weeks owing to preeclampsia. This infant had hyaline membrane but recovered without complications. The other two were due to idiopathic premature labor. One pre-term infant whose mother received chemotherapy 2 days prior to delivery had transient leucopenia but no infectious complications. Two infants required oxygen for transient tachypnea of the newborn that resolved within 48 hours. Two cases of postpartum endometritis resolved with IV antibiotic treatment. Zemlickis and colleagues reported from a case-control study that pregnant women with breast cancer are more likely to have a premature infant, and after adjusting for gestational age, the infants had a statistically lower mean birth weight.[17] In the retrospective case series of 20 pregnant breast cancer patients (n = 20) reported by Giacalone and colleagues, the mean gestational age at delivery was 34.7 weeks among the 17 live births.[99] In the series of 14 patients reported by Ebert and colleagues, 3 of the 8 live born infants without congenital anomalies were premature.[71]

BREASTFEEDING

Breastfeeding is contraindicated in women who are receiving chemotherapy. For most cytotoxic agents there is no specific information, but doxorubicin and cyclophosphamide are known to be excreted in breast milk.[100] A case of neonatal neutropenia in a breastfed infant whose mother was being treated with cyclophosphamide has been reported.[101] Women who have had a lumpectomy and/or recent chemotherapy may have a reduced milk supply.[82,102] Also, radiation treatment can cause changes to the nipple and milk ducts that may compromise lactation.[102]

LONG-TERM FOLLOW-UP OF CHILDREN EXPOSED IN UTERO TO CYTOTOXIC AGENTS

There are little data on long-term effects of in utero exposure to cytotoxic agents on the development and health of children. Most published reports consider children of women treated for hematological malignancies. Aviles and colleagues followed 84 children born to such mothers, 38 of whom were treated during the first trimester.[103] No deficits in physical health, neurology, development, or hematologic and cytogenetic assessments were found with a median follow-up of 18.7 years.[103] There were also no problems reported in 12 second-generation children. Another series of 50 live births to women with acute leukemia reported long-term follow-up for 7 children, up to the age of 17 years. All were growing and developing normally.[104] One other child from this series constitutes the only published report of malignancy developing in a child exposed in utero to chemotherapy. This child had congenital abnormalities at birth, and later developed a neuroblastoma and thyroid carcinoma. However, his fraternal twin who was exposed to the same agents in utero had no congenital abnormalities and did not develop malignant disease, so the role of the chemotherapy as a causative agent is highly questionable.

There are more limited reports of long-term follow-up of children whose mothers were treated in pregnancy for breast cancer. In the prospective study by Berry and colleagues, there were no developmental abnormalities in the 24 children born to mothers who received FAC chemotherapy for breast cancer during pregnancy at a median age of 4.5 years.[82] In the retrospective case series reported by Giacalone and colleagues, the 16 children who survived the neonatal period had all reached normal developmental milestones at a mean follow-up of 42.3 months.[99] Cardonick and Iacobucci report follow-up on 55 children born to mothers receiving chemotherapy, 35 of whom were being treated for breast cancer and the others for a variety of malignancies.[76] The oldest child at follow-up is 7 years, and 53 of the 55 children are displaying normal development and growth. The other 2 children had periventricular leukomalacia, one diagnosed soon after birth and the other at 2 months. They were both born to mothers who received doxorubicin and cyclophosphamide in the third trimester for breast cancer, but possible alternative etiologies for their neurologic problems were identified.

Reynoso and colleagues in 1987 urged that "a central registry is strongly advised in order to document the long-term complications arising in children exposed to chemotherapy in utero."[104] A registry is currently being developed by the Motherisk Program in Canada, and they hope that all oncologists treating pregnant patients with cancer will forward case details to them.[105] With the available information, children exposed to chemotherapy in utero who have no congenital abnormality and survive the neonatal period appear to have little risk of long-term developmental or physical health problems. However, it must be noted that the longest published follow-up period is a median of 18.7 years, and there may be as yet unknown effects later in life.[7,103]

FOLLOW-UP FOR BREAST CANCER AND PROGNOSIS

Women with a history of breast cancer during pregnancy can be followed according to the same guidelines established by the American Society of Clinical Oncology and the National Comprehensive Cancer Network for all women with breast cancer.[106,107] There is controversy regarding the prognosis for these patients. It was previously believed that these women had a significantly worse prognosis.[108] However, a number of studies over the past 20 years have shown that, when matched for stage and age, pregnant patients have an equivalent outcome to non-pregnant patients.[2] If this is so, the perceived worse prognosis may be due to the later stage at diagnosis. However, there are some studies that have found pregnancy at the time of breast cancer diagnosis to be an independent negative prognostic factor.[109] In a review of the literature, Kroman and Mouridsen concluded that available studies cannot allow a definite assessment of the prognosis of these women owing to small sample sizes and short follow-up periods.[109]

SUMMARY

Breast cancer diagnosed during pregnancy is rare, but its incidence is expected to increase as more women delay childbearing. The most common presentation is a painless mass. Full evaluation with clinical examination, diagnostic imaging, and biopsy must be performed. Mammography with abdominal shielding in pregnancy is safe, but the physiologic increase in breast density may compromise sensitivity. Breast ultrasound is useful as an adjunct to mammography. Staging of breast cancer can safely include physical examination, chest radiography with abdominal shielding, and liver ultrasonography. Bone scan with special precautions or screening MRI of the thoracic and lumbosacral spine can be used in patients with symptoms of bone metastases, or those deemed to be at high risk owing to locally advanced disease.

Breast radiotherapy is relatively contraindicated in pregnancy as the fetus may be exposed to hazardous radiation doses. A modified radical mastectomy is the most common surgical option for women with breast cancer during pregnancy as it may avoid the need for adjuvant radiotherapy. Breast-conserving surgery can be considered if (1) surgery is performed late in the third trimester, and radiotherapy can be delivered postpartum without significant delay, (2) neoadjuvant chemotherapy is given, and surgery is thereby delayed to the third trimester or the postpartum period, or (3) the diagnosis is made in or beyond late first trimester, and surgery can be followed by adjuvant chemotherapy in the second and third trimesters with radiotherapy administered postpartum (Figure 29–1). Although not standard of care, sentinel lymph node biopsy may be considered in lieu of axillary dissection in pregnant women. Termination of pregnancy does not appear to improve survival and should not be considered as a therapeutic option.

Although most of the information regarding the use of chemotherapy in pregnant breast cancer patients is derived from case-series and case-control studies, there is a significant body of evidence supporting the relative safety of anthracycline-containing chemotherapy regimens after the first trimester.

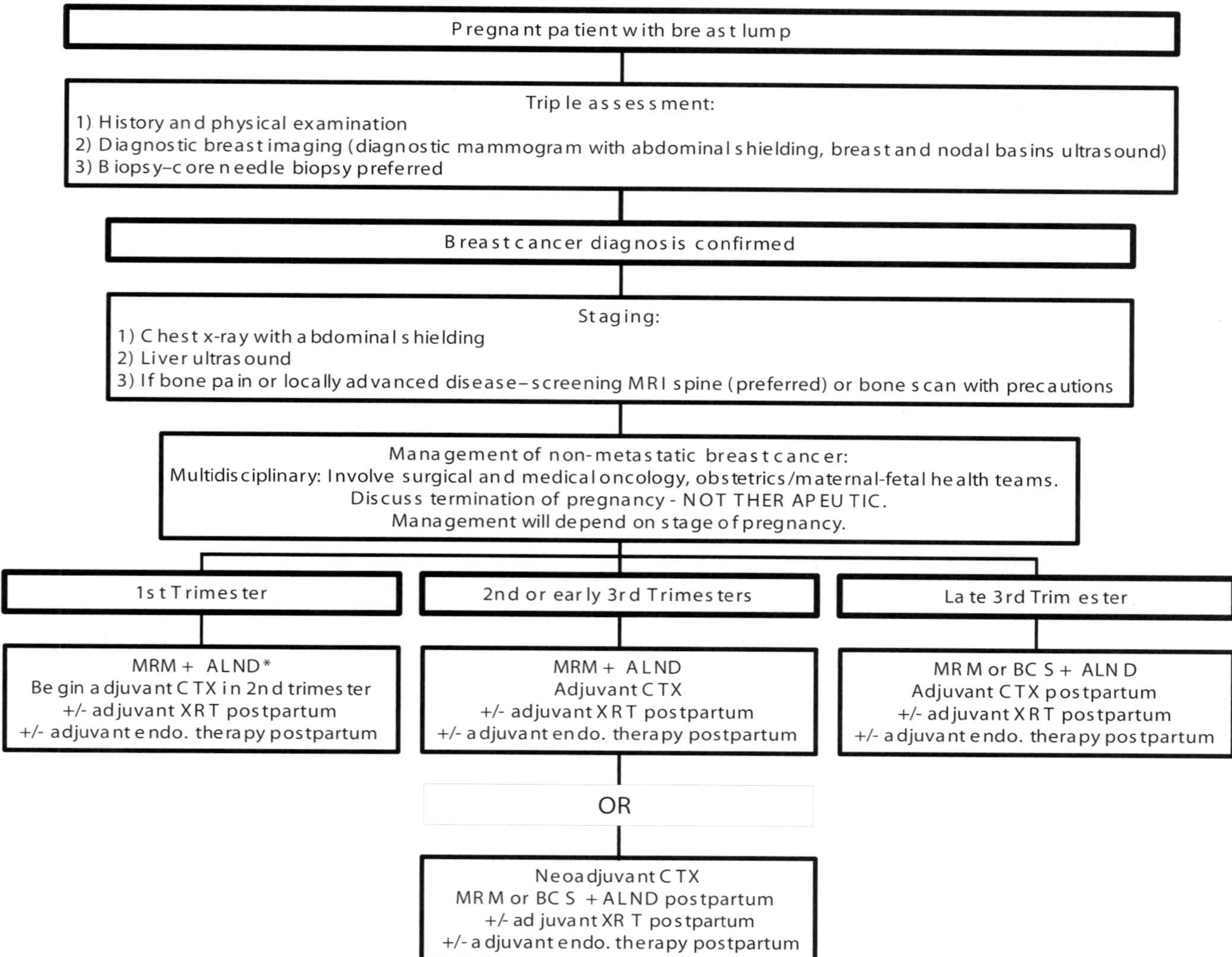

Figure 29–1. Management of primary breast cancer during pregnancy. *If late 1st trimester, may be possible to do BCS, rather than MRM, with adjuvant CTX commencing in the second trimester and post partum adjuvant radiotherapy. ALND = axillary lymph node dissection; BCS = breast-conserving surgery; CTX = chemotherapy; endo. = endocrine; MRM = modified radical mastectomy; XRT = radiotherapy. Note that standard indications for adjuvant radiotherapy apply, but it should be administered postpartum.

Based on the only prospective study available, FAC (fluorouracil, Adriamycin, and cyclophosphamide) used in the second and third trimesters can be considered the chemotherapy regimen of choice. There are insufficient data to support the routine use of taxanes for the treatment of breast cancer during pregnancy. Available evidence suggests that tamoxifen use during pregnancy is unsafe.

REFERENCES

1. Reis LAG, Hankey BF, Miller BA, et al. Cancer statistics review 1973-1988. Bethesda, MD: National Cancer Institute, NIH Publication III; 1991.39, 91-2789.
2. White TT. Prognosis of breast cancer for pregnant and nursing women: analysis of 1413 cases. Surg Gynecol Obstet 1955;700:661–6.
3. Saunders CM, Baum M. Breast cancer and pregnancy: a review. J R Soc Med 1993;86:162–5.
4. Woo JC, Yu T, Hurd TC, et al. Breast cancer in pregnancy—a literature review. Arch Surg 2003;138:91–8.
5. Wallack MK, Wolf JA Jr, Bedwineck J, et al. Gestational carcinoma of the female breast. Curr Probl Cancer 1983; 7:1–58.
6. Smith LH, Dalrymple JL, Leiserowitz GS, et al. Obstetrical deliveries associated with maternal malignancy in California, 1992 through 1997. Am J Obstet Gynecol 2001;184:1504–12.
7. AJ Keleher, Theriault RL, Gwyn KM, et al. Multidisciplinary management of breast cancer concurrent with pregnancy. J Am Coll Surg 2001;194:54–6.

8. Ventura SJ. First births to older mothers, 1970-86. AJPH 1989;79:1675–7.
9. Kelsey JL, Berkowitz GS. Breast cancer epidemiology. Cancer Res 1988;48:5615–23.
10. Martin JA, Hamilton BE, Sutton PD, et al. Births: Final data for 2002. National vital statistics report. National Center for Health Statistics; 2003. Vol 52, No 10. http://www.cdc.gov/nchs/births.htm (accessed Nov 11, 2004).
11. King RM, Welch JS, Martin JK Jr, Coulam CB. Carcinoma of the breast associated with pregnancy. Surg Gynecol Obstet 1985;160:228–32.
12. Tobon H, Horowitz LF. Breast cancer during pregnancy. Breast Dis 1993;6:127–34.
13. Ribeiro G, Jones D, Jones M. Carcinoma of the breast associated with pregnancy. Br J Surg 1986;73:607–9.
14. Scott-Connor C, Schorr S. The diagnosis and management of breast problems during pregnancy and lactation. Am J Surg 1995;170:401–5.
15. Ishida T, Yokoe T, Kasumi F, et al. Clinicopathological characteristics and prognosis of breast cancer patients associated with pregnancy and lactation: analysis of case-control study in Japan. Jpn J Cancer Res 1992;83:1143–9.
16. Petrek JA, Dukoff R, Rogatko A. Prognosis of pregnancy-associated breast cancer. Cancer 1991;67:869–72.
17. Zemlickis D, Lishner M, Degendorfer P, et al. Maternal and fetal outcome after breast cancer in pregnancy. Am J Obstet Gynecol 1992;166:781–7.
18. Anderson BO, Petrek JA, Byrd DR, et al. Pregnancy influences breast cancer stage at diagnosis in women 30 years of age and younger. Ann Surg Oncol 1996;3:204–11.
19. Bonnier P, Romain S, Dilhuydy JM, et al. Influence of pregnancy on the outcome of breast cancer: a case-control study. Int J Cancer1997;72:720–7.
20. Nettleton J, Long J, Kuban D, et al. Breast cancer during pregnancy: quantifying the risk of treatment delay. Obstet Gynecol 1996;87:414–8.
21. Rosene-Montella K, Larson L. Obstetric monitoring: maternal and fetal testing: diagnostic testing. In: Lee RV, Rosene-Montella K, Barbour LA, et al, editors. Medical care of the pregnant patient. Philadelphia: American College of Physicians; 2000. p. 103–16.
22. Nicklas A, Baker M. Imaging strategies in pregnant cancer patients. Semin Oncol 2000;27:623–32.
23. Ahn BY, Kim HH, Moon WK, et al. Pregnancy- and lactation-associated breast cancer: mammographic and sonographic findings. J Ultrasound Med 2003;22:491–7.
24. Talele AC, Slanetz PJ, Edmister WB, et al. The lactating breast: MRI findings and literature review. Breast J 2003;9:237–40.
25. Max MH, Klamer TW. Breast cancer in 120 women under 35 years old: a 10-year community wide survey. Am Surg 1984;50:23–25.
26. Liberman L, Giess CS, Dershaw DD, et al. Imaging of pregnancy-associated breast cancer. Radiology 1994;191: 245–8.
27. Samuels TH, Liu FF, Yaffe M, et al. Gestational breast cancer. Can Assoc Radiol J 1998;48:172–80.
28. Huisman TA, Martin E, Kubik-Huch R, Marincek B. Fetal magnetic resonance imaging of the brain: technical considerations and normal brain development. Eur Radiol 2002;12:1941–51.
29. Shellock FG, Kanal E. Safety of magnetic resonance imaging contrast agents. J Magn Reson Imaging 1999;10: 477–84.
30. Talele AC, Slanetz PJ, Edmister WB, et al. The lactating breast: MRI findings and literature review. Breast J 2003; 9:237–40.
31. Byrd BF Jr, Bayer DS, Robertson JC, Stephenson SE Jr. Treatment of breast tumors associated with pregnancy and lactation. Ann Surg 1962;155:940–7.
32. Carol EH, Conner S, Schorr S. The diagnosis and manangement of breast problems during pregnancy and lactation. Am J Surg 1995;170:401–4.
33. Merkel DE. Pregnancy and breast cancer. Semin Surg Oncol 1996;12:370–5.
34. Bottles K, Taylor RN. Diagnosis of breast masses in pregnant and lactating women by aspiration cytology. Obstet Gynecol 1985;66 Suppl:76–8.
35. Gupta RK, McHutchinson AGR, Dowle CS, et al. Fine-needle aspiration cytodiagnosis of breast masses in pregnant and lactating women and its impact on management. Diagn Cytopathol 1993;19:156–9.
36. Gupta RK. The diagnostic impact of aspiration cytodiagnosis of breast masses in association with pregnancy and lactation with an emphasis on clinical decision making. Breast J 1997;3:131–4.
37. Schackmuth EM, Harlow CL, Norton LW. Milk fistula: a complication after core breast biopsy. AJR Am J Roentgenol 1993:161:790–4.
38. Collins JC, Liao S, Wile AG. Surgical management of breast masses in pregnant women. J Reprod Med 1995;40:785–8.
39. Miller RW, Mulvihill JJ. Small head size after atomic radiation. Teratology 1976;14:355–8.
40. National Council on Radiation Protection and Measurements (NCRP) (1994). Considerations regarding the unintended radiation exposure of the embryo, fetus or nursing child. NCRP commentary no. 9., Bethesda, MD: NCRP Publications; p. 11–2.
41. Damilakis J, Perisinakis K, Dimovasili E, et al. Conceptus radiation dose and risk from chest screen-film radiography. Eur Radiol 2003;13:406–12.
42. Damilakis J, Perisinakis K, Voloudaki A, et al. Estimation of fetal radiation dose from computed tomography scanning in late pregnancy: depth-dose data from routine examinations. Invest Radiol 2000;35:527–33.
43. Baker J, Ali A, Groch MW, et al. Bone scanning in pregnant patients with breast carcinoma. Clin Nucl Med 1987; 12:519–24.
44. Donegan WL. Breast carcinoma and pregnancy. In: Donegan WL, Spratt JS, editors. Cancer of the breast. 4th ed. Philadelphia, PA: Saunders; 1995. p. 732–41.
45. Gosfield E, Alavi A, Kneeland B. Comparison of radionuclide bone scans and magnetic resonance imaging in detecting spinal metastases. J Nucl Med 1993;34:2191–8.
46. Flickinger FW, Sanal SM. Bone marrow MRI. Techniques and accuracy for detecting breast cancer metastases. Magn Reson Imaging 1994;12:829–35.
47. Hamaoka T, Madewell JE, Podoloff DA, et al. Bone imaging in metastatic breast cancer. J Clin Oncol 2004;22(14): 2942–53.
48. Gwyn K. Management of breast cancer in pregnancy. In: Singletary SE, Robb GL, Hortobagyi GN, editors. Advanced

therapy of breast disease. 2nd ed. Hamilton, ON: BC Decker Inc; 2004. p. 650–8.

49. Elledge RM, Ciocca DR, Langone G, McGuire WL. Estrogen receptor, progesterone receptor, and HER-2/neu protein in breast cancers from pregnant patients. Cancer 1993;71:2499–506.
50. Aziz S, Pervez S, Khan S, et al. Case control study of novel prognostic markers and disease outcome in pregnancy/lactation-associated breast carcinoma. Pathol Res Pract 2003;199:15–21.
51. Middleton PL, Amin M, Gwyn K, et al. Breast carcinoma in pregnant women: assessment of clinicopathologic and immunohistochemical features. Cancer 2003;98:1055–60.
52. Reed W, Hannisdal E, Skovlund E, et al. Pregnancy and breast cancer: a population-based study. Virchows Arch 2003;443:44–50.
53. Shousha S. Breast carcinoma presenting during or shortly after pregnancy and lactation. Arch Pathol Lab Med 2000;124:1053–60.
54. Kuczkowski KM. Nonobstetric surgery during pregnancy: What are the risks of anesthesia? Obstet Gynecol Surv 2004;59:52–6.
55. Gianopoulos JG. Establishing the criteria for anesthesia and other precautions for surgery during pregnancy. Surg Clin North Am 1995;75:33–43.
56. Duncan PG, Pope WDB, Cohen MM, et al. Fetal risk of anesthesia and surgery during pregnancy. Anesthesiology 1986;64:790–4.
57. Mazze RI, Kallen B. Reproductive outcome after anesthesia and operation during pregnancy: a registry study of 5405 cases. Am J Obstet Gynecol 1989;161:1178–85.
58. Mazonakis M, Vaveris H, Damilakis J, et al. Radiation dose to conceptus resulting from tangential breast radiation. Int J Radiat Biol Phys 2003;55:386–91.
59. Woo SY, Fuller LM, Cundiff JH, et al. Radiotherapy during pregnancy for clinical stages IA–IIA Hodgkin's disease. Int J Radiat Oncol Biol Phys 1992;23:407–12.
60. Kuerer HM, Cunningham JD, Bleiweiss IJ, et al. Conservative surgery for breast carcinoma associated with pregnancy. Breast J 1998;4:171–6.
61. Kuerer HM, Gwyn K, Ames FC, et al. Conservative surgery and chemotherapy for breast carcinoma during pregnancy. Surg 2002;131:108–10.
62. Kelley MC, Hansen N, McMasters KM. Lymphatic mapping and sentinel lymphadenectomy for breast cancer.Am J Surg. 2004 Jul;188:49–61.
63. Morita ET, Chang J, Leong S. Principles and controversies in lymphoscintigraphy with emphasis on breast cancer. Surg Clin North Am 2000;80:1721–37.
64. Gentilini O, Cremonesi M, Trifiro G, et al. Safety of sentinel node biopsy in pregnant patients with breast cancer. Ann Oncol 2004;15:1348–51.
65. Schwartz JL, Mozurkewich EL, Johnson TM. Current management of patients with melanoma who are pregnant, want to get pregnant, or do not want to get pregnant. Cancer 2003;97:2130–3.
66. Schwartz GF, Giuliano AE, Veronesi U. Consensus Conference Committee. Proceedings of the consensus conference on the role of sentinel lymph node biopsy in carcinoma of the breast, April 19–22, 2001, Philadelphia, PA. Cancer 2002;94:2542–51.
67. Early Breast Cancer Trialists' Collaborative Group. Polychemotherapy for early breast cancer: an overview of the randomized trials. Lancet 1998;352:930–42.
68. Carlson RW. Update: NCCN practice guidelines for the treatment of breast cancer. Oncology 1999;13:187–212.
69. Goldhirsch A, Wood WC, Gelber RD, et al. Meeting highlights: updated international expert consensus on the primary therapy of early breast cancer. J Clin Oncol 2003;21(17):3357-65. http://www.gpo.gov/procurement/ditsg/emag.html. Epub 2003 Jul 07.
70. Doll DC, Ringenberg S, Yarbro JW. Antineoplastic agents and pregnancy. Semin Oncol 1989;16:337–46.
71. Ebert U, Loffler H, Kirch W. Cytotoxic therapy and pregnancy. Pharmacol Ther 1997;74:207–20.
72. Grohard P, Akbaraly JP, Saux MC, et al. [Transplacental passage of doxorubicin] J Gynecol Obstet Biol Reprod 1989;18:595–600.
73. Karp GI, von Oeyen P, Valone F, et al. Doxorubicin in pregnancy: possible transplacental passage. Cancer Treat Rep 1983;67:773–7.
74. Turchi JJ, Villasis C. Anthracyclines in the treatment of malignancy in pregnancy. Cancer. 1988;61(3):435–40.
75. Germann N, Goffinet F, Goldwasser F. Anthracyclines during pregnancy: embryo-fetal outcome in 160 patients. Ann Oncol 2004;15:146–50.
76. Cardonick E, Iacobucci A. Use of chemotherapy during human pregnancy. Lancet Oncol 2004;5:283–91.
77. Peccatori F, Martinelli G, Gentilini O, Goldhirsch A. Chemotherapy during pregnancy: what is really safe? Lancet Oncol 2004;5:398.
78. Muller T, Hofmann J, Steck T. Eclampsia after polychemotherapy for nodal-positive breast cancer during pregnancy. Eur J Obstet Gynecol Reprod Biol 1996;67:197– 8.
79. Gadducci A, Cosio S, Fanucchi A, et al. Chemotherapy with epirubicin and paclitaxel for breast cancer during pregnancy: case report and review of the literature. Anticancer Res 2003;23:5225– 9.
80. Goldwasser F, Pico JL, Cerrina J, et al. Successful chemotherapy including epirubicin in a pregnant non-Hodgkin's lymphoma patient. Leuk Lymphoma 1995;20:173–6.
81. Andreadis C, Charalampidou M, Diamantopoulos N, et al. Combined chemotherapy and radiotherapy during conception and first two trimesters of gestation in a woman with metastatic breast cancer. Gynecol Oncol 2004;95:252–5.
82. Berry DL, Theriault RL, Holmes FA, et al. Management of breast cancer during pregnancy using a standardized protocol. J Clin Oncol 1999;17:855–61.
83. De Santis M, Lucchese A, De Carolis S, et al. Metastatic breast cancer in pregnancy: first case of chemotherapy with docetaxel. Eur J Cancer Care 2000;9:235–7.
84. Sood AK, Shahin MS, Sorosky JI. Paclitaxel and platinum chemotherapy for ovarian carcinoma during pregnancy. Gynecol Oncol 2001;83:599–600.
85. Mendez LE, Mueller A, Salom E, Gonzalez-Quintero VH. Paclitaxel and carboplatin chemotherapy administered during pregnancy for advanced epithelial ovarian cancer. Obstet Gynecol 2003;102(5 Pt 2):1200–2.
86. Gonzalez-Angulo AM, Walters RS, et al. Paclitaxel chemotherapy in a pregnant patient with bilateral breast cancer. Clin Breast Cancer 2004;5:317–9.
87. Cullins SL, Pridjian G, Sutherland CM. Goldenhar's syn-

drome associated with tamoxifen given to the mother during gestation. JAMA 1994;271:1905–6.
88. Isaacs RJ, Hunter W, Clark K. Tamoxifen as systemic treatment of advanced breast cancer during pregnancy—case report and literature review. Gynecol Oncol 2001;80:405–8.
89. Tewari K, Bonebrake RG, Asrat T, Shanberg AM. Ambiguous genitalia in infant exposed to tamoxifen in utero. Lancet 1997;350:183.
90. Clark S. Prophylactic tamoxifen. Lancet 1993;342:168.
91. Chamness GC, Bannayan LA, Landry JR, et al. Abnormal reproductive development in rats after neonatally administered antiestrogen (tamoxifen). Biol Reprod 1979;21:1087–90.
92. Iguchi T, Hirokawa M, Takasugi M. Occurrence of genital tract abnormalities and bladder hernia in female mice exposed neonatally to tamoxifen. Toxicology 1986;42:1–11.
93. Diwan BA, Anderson LM, Ward JM. Proliferative lesions of oviduct and uterus in CD-1 mice exposed prenatally to tamoxifen. Carcinogenesis 1997;18:2009–14.
94. Jimenez-Gordo AM, Espinosa E, Zamora P, et al. Pregnancy in a breast cancer patient treated with a LHRH analogue at ablative doses. Breast. 2000;9:110–2.
95. Holleb AI, Farrow JH. The relation of carcinoma of the breast and pregnancy in 283 patients. Surg Gynecol Obstet 1962;115:65–71.
96. Deemarsky LJ, Neishtadt EL. Breast cancer and pregnancy. Breast 1981;7:17–21.
97. Clark RM, Chua T. Breast cancer and pregnancy: the ultimate challenge. Clin Oncol 1989;1:11–8.
98. Carol EH, Conner S, Schorr S. The diagnosis and management of breast problems during pregnancy and lactation. Am J Surg 1995;170:401–4.
99. Giacalone P-L, Laffargue F, Benos P. Chemotherapy for breast cancer during pregnancy. Cancer 1999;86:2266–72.
100. Physician's desk reference. Available at: http://www.pdr.net (accessed Nov 11, 2004).
101. Durodola JI. Administration of cyclophosphamide during late pregnancy and early lactation: a case report. J Natl Med Assoc1979;71:165–6.
102. Higgins S, Haffty B. Pregnancy and lactation after breast-conserving therapy for early stage breast cancer. Cancer 1994;73:2175–80.
103. Aviles A, Neri N. Hematological malignancies and pregnancy: a final report of 84 children who received chemotherapy in utero. Clin Lymphoma 2001;2:173–7.
104. Reynoso EE, Shepherd FA, Messner HA, et al. Acute leukemia during pregnancy: the Toronto Leukemia Study Group experience with long-term follow-up of children exposed in utero to chemotherapeutic agents. J Clin Oncol 1987;5:1098–106.
105. The Motherisk Program. International Registry of Cancer in Pregnancy. Available at: http://www.motherisk.org/ cancer/index.php (accessed Nov 11, 2004).
106. Smith TJ, Davidson NE, Schapira DV, et al. American Society of Clinical Oncology 1998 update of recommended breast cancer surveillance guidelines. J Clin Oncol 1999;17:1080–2.
107. NCCN clinical practice guidelines in oncology v.1, 2004. Available at: http://www.nccn.org (accessed Nov 11, 2004).
108. Haagensen C, Stout A. Carcinoma of the breast. Ann Surg 1943;118:859–70.
109. Kroman N, Mouridsen HT. Prognostic influence of pregnancy before, around, and after diagnosis of breast cancer. Breast 2003;12:516–21.

30

Hormone Therapy and Breast Cancer

TONCRED MARYA STYBLO
CATHERINE A. MADORIN
WILLIAM C. WOOD

In recent years, hormone replacement therapy (HRT) with either estrogen alone (viz, estrogen replacement therapy [ERT]) or estrogen plus progesterone has been commonly recommended to healthy postmenopausal women, to alleviate the symptoms of menopause. Studies indicating long-term benefits on bone density, fracture prevention, genitourinary symptoms, dementia, and a perceived reduction of coronary artery disease (CAD) have further strengthened the popularity of hormone therapy.[1–4]

In contrast, the use of ERT/HRT has been discouraged in women with a history of breast cancer, fearing that estrogen could contribute to the development or recurrence of breast cancer. Observational studies suggest that using estrogen plus progesterone over estrogen alone may further increase the risk of developing breast cancer.[5] These observations, in addition to data from laboratory models, suggest that progesterone may also contribute to the risk of breast cancer development and recurrence.

Multiple studies strongly support the association of ERT/HRT use with an increased risk of breast cancer. A meta-analysis of data from 51 epidemiologic studies of over 52,000 women with breast cancer, and over 108,000 women without, reported a 1.31 relative risk for long-term HRT users[6] (Figure 30–1) Subsequent studies further implicate progesterone use as a risk factor for breast cancer (Table 30–1).[5–9] In the meta-analysis study described above, among current or recent hormone users, the risk of breast cancer was 53% higher for combination therapy and 34% higher for estrogen alone compared with no hormone use.[6,7]

The results of the randomized Women's Health Initiative (WHI), published in 2002 and 2003, have strongly challenged previously held findings on the benefits of ERT/HRT and have discouraged the use of HRT in postmenopausal women.[10] The observed risks so greatly exceeded the benefits that the part of the WHI trial comparing HRT with placebo was stopped early. Observed risks included increased rather than decreased CAD, increased strokes, increased pulmonary emboli, increased invasive breast cancers, and increased dementia in women over 65 years of age.[10,11]

Paradoxically, the WHI trial of unopposed estrogen in hysterectomized women has shown a reduced risk of breast cancer development, but maintains an increased risk of CAD, stroke, and pulmonary emboli. The trial of unopposed estrogen versus placebo was also stopped early because of increased risk of a cardiovascular event.[12]

The results of the WHI trials strengthen the rationale for discouraging the use of ERT/HRT in women

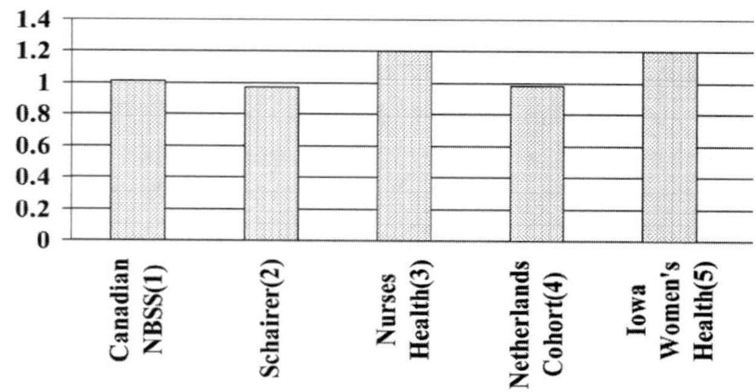

Figure 30–1. Relative risk (RR) of breast cancer in ever-users with never-users of HRT in prospective trials.

Table 30–1. ESTROGEN PLUS PROGESTERONE INFLUENCE ON CHRONIC DISEASE IN THE WOMEN'S HEALTH INITIATIVE (WHI) RANDOMIZED CLINICAL TRIAL FOR WOMEN AGED 65 YEARS OR OLDER IN AN ANCILLARY STUDY

Outcome	Hazard Ratio (95% CI)	Excess Events/10,000 Women-Years on MET
Coronary heart disease	1.29 (1.02–1.63)	7 more
Stroke	1.41 (1.07–1.85)	8 more
Pulmonary embolism	2.13 (1.39–3.25)	7 more
Invasive breast cancer	1.26 (1.00–1.59)	8 more
Endometrial cancer	0.83 (0.47–147)	No difference
Colorectal cancer	0.63 (0.43–0.92)	6 fewer
Hip fracture	0.66 (0.45–0.98)	5 fewer
Global Index	1.15 (1.03–1.28)	19 more
Dementia*	2.05 (1.21–3.48)	

Chlebowski RT.[31]
Writing Group for the Women's Health Initiative Investigators.[9]
Shumaker SA et al.[10]
CI = confidence interval; MET = menopausal estrogen therapy.

with a history of breast cancer. Although a group of case series, uncontrolled studies, and small case-controlled studies have suggested that ERT/HRT in women with a prior diagnosis of breast cancer might be safe or even protective, recent data from at least one small randomized study dispute these findings.[12]

A more thorough review of the short- and long-term effects of ERT/HRT in healthy women as well as those with a history of breast cancer is warranted to clarify inconsistent study results.

HRT IN WOMEN WITH NO HISTORY OF BREAST CANCER

Physiology of Menopause

Menopause occurs when the ovaries stop secreting estradiol and follicles fail to develop. It occurs at a mean age of 51 years in the United States. The removal of estradiol's positive feedback on the pituitary leads to increased serum levels of the gonadotropins, follicle stimulating hormone (FSH) and luteinizing hormone (LH). Menopause heralds the onset of a variety of symptoms that decrease quality of life, including hot flashes, vaginal dryness, urinary symptoms, skin and hair changes, difficulty sleeping, mood changes, and possibly reduced cognitive function. Menopause is also associated with bone and heart disease. Bone turnover increases and bone resorption exceeds bone formation, leading to an increased incidence of osteoporosis and fractures. Data from the Nurses' Health Cohort Study indicates that women who undergo bilateral oophorectomy without ERT have a significant increase in CAD, suggesting that the loss of estrogen production in menopause may contribute to heart disease.

Documented Benefits of ERT/HRT

Treatment for Menopausal Symptoms

ERT/HRT is an effective treatment for many menopausal symptoms. Estrogen is effective in controlling hot flashes, according to multiple studies.[13–15] Schiff and colleagues indicated that oral medroxyprogesterone is superior to placebo in controlling vasomotor symptoms.[14] Yet another study showed that transdermal estradiol and norethisterone acetate improves subjective quality of life in postmenopausal women.[15] In contrast, the WHI showed little improvement in quality of life in women randomized to HRT; however, this is most likely a reflection of the low number of women with menopausal symptoms randomized to the study. In women who did have menopausal symptoms, the WHI found an improvement in quality of life measures related to vasomotor and genitourinary symptoms.[16] It follows that relief of symptoms may be realized with the use of estrogen with or without progesterone. Progesterone alone may also relieve symptoms. There have been no direct comparisons of estrogen and progesterone in terms of vasomotor symptom control or quality of life.

Osteoporosis

Multiple studies indicate that the use of ERT/HRT is useful in the prevention of osteoporosis. Results from the WHI randomized trial demonstrate that estrogen plus progesterone increases bone mineral density and decreases the risk of fracture (hazard ratio [HR], 0.76; 95% CI, 0.69–0.83).[1] Likewise, the WHI trial, comparing unopposed estrogen to placebo, showed a reduction in hip fracture (HR, 0.61; 95% CI, 0.41–0.91).[10] Additionally, a meta-analysis of 22 estrogen trials, cohort studies, the WHI trial, and trials with bone density outcomes concluded that HRT is protective against osteoporotic fractures.[17] Estrogen is approved in many countries for osteoporosis prevention.

Colon Cancer

There is substantial evidence indicating that ERT/HRT reduces the risk of colon cancer.[18] In contrast to cardiovascular disease and dementia, the WHI findings have confirmed the conclusions of observational studies that ERT/HRT reduces the risk of colon cancer by nearly one half. The WHI study found that women on hormone replacement had a HR of 0.63 (95% CI, 0.43–0.92).[19] A surprising outcome of the study was the finding that colon cancers were diagnosed at a higher stage in women taking estrogen plus progesterone. Women on HRT had a greater number of positive lymph nodes (mean ± SD, 3.2 ± 4.1 versus 0.8 ± 1.7; $p = .002$) and had more advanced disease (regional or metastatic disease, 76.2% versus 48.5% in placebo group; $p = .004$). Histologic features and grade were similar between the HRT and placebo groups. In the HRT group, women with vaginal bleeding had a greater number of positive nodes than women who did not have vaginal bleeding, suggesting that confusion regarding the etiology of vaginal and colorectal bleeding may delay diagnosis.

Documented Risks of ERT/HRT

Cardiovascular Disease

The use of ERT/HRT is associated with an increased incidence of adverse cardiovascular events. The potential risk of venous thromboembolic events (VTEs), deep venous thrombosis, or pulmonary embolism is well recognized. The WHI found an HR of 2.11 (95% CI, 1.58–2.82) for VTEs. A meta-analysis of 12 studies that used a variety of ERT/HRT regimens found that current use of hormones increase the relative risk (RR) of VTEs to 2.14 (95% CI, 1.64–2.81).[20–22]

The use of HRT appears to increase the risk of stroke. The WHI found an overall HR of 1.41 (95% CI, 1.07–1.85) after 5.2 years of follow-up. The HRT users had an increased risk for nonfatal stroke (HR 1.50; 95% CI, 1.08–2.08) but not for fatal stroke (HR, 1.18; 95% CI, 0.58–2.50). A subanalysis of the WHI trial found that HRT was associated with an increased risk of ischemic stroke (HR, 1.44; 95% CI, 1.09–1.90), but not for hemorrhagic stroke (HR, 0.82; 95% CI, 0.43–1.56).[23] The Women's Estrogen for Stroke Trial is the only randomized, placebo-controlled trial studying the effect of estrogen alone on stroke. An increased RR of any stroke (RR, 2.30; 95% CI, 1.1–5.0) was observed, but there were no significant differences in fatal versus nonfatal stroke.

Studies have failed to prove that ERT/HRT plays a protective role in primary or secondary coronary heart disease (CHD). The WHI reported an HR of 1.29 (95% CI, 1.02–1.63) for CHD (fatal and nonfatal myocardial infarction) with use of HRT. The risk was greatest in the first year of use (HR, 1.78). The secondary prevention Heart and Estrogen/progesterone Replacement Study (HERS) trial also found an early increased risk that decreased with continued HRT use.[21] A meta-analysis of previous observational studies showed a decreased relative risk for CHD (RR, 0.80; 95% CI, 0.64–0.78) with ERT/HRT use, but the statistical significance of these studies disappeared when adjusted for socioeconomic status.[24]

Dementia and Alzheimer's Disease

Previously thought to prevent dementia, the latest results of the WHI strongly suggest that ERT/HRT increases the risk of developing dementia after menopause.[25] The Women's Health Initiative Memory Study (WHI-MS) demonstrated that women aged 65 to 79 years receiving estrogen plus progesterone suffered double the risk of dementia. It is possible that the increased risk of dementia reflects the adverse effects of HRT on cerebral vasculature. The WHI has not published any results on the effects of estrogen alone on the development of dementia. It has indicated an increased incidence of stroke in women receiving estrogen alone (HR, 1.39; 95% CI, 1.10–1.77).

Ovarian Cancer

The WHI randomized trial suggests that estrogen plus progesterone increases the risk of ovarian cancer and other gynecologic cancers, including primary peritoneal and fallopian tube cancers. However, there were insufficiently numerous events to meet statistical significance, and therefore, one cannot draw definitive conclusions about the relationship of HRT to ovarian and other gynecologic cancers. The WHI trial of estrogen alone versus placebo has not yet reported on rates of gynecologic cancer.

Breast Cancer

A large body of data indicates that HRT use increases the risk of developing breast cancer. Over 50 case-controlled and cohort studies have been carried out, and an RR of 1.3 to 1.4 associated with the long-term use of ERT/HRT has emerged.[5] The collaborative analysis of data from 51 epidemiologic studies of over 52,000 women with breast cancer and over 108,000 women without breast cancer found an RR of 1.31 for long-term HRT users. Now, data from the WHI randomized prospective trial of estrogen plus progesterone has also found an increase in the incidence of breast cancer with hormone use.

The WHI was the first randomized, placebo-controlled trial that looked at the effect of HRT on the risk of invasive breast cancer. The study found an overall HR of 1.26 (95% CI, 1.00–1.59) after an average of 5.2 years of follow-up. The increased risk of breast cancer was seen only in a subset of women with prior use of HRT. The HR was 1.06 (95% CI, 0.81–1.38) among never users, 2.13 (95% CI, 1.15–3.94) for women with under 5 years of previous use, 4.61 (95% CI, 1.01–21.02) for women with 5 to 10 years of use, and 1.81 (95% CI, 0.60–5.43) for women with over 10 years of prior use. These findings suggest that prolonged exposure may be necessary before a significant increase in risk occurs.

It appears that the addition of a progestational agent to HRT further increases the risk of breast cancer (see Table 30–1).[5–7,26] The collaborative analysis found that among current or recent hormone users, the risk of breast cancer was 53% higher for combination therapy, and 34% higher for estrogen alone compared with no hormone use.[5] The Million Women Study, a large cohort study conducted by the National Health Service Breast Screening Program in the United Kingdom, confirms these findings. Out of 1,084,110 women, 9,364 incident invasive breast cancers were seen, and HRT use was associated with significantly increased breast cancer incidence and breast cancer mortality (RR, 1.22; 95% CI, 1.05–1.41; $p = .05$). The increased incidence of breast cancer was seen after only 1 year of HRT use and up, and was independent of method of use (oral, transdermal, or implant). The Million Women Study found that breast cancer risk was higher in women on combination estrogen and progesterone therapy than in women on estrogen alone.

Breast cancers developing during HRT appear to be diagnosed at a more advanced stage. The WHI found that breast cancers in women taking HRT compared with placebo were similar in grade, receptor status, and histology, but were larger and more often associated with positive lymph nodes (Table 30–2). The findings of the WHI contest those of earlier observational studies that had suggested that breast cancers developing on hormone therapy are found at an earlier phase and that HRT use affects receptor status.

Women using HRT experience a greater incidence of abnormal mammograms. The WHI required that mammograms be performed, and the frequency of mammograms was comparable in the hormone therapy and placebo groups. After 1 year of estrogen plus progesterone use, there was a 4% increase in abnormal mammogram frequency. This difference rose to a 13% increased chance of having an abnormal mammogram in women taking hormones for 5.6 years. HRT has been found to increase mammographic breast density.[27,28] It is estimated that 120,000 women per year in the United States have abnormal mammograms related to combined hormone therapy, based on the frequency of HRT use in 2002.[29] The

Table 30–2. ESTROGEN PLUS PROGESTERONE INFLUENCE ON BREAST CANCER AND MAMMOGRAMS IN THE WOMEN'S HEALTH INITIATIVE

	Estrogen + Progesterone	Placebo	Hazard Ratio (95% CI)	*p*-Value
Women Entered	8,506	8,102		
Breast Cancer				
Total	245	185	1.24 (1.02–1.50)	< .001
Invasive	199	150	1.24 (1.01–1.54)	< .001
In situ	47	371.18 (0.77–1.82)	0.09	
Breast Cancer Characteristics				
Size, cm (± SD)	1.7 (1.1)	1.5 (0.9)	–	.04
Lymph nodes positive	25.9%	15.8%	–	.03
SEER stage (regional/metastatic)	25.4%	16.0%	–	.04
Receptor Status				
Estrogen receptor-positive	158(86.8%)	112(88.2%)	.72	
-negative	24(13.2%)	15(11.8%)		
Progesterone receptor-positive	135 (75.0%)	86 (69.9%)	.33	
-negative	45 (25.0%)	37 (30.0%)		
Abnormal Mammograms Number (%)				
After 1 year	716 (9.4%)	398 (5.4%)	–	< .001
Cumulative	2,601 (34.5%)	1,677 (21.2%)	–	< .001

CI = confidence interval; SD = standard deviation; SEER = Surveillance, Epidemiology, and End Results.
Adapted from Chlebowski RT.[31]

interference of HRT with mammography may mask developing breast cancers, providing a possible explanation of why women who develop breast cancer on HRT are diagnosed at a higher stage.[30]

The effects of estrogen alone on breast cancer risk are less certain. Both the Million Women Study and the collaborative analysis of 51 epidemiologic studies found an increased incidence of breast cancer in women taking estrogen alone versus placebo. In stark contrast to these findings, the WHI trial of estrogen alone versus placebo found a reduced risk of breast cancer, after almost 7 years of follow-up. The incidence of breast cancer was 23% lower in the estrogen group; however, the data narrowly missed statistical significance (Table 30–3).[11]

In four major trials, tamoxifen was shown to reduce the incidence of estrogen receptor (ER)-positive breast cancers by about 50%, with little effect on ER-negative breast cancers, with a 38% overall reduction in breast cancer.[31] Likewise, aromatase inhibitors (AI) may have shown a reduction in new breast cancer in patients treated for breast cancer. In four adjuvant trials on the use of three different AIs for postmenopausal women with breast cancer, a consistent reduction in the rates of contralateral breast cancer was found.[32–36] A review of these trials suggests that AIs may reduce ER-positive breast cancer incidence by 40 to 50%.[37] Current ongoing trials of AIs for the prevention of breast cancer in otherwise healthy women will shed further light on what may be a major shift from estrogen addition to estrogen suppression for chronic disease risk reduction.

A number of studies indicate that the combination of HRT and a selective estrogen-receptor modulator such as tamoxifen may reduce the risks (viz, breast cancer, endometrial cancer, and VTE), while retaining the benefits of either agent alone.[38,39] The HRT Opposed by Tamoxifen (HOT) study, a phase III trial addressing this issue, has recently been launched in Italy.[40] As of March 31, 2005, approximately 1,650 healthy postmenopausal women on HRT have been randomized to receive tamoxifen 5 mg/day or placebo for 5 years. The study is powered to detect a 40 to 50% reduction in the incidence of invasive breast cancer and ductal carcinoma in situ in the tamoxifen arm.

HORMONE REPLACEMENT THERAPY IN WOMEN WITH A HISTORY OF BREAST CANCER

Routine use of HRT in women with a prior diagnosis of breast cancer is not recommended. The association of ERT/HRT with increased breast cancer incidence precludes its use in women with a history

Table 30–3. ESTROGEN INFLUENCE ON CHRONIC DISEASE IN WOMEN'S HEALTH INITIATIVE (WHI) RANDOMIZED CLINICAL TRIAL

Outcome	Hazard Ratio (95% CI)	Excess Events/10,000 Women-Years on ERT
Coronary heart disease	0.9 (0.75–1.12)	5 fewer
Stroke	1.39 (1.10–1.77)	l2 more
Venous thrombolic disease	1.39 (0.91–2.12)	7 more
Invasive breast cancer	0.77 (0.59–1.01)	7 fewer
Colorectal cancer	1.08 (0.75–1.55)	1 more
Hip fracture	0.61 (0.41–0.91)	6 fewer
Global Index	1.01 (0.91–1.12)	

CI = confidence interval; ERT = estrogen replacement therapy.
Adapted from The WHI Steering Committee.[11]

of breast cancer. In fact, ovarian ablation significantly reduces recurrence and death, presumably by removal of estrogen, according to the Oxford meta-analysis.[41] Likewise, estrogen blocking and suppression through the use of tamoxifen and AIs has been shown to reduce the risk of recurrence and death.[39] However, most of the 2.5 million breast cancer survivors in the United States are postmenopausal, and 70% of those who are not will develop premature menopause from adjuvant chemotherapy. These women may seek treatment to relieve the symptoms and complications of menopause.[42,43]

Well-designed studies on the relationship between HRT and breast cancer recurrence are scarce. One randomized trial, Hormonal Replacement Therapy After Breast Cancer—Is It Safe? (HABITS), investigated the effect of HRT in women with a low to intermediate risk of breast cancer recurrence. HABITS was designed as a noninferiority study to exclude a relative hazard (RH) of 1.36 for new breast cancer events. Up to 434 women were randomized to either ERT/HRT or control and were followed up for 2.1 years (follow-up n = 345) with a primary end point of any new breast cancer event. The trial was stopped early because of a significant increase in breast cancer events (RH, 3.30; 95% CI, 1.5–7.4). In early 2004, safety data from the HABITS study was pooled with the Stockholm trial, a similar study, which actually had found a nonsignificant decrease in risk (RH, 0.82; 95% CI, 0.35–1.9).[12] The pooled data found a weighted RH of 1.80 (95% CI, 1.03–3.31). The reason for the discrepancy in findings between the two trials is unclear.[44] However, when taken together with the results of the WHI, the collective body of data demonstrate reduced disease-free and overall survivals in women with a prior diagnosis of breast cancer, who use combined estrogen and progesterone and perhaps estrogen alone.

Several small studies on the use of ERT/HRT in breast cancer survivors have been conducted. Many of these studies have found no increased risk of recurrence associated with ERT/HRT. However, most of these studies are case studies with no matched control groups. A meta-analysis of 11 studies (4 control-matched), with a total of 214 participants, found no significant effect on breast cancer recurrence after a mean follow-up of 22 months. These findings were based on observational data subject to a variety of biases.[45] There have been several other case-controlled, case-cohort, and case studies, all of which are plagued by methodologic limitations, including small sample size, varying duration of therapy, and short mean follow-up.[44–46]

Surveys of patient opinions suggest that women are willing to take HRT despite an increased risk of recurrence. A survey of 224 randomly selected women with breast cancer found that 80% had taken HRT at some point following their cancer diagnosis.[47] Despite a fear of increasing the risk of recurrence, these women sought to reduce the risk of osteoporosis and heart disease. According to surveys, between 30 and 44% of women with a prior diagnosis of breast cancer indicated that they would be willing to take estrogen replacement under medical supervision.[9,47]

The use of menopausal HRT has been challenged by the findings of the WHI study. The WHI results indicate increased breast cancer risk (HR, 1.26; 95% CI, 1.00–1.59) for women using estrogen combined with progesterone after 5.2 years.[48] Trend data indicate increasing risk with increasing duration of use. The WHI fails to demonstrate CHD protection, reporting an increased risk for nonfatal myocardial infarction (HR, 1.32; 95% CI, 1.02–1.72) but no increased risk for CHD death or coronary artery bypass graft surgery or percutaneous transluminal coronary angioplasty among estrogen users. Potential for serious illness (breast cancer and heart disease) may outweigh the benefits, such as prevention of fracture and colorectal cancer. As always, this underscores the importance of discussion between the patient and their physician.

There have been no randomized clinical trials of sufficient size, addressing menopausal hormone use among breast cancer survivors, to provide reliable estimates of its influence on breast cancer recurrence, development of second primary breast cancers, or mortality. Observational studies of breast cancer survivors treated with estrogen or estrogen and progesterone therapy versus no hormonal therapy are summarized in Table 30–4. These reports are based on small numbers of breast cancer survivors, with few breast cancer events during their limited observation periods. The suggestion that short-term menopausal hormonal therapy may be safely offered to these patients is tempered by the potential bias inherent in nonrandomized observational studies.

TREATMENT ALTERNATIVES

The management of estrogen deficiency symptoms in breast cancer survivors can be challenging. Increased numbers of women diagnosed with breast cancer face estrogen deficiency symptoms as compared to women treated in the past. This is in part due to the risk of chemotherapy induced amenorrhea. Numerous breast cancer trials have suggested that reducing estrogen levels through the use of hormone based therapies in both pre and post menopausal women improves clinical outcome. The most prudent approach to treat breast cancer survivors or high-risk patients suffering from short term or long term symptoms of menopause would be to recommend non-hormonal alternatives.

Osteoporosis

Osteoporosis can be treated with therapy other than ERT/HRT. Bisphosphonates including Didronel, alendronate, and risedronate have been shown to inhibit bone resorption and normalize bone turnover.[49,50] Tamoxifen has also been shown to increase bone mass and reduce fractures in postmenopausal women.[51–53] Raloxifene, another selective estrogen-receptor modulator, is now approved for the treatment and prevention of osteoporosis; it has also been shown to favorably influence lipid profiles.[53,54] Data from studies designed to study raloxifene's effect on osteoporosis suggest that raloxifene may be preventative against breast cancer. A large randomized trial of raloxifene versus tamoxifen for the prevention of breast cancer (The National Surgical Adjuvant Breast and Bowel Project Study of Tamoxifen and Raloxifene) is ongoing at the time of this writing.

Coronary Artery Disease

Coronary artery disease can be controlled through modulations in diet, exercise, smoking cessation,

Table 30–4. COMPARISON OF BREAST CANCER RECURRENCE RATES AMONG MENOPAUSAL HORMONE THERAPY USERS AND NONUSERS IN REPRESENTATIVE REPORTS

	No. Breast Cancer Patients			No. Cancer Recurrences		
Study	MHT	No MHT	Follow-Up (Months)	MHT	No MHT	Relative Risk of Recurrence
Ursic-Vrxcaj	21	42	38	4	5	1.6
Vassilopoulou-Sellin	39	280	55	1	14	0.51
O'Meara	174	695	44	16	101	0.50
Beckmann	64	121	37	6	17	0.67
Durna	286	836	70	44	247	0.62
Total	584	1,974		71	384	0.63

MHT = menopausal hormone therapy.

and by pharmacologic treatment with anti-hypertensives and lipid-lowering drugs.[55–57]

Colon Cancer

Data strongly suggests that aspirin and other nonsteroidal anti-inflammatory drugs are preventative against colon cancer.[58]

Genitourinary Symptoms

Vaginal dryness and other local genitourinary symptoms can be reduced with use of lubricants, Replens, vaginal estrogen creams, and Estring.[59,60] Vaginal absorption of estrogen via creams may be comparable to level achieved with oral use, whereas Estring has lower, but still substantial, systemic absorption.[60,61] Thus, local estrogen administration may carry some systemic risks.

Vasomotor Symptoms

There are a number of drugs being evaluated for the alleviation of hot flashes. In a series of trials conducted by the Mayo Clinic together with the North Central Cancer Treatment Group (NCCTG), there was a considerable placebo effect, with a 20 to 25% reduction in hot flashes over a 4-week period.[62–66]

The NCCTG found that clonidine reduces hot flashes by 15% more than placebo; however, it is associated with considerable toxicity.

A second NCCTG finding was that a low dose of megestrol acetate was associated with an 80% reduction in hot flashes.[67] The therapy was well tolerated and has been shown to control hot flashes for up to 3 years.[66] However, progestational agents should probably be used with caution in breast cancer survivors, as it may increase the risk of recurrence.

A third NCCTG trial found that vitamin E (900 IU/day) showed a statistically significant decrease in hot flashes.[65] However, this decrease is only around one hot flash per person per day.

Selective serotonin reuptake inhibitors (SSRIs) are a promising potential treatment for hot flashes. A Mayo Clinic trial found that a low dose of venlafaxine may decrease hot flashes by about 50%.[67] A subsequent dose-finding trial found that 75 mg/d is the most effective does.[68] Other SSRIs, including fluoxetine, decrease hot flashes.[69]

Black cohosh and Bellergal have been used to treat hot flashes but have not undergone placebo-controlled trials. An NCCTG trial of soy phytoestrogen found no reduction in hot flashes over placebo.[66]

CONCLUSIONS

Randomized data as well as observational studies suggest that combination therapy with estrogen and progesterone increase the risk of breast cancer more that estrogen alone does. The absolute excess risk of primary invasive breast cancer is low, but increases with continued use. There have been two randomized trials evaluating hormonal replacement therapy after breast cancer. One of the studies was stopped early because of a significant increase in breast cancer events. The other study failed to demonstrate a significant increase in risk.

Most of the 2.5 million breast cancer survivors in the United States are postmenopausal. These women will benefit from hormonal treatment for vasomotor symptoms as well as osteoporosis prevention. In view of the small trials that have been completed in women with a personal history of breast cancer, additional trials examining hormonal therapy should be completed. However, given that women with breast cancer will accept anticancer treatment for a small benefit, and are usually unwilling to consider estrogen replacement therapy, many women may be hesitant to enter a trial evaluating risk of recurrence in order to take HRT.[70,71]

REFERENCES

1. Lufkin EG, Wabner HW, O'Fallon WM, et al. Treatment of postmenopausal osteoporosis with transdermal estrogen. Ann Intern Med 1992;117:1–9.
2. Cauley JA, Seeley DG, Ensrud K, et al. Estrogen replacement therapy and fractures in older women. Ann Intern Med 1995;122:9–16.
3. Paganini-Hill A, Henderson VW. Estrogen deficiency and risk of Alzheimer's disease in women. Am J Epidemiol 1997;140:256–61.
4. Grodstein F, Stampfer MJ, Colditz GA, et al. Postmenopausal hormone therapy and mortality. N Engl J Med 1997; 336:1769–75.
5. Early Breast Cancer Trialists' Collaborative Group. Breast cancer and hormone replacement therapy: collaborative reanalysis of data from 51 epidemiological studies of

52,705 women with breast cancer and 108,411 women without breast cancer. Lancet 1997;350:1047–59.
6. Willett CG, Colditz GA, Stampfer MJ. Postmenopausal estrogens: opposed, unopposed, or none of the above. JAMA 2000;283:534–5.
7. Persson I, Weiderpass B, Bergkvist L, et al. Risks of breast and endometrial cancer after estrogen and progestin replacement. Cancer Causes Control 1999;10:253–60.
8. Ross RK, Paganini-Hill A, Wan PC, Pike MC. Effect of hormone replacement therapy on breast cancer risk: estrogen versus estrogen plus progestin. J Natl Cancer Inst 2000; 92:328–32.
9. Writing Group for the Women's Health Initiative Investigators. Risks and benefits of estrogen plus progestin in healthy postmenopausal women. Principal results from the Women's Health Initiative randomized controlled trial. JAMA 2002;288:321–33.
10. Shumaker SA, Legault C, Thai L, et al. Estrogen plus progestin and the incidence of dementia and mild cognitive impairment in postmenopausal women: the Women's Health Initiative memory study: a randomized controlled trial. JAMA 2003;289:2651–62.
11. The Women's Health Initiative Steering Committee. Effects of conjugated equine estrogen in postmenopausal women with hysterectomy: the Women's Health Initiative randomized controlled trial. JAMA 2004;291:1701–12.
12. Holmberg L, Anderson H. HABITS (hormonal replacement therapy after breast cancer—is it safe?), a randomized comparison: trial stopped. Lancet 2004;363:453–55.
13. Daly E, Gray A, Barlow D, et al. Measuring the impact of menopausal symptoms in quality of life. BMJ 1993;307: 836–40.
14. Schiff I, Tulchinsky D, Cramer D, Ryan U. Oral medroxyprogesterone in the treatment of postmenopausal symptoms. JAMA 1980;224:1443–5.
15. Wiklund I, Berg G, Hanimar M, et al. Long-term effect of transdermal hormonal therapy on aspects of quality of life in postmenopausal women. Maturitas 1992;l4:225–36.
16. Hays J, Ockene JK, Brunner RL, Effects of estrogen plus progestin on health-related quality of life. N Engl J Med 2003;348:1839–54.
17. Nelson HD, Humphrey LL, Nygren P, et al. Postmenopausal hormone replacement therapy: scientific review. JAMA 2002;288:872–81.
18. Calle EE, Miracle-McMahill HL, Thun MJ, Heath CWJ. Estrogen replacement therapy and risk of fatal colon cancer in a prospective cohort of postmenopausal women. J Natl Cancer Inst 1995;87:517–23.
19. Chlebowski RT, Wactawski-Wende J, Ritenbaugh C, et al. Estrogen plus progestin and colorectal cancer in postmenopausal women. N Engl J Med 2004;350:991–1004.
20. Miller J, Chan BK, Nelson HD. Postmenopausal estrogen replacement and risk for venous thromboembolism: a systematic review and meta-analysis for the U.S. Preventive Services Task Force. Ann Intern Med 2002;136:680–90.
21. Hulley S, Grady D, Bush T, et al. Randomized trial of estrogen plus progestin for secondary prevention of coronary heart disease in postmenopausal women. Heart and Estrogen/progestin Replacement Study (HERS) Research Group. JAMA 1998;280:605–13.
22. Herrington DM, Reboussin DM, Brosnihan KB, et al. Effects of estrogen replacement on the progression of coronary-artery atherosclerosis. N Engl J Med 2000;343:522–9.
23. Wassertheil-Smoller S, Hendrix S, Limacher M, et al. Effect of estrogen plus progestin on stroke in postmenopausal women: the Women's Health Initiative: a randomized trial. JAMA 2003;289:2673–84.
24. Humphrey LL, Chan BKS, Sox HC. Postmenopausal hormone replacement therapy and the primary prevention of cardiovascular disease. Ann Intern Med 2002;137:273–84.
25. Gleason CE, Cholerton B, Carlsson CM, et al. Neuroprotective effects of female sex steroids in humans: current controversies and future directions. Cell Mol Life Sci 2005; 62:299–312.
26. Colditz GA, Rosner B, Nurses' Health Study Research Group. Use of estrogen plus progestin is associated with greater increase in breast cancer risk than estrogen alone. Am J Epidemiol 1998;147:645.
27. Persson I, Thurfjell E, Holmberg L. Effect of estrogen and estrogen-progestin replacement regimens on mammographic breast parenchymal density. J Clin Oncol 1997; 15:3201–7.
28. Greendale GA, Reboussin BA, Sie A, et al. Effects of estrogen and estrogen-progestin on mammographic parenchymal density. Ann Intern Med 1999;130:262–9.
29. Chlebowski RT, Hendrix SU, Langer RD, et al. Influence of estrogen plus progestin on breast cancer and mammography in healthy postmenopausal women: the Women's Health Initiative randomized trial. JAMA 2003;289: 3243–53.
30. Chlebowski RT. Menopausal hormone therapy and breast, colon and gynecologic cancer risk: Women's Health Initiative results. American Society of Clinical Oncology; 2004. p. 550–5.
31. Cuzick J, Powles T, Veronesi U, et al. Overview of the main outcomes in breast-cancer prevention trials. Lancet 2003;361:296–300.
32. Baum M, Buzdar A, Cuzick J, et al. Anastrozole alone or in combination with tamoxifen versus tamoxifen alone for adjuvant treatment of postmenopausal women with early-stage breast cancer: results of the ATAC (Arimidex, Tamoxifen Alone or in Combination) trial efficacy and safety update analyses. Cancer 2003;98:1802–10.
33. Baum M, Buzdar AU, Cuzick J, et al. Anastrozole alone or in combination with tamoxifen versus tamoxifen alone for adjuvant treatment of postmenopausal women with early breast cancer: first results of the ATAC randomised trial. Lancet 2002;359:2131–9.
34. Coombes RC, Hall E, Gibson LJ, et al. A randomized trial of exemestane after two to three years of tamoxifen therapy in postmenopausal women with primary breast cancer. N Engl J Med 2004;350:1081–92.
35. Boccardo F, Rubagotti A, Amoroso D, et al. Anastrozole appears to be superior to tamoxifen in women already receiving adjuvant tamoxifen treatment [abstract]. Breast Cancer Res Treat 2003;82 Suppl:6.
36. Goss PE, Ingle JN, Martino S, et al. A randomized trial of letrozole in postmenopausal women after five years of tamoxifen therapy for early-stage breast cancer. N Engl J Med 2003;349:1793–802.

37. Cuzick J. Aromatase inhibitors for breast cancer prevention. J Clin Oncol 2005;23:1636–43.
38. Veronesi U, Maisonneuve P, Rotmensz N, et al. Italian randomised trial among women with hysterectomy: tamoxifen and hormone-dependent breast cancer in high-risk women. J Natl Cancer Inst 2003;95:160–5.
39. Cuzick J, Forbes J, Edwards R, et al. First results from the International Breast Cancer Intervention Study (IBIS-I): a randomised prevention trial. Lancet 2002;360:817–24.
40. Guerrieri-Gonzaga A, Galli A, Rotmensz N, et al. The Italian breast cancer prevention trial with tamoxifen: findings and new perspectives. Ann NY Acad Sci 2001;949:113–22.
41. Early Breast Cancer Trialists' Collaborative Group. Ovarian ablation in early breast cancer: overview of the randomised trials. Lancet 1996;348:1189–96.
42. Chlebowski RT, Col N. Menopausal hormone therapy after breast cancer. Lancet 2004;363:410–1.
43. Col NF, Hirota LK, Orr RK, et al. Hormone replacement after breast cancer: a systematic review and quantitative assessment of risk [meta-analysis]. J Clin Oncol 2001; 19:2357–63.
44. DiSaia PJ, Brewster WR, Ziogas A, Anton-Culver H. Breast cancer survival and hormone replacement therapy: a cohort analysis. Am J Clin Oncol 2000;23:541–5.
45. Peters GN, Fodera T, Sabol J, et al. Estrogen replacement therapy after breast cancer: a 12-year follow-up. Ann Surg Oncol 2001;8:828–32.
46. Natrajan PK, Gambrell RD Jr. Estrogen replacement therapy in patients with early breast cancer. Am J Obstet Gynecol 2002;187:289–94; discussion 294–5.
47. Vassilopoulou-Sellin R, Zolinski C. Estrogen replacement therapy in women with breast cancer: a survey of patient attitudes. Am J Med Sci 1992;304:145–9.
48. Couzi RJ, Helzlsouer U, Fetting JH. Prevalence of menopausal symptoms among women with a history of breast cancer and attitudes toward estrogen replacement therapy. J Clin Oncol 1995;13:2737–44.
49. Liberman UA, Weiss SR, Broll J, et al. Effect of oral Alendronate on bone mineral density and the incidence of fractures in postmenopausal osteoporosis. The Alendronate Phase II Osteoporosis Treatment Study Group. N Engl J Med 1995;333:1437–43.
50. Delmas PD, Balena R, Carfraveus E, et al. Bisphosphonate risedronate prevents bone loss in women with artificial menopause due to chemotherapy of breast cancer: a double-blind placebo-controlled study. J Clin Oncol 1997;15: 955–63.
51. Fornander T, Rutqvist LE, Sjoberg HE. Long-term adjuvant tamoxifen in early breast cancer: effect on bone mineral density in postmenopausal women. J Clin Oncol 1990;8: 1019–24.
52. Love RR, Barden HS, Mazess RB, et al. Effect of tamoxifen on lumbar spine bone mineral density in postmenopausal women after 5 years. Arch Intern Med 1994; 154:2585–8.
53. Ettinger B, Black DM, Mitlak BH, et al. Reduction of vertebral fracture risk in postmenopausal women with osteoporosis treated with raloxifene (results from a 3-year randomized trial). JAMA 1999;282:637–45.
54. Walsh BW, Kuller LH, Wild RA, et al. Effects of raloxifene on serum lipids and coagulation factors in healthy postmenopausal women. JAMA 1998;279:1445–85.
55. Eagles CJ, Gulait R, Martin U. Non-pharmacological modification of cardiac risk factors. J Clin Pharm Ther 1996;21: 289–96.
56. Hebert PR, Gaziano TM, Chan KS, Hennekens CH. Cholesterol lowering with statin drugs, risks of stroke, and total mortality. JAMA 1997;278:313–21.
57. Vaughan CJ, Murphy MB, Buckley BM. Statins do more than just lower cholesterol. Lancet 1996;348:1079–82.
58. Thun MJ. NSAID use and decreased risk of gastrointestinal cancers. Gastroenterol Clin North Am 1996;25:333–48.
59. Law M, Loprinzi CL, Kugler J, et al. Double-blind crossover trial of Replens versus KY Jelly for treating vaginal dryness and dyspareunia in breast cancer survivors [abstract]. Proc Am Soc Clin Oncol 1996;15:241.
60. Henriksson L, Stjernquist M, Boquist L, et al. A one-year multi-center study of efficacy and safety of a continuous, low dose estradiol-releasing vaginal ring. Am J Obstet Gynecol 1996;174:85–92.
61. Sitruk-Ware R. Estrogen therapy during menopause. Practical treatment recommendations. Drugs 1990;39:203–17.
62. Goldberg RM, Loprinzi CL, O'Fallon JR, et al. Transdermal clonidine for ameliorating tamoxifen-induced hot flashes. J Clin Oncol 1994;12:155–8.
63. Loprinzi CU, Pisansky T, Fonseca R, et al. Pilot evaluation of Venlafaxine hydrochloride for the therapy of hot flashes in cancer survivors. J Clin Oncol 1998;16:2377–381.
64. Quella SK, Uoprinzi CL, Sloan JA, et al. Vaught NU, DeKrey WU, Fischer T, Finck G, Pierson N, Pisansky T: Long term use of megestrol acetate for treatment of hot flashes in cancer survivors. Cancer 1998;82:1784–8.
65. Barton D, Loprinzi CL, Quella SK, et al. Prospective evaluation of vitamin E for hot flashes in breast cancer survivors. J Clin Oncol 1998;16:495–500.
66. Quella SK, Loprinzi CL, Barton DL, et al. Evaluation of soy phytoestrogens for the treatment of hot flashes in breast cancer survivors: a north central cancer treatment group trial. J Clin Oncol 2000;18:1068–74.
67. Loprinzi CL, Michalak JC, Quella SK, et al. Megestrol acetate for the prevention of hot flashes. N Engl J Med 1994;331:347–52.
68. Loprinzi CU, Kugler JW, Sloan JA, et al. Venlafaxine in management of hot flashes in survivors of breast cancer: a randomized controlled trial. Lancet 2000;356:2059–63.
69. Loprinzi CL, Sloan JA, Perez EA, et al. Phase III evaluation of fluoxetine for treatment of hot flashes. J Clin Oncol 2002;20:1578–83.
70. Dhodapkar MV, Ingle IN, Ahxnann DL. Estrogen replacement therapy withdrawal and regression of metastatic breast cancer. Cancer 1995;75:43–6.
71. Ganz PA, Greendale G, Kahn B, et al. Are older breast cancer survivors willing to take hormone replacement therapy? Cancer 1999;86:814–20.

31

Male Breast Cancer

WILLIAM L. DONEGAN
PHILIP N. REDLICH

Breast cancer is said to be a disease of women, but the vestigial breasts of men also develop cancer. Breast cancer in men is a serious disease; fortunately, it is infrequent. Only 0.8% of all cases of breast cancer in the United States occur in males. In the year 2005, 1,690 men in the United States are expected to develop breast cancer and 460 are expected to die from it. By comparison, an estimated 211,240 women shall develop breast cancer in this same year and deaths are estimated at 40,410. Men account for 1.1% of deaths from breast cancer.[1] Barely 0.2% of all cancers in men arise in the breast, but these cancers will cause 0.16% of the total deaths from cancer in men, a statistic that suggests high lethality. The incidence of male breast cancer may be increasing. The National Cancer Institute Surveillance, Epidemiology and End Results (SEER) data indicate that the age-adjusted incidence increased significantly from 0.86 to 1.08/100,000 population between 1973 and1998.[2,3]

BACKGROUND

The first generally accepted mention of breast cancer, which dates from the *Edwin Smith Surgical Papyrus* 2,500 to 3,000 years ago, was described in a man.[4] In modern times, Holleb and colleagues attributed the first documented case of male breast cancer to John of Arderne in England in the fourteenth century,[5] whereas Meyskens and colleagues attributed the first report to William Fabry of Germany in the sixteenth century.[6] In the early 1800s, clinical descriptions of cancer arising in the male breast began to appear in medical journals in France and England, and it was considered a curiosity. The problem received little attention until the late nineteenth century when small collections of cases were published.[7] In 1883, Porier provided a detailed clinical description of breast cancer in males. Further knowledge of this clinical entity was advanced by Wainwright's landmark collection and analysis of 418 cases in 1927.[7] Wainwright described the poor prognosis associated with high histologic grade, cutaneous ulceration and axillary lymph node involvement. Postoperative mortality at that time was 6.1%, and only 19% of 111 cases with complete follow-up survived 5 years. Wainwright concluded that the prospect for cure was not as good in men as in women.

Reports from numerous countries now document the ubiquity of male breast cancer, but the incidence remains low, and few physicians have personal experience with more than one or two cases. Information on the subject is based largely on case reports or retrospective reviews. Sizeable numbers are only collected over many years.[3,] Randomized trials of treatment of men are nonexistent, and treatment is largely based on extensive studies of women with this disease.

RISK

Although the etiology of breast cancer remains obscure, a considerable amount is known about risk for developing the disease. Most who are affected, men or women, are not at high risk according to accepted criteria. Most factors identified with increased risk for men are fragmentary and often tenuous. They suggest genetic, hormonal, and environmental influences; in many instances, they reflect risk patterns known for women (Table 31–1). Men share none of the early, prominent breast development and reproductive functions so prominently linked to risk for breast cancer in women. In many respects, therefore, the disease in men is more akin to that of postmenopausal women.[8,3] For example, the age-specific incidence of breast cancer in men rises gradually throughout life, lacking the early, steep rise seen in pre-menopausal women.[9]

Risk increases with age. Although age at diagnosis ranges from 10 to 103 years, only 0.9% of male breast cancers are diagnosed before 34 years of age and more than half after age 65.[3] The mean or modal ages at diagnosis in large series cluster around 65 years, 5 to 8 years older than the average age of women at diagnosis.[10–12] The incidence in various countries parallels that of women.[13,14] Hence, high rates are reported in England and Wales and low rates in Japan and Finland. Black races in sub-Saharan Africa have a high frequency of affected males, often attributed to a high prevalence of liver disease with alterations in estrogen metabolism. Males account for 7% of cases of breast cancer in Tanzania[15] and 9% of cases in Nigeria.[16] The lower average age at diagnosis in African counties than elsewhere suggests an earlier onset.

Table 31–1. RISK FACTORS FOR BREAST CANCER IN MEN
Genetic
First-degree relatives with breast cancer
Ashkenazi Jewish descent
BRCA2 or *BRCA1* gene mutations
Klinefelter's syndrome
XX male (SRY Syndrome)
Androgen insensitivity syndrome
Environmental exposures
Ionizing radiation to the breast
Medications
Estrogens
Anti-androgens (flutamide)
Cimetidine
Spironolactone
Occupational exposures
Soap and perfume workers
Blast furnace workers and steelworkers
Reduced testicular function
Mumps orchitis
Inguinal herniorrhaphy
Undescended testes
Gynecomastia
Childlessness
Hyperprolactinemia
Head trauma
Hyperprolactinoma
Other
High body weight early in life
High socioeconomic status
Higher education

Case control studies associate increased risk among men with high socioeconomic status, advanced levels of education, Ashkenazi Jewish descent, childlessness, obesity, limited exercise, tallness, and consumption of red meat.[17,18] Linkage between male breast cancer and exposure to low frequency electromagnetic fields has not been confirmed.[19]

Heredity and genetics contribute to risk. From 11 to 27% of affected males report a family history of breast cancer.[20–23] Families with high rates of breast cancer sometimes include multiple affected males and males in more than one generation.[24] Female descendents of males with breast cancer are at increased risk, indicating transmission through the male line. Between 35 and 45% of familial breast cancer can be attributed to *BRCA2* mutations, often including families in which both males and females are affected. In males, inheritance of breast cancer risk has been linked to germline mutations in the *BRCA2* gene, less frequently to the *BRCA1* gene. About 14% of affected males have *BRCA2* mutations, as high as 33% in some series, whereas only 1% have *BRCA1* mutations.[25] Mutations in *BRCA1* or *BRCA2* carry an estimated 56 to 85% lifetime risk of breast cancer for females who are members of high-risk families. The risk for men may be similar. Up to 85% of males with breast cancer and a *BRCA2* mutation have a family history of breast cancer.[21,26,27] Mutations in the androgen-receptor (AR) gene, which are associated clinically with androgen insensitivity syndrome, are also linked to male breast cancer.[28,29] Dissimilar amplification of various genes suggests to some researchers basic differences in the pathogenesis of male and female breast cancer. Frequent amplification of *CCND1* in males, which is associated with estrogen-receptor (ER) positivity, tends to confirm the role of hormonal regulation in the development of male breast cancer.[30]

Feminization through reduced androgen or increased estrogen stimulation promotes the disease in men. These influences are sometimes genetic. Men with Klinefelter's syndrome (obesity, hypogonadism, aspermatogenesis, increased urinary gonadotropins, infertility, and gynecomastia), identified by an XXY sex chromosome, are believed to have a 20- to 50-fold increase in risk for breast cancer and a 3% lifetime risk.[31–34] The frequency of Klinefelter's syndrome in reports on males with breast cancer varies widely, from 0 to 7.5%. An SRY positive (*s*ex-determining *r*egion of the *Y* chromosome) XX sex genotype owing to transposition has been reported in a man with breast cancer. Such men have short stature, gynecomastia, and genital abnormalities, and they are infertile.[35]

The male breast responds to hormones, and many associations exist between excess estrogens and cancer. The natural decline in testosterone associated with aging creates a subtle excess of estrogens, and parallels the gradual rise in the age-specific incidence of breast cancer in men. Obesity causes increased aromatization of adrenal androgens to estrogens, and cirrhosis of the liver interferes with estrogen catabolism. These conditions are associated with male breast cancer in Denmark and in Africa, respectively.[36,37] Breast cancer has been reported in three male transsexuals treated with orchiectomy and estrogen to enhance breast development.[38,39] Cancer in the breasts of men under estrogenic treatment for prostate cancer is reported,[40,41] although metastatic carcinoma from the prostate is possible in such cases. Both breast and prostate cancers have androgen receptors and prostate specific antigen (PSA). Only prostate cancer stains strongly for prostate specific acid phosphatase (PSAP).[42] Androgen deficiency is suggested by the frequent histories of orchitis, inguinal herniorrhaphy, mumps infections in adulthood, orchiectomy, and testicular injury reported by men with breast cancer.[43] Frequent reports of occupational exposure to high temperatures and chemicals are also suggestive of impaired testicular function.

Associations have been made between male breast cancer and chronic hyperprolactinemia and a history of prolactinoma or head injury.[44,45] The role of prolactin and any associated endocrine disturbances is undetermined.

Case reports document primary breast cancer in men after exposure of the breast to ionizing radiation, in one case to treat pubertal gynecomastia.[46,47] Radiation is a known carcinogen for the breasts of women, particularly with exposure early in life. Women exposed to atomic radiation or to multiple fluoroscopies in the course of treatment for tuberculosis, or who have been irradiated for mastitis or Hodgkin's disease, are at increased risk. Reid and colleagues found a prior history of breast irradiation in 3.1% of 229 men with breast cancer.[12]

The relationship between gynecomastia and male breast cancer is not well established since gynecomastia can be a clinical or a pathologic diagnosis. True gynecomastia (breast enlargement owing to increased glandular development) is not considered premalignant but may well place males at increased risk. Proliferation of ductal and lobular elements is evidence of an unbalanced estrogen effect, and the enlarged parenchyma offers expanded substrate for carcinogenesis. Noteworthy is the gynecomastia associated with high-risk syndromes and the parallel increase of breast cancer and gynecomastia with aging. Ductal hyperplasia is often seen in association with ductal carcinoma in males, and evolution to in situ and invasive lobular carcinoma is reported in the gynecomastia of Klinefelter's syndrome.[48] Medications that cause true gynecomastia as a side effect (eg, cimetidine and spironolactone) have been linked to male breast cancer.[49,50]

For the great majority of men, a preventive strategy consists of avoiding recognized mammary carcinogens and aspiring to a low-risk profile. Fortunately, ionizing radiation is no longer used to treat pubertal gynecomastia, acne, and other benign conditions of youth. Exogenous estrogens, obesity, and hepatic toxins are largely avoidable. Prophylactic mastectomy is an option for men with an inherited high risk for breast cancer.[51] Periodic breast self-examinations during bathing seems a reasonable practice for earlier detection as does including breast examination in routine physical examinations, although benefits are unproved at this point.

PATHOLOGY

Similar histologic types of breast cancer occur in men and women, but the frequencies of the types vary (Table 31–2). Noninvasive ductal carcinoma has been described both in pure form and mixed with an invasive component.[52,53] Ductal carcinoma in situ (DCIS) comprises approximately 5% of all cases of male breast carcinoma but ranges as high as 17% in some series.[53] The median age of occurrence of DCIS is usually the mid- to late fifties but DCIS has been reported in men under the age of 40 years. The most frequent histologic pattern is the papillary subtype, with the majority of cases being of low or intermediate grade. Paget's disease of the nipple is often a feature in males diagnosed in the fifth to sixth decade of life and is associated with a palpable mass in 50% of cases.[54]

Virtually all known histologic types of invasive breast cancer have been identified in men. Invasive ductal carcinomas predominate, accounting for up to 90% of cases, but special histologic types also occur. Both invasive lobular carcinoma and lobular carcinoma in situ (LCIS) have been reported in men, but they are much less common than in women. Neuroendocrine differentiation can be seen. Sarcomas comprise a minority of reported invasive breast cancers; a variety of types occur. Metastatic cancer to the breast must be included in the differential diagnosis of breast masses. Cancers of the lung, liver, and prostate have metastasized to the male breast.[55,56]

Table 31–2. HISTOLOGIC TYPES OF BREAST CANCER IN MEN
Noninvasive Carcinoma
Ductal carcinoma in situ
Lobular carcinoma in situ
Paget's disease of the nipple
Papillary carcinoma in situ
Invasive Carcinoma
Argyrophilic neuroendocrine carcinoma
Colloid carcinoma
Inflammatory carcinoma
Intracystic papillary carcinoma
Invasive ductal carcinoma
Invasive lobular carcinoma
Invasive papillary carcinoma
Medullary carcinoma
Mucinous carcinoma
Oncocytic carcinoma
Secretory carcinoma
Sarcoma
Phyllodes tumor
Fibrosarcoma
Leiomyosarcoma
Lymphosarcoma
Myxoliposarcoma
Osteosarcoma
Spindle cell sarcoma

Adapted from Donegan WL and Redlich PN.[78] Breast cancer in men. Surg Clin North Am 1996;76:343–63.

CLINICAL PRESENTATION AND EVALUATION

Men with breast cancer regularly present with a breast-related complaint, and physical signs ordinarily are present.[12,23,57–69] A history of trauma to the breast is reported in 5 to 10% of cases. The left breast tends to be affected slightly more often than the right.[10,69] Cancer is present in both breasts in < 1% of cases, although in one series, 7% of patients were found to have bilateral disease.[10,61] The most common presenting complaint is a breast mass with or without axillary adenopathy. A palpable mass is present in > 70% of cases, and axillary adenopathy in 30 to 55% (Figure 31–1). In cases of DCIS, a subareolar mass and nipple discharge are the two most common signs, occurring in 58 and 35% of patients, respectively.[53] Paget's disease thickens, excoriates, or darkens the surface of the nipple.[70] Location of the tumor centrally, under, or adjacent to the nipple is the rule. When the mass is eccentric, it is most often toward the upper outer quadrant, less commonly in other quadrants. In locally advanced cases, nipple retraction, infiltration, and ulceration are seen as is attachment to underlying muscle. The breast may develop signs of inflammation. Occasionally, patients complain of pain in the breast. Bone pain, headaches, and hepatomegaly suggest dissemination, and further evaluation may demonstrate metastases in the bones, lungs, brain, and liver.

Significant delay in diagnosis is a regular feature with males. In early series, the mean duration of symptoms was more than 14 months. More recently, the mean duration has declined to a range of 3 to 6 months.[59,61,63,69] Gynecomastia coexists in 7 to 23% of cases.[12,23,61] True gynecomastia is suggested clinically as an area of glandular-feeling tissue of variable dimensions centered on the nipple, which may or

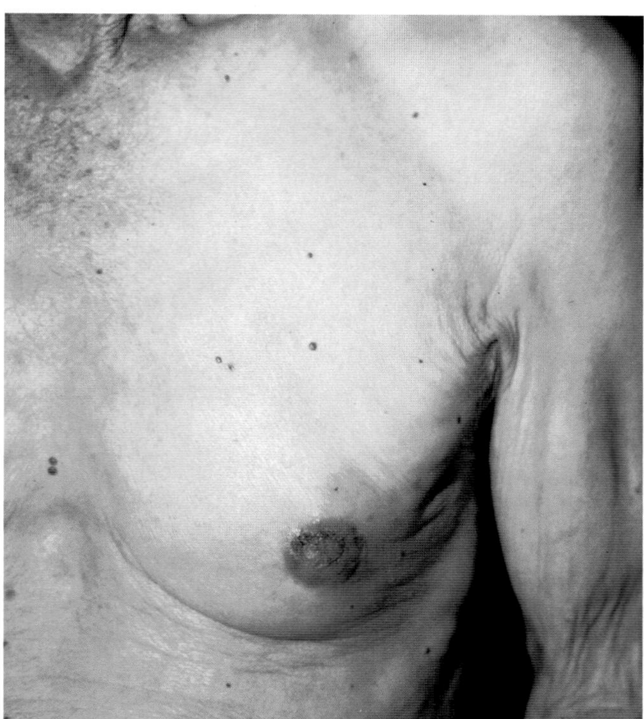

Figure 31–1. An elderly man with cancer of the left breast presenting as a non-tender, palpable sub-areolar mass. The nipple is fixed to the mass, thickened, and ulcerated.

may not cause obvious enlargement of the breast. Cancers have an average diameter of 2.5 to 3.0 cm, with a range of 0.5 to 12 cm. In surgical series, histologically proven axillary metastases are found in up to 70% of affected men, but more representative figures are in the range of 40 to 60%. The stage of disease at presentation varies considerably between reports and may not be entirely comparable among series owing to large time spans involved and periodic modification of staging systems (Table 31–3).

Evaluation of breast lesions includes the use of bilateral mammography, ultrasonography, fine-needle aspiration cytology (FNAC), needle core biopsy, and open surgical biopsy. Characteristics of male breast cancer on mammography are a radiodense mass with spiculated margins, with or without microcalcifications (Figure 31–2).[71–73] Malignant-appearing calcifications in the absence of a mass can also betray the presence of cancer. Gynecomastia, when present, is visible radiographically as architecturally benign-appearing fibroglandular tissue beneath and confluent with the nipple. Gynecomastia may or may not be present or of similar extent bilaterally and can obscure tumors, depending on its density.[71] Secondary radiologic signs of malignancy include architectural distortion, nipple and skin changes, and enlarged axillary nodes.[71]

Sonography (ultrasound) should be regarded as complementary to mammography. The sonographic features of male breast cancer often permit it to be distinguished from benign entities such as gynecomastia, lipomas, and fat necrosis.[73] Typically, cancer appears as a hypoechoic lesion with irregular margins (Figure 31–3). The lesion is characteristically at least as tall as it is wide. Distortion of surrounding normal breast tissue and subcutaneous fat may be present. Ultrasonic imaging is useful for distinguishing benign cysts from solid tumors, for characterizing solid masses, and for image-guided needle biopsy. It is less useful for men than for women since cysts are rare in the male breast and cancers are easily accessible for biopsy.

Ultimately, the diagnosis of invasive or in situ cancer is based on histologic confirmation, but the first diagnostic step in the evaluation of a breast mass is often FNAC. Cytologic features of male breast cancer are similar to those seen in the female and allow this modality to be a useful means of assessment.[74] Caveats pertaining to FNAC include confusing the epithelial hyperplasia of gynecomastia with cancer, inability to distinguish non-invasive from invasive cancer, and difficulty differentiating primary from metastatic lesions of the breast.[74] The accuracy of FNAC, combined with physical examination for evaluation of palpable breast masses, in

Table 31–3. STAGE OF CANCER AT PRESENTATION

	Frequency (%)	
AJCC Stage	SEER	NCDB*
0	10.5	7.1
I	29.4	36.9
II	38.5	41.9
III	7.5	9.6
IV	5.7	4.5
Unknown	8.5	

Stage of male breast cancer at diagnosis according to two large collected series from the National Cancer Institute's Surveillance, Epidemiology and End Results (SEER) data base and the National Cancer Data Base (NCDB) involving 2,524 and 4,755 cases, respectively.[3,10] AJCC = American Joint Committee on Cancer.

*These cases were selected for their ability to be matched with female patients with breast cancer.

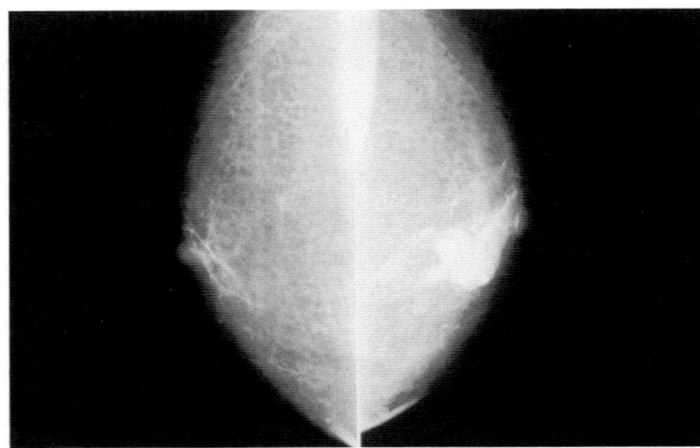

Figure 31–2. Mammogram of a male patient with breast cancer. The paired cephalocaudal (CC) views show a dense, spiculated mass near the nipple of the left breast (right side of the figure) that is characteristic of malignancy. A lead marker indicates the location of the nipple.

males is high and can reduce patient charges compared to routine open biopsy.[75] Optimal diagnosis with cytology mandates adequate sampling and an experienced cytopathologist. Core needle biopsy, on the other hand, can provide a definitive histologic diagnosis and often avoids the need for open biopsy.[76] False negatives are unusual, but areas of invasion can be missed with core biopsy in cases of DCIS. Open surgical biopsy should be performed in all cases in which diagnosis is not secure. Ultimately, a histologic diagnosis of cancer or proven benignity is necessary for masses or other suspicious changes. Diagnostic tissues likely to show cancer should be accompanied by a request for appropriate tumor markers.[69,77]

PROGNOSIS

The most important predictors for survival of men with undisseminated breast cancer are age at diagnosis, tumor size, and axillary node status.[3] Age is a prominent factor in the survival of men because of men's short life expectancy after 65 years of age owing to high rates of comorbid disease in the form of heart disease, second cancers, and stroke.[78] Age-related competing causes of death, combined with more advanced age at diagnosis, contribute to the poor observed survival of men with breast cancer. Overall observed survivals for men in large series range from 53 to 70% at 5 years and 38 to 53% at 10 years.[3,10,63,79,80] When corrections are made for natural mortality (relative survival) where only deaths from breast cancer are counted (disease-specific survival or DSS), 5- and 10-year survivals increase to 76 and 42% and to 74 and 51%, respectively.[63,81]

Among tumor-related prognostic factors, tumor size and the presence of axillary metastases are the most important.[62,81–85] A direct correlation exists between the size of the primary tumor and the involvement of axillary lymph nodes.[82,84] Guinee and colleagues found a progressive drop in 5-year survival from 94% for cases with tumors 0 to 10 mm in diameter to 39% in cases with tumors > 51 mm in diameter.[60] Tumor size was important prognostically independent of axillary node status. In node-negative cases, the relative risks of death associated with T0–T1, T2, and T3–T4 cases were 1.0, 2.0, and 3.2, respectively.[63] Skin and nipple involvement are associated with adverse survival.[81] Skin ulceration becomes insignificant, however, when tumor size is considered, and fixation to skin and chest wall are not important prognostically when size and nodal status are taken into account.[60]

The presence of axillary metastases is a potent and complicated prognostic indicator of survival for males. Crichlow reported 5-year survival rates of 79 and 28% for 143 patients without and with pathologic axillary metastases, respectively.[34] In a review

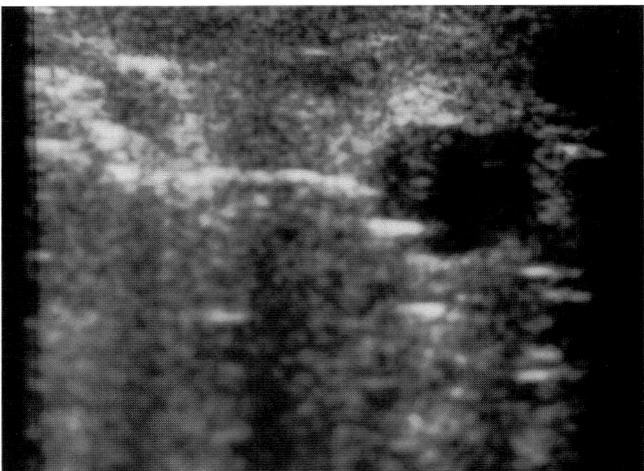

Figure 31–3. Ultrasonic image of breast cancer in a man. The lesion in the center of the field has irregular margins and reduced echoes within (hypoechoic), making it appear relatively dark. The white line to the left of the lesion represents a needle.

of 397 undisseminated cases, 5-year DSS of 77 and 51% for cases with histologically uninvolved and involved nodes, respectively, were reported.[63] The absolute number of involved nodes is inversely related to survival. In 335 collected cases, Guinee and colleagues demonstrated that the 5-year survival for patients with negative nodes was 90%. For those with one to three positive nodes it was 73%, and for those with four or more positive nodes it was 55%.[60] Others have found the same relationship[68,69] (Figure 31–4). Unequal proportions of involved nodes likely contribute to the varied prognoses reported for "node-positive" cases.

The clinical and pathologic stages at diagnosis are directly related to prognosis. (Figure 31–5). The international staging system based on a description of the primary tumor (T), the regional lymph nodes (N) and distant metastasis (M) is used by the American Joint Committee on Cancer (AJCC) for staging both men and women with breast cancer. However, the AJCC's TNM staging system may not be entirely appropriate for male breast cancer. The diminutive breasts of men allow even small tumors to readily reach underlying muscle and overlying skin and nipple.[11] Pivot and colleagues found skin or muscle involvement in 45% of 85 cases, and even small cancers were associated with a high frequency of regional metastases.[82] Forty-five percent of tumors < 2 cm in diameter had produced nodal metastases, and all tumors > 5 cm in diameter had produced nodal metastases. Since the prognosis was similar for T3 and T4 tumors, these investigators proposed a reduced T1, T2, and T4 classification for men.

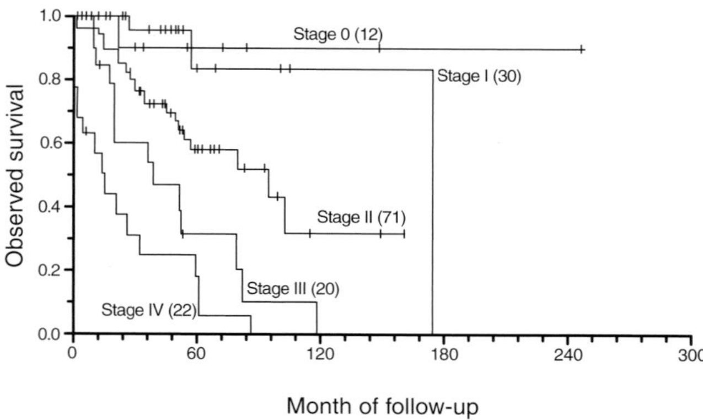

Figure 31–5. Survival of men with breast cancer stratified by TNM stage. The number of cases is shown parentheses. Reprinted with permission from Donegan WL et al.[69]

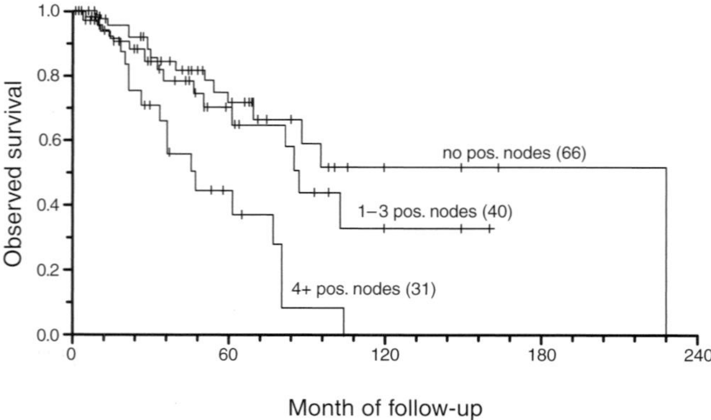

Figure 31–4. Survival of men with breast cancer stratified by number of axillary nodes with metastases. The number of cases is shown in parentheses. Reprinted with permission from Donegan WL et al.[69]

The influence of hormone receptors on the prognosis of men is controversial. ER positivity, which is regularly more frequent in men than in women and increases in frequency with age, is a weak but favorable prognostic sign for women. In men, ER positivity has been associated with both increased and decreased survival.[69,79,85,86] High tumor grade and aneuploidy are both associated with shortened survival.[79,87] The majority of breast cancers in men are histologically grade II or III. A significantly worse survival was reported in two series for grade III versus grade II cancers.[79,88] Visfelt and Scheike graded 150 male breast carcinomas according to the degree of tubule formation, mitoses, and atypia and found 5-year survivals of 60, 40, and 5% in men with cancers graded I, II, and III, respectively.[89] For males with diploid tumors, Pich and colleagues found a median survival of 77 months versus only 38 months for those with aneuploid tumors.[87] The mean S-phase fraction of male breast cancers (7.2%) approximates that of females.[90] Winchester and colleagues found high S-phase fraction (SPF) to be a significant indicator of poor disease-free survival for men.[85] Various growth accelerators are associated with inferior survival. Over-expression of *p53* cellular protein shortens median survival and disease-free survival.[87,91] In a study of 27 male breast cancers, Pich and colleagues found that strong staining for argyrophilic nuclear organizer regions and for proliferating cell nuclear antigen (PCNA) were correlated with inferior survival.[88] The frequency of tumor markers in male breast cancers, with and without established prognostic links, is shown in Table 31–4.

Many have sought to determine whether the relatively poor survival of men with breast cancer compared to women indicates that men have more aggressive cancers or is the result of older age, delayed diagnosis, and other inequities. In these comparisons, some have found men at a persistent disadvantage.[62,80,92] Others have concluded that, with appropriate adjustments, the survival of men with breast cancer may be no worse than that of women.[10,58,61,83] Guinee and colleagues came to this conclusion when male and female patients were stratified on the basis of histologically positive nodes.[60] A comparable prognosis for male and female patients, when analyzed for disease-specific survival and by tumor size and axillary node involvement, has been reported by other investigators.[61,63,93] In a review by Scott-Conner and colleagues, 4,755 cases of male breast cancer collected in the National Cancer Data Base between 1985 and 1990 were compared with 624,174 cases of female breast cancer.[10] Males and females were matched for age and ethnicity, and results were compared by AJCC stage. Men presented in more advanced stages than women, and their observed 5-year survival was lower in each stage. But when survival was adjusted for natural mortality (relative survival), the survival of men was similar to that of women for all stages except stages III and IV, in which men still fared less well (Table 31–5). This difference was most obvious in cases with similar surgical treatment.

Table 31–4. TUMOR MARKERS IN MALE BREAST CANCERS

Marker	Present or Enhanced % of Cases	Prognosis	Reference
ER+	64–93	Controversial	114,115,85,79,63
PR+	73–96		114,115,85,63
pS2+	44–50		79,117
Cathepsin D	48–72		79,117
AR+	95		79
HER2/neu+	15–50	Unfavorable	114–116,85,79,91
FISH+	11		91
p53+	21–58	Unfavorable	114–117,85,79,88,94
MIB-1+	38–40	Unfavorable	114,115
Bcl-2+	78–93		114,117
EGFR+	20		115
High SPF	7.2 (mean)	Unfavorable	91,85
Grade III	33–73	Unfavorable	115,91,79,68
Aneuploid	57	Unfavorable	91,88
Ki-67+	100		117
AgNOR+		Unfavorable	88
pcna+	100	Unfavorable	88,117

AgNOR = argyrophilic nuclear organizer regions; AR = androgen receptor; ER = estrogen receptor protein; EGFR = epidermal growth factor receptor; FISH = Fluorescence In Situ Hybridization testing for *HER2/neu* gene amplification; Grade III = histologic grade; HER2/neu = transmembrane oncoprotein; pcna = proliferating cell nuclear antigen; PR = progesterone receptor protein; pS2 = estrogen-dependent protein.

TREATMENT OF LOCALIZED DISEASE (TMN STAGES 0, I, II, AND III)

With few exceptions, the surgical treatment of males with breast cancer is a multi-disciplinary task, often combining surgery, radiation, hormonal therapy, and cytotoxic therapy. Surgical treatment of invasive cancer in early stages is mastectomy.[78] Modified radical mastectomy (total mastectomy plus axillary lymph node dissection without removal of the pectoralis major muscle) is currently the procedure of choice. Reports reflect an increasing number of patients treated with this operation.[11,22,61–63,69,92] (Figure 31–6). In one multi-institutional survey, 82% of patients diagnosed since 1986 were treated with modified radical mastectomy.[69] Other surgical operations reported include radical mastectomy (removal of the pectoralis major muscle en bloc with the breast and axillary nodes), simple mastectomy

Table 31–5. 5-YEAR SURVIVAL OF AGE-MATCHED AND ETHNICITY-MATCHED MEN AND WOMEN WITH BREAST CANCER BY AJCC STAGE

AJCC Stage	Survival %			
	Men		Women	
	Observed	Relative	Observed	Relative
0	82	97	93	100
I	78	98	85	98
II	68	88	70	81
III	51	67	56	66
IV	11	14	20	23

Adapted from Scott-Conner CE et al.[10] Data are based on 1,423 male and 983 female patients. The survival of men compares least favorably with that of women in stage IV. AJCC = American Joint Committee on Cancer.

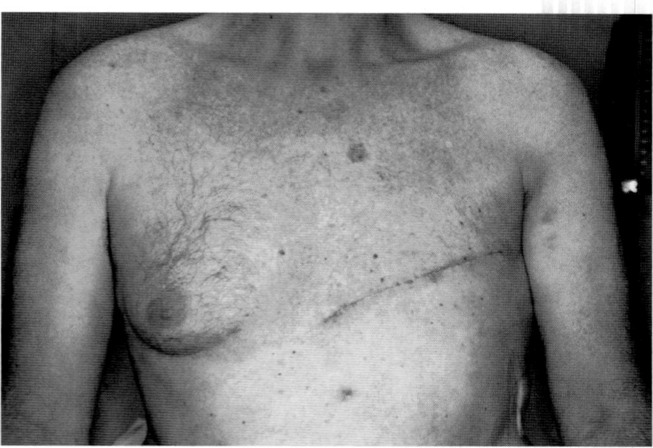

Figure 31–6. A man treated with modified radical mastectomy for cancer of the left breast. The right breast shows moderate gynecomastia.

(removal of the breast alone without muscle or axillary nodes), and lumpectomy (subtotal removal of the breast). The choice of operation likely reflected the extent of the disease and the patient's general condition, among other influences. The use of routine radical mastectomy has disappeared in recent decades. No significant difference in outcome for patients who underwent radical mastectomy compared to modified radical mastectomy was found in a number of series.[23,94] There is evidence that local recurrence is more frequent after lumpectomy than after mastectomy.[63]

Removal of the entire breast is generally necessary for men with invasive or in situ cancer because the breast is small and cancers are regularly located beneath or close to the nipple. Preservation of the pectoralis major muscle is a cosmetic advantage for men, leaving a near-normal contour of the anterior chest wall. Removal of the pectoralis major muscle is not necessary unless it is involved with direct tumor growth and en bloc removal of all or part of the muscle is needed to obtain cancer-free surgical margins. Lumpectomy offers little cosmetic advantage for men because of the small size of the breast. It might be an option, when desired, for very small carcinomas located eccentrically in the breast, provided widely uninvolved surgical margins can be obtained without sacrifice of the nipple and postoperative irradiation is planned. It is also acceptable as a palliative measure.

Axillary dissection is part of the surgical treatment of invasive breast cancer. Cutuli and colleagues reported a statistically significant reduction in the nodal recurrence rate of patients with routine axillary dissection compared to those without: 1.2% of 320 patients with axillary dissection had a regional recurrence, compared to 13% of 77 patients without axillary dissection.[63] An axillary dissection is not required in cases of pure DCIS. In cases of invasive cancer with a clinically negative axilla, sentinel lymph node biopsy (SLNB) is an alternative to routine axillary dissection in the hands of surgeons experienced with this procedure. SLNB involves lymphatic mapping, either with lymphoscintigraphy and an intra-operative gamma probe, or with visible isosulfan blue, or both, injected into the breast to identify the first draining node in the axillary chain. Removal and careful examination of this node (the sentinel lymph node, or SLN) intra-operatively can determine whether a metastasis is present, and hence, whether an axillary dissection should be performed. Omitting an axillary dissection when the SLN is "negative" spares patients needless morbidity. SLNB has proved highly accurate in women; SLNs (average 2.4) are found in almost all cases, false negatives are few, and recurrences in the undissected axilla are rare.[64] Limited experience indicates that SLNB is also appropriate for men.[65–67] In one of the larger series of 16 such cases in men, no SLNs were falsely negative.[65] Approximately 50% of cases with a positive SLN have additional nodes with metastases.

Postoperative radiation therapy to the chest wall is used as adjuvant therapy for male breast cancer with indications similar to those used for women, (ie, large cancers), narrow surgical margins, or multiple involved axillary nodes. A decrease in local-regional recurrences after postoperative radiation therapy is noted in some reports,[63,83] whereas no efficacy is noted in others.[23,94] Chest wall radiation offers no survival benefit,[23,93] but it is believed to reduce the local recurrence rate and should be considered as part of the overall treatment plan for cases at high risk for local or regional recurrence.[63,95]

Systemic adjuvant therapy, either chemotherapy, hormonal therapy, or both, is used for male patients with indications similar to those for females. Estrogen receptors are so regularly present in the breast cancers of men, reaching 87% in some series, that hormone therapy is usually an option.[93] Tamoxifen is most often chosen for postoperative adjuvant hormonal therapy in cases with positive estrogen receptors.[57,61,96,97] Tamoxifen is generally well tolerated by men; only occasionally do side effects require termination of treatment.[96,97] Orchiectomy has been reported in a few series but is used in no more than 3% of cases.[12,23,61] Experience with combination chemotherapy as an adjuvant is the subject of a number of reports.[12,63,69] The combination of cyclophosphamide, methotrexate, and 5-fluorouracil (CMF) was used at the National Cancer Institute in a series of 24 patients with stage II disease. The projected 5-year survival rate was > 80%, representing an improvement over survival rates reported in other series.[98] In another report, 5-fluorouracil, doxorubicin, and cyclophosphamide (FAC) or CMF was administered, with a projected 5-year survival > 85%.[99] The toxicity of these regimens and comorbidities sometimes limit the ability of patients to tolerate all of the planned treatments. In a multi-institutional study of male breast cancer in Wisconsin, no overall improvement in observed survival was associated with adjuvant chemotherapy, hormonal therapy, or combinations of both[69]; however, improved DSS was found in patients with ER positive cancers who had axillary lymph node metastases.

Treatment of soft tissue sarcomas of the breast follows the same principles as treatment of sarcomas located elsewhere in the body. Follow-up schedules after treatment are the same for male as for female patients.

TREATMENT OF ADVANCED DISEASE (TNM STAGE IV)

Stage IV designates patients with metastases beyond the breast and its regional lymph nodes. Men with breast cancer present with stage IV disease in from 11 to 16% of cases.[23,57,58,61,69] The pattern of spread in male patients is similar to that seen in female patients; metastases are most often to bone, lung, liver, skin, and brain.[12,23,61,62,68] Recurrences also are predominantly at these distant sites, with fewer being local or regional.

The objective of therapy is palliation in the form of extended survival and symptom control. Hormone therapy is the initial intervention in cases with ER positive cancers.[100,101] Endocrine surgery for advanced disease (ie, orchiectomy, adrenalectomy, and hypophysectomy) has been abandoned in favor of less morbid and equally effective hormonal treatment. But it is worth remembering that favorable responses to orchiectomy range from 30 to 60%,[58,102–104] and responses to secondary endocrine procedures in selected cases exceed 50%.[103]

Reid and colleagues reported the use of hormonal therapy in 73% of patients treated for metastatic disease.[12] The intervention of choice is tamoxifen.[12,61,103,104] Favorable responses to tamoxifen of 25 to 58% are reported in various series, the mean duration of response being 9 to 12 months. It is clear that responses to tamoxifen occur almost exclusively in patients with ER positive cancers; patients with receptor negative tumors do not respond.[101,105] If estrogen receptors remain positive in tamoxifen failures, secondary hormone treatments in the form of aromatase inhibitors may be effective. Both anastrozole (Arimidex ® AstraZeneca, Wilmington, DE) and letrozole (Femara® Novartis, East Hanover, NJ), second generation, non-steroidal aromatase inhibitors, have produced tumor regressions.[106,107] Other hormonal manipulations of occasional benefit include androgen therapy, estrogen therapy and luteinizing hormone-releasing hormone agonist analogue therapy.[78]

Systemic chemotherapy produces an overall response rate of 30 to 40%.[33,77,103,108–110] Chemotherapy is considered in cases that present initially with ER negative cancers or after failure of hormone therapies. Use of combination chemotherapy such as CMF or doxorubicin-containing regimens has been reported.[77,103,109,111] Metastases to the brain are treated with corticosteroids and whole-brain irradiation.[112]

ASSESSMENT OF PROGRESS

During the last century, clinical acumen, classification systems, techniques of pathologic examination, treatments, and methods for reporting results have undergone extensive changes. The validity of comparing time periods is questionable, particularly when data are few and incomplete as is the case for male breast cancer. Nevertheless, progress seems evident in a number of respects. The average symptomatic interval prior to diagnosis in Wainwright's

1927 review was 2.4 years; skin ulceration was observed in 38% of cases, and 68.9% of patients had involved axillary lymph nodes.[7] Overall 5-year survival was only 19%.[23] By comparison, the age of male patients has not declined, but shorter symptomatic intervals of 3 to 8 months have recently been reported.[20,113] Average tumor sizes continue to remain at 2.0 to 2.5 cm, but skin ulceration is seen now in only 12 to 13% of cases.[42,60] Dissemination at diagnosis still exceeds that of females, but as many as 10.5% of cancers are now diagnosed in situ.[3,60] The frequency of metastasis to axillary nodes remains high, although in some reports the rate is as low as 33%.[42,63] Men are now effectively treated with modified radical mastectomy rather than with radical mastectomy, a cosmetic improvement. Adjuvant systemic therapy is used more often with inferred benefits. Current 5-year survivals of 47 to 51% overall, and as high as 76% in undisseminated cases, compare favorably with results reported early in the twentieth century.

Reviews are mixed about whether recent changes are associated with an improved prognosis for men. In a report from the Mayo Clinic comparing experience with male breast cancer from the period 1933 to 1958 with the period 1959 to 1983, fewer radical operations and a higher frequency of adjuvant systemic therapy were found, but without improvement in median survival (5.5 years versus 6.3 years, respectively) or in 5-year disease-free survival (52 versus 47%).[23] In a more recent 10-year span from 1986 to 1995 compared with the period 1953 to 1985, investigators at the Medical College of Wisconsin noted a change to modified radical mastectomy and increased use of systemic adjuvant therapy and found a significant improvement in observed 5-year survival of males treated in Wisconsin hospitals from 42 to 59%.[69]

SUMMARY

Breast cancer in men is rare and occurs in an older population than does the disease in women. Men usually present with symptoms and often in advanced stages of disease. The low incidence, late age at diagnosis, juxta-areolar origin of the tumor, and presentation in advanced stages can be attributed largely to the small male breast and the scant attention it receives. The cancers of men express estrogen and progesterone receptors in a high percent of cases. Treatment trends are toward less radical surgery and increased use of systemic adjuvant therapy, especially hormone therapy. Prominent determinants of prognosis are AJCC stage, tumor size, and axillary node involvement. In potentially curable cases, prognosis declines with increasing numbers of involved axillary nodes. Although the prospects of men for surviving breast cancer approaches that of women in comparable stages, delayed diagnosis and the disproportionately high comorbidities of aging men contribute to an overall survival that remains inferior.

REFERENCES

1. Jemal A, Murray T, Ward E, et al. Cancer Statistics 2005. CA Cancer J Clin 2005;55:10–30
2. Hodgson NC, Button JH, Francaschi D, et al. Male breast cancer: is the incidence increasing? Ann Surg Oncol 2004;11:751–5.
3. Giordano SH, Cohen DS, Buzdar AU, et al. Breast carcinoma in men: a population-based study. Cancer 2004;101: 51–7.
4. Breasted JH. The Edwin Smith surgical papyrus. Vol. I. Chicago: University of Chicago Press; 1930. p. 403–6.
5. Holleb AI, Freeman HP, Farrow JH. Cancer of the male breast. I and II. NY State J Med 1968;68:544, 656.
6. Meyskens FL Jr, Tormey DC, Neifeld JP. Male breast cancer: a review. Cancer Treat Rev 1976;3:83–93.
7. Wainwright JM. Carcinoma of the male breast. Arch Surg 1927;14:836–59.
8. Anderson WF, Althuis MD, Brinton LA , Devesa SS. Is male breast cancer similar or different than female breast cancer? Breast Cancer Res Treat 2004;83:77–86.
9. Cutler SJ, Young JL Jr, editors. Third National Cancer Survey: incidence data. National Cancer Institute Monograph 41, March 1975. DHEW Publication No (NIH) 75–787. US Department of Health, Education, and Welfare. Public Health Service. National Institutes of Health. National Cancer Institute. Washington: US Government Printing Office; p. 106–7.
10. Scott-Conner CE, Jochimsen PR, Menek HR, Winchester DJ. An analysis of male and female breast cancer treatment and survival among demographically identical pairs of patients. Surgery 1999;126:775–80.
11. Schultz MZ, Coplin M, Radford D, et al. Outcome of male breast cancer (MBC) in the Department of Veterans Affairs (DVA) [abstract]. Proc Annu Meet Am Soc Clin Oncol 1996;15:257.
12. Goss PE, Reid C, Pintilie M,, et al. Male breast carcinoma: a review of 229 patients who presented to the Princess Margaret Hospital during 40 years: 1955-1996. Cancer 1999; 85:629–39.

13. Ewertz M, Homnberg L, Kajjalaninen S, et al. Incidence of male breast cancer in Scandinavia 1943-1982. Int J Cancer 1989;43:27–31.
14. Schottenfeld D, Lilienfeld AM, Diamond H. Some observations on the epidemiology of breast cancer among males. Am J Pub Health 1963;52:890–7.
15. Amir H, Makways CK, Moshiro C, Kwesigabo G. Carcinoma of the male breast a sexually transmitted disease? East Afr Med J 1996;73:187–90.
16. Hassan I, Mabogunje 0, Cancer of the male breast in Zaria, Nigeria. East Afr Med J 1995;72:457–8.
17. Hsing AW, McLaughlin JK, Cocco P, et al. Risk factors for male breast cancer (United States). Cancer Causes Control 1998;9:269–75.
18. D'Avanzo B, LaVecchia C. Risk factors for male breast cancer. Br J Cancer 1995;71:1359–62.
19. Stenlund C, Floderus B. Occupational exposure to magnetic fields in relation to male breast cancer and testicular cancer: a Swedish case-control study. Cancer Causes Control 1997;8:184–91.
20. Donegan WL, Perez-Mesa CM. Carcinoma of the male breast. Arch Surg 1973;106:273–9.
21. Olsson H, Andersson H. Johansson O, et al. Population-based cohort investigations of the risk for malignant tumors in first-degree relatives and wives of men with breast cancer. Cancer 1993;71:1273–8.
22. Friedman LS, Gayther SA, Kurosaki T, et al. Mutation analysis of *BRCA1* and *BRCA2* in a male breast cancer population. Am J Hum Genet 1997;60:313–9.
23. Gough DE, Donohue JH, Evans MM, et al. A 50-year experience of male breast cancer: is outcome changing? Surg Oncol 1993:2:325–33.
24. Everson RB, Fraumeni JF Jr, Wilson RE. Familial male breast cancer. Lancet 1976;3:9–14.
25. Winchester DJ. Male breast cancer. In: Donegan WL, Spratt JS, editors. Cancer of the breast, 5th ed. Philadelphia: W.B. Saunders; 2002. p. 951–8.
26. Couch FJ, Farid LM, DeShano ML, et al. *BRCA2* germline mutations in male breast cancer cases and breast cancer families. Nat Genet 1996;13:123–5.
27. Haraldsson K, Loman N, Zhang QX, et al. *BRCA2* germ-line mutations are frequent in male breast cancer patents without a family history of the disease. Cancer Res 1998; 58:1367–71.
28. Hiort O, Naber SP, Lehners A, et al. The role of androgen receptor gene mutations in male breast carcinoma. J Clin Endocrinol Metab 1996;81:3404–7.
29. Poujol N, Lobaccaro JM, Cliche L, et al. Functional and structural analysis of R607Q and R6O8K androgen receptor substitutions associated with male breast cancer. Mol Cell Endocrinol 1997;130:43–51.
30. Barlund M, Kuukasjarvi T, Syrjakoski K, et al. Frequent amplification and overexpression of *CCND1* in male breast cancer. Int J Cancer; 2004;111:968–71.
31. Klinefelter HF Jr, Reifenstein EC Jr, Allbright F. Syndrome characterized by gynecomastia, aspermatogenesis without A-leydigism and increased excretion of follicle-stimulating hormone. J Clin Endocrinol 1942; 2:615–27.
32. Hultborn R, Hanson C, Kopf I, et al. Prevalence of Klinefelter's syndrome in male breast cancer patients. Anticancer Res 1997;17(6D):4293–7.
33. Volm MD, Gradishar WJ. How to diagnose and manage male breast cancer. Contemp Oncol 1994;4:17–28.
34. Evans DB, Crichlow RW. Carcinoma of the male breast and Klinefelter's syndrome: is there an association? CA Cancer J Clin 1987;37:246–51.
35. Hado HS, Helmy SW, Klemm K, et al. XX male: a rare cause of short stature, infertility, gynaecomastia and carcinoma of the breast. Int J Clin Pract 2003;57:844–5.
36. Casagrande JT, Hanisch R, Pike MC, el al. A case control study of male breast cancer. Cancer Res 1988;48:1326–30.
37. Srensen HT, Fris S, Olsen JH, et al. Risk of breast cancer in men with liver cirrhosis. Am J Gastroenterol 1998; 93:231–3.
38. Symmers WC. Carcinoma of the breast in transsexual individuals after surgical and hormonal interference with the primary and secondary sex characteristics. Br Med J 1968;2:83–5.
39. Pritchard TJ, Pankowsky DA, Crowe JP, et al. Breast cancer in a male-to-female transsexua1. JAMA 1988;259:2278–80.
40. Crichlow RW, Kaplan EL, Keamey WH. Male mammary cancer: an analysis of 32 cases. Ann Surg 1972:175; 489–94.
41. Karamanakos P, Mitsiades CS, Lembessis, et al. Male breast adenocarcinoma in a prostate cancer patient following prolonged anti-androgen monotherapy. Anticancer Res 2004;24:1077–81.
42. Kidwai N, Gong Y, Sun X, et al. Expression of androgen receptor and prostate-specific antigen in male breast carcinoma. Breast Cancer Res 2004;6:R18–23.
43. Mabuchi K, Bross DS. Kessler II. Risk factors for male breast cancer. J Natl Cancer Inst 1985;74:371–5.
44. Karamanakos P, Aposiolopoulos V, Fafouliotis S, et al. Synchronous bilateral primary male breast carcinoma with hyperprolactinemia. Acta Oncol 1996;35:757–9.
45. Volm MD, Talamonti MS, Thangavelu M, Gradishar WK. Pituitary adenoma and bilateral male breast cancer: an unusual association. J Surg Oncol 1997;64:74–8.
46. Thompson DK, Li FP, Cassady JR. Breast cancer in a man 30 years after radiation for metastatic osteogenic sarcoma. Cancer 1979;44:2362–5.
47. Lowell DM, Marineau RG, Luria SB. Carcinoma of the male breast following radiation. Cancer 1968;22:581–6.
48. Sanchez AG, Villanueva AG, Redondo C. Lobular carcinoma of the breast in a patient with Klinefelter's syndrome. Cancer 1986;57:1181–3.
49. San Miguel P, Sancho M, Enriquez JL, et al. Lobular carcinoma of the male breast associated with the use of cimetidine. Virchow Arch 1997;430:261–3.
50. Lamy O, Elmiger H, Fiche M, et al. Acquired hemophilia as first manifestation of breast carcinoma in a man under long-term spironolactone therapy. Int J Clin Oncol 2004; 9:130–3.
51. Daltry JR, Eeles RA, Kissin MW. Bilateral prophylactic mastectomy: not just a woman's problem. Breast 1998; 7:236–7.
52. Cutuli B, Dilhuydy JM, DeLafontan B, et al. Ductal carcinoma of the male breast: analysis of 31 cases. Eur J Cancer 1997;33:35–8.

53. Hittmair AP, Lininger RA, Tavassoli FA. Ductal carcinoma in situ (DCIS) in the male breast. Cancer 1998;83:2139–49.
54. Desai DC, Brennan EJ Jr, Carp NZ. Paget's disease of the male breast. Am Surg 1996;62:1068–72.
55. Muttarak M, Nimmonrat A, Chaiwun B. Metastatic carcinoma of the male and female breast. Australas Radiol 1998;42:16–9.
56. Lo HC, Lee KF, Yeh CN, Chen MF. Breasts metastasis from hepatocellular carcinoma. Hepatogastroenterology 2004; 51:387–90.
57. Ribeiro, G. Male breast carcinoma—A review of 301 cases from the Christi Hospital & Holt Radium Institute, Manchester. Br J Cancer 1985;51:115–9.
58. van Geel AN, van Slooten EA, Mavrunac M, Hart AAM. A retrospective study of male breast cancer in Holland. Br J Surg 1985;72:724–7.
59. Hultborn R, Freiberg S, Hultborn KA. Male breast carcinoma. I. A study of the total material reported to the Swedish Cancer Registry 1958-1967 with respect to clinical and histopathologic parameters. Acta Oncol 1987;26:241–56.
60. Guinee VF, Olsson H, Moller T, et al. The prognosis of breast cancer in males. Cancer 1993;71:154–61.
61. Borgen PI, Wong GY, Vlamis V, et al. Current management of male breast cancer: a review of 104 cases. Ann Surg 1992;215:451–9.
62. Salvadori B, Saccozzi R, Manzari A, et al. Prognosis of breast cancer in males: an analysis of 170 cases. Eur J Cancer 1994;30A:930–5.
63. Cutuli B, Lacroze M, Dilhuydy JM, et al. Male breast cancer: results of the treatments and prognostic factors in 397 cases. Eur J Cancer 1995;31A:1960–4
64. Naik AM, Fey J, Gemignani M, et al. The risk of axillary relapse after sentinel lymph node biopsy for breast cancer is comparable with that of axillary lymph node dissection: a follow-up study of 4008 procedures. Ann Surg 2004;240:462–71.
65. Port ER, Fey JV, Cody HS, et al. Sentinel lymph node biopsy in patients with male breast carcinoma. Cancer 2001; 91:319–32.
66. De Cicco C, Baio SM, Veronesi P, et al. Sentinel node biopsy in male breast cancer. Nucl Med Commun 2004;25:139–43.
67. Cimmino VM, Degnim AC, Sabel MS, et al. Efficacy of sentinel lymph node biopsy in male breast cancer. J Surg Oncol 2004;86:74–7.
68. McLachlan SA, Erlichman C, Liu FF, et al. Male breast cancer: an 11 year review of 66 patients. Breast Cancer Res Treat 1996;40:225–30.
69. Donegan WL, Redlich PN, Lang PJ, Gall MT. Carcinoma of the breast in males: a multi-institutional survey. Cancer 1998;83:498–509.
70. Perez A, Sanchez JL, Colon AL. Pigmented mammary Paget's disease in a man. Bol Asoc Med P R 2003;95:36–9.
71. Dershaw DD, Bergen PI, Deutch BM, Liberman L. Mammographic findings in men with breast cancer. AJR 1993; 160:267–70.
72. Cooper RA, Gunter BA, Ramamurthy L. Mammography in men. Radiology 1994;191:651–6.
73. Stewart RAL, Howlett DC, Hern FJ. Pictorial review: the imaging features of male breast disease. Clin Radiol 1997; 52:739–44.
74. Sneige N, Holder PD, Katz RI, et al. Fine-needle aspiration cytology of the male breast in a cancer center. Diagn Cytopathol 1993;9:691–7.
75. Vetto J, Schmidt W, Pommier R, et al. Accurate and cost effective evaluation of breast masses in males. Am J Surg 1998;175:383–7.
76. Westenend PJ. Core needle biopsy in male breast lesions. J Clin Pathol. 2003;56:863–5.
77. Bezwoda WR, Hesdorffer C, Dansey R, et al. Breast cancer in men: clinical features, hormone receptor status and response to therapy. Cancer 1987;60:1337–40.
78. Donegan WI, Redlich PN. Breast cancer in men. Surg Clin North Am 1996;76:343–63.
79. Bruce DM, Heys SD, Payne S, et al. Male breast cancer: Clinico-pathological features, immuno-cytochemical characteristics and prognosis. Eur J Surg Oncol 1996;22:42–6.
80. Caton J, Reardan T, Ellis R. Male breast cancer: the Department of Defense (DOD) experience [abstract]. Proc Annu Meet Am Soc Clin Oncol 1995;14:140.
81. Joshi MG, Lee AK, Loda M, et al. Male breast carcinoma: an evaluation of prognostic factors contributing to a poorer outcome. Cancer 1996:77:490–8.
82. Pivot X, Llombart-Cussac A, Rohr-Albarddo A, et al. Clinical staging for male breast cancer: an adaptation of the international classification (TNM) [abstract]. Proc Annu Meet Am Soc Clin Oncol 1997;16:655.
83. Lartigau E, El-Jabbour JN, Dubray B, Dische S. Male breast carcinoma: a single center report of clinical parameters. Clin Oncol 1994;6:162–6.
84. Yap HY, Tashima CK, Blumenschein GR, Eckles NE. Male breast cancer: a natural history study. Cancer 1979;44: 748–54.
85. Winchester DJ, Goldschmidt RA, Khan SI, et al. Flow cytometric and molecular prognostic markers in male breast carcinoma patients [abstract]. Presented at the 46th Annual Cancer Symposium of the Society of Surgical Oncology, 1993 Mar 18–21, Los Angeles: 1993.
86. Winchester DJ. Male breast cancer. Semin Surg Oncol 1996; 12:364–9.
87. Pich A, Margaria E, Chiusa L, et al. DNA ploidy and *p53* expression correlate with survival and cell proliferative activity in male breast carcinoma. Hum Pathol 1996;27: 676–82.
88. Pich A, Margaria E, Chiusa L. Proliferative activity is a significant prognostic factor in male breast carcinoma. Am J Pathol 1994;145:481–9.
89. Visfelt J, Scheike O. Male breast cancer. I. Histologic typing and grading of 187 Danish cases. Cancer 1973;32:985–90.
90. Jonasson JG, Agnarsson BA, Thorlacius S, et al. Male breast cancer in Iceland. Int J Cancer 1996;65:446–9.
91. Rudlowski C, Friedrichs N, Faridi, et al. Her-2/neu gene amplification and protein expression in primary male breast cancer. Breast Cancer Res Treat 2004;84:215–23.
92. Ciatto S, Iossa A, Bonardi R, Pacini P. Male breast carcinoma: review of multicenter series of 150 cases. Tumori 1990:76:555–8.
93. Borgen PI, Senie RT, McKinnon WM, Rosen PP. Carcinoma of the male breast: analysis of prognosis compared with matched female patients. Ann Surg Oncol 1997;4:385–8.
94. Hultborn R, Friberg S, Holtborn DA, et al. Male breast car-

cinoma. II. A study of the total material reported to the Swedish Cancer Registry 1958–1967 with respect to treatment, prognostic factors and survival. Acta Oncol 1987;26:327–41.

95. Schuchardt U, Seegenschmiedt MH, Kirschner MJ, et al. Adjuvant radiotherapy for breast carcinoma in men: a 20-year clinical experience. Am J Clin Oncol 1996;19: 330–6.
96. Anelli TFM, Anelli A, Tran KN, et al. Tamoxifen administration is associated with a high rate of treatment-limiting symptoms in male breast cancer patients. Cancer 1994; 74:74–7.
97. Ribeiro G, Swendell R. Adjuvant tamoxifen for male breast cancer. Brit J Cancer 1992;65:252–4.
98. Bagley CS, Wesley MN, Young RC, Lippman ME. Adjuvant chemotherapy in males with cancer of the breast. Am J Clin Oncol 1987;10:55–60.
99. Patel HZ, Buzdar AU, Hortobagyi GN. Role of adjuvant chemotherapy in male breast cancer. Cancer 1989;64: 1583–5.
100. Becher R, Höffken K, Pape H, Schmidt CG. Tamoxifen treatment before orchiectomy in advanced breast cancer in men. N Eng J Med 1981:305:169–70.
101. Ribeiro GG. Tamoxifen in the treatment of male breast carcinoma. Clin Radiol 1983;34:625–8.
102. Patel JK, Nemoto T, Dao TL. Metastatic breast cancer in males: assessment of endocrine therapy. Cancer 1984; 53:1583–5.
103. Jaiyesimi IA, Buzdar AU, Sahin AA, et al. Carcinoma of the male breast. Ann Intern Med 1992;117:771–7.
104. Kantarjian H, Yap H-Y, Hortobagyi G, et al. Hormonal therapy for metastatic male breast cancer. Arch Intern Med 1983;143:237–40.
105. Patterson JS, Batersby LA, Back BK. Use of tamoxifen in advanced male breast cancer. Cancer Treat Rep 1980;64: 801–4.
106. Italiano A, Largillier R, Marcy PY, et al. Complete remission obtained with letrozole in a man with metastatic breast cancer. Rev Med Interne 2004;25:323–4.
107. Giordano SH, Valero V, Buzdar AU, et al. Efficacy of anastrozole in male breast cancer. Am J Clin Oncol 2002; 25:235–7.
108. Kraybill WG, Kaufman R, Kinne D. Treatment of advanced male breast cancer. Cancer 1981;47:2185–9.
109. Sandler B, Carman C, Perry RR. Cancer of the male breast. Am Surg 1994;60:816–20.
110. Yap HY, Tashima CK, Blumenschein GR, et al. Chemotherapy for advanced male breast cancer. JAMA 1980;243:1739–41.
111. Lopez M, DiLauro L, Papaido P, et al. Chemotherapy in metastatic male breast cancer. Oncology 1985:452:205–9.
112. Nieder C, Jost PJ, Grosu AL, et al. Report of a male patient with brain metastases from breast cancer. Breast 2003; 12:345–7.
113. Stierer M, Rosen H, Weitensfelder W, et al. Male breast cancer: Austrian experience. World J Surg 1995;19:687–92.
114. Rayson D, Erichman C, Wold LE, et al. Molecular markers in male breast cancer [abstract]. Proc Annu Meet Am Soc Clin Oncol 1997;16:477.
115. Willsher PC, Leach IH, Ellis IO, et al. Male breast cancer: pathological and immunohistochemical features. Anticancer Res 1997;17:2335–8.
116. Bines J, Goss B, Hussong J, et al. c-erbB2 and *p53* overexpression as predictors of survival in patients with male breast cancer [abstract]. Proc Annu Meet Am Soc Clin Oncol 1997;16:558.
117. Temmim L, Luqmani YA, Jarallah M, et al. Evaluation of prognostic factors in male breast cancer. Breast 2001; 10:166–75.

32

Management of Locoregional Recurrences

STEFAN AEBI
IRENE WAPNIR

Locoregional recurrences (LRR) after breast-conserving surgery (BCS) or mastectomy predict a poor outcome in many patients. Local treatment algorithms have consistently included surgery and/or radiotherapy, whereas the use and benefit of systemic therapies in this population remains controversial. Overall, 10 to 20% of patients with stages I–III breast cancer will develop a locoregional recurrence alone or as a component of their disease recurrence during the first 10 years.[1–4] Specifically, the majority of local relapses occur as isolated events, and a small proportion present with concurrent metastatic disease or following distant metastasis.[5,6] In some instances, the time interval between recurrence and the detection of metastasis is quite short, resulting in the inconsistent grouping of these failures as either LRR or metastatic disease.[4] Local and regional recurrences represent about one-third of all relapses after mastectomy (without radiation therapy) and breast-conserving therapy (surgery plus radiation therapy).[7]

Isolated locoregional failures are commonly subdivided into chest wall recurrences after mastectomy, ipsilateral breast tumor recurrences (IBTR) after breast-conserving therapy, and recurrences in regional lymph nodes or extranodal tissues. Skin recurrences can be the sole form of relapse after both types of surgery. For our purposes, contralateral breast cancer is not considered an isolated locoregional recurrence but as a second primary breast cancer. The distinction between IBTR and an ipsilateral new primary tumor may be difficult, but most IBTRs occur in the same quadrant as the primary cancer and resemble the histopathologic characteristics of the primary.[8,9] Non-invasive IBTR is reported in about 10% or less of cases and is associated with better prognosis and lower death rates than invasive recurrences.[10]

Total mastectomy, with or without nodal staging surgery, used to be the most commonly performed operation for breast cancer in the United States.[11] Skin-sparing and nipple-areolar–sparing mastectomies are increasingly used because of superior cosmetic outcomes for patients undergoing immediate breast reconstruction.[12] As well, breast-conserving therapy may be changing as techniques of accelerated partial breast irradiation undergo prospective validation. Both of these approaches could alter the rates of local failure and influence management after LRR. The extent of local involvement determines the likelihood that surgery will successfully remove all visible disease after LRR. A recurrence is deemed operable if the tumor is not fixed to the chest wall and if the skin is not extensively involved. Surgical excision and radiotherapy are the most commonly used treatments in these patients. Palliative procedures can be undertaken to ameliorate symptoms of pain, ulceration, or bleeding even if metastases are present with LRR.

Conceptually, LRR may be a marker of disseminated disease or itself a source of metastasis. Arguments for the first hypothesis are based on the observation that the omission of radiation therapy after

BCS leads to higher IBTR rates; but the survival as a group was equal whether or not radiation therapy was used although the prognosis of the individual patients with IBTR was poor.[13,14] The counterargument is based on the observation of slightly better survival after breast irradiation in a meta-analysis.[15] Accordingly, the benefit of local and adjuvant therapies after IBTR or LRR is unknown.

The management of the patient with LRR after mastectomy or BCS for primary breast cancer is dependent on an understanding of the probability of relapsing at distant sites and the risk of developing second locoregional failures. In this chapter, the prevalence of IBTR, locoregional recurrences, modes of presentations, therapeutic approaches, and prognosis will be summarized.

IPSILATERAL BREAST TUMOR RECURRENCE AFTER LUMPECTOMY

Predictors of IBTR after Lumpectomy

Numerous studies have addressed the risk of local recurrence in retrospective and prospectively collected series. However, it is virtually impossible to summarize these owing to different definitions of LRR and to variations in statistical design and analysis. Nevertheless, the results are broadly comparable, and a few key studies are summarized in Table 32–1. Clinical predictors of IBTR after lumpectomy include age, tumor size, involvement of axillary lymph nodes, and histologic features such as grade and extensive intraductal component.[5] The Gustave Roussy series is of particular interest since their observations are not confounded by the use of adjuvant systemic treatments, as is the case in other retrospective series.[16] Young age was the most significant predictor of locoregional relapse with patients below the age of 40 having a fivefold risk compared to older patients. A systematic review of the effect of age on recurrence rates confirmed a consistent pattern with younger patients being at a higher risk both after BCS with radiation therapy and after mastectomy.[17] Neither genomic nor molecular predictors of local recurrence have been reliably identified, with the possible exception of the proliferation fraction as measured by Ki67 (MIB-1).[18] Patients with mutations of *BRCA1* or *BRCA2* appear to have a short-term risk of IBTR similar to age and stage-matched patients without such mutations; however, the development of new primaries in the ipsilateral (and contralateral) breast is consistently elevated.[19] Therefore, traditional clinical-pathologic and demographic discriminants remain predictive markers for local failure.

Omission of adjuvant breast irradiation is a highly significant predictive factor for IBTR. A meta-analysis of 15 randomized controlled trials reported a relative risk for local recurrence of 3.0; this was accompanied by a smaller relative increase in mortality of 8.6%.[15] The use of boost radiation therapy to the tumor bed, in addition to standard whole breast radiation therapy, reduces the rate of local failure, particularly in young patients.[20] In contrast, older women > 70 with small estrogen-receptor (ER)-positive tumors have low rates of IBTR even without radiotherapy, thus underscoring the indolent behavior of some tumors.[21,22] Adjuvant chemotherapy and hormonal therapy with either tamoxifen or aromatase inhibitors are associated with lower rates of local failure.[23,24]

Lumpectomy Margins and IBTR

BCS achieves local control of disease and maintains cosmesis. The importance of tumor-free margins after lumpectomy is underscored by the observed high local recurrence rates before routine microscopic examination of margins.[25,26] The definitions of positive and negative lumpectomy margins are inconsistent. Overall, higher rates of local recurrence have been reported with positive margins (Table 32–2). However, these results are confounded by variations in radiation dose to the tumor bed in some studies. Negative margins are defined as the absence of tumor cells at the margin or, by some authors, as within 1 to 2 mm from the edge of the specimen. IBTR rates for negative margins measuring > 1 mm are 2 to 7% versus 3 to 24% for close margins.[27] Freedman and colleagues showed that cumulative IBTR rates at 10 years were approximately doubled for patients with close or positive margins versus negative margins.[28] Conversely, virtually identical recurrence rates were observed by others for close versus negative margins.[29,30]

Table 32–1. PREDICTORS OF IBTR AFTER BREAST CONSERVING SURGERY + XRT

Study, Author	Patients Median Follow-up	Age or Menopausal Status Nodal status	Systemic Therapy	Cumulative Risk of IBTR	Predictors of IBTR: Tumor Size	Nuclear Grade	EIC	Young Age	Nodal Status	LVI
NSABP B-06, Fisher et al[13,14]	731 > 20 yr	40% ≤ age 50 62% N–	N+: L-PAM+5- FU	14.3% (17.0% N–, 8.8% N+)	+	+				+
NSABP B-21, Fisher et al[23]	1009 7.2 yr	20% < age 50 100% N–	Randomized tam	XRT: 9.3% tam: 16.5% XRT + tam: 2.8%	+			+		
Milan et al[33]	2,233 > 10 yr	58% pre-menopausal, 65% N–	N+: CMF for most patients	5.3%	+		+	+		+
EORTC and DBCG, Voogd et al[79]	879 9.8 yr	43 % ≤ age 50 62% N–		10%			+	+		+
Gustave et al[16]	717 20 yr	48% ≤ age 50	None	≈ 10%		+		+	+	
Karolinska, Dalberg et al[80]	759 10 yr	38% ≤ age 50 84% N–	Tam in 15%, CMF in 2%	12%				+	+	
EORTC, Bartelink, et al[20]	2657 5.1 yr	33% ≤ age 50	Chemotherapy in 12%, tam in 18%	5 yr: 7.3% without, 4.3% with XRT boost	+			+		

CMF = cyclophosphamide, methotrexate, fluorouracil; DBCG = Danish Breast Cancer Cooperative Group; EIC = extensive intraductal component; EORTC = European Organization for Research and Treatment of Cancer; FU = follow-up; IBTR = ipsilateral breast tumor recurrences; L-PAM = melphalan; LVI = lymphovascular invasion; N = normal; NSABP = National Surgical Adjuvant Breast and Bowel Project; tam = tamoxifen; XRT = adjuvant radiation therapy.

Table 32–2. IBTR RATES AS A FUNCTION OF LUMPECTOMY MARGINS

Author	N	Time Interval (yr)	Resection Margins			
			Negative	Close	Focally Positive	Positive
Borger et al[81]	1,026	5.5	2	6		16
Dewar et al[82]	757	9	6			14
Freedman et al[28]	1,262	6.3	7	14		12
Park et al[30]	533	10.6	7	7	14	27
Smitt et al[83]	303	6	2	16	0	9
Peterson et al[84]	1,021	6.8	9	17		11
Wazer et al[85]	498	6	2	2		15
Fyles et al[21]	386	5	0.4			

IBTR = ipsilateral breast tumor recurrences.

Singletary points out, in an overview of 34 published reports, that wider margins do not proportionally predict lower rates of recurrence.[27] Moreover, although positive margins denote a predisposition for local failure, 70% or more of patients in this category experienced no IBTR. Some authors have proposed that positive margins are independent prognosticators of distant disease.[31]

Re-excisions to achieve microscopically negative margins have become increasingly common after BCS. Ultrasound, frozen section, or touch-prep cytology have been tested to determine margin status intraoperatively.[27] Some pathologists favor frozen section analysis, whereas others prefer touch-prep technique, which is reported to have 100% sensitivity and specificity in the evaluation of margins.[32] Inking of specimen is valuable as it provides a guide for surgical re-excision in the event of positive margins.

Diagnosis and Treatment

Detection of IBTR

The annual risk of IBTR in women who are treated by breast conservation is 1 to 2% per year; the risk is highest in the first few years after local treatment, leveling off after about 5 years.[13,33] Physical exam every 3 to 6 months and annual mammography are the recommended methods of surveillance after BCS.[34] Detection of recurrent cancer in the irradiated, conserved breast and, specifically, the lumpectomy scar can be challenging owing to the presence of postoperative parenchymal induration and skin thickening. As many as 50 to 86% of recurrences are palpable, with or without associated mammographic abnormalities.[33,35] The majority of ipsilateral recurrences occur in the vicinity of the lumpectomy site and measure < 2 cm. Recurrences away from the lumpectomy site are potentially considered second primaries, especially those that appear histologically different from the index lesion.[8] Modern molecular techniques may facilitate the distinction between recurrences arising from the original malignant clone versus new primaries.[36] The utility of this distinction for the management of this event needs further study.

Skin recurrences (Figure 32–1) in the conserved breast without parenchymal involvement are rare. Several patterns of skin involvement are recognized: single or multiple erythematous nodules, diffuse edema, or erythema (inflammatory) changes. Gage and colleagues reported 18 cases of skin recurrence among 1,624 women treated with BCS.[37] This pattern constituted 8% of all IBTRs. Metastatic disease developed in 44% of cases within 2 months of diagnosis. Compared to other types of in-breast recurrences, the time interval from diagnosis to skin recurrence was shorter, 38 months versus 60 months.

Mammographic evaluation of lumpectomy scars is difficult because of architectural distortion or spiculation at the site of the previous cancer. Recurrent carcinoma may mimic a lumpectomy scar. Increasing density, or distortion, and new microcalcifications in the area of the lumpectomy can indicate tumor recurrence since, typically, scars attenuate over time. New calcifications can appear in the area of the scar in about 18% of cases. The majority are benign, presenting as scattered or coarse calcifications. Recurrent cancer is present in 40 to 66% of

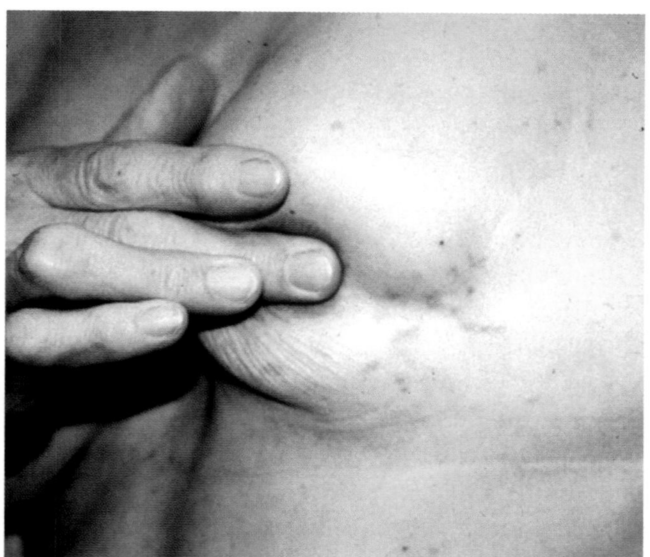

Figure 32–1. Skin recurrence. Erythematous papules recurring in the skin of the breast and chest wall after lumpectomy and breast irradiation.

cases with isolated new microcalcifications. The sensitivity and specificity of mammography after lumpectomy and radiation has been reported as 50 and 75%, respectively.[38] Mumtaz and colleagues recognized that only 7 of 14 IBTR were not mammographically detected and 2 of the 7 were retrospectively present one year before diagnosis. Chen and colleagues studied 125 women with ipsilateral breast tumor recurrences and found that the method of detection of the primary predicted the method of detection of the recurrence.[39] Mammography and physical exam independently detected 38 and 37% of recurrences, respectively. The remaining 25% were discovered by the two modalities. Interestingly, among patients whose primary tumors were discovered by physical exam, 24% of their corresponding IBTRs were detected by mammography only, irrespective of age and time to recurrence.

Biopsies of the irradiated, conserved breast are undertaken whenever recurrent carcinoma is suspected clinically or detected by routine imaging studies. Solin and colleagues reported in 1990 that 10% of 1,416 women treated with BCS underwent a subsequent diagnostic biopsy procedure using fine-needle aspiration cytology, tissue core, incisional, or excisional biopsy.[40] Recurrent carcinoma was detected in 52%. Of these, 4% diffusely involved the breast and 30% were not in the vicinity of the primary tumor or lumpectomy scar.

Magnetic resonance imaging (MRI) may be superior to film screen mammography as it identified 13 of 14 recurrences, whereas mammography identified only seven. However, inflammatory changes resulting from a recent biopsy can hamper the accuracy of MRI. Positron emission tomography (PET) or PET/computed tomography (CT) may prove useful in the characterization of breast lesions or evaluation of the lumpectomy scar, but thus far there has been limited testing and validation of this imaging modality.[41]

Salvage Surgery after IBTR

The majority of recurrent cancers in the conserved breast are relatively small and readily operable. Fewer than 10% of local failures are inoperable by virtue of the presence of diffuse skin involvement, extensive nodal disease, or chest wall fixation, which do not lend themselves to complete surgical excision.[42–45] Close to 90% of recurrences can be treated surgically, excluding those cases with antecedent or simultaneous metastases.[35] Up to half of the patients suffering skin recurrences are resectable, based on limited skin involvement.[37] Mastectomy remains the most common type of salvage surgery performed for IBTR.[46] Repeat lumpectomy has been embraced selectively as an alternative approach. Kurtz and colleagues were one of the first groups to present their favorable long-term experience with local re-excision.[35] This form of surgical therapy is gaining momentum[47] but has not been formally compared to salvage mastectomy. Durable local control after salvage surgery is not achieved in many instances. Kurtz and colleagues found that 12% of patients failed again after salvage mastectomy, compared to 36% for women who had a second breast-conserving procedure.[35] Chest wall recurrence or distant relapse occurred in 12 of 25 patients treated by salvage mastectomy following BCS without radiotherapy.[48] Kuerer and colleagues summarized the experience with salvage mastectomy abstracted from 14 reports and noted that 3 to 32% of patients went on to suffer a second local failure in the form of chest wall recurrence.[47] Re-radiation of the entire breast or, alternatively, conventional doses limited to the site of recurrence have been employed.[49] Brachytherapy or external beam dose of 50 Gy are possible with satisfactory long-term results. At the University of Pittsburgh, 31 women with invasive and 8 with in situ IBTRs received 5,000 cGy with 6–14 MeV electron beam.[50] After a median follow-up of 52 months, only 21% developed a second IBTR, and 8 failed with distant metastasis. Local control without evidence of disease was achieved in 76.9% at 51.5 months, median follow-up.

Re-exploration of the axilla in the absence of clinical or radiologic findings is unnecessary.[51] However, repeat axillary dissection is possible even if the original operation included a standard axillary dissection. Additional lymph nodes are frequently found. Completion axillary dissection at the time of IBTR for women initially staged by sentinel node biopsy is a reasonable approach.

Survival after IBTR

The prognostic significance of in-breast recurrences was not appreciated initially as these were largely considered cosmetic failures. This view was based on the fact that survival was not affected in lumpectomy trials in spite of three- to fourfold higher IBTR rates for patients who did not receive breast irradiation.[14,52] Fisher and colleagues performed an analysis on patients from the National Surgical Adjuvant Breast and Bowel Project (NSABP) protocol B-06 and found that an isolated IBTR was the most significant predictor of distant relapse.[13] Specifically, there was a 3.41-fold increase in the risk of developing metastatic disease in patients who had an IBTR compared to those who did not. Other groups confirmed this observation by demonstrating that survival is decreased in patients with IBTR and that this event is an independent factor predicting systemic failure.[29,53,54]

Five-year survival after IBTR ranges from 52 to 68%.[5] However, some studies include cases with ductal carcinoma in situ or metastatic disease, which undoubtedly skew the survival data. Operable recurrences, as expected, have a dramatically more favorable outcome than inoperable cases. Kurtz and colleagues reported their experience on 1,593 patients treated by lumpectomy and radiotherapy from 1963 to 1982 (681 had axillary dissection) and noted no detrimental influence on survival for early, operable recurrences.[35] Ten years after salvage treatment, 57% were alive. The median survival, however, for patients with inoperable recurrences was only 7 months, compared to 71 months for operable disease.[44]

Shorter time interval to recurrence portends a worse survival after IBTR.[5,13,35] Specifically, 5-year survival for women having IBTR within 2 years of diagnosis range from 48 to 69%. Veronesi and colleagues calculated that the risk of developing a distant failure was 6.6 times higher if an IBTR occurred during the first year after the diagnosis of cancer, compared to after the third year.[33] The NSABP performed a preliminary analysis on patients with node positive cancer entered into five clinical trials (B-06, B-15, B-16, B-22, B-25) and studied the annual mortality independent of the time interval from initial diagnosis to IBTR. This group examined the annual death rate during the first 5 years after IBTR and calculated this to be 14.5%.[46]

Diffuse involvement of the breast parenchyma and skin recurrences are associated with poor prognosis.[37,55] Five-year actuarial rates demonstrate that only 22% of women with skin recurrences versus 58% with non-breast skin recurrences were alive without evidence of metastatic disease, suggesting that recurrences in the skin of the conserved breast behave very similar to postmastectomy skin relapses.[37]

Twenty-year follow-up on the results of NSABP B-06 randomized trial, comparing lumpectomy with lumpectomy plus radiotherapy, show no differences in distant disease-free survival or overall survival.[14] Some investigators have postulated that IBTR may indeed contribute to disease dissemination rather than be an indicator of metastatic risk. Fortin and colleagues hypothesized that if metastatic disease results from local failure, then the time interval from diagnosis to distant relapse in patients without a local failure must be shorter because the metastases were present at the time of surgery for the index tumor.[55] In their study, 172 of 2,030 patients experienced a local failure. Their survival was 55%, as compared to 75% without a local failure at 10 years.

A second mortality peak was seen in patients with local failure at 5 to 6 years of follow-up, possibly caused by later-appearing metastasis that were due to the IBTR.

Successful local control after salvage surgery is associated with an overall survival of 78 versus 21% for patients who do not achieve local control by salvage surgery or nonoperative methods.[56] Larger tumor recurrences (eg, measuring over 3 cm) portend a worse survival than non-palpable mammographically detected recurrences.

LRR AFTER MASTECTOMY

Predictors of LRR after Mastectomy

Five major analyses deserving mention are summarized in Table 32–3. Identification of factors predictive for chest wall recurrences is complicated by the lack of uniform definitions. Nevertheless, axillary node involvement, low number of resected axillary nodes, and tumor size emerge as predictors of recurrence in most studies, whereas other factors such as age, estrogen receptor expression, or vascular invasion were less consistently predictive or were not investigated. Similar results were observed in a recent retrospective study of patients treated at the M.D. Anderson Cancer Center: node negative status, low nuclear grade, early-stage disease, and hormone receptor positivity of the primary tumor were predictors of better outcomes. Three independent factors were used to stratify patients into risk categories. Low risk was defined by node negative status of primary tumor, use of radiation therapy, and time interval to recurrence greater than 24 months.[57] The overexpression of HER-2 may predict LRR.[58] Additional systemic adjuvant therapy and chest wall irradiation decrease the risk of locoregional relapse after mastectomy.[59,60] Molecular markers associated with recurrence would be desirable but have not yet been defined.

Diagnosis and Local Treatment of Chest Wall Recurrences

Almost half of all local recurrences following mastectomy are diagnosed in asymptomatic patients during routine follow-up examinations. Isolated chest wall recurrences represent approximately 50 to 60% of all locoregional relapses, with supraclavicular and axillary lymph nodes being much less common. About half of all chest wall recurrences appear within the mastectomy scar, and one-quarter present as solitary nodules.[61] Other clinical manifestations of chest wall recurrences range from rash-like skin involvement to ulcerating/bleeding or fixed masses that infiltrate intercostal muscles and periosteum. Although it is well recognized that chest wall recurrences can present as late as 40 years after radical mastectomy, the median time between the resection of the primary tumor and locoregional recurrence ranges from 2 to 3 years.[6,62,63] Detection of local failures in patients who have had postmastectomy autologous tissue reconstructions or implants may be more challenging.[64] Survival after recurrence was 61% for subcutaneous and 45% chest wall failures, with mean follow-up of 80.8 months. Metastatic disease developed in 57 versus 91% of cases. Carlson and colleagues reported a 77% distant failure rate with recurrence after skin-sparing mastectomy and reconstruction.[65]

Aside from physical examination, computerized tomography is the most readily available, cost-effective imaging modality for LRR following mastectomy.[66] Imaging studies may be useful to document the extent of disease and, therefore, the operability of patients. MRI is especially well suited to evaluate brachial plexus involvement in axillary recurrences. The role of 18-F-fluorodeoxyglucose PET is expanding and may have the greatest impact in altering management in as many as 44% of patients with suspected locoregional disease.[67] Moreover, it may be particularly useful in detecting nodal disease in the internal mammary chain and mediastinum.[68] In any case, preoperative assessment of metastatic disease is appropriate.

Patients with localized recurrences are candidates for complete excision of all visible tumor including chest wall resection. Second local failures are observed in 60 to 70% of patients who have been treated by excision alone.[69] Although no randomized clinical trial has ever been completed to show that combined surgery and radiation therapy improves prognosis, there is little doubt that

Table 32–3. PREDICTORS OF CHEST WALL RECURRENCE AFTER MASTECTOMY

Study, Author	Patients, Median Follow-up	Age, Nodal Status	Systemic Therapy	Cumulative 10-yr Risk of Isolated LRR	Predictors of LRR				
					Tumor Size	Nuclear Grade	Young Age	Nodal Status	LVI
ECOG; Recht[62]	2,016 12.1 yr	53% pre-menopausal 100% N+	CMF and doxorubicin containing regimens. tam in a proportion of patients	12.6%				+	
M.D. Anderson Cancer Center, Katz[63]	1,031 9.7 yr	48% premenopausal 86% N+	Doxorubicin containing regimens. tam if ER+	14%	+			+	
Institut Gustave Roussy, Arriagada[16]	1,289 20 yr	40% ≤ age 50 52% N+	Chemotherapy 3%, oophorectomy in premenopausal patients with ER+ tumors	7.5%		+		+	
IBCSG, Wallgren[86]	5,352 >12 yr	57% premenopausal 76% N+	CMF chemotherapy 70%, tam for postmenopausal patients	6–25%	+	+		+	+
NSABP, Taghian[6]	5,758 11.1 yr	45% premenopausal) 100% N+	Doxorubicin containing 90% or CMF. Tam for postmenopausal and premenopausal patients with ER+ tumors	12.4%	+	+		+	

CMF = cyclophosphamide, methotrexate, fluorouracil; ECOG = Eastern Cooperative Oncology Group; ER = estrogen receptor; IBCSG = International Breast Cancer Study Group; LRR = Locoregional recurrences; LVI = lymphovascular invasion; N+ = node positive; NSABP = National Surgical Adjuvant Breast and Bowel Project; tam = tamoxifen.

radiation therapy after primary mastectomy reduces the risk of local relapse.[7,60] By analogy, it is very likely that at least further local recurrences can be averted by radiation therapy. Thus, chest wall irradiation is strongly recommended after resection of chest wall recurrences.[70]

Palliative local surgery may be indicated even in the presence of metastatic disease. For instance, resection of an ulcerating tumor may improve local management of the disease, or debulking of some lesions could conceivably enhance pain control. Extensive surgery, including resection of ribs, sternum, muscle and even lung or diaphragm, has been used with the goal of palliation. However, this is not typical and may necessitate complex reconstructive approaches in a patient population with a markedly limited prognosis.

Diagnosis and Treatment of Axillary Recurrences

The rate of axillary recurrences after traditional levels I–III axillary node dissection is reported between 0.5 to 3%.[21] On the other hand, incomplete axillary dissections are associated with high relapse rates of 17 to 19%[71]; Weir reported a direct relationship between the number of axillary nodes removed and the risk of regional recurrence with more than 5% for < 6 nodes and about 1% for >10 lymph nodes.[72]

The short-term follow-up on sentinel node biopsy for clinically node-negative patients reveals low axillary failure rates. Naik and colleagues observed 10 axillary recurrences among 4,008 sentinel node biopsy-guided axillary dissections, but only 3 cases represented isolated relapse events.[73]

Nearly all axillary recurrences present as palpable masses and are readily accessible for fine-needle biopsy. Other clinical features of recurrence may be new onset of upper extremity lymphedema, pain, or limited arm mobility. Imaging studies such as CT or magnetic resonance may be helpful in delineating the extent of disease, invasion into surrounding anatomic areas, and resectability. Repeat exploration of the axilla may yield nodes from areas not previously dissected, for example, the axillary arch, and may enhance ultimate local control. With today's widespread use of sentinel node biopsy, it is our recommendation to perform completion axillary dissection after an axillary failure.

Diagnosis and Treatment of Extra-Axillary Nodal Recurrences

Extra-axillary nodal recurrences refer to supraclavicular, infraclavicular (level III or interpectoral nodes), or internal mammary nodes. Supraclavicular nodal involvement is commonly considered regional disease, although prior to the recent revision by the AJCC, it was synonymous to stage IV disease.[74] In retrospective analyses, LRR are located in supraclavicular lymph nodes in 10 to 15% of cases, whereas the internal mammary nodes are affected in about 5%.[75] Treatment typically includes surgical resection of all gross disease and radiation therapy for patients who did not receive prior radiotherapy.

Survival after LRR

The prognosis after locoregional recurrence has been investigated in many retrospective studies.[5] The 5- to 10-year recurrence-free survival after LRR is 24 to 48%. Pathologic characteristics of the *primary* tumor, such as nodal status, tumor size, steroid hormone receptors, and histologic grade, are predictive of outcome after LRR. In addition, a short interval between the primary therapy and the first recurrence is an adverse prognostic factor.[4] Site-specific outcomes vary markedly. For example, Kamby and Sengelov reported a 10-year cumulative incidence of distant metastases of 59% in patients with chest wall recurrences and 68% after relapse in regional nodes.[76] Similarly, 5-year survival after chest wall, axillary, or internal mammary recurrences was 44 to 49%; supraclavicular recurrences or patients with a combination of nodal disease and chest wall did worse, with a 21 to 24% 5-year overall survival.[75] Mortality during the first 5 years after an isolated and localized axillary recurrence is 39 to 50%.[5]

SYSTEMIC THERAPIES AFTER IBTR AND LRR

Adjuvant hormonal therapy and chemotherapy reduce the risk of recurrence after primary breast cancer. In addition, adjuvant perioperative and postoperative chemotherapy decreases not only the risk of distant recurrence but also the likelihood of local relapse.[24,59] It would seem obvious to postulate that a second course of adjuvant therapy could also diminish the risk of recurrence after rendering patients free of local disease. However, this concept has not been adequately evaluated in a randomized controlled trial.[77] The role of adjuvant systemic therapy after local or regional recurrence has been investigated in a few trials; however, only one randomized trial of contemporary adjuvant systemic therapy has been completed. The Swiss Association for Clinical Cancer Research (SAKK) reported a randomized trial comparing tamoxifen with observation in 167 patients with small (≤ 3 cm, or ≤ 3 discrete nodules) ER positive or unknown local or regional recurrences.[78] Seventy-nine percent of the patients were postmenopausal at randomization. After a median follow-up period of 11.6 years, post-recurrence disease-free survival was 6.5 years with tamoxifen and 2.7 years with observation ($p = .053$). Tamoxifen increased the 5-year disease-free survival from 33 to 61% ($p = .006$) in post-menopausal women, whereas no advantage was noted in premenopausal women. This observation was mainly attributed to reduction of further local relapses ($p = .011$) as survival was not improved.

CURRENT CLINICAL TRIALS OF ADJUVANT THERAPY

At present, two randomized controlled clinical trials are being conducted (Table 32–4): The Fédération Nationale des Centres de Lutte Contre le Cancer is comparing the use of three courses of FEC100 (fluorouracil, epirubicin, cyclophosphamide) followed by 3 courses of docetaxel with observation in patients with radically resected IBTR. Similarly, the International Breast Cancer Study Group (IBCSG), in collaboration with NSABP and the Breast International Group, is comparing chemotherapy with no chemotherapy in patients with radically resected locoregional recurrence after mastectomy or breast conserving primary surgery. In this pragmatic trial (BIG-01-02/IBCSG 27-02/NSABP B-37/MAC.8), the chemotherapy regimen is selected by the participating investigator (<www.nsabp.org; www.ibcsg.org>). It is the aim of such efforts to provide answers regarding the outcome and utility of systemic therapies in patients suffering isolated LRR.

CONCLUSION

In summary, IBTR and locoregional recurrences portend a poorer prognosis and may predict the development of systemic disease and mortality. Those patients with resectable recurrences have an improved

Table 32–4. CURRENT RANDOMIZED CONTROLLED CLINICAL TRIALS FOR PATIENTS WITH RADICALLY RESECTED LOCOREGIONAL RECURRENCE OF BREAST CANCER

Trial	Inclusion	Intervention	Concomitant Therapy	Primary End Point, *N*
PACS 03	IBTR following breast-conserving surgery and radiation therapy. Absence of distant metastasis	3 courses of FEC100 (fluorouracil, epirubicin, cyclophosphamide) followed by 3 courses of docetaxel versus no chemotherapy	Hormonal therapy[1]; radiation therapy if the patient had no prior radiation therapy	Disease-free survival (50 versus 65% at 5 years), one-sided test. *N* = 370
IBCSG 27-02/BIG 01-02/NSABP B-37/ MAC.8	IBTR following breast-conserving surgery and radiation therapy *or* chest wall recurrence following mastectomy *or* regional lymph node recurrence. Absence of distant metastasis	Chemotherapy as selected by the investigator (recommendation for ≥ 2 drugs, 3 to 8 courses) versus no chemotherapy	Hormonal therapy*; radiation therapy if the patient had no prior radiation therapy and for microscopically positive margins; elective trastuzumab if HER-2 is amplified or $p^{185/HER-2}$ is overexpressed	Disease-free survival (50 versus 60% at 5 years), two-sided test. *N* = 973

IBTR = ipsilateral breast tumor recurrences. *Identical hormonal therapies for patients with estrogen receptor positive recurrences.

survival. Although not confirmed by randomized clinical trials, radiation therapy following resection of recurrent disease is recommended, based upon the known reduction of local recurrence following principle therapy. Chemotherapy and hormonal therapy should be considered for ER-negative and ER-positive tumor recurrences respectively. However, only tamoxifen has been shown to significantly reduce subsequent relapses. Prospective randomized studies are ongoing to define the worth of chemotherapy in patients with isolated IBTR and LRR.

REFERENCES

1. Andry G, Suciu S, Vico P, et al. Locoregional recurrences after 649 modified radical mastectomies: incidence and significance. Eur J Surg Oncol 1989;15:476–85.
2. Arriagada R, Le MG, Rochard F, et al. Conservative treatment versus mastectomy in early breast cancer: patterns of failure with 15 years of follow-up data. Institut Gustave-Roussy Breast Cancer Group. J Clin Oncol 1996;14: 1558–64.
3. Fisher B, Anderson S, Wickerham DL, et al. Increased intensification and total dose of cyclophosphamide in a doxorubicin-cyclophosphamide regimen for the treatment of primary breast cancer: findings from National Surgical Adjuvant Breast and Bowel Project B-22. J Clin Oncol 1997;15:1858–69.
4. Schmoor C, Sauerbrei W, Bastert G, et al. Role of isolated locoregional recurrence of breast cancer: results of four prospective studies. J Clin Oncol 2000;18:1696–708.
5. Clemons M, Danson S, Hamilton T, et al. Locoregionally recurrent breast cancer: incidence, risk factors and survival. Cancer Treat Rev 2001;27:67–82.
6. Taghian A, Jeong JH, Mamounas E, et al. Patterns of locoregional failure in patients with operable breast cancer treated by mastectomy and adjuvant chemotherapy with or without tamoxifen and without radiotherapy: results from five National Surgical Adjuvant Breast and Bowel Project randomized clinical trials. J Clin Oncol 2004;22:4247–54.
7. Early Breast Cancer Trialists' Collaborative Group. Favourable and unfavourable effects on long-term survival of radiotherapy for early breast cancer: an overview of the randomised trials. Lancet 2000;355:1757–70.
8. Smith TE, Lee D, Turner BC, et al. True recurrence vs. new primary ipsilateral breast tumor relapse: an analysis of clinical and pathologic differences and their implications in natural history, prognoses, and therapeutic management. Int J Radiat Oncol Biol Phys 2000;48:1281–9.
9. Huang E, Buchholz TA, Meric F, et al. Classifying local disease recurrences after breast conservation therapy based on location and histology: new primary tumors have more favorable outcomes than true local disease recurrences. Cancer 2002;95:2059–67.
10. Fisher ER, Anderson S, Redmond C, et al. Ipsilateral breast tumor recurrence and survival following lumpectomy and irradiation: pathological findings from NSABP protocol B-06. Semin Surg Oncol 1992;8:161–6.
11. Morrow M, White J, Moughan J, et al. Factors predicting the use of breast-conserving therapy in stage I and II breast carcinoma. J Clin Oncol 2001;19:2254–62.
12. Gerber B, Krause A, Reimer T, et al. Skin-sparing mastectomy with conservation of the nipple-areola complex and autologous reconstruction is an oncologically safe procedure. Ann Surg 2003;238:120–7.
13. Fisher B, Anderson S, Fisher ER, et al. Significance of ipsilateral breast tumour recurrence after lumpectomy. Lancet 1991;338:327–31.
14. Fisher B, Anderson S, Bryant J, et al. Twenty-year follow-up of a randomized trial comparing total mastectomy, lumpectomy, and lumpectomy plus irradiation for the treatment of invasive breast cancer. N Engl J Med 2002;347:1233–41.
15. Vinh-Hung V, Verschraegen C. Breast-conserving surgery with or without radiotherapy: pooled-analysis for risks of ipsilateral breast tumor recurrence and mortality. J Natl Cancer Inst 2004;96:115–21.
16. Arriagada R, Lê MG, Contesso G, et al. Predictive factors for local recurrence in 2006 patients with surgically resected small breast cancer. Ann Oncol 2002;13:1404–13.
17. Zhou P, Recht A. Young age and outcome for women with early-stage invasive breast carcinoma. Cancer 2004;101: 1264–74.
18. Dalberg K, Eriksson E, Kanter L, et al. Biomarkers for local recurrence after breast-conservation—a nested case-control study. Breast Cancer Res Treat 1999;57:245–59.
19. Haffty BG, Lannin D. Is breast-conserving therapy in the genetically predisposed breast cancer patient a reasonable and appropriate option? Eur J Cancer 2004;40:1105–8.
20. Bartelink H, Horiot JC, Poortmans P, et al. Recurrence rates after treatment of breast cancer with standard radiotherapy with or without additional radiation. N Engl J Med 2001;345:1378–87.
21. Fyles AW, McCready DR, Machul LA, et al. Tamoxifen with or without breast irradiation in women 50 years of age or older with early breast cancer. N Engl J Med 2004;351: 963–70.
22. Hughes KS, Schnaper LA, Berry D, et al. Lumpectomy plus tamoxifen with or without irradiation in women 70 years of age or older with early breast cancer. N Engl J Med 2004;351:971–7.
23. Fisher B, Bryant J, Dignam J, et al. Tamoxifen, radiation therapy, or both for prevention of ipsilateral breast tumor recurrence after lumpectomy in women with invasive breast cancers of one centimeter or less. J Clin Oncol 2002;20:4141–49.
24. Baum M, Budzar AU, Cuzick J, et al. Anastrozole alone or in combination with tamoxifen versus tamoxifen alone for adjuvant treatment of postmenopausal women with early breast cancer: first results of the ATAC randomised trial. Lancet 2002;359:2131–9.
25. Jacobson JA, Danforth DN, Cowan KH, et al. Ten-year results of a comparison of conservation with mastectomy in the treatment of stage I and II breast cancer. N Engl J Med 1995;332:907–11.
26. Schnitt SJ, Abner A, Gelman R, et al. The relationship between microscopic margins of resection and the risk of

local recurrence in patients with breast cancer treated with breast-conserving surgery and radiation therapy. Cancer 1994;74:1746–51.
27. Singletary SE. Surgical margins in patients with early-stage breast cancer treated with breast conservation therapy. Am J Surg 2002;184:383–93.
28. Freedman G, Fowble B, Hanlon A, et al. Patients with early stage invasive cancer with close or positive margins treated with conservative surgery and radiation have an increased risk of breast recurrence that is delayed by adjuvant systemic therapy. Int J Radiat Oncol Biol Phys 1999;44:1005–15.
29. Touboul E, Buffat L, Belkacemi Y, et al. Local recurrences and distant metastases after breast-conserving surgery and radiation therapy for early breast cancer. Int J Radiat Oncol Biol Phys 1999;43:25–38.
30. Park CC, Mitsumori M, Nixon A, et al. Outcome at 8 years after breast-conserving surgery and radiation therapy for invasive breast cancer: influence of margin status and systemic therapy on local recurrence. J Clin Oncol 2000; 18:1668–75.
31. Meric F, Mirza NQ, Vlastos G, et al. Positive surgical margins and ipsilateral breast tumor recurrence predict disease-specific survival after breast-conserving therapy. Cancer 2003;97:926–33.
32. Klimberg VS, Westbrook KC, Korourian S. Use of touch preps for diagnosis and evaluation of surgical margins in breast cancer. Ann Surg Oncol 1998;5:220–6.
33. Veronesi U, Marubini E, Del Vecchio M, et al. Local recurrences and distant metastases after conservative breast cancer treatments: partly independent events. J Natl Cancer Inst 1995;87:19–27.
34. Smith TJ, Davidson NE, Schapira DV, et al. American Society of Clinical Oncology 1998 update of recommended breast cancer surveillance guidelines. J Clin Oncol 1999;17:1080–2.
35. Kurtz JM, Amalric R, Brandone H, et al. Local recurrence after breast-conserving surgery and radiotherapy. Frequency, time course, and prognosis. Cancer 1989;63:1912–7.
36. Schlechter BL, Yang Q, Larson PS, et al. Quantitative DNA fingerprinting may distinguish new primary breast cancer from disease recurrence. J Clin Oncol 2004;22:1830–38.
37. Gage I, Schnitt SJ, Recht A, et al. Skin recurrences after breast-conserving therapy for early-stage breast cancer. J Clin Oncol 1998;16:480–6.
38. Mumtaz H, Davidson T, Hall-Craggs MA, et al. Comparison of magnetic resonance imaging and conventional triple assessment in locally recurrent breast cancer. Br J Surg 1997;84:1147–51.
39. Chen C, Orel SG, Harris EE, et al. Relation between the method of detection of initial breast carcinoma and the method of detection of subsequent ipsilateral local recurrence and contralateral breast carcinoma. Cancer 2003;98:1596–602.
40. Solin LJ, Fowble BL, Schultz DJ, et al. The detection of local recurrence after definitive irradiation for early stage carcinoma of the breast. An analysis of the results of breast biopsies performed in previously irradiated breasts. Cancer 1990;65:2497–502.
41. Goerres GW, Michel SC, Fehr MK, et al. Follow-up of women with breast cancer: comparison between MRI and FDG PET. Eur Radiol 2003;13:1635–44.
42. Recht A, Silver B, Schnitt S, et al. Breast relapse following primary radiation therapy for early breast cancer. I. Classification, frequency and salvage. Int J Radiat Oncol Biol Phys 1985;11:1271–6.
43. Fisher ER, Sass R, Fisher B, et al. Pathologic findings from the National Surgical Adjuvant Breast Project (protocol 6). I. Intraductal carcinoma (DCIS). Cancer 1986;57: 197–208.
44. Kurtz JM, Jacquemier J, Brandone H, et al. Inoperable recurrence after breast-conserving surgical treatment and radiotherapy. Surg Gynecol Obstet 1991;172:357–61.
45. Salvadori B, Marubini E, Miceli R, et al. Reoperation for locally recurrent breast cancer in patients previously treated with conservative surgery. Br J Surg 1999;86:84–7.
46. Wapnir I, Anderson S, Tan-Chiu E, et al. Ipsilateral breast tumor recurrence (IBTR) and survival in NSABP node-positive breast cancer protocols [abstract]. Proc Am Soc Clin Oncol 2000;19:82.
47. Kuerer HM, Arthur DW, Haffty BG. Repeat breast-conserving surgery for in-breast local breast carcinoma recurrence: the potential role of partial breast irradiation. Cancer 2004;100:2269–80.
48. Cajucom CC, Tsangaris TN, Nemoto T, et al. Results of salvage mastectomy for local recurrence after breast-conserving surgery without radiation therapy. Cancer 1993; 71:1774–9.
49. Resch A, Fellner C, Mock U, et al. Locally recurrent breast cancer: pulse dose rate brachytherapy for repeat irradiation following lumpectomy—a second chance to preserve the breast. Radiology 2002;225:713–8.
50. Deutsch M. Repeat high-dose external beam irradiation for in-breast tumor recurrence after previous lumpectomy and whole breast irradiation. Int J Radiat Oncol Biol Phys 2002;53:687–91.
51. Kurtz JM, Amalric R, Brandone H, et al. Results of wide excision for mammary recurrence after breast-conserving therapy. Cancer 1988;61:1969–72.
52. Veronesi U, Cascinelli N, Mariani L, et al. Twenty-year follow-up of a randomized study comparing breast-conserving surgery with radical mastectomy for early breast cancer. N Engl J Med 2002;347:1227–32.
53. Whelan T, Clark R, Roberts R, et al. Ipsilateral breast tumor recurrence postlumpectomy is predictive of subsequent mortality: results from a randomized trial. Investigators of the Ontario Clinical Oncology Group. Int J Radiat Oncol Biol Phys 1994;30:11–6.
54. Vicini FA, Kestin L, Huang R, et al. Does local recurrence affect the rate of distant metastases and survival in patients with early-stage breast carcinoma treated with breast-conserving therapy? Cancer 2003;97:910–9.
55. Fortin A, Larochelle M, Lavertu S, et al. Local failure is responsible for the decrease in survival of patients treated with conservative surgery and postoperative radiotherapy. J Clin Oncol 1999;17:101–9.
56. Dalberg K, Liedberg A, Johansson U, et al. Uncontrolled local disease after salvage treatment for ipsilateral breast tumour recurrence. Eur J Surg Oncol 2003;29:143–54.
57. Chagpar A, Meric-Bernstam F, Hunt KK, et al. Chest wall

recurrence after mastectomy does not always portend a dismal outcome. Ann Surg Oncol 2003;10:628–34.

58. Haffty BG, Hauser A, Choi DH, et al. Molecular markers for prognosis after isolated postmastectomy chest wall recurrence. Cancer 2004;100:252–63.
59. Goldhirsch A, Gelber RD, Price KN, et al. Effect of systemic adjuvant treatment on first sites of breast cancer relapse. Lancet 1994;343:377–81.
60. Whelan TJ, Julian J, Wright J, et al. Does locoregional radiation therapy improve survival in breast cancer? A meta-analysis. J Clin Oncol 2000;18:1220–9.
61. Freedman GM, Fowble BL. Local recurrence after mastectomy or breast-conserving surgery and radiation. Oncology (Williston Park) 2000;14:1561–81
62. Recht A, Gray R, Davidson NE, et al. Locoregional failure 10 years after mastectomy and adjuvant chemotherapy with or without tamoxifen without irradiation: experience of the Eastern Cooperative Oncology Group. J Clin Oncol 1999;17:1689–700.
63. Katz A, Strom EA, Buchholz TA, et al. Locoregional recurrence patterns after mastectomy and doxorubicin-based chemotherapy: implications for postoperative irradiation. J Clin Oncol 2000;18:2817–27.
64. Langstein HN, Cheng MH, Singletary SE, et al. Breast cancer recurrence after immediate reconstruction: patterns and significance. Plast Reconstr Surg 2003;111:712–20.
65. Carlson GW, Styblo TM, Lyles RH, et al. Local recurrence after skin-sparing mastectomy: tumor biology or surgical conservatism? Ann Surg Oncol 2003;10:108–12.
66. Cheng JC, Cheng SH, Lin KJ, et al. Diagnostic thoracic-computed tomography in radiotherapy for loco-regional recurrent breast carcinoma. Int J Radiat Oncol Biol Phys 1998; 41:607–13.
67. Eubank WB, Mankoff D, Bhattacharya M, et al. Impact of FDG PET on defining the extent of disease and on the treatment of patients with recurrent or metastatic breast cancer. AJR Am J Roentgenol 2004;183:479–86.
68. Bellon JR, Livingston RB, Eubank WB, et al. Evaluation of the internal mammary lymph nodes by FDG-PET in locally advanced breast cancer (LABC). Am J Clin Oncol 2004;27:407–10.
69. Clemons M, Hamilton T, Goss P. Does treatment at the time of locoregional failure of breast cancer alter prognosis? Cancer Treat Rev 2001;27:83–97.
70. Schuck A, Konemann S, Matthees B, et al. Radiotherapy in the treatment of locoregional relapses of breast cancer. Br J Radiol 2002;75:663–69.
71. McKinna F, Gothard L, Ashley S, et al. Lymphatic relapse in women with early breast cancer: a difficult management problem. Eur J Cancer 1999;35:1065–9.
72. Weir L, Speers C, D'Yachkova Y, et al. Prognostic significance of the number of axillary lymph nodes removed in patients with node-negative breast cancer. J Clin Oncol 2002;20:1793–9.
73. Naik AM, Fey J, Gemignani M, et al. The risk of axillary relapse after sentinel lymph node biopsy for breast cancer is comparable with that of axillary lymph node dissection: a follow-up study of 4008 procedures. Ann Surg 2004; 240:462–8.
74. Singletary SE, Allred C, Ashley P, et al. Revision of the American Joint Committee on Cancer staging system for breast cancer. J Clin Oncol 2002;20:3628–36.
75. Halverson KJ, Perez CA, Kuske RR, et al. Survival following locoregional recurrence of breast cancer: univariate and multivariate analysis. Int J Radiat Oncol Biol Phys 1992; 23:285–91.
76. Kamby C, Sengelov L. Pattern of dissemination and survival following isolated locoregional recurrence of breast cancer. A prospective study with more than 10 years of follow up. Breast Cancer Res Treat 1997;45:181–92.
77. Rauschecker H, Clarke M, Gatzemeier W, et al. Systemic therapy for treating locoregional recurrence in women with breast cancer. Cochrane Database Syst Rev 2001: CD002195.
78. Waeber M, Castiglione-Gertsch M, Dietrich D, et al. Adjuvant therapy after excision and radiation of isolated postmastectomy locoregional breast cancer recurrence: definitive results of a phase III randomized trial (SAKK 23/82) comparing tamoxifen with observation. Ann Oncol 2003;14:1215–21.
79. Voogd AC, Nielsen M, Peterse JL, et al. Differences in risk factors for local and distant recurrence after breast-conserving therapy or mastectomy for stage I and II breast cancer: pooled results of two large European randomized trials. J Clin Oncol 2001;19:1688–97.
80. Dalberg K, Mattsson A, Rutqvist LE, et al. Breast conserving surgery for invasive breast cancer: risk factors for ipsilateral breast tumor recurrences. Breast Cancer Res Treat 1997;43:73–86.
81. Borger J, Kemperman H, Hart A, et al. Risk factors in breast-conservation therapy. J Clin Oncol 1994;12:653–60.
82. Dewar JA, Arriagada R, Benhamou S, et al. Local relapse and contralateral tumor rates in patients with breast cancer treated with conservative surgery and radiotherapy (Institut Gustave Roussy 1970-1982). IGR Breast Cancer Group. Cancer 1995;76:2260–5.
83. Smitt MC, Nowels KW, Zdeblick MJ, et al. The importance of the lumpectomy surgical margin status in long-term results of breast conservation. Cancer 1995;76:259–67.
84. Peterson ME, Schultz DJ, Reynolds C, et al. Outcomes in breast cancer patients relative to margin status after treatment with breast-conserving surgery and radiation therapy: the University of Pennsylvania experience. Int J Radiat Oncol Biol Phys 1999;43:1029–35.
85. Wazer DE, Schmidt-Ullrich RK, Ruthazer R, et al. Factors determining outcome for breast-conserving irradiation with margin-directed dose escalation to the tumor bed. Int J Radiat Oncol Biol Phys 1998;40:851–8.
86. Wallgren A, Bonetti M, Gelber RD, et al. Risk factors for locoregional recurrence among breast cancer patients: results from International Breast Cancer Study Group trials I through VII. J Clin Oncol 2003;21:1205–13.

33

Breast Cancer and Multiethnic/Multiracial Populations

LISA A. NEWMAN

EPIDEMIOLOGY OF BREAST CANCER WORLDWIDE

Breast cancer incidence and mortality rates vary substantially in conjunction with ethnic background and country of origin. Western industrialized nations characterized by diets that are relatively high in fat and meat content, and where women begin childbearing at relatively older ages (or not at all), tend to have the heaviest breast cancer burden. In contrast, breast cancer is less common in underdeveloped areas where dietary fat consumption is lower and where childbearing patterns are shifted toward younger ages and larger families.[1,2] Nations such as Japan and China that have experienced a relatively recent expansion of their urbanized and industrialized cities have been experiencing a concomitant increase in the risk of breast cancer faced by their female populations. Similarly, migrant studies reveal that individuals from low-risk regions who relocate to high-risk countries tend to assume increased breast cancer risks that reflect the adopted countries; this risk is likely to be maximized by the second generation, when assimilation into the high-risk environment is more complete.[3] Examples of the variation in international breast cancer incidence and mortality rates are shown in Figure 33–1.[4]

The patterns described above indicate that environment and culture exert a strong influence on breast cancer risk by modulating lifetime estrogen exposure. For example, the greater prevalence of women pursuing professional careers contributes to the tendency to delay pregnancy and to have fewer children. Furthermore, the lifestyle and dietary habits of industrialized countries promote sedentary, obesity-prone populations. This in turn leads to higher breast cancer risk secondary to the increased estrogen load of postmenopausal obesity, as the breasts are then exposed to higher levels of estrone via extraglandular conversion of adrenal gland hormones by enzymes originating in adipocytes. The sedentary environment also yields fewer adolescents experiencing exercise-related irregular menses/anovulatory cycles, further contributing to an increased number of estrogenic cycles seen by the mammary tissue. It has been proposed that various reproductive and lifestyle risk factors explain most of the reported international variation in breast cancer incidence.[5]

Although lifestyle accounts for much of the worldwide variation in breast cancer epidemiology, genetic factors contribute to international differences in risk as well. Hereditary breast cancers result from inherited abnormalities in the genetic sequence for proteins that result in increased susceptibility to certain cancers. Founder mutations are particular germline mutations that are preserved within communities belonging to a particular ethnic background. Whether due to cultural preference or geographic isolation, these communities are notable for their strong ethnic homogeneity, resulting in a particularly strong prevalence of these founder mutations. Founder mutations in the *BRCA* genes associated with Ashkenazi Jewish, African American, Filipino, Chinese, Japanese, and numerous other ethnic groups have been described.[6] Additional disease-associated founder mutations in the *BRCA* genes may

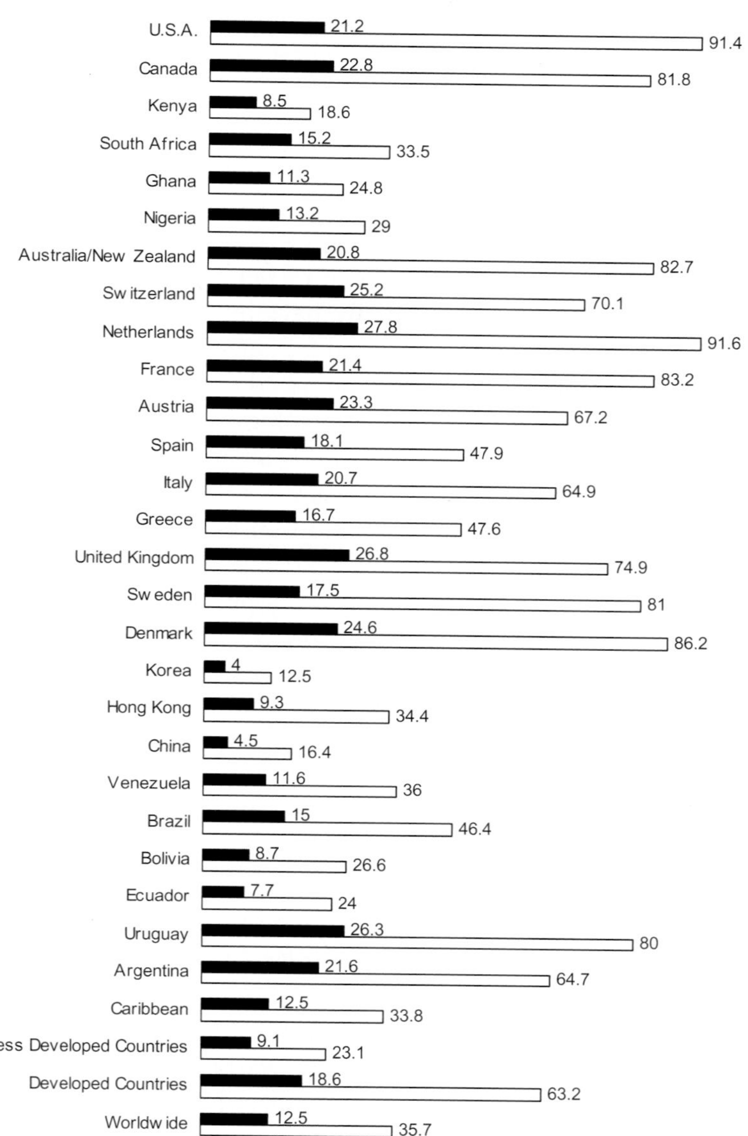

Figure 33–1. Breast cancer (rates per 100,00) worldwide incidence and mortality rates. Adapted from Globocan.[4]

also exist, and it is similarly possible that they may be present in breast cancer susceptibility genes that have simply not yet been characterized. The prevalence and the penetrance of these various founder mutations may affect observed patterns of breast cancer incidence within different ethnic groups.

EPIDEMIOLOGY OF BREAST CANCER IN THE UNITED STATES: DATA COLLECTION, RISK FACTORS, AND OUTCOME IN A MULTIETHNIC POPULATION

The ethnic and cultural diversity of the American population is readily apparent, resulting from a tumultuous 400-year history of British and European settlements among North American territories previously inhabited by Native American tribal groups. Slave laborers, predominantly from Western Africa, were also brought to the Americas during this pioneer and colonization era. Contemporary American society includes descendents of these different populations. American history is also notable for the launching of the industrial revolution and capitalism. Although this background has led to the evolution of the United States into one of the wealthiest and most powerful nations in the world, substantial disparities unfortunately exist regarding the socioeconomic resources available to different population subsets. The epidemiology of breast cancer among American women therefore reflects the combined influences of genetic, dietary, lifestyle, socioeconomic, and environmental risk factors.

The Surveillance Epidemiology and End Results (SEER) Program was established in 1973 as a means of generating population-based incidence and mortality data on various cancers in the United States. This is accomplished by selecting representative sites that are comparable to the general population of the United States with regard to socioeconomic status and geographic region. The selected sites must also be capable of maintaining a high-quality data collection and reporting system. The original nine SEER registries included four cities: Detroit, Michigan; Atlanta, Georgia; San Francisco-Oakland, California; and Seattle-Puget Sound, Washington. In addition, there were five statewide sites: Connecticut, Hawaii, Iowa, New Mexico, and Utah. In 1992, the SEER Program expanded to 12 sites with the inclusion of Los Angeles and San Jose-Monterey, California as well as the Alaska Native Tumor Registries.

In recognition of the need to obtain better and more representative data on minority ethnicity and medically underserved communities, the National Cancer Institute announced plans in 2001 for a near-doubling of the population covered by the SEER data collection. In particular, there was a lack of information regarding the cancer burden of rural African Americans as well as diverse ethnic subsets of Hispanic Americans and Native Americans to address this deficiency. The most recent expansion has involved the addition of four states as SEER sites: Louisiana, Kentucky, New Jersey, and California (by adding coverage of areas previously not included within the SEER Program). This present system should account for cancer case ascertainment on 26% of the American population (65 million people), representing an increase from 14% of the population (35 million). Furthermore, this system is expected to cover 24% of African Americans, 44% of Hispanic Americans, 42% of Native Americans/Alaskan Natives, and 59% of Asian Americans/Pacific Islanders.[7]

The SEER Program estimates regional and national incidence and mortality rates by using the tumor registry case ascertainment data in conjunction with population data from the US Census Bureau. One potential but unavoidable source of inaccurate data is related to the assignment of ethnic identity. The diversity of the American population has resulted in substantial heterogeneity in ethnic background that may or may not be reflected in the individual's self-reported ethnicity. For example, a woman who identifies herself as an African American because one or both of her parents are African American may actually have any number of white Americans in her extended ancestry. The study of ethnicity related population admixture and how it is related to cancer epidemiology is an exciting and rapidly growing field, but is an area of research that is nonetheless in its infancy.[8–12] Hence, the impact of ancestral ethnic admixture on breast cancer risk is undefined at present.

Despite the complex issues described above, SEER data regarding the breast cancer burden among various ethnic subsets of the United States reveal provocative patterns that are similar to international variations observed in breast cancer incidence and mortality.[13] As shown in Figure 33–2, breast cancer incidence is highest among white Americans (the majority of whom are probably of Anglo-Saxon descent) but relatively lower among Hispanic Americans and Asian Americans; this mirrors the breast cancer burden of Great Britain compared to Spain and Asia.

The independent effects of ethnicity on breast cancer outcome in American women are difficult to disentangle from other characteristics that also affect breast cancer risk, and which are independently associated with particular ethnic groups. Socioeconomic status and dietary preferences are prime examples of these confounding factors. Minority ethnic groups in the United States tend to be disproportionately weighted with indigent and medically underserved individuals. These socioeconomic disadvantages result in barriers to accessing the health care system, leading to more advanced stage distributions and increased mortality rates.[14] As shown in Figure 33–3, poverty rates and the likelihood of being medically uninsured are approximately two to three times higher for African Americans, Hispanic Americans, and Asian Americans/Pacific Islanders compared to white (non-Hispanic) Americans.[15,16] Ward and colleagues have demonstrated the significant adverse effect of poverty on cancer outcome within the "distinct" ethnic groups of non-Hispanic Whites, African Americans, American Indian/Alaskan Natives, Asian/Pacific Islanders, and Hispanic/Latin Americans, based on data from the SEER Program and the US Census Bureau.[17] However, even after stratifying by ethnic background and poverty rates, trends are observed for lower cancer-specific survival rates among even the most affluent African Americans and American Indian/Alaskan Natives compared with white Americans, Asian Americans/Pacific Islanders, and Hispanic/Latin Americans.

Few studies have evaluated breast cancer in truly multiethnic populations, where two or more population subsets are compared to white American patients. Findings from some of these studies are presented in Table 33–1, and demonstrate our strong reliance on the SEER Program in providing most of the data for analysis.[18–23] The patterns identified can be summarized as follows: (1) white Americans and Asian Americans tend to present with earlier stage disease compared to African American, Native American, and Hispanic American breast cancer patients; (2) hormone receptor-negative and high-grade tumors are most prevalent among African Americans and Native Americans, least prevalent among white Americans, and intermediate in prevalence among Hispanic Americans; (3) screening mammography is used most consistently among white American women compared with all minority ethnicity women; and (4) breast cancer survival rates are highest among white American and Asian American breast cancer patients, outcome is poorest among African Americans and Native Americans, and Hispanic breast cancer patients face an intermediate mortality hazard.

Insights regarding the associations between hormone metabolism, nutrition, and breast cancer risk are gradually evolving. Available data suggest that complex relationships exist between increasing levels of sex steroid hormones, insulin-related growth factors, insulin resistance (with corresponding hyperinsulinemia), and breast cancer risk. All of these metabolic features are associated with obesity, which compounds their breast tissue carcinogenic effects. Ethnicity associated variation in the prevalence of these hormonal variations as well as obesity

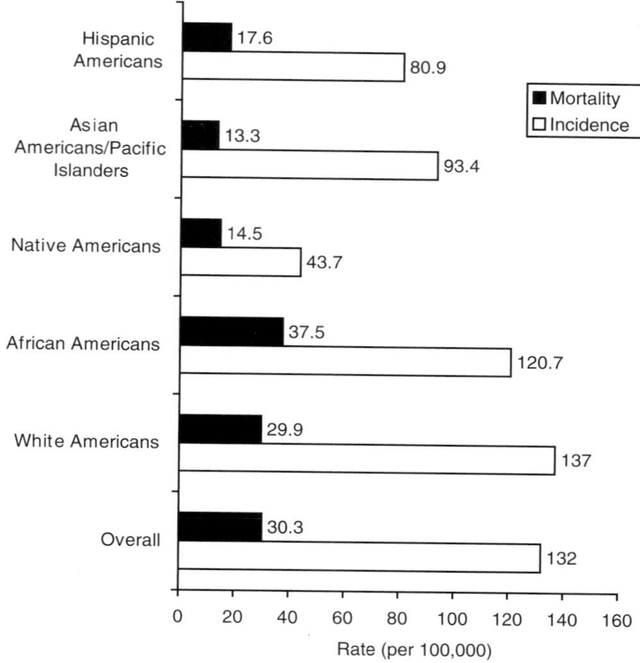

Figure 33–2. Surveillance, Epidemiology, and End Results Program; Breast cancer incidence and mortality rates by ethnicity, 11 registries, 1990–99. Reproduced with permission from SEER.[13]

rates have been demonstrated by several investigators.[24–26] Whether obesity/body mass index (BMI) or circulating hormone levels are the dominant features in ethnicity related variation in breast cancer risk is unclear at present.

Flegal and colleagues analyzed the Third National Health and Nutrition Examination Survey (NHANES III) and found that more than half of African American women over the age of 40 years were obese (BMI $\geq$ 30) and more than 80% were

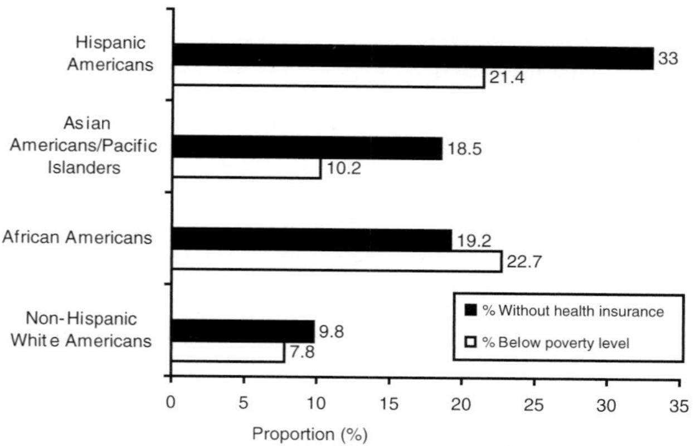

Figure 33–3. Poverty and health insurance coverage rates, by ethnicity.

Table 33–1. SELECTED PUBLISHED STUDIES OF ETHNICITY-RELATED VARIATION IN BREAST CANCER WITHIN THE UNITED STATES

Study	Dataset	Feature	White Americans	African Americans	Asian Americans/ Native Americans	Pacific Islanders	Hispanic Americans
Li et al, 2003[19]	SEER	*N*	97,999	10,560	322	8,834	7,219
		Stage (%) I	50.4	35.4	41.0	47.3	36.0
		III/IV	11.3	18.9	17.7	10.7	15.4
		High-grade tumors (%)	32.1	43.2	37.6	36.0	40.7
		Tumor ≥ 5 cm (%)	8.0	15.0	11.5	10.0	13.9
		Node-negative (%)	53.9	42.6	42.6	56.4	46.7
		ER-negative (%)	22.0	39.2	32.4	25.5	31.3
		PR-negative (%)	31.7	46.6	40.5	32.2	39.2
		Mortality hazard* (95% CI)	1.0	1.5	1.7	0.9	1.1
			(ref)	(1.4–1.6)	(1.3–2.3)	(0.8–1.0)	(1.0–1.1)
Li et al,[18] 2002	SEER, age ≥ 50 years	*N*	75,978	6,915	203	5,750	4,471
		Stage (%) I	53.2	39.1	47.8	51.6	41.5
		III/IV	11.1	19.1	17.8	10.7	14.6
		High-grade tumors (%)	29.0	37.6	31	33.1	35.1
		Tumor ≥ 5 cm (%)	7.4	14.1	9.4	9.2	11.3
		Node-negative (%)	54.3	43.2	44.8	57.8	49.6
		ER-negative (%)	15.2	24.1	24.1	19.0	17.8
		PR-negative (%)	23.8	30.4	62.5	26.5	25.3
Shavers et al, 2003[20]	SEER, age < 35 years	*N*	2,638	724	NR	NR	616
		Stage (%) I	26.7	16.4	NR	NR	15.9
		III/IV	12.3	16.7			17.9
		High-grade tumors (%)	43.3	54.8	NR	NR	51.5
		Median tumor size (cm)	2.5	2.8	NR	NR	3.0
		Node-negative (%)	44.6	36.5	NR	NR	32.6
		ER-negative (%)	33.1	34.4	NR	NR	32.0
		PR-negative (%)	35.4	35.6	NR	NR	32.5
		Mastectomy (%)	53.2	53.7	NR	NR	54.3
		5-year disease-specific survival	76.5	66.6	NR	NR	64.7
		Mortality hazard† (95% C I)	1.0	1.3	NR	NR	1.0
			(ref)	(1.0–1.6)			(0.8–1.3)
Elledge et al, 1994[21]	San Antonio database ‡	*N*	4,885	1,016	NR	NR	777
		Age > 50 years (%)	76.1	62.6	NR	NR	45.9
		p53-positive (%)	50.9	54.9	NR	NR	54.2
		Tumor ≥ 5 cm (%)	10.9	27.7	NR	NR	16.6
		Node-negative (%)	57.9	48.8	NR	NR	45.9
		ER-negative (%)	22.1	37.9	NR	NR	29.9
		PR-negative (%)	44.0	59.2	NR	NR	49.4
		HER2/neu-positive (%)	16.1	13.8	NR	NR	20.9
		5-year overall survival (%)	75	65	NR	NR	70
		Median survival (months)	166	117	NR	NR	156
Boyer-Chammard et al, 1999[22]	Southern California	*N*	10,937	185	NR	412	875
		Localized disease (%)	61.4	50.8	NR	59.7	52.2
		Median age (years)	64	52	NR	50	55
		Mortality hazard§	1.0	2.32	NR	1.18	1.28
			(ref)	(1.76–3.07)		(0.93–1.50)	(1.10–1.50)
Clegg et al, 200223	SEER, age ≥ 50 years	2-year mammography screening rates (%)	70	67	51	63	61

CI = confidence interval; ER = estrogen receptor; *HER2/neu* = *HER2/neu* gene/protein biomarkers; *N* = number of patients; NR = not reported; *p53* = *p53* tumor repressor gene marker; PR = progesterone receptor; SEER = Surveillance Epidemiology and End Results Program.

*Adjusted for age, stage, hormone receptor status, and treatment.

†Adjusted for age, stage, grade, treatment, and socioeconomic status.

‡Thirty-one contributing hospitals throughout the United States.

§Adjusted for age, stage, histology, and treatment.

overweight (BMI ≥ 25).[25] Obesity rates were also elevated for Mexican American women in this age range (> 40%) and were lowest for white American women (approximately one-third of participants). Since postmenopausal obesity is a well-established risk factor for breast cancer, these findings suggest that public health messages regarding dietary and exercise practices should be strengthened in communities of minority ethnicity. Kumanyika has reviewed the significance of body fat distribution as it pertains to health risks, and found that the high-risk body fat distribution (upper body, central obesity) is more prevalent among populations of minority ethnicity.[26]

Dietary soy, mammographic density, and genetic polymorphisms have also been proposed as factors associated with ethnicity related variation in breast cancer risk. Phytoestrogens consumed from soy products have been suggested as putative protective substances against breast neoplasia, based on observations of very high soy intake in the low breast cancer risk Asian populations, and based on some limited evidence of antiangiogenic effects in laboratory models.[27] However, studies of soy intake among American population subsets have been unsuccessful in demonstrating breast cancer risk reduction effects, at least within the ranges of soy consumption commonly seen in the United States.[28,29] Whereas mammographic density has been correlated with breast cancer risk by some investigators, studies attempting to correlate ethnicity related variations in mammographic density with differences in breast cancer incidence have been largely inconclusive.[30–32] Prevalence of polymorphisms in genes coding for essential detoxifying enzymes has also been shown to vary between different ethnic groups.[24,33–35] In particular, ethnicity related variation in cytochrome P-related enzymes (CYP polymorphisms) have been studied extensively, because these enzymes can have downstream effects on the metabolism of many different medications, including several that are used in breast cancer management.

While efforts to improve the efficacy and tolerability of breast cancer treatments are extremely important, research efforts aimed at primary disease prevention are also worthwhile. Tamoxifen is currently approved by the Food and Drug Administration for chemoprevention in high-risk women, based on findings from the National Surgical Adjuvant Breast Project (NSABP) P-01 Study and the Breast Cancer Prevention Trial (BCPT), demonstrating a nearly 50% risk reduction associated with tamoxifen use compared with placebo.[36] Studies of the selective estrogen receptor modulator (SERM) raloxifene for management of osteoporosis, and the aromatase inhibitor (AI) anastrozole as adjuvant therapy for breast cancer, suggest that these medications are also promising chemopreventive agents.[37,38] Any chemopreventive agent will be associated with risks for adverse events; for example, thromboembolic phenomena, uterine cancer, and vasomotor effects for SERMs, and osteoporotic complications for AIs. It is therefore incumbent upon us to accurately identify women facing a substantially elevated breast cancer risk that would justify assuming the morbidity risks of chemoprevention. The incidence of breast cancer varies with ethnicity, and similar variations can be demonstrated with respect to incidence of the various chemoprevention-associated health risks. The efficacy of various chemoprevention agents within different ethnic groups must therefore be carefully scrutinized.

Unfortunately, little is known about breast cancer risk assessment in non-white American populations. The Gail model is a logistic regression equation that permits estimation of the absolute likelihood that an individual woman will develop breast cancer over a fixed interval of time.[39] The conventionally established cutoff point for the designation of "high risk" is a Gail model 5-year breast cancer risk estimate of at least 1.67%; this value is used to identify women who would benefit from risk reduction counseling, and to determine eligibility for the NSABP chemoprevention trials. The risk factors incorporated into the Gail model were derived from analyses of a case-control subset of women participating in the Breast Cancer Detection and Demonstration Project (BCDDP), a mammography screening program. Since the vast majority of BCDDP participants were white American, the model was specifically described as a risk assessment tool for white American women receiving with annual mammographic screening.[39] Although the accuracy of the Gail model has been validated in three different populations of white American women, its performance in women of other ethnic backgrounds is less well understood.[40–44]

As discussed above, ethnicity is associated with many features that influence breast cancer risk, ranging from reproductive experiences to hereditary factors, and including diet as well as socioeconomic status and cultural practices. All of these issues are likely to account for documented differences in breast cancer outcome between the diverse subsets of the American population, as discussed below.

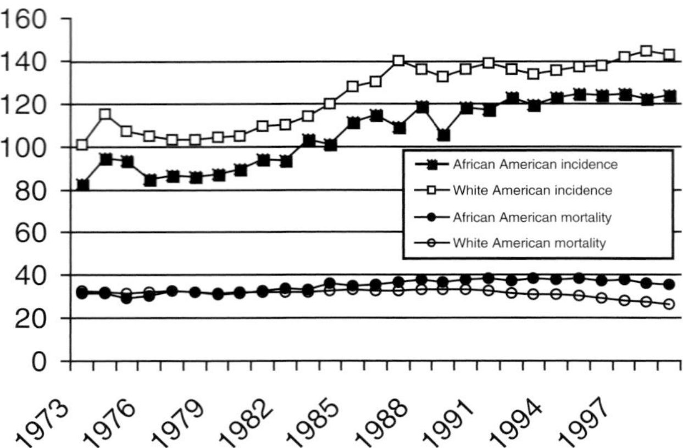

Figure 33–4. SEER data: breast cancer incidence and mortality rates, African Americans and white Americans.

African Americans

An intriguing paradox is seen for the breast cancer burden experienced by African American women compared with most other populations. As shown in Figures 33–1 and 33–2, for most population subsets (worldwide as well as regionally), there is a direct correlation between breast cancer incidence and mortality rates, so that the ethnic groups with the highest incidence rates also have the highest mortality rates. African American women, however, face a higher risk of dying from breast cancer despite having a relatively lower risk of being diagnosed with the disease (Figure 33–4).

Another relatively unique aspect of breast cancer in African American women is the age-incidence curve in comparison to white American women (Figure 33–5). As noted previously, breast cancer incidence overall is lower for African Americans compared to white Americans; however, for women under the age of 40 years, the incidence is greater for African Americans. The absolute magnitude of the incidence rates for both ethnic subsets in this young age range however is fairly low (≤ 100/100,000 women), as the major increase in breast cancer risk associated with age occurs at the perimenopausal age of 50 years, when rates exceed 250 of 100,000 women.[13] The difference in age distribution becomes more relevant in the clinical setting, where practicing oncologists may readily observe that approximately one-third of their African American breast cancer patients are younger than 50 years, compared to only one-fifth of the white American patients.

African American breast cancer patients have a more advanced-stage distribution at the time of diagnosis compared with white American women; approximately one-third and one-half, respectively, present with stage I disease.[19] The impact of breast health awareness messages and screening mammography are starting to become stronger, however, as evidenced by the rising rates of ductal carcinoma in situ among African American women over the age of 50 years.[13] As shown in Table 33–1, several investigators have also reported a higher prevalence of adverse primary tumor features (hormone receptor negativity, aneuploidy, etc) among African American breast cancer patients compared with women of other ethnic backgrounds. In addition, Poola and colleagues have shown that expression of the estrogen receptor beta isoform, which may be protective against abnormal proliferative changes in mammary epithelial tissue, may be disproportionately low in African American women.[45]

Similarities between breast cancers detected in African American women and native African women as well as hereditary breast cancer patients have

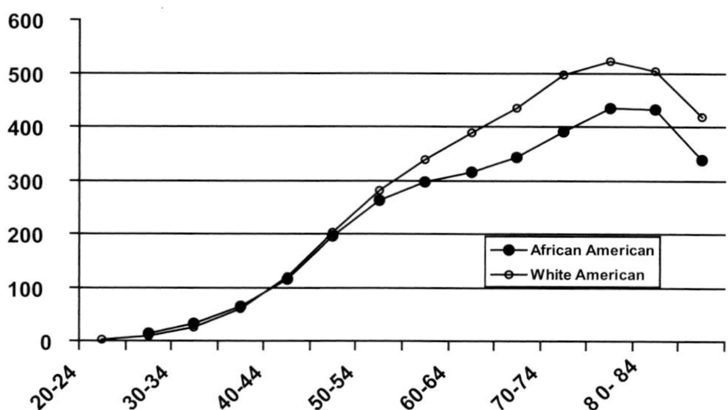

Figure 33–5. SEER data: age-specific incidence of breast cancer in African American and white American women.

prompted speculation that genetic factors may account for the increased biologic aggressiveness seen in these tumors. Women from the continent of Africa face a relatively low risk of developing breast cancer compared with most other regions of the world, but a younger age distribution and increased prevalence of aneuploid, hormone receptor-negative disease is also reported.[46–49]

Furthermore, *BRCA*–mutation-associated breast cancers are characterized by younger age at onset, increased prevalence of hormone receptor negativity, aneuploid tumors, and medullary histology, and all of these features have been noted among African American breast cancer patients. Several *BRCA* mutations have been detected within African American breast cancer patients[50,51]; Gao and colleagues and Mefford and colleagues have identified founder mutations in the *BRCA* genes that are expressed within African American families, and multicenter trials are currently underway to determine the population-based prevalence of *BRCA* mutations within the African American community.[50,52,53] It is possible that other founder mutations, perhaps in different breast cancer susceptibility genes, remain to be characterized.

Pathak and colleagues have proposed an alternative explanation for the younger age distribution in conjunction with the overall diminished incidence of breast cancer in African American women, related to reproductive risk factors.[54] These investigators note that there is a short-term increase in breast cancer risk that occurs in the immediate postpartum period, and population-based data reveal that African American women are more likely to begin childbearing at younger ages compared with white American women. Pathak and colleagues have proposed that the overall lower incidence and younger age distribution for breast cancer among African American women results from lifetime protective effects of early childbearing balanced against the increased postpartum risks expressed in young women. The dual effect of parity on the breast cancer age-incidence curve in African American women has been supported by findings from Palmer and colleagues in an analysis of the Black Women's Health Study (BWHS).[55] The BWHS is a prospective database of self-reported medical information contributed by subscribers to the magazine *Essence*, which targets a predominantly African American and female readership audience. In contrast, an analysis of breast cancer risk factors among participants of the case-control Women's Contraceptive and Reproductive Experience (CARE) Study failed to demonstrate an association between parity and early-onset breast cancer.[56]

The younger age distribution of breast cancer in African Americans is a particularly disturbing pattern because of the general impression that breast cancer in premenopausal women tends to be a biologically more aggressive disease, associated with an increased risk of nodal metastases, higher rates of estrogen receptor negativity, and increased treatment failure rates. This then prompts the question of whether or not the greater prevalence of early-onset disease among African American women contributes to the observed survival disparities between African American and white American breast cancer patients. Newman and colleagues addressed this question in a study based on African American and white American breast cancer patients under age 40 years, identified through the Detroit SEER-based tumor registry.[57] Their study revealed that among all of these similarly young women, the African Americans had even higher rates of adverse prognostic features such as hormone receptor negativity and aneuploid tumors. Furthermore, the Cox proportional hazards survival analysis (adjusted for age, tumor size, nodal status, and hormone receptor status) revealed a significantly elevated mortality risk for the young African American breast cancer patients compared with the young white American breast cancer patients. Even among patients presenting with localized disease, the mortality hazard for the African American women was 1.94 (95% CI, 1.23–3.05). Shavers and colleagues had similar findings in a study of African American compared with white American breast cancer patients under age 35 years.[20]

One obvious explanation for the increased breast cancer mortality rates among African American women would be related to socioeconomic status (SES) and access to health care. Poverty rates and lack of insurance are found at alarmingly high rates within the African American community, and these disadvantages undoubtedly contribute to the more advanced-stage distribution and poor outcomes that are seen among African American breast cancer patients. Whether these socioeconomic issues completely explain the survival disparity, however, remains unclear. Numerous studies have revealed that the independent effect of African American ethnicity on breast cancer mortality is diminished after some measure of SES is taken into account, suggesting that ethnicity is merely a surrogate marker for risk of poverty and lack of health care access. However, findings from a recent meta-analysis have indicated that African American ethnicity remains a statistically significant predictor of adverse outcome even after SES has been taken into account.[58]

The strength of a meta-analysis as a statistical tool is the ability to increase the robustness of a particular measure of association by the increased sample size of pooled data. Studies of breast cancer in African Americans are frequently limited by relatively small datasets within individual institutions. The ability to adequately assess the independent effects of SES versus ethnicity is particularly challenging, because of the even smaller subset of affluent African American breast cancer patients. Newman and colleagues identified 14 studies published over the past two decades that provided proportional hazards survival analyses of breast cancer outcome in African American and white American breast cancer patients, and that also included outcome adjustment for SES.[58–72] This meta analysis yielded 10,001 African American and 42,473 white American breast cancer patients for evaluation.[58] In the pooled survival analysis (adjusted for age, stage of disease, and SES), ethnicity emerged as an independent and statistically significant predictor of breast cancer mortality risk (mortality odds ratio, 1.22; 95% CI, 1.13–1.30). Figure 33–6 demonstrates the general findings of this meta-analysis.[58]

This meta-analysis also revealed that SES is usually a poorly measured variable. Most studies relied upon area-level measures to assign SES status to individual patients rather than self-reported data. Use of census blocks and census tracts is generally a valid surrogate for SES when individualized data are unavailable[73]; however, it may be less reliable in studies of the African American community, as demonstrated by Bassett and Krieger.[59] Census blocks and census tracts may comprise several thousand people, and assignment of the most prevalent income category within this size area to all individuals within that area is unlikely to capture the SES heterogeneity that may exist within the African American neighborhoods. Many affluent African American families may

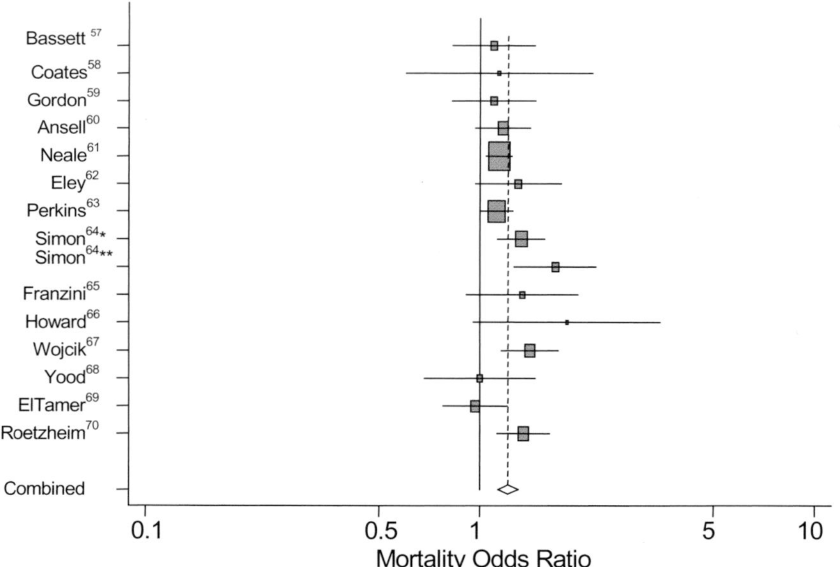

Figure 33–6. A meta-analysis of 14 studies on breast cancer outcomes in African American and white American breast cancer patients. Reproduced with permission from Newman LA et al.[58]

choose to reside in a predominantly African American community rather than a white American community, despite the fact that the average SES status of the white American community may be more similar to their own. In summary, although it is intuitively clear that SES disadvantages are likely to delay cancer care and have an adverse effect on outcome, it is not at all clear that ethnicity does not also contribute independent effects on breast cancer outcome.

Nutrition and differences in treatment response are other factors that warrant further investigation in the study of breast cancer outcome among African Americans. Forshee and colleagues reported that obesity, physical inactivity, and lack of a balanced diet appeared to be particularly significant health issues among African American women, based on analysis of the NHANES III.[74] A provocative study reported by Hershman and colleagues demonstrated that African American breast cancer patients were more likely to experience delays in completion of adjuvant chemotherapy regimens related to neutropenia, and that this prolongation of treatment may correlate with diminished overall dose intensity.[75] Interestingly, the clinical relevance of ethnicity related neutropenia is poorly understood, as baseline neutrophil counts were lower among the African American patients; this hematologic pattern has been noted among the general population as well.

Unfortunately, disparities in delivery of treatment to African American breast cancer patients have also been reported, raising the concern that discriminatory practices in the health care system may also contribute to outcome disparities.[76] These disparities may be unintentional and related to miscommunication between patient and health care provider, or they may be related to socioeconomic issues. Chu and Freeman reported that the magnitude of difference in breast cancer outcome between African American and white American patients was minimized among women age 65 years or older, suggesting that Medicare insurance eligibility was associated with improved survival.[77]

Standardization of care through the clinical trial mechanism would be expected to abolish the influence of ethnicity related treatment and/or socioeconomic disparities on breast cancer outcome, thereby providing a "pure" assessment of ethnicity related survival. Roach and colleagues examined breast cancer survival among African American and white American participants of a Cancer and Leukemia Group B phase III study of node-positive disease, and found worse outcome for the African Americans in a univariate analysis.[78] The investigators were able to eliminate the statistical significance of this association by performing a multivariate logistic regression analysis that included age, hormone receptor expression, number of metastatic nodes, and chemotherapy dose. This latter analysis was clearly affected by progressive loss of robustness related to small subset sample sizes.

In a recent and very robust study of multiple prospective randomized breast cancer clinical trials conducted by the Southwest Oncology Group, Albain demonstrated that African American ethnicity was a statistically significant and independent predictor of mortality risk in multivariate survival analyses of both pre- and postmenopausal breast cancer patients, even after accounting for SES.[79] Data from the Women's Health Initiative (WHI) have also demonstrated significant outcome disadvantages for African American breast cancer patients within the clinical trials context. The WHI was a placebo-controlled, prospective, randomized trial designed to evaluate the impact of hormone replacement therapy on cancer and cardiovascular risk in postmenopausal women; this study definitively established the increased risk of breast cancer that is conferred by exogenous, combination estrogen-progestin therapy.[80] The WHI investigators have extended their work by evaluating study participants that developed breast cancer, and they recently reported that African American ethnicity was associated with an unexplained excess in risk for node-positive disease and worse outcome.[81]

The disproportionately high breast cancer mortality risk faced by African American women increases the appeal of chemoprevention for this population. As noted previously, tamoxifen is now an accepted breast cancer risk reduction intervention; however, available data provide conflicting messages regarding the potential efficacy of tamoxifen for pure chemoprevention in African American women. On the other hand, tamoxifen is associated with a lower risk for major adverse reactions in young women, and African Americans face an increased risk of early-onset breast cancer. Tamoxifen is also only effective at preventing estrogen receptor-positive disease, and African American women are at increased risk for developing estrogen receptor-negative tumors. Most unfortunately, however, only 1.7% of the BCPT participants were African American[36]; data are therefore lacking regarding the risk-benefit value of tamoxifen in high-risk African American women. One reason for the low accrual of African Americans to the BCPT was related to the risk assessment and eligibility criteria, based on Gail model risk estimates, which may underestimate risk among African Americans.[44]

Asian Americans

Breast cancer incidence has historically been relatively low among women whose place of birth, ethnic ancestry, and residence is within an Asian nation. Incidence rates for breast cancer in American women are typically 4 to 7 times greater than those for women from Japan or China. However, the adoption of westernized cultural practices among these countries, particularly in the urban areas, is resulting in a corresponding increase in breast cancer risk. In Japan, for example, the incidence of breast cancer has more than doubled between the years of 1959 to 1960 and 1983 to 1987.[82] Although reproductive and dietary practices have been presumed to account for these trends, data to support these theories are limited.[83] Ijuin and colleagues found that Japanese women had significantly higher BMI compared to premenopausal women[84]; however, the community-based Takayami Study reported the opposite relationship, and found only modest weight gains in Japanese women.[85] Furthermore, Nagata and colleagues reported that changes in the four major population-based breast cancer risk factors (age at menarche, age at first live birth, age at menopause, and parity) accounted for < 40% of the observed increases in breast cancer risk seen over the past 40 years.[82]

Studies of Asian women migrating to the United States have confirmed a direct correlation between breast cancer risk and duration of residence in America. For Asian American women born in the United States, risk is increased with the number of generations that have also lived in the United States. Much of the published data on breast cancer in Asian American women has focused on communities on the west coast and in Hawaii. Ziegler and colleagues conducted a population-based study of breast cancer among women residing in San Francisco-Oakland and Oahu, who were of Chinese, Japanese, and Filipino ethnic descent.[86] This analysis of 597 breast cancer cases compared with 966 controls revealed a sixfold gradient in breast cancer risk associated with migration patterns; progressive increases in risk were seen with increasing length of time and increasing number of generations residing in the United States.

The Japanese American population, probably the oldest and most strongly acculturated Asian American community, has been experiencing the largest increases in breast cancer incidence when compared to Chinese Americans and Filipino Americans, as demonstrated by Deapen and colleagues in a study from Los Angeles County[87]; however, incidence is rising for all three ethnic groups. Increasing similarities in prevalence of gynecologic risk factors between later-generation Asian American women and white American women have also been documented, and reveal that Asian American women begin experiencing menarche at younger ages, start childbearing at older ages, and complete fewer pregnancies when compared to native Asian women who have recently migrated to the United States.[88]

As demonstrated by Li and colleagues, breast cancer stage distribution varies among the different ethnic subsets of Asians and Pacific Islanders.[19] The proportion of patients with stage I disease ranges from a low of 34% for Indian/Pakistani Americans and 39% for Vietnamese Americans, to a high of 58% for Japanese Americans. Filipino, Chinese, Hawaiian, and Korean Americans have an intermediate proportion of stage I disease, ranging from 42 to 47%. There is a corresponding range of mortality risks for these communities. The age-adjusted mortality hazard for Japanese Americans is 0.6 (95% CI, 0.5–0.7) compared with outcome in non-Hispanic White Americans. Vietnamese American and Indian/Pakistani American breast cancer patients face increased mortality risks, with hazard ratios of

1.3 (95% CI, 1.0–1.7) and 1.2 (95% CI, 0.8–1.6), respectively. Adjustments for stage, hormone receptor status, and treatment reduce the magnitude of variation in the mortality risks; however, significantly improved outcomes for Japanese American breast cancer patients (mortality hazard ratio, 0.6; 95% CI, 0.5–0.8) continue to be observed and the survival disadvantage for Hawaiian American breast cancer patients persists (hazard ratio, 1.3; 95% CI, 1.0–1.2). Access to cancer screening and health care for any member of these ethnic subsets will of course be influenced by availability of cultural and linguistic support services, particularly in the cases of non–English-speaking patients.

Hispanic Americans

The breast cancer burden of native Spanish women is intermediate between the high risk that is seen in Scandinavian countries and the low risk seen in native Asian women. Diets that are rich in monounsaturated fatty acids have been purported to be protective against breast cancer.[2,89] The diets of Mediterranean populations, such as those in Spain, Greece, and Italy, tend to be characterized by a relatively high olive oil content, which may account for the lower breast cancer incidence seen in these countries. In parallel with the data on breast cancer in Spanish European women, the incidence and mortality rates for the disease in Hispanic American women are intermediate between those seen in non-Hispanic white Americans and Asian Americans (see Figure 33–2).

The Hispanic American community is the most rapidly growing minority ethnicity group in the United States, and represents 12% of the US population.[90] However, evaluation of the epidemiology of breast cancer in Hispanic women is particularly difficult because of several issues. First, socioeconomic disadvantages are highly prevalent among Hispanic Americans; 12% live below the poverty line and 33% are medically uninsured.[15,16] These problems lead to unavoidable barriers regarding access to the health care system, and are confounding factors in studies of ethnicity and breast cancer outcomes. Second, there is extensive diversity within the Hispanic American population, comprised of Cuban Americans (4%), Puerto Ricans (9%), Mexican Americans (66%), Central/South Americans (15%), and women of other Hispanic backgrounds, including those of European/Spanish descent (6%).[90] These disparate geographic origins are associated with a corresponding heterogeneity in ethnic descent (which will include varying mixtures of European, African, and Native American/Indian bloodlines), as well as cultural and dietary practices. Last, many Hispanic American communities also include varying proportions of illegal immigrants and non–English-speaking individuals; these issues will also influence studies of breast cancer risk. The ethnic and cultural heterogeneities encompassed by the terms "Latino" and "Hispanic" American are addressed in a 2002 commentary by Selinkoff.[91]

Heterogeneity within the overall Hispanic American community is also apparent in studies of different subsets of Hispanic American breast cancer patients. As noted above, national population-based statistics reveal lower breast cancer incidence and mortality rates for Hispanic Americans compared with white Americans, yet this outcome advantage is not consistently seen in all patient populations. A study from the Department of Defense (DOD) Health Care System evaluated 182 Hispanic American and 6,134 white American breast cancer patients treated between 1980 and 1992.[92] The DOD system would theoretically have diminished effects secondary to access issues. This study found Hispanic breast cancer patients to be younger than white American patients (median age 51 years versus 58 years) and to have more advanced stage of disease at diagnosis. Biffl and colleagues have also demonstrated a younger age distribution for Hispanic American breast cancer patients from Colorado, and found a lower breast cancer survival rate for these women (5-year survival, 63% versus 83% seen for non-Hispanic patients).[93]

The New Mexico Women's Health Study was developed as a case-control-type analysis of breast cancer among Hispanic and non-Hispanic white American women diagnosed between 1992 and 1994. Selection of cases was based on the New Mexico Tumor Registry, a component of the SEER Program. Werter and colleagues used this database specifically to address the association between obesity and breast cancer risk among Hispanic American women.[94] These investigators found that obesity was a particularly strong risk factor for breast cancer and Hispanic women, and this correlation was seen regardless of menopausal status, whereas obesity as a breast cancer risk factor among white Americans was only significant for postmenopausal women. The significance of this finding amplified that obesity may be culturally more acceptable among Hispanic American communities against the background information that obesity is a potentially modifiable risk factor, and obesity may be more prevalent among Hispanic women. It has also been suggested that obesity may be culturally more acceptable among Hispanic American communities.[95]

Data from the New Mexico Women's Health Study have also demonstrated that long-term (more than 140 months) estrogen replacement therapy is also a significant risk factor for breast cancer among postmenopausal Hispanic women (odds ratio, 2.57; 95% CI, 1.25–5.28).

NATIVE AMERICANS

Of all the minority ethnicity groups in the United States, data on breast cancer incidence and outcome are probably the most limited for Native Americans. Kaur and Burhansstipanov have individually reviewed the impact of Native American migration patterns on breast cancer risk within this community, and have delineated some of the reasons for the paucity of data regarding overall cancer case ascertaining for this subset of the American population.[96,97] Historically, cancers have been thought to be relatively rare among Native American tribes. The introduction of European lifestyles and exposures (eg, alcohol, tobacco) has likely resulted in a significant increase in generalized risk for neoplastic events.

More than half of all Native Americans currently live in urban areas.[97] This "urbanization" has encased and promoted the difficulties of evaluating breast cancer among this community. It has been stated that data on health statistics among Native Americans are "undercounted" by approximately 38%, and many more Native Americans from urban areas are classified as white or even "Hispanic white" on health records.[97] This problem is magnified by the fact that in many Native Americans from the California west were "given" Hispanic surnames when they lived and worked in California during the periods of Spanish and missionary rule. More detail-oriented investigations of cancer risks in the diverse Native American and Alaskan Native communities, based on medical records as well as death certificates for populations residing in different geographic areas, are currently underway and are likely to be substantially more valuable than past studies.[98–100]

The Indian Health Service (IHS) is available to compensate for the health care needs of Native Americans and Alaskan Natives. Unfortunately, many Native Americans residing in urban areas may be unaware of these benefits, do not have access to an IHS facility/referral center, or become ineligible for IHS support because of tribal policies denying services to members who have been off of the reservation for more than 6 months.[97]

There are also some unique cultural considerations that arise for some Native American breast cancer patients. Many will desire a temporary return to the Indian reservation so that the traditional tribal "healers" can incorporate special ceremonies into the treatment sequence.[97] Welty and colleagues have evaluated the health care needs of the Sioux tribes, and emphasize the importance of having female health care providers available to administer breast cancer screening programs.[101]

SUMMARY AND CONCLUSIONS

In summary, it is clear that breast cancer incidence and mortality risk are influenced by ethnic background and country of origin, based on studies of international variation in breast cancer burden as well as studies of the ethnically diverse subsets of the American population. The collective effects of lifestyle and the environment in the United States result in increased breast cancer risks for American women. The effects of ethnicity continue to be seen, however, in risk for breast cancer mortality, and it is therefore essential that research efforts be continued to disentangle lifestyle, dietary, and reproductive risk factors from genetically associated ethnic risk factors. Disparities in access to care and socioeconomic resources must also be eliminated.

REFERENCES

1. Boffetta P, Parkin DM. Cancer in developing countries. CA Cancer J Clin 1994;44:81–90.
2. Kushi L, Giovannucci E. Dietary fat and cancer. Am J Med 2002;113 Suppl 9B:63S–70S.
3. Lacey JV Jr, Devesa SS, Brinton LA. Recent trends in breast cancer incidence and mortality. Environ Mol Mutagen 2002;39:82–8.
4. Globocan. Globocan 2000: Cancer incidence, mortality and prevalence worldwide. Vol 2003. Lyon: IARC Press; 2001.
5. Henderson BE, Bernstein L. The international variation in breast cancer rates: an epidemiological assessment. Breast Cancer Res Treat 1991;18 Suppl 1:11–7.
6. Olopade O. Breast cancer genetics: toward molecular characterization of individuals at increased risk for breast cancer. In: DeVita VHS, Rosenberg S, editors. Updates, principles and practice of oncology. Vol 12. Philadelphia: Lippincott; 1998. p. 1–12.
7. SEER. SEER 2001 expansion. National Cancer Institute; 2001. Available at: http://seer.cancer.gov/about/expansion.htm (accessed September 2005).
8. Barnholtz-Sloan JS, de Andrade M, Dyer TD, Chakraborty R. Admixture effects in the traditional linkage analysis of admixed families. Ethn Dis 2002;12:411–9.
9. Barnholtz-Sloan JS, de Andrade M, Chakraborty R. The impact of population admixture on traditional linkage analysis. Ethn Dis 2001;11:519–31.
10. Shriver MD, Parra EJ, Dios S, et al. Skin pigmentation, biogeographical ancestry and admixture mapping. Hum Genet 2003;112:387–99.
11. Smith MW, Lautenberger JA, Shin HD, et al. Markers for mapping by admixture linkage disequilibrium in African American and Hispanic populations. Am J Hum Genet 2001;69:1080–94.
12. Zhao H, Pfeiffer R, Gail M. Haplotype analysis in population genetics and association studies. Pharmacogenomics 2003;4:171–8.
13. SEER. SEER incidence age-adjusted rates, 11 registries, 1992–99. Vol 2003. National Cancer Institute; 2003.
14. Naik AM, Joseph K, Harris M, et al. Indigent breast cancer patients among all racial and ethnic groups present with more advanced disease compared with nationally reported data. Am J Surg 2003;186:400–3.
15. Health insurance coverage: 2001. Vol 2003. U.S. Census Bureau; 2001.
16. Proctor B. Current population reports: poverty in the United States: 2001. Washington (DC): U.S. Government Printing Office; 2002. p. 60–219.
17. Ward E, Jemal A, Cokkinides V, et al. Cancer disparities by race/ethnicity and socioeconomic status. CA Cancer J Clin 2004;54:78–93.
18. Li CI, Malone KE, Daling JR. Differences in breast cancer hormone receptor status and histology by race and ethnicity among women 50 years of age and older. Cancer Epidemiol Biomarkers Prev 2002;11:601–7.
19. Li CI, Malone KE, Daling JR. Differences in breast cancer stage, treatment, and survival by race and ethnicity. Arch Intern Med 2003;163:49–56.
20. Shavers VL, Harlan LC, Stevens JL. Racial/ethnic variation in clinical presentation, treatment, and survival among breast cancer patients under age 35. Cancer 2003;97:134–47.
21. Elledge RM, Clark GM, Chamness GC, Osborne CK. Tumor biologic factors and breast cancer prognosis among white, Hispanic, and black women in the United States. J Natl Cancer Inst 1994;86:705–12.
22. Boyer-Chammard A, Taylor TH, Anton-Culver H. Survival differences in breast cancer among racial/ethnic groups: a population-based study. Cancer Detect Prev 1999;23:463–73.
23. Clegg LX, Li FP, Hankey BF, et al. Cancer survival among US whites and minorities: a SEER (Surveillance, Epidemiology, and End Results) Program population-based study. Arch Intern Med 2002;162:1985–93.
24. Maskarinec G. Breast cancer: interaction between ethnicity and environment. In Vivo 2000;14:115–23.
25. Flegal KM, Carroll MD, Ogden CL, Johnson CL. Prevalence and trends in obesity among US adults, 1999–2000. JAMA 2002;288:1723–7.
26. Kumanyika SK. Special issues regarding obesity in minority populations. Ann Intern Med 1993;119:650–4.
27. Newman LA, Kuerer HM, Harper T, et al. Special considerations in breast cancer risk and survival. J Surg Oncol 1999;71:250–60.
28. Wu AH, Ziegler RG, Nomura AM, et al. Soy intake and risk of breast cancer in Asians and Asian Americans. Am J Clin Nutr 1998;68 Suppl:1437–43.
29. Horn-Ross PL, John EM, Lee M, et al. Phytoestrogen consumption and breast cancer risk in a multiethnic population: the Bay Area Breast Cancer Study. Am J Epidemiol 2001;154:434–41.
30. Yaffe MJ, Boyd NF, Byng JW, et al. Breast cancer risk and measured mammographic density. Eur J Cancer Prev 1998;7 Suppl 1:47–55.
31. Boyd NF, Lockwood GA, Byng JW, et al. Mammographic densities and breast cancer risk. Cancer Epidemiol Biomarkers Prev 1998;7:1133–44.
32. El-Bastawissi AY, White E, Mandelson MT, Taplin S. Variation in mammographic breast density by race. Ann Epidemiol 2001;11:257–63.
33. Ma MK WM, McLeod HL. Genetic basis of drug metabolism. Am J Health Syst Pharm 2002;59:2061–9.
34. Xie HG PH, Kim RB, Stein M. CYP2C9 allelic variants: ethnic distribution and functional significance. Adv Drug Deliver Rev 2002;54:1257–70.
35. Ingelman-Sundberg M. Genetic susceptibility to adverse effects of drugs and environmental toxicants: the role of the CYP family of enzymes. Mutat Res 2001;482:11–9.
36. Fisher B, Costantino JP, Wickerham DL, et al. Tamoxifen for prevention of breast cancer: report of the National Surgical Adjuvant Breast and Bowel Project P-1 Study. J Natl Cancer Inst 1998;90:1371–88.
37. Cummings SR, Eckert S, Krueger KA, et al. The effect of raloxifene on risk of breast cancer in postmenopausal women: results from the MORE randomized trial. Multiple Outcomes of Raloxifene Evaluation. JAMA 1999;281:2189–97.
38. Baum M, Buzdar A, Cuzick J, et al;. The ATAC Trialists' Group. Anastrozole alone or in combination with tamoxifen versus tamoxifen alone for adjuvant treatment of postmenopausal women with early breast cancer: first results of the ATAC randomised trial. Lancet 2002;359:2131–9.

39. Gail MH, Brinton LA, Byar DP, et al. Projecting individualized probabilities of developing breast cancer for white females who are being examined annually. J Natl Cancer Inst 1989;81:1879–86.
40. Gail MH, Costantino JP. Validating and improving models for projecting the absolute risk of breast cancer. J Natl Cancer Inst 2001;93:334–5.
41. Bondy ML, Lustbader ED, Halabi S, et al. Validation of a breast cancer risk assessment model in women with a positive family history. J Natl Cancer Inst 1994;86:620–5.
42. Rockhill B, Spiegelman D, Byrne C, et al. Validation of the Gail et al. model of breast cancer risk prediction and implications for chemoprevention. J Natl Cancer Inst 2001;93:358–66.
43. Spiegelman D, Colditz GA, Hunter D, Hertzmark E. Validation of the Gail et al. model for predicting individual breast cancer risk. J Natl Cancer Inst 1994;86:600–7.
44. Newman LA, Rockhill B, Bondy ML, et al. Validation of the Gail Breast Cancer risk assessment model in African American women based on a multi-center case-control study of 3,283 African American and 5,974 White American women. In: Proceedings of the 38th Annual Meeting of the American Society of Clinical Oncology; 2002 May 19; Orlando, Florida. Vol 21(1). ASCO; 2002.
45. Poola I, Clarke R, DeWitty R, Leffall LD. Functionally active estrogen receptor isoform profiles in the breast tumors of African American women are different from the profiles in breast tumors of Caucasian women. Cancer 2002;94: 615–23.
46. Adebamowo CA, Adekunle OO. Case-controlled study of the epidemiological risk factors for breast cancer in Nigeria. Br J Surg 1999;86:665–8.
47. Adebamowo CA, Ajayi OO. Breast cancer in Nigeria. West Afr J Med 2000;19:179–91.
48. Ihekwaba FN. Breast cancer in Nigerian women. Br J Surg 1992;79:771–5.
49. Ikpatt OF, Kuopio T, Ndoma-Egba R, Collan Y. Breast cancer in Nigeria and Finland: epidemiological, clinical and histological comparison. Anticancer Res 2002;22:3005–12.
50. Olopade OI FJ, Dunston G, Tainsky MA, et al. Breast cancer genetics in African Americans. Cancer 2002;97:236–45.
51. Panguluri RC BL, Modali R, Utley K, et al. BRCA mutations in African Americans. Hum Genet 1999;105:28–31.
52. Gao Q, Neuhausen S, Cummings S, et al. Recurrent germline BRCA1 mutations in extended African American families with early-onset breast cancer. Am J Hum Genet 1997;60:1233–6.
53. Mefford HC BL, Panguluri RCK, Whitfield-Broome C, et al. Evidence for a BRCA founder mutation in families of West African ancestry. Am J Hum Genet 1999;65:575–8.
54. Pathak DR, Osuch JR, He J. Breast carcinoma etiology: current knowledge and new insights into the effects of reproductive and hormonal risk factors in black and white populations. Cancer 2000;88:1230–8.
55. Palmer JR, Wise LA, Horton NJ, et al. Dual effect of parity on breast cancer risk in African-American women. J Natl Cancer Inst 2003;95:478–83.
56. Ursin G, Bernstein L, Wang Y, et al. Reproductive factors and risk of breast carcinoma in a study of white and African-American women. Cancer 2004;101:353–62.
57. Newman LA, Bunner S, Carolin K, et al. Ethnicity related differences in the survival of young breast carcinoma patients. Cancer 2002;95:21–7.
58. Newman LA, Mason J, Cote D, et al. African-American ethnicity, socioeconomic status, and breast cancer survival: a meta-analysis of 14 studies involving over 10,000 African-American and 40,000 White American patients with carcinoma of the breast. Cancer 2002;94:2844–54.
59. Bassett MT, Krieger N. Social class and black-white differences in breast cancer survival. Am J Public Health 1986;76:1400–3.
60. Coates RJ, Clark WS, Eley JW, et al. Race, nutritional status, and survival from breast cancer. J Natl Cancer Inst 1990; 82:1684–92.
61. Gordon NH, Crowe JP, Brumberg DJ, Berger NA. Socioeconomic factors and race in breast cancer recurrence and survival. Am J Epidemiol 1992;135:609–18.
62. Ansell D, Whitman S, Lipton R, Cooper R. Race, income, and survival from breast cancer at two public hospitals. Cancer 1993;72:2974–8.
63. Neale AV. Racial and marital status influences on 10 year survival from breast cancer. J Clin Epidemiol 1994;47: 475–83.
64. Eley JW, Hill HA, Chen VW, et al. Racial differences in survival from breast cancer. Results of the National Cancer Institute Black/White Cancer Survival Study. JAMA 1994;272:947–54.
65. Perkins P, Cooksley CD, Cox JD. Breast cancer. Is ethnicity an independent prognostic factor for survival? Cancer 1996;78:1241–7.
66. Simon MS, Severson RK. Racial differences in survival of female breast cancer in the Detroit metropolitan area. Cancer 1996;77:308–14.
67. Franzini L, Williams AF, Franklin J, et al. Effects of race and socioeconomic status on survival of 1,332 black, Hispanic, and white women with breast cancer. Ann Surg Oncol 1997;4:111–8.
68. Howard DL, Penchansky R, Brown MB. Disaggregating the effects of race on breast cancer survival. Fam Med 1998;30:228–35.
69. Wojcik BE, Spinks MK, Optenberg SA. Breast carcinoma survival analysis for African American and white women in an equal-access health care system. Cancer 1998;82: 1310–8.
70. Yood MU, Johnson CC, Blount A, et al. Race and differences in breast cancer survival in a managed care population. J Natl Cancer Inst 1999;91:1487–91.
71. El-Tamer MB, Homel P, Wait RB. Is race a poor prognostic factor in breast cancer? J Am Coll Surg 1999;189:41–5.
72. Roetzheim RG, Gonzalez EC, Ferrante JM, et al. Effects of health insurance and race on breast carcinoma treatments and outcomes. Cancer 2000;89:2202–13.
73. Krieger N. Overcoming the absence of socioeconomic data in medical records: validation and application of a census-based methodology. Am J Public Health 1992;82:703–10.
74. Forshee RA, Storey ML, Ritenbaugh C. Breast cancer risk and lifestyle differences among premenopausal and postmenopausal African-American women and white women. Cancer 2003;97:280–8.
75. Hershman D, Weinberg M, Rosner Z, et al. Ethnic neutrope-

nia and treatment delay in African American women undergoing chemotherapy for early-stage breast cancer. J Natl Cancer Inst 2003;95:1545–8.

76. Breen N, Wesley MN, Merrill RM, Johnson K. The relationship of socio-economic status and access to minimum expected therapy among female breast cancer patients in the National Cancer Institute Black-White Cancer Survival Study. Ethn Dis 1999;9:111–25.
77. Chu KC, Lamar CA, Freeman HP. Racial disparities in breast carcinoma survival rates: seperating factors that affect diagnosis from factors that affect treatment. Cancer 2003; 97:2853–60.
78. Roach M III, Cirrincione C, Budman D, et al. Race and survival from breast cancer: based on Cancer and Leukemia Group B trial 8541. Cancer J Sci Am 1997;3:107–12.
79. Albain K, KS A, JM U, LF H, SE R, S M, et al. Outcome of African Americans on Southwest Oncology Group (SWOG) breast cancer adjuvant therapy trials. Abstract #21. 2003 San Antonio Breast Cancer Symposium. San Antonio, TX; 2003.
80. Rossouw JE, Anderson GL, Prentice RL, et al. Risks and benefits of estrogen plus progestin in healthy postmenopausal women: principal results From the Women's Health Initiative randomized controlled trial. JAMA 2002;288:321–33.
81. Chlebowski RT, Chen Z, Anderson GL, et al. Ethnicity and breast cancer: factors influencing differences in incidence and outcome. J Natl Cancer Inst 2005;97:439–48.
82. Nagata C, Kawakami N, Shimizu H. Trends in the incidence rate and risk factors for breast cancer in Japan. Breast Cancer Res Treat 1997;44:75–82.1
83. Tung HT, Tsukuma H, Tanaka H, et al. Risk factors for breast cancer in Japan, with special attention to anthropometric measurements and reproductive history. Jpn J Clin Oncol 1999;29:137–46.
84. Ijuin H, Douchi T, Oki T, et al. The contribution of menopause to changes in body-fat distribution. J Obstet Gynaecol Res 1999;25:367–72.
85. Nagata C, Takatsuka N, Kawakami N, Shimizu H. Weight change in relation to natural menopause and other reproductive and behavioral factors in Japanese women. Ann Epidemiol 2002;12:237–41.
86. Ziegler RG, Hoover RN, Pike MC, et al. Migration patterns and breast cancer risk in Asian-American women. J Natl Cancer Inst 1993;85:1819–27.
87. Deapen D, Liu L, Perkins C, et al. Rapidly rising breast cancer incidence rates among Asian-American women. Int J Cancer 2002;99:747–50.
88. Wu AH, Ziegler RG, Pike MC, et al. Menstrual and reproductive factors and risk of breast cancer in Asian-Americans. Br J Cancer 1996;73:680–6.
89. Willett WC. Specific fatty acids and risks of breast and prostate cancer: dietary intake. Am J Clin Nutr 1997;66 Suppl:1557–63.
90. Thierrien M RR. The Hispanic population in the United States: March 2000. In: Current population reports. Washington (DC): U.S. Census Bureau; 2000. p. 20–535.
91. Selinkoff PM. Breast cancer in young Latinos. Am J Surg 2002;184:660; author reply 660–1.
92. Zaloznik AJ. Breast cancer stage at diagnosis: Caucasians versus Hispanics. Breast Cancer Res Treat 1997;42:121–4.
93. Biffl WL, Myers A, Franciose RJ, et al. Is breast cancer in young Latinas a different disease? Am J Surg 2001;182: 596–600.
94. Wenten M, Gilliland FD, Baumgartner K, Samet JM. Associations of weight, weight change, and body mass with breast cancer risk in Hispanic and non-Hispanic white women. Ann Epidemiol 2002;12:435–4.
95. Felts WM, Parrillo AV, Chenier T, Dunn P. Adolescents' perceptions of relative weight and self-reported weight-loss activities: analysis of 1990 YRBS (Youth Risk Behavior Survey) national data. J Adolesc Health 1996;18:20–6.
96. Kaur JS. Migration patterns and breast carcinoma. Cancer 2000;88:1203–6.
97. Burhansstipanov L. Urban native American health issues. Cancer 2000;88:1207–13.
98. Espey D, Paisano R, Cobb N. Regional patterns and trends in cancer mortality among American Indians and Alaska Natives, 1990–2001. Cancer 2005;103:1045–53.
99. Paskett ED, Tatum C, Rushing J, et al. Racial differences in knowledge, attitudes, and cancer screening practices among a triracial rural population. Cancer 2004;101:2650–9.
100. Petereit DG, Rogers D, Govern F, et al. Increasing access to clinical cancer trials and emerging technologies for minority populations: the Native American Project. J Clin Oncol 2004;22:4452–5.
101. Welty TK, Zephier N, Schweigman K, et al. Cancer risk factors in three Sioux tribes. Use of the Indian-specific health risk appraisal for data collection and analysis. Alaska Med 1993;35:265–72.

34

Image-Guided Ablation for Breast Cancer

TARA L. HUSTON
RACHE M. SIMMONS

There is a growing need for minimally invasive surgical intervention as part of a multidisciplinary approach to the treatment of breast cancer. Current minimally invasive techniques include cryoablation, radiofrequency ablation, interstitial laser ablation, focused ultrasound ablation, and microwave ablation. All of these techniques are guided by ultrasound, stereotactic mammography, or magnetic resonance (MR) imaging. Most ablation procedures can be performed in the office or in an ambulatory surgery setting. It should be noted that none of these techniques is the standard of care at this time. They are to be used in the breast cancer patient only in the setting of a clinical trial.

Percutaneous ablation is not a novel concept. Ablative techniques have successfully been used to treat metastatic hepatic tumors for several years. However, it is only recently they have been applied to malignancies in the breast, lung, bone, central nervous system, kidney, and prostate.[1] With a superficial location on the thorax and lack of intervening organs between it and the skin, the breast is an ideal organ for these therapies.

Since the ablation-induced apoptosis makes adequate pathologic determination of markers impossible, a pre-ablation core biopsy of the breast tumor is standard practice. This affords determination of estrogen and progesterone receptors, *HER2/neu*, as well as markers of proliferation, apoptosis, differentiation, and cell regulation.[2]

CRYOABLATION

The only ablative therapy to not use heat, cryoablation destroys tissue through multiple cycles of localized freezing (Figure 34–1). The target temperature with each cycle for effective tissue destruction falls between –160° and –190°C.[2–4] The number of necessary cycles is determined by the overall volume and dimensions of the tumor.[2–6] Gross determination of tissue death is challenging in the first week following the procedure. If postprocedural resection is planned, then most surgeons recommend waiting at least 1 week in order to obtain adequate resection margins and to perform an accurate histologic analysis.[2]

Cryoablation can be performed in the office setting with very little discomfort to the patient. First, the tumor is located by ultrasound and the overlying skin is numbed with a local anesthetic. Next, a small skin incision is created, through which the cryoprobe is inserted. The cryoprobe itself is entirely insulated except for a small, sharp area at the tip that

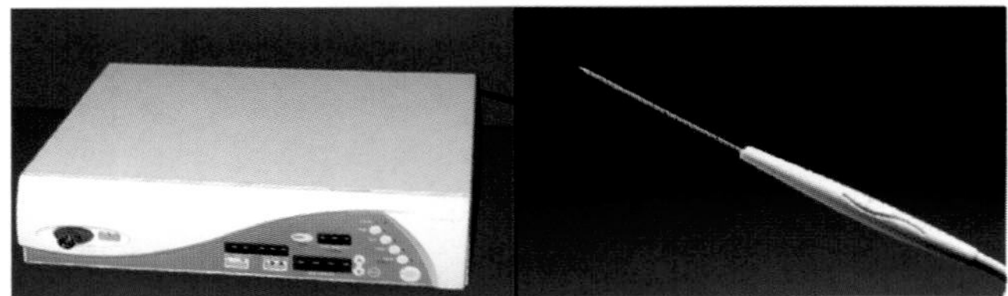

Figure 35–1. Cryoablation device and cryoprobe. Reproduced with permission from Sanarus Medical, Inc, Pleasanton, CA, USA.

is placed directly into the tumor. Since the freezing procedure itself acts as an anesthetic on the breast tissue, no anesthesia is needed for the remainder of the procedure. Patients remain completely awake and many view their procedure on the ultrasound monitor along with their physician.[5] On ultrasound, the sonographic freezeball created by the liquid nitrogen or argon gas can be seen, due to a highly echogenic interface between frozen and unfrozen tissue (Figures 34–2, 34–3, and 34–4).

Early pilot studies demonstrated that dermal may occur if the freezeball is too superficial. Therefore, to maintain a suitable distance, saline can be injected into the breast tissue between the tumor and the skin to create a separation. Alternatively, room temperature saline or water can be dripped directly onto the skin surface to protect it.[5] Saline can also be used to create a safe distance between the pectoralis muscle and a deep breast tumor.

The first documented use of cryoablation in the treatment of breast cancer was published 20 years ago by Rand and colleagues.[7] The patient was a 77-year-old woman with a 2 cm palpable mass, harboring malignant characteristics on the mammogram. Using sonographic guidance, a 0.5 cm cryoprobe was inserted into the lesion and five freeze cycles were performed. Following resection, no viable tumor cells were identified in the pathologic specimen. The patient had a brief and uneventful recovery and, 2 years later, was clinically and mammographically disease free.[7]

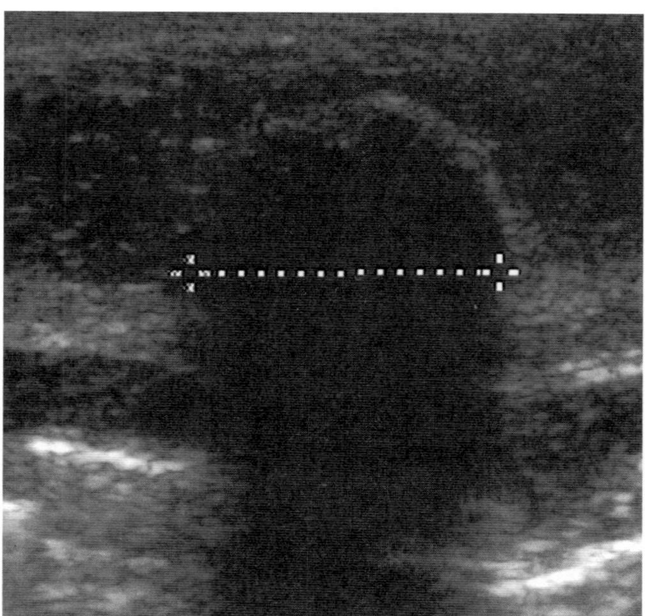

Figure 34–2. Freezeball visualized on ultrasound during cryoablation procedure.

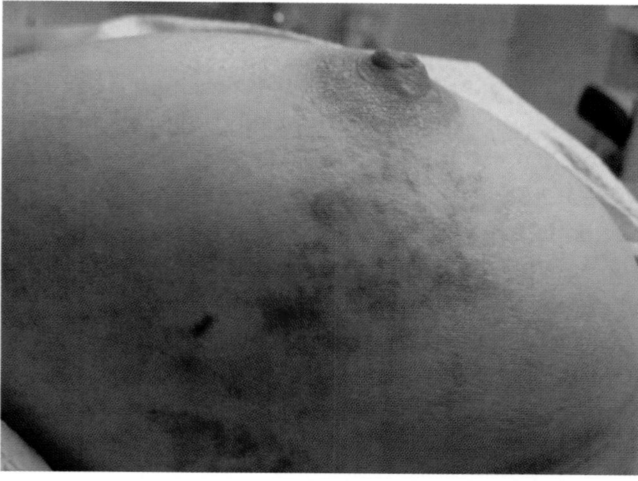

Figure 34–3. A patient with ecchymoses, 1 week following cryoablation.

Staren and colleagues were the first to perform cryoablation without postprocedural resection and give one of the only examples of the natural history of cryoablated breast cancers.[4] This patient was a 76-year-old woman, who had two foci of infiltrating lobular carcinoma (0.5 cm and 0.8 cm) in the same quadrant, confirmed by ultrasound-guided core nee-

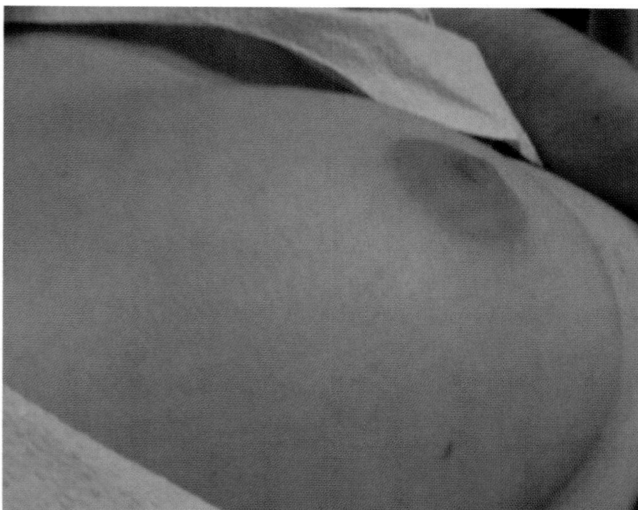

Figure 34–4. The same patient as in Figure 34–3, 3 months after cryoablation.

dle biopsy. Cryoablation was performed separately on both tumors via sonographic guidance and the masses were not resected. Core needle biopsy at 4 weeks and 12 weeks post-ablation revealed tissue necrosis, inflammatory cells, and cellular debris, but were negative for persistent tumor. Shortly after the procedure, the patient developed a nondescript 2 cm firmness in the area between the two cryoablation zones, but this spontaneously resolved within 12 weeks.[4]

Stocks and colleagues published a series of 11 women with invasive breast cancer, who underwent cryoablation followed by resection within 1 to 3 weeks. In this study, mean tumor size was 1.3 cm (range, 0.7–2.2 cm). In each case, a sonographic freezeball surrounded the tumor as well as a 1 cm margin of normal appearing breast parenchyma. Ten of 11 (91%) tumors showed complete ablation. One tumor demonstrated residual ductal carcinoma in situ (DCIS) at the margin of the ablation zone. Two of the women sustained minor dermal injuries; however, this was prior to the use of saline injection for superficial tumors.[8]

Pfleiderer and colleagues further investigated the potential of ultrasound-guided cryotherapy in a series that included 15 women with 16 breast cancers, averaging 2.1 cm.[9] They used a 0.3 cm cryoprobe with two freeze–thaw cycles of 7 to 10 minutes and 5 minutes, respectively. The mean freezeball diameter was 2.8 cm. All tumors were resected 5 days following cryoablation. No severe side effects were observed. The five tumors < 1.6 cm had no evidence of invasive cancer after treatment; however, two did have DCIS in the surrounding nonablated breast parenchyma. In the 11 tumors ≥ 2.3 cm, histologic examination revealed incomplete necrosis. Overall, this demonstrated how invasive components of small tumors can be treated using cryotherapy. However, significant amounts of in situ carcinoma, which may not be detected prior to ablation, represent a relative contraindication to cryoablation.[9]

Sable and colleagues performed cryoablation on 29 women with core biopsy proven, ultrasound visible invasive breast cancers, measuring ≤ 2 cm.[10] The cryoablation procedure consisted of two freeze–thaw cycles in each patient and was followed by planned surgical resection between 1 week and 1 month later. All tumors < 1 cm were fully ablated. In primary tumors measuring 1 to 1.5 cm, only those without an extensive intraductal component were destroyed. Tumors > 1.5 cm were not reliably eradicated with cryoablation. Specifically, it was found that the noncalcified type of DCIS caused the most treatment failures in the patients with larger tumors. No patient had pain severe enough to require postprocedural narcotics. Although these authors also successfully demonstrated cryoablation to be safe and effective, they recommended it be limited to invasive ductal cancers of ≤ 1.5 cm, containing < 25% DCIS on core biopsy.[10]

Most recently, the cryoprobe has been used as an alternative to needle localization in order to obtain more accurate margins when excising small, nonpalpable, ultrasound-visible tumors. Tafra and colleagues concluded that cryoprobe-assisted lumpectomy is a viable alternative to the preoperative wire localization because it facilitates an easier and more precise resection while decreasing the incidence of positive margins.[11] In 24 procedures, a cryoprobe was used to create a freezeball encompassing the tumor along with 0.5 to 1 cm of sonographically normal surrounding parenchyma. On pathologic sectioning, the tumor size ranged from 0.7 to 2 cm and the average freezeball margin was 0.8 cm in all directions. Among patients with at least a 0.6 cm rim of cryoablated tissue beyond the tumor, the margin reexcision rate was only 5.6%.[11] Using cryoablation in place of wire localization is an interesting new option for the treatment of women with nonpalpable breast cancer, and clinical trials to further evaluate this method are underway.[12]

The above studies indicate that cryoablation of breast cancers is a promising technique; however, more research needs to be done. In two of the studies, the presence of DCIS at the margin of the ablation zone resulted in incomplete tumor necrosis. Thus, patients with DCIS may not be good candidates for cryotherapy. Since cryoablation procedures are generally guided by ultrasound, this may represent the limitation of ultrasound to define DCIS at the perimeter of the malignancy. Major advantages to this technique are the avoidance of anesthesia administration and the ability to perform an office-based procedure under real-time ultrasound guidance. Prospective, randomized trials are needed to determine the long-term effectiveness of cryoablation on breast cancer.

RADIOFREQUENCY ABLATION

The most widely studied form of ablation is radiofrequency (RF) ablation. RF ablation uses a high-frequency alternating current, which causes ions in close proximity to oscillate, creating friction and generating heat that destroys tumor cells.[13] RF ablation is generally performed in the operating room with mild sedation or general anesthesia and has been followed by standard surgical resection.[14] Preoperatively, the tumor is identified by stereotactic mammography or ultrasound, and a grounding pad is applied to the patient's skin in order to prevent electric shock.[2,15] The skin is injected with local anesthetic, a small incision is made, and an insulated 15-gauge probe is inserted. Once the probe is in its proper position, a star-like array of prongs is deployed, which evenly distribute the thermal energy (Figures 34–5 and 34–6).[2,15] With varying deployment of these prongs, a spherical ablation zone of anywhere between 3 and 5 cm in diameter can be created.[16] Temperature sensors located within the prongs monitor the temperature of the surrounding breast tissue. The usual RF ablation procedure achieves a target temperature of 95°C within 5 to 7 minutes, is maintained for 15 minutes, and is then followed by a 1-minute cool-down period.[2]

On a cellular level, RF ablation causes coagulative necrosis and protein denaturization.[5] Although the basic architecture of the ablated tumor can be discerned, the assessments of tumor grade and lymphovascular invasion are hindered by the heat destruction.[17] This is why obtaining a preprocedural core biopsy is crucial with ablative therapies. Grossly, the ablated region is firm, chalky, and yellow-white in the center, with a hyperemic red ring marking the edge of tissue destruction (Figure 34–7). It takes approximately 48 hours for these changes to manifest; therefore, a specimen examined immediately post-ablation will likely not reveal this characteristic pattern. Nicotinamide adenine dinucleotide (NADH)-diaphorase staining is used to evaluate cell viability. The NADH causes an oxidation reaction in the cytoplasm, which turns viable tissue dark-blue and leaves nonviable tissue pale-gray.[1,2]

One of the earliest pilot studies to evaluate breast cancer cell destruction following RF ablation was undertaken by Jeffrey and colleagues.[18] Five locally advanced breast cancer patients, with tumors

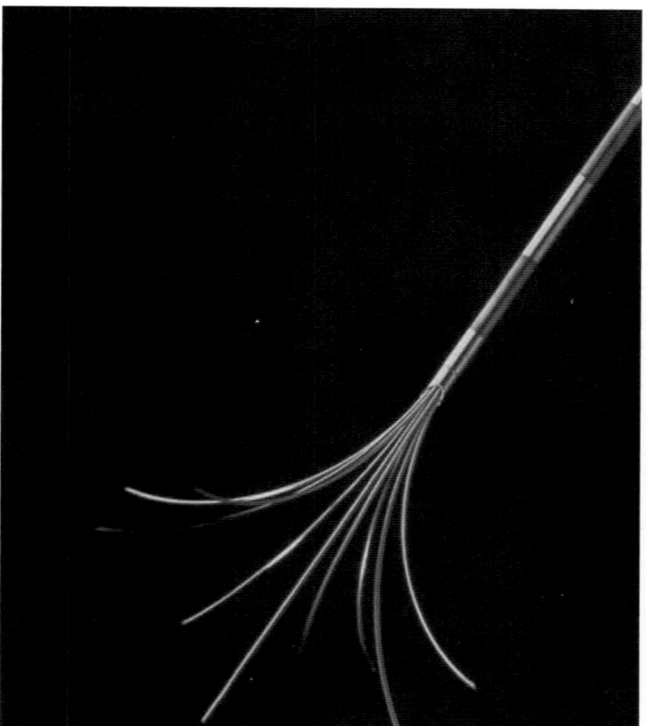

Figure 34–5. Radiofrequency ablation probe with prongs deployed as they would be inside a tumor.

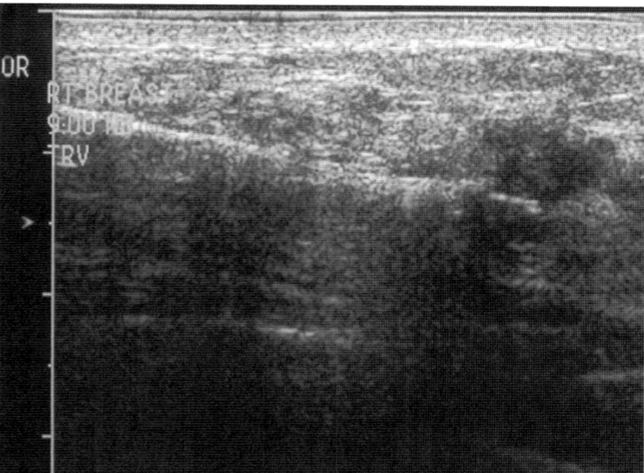

Figure 34–6. Radiofrequency ablation probe inserted in a tumor, as visualized on ultrasound.

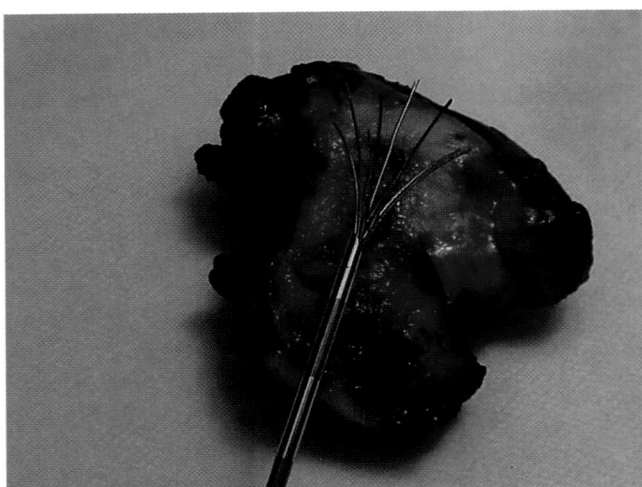

Figure 34–7. Radiofrequency ablation probe overlying the zone of ablation on a resected specimen. Note the hyperemic red ring defining the margin of the ablation zone.

ranging from 4 to 7 cm, underwent RF ablation immediately prior to planned mastectomy. Pathologically, all tumors showed some degree of tumor necrosis, and there was a concentric zone of ablation extending between 0.8 and 1.8 cm from the tip of the RF probe. NADH staining revealed complete cell death within the ablated zone in four of the patients. The fifth specimen harbored a single focus of viable cells of < 0.1 cm; however, they were partially lining a cyst and thus may have been protected from the heat. All patients tolerated the procedure well without complications related to the RF ablation.[18]

Izzo and colleagues reported on 26 women with needle core biopsy proven T1 and T2 tumors averaging 1.8 cm (range, 0.7–3 cm).[19] All had RF ablation followed by immediate resection of the primary tumor. NADH staining revealed cell viability in only 1 of the 26 patients (4%). Additionally, one woman sustained a full-thickness burn in the skin overlying the treatment zone. However, this was excised during the subsequent mastectomy without complication.[19]

RF ablation has been successfully performed with the assistance of stereotactic guidance. A 71-year-old woman with a 1.6 cm infiltrating ductal carcinoma, diagnosed by stereotactic core needle biopsy, underwent RF ablation, after which a metallic clip was left in place. One month later, needle-localized surgical resection was performed with successful retrieval of the clip. The patient tolerated the procedure well and no viable tumor was found. This case highlights a promising use for RF ablation in early breast cancers that are mammographically detected and then diagnosed with stereotactic core needle biopsy.[20]

In addition to stereotactic mammography, pre- and post-ablation MR imaging can also be used in conjunction with RF ablation in order to predict histologic findings in ablated breast tissue. Burak and colleagues studied 10 women with core biopsy proven invasive breast carcinoma, who underwent RF ablation and then surgical excision 1 to 3 weeks later, in order to allow the "true" zone of coagulation necrosis to mature.[21] Prior to RF ablation, MR imaging revealed tumor enhancement in 9 of the 10 (90%) tumors. In the tenth, a hematoma from a previous core biopsy precluded visualization. Post-RF ablation, MR imaging demonstrated an absence of residual lesion enhancement in 8 of the 9 (89%) initially visualized tumors. The zone of ablation was evident in all 10 tumors. The ablated lesions demonstrated the spectrum of histology, ranging from no residual tumor to coagulation necrosis with recognizable malignant cells; however, all cells tested were proven nonviable. The single patient with post-ablation MR imaging enhancement was found to have viable tumor on pathologic analysis. This case series suggests that MR imaging may be a valuable tool for the assessment of tumor response to RF ablation.[21]

Two studies from the M.D. Andersen Cancer Center have demonstrated that neoadjuvant chemotherapy may be a relative contraindication to RF ablation. The first series included 17 women and demonstrated complete tumor cell death in 94% of cases upon microscopic examination of the resected specimen. The single unsuccessful ablation was in a patient who had undergone neoadjuvant chemotherapy prior to ablation, which had resulted in nonconcentric tumor regression.[14] In the second series, ultrasound-guided RF ablation was performed on 21 invasive breast tumors of < 2 cm, immediately prior to scheduled lumpectomy or mastectomy. Here, the goal was total destruction of tumor with an adequate margin, as determined by NADH staining. In all 21 tumors, complete ablation was demonstrated by postprocedural ultrasound. However, in one woman who had undergone neoadjuvant chemotherapy for what was originally considered a T2 tumor, residual mammographically and sonographically occult invasive carcinoma was found on histopathologic examination.[22]

Not all groups have shown such a high level of success with their RF ablation trials. Hayashi and colleagues studied 22 postmenopausal women, > age 60 years, with clinical T1N0 breast cancers and tumors < 3 cm.[17] All underwent RF ablation followed by surgical resection within the following 2 weeks. In 19 of 22 patients, the specimens demonstrated complete coagulation necrosis. However, in the remaining three patients, residual disease was found at the ablation zone margin. One woman's dense breast tissue bent the probe tips, another's tumor was at the chest wall, and in the third, ultrasound significantly underestimated the size of the tumor. In five patients, the tumor was found to be multifocal and distant to the ablation zone. Of these five, two had multifocal cancer, two had extensive DCIS, and the last had in-transit metastasis. A retrospective review of these five preprocedural mammograms had failed to identify the sites of multifocal disease. RF ablation alone would have been insufficient and would have led to a high rate of local failure in these five cases, equaling 23% of this study group. Overall, patient satisfaction was high with minimal pain noted during the procedure itself, and 95% of the women said they would be willing to have RF ablation again. [17]

One of the strengths of RF ablation is its ability to produce reliable complete tumor cell death. Similar to the other ablative therapies, extensive DCIS and neoadjuvant chemotherapy are relative contraindications to its use. As a result of the successful treatments with RF ablation, a few trials are now investigating the use of RF alone, not followed by resection. These protocols will likely exclude patients with large tumors, those with a high likelihood of harboring multifocal disease, or patients who have received neoadjuvant chemotherapy. The natural history of RF-treated breast tumors without resection remains unknown and justifies further evaluation.

INTERSTITIAL LASER ABLATION

Interstitial laser ablation (ILA) uses heat to destroy breast cancer cells. In order to perform this technique, the tumor must first be visualized by mammography, MR imaging, or ultrasound (Figure 34–8). Mammographic guidance is used for microcalcifications or tumors seen solely on the mammogram, whereas MR imaging tends to be used for other lesions. In addition, ideal tumors for this technique are well circumscribed and measure < 1.5 cm.[23]

ILA is usually performed in the radiology suite, as general anesthesia is not necessary. Following the administration of a mild sedative, the breast is immobilized on the stereotactic table, the skin numbed, and a field block is performed directly at the site of the tumor.[16,24] A small skin incision is then made, through which a hollow needle is inserted. Next, a 16- to 18-gauge laser-emitting optic fiber is deposited through the hollow needle.[2,24] Parallel to the stereotactic needle, approximately 1 cm away, a multisensing probe is positioned to monitor the temperature of the surrounding breast tissue. Within 20 minutes, approximately 1,400 joules of laser energy per cubic centimeter of calculated tissue are delivered at a rate of 5 to 7 W/s.[16,23] The target temperature at the center is between 80° and 100°C, which correlates to around 60°C on the multisensing probe at the periphery. At this temperature, a spherical zone of ablation measuring 2.5 to 3 cm, encompassing a 1 to 1.5 cm tumor, is achieved.[24] Saline is continuously dripped from the tip of the laser to prevent overheating.[16] If using MR imaging, then detailed temperature grids can be generated that outline the area of ablation and help to monitor the temperature of the surrounding breast tissue.[25] Postprocedurally, contrast-enhanced Doppler can be used to see the absence of blood flow in the ablated area.[23]

At Rush University, Bloom and colleagues reported an ILA series of 40 patients with mammographically detected breast cancers, all measuring ≤ 2 cm.[26] Following stereotactically guided ablation, all tumors were excised within 5 to 42 days. Upon pathologic evaluation, all revealed a characteristic series of five concentric zones surrounding the cavity left by the laser needle tip. Zone one demonstrated charred tissue within the cavity; zone two appeared coagulated with "wind-swept" nuclei, similar to those seen in cautery artifact; zone three was a gray-tan ring, which histologically showed recog-

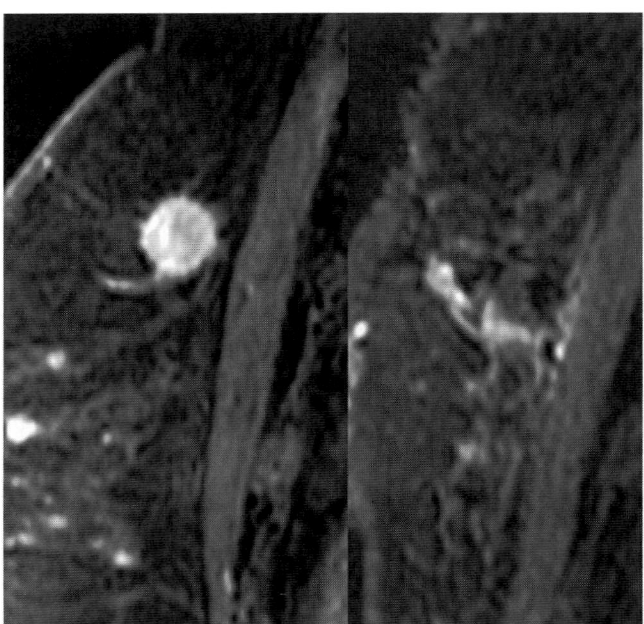

Figure 34–8. A magnetic resonance image demonstrating a breast tumor before (left) and after (right) interstitial laser ablation. Reproduced with permission from Steven Harms, MD.

nizable tumor but did not express cytokeratin 8/18 (a viability marker); zone four was a ring of red-tan tissue in which the tumor architecture was evident but the cytoplasm and nuclear characteristics had been erased; and zone five was grossly hyperemic while histologically consisting of a rim of vascular proliferation with fat necrosis interspersed with aggregates of inflammatory cells and macrophages. It is this outer zone of fat necrosis that delineates the area of effective ablation. Interestingly, the classic zones were present in all patients regardless of the time that had elapsed between ablation and resection.[26]

Dowlatshahi and colleagues studied the effect of stereotactically guided ILA on 56 women with breast cancers of < 2.3 cm.[23] The tumors were resected within 8 weeks in all but two of these patients, both treated outside of the protocol. Sixteen patients harbored residual tumor following ablation: four were early (learning curve) and not given sufficient laser energy; two were oversedated and moved involuntarily; four failed due to technical problems with the equipment; five had suboptimal target visualization due to excessive fluid infusion or needle-biopsy hematomas; and one had a tumor > 2 cm. Difficult target visualization was subsequently overcome by inserting metallic markers around the tumor after numbing the skin, but prior to the infusion of peritumoral anesthesia. The two patients without resection were monitored by mammography, ultrasonography, and needle core biopsy for 2 years. In both, the laser-treated tumors first regressed and were then replaced by a 2 to 3 cm oil cyst. Subsequent biopsies after the cysts resolved identified fibrosis only.[23] The Dowlatshahi group currently has a protocol treating selected patients solely with laser and then closely monitoring them with radiologic imaging and clinical examination, performing needle biopsies when indicated. At this time, with a median follow-up of 21 months (range, 6 to 48 months), 6 of 7 patients show no evidence of local or distant recurrence.[27]

ILA of breast cancers can also be done with MR guidance. Harms and colleagues performed MR-guided ILA on 22 invasive cancers in 12 patients in order to test the feasibility of this approach.[28] In this study, a needle was placed within the lesion under MR guidance and the ablative therapy interactively controlled by continuous images with energy delivery correlated to tumor dimensions. The appearance of a hypointense zone on the MR image correlated with the effectiveness of the treatment.[28] In the three patients with tumors of < 3 cm, the goal was total ablation, whereas in the other nine with tumors > 3 cm, ablation was only attempted on portions of tumors. The laser-treated area was resected in all patients. The zone of ablation, measured as the width of the hyperemic ring, underwent hematoxylin-eosin (H + E) as well as proliferating cell nuclear antigen (PCNA) staining for tumor viability. In all tumors < 3 cm, tumor destruction was complete. The most frequent complaint from patients in this study was discomfort from compression of the MR coils, but not related to the laser itself. The study concluded that MR-guided ILA is a safe and feasible technique for breast tumors measuring < 3 cm.[28]

Korourian and colleagues, also from the University of Arkansas, evaluated 29 invasive breast carcinomas, ranging from 1.8 to 4 cm, that had been treated with rotating delivery of excitation off resonance (RODEO) MR-guided ILA and then resected.[29] Tumor viability was assessed by the determination of PCNA staining, where staining intensity correlates with the proliferative capacity of tumor cells. The foci of the tumor treated with ablation revealed coagulative necrosis at the center, whereas reduced PCNA activity was seen in the cells immediately surrounding the site. PCNA expression gradually increased at radial intervals farther from the tumor ablation site. [29]

ILA, although less common than cryoablation and RF ablation, is a promising technique for the minimally invasive treatment of selected breast cancers. A major advantage to this technique is the ability to precisely determine the margins of ablation, if using MR guidance. Furthermore, since ILA does not require general anesthesia, it may be performed in the outpatient setting. There is little data on the natural history of ILA-treated breast cancers. Until such data are evident, this technique is only available on protocol.

FOCUSED ULTRASOUND ABLATION

Focused ultrasound (FUS) ablation is another technique that destroys tumor tissue with heat. Since MR imaging is used to guide this technique, FUS is best for cancers visible in this manner. In addition, MR imaging affords excellent anatomic resolution and allows the physician to monitor the ablation in real time.[30]

In order to perform FUS ablation, the patient is placed prone on an FUS table inside of an MR imaging magnet. An anxiolytic is administered intravenously to reduce movement inside the MR tube and an analgesic is given to reduce the associated discomfort. This procedure is unlike the others in that no skin incision is needed because the ablation is directed transcutaneously. The transducer is then positioned such that the ultrasound beam is focused directly on specific points within the tumor. The ultrasound penetrates the soft tissue, producing temperature elevations of between 55° and 90°C in the targeted breast tissue. The treatment consists of a series of sonications throughout these points within the tumor itself plus a surrounding margin. Dose calculations are based upon tumor size and the length of the ultrasound pathway.[31] The boundaries of the treatment area are sharply demarcated without damage to the surrounding parenchyma. Upon histologic assessment of resected specimens, the treated areas show a yellow-white area of central necrosis surrounded by a red hemorrhagic ring. Microscopically, this results in coagulation necrosis via protein denaturation.[30]

The first single-patient pilot study on FUS was performed by Huber and colleagues on a woman with a 2.2 cm centrally located invasive ductal carcinoma.[31] Following FUS, MR imaging was performed to evaluate the extent of tissue destruction. There was a zone without contrast in the targeted area, suggesting complete interruption of the blood supply. Interestingly, no anesthesia was needed, and the patient did not experience pain during the procedure. Within a week of ablation, the specimen was resected. Pathologic examination revealed both lethal and sublethal damage to the tumor. This was the first demonstration of a noninvasive therapy of breast cancer that was feasible and safe.[31]

Gianfelice and colleagues used FUS ablation to treat 12 women with invasive breast cancers < 3.5 cm.[30] All ablations were followed by surgical excision of the tumor and zone of ablation. The volumes of necrosed and residual tumor were compared in the specimens. Two patients sustained minor skin burns, but no other complications were reported. In three patients treated with the first-generation FUS technology, a mean of 46.7% of the tumor was within the targeted zone and a mean of 43.3% of the cancer tissue was necrosed. In nine patients treated with the more advanced second-generation FUS system, a mean of 95.6% of the tumor was within the targeted zone and a mean of 88.3% of the cancer tissue was necrosed. In all specimens, residual tumor was identified predominantly at the periphery of the tumor mass. In time, the authors also noted that by increasing the total targeted area with an increased number of sonications, a greater tumor volume could be destroyed.[30]

The largest prospective, randomized clinical trial to date on FUS for invasive breast cancer was recently published.[32] The 48 subjects were randomized to undergo modified radical mastectomy or FUS followed by modified radical mastectomy 1 to 2 weeks later. To be eligible, tumors had to be > 2 cm from the nipple and > 0.5 cm from the chest wall or skin. During the procedure, the tumor plus a rim of 1.5 to 2 cm of normal-appearing tissue were ablated. Although the main physical finding seen after FUS was breast edema, this resolved in all patients by 10 days after the procedure. Fourteen of the 23 FUS patients experienced minor local pain, warmth, or a sensation of heaviness; however, only four required prescription oral analgesics. In the operating room, the ablated area was noted to be firm, with a visible rim of congestion representing an inflammatory reaction to the FUS. On histologic examination, tumors demonstrated coagulative necrosis, nuclear destruction, vascular disruption, and vessel occlusion. Immunohistochemical testing with PCNA for proliferation, cell adhesion molecule CD44v6 for invasion, and matrix metalloproteinase MMP-9 for metastasis, revealed the nonviability of all cells within the treated area.[32]

Advantages of FUS ablation include absence of skin incision and the ability to continually change the focal point throughout the treatment, allowing great flexibility in matching the size of the treatment zone to the targeted volume of the tumor in three dimensions. Additionally, the ultrasound beams penetrate soft tissue and can be directed at tissue volumes as small as a few cubic millimeters.[30] MR-guided FUS may represent a noninvasive strategy for the neoadjuvant, adjuvant, or palliative treatment in selected breast cancer patients. As with the other ablative therapies, significantly more research into the safety, efficacy, and long-term outcome of the procedure is warranted before it can be used outside of a clinical trial.

MICROWAVE ABLATION

Microwave ablation also involves thermal tissue destruction. Since breast cancers have higher water content than surrounding normal parenchyma, the cancer heats more rapidly than healthy tissue during microwave ablation. During the procedure, the breast is compressed between two acrylic plates (technically referred to as microwave phased array wave guide applicators), which allow penetration of microwave energy while minimizing patient movement. Similar to other techniques, a temperature probe is placed at the center of the tumor, where the microwaves are focused, to regulate the target temperature of 43°C. To avoid burning the overlying skin, noninvasive surface temperature probes are applied while fans provide constant air cooling.[33]

Microwave ablation has shown success in reducing the volume of tumor preoperatively. Gardner and colleagues used focused microwaves on 10 women who were scheduled to undergo mastectomy.[33] The treatment averaged 34.7 minutes with a mean peak temperature of 44.9°C. All patients then underwent mastectomy within 18 days. Sonographic measurements before and after microwave therapy demonstrated that the tumor size was reduced an average of 41% (range, 29 to 60%). Upon pathologic analysis, tumor necrosis was noted in 4 of 10 specimens, whereas only apoptosis was seen in 6. It is important to point out that 3 of 10 women suffered flap necrosis following mastectomy, likely resulting from the elevated skin temperature during the microwave therapy.[33] Fujimoto and colleagues recently used hyperthermic tumor ablation (HTA) on a group of nine patients with advanced breast carcinoma, undergone as a preoperative adjunct to demonstrate the decrease in tumor volume.[34] With a target temperature above 50°C, tumor size was decreased an average of 33%.[34] Overall, both of these studies show that there is success in tumor volume reduction; however, the level of cancer cell destruction is not adequate to begin using this procedure without post-ablation resection.

Most recently, Vargas and colleagues completed a prospective, nonrandomized study of 25 women with invasive breast cancers (mean, 1.8 cm) who had undergone microwave ablation.[35] Tumoricidal temperatures were attained in 23 patients (92%). Some pathologic necrosis was only demonstrated in 17 patients (68%). These researchers concluded that microwave therapy could successfully cause tumor necrosis, the degree of which was a function of the thermal dose.[35]

Considerable additional research is needed regarding microwave ablation. Although it has been shown to shrink tumors and may be useful in the neoadjuvant setting, data regarding effective tumor cell killing are lacking. Another promising use for microwave ablation is as an adjunct to chemotherapy. Gardner and colleagues showed that the addition of microwave ablation to Adriamycin/Cytoxan enhanced the chemotherapy's tumoricidal effects.[36] Current large-scale multi-institutional prospective trials are underway to determine the safety and efficacy of this technique for neoadjuvant treatment of locally advanced breast cancers and the sole treatment of small early-stage tumors.[36]

CONCLUSION

This chapter provides the clinician with a broad understanding of the minimally invasive strategies under investigation for breast cancer treatment. Currently, the "gold standard" treatment for local control of small invasive and noninvasive breast cancers remains surgical excision followed by radiation therapy to the tumor bed, if clinically appropriate. We remain cautiously optimistic that ablative therapies will be used as a routine adjunct in the future to treat selected breast cancers.

The long-term oncologic and esthetic outcomes of ablative therapies will become clear as more clinical trials are completed. At this time, ablative therapies are approved for the treatment of breast malignancies as part of ongoing clinical trials only. Some of the challenges to be faced prior to mainstream acceptance and application of these technologies include widespread education of clinicians regarding the use of techniques; accurate three-dimensional reconstruction of breast tumors before, during, and after the procedure; determination of the degree of in situ carcinoma; and the definition of methods to accurately assess pathologically complete responses. Only when these issues are resolved and results from prospective, randomized trials are available can ablative therapies be considered for widespread clinical use.

Numerous methods of image-guided breast cancer ablation are currently being investigated in clinical trials. Hopefully, the data generated from these ongoing clinical trials will allow incorporation of these minimally invasive ablative techniques into the repertoire of the clinical treatment of breast cancer in a responsible manner.

REFERENCES

1. Mirza AN, Fornage BD, Sneige N, et al. Radiofrequency ablation of solid tumors. Cancer J 2001;7:95–102.
2. Simmons RM, Dowlatshahi K, Singletary SE, Staren ED. Ablative therapies for breast cancer. Contemp Surg 2002;58:61–72.
3. Rand RW, Rand RP, Eggerding FA, et al. Cryolumpectomy for breast cancer: an experimental study. Cryobiology 1985;22:307–18.
4. Staren ED, Sabel MS, Gianakakis LM, et al. Cryosurgery of breast cancer. Arch Surg 1997;132:28–33.
5. Kaufman CS, Bachman B, Littrup PJ, et al. Office based ultrasound-guided cryoablation of breast fibroadenomas. Am J Surg 2002;184:394–400.
6. Rui J, Tatsutani KN, Dahiya R, Rubinsky B. Effect of thermal variable on human breast cancer in cryosurgery. Breast Cancer Res Treat 1999;53:185–92.
7. Rand RW, Rand RP, Eggerding FA, et al. Cryolumpectomy for carcinoma of the breast. Surg Gynecol Obstet 1987;165:392–6.
8. Stocks LH, Chang HR, Kaufman CS, et al. Pilot study of minimally invasive ultrasound-guided cryoablation in breast cancer [abstract]. Am Soc Breast Surg 2002.
9. Pfleiderer SO, Freesmeyer MG, Marx C, et al. Cryotherapy of breast cancer under ultrasound guidance: initial results and limitations. Eur Radiol 2002;12:3009–14.
10. Sabel MS, Kaufman CS, Whitworth PW, et al. Cryoablation of early stage breast cancer: work in progress report of a multi-institutional trial. Ann Surg Oncol 2004;11:542–9.
11. Tafra L, Smith SJ, Woodward JE, et al. Pilot trial of cryoprobe-assisted breast-conserving surgery for small ultrasound-visible cancers. Ann Surg Oncol 2003;10:1018–24.
12. Simmons RM. Freezing breast cancers to enhance complete resection. Ann Surg Oncol 2003;10:999.
13. Dickson J, Calderwood S. Thermosensitivity of neoplastic tissue in vivo. In: Storm F, editor. Hyperthermia in cancer therapy. Boston: GK Hall Medical; 1983. p. 63–140.
14. Singletary SE, Fornage BD, Sneige N, et al. Radiofrequency ablation of early-stage invasive breast tumors: an overview. Cancer J 2002;8:177–80.
15. Dowlatshahi K, Francescatti D, Bloom KJ, et al. Image guided surgery of small breast cancers. Am J Surg 2001;182:419–25.
16. Edwards MJ, Dowlatshahi K, Robinson D, et al. 2001 Image-guided percutaneous breast cancer ablation meeting at the American Society of Breast Surgeons. Am J Surg 2001;182:429–33.
17. Hayashi A, Silver SF, van der Westhuizen NG. Treatment of invasive breast carcinoma with ultrasound-guided radiofrequency ablation. Am J Surg 2003;185:429–35.
18. Jeffrey SS, Birdwell RJ, Ikeda DM, et al. Radiofrequency ablation of breast cancer. Arch Surg 1999;134:1064–8.
19. Izzo F, Thomas R, Delrio P, et al. Radiofrequency ablation in patients with primary breast carcinoma: a pilot study of 26 patients. Cancer 2001;92:2036–44.
20. Elliot R, Rice PB, Suits JA, et al. Radiofrequency ablation of a stereotactically localized nonpalpable breast carcinoma. Am Surg 2002;68:1–5.
21. Burak WE, Angese MA, Povoski SP, et al. Radiofrequency ablation of invasive breast carcinoma followed by delayed surgical excision. Cancer 2003;98:1369–76.
22. Fornage BD, Sneige N, Ross MI, et al. Small (≤ 2 cm) breast cancer treated with US guided radiofrequency ablation: feasibility study. Radiology 2004;231:215–24.
23. Dowlatshahi K, Francescatti D, Bloom KJ. Laser therapy for small breast cancers. Am J Surg 2002;184:359–63.

24. Dowlatshahi K, Fan M, Gould VE, et al. Stereotactically guided laser therapy of occult 1breast tumors, work in progress. Arch Surg 2000;135:1345–52.
25. Harms S. Percutaneous ablation of breast lesions by radiologists and surgeons. Breast Dis 2001;13:67–75.
26. Bloom KJ, Dowlatshahi K, Assad L. Pathologic changes after interstitial laser therapy of infiltrating breast carcinoma. Am J Surg 2001;182:384–8.
27. Kepple J, Van Zee KJ, Dowlatshahi K, et al. Minimally invasive breast surgery. J Am Coll Surg 2004;199:961–75.
28. Harms S, Mumtaz H, Hyslop B, et al. RODEO MRI guided laser ablation of breast cancer. SPIE 1999;3590:484–9.
29. Korourian S, Klimberg S, Henry-Tillman R, et al. Assessment of proliferating cell nuclear antigen activity us1ing digital image analysis in breast carcinoma following magnetic resonance-guided interstitial laser photocoagulation. Breast J 2003;9:409–13.
30. Gianfelice D, Khiat A, Amara M, et al. MR imaging-guided focused US ablation of breast cancer: histopathologic assessment of effectiveness—initial experience. Radiology 2003;227:849–55.
31. Huber PE, Jenne JW, Rastert R, et al. A new noninvasive approach in breast cancer therapy using magnetic resonance imaging-guided focused ultrasound surgery. Cancer Res 2001;61:8441–7.
32. Wu F, Wang ZB, Cao YD, et al. A randomised clinical trial of high-intensity focused ultrasound ablation for the treatment of patients with localised breast cancer. Br J Cancer 2003;89:2227–33.
33. Gardner RA, Vargas HI, Block JB, et al. Focused microwave phased array thermotherapy for primary breast cancer. Ann Surg Oncol 2002;9:326–32.
34. Fujimoto S, Kobayashi K, Takahashi M, et al. Clinical pilot studies on pre-operative hyperthermic tumour ablation for advanced breast carcinoma using an 8 MHz radiofrequency heating device. Int J Hyperthermia 2003;19:13–22.
35. Vargas HI, Dooley WC, Gardner RA, et al. Focused microwave phases array thermotherapy for ablation of early-stage breast cancer: results of thermal dose escalation. Ann Surg Oncol 2004;11:139–46.
36. Gardner RA, Heywang-Kobrunner SH, Dooley WC, et al. Phase II clinical studies of focused microwave phased array thermotherapy for primary breast cancer: a progress report. Am Soc Breast Surg 2002.

35

Lymphedema

JOSEPH L. FELDMAN
DAVID J. WINCHESTER

ANATOMY

The lymphatic system carries excess fluid from the interstitial spaces—the interstitium—back to the blood vascular system. The interstitium contains collagen fibers and proteoglycan filaments (Figure 35–1). The interstitial fluid has the characteristic of a gel. The dermal lymphatic capillaries are endothelial ducts of overlapping flat cells attached by proteoglycan filaments to the surrounding connective tissue (Figure 35–2). The overlapping flat cells act as flap valves. Excess interstitial fluid will pull the proteoglycan filaments taut, opening a space between the interendothelial junctions, thus allowing interstitial fluid to enter the lymph system. Lymph moves from the lymph capillaries to the precollectors, which are located deeper in the dermis. Their endothelial cells have a tighter junction than the capillaries and contain smooth muscle fibers.

The precollectors drain into the collecting lymphatics, which are in the superficial subcutaneous tissues. The wall of a collecting lymphatic has three layers: the intima, the media, and the externa. The media contains smooth muscle, predominately in the intervalvular portion. The collecting lymphatics have bicuspid valves placed every few millimeters to prevent back flow (Figure 35–3). The collecting lymphatics drain into lymph trunks and may connect to adjacent collectors. The segment of a collector between a proximal and distal valve is termed a lymphangion or the "heart" of the lymph system. Lymphangions are innervated by autonomic nerve fibers, and they pulsate at a rate of 10 to 20 per minute, propelling lymph through the bicuspid valve into the next proximal lymphangion.

The lymph trunks, which are near the deep fascia, join the thoracic duct or the right lymphatic duct. The thoracic duct is the common trunk of all lymphatic vessels in the body except for those in the right side of the head, neck, thorax, and right upper extremity. These areas are drained by the right thoracic duct. The right lymphatic duct and the thoracic duct drain into the right and left jugulo-subclavian junction, respectively.

There are superficial and deep lymphatic systems in the extremities and connections between the two systems. The deep lymphatic vessels accompany the deep blood vessels. In the upper extremities, they

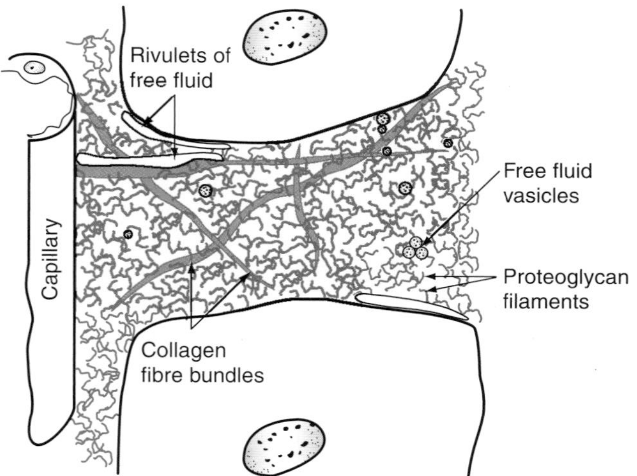

Figure 35–1. Structure of interstitium. Proteoglycan filaments are everywhere in the spaces between the collagen fiber bundles. Free fluid vesicles and the small amount of free fluid in the form of rivulets occasionally also occur. Reproduced with permission from Guyton AC.[2]

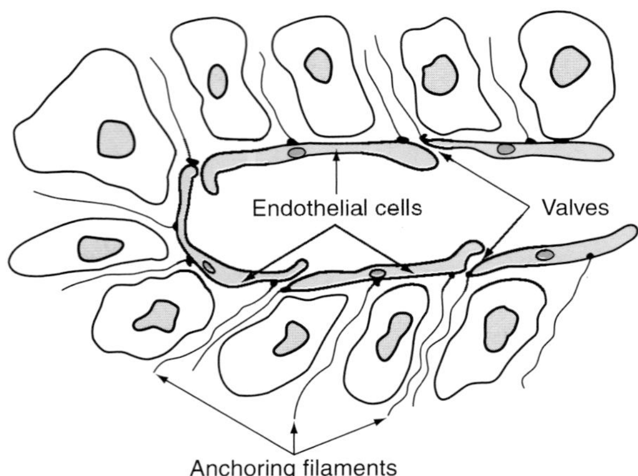

Figure 35–2. Special structure of the lymphatic capillaries that permits the passage of substances of high molecular weight into the lymph. Reproduced with permission from Guyton AC.[2]

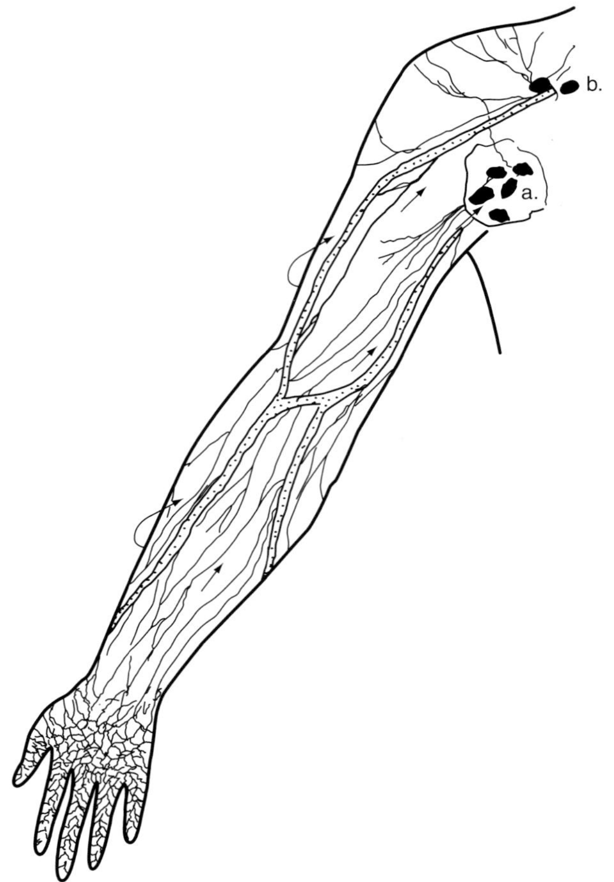

Figure 35–4. Drainage of the arm showing lymphatic pathways through the axillary nodes (a) and through the deltoid-pectoral cephalic chain (b). The dotted lines are veins. Reproduced with permission from Casely-Smith JR.[72]

drain predominately into the axillary lymph nodes (Figure 35–4). Some superficial vessels drain into the supraclavicular and posterior scapular nodes. Leduc and colleagues injected dye into the upper limb lymphatic vessels of 300 cadavers.[1] They found numerous potential substitution lymphatic pathways, including the supraclavicular pathway in 36% of the cases and a dorsoscapular pathway in 36%. In 76% of the cases, collecting lymphatic vessels from the posterior cutaneous thoracic region were found crossing midline and reaching additional contralateral substitution pathways.

PHYSIOLOGY

The forces controlling fluid exchange between blood and the interstitium were described by E.H. Starling in the 1890s (Figure 35–5). The capillary wall behaves as a leaky, semipermeable membrane, permeable to water, electrolytes, and glucose but relatively impermeable to plasma proteins. The plasma proteins exert osmotic pressure across this membrane. Albumin is the most osmotically active protein, accounting for about 80% of the total colloid osmotic pressure. The outward pressure causes a continual leakage of plasma ultrafiltrate out of the capillaries into the interstitial spaces. The interstitial fluid pressure, when positive, forces fluid through the capillary membrane. The colloid osmotic pressure draws fluid inward through the capillary membrane, whereas the interstitial fluid colloid osmotic pressure causes osmosis of fluid through the capillary membrane into the interstitium. At the arterial end of the blood capillary, the effective ultrafiltering pressure exceeds the effective reabsorption pressure, resulting in ultrafiltration. The low capillary pres-

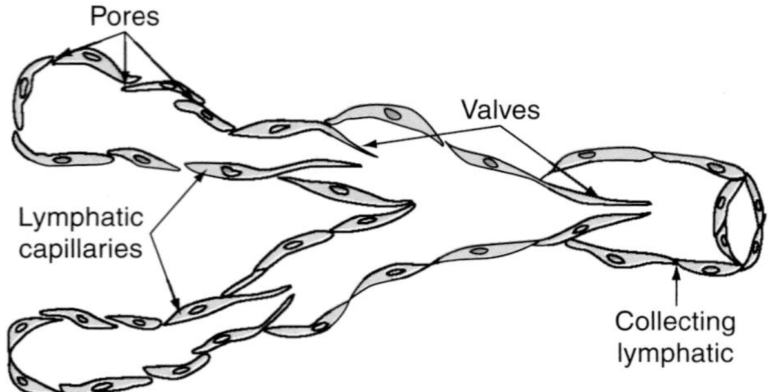

Figure 35–3. Structure of lymphatic capillaries and a collecting lymphatic, showing also lymphatic valves. Reproduced with permission from Guyton AC.[2]

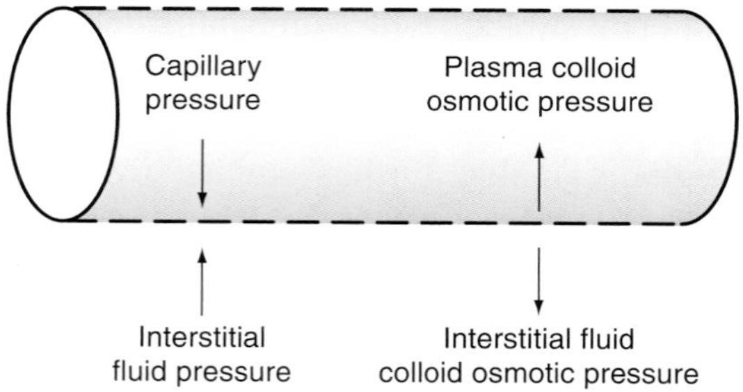

Figure 35–5. Fluid pressure and colloid osmotic pressure forces operate at the capillary membrane, tending to move fluid either outward or inward through the membrane pores. Reproduced with permission from Guyton AC.[2]

sure at the venous end of the capillary changes the balance of forces in favor of resorption. The mean forces moving fluid outward almost equals the mean force moving fluid inward. This is known as the Starling equilibrium (Table 35–1). There is a slight net outward force. The lymphatics return the excess fluid to the circulation.

Guyton demonstrated that in loose subcutaneous tissue the interstitial fluid pressure is a few mm Hg less than the atmospheric pressure.[2,3] This negative pressure holds some of the body tissues together. The lymphatic system clears free fluid and excess proteins from the tissues, maintaining the negative pressure. Lymph flow is discontinuous. Total lymph flow is approximately 120 mL/hour or 2 to 3 L/day. A negative interstitial fluid pressure slows lymph flow, whereas a pressure greater than atmospheric pressure can increase lymph flow greater than 20-fold. Interstitial fluid pressure in the positive range results in accumulation of free fluid in the tissue, which pushes the proteoglycan filaments apart. The interstitial gel becomes diluted, and pools of displaceable fluid form. This state allows for pitting edema. Compression of the skin pushes fluid out of the way, leaving a pit for a few seconds. When the interstitial spaces become fibrotic in chronic lymphedema, the edema becomes non-pitting. Pitting edema is present when there is an accumulation of the free fluid in the tissues.

Table 35–1. THE STARLING EQUILIBRIUM

Mean forces moving fluid outward	mmHg
Mean capillary pressure	17.3
Negative interstitial fluid pressure	3.0
Interstitial fluid colloid osmotic pressure	28.0
Total Outward Force	28.3
Mean force tending to move fluid inward	
Plasma colloid osmotic pressure	28.0
Total Inward Force	28.0
Summation of mean forces	
Outward	28.3
Inward	28.0
Net Outward Force	0.3

PATHOLOGY

Weissleder and Schuchhardt discussed the pathologic changes seen in postmastectomy lymphedema.[4] Proximal to the edema, there are fibrous vessel alterations with varying reductions in diameter and dilated prestenotic lymph collectors. Perilymphatic fibrosis is, at times, pronounced. Koshima and colleagues reported on the histologic changes in patients who underwent microsurgical lymphaticovenous anastomoses, six of whom had upper extremity lymphedema.[5] Thirty-three biopsied lymphatic trunks with lymphedema were evaluated histologically by light and electron microscopy. Perilymphatic fibrosis was often observed. In the initial stage of lymphedema, there is destruction of both endothelial and smooth muscle cells in the proximal level of the lymphatic trunks. Some of the proximal trunks are occluded, but the distal lymphatics remain patent. The results suggest that the occlusions of the lymphatic trunks and degeneration of smooth muscle cells may start from the proximal ends of the extremities. The smooth muscle degeneration in the proximal lymphatic trunks weakens the lymph drainage capacity.

PATHOPHYSIOLOGY

Lymphedema is excess fluid collection in the interstitium caused by a low output failure of the lymph vascular system. Lymphedema is categorized as a high protein, inflammatory edema. The most important cause of breast cancer therapy–related lymphedema is the disruption of lymph drainage from the ipsilateral arm and trunk. The extirpation of axillary lymph nodes, with or without irradiation, can produce a low output failure of regional lymph flow and a disturbance in interstitial-vascular osmotic equilibrium. Contributing factors include cicatrization, resulting in further lymphatic obstruction, immediate complications of surgery (such as wound infection and healing by secondary intention), infections, radiation, venous obstruction, and obesity.

Stanton and colleagues noted that the traditional theory of drainage to the lymphatic system causing edema in a "stopcock" manner leaves several puzzling questions.[6] Why do only some at-risk individuals develop edema? Why do some patients develop lymphedema in the hand or other parts of the arm and others do not? Why is the latent period so variable before lymphedema is apparent? Why does the quality of the tissue swelling vary between patients?[6,7]

In an attempt to answer these questions, Bates and colleagues published several papers. They found a lower concentration of interstitial fluid protein in the swollen forearm and, hence, a lower interstitial colloid osmotic pressure when compared to the normal forearm of the same patient.[8] The explanation was that a rise in internal capillary blood pressure measured micro-vascular fluid filtration. Capillary permeation of plasma proteins was reduced, or degradation of interstitial protein by macrophages increased. The net capillary filtration was studied in the edematous forearm and found to be lower rather than higher; but when the difference in arm volume on the two sides was taken into account, the total fluid load in the lymphatic system of each arm was not significantly different.

Földi criticized the methodology used in this study, including the wick method to obtain edema fluid and the truncated cone formula to measure volume in a misshapen lymphedematous extremity.[9] Mortimer and colleagues defended the validity of their methodology.[10] Mellor and colleagues studied forearm dermal lymphatic capillaries with fluorescence microlymphography in 16 patients with lymphedema and 19 breast cancer treated patients without lymphedema.[11] They concluded that microlymphatic changes occur in the swollen arm with a local superficial rerouting of lymph drainage and either lymphangiogenesis and/or increased recruitment of dominant lymphatic vessels. Their working hypothesis is that active contractible lymphatic collectors of the arm have to work against increased resistance following the axillary irradiation and surgery. Furthermore, the distribution of swelling with a limb ultimately depends on the fatigue and the eventual pump failure of the weakest vessels, which may be those draining the mid-arm region. Finally, further studies were recommended to test this hypothesis.

RISK FACTORS

Surgery

The risk of lymphedema is directly related to the extent of the surgical intervention. Although breast surgery also increases the risk of arm and breast edema, lymphedema risk is modulated primarily by the axillary component of the surgical intervention. Axillary surgery includes axillary dissection, node sampling, and sentinel node biopsy. In a review of 475 patients, a complete axillary dissection was associated with a 37% risk of lymphedema, as compared to an 8% risk for a low dissection and a 5% risk for node sampling. This risk also varies with the number of axillary nodes removed. If more than 10 nodes are harvested, the risk of lymphedema is 28%, as compared to 9% for 1 to 9 nodes removed.[12]

A standard axillary dissection can be arbitrarily divided into three levels based upon the relationship to the pectoralis minor muscle. Level I lymph nodes are located inferior and lateral to the muscle. Level II nodes are located posterior to the muscle, and level III nodes are superior and medial to the muscle. All but approximately 1% of involved axillary lymph nodes are located in levels I and II. Including level III within a node dissection offers only a 1% advantage over a level I/II dissection to identify involved nodes.[13–15]

Just as the probability of encompassing nodal disease varies according to the level of dissection, the risk of lymphedema also varies. The difference between these two end points is that the incremental benefit of axillary dissection is much lower with the inclusion of level III nodes relative to the incremental increase in the risk of developing lymphedema. Taking into account the small incremental benefit of including level III and a substantially increased risk of lymphedema, most patients should have a level I/II axillary dissection for staging and therapeutic purposes, unless extensive nodal disease or clinically suspicious level III nodes are identified.

Although a level I/II node dissection provides a balanced choice between more extensive sampling and an increased risk of lymphedema, it has become a necessary exercise only for patients undergoing a therapeutic node dissection for histologically involved nodes or as a staging operation for patients who do not have an identifiable sentinel lymph node. The risk of lymphedema with sentinel node biopsy was initially perceived to be negligible based upon the early experience of investigators. As observed with patients undergoing axillary dissection, the risk of lymphedema varies according to the definition of lymphedema and the scrutiny of the investigator. Volumetric measurement of the limb provides the most objective assessment of arm lymphedema but should include a comparison to the preoperative limb volume as well as the contralateral limb to implicate any difference as morbidity of the therapy. Other assessments, including arm circumference, are more easily obtained. Symptoms of arm fullness may also be included within the definition without volumetric or circumference difference.

With careful, prospective evaluation, lymphedema following sentinel node biopsy has been estimated to be 3 to 6%. Sener and colleagues found a 3% incidence of lymphedema following breast conservation and sentinel node biopsy as compared to a 17% risk during the same time period for patients undergoing a level I/II axillary dissection. This figure for sentinel node biopsy included a 1% risk of breast edema and a 2% risk of arm edema.[16] In a retrospective study analyzing women treated with mastectomy, 16% developed lymphedema as compared to none undergoing sentinel node biopsy.[17] In a study at the Mayo Clinic, 34% of patients undergoing axillary dissection developed lymphedema as compared to 6% for those undergoing a sentinel node biopsy.[18] Although there is a range of reported values of lymphedema for sentinel node biopsy, there is a significant reduction in risk as compared to axillary dissection. Sentinel node biopsy has provided patients with a less morbid axillary staging procedure. However, there are occasions when sentinel nodes are not identified. In a review of 1,094 patients, 5.7% failed to have identification of sentinel nodes. In patients with more than 10 involved lymph nodes, the risk of nonmapping was 41%. For those with no histologic nodal involvement, the risk of nonmapping was 5.3%.[19] This observation suggests that the failure to map is a risk factor for extensive nodal disease and should prompt consideration of a complete axillary dissection, despite the risk of lymphedema.

The presence of nodal disease is also a risk factor for lymphedema in several reports.[20–22] In addition, patients presenting with locally advanced breast cancer may have lymphedema as their presenting symptom. It therefore follows that a therapeutic node dissection may provide excellent regional control without increasing the risk of developing lymphedema in an otherwise untreated axilla.

It is also plausible that the risk of lymphedema in the setting of sentinel node biopsy is related to other treatment factors. In an analysis of long-term complications following breast conservation therapy, 3% of women having lumpectomy will develop arm lymphedema without any axillary surgery.[23] Larson also reported a 4% incidence of lymphedema in 235 patients not undergoing any axillary surgery.[12] The extent of the breast surgery also impacts on the risk of lymphedema. Thus, in the infrequent event that lymphedema develops following sentinel node biopsy, it may be related to either the breast procedure or the use of postoperative radiation therapy.

Radiation

Normal lymphatic vessels are relatively insensitive to radiation. Lymph nodes are radiosensitive to conventional doses of radiotherapy. The lymphatic vessel constriction seen late in post-radiotherapy may be due to the development of surrounding fibrous tissue.[24]

The inclusion of radiation therapy has a more than additive effect on the risk of developing lymphedema.[10] Kissin and colleagues found that combined therapy increased the risk from 7.4 to 38% over axillary clearance alone. In a more recent report evaluating the interaction between sentinel node biopsy and radiotherapy, the use of radiation increased the risk of lymphedema by 2.4-fold.[25] Breast radiotherapy can increase the risk of axillary node dissection patients by approximately 7%, possibly owing to incidental radiation to the axilla.

Infection

Infection has long been recognized as a precipitating cause of lymphedema (Figure 35–6). Halsted reported that "the element of infection is the one essential and determining factor of elephantiasis."[26] Mozes and colleagues contended that infection, in one form or another, is the most important factor in the formal appearance of lymphedema.[27] Contributing factors include radiation fibrosis, postoperative scarring, and, of course, post-surgical lymphatic obstruction. Noninfectious inflammatory conditions, such as rheumatoid and psoriatic arthritis and chronic dermatitis, have been associated with lymphedema and are comorbid factors in patients at risk for developing lymphedema.

Venous Obstruction

Consideration of venous obstruction as a cause of post-mastectomy lymphedema dates back to early reports. Veal felt that the incidence of lymphedema was only 10% of swollen arms and attributed the rest to venous obstruction and that most lymphedema appeared in the presence of superimposed infection.[28] He mistakenly believed that only patients with brawny edema had lymphatic obstruction. Hughes and Patel, after lymphangiography and bilateral venography in radical mastectomy patients, found various degrees of venous obstruction without adequate collateral circulation.[29] Reduction in arm size was achieved after axillary vein decompression and maintained at 1- to over 2-year follow-up. The cause of obstruction was found to be fibrosis blocking the axillary vein. Kinmonth reported that axillary exploration to remove scar tissue causing venous obstruction may result in improved shoulder mobility but that venous decompression by itself was never sufficient to reduce the size of the limb.[30]

Larson and Crampton performed venograms in normal controls and 14 postmastectomy patients with the arm adducted and in 90 degrees of abduction.[31] In adduction, the axillary vein was normal in only 22.8% of the controls, was narrowed in 42.9%, and was positionally totally obstructed in 34.3%. The axillary vein visualized normally in abduction in 100%. There was no edema in the control patients since their lymphatic system was intact. Nine postmastectomy patients who showed complete obstruction in the adducted position had axillary-subclavian venolysis. Five of the 8 had "excellent" results with up to 6-year follow-up. Follow-up phlebography in these patients showed a normal axillary system runoff in adduction and abduction.

Svensson and colleagues used color duplex Doppler imaging in 81 patients with breast cancer–related lymphedema and no signs of recurrent cancer.[32] Only 38% of the swollen arms had normal venous outflow, whereas 57% had evidence of venous obstruction and 14% of venous congestion. Martin and Földi documented axillary-subclavian occlusion in 14.5% of 48 women who had unilateral arm edema after breast cancer surgery.[33] Forty patients also had irradiation. Arterial inflow was increased in 45%. The authors concluded that hemodynamic alterations are a consequence of either the treatment of breast cancer or a response to skin and subcutaneous edema itself or possibly a response to smoldering inflammation in the lymphedematous arm.

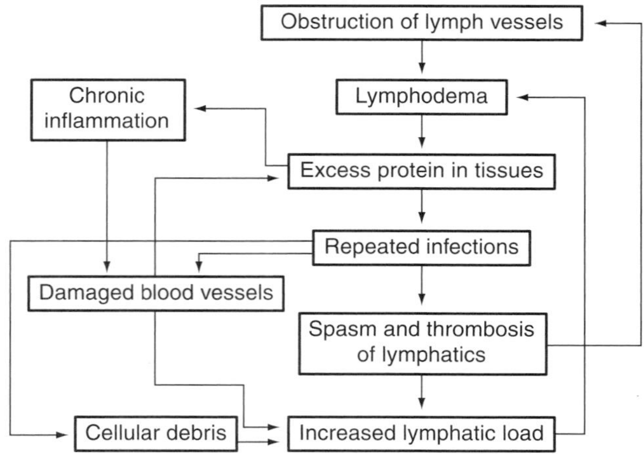

Figure 35–6. The mutual interactions of lymphedema and infection. Adapted with permission from Casely-Smith JR.[72]

Obesity

See "Risk Reduction" below.

Stages of Lymphedema

The International Society of Lymphology (ISL) describes a four-stage scale for the classification of a lymphedematous limb.[34] The stages refer only to the physical condition of the extremity, not to the pathophysiologic mechanisms of lymphedema. Stage 0 refers to lymphostasis, a latent or subclinical condition where swelling is not evident despite impaired lymph transport. Lymph flow is slowed down or stopped at different levels of the lymph vessel system. Stage I represents an early accumulation of fluid relatively high in protein content. The edema usually decreases with elevation, and pitting may occur. Stage II signifies that limb elevation does not significantly reduce the edema. In late stage II, there is little, if any, pitting and the tissues are increasingly fibrotic. Stage III encompasses lymphostatic elephantiasis, where pitting is absent and there are trophic changes, such as acanthosis, fat deposits, and verrucous hyperplasia. With each stage, severity based on volume can be assessed as minimal (< 20% increase) in limb volume, moderate (20 to 40% increase) or severe (> 40% increase).

Diagnosis of Lymphedema

A transient edema may occur within the first 3 months after breast cancer treatment. Browse and colleagues state that approximately 7% of breast cancer patients develop a transient edema within 2 months of their surgery or radiation.[35] It is not known if this transient edema will later progress to lymphedema. This early edema is caused by a surgical disruption of lymph flow and is improved by the development of collateral lymphatic vessels and drainage across watershed pathways toward the contralateral axilla and ipsilateral groin.[36]

The diagnosis of lymphedema is usually straightforward in a patient with a history of breast cancer therapy. The patient may have symptoms that precede objective evidence of lymphedema. These include a sensation of fullness, tightness, or heaviness of the arm or adjacent trunk.[37] The onset of edema may be insidious, and the swelling may initially be noted by others. Some patients will report the onset of edema during air travel, sitting in a hot tub, after heavy lifting or venepuncture. Cellulitis may both trigger clinical lymphedema and aggravate pre-existing edema. The edema may be reported to first occur in the hand, the forearm, the upper arm, or the trunk and then spread to other segments of the extremity. The physical findings can be obvious or subtle. They include any detectable swelling or enlargement of the arm or trunk (with or without pitting), an increase in the thickness of the skin-folds in the trunk or arm, an increase in the texture or consistency of the skin, or an asymmetric increase in subcutaneous adipose tissue. The skin-fold sign of Stemmer is considered specific for the presence of chronic lymphofibrotic edema.[38] The cutaneous folds on the dorsum of the swollen digits are hard, thickened, and difficult to lift. The absence of a Stemmer sign does not exclude the diagnosis of lymphedema. Apart from radiation erythema, the color of the skin is usually normal. A chronic, non-infectious, splotchy erythema may occasionally be present. The temperature of the skin may be normal or slightly increased. Diagnostic studies are useful to exclude other comorbidities, such as recurrent malignancy or deep vein thrombosis. These studies include magnetic resonance imaging (MRI), computed tomography (CT) scan, and venous Doppler ultrasonography. A lymphoscintigram is indicated only where doubt exists regarding the diagnosis.

When lymphedema first develops, an initial, reversible stage is common. The patient reports that the edema has "disappeared," but the clinician needs to recognize that the edema is hovering between stage 0 and stage I. Risk precautions should be followed, and the patient should be referred for complete decongestive therapy in an effort to prevent or delay the onset of irreversible lymphedema.

Adverse Effects of Lymphedema

Lymphedema is a disease, not a symptom, arising as a consequence of a low output failure of the lymphatic system.[39] Lymphedema can cause adverse effects owing to altered anatomy and physiology of the involved limb and adjacent trunk. Adverse effects include musculoskeletal dysfunction, cording, cellulitis, pain, and angiosarcoma.

Musculoskeletal Dysfunction

The shoulder is a complex joint. Normal scapulohumeral rhythm is required to accomplish full active shoulder movement. There is a 2:1 ratio of movement of the humerus to movement of the scapula when abducting the arm. During the first 15 to 30 degrees of abduction, the scapula may remain fixed, with the 2:1 ratio applying to abduction beyond 15 to 30 degrees. Shoulder movements require the synergistic action of shoulder muscles.

Individuals with lymphedema may experience shoulder pain in a heavy arm owing to traction on the joint. This can lead to tendinitis, bursitis, and adhesive capsulitis. Many of these individuals have a kyphotic posture, which lowers the coracoacromial hood and causes internal rotation of the humerus. This leads to impingement of the humerus against the coracoacromial ligament. Tight axillary soft tissue from surgery or radiation can limit active range of motion. This is most common in the anterior axillary fold.

Posture exercises and shoulder range of motion exercises are important components of a lymphedema exercise program. Other therapeutic measures include modalities such as soft tissue mobilization, cold or iontophoresis, and analgesics or non-steroidal anti-inflammatory medications. Steroid injections should be a last resort, and the patient should be covered with oral antibiotics. Heat can aggravate the edema.

Cording

Cording (axillary web syndrome) is the development of visible cordlike bands in the chest wall and axilla, which can extend down the arm. The cords are tender and can restrict range of motion. Cording occurs after surgery or during irradiation and is not necessarily associated with lymphedema. The incidence of cording is unknown. Moskovitz and colleagues reported a 6% occurrence rate in 750 patients, most of whom had level 1 and 2 axillary lymph node dissection (ALND).[40] Four patient with sentinel lymph node dissection (SLND) and lumpectomy developed cording. Cording may result from lymphangitis, lymphatic thrombosis, and/or venous thrombosis. Cording usually resolves within 1 to 2 months. Therapy, including passive stretch, soft tissue mobilization, and manual lymphatic drainage, is indicated to improve comfort and shoulder range of motion.

Cellulitis

There are various terms in the literature for acute inflammatory episodes (AIE), including cellulitis, erysipelas, and dermatolymphangioadenitis (DLA). Cellulitis is the most commonly used term and describes an acute, diffuse, spreading inflammation within subcutaneous tissues characterized by erythema, pain, tenderness, and edema (Figure 35–7). The most common cause of cellulitis associated with lymphedema is *Streptococcus pyogenes* (Group A β-hemolytic strep). *Staphylococcus aureus*, *Escherichia* coli, and *Pseudomonas* infections are less common. Erysipelas is a superficial cellulitis with lymphatic vessel involvement usually caused by *S. pyogenes*. Classic erysipelas is characterized by well-defined raised margins. Cellulitis may extend superficially, whereas erysipelas may extend deeply, but it may be difficult to differentiate the two. The onset of cellulitis can be dramatic with flu-like symptoms—fever, chills, myalgia—and a spreading erythema, either involving the chest wall or the ipsilateral extremity. At times, the cellulitis begins as a few red spots or blotchy areas that spread and coalesce. Increased limb edema and pain are common.

Simon and Cody reported cellulitis in 15 of 273 patients (6%) over 42 months following ALND.[41] All of the patients had lymphedema. The mean interval between ALND and the onset of cellulitis was 38 months. Hughes and colleagues observed initial episodes of cellulitis in patients with breast-conserving surgery occurring before, during, and after breast irradiation.[42] Cellulitis usually involved the whole breast. The authors hypothesized that impaired lymphatic circulation after excision, axillary dissection and/or irradiation predisposed the patient to breast and adjacent soft tissue cellulitis. A

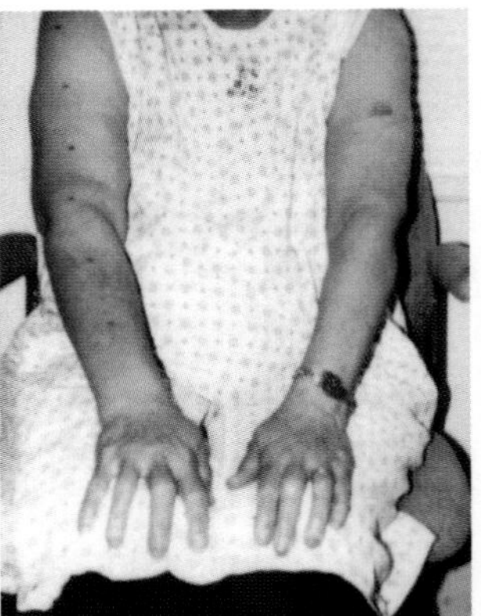

Figure 35–7. Lymphedema and acute cellulitis.

retrospective study on the incidence of cellulitis and lymphedema found a 1% incidence of cellulitis in stage I, 27% in stage II, and 72% in stage III.[43]

The management of cellulitis requires antibiotics, rest, and elevation. In a mild case, treatment with an anti-staphylococcal penicillin, oral macrolide, or a first generation cephalosporin is appropriate. Patients with systemic infection are usually hospitalized and put on intravenous (IV) antibiotics such as vancomycin hydrochloride and anti-pseudomonal penicillins. Patients with recurrent cellulitis will require prophylactic antibacterial therapy (eg, 0.5 gm penicillin IV daily). Patients allergic to penicillin can take erythromycin 0.25 to 0.5 gm/day. Patients are frequently able to recognize the symptoms and signs of cellulitis. They are advised to keep antibiotics available for prompt treatment. In one study, patients reported a decrease in the incidence of infection in upper and lower extremity lymphedema from 1.10 infections/patient/year to 0.65 infections/patient/year after a course of complete decongestive therapy (CDT).[44]

Pain

Pain control improves quality of life and compliance with lymphedema management. Lymphedema is usually not painful. However, some patients report symptoms associated with lymphedema such as a feeling of the arm being achy, heavy, tight, or any combination of the above. Use of the affected limb may exacerbate these symptoms. The degree of discomfort is usually proportional to the severity of the edema. Carroll and Rose reported that the ten most common descriptive words chosen from the McGill Pain Questionnaire were tight, tiring, throbbing, heavy, nagging, aching, shooting, tingling, hot, and annoying.[45] In addition to lymphedema, other causes of pain include adhesive capsulitis of the shoulder, tendinitis, entrapment neuropathies, myofascial pain, infection, and neuropathic pain. Neuropathic pain can be caused by chemotherapy, post-radiation fibrosis, post-mastectomy intercostal neuralgia, radiation plexopathy, and tumor recurrence. A significant reduction in pain was reported with lymphedema management. Twycross, in a comprehensive discussion of pain in lymphedema, advocates a multimodal approach to pain management, including discussion to reduce the emotional impact of pain, analgesics, physical therapy, decongestive therapy, and, when necessary, cognitive-behavioral therapy.[46]

Angiosarcoma (Stewart-Treves Syndrome)

Angiosarcoma is a malignant tumor of the skin that develops in chronic primary or secondary lymphedema. The mean time of onset in post-mastectomy lymphedema is 10 years, as opposed to approximately 20 years in other types of lymphedema. The malignancy arises in the endothelial cells of blood vessels, so the older term "lymphangiosarcoma" is not correct.[47] Fortunately, angiosarcoma is uncommon, since it is usually fatal. The risk of angiosarcoma in breast cancer patients is less than 0.5% within 10 years of definitive treatment for breast cancer.[48,49] Most cases of angiosarcoma arise in patients with chronic lymphedema who had irradiation; however, in some cases, angiosarcoma develops in the radiation field in the absence of breast or arm edema. The patient complains of reddish blue or blackish blue lumps that increase rapidly in size, bleed easily, ulcerate, and become infected. The nodules will penetrate the subcutis and spread to the trunk.[50] The treatment of angiosarcoma mainly has been amputation or wide excision. The role of chemotherapy and radiation therapy is not well defined. Pulmonary, intra-abdominal, brain, and bone metastases may occur. Chemotherapy, radiation therapy, and amputation are usually unsuccessful, and the median survival is less than 3 years. Fineberg and Rosen and Sener and colleagues discussed the spectrum of abnormalities in the mammary skin after lumpectomy, axillary staging, and radiotherapy.[51,52] These abnormalities included lymphangiectasis, atypical vascular lesions, and angiosarcoma. Angiosarcoma and variants of atypical vascular lesions may be difficult to diagnosis when superimposed in the ubiquitous clinical changes of radiation dermatitis.

Risk Reduction

Risk reduction is an important concept in lymphedema management. It applies to those at risk of developing lymphedema, as well as those living with lymphedema. The phrase "risk reduction" is preferred over "prevention," since those at risk cannot be given ironclad assurance that lymphedema can be prevented. The goals of the risk reduction precautions are to avoid an increased lymphatic load (Table 35-2) and reduced lymph transport capacity. The precautions achieve these goals by reducing the risk of infection, inflammation (Table 35–3), injury to the veins and superficial lymphatic vessels, and by increasing arterial blood flow, which may result in increased interstitial fluid.

Although some of these precautions have been criticized for not being evidence based, most of them have a solid physiologic basis. Földi states that there are cases in which anecdotal observations are in harmony with scientific facts and established knowledge.[53,54] Patients who develop lymphedema after minor trauma, sitting in a hot tub, flying or exercising most likely had stage 0 latent lymphedema (lymphostasis). It is important for health professionals to know that these are lifetime precautions since lymphedema can occur even 20 to 30 years after surgery.

There should be a pre-surgical discussion about lymphedema risk and precautions. These precautions are recommendations, and precautions concerning activity should be tailored to the patient's lifestyle. Three areas of risk are discussed in more detail: obesity, airline travel, and exercise.

Obesity

Obesity has been cited as a risk factor in lymphedema.[55] Clinically, the obese patient with large, flabby arms and trunk is noted to be more prone to develop lymphedema, and the lymphedema is more difficult to control. MacDonald and Osman cited obesity as a commonly recognized fact for predisposing the arm to swelling.[56] They found that 7 thin persons had slight to moderate swelling whereas 30 average or obese persons had moderate to severe swelling. They suggested the following sequence influencing the development of swelling in the obese: fat necrosis, secondary infection, regional lymphangitis, and obstruction.

Table 35–2. PRECAUTIONS TO REDUCE RISK OF INCREASED LYMPHATIC LOAD
Avoid blood pressure measurements in the affected arm. If both arms are at risk, use a leg cuff or the arm less at risk.
Avoid hot tubs or saunas.
Brassiere straps should be wide, padded, and should not cut into the skin.
The prosthesis should be as light as possible.
Avoid tight jewelry.
Avoid repetitive, heavy lifting—generally over 10 to 15 lbs. Wear a compression sleeve if lifting is necessary.
Avoid carrying heavy luggage or bags.
Avoid slinging bags/purses over the shoulder.
Wear a compression sleeve when flying.
Wear a compression sleeve when exercising.
Maintain ideal body weight.
Avoid salty foods.

Table 35–3. TO REDUCE THE RISK OF INFECTION AND INFLAMMATION
Avoid venepuncture and injections in the involved extremity except in case of an emergency. If both arms are at risk, use a leg for venepuncture. If this is not possible, use the arm less at risk.
Keep the skin clean and moist. Use non-greasy moisturizers.
Wash bandages and compression garments each day.
Do not cut the cuticles.
Use an electric razor.
Wear work gloves to avoid wounds.
Use insect repellent.
Avoid sunburns.
Avoid acupuncture in the at-risk arm and the ipsilateral trunk.
Use care when cooking, ironing, and sewing.

Werner and colleagues studied edema risk factors in 282 patients who had conservative breast cancer management with local excision, axillary dissection, and primary single dose radiation therapy.[57] The authors prospectively measured differences in upper and lower arm circumferences prior to radiation and at intervals thereafter. The only predictor that held up to multivariate analysis was body mass index (BMI). A greater BMI suggested a greater risk of arm edema as well as an increased risk of severe arm edema.

Weight control can be a challenge in the breast cancer patient. Inactivity, obesity, depression, hyperphagia, and complications of adjuvant chemotherapy, such as induced menopause and fluid retention, have been cited as causes of weight gain. In addition, some patients may have pre-existing conditions, such as osteoarthritis and cardiopulmonary disease that reduce their activity level. Harvie and colleagues found resting energy expenditure depressed 3% during adjuvant chemotherapy and remained depressed until at least 3 months posttreatment.[58] The conclusion was that treatment with adjuvant chemotherapy causes gain of body fat because of reduced energy expenditure and the failure of women to reduce their energy intake to compensate for the decline in energy requirements during the 6 months post-treatment. Freedman and colleagues found no significant differences in weight changes when compared with controls during the first year of treatment.[59] There was, however, increased body fat and a decreased percentage of lean soft tissue and skeletal mass.

Air Travel

Anecdotally, patients report new onset lymphedema or aggravation of existing lymphedema after air travel. In a retrospective study, Casley-Smith sent questionnaires to 1,020 Australian lymphedema patients.[60] Responses were received from 490 secondary lymphedema patients. One hundred sixty-two of the responses were from breast cancer surgery patients. In 27 of the 490, swelling began during an airplane flight (15 legs and 12 arms) and 9 from a long bus or car trip. Most of the flights were long-haul and lymphedema developed when the patient was in the air. The presumed triggers during flight are lower cabin pressure, dehydration, and stasis.

A 2004 National Lymphedema Network <www.lymphnet.org> position paper recommends that individuals at risk wear a 20 to 30 mm Hg upper extremity support garment and either a detachable gauntlet or glove.[61] The garment should be worn from point of departure to the destination. Other measures include adequate hydration and limbering up by walking in the aisle of the airplane or stretching. The individual with a confirmed diagnosis of lymphedema should wear short-stretch compression bandages or a well-fitted garment depending on the severity of the edema. While away from home, the regular schedule of garment wear and/or bandaging should be maintained.

Exercise

Exercises are important to a healthy lifestyle. Exercises promote lymph flow in the normal limb.[62] In the limb at risk, there is concern that vigorous exercise can produce lymph overload and cause lymphedema. The literature is mixed as to the risks of exercise. Stillwell advocated isometric exercises.[63] He noted that minimal joint movement makes the activity less obtrusive and more efficient. Patients contracted the muscles for 1 to 2 seconds with 2- to 3-second rest periods for 20 repetitions. He cautioned against excessive use of the muscles of the limb so as to avoid increased blood flow and an increase in swelling. Browse and colleagues state that isotonic exercises are ideal because they create adequate pressure to expel lymph from a segment of lymph vessel and an equal period of relaxation to allow filling.[64] Hence, they believe sustained contractions of isometric exercises are undesirable. They agree that overexertion and excessive static exercise are counterproductive because they increase capillary blood flow with a resultant increase in capillary filtration.

There are studies in the literature whose authors do not subscribe to the prohibition against vigorous exercise. Harris and Niesen-Vertommen examined 20 breast cancer treated women who had received axillary dissection and who were in an upper extremity strengthening and aerobic conditioning program to prepare for dragon boat racing (rowing).[65] As a precautionary measure, the women wore a compression sleeve during training and paddling. At the end of the season 7 months later, the lymphedema of two patients with preexisting lymphedema increased whereas the arm volumes of the remaining 18 women were not increased. Földi believes that the 7-month follow-up is too early to draw the conclusion that vigorous exercise does not cause lymphedema.[66]

Johansson and colleagues reported a match pair case-controlled study.[67] Seventy-one breast cancer treated women with arm lymphedema lasting more than 6 months, but less than 2 years, were matched to women similarly treated for breast cancer, but without lymphedema. Patients who exercised engaged in a wide range of sports such as jogging, swimming, tennis, golf, walking, cycling, physical training, and others. The conclusion was that even vigorous physical activity is unlikely to promote arm lymphedema. The research was based on response to a questionnaire, so the controls were not examined for early lymphedema. The matching factors included axillary node status, time after axillary dissection, and age. There were no statistically significant differences between the controls and the lymphedema patients as to whether or not they exercised. Földi criticized the paper, noting that a group of patients who suffered a sports injury, which could trigger lymphedema, was missing from the study. He also felt that 2 years was too short an observation time since lymphedema can develop 20 to 30 years after surgery.

Given the conflicting literature, the patient's exercise program should be individualized. It is important to draw a distinction among the various types of exercise. Active range of motion and stretching exercises hold little risk. Working out with light weights, generally 5 pounds and under, is less risky than vigorous arm exercises. Aerobic conditioning in moderation is beneficial for cardiovascular reconditioning. Rest periods between exercise sets are advisable. The patient should wear an elastic garment while performing land-based exercises.

MEASUREMENTS OF LYMPHEDEMA

There are no universally accepted standards for measuring lymphedema. This makes it difficult to compare epidemiologic and outcome studies. Some clinicians define lymphedema as the treated side being 2 or 2.5 cm larger; others believe a 3 cm to 4 cm difference is significant. There is also no agreement on what constitutes a significant volume difference.

Measurements are important to track changes during cancer therapy and to assess the effectiveness of lymphedema therapy. Circumferential measurements should be taken prior to cancer therapy and the limbs re-measured during return visits. Bilateral arm measurements are recorded to compensate for changes in weight, muscle mass, and fluid retention that can affect both arms. The weight should be recorded at each visit, since both the volume and tape measurements will fluctuate with changes in weight. Tape measurements are the most commonly used assessment tool. There is no standardized measuring template. Some clinics measure the limb at 4 cm intervals, some at 10 cm, and others divide the forearm and upper arm into thirds in addition to measuring the hand and wrist circumferences. The 10 cm and 4 cm methods give comparable results and are equally valid. The 4 cm method should be used in large limbs with numerous complex bulges and sulci.[68] Tape measurements are subject to error owing to variations in tape tension and the difficulty in measuring at the same point each time. The use of a Gulick anthropometric tape , which is attached to a spring tension device, will allow for consistent tension. Marking the skin and measuring at an identical distance from bony prominences improves the accuracy of tape measurements. Another option is to use a measuring board. Skin-fold calipers can be used to measure posterior axillary fold edema.

Limb volume can be measured directly by placing the arm in a volumeter and measuring the volume of the displaced water (Figure 35–8). A dowel rod is set at different depths so that most of the arm can be submerged with the hand resting on the dowel rod. Although reliable, the drawback of direct volumetry is the extra time it takes to fill and empty the volumeter. Hygiene is a concern, and direct volumetry cannot be used in patients with skin lesions or infections.[69] Limb volume can be calculated from a number of circumferential measurements. The limb is measured at 4 cm intervals, and each pair of measurements give the top and bottom of a truncated cone. The volume can be calculated by the equation:

$$\text{Volume}_{\text{limb}} = \Sigma x^2 + y^2 + xy / 3\Pi$$

where x is the circumference at one point and y is the circumference at a point 4 cm up the arm from x.[70] Casley-Smith found no significant difference between using 4 cm and 10 cm intervals. There are software programs available to calculate limb volume.[69]

Optoelectronic volumetry depends on the interruption of infrared light beams by the limb.[71] The principle is similar to computer assisted tomography but uses light instead of x-ray. The form of the distal extremity is not ideal for this type of measurement. The availability of optoelectronic volumetry is limited since the equipment is expensive.

Other methods to measure the limb, including tonometry and bioelectrical impedance, are not in wide use.

THERAPY

Complete Decongestive Therapy

Alexander Von Winiwarter described conservative therapy for lymphedema in 1892.[72] The regimen

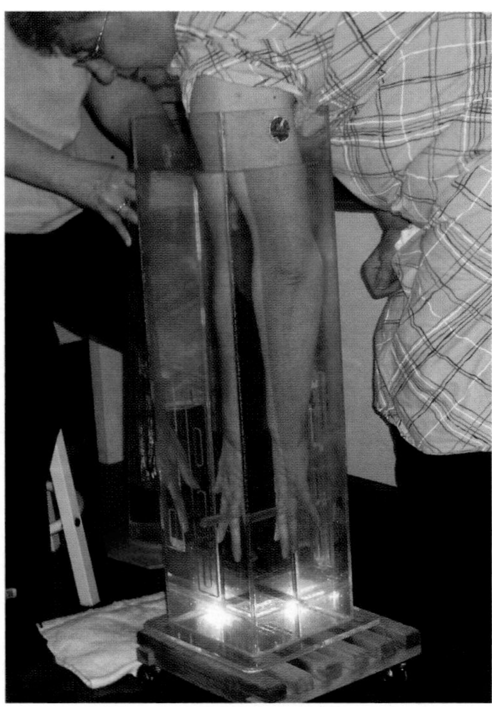

Figure 35–8. Direct volumetry.

included bed rest, elevation, bandaging, exercises, proximal to distal light pressure massage techniques, and skin care. The therapy regimen fell out of use. In the 1930s, Dr. Emil and Estrid Vodder presented their refinement of Winiwarter's techniques. Vodder used a light massage technique and manual lymphatic drainage to improve lymph flow.[73] These techniques were initially directed toward making normal lymphatics work better (eg, to reduce traumatic edema). During World War II, Vodder used massage to drain the lymphatics in patients with infection-related enlarged cervical nodes. Vodder's technique was refined by Asdonk in 1963. In 1969, Asdonk established the first school for manual lymph drainage in Germany with Emil and Astrid Vodder as instructors. The Vodders subsequently started their own school in Austria in the early 1970s. In the same decade, Földi developed and refined complete decongestive therapy and founded his own school of lymphology in Germany in 1981.

In the United States, Stillwell and others also noted that the coordinated application of long-recognized edema reduction measures produced better results than the casual application of one or two of the components.[74] These measures included elevation, massage, exercise, and elastic support. Stillwell mentioned firm kneading and centripetal manual massage to help mobilize edema fluid. The limb was worked in segments, beginning proximally and progressing distally. Differing from Vodder and others, he noted that massaging the distal parts first seemed to work as well. Pneumatic massage machines (pumps) were used in the initial mobilization of the fluid. A reduction of 30% or more of the swelling was noted by more than 50% of the patients whose treatment included the use of a pump. The use of an external elastic support was "the most important single part of the treatment program." The use of lymphatic drainage lay dormant until Földi, LeDuc, Casley-Smith, and others explained the rationale for this treatment in the 1970s. Földi advocated manual lymphatic massage, skin care, infection control, and compression bandaging.

Several circumstances have resulted in the increased availability of complete decongestive therapy in the United States. The founding of the National Lymphedema Network (NLN) by Saskia R.J. Thiadens, R.N. in 1988 increased public and professional awareness of lymphedema through the NLN newsletter, a biennial international lymphedema conference, and the NLN Web site, www.lymphnet.org. To satisfy a growing demand for lymphedema therapy, the number of comprehensive complete decongestive therapy training programs has grown since the late 1980s. Concern was expressed at a 1998 American Cancer Society Lymphedema Workshop that "there are no guidelines or certification to assure that specific treatments or treatment facilities meet state-of-the-art criteria."[e75] The Lymphology Association of North America (LANA), incorporated in 1999, established a voluntary North American certification board for lymphedema therapists and set minimum basic science and training eligibility requirements.

Lymphedema therapists represent several health care professions and are usually physical therapists, occupational therapists, massage therapists, and, occasionally, nurses and physicians.

Complete decongestive therapy (CDT) is a multimodality approach to reducing and controlling lymphedema. CDT is also effective for treating phlebolymphedema and lipedema. CDT is divided into

Phase I (Treatment) and Phase II (Maintenance) (Table 35–4).[76] There is no sharp demarcation between Phase I and Phase II; Phase I flows into Phase II.

CDT conforms to the Starling equilibrium. External compression and manual lymphatic drainage (MLD) increase the interstitial tissue pressure, and MLD also moves lymph fluid and excess protein. CDT is not used if the patient is unwilling or unable to follow through with bandaging and wearing a compression garment. Patients with mild non-progressive edema may be satisfied with no treatment or may prefer to wear a sleeve and forego the other components of CDT. The therapy program should be individualized to improve compliance and contain costs. Treatment frequently will depend on the severity and stage of the edema. Phase I lays the groundwork for a successful self-management program. A discussion of risk factors and the rationale for CDT improves compliance.

Table 35–4. PHASES OF COMPLETE DECONGESTIVE THERAPY

Phase I: Treatment
Patient education Meticulous skin and nail care Manual lymphatic drainage (MLD) 24-hour compression bandaging with non-elastic bandages Compression garment after the limb reduction stabilizes
Phase II: Maintenance
Compression garment Compression bandages or a rigid appliance at night in cases of moderate to severe lymphedema Lymphedema exercises in garment or bandages

Skin Care

Proper care is essential to maintain healthy skin and reduce the risk of bacterial and fungal infections.[77,78] This can be accomplished with meticulous hygiene, moisturization of the limb and trunk with emollients, and periodic inspection of the skin and adjacent trunk. Emollients moisturize and soothe dry, irritated skin. There are three emollient categories: bath oil, soap substitutes, and moisturizers. Fungal infections and lymphorrhea, skin complications, commonly seen in lower extremity lymphedema, are less common in upper extremity lymphedema. Skin sensitivity, even contact dermatitis, is common in upper extremity and chest wall lymphedema.

Compression garments and bandages may irritate the skin, and, rarely, patients will develop contact dermatitis owing to the dyes or latex in some of the fabrics. Prolonged use of compression bandages can cause miliaria (prickly heat), requiring a change in the treatment regimen and, at times, a topical steroid. Compression garments can cause focal areas of skin irritation, most commonly in the antecubital fossa, and will require the addition of an elbow cover.

Patients with pendulous breasts frequently develop intertriginous skin irritation and candidiasis. Nystatin cream, Miconazole 2% cream or lotion, or Clotrimazole 1% cream can be used to treat the fungal infection and a trunk support garment used to keep the skin folds separated

Elevation

Elevation reduces the swelling by reducing the venous pressure and is more effective in venous edema than lymphedema. There is no objective evidence that elevation improves the rate of drainage. Gravity drains the fluid to lower parts of the elevated limb into areas with better lymph drainage, for example, the trunk. Although elevation may reduce stage I lymphedema, as a practical matter elevation is generally used at night with the arm positioned at or above heart level on pillows or a foam wedge. By morning, patients frequently find their arm is no longer elevated.

MLD

The goal of MLD, also known as manual lymphatic treatment (MLT), is to increase the transport capacity of the lymph collectors, thus increasing protein absorption. The sequence and direction of the strokes stimulate lymphatic flow and drainage from congested areas. MLD is a gentle pressure technique used in stage I lymphedema because the superficial lymphatics are fragile. Greater mobilization pressure is used on fibrotic tissue, but skin redness and pain is avoided. MLD is effective only if there are some lymphatics left so that they can be activated.[79] MLD usually begins by stimulating lymph drainage within the normal, contralateral quadrant of the trunk to suck fluid across watershed pathways. Next, the congested trunk is massaged to move fluid along skin and subcutaneous collaterals. The rest of the limb is then cleared in a proximal to distal gradient. The sequence and direction of massage stimulates lymphangiomotorici activity and drainage from congested areas, thereby increasing the transport capacity of the lymph collectors. Protein absorption is increased. The gentle pushing and stretching strokes create a pumping action. Except in cases of mild stage I lymphedema, MLD is never used as a sole modality of treatment. MLD is contraindicated in the presence of cellulitis, radiation dermatitis, venous thrombosis, and directly over cancerous tissue. Földi addresses the issue of whether or not CDT causes metastases in cases of lymphedema appearing after cancer therapy or in the case of malignant lymphedema.[80] His answer is, "No." He notes that the biological properties of cancer cells and the condition of the immune system are the cause of metastasis, not external mechanical factors.

Compression Bandaging

Multilayered compression bandaging is an integral part of CDT. Compression bandages maintain the therapeutic results of manual lymph decongestive therapy. The concept of resting and working pressure is germane to understanding the action of the compression bandages (Figure 35–9). The resting pressure is the external force applied against the tissues when the limb is relaxed. The highest resting pressure is achieved with high-stretch bandages. A prolonged high pressure hinders refilling of the superficial vessels. Working pressure is a temporary pressure generated by contracting muscles pushing the tissue against the resisting bandages, compressing blood and lymph vessels. Working pressure is highest with rigid, low-stretch bandages, which, conversely, have the lowest resting pressure. Therefore, low-stretch bandages are preferred for multilayered compression bandaging. In accordance with the Law of Laplace, regions with bumps and curves, such as a bony prominence, will be subjected to more pressure. These areas require extra padding. Flattening out irregularly shaped areas will permit

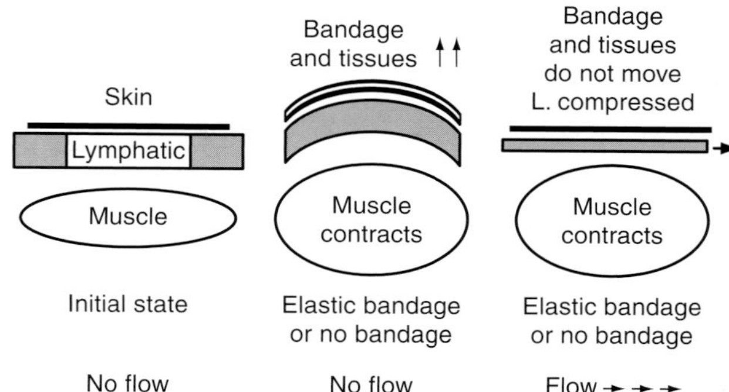

Figure 35–9. The importance of low-stretch bandages for pumping by lymphatics during muscle contraction. On the left is a relaxed muscle with lymphedema between it and the skin. In the center, the muscle has contracted but the compression garment is too elastic or non-existent. The subcutaneous tissue just moves away from the muscle; there is little compression and minimal lymphatic pumping. On the right, the muscle compresses the dilated lymphatics between it and a low-elastic compression garment or bandage. This makes the lymphatics pump, and the lymph flows on to the more proximal lymphatics. Adapted with permission from Casely-Smith JR.[72]

more effective gradient pressure. The proper application of compression bandages is important, or they will do more harm than good (Figure 35–10). Patients and caregivers need adequate training to safely apply the bandages at home.

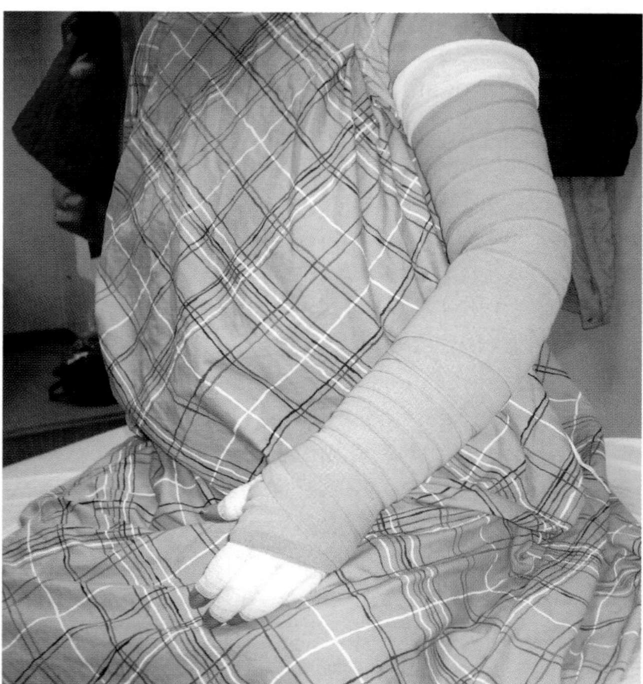

Figure 35–10. Multilayered compression bandaging with low-stretch bandages.

Compression Garments

Compression garments are the common denominator of edema therapy. A properly fitted garment can maintain the edema reduction achieved through decongestive therapy and compression bandaging. An ill-fitting garment can do more harm than good and increase edema. A compression garment should be fitted by an experienced lymphedema therapist or a certified fitter. Elastic sleeves are ready-fit or custom-fit. The ready-fit sleeves cost less and are generally sufficient for patients with mild to moderate lymphedema. Individuals with short, long, or bulky arms or with moderate to severe edema will need a custom-fit garment. Elastic garments are either circular or flat knit.[81] Originally, only natural rubber was used as an elastic material in compression garments. Although rubber has excellent elastic properties, it deteriorates under the effects of oil, sweat, chemicals, ointments, heat, light, and mechanical stress. Since the mid-1960s, synthetic elastic polyurethane has supplanted rubber yarns. The polyurethanes are more sensitive to hypochlorites and long-term exposure to moisture. Circular knit garments are produced in one piece and have no seam. Effective compression is determined by the strength of the interwoven threads and the manner in which they are interwoven, as well as the characteristic of the threads used in knitting. These garments are thinner and smoother than flat knit garments. However, in large arms, the circular knit garments can bind on skin-folds and over the elbow and wrist.

The basic advantage of flat knitting is that the width of the knitted fabric can be almost infinitely varied, and a garment of any desired size and shape can be manufactured. The flat knit garment has a seam and a coarser appearance and is usually custom fitted. The clinician should be familiar with the definition of compression classes. The distribution of pressure beneath the compression garment is determined by the Law of Laplace: $P = S/r$, where P = Pressure, S = Tension in the sleeve, and R = radius.

The sub-bandage pressure will be inversely proportional to the circumference of the limb. The pressure exerted by the compression sleeve decreases in a distal to proximal gradient, the greatest pressure being at the wrist. The pressure in the upper arm is 40 to 50% less than the pressure at the wrist.

There are four compression classes available to treat lymphedema and associated conditions.[82]Compression garments less than 20 mm Hg are not used to treat lymphedema but are used to treat mild benign postural edema, mild venous edema, or as anti-embolism stockings. The compression class (CCl) or compression range a is usually stamped inside the garments or on a label (eg, CCl 2). In North America, most manufacturers use the compression classes shown in (Table 35–5).

The success of compression therapy will depend on selecting the appropriate garment compression class. Lymph fluid will seek the path of least resistance, so a sleeve that is too tight will push fluid distally into the hand or proximally in the shoulder and adjacent trunk.

Garment Styles

Typically, a full arm sleeve and gauntlet are worn and, when necessary, a glove. The sleeve extends from the wrist to the upper arm but not into the axilla. Although the proximal band in most sleeves is circular, a custom-fit, flat-weave garment has an oblique band. At times, the proximal band of the sleeve will slip down, necessitating the use of a water soluble skin adhesive or a silicone band. Sleeves with shoulder flaps are available. These sleeves are anchored to the bra strap or by straps across the trunk. The advantage of the shoulder flap is the absence of a proximal elastic band. However, most patients prefer to avoid straps across the chest and back.

Compression gauntlets and gloves are available to control hand edema. Patients usually prefer detachable gauntlets and gloves, although one-piece arm and hand garments are available. The one-piece garment minimizes overlapping garment compression at the wrist. Gauntlets are effective if there is

Table 35–5. COMPRESSION CLASSES

International Standard	Indication
CCl 1 20–30 mm Hg	Prevention and mild to moderate arm lymphedema.
CCl 2 30–40 mm Hg	Moderate to severe arm lymphedema
CCl 3 40–50 mm Hg	Severe arm lymphedema
CCl 4 50–60 mm Hg	Severe lymphedema, rarely used for arms

mild proximal hand edema but little, if any, finger edema. Gloves are necessary if the fingers are edematous. Partial gloves, extending to the distal interphalengeal joints, are preferred to allow finger tip sensation. Dorsal hand edema can be difficult to control; foam pads can be placed over the dorsum of the hand for additional compression.

Chest wall and breast lymphedema are more difficult to control with compression garments. The brassiere should be wireless and with wide, padded straps. Sport bras have wider side panels and offer better chest wall compression. There are custom-fit, post-mastectomy supportive brassieres available. Some women prefer a camisole containing Lycra for chest wall support.

A variety of non-elastic containment appliances are available for nighttime compression. These are generally easier to slip into than the compression bandages. Most have a foam core and an elasticized jacket or use non-elastic straps tightened over a foam liner. Some patients have successfully used a section of elasticized tubular bandage to control mild arm or chest wall edema. This material is inexpensive and available in most therapy departments.

Lymphedema Exercises

Exercises are an integral component of the CDT program. The goal of exercise is to promote lymph flow, mobilize the joints, and strengthen the muscles. Patients participate in exercises during both the initial treatment phase and the maintenance phase. The exercises are performed while wearing a compression garment or bandages. The exercise program should be individualized. Lymphedema exercises are designed to follow a sequence. The first exercises empty the more central lymph reservoirs. The rest of the exercises make any surviving lymphatics work more efficiently. They help to mobilize joints and strengthen the limb. Posture exercises are important since many breast cancer patients have a round-shouldered, kyphotic posture that can impair shoulder range of motion and cause cervicobrachial pain. Exercise sets should be short and effective. A slow rhythm is preferred.

During the maintenance phase, exercise programs should be individualized. Light (5 pounds or less) upper extremity resistive exercises wearing a compression garment can be introduced. Some patients can tolerate higher resistance.

Exercise programs, such as yoga, Feldenkrais, Tai Chi, and aquatic therapy, can be incorporated into the lymphedema exercise program. Most patients can return to recreational sports such as swimming, cycling, and golf. McKenzie and Kalda found that participation in an upper-body exercise program caused no changes in arm circumference or arm volume in women with breast cancer therapy-related lymphedema.[83] The exercise programs may have to be modified to avoid extremity over-exertion and an increased lymphatic load.

Effectiveness of CDT

Studies to assess the effectiveness of CDT are quite varied in methodology and outcome. Badger and colleagues, while reviewing therapies to treat lymphedema, looked at randomized controlled clinical trials that tested physical therapies with a follow-up period of at least 6 months.[84] Only three studies were included, and none studied the same intervention. One trial of arm lymphedema patients looked at elastic support garments versus no treatment and had a high dropout rate, particularly in the control group. The authors concluded that wearing a compression sleeve is beneficial.

A bandage-plus-hosiery versus hosiery alone trial in both leg and arm lymphedema patients concluded that bandage-plus-hosiery resulted in almost twice the reduction of excess limb volume than hosiery alone over a 24-week period.

An MLD 12-month study of 42 participants randomized 22 patients to the MLD and sleeve group and 20 to the sleeve group alone.[85] Eight MLD sessions were followed by self-massage for the remainder of the 12-month trial. At the end of the trial, there was no significant difference in excess limb volume between the two groups. The authors concluded that MLD provided no extra benefit at any point during the trial and that improvements were attributable to the use of compression sleeves. Badger and colleagues, in their evaluation of this study, noted that the median excess volume at the start of the trial is reported as the absolute volume rather than as a percentage, so it is difficult to judge how serious the participants' edema was.[84] Földi criticized this study.[86] He noted that the "dubious practice" of self-massage is not a part of CDT. The first phase, which included MLD, was ended without any physical examination of the patients to define the extent of decongestion.

Another randomized crossover trial comparing sleeves with and without MLD found that the group who received MLD achieved a significantly higher reduction in arm volume, a reduction in edema in the posterior axillary fold, and a reduction in skin thickness measured by high-resolution ultrasonography.[87] Boris and colleagues reported on the effectiveness of lymphedema reduction after CDT.[88] Among 56 patients with lymphedema of one arm, lymphedema decreased by an average of 62.6% following 30 days of intensive CDT. Lymphedema declined during follow-up and reached maximum reduction of 97.3% at 18 months following treatment. At 36 months, the reduction averaged 63.8%. Upon completion of CDT, patients were instructed to wear a compression garment 24 hours a day and perform lymphedema exercises twice daily for 15 to 20 minutes. Individuals who were noncompliant maintained an average of 43% subsequent reduction, varying with the percentage of compliance. In patients who were 100% compliant, lymphedema reduction increased to 79%. Thus, CDT produced a rapid decrease in all stages of lymphedema. Compliant patients achieved better long-term results (Figure 35–11).

Pressotherapy (Pneumatic Massage)

During pressotherapy, the extremity is inserted into an inflatable appliance placed over a limb which is then intermittently filled with air by a pump, compressing the extremity. The pumps have an on/off, compression/decompression cycle. The original pumps had a one-cell appliance that distributed pressure equally over the limb. In the 1970s, sequential pneumatic pumps were developed. These pumps use a multi-cell, inflatable appliance ranging from 3 to 12 cells, depending on the pump design. The compression wave moves in a distal to proximal gradient. Some pumps are gradient pressure with at least a 10 mm Hg decrease in pressure between adjacent cells. These pumps are purported to improve lymph flow. In the United States, the use of pneumatic compression pumps increased after the founding of the Jobst Institute in 1950. The Jobst intermittent pneumatic compression pump and gradient pressure elastic garments became available in most therapy departments for edema therapy. Pump pressures as high as 110 mm Hg were used on an arm, avoiding pressure above the systolic blood pressure. No comparative studies have been published to determine the most effective pumping time, pressure levels, or kind of pump.[89]

Pump therapy, if used, must be supervised by a lymphologist or experienced lymphedema therapist to avoid complications. The pumps are believed to have little value in stage II or stage III lymphedema

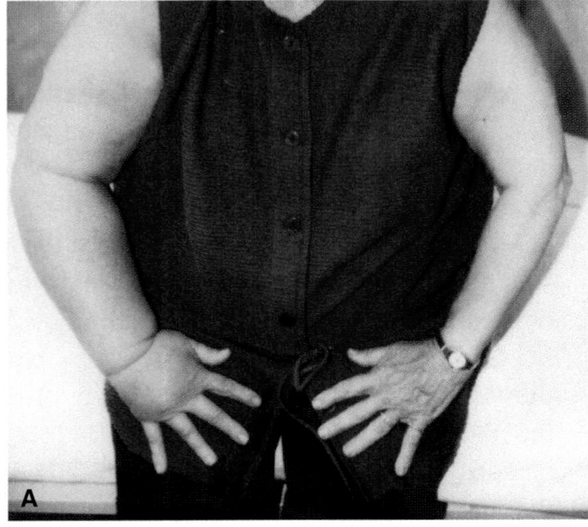

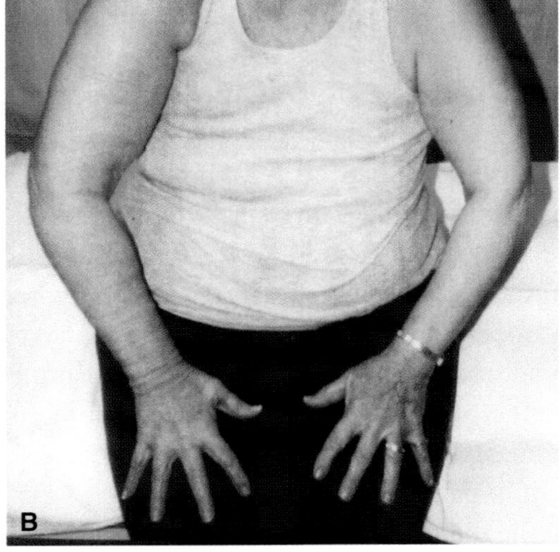

Figure 35–11. Complete decongestive therapy. *A*, Before; *B*, 2-months posttreatment.

because of the presence of scar and fibrous tissue.[90,91] Pressotherapy can enhance the resorption of fluid but rarely does it affect the resorption of protein. The pressure should not exceed 40 mm Hg.[92,93] Greater pressure will cause collapse of the superficial lymphatic vessels. Although pumps are promoted as easier to use than compression bandages, pumps are more expensive than the low-stretch bandages.

Patients must wear compression bandages or an elastic sleeve after pumping, or the edema fluid will soon return. Whereas some clinicians found pressotherapy effective, others warned of risks, such as pushing fluid into the adjacent trunk.[94,95] Schuchhardt and colleagues, after a review of literature, concluded that intermittent pneumatic compression is not suitable as an exclusive decongestive measure to treat chronic lymphedema.[96]

Medications

Diuretics. Diuretics have little effect on uncomplicated lymphedema.[89] They cause hemoconcentration but do not help in the transport of excess interstitial fluid protein. Patients on a diuretic for treatment of hypertension or other medical conditions find them ineffective in reducing upper extremity lymphedema. A trial of diuretics should be considered if there is a component of venous edema or if the patient is on medications that may cause fluid retention.

Benzopyrenes. Benzopyrenes include the coumarins and bioflavonoids. They increase the number of macrophages at the site of a high-protein edema, resulting in increased proteolysis.

A Mayo Clinic study reported lack of effect of coumarins in women with lymphedema.[97] A 6% hepatotoxicity rate has been reported. Coumarin is not Food and Drug Administration (FDA) approved and was banned in Australia owing to concern about the incidence of hepatotoxicity. Another randomized controlled crossover trial of oxerutins found reduced arm volume by a statistically significant, but clinically unimportant, amount (4%).[98]

Surgical Management

There is extensive scientific literature on the surgical management of primary and secondary lymphedema dating back at least a century. The operations fall into two categories: resection (debulking) and lymphatic drainage. Continued use of a compression garment is necessary after these operations.

Resection (Debulking)

An early debulking operation was the Charles procedure (1912) in which all of the swollen tissue down to the deep fascia or muscle is excised and the skin covered with free skin grafts.[99] It was designed for the treatment of filarial elephantiasis, and Kinmonth noted that it was of benefit to the minority of severe cases where the skin is too degraded for local flap operations. Kinmonth abandoned this procedure owing to poor results in the hand from destruction of superficial veins. Thompson (1962)[100] described excision of the subcutaneous tissue and implantation of a shaved flap of skin between the muscles and near the deep vessels so that physiologic drainage may be improved. Homan (1936)[101] used local flap grafts after excision.

Lymph Drainage

Several operations have been described to bypass obstructed lymph flow. These include procedures developed by Kondoleon (1912),[102] Handley (1908),[103] and Goldsmith (1967).[104] The Kondoleon operation was designed to improve lymph drainage by excising a window of deep fascia from the affected limb to allow skin lymphatics to reconnect with deep lymphatics. The fascial defects healed over so the procedure failed to achieve its goal; however, quantities of edematous tissue were removed, which produced improvement.[105] Handley inserted silk threads in the subcutaneous tissues to act as wicks in an attempt to carry lymph past an obstruction. Goldsmith used pedicle grafts of omentum drawn down into the base of the limb to act as a lymph bridge. The results were inconsistent, with only half of the patients improving. Nielubowicz and Olszewski developed a lymphovenous shunt by anastomosing a vein into a transected lymph node so that lymph may enter the blood below a level of obstruction. This procedure was used in patients with lower extremity primary lymphedema.[106]

O'Brien (1979) recommended the lymphovenous shunt, in which congested lymph vessels are connected to veins.[107] Földi and Clodius reported that relapses are inevitable because the lymph vessels are affected by lymphostatic lymphangiopathy, with lymphatic pressure falling below the venous pressure.[108]

Baumeister and colleagues described autologous lymph vessel transplantation.[109,110] In postmastectomy patients, a few normal lymph vessels are removed from the thigh and are transplanted into the proximal arm and cervical lymphatics. Most patients with arm edema experienced a decrease in volume measurements. Browse and colleagues noted that graft patency was followed by only short-term clinical improvement.[111] Merely one-third of the operated patients can dispense with compression treatment.

Only some of the operations designed to alleviate or cure lymphedema have been described, and many of these procedures were for lower extremity edema. The International Society of Lymphology Consensus Document states that "operations designed to alleviate peripheral lymphedema by enhancing lymph return have not as yet been accepted worldwide and often require combined physiotherapy after the procedure to maintain edema reduction."[112] One justification for surgery has been the failure of lymphedema therapy, but the older procedures were developed before complete decongestive therapy was available. Even now, the most important causes of unsuccessful therapy are a shortage of well-trained therapists and poor patient compliance.

The growth of breast and lymph node conservation surgery, as well as the increased availability of lymphedema treatment facilities, will make most of these procedures of historic interest in breast cancer–related lymphedema.

Liposuction

Brorson has used liposuction to achieve a reduction of arm swelling in conjunction with compression bandages or garments.[113] Liposuction removes subcutaneous fat. Chronic lymphedema in the arm appears to stimulate fat cell growth and fat accumulation, so there is more fat to suction out than in the normal arm. Thirty to 40 incisions are made, through which cannulas are inserted, to suction out the fat, which has only a minor effect on limb size, unless there is excess fat.[64,114] Liposuction causes rapid and considerable volume reduction but damages the lymphatic system. The edema will rapidly return if compression is not applied after surgery. Földi, citing a cadaver study, states that "following liposuction, as a consequence of the destruction of lymphatics, the extremity must be kept permanently under compression, day and night, for the rest of the patient's life.[115] Otherwise, edema will recur within a couple of days."[115]

BREAST EDEMA

There is an increased awareness of breast lymphedema after breast-conserving surgery.[35] Persistent edema is more likely to follow radiation of the breast. The breast becomes swollen, heavy, and larger than the normal breast. The inferior portion of the pendulous breast is usually more edematous than the upper breast. Women with large breasts are more at risk. One study reviewed breast edema in 57 breast cancer patients with breast-conserving therapy who had sentinel node biopsy (SNB) and 103 who underwent axillary clearance (AC) one year after surgery. On clinical examination, breast edema was present in 48% of patients in the AC positive group, 35% in the AC node negative group, and 23% in the SNB group. Breast lymphedema was less common in the SNB group. Ultrasonography revealed subcutaneous edema in the operated breast in 69 to 70% of the AC group and in 28% of the SNB group. Contributing factors to the development of breast edema are the extent of the axillary dissection, infection, radiation, and breast size.[116]

CDT is an effective treatment for breast lymphedema. Various support garments can help support the breast. These include sport bras, camisoles containing Lycra (elastine), and custom-fitted support vests. The heavy breast can cause discomfort, and skin irritation in the underside of the breast is common. Candida infections can be treated with topical nystatin, the imidazoles, or ciclopirox olamine. These agents will suppress both dermatophyte and candidal skin infections.

Manual lymphatic drainage has been beneficial to patients after breast reconstruction. Casas and DePoli reported a shorter recovery phase in cosmetic surgery patients receiving postoperative manual lymphatic drainage treatments.[117] Patients who received manual lymphatic drainage progressing to deep tissue release resolved swelling and fibrosis in 6 weeks to 3 months. Patients not receiving manual lymphatic drainage resolved swelling and fibrosis in 9 to 18 months.

ADVANCED CANCER AND PALLIATIVE TREATMENT

Breast cancer patients with metastatic disease may develop proximal venous obstruction from extrinsic compression by the tumor, leading to or aggravating arm edema. Malignant lymphedema is a form of lymphedema that has an acute onset and has a central to peripheral progression. The swelling can expand rapidly, the limb becoming tense and hard. The skin can be inflamed or develop a bluish tinge caused by the many dilated intradermal and subcutaneous veins. There can be pain and loss of joint motion. Metastatic disease may be present in the chest wall.

Tumor infiltration or irradiation can cause brachial plexopathy with resultant sensory impairment and muscular weakness. The loss of muscle contraction will increase the edema and make it more difficult to get into a compression garment.

The goals of palliative treatment are to control pain, improve function, and provide psychosocial support to the patient and family.

Complete decongestive therapy can decrease swelling, pain, and improve quality of life. Compression bandaging is the most effective modality for reducing edema. Even in severe cases of combined venous and lymphedema, the tissue will usually soften. When necessary, an occupational therapist can recommend modifications to activities of daily living to improve function. If the compression bandages reduce the edema, then an elastic sleeve can be fitted.

PSYCHOSOCIAL CONSIDERATIONS

As is true for any chronic illness, lymphedema can adversely affect an individual's quality of life. Quality of life is a subjective impression perceived by individuals about their own situation. Dimensions of quality of life include physical health, mental health, socioeconomic functioning, and general well-being.[118] Lymphedema affects one's body image and can lead to self-consciousness, embarrassment, anxiety, and even depression. Some individuals will refuse to wear compression garments outside of the home to avoid inquiries about their health. Other problems include increased arm weight, impaired arm strength and range of motion, pain, infection, and impairment of daily activities. Tobin and colleagues found that, matched with controls without swelling, 50 patients with lymphedema had greater psychological morbidity and difficulty in the vocational, domestic, social, and sexual domains.[119]

Passek and McDonald reviewed the literature on the psychosocial aspects of lymphedema in women.[119] They evaluated predictors of psychological and functional morbidity since not every individual who develops lymphedema will have problems adjusting.[120]

They concluded that women who have poor social support, pain, lymphedema in the dominant hand, and/or a passive and avoidant coping style report the highest level of disability. The clinician needs to be sensitive to a patient's concerns about developing and treating lymphedema. One of the biggest complaints heard by the lymphologist and therapist is that "the doctor did not tell me my arm could swell." Experience has taught that responses such as "Do not worry about it" or "You will not get lymphedema" leave the patient unsatisfied, angry, and anxious, and they frequently will seek out lymphedema professionals or support groups on their own. The web search engines provide patients with ready information and resources. The clinician should share basic information about lymphedema with the patient and, if necessary, refer the patient to a lymphedema professional or the National Lymphedema Network (<www.lymphnet.org>).

REFERENCES

1. Leduc A, Caplan I, Leduc O. Lymphatic drainage of the upper limb. European Journal of Lymphology 1993;4:11–7.
2. Guyton AC, Hall JE, editors. The microcirculation and the lymphatic system: capillary fluid exchange, interstitial fluid, and lymph flow. In: Textbook of medical physiology. 10th ed. Philadelphia: WB Saunders (Elsevier); 2000. p. 162–74.
3. Guyton AC, Hall JE, editors. The body fluid compartments: extracellular and intracellular fluids; interstitial fluid and

edema. In: Textbook of medical physiology. 10th ed. Philadelphia: WB Saunders (Elsevier); 2000. p.264–78.
4. Weissleder H, Schuchhardt C. Lymphedema of the arm following breast cancer therapy. In: Weissleder H, Schuchhardt C, editors. Lymphedema—diagnosis and therapy. Köln (Germany): Viavital Verlag; 2001. p. 191.
5. Koshima I, Kawada S, Moriguchi T, Kajiwara Y. Ultrastructural observations of lymphatic vessels in lymphedema in human extremities. Plast Reconstr Surg 1996;97:397–405.
6. Stanton AWB, Levick JR, Mortimer PS. Current puzzles presented by post-mastectomy breast cancer related lymphedema. Vasc Med 1996;1:213–25.
7. Stanton AWB, Svensson WE, Mellor RH, et al. Differences in lymph drainage between swollen and non-swollen regions in arms with breast-cancer-related lymphedema. Clin Sci 2001;101:131–40.
8. Bates DO, Levick JR, Mortimer PS. Starling pressure in the human arm and their alterations in postmastectomy oedema. J Physiol 1994;477(Pt 2):355–63.
9. Földi M. On the pathophysiology of arm lymphedema after treatment for breast cancer. [letter]. Lymphology 1995; 28:151–6.
10. Mortimer PS, Levick JR, Stanton AWB. [Reply to Dr. Földi's letter]. Lymphology 1995;28:156–8.
11. Mellor RH, Stanton AWB, Azabore P, et al. Enhanced cutaneous lymphatic network in the forearms of women with postmastectomy oedema. J Vasc Res 2000;37:501–12.
12. Larson D, Weinstein M, Goldberg I, et al. Edema of the arm as a function of the extent of axillary surgery in patients with stage I-II cancer of the breast treated by primary radiotherapy. Int J Radiat Oncol Biol Phys 1986;12:1575–82.
13. Boova RS, Bonanni R, Rosato FE. Patterns of axillary nodal involvement in breast cancer. Predictability of level one dissection. Ann Surg 1982;196:642–4.
14. Rosen PP, Lesser ML, Kinne DW, Beattie EJ. Discontinuous or "skip" metastases in breast carcinoma. Analysis of 1,228 axillary dissections. Ann Surg 1983;197:276–83.
15. Veronesi U, Rilke F, Luini A, et al. Distribution of axillary node metastases by level of invasion. An analysis of 539 cases. Cancer 1987;59:682–7.
16. Sener SF, Winchester DJ, Martz CH, et al. Lymphedema after sentinel lymphadenectomy for breast carcinoma. Cancer 2001;92:748–52.
17. Langer S, Guenther JM, Haigh PI, Difronzo LA. Lymphatic mapping improves staging and reduces morbidity in women undergoing total mastectomy for breast carcinoma. Am Surg 2004;70:881–5.
18. Blanchard DK, Donohue JH, Reynolds C, Grant CS. Relapse and morbidity in patients undergoing sentinel lymph node biopsy alone or with axillary dissection for breast cancer. Arch Surg 2003 138:482–7.
19. Sener SF, Winchester DJ, Brinkmann E, et al. Failure of sentinel lymph node mapping in patients with breast cancer. J Am Coll Surg 2004;198:732–6.
20. Kissin MW, Querci della Rovere G, Easton D, Westbury G. Risk of lymphoedema following the treatment of breast cancer. Br J Surg 1986;73:580–4.
21. van der Veen P, De Voogdt N, Lievens P, et al. Lymphedema development following breast cancer surgery with full axillary resection. Lymphology 2004;37:206–8.
22. Kasse AA, Diop M, Dieng M, et al. [Risk factors for lymphedema of the arm after mastectomy for breast cancer] [Fr] Dakar Med 1999;44:32–5.
23. Meric F, Buchholz TA, Mirza NQ, et al. Long-term complications associated with breast-conservation surgery and radiotherapy. Ann Surg Oncol 2002;9:543–9.
24. Meek AG. Breast radiotherapy and lymphedema. Cancer 1998;83:2788–97.
25. Schijven MP, Vingerhoets AJ, Rutten HJ, et al. Comparison of morbidity between axillary lymph node dissection and sentinel node biopsy. Eur J Surg Oncol 2003;29:341–50.
26. Halsted WS. Swelling of arm after operation for cancer of breast—elephantiasis chirurgica—its causes and prevention. Bull Johns Hopkins Hosp 1921;32:309–13.
27. Mozes M, Paysa Z, Karasik A, et al. The role of infection in post-mastectomy lymphedema. Surg Ann 1982;14:73–83.
28. Veal JR. Swelling of the arm following radical mastectomy: the role of the axillary vein in production of edema following radical removal of the breast. JAMA 1937;108:1236–45.
29. Hughes JH, Patel AR. Swelling of the arm following radical mastectomy. Br J Surg 1966;53:4–15.
30. Kinmonth JB. The lymphatics. London: Edward Arnold; 1982. p. 152.
31. Larson NE, Crampton AR. A surgical procedure for postmastectomy edema. Arch Surg 1973:106:475–81.
32. Svensson WE, Mortimer PS, Tohno E, Cosgrove DO. Colour doppler demonstrates venous flow abnormalities in breast cancer patients with chronic arm swelling [abstract]. Eur J Cancer 1994;30:657–60.
33. Martin KP, Földi E. Are hemodynamic factors important in arm lymphedema after treatment of breast cancer. Lymphology 1996;29:155–7.
34. International Society of Lymphology Consensus Document. The diagnosis and treatment of peripheral lymphedema. Lymphology 2003;36:84–91.
35. Browse N, Burnand KG, Mortimer PS, editors. Diseases of the lymphatics. London: Arnold; 2003. p. 235.
36. Földi M, Földi E. Physiology and pathophysiology of the lymphatic system. In: Földi M, Földi E, Kubik S, editors. Textbook of lymphology. München: Urban & Fischer; 2000. p. 274–5.
37. Rockson SG, Miller LT, Senie R, et al. Diagnosis and management of lymphedema. Cancer 1998;83(12 Suppl): 2882–5.
38. Stemmer R. Ein klinisches zeichen zur früh- und differentialdiagnose des lymphödems. Vasa 1976; 5:261–2.
39. Földi E. The treatment of lymphedema. Cancer 1998;83 (12 Suppl);2833–4.
40. Moskovitz AH, Anderson BO, Yeung RS, et al. Axillary web syndrome after axillary dissection. Am J Surg 2001;81: 434–9.
41. Simon MS, Cody R. Cellulitis after axillary lymph node dissection for carcinoma of the breast. Am J Med 1992;93: 543–8.
42. Hughes LL, Stybo T, Thorne W, et al. Cellulitis of the breast as complication of conserving radiation. Am J Clin Ortho 1997;20:338–41.
43. Benda K, Svestlova S. Incidence rate of recurrent erysipelas in our lymphedema patients. Lymphology 1994;27 (Suppl):519–22.

44. Ko DSC, Lerner R, Klose G, Cos M. Effective treatment of lymphedema of the extremities. Arch Surg 1998;133:452–8.
45. Carroll D, Rose K. Treatment leads to significant improvement: effect of conservative treatment in pain in lymphoedema. Prof Nurse 1992;8:32–6.
46. Twycross R. Pain in lymphoedema. In: Twycross R, Jenns K, Todd J, editors. Lymphoedema. Oxon (England): Radcliffe Medical Press Ltd; 2000.
47. Földi E, Földi M. Lymphostatic disease. In: Földi M, Földi E, Kubik S, editors. Textbook of lymphology. München (Germany): Urban & Fischer; 2001. p. 274–5.
48. Karlsson P, Holmberg E, Samuelsson A, et al. Soft tissue sarcoma after treatment for breast cancer – a Swedish population-based study. European Journal of Cancer 1998;34: 2068–75.
49. Taghian A, deVathaire F, Terrier P, et al, Long-term risk of sarcoma following radiation treatment for breast cancer. Int J Radiat Oncol Biol Phys 1991;21:361–7.
50. Steward NJ, Pritchard DS, Naseimento FG, Lang Y. Lymphangiosarcoma following mastectomy. Clin Orthopedics and Related Research. 1995;320:135–41.
51. Fineberg S, Rosen PP. Cutaneous angiosarcoma and atypical vascular lesions of the skin after radiation therapy for breast carcinoma. Am Clin Path 1994;102:757–63.
52. Sener SF, Milos S, Feldman J, et al. The spectrum of vascular lesions in the mammary skin, including angiosarcoma, after breast conservation treatment for breast cancer. J Am Coll Surg 2001;193:24–8.
53. Földi M. Are there enigmas concerning the pathophysiology of lymphedema after breast cancer treatment? National Lymphedema Network Newsletter 1998;10:1–4.
54. Földi E, Földi M, Clodius L. The lymphedema chaos: a lancet. Am Plast Surg 1989;22:505–15.
55. Treves N. An evaluation of the etiological factors of lymphedema following radical mastectomy: an analysis of 1,007 cases. Cancer 1957;10:444–59.
56. MacDonald I, Osman K. Post mastectomy lymphedema. Am J Surg 1955;90:281–6.
57. Werner RS, McCormick B, Petrek J, et al. Arm edema in conservatively managed breast cancer: obesity is a major predictive factor. Radiology 1991;180:177–84.
58. Harvie MN, Campbell IT, Baildam A, Howell A. Energy balance in early breast cancer patients receiving adjuvant chemotherapy. Breast Cancer Res Treat 2004;83:201–10.
59. Freedman RJ, Aziz N, Albanes D, et al. Weight and body composition changes during and after adjuvant chemotherapy in women with breast cancer. J Clin Endocrinol Metab 2004;89:2248–53.
60. Casley-Smith JR, Casley-Smith JR. Lymphedema initiated by aircraft flights. Aviat Space Environ Med 1996;67:52–6.
61. National Lymphedema Network . position papers – topic: air travel 1994. Available at: www.lymphnet.org (accessed Sept 13, 2005)
62. Elkins EC, Harrick JH, Grindly JH, et al. Effect of various procedures on the flow of lymph. Arch Phys Med Rehabil 1953;34:31–9.
63. Stillwell GK. Treatment of post-mastectomy lymphedema. Mod Treat 1969;6:396–412.
64. Browse N, Burnand KG, Mortimer PS, editors. Disease of the lymphatics. London: Arnold; 2003. p. 167–68, 237.
65. Harris SR, Niesen-Vertommen SL. Challenging the myth of exercise-induced lymphedema following breast cancer: a series of case reports. J Surg Oncol 2000;74:95–8.
66. Földi M, Földi E, Kubik S, editor. Textbook of lymphology. München: Urban & Fischer. 2003; p. 277–8.
67. Johansson K, Ohlsson K, Ingvar C, et al. Factors associated with the development of arm lymphedema following breast cancer treatment: a match pair case-controlled study. Lymphology 2002;35:59–71.
68. Latchford S, Casley-Smith JR. Estimating limb volumes and alterations in peripheral edema from circumferences measured at different intervals. Lymphology 1997;30: 161–4.
69. Casley-Smith JR, Casley-Smith JR, editors. Measuring and representing lymphedema. In: Modern treatment for lymphedema. 5th ed. Adelaide: Terrace Printing; 1997. p. 102–10.
70. Burnand KG, Mortimer P, Partsch H. Diagnosis and investigation of lymphoedema. In: Browse N, Burnand KG, Mortimer PS, editors. Diseases of the lymphatics. London: Arnold; 2003. p. 115–17.
71. Petlund CF. Volumetry of limbs. In: Olszewski WL, editor. Lymph stasis: pathophysiology, diagnosis and treatment. Boca Raton: CRC Press; 1991. p. 448–9.
72. Von Winiwater A. Chirurgischen krank heiten der Haut. In: Deuthsche Chirurgie. Stuttgart: Enke; 1892.
73. Vodder E. Le drainage lymphatique, une nouvelle méthode thérapeutique. Revue d'Hygiène individuelle Santé pour Tous Paris, 1936.
74 . Stillwell GK. Physical medicine in management of patients with postmastectomy lymphedema. JAMA 1959;171: 2285–91.
75. Walley DR, Augustine E, Saslow D, et al. Workgroup IV. Lymphedema treatement resources-professional education and availability of patient services. In: Petrek J, Pressman PI, Smith RA, editors. Results from a workshop on breast cancer treatment-related lymphedema and lymphedema resource guide. Cancer 1998; 83:2886–7.
76. Dicken SCK, Lerner R, Klose G, Cosini AB. Effective treatment of lymphedema of the extremities. Arch Surg 1998; 133:452–8.
77. Kelly, DG. A primer on lymphedema. Upper Saddle River (NJ): Prentice Hall; 2002.
78. Casley-Smith JR, Casley-Smith, JR. Modern treatment for lymphedema. 5th ed. Adelaide (Australia): Terrace Printing; 1997. p. 132.
79. Leduc O, Bourgeois P, Leduc A. Manual lymphatic drainage: scintigraphic demonstration of its efficacy on colloidal protein re-absorption. In: Partsh H, editor. Progress in lymphology. IX. Excerpta medica. Amsterdam: Elsevier; 1988.
80. Földi M, Földi E. Lymphedema. In: Földi M, Földi E, Kubik S, editors. Textbook of lymphology. München (Germany): Urban & Fischer; 2001. p. 283–4.
81. Weber G. Manufacture, characteristics, testing and care of medical compression hosiery. In: Hohlbaum GG, editor. The medical compression stocking. Stuttgart (Germany): Schattauer; 1989. p. 79–105.
82. Zuther J. Lymphedema Management. New York: Thieme; 2005. p. 114–20.
83. McKenzie DC, Kalda AL. Effect of upper extremity exercise

in secondary lymphedema in breast cancer patients: A pilot study. J Clin Oncol 2003;21:463–8.

84. Badger C, Preston N, Seers K, et al. Physical therapies for reducing and controlling. lymphoedema of the limbs. The Cochrane Library; 2004. Cochrane database of systemic reviews Ovid does not list a location.
85. Andersen C, Horis I, Erlandsen M, Andersen J. Treatment of breast-cancer–related lymphedema with or without manual lymphatic drainage—a randomized study. Acta Oncol 2000;39:399–405.
86. Földi M, Földi E, Kubik S, editors. Disease of the lymphatics. München: Urban & Fischer; 2003. p. 287.
87. Williams AF, Vadgama A, Franks P, Mortimer PS. A randomised controlled crossover study of manual lymphatic drainage therapy in women with breast cancer related lymphedema. Eur J Cancer Care 2002;11:254–61.
88. Boris M, Weindorf S, Lasinski B. Persistence of lymphedema reduction after non-invasive complex lymphedema therapy. Oncology 1997;11:99–109.
89. Harris SR, Hugi, MR Olivotto IA, Levine M. Clinical practice guidelines for the care and treatment of breast cancer: 11. Lymphedema. CMAJ 2001;164:191–205.
90. Lerner R. Complete decongestive physiotherapy and the Lerner Services Academy of Lymphatic Studies (The Lerner School). Cancer 1998;83(12 Suppl):2861–3.
91. Leduc O, Leduc A, Bourgeois P, Belgrado J. The physical treatment of upper limb edema. Cancer 1998;83(12 Suppl): 2835–9.
92. Eliska O, Eliskova M. Are peripheral lymphatics damaged by high pressure manual massage. Lymphology 1995;28: 21–30.
93. Földi, M. Massage and drainage to lymphatics [editorial]. Lymphology 1995;28:1–3.
94. Pappas CJ, O'Donnell T. Long-term results of compression treatment of lymphedema. J Vasc Surg 1992;16:555–64.
95. Casley-Smith JR, Casley-Smith JR, Lasinski B, Boris M. The dangers of pumps in lymphedema therapy. Lymphology 1996;29Suppl:232-4.
96. Schuchhardt C, Pritschow H, Weissleder H. Therapy I Concepts–pneumatic compression treatment In: Weissleder H, Schuchhardt C, editors. Lymphedema diagnosis and therapy. Koln: Viavital Verlag GmbH; 2001. p. 346–51.
97. Loprenzi CL, Kugler JW, Sloan JA, et al. Lack of effect of coumarins in women with lymphedema after treatment for breast cancer. N Eng J Med 1999;340:346–50.
98. Taylor JM, Rose KE, Twycross RG. A double blind clinical trial of hydroxyethylrutosides in obstructive arm oedema. Phlebology 1993;8Suppl:22–8.
99. Charles H. A system of treatment, Vol 3. Latham A, English TC, editors. London: Churchill; 1912.
100. Thompson N. Surgical treatment of chronic lymphoedema of the lower limb. Brit. Med. Journal 1962; 2:1566-9.
101. Homans J. Treatment of elephantiasis of legs. N Eng J Med 1936; 215:1099.
102. Kondoleon E. Die chirurgische behandlung der elephantiastichen oedeme. Münch.med. Wschr 1912;59:525,2726.
103. Handley WS. Lymphangioplasty. Lancet 1908;1:783–84.
104. Goldsmith HS, de los Santos R, Beattie EJ. Relief of chronic lymphoedema by omental transposition. Ann Surg 1967; 166:573–85.
105. Kinmonth JB. Operations for lymphedema of the lower limbs. In: The lymphatics. London: Edward Arnold Ltd.; 1982. p. 159–91.
106. Nielubowicz J, Olsewski W. Surgical lymphaticovenous shunts in patients with secondary lymphedema. Br J Surg 1968;55:440–2.
107. O'Brien BM, Shafiroff BB. Microlymphaticovenous and resectional surgery in obstructive lymphedema. World J Surg 1979;3:121–3.
108. Földi M, Földi E, Kubik S, editors. Textbook of lymphology. München: Urban & Fischer; 2003. p. 297.
109. Baumeister RG, Sinda S, Bohmert H, Moser E. A microsurgical method for reconstruction of interrupted lymphatic pathways: autologous lymph-vessel transplantation for treatment of lymphedemas. Scand J Plast Reconstr Surg 1986;20:141–6.
110. Baumeister RGH, Fink U, Tatsch K, Vick A. Microsurgical lymphatic grafting: first demonstration of patent grafts by indirect lymphography and long term follow-up studies. Lymphology 1994; 27(Suppl):787–89.
111. Browse N, Burnand KG, Mortimer PS, editors. Diseases of the lymphatics. London: Arnold; 2003. p. 195–6.
112. The diagnosis and treatment of lymphedema. International Society of Lymphology Consensus Document. Lymphology 2003;36:89–90.
113. Brorson H. Liposuction gives complete reduction of chronic large arm lymphedema after breast cancer. Acta Oncol 2000;39:407–20.
114. Weissleder H, Schuchhardt C, Gsell F. Liposuction. In: Weissleder H, Schuchhardt C, editors. Lymphedema: diagnosis & therapy. Köln (Germany): Viavital Verlag; 2001. p. 385–400.
115. Földi M, Földi E, Kubik S, editors. Text of lymphology. München (Germany). Urban & Fischer; 2003. p. 296.
116. Rönka RH, Pamilo MS, Von Smitten KA, Leideruis MH. Breast lymphedema after breast conserving surgery. Acta Oncol 2004;43:551–7.
117. Casas L., DePoli P. Manual lymphatic drainage therapy: an integral component of post-operative care in plastic surgery patients. Proceedings of the American Society of Lymphology Conference: 1999 Aug; Chicago.
118. Woods M. Psychological aspects of lymphoedema. In: Twycross R, Jenns K, Todd J, editors. Lymphoedema. Oxon (England): Radcliffe Medical Press Ltd; 2000. p. 90–6.
119. Tobin MB, Lacy HJ, Meyer L, Mortimer PS. The psychological morbidity of breast cancer-related arm swelling. Psychological morbidity of lymphoedema. Cancer, 1993; 72:3248–52.
120. Passek SD, McDonald MV. Psychosocial aspects of upper extremity lymphedema in women treated for breast carcinoma. Cancer 1998;83(12 Suppl):2817–20.

36

Surveillance Strategies for Breast Cancer Survivors

LAURA P. MCGARTLAND
WILLIAM J. GRADISHAR

Breast cancer is the most commonly diagnosed malignancy in women. In 2004, it was estimated that there were 217,440 new cases of breast cancer diagnosed, with the vast majority of these cases (215,990) occurring in women.[1] The number of deaths from breast cancer in 2004 was estimated to be 40,580. Changes in both the incidence of invasive breast cancer and survival rates have led to an increased prevalence of patients considered at risk for breast cancer recurrence.

A relatively stable incidence of invasive breast cancers was observed between 1973 and 1980, with an increase then of 3.7% per year between 1980 and 1987, and a smaller increase of 0.4% per year from 1987 and 2001.[2] This increase reflects a number of factors, including changing reproductive patterns, such as delayed childbearing and reduced parity, as well as the well-accepted mammography screening program.[3]

Survival rates have also improved, with an overall improvement of 13% since the mid-1970s to a 2.3% decline in mortality between 1990 and 2001. These gains can be attributed to early detection with screening mammography and the improvement in adjuvant therapy, with increased use of hormonal agents and adjuvant chemotherapy.[2] The overall 5-year survival for breast cancer is now 85%, with a 15-year survival of 61%.

These increases in incidence and survival translate into an estimated 2 million breast cancer survivors in the United States. Therefore, issues of surveillance and primary care for this population have become increasingly important.[4] Surveillance of breast cancer survivors addresses myriad issues, from early detection of recurrence, both locoregional and systemic, to diagnosing second primary breast cancers, to screening for long-term adverse effects of therapy.

RECURRENCE RISK

Breast cancer recurrence occurs both locoregionally and systemically. Women with a personal history of breast cancer are also at increased risk of malignancy in the contralateral breast. The risk of a second primary breast cancer in the contralateral breast is estimated to be approximately 0.5 to 1.0% per year. The risk of recurrence after primary breast cancer treatment does decline over time, but women should certainly be considered at risk for recurrent disease throughout their lifetime.

Patients with early-stage disease maximally treated for curative intent still have a significant chance of relapse, from 10 to 20% for stage I disease and 40 to 50% for stage II.[5] A total of 3,585 patients who had been enrolled in 7 different trials conducted by the Eastern Cooperative Oncology Group (ECOG) of adjuvant therapy were evaluated for rates of recurrence.[6] The patient population included both premenopausal and postmenopausal women, and the majority of patients had lymph node-positive disease. The total number of patients diagnosed with recurrence was 1,625, which was 45% of the analyzed population.

Peak recurrence for all patients analyzed was greatest in the first 2 years following surgery and then decreased consistently between 2 and 5 years. Hazards of recurrence, did persist, at approximately 4.7% per year for years 5 through 8 and 3.4% in years 8 through 12. (Figure 36–1) The hazard of recurrence did not reach zero by year 12. Analysis of estrogen receptor status revealed an ongoing hazard of recurrence for estrogen receptor negative as well as estrogen receptor positive patients, although the patterns of recurrence differed. Overall, the hazard of recurrence was higher in the estrogen receptor negative population, primarily accounted for by their increased recurrence hazard in the first 5 years compared with estrogen receptor positive patients. (Figure 36–2). These data contribute to the idea that surveillance for recurrent disease or a new primary breast cancer should be frequent in the first 5 years following primary therapy, when recurrence rates are expected to be highest. This analysis also suggests that there is a continuous, albeit declining, risk of breast cancer recurrence many years after primary therapy, thus reinforcing the importance of continued surveillance in breast cancer survivors.[3]

What makes an effective surveillance program, both from a cost-benefit viewpoint and from a survival and quality-of-life perspective, has been the subject of a number of retrospective and at least two large prospective, randomized trials. Follow-up programs have been developed and evaluated, with the primary goals of early detection of breast cancer recurrence, generally at an asymptomatic stage. It is important not just to detect recurrent disease but to detect it at a stage where curative intent may be possible, with an impact on overall survival.[5] The evaluation of follow-up programs involves determining the efficacy of a number of clinical modalities, from history and physical examination to imaging and laboratory studies.

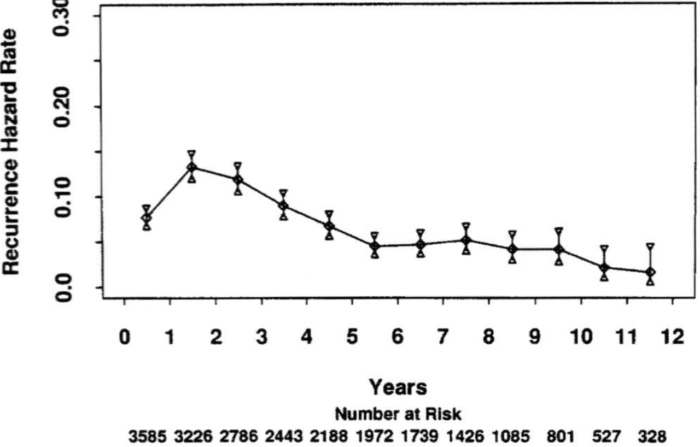

Figure 36–1. Annual hazard of recurrence for 3,585 patients entered on seven ECOG studies. The median follow up was 8.1 years. Reproduced with permission from Saphner et al.[6]

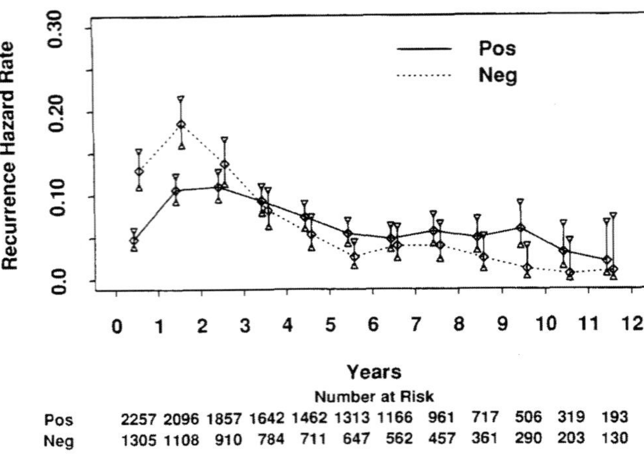

Figure 36–2. Annual hazard of recurrence of 3,562 patients separated by ER status. The mean follow up times for ER-positive and ER-negative patients were 8.1 and 8.0 years, respectively. Reproduced with permission from Saphner et al.[6]

History and Physical Examination

The value of the history and physical examination in the follow-up of breast cancer patients who have completed primary therapy has been supported in a number of studies.[7–9] A total of 857 patients who had entered two ECOG adjuvant trials were evaluated in a retrospective analysis of the earliest indicators of recurrent disease.[8] ECOG studies 5177 and 6177 were both trials of adjuvant therapy following radical or modified radical mastectomy in patients with positive lymph nodes, evaluating different chemotherapeutic regimens in premenopausal and postmenopausal women, respectively.

After a median duration of follow-up of 36 months (range, 5 to 56 months), 208 recurrences were diagnosed. Seventy-four relapses were diagnosed in the first year, 95 in the second year, and the remainder in year 3. Of these relapses, 36% were diagnosed based on reported symptoms, and 18.3% were found by patient self-examination. An additional 19.4% of relapses were discovered by physician physical examination, bringing the total to 73.7% of all relapses detected clinically.

Another retrospective analysis of 1,230 patients treated for cure of invasive breast cancer observed 248 cases of recurrent disease.[10] Of all recurrences, 36% were discovered in an asymptomatic patient at the time of a scheduled physician follow-up by examination, laboratory studies, or chest radiography. Recurrence in bone was the most common (28%), followed by local recurrence (19%), pulmonary (16%), and visceral (5.2%).

There was a detectable difference in median survival in those patients with asymptomatic compared with symptomatic recurrence (29 months versus 17 months; $p = .0017$). Although a difference in median survival was detected, and thus appears to support the value of regularly scheduled follow-up, this advantage may be only a reflection of lead time bias or simply an awareness of the diagnosis of recurrent disease for a longer period of time, but there is no true difference in overall survival. This is a bias that often hinders the interpretation of retrospective studies.

In this study, it was not clear if recurrence was discovered by history and physical examination or by laboratory studies and imaging ordered on an asymptomatic patient. This study did reflect the importance of history; while 36% of patients were asymptomatic at the time of diagnosed recurrence, more than 65% experienced symptoms prompting investigations. As the overwhelming number of relapses will be diagnosed based on patient symptoms or physician examination, it is clear that patient education about symptoms of recurrence and scheduled physician follow-up with thorough physical examination form the foundation of an effective breast cancer surveillance program (Table 36–1). Patients should be aware that new symptoms of potential recurrence should prompt contact with their physician, even in the interval between scheduled follow-up.

Table 36–1. SIGNS AND SYMPTOMS CONSISTENT WITH BREAST CANCER RELAPSE

Locoregional Recurrence
Mass in the ipsilateral breast following breast conserving therapy
Mass in the chest wall after mastectomy
Nipple discharge in the treated breast following breast conserving therapy
Rash localized to the treated breast or chest wall
Axillary, supraclavicular, infraclavicular, or cervical lymph node enlargement
Systemic Recurrence
Skeletal relapse – localized, progressive bone pain, or tenderness
Pulmonary metastasis – pleuritic chest pain, cough, dyspnea
Liver relapse – right upper quadrant discomfort, fullness, or pain; weight loss; anorexia
CNS metastasis – persistent headache, mental status changes, new onset seizure, focal motor sensory loss, bladder or bowel dysfunction

CNS = central nervous system.

Imaging in Surveillance

A number of imaging studies can be employed in the follow-up of breast cancer patients. As techniques of imaging evolve, questions about their use in the early detection of recurrence continue to arise. There are some data available for the use of traditional imaging, such as chest radiography, and emerging results on newer modalities, such as positron emission tomography scans.

Pulmonary metastases are a common site of disease recurrence. Thus, there has been interest in chest radiography as a means of early detection of recurrent disease. After locoregional and bone recurrence, intrathoracic disease is the most common pattern of recurrent breast cancer. In a study of 401 patients with first recurrence of breast cancer, isolated pulmonary metastases were detected in 8%.[11] Pulmonary disease was more often part of multiple systemic metastases, with nearly 40% of patients with metastatic disease having pulmonary involvement.

The value, in terms of overall survival outcome and cost-benefit ratio, of incorporating scheduled chest radiography into routine follow-up was evaluated in 280 patients treated for stage II breast cancer.[12] Chest radiographies were performed at 6 and 12 months in the first year following treatment and then yearly thereafter, to 6 years of follow-up. Of the 280 patients, 17 patients (6.0%) had evidence of asymptomatic metastatic disease on scheduled imaging studies. Symptomatic pulmonary metastatic disease was diagnosed in 26 patients (9.0%) between the scheduled yearly chest radiography.

Although this was a small population of patients, there was no difference in median survival in those patients with disease found in the asymptomatic stage at scheduled follow-up compared with those presenting with symptoms ($p = .26$).

Another small prospective study evaluated scheduled chest radiographies as well as bone scans in the follow-up of breast cancer patients. This study involved 241 women who had undergone modified radical mastectomy and had findings of axillary node involvement. They were part of a prospective, randomized trial of an adjuvant chemotherapy protocol. Serial chest radiographies and bone scans were performed in the first 2 years of follow-up after primary therapy. Chest radiography detected an asymptomatic recurrence in only 3% of the evaluated patients.[13]

A significant proportion of recurrent disease manifests as skeletal metastases, with anywhere from 30 to 60% of patients recurring with bone-only disease.[5] A retrospective analysis was undertaken of 2,697 patients entered onto the National Surgical Adjuvant Breast and Bowel Project (NSABP) B-09 protocol, which required scheduled bone scans every 6 months for 3 years after mastectomy and then annually thereafter.[14] This analysis found that 163 patients (6.0%) had skeletal-only metastases as the site of first recurrence, with 207 (7.6%) having skeletal and other sites simultaneously. A number of nonscheduled scans were performed in the interval between those required to follow up on symptoms, physical findings, or laboratory tests. A total of 7,984 bone scans were performed, with only 52 (0.6%) of these detecting metastatic skeletal lesions in an asymptomatic patient, thus making routine bone scans in follow-up likely not worthwhile from a cost-benefit analysis. Of clinical importance is the lack of evidence that treating asymptomatic patients found to have skeletal metastases results in improved survival. NSABP trials have changed surveillance protocols to require bone scans only as clinically indicated.

RANDOMIZED TRIALS OF FOLLOW-UP PROGRAMS

A number of randomized trials have been designed to evaluate symptom-driven compared with "intensive" follow-up strategies.[15,16] An Italian multicenter study enrolled 1,243 pre- and postmenopausal patients who had been treated for stages I, II, and III unilateral breast cancers.[15] The patients were randomized to an "intensive" or clinical follow-up strategy after completion of treatment for histologically confirmed invasive, but not metastatic, breast cancer. The "intensive" follow-up protocol involved a history and physical examination every 3 months for the first 2 years and then every 6 months the following 3 years, a bone scan and chest radiography every 6 months, and annual mammography. The clinical follow-up scheme consisted of the same schedule for history, physical examination, and mammography. Other diagnostic tests were used only if deemed necessary, to address signs or symptoms. The planned end point of this study was overall survival.

A total of 393 recurrences were observed between the two groups. There was a statistically significant increase in relapse-free survival in the intensive follow-up group. However, there was no difference in overall survival at 5 years between the "intensive" and symptom-driven follow-up regimens (18.6% versus 19.5%, respectively) despite earlier detection of recurrence in the "intensive" follow-up group.

Another multicenter study evaluated two similar follow-up regimens and focused on overall survival as well as health-related quality-of-life outcomes.[16] A total of 1,320 women who had been treated for stage I, II, or III breast cancer were randomized to an "intensive" or clinical follow-up program. As in the previous randomized study, the "intensive" program consisted of history, physical examination, bone scan, and chest radiography at predefined intervals, as well as laboratory studies (not defined by the authors) and liver ultrasonography. The control regimen was a physician visit with history and physical examination at the same interval as the "intensive" group. Both follow-up regimens included yearly mammography.

At a median follow-up of 71 months, there was no difference in overall survival between the two groups. Patients had been stratified initially according to nodal status, and no statistical difference was seen in survival of node-positive versus node-negative women based on the follow-up regimen. Of equal importance was the evaluation of health-related quality of life. Although patients often, and not surprisingly, express a preference for a more intensive follow-up regimen, this study found that health-related quality of life was not affected by the type of program used.

One well-designed randomized study has suggested that follow-up care of early-stage breast cancer patients may be effectively administered in the primary care setting as opposed to specialist-centered surveillance.[17] In this trial, 296 patients were randomized to either usual hospital follow-up in specialty clinics or to follow-up by their primary care physician. Women with stage I disease represented 45.6% of the enrolled patients, whereas 50.3% of patients had stage II disease and the remaining 4% had stage III disease. All patients had completed primary treatment at least 3 months prior to enrollment and had no evidence of distant metastases. Patients under surveillance in the primary care setting followed the same frequency of physician visits as those patients in the specialist clinics. There was no delay in time to diagnosis of recurrence in the two groups and, again, most recurrences were detected by patients through symptoms or self-examination, prompting a physician evaluation in the interval between scheduled visits.

GUIDELINES

To develop its breast cancer surveillance guidelines, the American Society of Clinical Oncology (ASCO) reviewed the literature to formulate an evidence-based approach to follow-up after primary breast cancer (Table 36–2).[18,19] The evidence for each recommendation was based on an assessment of the level of evidence and a grading of the available evidence, following a guidelines process established by the Canadian Medical Association (Table 36–3).[20] The most recent update of the ASCO guidelines, published in 1999, continues to recommend surveillance with history and physical examination every 3 to 6 months for the first 3 years after primary treatment, followed by every 6 to 12 months for the next 2 years, and then annually thereafter.[19] The frequency of recommended visits is based on the knowledge that the highest risk of recurrence occurs in the first 5 years, although the optimal interval of visits has not been established in a randomized clinical trial.[5]

Mammography also plays an important role in the ASCO guidelines, to be performed 6 months after irradiation in those women who have had breast-conserving treatment, and annually thereafter. There has not been a randomized trial evaluating whether mammography impacts disease stage at discovery or overall survival after diagnosis of a second breast primary cancer. However, women who have been treated for invasive breast cancer have a clear risk of a second breast cancer above that of the general population, estimated to be between a three- to fivefold increased risk.[21] Randomized trials have

Table 36–2. AMERICAN SOCIETY OF CLINICAL ONCOLOGY RECOMMENDATIONS FOR FOLLOW-UP OF BREAST CANCER PATIENTS AFTER PRIMARY THERAPY

Recommended Procedure	Frequency	Level of Evidence*
History and physical examination	Every 3–6 months for 3 years, then every 6–12 months for next 2 years, then annually	IIIb, except consensus
Mammography	Annually	
Contralateral		Ia
Ipsilateral		IVc
Breast self-examination	Monthly	IIId, except consensus
Not Recommended (unless indicated by history and physical examination)		
Complete blood count, chemistry studies		Ia
Tumor markers (CA 15-3, CEA)		III, except consensus
Chest radiography		Ia
Bone scans		Ia
CT scans		Vd

CEA = carcinoembryonic antigen; CT = computed tomography.
*See Table 36–3 for description
Adapted from American Society of Clinical Oncology.[19]

Table 36–3. TYPE AND GRADING OF EVIDENCE FOR RECOMMENDATIONS

Level	Type of Evidence for Recommendation
I	Evidence obtained from meta-analysis of multiple well-designed controlled studies; randomized trials with low false-positive and low false-negative errors (high power)
II	Evidence obtained from at least one well-designed experimental study; randomized trials with high false-positive and/or false-negative errors (low power)
III	Evidence obtained from well-designed quasi-experimental studies, such as nonrandomized, controlled, single-group, pre-past, cohort, time, or matched case-control series
IV	Evidence from well-designed nonexperimental studies, such as comparative and correlation descriptive and case studies
V	Evidence from case reports and clinical examples
Category	**Grade of Evidence**
A	There is evidence of type I or consistent findings from multiple studies of types II, III, or IV
B	There is evidence of types II, III, or IV and findings are generally consistent
C	There is evidence of types II, III, or IV but findings are inconsistent
D	There is little or no systematic empirical evidence
NG	Grade not given

demonstrated that mammography does reduce breast cancer mortality in women over age 50 years at average risk. Therefore, inclusion of mammography to promote early detection of a second primary breast cancer in high-risk women is considered a reasonable recommendation.[3]

Monthly breast self-examination is recognized as a prudent recommendation as well. Based on the available evidence, ASCO guidelines state that there is insufficient evidence to recommend routine laboratory studies, chest radiography, bone scan, ultrasonography, or computed tomography in breast cancer surveillance, but that the decision to obtain these tests should be driven by a patient's history and physical examination. Guidelines are recommendations and certainly should be tailored based on the clinical judgment of the physician and the individual patient's circumstances.

ASCO has also specifically addressed the use of tumor markers in routine surveillance of early-stage breast cancer patients. CA 15-3, CA 27-29, and carcinoembryonic antigen (CEA) are three serum markers associated with breast cancer, and they rise in accordance with increasing disease burden.[22,23] CA 27-29 and CA 15-3 are tumor-associated antigens that are products of the *MUC1* gene.[24] This gene has been cloned from a number of cell lines, including breast carcinoma. The detection of the *MUC1* gene product (the CA 27-29 antigen) is most sensitive in the metastatic stage of breast cancer. The question is not whether the quantitative rise in tumor marker correlates with increasing stage of disease, but rather whether early detection of this rise, and therefore early detection of recurrent disease, translates into a clinical benefit.

In a prospective trial of 166 patients who had completed therapy for stages II and III breast cancers, serial CA 27-29 levels were measured.[25] The recurrence rate in these 166 patients was 15.7%, and the CA 27-29 assay demonstrated a sensitivity of 57.7% and specificity of 97.9%. The positive and negative predictive values were 83% and 92.5%, respectively. The study found that the measurement of the tumor marker was useful in detecting both locoregional and systemic recurrence, and was elevated an average of 5.3 months prior to the appearance of symptoms or detection of recurrence by other tests. However, this study was not designed to evaluate a survival outcome, disease-free survival, or quality-of-life difference made by the earlier detection of the recurrent disease, and there has not been a demonstrated impact on these important clinical outcomes. With this information, and the lack of a clear clinical benefit, ASCO does not recommend the routine use of CA 27-29, or other tumor markers, in surveillance of recurrent disease.

The coordination of care for the breast cancer survivor is also addressed in the ASCO guidelines. The 1999 update of the ASCO breast cancer surveillance guidelines acknowledged that in the previously discussed well-designed, randomized trial conducted by Grunfeld and colleagues, the women assigned to follow-up in the primary care setting did not experience a delay in diagnosis of recurrence, increased anxiety, or deterioration in health-related quality of life.[17,19] However, the recommendation maintains that breast cancer patients have a right to indefinite continued treatment by an oncologist after their diagnosis and initial therapy, as this question of surveillance by the primary care physician as opposed to a specialist has not been otherwise rigorously evaluated.[19]

The National Comprehensive Cancer Network (NCCN) also published clinical practice guidelines in oncology.[26] Based on the available evidence on surveillance, these guidelines also emphasize the importance of history and physical examination, although at slightly different intervals than suggested by the ASCO. The NCCN recommends physician follow-up with history and physical examination every 4 to 6 months for the first 5 years after primary therapy, and then annually. Mammography is recommended annually, starting 6 months after irradiation in women who have undergone breast-conserving therapy. The NCCN does not recommend routine laboratory studies (specifically liver function tests and alkaline phosphatase), tumor markers, or bone scans in an asymptomatic patient, based on the consensus that monitoring of these studies in an asymptomatic patient offers no survival advantage.

Although the guidelines encourage history and physical examination as the foundation of surveillance, and many studies have reinforced these modalities as the primary detectors of recurrence, patients may not always be aware of the important role that these strategies play in their follow-up.[8,15,16] In a survey of 102 patients with breast cancer, both localized and metastatic, most patients expressed a desire to have a physical examination at each follow-up visit and felt it was important for their physician to ask about pain at each visit as well.[27] Despite their desire for physical examination and symptom-directed questions, only approximately one-third of patients felt that history contributed to the detection of recurrent disease, although physical examination was felt to be valuable by nearly two-thirds of patients interviewed. Laboratory studies, chest radiographies, and routine scans were believed to be much more valuable than history in recurrence detection. Once recurrence was detected, 92% of patients believed that their long-term outlook was positively affected by early detection. Despite these perceptions, the data do not support the conclusion that early detection of recurrent disease positively impacts overall survival.

Surveillance programs for recurrent disease in a patient treated for invasive breast cancer should focus on patient education and scheduled physician visits, more frequently in the first 5 years, when the risk of relapse is highest. Data do not yet support that "intensive" surveillance programs, involving scheduled laboratory studies, routine nonsymptom-driven imaging studies, and the measurement of serial tumor markers, improve the overall survival outcome of women who experience disease recurrence. As salvage therapies for recurrent disease continue to evolve and improve, it is hoped that eventually earlier detection will translate into a survival advantage.

REFERENCES

1. Jemal A, Tiwari RC, Murray T, et al. Cancer statistics, 2004. CA Cancer J Clin 2004;54:8–29.
2. Jemal A, Clegg LX, Ward E, et al. Annual report to the nation on the status of cancer, 1975–2001, with a special feature regarding survival. Cancer 2004;101:3–27.
3. Emens LA, Davidson NE. The follow-up of breast cancer. Semin Oncol 2003;30:338–48.
4. Burstein HJ, Winer EP. Primary care for survivors of breast cancer. N Engl J Med 2000;343:1086–94.
5. Tomiak E, Piccart M. Routine follow-up of patients after primary therapy for early breast cancer: changing concepts and challenges for the future. Ann Oncol 1993;4:199–204.
6. Saphner T, Tormey DC, Gray R. Annual hazard rates of recurrence for breast cancer after primary therapy. J Clin Oncol 1996;14:2738–46.
7. Schapira DV, Urban N. A minimalist policy for breast cancer surveillance. JAMA 1991;265:380–2.
8. Pandya KJ, McFadden ET, Kalish LA, et al. A retrospective study of earliest indicators of recurrence in patients on Eastern Cooperative Oncology Group adjuvant chemotherapy trials for breast cancer. Cancer 1985;55:202–5.
9. Hannisdal E, Gundersen S, Kvaloy S, et al. Follow-up of breast cancer patients stage I–II: a baseline strategy. Eur J Cancer 1993;29A:992–7.
10. Tomin R, Donegan WL. Screening for recurrent breast cancer—its effectiveness and prognostic value. J Clin Oncol 1987;5:62–7.
11. Kamby C, Vejborg I, Kristensen B, et al. Metastatic pattern in recurrent breast cancer. Special reference to intrathoracic recurrences. Cancer 1988;62:2226–33.
12. Logager VB, Vestergaard A, Herrstedt J, et al. The limited value of routine chest x-ray in the follow-up of stage II breast cancer. Eur J Cancer 1990;26:553–5.

13. Chaudary MM, Maisey MN, Shaw PJ. Sequential bone scans and chest radiographs in the post-operative management of early breast cancer. Br J Surg 1983;70:517–20.
14. Wickerham L, Fisher B, Cronin W, et al. The efficacy of bone scanning in the follow-up of patients with operable breast cancer. Breast Cancer Res Treat 1984;4:303–7.
15. Del Truco MR, Palli D, Cariddi A, et al. Intensive diagnostic follow-up after treatment of primary breast cancer: a randomized trial. JAMA 1994;271:1593–7.
16. Impact of follow-up testing on survival and health-related quality of life in breast cancer patients: a multicenter randomized controlled trial. The GIVIO Investigators. JAMA 1994;271:1587–92.
17. Grunfeld E, Mant D, Yudkin P, et al. Routine follow-up of breast cancer in primary care: randomized trial. BMJ 1996;313:665–9.
18. American Society of Clinical Oncology. Recommended breast cancer surveillance guidelines. J Clin Oncol 1997; 15:2149–56.
19. American Society of Clinical Oncology. American Society of Clinical Oncology 1998 update of recommended breast cancer surveillance guidelines. J Clin Oncol 1999;17:1080–92.
20. Temple LKF, Wang EEL, McLeod RS, et al with the Canadian Task Force on Preventive Health Care. Preventive health care, 1999 update: 3. Follow-up after breast cancer. CMAJ 1999;16:1001–8.
21. Mellink WAM, Holland R, Hendriks JH, et al. The contribution of routine follow-up mammography to an early detection of asynchronous contralateral breast cancer. Cancer 1991;67:1844–8.
22. Bast RC, Ravdin P, Hayes DF, et al. 2000 update of recommendations for the use of tumor markers in breast and colorectal cancer: clinical practice guidelines of the American Society of Clinical Oncology. J Clin Oncol 2001;19:1865–78.
23. Molina R, Zanon G, Filella X, et al. Use of serial carcinoembryonic antigen and CA 15.3 assays in detecting relapses in breast cancer patients. Breast Cancer Res Treat 1995;36:41–8.
24. Stearns V, Yamauchi H, Hayes DF. Circulating tumor markers in breast cancer: accepted utilities and novel prospects. Breast Cancer Res Treat 1998;52:29–59.
25. Chan DW, Beveridge RA, Muss H, et al. Use of Truquant BR radioimmunoassay for early detection of breast cancer recurrence in patients with stage II and stage III disease. J Clin Oncol 1997;15:2322–8.
26. National Comprehensive Cancer Network (NCCN). Clinical practice guidelines in oncology. Available at http://www.nccn.org/professionals/physician (accessed April 2005).
27. Muss HB, Tell GS, Case LD, et al. Perceptions of follow-up care in women with breast cancer. Am J Clin Oncol 1991; 14:55–9.

37

A Patient's Perspective

RUTH SILVERMAN

Without the patient, there would be no work for anyone in medicine. That is especially true with cancer. We are not likely to see a complete end to that conventional arrangement in our lifetimes.

Without all the doctors and the members of their staffs, there would be no treatment, no options, and no decisions. What is most helpful is that all involved should recognize that they must forge a long-term working relationship. In doing so, many will also build the kind of personal connections that too often are frowned upon in medical schools.

After all, getting too close means acknowledging feelings, and that could conceivably lead to disappointment or sadness. However, I made it a point to seek excellent practitioners who were not afraid to smile, laugh, hug hello, and find the time to listen to occasional personal stories, as well as medical concerns.

I now realize that I am probably part of a very small group of patients who have tried to change things, but if my methods worked for me, they might just work for others. If they did not interfere with the treatment plan, then they must have been acceptable to my doctors and their staff members, who also have to be willing to understand that not all patients are cut from the same cloth.

And, not all doctors, other medical practitioners, and students are ready to learn that the word "doctor" is not a synonym for "God."

As I think back over my more than 2 years of diagnosis, treatment, and follow-up, I am sometimes puzzled that friends and family act surprised when I share comments, feelings, and more with them—especially when I mention that I am looking forward to seeing one or more of the doctors on my team.

In today's world of instant communication, it is easier for those who find a lump, or who get the word about one from a family physician, to build such a team and to participate in all decisions.

When I found a lump on the outside of my left breast, while showering after a Pilates class, I think I knew the results even before I went to doctors, so I was not completely surprised when the diagnosis confirmed my hunch; however, I still had to decide on a plan of action.

Between the contacts I had made writing medical stories occasionally, during my 25 years as a freelance writer for a daily newspaper, and the contacts in my family, I had to place only a couple of phone calls to get started.

I began with my kids' pediatrician. The girls were grown, but he and I had stayed in touch occasionally, and I was comfortable talking to him. My cousin, a breast-imaging specialist in Boston, was the son of the obstetrician who delivered this pediatrician's children.

Later, as a chief of pediatrics, my children's pediatrician functioned at the level I sought in the doctors I wanted to treat me throughout all that was to come. Most people probably do not have well-known doctors in their families, but that should not stop them from networking through friends, support groups, and the Internet.

In the same way as I did, through family networking, most patients should be looking for "The Best." But, what does that really mean? And, how do they do it when they do not have such family networks?

Titles do not necessarily define those who are in that category. It is almost easy to be a fine practitioner. Being willing to take the time to be understanding and empathetic is more difficult and I would imagine refining those techniques takes as much–or more–practice as it does to develop and hone technical skills and apply pure scientific knowledge.

The pediatrician mentioned to me that when doctors need medical assistance in areas other than their own fields, they network with other doctors, generally at their own levels of excellence. So, he reasoned, patients should start at the top, too. They can simply call a teaching hospital and ask to talk to a chief of a department. From that person, they can find others.

Before I made a first appointment, I spent hours with friends and family in person and on the phone and plenty of time e-mailing and instant messaging to learn what questions to ask of prospective doctors. Each resource had something of value to add to my rapidly growing bank of knowledge.

Again, in today's world, people are only a keystroke away from others who can help.

The first recommendation I needed was the name of a surgeon at a teaching hospital, who could do a biopsy to determine the nature of the lump. When all other qualifications and skills were equal, I decided I would go with the person who could communicate well. This proved to be a wise idea, because we would be making some important decisions together in the course of the next 2 years.

I imagine not all patients arrive for appointments that will likely change their lives, forever, in a relaxed frame of mind. Although I had a few trepidations, I was confident that I was in good hands and could relax—a state that is also helpful to medical professionals.

Preliminary palpation and radiologic tests confirmed what I already knew. I would need the biopsy to determine the nature of the lump.

As expected, the biopsy confirmed the diagnosis. The surgeon and the oncologist decided we would need to do chemotherapy and irradiation to reduce the chance of metastasis. I would have to plan on two 12-week rounds of chemo before the irradiation. I guess I was among the lucky ones, since I did not get sick from the chemo, although I did get tired easily.

Each day after chemo, I would return home to the care of my young Burmese cats, who decided their role would be to lick the infusion site, to make it better, as is the practice of most cats who must deal with injuries to members of their families. I still laugh when I remember sharing this information with my oncologist.

His reaction reflected barely suppressed amazement. "They're doing what?" he asked, and he voiced concern about infection, which I just laughed off.

My cousin shouted, "Toxoplasmosis!" I had to reassure him that they do not go out, so they are not likely to be near rat droppings.

I had actually read that cats can be very important in the healing process; that their purring has the same effect on the body as meditation. This was confirmed by another member of my team, a specialist in integrative medicine. Whenever they leaned against me, or slept in my arms, their purring precipitated a slower rate of respiration and a feeling of great well being.

I think doctors need to understand that even the most well-informed and well-educated patients, today, will come armed with more than "purely" scientific information and opinions. If these do no harm, they should not be dismissed.

As I lost my hair, the cats had a new, self-selected responsibility. They began to lick my head, giving me another source of laughter. Once, I even found one grooming my wig. If they could accept it, so could I.

My response to chemotherapy was excellent. To further refine the nature and extent of the cancer, a lumpectomy would be next.

When I woke up, although still groggy, I wanted to know the results of the surgery. Two sentinel nodes confirmed that there was no nodal involvement, but several days later, I was informed that 4 of 6 of the margins in remaining breast tissue still showed cancer cells.

My response was, "OK. If that's what we've got, let's just lop it off."

Undoubtedly taken aback by my casual choice of words, the surgeon suggested that we consider all options prior to making a decision. We did, but my resolution to be rid of the invader remained unchanged.

We scheduled the mastectomy for early in the morning, a few weeks after I had healed from the first procedure. Years back, mastectomies required several days in the hospital. Now, they are almost as routine as lumpectomies. We scheduled it for early in the week, so that my regular attendance at Shabbat services on

Saturdays would not be interrupted. I was home that same night, once again, in the care of my cats.

As medical professionals, you should be open to something like that, as much as you are to new surgical and treatment options. I slept with a pillow over my chest, so that the cats would not accidentally do any damage. They slept right beside me, even if I was simply taking a nap.

I became proficient at keeping track of drainage tubes and their output. I also invented new ways to hide them with loose tops over pants. Since I refused to join support groups, I sometimes asked my doctors to answer questions that those groups might have answered. Not once did they complain. They were my support group because that was what I wanted. The result: we forged friendships that undoubtedly break the old rules in Patient Relations 101 in most medical schools.

Since my primary reaction to all the chemo, radiation, and surgeries was cumulative fatigue, I was not doing my usual running around to interviews, openings, events, and the like. So, my day-to-day pattern of being with friends in the media and new friends, made in the course of stories I was writing, was interrupted. My grown children live in other cities and, because I am an only child, I do not have siblings to call upon for support.

Once again, today's modern world of technology came to the rescue. It is OK if you suggest to your patients that they join online special interest groups. There are hundreds of them and they are only as far away as the computer.

My friends in the groups to which I began to contribute fairly regularly live all over the world. But, they always asked how I felt and they bolstered me with good and bad jokes, lots of intellectual stimulation, and a shared interest in whatever the group was discussing at a given moment in time. Not once was one of these groups solely devoted to breast cancer, but off-list, many had great suggestions on what to ask doctors on follow-up appointments. We still compare notes on brands of green tea and on antioxidant effectiveness in blueberry juice versus pomegranate juice.

Although we have never met, in person, these people who are scattered throughout the world became my at-home support group. Occasionally, we have spoken by phone, but for the most part, we have connected electronically. I cannot recommend enough how important it is that you consider suggesting this new kind of support to your patients.

While at the computer, of course, I began to become proficient at medical research, and with the advent of google, I realized I could engage in "med-speak" with all my doctors. They were always open to discussions precipitated by my latest finds.

Now, as a beta-tester for the new Google-alerts, I can sit back and let the latest information come to me, not only for me, but also for others with different health problems. When a friend was having problems bringing his latest bout of inflammatory bowel disease under control, and suddenly developed vision problems at the same time, I entered an alert request and quickly learned that he might in fact want to consult someone regarding a different diagnosis than the one he had been given about 20 to 25 years earlier.

I was not about to play doctor, but my friend finally agreed to meet with a new consultant. He came back with a new and more accurate diagnosis, new medicines, and new hope.

When I asked him what he planned to do with the doctor in whom he had put his trust for so many years, he wryly said, "First, I'm going to listen to what he has to say; then, if I don't like it, I'll rip him up one wall and down the other."

Be prepared. Your patients will lose patience with you, too, if you cannot or prefer not to work with them as a teammate.

For years, people have debated on whether practicing medicine is more of an art than a science. In my view, it is both. I think it is probably easier to learn the science. For some people, learning the art of conversation can take as much practice as learning how to insert catheters and perform surgery.

Even if a medical school does not take a course in role-play, in which students can take both roles of doctor and patient, students can engage in that technique on their own. Results can be enlightening, satisfying, and even humorous.

That brings up another important idea. It is OK to laugh with a patient. Being too dour equates with arrogance in the minds of many.

THE PATIENT

P

First of all, the PATIENT is a PERSON, not a page in a text or an experiment in a lab.

Second, ask yourself some questions. Think about how you might feel if you were the patient and not the doctor. All patients come in for their appointments feeling a variety of emotions. They might not convey all of them, but you can bet they are there.

How would you feel if you were facing a diagnosis of cancer?

The word PATIENT also calls to mind a similar word: PATIENCE. I think it might be a good idea to cultivate patience. If patients feel rushed, they will also feel that their doctors and other practitioners do not care about them. Not all will need more time than your practice administrators are willing to budget, but some will want and should get a few more words and explanations than others.

Today's patient is not your parents' patient. Even the most tentative will begin treatment armed with some basics that were not available just a few years ago.

Add to the mix a healthy dose of respect. If you respect your patient, your patient will be more likely to respect you. With mutual respect, the outcome will probably be better, too.

A

ANSWERS: Providing them means it is a good idea to think beyond the texts. And, you do not necessarily have to have all the answers. Remember, you are human, too.

Today's patients are well versed in both conventional and alternative methods of treatment. If you are quick to discard the value of something a patient brings to an appointment, then there will likely be repercussions down the road.

If a patient complains of itchy skin, do not necessarily reach for the prescription pad. The last thing some patients want is cortisone, unless and until it is absolutely necessary. Yes, the pharmaceutical houses want you to use their products, but are you there to serve them or are you there to serve and help your patients? There are plenty of ALTERNATIVES (another "A" word) out there—and some do work. When another patient complains about feeling nervous or uneasy, prescribe meditation, massage, or a healthy dose of a purring cat.

Among the many e-mails that I receive each day are some from noted integrative practitioners. Their Web sites are well designed and inviting, and answer just about every question that patients ask. If you are fortunate enough to have an integrative medical practitioner at the hospital where you practice, get to know that person. Take some hints from the way that those offices are configured.

In my case, I love going there because I am greeted by a highly trained physician who is equally informed about alternatives. The décor in her office features soft music and lighting. She prefers Indian silk scarves over soft knit pants and tops, to lab coats. If she were to count the respiration rates of her patients, these would probably be much slower than those that the same people would show in a conventional office.

T

TREATMENTS can include everything from conventional to unconventional. Prepare to be open to printouts of reports from throughout the world, brought to your attention by your patients.

I

Again, the familiar first-person pronoun is not a synonym for God. Doctors are people, not gods. There was a time when the opposite might have been the case. Patients came into an office, quietly sat down and addressed their physicians as "Doctor." Today, many come in with folders packed with INFORMATION. They are INFORMED. It might be a good idea to learn to use the pronoun WE, instead of I. Appointments often begin, for those who are open enough, with first-name greetings and mutual hugs.

"I" is also for INTERNET. For good or for ill, computers have played a major role in helping people connect to others with similar problems. With the push of a button, they learn all about someone's Aunt Tillie, or a thirty-second cousin twice-removed and what their experiences have been.

And, of course, all will have had the "BEST" or the "WORST" oncologists, surgeons, radiation experts, and other specialists. Those who can maneuver well online will try to sort out fact from fiction. Others will ask friends, relatives, and anyone else they know for input.

Nobody would suggest that I am practicing medicine without a license; just alerting those, whose doctors might be too busy to be at a computer all day, of the newest reports before they get to read them. So, when patients come in with information, it might be worthwhile to give it some thought.

E

EMPATHY is not the same as sympathy. It is really about compassion and understanding. Family members and in-person or online support groups can be sympathetic. Sometimes, a patient is too fatigued to even attend a support group meeting. Too often, those meetings can degenerate into a "who can top this" scenario, with members wallowing in tales of woe. My advice is to suggest to patients that they seek out real-life and online groups that are not necessarily dedicated to the disease and its complications and treatment. It is healthy for them to attend religious services, meetings of upbeat people, and even pet shows, where they can reach out to give and receive love from little creatures who do not care if those doing the reaching have no hair or are often too tired to open a book or newspaper.

It is OK to show EMOTION. If you stand there like a stone, people will think of you as being hard-hearted. Perhaps you are. But, probably one of the things that brought you into medicine in the first place was your desire to help people and to make a difference in their lives. It is OK to get in touch with that side of you, too. If you are afraid that doing that will leave you too vulnerable to pain, consider the physical and emotional pain that your patients must endure. Yes, they only do so when it involves their own issues, and you are seeing many patients each week, but not all patients will need that emotional connection from you.

How do you protect yourself from total meltdown? Talk to other medical professionals; talk to patients who have been there and have had a good outcome. Share concerns. Be open to being human. You will grow from the experience.

EXERCISE: Many patients find they are too tired to engage in strenuous exercise, but if patients can do a little Pilates or a little yoga, or take a walk in a shopping center, they might find those options are helpful, not only physically but emotionally as well.

Even walking in a shopper-friendly store provides a boost, whether or not patients make any purchases. For me, after hospital procedures, a visit to an area department store, where sales associates always greet familiar people by name, was great fun and made me feel that I was among the living.

Going from one department to another was about as much exercise as I could take on some days and I took advantage of seats in the shoe department and in the café, when I needed a rest. On nice days, I ventured a little beyond the store and enjoyed the beauty of the outdoor mall.

Now that I am back to hard workouts on the Pilates Reformer, I find that the more I do, the stronger I feel—even on days when the medications I take might make me want to stay in bed for an extra hour of sleep, in the morning. Tell your patients about that, so that they will realize there is a light at the end of the tunnel.

"E" also stands for EATING.

Having had breast cancer pushed me to learn more about healthy eating. I am now an advocate of green tea, rough-cut oatmeal, splashes of wild blueberry or pomegranate juice in water, almonds, and dark-green vegetables; and I keep on top of other healthy options to include in my daily meal plans.

Adding such new information to a storehouse of knowledge also helps to keep the "chemo-fog" that descends on many patients, from taking over the mind completely.

N

Never say NEVER.

T

TEAMWORK is the order of the day. Those on the team are not only your coworkers in medicine. They also include your patients.

Index

Page numbers followed by f indicate figure. Page numbers followed by t indicate table.